Fodors91

Budget Europe

Fodor's Travel Publications, Inc.
New York and London

ISBN 0-679-01886-7

Fodor's Budget Europe

Editors: Christopher Billy, Linda K. Schmidt

Editorial Contributors: Frances Arnold, Anne Campbell-Lord, Nancy Coons, Thomas Cussans, Donna Dailey, Nigel Fisher, Asgeir Fridgeirsson, Cliff Gaw, George Hamilton, Emma Harris, Charles Hebbert, Simon Hewitt, Allanah Hopkin, Lisa Kagel, Helmut Koenig, Graham Lees, Alan Levy, Susan Lowndes, Delia Meth-Cohn, Richard Moore, Anita Peltonen, Karina Porcelli, Philip Ray, Eric Sjogren, Linda Stout, Robert Tilley, Barbara Walsh-Angelillo

Cartography: Brian Denyer, Jeremy Ford, Alex Murphy, Swanston Graphics, Bryan Woodfield

Cover Photograph: R. Doisneau/Photoresearchers

Cover Design: Vignelli Associates

Special Sales

MANUFACTURED IN THE UNITED STATES OF AMERICA
10 9 8 7 6 5 4 3 2 1

CONTENTS

CONTENTS

FOREWORD

At the risk of stating the obvious, the key component in any budget vacation is how far your money will stretch. Nine times out of ten, this is almost indecently dependent on the prevailing rate of exchange. The middle 1980s were boom years in this respect. As the dollar rose seemingly unstoppably, so Europe's currencies shrank in its shadow and Americans streamed across the Atlantic in unprecedented numbers. Since 1987, by comparison, the dollar has been in a much less virile state, with the inevitable result that the transatlantic tourist flood dwindled dramatically.

As we write at Easter 1990, forecasting the likely strength or otherwise of the dollar in 1991 against Europe's elastic currencies is a job to shatter a crystal ball. But if there is any one piece of advice that can be given with at least a degree of confidence it is that you should be flexible in your travel planning. Try not to tie yourself down at too early a stage to rigid schedules and dates and, above all, shop around for the best buy.

"Budget" is in any case a very relative term. One man's budget is another man's splurge—and in this book we have, from year to year, tried to suggest that budget traveling is more a state of mind than anything else. It can best be summed up in the phrase "look before you leap." It means searching out every permutation and combination of transport to be sure that you will not find yourself sitting next to someone on the plane over who has paid less for his ticket than you have. It means carefully casing every restaurant before you go in, reading the menu posted outside, to know what the meal is likely to cost. It covers making sure which extras are—or aren't—included in the price of a hotel room before settling in. It means *never* making a long-distance call from your hotel room, where the cost can be astronomical, but going down the road to the post office.

In other words, a budget traveler counts his hard-earned cents and makes sure he is getting value for them. One thing we very seriously urge is that the budget traveler keep an eagle eye on exchange fluctuations, both before starting out and while on the trip. Considerable changes can occur overnight.

*

The plan of this book is first of all to give you background information to help you plan your trip. We have divided it into general travel material—giving suggestions on air, sea, road and rail travel to and around the Continent; sources of information to help you delve deeper into the particular aspect of the trip that interests you most; and some background hints that should help you to keep more closely within your budget. We then cover all the main European countries, in 27 chapters, concentrating mainly on the capital—or chief city—and then looking at some of the other sections of each country which are worth visiting on a budget.

Naturally, in a book of this size, we cannot cover the whole of every country. Should you wish for more information than we have space for here, all of the countries are covered by books in our main series, which themselves contain much information useful to the budget traveler.

*

While every care has been taken to assure the accuracy of the information in this guide, the passage of time will always bring change, and consequently the publisher cannot accept responsibility for errors that may occur.

All prices and opening times quoted in this guide are based on information supplied to us at press time. Hours and admission fees may change, however, and the prudent traveler will avoid inconvenience by calling ahead.

Fodor's wants to hear about your travel experiences, both pleasant and unpleasant. When a hotel or restaurant fails to live up to its billing, let us know and we will investigate the complaint and revise our entries where the facts warrant it.

Send your letters to the editors of Fodor's Travel Publications, 201 E. 50th Street, New York, NY 10022.

FACTS AT YOUR FINGERTIPS

PLANNING YOUR TRIP

WHAT WILL IT COST

If you go to Europe on any sort of package tour or pre-arrangement, you have a pretty accurate idea of what it is going to cost you. If you choose to travel independently, however, your costs will be mainly a function of two things, how you choose to live and which countries you visit.

The first of these obviously is difficult to predict because individual requirements vary greatly, and you may in any case not know what you want until after you have done some experimenting. A medium-level accommodation in a city in Scandinavia will be very different from a medium-level accommodation in a village in rural Turkey, for example. If you are traveling with a fairly open schedule, you can afford to spend the first couple of days in any country looking around and making comparisons and getting to know the conditions of that particular country. Then you can decide what kind of trade-off you yourself want to make, what kind of balance you are willing to strike between comfort and economy. It rarely takes more than a couple of days in a place to learn the signals, that is to get to know both what kind of comfort you will find behind a particular facade and what you can reasonably expect in a given price range. In other words, you begin to think in local terms.

Though it's probably true to claim that no European countries are beyond the range of anyone armed with dollars, it's also true that the farther south you go in Europe the cheaper it becomes. Fifteen dollars in Greece will take you farther than fifteen dollars in Switzerland or Sweden. Furthermore, there will be variations within a single country in that the main cities will be more expensive than the small towns and some regions will be more expensive than others. In France, for example, the Riviera will be more expensive than the mountains of Auvergne or the villages of Languedoc.

Belgium, Great Britain and West Germany are fairly expensive countries. In around the same range come Switzerland and Scandinavia, although they are less expensive than their reputations would suggest. France, once you are outside Paris and the trendier centers; Italy, again outside the main cities; and Austria all offer excellent chances for budget living. Spain is spiralling upwards into the company of the middle-cost countries—fuelled by higher demands from the work force—as are Greece and Ireland. Portugal is still low in the cost scale as are Cyprus and, especially, Turkey.

In southern Europe particularly there is a greater variety available in the lower end of the spectrum, which means that you can experiment more and find your own particular level and trade-off. And if you go camping or hosteling your calculations are in a wholly different frame of reference anyway.

In Eastern Europe, Poland and Bulgaria are the cheaper countries, Czechoslovakia, Hungary and Romania are more expensive. In most of these countries you are required to spend a fixed minimum per day in any case.

The words "expensive" and "inexpensive" are relative terms—relative to whatever the current value of the dollar and the pound is against any other currency. Yet, regardless of the strength of the dollar, it's still vital to watch exchange rates, both before and during the vacation. It's a boring and slightly depressing way to have to live, but if you can psych yourself into a state of mind where watching the pennies can actually be a kind of game, then you are home and dry.

One excellent way to minimize costs is to travel off-season, which has definite advantages over touring during the peak summer months. In cases where prices remain the same, the pressure is off, and you will have a wider choice of accommodations. And you'll be very much helped by the considerable discounts and other cost-saving benefits that all National and Regional tourist offices organize for the

1

off-season period. Similarly, many hotels, restaurants and travel firms (rail companies, airlines and so on) offer considerable savings. Investigate these and other savings through your travel agent or the National Tourist Office of the country concerned.

Other off-season benefits are that cheaper hotel rooms will be available, restaurants still open, and you'll gain a more intimate knowledge of the countries you
visit, seeing their people in their normal routine of making and enjoying a living.
The great cities and capitals of Europe bloom in the winter and fall, rather than
in the summer, while spring is gloriously festive virtually all over. The theaters
open, the concert and opera seasons begin, the circus comes to town, new scenes
emerge. Even if you're not a member of that mass movement that converges annually with the first fall of snow on the ski slopes of the Alps, check the calendar later
in this section and think about "out-of-season" travel this year in Europe.

Whenever you come, you can count on a glorious adventure. Europe awaits you,
even more precious for showing many signs of new vitality and growth. You can
still trace the history of man's adventure on this earth from the Caves of Altamira
to the Chapel of Matisse at Vence, from the Agora in Athens to the Forum in Rome
or to the Palace of Westminster. Though budget air travel has made Europe accessible as never before, her ancient spell is undiminished.

TAKING MONEY ABROAD

Travelers checks and credit cards are probably still the safest and simplest ways
to carry money. There are several brands of travelers checks, but best known are
American Express, Barclays' and *Cook's*, all of which charge a 1% commission. The
American Automobile Association (see page 14) provides *American Express* traveler's checks free to its members.

Important. Avoid exchanging money on weekends or at hotels and restaurants.
You'll pay a big premium for the convenience. Wait for the banks to open. Also,
always keep a written record of the check numbers in a place other than that where
you carry the checks, or give the numbers to a companion or friend. In the event
the checks are lost or stolen this will greatly facilitate obtaining replacement checks.

American Express sells travelers checks in French francs and other foreign
monies. It might be wise to purchase foreign travelers checks before your departure.
If you are really traveling on a limited or careful budget, you won't need a credit
card for most purposes because the inexpensive places don't accept them. But some
credit cards allow you to draw cash or write personal checks up to a certain amount,
and that can come in handy as a back-up to your travelers checks.

To avoid having to change money at a strange airport or trying to pay an Italian
cab driver in American quarters or British 50p pieces buy a prepack, sometimes
called a tip pack, of foreign currency from your bank before you depart. Having
$50–$100 in local currency in your pocket not only saves the trouble and expense
of converting your money for the tips and transportation you'll need when you first
arrive, it will also help you to become familiar with the look and denominations
of the currency. *MTB Banking Corporation* (tel. 800–221–9830 or, in New York,
212–775–1440) sells travel packs—approximately $50 in small denomination notes
and coins—in 15 currencies. Each pack comes with a currency conversion card and
tipping hints. **Warning:** You'll never get exactly as much for your dollar or pound
as the official daily exchange rate.

In Eastern Europe. You usually cannot bring any local currency with you into
a communist country (except Yugoslavia and Hungary, small amounts). Never try
to do so illegally, either in Eastern Europe or anywhere else. If caught you can expect confiscation of the money and even imprisonment.

If you should lose your money or run short, some British consulates may cable
home for you; but we regret to say that many American tourists have found their
own consular authorities of no help at such times. Thus, it's best to guard against
such an eventuality yourself: if your bank has a foreign branch it will be able to
forward funds to you, or you can use the services of a worldwide agency like *American Express* or *Thomas Cook Travel Agency*.

Credit Cards

Credit cards are now an integral part of the Western financial way of life, and, in theory at least, are accepted all over Europe. But, while the use of credit cards can smooth the traveler's path considerably, they should not be thought of as a universal answer to every problem.

Firstly, there is a growing resistance in Europe to the use of credit cards, or rather to the percentage that the credit card organizations demand from establishments taking part in their schemes. Not so long ago 200 restaurants in Paris refused to accept credit cards—and some of them still refuse—simply because they feel that the benefit credit cards bring is all on the side of the customer. If you intend to use your credit cards in Europe, you would be well advised to get one of the directories that the companies put out, listing the firms that will accept their particular cards.

Another point that should be watched with those useful pieces of plastic is the problem of the rate at which your purchase may be converted into your home currency. We have ourselves had two purchases made on the same day in the same place charged ultimately at two totally different rates of exchange. If you want to be certain of the rate at which you will pay, insist on the establishment entering the current rate onto your credit card charge at the time you sign it—this will prevent the management from holding your charge until a more favorable rate (to them) comes along, something which could cost you more dollars than you counted on. (On the other hand, should the dollar or pound be revalued upward before your charge is entered, you could gain a little.)

We would advise you, also, to check your monthly statement very carefully indeed against the receipts you got at the time of your purchase. It has become increasingly common for shops, hotels or restaurants to change the amounts on the original you signed, if they find they have made an error in the original bill. Sometimes, also, unscrupulous employees make this kind of change to their own advantage. The onus is on you to report the change to the credit card firm and insist on sorting the problem out.

Credit cards are easily usable in most of Europe, but there are three fairly weak spots, Austria, Norway, and Germany, where use is less general.

VACATION TRAVEL INSURANCE

Travel insurance can cover everything from health and accident costs, to lost baggage and trip cancellation. Sometimes they can all be obtained with one blanket policy; other times they overlap with existing coverage you might have for health and/or home; still other times it is best to buy policies that are tailored to specific needs. But, insurance is available from many sources and many travelers unwittingly end up with redundant coverage. Before purchasing separate travel insurance of any kind, be sure to check your regular policies carefully.

Generally, it is best to take care of your insurance needs *before* embarking on your trip. You'll pay more for less coverage—and have less chance to read the fine print—if you wait until the last minute. Best of all, if you have a regular insurance agent, he is the person to consult first. Flight insurance, often included in the price of the ticket when the fare is paid via American Express, Visa or certain other major credit cards, is also frequently included in package policies providing accident coverage as well. These policies are available from most tour operators and insurance companies. While it is a good idea to have health and accident insurance, be careful not to spend money to duplicate coverage you may already have . . . or to neglect some eventuality that could end up costing a small fortune. For example, basic Blue Cross Blue Shield policies cover health costs incurred while traveling. They will not, however, cover the cost of emergency transportation, which can often add up to several thousand dollars. Emergency transportation *is* covered, in part at least, by many major medical policies such as those underwritten by *Prudential, Metropolitan, Mutual of Omaha,* and *New York Life.* Again, check any policy carefully before buying. Another important example: Most insurance issued specifically for travel does not cover pre-existing medical conditions.

Several organizations offer coverage designed to supplement existing health insurance and to help defray costs not covered by many standard policies, such as emergency transportation. Some of the more prominent are:

Travel Assistance International, the American arm of Europ Assistance, offers a comprehensive program offering immediate, on-the-spot medical, personal and financial help. Trip protection ranges from $40 for an individual for up to eight days to $200 for an entire family for a year. Full details from travel agents or insurance brokers, or from Europ Assistance Worldwide Services, Inc., 1133 15th St., N.W., Suite 400, Washington, D.C. 20077–2166 (800–821–2828). In the U.K., contact Europ Assistance Ltd., 252 High St., Croydon, Surrey CRO 1NF (081–680 1234).

Carefree Travel Insurance, c/o ARM Coverage Inc., P.O. Box 310, 120 Mineola Blvd., Mineola, N.Y. 11501, underwritten by the Hartford Accident and Indemnity Co., offers a comprehensive benefits package that includes trip cancellation and interruption, medical, and accidental death/dismemberment coverage, as well as medical, legal, and economic assistance. Trip cancellation and interruption insurance can be purchased separately. (Tel. 800–654–2424 for additional information.)

International SOS Assistance Inc., P. O. Box 11568, Philadelphia, PA 19116, has fees from $15 a person for seven days, to $195 for a year (tel. 800–523–8930).

IAMAT (International Association for Medical Assistance to Travelers), 417 Center St., Lewiston, N.Y. 14092 in the U.S.; or 188 Nicklin Rd., Guelph, Ontario NlH 7L5 in Canada.

The Association of British Insurers, Aldermary House, 10–15 Queen St., London EC4N 1TT (tel. 071–248 4477), will give comprehensive advice on all aspects of vacation travel insurance from the U.K.

Loss of baggage is another frequent inconvenience to travelers. It is possible, though complicated, to insure your luggage against loss through theft or negligence. Insurance companies are reluctant to sell such coverage alone, however, since it is often a losing proposition for them. Instead, this type of coverage is usually included as part of a package that also covers accidents or health. Should you lose your luggage or some other personal possession, it is essential to report it to the local police immediately. Without documentation of such a report, your insurance company might be very stingy. Also, before buying baggage insurance, check your homeowner's policy. Some such policies offer "off-premises theft" coverage, including the loss of luggage while traveling.

Trip cancellation coverage is especially important to travelers on APEX or charter flights. Should you be unable to continue your trip during your vacation, you may be stuck having to buy a new one-way fare home, plus paying for the charter you're not using. You can guard against this with "trip cancellation insurance." Most of these policies will also cover last minute cancellations.

NATIONAL TOURIST OFFICES

Most countries maintain official tourist information bureaus in important cities—New York, Chicago, Los Angeles, San Francisco, London, Paris, Toronto and many others. Upon request, they will send free printed matter to help you plan your trip. They are always willing to give you any additional special information without charge for the service. However, they do *not* issue tickets or make hotel reservations.

Addresses of some of the principal European tourist offices in the United States, Canada and Great Britain are:

United States

Austrian National Tourist Office: 500 Fifth Ave., 20th Floor, New York, N.Y. 10110; 11601 Wilshire Blvd., Suite 2480, Los Angeles, CA 90025; 500 N. Michigan Ave., Suite 1950, Chicago, IL 60611; 1300 Post Oak Blvd., Suite 960, Houston, TX 77056.

Belgian National Tourist Office: 745 Fifth Ave., Suite 714, New York, N.Y. 10151.

British Tourist Authority: 40 West 57th St., New York, N.Y. 10019; 625 N. Michigan Ave., Suite 1510, Chicago, IL 60611; World Trade Center, 350 S. Figueroa St., Suite 450, Los Angeles, CA 90071; 2305 Cedar Springs Rd., Suite 210, Dallas, TX 75201.

Bulgarian National Tourist Office (Balkan Holidays): 161 East 86th St., New York, N.Y. 10028.

Cyprus Tourism Organization (Republic of Cyprus): 13 East 40 St., New York, N.Y. 10016.

Czechoslovak Travel Bureau (Cedok): 321 E. 75th St., New York, N.Y. 10021.

Danish Tourist Board: 655 Third Ave., New York, N.Y. 10017.

Finnish Tourist Board: 655 Third Ave., New York, N.Y. 10017.

French Government Tourist Office: 610 Fifth Ave., New York, N.Y. 10020; 645 North Michigan Ave., Chicago, IL 60611; 9454 Wilshire Blvd., Beverly Hills, CA 90212; 2305 Cedar Springs Rd., Dallas, TX 75201.

German National Tourist Office (West Germany): 747 Third Ave., New York, N.Y. 10017; 444 South Flower St., Suite 2230, Los Angeles, CA 90071.

Greek Nat'l Tourist Organization: 645 Fifth Avenue., New York, N.Y. 10022; 611 West 6th St., Suite 2198, Los Angeles, CA 90017; 168 N. Michigan Ave., Chicago, IL 60601.

IBUSZ Hungarian Travel Company, 1 Parker Plaza, Ft. Lee, N.J. 07024.

Icelandic Tourist Board: 655 Third Avenue, New York, N.Y. 10017.

Irish Tourist Board: 757 Third Ave., New York, N.Y. 10017.

Italian Gov't. Travel Office (ENIT): 630 Fifth Ave., Suite 1565, New York, N.Y. 10111; 500 N. Michigan Ave., Chicago, IL 60611; 360 Post St., Suite 801, San Francisco, CA 94108.

Luxembourg National Tourist Office: 801 Second Ave., New York, N.Y. 10017.

Malta Consulate, 249 East 35 St., New York, N.Y. 10016.

Monaco Gov't. Tourist Office: 845 Third Ave., New York, N.Y. 10022.

Netherlands Board of Tourism: 355 Lexington Ave., New York, N.Y. 10017; 225 N. Michigan Ave., Suite 326, Chicago, IL 60601; 90 New Montgomery St., Suite 305, San Francisco, CA 94105.

Norwegian Tourist Board: 655 Third Ave., New York, N.Y. 10017.

Polish National Tourist Office (Orbis): 500 Fifth Ave., New York, N.Y. 10110; 333 N. Michigan Ave., Chicago, IL 60601.

Portuguese National Information Office (Casa de Portugal): 590 Fifth Ave., New York, N.Y. 10036.

Romanian Nat'l Tourist Office: 573 Third Ave., New York, N.Y. 10016.

Spanish Nat'l Tourist Office: 665 Fifth Ave., New York, N.Y. 10022; 845 N. Michigan Ave., Chicago, IL 60611; San Vicente Plaza Bldg., 8383 Wilshire Blvd., Ste. 960, Beverly Hills, CA 90211.

Swedish Tourist Board: 655 Third Ave., New York, N.Y. 10017.

Swiss National Tourist Office: 608 Fifth Ave., New York, N.Y. 10020; 260 Stockton St., San Francisco, CA 94108–5387.

Turkish Culture & Information Office: 821 U.N. Plaza, New York, N.Y. 10017.

Yugoslav National Tourist Office: 630 Fifth Ave., Suite 280, New York, N.Y. 10111.

Canada

Austrian National Tourist Service, 200 Granville St., Suite 1380, Vancouver, British Columbia V6C 1S4; 2 Bloor St. E., Suite 3330, Toronto, Ontario, M4W 1A8; 1010 Sherbrooke St. W., Suite 1410, Montreal, Quebec, H3A 2R7.

British Tourist Authority, 94 Cumberland St., Suite 600, Toronto, Ontario, M5R 3N3.

Danish National Tourist Office, Box 115, Station N, Toronto, Ontario, M8V 3S4.

Finnish Tourist Board, 1200 Bay St., Suite 604, Toronto, Ontario, M5R 2A5

French Government Tourist Office, 1981 McGill College, Suite 490, Montreal, Quebec, H3A 2W9; 1 Dundas St. W., Suite 2405, Toronto, Ontario, M5G 1Z3.

German National Tourist Office, 175 Bloor St. E., Suite 604, Toronto, Ontario M4W 3R8.

Greek National Tourist Organization, 1233 Rue de la Montagne, Suite 101, Montreal, Quebec H3G 1Z2; 1300 Bay St., Toronto, Quebec, M5R 3K8.

Irish Tourist Board, 10 King St. East, Toronto, Ontario M5C 1C3.

Italian Government (ENIT) Travel Office, 1 Place Ville Marie, Suite 1914, Montreal, Quebec, H3B 3M9.

Netherlands National Tourist Office, 25 Adelaide St. E., Suite 710, Toronto, Ontario M5C 1Y2.

Portuguese National Tourist Office, 2180 Yonge St., Toronto, Ontario, M4S 2B9.

Spanish National Tourist Office, 102 Bloor St. W., Suite 1400, Toronto, Ontario M5S 1M8.

Swiss National Tourist Office, 154 University Ave., Suite 610, Toronto, Ontario M5H 3Y9.

Great Britain

Austrian National Tourist Office, 30 St. George St., London W1R OAL.

Belgian National Tourist Office, Premier House, 2 Gayton Rd., Harrow, Middlesex HA1 2XU.

British Tourist Authority, Thames Tower, Blacks Rd., Hammersmith, London W6 9EL.

Bulgarian National Tourist Office, 18 Princes St., London W1R 7RE.

Cyprus National Tourism Organization, 213 Regent St., London W1R 8DA.

North Cyprus Tourist Office, 28 Cockspur St., London SW1Y 5BN.

Czechoslovak Travel Bureau (Cedok), 17–18 Old Bond St., London W1X 4RB.

Danish Tourist Board, 169–173 Regent St. (6th floor), London W1R 8PY (entrance in New Burlington St.)

East German Information (Berolina Travel), 22 Conduit St., London WIR 9TB.

Finnish Tourist Board, 66–68 Haymarket, London SW1Y 4RF.

French Tourist Office, 178 Piccadilly, London W1V OAL.

German National Tourist Office, 65 Curzon St., London WIY 7PE.

National Tourist Organization of Greece, 195–197 Regent St., London W1R 8DL.

Hungarian State Tourist Office, Danube Travel (IBUSZ), 6 Conduit St., London W1R 9TG.

Iceland Tourist Information Bureau, 3rd floor, 172 Tottenham Court Rd., London W1P 9LG.

Irish Tourist Board, Ireland House, 150–151 New Bond St., London W1Y OAQ.

Italian State Tourist Office, 1 Princes St., London W1R 8AY.

Liechtenstein (see Switzerland).

Luxembourg National Tourist Office, 36–37 Piccadilly, London W1V 9PA.

Malta National Tourist Office, Suite 207, College House, Wright's Lane, London W8 5SH.

Netherlands National Tourist Office, 25–28 Buckingham Gate, London SW1E 6LD.

Norwegian National Tourist Office, Charles House, 5/11 Regent St. (Lower), London SW1Y 4LR.

Poland National Tourist Office (Orbis), 82 Mortimer St., London W1N 7DE.

Portuguese National Tourist Office, New Bond St. House, 1–5 New Bond St., London W1Y ONP.

Romanian National Tourist Office (Carpati), 29 Thurloe Pl., London SW7 2HP.

Spanish National Tourist Office, 57 St. James's St., London SW1A 1LD.

Swedish National Tourist Office, 29–31 Oxford St., 5th Floor, London W1R 1RE.

Swiss National Tourist Office, Swiss Center, 1 New Coventry St., London W1V 8EE.

Turkish Tourism Information Office, Egyptian House (1st floor), 170–173 Piccadilly, London W1V 9DD.

Yugoslavian National Tourist Office, 143 Regent St., London W1R 8AE.

Many countries also maintain National Tourist Offices in principal cities within Continental Europe, which may prove useful if you suddenly decide to change your itinerary and want to collect a few brochures and last-minute information.

TRAVEL AGENTS

The critical issues in choosing a travel agent are how knowledgeable that person is about travel and how reliable his or her bookings are, regardless of whether you are looking for a package tour or planning to go it independently. The cost will be substantially the same whether you go to a major tour operator such as *Maupintour, American Express, Thomas Cook & Son* and *Olson's* or to the small agency around the corner: most commissions are paid by airlines, hotels and tour operators. In Europe there may be a small general service charge or fee-per-reservation; in the U.S. the only additions are for out-of-the-ordinary telephone or telex charges.

The importance of a travel agent is not merely for the making of reservations, however. Most of us could readily call an airline and book a reservation, but, as periodic experiments have proved, we could also call the same airline seven different times, reach seven different reservations clerks and get seven different prices quoted for the same "economy" fare coach seat on the exact same flight. A good travel agent booking a flight for a customer, for example, will know what general discount fares are available based on how long your stay will be, how far in advance you are able to make your reservations, whether you are making a simple round trip or adding extra stops and other factors. He will then get prices from several different airlines. The agent should have a frame of reference against which to judge the prices quoted, and will also often be able to suggest suitable accommodations, tie passage and lodging into a specially designed package, know which airline has deals available for inexpensive rental cars, or which has a special deal for skiers that includes all lift tickets. These are the sorts of ways in which a truly professional travel agent provides service.

In the case of package tours, you want to be sure that the tour operator can deliver the package being offered. Here again, a local travel agent can be helpful by advising you on the reliability of a tour operator and how realistic a given tour prospectus is. Certainly the organizations named above have established their reputations based on reliability—the inevitable occasional foul-up notwithstanding. If there is any doubt, there are trade organizations that can be consulted about specific questions.

Not all U.S. travel agents are licensed, as the laws vary from state to state, but membership in the *American Society of Travel Agents* (ASTA) or the *Association of British Travel Agents* (ABTA) is a safeguard. All ABTA tour operators and travel agents are bonded for your protection. In addition, the Air Travel Trust, administered by the Civil Aviation Authority, gives further financial protection to air travelers on charter or part-charter flights if the air travel operator is unable to meet his financial commitments. ASTA polices its membership through a Consumer Affairs Committee. In addition, a number of the larger and most responsible American tour operators have formed the United States Tour Operators Association, whose members post a bond to reimburse consumers if a tour operator fails or goes bankrupt. For a list, write to USTOA at 211 E. 51st St., Suite 12B, New York, N.Y. 10022.

First try to iron out any difficulties with the travel agent, himself, before contacting ASTA or ABTA. If a hotel does not live up to standards or some facet of the trip goes sour, contact the agent who did the booking and arranging. Get him to do something about it. Any agent worth his salt will follow through either directly or via the ASTA national office or ABTA chapter. ASTA's free brochure, *Avoiding Travel Problems,* is a good primer on avoiding the most common travel pitfalls. Send an SAE to ASTA at the address below.

As a last resort, contact ASTA, 1101 King St., Alexandria, VA 22314, or ABTA, 55–57 Newman St., London W1P 4AH, and refer your grievance directly to the committee.

Read this book thoroughly, paying attention to the information on package tours, the country-by-country hotel and restaurant prices (always subject to inflation and variations in exchange rates) and the suggestions on travel.

Write to the tour operators, national tourist offices and airlines for literature on areas that interest you. Learn where the bargains are and how to speak travel jargon. You will then know if your travel agent is doing a good job.

INDEPENDENT TRAVEL VS. PACKAGE TOURS

Time, convenience and cost are the factors to consider when it comes to choosing an all-inclusive, fully escorted tour, a loose plan-your-own-itinerary package tour, or totally independent travel.

Package tours are the easiest to arrange, and are probably the most economical and efficient way for a first-time traveler to Europe to get a broad overview of the most famous sights. "If it's Tuesday this must be Belgium" is how the joke and the movie title go, but if you only have a limited amount of time and are more interested in getting a taste of many places than exploring one city or country in depth, a well-constructed package tour will minimize your travel time and costs. The operator will arrange for all plane, rail, motorcoach and other transportation, transfers wherever needed, well-versed tour guides and generally commodious accommodations. For those seeking rest and relaxation at one of Europe's numerous shoreline resort areas, packages offered by airlines, travel agencies or tour operators—and including transportation and hotel—are often cheaper than either would be if booked independently.

Package tour operators have the advantage of booking transportation, lodging and in some instances food for great numbers of people at what might be considered "wholesale" prices. Additionally, as a client of a tour operator, you can pretty well rest assured that all your reservations will be honored—hotel owners and airlines are reluctant to "bump" tour members for fear of alienating the operator, who virtually guarantees full flights and fully-booked rooms for extended periods, as one tour rolls into the next. (And if, by chance, your room isn't what you'd anticipated, voice your displeasure in a friendly manner at the tour operator's desk and/or to the concierge; even if a change isn't possible that day, the hotel will usually make every effort to improve your situation as soon as another room becomes available.)

Sometimes, package tours are also an excellent way to take advantage of a given city for a week or two at a time. Flight-plus-lodging for many one-city tours often works out to be less expensive than the flight alone would be if booked as a regular economy fare. Thus, even if you prefer arranging for accommodations at someplace other than those offered by the tour operator, and even if you have no intention of participating in any group sightseeing or other package activities, it may still be in your best interest to buy the entire package. Some packagers offer flights independent of lodging, but the savings are usually minimal.

European travelers are somewhat more accustomed to the notion of package tours than are Americans, for whom there is sometimes a stigma associated with the idea—as though only those who can't take care of themselves would ever leave the arrangements in someone else's hands. We can only stress that, within the limits of group transportation, you are as free as you would be in any other mode of travel. The price advantage for any budget traveler is almost always worth a few concessions in your scheduling, provided, of course, that you have such flexibility in the first place.

A good travel agent can make all reservations in advance for "GIT" (Group Inclusive Travel plans, which are built around transportation and lodging only) and "FIT" (Foreign Independent Travel, as it is known in the U.K.) travelers. In Europe there is sometimes a fee for these services; in the U.S. the fees—except for any necessary long distance telephone calls or other out-of-the-ordinary expenses—are almost always paid by the airlines, hotels and other businesses.

Traveling independently allows for greater freedom than does tour travel, but it is also almost always more expensive. For example, booking all the same travel and lodging arrangements as a packager will cost the individual (or couple or family) *at least* 20% more—and often much more than that—than it will cost the operator. On the other hand, you might prefer staying at pensions or bed and breakfasts rather than at more formal hotels; if you use this method to follow the same route as a tour might take, your final cost could be the same, but don't forget that there is a considerable tradeoff between the charm and intimacy of simple settings and such hotel services as telephones or televisions in the room, the availability of a concierge and the like.

The truly free-spirited traveler may prefer making no advance reservations at all—might want to hop onto the first available flight as a standby, regardless of where it's going, and follow his or her nose thereafter. That's an extreme, but it too can be a viable option. It is a good idea to have a first night's lodging booked ahead, particularly after a wearying transatlantic flight that leaves you at one of the world's busiest capitals.

One of the keys to successful budget traveling is to avoid situations where, because you're tired and wornout, you succumb to the temptation of the first available bed— which invariably costs twice what you had allotted for a room.

Throughout Europe, however, the best starting point for accommodations for those who have just arrived in town are the information kiosks at rail, ship and air terminals. The people who man these booths will know the availability of rooms at hotels, hostels, pensions and even private homes. During peak tourist periods (Oktoberfest in Munich, the summer music festival in Salzburg, etc.) they may be forced to find you someplace some miles from your desired destination, but to the independently-minded traveler that itself is one of the challenges (and rewards) of going on your own. The only time when this is especially difficult—and sometimes *verboten* (not to mention interdict)—is when traveling in Eastern Europe, where it is frequently necessary to possess reservations (and return tickets) in order to be admitted to a country in the first place.

Our recommendation. Unless you have been overseas several times already, or have a strong taste for adventure, select a package tour. Some packages are flexible enough to suit every taste—besides, you can always go off on your own for a bit and rejoin the tour as it leaves for the next city. "FIT"s can be expensive to arrange and freelance independent travel should be for those who either want to go without reservations altogether (not recommended during the summer months), stay more than one month, or have an itinerary and a special objective not available on some package tour.

SPECIAL INTEREST TOURS FROM THE U.S.

The specific details of Special Interest tours change just as much from year to year as do those of ordinary package tours. Here we give you an idea of the amazing variety of special interests catered to, and in many cases the main sources and specialists for tours in those fields. The current issue of the *Specialty Travel Index,* a directory of special interest travel, lists more than 150 activities worldwide: here are the ones that are both relevant to Europe and that tend to be stable over the years, together with the specialists to consult.

At first glance, special interest tours are likely to be more expensive than most budget-minded travelers have in mind. Once again you must balance your touring priorities against what your wallet will allow. Remember, though, that sometimes the tour operator's buying power will be better than yours, and that despite the seemingly high price tag, he may be getting you a good deal. With opera tours, for example, good seats are generally part of the package, and these are often difficult to secure, let alone at a discount. Therefore, we suggest sitting down with a travel agent and comparing what it would cost to do similar specialized tours on your own as against the organized packages listed below.

In seeking specialized advice remember that in many cases national airlines and tourist offices are your best places to start.

Archeology. Greatest interest centers on the Mediterranean, Aegean and Near East, with *Maupintour,* Box 807, Lawrence, KS 66044; *Swan Hellenic Tours,* represented in the U.S. by Esplanade Tours, 581 Boylston St., Boston MA 02116; and *Far Horizons,* Box 1529, 16 Fern Lane, San Anselmo, CA 94960, among the specialists. There is also a considerable amount of archeology in Britain, but tours for it originate there rather than in the U.S. Consult either Fodor's volume on Great Britain or the British Tourist Authority.

Art. Literally all of Europe will be of note, with the Balkans, Soviet Union and Turkey increasingly coming into their own in the tour repertory, and with Belgium a treasure house that has not been entirely appreciated so far. *Swan Hellenic Tours* is probably the leading art tour operator, with about 30 different offerings that cover such lesser known areas as Albania, Crete, and Sicily as well as more commonly visited sites. *Maupintour's* Flemish Art Treasures concentrates on the masterpieces of Belgium and the Netherlands.

Biking. Seeing Europe on two wheels is not only great fun, but it can be quite economical. If, however, your preference is for gourmet meals and fine lodgings, many tours take the high (deluxe) road. *Bicycle France Ltd.,* 2104 Glenarm Place, Denver, CO 80205, specializes in one country, France. Others, such as *Forum Travel International,* 91 Gregory Lane, #21, Pleasant Hill, CA 94524; *Country Cycling Tours* 140 W. 83rd St., New York, N.Y. 10024; and *Butterfield & Robinson,* 70 Bond St., Suite 300, Toronto, Ontario, M5B 1X3, go almost everywhere. Cyclists ride an average of 25–35 miles a day and are followed by a support van, or "sag van", which transports gear and weary cyclists. Meals, accommodations, guides, and baggage handling are included.

Golf. You can play golf just about anywhere these days, and we suggest that in addition to the obvious choice of Scotland, Ireland is extraordinarily well equipped for golfers—with 20-odd courses in and around Dublin alone. Golf in Scandinavia has made rapid strides in recent years and there are now almost 200 courses in Sweden alone, most in the southern part of the country. Portugal's Algarve area is an up and coming golf center and Greece has good courses in Glyfada (15 miles outside Athens), Rhodes, Corfu, and Pórto Carrás.

There are a lot of package deals for golfers on offer—many of them budget ones. For Ireland, there are those by *Lismore Travel,* 106 E. 31st St., New York, N.Y. 10016; and by *Aer Lingus* with various operators. *B.T.H. Holidays,* the U.S. representative of the British Transport Hotels chain, offers tours in Ireland, England, Scotland, and Wales, 185 Madison Ave., New York, N.Y. 10016.

Hang Gliding. Those wishing to get the hang of this testing and exciting sport can practice 1000 meter glides down into the valleys of the Black Forest. Lessons, equipment, accommodation and, of course, insurance can all be obtained in advance from *Drachenflugschule Schwaebish-Alb,* Hartwaldstrasse 83, 700 Stuttgart 50, West Germany. For other parts of West Germany, contact the *Deutscher Aero Club,* Lyoner Strasse 16, 600 Frankfurt, West Germany.

Horseback Riding. In Spain you travel into the mountains, in Hungary across the plains around Lake Balaton, in Iceland across spectacular landscapes and in Ireland around castles or formal riding schools. Details from the *Irish Tourist Board* (757 Third Ave., New York, N.Y. 10017), and *IBUSZ Hungarian Travel Company,* 1 Parker Plaza, Ft. Lee, N.J. 07024.

Music and Drama. The major festivals are listed in a calendar a little later on, but it is worth noting here that between May and October there are about 45 major music festivals in Europe, and about 70 others of various proportions. Many of them sell out well in advance, so it is wise to plan ahead.

Dailey-Thorp Travel Inc., 315 W. 57th St., New York, N.Y. 10019 (tel. 212/307–1555), runs tours to such major cultural centers as Vienna, Budapest, Munich, Salzburg, Bayreuth, London and Edinburgh as well as many others. They offer a wide variety of tours, particularly emphasizing opera. All accommodations are deluxe, seat reservations the best. Most tours are about 2 weeks. Although this may not sound "budget", it is worth investigating.

TWA and *British Airways* offer theater packages to London; while *Keith Prowse,* 234 W. 44th St., New York, N.Y. 10036, can procure prime theater tickets, but does not handle travel arrangements.

Nature and Ecology. Offerings in this area tend to be very specialized and to change greatly from one year to the next, with destinations in Europe only a small part of what is available. They are rarely for budget travelers. Chances are that if your interests are here you belong to some professional or hobbyist societies; check their publications for current tour offerings. *Swan Hellenic (Esplanade Tours* in the U.S.) has botanical expeditions to the Po Valley and the Dolomite region of Italy, and *Travel Plans International,* Box 3875, Oak Brook, IL 60521, will custom-design tours for specific nature interests in Europe.

Pilgrimages. Your own minister, priest or rabbi is likely to have announcements of pilgrimages being organized for his own sect or denomination, but in addition we suggest *Travelink Tours International,* 401 S. Milwaukee Ave., Wheeling, IL 60090; *Sky Harbor Tours,* Box 297, New Lebanon, N.Y. 12125; and *Fatima Travel,* 360 Belvidere Ave., Washington, N.J. 07882.

Singles. More and more people of all ages and social situations are choosing to travel by themselves. The great disadvantage is the punishing extra expense of the single supplement, a surcharge that can run up to as much as 50% above the basic price of the trip. Several travel agencies now specialize in finding ways to beat the extra expense and to introduce people of similar tastes and interests. The largest is *Gramercy Travel System, Inc.,* 401 Theodore Frend Ave., Rye, N.Y. 10580, with its *Singleworld Tours* (914–967–3334). Some others are: *Trafalgar Tours,* 21 E. 26th St., New York, N.Y. 10010 (tel. 212–689–8977 or 800–854–0103); *Travel Mates,* 49 W. 44th St., New York, N.Y. 10036 (212–221–6565); *Travel Companion Exchange,* Box 833, Amityville, N.Y. 11701 (516–454–0880).

Another possibility is *Club Méditerranée,* with its own year-round "summer villages" all over the Mediterranean, Near East, North Africa, France and Switzerland. Tours include transfers, double occupancy rooms (they'll assign roommates arbitrarily), all meals, wine, sports facilities and entertainment. For an untrammeled holiday Club Med is hard to beat—the organization hails its system as a new way of life, and it may well be. European packages are available at Puerto Maria in Spain, Porto Petro on Mallorca, Corsica, Corfu, and Pompadour in central France (an equestrian village). There are Club Med villages throughout Europe, some rather primitive, others more elegant.

Club Med ski resorts are located in St. Moritz, Chamonix, Villars, Engelberg, Leysin, Cortina, Superbagnères, Val d'Isère, Tignes and Serre Chevalier, Livigno and Zinal. Except for St. Mortiz and Chamonix, only French is spoken in all ski villages. The two exceptions are bi-lingual (English).

Check with your travel agent about a Club Med trip. Club Med villages are also located in Bulgaria, Morocco, Tunisia, Egypt, Israel, Turkey, Romania, Greece, Yugoslavia, Ivory Coast, Italy, Switzerland, Spain, Austria and France.

Skiing. Best to check the national airlines going where you wish to go—*Swissair, Air France* and others offer outstanding values that include air fare, accommodations and transfers to resorts: ski passes are usually extra.

Winetasting and Gourmet Foods. This, too, we must admit is not usually "Budget" touring. The *German National Tourist Office,* 747 Third Ave., New York, N.Y. 10017 can put you in touch with the Wine Seminars that are now available in some of the principal centers of the Rhine-Moselle wine country of Germany. Air France, Swissair, and Alitalia sometimes run wine and gourmet tour packages too, but these are not offered consistently from year to year.

Sampling the food and wine of a region is one of the very happiest ways of wandering with a purpose. You can meander through the countryside, stopping here for a glass, there for lunch, and gradually become an expert.

SPECIAL INTEREST TOURS FROM BRITAIN

Anchors Aweigh. The Norwegian Coastal Voyage, a coast-hugging journey from Bergen, Norway, up to the North Cape beyond the Arctic Circle in the land of the Midnight Sun, is a truly spectacular cruise. June departures are best (but also most costly—Nov. and Dec. see a significant price-drop, and an even more significant decrease in the daylight hours), and the cruise usually lasts 11 days. To give an idea of cost, a mid-September voyage in an inside cabin with bunks and washbasin starts at £540 per person from Bergen, £825 per person including flight from Gatwick or Manchester. For details, *Fred Olsen Holidays,* Crown House, Crown St., Ipswich IP1 3HB (tel. 0473–233022). Book a long time in advance.

Art and Archeology. Long the leaders in this field are *Swan Hellenic Art Treasures Tours Ltd.,* 77 New Oxford St., London WC1A 1PP (tel. 071–831 1616). The company offers a series of tours, complete with guest lecturers, taking in some of the most glorious parts of Europe's heritage—though they don't come cheap. Not all holidays follow the beaten track; for example, there is a 14-day tour of the Italian hill towns from £1865, and visit to Romania and the Danube Delta (15 days from £985).

Among the other U.K. operators specializing in painting and art appreciation are *Artscape Painting Holidays,* Artists' Home Supplies Ltd., Units 40/41 Temple Farm Industrial Estate, Southend-on-Sea, Essex SS2 5RZ (tel. 0702–617900). Choice of centers varies from year to year, but could include Bruges (a week from £379) or Italy, Spain, Crete, or Provence, as well as a number of U.K. locations. *Prospect Music and Art Tours,* 10 Barley Mow Passage, Chiswick, London W4 4PH (tel. 081–995 2163), offer a nine-day trip to Umbria and the Marshes from £750 (price includes bed, breakfast, and six dinners), and five days in Paris for students of 19th-century Paris (from £395, including bed, breakfast, and one dinner).

Castles and Gardens. Within Britain, there is a wide choice of coach holidays to the country's gardens and stately homes. *Prospect Music and Art Tours.* (see above) have a three-day excursion to the castles of Yorkshire from £160 (half-board), as well as various three- and four-day Country Houses Explorations (from £180 half-board).

Horseback Riding. *Cavalry Tours,* 14 Cromwell Crescent, London SW5 9QW, (tel. 071–602 8433), offers escorted packages for *experienced* riders to destinations in Italy, Spain, France, Portugal, Austria, and Hungary. A week's riding in the Dordogne in France, for example, costs £799, which, though not inexpensive, includes the flight from London and fullboard accommodations. In Spain, riding holidays in the mountains south of Granada are organized by *Ventura Holidays,* Apartado 21, Orgiva (Granada), Spain. U.K.-based riding holidays are naturally less expensive. *Northumbria Horse Holidays,* East Castle, Annfield Plain, Stanley, Co. Durham (tel. 0207–235354), are one of the biggest operators in the U.K., and cater for all age groups and levels of proficiency, with fully inclusive packages starting at £115. The *Youth Hostels Association,* Trevelyan House, 8 St. Stephen's Hill, St. Albans, Herts AL1 2DY (tel. 0727–45047), offers seven-day trail rides in the Black Mountains (Wales) from £185, and in the Yorkshire Dales from £219. Pony-trekking trips for ages 12–15 start at £199. Prices are fully inclusive.

Motor Racing. Specialist in the U.K. for trips to all the major Continental championship grands prix are *Page & Moy,* 136–140 London Rd., Leicester LE2 1EN (tel. 0533–552521).

Music. *Prospect Music and Art Tours* (see Art and Archeology, above) offers music and opera holidays to many cities throughout Europe and the United Kingdom.

Naturism. The popular place to take off your clothes is along Yugoslavia's sunny Dalmatian coast. *Yugotours,* 150 Regent St., London W1R 6BB (tel. 071–439 7233) have a number of half-board packages including flights and accommodations. Reckon on from £148 (seven days) and £190 (14 days) in the low season, and £225, £312 in high season. Largest and most popular of the resorts used by *Peng Travel,* 86 Station Road, Gidea Park, Essex RM2 6DB (tel. 04024–71832), is at Cap d'Agde in the south of France, where you can soak up the sun for £148 (seven days) or £198 for two weeks (prices are per person for two people traveling by rail and sharing self catering accommodations).

TRAVEL DOCUMENTS

Passports

Americans. Major post offices throughout the country are now authorized to process passport applications; check with your local post office for the nearest one. You may also apply in person at U.S. Passport Agency offices in various cities; addresses and phone numbers are available under governmental listings in the white or blue pages of local telephone directories. Applications are also accepted at most county courthouses. Renewals can be handled by mail (form DSP-82) provided that your previous passport is not more than 12 years old. In addition to the completed application (form DSP-11), new applicants will need:

1. A birth certificate or certified copy thereof (giving your name, date and place of birth, and showing clearly the seal and signature of the registrar of births) or other proof of citizenship;
2. Two identical photographs 2 inches square, full face, black and white or color, on nonglossy paper, and taken within the past six months;
3. $35 for the passport itself, plus a $7 processing fee if you are applying in person (no processing fee when renewing your passport by mail). For those under 18 the cost is $20 for the passport, plus a $7 processing fee.
4. Proof of identity that includes your signature and a current photo, such as a driver's license, employment ID card, copy of an income tax return, previous passport, governmental ID card.

U.S. passports issued after Jan. 1, 1983 are valid for 10 years; passports issued for those under 18 are valid for five years only. You should allow a month to six weeks for your application to be processed, but in an emergency, Passport Agency offices can have a passport readied within 24–48 hours.

If you expect to travel extensively, request a 48- or 96-page passport rather than the usual 24-page one. There is no extra charge. Record your passport's number and date and place of issue in a separate, secure place. When you have pictures taken for passports, have extra copies made, especially if you plan to travel extensively. You'll need photos for your International Driver's License and for visas for Poland, Hungary and Czechoslovakia. The loss of a valid passport should be reported immediately to the local police and to the Passport Office, Dept. of State, 1425 K St. N.W., Washington, D.C. 20524; if your passport is lost or stolen while abroad, report it immediately to the local authorities and apply for a replacement to the nearest U.S. embassy or consular office.

Britons. Apply for passports on special forms obtainable from your travel agency or from the main post office in your town. The application should be sent to the Passport Office in your area (as indicated on the guidance form) or taken personally to your nearest main post office. It is advisable to apply for your passport 4–5 weeks before it is required, although it will be issued sooner if you call at the office in person. The regional Passport Offices are located in London, Liverpool, Peterborough, Glasgow and Newport. The application must be countersigned by your bank manager, or by a solicitor, barrister, doctor, clergyman or Justice of the Peace who knows you personally, or by someone who has known you for a number of years. You will need two photos. The fee is £15. A larger, 94-page passport can be obtained for £30.

British Visitor's Passport. This simplified form of passport has advantages for the once-in-a-while tourist to most European countries (Yugoslavia and Eastern European countries presently excepted). Valid for one year and not renewable, it costs £7.50 at press-time. Application may be made at a local post office (in Northern Ireland at the Passport Office in Belfast); you will need identification plus two passport photographs—no other formalities.

Canadians. Canadian citizens living in Canada may obtain application forms for passports at any post office or passport office; these are to be sent to the Bureau of Passports, External Affairs, Ottawa, Ont. K1A OG3 with a remittance of $25, two photographs, a guarantor, and evidence of Canadian citizenship. You may apply in person to the regional passport offices in Edmonton, Halifax, Montreal, Toronto, Vancouver or Winnipeg. Canadian passports are valid for five years and are non-renewable.

Visas

Of the 27 countries covered in this guide, the following require a visa from **American** and **Canadian** citizens: Albania, Andorra, Bulgaria, Czechoslovakia, France, Hungary, Monaco, Poland, Romania, and Yugoslavia (in Romania and Yugoslavia you get a free visa on arrival). **British** citizens from the United Kingdom must have visas for Albania, Czechoslovakia, Hungary, Poland and Romania (issued on arrival but sometimes, as in Romania, with some delay).

Potential visitors to Eastern European countries should ask their passport agency to provide them with the addresses of consular offices of the countries they intend to visit in order to check on last-minute details concerning documentation, though visa regulations are considerably eased in some of these countries. It is often much easier to get visas in Europe than in North America. Vienna is a particularly good place for this.

Commonwealth members sometimes require visas where United Kingdom "patrial" residents do not. Visas may usually be procured through the consulates of the countries you wish to visit, either in your country or abroad.

In order to visit certain Eastern European countries, you must plan in advance and often pay that way too. To obtain your tourist visa, you'll have to make all your hotel reservations, paying ahead for your entire stay. You will also be required to pre-pay meals, and guide and interpreter services, private cars or buses and theater tickets. You make this pre-payment to the accredited travel agent in your country acting for the national tourist bureaus. Usually they will also secure your visa. Check with your travel agent for more details.

General warning: Refusal of entry may occur (no appeal possible) if the Immigration Officer isn't happy about the amount of money you are carrying or if you don't have a valid ticket out of a country. You've got to prove that you can support yourself or you're not admitted into the country.

Other Documents

American Residents. If you are an alien (as opposed to a permanent resident), you'll need *Treasury Sailing Permit,* Form 1040C, or the shorter Form 2063. This certifies that your Federal taxes have been paid. Apply to your District Director of Internal Revenue for this. You will have to present: 1) blue or green alien registration card; 2) passport; 3) travel tickets; 4) filed 1040 forms for the last two years; 5) W-2 forms for the most recent full year; 6) most recent current payroll stubs or letter; and 7) receipts to verify your tax returns. Check to be sure this is all! Noncitizens who expect to remain abroad longer than one year will have to have a *reentry permit.* Apply for it in person, six weeks prior to departure, at the nearest office of the Immigration and Naturalization Service, or by mail to the agency headquarters, Washington, D.C.

International Driving Permit. Issued by the American Automobile Association, 1000 AAA Drive, Heathrow, FL 32746, and affiliated auto clubs. You'll need the form plus two passport-sized photos (signed on the back), a valid U.S. driver's license, and $10. The *International Driving Permit* is good for one year from its date of validation. Most European countries accept your usual driving license, but best take this international permit, in case. Note: you do *not* have to belong to AAA.

Certificate of Registration for Personal Effects Taken Abroad. For registering your previously bought foreign goods, such as cameras, so that you can get them *back into the U.S.,* without paying duty. This can be done at the customs office at the airport prior to departure.

International Student Identity Card. Indispensable for the Budget Traveler. For details, see the section on Youth Travel.

HEALTH

Unless you're allergic to garlic you are just as safe in Europe as you are in the U.S. or Britain. Water is generally safe. In some southern countries, stay with mineral water, coffee, tea, soft drinks and beer. Food is as safe as it looks or as you see it handled. Generally speaking, only independent travelers going off into unknown territory—a really under-developed Greek island or a village in North Africa or eastern Turkey—need worry about the food.

Glasses. If you wear them, bring along an extra pair. You might wish to carry a photocopy of your prescription with you.

Those with diabetes, people who are allergic to penicillin or other common drugs, and those with a rare blood type should wear a tag or bracelet or carry a wallet card indicating this. *Drugstore items* are commonly available, often in the same brands as in the U.S. or U.K. *Prescription medicines,* however, can be obtained with your home prescription only rarely. If you take a prescription medicine regularly, bring enough to last the trip. If you have any kind of medical problem you will find it useful to have a Medical Passport, containing forms to be filled out by you and your doctor, giving a detailed up-to-date record of your medical history.

Medical Attention. Your hotel management will generally know the name of a local doctor who speaks English. The *International Association for Medical Assistance to Travelers, Inc.* (IAMAT), 417 Center St., Lewiston, N.Y. 14092, or 40 Regal Rd., Guelph, Ontario N1K 1B5, makes available a free list of English-speaking doctors throughout Europe. Donations are solicited to promote the organization's educational projects. In Europe IAMAT has an office at: 57 Voirets, 1212 Grand-Lancy-Geneva, Switzerland.

Comprehensive medical insurance is available from *Travel Assistance International* and *Europ Assistance;* see "Vacation Travel Insurance" on page 3.

British public health services are free, even for tourists, but not for long-term treatment. In Scandinavia you can get an inoculation (smallpox) free.

Students can get special insurance at bona fide student travel organizations (those operating under the aegis of the ISTC).

Health Certificates

Not needed for entry to any European country covered in this book. However, any country may demand vaccination certificates periodically and temporarily. Best check in advance of your trip.

Rabies. Being an island, Britain is one of the few rabies-free areas in the world, and intends to stay that way. Dogs, cats, and other warm-blooded animals arriving from abroad must be put in quarantine for six months. Persons attempting to smuggle pets into Britain face huge fines and up to one year's imprisonment, and their pets will be destroyed.

HANDICAPPED TRAVEL

One of the newest, and largest, groups to enter the travel scene is the handicapped, literally millions of people who are in fact physically able to travel and who do so enthusiastically when they know that they can move about with safety and comfort. Generally these tours parallel those of the non-handicapped traveler, but at a more leisurely pace, with everything checked out in advance to eliminate all inconvenience, whether the traveler happens to be deaf, blind or in a wheelchair.

For a complete list of tour operators who arrange such travel, send an SAE to the *Society for the Advancement of Travel for the Handicapped,* International Office, 26 Court St., Brooklyn, N.Y. 11242; or become a member of this nonprofit organization for $40 a year, or $25 for senior citizens and students, and receive a newsletter and updates on trips for the handicapped. One publication giving valuable information about facilities for the handicapped is Louise Weiss' *Access to the World: A Travel Guide for the Handicapped,* published by Henry Holt & Co. It can be ordered through your local bookstore. This book covers travel by air, ship, train, bus, car, recreational vehicle; hotels and motels; travel agents and tour operators; destinations; access guides; health and medical problems; and travel organizations. Another major source of help is the Travel Information Service, Moss Rehabilitation Hospital, 12th St. and Tabor Road, Philadelphia, PA 19141. Another helpful contact is the *Information Center for Individuals with Disabilities,* 27–43 Wormwood St., Boston MA 02210, which publishes "Tips on Planning a Vacation," with information on renting automobiles, driving your own car if you have a disability, buses, trains, hotels and restaurants, travel insurance, travel companions, medical preparations, and a list of books of interest to the handicapped traveler.

From the U.K.: *The Air Transport Users' Committee,* 2/F, Kingsway House, 103 Kingsway, London WC2B 6QX, publishes a very useful booklet for the disabled traveler entitled *Care in the Air,* free of charge.

The *Royal Association for Disability and Rehabilitation* (RADAR), 25 Mortimer St., London W1N 8AB, publishes several titles of interest, among them *Holidays and Travel Abroad,* which covers 45 countries (£3 including postage and packing),

Holidays in the British Isles (£4.50 including postage and packing)—both of them available from RADAR or W.H. Smith—and *Motoring and Mobility for Disabled People* (£5 including postage), which covers just the U.K.

RADAR also stocks many Access booklets (not to be confused with other guide books bearing the same title). These give details of accommodations, restaurants, theaters and other tourist attractions offering facilities for the handicapped holiday-maker throughout Europe—and, in the case of the *Brittany* guide, of access to beaches, too. Titles currently in print include the *Channel Ports, Jersey,* and an extensive *London* (new edition 1989). Write (address above) for a complete list of titles carried.

Free advice and information on travel within Britain and on the Continent is available to the disabled from *Holiday Care Service,* 2 Old Bank Chambers, Station Rd., Horley, Surrey RH6 9HW (tel. 0293–774535).

PRACTICAL BAGGAGE TIPS

Always pack your passport separately. Do the same with money (both travelers' checks and some local currency to use upon arrival) and any medications you may need, and have them readily available, preferably on your person. Take along copies of all medical prescriptions, including glasses, in case you need a refill or replacement. Pack film separately or in special lined bags (for example, *Filmashield*) for protection against airport-security X-rays.

Don't buy cheap luggage. Borrow if you must, but have bags whose construction and locks you can trust. Never leave your luggage unlocked anywhere, anytime. Airlines will not take luggage that is not tagged with your name and home address. Put on your destination address as well, with dates of arrival and departure, in case your bags go astray and have to be forwarded. Put your identification inside, too; special stickers are free from any airline. Remove all old tags; they just confuse things. Near the handle put a piece of some bright-colored tape to help pick out your bag from all the similar models on your plane, train, or bus.

With porters very thin on the ground, it is wise to have two small bags rather than one large one. This will mean an evenly distributed load when you are forced to carry them for any distance.

At airports, watch to be sure that your bags go on the conveyor belt, and keep your stubs until you have carefully compared the numbers; those stubs are your receipts. Lost luggage must be reported within four hours after arrival. Remember that the carrier's liability is limited, so carry extra baggage insurance if you need it. It's available from travel agents.

If your baggage is oversize on your return trip, get the rates for shipping the excess separately by Air Freight instead of paying the higher rates for excess baggage.

Whenever you can, on short sections of your trip, try to make do with just your on-flight bag. If you are on a weekend jaunt, this will save you having to wait around for hours to claim your baggage at the airport.

CONVERSION CHARTS

Simplified: 1 inch = 2.54 centimeters; 1 foot = 12 inches = 30.48 centimeters; 1 yard = 3 feet = 0.9144 meters.

1 ounce = 28.35 grams; 1 pound = 453.5924 grams. 2.2 pounds = 1 kilo.

1 U.S. gallon = 3¾ liters; 1 English gallon = 4½ liters.

Length		Weights	
centimeters	*inches*	*gram(me)s*	*ounces*
5	2	100	3.33
10	4 (under)	200	6.67
20	8 (under)	250	8.03
30	11¼	500	16.07
40	15¼	1 kilogram (kilo) = 2.2046 lbs.	
50	19¼		
1 meter = 39.37 inches			

Clothing

Although you may see several charts with comparative U.S.-British-Continental sizings, in our experience these are not truly standardized. Best take along a tape measure, or rely on the shop assistant's assessment (in the first place) of your sizing. Always try on a garment before purchasing: an apparently correct sizing may prove to have arm-holes too wide or too narrow, sleeves too long or too short. After all, each country sizes according to the average measurements and proportions of its nationals, just as in the States and Gt. Britain. Dress fabrics, usually 1 meter (100 cm.) wide.

Kilometers into Miles

This simple chart will help you to convert to both miles and kilometers. If you want to convert from miles into kilometers read from the center column to the right, if from kilometers into miles, from the center column to the left. Example: 5 miles = 8.0 kilometers, 5 kilometers = 3.1 miles.

Miles		Kilometers	Miles		Kilometers
0.6	1	1.6	37.3	60	96.6
1.2	2	3.2	43.5	70	112.3
1.9	3	4.8	49.7	80	128.7
2.5	4	6.3	55.9	90	144.8
3.1	5	8.0	62.1	100	160.9
3.7	6	9.6	124.3	200	321.9
4.3	7	11.3	186.4	300	482.8
5.0	8	12.9	248.5	400	643.7
5.6	9	14.5	310.7	500	804.7
6.2	10	16.1	372.8	600	965.6
12.4	20	32.2	434.9	700	1,126.5
18.6	30	48.3	497.1	800	1,287.5
24.8	40	64.4	559.2	900	1,448.4
31.0	50	80.5	621.4	1,000	1,609.3

Gallons Into Liters

Gallon	U.S. Liters	Gallon	Imperial (British) Liters
1	3.78	1	4.54
2	7.57	2	9.09
3	11.36	3	13.63
4	15.14	4	18.18
5	18.93	5	22.73
6	22.71	6	27.27
7	26.50	7	31.82
8	30.28	8	36.36
9	34.07	9	40.91
10	37.85	10	45.46

There are 5 Imperial (British) gallons to 6 U.S. gallons.

FESTIVALS AND SPECIAL EVENTS

The variety, quantity, and quality of Europe's festival, artistic and sports life are unequaled anywhere else in the world. From operas to wine-tasting, ballet to bull-fights, masses to motorcycle races, plus coronations, revolutions and newborn lambs—just about everything you can think of is celebrated, observed or commemorated somewhere, sometime, in these culturally varied and highly developed countries, each with its own history, traditions, customs, art, architecture, and special products.

There is far too much to list here completely, and such a catalogue would run to a thick volume in itself. France alone lists over 200 art, music, and folklore festivals each year, and that does not include sports events, trade fairs, or political and religious observances. But we can give you a taste of the kinds of fun, adventure and memories that Europe's rich and fascinating festival life holds for you as a visitor.

Where and when? The question of dates can be a nuisance, for the precise times of many of these events change from year to year. Political holidays have specific dates and are easy to plan for. A good example would be the French national holiday, July 14, commemorating the fall of the Bastille in 1789. Likewise for the birthdays of founding fathers, great patriots, and reigning monarchs. Religious holidays may vary or not; Christmas and saints' days are fixed, Easter is variable.

By and large, cultural events sprawl conveniently. For example, somewhere along the Yugoslav coast, there's a festival devoted to music, drama, folklore or all three, almost any time from June through September. Rome's July-August summer opera season is another example. The Baths of Caracalla are the world's largest stage; but if you want to see only *Aida,* with all those real horses, you have to choose your night. Thus, for a great many events it is difficult to give precise dates that can be valid from one year to the next.

The big Trade Fairs in summer and fall are in Paris, Leipzig, Hannover, Brussels, Copenhagen (for Scandinavian furniture, furs and fashions), and Frankfurt (for books); the Milan Fair is in April. There are flower festivals in Stuttgart, Istanbul, Nantes, and all over the Netherlands. Sports in Europe are year-round, from midnight golf in Norway to alpine high ballooning in Switzerland. There are a number of film festivals of various kinds other than those at Cannes and Venice. And to end it all with either a bang or a splash, in September the wine and beer festivals in Germany, Spain, Greece and Belgium culminate in Munich's famous Oktoberfest, a two-week bash that begins on the third Saturday in September.

Although many of the specific events referred to above happen to fall in the summer, which is the peak tourist season in Europe, remember that the festival calendar goes on all year. There are seasonal variations; skiing in the winter and yacht racing in the summer, for example, or harvest festivals in autumn and planting ones in the spring; but you will find a rich and varied choice whenever you go, and there is really no "off-season" that you should worry about. Of course, festival times are big business for local entrepreneurs, and make the life of the budget traveler less easy. But with careful planning and a sharp eye on the increased costs, you should get by comfortably. One hint is to stay in a smaller place outside the festival venue and travel in and out by local bus.

For more detailed listings see the Fodor individual country, city, and regional guides; for Europe there are currently 41 of these books covering all the important places in the entire continent, from Austria to Yugoslavia. For a fairly detailed overall listing for any current year, write to the *European Travel Commission,* 630 Fifth Ave., Ste. 565, New York, N.Y. 10111 (tel. 212-307-1200); and for the most detailed possible coverage of any individual country write to that country's national tourist office. Information about Europe's major music festivals may be obtained by writing to: *European Association of Music Festivals,* 122 rue de Lausanne, Geneva, Switzerland; or *Specialised Travel P.A. Ltd.,* 4 Hanger Green, London W5 3EL.

Though we have made every effort to insure the accuracy of the dates given below, there may be slight variations in any given year. Be sure to check again for any particular event when you make your plans and reservations.

January

Austria. Vienna Carnival *(Fasching)* season begins, continuing with gala festivities until Shrove Tuesday, 46 days before Easter. Mozart week, Salzburg. Exhibition of Christmas cribs and figurines in Ebensee (Upper Austria). Ski-jumping events.

France. International Boat Show, mid-January, Paris. Prix d'Amérique horse race, Paris. Festival du Film Fantastique, Avoriaz.

Germany. Carnival month, especially festive in Köln, Düsseldorf, Mainz and Munich, until Shrove Tuesday. International Boat Show, "BOOT", Düsseldorf, through first few days of February—world's largest boat show. International Green Week *(Grüne Woche),* Berlin, through first week in February. World Cup Downhill Ski-racing, Garmisch-Partenkirchen.

Great Britain. International Boat Show, Earl's Court, London.

Greece. Epiphany, nationwide, January 6; Blessing of Waters ceremony, especially impressive at Piraeus.

Iceland. National Theater of Foreign and Icelandic Drama, Reykjavik, through June.

Italy. La Scala opera season, Milan, through May. Epiphany celebrations (Jan. 6), nationwide.

Norway. Monolith Ski Race, Oslo.

Poland. "Golden Washboard" Traditional Jazz Meet, Warsaw.

Portugal. Gulbenkian Music and Ballet Festival.

Switzerland: Inferno Ski Race, Mürren. Vogel Gryff Festival, Basel. International Hot Air Balloon Week, Château-d'Oex-Vaud. Lauberhorn International Ski Races.

Turkey: Camel wrestling, Selçuk (Ephesus), mid-January.

February

Austria. Carnival continues with the Philharmonic and Opera gala balls and ends with *Heringsschmaus,* a dinner consisting of delicate fish dishes.

Belgium. Carnival of the Gilles, Binche.

Bulgaria. Trifon Zarezan, winegrowers' feast day, February 14.

France. Feast of Sainte Bernadette, Lourdes, February 18. Mardi Gras Carnival and the Battle of Flowers, Nice. Lemon Festival, Menton. Mimosa Festival, Cannes.

Germany. International Toy Fair, Nürnberg. Berlin Film Festival. Frankfurt Trade Fair. Black Forest Ski Marathon.

Great Britain. Cruft's Dog Show, Earl's Court, London, early February.

Holland. Carnival celebrations, seven weeks before Easter, in the provinces of North Brabant, Limburg, Gelderland and Overijssel. Celebration of five-day "Carnival in the South".

Hungary. Gypsy Festival, Budapest.

Iceland. Thorr: Food Festival nationwide.

Italy. Carnival at Venice and Viareggio. Folklore Festival, Agrigento.

Malta. Feast of St. Paul's shipwreck, February 10. Valletta Carnival.

Poland. Highland Carnival in the Tatra Mountains, Bukowina Tatrzańska. "Jazz on the Odra" Student Festival, Wrocław. Festival of Modern Polish Music, Wrocław.

Portugal. Carnival Festival, Loulé, Ovar and Estoril, Monday and Tuesday before Lent.

Sweden. Great Lapp Winter Fair, Jokkmokk.

Switzerland. Carnival, Luzern. Fasnacht Carnival, Basel. Snow Sculpture Contest, Hoch-Ybrig-Schwyz.

Turkey. Folkdance Festival, Ankara, late February.

Yugoslavia. Fest Film Festival, Belgrade.

March

Austria. Easter Festival, Salzburg. Annual Spring Fair, Graz, second week in March. Spring Trade Fair, Vienna. Haydn Festival, Vienna.

Belgium. *Rat mort* masked ball, Oostende. Religious processions, Veurne, Fridays.

Finland. Salpausselkä International Winter Games, Lahti. Lady Day Church Festival, Enontekiö. Ounasvaara International Winter Games, Rovaniemi.

France. International Contemporary Music Festival, Royan. Prix du Président de la République horse race, Auteuil, Paris. Paris opera season opens.

Germany. Munich Fashion Week. *Starkbier* (Strong Beer) Festival, Munich. Berlin Tourist Fair. International Trade Fair, Leipzig, March 12–15.

Great Britain. Ideal Home Exhibition, Earl's Court, London. Grand National horse race, Aintree, Liverpool, end of March. Oxford v. Cambridge University Boat

Race, Putney to Mortlake, London, end March or beginning April depending on tides.

Greece. Annunciation and National Holiday, March 25; military parades in major towns. Easter processions nationwide.

Holland. Keukenhof Flower Exhibition, Lisse, through mid-May. Amsterdam Art Weeks, cultural events (many free).

Hungary. Spring Festival, Budapest. International Tourist Exhibition, Budapest.

Ireland. St. Patrick's Week. World Irish Dancing Championships, Limerick.

Italy. Passion Play, Sezze Romano, Good Friday. Easter Sunday festivities, Rome, special blessing from Pope.

Malta. Freedom Day, March 31.

Norway. Holmenkollen Ski Festival and international ski competitions and events, Oslo. Easter Sami Weddings, Karasjok and Kautekeino. Interesting ceremonies followed by reindeer races.

Poland. Jazz Festival and International Festival of Student Theaters, Wrocław.

Portugal. *Feira de Março,* Aveiro: handicraft fair; music and dancing on boats in the Rias. Holy Week processions in Braga, and many other parts of the country, especially the North.

Romania. The Kiss Fair, Arad.

Spain. *Fallas* of San José, Valencia: carnivals, flower-decked floats and burning of effigies. Holy Week religious processions nationwide, but especially Seville. Major bullfights nationwide, Easter Sunday.

Sweden. Vasaloppet long-distance ski race from Sälen to Mora, Dalarna.

Switzerland. International Motor Show, Geneva. Swiss Industries Fair, Basel. Engadine Ski Marathon. Easter Festival, Luzern.

April

Austria. Viennale Film Festival, Vienna.

Belgium. International Fairs, Liège and Brussels, throughout April. Flanders Spring and Summer Music Festival, in various towns and cities, to mid-September.

Denmark. Numus Festival of contemporary music, Århus, end of April.

Finland. *Vapunaatto* (Walpurgis Night), April 30, student celebrations with bonfires and dancing to mark the arrival of spring.

France. Le Mans 24-Hour motorcycle race.

Germany. May Fair-Folk Festival, Mannheim. Walpurgis Night celebrations, Harz Mountains. "Flowering Baroque" garden show at Ludwigsburg Castle (through October). Frankfurt Fur Fair. *Leonhardiritt* equestrian procession, Fürth im Wald. Jazz Festival, Stuttgart.

Great Britain. Start of season at Royal Shakespeare Theater, Stratford-upon-Avon (until following January). International Folk Festival, Eastbourne. Oxford and Cambridge Boat Race, River Thames, in March or April depending on tides. London Marathon.

Greece. *Son et lumière* performances, Athens and Rhodes, April 1 through October 31.

Holland. Queen's birthday celebrations, April 30. Flower parade, Haarlem, April 30.

Iceland. Ski events.

Ireland. Irish Grand National horse race, Fairyhouse, Co. Meath. International Choral and Folk Dance Festival, Cork.

Italy. May Calends, Assisi, April 30 through May 1; medieval pageant welcomes return of spring.

Luxembourg. Octave Festival, religious celebrations dating back to 1628.

Poland. National Student Song Festival, Cracow.

Spain. Seville Fair.

Sweden. Walpurgis Night celebrations, nationwide, April 30.

Switzerland. International Choral Festival, Montreux. European Watch and Jewelry Fair, Basel. Sechselauten Spring Festival, Zürich. Annual J.S. Bach Festival, Schaffhausen.

May

Austria. International Music and Drama Festival, Vienna, late May through mid-June. Whitsun concerts, Salzburg.

Belgium. Cat Festival, Ieper. Golden Chariot Procession, Mons.

Bulgaria. Labor Day parades, nationwide, May 1. Day of Bulgarian Culture, parades with emphasis on youth and culture, May 24. International Trade Fair, Plovdiv. Festival of Humor and Satire, Gabrovo. Sofia Music Weeks, through June. Festival of Arts, Roman Theater, Plovdiv, through June.

Czechoslovakia. Prague Music Festival, through early June.

Denmark. End of May Carnival, Copenhagen.

Finland. *Vappu* (May Day) celebrations, May 1.

France. Bordeaux Festival of Music, Ballet and Theater. Festival of the Gypsies, Saintes-Maries-de-la-Mer, southern France. International Film Festival, Cannes, early May. French Open Tennis Championship, Paris. Theater Festival, Nancy. National Wine Fair, Mâcon. Joan of Arc Festival, Orléans, Rouen.

Germany. International Theater Festival, Wiesbaden. Annual Summer Festival, Bonn. Spring Folk Festival, Stuttgart. International Aerospace Exhibition, Hannover.

Great Britain. Brighton Festival, early May. Mayfest, Glasgow, early May. Glyndebourne Festival Opera, mid-May through mid-August. Royal Windsor Horse Show, early May. Chelsea Flower Show, London, late May. Pitlochry Festival Theater Season, Pitlochry, Scotland, May to October.

Greece. *Son et lumière* performances, Corfu and Rhodes, May 15 through September 30. Flower Festival, Edessa (Macedonia), lasts two weeks.

Holland. Commemoration of Liberation Day, May 5. National Windmill Day, May 12. Flag Day in the ports of Scheveningen, IJmuiden and Vlaardingen, with an exciting race back to port with the first new salted herring.

Hungary. International Trade Fair, Budapest. Film Festival, Miskolc, through June.

Ireland. Royal Dublin Society Spring Show, Dublin. Norman Festival, Cahir, Co. Tipperary. Pan Celtic Festival, Killarney.

Italy. Festival of Sant'Efisio, Cagliari, Sardinia, religious pageant with costume and special events, May 1–4. Maggio Musicale (opera, ballet, concerts, drama), Florence, through late June. Festival of the Ceri (folklore), Gubbio. *Inforiata* flower festival, Geuzano, Corpus Christi, May 30.

Luxembourg. Broom-Flower Festival, parades, pageantry and balls, Wiltz. Dancing procession in honor of St. Willibrord of Northumberland, Echternach.

Monaco. Grand Prix (for Formula One automobiles), May 23–26).

Norway. Midnight sun, North Cape, first day of the season with round-the-clock daylight, May 14. Bergen International Festival, music, drama, folklore and concerts at Grieg's home.

Poland. Chopin Music Concerts, Łazieuki Park, Warsaw; and Żelazowa Wola (Chopin's birthplace), through September. "Juvenalia" Traditional Student Carnival, Cracow. International Chamber Music Festival, Łancut. Festival of Contemporary Polish Drama, Wrocław. International Book Fair, Warsaw.

Portugal. Largest pilgrimage of the year, to Fatima, May 12–13. *Romaria* (country fair), Penha Longa, between Estoril and Sintra, Whit Monday. *Festa das Cruzes,* fair and fireworks, Barcelos.

Romania. Week of the Lads, Braşov.

Spain. Feast of San Isidro, major bullfights, Madrid. Horse Fair, Jerez de la Frontera. Whitsuntide pilgrimage to shrine of Virgen del Rocio, Almonte (Huelva).

Switzerland. Golden Rose TV Festival, Montreux. Annual folklore festival, Vevey.

Turkey. Festival of Ephesus, early May. Festivals of Silifke and Bergama (Pergamon), end of month.

Yugoslavia. Peasant Wedding, Plitvice. Belgrade Spring (pop and rock music).

June

Austria. Pageants, nationwide, Corpus Christi. International Youth Music Festival, Vienna. Styriarte Music Festival, Graz. Jazz Festival, Graz. Schubertiade, Hohenems. Bonfires, nationwide, Midsummer's Day.

Belgium. Ascension Day procession of the Holy Blood, May 9, Bruges. Annual Chamber Music Festival, Chimay. Flanders Festival, music, ballet, theater, through mid-September.

Bulgaria. Festival of Roses, Karlovo and Kazanlak. Varna Summer International Festival of Music, through July.

Czechoslovakia. Festival of Brass Music, Kolín. Folk Art Festival, Strážnice.

Denmark. Viking Festival, Frederikssund. Midsummer Eve (St. Hans Aften), bonfires and fetes, nationwide, June 23. International Organ Festival, Soro, every Wednesday through mid-September. Riverboat Jazz Festival, floating concerts on the lakes, Silkeborg.

Finland. Dance and Music Festival, Kuopio. Vaasa Festival (International Puppet Theater), Vaasa. Ilmajoki Music Festival (classical, light, folklore) Naantali Music Festival (chamber music), Jyväskylä Arts Festival, through July. Joensuu Song Festival. Midsummer celebrations, nationwide, June 25–26.

France. 24-Hour Endurance Race for sports cars, Le Mans. Tour de France cycling race begins. International Festival, Strasbourg. Marais Music and Theater Festival, Paris, through mid-July. *Son et lumière* performances start in Loire Valley châteaux, through August. Fêtes musicales in Touraine châteaux. Gascony Festival, Auch. Versailles Festival. Theater Festival, Provins. Music Festival, Sully-sur-Loire. Music, theatrical and literary folklore festival, Nohant. National Music and Dance Festival, Bellac. *Festival de l'Image,* Epinal. International Music Festival, Strasbourg. Music and Theater Festival, Lyon. Music Festival, Vienne. Theater Festival, Pau. Music, Theater and Dance Festival, Angers.

Germany. Mozart Festival, Wurzburg. European Music Weeks, Passau. Franco-German Folk Festival, Berlin. Pied Piper Festival, Hameln, through September. Film Festival, Munich. Ballet Festival, Stuttgart. Lower Rhine Music Festival, Köln. Kiel Week Yachting Regatta. Castle illuminations, with fireworks, Heidelberg, also July and September. Handel Festival, Karlsruhe. *Landshut Wedding 1475,* open-air historic play, Landshut, through July. Open-air summer concerts begin in many large cities.

Great Britain. The Derby and the Oaks horse races, Epsom. Royal Ascot horse race meet. Trooping the Color, London, official birthday of Queen Elizabeth. Wimbledon Lawn Tennis Championship, London, late June through early July. Festival of Music and the Arts, Aldeburgh.

Holland. Holland Festival, three weeks of opera, ballet, theater and concerts, Den Haag, Amsterdam and Rotterdam. International rose-growing competition, Westbrock Park, Den Haag. International yacht race from Harlingen to Terschelling.

Hungary. Beethoven Memorial Concerts, Martonvásár, through July. Film Festival, Miskolc. "Musical Summer", Györ, through July. Sopron Festival Weeks, through July. Chamber Music Festival, Veszprém, through July.

Iceland. National Independence Day celebrations, June 17.

Ireland. Irish Derby run at Curragh, Co. Kildare. Literary Festival, Dublin—Bloomsday. Irish Open Golf Championships, Dublin.

Italy. Festival of Two Worlds, opera, ballet, theater, concerts, Spoleto, through early July. Corpus Domini religious-historical procession, Orvieto. Venice Regatta.

Luxembourg. Ancient and Classic Automobile Meet. Remembrance Day, Ettelbruck. International music festival at Echternach and Luxembourg City, mid-June through mid-July.

Malta. Mnarja Folk Festival, June 29.

Norway. Midnight Cup Golf Tournament, Trondheim. Carnival, Oslo. Arts Festival, Harstad.

Poland. Art Festival, Cracow. Carnival on the Vistula River, Warsaw and Cracow. Festival of Folk Bands and Singers, Kazimierz. Organ Music Festival, Frombork. International Trade Fair, Poznań. Polish Song Festival, Opole. Midsummer "Wianki" celebrations, nationwide, June 23.

Portugal. International Fair, Lisbon. Feast days in Lisbon, Oporto, Vila Real and Braga: St. Anthony's (June 13), St. John's (June 23), St. Peter's (June 29). Agricultural Fair, Santarem. *Feira de S. João,* handicraft fair, folk music and dancing, Evora. Corpus Christi procession with mock fight between St. George and "Coca", symbolizing evil.

Spain. International Festival of Music and Dance, Granada, late June through early July. Corpus Christi processions, Toledo and Sitges.

Sweden. Midsummer celebrations, nationwide, June 21–22.

Switzerland. International Music, Theater and Art Festival, Zürich. Art Fair, Basel. *Wilhelm Tell* play, Interlaken, through September. High Alpine Ballooning Weeks at Murren.

Turkey. Rose festival, Konya, early June. Istanbul Festival, ballet, theater, concerts, through July.

Yugoslavia. International Jazz Festival, Ljubljana. Summer Festival, Opatija, through September. Zagreb Summer, through August.

July

Austria. Trade Fair, Dornbirn. Bregenz Festival, on floating stage on Lake Constance. Salzburg Festival, through August. Carinthian Summer, local open-air theater nationwide.

Belgium. International Music Festival, Bruges. *Foire du Midi,* Brussels. International Festival of Folk Dancing, Schoten. Bruges and Malines Carillon Festivals, through September. Cherry Festival, St. Truiden. Procession of the Penitents, Veurne.

Bulgaria. Song and Dance Festivals, Golden Sands (through August).

Czechoslovakia. Východná Folk Festival. Brno Grand Prix Motor Rally. Karlovy Vary International Film Festival (every two years, next in 1991). Bratislava Music Summer, through August.

Denmark. Rebild Festival marking American Independence Day, Aalborg and Jutland, July 4. Hans Christian Andersen Festival, Odense. Roskilde jazz, folk and rock festival. Copenhagen Jazz Festival. Copenhagen Summer Festival for young Danish musicians.

Finland. Pradznik Festivals, traditional Orthodox Church and folk festivals, through September, main event in Ilomaatsi in July. Aleksis Kivi Festival, Numijärvi. Bomba Festival Weeks, Karelian folklore, Nurmes. Opera Festival, Savonlinna. International Jazz Festival, Pori. Chamber Music Festival, Kuhmo. Folk Music Festival, Kaustinen.

France. Bastille Day, nationwide, July 14, best in Paris. International Festival of Music, Aix-en-Province. Bagpipe Great Celtic Festival, Quimper (Brittany). Avignon Festival. Festival Estival, Paris. Prades Music Festival. Jazz Festival, La Grande Motte and Nîmes. Corridas, Ales. *Festival de Folklore International,* Vaison-la-Romaine. International Music Festival, Gourdon. Lyric Festival, Orange. Ancient Music Festival, Saintes. International Regatta, Le Havre. Grand Prix de France, Le Castellat.

Germany. Wagner Festival, Bayreuth. Opera Festival and Schleissheim Palace concerts, Munich, through August. Opera Festival, Bregenz.

Great Britain. Henley Royal Regatta, Henley-on-Thames, early July. Llangollen International Musical Eisteddfod, Llangollen, North Wales, early July. Music Festival, Cheltenham. British Grand Prix (cars), Brands Hatch or Silverstone. Royal Tournament, Earl's Court, London, last 2½ weeks of July.

Greece. Athens Festival, opera, ancient drama, ballet and concerts, through September. Epidaurus Festival, ancient drama and concerts in antique theaters throughout the country. Wine Festival, Daphni, near Athens, through September.

Holland. International Organists' Competition, St. Bavo Church, Haarlem.

Hungary. Haydn and Mozart Concerts, Esterházy Palace, Fertöd, through August. Open-Air Opera and Drama Festival, Szeged. Bartók Choral Festival, Debrecen. Film Week, Siófok. Jazz Festival, Debrecen. Chamber Music Festival, Festetich Palace, Keszthely. International Equestrian Day, Szilvásvárad.

Italy. Opera at Baths of Caracalla, Rome; and at Arena, Verona, both through mid-August; and at Sferisterio (Macerata). Medieval horse race—the Palio—in Siena. Feast of the Redeemer, Venice.

Luxembourg. International Open-Air Theater and Music Theater Festival, Wiltz, through early August.

Norway. International Jazz Festival, Molde. International Sea Fishing Festival, Harstad.

Portugal. Festival of the *Colete Encarnado* (Red Waistcoat), bullruns through the streets, fireworks, suppers, Vila Franca de Xira. *Festa da N. Senhora do Carmo,* one of the largest fairs in the Algarve, processions, etc., Faro, July 16. *Festas da Rainha Santa,* processions in honor of St. Elizabeth of Portugal, funfair, dancing, Coimbra. *Romaria da Senhora,* processions, funfair, bullfights, Nazaré.

Spain. Running the bulls in Pamplona in honor of San Fermín. St. James's Day celebrations in Santiago de Compostela.

Sweden. Visby Festival in medieval cathedral ruin. Halsinge Hambo (a hambo dance competition with more than 1500 couples), Abra-Järvsö.

Switzerland. International Jazz Festival, Montreux. International Rowing Regatta, Luzern. Wrestling festivals, central Switzerland.

Turkey. Wrestling matches, Edirne. Folklore Festival, Bursa.

Yugoslavia. Dubrovnik Festival, music, drama, folklore, through late August. International Review of Original Folklore, Zagreb. Peasant Weddings, Galicnik, Bled, and Mohinj. Moreska Sword Dance, Korcula, Thursdays throughout the summer.

August

Austria. Operetta weeks, Ischl (near Salzburg) and on floating stage on Lake Neusiedl, Mörbisch. Palace and Park Concerts, Vienna.

Belgium. Flemish painting pageant, Koksijde. *Son et lumière* festival, Bruges.

Czechoslovakia. Chopin Music Festival, Marianské Lázne. Dvořák Festival, Karlovy Vary.

Denmark. Ronne Music Festival. Tonder Jazz and Folk Festival, south Jutland.

Finland. Music Festival, Turku. Organ Festival, Lahti. Tampere Theater Summer. Helsinki Festival of music, drama, and ballet, through mid-September.

France. Major parades and other celebrations, especially at Lourdes, Assumption Day, August 15. Napoleon's birthday celebrations, Corsica. National Show Jumping Competition, Brantôme. *Joutes Nautiques,* Agde. Music Festival, Cordes. Chamber Music Festival, Menton. Wine Fair, Colmar. Grand Prix horse racing, Deauville.

Germany. The Rhine in Flames, from Braubach to Koblenz, illumination of the castles and towns along the river. Open-air theater, Heidelberg. German Grand Prix (cars), Hockenheim (near Mannheim).

Great Britain. Edinburgh International Festival, mid-August for three weeks. Royal National Eisteddfod, Newport, Gwent, Wales, first week August. Three Choirs Music Festival, alternating between Gloucester (1989 venue), Hereford and Worcester.

Greece. National pilgrimage to the Aegean island of Tinos, Assumption Day, August 15.

Holland. Sneek Week, Sneek Friesland Regatta.

Hungary. Ethnic Folk Festival, Keszthely. Horse Show, Bugac Puszta. National Flower Festival, Debrecen. Summer Music Festival, Békéscsaba. Constitution and St. Stephen's Day, sporting events, water parade on the Danube, fireworks, Budapest, August 20.

Ireland. Dublin Horse Show. Birr Vintage Week, entertainment from the past. Connemara Pony Show. Puck Fair, Killorgin, Co. Kerry. Antique Dealers' Fair, Dublin. International Busker's Festival, Clonakilty.

Italy. Quintana historical pageant, Ascoli Piceno. Feast of the Redeemer, Nuoro. Final of the Palio, Siena, and parades next day. Venice Film Festival.

Luxembourg. Beer Festival, Clausen/Luxembourg City, mid-August. World Moto-Cross Meet, 500cc, Ettelbruck. Luxembourg City Kermesse, celebrated since 1340. Folkloric events.

Poland. International Song Festival, Sopot. Chopin Festival, Duszniki Zdrój.

Portugal. Music and Ballet Festival and craft fair at the Casino, Estoril. *Festas da Nossa Senhora da Agonia,* religious festival, fair, fireworks, Viana do Castelo. *Festas de Santa Barbara,* festival with local pauliteiros dance, Miranda do Douro. Bullfights and bullruns through the streets, Alcohete and Barrete Verde.

Spain. Mystery Play celebrating the Assumption, Elche, near Alicante, August 15. Semana Grande celebrations, fireworks, jazz, carnival, San Sebastián.

Sweden. Swedish–American celebrations, Stockholm and Växjö.

Switzerland. International Music Festival, Montreux, late August through early October. International Festival of Music, Luzern, mid-August through early September. *Fêtes de Genève* (festival with fireworks), Geneva. Yehudi Menuhin Festival, Gstaad. International Jazz Festival, Willisa-Luzern. Wrestling Festival, Canton Bern. Swiss National Day, August 1.

Turkey. Trojan Horse Festival, Çanakkale, second week in August. International Fair, Izmir, August 20 through September 20.

Yugoslavia. International Poetry Evenings, Struga. Alka, traditional equestrian event, Sinj.

September

Austria. Bruckner Festival, Linz. Autumn trade fairs, Vienna and Graz. Harvest and grape festivities in many villages. Opera, theater and concert season through June 30. Ars Electronica, Linz, September 12–16.

Belgium. Festival of Wallonia. International Music Festival, "September Nights", Liège. Beer Festival, Wieze.

Bulgaria. International Arts Festival, Plovdiv. Apollonia Arts Festival and International Plein Air of Marine Painters, Sozopol, through October.

Czechoslovakia. Znojmo Wine Festival. International Music Festival, Bratislava, through October. International Music Festival, Brno, through October.

Denmark. Royal Theater season starts, Copenhagen, September 1, ballet, opera and drama alternate. Arhus Festival Week of opera, ballet, concerts and art, second week in September. Holstebro Jazz Festival, Jutland, end of September.

Finland. Cultural Festival, Aland, Mariehamn.

France. Chamber music concerts, Royaumont château. J.S. Bach Festival, Mazamet. Berlioz Festival, Lyon. Music Festival, Biarritz and Côte Basque.

Germany. Beethoven Festival, Bonn. Berlin Art Festival, through October. International Horse Show, Aachen. German Wine Festival, Dürkheim. *Backfischfest* wine festival, Worms. *Oktoberfest* beer festival, Munich. Canstatt Festival, Stuttgart. International Radio and Communications Exhibition, Berlin.

Great Britain. Braemar Royal Highland Gathering, Scotland, first Saturday of month. International opera season, Covent Garden, London (through to following summer).

Greece. International Trade Fair, Thessaloniki, followed by Film Festival and Festival of Light Song. Demetria Festival of theater, music and ballet, through October.

Holland. Opening of Dutch Parliament by the Queen, September 20. International Show Jumping, Rotterdam.

Hungary. International Trade Fair, Budapest, September 22. Budapest Arts Weeks.

Ireland. Waterford International Festival of Light Opera. Oyster Festival, Galway.

Italy. Historical pageant, Venice. Saracen Joust, Arezzo. *Sagra Musicale Umbra,* Umbrian music festival, Perugia and other towns. Palio of Asti, pageant and race.

Luxembourg. Grape and Wine Festival, Grevenmacher and other towns in the Mosel valley.

Malta. Carnival commemorating end of Great Siege of 1565 and World War II, September 8.

Poland. International Festival of Contemporary Music, Warsaw. International Festival of Highland Folklore, Zakopane. Feature Film Festival, Warsaw. Oratorio and Cantata Festival, Wrocław. International Festival of Song and Dance Ensembles, Zielona Góra.

Portugal. Port wine grape harvest along the Douro river, late September to early November. Wine vintage festivals nationwide. *Romaria da Nossa Senhora dos Remedios,* processions, fair, fireworks, Lamego, September 3–4. Feira de S. Mateus, handicraft and agricultural fair, Viseu, first three weeks of September. *Feira de S. Mateus,* riding, bullfights, singing and dancing, Elvas. "New Fair", held since the 12th century, folk music and dancing, Ponte de Lima.

Romania. Folklore Festival, Bucharest.

Spain. Vintage Festival, Jerez de la Frontera. International Music Festival and celebrations of the Feast of the Merced, Barcelona, through October. International Contemporary Music Festival, Alicante. International Film Festival, San Sebastián.

Switzerland. Vintage festivals begin, Canton Neuchâtel.

Turkey. Cappadocian Grape Harvesting Festival, Urgup.

Yugoslavia. International Autumn Fair (science and technology), Zagreb. Belgrade International Theater Festival.

October

Austria. Styrian Autumn Festival, Graz, mid-October. *Salzburg Kulturtage.*

Czechoslovakia. Pardubice Grand Steeplechase.

France. The International Auto Show, Paris. Rosary Pilgrimage to Lourdes. Prix de l'Arc de Triomphe horse race, Longchamp, Paris. Corridas Film Festival, Montpellier.

Germany. International Film Festival, Mannheim. Vintners' Festival, Boppard, Koblenz and Neustadt. Frankfurt Book Fair. Berlin International Marathon.

Holland. Art and antique dealers' fair, Delft. *Herfstflora* fall flower show, Laren.

Hungary. Limestone Cave Concerts, Aggtelek. Sopron Vintage Days.

Iceland. Leif Ericson's Day (October 9), marking the discovery of North America.

Ireland. Dublin Theater Festival. Wexford Opera Festival. Dublin International Marathon Road Race, October 29. Kinsale Gourmet Festival, Co. Cork. International Jazz Festival, Cork.

Italy. Wine festivals, nationwide.

Norway. Opening of Parliament by King Olav V, Oslo.

Poland. International Jazz Festival and Jazz Jamboree, Warsaw.

Portugal. Folklore festival, Nazaré. Last big pilgrimage of the year, to Fatima, October 12–13. *Feira de Santa Iria,* lively traditional fair, Faro. *Feira do Outubro,* handicrafts, livestock, etc., Monchique.

Turkey. Art and Culture Festival, Antalya. Turkish Republic Day, October 28–29.

Yugoslavia. BEMUS Musical Festival, Belgrade.

November

Austria. St. Leopold's Day and Vintage Festival, Klosterneuburg, November 15. Schubertiade, Vienna. Antiques fair, Vienna.

France. International Dance Festival, Paris, through December. *Les Trois Glorieuses* (wine festivals), Nuits-Saint-George, Beaune and Meursault. Gastronomic Fair, Dijon. Santons Fair, Marseilles. Tour de Corse, automobile race, Corsica. International Food Fair, Dijon.

Germany. Jazz Festival, Berlin. Folk Festival, Hamburg. Carnival season begins, Rhineland, November 11. International Six-Day Cycle Race, Munich.

Great Britain. Lord Mayor's Show and Procession, London. State Opening of Parliament. London–Brighton Veteran Car Run, first Sunday of month.

Holland. Arrival of "St. Nicholas"; in Amsterdam he is welcomed by the mayor.

Italy. Feast of the Salute, Venice, November 21. Opera season begins, Turin, Parma, Bologna.

Portugal. São Martinho Horse Fair, Golegã, November 10–12.

December

Austria. "Silent Night, Holy Night" celebrations, 24.

Germany. Christ-Kindl markets with Christmas outdoor toy fairs, Nürnberg, Munich, Heidelberg, Rothenburg and Stuttgart. Christmas Fair, Nürnberg.

Ireland. Wren Boys Festivities, Co. Cork and Co. Kerry. Horse racing, Leopardstown.

Italy. La Scala opera season begins, Milan. Christmas masses in Rome's basilicas.

Portugal. Funchal Bay Festivities, Madeira, with fireworks on December 31.

Romania. Winter and New Year festivals with colorful costumes and masks in many rural areas, especially Sighetu Marmatiei (Maramures) and Vatra Dornei spa (Bukovina).

Sweden. Santa Lucia Day (December 13), Stockholm.

Turkey. Rites of the Whirling Dervishes, Konya, December 14–17.

GETTING TO EUROPE

BY AIR

The air lanes between the U.S.A. (and Canada) and Europe are the busiest intercontinental routes in the world with nearly forty airlines both on scheduled and charter services linking the two continents. Competition for passengers is accordingly extremely fierce, and fares therefore generally reasonable. But nothing can be guaranteed, so keep an eagle eye on what fares are available—check regularly with your travel agent—and remember that even in the peak of the summer (by some considerable margin the busiest, and hence most expensive, period to fly to Europe) there are nearly always bargains to be had if you are prepared to shop around. Never take the first fare offered.

In addition, be warned that although flights may be numerous and fares low, long-distance flying today is no bed of roses. Indeed the glamor of air travel, if it ever existed, is very much a thing of the past. Lines and delays at ever more crowded airports, perfunctory in-flight service and shrinking leg-room on board a giant jet with 400 other people, followed by interminable waits for your luggage when you arrive, the whole compounded by jet-lag and fatigue, make flying to Europe a process to be endured rather than enjoyed. These problems are every bit as bad on the major airlines as on the newer, cut-price operators. It is quite untrue to suggest that simply because an airline is expensive or has been in business for many years that it will be more comfortable, more efficient or more reliable than a budget airline like, for example, *Virgin Atlantic*. Some of the larger carriers can in fact be less convenient in that they fly to larger and busier airports—J.F.K. rather than Newark, for instance—which, by their very nature, are more crowded and thus less efficient.

But whichever airline you choose, there's really no point in expecting good service and comfort because you won't get them. Think of your flight simply as a means of getting from A to B.

Fares

The vast bulk of passengers fly by scheduled services, as all airlines offer varied fare structures on their routes aimed at different markets. There are still a number of charter services originating on both sides of the Atlantic, but these are in the minority. In all cases aircraft and their crews must meet the same U.S. Federal Government standards of maintenance, safety and reliability.

As to actual costs, fixed-date charter flights are usually slightly cheaper than on scheduled services although the margin is not always very big. Charters however often tend to "throw in" free wine and drinks, free in-flight entertainment etc., which have to be paid for on scheduled services.

In the economy fares section all airlines offer a choice of tickets. For the round trip the APEX fare is the best buy if you have definite fixed dates on which you want to travel. Bookable at least 21 days before travel there is usually a minimum length of stay of at least seven days on the other side of the Atlantic. Maximum stay can vary but is usually 6 months at most.

The number of APEX fares is limited on each flight so the earlier you book the better. It is also possible to book open-jaw tickets, which allow you to fly into one destination and back from another. This usually means utilizing the same airline for both flights. The cost is generally based on half the APEX fare to both destinations.

Most airlines also offer what has come to be known, rather euphemistically, as *Full fare economy* returns, which allow complete flexibility of arrangements and do not require advance booking. And you can change your plans with little notice either without any additional charge or only a small one. These fares are generally expensive, however.

For the average budget traveler we suggest that the APEX or fixed-date charter flights are the best buy, particularly so as you know exactly when you will travel both ways and at what cost.

Here are some approximate air fares for North Atlantic travel. All are estimates and should be taken only as an indicator. The prices are minimum and maximum, according to date. Be sure to check with your travel agent or the relevant airlines for the most up-to-date fares.

APEX (return) New York to London $500–$850 (approx)
Los Angeles to London $700–$950
Chicago to London $420–$850

Do not forget to allow for airport taxes, security and customs charges—around $30.

Children aged 2 to 11 years must occupy a separate seat and pay 50% of the adult fares, except in Standby where there is no reduction. Children under 2 not occupying a seat pay 10% of adult fare in all cases.

Fares are calculated on dates of departure east and west bound. These are *low* season in both directions November to March except over Christmas and New Year period; *shoulder* season—April and May eastbound (also June westbound), mid-August to end October eastbound (from mid-September only on westbound) and the Christmas and New Year holidays; *peak*—June–mid-August eastbound, July–mid-September westbound.

You will find some hints on how to deal with baggage under *Practical Baggage Tips.*

BY SEA

There are now very few transatlantic liners left in operation. The recently modernized—and extremely expensive—*QE2* operates the route from June to November, and during that time she also undertakes several cruises from the U.K. She normally makes nine round trips between New York and Southampton (with calls on most voyages at Cherbourg). It takes five days each way. The liner operates on the Atlantic as a two-class vessel but this division is largely reflected in the style of cabin and the food in the restaurant, most of the ship's other facilities being available to both classes.

Traveling on the QE2 is a great experience but, alas, expensive, costing from about $1,350 to $8,500 for a one way ticket, plus tips—not remotely a budget trip. Full information from *Cunard Line,* 555 Fifth Avenue, New York, N.Y. 10017.

The 15,000-ton Polish liner *Stefan Batory,* which sailed one round trip a month from May to October, has been taken out of service and no replacement had been announced at the time of going to press. For current information contact *McLean Kennedy Ltd.,* General Agents, U.S.A. & Canada, 410 St. Nicholas St., Montreal H2Y 2P5, P.Q.

Polish Ocean Lines operates weekly departures for its freighters between various North American east coast ports and France, Holland and Germany. A 28-day, uninterrupted round-trip is about $1,580; one-way is about $790. Children 6–12 go half-fare; those under 6 are not accepted. Contact *Gdynia American Line,* 39 Broadway, 14th floor, New York, N.Y. 10006.

The freight shipping companies are making more berths on their container ships available to passengers. But as the number of people carried is usually not more than 12, it is essential to book well in advance. It can take up to a year ahead to secure a berth. Costs are higher than going economy class by air, although you do get well fed for the eight to ten day voyage. For those on budget holidays however we would recommend air rather than sea travel.

But if you wish to know more about possible freighter trips send a stamped, self-addressed envelope to:

Pearl's Freighter Tips, PO Box 188, 16307 Depot Road., Flushing, N.Y. 11358.

TRAVEL IN EUROPE

EUROPE BY AIR

Although there is not the intensity of air services within Europe that there is in the U.S.A. the air network is much more extensive than is generally realized. Indeed most cities and large towns either have their own airport or are within no more than three hours' drive (generally much nearer) of an airport with scheduled services. The vast majority of services are by jet with some being operated by modern turbo-prop aircraft.

Most airlines in Europe are state-owned or at least have the state as a major stock holder. The U.K. is the exception to this where all the leading airlines, including the giant *British Airways,* are private organizations, fighting hard for profits and routes.

Taken over-all air fares within Europe are higher than in the U.S.A. But major efforts to get these made more reasonable are beginning to bear fruit. The introduction of excursion fares of various kinds (all involve restrictions of one kind or another) have been brought about on many routes such as London to Paris, Rome, Madrid, Amsterdam, Venice and Munich. Of greater significance is a major move to deregulate certain air routes—the upsurge in competition is already seeing a drop in air fares in parts of Europe. Air fares will not stabilize for some time to come, so check with your travel agent.

We strongly advise that if you plan to fly within Europe you check carefully first what tickets are available on the route (or routes) you have chosen. Do not accept the first figure given if it seems unduly high as often there are many special bargains available.

As fares are constantly changing we have decided not to give these in any detail (it would require many pages of the guide and much would be out of date by the time it was published) but instead just select a very few as examples. These are—

London to Paris—Least expensive on some off-peak flights is around £78–£84 (APEX) return.

London to Madrid—APEX fares range from £99–£174 return.

London to Venice—APEX fares range from £185–£216 return.

You may find a charter seat at lower cost to some destinations. These operate from Luton, Gatwick and Standsted airports (no charter to or from Heathrow) and you fly on holiday charter flights. They are, however, more restricted in number and flexibility. Charter flights with travel-only tickets are not valid to Greece.

Details of these flights can be obtained from travel agents in the U.K. or in the Continental countries where they originate. Along the same lines are charter tickets which also include "nominal" accommodation which you need not take up unless you wish. These also are cheaper than scheduled flights.

For up-to-date information on what cheap flights are available consult the small adverts in the national press (especially in the U.K. and London in particular) and also in various weekly magazines, particularly those giving information on entertainment and travel. These ads are inserted by "bucket shop" owners—that is entrepreneurs who sell cut price tickets. These are very much frowned upon by the registered travel agents and it could be that regulations governing them will be introduced. But for air travel bargains they are worth seeking out. However, some bucket shops are less than 100% reliable and it is always smart to seek out those that have been in business for some time. And don't hand over all the money until you see the ticket.

Students of course should always check with their own travel organizations and travel offices in universities and colleges. They are always up-to-the-minute with cheap fares applicable to the general student body.

Remember, too, that for journeys of around 250 miles and less in Continental Europe and the U.K. (except where cross-Channel and cross-North-Sea travel is involved) it is usually quicker and cheaper to take the train.

EUROPE BY RAIL

In the last couple of years, train travel in Europe, from Sweden to southern Spain and Ireland to Italy, has enjoyed substantial improvements in the realm of 2nd-class travel. Many countries have introduced modern rolling stock, much of it air-conditioned, all for the 2nd-class ticket holder. This has not just been restricted to the leading international express trains, but is also filtering through to semi-fast trains on secondary lines and to many commuter services. Indeed, the French *Trains à Grande Vitesse* (TGVs)—the world's fastest—British Rail's *High Speed Trains,* Swiss Railways' *Trains Interville,* Germany Railways' *Inter-City* expresses and the international rolling stock on many cross-frontier trains all offer standards of comfort and design which twenty years ago would have warranted the first class label.

Not all 2nd-class travel is of this standard—in some countries on the less important routes some of the older rolling stock trundles on, but it is now well in the minority—even in Italy, which of all the west European nations still has a substantial amount of vintage stock running.

If you have never traveled by train on the Continent or in Britain, you will be pleasantly surprised by what you find—with one major proviso. At peak holiday periods second class does get very busy indeed, especially on trains which do not have reservations—only accommodations. Several summers ago, one of our revisors stood for well over 200 kilometers in Italy on a very hot day—and he had a 1st class ticket.

The other thing which has improved greatly of late is the high speeds which now prevail on many express routes. In the vanguard of this is the previously mentioned French TGV service from Paris to Lyons and beyond, which links these two cities in two hours flat as compared to the previous four-hour trip—not bad at all for 450 kilometers (281 miles) traveling over long distances at 162 m.p.h. Even higher speeds are reached on the new TGV Atlantique line to Nantes and Bordeaux. And many other trains in France average 90 m.p.h. over long distances.

In Germany, too, there has been a speeding up of services while the Italian Railways have opened a further stretch of their fast *direttissima* line which will link Florence and Rome. Swedish Railways has stepped up the speed and reduced the time for their fast trains linking Stockholm with Gothenburg and Malmo. In Great Britain the High Speed Trains have been introduced on certain crosscountry routes such as Newcastle via Sheffield, Birmingham to Bristol and between Newcastle and Plymouth. All of these trains carry both 1st and 2nd class.

The TEE system has been swept away and replaced by a comprehensive new network of fast, air-conditioned express trains called Euro-City. These trains are open to both first- and second-class passengers, and most have full restaurant facilities. Book your reservation in advance.

By night there has also been a noticeable improvement for the 2nd-class passenger. The newest couchette coaches (these offer a simple form of bed, six to a compartment) are fully air-conditioned and remarkably quiet, while the Tourist Sleepers (two or three berths per cabin) are very comfortable indeed. The latter are admittedly more expensive, from $24–$64 a night (prices vary with distance) per berth while a couchette is around $14 a night (no matter what the distance).These are, of course, in addition to the rail travel ticket for the distance.

The sleeping cars (night trains carry both 1st- and 2nd-class carriages) belong either to the *Wagons-Lits* company (an international concern with many ramifications in the transport and tourist industries), to the railway itself (as in Great Britain), or to a railway-owned subsidiary (as in Germany). Many of the *Wagons-Lits* services, including all the international routes, are operated in pool under the marketing slogan *TEN* which stands for *Trans Europ Nacht*—or *Nuit,* or *Notte* depending on the country of origin.

Many trains in Europe carry dining or buffet cars or refreshment services. The traditional formal dining car is losing out largely to the buffet or cafeteria car for economic reasons. This is also good news for the budget traveler as a full meal in a dining car is expensive ($35 upwards) while a substantial snack can cost just half that. It is significant that expresses on comparatively short distances (e.g. 55 to 100 miles) carry buffet or refreshment services in many countries. But always check before you leave, or you may find yourself in for a long, hungry trip.

Why take the train at all?

Well, leaving aside the economic considerations (2nd-class travel is generally—although not always—cheaper than economy class by air), train travel really does give you much of the "feel" of the country in a way that flying never can. And by day you see the landscape as it is, not a hazy impression of it from 30,000 feet or a few side-ways glances as you concentrate on the traffic packed road ahead. With a little planning and careful selection of routes, rail travel can add immeasurably to the enjoyment of your holiday.

Fares

It is not practical to give a generalization about rail travel costs in Europe with any degree of accuracy. For a start, fare policies vary from one country to another; some subsidize their railways very heavily, others rely more on market forces to set costs. In addition, the fluctuation of exchange rates makes accuracy difficult, if not impossible. But it is fair to say that the further you go, the cheaper the cost per mile or kilometer.

For example, a ticket from say London to Vienna (2nd class) would be about £120 for the entire journey including the Dover-Oostende ferry. But you could break your journey at, for example, Brussels, Köln, Frankfurt, Munich and Salzburg at no extra cost. Book individual tickets between each and the cost would be twice as much. But a word of warning about this. Tickets issued in Europe are restricted in the time of their use, which can be from one day to one month. If bought in the U.S.A. or Canada, they are valid six months from date of purchase.

Roughly speaking 2nd class is always cheaper than the equivalent air fare on the Continent, although various charter and low-price scheduled tickets linking the U.K. and the Continent can be less expensive than standard rail tickets. 1st-class fares are anything from 30% to 50% above those for 2nd class, so you are warned!

As we said at the beginning of this section the improvement in 2nd-class travel is most noticeable—but always be prepared for it to be pretty busy. It can and does happen that even if you have a reserved seat you find yourself standing at peak periods simply because you can't get near the seat. On the plus side, travel in 2nd class is usually relaxed and you make friends easily, particularly if you are in the younger age group.

If you are taking kids, remember that there are reductions for them in every country. This, however, varies considerably with no fewer than 14 different rates depending on age. Basically, children under three (four or five in some cases) go free while those under 12, 14 or even 16 get half fare. Always check. On most international tickets, the children's 50% reduction applies from four to 11 inclusive, with the under fours going free.

Supplementary fares are charged on a number of European express trains, details of which are given under each country later in the guide. These supplements should always be paid for in advance, rather than on the train. In addition, other expresses have limited accommodation and reservation is obligatory. Always check on this.

Reduced Rate Tickets. The number and scale of these in most of Europe is very extensive indeed. Here we have given a basic selection, highlighting those which we are sure will be of most use to budget travelers. But it is always worthwhile asking at railway information offices or local tourist offices in each country what rail bargains are available during your stay.

Eurailpass. Ideal if you plan to do a great amount of rail travel as it covers 16 European countries (not the U.K.) and over 100,000 route miles of railway plus some bus routes, many river and lake steamer services, rail-operated ferries and several Mediterranean ferry routes. Issued for 1st class only it gives unlimited travel for the period of the ticket's validity; and it includes surcharges for EuroCity travel and other supplementary fares. The Eurailpass is available only if you live outside Europe or North Africa and *must* be purchased *beforehand* from an issuing agent in North America, South America, South Africa, Australasia or Japan. Major travel agents will be able to get one for you. It must be used within six months of the date of issue and be date-stamped on the first day of use. It is then valid for the appropriate period as issued.

Costs are as follows—15 days, $340; 21 days, $440; 1 month, $550; 2 months, $750, and 3 months, $390.

In addition children under 12 get half fare in all cases and those under four go free of charge if accompanied by a Eurailpass holder on a ratio of one to one.

Two new versions of the standard Eurailpass expand your travel options. The *Eurail Saverpass* is ideal for shorter holidays and is available to small groups (3 or more). Two people traveling together can use it out of season (November through March). It costs $240 per person and gives 15 days' unlimited 1st-class travel as with the Eurailpass. The *Eurail Flexipass* ($360) gives 9 days' rail travel, which can be used consecutively or not, over 21 days. There is also a 15-day Flexipasses ($198) giving you five days' travel, and a one-month pass ($458) good for 14 days' travel. The *Hertz Eurail-Drive Escape* combines four days of rail travel with 3 days' car rental, all in a 21-day period, and includes unlimited mileage, tax, and basic insurance, as well as a variety of dropoff options. The cost is $229 per person, with a minimum of two people traveling together.

For details, contact Eurail, c/o French National Railways, 610 Fifth Ave., New York, N.Y. 10020; 1500 Stanley St., Montreal, Quebec H3A 1R3; or 409 Granville St., Suite 452, Vancouver, B.C. B6C 1T2.

Inter Rail Card. This ticket is issued in Europe and can be bought by those under the age 26 on the date of commencement of the ticket's validity. Sadly, this ticket is *not* available to residents of the U.S. or Canada, unless you have been resident in Europe for six months. It gives unlimited travel by rail, on buses that are substituted for trains, and on some river and lake steamers. The train ferry routes between Denmark and Sweden are included. However, the ticket does not include express train supplements and these must be paid before boarding or you will be charged a penal rate. Also note that the Inter Rail card does not cover many of the small European private railways.

It covers 21 European countries plus Morocco and includes Hungary, Czechoslovakia, Yugoslavia and Romania. It gives half fare in the country in which it is issued and gives up to 50% discount on Hovercraft, Jetfoil and ferry routes between the U.K. and the Continent and Ireland if the ticket is bought in the U.K. or the Republic of Ireland. Available from many mainline stations in Europe and the British Isles as well as travel agencies which issue rail tickets, the current cost is around $248 or £155 in the U.K. There is also an InterRail + Boat ticket that gives free "deck" travel on certain Irish Sea, Scandinavian and Mediterranean ferry lines. The extra cost is only really worth it if traveling from Italy to Greece, or from France to Ireland. Cost around £180. These prices vary according to the rate of exchange in the country of purchase.

Youthpass. The conditions and application of this pass are like those of the Eurailpass—with the following differences. It is only issued to those who are under 26 on the date it starts and is for 2nd-class travel. In addition it is issued only for one and two month periods costing respectively $380 and $500.

For fuller information on the Eurailpass and the Youthpass write to the following addresses—

Eurailpass, 610 5th Ave., 5th floor, New York, N.Y. 10020.

French National Railways, (Eurailpass), 610 Fifth Ave., New York, N.Y. 10020.

Germanrail, (Eurailpass), 747 Third Ave., New York, N.Y. 10017; or 1290 Bay St., Toronto, Ontario, M5R 2C3.

Italian State Railways, (Eurailpass), 666 Fifth Ave., New York, N.Y. 10103.

Swiss Federal Railways, (Eurailpass), Swiss National Tourist Office 608 Fifth Ave., New York, N.Y. 10020.

Individual Country Tickets. Many European railway systems issue unlimited travel tickets covering their whole network. Again these are well worthwhile if you plan to do a lot of traveling within the period. But should you just wish to make, say, two or three excursion trips, it is more economical to buy individual tickets at excursion rates. If you are "staying-put" in one city or town or resort then a "runabout ticket" based on that center would be the best buy for you. Decide exactly what your requirements are before you purchase any "runabout" ticket.

The following countries issue these tickets—Belgium, Benelux nations (Belgium, Netherlands, Luxembourg combined), Denmark, Finland, France, Germany

(West), Great Britain (including Scotland), Ireland, Italy, Netherlands (Holland), Portugal, Scandinavia (Norway, Sweden, Denmark and Finland), Spain and Switzerland.

Details of reduced fares tickets will be found in the individual chapters for each country.

Sources of Rail Information

The *International Railway Union* (Union Internationale des Chemins de Fer) or UIC represents the majority of Europe's railways as well as many throughout the world. Its headquarters are at UIC, 14 rue Jean Rey, F–75015 Paris, France.

However for the most up-to-date information on rail travel in Europe (including the U.K. and Ireland) there is no better publication than the *Thomas Cook European Timetable*. Packed with reliable facts and figures, checked and corrected for every edition, it is published monthly. It contains not only timetables of all the main and many secondary railway services, it also covers ferry and lake steamer services, some bus routes, notes on visa requirements, sketch maps and hundreds of addresses for more detailed information. Its cost, at time of writing, was £6.10 sent 1st-class post, £5.85 2nd-class; in the U.S., $19.95 including postage and handling. It can be bought directly from any Thomas Cook branch throughout the world. The U.K. address, if ordering through the post, is *Thomas Cook Ltd.*, Timetable Publishing Office, P.O. Box 36, Thorpe Wood Peterborough, England PE3 6SB (tel. 0733–268937). In the U.S.A. and Canada write to *Stephen Forsyth Travel Library*, P.O. Box 2975, 9154 West 57th St., Shawnee Mission, KS 66201.

Selected Rail Routes

There are, at a conservative estimate, around 250 scenic or above average interest main rail routes in Europe. From these we have selected a few which show the range. In each case the trains carry both 1st- and 2nd-class carriages, dining facilities of some kind (mainly buffet or self-service cafeteria) and, on overnight services, either couchette cars or sleeping cars or both. In some cases supplementary fares are payable all or part of the way (check on this). Reservations where not mandatory are advisable except for short distances.

This list also includes several EuroCity and Inter-City trains for fast connections between main cities. All timings are approximate.

Arlberg Express—Paris - Zürich - Innsbruck - Vienna. Leaves Paris late evening (connection from London via Dover-Calais) traveling overnight to Switzerland. Through Alps in daylight. Takes about 21 hours.

Catalan Talgo—Barcelona - Perpignan - Narbonne - Avignon - Lyon - Geneva. Morning departures from either end taking about 10 hours. A very comfortable TALGO train, with good restaurant facilities.

Cornish Riviera—London (Paddington) - Exeter - Plymouth - Penzance. One of England's most famous trains operated by a High Speed Train (HST). Very scenic route most of the way. Takes about five hours. Weekdays only.

Edelweiss—Brussels - Luxembourg - Strasbourg - Basel - Zürich. Four-nation express with afternoon departure southbound, early morning northbound. Takes about 7½ hours.

Flying Scotsman—London (Kings Cross) - Newcastle - Edinburgh. Most famous train in the U.K. The East Coast line has been electrified and the 395-mile trip now takes a little over four hours. Limited accommodation.

Foguete—Lisbon - Coimbra - Oporto. Three times daily linking Portugal's two main cities and also its leading university city (Coimbra). Limited accommodation. Reservation essential.

Freccia della Laguna—Rome - Florence - Bologna - Venice. Fast service. Leaves Rome at lunch time taking just under six hours. Runs daily.

Henrik—Bergen - Voss - Finse - Geilo - Oslo. A most scenic route traveling through western Norway. Takes under seven hours for 295 mile journey. Early morning departure. Opposite train taking same time called **Pernille**.

Lemano—Geneva - Lausanne - Brig - Stresa - Milan. A scenic route most of the way going through Simplon Tunnel. Takes about 4½ hours.

Lisbon Express—Madrid - Talavera - Encontronamento - Lisbon. Runs daily through the heartland of both countries in each direction. Takes 9 hours for the 425 mile trip.

Lorely—Hook of Holland - Rotterdam - Köln - Mainz - Mannheim - Basel, with through carriages to Chiasso. One of the new EC trains.

Mont Cenis—Milan - Turin - Chambéry - Lyons. Early morning departure on this scenic route through the Mont Cenis Tunnel. Evening run the other way. Takes about 6 hours.

Night Aberdonian—London (Kings Cross) - Dundee - Aberdeen. Popular overnight train with new airconditioned sleepers in both classes. Takes about 9 hours 40 minutes for 526 mile journey. Not Saturdays.

Nord-West Express—Hook of Holland - Rotterdam - Utrecht - Bremen - Hamburg - Lubeck - Copenhagen (also serves Amsterdam). Overnight service in each direction with couchettes.

Norgepilen and Sverigepilen—Oslo - Stockholm. Twin trains connecting the two Scandinavian capitals. Lake and woodland scenery most of the way. About 6½ hours.

Nymphenburg—Hannover - Dortmund - Köln - Bonn - Wiesbaden - Frankfurt - Munich. An interesting route following the Rhine part of the way. Takes under nine hours for the 596 miles.

Palatino—Paris - Turin - train divides here with one section to Genoa - Pisa - Rome; the other to Bologna - Florence. Leaves either end each evening with buffet car service, sleeping and couchette cars (2nd class) only. Combined rail-sleeper tickets issued for this service.

Peloritano—Rome - Naples - Salerno - Messina - Palermo. Links the capital of Italy with the chief city in Sicily. Runs beside the sea for long stretches—crosses Straits of Messina on ferry. Takes about 11 hours. 1st class only.

Transalpin—Vienna - Linz - Salzburg - Innsbruck - Zürich - Basel. One of Europe's finest trains for mountain scenery mainly in daylight throughout the year. Takes about 10 hours.

Sevilla Express—Madrid - Cordoba - Seville. Main overnight connection linking these cities. Carries both 1st and 2nd class sleepers and 2nd class couchettes. Takes about nine hours for full journey, two hours less to Córdoba.

Sud Express—Paris - Bordeaux - Biarritz - Lisbon. Excellent through train to Lisbon with good sleeping facilities, 1st and 2nd class. Takes about 22 hours.

Venezia—Venice - Udine - Villach - Klagenfurt - Vienna. Links these two romantic cities in about 10 hours of scenic travel. Operates May to September only.

EUROPE BY CAR

It is no longer true to say that Britain is the best place in which to start a budget motoring holiday, because the car rental tariffs are now lower in several other Continental countries, notably and usefully, Belgium.

It is also less easy to argue the case for traveling by car at all, unless there are four people in it to cover the cost of gas, which is significantly higher than in the United States. You also need to have a bit of local information to make a go of Continental motoring, as gas and hire charges can vary greatly in neighboring areas. It is as well, for example, for American travelers to discard their natural instinct for large cars and go along with the majority of European drivers with whom medium-sized cars—i.e. about 14 ft.—are popular. The best selling cars in Britain for several years have all been around this size, for which reason the cross channel ferry companies have actually arranged their rates so that cars of this size get a very good deal. You can also reckon to get 35 m.p.g. out of one, and with feather-footing even more. It is possible to hire automatics, but they come a little more expensive and are thirstier.

There is, too, the question of roads and parking. Owners of big cars often have quite a job fitting their machines into a standard meter space, and the most rewarding roads for motor tourists, anywhere in Europe, are the small ones. In a few cases they may be a bit rough, but not many or very. Of course big cars are good for motorways, but they also generate higher costs. If you really tried, you could live for two days on the tolls charged to drive from the north of France to the south along the autoroute, and for even longer if you did the same thing on the Italian autostrada.

But the question of which form of transport to use for a European holiday does not hinge solely on cost, even in a Budget Guide. It is a matter of values. Truly a plane gets you anywhere quicker than anything else—providing it gets off the ground at all, but no one could claim that air travel in the 80s is exactly a cultural experience. Rail travel is much better, because at least you can see something, but to the dedicated motorist there is nothing to compare with the ease, comfort, convenience and freedom of having your own transport. No timetables, no predetermined routes, no advance bookings. You are at liberty to come and go how, when and where you like. Or not to go anywhere if the place where you are—the absurdly cheap, small hotel discovered on a country road—proves irresistible. That way you might even save enough to buy a case of wine or some other unwieldy object prohibited to public transport passengers.

You can save more money by having pleasant picnic lunches instead of being condemned to the Continental equivalent of a Wimpy Bar or to a squashed sandwich on a park bench. Neither do you have to battle your way on and off buses or try not to be outwitted by taxi drivers.

Against all this there is the bother of disposing of the car in towns when you don't want it, but this is much easier in countries other than Britain, where authority regards the motorist as only a pest from which to extract money. Then again there is always the chance that a car will break down, but if you rent from one of the giants such as *Avis, Hertz* or *Eurocar* you will be given a replacement almost at once; or with a small, cheaper firm you can take out insurance against the same eventuality.

Incidentally there are many perfectly reliable small car rental firms in England who offer the same facilities as the giants but at considerably less cost, often making no extra charge for taking the car abroad. Some will even make ferry bookings. Their names and addresses can always be found in the British Tourist Authority's monthly publication, *In Britain,* obtainable from bookstalls and B.T.A. offices in Britain and America (addresses, see pages 4–6).

At the present time travelers may drive in any country of Western or Eastern Europe except Albania. Motoring in Hungary, Yugoslavia, Romania and Bulgaria is without official restrictions though it is wise not to poke your nose between barbed wire or over high walls, and cameras should be pointed only at the patently innocuous, which does *not* include people in uniform. The one unintentional restriction common to all these countries except Yugoslavia is the lack of accommodation, which forces one to make advance reservations in more substantial hotels than one would, possibly, use in the West. There are various little rules and regulations in East European countries which may sometimes be helpful—as in the case of Romania, which entices motorists with offers of free gasoline. But it is as well to know all about them before arriving at the frontier, the crossing of which is invariably slow even when everything goes smoothly.

Travel hold-ups in any country always result in unexpected expenses. And when leaving any Communist country make a point of unloading your local currency before reaching the frontier, because you will not be allowed to take it out with you. Even if you could, it would be useless; and in any case, the exchange bureaux at the border crossing points have been known to run out of Western monies and to offer all sorts of bizarre items in payment for what you hand over.

In East European countries some 1st-class roads tend to be a bit second class, and second class better left alone, although there are some very good and expanding sections of motorway and some perfectly adequate 2nd-class roads. In Western Europe there is no need to fear even unclassified roads, except in Spain, Yugoslavia, Finland and the north of both Norway and Sweden. In mountainous areas such as Austria, Switzerland, the French Alps and Italian Dolomites the roads are narrow and can be a bit scary, but the surfaces are tolerable.

British roads are not so atrocious as many Americans fear. There are now several hundred miles of excellent motorways, the trunk roads have been greatly improved, and the "B" roads, providing that you are not in a hurry, are a delight. And that goes for the wilds of Scotland and Wales as well.

The secret of successful budget touring in Europe is flexible planning. Decide where you want to go and at least roughly what route to take, and how much time you will need. In this way you avoid arriving at midnight in some very expensive city, at the mercy of your own exhaustion and every shark around. In most European countries if you plan to cover 200 miles a day you will be taking it very easy with plenty of time to look around. That also will save gasoline, of course. If you do 400 a day you are going to be working hard. This is just a generalization. In Norway motoring is always very slow; in Germany it can be very fast. A much-used general yardstick is that one kilometer per minute (60 kmph or 37 mph) is a reasonable average. But remember also that the center of Europe is extremely mountainous and many of the passes will be closed some time between October and March.

Even free motorways generate costs because one drives faster, the gas stations charge peak prices, and so do the eating places. In countries where there is very heavy commercial traffic it is quicker to use secondary roads rather than trunk roads, in addition to it being pleasanter. For this reason it is worth the money to equip yourself with good maps, not just the small-scale handouts from national tourist offices. Most of tourist Europe is covered by excellent road maps.

Small roads invariably lead to small hotels where you get the small bills. In Western Europe you can quite safely make overnight stops at these. They may not look much and possibly no one will be able to speak English, but they will be acceptable and interesting. When a service charge is added to the bill you are absolutely not expected to tip as well, except in Austria. Read the menus displayed outside restaurants carefully, or you could be caught eating a very expensive meal in unpretentious surroundings.

On the other hand, restaurants carrying the round blue/red sign Les Routiers offer good plain food and wine at realistic prices. They originated in France, mostly for truck drivers, but are now spreading to neighboring countries and are much frequented by impecunious motorists. Many have a few, inexpensive simple rooms, the only drawback being that they tend to be on the main thoroughfares and therefore subjected to almost continuous traffic roar. The popular ones also fill up rather early in the evening.

If keeping down costs for yourself sounds too much like hard work, there is another way to do it, although they won't be quite so low: treat yourself to a motoring package. These are on offer from the following organizations:

The Automobile Association, Fanum House, Basingstoke, Hants RG21 2EA, through its subsidiary, AA Motoring Holidays, who have simple budget packages—most of them in France, but some also in Spain.

And *Car Holidays Abroad,* Canvas Holidays, Bull Plain, Hertford, Herts SG14 1DY (tel. 0992–553535), whose packages cover cross-Channel ferries, destination hotels or, en route hotels with dinner, bed and breakfast, travel insurance and car rescue, which all means that you know exactly what the holiday will cost except for lunches, drinks, amusements and gasoline.

The net result of using such agents is that you stay in their recommended hotels for less than you would pay individually, but you could find cheaper places for yourself if you cared to make the effort, except in the case of *Car Holidays Abroad* who really have got a line on economy. Besides these operators, many of the ferry companies offer packages attached to their own services, particularly the Scandinavian ones, while the Channel ferry companies promote short breaks of just two to five days, mostly with free carriage of the car if you have four paying passengers. These little trips are very good value and serve as a sort of taster for people who don't want to commit themselves too heavily without knowing whether or not they will enjoy it.

Budget-conscious Americans and Britons who start their holidays in Britain and then take themselves and their cars across to the Continent need to find the most economical buy among the car ferries. If it is just a matter of crossing the channel, the cheapest routes are out of Dover and Ramsgate, and then driving your own car to wherever. It has to be extravagant to buy a ticket to transport a car, which is itself a transporter, by ship or train, so keep the voyage as short as possible. To Scandinavia, which is expensive and on the far side of so much water, it is advisable to take one of the ferry companies' packages. Information about the short sea crossings follows, and details about longer crossings are in the chapters on the countries concerned.

Crossing to France, Belgium or Holland at night can be a great time saver when the ships dock around 07.00, thus providing a springboard for a long day's driving. In such circumstances it is legitimate to accept the cost of a cabin, which is cheaper than an overnight hotel and will land you refreshed and ready for action. A full passenger-load also greatly reduces the per capita cost. On such considerations the success of Budget Motoring is built.

European Roads and Regulations

All over Europe, there is now a network of International Highways, designated with the letter "E" and then the road number, in black on green. E5, for instance, runs from Oostende, Belgium to Istanbul, Turkey, by way of Germany, Austria, Hungary, Yugoslavia and Greece. These roads are not, by any means, all express-ways or motorways or all of the same standard, but the various countries are concerned to see that they eventually become so. Road maps are available, free, from every national tourist office, or are on sale in offices of the AA, RAC and the AAA. Several petroleum companies also supply not very good maps.

Traffic Regulations. For the most part, the old rule, "priority of traffic from the right" *(priorité à droite)*, is no longer practiced on country roads, but is still maintained to varying degrees in cities. Never, however, rely on a car, cart or bicycle to refrain from darting out in front of you if its driver has a will to do so. Where two country roads of equal importance cross one another, traffic from the right *usually* has right of way, but most such cross roads have signs to indicate who has priority. In France, however, it is *always* priority of traffic from the right, country roads or not, *unless* the road coming from the right has a stop signal (or obviously unless a small secondary road crosses a main thoroughfare, but there are *always* signs), or unless entering a traffic circle, where traffic already on the traffic circle has priority. For detailed instruction on such matters see the AAA, RAC or AA handbooks. Priority from the right is not the rule in Britain except on roundabouts (circles).

In many countries, it is obligatory to carry a portable, red reflective triangle, which must be put out on the road well behind a car which has broken down and is in danger of causing an obstruction. Such triangles can be hired at border points, but it is cheaper and easier to buy one for about $6.50.

Police Fines. In several countries, police are authorized to make on the spot fines for infringements of the traffic regulations. These may be as low as $1.50 or as high as $220, depending on the country. *This goes for jay-walkers, too, in some places.* Among countries with spot-fining are: Andorra, Austria, Denmark, France, Germany, Holland, Italy, Luxembourg, Portugal, Spain.

Drinking and Driving. Laws on this are strict in many continental countries, with heavy fines or imprisonment. Scandinavia is particularly strict. The legal limits of the blood alcohol level vary according to country, so check with your motoring association before setting out. *Better still, don't drink and drive.*

Gasoline (Petrol). Most of the brands familiar to both American and British drivers are to be found on the continent at differing prices. Very few countries have more than two octane ratings—*super* (or premium) and *ordinary* (or regular)—and only super is recommended for most American and British cars. Owners of cars which will go on lower octane ratings are always aware of it, and will know that their petrol will cost slightly less. Oil brands common to all countries invariably cost more than they do in Britain. Tourist gas coupons, giving a discount, are available only in Italy and some Communist countries. They are obligatory in Bulgaria and Romania and must be paid for in hard currency.

Information on Driving. *American Automobile Association (AAA),* World-Wide Travel, Inc., 12600 Fair Lake Circle, Fairfax, VA 22033.

Automobile Association (AA), address—see page 36.

Canadian Automobile Association, 2 Carlton St., Toronto, Ontario M5B 1K4.

Royal Automobile Club (RAC), RAC House, P.O. Box 100, 7 Brighton Rd., S. Croydon, Surrey CR2 6XW.

See also the big red *Europa Touring,* an 820-page atlas published by Hallwag (Germany) and available at U.S. bookstores for about $6.95. Michelin road maps are excellent.

Papers Needed. For yourself, of course, a passport, and a driving license. It is wise to get an *International Driving Permit* (cost $5—not likely to rise—in the U.S., and £3 in the U.K.). Take your money, a valid national license, and two passport-type photographs to the AAA, AA or RAC for the Permit. The IDP remains good for one year from the date of validation. For the car, a nationality plate (USA or GB for example), and an international comprehensive motor insurance card, known as the *Green Card,* are advisable. The latter is valid in all West European countries and in a few Eastern European countries. Green Cards are normally issued by the car owner's insurance company, at widely differing rates starting from around $15, according to the type of car and record of the driver. Insurance bought in a frontier is for minimum legal cover only, and usually works out to be rather expensive. Get details from the AAA. For Spain, it is advisable to have also a Bail Bond since an accident might otherwise result in the car, or even yourself, being impounded. France, too, has lately taken to demanding the actual car registration document and levying large, instant fines on anyone who can't produce one.

AAA World-Wide Travel's booklet, *Motoring in Europe,* has the latest information about motoring in Europe, and can provide you with all the documents European countries require. Write to *AAA World-Wide Travel, Inc.,* 1000 AAA Drive, Heathrow, FL 32746, attn: Foreign Motoring Division. Order AAA's booklet *Offices to Serve You Abroad* which lists AAA affiliates in Europe: it's free to members.

Circular signs indicate regulations; triangular mean danger, and square are informative. Colors are usually red and black on white.

Note: You must have your driving license, Green Card or Vehicle Registration Card with you at all times you are driving. In the event that you are stopped by the authorities, you are *not* allowed to "go back to the hotel and get them."

Renting a Car

Most well-known car rental firms operate all over western Europe, with *Avis,* at least, covering all the communist countries as well. They will reserve you a car in advance of your departure through their office nearest you or through your travel agent and tour operators. Many airlines offer a fly-and-drive holiday package that includes airfare, use of a car, and bed-and-breakfast accommodations (see Package Tour section).

The cost of car rental (for cheapest cars) varies from around $20 per day in Portugal to $35 in Switzerland, with special rates for Paris, plus mileage charge and local hire tax. Fuel, of course, is extra, and is generally twice the price that it is in the U.S. Rates for renting by the week are much more economical, often dispensing with a mileage charge and including the hire tax, which incidentally can be so high that it is worth planning to rent in a low levy country whenever possible. Some firms also offer reduced "holiday hire" rates for 14 days.

Reputable agencies will also often charge you the cheaper rate—day/miles versus week/unlimited mileage—though it is always good to check their figures. Also beware of what will most likely happen if you charge your car on a credit card that is billed to you in a currency other than that of the country in which you rented. Given exchange rates and the amount involved, you may well wish to pay cash, if possible, or via international money order drawn on a local bank.

Names of accredited car rental firms can be had from the AAA, RAC or AA or from branches of Thomas Cook. If you require a car with automatic transmission, be sure to specify so well in advance; most Europeans still use standard transmissions with clutch, and that is the norm at most rental agencies. You may also have to pay a premium for this "extra."

There are many little dodges that operate locally which are of use to the budget motorist. For example, a car picked up at the railway station in Edinburgh, Scotland, will cost more than the identical vehicle picked up from the same firm's downtown office. It pays to shop around and take local advice.

EUROPE BY BUS

Although there is no European equivalent of the American Greyhound or Canadian Trailways network, the standard of bus travel both on the Continent and in the U.K. has improved immensely in the last few years and now provides excellent road travel in every way, whether you are using the bus for an inclusive holiday tour or just as a means of transport. Of course there are still some rather-less-than-satisfactory operators—so choose with care.

Firstly, let us sort out the use of the words "bus" and "coach" in Europe and the U.K. On the Continent "bus" usually means scheduled services, generally, although not always, excluding accommodations. "Coach" on the other hand tends to be used for organized tours. But in the U.K. "coach" means any long distance travel while "bus" tends to refer to local services, although oddly enough in Scotland "bus" is used for all public transport. For the purposes of this guide we have used "bus" throughout, except where it applies to an organized, inclusive coach tour.

There is now a marketing consortium of bus operators throughout much of western and central Europe and extending right into the Balkans. Called *National Express-Eurolines* in the U.K. and *Supabus/Europabus* in Continental Europe, it combines the services of both state-owned and privately-operated companies. As we went to press, over 160 cities and towns were linked by this system, with either through services or connecting routes. Further developments are in the pipeline, so contact *National Express-Eurolines* for the latest information.

Its biggest advantage is in ticketing on international routes whereby one ticket (or at least a series of linked tickets) can be issued, ensuring a smooth journey without bureaucratic hassle. For example, tickets can be issued from Edinburgh in Scotland through to Rome with a fixed fare. Many of these routes on the longer distances do not have an overnight stop, but there are both meal and comfort stops on all routes. In some cases you have to spend a night en route. Some of the services are seasonal but the majority are year-round with varying timetables. However, international buses are infrequent when compared with train and airline services. On many international runs there are only a couple of departures a week.

In addition to this system there are networks of bus routes within each country. These are sometimes run in conjunction with the railway system, often serving areas not reached by the train. Switzerland, with its post bus routes, and the Republic of Ireland are good examples.

As to costs, these vary, but are either equivalent to or cheaper than 2nd class rail travel. Round-trip tickets are usually cheaper than two one-way tickets. There are reduced rates for children on all routes, and often reduced rates for students.

Details of these services can be obtained from travel agents, most of whom can make reservations. In the U.K. contact *National Express-Eurolines,* 13 Lower Regent St., London SW1Y 4LR (071–730 0202), or most bus stations. On the Continent local tourist offices are good sources of information, but don't usually take reservations.

In Continental Europe the main international services are run by *Europabus,* which is controlled by the various national railways. Details from *SCETA Europabus,* 7 rue Pablo-Neruda, 92532 Levallois-Perret, Cedex, France, and from Deutschen Touring Gmbh, Am Romerhof 17, 6000 Frankfurt am Main 90, West Germany.

Apart from International Express, there are a number of sizable independent bus companies operating from the U.K., mostly out of London, offering all-inclusive Continental holidays. Among the most prominent are *Global Tours,* 29–31 Elmfield Rd., Bromley, Kent BR1 1LT (tel. 081–464 7515); *Frames Rickards,* 11 Herbrand St., Russell Square, London WC1N 1EX (tel. 071–637 4171); *Thomas Cook,* 45 Berkeley St. London W1A 1EB (tel. 071–499 4000), and elsewhere; *Thomson Holidays,* 1st Floor, Greater London House, Hampstead Rd., London NW1 7SD (tel. 071–387 9321); *Trafalgar Tours,* 15 Grosvenor Place, London SW1X 7HH (tel. 071–235 7090); and *Glenton Tours,* 114 Peckham Rye, London SE15 4JE (tel. 071–639 9777).

In extent these bus tours from the U.K. range from three-day (two-night) "shorties" to places like Brussels, Amsterdam and Paris to marathon 28-day tours of much of Europe.

There are of course also many bus tour operators in Continental countries such as *CIAT, SATI* and *SAD* (an unfortunate name for a company) in Italy; *CHAT* in Greece; *Transbus* and *Brabena* operating from the Netherlands to all of Benelux, France, Germany, Austria, Switzerland and Italy; *Marsans* in Spain (they also go over to Morocco); *West Belgian Coach Company* and *Generalcar,* both in Belgium but operating extensive tours.

We emphasize that this is only a brief selection. New companies come into the market regularly. Check with your own travel agent or when you arrive in the country.

Mention must be made of the excellent *Postbus* services operated by the post office administrations in Switzerland, Austria, southern Germany, northern Italy and the Alpine regions of France. Reliable, comfortable and with an excellent safety record, they reach places which are often well away from the usual tourist trails, linking in most cases with rail services, particularly so in Switzerland and Austria. The distinctive yellow buses with their melodic Alpine-horn klaxon are very much part of the travel scene in the mountains. Accommodation is limited and advance reservation is advisable at all times and essential in the peak season. Some carry the mail on the bus itself, while in other cases it is towed behind in a trailer. Details from national tourist offices and local offices in the areas served.

At the majority of resorts there are good—or at least reasonably good—local bus services. This is particularly true, for example, around the Bay of Palma in Majorca, on the Costa Blanca from Benidorm, on the Costa del Sol in southern Spain, on both the Italian and French Rivieras, on the Adriatic coast of Italy linking Rimini, Cattolica and Riccione, and in Corfu, Crete and Rhodes. Local tourist offices generally display timetables as do holiday hotels. Make use of these local buses. They are cheap, amusing and give a true flavor of the area—even if they are usually packed solid!

EUROPE BY WATER

Seeing Europe from the deck of a comfortable river or lake steamer or a converted and spacious barge or your own motor cruiser is, to put it mildly, pleasant. And there is certainly a tremendous range, from the large vessels that ply the Rhine to two-berth cruisers in some quiet backwater of the renowned Norfolk Broads in England. Or again a long cruise on the mighty Volga then by canal across to the River Don. Or taking it gently but eating superbly well and at moderate cost on a cruising barge on the Canal du Midi in France.

The Rhine is the classic example. You can cruise all the way from Rotterdam or Amsterdam right up to Basel, a 480-mile water-borne odyssey. Alternatively, you can do it in sections such as from Nijmegen in the Netherlands to Mainz, or just do a day trip between Koblenz and Mainz—the most scenic part of the Rhine. Should you opt for a proper cruise this can be for three, five or seven days.

These are by fully equipped vessels, some even with their own swimming pools, cabins with private shower and toilet and dining rooms. Some are German owned and operated, others Dutch and one or two British. But all have equal facilities. Full details from travel agents.

The regular service of boats on the Rhine is operated by the long-established *KD German Rhine Line* whose fleet of 17 vessels operate from April to October with the full route being from Dusseldorf to Mainz and some service going up the River Main to Frankfurt. These boats offer both fast and slow services, the latter stopping at all points. They are large, comfortable, spotlessly clean and all have restaurant or buffet facilities on board. An ideal way to view the splendors of this great river, they are very popular, especially in the peak summer weeks and during the wine festival periods in the autumn. The company also operates a similar but less frequent service on the River Moselle from Koblenz. Full details of service from travel agencies and KD offices and agencies in many German cities.

Europe's other great river, the Danube, also has steamer and hydrofoil services. The Russian owned *Soviet Danube Line* has a route that goes from Passau on the Austro-German border via Vienna, Budapest, Belgrade and Giurgiu to Ismail at the mouth of the river. Down stream this takes nine days, 13 days upstream, with connections by sea-going ship at Ismail to Yalta in the Crimea, and also to Istanbul. The Austrian *First Danube Steamship Co.* operates from Passau to Linz and also on to Vienna, while the Romanian *Danube Line* offer week-long cruises between Vienna and Cernavoda in Romania. Peter Deilmann, a German tour operator, offers week-long Danube cruises from Passau to Budapest and back: U.K agents are Fred Olsen Ltd., Crown House, Crown St., Ipswich IP1 3HB (tel. 0473–233022). Most are summer only services—April to October as a rule.

In Sweden, on the Gota Canal between Gothenburg and Stockholm, there are three days cruises from mid-May to early September; while in England there are cruises on the River Thames and through the network of canals. Similarly there are canal cruises in France from Brittany right down to Provence, and many opportunities for cruising the lakes of Finland.

An increasingly popular water-borne holiday is to hire your own cruiser and travel on canals, lakes, rivers and other inland waterways. Among the places you can do that are France, England, Scotland and Ireland.

And, of course, there are numerous cruises from three days to two weeks in the Mediterranean. The Greek islands are extremely busy in summer with all kinds of craft from cruise ships to two-man skiffs. Flotilla holidays, where yachts go around in small "fleets" supervised by experts, are now a fast growing business around the Greek islands both in the Aegean and the Ionian Seas; as well as on Yugoslavia's Adriatic coast.

For information on many aspects of river and canal travel in England, Holland, Belgium, and France, contact *Floating Through Europe,* 271 Madison Ave., New York, N.Y. 10016 (212–685–5600). Though rates for some of these hotel barge cruises are high for budget travel, they include accommodations, transfers, land tours, all meals and wine. And the company has a fine reputation. For water-borne holidays both in, and from, the U.K., two of the main operators are the long-established *Blakes Holidays,* Wroxham, Norwich NR12 8DH, Britain's biggest boat-holiday company (with vacations in Ireland, Scotland, France, Denmark and Holland, as well, of course, as the Norfolk Broads); and *Hoseasons Holidays,* Sunway House, Lowestoft, Suffolk NR32 3LT, whose catalog includes—along with the Norfolk Broads again—Friesland in Holland, the Baltic, Limfjorden on Danish Jutland, and a number of locations in France.

Ferries

Not only is Continental Europe crisscrossed by a vast network of waterways, many of which are navigable and offer an enjoyable new dimension to a vacation, but the coastal waters are also full of available shipping—from plodding old steamers to swift hovercrafts. The surge of air services in the last couple of decades has only marginally reduced the ferry traffic. Indeed, on some of the routes, notably those across the Channel from Britain to the Continent, there has been an enormous increase in ferry services.

If you're traveling by car, many of the ferry routes in the Aegean, across from Italy to Greece, or in the Baltic, are not a budget way of getting from one spot to another. But, for the foot passenger who is prepared to make do without a cabin and rough it on deck, or sleep wherever he can find shelter, it can be both cheap and enormously rewarding. To cross from the Greek mainland to one of the islands, Crete for example, and see dolphins playing beside the elderly ferryboat while the deck is piled high with crates, animals and noisy, gesticulating passengers, is one of the more exciting ways of seeing the world.

We outline the ferry crossings from Britain to the Continent elsewhere (under the next section), so here we will suggest some of the other routes that are possible elsewhere in Continental waters.

The Greek mainland is connected to the islands by half-a-dozen or so lines, mostly from Piraeus—*Naias Shipping, Minoan Lines, Lemnos Maritime, Naxos Maritime, Sol Maritime* —which are often car ferries, but take foot passengers. A very good spot to leave from, since it is much less busy, is Rafina, on the east coast only a dozen miles from Athens. From there you can get to Andros, Mykonos, Tinos, etc.

The western Mediterranean is also a happy hunting ground for the ferry addict. Spain, the South of France, Italy, Sicily and North Africa are all connected by lines. Not all of them are cheap, of course, and it would be well to investigate both the latest availability and fares. It is possible that the opening of the frontier between Gibraltar and Spain may well give companies that had to shut down their operations between, say, Gibraltar and Algeciras, the chance to sail again. All the islands, large and small, in this part of the Mediterranean, Corsica, Sicily, Elba, the Balearics, can be reached by boat, indeed this is frequently the best and cheapest way to do so. Also they are reachable from several ports, with many boats doing a hopping route along the coast. It is possible to get a discount fare on some lines if booked through British car ferry companies.

This coastal kind of trip can be a holiday all to itself. The Dalmatian coast of Yugoslavia provides a splendid voyage, running from Rijeka through Rab, Zadar, the ancient city of Split, the island of Hvar, Dubrovnik, jewel of the region, and sometimes continues on to Corfu. The overnight service with a cabin from Rijeka to Corfu starts at $115 per person, including meals: deck passengers pay less. The operator for this service is *Jadrolina (Jadranska Linijska Plovidba);* their general agent in the U.S. and Canada, is the *International Cruise Center,* 250 Old Country Rd., Mineola, N.Y. 11501. The Adriatic fares are moderate, especially for deck passengers.

In the north of Europe the routes are just as numerous, but tend to be a little more costly, though the services are usually of a higher standard than in the warmer southern waters. The Baltic is a happy hunting ground for the ferry freak, and the boats can give many insights into cultural differences, since they are run by the Soviet Union, Finland and a mixture of Scandinavian and German companies. Not only do the ferries serve the bigger cities fringing the Baltic, but they potter about among the thousands of islands that nestle along the shorelines—as, for example, around the southeastern edge of Finland. For really good ferry-cruise discounts, and last-minute cruise offers at exceptional prices, contact *Cruise World,* 10 Birches Bridge Shopping Center, Wolverhampton Road, Codsall, Wolverhampton, Staffs WV8 1PD (tel. 09074–5000).

GETTING TO THE CONTINENT FROM BRITAIN

BY AIR

There are direct (or through) plane services from no fewer than 18 airports in the U.K., from Aberdeen to Exeter, to the Continent. From London (Heathrow and Gatwick) every capital (except Tirana in Albania) has a direct air link, with the services to nearer cities like Paris, Brussels, Amsterdam and Dusseldorf being very well served, the Paris route being the busiest in Europe. Most of these are scheduled services but there are a number of regular charter routes (e.g. Gatwick to Geneva, Luton to Dusseldorf or Frankfurt) in operation. The price range is very wide although British Airways no longer offer first class which will be no trial to budget travelers. Flying times can be as short as 30 minutes (Southend near London to Oostende in Belgium) or as long as 4½ hours to Larnaca in Cyprus.

All European national airlines (except Albania and East Germany) serve London.

BY HOVERCRAFT

Although designed for the haulage of cars and motor coaches (buses) these air-cushioned craft carry a very large number of foot passengers who arrive at the Hoverports—Dover in England, Calais and Boulogne in France—by train or bus. The "flights" across the Channel take 35 to 40 minutes. No food is served on the crossing but duty-free drinks are sold on board. Two new large terminals serve travelers at Dover and Calais, with a smaller one at Boulogne.

All these services are operated by one company, *Hoverspeed: British Ferries.* They run all the year round from Dover to both Calais and Boulogne.

Passenger fares are about £23 one way with through tickets from London by rail using the CityLink service costing around £60 in 1st and £46 in 2nd class (single). Their integrated CitySprint bus service is excellent value at about £23 single.

In summer there is a high frequency of services from Dover to Calais, with some services to Boulogne. The problem is that hovercraft services are easily canceled with the onset of bad weather.

BY TRAIN

Foot passengers have a choice of routes if taking the train from London to the Continent using cross-Channel or cross-North Sea ferries. Which you choose will depend on your ultimate destination but the cheapest (by a small margin) from London to Paris for example is via Newhaven and Dieppe, a 10-hour journey of which just under 4 are at sea.

Other routes are London (Victoria Station) to Paris via Folkestone (about 7½ hours) or via Dover (overnight service about 10 hours); London to Brussels via Dover and Oostende (about 7½ hours by conventional ferry or 5½ hours by Jetfoil across the Channel); London (Liverpool Street Station) to Rotterdam/Amsterdam via Harwich and the Hook of Holland (about 11 or 12 hours); London (Waterloo Station) to Paris via Portsmouth and Le Havre (bus links at the ports, taking about ten hours in all, overnight service only); London (Liverpool St. Station) to Copenhagen via Harwich and Esbjerg (about 28 hours).

Note also that all the car ferries (see next section) carry foot passengers and most of these ports can be reached by train from London.

For train travel beyond the Continental Channel ports the services are as follows—from Calais and/or Boulogne to southern France, Italy, Switzerland, Austria, Spain (no through trains—change at Paris) and Yugoslavia (change in Milan or Venice); from Oostende to Germany (West and East), Poland, the U.S.S.R., Austria, Czechoslovakia and Denmark; from the Hook of Holland to northern Germany, Berlin, East Germany, Poland, the U.S.S.R., Scandinavia; from Dieppe and Le Havre—same destinations as from Calais/Boulogne but all involving a change in Paris; from Esbjerg to Norway and Sweden with a change in Copenhagen.

BY BUS

Hoverspeed operates express daytime bus services from London Victoria coach station to Amsterdam, Antwerp, Brussels, Mons, Paris and Rotterdam. These CitySprint services are part of the *National Express-Eurolines* network. All are excellent value and are almost as fast as by train/ship. For those who don't mind a disturbed night, *National Express-Eurolines* also operates overnight services.

There are long-distance bus services from London Victoria coach station to various destinations in France, West Germany, Greece, Ireland, Italy, Holland, Spain, Scandinavia and Turkey. These are also run by various companies as part of *National Express-Eurolines.*

The most important group of intercity buses in mainland Europe is operated by *Europabus,* but these can be infrequent and poorly timed.

BY CAR

Some of the larger ferries on the longer crossings have very comfortable accommodations. All ferries these days have drive on/off systems for cars. Look out for bargain offers by all the companies—ie., 1–5-day or longer period packages. Standard fares can be reduced if you choose your crossing carefully, or more costly if you insist on traveling at peak weekends. Children are mostly carried at half price, but the age at which they are deemed to become adult varies between 13 and 18.

The fares listed below are the standard single summer rates for a driver and one passenger and a car up to 4.5 m. long.

To France: Dover–Calais, *Sealink,* 90 minutes; Folkestone–Boulogne, 1¼ hours; £93. Up to 24 combined sailings daily.

Dover–Calais, *P & O European Ferries,* 75 minutes; £99. 15 crossings daily.

Dover–Calais/Boulogne, *Hoverspeed: British Ferries,* 35–40 minutes; £117. Up to 23 flights daily to Calais, six to Boulogne.

Ramsgate–Dunkerque, *Sally Viking,* 2½ hours; £92. Up to three day, two night sailings.

Folkestone–Boulogne, *Sealink,* 1 hour and 50 minutes; £93. Up to four sailings a day, two night sailings.

Newhaven–Dieppe, *Sealink,* 4–5 hours, £95. Up to two sailings a day, two night crossings.

To Belgium: Dover–Oostende, *P & O European Ferries/R.T.M.* 4 hours; £89, berth £6. Up to four daytime sailings plus four night sailings in summer.

Dover–Zeebrugge, *P & O European Ferries,* 4–4½ hours; £89, 2 berth cabin £12. Up to three sailings per day, three per night.

Felixstowe–Zeebrugge, *P & O European Ferries,* five hours; £94, berth £11.50. One daytime, one overnight sailing.

Hull–Zeebrugge, *North Sea Ferries,* 14 hours; £150 including berths and all meals. One overnight sailing.

To Holland: Sheerness–Vlissingen, *Olau Line,* 7 hours day, 8 hours overnight; £79 day, £94 night, couchette £4. One day, one night sailing.

Harwich–Hook of Holland, *Sealink,* 7–8 hours; £87–£108, "Night Rest" chair £3. One day, one night sailing. First class available.

Hull–Rotterdam, *North Sea Ferries,* 14 hours; £150 including berths and all meals. One overnight crossing.

To Germany: Harwich–Hamburg, *Scandinavian Seaways* (formerly known as DFDS), 20 hours; £214, including berths. Sailings on alternate days.

To Denmark: Harwich–Esbjerg, *Scandinavian Seaways,* 19–20 hours; £196 including couchette. Daily from March to November; three times a week in winter.

To Sweden: Harwich–Gothenburg, *Scandinavian Seaways,* 23½ hours; £244 including cheapest berth. Sailings every other day in summer; three times a week in winter.

Newcastle–Gothenberg, *Scandinavian Seaways,* 26 hours; £264 including berth in 4-berth cabin plus shower/wc. Summer only, one sailing a week.

To Norway: Newcastle–Stavanger/Bergen, *Norway Line,* 20–26 hours; £138–£198 including reclining seat: good discounts for students. Two/three weekly, mid-March through October.

Harwich–Oslo, *Fred Olsen Lines,* around 38 hours; £174 including berth. One sailing weekly.

Harwich–Kristiansand, *Fred Olsen Lines,* 24½ hours; £126 including berths. Mid-June to mid-August only. One sailing a week.

Aberdeen/Scrabster–Stromness/Lerwick. *P&O* sail throughout the year from Aberdeen and Scrabster to Stromness in the Orkneys and Lerwick (Shetlands). For Lerwick *Smyril Line* sail direct to Bergen (Norway), and via Torshavn to Hanstholm (Denmark).

To Spain: Plymouth–Santander, *Brittany Ferries,* 24 hours; £239, 2-berth cabin £54. Two sailings per week.

STUDENT AND YOUTH TRAVEL

SOURCES OF INFORMATION

In the U.S. The following agencies are good sources of general information about, or can actually book, the following services for you: worldwide student and youth flight discounts; International Student ID Card; International Youth ID Card; Eurail passes, Britrail passes and other rail discounts; travel insurance; educational tours in Western and Eastern Europe, and the U.S.S.R.; car leasing and rentals; and accommodations. They also have information about work opportunities abroad, voluntary service projects, language courses, study programs, and other student/youth travel details.

The Council on International Educational Exchange (CIEE), 205 East 42 St., 16th floor, New York City, N.Y. 10017, for study, travel and work abroad programs, and travel and services for college and high school students and other budget travelers. Write for a free copy of CIEE's annual Student Travel Catalog. Another CIEE publication, *Work, Study, Travel Abroad: the Whole World Handbook* ($9.95 plus $1 postage) is the best listing. There is also CIEE's *Teenager's Guide to Study,*

Travel and Adventures Abroad ($9.95 plus $1 postage), and *Volunteer! The Comprehensive Guide to Voluntary Service in the U.S. and Abroad* ($6.95 plus $1 postage), which is compiled every two years by CIEE and the Commission on Voluntary Service and Action, and lists over 100 organizations looking for volunteers for help with projects worldwide. CIEE also assists students with voluntary service projects in more than 12 countries. CIEE maintains offices, known as Council Travel Services, in many U.S. cities.

The Institute of International Education, 809 United Nations Plaza, New York, N.Y. 10017, provides information on study opportunities abroad and administers scholarships and fellowships for international study and training. Their *Vacation Study Abroad* is an annually-revised guide to over 1,100 courses offered by both foreign and American colleges and universities. It costs $24.95 *Academic Year Abroad* costs $29.95 and gives details on foreign study programs run by American schools and for academic credit during the regular academic year. Most European student organizations have information on work camps as well as other student jobs in their own countries.

Also check with the *Educational Travel Center,* 438 N. Frances, Madison, WI 53703.

In Canada. *Canadian Federation of Students-Services,* 243 College St., Toronto, Ontario M5T 1R5 is a non-profit student service cooperative owned and operated by over 50 college and university student unions. Its travel bureau, Travel Cuts, can arrange transportation, tours, and work programs abroad. Try also *TOURBEC,* 535 Ontario E., Montreal, Quebec H2L 1N8.

In Britain. Student travel arrangements may be made through the following organizations:

STA Travel (Student Travel Australia), 74 Old Brompton Rd., London SW7 3LQ.

USIT (Union of Student International Travel)/*London Student Travel,* 52 Grosvenor Gdns., London SW1W 0AG.

YHA Travel, 14 Southampton St., London WC2E 7HY.

Foreign Sources in the U.S. Austria: *Information for Foreign Students at Austrian Universities, Salzburg Summer School, Summer Courses in Austria,* annual, available from the Austrian Institute, 11 East 52nd St., New York, N.Y. 10022.

Denmark: Fact Sheet & Reference List of Universities, etc. Available from the Danish Embassy, 3200 Whitehaven St., NW, Washington, D.C. 20008–3683.

Finland: *Courses in Finnish Language and Culture.* Available from the Finnish Consulate General, 540 Madison Ave., New York, N.Y. 10022.

France: *Specialized Summer Courses for Foreigners in France offered by French Universities—Summer or (Academic Year). Schools & Camps & Specialized Summer Studies. Higher Education in France. Elementary & Secondary Schools in France, Study of The Arts.* Available from the French Cultural Services, 972 Fifth Ave., New York, N.Y. 10021.

Great Britain: *Study in Britain. Short Courses and Summer Schools in Britain.* Annual. Available from the British Information Services, 845 Third Ave., New York, N.Y. 10022. The excellent book (published 1987), *Guide for Young Visitors to Britain,* compiled by the Central Bureau for Educational Visits and Exchanges, Seymour Mews House, Seymour Mews, London W1H 9PE, is packed with information about access to education, work possibilities, welfare provisions, etc., etc. Price £2.45 by post. Their annual publication *Working Holidays* is most useful. Price £7.70 by post.

Italy: *Rules for the Admission of Foreign Students to Italian Universities, Art Courses in Italy; Schools for Foreigners in Italy.* Available from the Italian Cultural Institute, 686 Park Ave., New York, N.Y. 10021.

Netherlands: *Basic Data on International Courses Offered in The Netherlands, The Dutch System of International Education, University Studies in the Netherlands.* Available from the Press and Cultural Section, Netherlands Consulate General, One Rockefeller Plaza, New York, N.Y. 10020.

Norway: *Foreign Students in Norway; International Summer School; The Technical University of Trondheim.* Norwegian Information Service, 825 Third Ave., New York, N.Y. 10022.

Portugal. *University of Lisbon and Coimbra Summer Courses.* Portuguese National Tourist Office, 590 Fifth Ave., New York, N.Y. 10036.

Scandinavia: *Scan* (quarterly bulletin of the American-Scandinavian Foundation). Available from the foundation at 127 East 73rd St., New York, N.Y. 10021.

Spain: On request, the Education Department of the Consulate General, 150 East 58th St., New York, N.Y. 10022, will send you *Study in Spain: General Information for Foreign University Students; Summer Courses in Spain; American Programs in Spain;* and similar things. Note that if you are not from the northeastern U.S. you should get information from the Spanish consulate nearest you, or from the Office of Cultural Relations for the Spanish Embassy, 2600 Virginia Ave., NW, Suite 214, Washington, D.C. 20037.

Sweden: *Study in Sweden: ISU at Lund; Summer Studies at Upsala University; Study Abroad in Stockholm; Swedish Programs; Studying in Sweden: Higher Education for Visiting Students.* Available from the Swedish Information Service, 825 Third Ave., New York, N.Y. 10022.

Switzerland: *Holiday Courses and Camps in Switzerland. American Schools and Colleges in Switzerland. Lodging for Students at University Cities in Switzerland.* Available from the Swiss National Tourist Office, 608 Fifth Ave., New York, N.Y. 10020.

Useful Publications

SATA stands for Student Air Travel Association, which is an affiliate of the International Student Travel Conference that operates a system of student transportation by train, plane and ship all over Europe and from there to Africa, the Middle East and Asia. Fares on SATA student charter flights can sometimes be as low as one-third those of ordinary commercial flights.

International Student Handbook, published annually by SATA, is free.

CIEE, a nonprofit organization of more than 200 U.S. university, college, and youth-service agencies, publishes several handbooks for students traveling abroad. *It Pays To Go Abroad* is a free annual brochure on overseas work programs for students in Europe, the south Pacific, Latin America and the Caribbean.

Let's Go Europe—General handbook for students traveling abroad. Lists student accommodations, universities to attend, restaurants, etc. for the touring student.

Student and Youth Travel Agencies

(Editor's Note: Here are the best-known specialists in the youth travel field. Although most of these travel agencies have excellent reputations, we cannot assume any responsibility for their operations.)

Bailey Travel Service, Inc., 123 East Market St., York, PA 17401. Student and youth group tours.

Campus Holidays, 242 Bellevue Ave., Upper Montclair, NJ 07043.

Council Travel Services, offices in 20 U.S. cities. (See CIEE on page 45.)

Harwood Tours & Travel, Inc., 2428 Guadalupe, Austin, TX 78705. Specializes in quality escorted, co-educational motorcoach tours to Europe for students in high school and college age. Equipment used for tours is private motorcoaches seating 30–40 students.

Osborne Travel Service, Inc., 3379 Peachtree Rd., N.E., Atlanta, GA 30326. College Visits to Europe Program is designed for both high school and college students; there is also a College Tour Program for ages 18–25. These are mainly quality trips, but some budget tours are available.

Travel Plans International, Inc., P.O. Box 3875, Oak Brook, IL 60521. Quality high school and college student tours abroad planned according to specifications.

INTERNATIONAL STUDENT IDENTITY CARD

The *International Student Identity Card* is available to all university and college students who are either full-time students or graduate students. It costs $10.

There are vital reasons for carrying an *International Student Identity Card (ISIC):*

1. You can get student discounts at most museums, bullfights, concerts, theaters, etc. In fact, you can flash the card almost anywhere and get some kind of discount.

2. The card secures student/youth discounts on scheduled as well as supplemental carriers in Europe.

3. An Identity Card is also required at student lodgings and restaurants, and on student trains and ships.

4. You'll need it if you want to join a student tour group, study group, camp or work camp group once you are in Europe.

5. Also, you'll have to prove that you're a student to get a student rail pass, and the *International Student Identity Card* is an easy way to prove it.

The *ISIC* can be obtained at all of the General Student Travel Service Organizations. You can also get it from the *Council on International Educational Exchange,* 205 East 42 St., New York, N.Y. 10017; and 312 Sutter St., San Francisco, CA 94108. Canadian students should apply to the *Canadian Federation of Students-Services,* 187 College St., Toronto, Ontario M5T 1P7. In the U.K. from *STA Travel,* 74 Old Brompton Rd., London SW7 3LQ, or *USIT,* 52 Grosvenor Gardens, London SWIW OAG. It is generally easier and cheaper to buy membership cards and passes *before* you leave home, for example, international student card, student rail pass, International Driving Permit, etc.

The *Federation of International Youth Organizations* (FIYTO) card gives those under 26 access to discounts on flights, student accommodations, and discounts on museum, etc., entrance fees. An information pack comes with the card detailing facilities. Cards are available from most student organizations or from *Worldwide Student Travel.*

YOUTH TRAVEL IN EUROPE

By Rail

If you are under 26 years (whether or not a student) you have the choice of a range of reduced fares in Europe. There is the *Eurail Youth Pass* for unlimited 2nd class rail travel throughout 16 countries for $380 and valid one month, or two months for $500; this may be bought in the U.S. or Canada before you leave for Europe or from agencies in London (*YHA Travel,* 14 Southampton St., London WC2E 7HY or *Touropa,* 52 Grosvenor Gdns., London SWIW 0NP).

The less-expensive *Inter Rail Card* and the *Inter-Rail + Boat Card* for European rail travel with one month validity, are not officially available to residents of the U.S.A. or Canada unless they have resided in one of the participating European countries for six months before purchase. *Transalpino/Eurotrain,* the largest youth rail operators in Europe, offer travelers under 26 reductions up to 50% to more than 2,000 destinations; you can break your journey as often as you like en route to your final destination, within the two months' validity of the ticket (six months' validity in Turkey and Morocco). There are *Transalpino/Eurotrain* offices in London and most European capitals as well as agencies in most large towns.

In making use of the *Eurail Youth Pass* or *Transalpino* rail tickets it is most useful to have a copy of *Thomas Cook's European Timetable* which contains every European railway timetable, together with diagrams showing railway routes throughout the Continent. It is published monthly in the U.K. at £6.10 (includes first-class postage) or £5.85 second class; in the U.S., $19.95 including postage: order from the Forsyth Travel Library (see page 33). It is also on sale at principal *Thomas Cook Travel Offices.*

A *Youth Hostel Membership Card* is also an entitlement to a range of cheaper European fares—by rail, bus, sea and air; details are set out in the *International YH Handbook,* published at the beginning of each year and on sale at U.S.A. and Canadian YH HQ Offices (see page 50).

There are *Run-about Rail Tickets* for under-26s for five days' unlimited travel within a 17-day period throughout Belgium at 1300 Belgian francs (Bfr); also a *Benelux Tourrail* ticket covering Belgium, Luxembourg and the Netherlands at Bfr 2690. Similarly, cards are available on West Germany's railroads. For under 23s (27 if a full-time student) there is the *Tramper-Monats* ticket valid for one month's unlimited travel on trains and DB bus services at 240 Deutschmarks (DM). In the

U.K., inquire at British Rail Travel Centers in the main tourist centers throughout the country.

By Bus

Long-distance bus travel in Europe is relatively expensive against train and air travel (charter and last-minute cheap flights). For example, from London to Munich return: *Eurotrain/Transalpino* £111; German Tourist Facilities scheduled air charter (student rate) £94; *Eurolines* bus £82. With a train ticket you can break your journey; buses do not have this flexibility. Discount bus fares to selected destinations for those under 25 with a valid Student Coach Card/ISIC.

By Air

Certain concessionary flights are available for full-time students under 30 in possession of an ISIC card, and under-26s with a FIYTO card. Details from *STA Travel*, 74 Old Brompton Rd., London SW7, *Campus Travel at YHA*, 14 Southampton St., London WC2E 7HY and *USIT*, 52 Grosvenor Gdns., London, SW1W 0NP, or from *Student Air Travel Association* offices in many European cities; a list of their addresses is available from the student travel organizations mentioned earlier.

Although scheduled flights for students under 25 years and for young persons under 21 years carry discounts up to 25%, it is often less expensive to buy flight excursion tickets "PEX" which are on offer to all, free of student status or age restriction. Some such tickets have to be booked and paid for one month in advance "APEX," but many others are not so restricted and can readily be bought over-the-counter at airline offices or travel agents, in London.

By Motorbike

As in America, biking is enormously popular with European students. Touring speed is about 35 miles an hour, and for long hauls you can put them aboard trains and ferries. Gasoline mileage is very economical. It's easier to buy than to rent them, so order yours from a European manufacturer's agent in the United States before you leave. This has several advantages. You save about $50. You save time getting organized when you get to Europe. Licensing and insurance are handled by the dealer. You pay here in dollars and save carrying more money abroad. By ordering in advance you have a better chance of getting the model and make that you want. Best locally made buys are in England or Germany; Japanese makes can be picked up almost anywhere. You'll use the same documents (full-coverage insurance, for sure!) as a car, and you can bring the motorcycle back in the same way as a car. Helmets and goggles are compulsory.

By Bicycle

You can buy one there, you can go on your own, you can go in twos and threes, you can go in a large group, you can set up an itinerary and stay at hostels and the like, or you can be spontaneous and stay wherever you drop. Anyway you want, the *American Youth Hostels* can help. Contact them early in the winter, join the organization, buy the books, and ask them anything not already answered in the printed text. Their prices are cheap, their experience extensive, their quality of advice and merchandise the highest. In addition, AYH sponsor a number of bicycle tours of their own, in both Europe and the U.S. If you plan to buy a bike in Europe and bring it back, there are two things to bear in mind. Spare parts for British bikes are the same as for American ones; but if you buy a continental bike be sure to get a model destined for the American market, so that you can get it fixed in the U.S. Remember too that in spite of the size limits on airline baggage, some airlines make special arrangements for bicycles or count them as your second piece of free baggage. Inquire before you buy your ticket.

There are some countries that seem made for cycling. Holland and Denmark are two obvious examples; they are small and compact, flat, and well organized. Sometimes the bicycle paths in Holland seem better than the roads that they parallel, in fact. You'll probably find it simpler to buy a bicycle in Europe than to try to get one across the Atlantic; when you do, ask what to expect if you try to sell it back at the end of your vacation. You can rent bicycles all over Europe, and in Belgium, France, Holland, Switzerland and Germany a particularly attractive feature is that at over 250 railway stations you can rent a bicycle for about $5 a day (less if you have a rail ticket), and not only use it in the immediate area then return it but even ride it away and return it in your *next* sight-seeing area.

In Britain you can rent a bicycle from £6 to £10 a day, or £36 to £60 a week (plus about £50 deposit), but you'll also need proof of identity. A useful address is *Bike UK*, 11 Lower Robert St., WC2N 6BH (tel. 071–839 2111). If you are planning a cycling tour, and can arrange things well ahead, contact the *British Cycling Federation*, 36 Rockingham Rd., Kettering, Northants, NN16 8HG (tel. 0536–412211). They produce several interesting publications. And good news, too, for budget travelers—British Rail carry bicycles free of charge on most trains (but not at rush hours or on 125 High Speed Trains) so you can get easily and cheaply to the area you wish to tour.

The various Scandinavian countries' national tourist offices have information sheets with titles like: Cycling in Sweden, Cycling Vacations in Norway, Rent a Bicycle in Copenhagen, etc.

Hitchhiking

Hitchhiking is a sport. There are people who say it's the only way really to experience "travel." They also say it's the best way of meeting the people and seeing the countryside, even better than driving your way through Europe. But it can be a somewhat hazardous sport, and you should be aware of this before you get too enthusiastic about using your thumb. (In fact, in Italy and some other European countries, you point your index finger down toward the road in the direction you wish to travel to signal your desire to hitch. The traditional American thumb pointed behind you may be interpreted as an obscene gesture by those unfamiliar with U.S. students).

It's not always easy to get a lift; sometimes a whole day will pass without a ride—while you get twelve lifts on the next day. But you can do certain standard things to get vehicles to stop for you. For one thing, you should look like you want a lift. Too much luggage will repel most drivers who will picture the time it will take to get it into the car.

Generally speaking, hitchhiking is safest in Western, Northeastern, and Central Europe. It is not recommended for women, especially in Spain, Italy, Greece and Turkey. You had better be warned, though, that France, Italy and West Germany have the highest accident rates in Europe because of excessively fast driving habits. Communist Europe may be the safest, as private cars mostly carry officials.

The best spot to get a lift is on the outskirts of the city, at the point where the highway going in your direction begins. There is usually a cluster of gas stations there. Otherwise, try the highway toll booths or gas stations.

Always check out the laws of the country in which you intend to hitch. It's illegal in certain areas and on some motorways. There are cities, Florence for instance, in which it is all right to hitchhike from the curb, but you'll get a ticket if you step down into the street.

The single most important piece of equipment you can have is a large, visible sign, hand-drawn, with thick, black letters announcing where you want to go. If possible, spell the name of the city in its native form: Firenze, not Florence; København, not Copenhagen. Most hitchhikers carry or sew on a flag, and for good reason. Drivers who are notoriously suspicious of an unknown rider are often reassured when the hitchhiker waves his mother country's flag.

It's highly unlikely that a driver would pick up two men. Two women can have better luck, or even a young couple, but men do better traveling alone than with another man.

Don't worry about the language barriers. It will take you a very short time to realize that people communicate very well without the least knowledge of each other's language. A drawing (it's a good idea to carry a pad and pencil), some hand signs and facial expressions are good basics for communication without language.

Limit your luggage.

HOSTELS

Student Hostels

Student hostels, usually to be found in the quiet neighborhood of universities in European cities, are often open to student visitors in out-of-term times. Accommodations are in small dormitories, sometimes in single rooms; married couples can occasionally be accommodated. Shower/bathroom, as well as kitchen and laundry rooms are often provided. Length of stay is not so restricted as in youth hostels and the standard of accommodations is superior; language difficulties are unlikely, too. Such accommodations cost $22 to $30 a night; an ISIC card is essential.

Youth Hostels

There are more than 3,000 youth hostels in Europe; they vary in standard from country to country, but they all offer simple accommodations for men and women in separate multi-bedded rooms, washing and toilet facilities and a common room. They are designed for communal living at minimum cost; you make your own bed and sometimes help with simple household tasks, such as washing-up. At many hostels, inexpensive meals are provided and most have a kitchen where you can cook your own food.

Youth hostels are not a cheap substitute for hotels, suitcases and smart clothes are out of place, and there is no staff to serve guests. If you have never visited a hostel before, try to get some experience in your own country before going abroad. You must use a *sheet* sleeping bag of approved pattern (can be bought from addresses given below, or rented at youth hostels). Occasionally other types of sleeping bag may be allowed, particularly in remote mountain hostels, but in most cases such bags are not permitted. Pillows and blankets (or duvets) are provided where you are required to use a sheet sleeping bag. In some countries, at peak periods, you may not usually stay more than three consecutive nights at any one hostel. Membership is essential and you can buy your *International Youth Hostel Membership Card* from—

American Youth Hostels, Inc., P.O. Box 37613, Washington, D.C. 20013	Junior US$10 Senior US$25 Senior citizen US$15	under 18 years over 18–54 years over 54
Canadian Hostelling Assoc., 1600 James Naismith Dr., Suite 608 Gloucester, Ont. K1B 5N4	Junior Can$12 Senior Can$21	under 17 years over 17 years
YHA England and Wales, 14 Southampton St., London WC2E 7HY	Adults 21 and over £7.60 (£4 for under-21s) Overseas visitors to U.K. £8 (can be paid in installments) Life membership £80 (again, can be paid in installments)	

You can also buy the *International YH Handbook* at these addresses; there are in fact two volumes, but the one you will want is Vol. 1, "Europe and Mediterranean," which costs £5.95 including postage in the U.K., and $8.95 in the U.S. It gives details of all permanent hostels in Europe, with miniature diagrams showing their location in the larger cities.

Although there is no fixed upper age limit (except in Bavaria, where the maximum is 27 years) some countries give preference to younger members. Many youth hostels in Europe, especially in Scandinavia, have separate accommodations for families with young children.

Motorists and motorcyclists are welcome, although priority is always given to walkers and cyclists.

The average cost of an overnight at a youth hostel ranges from $5–$20. Meals, where provided, cost from $3–$6. If you buy and cook your own food the cost can be less. Allow $20–$25 per day to cover bed and three simple meals.

YMCA/YWCA Hostels

There are YMs and YWs throughout Europe, mostly in cities, not all of them segregated or strictly religious. Their handbook, *Pack for Europe,* listing addresses, availabilities, charges, etc., is available from the *YWCA in the U.S.A.,* 726 Broadway, New York, N.Y. 10003 ($3); in U.K., *YWCA,* Clarendon House, 52 Cornmarket St., Oxford OX1 3EJ (£1.50 plus 25p post/packing).

CAMPING

For tourists from the U.S., it is less expensive and probably better value to buy lightweight camping equipment in London, where a number of good specialist camping shops stock selections of such gear. For outdoor types, lightweight camping in Europe is the least expensive and most rewarding means of touring and securing accommodations with little constraint. A lightweight tent, large enough for two, is light and compact enough to be carried in a back pack. Touring with a partner has economic benefits—initial costs are shared, overnights at camp sites and everyday expenses are reduced. Although it is prudent to seek out official camp sites rather than setting up camp on what may appear to be common land, it is often necessary to possess a *Carte de Campeur* or *International Camping Carnet.* Such a document, verifying your status as a bona-fide camper is issued by the AA or RAC to their members on application. In the U.S.A. apply to *National Campers and Hikers Association,* 4804 Transit Rd., Bldg. 2, Depew, N.Y. 14043; in the U.K. to the *Automobile Association,* Fanum House, Basingstoke, Hants RG21 2EA (£2.30 for those with AA Insurance), the *Royal Automobile Club,* RAC House, P.O. Box 100, 7 Brighton Rd., S. Croydon, Surrey CR2 6XW, or for cyclists to the *Cyclists' Touring Club,* 69 Meadrow, Godalming, Surrey GU7 3HS. Price £4.75 (members only; membership £18.50, and £9.25 for under-21s).

Facilities offered at camp sites in Europe vary from country to country, so too do the length of season and cost of overnights. In Northern Europe the season opens in early June and closes by mid-September, whereas in Mediterranean countries most camp sites stay open year-round. Many camp sites in north west Europe are excellently equipped, those in Germany best of all; in Southern European countries standards are not always as satisfactory as they might be. In France, where camping is so popular, camp sites abound but standards can range from excellent to deplorable, and so it is prudent to make local inquiries before making reservations.

Inquire at European Government Tourist Offices in the U.S. and Canada for advice on camping in their own countries; such offices provide detailed literature on their camp sites, showing locations, costs and facilities offered—together with maps showing their whereabouts. Rates for overnights vary from about U.S. $2 to U.S. $5 per person; visitors intending to stay more than one night are advised to make prior reservations.

You should join your own National Camping Association before setting out for Europe; they are authorities on European camping, too, and their advice is freely available to their members. In the U.S.A. apply to—*The National Campers and Hikers Association* (address above).

Names and addresses of National Camping Associations in Europe to whom it would be useful to write for information are as follows—

Austria: *Osterreichischer Camping Club,* Schubert Ring 1, A 1010 Vienna

Belgium: *Royal Camping et Caravanning Club de Belgique,* 31 rue Madeleine, 1000 Brussels

Bulgaria: *Bulgarischer Touristenverband Zentralrat,* Boul. Tolbuchin 18, Sofia

Czechoslovakia: *"Cedok,"* Na Prikope 18, 11135 Prague 1

Denmark: *Dansk Camping Union,* Gl. Kongevej 74-D, 1850 Copenhaven V

Finland: *Travel Association,* Mikonkatu 25, Helsinki

France: *Camping Club de France,* 218 boulevard St. Germain, Paris 7

Germany: *German Camping Club,* Mandelstrasse 28, D 8000 Munich 23

Great Britain: *Camping and Caravanning Club Ltd.,* 11 Lower Grosvenor Place, London SW1W OEY

Hungary: *Magyar Camping Club,* Kalvin Ter. 9, Budapest H-1091.

Iceland: *Iceland Camping Club,* Bogartun 33, Reykjavik, ISC 105.

Ireland: *Irish Tourist Board,* 757 Third Ave., New York, N.Y. 10017

Italy: *FIC,* Costa de Magnoli 30, Florence

Luxembourg: *National Tourist Office,* P.O. Box 1001, Luxembourg City

Netherlands: *Nederlandse Kampeerraad,* Daendelstraat 11, Den Haag

Norway: *NAF,* Storgt. 2, P.O. Box 494, Sentrum, Oslo 1

Poland: *"Orbis,"* 16 Braca St., Warsaw

Portugal: *Federacao Portuguesa de Campismo e Caravanismo,* Rua Voz do Operario 1, 1100 Lisbon.

Romania: *"Carpati,"* 7 Blvd. General Magheru, Bucharest

Spain: *Spanish National Camping Association,* Calle de Duque de Medinaceli 2, Madrid 14

Sweden: *SCR,* P.O. Box 255, 45117 Uddevalla

Switzerland: *Swiss Camping Association,* Bertastrasse 72, 8003 Zurich

Yugoslavia: *Turisticki Savez Jugoslavije,* Mose Pijade 8, Belgrade

LEAVING EUROPE

CUSTOMS ON RETURNING HOME

If you propose to take on your holiday any *foreign-made* articles, such as cameras, binoculars, expensive timepieces and the like, it is wise to put with your travel documents the receipt from the retailer or some other evidence that the item was bought in your home country. If you bought the article on a previous holiday abroad and have already paid duty on it, carry with you the receipt for this. Otherwise, on returning home, you may be charged duty (for British residents, Value Added Tax as well). In other words, unless you can prove prior possession, foreign-made articles are dutiable *each time* they enter the U.S. The details below are correct as we go to press. It would be wise to check in case of change.

U.S. residents may bring in $400 worth of foreign merchandise as gifts or for personal use without having to pay duty, provided they have been out of the country more than 48 hours and provided they have not claimed a similar exemption within the previous 30 days. Every member of a family is entitled to the same exemption, regardless of age, and the exemptions can be pooled.

The $400 figure is based on the fair retail value of the goods in the country where acquired. Included for travelers over the age of 21 are one liter of alcohol, 100 cigars (non-Cuban) and 200 cigarettes. Any amount in excess of those limits will be taxed at the port of entry, and may additionally be taxed in the traveler's home state. Only one bottle of perfume trademarked in the U.S. may be brought in. Unlimited amounts of goods from certain specially designated "developing" countries may also be brought in duty free; check with U.S. Customs Service, Box 7407, Washington, D.C. 20044. Write to the same address for information regarding importation of automobiles and/or motorcycles. You may not bring home meats, fruits, plants, soil or other agricultural items.

Gifts valued at under $50 may be mailed to friends or relatives at home duty free, but not more than one per day (of receipt) to any one addressee. These gifts must not include perfumes costing more than $5, tobacco or liquor.

If you are traveling with such foreign made articles as cameras, watches or binoculars that were purchased at home, it is best either to carry the receipt for them with you or to register them with U.S. Customs prior to departing. This will save much time (and potentially aggravation) upon your return.

Military personnel returning from abroad should check with the nearest American Embassy for special regulations pertaining to them.

Canadian residents. In addition to personal effects, the following articles may be brought in duty free: a maximum of 50 cigars, 200 cigarettes, 2 pounds of tobacco and 40 ounces of liquor, provided these are declared in writing to customs on arrival and accompany the traveler in hand or checked-through baggage. These are included in the basic exemption of $300 a year. Personal gifts should be mailed as "Unsolicited Gift—Value Under $40". Canadian customs regulations are strictly enforced; you are recommended to check what your allowances are and to make sure you have kept receipts for whatever you have bought abroad. For details ask for the Canada Customs brochure, "I Declare."

British residents. There are two levels of duty-free allowance for people entering the U.K.: one, for goods bought outside the EC or for goods bought in a duty-free shop within the EC; two, for goods bought in an EC country but not in a duty-free shop.

In the first category you may import duty free: 200 cigarettes or 100 cigarillos or 50 cigars or 250 grams of tobacco (*Note:* if you live outside Europe, these allowances are doubled); two liters of still table wine plus one liter of alcoholic drinks over 22% vol. (38.8% proof) or two liters of alcoholic drinks not over 22% vol. (e.g. fortified or sparkling wine) or a further two liters of still table wine; (in other words, you could—if you chose to forego your spirits allocation—bring in four liters of still table wine); plus 50 grams (two fl. oz.) of perfume; plus 1/4 liter (nine fl. oz.) of toilet water; plus other goods to the value of £32.

In the second category you may import duty free: 300 cigarettes or 150 cigarillos or 75 cigars or 400 grams of tobacco; five liters of still table wine plus 1½ liters of alcoholic drinks over 22% vol. (38.8% proof) or three liters of alcholic drinks not over 22% vol. (e.g. fortified or sparkling or still table wine) or a further three liters of still table wine (i.e. up to eight liters of still table wine if no spirits); plus 75 grams of perfume; plus 3/8 liter (13 fl. oz.) of toilet water; plus other goods to the value of £250. (*Note:* though it is not classified as an alcoholic drink by EEC countries for Customs' purposes and is thus considered part of the "other goods" allowance, you may not import more than 50 liters of beer).

In addition, *no animals or pets of any kind* may be brought into the U.K. The penalties for doing so are severe and are strictly enforced; there are *no* exceptions. Similarly, fresh meats, plants and vegetables, controlled drugs and firearms and ammunition may not be brought into the U.K. There are no restrictions on the import or export of British and foreign currencies.

Anyone planning to stay in the U.K. for more than six months should contact H.M. Customs and Excise, Dorset House, Stamford St., London SEI 9PS (tel. 01-928 0533) for further information.

DUTY FREE

Duty free is not what it once was. You may not be paying tax on your bottle of whiskey or perfume, but you are certainly contributing to somebody's profits. Duty-free shops are big business these days and markups are often around 100 to 200%. So don't be seduced by the idea that because it's duty free it's a bargain. Very often prices are not much different from your local discount store and in the case of perfume or jewelry they can be even higher. It is, however, worth buying cosmetics, perfume, liquor and tobacco in duty-free shops before entering any Scandinavian country, as local taxes on these goods are extremely high and many items cost two or three times as much as in duty-free stores.

As a general rule of thumb, duty-free stores on the ground offer better value than buying in the air. Also, if you buy duty-free goods on a plane, remember that the range is likely to be limited and that if you are paying in a different currency to that of the airline, their rate of exchange often bears only a passing resemblance to the official one.

EUROPE
COUNTRY
BY
COUNTRY

Austria

Once the heart of a vast empire that stretched to the New World, Austria today is an attractive amalgam of the rich vestiges of its proud past and a balanced attitude to the modern world. Vienna, for example, contains both the Hofburg, with its Burgundian treasure, and the modern UN Vienna International Center, which houses the International Atomic Energy Agency. This juxtaposition of the old and the new makes Austria a fascinating place to visit. So, too, does the fact that it is poised between East and West, sharing its cultural heritage with Europe, and yet having very obvious affinities with the lands that lie beyond. It was Metternich who said that "Asia begins at the Landstrasse", encapsulating thus the crucial role of Vienna as the meeting place of East and West for two thousand years.

But, as with most countries, the capital is only a small part of what Austria has to offer. Indeed, most visitors will see only a part of the wide variety, geographical and cultural, that is available. Whether you are looking for a quiet holiday in the green depths of the countryside, exciting skiing, music and drama festivals, churches, museums and galleries, the chance to extend your skills in a "hobby holiday", or if you want to improve your health in one of the many spas, Austria can supply exactly what you want.

Although it is one of Europe's smallest countries, Austria manages to pack within its borders as many mountains, lakes and picturesque cities as countries five times its size. On top of which it can boast a people as welcoming and friendly as any in the world, who insist on real comforts in all aspects of life. Sports rank high and skiing highest, with innumerable ski lifts, cable cars, mountaintop lodges, highways. Though the currency has stopped appreciating, the inflation rate is still one of Europe's lowest. Thus Austria remains the most economical of skiing's Big Three (Austria, France and Switzerland).

For most people Austria is Vienna or Innsbruck or Salzburg or the Tirol region generally. These places have the grandeur and all that is superlative in style and scenery. But there are some half dozen other superb vacation areas from the splendid Vorarlberg to the warm Carinthia, and remote Burgenland and Styria, for instance—and there is a case for spending some time in these areas rather than slavishly doing the grand tour. In fact, you will find that many of the smaller country towns reproduce in miniature the glories of the great centers, and also provide budget places to stay and atmospheric places to eat.

As the National Tourist Office is always coming up with new ideas for imaginative sports and hobby holidays, we suggest that you contact them when you begin to plan your vacation.

PRACTICAL INFORMATION FOR AUSTRIA

WHAT WILL IT COST. Austria is, like it or not, one of Europe's more expensive countries. True, you'll get value for money here, and true, prices may not yet be generally as high as in Germany, say, or the Scandinavian countries. But for the most part, Austria is not a land in which your dollar will stretch far.

But don't immediately cross this lovely country off your list. There are plenty of practical steps you can take to help keep costs low. First, and most obvious, limit your time in the major cities and centers. These are the most expensive places, but towns like Graz, Linz, Krems or Hallstatt, for example, all offer history and comfort at much lower rates.

Take advantage of the cheaper weekly rates offered by most winter and summer resorts and several hotels in the various cities including Vienna and Salzburg. The Austrian National Tourist Office provides a list, in English, of such places and also notes where ski resort prices include ski lift expenses.

The public transportation systems in all larger towns and cities are excellent, and make taking expensive taxis quite unnecessary. Tickets (in Vienna and Innsbruck) can be bought in blocks of five at a cheaper rate at most tobacco shops *(Tabak-Trafik)*. If you plan to do a lot of traveling in Vienna in one day, buy a day's ticket for 40 AS, which entitles you to limitless riding within that day.

The monetary unit is the Austrian Schilling (AS), subdivided into 100 Groschen. The AS 500 and 100 notes look similar in color and design; confusion can be expensive. Exchange rate at presstime (spring '90) was about 12 AS to the U.S. dollar and 20 AS to the pound sterling. Foreign currency and Austrian Schillings may be brought into Austria in unlimited quantities. Officially you must not take out more than 100,000 AS.

Sample Costs. The extras can add up quickly. These will run for a movie seat, around 60AS; theater seat, from 50–600; museum entry, 15 upwards (try for the free days); coffee, from 20–40. For other food prices see under *Restaurants.*

NATIONAL TOURIST OFFICE. For all information concerning your holiday in Austria, contact the *Austrian National Tourist Office,* Österreich-Information, Margaretenstrasse 1, Vienna 1040. Tel.(0222) 588–660. Other information can be obtained from the *Verkehrsvereine* (local tourist offices) in most towns. Each province has its own tourist board.

Addresses of the Austrian National Tourist Office overseas are:

In the U.S.: 500 Fifth Ave., New York, N.Y. 10110 (tel. 212–944–6880); 11601 Wilshire Blvd., Los Angeles, CA 90025 (tel. 213–477–3332); 500 N. Michigan Ave., Chicago, IL 60611 (tel. 312–644–5556); 4800 San Felipe, Houston, TX 77056 (tel. 713–850–8888).

In Canada: 2 Bloor St., E., Suite 3330, Toronto, Ontario M4W 1A8 (tel. 416–967–3348); 1010 Sherbrooke St. W., Suite 1410, Montreal, P.Q. H3A 2R7 (tel. 514–849–3709); 736 Granville St., Suite 1220, Vancouver Block, Vancouver, B.C. V6Z 1J2 (tel. 604–683–8695).

In the U.K.: 30 St. George St., London W1R OAL (tel. 071–629 0461).

WHEN TO COME. Austria has two tourist seasons; one in the summer from May to September and one in the winter, for skiing, from December to April. Skiing in high altitudes lasts from November to June. Glacier skiing goes year round.

Average afternoon temperatures in degrees Fahrenheit and centigrade:

Vienna	Jan.	Feb.	Mar.	Apr.	May	June	July	Aug.	Sept.	Oct.	Nov.	Dec.
F°	34	38	47	57	66	71	75	73	66	55	44	37
C°	1	3	8	14	19	22	24	23	19	13	7	3

SPECIAL EVENTS. *New Year* is of course a time for merriment, and in some fashionable winter resorts, such as Zürs in Vorarlberg and Seefeld in Tirol, its beginning is celebrated with such unusual features as torchlight ski races; Vienna offers the *Fledermaus* in both Opera Houses, a choice of superb concerts, and the Kaiserball in the Hofburg—the first of the glittering balls. The Three Magi singing is observed almost everywhere in the countryside and special masked processions can be seen around Twelfth Night and in mid-*January* in some localities of Styria where they are known by the name of Glöckerllauf, as well as in the Pongau area of Land Salzburg where they are called Perchtenlauf. In Salzburg there is a Mozart week.

Carnival, or Fasching, celebrations get under way immediately afterwards and continue, crescendo, officially until Ash Wednesday; if the season is short, then the partying continues on into Lent. The activities include hundreds of balls in Vienna, culminating in the grand gala Opera Ball and the Philharmonic Ball; mummers' parades with old woodcarved masks in several localities in Tirol, masked dances and parties everywhere.

Easter is celebrated everywhere, with a music festival in Salzburg and many fine masses sung in major churches all over Austria.

The first weekend of *May* is most energetically celebrated at Zell am Ziller, in the Ziller valley of Tirol, which is thronged with visitors to the Gauderfest. The many attractions of this festival include Preis-Rangeln (a folk type of wrestling), folk dancing, the serving of a special beer and a tremendous outburst of Gemütlichkeit. May also marks the beginning of the season for three famous trips that can be made until October—the exploration of the largest ice caves in Europe, at Werfen and on the Dachstein above Halstatt, and the trip over the Grossglockner Alpine road. The Vienna Festival begins during the second half of May and lasts through mid-June.

On Midsummer's Day (*June* 21) great bonfires burn almost everywhere throughout the country.

At the height of the season, in *July* and *August,* the Salzburg Festival, one of the world's most prestigious, attracts a cosmopolitan audience. In the same months, opera and operettas are performed on water stages at Bregenz on Lake Constance, and at Mörbisch on Neusiedler Lake in Burgenland. The Danube Arts Festival is held in Lower Austria and the Lockenhausen Music Festival in Burgenland. Classical plays are presented in the courtyards of the Dominican Convent of Friesach and Porcia Palace, Spittal/Drau, both in Carinthia. In August, Klagenfurt holds its Wood Fair. Styria and Tirol hold brass band and folk festivals in summer.

In *September,* musical interest shifts to Linz, where the Bruckner Festival is accompanied by an exposition of modern art. There are trade fairs in Vienna and Innsbruck. Many villages have their own harvest or grape festivities throughout this month and *October.* The Graz music and drama festival called Steirischer Herbst (Styrian Autumn) takes place from early October to mid-November.

St. Nicholas Day, the 6th of *December,* as in many countries of Europe, is the real beginning of the Christmas season.

National Holidays. Jan. 1 (New Year's Day); Jan. 6 (Epiphany); Mar. 31, Apr. 1 (Easter); May 1 (May Day); May 9 (Ascension); May 20, 21 (Whitsun); Aug. 15 (Assumption); Oct. 26 (National Day); Nov. 1 (All Saints); Dec. 8 (Immaculate Conception); Dec. 25, 26.

VISAS. Citizens of the United States, all E.C. countries including Britain, and Canada do not need visas to visit Austria. However, you must of course have a valid passport.

HEALTH CERTIFICATES. Not required for entry into Austria.

GETTING TO AUSTRIA. By Plane. *Austrian Airlines* offers a non-stop service between Vienna and New York, five or six times weekly. *Pan Am* have flights between JFK and Vienna. There are excellent connecting flights from all the major European cities, London included, by *Austrian Airlines,* who also have a London/Salzburg route. For the Tirol it is more convenient to fly to Munich and go on by road or rail to Innsbruck. There are good train connections from Zürich airport to Innsbruck and Bregenz. Southern Austria has its own airport at Klagenfurt, and a sizable internal air-network operates between most of the provincial capitals. *Rheintalflug* fly from Vienna to Friedrichshafen, Germany, on weekdays, with a free transfer service to main cities in Vorarlberg.

There are international air services from most European capitals to Vienna and also from major cities in Germany. Like its neighbor Switzerland, Austria really is a junction of European routes.

By Train. From the U.K. the best routes are via Oostende. The long-running express the *Oostende-Vienna* links the two cities in about 22 hours running via Brussels, Köln, Frankfurt, Passau and Linz. Immediate connection at Oostende with ferry service from Dover (departs London around 9 A.M.) and reaches Vienna just after breakfast. The train carries 1st and 2nd class sleepers, 2nd class bunk beds, 1st and 2nd day coaches; light refreshment services part of the way. Similar service also from Oostende, leaving mid-evening (connections from Dover and London) arriving in Salzburg (about 9.45 A.M.) via Cologne and Munich. Sleepers (both classes) and 2nd class bunk beds, Oostende to Salzburg. Reservations are advisable for both trains.

From Paris the Orient Express runs overnight from the Gare de l'Est, arriving in Vienna at 3.17 P.M. A daytime train leaves Paris at 7.55 A.M, and reaches Vienna at 10 P.M.

For the Tirol from the U.K. the best route is by the through service from Calais to Innsbruck (bunk beds and day carriages) which leaves London (Victoria) at 2.30 P.M. and goes via Dover–Calais, Lille, Mulhouse, Basel and Zürich into Austria, terminating at Innsbruck (for Kitzbühel) just before midday.

There are excellent rail services to Austria, especially from neighboring Switzerland, Germany, and Italy.

By Bus. At present no through bus services run from the U.K. to Austria. *Eurolines,* as part of International Express, run a daily service in summer to Munich. It leaves London mid-evening, arriving in Munich some 23 hours later. Return fare to Munich is about £100, £90 for students. Onwards from Munich, *R.V.O.* runs buses three times a day on Fridays to Sundays that arrive in Innsbruck after three hours. The fare is DM 42.60.

CUSTOMS. There are two levels of duty-free allowance for goods imported to Austria. Travelers coming from a European country may import 200 cigarettes or 50 cigars or 250 gr. of tobacco; 2 liters of wine and 1 liter of spirits; 1 bottle of toilet water, 50 gr. of perfume. Travelers coming from non-European countries may import 400 cigarettes or 100 cigars or 500 gr. tobacco; 2 liters of wine and one liter of spirits; 1 bottle of toilet water, 50 gr. of perfume.

HOTELS. Hotel prices are high but even the simplest establishments, as well as accommodations in private homes, which are available in all country resorts, are clean with very polite service. Pre- and post-season rates (May/June and September) are 15 to 25% cheaper and off-season rates 20 to 40%, but many resort hotels close then. Prices always include breakfast.

Many towns and resorts are expensive, but inexpensive accommodations can still be found even at the most chic ski villages. Equally comfortable accommodations and excellent food can be found at half the price in the same category in the numerous lesser yet still attractive resorts. This accounts for the very wide price ranges in each category.

Price ranges for a double room are: Moderate (M) 900–1,500 AS; Inexpensive (I) 500–900 AS.

Under the official rating system two to three stars will usually correspond to our (M) and (I) categories. You may even find Moderate prices in some four-star hotels, but always check.

In the countryside and occasionally in the towns, various local terms are common: *Gasthof,* German for a country and small town type of a good-size hotel combined with a fairly large eating and drinking establishment. In bigger cities they are usually old, often colorful but unpretentious; in the resorts, *hof* frequently forms part of the names of even deluxe modern establishments. *Gasthaus,* a country inn (but found also in the cities), smaller in size than Gasthof, but usually with at least a few beds; the emphasis is on the eating and drink services. *Frühstücks-pension,* a guest house usually offering rooms with breakfast, and occasionally a small evening snack.

The expression *garni* means simply bed and breakfast.

Youth Hostels. Members of the International Youth Hostels Federation are welcome at all Austria's Youth Hostels. Details from *Osterreichischer Jugendherbergsverband,* Gonzagagasse 22, A-1010, Vienna. The Austrian Camping Club (Johannesgasse 20, A–1010 Vienna) offers a wide choice of camping in summer and winter.

RESTAURANTS. Lunch is served usually between 12 noon and 2 P.M. and dinner between 6 and 9 P.M., except in late-hour restaurants, where it is served much later.

It is possible to have really excellent meals all over Austria for a modest cost—even in Vienna and Salzburg. Among the good places to eat are the wine cellars, which not only provide low cost meals with delicious wine by the glass and large helpings, but also will satisfy even the most blasé seeker after atmosphere.

A Moderate meal will cost around 250–400 AS, less if you take the set-menu meals that are usually offered at noon (the main meal in Austria). An Inexpensive meal will cost around 90–200 AS, although there can be a considerable overlap between the two kinds of meal. We grade restaurants (M) for moderate and (I) for inexpensive—but you could easily get an inexpensive meal in a moderate place, especially in the wine cellars.

A bottle of wine costs about 150–250 AS (more, of course, for special vintages), but the open wines are very good and cost about 25–35 AS per ¼-liter carafe. A glass (half liter) of beer varies from 24 to 30 AS depending on the establishment; coffee varies from 20 to 40 AS; whiskey about 55–90 AS; schnaps from 15 to 30; a cocktail in a first-class bar will cost at least 90 AS. Mineral water, apple juice, cola, and similar drinks cost about 17 AS, all inclusive of taxes.

Food and Drink. Austrian specialties include several marvelous soups: *Leberknödelsuppe* (meat broth with liver dumplings); *Fischbeuschlsuppe* (thick, spicy and Viennese, and made from freshwater fish); and *Gulaschsuppe* (paprika-hot and Hungarian). Fish, too, from Austrian lakes and rivers, are excellent, especially *Fogosch* (pike) and *Forelle* (trout). And, of course, there are numerous types of *Schnitzel*. Pork comes in many disguises (*Schwein* is the name to seek out) and is truly succulent. Steaks are often good but expensive, while *Tafelspitz* (boiled beef) is delicious and good value. Noodles and dumplings are staple items, and these in soup make a perfect budget meal.

Coffee and cakes or desserts are the highlight of Austrian culinary art but they do run away with the money. *Strudel* ought to be tried though, because it is lighter in Austria than anywhere else. *Torte* usually means a cake and the most famous is one flooded in chocolate and jam called *Sachertorte;* it originates from the Hotel Sacher in Vienna and has made its way in paler forms to all the patîsseries of the world.

Wine and beer are the main drinks, both available very reasonably on draft in most restaurants. Wine quality ranges from good to outstanding. The white wines, especially, are quite delicious and far too little known outside Austria.

TIPPING. Most hotels and restaurants (among the few exceptions are smaller country inns) include service charges in their rates. For restaurants this includes 10% service and all the various taxes, but it is customary to give a little extra (about 5–7 AS, or 5% on a larger bill). Round taxi fares up to nearest 5 AS.

MAIL. Letters within Austria cost 5 AS, to other countries within Europe 6 AS. Postcards within the country cost 4 AS, to other European nations 5 AS, and to the U.S. 7.50 AS. Letters to the U.S. are either weighed and charged accordingly, or else sent via air-letters available at all post offices for 11 AS.

TELEPHONE. The Austrian telephone system is being reorganized, and numbers will be changing for years to come. We make every effort to keep numbers up to date, but check on the spot should you find it difficult to make your connection.

CLOSING TIMES. Stores open from 9 to 6, close 12.30 or 1.00 on Saturdays, except for the first Saturday in the month, when many stay open until 5 or 6. Banking hours vary in each town so check on the spot. Banks are always closed Sat. Outside Vienna most shops close for lunch till 3 P.M. Hairdressers close Mon.

GETTING AROUND AUSTRIA. By Train. With a remarkably extensive railway network (almost totally electrified) getting about by train is easy. Services are frequent, the trains clean and usually punctual. Austria, oddly enough, is the last country in Continental Europe still building traditional full-scale dining cars as opposed to the current trend to buffet or cafeteria cars.

Austrian Railways (OBB) no longer offer any runabout tickets combining rail and bus travel. If you intend using trains a lot consider buying the *Bundesnetzkarte,* which gives unlimited rail travel for 9 or 16 days or one month at 1,440 AS, 1,960 AS, and 3,100 AS respectively throughout Austria in 2nd class. At these prices EurailPass, YouthPass, and InterRail would be a better bet, if you qualify! For local travel the 18 *Regional-Netzkarten* are good value. They can be bought for periods of 4 to 10 days at 400 AS to 760 AS. With a *Rabbit* card, on any of four days during a ten-day period, you can travel anywhere for 1,290 AS first class, 890 AS second; if you're under 27, the prices are 690 AS and 490 AS. You'll need a passport photo and identification.

By Bus. In addition to the Post Buses (a good service but mainly serving rural areas) there are a number of long distance bus routes in Austria. The cities have excellent public transport, which serves not only the central zones but goes far out into the suburbs. Local tourist offices will give you full details.

Vienna

There are three cheap ways to get a good bird's-eye view of Austria's great capital: climb the 345 steps of the "Old Steffel," the south steeple of Saint Stephen's Cathedral (or take the elevator to the observation platform at the top of the much smaller second tower if you prefer the easy way); visit the Big Wheel of *The Third Man* fame in the Prater; or take the half-hour streetcar ride (#38 from Schottentor) to Grinzing plus the 15-minute bus trip to the Kahlenberg, Kobenzl, or Leopoldsberg. From any one of these hills in the Vienna Woods, you will get a very good idea of the layout of the city.

Most of Vienna lies in an arc along the southern bank of the Danube. Its heart, the Innere Stadt (Inner City), is bounded by the Ringstrasse (Ring), built in the 19th century on the site of the moats and ramparts of medieval Vienna. The Danube Canal, diverted from the main river just above Vienna and flowing through the city to rejoin the parent stream just below it, completes the Ring. About a mile beyond the Ring runs the roughly parallel line of the Gürtel (Beltway), which until 1890 formed the outer fortifications, or Linien-wall. It was at the height of Vienna's imperial prosperity that the Ringstrasse became one of the most handsome streets in all Europe, studded with such imposing buildings as the Opera House, Museum of Fine Arts, Museum of Natural History, the "New Wing" of the Hofburg, Parliament, the Rathaus, the Burgtheater, the University, and the Votivkirche. An easy way to see much of the city is to take the full circuit of the No. 1 or No. 2 streetcar around the Ring.

Bus tours of the city and vicinity are offered by several enterprises, and you can also take a boat tour along the Danube and the Danube Canal. However, the best way to explore the Inner City, that vital square mile that includes Vienna's greatest treasures of art and architecture, is on foot—this is essentially a city for walking. The best weather for that is from spring to about halfway through fall, but the winter (which can be quite severe) does give an extra sparkle to the glittering interiors of theaters and Baroque palaces.

The main artery is the three-quarter mile of the Kärntnerstrasse-Rotenturmstrasse that runs straight through from the Opernring past the Staatsoper (Opera House) to the Danube Canal. Halfway down, where the street changes its name, is Stephansdom (Saint Stephen's Cathedral), the main landmark of Vienna. Left of the cathedral is the square-like street of Graben with its famous and stunningly restored Plague Column, and if you turn left again at the end of Graben, you proceed through Kohlmarkt to the Michaeler Platz, where you see the main entrance—now in gilded splendor, fully restored—to the Hofburg (Imperial Palace).

Take in a performance of the Spanish Riding School in the beautiful Baroque manège of the Hofburg. Here, under the glittering chandeliers, the famous white stallions called Lippizaner go through their *courbettes, levades,* and *caprioles* to the music of Mozart, Schubert, and Johann Strauss from March through June and from

September to mid-December. You can watch the horses training daily from 10 to 12 P.M., holidays excepted. Entrance and tickets on the Josefsplatz.

Saint Stephen's Cathedral, Vienna's most famous landmark, merits a long visit. Being Gothic, the contrast with almost all other Viennese treasures is memorable. Apart from the Hofburg, two other palaces should be on the list for "must" visiting—the Belvedere, easily reached via streetcar "D" or on foot from the center, with its wonderful view over the city and its fine collection of art; and Schönbrunn, on the edge of town, but with excellent subways links. (take the U–4 subway) Schönbrunn will provide the best part of a day's outing, with its lovely grounds, small zoo, and magnificent rooms, although it could be done in half a day.

One of the joys of Vienna is to find the small churches, tiny hidden courtyards and fine architectural features all of which will turn a casual stroll into a treasure hunt. It may not be a city pulsating with modernity, but for the traveler who enjoys quiet pleasures it has much to offer.

All buildings of historic interest are marked by explanatory shields (in summer festooned with red-white banners); a guide in English *(Vienna from A to Z)* to these shields can be bought from the Tourist Office or bookshops. In most churches of importance there are coin-operated tape machines that will give you an excellent commentary on the history and architecture of the building in English.

PRACTICAL INFORMATION FOR VIENNA

HOTELS. From Easter through October the hotels are kept busy. For budgeteers *pensions* are often best, though they usually only offer bed and breakfast and standards vary greatly. In addition, pensions are sometimes on the upper floors of large buildings and the elevator is occasionally out of order—a point to remember if you are daunted by stairs.

Unless you have a car, it is most convenient to stay in the Inner City (1st district, postal code 1010). On the other hand, many of the most pleasant small hotels and pensions are a little way out; if you don't mind riding quite a bit on public transport, they offer good value.

Moderate

In the Inner City —Austria, Wolfengasse 3, 1010 (tel. 51 5 23). 51 rooms. On a quiet side street, friendly. Recommended.

Capri, Praterstrasse 44–46, 1020 (tel. 24 84 04). 40 rooms. Across the Danube Canal, but only minute's walk from the center.

Fuchs, Mariahilfer Str. 138, 1150 (tel. 83 12 10). 83 rooms. Close to the Westbahnhof rail station, streetcar to city center.

Kärntnerhof, Grashofgasse 4, 1010 (tel. 512 19 23). 45 rooms. Central, but on a quiet side street. Recommended.

Tigra, Tiefer Graben 14, 1010 (tel. 63 96 45). 45 rooms, all with bath. Small rooms, but modern.

Wandl, Petersplatz 9, 1010 (tel. 53 45 50). 138 rooms. Just off the Graben, splendid location if short on elegance.

Zur Wiener Staatsoper, Krugerstrasse 11, 1010 (tel. 513 12 74). 22 rooms. As the name implies, within sight of the opera house.

Pensions —Christina, Hafnersteig 7, 1010 (tel. 533 29 61). 33 rooms, all with bath or shower. Popular with the young crowd.

Elite, Wipplingerstr. 32, 1010 (tel. 533 25 18, 533 51 13). 26 rooms. Nice rooms, upstairs in a lovely old building.

Franz, Währinger Str. 12, 1090 (tel. 34 36 37). Pleasant rooms and good location close to university and transportation.

Nossek, Graben 17, 1010 (tel. 533 70 41). 27 rooms. A recommended favorite for friendly service and central location. Book ahead.

Pertschy, Habsburgergasse 5, 1010 (tel. 533 70 94). 43 rooms, all with bath or shower. Central but quiet. Recommended.

Post, Fleischmarkt 24, 1010 (tel. 51 58 30). 107 rooms, 77 with bath or shower. Friendly, older house. Recommended.

Suzanne, Walfischgasse 4, 1010 (tel. 513 25 07). 19 rooms, all with bath or shower. More modern, superb central location.

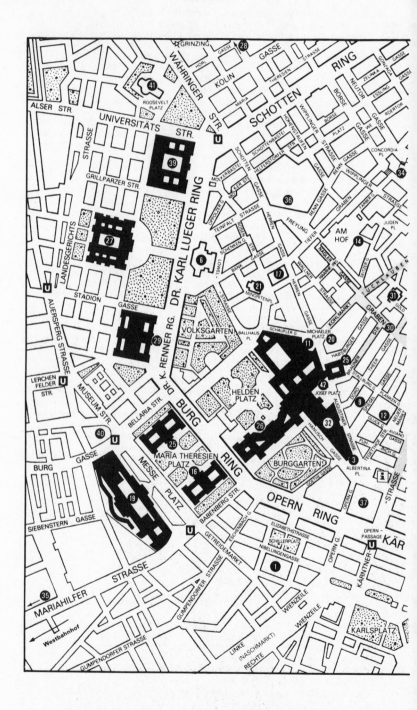

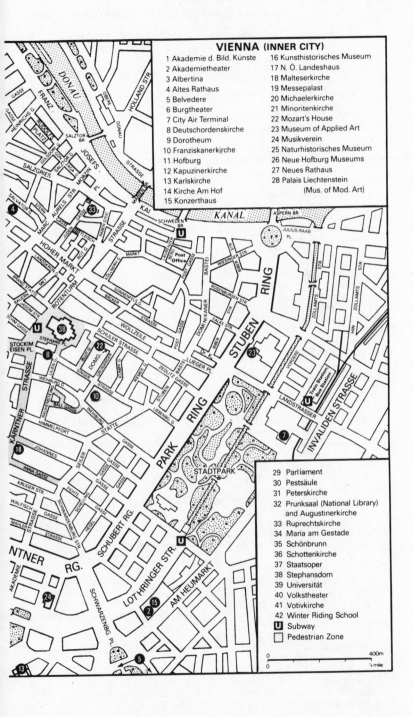

VIENNA (INNER CITY)

1 Akademie d. Bild. Künste
2 Akademietheater
3 Albertina
4 Altes Rathaus
5 Belvedere
6 Burgtheater
7 City Air Terminal
8 Deutschordenskirche
9 Dorotheum
10 Franziskanerkirche
11 Hofburg
12 Kapuzinerkirche
13 Karlskirche
14 Kirche Am Hof
15 Konzerthaus
16 Kunsthistorisches Museum
17 N. Ö. Landeshaus
18 Malteserkirche
19 Messepalast
20 Michaelerkirche
21 Minoritenkirche
22 Mozart's House
23 Museum of Applied Art
24 Musikverein
25 Naturhistorisches Museum
26 Neue Hofburg Museums
27 Neues Rathaus
28 Palais Liechtenstein
   (Mus. of Mod. Art)

29 Parliament
30 Pestsäule
31 Peterskirche
32 Prunksaal (National Library)
   and Augustinerkirche
33 Ruprechtskirche
34 Maria am Gestade
35 Schönbrunn
36 Schottenkirche
37 Staatsoper
38 Stephansdom
39 Universität
40 Volkstheater
41 Votivkirche
42 Winter Riding School
U Subway
☐ Pedestrian Zone

400m
¼ mile

In the Outer Districts—**Albatros,** Liechtensteinstrasse 89, 1090 (tel. 34 35 08). 70 rooms near the U.S. embassy.

Alpha, Boltzmangasse 8, 1090 (tel. 31 16 46). Also near the U.S. embassy.

Cortina, Hietzinger Hauptstrasse 134, 1130 (tel. 82 74 06). 34 rooms. Attractive hotel near Schönbrunn.

Fürstenhof, Neubaugürtel 4, 1070 (tel. 93 32 67). Old-fashioned atmosphere but comfortable and excellent value.

Savoy, Lindengasse 12, 1070 (tel. 93 46 46). 43 rooms, all with bath. Modern, recommended.

Westbahn, Pelzgasse 1, 1150 (tel. 92 14 80). Near the West station.

Westminster, Harmonieg. 5–7, 1090 (tel. 34 66 04). Efficient and friendly.

Pension—Zipser, Lange Gasse 49, 1080 (tel. 42 02 28). 47 rooms, all with bath or shower. A favorite with regular guests, so book ahead. Recommended.

Inexpensive

Most (I) hotels are located away from the center, but there is a choice of pensions in particular for those who want to be in the middle of activities:

Aclon, Dorotheergasse 6–8, 1010 (tel. 512 79 49). 22 rooms. Pension.

Am Schottenpoint, Währinger Str. 22, 1090 (tel. 31 85 00). 17 rooms with shower. Close to university, transportation.

Central, Taborstr. 8a, 1020 (tel. 24 24 05). Just over the canal from the first district.

City, Bauernmarkt 10, 1010 (tel. 63 95 21). 19 rooms, newly redone, all amenities. Central, recommended.

Neuer Markt, Seilergasse 9, 1010 (tel. 512 23 16). 37 rooms. Pension. Central, offers meals as well. Recommended.

Rathaus, Lange Gasse 13, 1080 (tel. 43 43 02). 37 rooms, most with shower. Convenient to museums.

In the Outer Districts —**Astra,** Alser Str. 32, 1090 (tel. 42 43 54). 22 rooms. Pension.

Edelweiss, Lange Gasse 61, 1080 (tel. 42 23 06). 20 rooms, with bath or shower. Near city hall. Pension.

Gabriel, Landstrasser Hauptstr. 165, 1030 (tel. 712 32 05). 29 rooms, most with bath or shower. Garden.

Hohe Warte, Steinfeldgasse 7, 1090 (tel. 37 32 12, 37 31 28). At the end of streetcar route 37, almost in the vineyards.

Haydn, Mariahilfer Str. 57–59, 1060 (tel. 587 44 14). 36 rooms with shower or bath. In the center of the shopping district.

Hospiz, Kenyongasse 15, 1070 (tel. 93 13 04). Close to rail station.

Mozart, Theobaldgasse 15, 1060 (tel. 587 85 05). 16 rooms. Adjacent to the main shopping district. Pension.

Quisisana, Windmühlgasse 6, 1060 (tel. 587 33 41). 16 rooms. Adjacent to the main shopping district. Pension.

Terminus, Fillgradergasse 4, 1060 (tel. 587 73 86). 46 rooms, most with bath or shower. Close to museums, shopping.

Vera, Alser Str. 18, 1090 (tel. 43 25 95). 9 rooms. Pension.

Student Homes

An excellent bargain are the student homes. These operate as hotels from July 1 to September 30.

Among the *Moderate* student homes are:

Academia, 1080 Pfeilgasse 3A (tel. 43 16 61). 320 rooms, all with bath, w.c., telephone and radio.

Atlas, Lerchenfelderstr. 1–3, 1080 (tel. 93 45 48).

Haus Burgenland 1, Wilhelm Exner. G. 4, 1090 (tel. 43 91 22). 72 rooms.

Haus Burgenland 2, Mittelg. 18, 1060 (tel. 596 12 47). 87 rooms.

Haus Burgenland 3, Bürgerspitalg, 17, 1060 (tel. 597 94 75). 66 rooms.

Haus Dr Schärf, Lorenz Müllergasse 1, 1200 (tel. 33 81 71–0).

Haus Margareten, Margaretenstr. 30, 1040 (tel. 588 15–0). 55 rooms.

Haus Niederösterreich, Untere Augartenstr. 31, 1020 (tel. 35 35 26).

Haus Panorama, Brigittenauer Lände 224–8, 1200 (tel. 35 15 41–0).
Josefstadt, Buchfeldg. 16, 1080 (tel. 43 52 11). 40 rooms, all with showers.
Among the *Inexpensive* student homes are:
Aquila, Pfeilgasse 1A, 1080 (tel. 43 16 61). 70 rooms, all with shower.
Auersperg, Auerspergstr. 9, 1080 (tel. 43 25 49). 80 rooms.
Auge Gottes, Nussdorfferstr. 75, 1090 (tel. 34 25 85). 67 rooms.
Avis, Pfeilg. 4, 1080 (tel. 42 63 74).
Haus Döbling, Gymnasiumstr. 85, 1190 (tel. 34 76 31). 537 rooms.
Jugendgästehaus Brigittenau, Friedrich Engelspl. 24, 1200 (tel. 33 82 94).
Jugendgästehaus der Stadt Wien, Schlossbergg. 8, 1130 (tel. 82 15 01).
Turnherberge Don Bosco, Lechnerstr. 12, 1030 (tel. 713 14 94). 50 beds.

RESTAURANTS. The *Speisekarten* posted outside most restaurants will give budgeters a clue as to price ranges as well as offerings. At noon, look for a "Mittags-menu," a fixed meal of at least soup, meat and a vegetable dish. These are particularly good value for money, in cafés as well, which otherwise usually are not as much a bargain for food as a regular restaurant or simpler *Gasthaus*. For budgeters, the restaurants in the department stores are also a find. Many butcher shops also offer prepared food dishes at noon and are a bargain, if you're prepared to put up with the inconvenience of often having to stand. And for just a quick coffee, unless you want the relaxation of a café, the best value by far is one of the shops—mainly those of the Eduscho chain—which offer coffee by the cup as well as in bean and ground form.

Moderate

Bastei Beisl, Stubenbastei 10, 1010 (tel. 512 43 19). Standard Viennese fare, attractive wood-paneled rooms. Closed Sun.
Ofenloch, Kurrentgasse 8, 1010 (tel. 533 72 68). Unique offerings from a Viennese grandmother's cookbook; delightful atmosphere in a series of small rooms, although occasionally too noisy and smoky for some guests. The *Vanillerostbraten* (rump steak with garlic) is superb. Closed Sun. Reservations essential, noon and evenings. Recommended.
Paulusstube, Walfischgasse 7, 1010 (tel. 512 81 36). A combination wine stube and restaurant; attractive garden outside in summer, although the added tables put a burden on the staff. Open daily, although evenings only from mid-Jan. to mid-March.
Smutny, Elisabethstr. 8, 1010 (tel. 587 13 56). Traditional Viennese fare with some Czech overtones, game in season, plus original Budweiser beer on tap. Particularly good soups and *Torte* (cakes) from their own kitchen. Service is usually better in the downstairs rooms. Open daily.
Stadtbeisl, Naglergasse 21, 1010 (tel. 533 33 23). Good Austrian cooking, game in season. The "garden" across from the restaurant in the pedestrian zone is a delight in summer. Open daily. Reservations useful in peak season.
Zu den drei Hacken, Singerstr. 28, 1010 (tel. 52 58 95). One of the few remaining genuine old Gasthäuser in the city center; Schubert and nearly everybody else dined here. An incredible list of standard Viennese dishes. The summer outside "garden" is attractive. Open Mon.–Fri. to midnight, Sat. to 3 P.M.; closed Sun.
Zum Laterndl, Landesgerichtsstr. 12, 1010 (tel. 43 43 58). Seasonal specialties including game, plus solid standard local fare in a cozy atmosphere. Outdoor "garden" in summer can be a splendidly Viennese finish after a concert in the nearby Rathaus courtyard. Closed Sat., Sun. Reservations useful.

Inexpensive

Figlmüller, Wollzeile 5 (passageway), 1010 (tel. 512 61 77). A Viennese tradition for its wines and the oversized Schnitzel; informal seating at long benches. Closed Sat. afternoons and Sun. No reservations.
Gulaschmuseum, Schulerstr. 20, 1010 (tel. 512 10 17). Spelled gulasch or guylas, more varieties of this Austro-Hungarian specialty would be hard to find—and all delicious. Open daily.
Langenloiser Stuben, Florianigasse 46, 1080 (tel. 43 23 92). Wide range of local dishes at particularly low prices. Closed Sat., Sun.

Mensa, Ebendorferstr. 8, 1010 (tel. 48 35 87). Student cafeteria, open to the public, with basic fare at bargain prices. Weekday noons from 11.30–2.

Naschmarkt, Schwarzenbergpl. 16, 1010 (tel. 505 31 15), open daily to 9 P.M.; Schottengasse 1, 1010 (tel. 533 51 86), open Mon.–Fri. to 7.30 P.M., Sat., Sun. to 5 P.M. Self-service cafeterias with a fair range of main dishes as well as salads, salad bar. Outdoor terrace at Schwarzenbergpl. in summer.

Reinthaler, Glückgasse 5, 1010 (tel. 512 33 66). Solid Viennese cooking and good wines in this typically local restaurant. The "garden" outside in summer is appealing. Open Mon.–Thurs. to 10 P.M., Fri. to 4 P.M. Closed Sat., Sun.

Stadtkeller, Singerstr. 6, 1010 (tel. 512 12 69). Cafeteria with standards plus daily specials. Open daily to 9 P.M.

Wine cellars. All of the cellars offer light foods; several have full food service. But be careful: you can quickly run up a substantial bill when combining keller food and drink. Recommended: **Antiquitäten-Keller,** Magdalenenstr. 32, 1060 (tel. 56 69 533). Fine wines amid a great atmosphere among genuine antiques. Open daily. Reservations recommended. **Melker Stiftskeller,** Schottengasse 3, 1010 (tel. 533 55 30). Known for its crispy knuckle of pork along with the wines. Closed Sun. **Urbani-Keller,** Am Hof 12, 1010 (tel. 63 91 02). Substantial food offerings along with wine and music. Closed Sun. in summer, holidays from 15 July to 15 Aug. Reservations useful. **Zwölf-Apostelkeller,** Sonnenfelsgasse 3, 1010 (tel. 512 67 77). Down, down, down into one of Vienna's oldest as well as deepest cellars. Fascinating, and wines are good too. Reservations may be useful.

GETTING AROUND VIENNA. Travelers with one eye on the budget would find it advisable to get acquainted with Vienna's public transport system. With any ticket other than that for a "short trip" (two stops on the subway, a designated stretch on buses and streetcars), passengers can change between any of the streetcars, buses, subway and the *Schnellbahn,* which mainly serves the suburban areas.

By Subway. The *U-Bahn* (subway) has four lines: the U1 from Reumannplatz to Zentrum Kagran (via Vienna International Center), the U2 from Schottenring to Karlsplatz, and the U4 from Heiligenstadt to Hütteldorf via Schönbrunn, and the U6 from Friedensbrucke/Heiligenstadt to Meidling. Another line, the U3, is under construction. The U-Bahn is easy to use, the plans using a clear system of colors.

By Streetcar and Bus. In most busy areas, such as would be frequented by a tourist, the streetcars tread on one another's heels. They start at an incredibly early hour of the morning and continue, usually, to between 11 and 12 at night. At each streetcar stop there is a sign that tells what cars stop there, where these cars are going and the times of the first and last trips of the day.

Special city buses, marked "A", operate in the Inner City weekdays 7 A.M.—8 P.M. and Sat., until 2 P.M. At weekends, night buses marked "N" run in all directions, departing from Schwedenplatz every 30 minutes; fare 25 AS.

If you can't figure out the system yourself, your hotel porter or desk clerk can steer you to the right stop and tell you how to proceed.

Tickets for buses, streetcars, subway and Stadtbahn cost 20 AS if bought singly; 14 AS if bought in advance in a block of five at a *Tabak-Trafik* (tobacco store). A three-day unlimited travel ticket can be bought in advance at a *Tabak-Trafik* for 102 AS and an eight-day ticket for 220 AS. With a single ticket, cars and means of transport can be changed if continuing in same direction. Some streetcars have automatic ticket machines in the first car (marked by a yellow sign). They swallow 5 and 10 schilling coins, so have them handy. Separate full-fare tickets are also available from automatic dispensers at U-Bahn stations; these machines also take 100 AS bills.

ENTERTAINMENT. Cinema. There are now several up-to-date movie centers offering comprehensive programs. Foreign films are dubbed in German, but the *Burgkino* at Opernring 19, *de France* at Schottenring/Hessgasse and *Top Kino Center* at Rahlgasse/Gumpendorfer Str. show films in English with German subtitles.

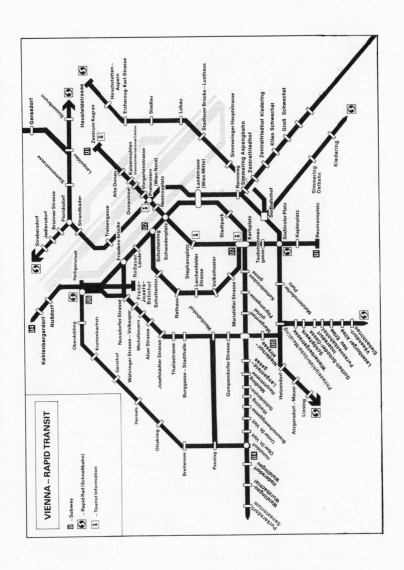

VIENNA – RAPID TRANSIT

U – Subway

S – Rapid Rail (Schnellbahn)

i – Tourist Information

Discos. Although the various night establishments of Vienna are plentiful, the city cannot boast of a real nightclub tradition. The average Viennese prefers to go to the opera, theater, and concerts for serious entertainment, and for an evening of merriment to a wine tavern or a Heuriger. Bars of every description have suddenly sprung up in the city center. They stay open well into the small hours and the prices are very reasonable. The Viennese love to dance, but the dancing is done mostly at the numerous balls during the season, in a few cafés with weekend music, and in dance-bars.

Other dance bars—*Chattanooga,* Graben 29 (tel. 533 50 00), and *Scotch,* Parkring 10 (tel. 512 94 17), *Casanova,* Dorotheerg., (tel. 512 98 45), where the accent is on night-club and striptease. *Volksgarten* (tel. 63 05 18); *Atrium,* Schwarzenbergplatz 10 (tel. 505 35 94), is frequented mostly by students, and offers 50 types of beer; *Take Five,* Annagasse 3A; *Queen Anne,* Johannesgasse 12 (tel. 512 02 03); *Lords Club,* Karlplatz 1 (tel. 65 83 08); and *Jazzland,* Morzinplatz (tel. 533 25 75), for first-class live jazz. *Papa's Tapas,* Schwarzenbergplatz 10 (tel. 65 03 11) has a daily program of spontaneous jazz, as does *Roter Engel,* Rabensteig 5 (tel. 535 41 05), where offerings run from song to instrumental groups. Also check *Opus One,* Mahlerstr. 11 (tel. 513 20 75).

Theaters. Among the most important are the still very imperial *Burgtheater;* the *Akademietheater,* Lisztstrasse 1, classical and modern plays; the *Theater in der Josefstadt,* Josefstädterstr. 26, the old theater of Max Reinhardt, classical and modern plays; the *Volkstheater,* Neustiftgasse 1, dramas, comedies and folk plays; and *Kammerspiele,* Rotenturmstrasse 20, modern plays.

The numerous small avant-garde theaters demand a good knowledge of German, as does the *Simpl,* Wollzeile 36, which pokes fun at Austrian and international politics, love and life in general. The *English Theater,* Josefsgasse 12, 1080, and *International Theater,* Porzellangasse 8/Müllnergasse, 1090, both offer excellent theater in English.

Opera. Opera performances are meat and drink to the Viennese. The *Opera* itself performs from September through June, and has a season of light operas and operettas in July and August, but can be fantastically expensive. Some cheaper seats are available with luck. There is standing room for 600 at 15–20 AS. If the performance is popular, standing room lines may start a day ahead. Tickets go on sale one hour before performance. Suit and tie are recommended for first performances and for better seats. In summer, some chamber opera performances are given in the *Schlosstheater* of Schönbrunn.

Light operas and operettas are presented during the season at the *Volksoper* on the corner of Gürtel and Währingerstrasse. The tradition of Strauss and Lehár continues in the city that gave them their greatest successes. Operettas and musical shows are also performed at *Theater an der Wien,* Linke Wienzeile 6. The *Raimundtheater,* 1060 Wallgasse, and *Ronacher,* 1010 Himmelpfortgasse/Seilerstätte, both present musicals. The *Sommerarena* in the Baden Kurpark offers operetta in the summer.

Concerts. Vienna is one of the greatest cities in the world for music. The two great orchestras of the capital are the *Vienna Philharmonic* and the *Vienna Symphony.* In addition to their performances, there is an abundance of concerts by soloists, choruses, and chamber music groups.

The most important concert halls in Vienna are in the building of the *Gesellschaft der Musikfreunde* (popularly called *Musikverein*), Dumbastr. 3 (tel. 505 81 90), the home of the Vienna Philharmonic, and in the *Wiener Konzerthaus,* Lothringerstr. 20 (tel. 712 12 11). Both of these contain a number of auditoriums for concerts of different types, and your ticket may be marked with the name of the particular hall in which the concert is being given.

Concerts are also given in the small *Figarosaal* of the Palais Palffy, the ORF broadcasting studio and the concert halls of the Music Conservatory.

In addition to the Vienna Festival, held late-May and June, there are special summer concerts in the Arkadenhof (Arcade Court) of the Rathaus, in Belvedere garden and Volksgarten, and in many palaces, the most notable being held in Palais Schwarzenberg, Schloss Schönbrunn.

Schubert fans can enjoy occasional piano concerts in the house of his birth, Nussdorferstr. 54.

Church music of high artistic value can be heard during Sunday morning Mass in the following churches in the downtown area—in the Cathedral of St. Stephen, in the Franciscan Church, Augustinerkirche, and in Hofburgkapelle where the famous Wiener Sängerknaben (Vienna Boys' Choir) sing at 9.15 A.M. from mid-Sept. to late June. Programs published on first of month on church door and in the Saturday papers. There are Wednesday evening organ concerts in St. Stephen's from early May to end Nov. Organ concerts are held every Friday evening in summer, at the Augustinerkirche, which houses both the city's finest organ and a newly constructed Bach organ. Tickets at the door.

Try to hear brass band music—there are concerts on various squares and in different parks throughout the summer.

Theater and concert tickets. Operas and concerts are often sold out, so it is advisable to buy tickets when they are put on sale one week before the performance. For the state theaters (Oper, Volksoper, Akademietheater and Burgtheater) the ticket office is across the Opera in a courtyard entered from Goethegasse 1 and Hanuschgasse 3. Order by phone and credit card up to six days ahead, tel. 513 15 13. Tickets for all other theaters can be purchased at the theater during business hours and one hour before the performance.

The various ticket agencies charge at least 20% commission, so are to be avoided by budgeteers. The least expensive seats are those in the gallery or at the back of the boxes, but standing room always presents the best deal.

MUSEUMS. There are over 50 museums and galleries in Vienna. Entrance charges are minimal, and there is usually free entrance on Sundays, with a small charge for guided tours. Some are open daily, others only certain days and halfdays. As these can change from season to season, check on the spot. "Seven-Day Museum Ticket" (150 AS) is good for all federal and city museums, at all opening hours. It is available at the pay desks of most museums. The City Information Office on the Kärntner Str. has a brochure listing all museums and their times of opening.

Albertina. Collection of Graphic Arts, Augustinerstrasse 1 (diagonally behind the Opera). Engravings, aquarelles, and drawings from Middle Ages to present day, among them particularly those of Dürer, and also of Raphael, Rembrandt, Rubens, Leonardo da Vinci, Michelangelo, Correggio, Fragonard, etc. Only a small part on display; rest available on request in the reading room for study purposes. The largest collection of this kind in the world; contains over 600,000 items.

Dom- und Diözesanmuseum. Museum of Religious Art, Stephansplatz 6, next to St. Stephen's. Religious paintings from Gothic, Baroque, and Biedermeier periods. Fine products of goldsmith's art.

Gemäldegalerie de Akademie der bildenden Künste, Schillerplatz 3, upstairs from the main entrance of the Academy of Fine Arts is a collection of about 150 paintings, among them Bosch, Titian, Cranach, Rubens, Rembrandt, van Dyck.

Herzgruft der Habsburger. Small Crypt with the Hearts of the Habsburgs, in Loretto Chapel of Augustine Church, Augustinerstr. 7. The hearts of the Habsburgs who died between 1619 and 1878 are here in 54 urns.

Historisches Museum der Stadt Wien. Vienna City Museum, at Karlsplatz. History of Vienna; art works from Vienna.

Hofburg. Imperial Apartments in the Amalien and Reichskanzlei wings. Apartments and reception halls of Emperor Franz Josef and Empress Elisabeth. The **Schatzkammer** (Treasury) has reopened after total renovation and extension. It now does full justice to the Habsburg treasures. **Waffensammlung** (Collection of Weapons) and **Sammlung alter Musikinstrumente** (Old Musical Instruments). The Musical Instruments collection is currently closed for renovation. Two sections of Kunsthistorisches Museum in Neue Hofburg, entrance from Heldenplatz. Ornamented suits of armor in Gothic, Renaissance, and Baroque styles and old weapons from the same periods; among some 1,400 guns are many masterpieces of artistic craftsmanship. The oldest among the instruments in the musical collection originate from the 16th and 17th centuries. The new and excitingly displayed **Ephesus Museum** is housed in the Hofburg, entrance in the Heldenplatz. It exhibits the finds from the dig at Ephesus with plans and models.

Kaisergruft. Imperial Crypt, under Capuchin Church, entrance at Tegetthofstr. 2. Guided tours daily. Most of Habsburg emperors and other members of the family are buried here; the most recent, Empress Zita, died in 1989.

Kunsthistorisches Museum. Museum of Art History (also referred to as the Museum of Fine Arts), Burgring 5, entrance Maria-Theresienplatz. This building houses 5 sections; Egyptian antiquities, among the most important collections in the world; Greek, Etruscan, and Roman antiquities, *The Youth from Magdalensberg, Athlete from Ephesus, Artemis from Larnaka;* plastic arts and *objets d'art;* collection of coins, and the famous gallery of paintings, one of the best in the world. The gallery owns some 10,000 paintings, but not all are exhibited. Among those on display, particularly well represented are Titian, Tintoretto, Veronese, Velazquez, Pieter Breughel, Rubens, Dürer, and both Cranachs.

Museum des XX. Jahrhunderts. 20th-century Gallery, Schweizergarten 3 near South Station and Belvedere Palace. A very representative collection of modern paintings and sculpture since the turn of the century.

Museum für moderne Kunst in the Liechtenstein Palace, Fürstengasse 1. A brand new collection of modern art of the last 30 years, housed in one of Vienna's great buildings. There's a useful cafeteria.

Museum für Völkerkunde. Ethnological Museum, Neue Hofburg, entrance from Heldenplatz. Collections from Mexico, including *feather crown and shield of Montezuma,* from Brazil, Peru, Argentina, and Africa.

Nationalbibliothek, Josefplatz 1. The Prunksaal, the great hall of the National library, is one of the most stunning Baroque interiors around. Opening hours can be tricky—in winter just from 11–12 in the morning.

Naturhistorisches Museum. Museum of Natural History, Burgring 7, entrance from Maria-Theresienplatz. Fossils, meteorites, prehistoric finds from Stone Age (*Venus of Willendorf,* about 20,000 B.C.) and from Hallstatt period (*Golden Dagger* and other fine weapons from Hallstatt smiths), botanical and zoological sections. You can park your offspring in the children's room, nurse in attendance.

Österreichische Galerie (Austrian Gallery) in **Belvedere Palace.** Contains—Museum of Medieval Austrian Art located in the Orangerie at Lower Belvedere; Museum of Austrian Baroque in Lower Belvedere; Austrian Gallery of 19th and 20th Centuries in Upper Belvedere (don't miss the Klimts, Schieles and Kokoschkas). The Baroque Belvedere Palace was built by Lukas von Hildebrandt. *Sound and Light* performances take place in Belvedere on summer evenings.

Römische Ruinen unter dem Hohen Markt, Hoher Markt 3. Roman foundations in the basement of modern buildings, showing something of the shape of houses in Roman Vienna.

Schönbrunn Palace. The Imperial apartments can be visited daily. Only some 40 of over 1,400 rooms are on display. Many of them have not been changed since the times of Maria Theresa. Baroque and Rococo interiors with crystal chandeliers, furniture from precious woods, gilded wall and ceiling decorations, miniature paintings, Chinese porcelain and cabinets, the *Million Room* (its décor cost a million florins). **Wagenburg** in Schönbrunn. Fine collection of various types of state coaches and sleighs, ranging from Baroque and Rococo to Biedermeier, and of the industrial period under Franz Josef. The oldest *zoo* in Europe is also here, as well as the *Palmenhaus,* a greenhouse with many exotic plants.

Uhrenmuseum. Clock Museum, Schulhof 2, off from Tuchlauben. A fascinating collection of old and ancient clocks and timepieces; be there at noon for the full effect. Housed in one of the city's oldest buildings.

SHOPPING. The finest shops in Vienna line Kärntnerstrasse from the Opera to St. Stephen's Cathedral, then run left through the Graben and again left, following Kohlmarkt to the Imperial Palace. A lot of this route follows the pedestrian precinct, which has turned the center of Vienna into a strollers' paradise, and driven the motorists berserk. Almost all the small side streets around here are crowded with good shops. Shops are open Mon.-Fri. 9–6 P.M.; Sat. 9–noon or 1 P.M.; most stay open until 5 or 6 P.M. on the first Saturday of the month. Food shops close at 6:30 P.M. Shops in the Westbahnhof, Südbahnhof, Wien Mitte/Landstrasse and other stations sell food, books, tobacco, and flowers (there are also beauty parlors and laundromats). They are usually open until 11 P.M. but prices are higher.

The Floh Markt (Flea Market) is open Saturday only, and the NaschMarkt—an open market place between the Rechte and Linke Wienzeile, opposite the Theater an der Wien—is one of the world's great food markets and a splendid place to sample specialties from all over the globe.

For the budget shopper on the look out for small attractive presents to take home, the very best bets are the food shops and the craftwork shops, both of which can offer very pretty items, candies, candles, little figurines, small embroidered bags, even playing cards with historical figures as the kings and queens. For while Vienna has some very chic, expensive shops, it also has lots of much less pricey merchandise, most of it worth looking at, with craftwork leading the parade. Steffl department store in the Kärntnerstrasse has good-quality merchandise at fair prices.

USEFUL ADDRESSES. Consulates: *British,* Jauresgasse 10 (tel. 755 61 17); *Canadian,* Dr Karl Lueger-Ring 10 (tel. 533 36 91); *United States,* Gartenbaupromenade 2 (in the Marriot building), (tel. 51 4 51).
Austrian National Tourist Office, Margaretenstr. 1, 1040 (tel. 588 66–0). Open Mon. to Fri., 9–5.30. *Austrian Travel Agency,* Opernring, corner Operngasse, opposite Opera (tel. 588 00 0); also downstairs in the Opernpassage (tel. 586 23 52). *Vienna Information,* Kärntnerstrasse 38 (tel. 513 88 92). Open daily 9–7. *Accommodations information* from the following offices:
Information-Zimmernachweis at Westbahnnof (West Station), open daily from 6.15 A.M. to 11 P.M.
Information-Zimmernachweis at Südbahnhof (South Station), open daily from 6.15 A.M. to 10 P.M.
Tourist information and room reservation office at the airport (tel. 7700 2828), open from 9 A.M. to 10.30 P.M.
American Express, Kärntnerstr. 21 (tel. 51 54 00); *Wagons Lits,* Kärntnerring 2 (tel. 501 600), also at Innsbruck, Linz, Salzburg.
Lost and Found, Wasagasse 22, 1090 (tel. 313 440).
If you need a doctor and don't speak any German, try *American Medical Society of Vienna,* Lazarettgasse 13 (tel. 42 45 68), or call your embassy. In case of an accident, call 133 for Police Accident Squad, and 144 for ambulance service. British tourists receive free emergency hospital in-patient treatment, if documented before leaving Britain with Form CM1 from local Social Security Office, plus passport.
Bicycle hire, Salztorbücke, 1010 (tel. 66 23 22) or Vivariumstr. 8, 1020 (tel. 22 66 44). An ever-growing network of cycle tracks is being built in Vienna.
Nationwide automobile emergency service, ÖAMTC, (tel. 120); ARBO (tel. 123).

Salzburg

This marvelous city lies on the bank of the Salzach River, pressed between two cliffs, the Mönchsberg or Old Town on the left shore, the Kapuzinerberg or New Town on the right shore. Architecturally it is a city in a single style: a riot of pure Baroque. And for at least a month a year, it is also a riot of music, at the annual Salzburg Festival (last week in July to the end of August), with daily performances of opera and concerts, and by no means overlooking Mozart, the 18th-century genius born here in 1756. Salzburg is a blend of cosmopolitanism in a small-town setting—exactly the sort of place travelers are always looking for. As with many festival cities, Salzburg can be expensive. We include it in this book because the great majority of our readers will want to go there, and a budget visit is certainly possible . . . with care.

There are conducted tours of the Festung Hohensalzburg, the great fortress that dominates the city, but you can get a splendid idea of this medieval stronghold by wandering around it yourself. Hike up, or take the cable railway. Don't miss St. George's Chapel, added to the ensemble in 1501. The 16th-century 200-pipe barrel organ plays daily during the summer. Not far from the fortress is the 1,200-year-old Nonnberg Convent. The Residenz, 17th-century city palace of the Salzburg archbishops, has conducted tours of the State Rooms.

The Salzburg Festival House, designed by Clemens Holzmeister, has a capacity for 2,400 people and the widest stage in the world; splendid acoustics. The beautiful 17th-century Felsenreitschule, once a riding academy, is a part of the Festspielhaus complex. Conducted tours of this, the Stadtsaal with ceiling paintings by Rottmayer and of the Felsenreitschule.

The Mozart Museum (Mozart's birthplace) contains Mozart's clavichord (Hammerklavier), family pictures, exhibition of staging of Mozart operas. Mozarteum (Music Academy): two concert halls, Bibliotheca Mozartiana (about 1,500 works by Mozart and about 1,500 books on Mozart in addition to several thousand other books and musical works), some Mozart letters; Zauberflötenhäuschen (tiny house in which Mozart is supposed to have composed *The Magic Flute*), is in the courtyard of the nearby Mozarteum.

St. Sebastian's Cemetery, Linzergasse 41. Wolf Dietrich's mausoleum, tomb of Paracelsus, 16th-century pioneer in medicine, and Mozart family grave, recently restored.

The 17th-century Salzburg Cathedral to one side of the Dom Platz is the first and one of the finest Baroque buildings north of the Alps. The superb Franciscan Church is at the other end of the Dom Platz. The Universitätskirche (University Church) is another outstanding example of Baroque, the work of Fischer von Erlach. See also the Benedictine Abbey of St. Peter, dating from 847, Romanesque with a Gothic cloister. Near the handsome Residenzplatz, with its 40-foot-high Residenz Fountain, and the Glockenspiel Tower (carillon concerts at 7 A.M., 11 A.M. and 6 P.M.) is the Alter Markt, colorful old market place.

The Schloss Mirabell was built in 1606 by Bishop Wolf Dietrich for his mistress, Salome Alt (what a name for a bishop's girl friend!). There are often candlelit chamber music concerts here.

Try to see a performance of the famous Salzburg Marionettes in the Marionette Theater (Schwarzstrasse 24), headquarters for Professor Hermann Aicher, whose family has been making and exhibiting these fabulous puppets for 200 years.

Hellbrunn Castle-Palace. Building dates from early 17th century, oldest Baroque park in Europe, with fountain water plays, natural rock theater, fine garden sculptures, Monatsschlösschen with folklore museum. Reachable by bus 55 or bus H.

For a splendid view over the city, take the easy climb up Kapuzinerberg, or drive up to Gaisberg. Even better, take the aerial cable car to the top of Untersberg (over 5,800 ft.), the valley station of which can be reached by bus from the city.

PRACTICAL INFORMATION FOR SALZBURG

HOTELS. High season is the Easter period and from July 1 to Sept. 1, when it's nearly impossible to find rooms. At any time of year, it's best to phone or write ahead for reservations. An alternative is to go to one of the villages outside of the city for more moderate lodgings. If you don't have rooms, check with the Tourist Office (*Stadtverkehrsbüro*), at Mozartplatz, tel. 84 75 68, or at the Zimmernachweis, downstairs at the railway station. If you want a private room (usually a bus ride to the outskirts, rural but cheap), contact Eveline Truhlar of Bob's Special Tours (06246/3377), which offers a private-room service.

Our categories are based on normal prices; during the high season, most hotels raise their rates and some may no longer qualify for the category as given here. For hotels open only during the high summer months, the categories apply as listed. Virtually all moderate hotel rooms are with bath or shower.

Moderate

Auersperg, Auerspergstr. 61 (tel. 71 7 21). 57 rooms.

Elefant, Sigmund-Haffner-Gasse 4 (tel. 84 33 97). 36 rooms. In the very heart of the old city.

Gablerbräu, Linzer Gasse 9 (tel. 73 4 41). 53 rooms. Well located across the river from the old city. Friendly staff.

Hohenstauffen, Elisabethstr. 19 (tel. 72 1 93). 27 rooms. Close to the railroad station.

Kasererbräu, Kaigasse 33 (tel. 84 24 45). 37 rooms. In the old city, tucked under Mönchsberg.

Markus Sittikus, Markus-Sittikus-Str. 20 (tel. 71 1 21). 41 rooms, some (I) without bath. Close to Mirabell gardens.

Pension am Dom, Goldgasse 17 (tel. 84 27 65). 15 rooms. In the very heart of the old city. Family run.

Stein, Giselakai 3–5 (tel. 74 3 46). 70 rooms, some (I) without bath. Overlooks the old city; rooms on the back are quieter. Roof garden restaurant. Closed Nov.–mid-Dec.

Weisse Taube, Kaigasse 9 (tel. 84 24 04). 33 rooms, some (I) without bath. In the old city.

Inexpensive

Adlerhof, Elisabethstr. 25 (tel. 75 2 36). 27 rooms, some with bath. Close to railroad station.

Amadeus, Linzer Gasse 43–45 (tel. 71 4 01). 28 rooms.

Blauer Gans, Getreideg. 43 (tel. 84 13 17). 45 rooms, some with bath. You can't find more atmosphere than in this centuries-old hostelry in the most picturesque part of the old city.

Goldene Krone, Linzer Gasse 48 (tel. 72 3 00). 27 rooms, some with bath.

Jahn, Elisabethstr. 31 (tel. 71 4 05). 24 rooms, some with bath. Modest, but so are the prices. Near the railroad station.

Stadtkrug, Linzer Gasse 20 (tel. 73 5 45). 25 rooms.

Trumer Stube, Bergstr. 6 (tel. 74 7 76). 22 rooms. Modest, but well located in the new city.

Hostels. Salzburg boasts a number of good hostels, better located than in many cities. Most, however, have a 10 P.M. curfew. Rates run around 80 AS, generally with breakfast. Meals, where available, run between 40 AS and 60 AS. Basic information is available from *Jugendgästehaus Salzburg,* Josef-Preis-Allee 18 (tel. 84 26 70). For accommodation, also try *Jugendherberg Aigen,* Aigner Str. 34 (tel. 23 2 48); *International Youth Hostel,* Paracelsusgasse 9 (tel. 73 4 60), splendidly located. *Jugendherberg Glockengasse,* Glockengasse 8 (tel. 76 2 41) is open Apr.-mid-Oct. *Jugendherberg Eduard-Heinrich-Haus,* Eduard-Heinrich-Str. 2 (tel. 25 9 76) and *Jugendherberg Haunspernstrasse,* Haunspernstr. 27 (tel. 75 0 30) are open July and Aug., as is the *Dependence St. Elisabeth,* Plainstr. 83.

Camping. Most camps are open from May through Sept. Rates run from 20 AS. As camping places are not particularly central, phone ahead to determine space availability and get directions. *Camping Kasern-Nord,* Jägerwirt, Kasern 1 (tel. 50 5 76); *Camping Ost-Gnigl,* Parscherstr. 2 (tel. 70 27 43); *Camping Aigen,* Aigen (tel. 22 0 79); *Camping Nord-Sam,* Samstr. 22a (tel. 66 06 11); *Camping West,* ASK, Karolingerstr. 4 (tel. 84 56 02); *Camping Stadtblick,* Rauchenbichlerstr. 23 (tel. 50 6 52).

RESTAURANTS. Salzburg has many good restaurants though it is always wise to make reservations and check on the closing days. The hotel restaurants are all up to standard, but the budget traveler will do better in a more modest *Gasthaus* or in one of the restaurants associated with the breweries.

Moderate

Brasserie, Kaigasse 7 (tel. 84 11 80), friendly, with good food including unusual dishes.

Festungsrestaurant (tel. 84 17 80), at the fortress with fine view from the outdoor section, folklore evenings mid-June to early Sept. on Tues., Thurs., Fri.

Schlossstube Mirabell, Mirabellplatz 4 (tel. 71 7 29), delicious Apfelstrudel.

Stieglbräu, Rainerstr. 14 (tel. 77 6 92), in hotel of the same name but with completely separate, rambling restaurant halls in modernized Salzburg style.

Stiftskeller St. Peter, in St. Peter's Abbey, (tel. 84 12 68), traditional *Peterskeller Teller* with good white Praelaten wine from the Abbey's own vineyards.

Tomasseli, Alter Markt 9 (tel. 84 44 88) is mainly a café, but as one of Salzburg's enduring institutions, it's not to be missed.

Weisses Kreuz, Bierjodlg. 6 (tel. 84 56 41), noted Balkan food. (At Herrengasse corner, near cogwheel car depot.)

Inexpensive

Augustiner Bräu, Augustinergasse 4 (tel. 31 2 46), where the Augustinian fathers sell their beer; in winter several large halls, in summer a pleasant shady garden, self-service with one-liter beer mugs, you bring your own cold snacks or buy them in tiny shops in one of the halls.

Krimpelstätter, Müllner Haupstr. 31 (tel. 32 2 74). At other end of Mönchsberg. Real local atmosphere, food and beer.

Sternbräu, a vast brewery restaurant, with entrances at Getreidegasse 34–6, and Griesgasse 23 (tel. 84 21 40), self-service garden and a semi-covered restaurant garden with music on Fri. and Sun. evenings; patronized particularly by country people.

Stieglkeller, Festungsgasse 10 (tel. 84 26 81), on the way to the fortress, very popular, excellent beer and low prices; early June to mid-Sept. on Wed. and Sat. folk music and dance show in the Grand Hall.

WHAT TO SEE AND DO. The Salzburg Festival is one of the most celebrated cultural events in Europe, and securing tickets for its many events as well as hotel accommodations is a major problem. The demand for tickets always exceeds the supply, so get them early through your travel agent or at the official Austrian tourist office in your country. Two specialist booking agents are *Mayfair Travel Service, Inc.,* 119 W. 57th St., New York 10019 and *International Services, Ltd.,* 7 Haymarket, London S.W.1, who are both agents for the Association of Music Festivals. Details also from the *Salzburger Festspiele,* Postfach 140, 5010 Salzburg (tel. 06 222/84 25 41). The snag is that tickets are rapidly becoming ludicrously expensive.

Nightlife. *Stieglkeller, Festungsrestaurant* and *Sternbräu* have folklore shows on some days of the week during summer. A number of wine taverns have local atmosphere and musical entertainment, among them: *Bacchus Stuben,* Rudolfskai 16; *Paracelsus Weinstube,* established 1541, Kaigasse 8; *Höllbräu Kerzenstübl,* Judengasse 15; *Steirische Weinstuben,* St.-Julienstr. 9, which also serves the best chicken in Salzburg. Try one of the many attractive bars, open into the small hours. These have collected in an area around Platzl and Steingasse, just in back of the Hotel Stein; look out for *Chez Roland, Bazillus,* or *Saitensprung.*

Discos. Try *Cloud,* Lederergasse 10; *Disco 7,* Gstättengasse 7; *Tyrol Disco,* Wolf-Dietrich-Str. 4. *Casanova,* Linzer Gasse 23 (tel 71 90 64) offers striptease. Some of Salzburg's evening establishments can run way over budget limits when a "hostess" invites you to invite her for a drink, so look before you leap.

The mortality of nightclubs in Salzburg is great; better inquire from the city tourist office or from the hotel porter (however, keep in mind that he probably gets a percentage from the places reserved by him and therefore your bill will run that much higher).

Museums. Admission times vary from season to season. You will be fairly safe if you keep to the week-day schedule of 9–12, 2–4, Sat. and Sun. mornings. But to be sure, check with the city tourist office or your hotel porter.

Carolino Augusteum, The City Museum dealing with the history of Salzburg. Open Tues. to Sun. 9–5; closed Mon.

Catacombs. Church of St. Peter. Conducted tours 10–12 and 1–5 May to Sept., and 11–12 and 1.30–3.30 Oct. to Apr.

Festspielhaus. Conducted tours through auditorium and stage. Closed because of rehearsals in July and Aug.

Festung (Fortress) Hohensalzburg. Cog-wheel cable car operating daily every 10 minutes between 7.30 A.M. and 7 P.M. (in summer until 9 P.M.). Conducted tours of the fortress; check that it's open before you set out. **Rainer-Regiments-Museum.** The historic memorabilia of one of the oldest Austrian Army regiments, located in the Fortress. Open May through Sept.

Hellbrunn Castle-Palace. Building dates from early 17th century, oldest Baroque park in Europe with fountain water plays, natural rock theater, fine garden sculptures, Monatsschlösschen with folklore museum. Conducted tours from Easter to late fall. Bus H from Salzburg.

Mozarteum. Music Academy: two concert halls, Bibliotheca Mozartiana (about 1,500 works by Mozart in addition to several thousand books and other musical works), some Mozart letters; *Zauberflötenhäuschen* (tiny house in which Mozart is supposed to have composed *The Magic Flute*) has been in the garden since 1950. Open weekdays; conducted tours only July and Aug.

Mozart Museum. Mozart's birthplace. Mozart's clavichord, Hammerklavier, his first violin, family pictures, exhibition of staging of Mozart operas, etc. Open weekdays.

Residenz. City palace of Salzburg archbishops since 12th century. Present building dates from early 17th century. Conducted tours through State Rooms. Various art exhibitions take place in the Residenz Gallery.

Rupertinum. Wiener Philharmonikerg 9. Modern paintings.

St. Sebastian's Cemetery. Linzergasse 41. Wolf Dietrich's mausoleum, tomb of Paracelsus, and Mozart family grave.

USEFUL ADDRESSES. *Stadtverkehrsbüro,* the official city tourist office, has its headquarters at Auerspergstr. 7 (tel. 80 72–0), and an attractive information center, in traditional Salzburg style, at Mozartplatz 5 (tel. 84 75 68). In addition it maintains an information office at the main railway station (tel. 71 7 12), also open all year, and 3 additional summer offices: *Informationsdienst Salzburg-Mitte,* at AGIP service station in Münchener Bundesstr. (tel. 32 2 28), *Informationsdienst Salzburg-West,* at BP service station in Innsbrucker Bundesstr. (tel. 85 24 52), and *Informationsdienst Salzburg-Süd,* Alpenstr. 67 (tel. 20 9 66).

Landesverkehrsamt, the official Salzburg State Tourist Department, has its offices at Mozartplatz 1 (tel. 8042/2232) and shares the above-mentioned information center at Mozartplatz 5 with the city tourist office.

For bus sightseeing tours: *Albus,* Makartplatz 9 (tel. 73 4 45), Mirabellplatz kiosk (tel. 71 7 73); *Autoreisebüro Salzkraft,* Mirabellplatz 2 (tel. 72 6 56).

American Express, Mozartplatz 5 (tel. 84 25 01); *Wagons Lits,* Münzgasse 1 (tel. 84 27 55).

U.K. Consulate, Alter Markt 4 (tel. 84 81 33); *U.S. Consulate,* Giselakai 51 (tel. 28 6 01).

Innsbruck

Sharing a narrow valley with the Inn river between two dominating mountain ranges, Innsbruck holds surprises with its picturesque charm around every corner. Arcaded walkways of centuries-old buildings line the narrow streets of the old city; the colorful Baroque decor is a fascination and a delight to the eye. And not incidentally, Innsbruck is the center of five outstanding ski areas, all close enough to the city so that you can ski the slopes by day and enjoy the varied attractions of the city in the evening.

The city tour is a quick way to get acquinted with Innsbruck, but since most of the highlights are in or adjacent to the old city—now completely a pedestrian zone—the best way to cover the main attractions is on foot.

PRACTICAL INFORMATION FOR INNSBRUCK

HOTELS. During the two main seasons of winter (Christmas through Feb.) and summer (late June through early Sept.), hotels generally must be booked well in advance, particularly the budget accommodations. Those with cars will do better either staying outside of town or choosing a hotel with parking.

Moderate

Grauer Bär, Universitätsstr. 5–7 (tel. 59 24). 103 rooms, all with bath. A five-minute stroll to the old city. Ask for a lower-priced room, as this is top of the "moderate" category.

Maximilian, Marktgraben 7–9 (tel. 59 9 67). 35 rooms, all with bath, in a new but comfortably standard house on the edge of the old city.

Sailer, Adamgasse 6–10 (tel. 53 63). 76 rooms, all with bath, close to main rail station. Garage.

Inexpensive

Goldene Krone, Maria-Theresien-Str. 46 (tel. 58 61 60). 35 rooms with bath. "Inside" rooms are quieter.

Hotel-Pension Binder, Dr.-Glatz-Str. 20 (tel. 42 2 36). 32 rooms, some with bath. Somewhat outside the center, but that's the price of economy. Reachable by bus.

Union, Adamgasse 22 (tel. 58 33 13). 58 rooms, all with bath. Postwar modern in style, close to the main rail station.

Weisses Kreuz, Herzog-Friedrich-Str. 31 (tel. 59 4 79). 34 rooms, all with bath. Charming centuries-old house tastefully modernized, directly in the center of the old city. Recommended.

Weisses Lamm, Mariahilfstr. 16 (tel. 83 1 56). 18 rooms, all with bath. Older, comfortable house across the river from the old city.

Hostels. Innsbruck's hosting of winter olympic games has meant that the city is well equipped with accommodations for hostelers and students, although the facilities tend to be located somewhat away from the city center. For availabilities, try Jugendherberge Innsbruck, Reichenauer Str. 147 (tel. 46 1 79); MK-Jugendzentrum, Sillgasse 8 (tel. 57 13 11); Torsten-Arneus-Schwedenhaus, Rennweg 17b (tel. 58 58 14); St. Paulus, Reichenauer Str. 72 (tel. 44 2 91); Volkshaus Reichenau, Radetzkystr. 47 (tel. 46 66 82). Student dormitories are available July–Sept. at about 330 AS per person per night, breakfast included. Try the Rössl in der Au, Höttinger Au 34 (tel. 86 8 46) or Internationales Studentenhaus, Rechengasse 7 (tel. 59 47 70); both are fairly centrally located, take credit cards, and most rooms have baths.

Camping. Year round: Camping Seewirt, Amras, Geyrstr. 25 (tel. 46 1 53); from Easter to mid-Oct.: Camping Reichenau, Reichenauer Str. (tel. 46 2 52).

RESTAURANTS. Good Tyrolean food remains basic for most budget dining, but newer restaurants offering international specialties are appearing. Check prices on the *Speisekarte* posted outside, and look for bargain fixed menus at noon. And note that many places are closed on Sundays. After hours, there's always a mobile frankfurter stand, one of which appears in the early evening in front of the *Goldenes Dachl.*

Moderate

Churrasco, Innrain 2 (tel. 58 63 98). Open daily to midnight. Italian specialties, also upstairs in la Mamma at the same location. Pleasant riverside garden in summer.

Hirschenstuben, Kiebachgasse 5 (tel. 58 29 79). Excellent Tyrolean food with emphasis on game; lovely old rooms in the heart of the old city. Closed Sun. Recommended.

Picnic, Fallmayerstr. 12 (tel. 58 38 59). Open to 1 A.M. Modern but comfortable, with helpful service.

Schwarzer Adler, Kaiserjägerstr. 2 (tel. 58 71 09). Elegant rooms, fine food, still at "moderate" prices if you watch your selection! Reservations suggested. Closed Tues.

Inexpensive

Al Dente, Meranerstr. 7 (tel. 58 49 47). Good Italian cuisine in a modern, attractive atmosphere. And open Sundays.

Bahnhof Restaurant, Sudtiroler Platz (tel. 58 20 24). Hardly elegant, but certainly budget, and open daily.

Gasthaus Steden, Anichstr. 15 (tel. 58 08 90). Anything but fancy, but lowest prices in town for typically local dishes. Closed Sat. eve, Sun.

Gasthof Innrain, Innrain 38 (tel. 58 89 81). Solid local food, in summer outdoors in a pleasant garden. Closed Sat.

Ottoburg, Herzog-Friedrich-Str. 1 (tel. 57 46 52). Excellent local dishes served in a warren of upstairs rooms. Open daily. Reservations advised in season. Recommended.

Stiegelbräu, Wilhelm-Greil-Str. 25 (tel. 58 43 38). Good beer along with solid local food in this vast complex. Open daily.

Weisses Rössl, Kiebachgasse 8 (tel. 58 30 57). Family-run, fine regional food served in just the right Tyrolean friendly atmosphere. Closed Sun. Recommended.

WHAT TO SEE AND DO. Winter sports enthusiasts will need no advice, but for those who come at other seasons, Innsbruck is now planning a summer music festival.

Nightlife. The nightclubs tend to be expensive, some of them wildly expensive. Unless you're prepared to break the budget entirely, head for a disco or a wine tavern instead.

Discos. Most are open from 8–9 P.M. to 4 A.M., a couple until 7 or even 8 A.M., starting about midnight or so. *Dorian Gray* (Valiergasse 10, tel. 47 9 28) for years has been Innsbruck's leading disco-dining center. Also recommended are *Pascha* (Anichstr. 7, tel. 58 24 20) and *Queen Anne* (Amraser Str. 6, tel. 57 51 55). *Café-Club Filou* (Stiftgasse 12, tel. 58 02 56) has an outdoor garden open to 10 P.M., dancing inside to 4 A.M.

Museums. Admission times vary from season to season, so check to be sure you'll get to see what you want.

Ferdinandeum, Museumstr. 15. Houses Austria's largest Gothic collection, plus arts and crafts, and art from the 19th and 20th centuries. Admission 20 AS. Open Tues.–Sat. 10–12, 2–5; Sun. 9–12, 2–5.

Hofburg, Rennweg 1. The rococo imperial palace, with its ornate reception hall decorated with portraits of Maria Theresa's ancestors. Admission 20 AS. Open 9–4, closed. Sun. and hols. from mid-Oct. to mid-May.

Hofkirche, Universitätsstr. 2. Maximilian's imperial church, built as his mausoleum, with the tomb minus the emperor surrounded by 24 marble reliefs portraying his life deeds and 28 oversized bronze statues by Dürer of his ancestors, including King Arthur. The Tyrolean patriot Andreas Hofer is buried here. The silver chapel with its ornate altar upstairs is best seen in the morning; the afternoon sun through the windows is blinding. Admission 18 AS. Combined ticket with Volkskunstmuseum, 25 AS. Open May–Sept. 9–5, Oct.–Apr. 9–12, 2–5.

Olympic Museum, Goldenes Dachl. Mainly videotapes of past Innsbruck winter olympics, plus some three-dimensional relics of those events. Admission AS 20. Open 10–5.30.

Tyroler Volkskunstmuseum (Tyrolean folk art museum). Universitätsstr. 2. Costumes, furniture, and a series of typical period country rooms. Alas, while not uninteresting, exhibits are poorly arranged and take a lot of guessing for those who do not understand German. Admission 15 AS. Open 9–12, 2–5; Sun. and hols. 9–12.

USEFUL ADDRESSES *Tourist Information.* Bozner Platz 7, 6010 Innsbruck (tel. 59 8 85); Burggraben 3, 6020 Innsbruck (tel. 53 56 0). Rooms can be booked at the *Zimmernachweis* in the railroad station from 9 A.M.–10 P.M. daily (tel. 58 37 66), or at designated points on the incoming West, East and South expressways. *American Express,* Brixner Str. 3 (tel. 58 24 91). *Wagon-Lits,* Brixner Str. 2 (tel. 52 0 79). UK Consulate, Matthias-Schmidt-Str. 12 (tel. 58 83 20). Police, (tel. 133). Ambulance, (tel. 144).

Belgium

Belgium's cosmopolitan culture reflects the fact that it shares borders with four countries. Yet this small country, celebrating only 160 years of nationhood, is no mere cocktail of France, Germany, Holland, and Luxembourg. Both Parisians and Amsterdammers tend to sneer at Belgium as a sub-standard version of 'pure' French or Dutch culture. However, Belgium has a very distinctive culture, or rather, two cultures, Flemish and Walloon. The north is Flemish-speaking, the south French-speaking, and Brussels is officially designated a dual-language area. Both ancient cultures run deeper than nationality and make for a regional diversity exceptional in a country the size of New Hampshire.

It was in the Ardennes that Hitler staged his final desperate counter-attack during the last days of World War II—the Battle of the Bulge. In fact, largely as a result of its geographical position, the territory that is now Belgium has long been the "cockpit of Europe," witnessing many great battles through the centuries—the greatest of which was the Battle of Waterloo, the historic victory over Napoleon in 1815.

At different times through history, Belgium has been ruled over by every major European power, from the Romans to the Nazis. But nowadays the Belgians have put their resultant international outlook and their geographical situation to good use: instead of being ruled over by European powers, their capital, Brussels, is now the center of European politics. This is the capital of the European Community (EC), and the European headquarters of NATO and hundreds of international bodies and associations.

As a result, Belgium is relatively expensive but provides good value. Southern Wallonia is slightly cheaper than northern Flanders. The budget traveler will find many excellent deals to offset high hotel prices. Outside the major cities, hotels tend to be cheaper but even in Antwerp and Brussels, many offer reduced weekend rates. Transport costs are low and there are many attractive train and tram deals. Castles and museums are inexpensive and the finest collections are often free. Restaurants have a reputation for being over-priced but apart from gourmet Michelin restaurants, most are comparable in price to neighboring countries, while offering world-class cuisine, dignified service, and huge portions.

The historic cities are the obvious start to any tour of Belgium. At first sight, the capital of Europe presents a somber, impersonal exterior but a little exploration reveals a domestic, small-town atmosphere seeping through the institutional brickwork. Walk across the Grand'Place during a *son et lumière* show and watch from a cozy bar, tables stacked high with pancakes or Duvel beer. Brussels is an odd mixture of provincial and international. Underneath the bureaucratic surface, the city is a subtle meeting of the Walloon and Flemish cultures. As the heart of the ancient Duchy of Brabant, Brussels retains its old sense of identity and civic pride.

Brussels and Antwerp are diametrically opposed. Antwerp is a dynamic, ambitious city, immortalized in Rubens' paintings of rich Jewish merchants and their voluptuous mistresses. Set in prosperous Flanders, Antwerp considers itself more artistic and politically aware than the sedate capital. Antwerp lives for today and has no fears about paying for it tomorrow. By contrast, Bruges is a perfectly preserved medieval museum, deservedly dubbed the Venice of the north. Strict building requirements keep the city preserved in aspic, but the independent locals refuse to be trapped in the past. Outside the major art cities, Belgium offers a sandy coastline, ravishing chateaux, and a wildly wooded interior in the provinces of Namur and Luxembourg. Limburg province is an unspoiled landscape of marshes, sand and broom. Its Kempen national park is also an open-air museum, a tribute to the rigors of the old peasant life.

Belgians do not let showers dampen their enthusiasm for the outdoor life, whether they are visiting the Zwin bird sanctuary, sailing near Antwerp, or canoeing down the Lesse River. A very cold winter can mean ice-skating in scenes reminiscent of Brueghel's paintings. A slight chill just means that every cozy bar from Antwerp to Bastogne is full of Belgians reviving themselves with hot chocolate, mulled wine, or the inevitable beer.

As befits a bourgeois culture, the Belgians are great believers in the quality of life. In practice, this means that meals, parks, cars, and homes are larger than necessary. Homes are highly individualistic yet very comfortable; trendy designer bars are cozy as well as chic. Except on the road, Belgians are generous and have time for old-fashioned courtesy.

Belgium's robust culture is celebrated in paintings by Breughel and Rubens, Magritte and Delvaux, by exciting Gothic, Renaissance and Art Nouveau architecture, and by the best jazz in Europe.

PRACTICAL INFORMATION FOR BELGIUM

WHAT WILL IT COST. A Belgian franc is divided into 100 centimes. The money comes in coins of 50 centimes, 1, 5, 20, and a recently introduced 50 francs. There are 100, 500, and 5,000 franc bank notes. You can bring in and take out unlimited foreign currency and Belgian francs. At the time of writing there were about 38 francs to the U.S. dollar and about 60 francs to the pound sterling. Belgian banks charge a considerable fee to exchange traveler's checks and this is often passed on by hotels. However, it is easily avoided by exchanging your checks with agents of the bank or company who issued the checks (American Express, Barclays etc.). Inquire beforehand if there is a charge.

Sample Costs. Food and drink in Belgium are reasonably priced if you buy in supermarkets or from market stalls for picnics or camping. Whiskey or gin and wine are much cheaper than in the U.K. Drinks are expensive in restaurants; a whiskey and soda will cost about 120 francs, but measures are generous. Sightseeing is not expensive; even stately homes and castles charge less than 75 francs entrance fee. Other sample costs are: cinema ticket 200 francs; theater ticket 500–700 francs; museum 80 francs; coffee 50 francs; beer 65 francs; ½-liter carafe of house wine 200 francs.

SOURCES OF INFORMATION. For information on all aspects of travel to Belgium, the Belgian National Tourist Office is invaluable. Its addresses are:

In the U.S.: Belgian National Tourist Office, 745 Fifth Ave., Ste. 714, New York, N.Y. 10151 (tel. 212–758–8130).

In the U.K.: Belgian National Tourist Office, Premier House, 2 Gayton Road, Harrow, Middlesex HA1 2XU (tel. 081–861 3000).

WHEN TO COME. The main tourist season runs from May to the end of September. Peak periods are July and August. Belgium divides her big festivals throughout the year so you will not lose out if you explore the country earlier or later in the year. Indeed it might prove advantageous. For example, the Ardennes are just as lovely in spring or fall and camping and caravan sites are a good deal less crowded than in the summer.

Average afternoon temperatures in degrees Fahrenheit and centigrade:

Brussels	Jan.	Feb.	Mar.	Apr.	May	June	July	Aug.	Sept.	Oct.	Nov.	Dec.
F°	42	43	49	56	65	70	73	72	67	58	47	42
C°	6	6	9	13	18	21	23	22	19	14	8	6

SPECIAL EVENTS. Belgian festivals are famous throughout Europe and provide unusual free entertainment. In *January* there are the parades of the Magi. *February* is the start of the carnival season, best at Eupen and Malmedy, and climaxing on Shrove Tuesday at Binche with the procession of the Gilles. In *April* there is an international fair at Liège. *May* sees the procession of the Holy Blood at Bruges (Ascension Day), the festival of the cats at Ypres and the Queen Elizabeth international music competition for young artists in Brussels. *June* is busy with the festival of the Lumeçon in Mons (Trinity Sunday), carillon concerts in Bruges and Mechelen (until September). In *July,* Brussels stages a historical cavalcade, the Ommegang, in its Grand'Place, and there are nightly sound and light performances in front of Tournai Cathedral; there is also a music festival in Bruges. In *August* comes the festival of the *Tapis de Fleurs,* when Brussels' Grand'Place is covered with a carpet of flowers. In *November,* the feast of St. Hubert is celebrated by huntsmen, especially in the Ardennes.

National Holidays. Jan. 1 (New Year's Day); April 1 (Easter Monday); May 1 (May Day); May 8 (Victory 1945); May 9 (Ascension); May 20 (Pentecost Monday); Jul. 21 (National Holiday); Aug. 15 (Assumption); Nov. 1 (All Saints); Nov. 11 (Armistice); Nov. 15 (King's Birthday, but stores, banks etc. not closed; some schools are); Dec. 25, 26 (Christmas).

VISAS. Nationals of the U.S.A., Canada, Australia, New Zealand, E.C. countries and practically all other European countries do not require a visa for entry into Belgium.

HEALTH CERTIFICATES. No vaccinations are required to enter Belgium from any country.

GETTING TO BELGIUM. By Plane. From North America there are direct flights from New York, Boston, Chicago, Atlanta, Anchorage, Toronto and Montreal, with the Belgian national carrier *Sabena* being in the vanguard. *PanAm, TWA,* and *American* also fly to Brussels.

From the U.K. *British Airways* and *Sabena* operate a high frequency of services between London (Heathrow) and Brussels daily while *Air Europe* offers a more limited but equally swift route from London (Gatwick) to Brussels. *Sabena* also flies from Heathrow to Antwerp. There are also services from Birmingham, Manchester, Glasgow, and Edinburgh direct to Brussels.

Brussels International Airport has an excellent train service into the center of the city and there is a direct express bus service to Antwerp, Ghent, and Liège.

By Bus. There are excellent coach services to Brussels and Antwerp from London Victoria coach station. The fastest is the City Sprint Hoverspeed service that leaves London at 10 A.M. arriving in Brussels at 6.20 P.M. Other overnight services run by *National Express-Eurolines* take the ferry.

By Train. The combination of rail and P&O Jetfoil to Belgium is unbeatable. The 11.40 A.M. departure from London Victoria station reaches Brussels at 5.55 P.M. Intermodel transfers at Dover and Oostende are easy, and the small supplement for the jetfoil is excellent value. Advance reservations are essential.

By Boat. There are no sailings for passengers from North America to Belgian ports.

From the U.K. there are good services to Belgium. From Dover, *RTM/P & O European Ferries* ply the Oostende route, while *P & O European Ferries* also sail to Zeebrugge. The crossings take between four and five hours depending on route. For rail and foot passengers the *P & O* Jetfoil to Oostende is worth the £6 supplement as this cuts the journey time to 100 minutes. An alternative is a fast and frequent *Hoverspeed* hovercraft from Dover to Calais, from which it is a short hop over the border. There are also car ferry services from Felixstowe to Zeebrugge by *P & O European Ferries,* and from Hull by *North Sea Ferries.* (See *Planning Your Trip* for further details.)

CUSTOMS. Visitors from overseas and other non-EC countries can bring in 200 cigarettes or 50 cigars or 250 grams of tobacco; 2 liters of still wine and 1 liter of spirits, or 2 liters of fortified wine (apéritifs); and 50 grams of perfume. Other goods may not exceed 2,000 francs in value.

Travelers from other EC countries can bring in 300 cigarettes or 75 cigars or 400 grams of tobacco; 5 liters of still wine and 1½ liters of spirits, or 3 liters of fortified wine; and 75 grams of perfume. Other goods from EEC countries may not exceed 17,000 francs in value.

There are no restrictions on the import or export of currency.

HOTELS. Within the major cities, the Moderate and Inexpensive hotels are usually comfortable, modern and centrally located, if lacking in charm. Hotels in the countryside and in the smaller historic cities are better value. In the Ardennes, rustic stone farmhouses are common while in Bruges or Ghent, a delightful canalside setting is affordable. On the coast, a family run pension with full or half-board is a popular option. Outside Brussels, prices and facilities are not just aimed at expense account travelers. If you plan to tour widely, ask the tourist office for its *Hotels 1991* guide. Outside Brussels, allow 2,500–4,000 francs for a double room in a Moderate hotel and 1,500–2,500 for a room in an Inexpensive hotel. Young people can stay in well-run youth hostels for 200–500 francs per night. A complete list of hostels, camp sites and holiday homes for young people is available from the National Tourist Office or from *Central Wallonne des Auberges de la Jeunesse,* rue Van Ost 52, Brussels and *Vlaamse Jeudgherbergcentrale,* Van Stralenstraat 40, Antwerp. They can also provide addresses and introductions to other youth associations. Caravan and camp sites are numerous and a family of four would pay between 400–800 francs per night.

RESTAURANTS. Restaurants can be expensive, but there are innumerable cafés and most places have their menus posted up outside or in a window so that you know what you are letting yourself in for. Many restaurants have set price menus (hors d'oeuvres, main course, dessert) or a special *plat du jour* or *dagschotel* (dish of the day). But watch out for some unscrupulous restaurants in tourist areas that advertise tourist menus or plats du jour, then say they're not available once you get inside. If this happens, just leave. Self-service cafeterias and snack bars are everywhere to be found, including in supermarkets and department stores, and you can eat a salad or a sandwich with a glass of wine or beer there for 200–250 francs. Many little cafés also serve sandwiches and hot dishes.

Perhaps the most delicious snack meal you can have is at a Belgian pâtisserie. It may not improve your figure but who can resist the creamy pastries, chocolates and waffles for which the country is famous? You may order omelet, toasted or cold sandwiches, salad, wine, beer, coffee, tea or chocolate. An omelet and a beer costs 180 francs. A large, freshly baked roll, a *pistolet,* with tomato and ham costs about 60 francs, but if you cannot resist the cakes and chocolates the price will soar.

It may not sound like much, but the Belgians happen to make the best french fries in the world *(frites).* They're served from stalls all over the place. Eat them the way the Belgians do—with mayonnaise (or *sauce béarnaise*). You can also buy another great Belgian specialty—waffles *(gaufres)*—at open-air stalls; best piping hot with syrup and cream. You can eat piping hot snails from open-air stalls as well, or try the Belgian open-sandwich of cream cheese and black radish at any café.

Food and Drink. Try sampling *Anguilles au vert*—young eels served hot or cold with a green sauce of shredded herbs. *Witloof* (endives or chicory) is grown and cooked in Belgium better than anywhere else in the world. Or try a *carbonnade,* Belgian beef stew made with beer; or a *waterzooi,* a type of creamy stew made with chicken or fish. One of the most reasonable meals around is a big bowl of steaming mussels served in a variety of sauces accompanied by the traditional "frites". Beer is the customary daily drink for the average Belgian. Nearly all the beers, such as

84 BELGIUM

Stella Artois, are a light lager type and served ice-cold. Among the 185 different brands brewed in Belgium, there are stronger ones such as *Kriek, Lambic,* and *Gueuse.* Several are made at monasteries, one being the Guinness-like brew from Orval Abbey. Some well known English beers are also available.

TIPPING. A 16% service charge will be added to your hotel bill. Restaurants add a 16% service charge too, as do nightclubs and taxis. Cinema usherettes expect 20 francs a head, while the fees are usually posted in washrooms, about 10 francs.

MAIL. Airmail letters and postcards to the U.S. and Canada go for 31 francs, to non-EC countries in Europe for 25 francs, and to EC countries at the domestic rate of 14 francs.

CLOSING TIMES. Banks are usually open from 9 to 4. Shops must close for 24 consecutive hours once a week and they post a notice to say which day this will be. The usual opening hours for shops are 9 to 6 or 6.30, but a number of small shops stay open later. For shopping centers and supermarkets, the hours are 9 to 8. Post offices are usually open from 9 to 5, although many, like banks and small shops, close for lunch for 1 to 2 hours.

GETTING AROUND BELGIUM. By Train. An extensive network covers the whole country. You'll find a high frequency of trains especially on trunk routes such as Oostende-Brussels-Liège; Brussels-Antwerp etc. All trains carry second class; however, avoid the new EuroCity trains, which carry a supplement—there are plenty of local trains.

There is a variety of budget ticket schemes, including a five-day ticket (used in a 17-day period) which costs 1,700 francs for those over 26, and 1,300 for those under 26. The *Benelux Tourrail* gives unlimited travel through Belgium, Holland, and Luxembourg for 5 out of 17 days and costs 2,490 francs for those over 26, and 1,790 for those under 26.

By Bus. There is a good network of local and regional bus services throughout Belgium. Details from most rail stations and all tourist information offices.

By Bicycle. Bicycles can be hired from many Belgian railway stations. Information can be obtained from railway stations and from *Belgian Railways,* rue de France 85, 8–1070 Brussels (tel. 02–525 21 11). Trains carry bikes for a fee of 150 francs per trip within Belgium.

Brussels

The Grand'Place is one of the most ornate market squares in Europe. The bombardment of the city by Louis XIV's troops left only the Hotel de Ville (Town Hall) intact. Civic-minded citizens rebuilt the Grand'Place immediately, but the highlight of the square remains the Gothic Town Hall. The central tower, combining boldness and light, is topped by a statue of St. Michel, the patron saint of Brussels. The square is encircled by historic guild houses. Many have been transformed into cafes, the ideal place from which to view the daily flower market or a *son et lumière* show. On summer nights, the entire square is flooded with music and colored lights.

Not far away, in the rue de l'Etuve, is an amusing bronze statue of the famous, if rather rude, little boy known as the Manneken-Pis. The present Manneken is a copy since the original one was kidnapped by 18th-century French and English invaders (both tourists and soldiers!). In the Maison du Roi, back in the Grand'Place, you can see a collection of his costumes, including a gold-embroidered suit from Louis XV. Cross the Grand' Place to the petite rue des Bouchers, an ancient street overflowing with restaurants. From here, explore the network of elegant galleries. Built in 1847, their harmonious glass-topped design was the first of its kind in Europe. Written on the central galleries is the motto *Omnibus Omnia,* "Everything for Everyone", not altogether appropriate given the designer prices.

From the galleries, take rue de la Montagne to Cathédrale St. Michel, the much-restored cathedral with its 16th-century stained glass windows. Nearby, in rue Montagne aux Herbes Potagères is a genuine beer hall. *La Mort Subite* (Sudden Death!) is the place for authentic beers, cream cheeses and Ardennes ham.

Continue downhill past the imposing Bourse (Stock Exchange) to place Sainte Cathérine with its crumbling 13th-century tower. Under the square runs the River Senne, channeled underground last century when the stench from the open sewers became too great. As a result of its watery past, Sainte Cathérine still holds the city's best seafood restaurants. If you are interested in renovation, visit neighboring place Saint Géry. Locals are gradually appreciating the charms of the 17th-century buildings in this old port setting.

Walk back through the Grand' Place to the Mont des Arts, a formal park leading to the place Royale, the site of the Coudenberg Palace, where the sovereigns once lived. Apart from a superb view of the lower town, the dignified square boasts the city's two finest museums, the Museums of Ancient and Modern Art. From here, the stately rue de la Régence leads north to the Palais Royal (Royal Palace) and south to the Grand Sablon, the city's most sophisticated square. Although awash with restaurants and antique shops, the square is dominated by the church of Notre Dame du Sablon, built in flamboyant Gothic style. At night, the brilliant church windows illuminate the Grand Sablon. Behind the church is a small garden, the Petit Sablon, surrounded by 48 statues representing the medieval guilds. Each craftsman carries an object that reveals his trade: the furniture maker holds a chair while the wine maker clasps a goblet.

At the end of rue de la Régence is the ugly Palais de Justice, the monolithic law courts. Down a steep hill from here is the working class Marolles district, where the artist Pieter Breughel died in 1569. His marble tomb is in the Gothic splendor of Notre Dame de la Chapelle. Take rue Blaes to the flea market in place du Jeu de Balle (See *Markets*). Until this century, bourgeois Belgians considered this labyrinth of small alleys a den of thieves and political refugees! Although the Marolles continues to welcome immigrants or outsiders, it has lost its danger but kept its slightly raffish character.

Keen shoppers can head back to the Sablon via the cobbled rue Rollebeek and its cluster of designer shops. For a complete change of scene, catch a 94 tram from the Sablon church to the city's rambling park, the Bois de la Cambre. In the center of the park is a lake; on the lake is an island; and on the island is an inviting Swiss chalet with the inevitable restaurant.

PRACTICAL INFORMATION FOR BRUSSELS

HOTELS. As far as price is concerned, do not rely upon the listings provided by the Brussels Tourist Office: the entire Benelux Classification system is undergoing re-organization and until this is complete, the four official hotel categories bear little relation to price and services. In general, finding accommodation is not difficult but, as an EEC and business center, Brussels has far more choice in the Very Expensive and Expensive ranges. Hotels below these categories are often comfortable but characterless. The main hotel districts are: the *ville basse,* old town center; near the Avenue Louise business district; near Zaventem airport and in Brussels 'Silicon Valley'. Avoid the cheap hotel districts near Gare du Midi and Gare du Nord train stations. Hotels can be booked at the Tourist Office on the Grand' Place (tel. 02–513 89 40). Reservations are free but a deposit is required (deductible from final hotel check).

Moderate

Alfa Louise, Rue Blanche 4 (tel. 02–537 92 10). Situated near the Avenue Louise business and shopping district, this convenient hotel is tucked away down a quietish side street. The hotel is modern, service is friendly and the facilities are above average for a hotel in this price bracket. It is close to a number of good bars and restaurants, including the Amadeus (See Dining). From nearby Avenue Louise, the 93 and 94 trams take you downtown or to the lovely Bois de la Cambre, the city's finest park. 83 rooms, most with bath.

Arenberg, Rue d'Assaut 15 (tel. 02–511 07 70). Recently renovated, this hotel enjoys a central location near the Cathedrale St. Michel (the Cathedral) and the Gare Centrale (Central Station). All rooms have color TV and radio. The noted restaurant offers lunch for only 450 francs. Special dietary requirements can be accommodated. 156 rooms with bath.

Delta, Chaussée de Charleroi 17 (tel. 02–539 01 60). This modern, rather anonymous-looking hotel is located within walking distance of the exclusive Place Louise shopping district, good bars and cinemas. The street itself is always busy so ask for a room at the back. Frequent trams from the Place Stephanie take you downtown to the Sablon area and the Avenue Louise metro is nearby. The hotel is comfortable and fairly convenient but rather colorless.

Inexpensive

Arlequin, rue de la Fourche 17–19 (tel. 02–514 16 15). This 60-room hotel can also be reached through an arcade from the restaurant-packed Petite rue des Bouchers, so the lack of a dining room is no problem. The owners are a friendly young couple, and the TV-equipped rooms have bath or shower.

Marie-José, rue du Commerce 73 (tel. 02–512–08–42). Each room is decorated in a different style, some with antiques, in this bargain hotel that is just a five-minute walk from the Parc de Bruxelles. The restaurant, *Chez Callens,* is moderately priced and good for seafood specialties. A typical meal costs 1,700 francs (M). There are 17 rooms with bath or shower.

Youth Hostels and Camping. Brussels provides many hostels. *Sleep Well,* rue de la Blanchisserie 27 (tel. 02–218 50 50). Near the busy City 2 shopping center, 136 beds, 3 lounges, a bar, garden and library. The dormitories are for 4–6 people; price (per person) is 330 francs per night, inclusive of shower and breakfast. Between the elegant Sablon and the authentic Marolles is the brand new *Auberge de J. Breughel,* rue St. Esprit 2, (tel. 02–511 04 36) a well-designed hostel with good facilities and a friendly atmosphere. 450 francs per night (per person) for rooms with 2–4 people. Also in the center, the *Auberge Jacques Brel,* rue de la Sablonnière 30 (tel. 02–218 01 87) charges 450 francs per person in a twin-bedded room, 375 francs in rooms for 3–4. Special rooms are available for handicapped people. Restaurant, bar, and parking facilities for bikes and motorcycles. There are camp sites at Huizingen and Beersel, outside the city. Huizingen, Provinciaal Domein, (tel. 02–380 14 93). Beersel, 12 kilometers from Brussels, is at Steenweg op Ukkel 75 (tel. 02–376 25 61).

Restaurants

Brussels offers an excellent spread of restaurants in all price categories. The local *cuisine Bruxelloise* is a rich and often imaginative variant on French cuisine. The ambience tends to be dignified and old-fashioned in the more exclusive restaurants and cozy or jovial in the simpler *brasseries.* Servings are plentiful. Restaurants abound, but the greatest number are in the Grand' Place area: wall to wall restaurants line the busy Petite rue des Bouchers. Although service is generally prompt and polite, this is not always the case in the Petite rue des Bouchers, something of a tourist trap. One neighboring alley is devoted entirely to fish restaurants, another to meat specialities; Italian, Greek and Lebanese food are also available nearby. For quieter, more elegant dining you could try try the Sablon area, or the Marolles for authentic, inexpensive dining. A fixed menu costs less than *à la carte.* In general, the (M) restaurants listed below offer à la carte between 1,000 and 1,700 francs and (I) between 700 and 1000 francs, including service but not wine.

Moderate

Amadeus, Rue Veydt 13 (tel. 02–538 34 27). This stylish, dramatic restaurant once belonged to the French sculptor Rodin. Trendy diners can choose to have a drink, *blinis,* and caviar in the romantic Wine and Oyster Bar. For something more substantial, the candlelit Amadeus restaurant offers spare ribs and unusual salads. Reservations advised.

Aux Armes de Bruxelles, Rue des Bouchers 13 (tel. 02–511 21 18). An island of restraint in a line of restaurants packed with displays of headless birds and vast fish. Service is fast and portions large. Specialties include *waterzooi de volaille* (a rich chicken stew) and *moules au vin blanc* (mussels in white wine). Order the *crêpes suzette* if you want to see your table engulfed by brandy flames! Closed Mon.

Livre Jaune-Chez Rachid, Rue du Bailli 51 (tel. 02–648 67 30). This is the place for Algerian and Moroccan cuisine in a friendly, courteous restaurant just off Avenue Louise. *Couscous* is the central dish, perhaps prepared with lightly cooked lamb, peppers, zucchini, fennel and spices. Closed Sat. lunch and Sun.

Ogenblik, Galerie des Princes 1 (tel. 02–511 61 51). This authentic bistro, with its marble-topped tables, sawdust-covered floors and green-shaded lamps, serves up specialties like saddle of lamb that would do a five-star restaurant proud. No reservations after 8 P.M., so plan to come early. Open till midnight. Closed Sun.

Les Petits Oignons, Rue Notre-Seigneur 13 (tel. 02–512 47 38). Unlike the tourist traps around the Grand' Place, this place appeals to locals. The 17th-century building is furnished with plants and bold modern paintings. There is even a garden for summer dining. Tasty game dishes, the fixed menus and the special lunch menu are good value. Closed Sun. and in July.

Inexpensive

Chez Leon, 18 rue des Bouchers (tel. 02–511 14 15.) In the heart of the restaurant quarter, this unpretentious restaurant is an institution. Its fame rests on its authentic local dishes and draft beer. In the mussels season, it is packed with locals, but since meals are consumed so quickly, you never have to wait long.

La Grande Porte, Rue Notre Seigneur 9 (tel. 02–539 21 32). A warren of interconnecting rooms. The jovial waiters make no concessions to fashion or style. Specialties include: *risotto à la provençale* (a simple but tasty risotto with tomato, cheese and onions); steaks (served with rice, French fries or both at once!); and *salade folle* (a meal in itself). Closed July.

La Maison d'Atilla, 36–44 Av. Prince de Ligne (tel. 02–375 38 05). Calling itself a Mongolian barbeque house, this crazy restaurant is popular with families or boisterous groups. Children pay according to their age. Adults eat and drink as much as they like. Since it is slightly out of town, you will need to budget for a cab, at least for the return journey.

Le Paradoxe, 329 Chaussee d' Ixelles (tel. 02–649 89 81). This self-proclaimed 'natural' restaurant serves unusual seafood and vegetarian dishes in a setting rather like an elegant greenhouse. Presided over by Lupe, a charming Brazilian, the friendly staff know most of their clients by name or by sight. Specialties include samosas with rice and scampi with kiwi fruit, and home-made desserts. Friday or Saturday evening there is live music. Reservations advised on musical evenings. Closed Sun. and three weeks in July–Aug.

Le Zavel, Place du Grand Sablon (tel. 02–512 03 49). Both a bar and a brasserie, the Zavel is a friendly, unpretentious bar in a very pretentious square. Specialities include: *Belgian waterzooi* and *salade Liègeoise* (a warm bacon salad), *tagliatelle au pistou* (noodles with pine kernels), Russian *borsch* (beetroot soup) and *piroghi* (pancakes). The meal can be accompanied by wine or by Belgian beer. Why not try a *bière trappiste,* a strong 'monastery' beer or a light *bière blanche* such as *Hoegaarden.* You can dine outside in summer.

Budget Tip. You can get a small book of coupons in conjunction with a hotel reservation that saves 10% on tickets for sightseeing, shopping, and meals in certain restaurants.

GETTING AROUND BRUSSELS. By Tram, Bus and Subway. Brussels has an extensive and comparatively inexpensive bus and tram system. It also has an adequate subway system, which consists essentially of two lines running north-south and one crosstown route. Maps of all Brussels public transport routes are available at tourist offices, as well as details of the various savings tickets. Individual bus, tram, or metro tickets cost 35 francs each, so the ten-ride ticket at 220 francs and the five-ride ticket at 155 francs are bargains. A special rover ticket, valid for an unlimited number of trips during a 24-hour period, is also a good deal for 140 francs. Transits or transfers to a connecting bus, tram, or metro are included in the price. For further details go to *Information Centre,* 61 rue Marché aux Herbes or inquire at any major metro station.

By Taxi. These are expensive, but your tip is included in the fare. To call a taxi, ring *Taxis Verts* (Green Cabs) on 02–511 22 44 or pick one up at one of the many stands.

Car Rental. Again, this is expensive. The better firms run better cars, but cost more. Back-street hiring may appear to be less expensive but can lead to greatly increased expenses with unreliable cars. Try *Hertz* (tel. 02–735 40 50) or *Avis* (02–724 06 25). They also have offices in the airport.

By Bicycle. Owing to Belgian driving habits (biggest vehicle wins) these are dangerous in Brussels traffic. Sightseeing is best done on foot.

From the Airport. Brussels is one of the increasing number of major European airports to be linked by fast rail services to the city center, and it was one of the first. Special electric trains run every 20 to 30 minutes from Central Station (stopping at Nord station en route) to the airport. Journey time just under 20 minutes. Trains start around 5.30 A.M. and run through to about 11.15 P.M. Fare is 70 francs one way. **Budget tip:** If you've time, try to buy your ticket from the window at the station; there's a 30-franc supplement if you pay on the train.

THE ARTS AND ENTERTAINMENT. An invaluable source of information is *The Bulletin,* the city's English language magazine. It comes out on Thursday and costs 65 francs.

Cinema. Movies are mainly shown in their original language so many are in English. The *Acropole* in avenue de la Toison d'Or, the *Vendome* in avenue Louise and the new 26-theater complex *Kinepolis* near the Atomium all show first-run U.S. and British imports. On Monday, tickets are reduced from 200 to 150 francs. For unusual movies or screen classics, visit the *Cinema Museum,* rue Baron Horta 9 (tel. 02–513 41 55). Five movies are shown daily, at only 50 francs each.

Music. Brussels is a major center for classical music and jazz. Classical concerts are often held at the *Palais des Beaux-Arts,* rue Ravenstein 23, (tel. 02–512 50 45). Alternatively, there are many free Sunday morning concerts at various churches, including the Cathedral and the Petite eglise des Minimes, rue des Minimes 62. Brussels lays claim to being Europe's jazz capital. Try the smooth *Brussels Jazz Club,* Grand' Place 13 (tel. 02–512 40 93), open every night except Wednesday and Sunday. While the Jazz Club attracts a sophisticated clientele, the *Bierodrome* is a smokey rough-and-ready club in Place Fernand Cocq 21 (tel. 02–512 04 56). Except for weekend tickets at the Jazz Club, most entrance prices are low (from 50–500 francs).

Dance and Opera. Both can be seen at the *Theatre Royal de la Monnaie,* Place de la Monnaie (tel. 02–218 12 02) but tickets are not cheap (500–2,000 francs). Mark Morris has successfully replaced Béjart as resident director-choreographer of the national dance company.

Theater. Brussels' 30 theaters perform in French, Flemish, and occasionally in English. The loveliest theater is the *Theatre du Residence Palace,* 155 rue de la Loi (tel. 02–231 03 05). Both plays and concerts are put on here. Be sure not to miss puppet theater. Visit the *Theatre Toone,* petite rue des Bouchers (tel. 02–513 54 86). Set in a medieval house, this intimate theater performs satirical plays in incomprehensible *Bruxellois* dialect.

Nightlife. Bars. The city's most typical nightlife. Rustic bars vie with designer bars, cozy bars, Art Deco bars, American bars, English or Irish bars, beer or wine bars. *La Fleur en Papier Doré,* rue des Alexiens, is an artistic bar that attracts a Bohemian audience to drink local beer and look at the ancient walls covered with surreal paintings and old etchings. *Falstaff,* 17 rue Henri Maus (tel. 02–511 98 77), is a famous Art Nouveau tavern that continues to draw a mixed crowd. *De Ultième Hallucinatie,* 316 rue Royale (tel. 02 217 06 14), is an Art Nouveau bar popular with the trendy Flemish community.
Discotheques and Nightclubs. The *Crocodile Club,* Royal Windsor Hotel, rue Duquesnoy, is a disco appealing to Eurocrats and visiting executives. *Le Garage,* rue Duquesnoy 16, attracts a younger, local crowd. Both closed on Sunday. *Le Cocoon Club,* 14 rue de la Montagne, is a trendy spot open on Friday and Saturday

after 10.30 P.M. Nightclubs are not always distinguishable from striptease shows but lack Parisian looks, verve, and high kicks. *Show Point,* place Stéphanie 14, does its best.

MUSEUMS. Most museums are open 10–12 and 2–5, if not longer, but closed Mon. Entry is generally under 100 francs.

Atomium, Laeken (Heysel Stadium metro). In 1958 when this model of a molecule was built, it was considered a clever feat of engineering—the Belgian answer to the Eiffel Tower. The vast 'atom balls' are being converted into a science museum. Open 9.30–4.

Autoworld, Parc du Cinquantenaire 11. This new museum claims to have one of the world's most handsome collection of vintage cars. Open 10–6.

Bruparck, Laeken (next to Atomium). This is the latest Brussels attraction, featuring Mini-Europe (1:25 scale models of 350 famous buildings) a village with pubs and shops, and the Kinepolis movie-theater complex.

Cantillon Brewery, rue Gheude 56. Here traditional methods are still used to make *Gueuze* and *Lambic* beer. Try the strange fruit beers, *Kriek* (cherry) and *Framboise* (raspberry). Open mid-Oct–mid-May and every Sat. from 10–5.

Comic Strip Museum, Les anciens magasins Waucquez, rue des Sables 20. This brand new museum celebrates the work of such famous Belgian graphic artists as Hergé, Tintin's creator. The display is housed in Victor Horta's splendid Art Nouveau building.

Erasmus' House, rue du Chapitre 31. This beautifully restored 15th-century house was where Erasmus, the great humanist, lived in 1521. The custodian considers he has failed if you do not leave enthused by the relevance of Erasmus' works to peace in our time. Open Wed., Thurs., Sat.–Mon.

Historium, Anspach Center (first floor), Place de la Monnaie. This is a waxworks museum and history museum for children. The romp through Belgian history is enlivened by sound effects. Open daily 10–6.

Horta Museum, rue Americaine 25. This was once the workshop designed by the Belgian master of Art Nouveau, Victor Horta. From the attic to the cellar, every detail of the house celebrates the exuberant curves of Art Nouveau style. Open Tues.–Sun. 2–5.30.

Museum of Ancient Art, rue de la Régence 3. Do not miss Breughel's dramatic *The Fall of Icarus* or light skating scenes. Bosch's malevolent *Last Judgment* and Rubens' voluptuous nudes are also highlights. Open Tues.–Sun. 10–12, 2–5.

Museum of Modern Art, place Royale 1. The surprise lies in the quality of Belgian modern art. See Magritte's luminous fantasies, James Ensor's masks, Permeke's deeply brooding *Fiancés* and Delvaux's Surrealist dreams of women, sex and trains. Open Tues-Sun 10–1, 2–5.

Museum of Musical Instruments, Petit Sablon 17. Over a thousand musical instruments are on display. Of these, half are unique and a few go back to the Bronze Age. Open Tues., Thurs., Sat. 2.30–4.30, Wed. 4–6, Sun. 10.30–12.30.

SHOPPING. Lace and chocolates are the best buys for the budget traveler but hand-blown Val-St.-Lambert lead crystal is an affordable luxury. Try *Art And Selection,* Marché-aux-Herbes 83, near the Grand' Place. For cut-price porcelain and china, visit the *Vaisselle au Kilo,* rue Bodenbroek 8. Open daily. For rich Belgian chocolates, try the brands made by Godiva, Neuhaus or Leonidas. Although Godiva is better known abroad, Leonidas is rated more highly by Belgians. Leonidas shops are found everywhere, including in boulevard Adolphe Max. As for lace, check whether it is machine-made or handmade. As preparation, visit the *Lace Museum,* 6 rue de la Violette (near the Grand' Place). *La Maison F. Rubbricht,* on the Grand' Place, sells authentic, handmade Belgian lace. For a large choice of old and modern lace, try *Manufacture Belge de Dentelles,* Galerie de la Reine 6–8. The *Tintin Shop* in the rue de la Colline off the Grand'Place sells all kinds of memorabilia and gift items inspired by the comic-strip boy reporter.

Markets. The flower market on the Grand'Place (daily except Mon.) makes a colorful diversion from museum visiting. Midi Market is very exotic (by Gare du Midi, Midi train station). On Sunday morning the whole area becomes a colorful souk: the city's large North African community gathers to buy and sell exotic foods

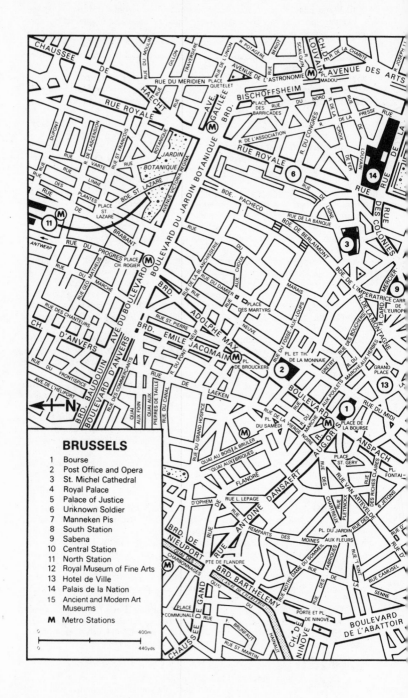

BRUSSELS

1 Bourse
2 Post Office and Opera
3 St. Michel Cathedral
4 Royal Palace
5 Palace of Justice
6 Unknown Soldier
7 Manneken Pis
8 South Station
9 Sabena
10 Central Station
11 North Station
12 Royal Museum of Fine Arts
13 Hotel de Ville
14 Palais de la Nation
15 Ancient and Modern Art
     Museums

M Metro Stations

400m
440yds

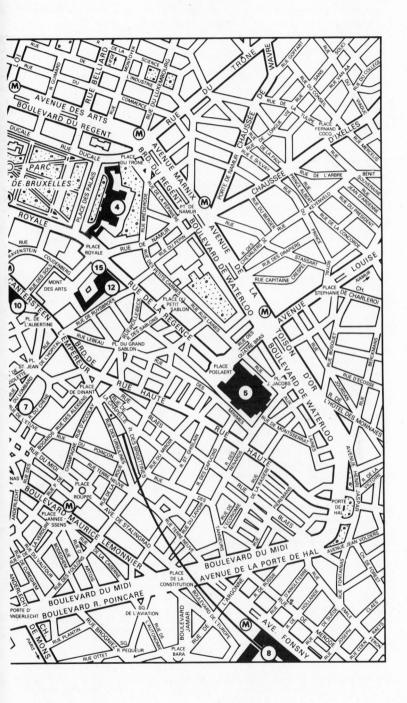

or household equipment. The Vieux Marché (Old Market) in Place Jeu de Balle is a daily flea market worth visiting for the authentic atmosphere of the working class Marolles district.

USEFUL ADDRESSES. *U.S. Embassy,* 27 blvd. du Régent (tel. 02–513 3830); *Canadian Embassy,* 2 ave. de Tervuren (tel. 02–735 60 40); *British Embassy,* 28 rue Joseph II (tel. 02–217 90 00); *Brussels Tourist Office,* Hôtel de Ville, Grand'Place (tel. 02–513 89 40); *Belgian Tourist Offices,* 61 rue Marchè-aux-Herbes (tel. 02–512 30 30); *Thomas Cook,* 4 Grand'Place (tel. 02–513 28 44); *American Express,* pl. Louise 2 (tel. 02–512 17 40); *Wagon-Lits Tours,* 144 ave. E. Plasky (tel. 02–736 60 07). All in center of Brussels. *Emergency,* dial 100 throughout the country; *Police,* 101.

Antwerp

Antwerp, lying on the Scheldt River, is the world's fifth largest port and the main city of Belgium's Flemish region. This bustling, sophisticated city has long been used to wealth. With its long tradition of merchants and an ancient diamond cutting trade, Antwerp has not looked back since the 1860s when it freed the port from Dutch control. Even on Sunday, the city is out on the streets: buying flowers or birds in the markets, visiting the fine art galleries, eating *warme wafels* with whipped cream at stalls, or just thronging the cafes in Kaasrui, off the Grote Markt.

PRACTICAL INFORMATION FOR ANTWERP

HOTELS. All the hotels are modern so expect comfort rather than period charm.

Moderate

Antwerp Docks, 100 Noorderlaan (tel. 03–541 18 50). 79 rooms with bath. Close to the port installations; good value.

Columbus, 4 Frankrijklei (tel. 03–233 03 90). 27 good rooms; close to diamond quarter.

Congress, 136 Plantin en Moretuslei (tel. 03–235 30 00). 66 rooms in modern building on city outskirts.

Drugstore Inn, 43 Koningin Astridplein (tel. 03–231 21 21). 27 rooms with bath; pleasant and centrally located.

Inexpensive

Arcade, 39 Meistraat (Theaterplein) (tel. 03–231 88 30). This modern, impersonal hotel overlooks the weekend marketplace and old district.

Boomerang, 58 Volksstraat (tel. 03–238 47 82) is a well-equipped youth hostel with dormitories and rooms for 2 to 4 persons. Free showers, restaurant, picnic lunches, bicycle rentals.

Florida, 59 De Keyserlei (tel. 03–232 14 43). 51 rooms, some with bath; no restaurant.

New International Youth Pension, 256 Provinciestraat (tel. 03–230 05 22). 30 beds, large annex; pleasant, friendly and well run.

Rubenshof, 117 Amerikalei (tel. 031–237 07 89). 20 rooms; no restaurant.

Tourist, 22 Pelikaanstraat (tel. 03–232 58 70). Situated next to the Central Station, this is a budget standby. 148 rooms, 126 with bath.

RESTAURANTS. Local specialties include herring and mussels dishes; *witloof* (endives) cooked in a variety of ways. As for drink, there are 20 local beers, a city gin called *jenever,* and a strong liqueur, *Elixir d'Anvers.*

Moderate

Het Fornuis, 24 Reyndersstraat (tel. 03–233 62 70). Country-style; in old quarter.

Rooden-Hoed, 25 Oude Koornmarkt (tel. 03–233 28 44). Seafood is a specialty of this cozy, traditional restaurant. Try the *paling in 't groen* (eel in green sauce) with Alsace wine. Closed Wed.–Thurs.

Inexpensive

In de Schaduw van de Kathedral, 17 Handschoenmarkt (tel. 03–232 40 14). Seafood dishes are served "in the shadow of the Cathedral." Closed Tues.
Mini-Lunch, 42 Sint Katelijnevest (tel. 03–232 61 16). Excellent midday snack bar.
't Peerd, Paardenmarkt 53 (tel. 03–234 09 76). Rustic decor; good value *dagschotel.*
Rubenshof, 9 Groenplaats (tel. 03–233 85 87). One of the better value places on the square by the Cathedral.

GETTING AROUND ANTWERP. By Metro. Antwerp now has a new underground "railroad"—unusual in that it consists of trams going through underground tunnels! Invest in a *toeristenkaart.*

By Bus. Bus routes thread through the city and the terminal station is in Franklin Rooseveltplaats. There are also bus services to such excursion places as the picture-book town of Lier, Schoten, 's Gravenwezel, Brasschaat, and Lillo.

By Taxi. Taxis are plentiful and all carry meters. Tips are included in the fare.

By Boat. Trips on the river Scheldt or visits to the port can be made on the *Flandria,* sailing at 10 A.M. and 2 P.M. from Steen landing stage (tel. 03–233 74 22).

WHAT TO SEE AND DO. Museums. These are generally open 10–5, but check at Tourist Office to be precise. Entry usually 50 francs.
Butchers Hall, 38–40 Vleeshouwerstraat. Council chamber of the butchers guild with lapidary department and old musical instruments.
Diamond Museum, Lange Herentalsestraat 30. Watch the cutters at work and see many fine examples of their art.
Mayer van den Bergh Museum, 19 Lange Gasthuistraat. Collection of old paintings including Breughel's famous *Mad Meg.*
National Maritime Museum (Steen), 1 Steenplein. Ship models, charts and navigation instruments.
Our Lady's Cathedral, 21 Groenplaats. Biggest Gothic church in Belgium.
Plantin Moretus Museum, 22 Vrijdagmarkt. House and 16th-century printing shop of the Plantin and Moretus families.
Rubens House, 9 Wapper. This magnificent house was designed by the artist himself in 1610. Wide ranging exhibition of paintings by the master and pupils.
Zoo (Dierentuin), 26 Koningin Astridplein. Antwerp Zoo is one of the world's most reputable. The complex includes a winter garden, a planetarium, a good cafe, and two natural history museums. Admission 280 francs, 180 francs for children.
There are many cinemas and places of entertainment. Antwerp is an excellent city for walkers. Try strolling around the winding streets of the Old Quarter by the Cathedral, or north to the barge docks. Antwerp has many night clubs and discos such as *Pop King Shake,* and *President* in Anneessenstraat. You can get up-to-date leaflets from the Tourist Office.

SHOPPING. Shoppers should head for the main thoroughfare, *De Keyserlei,* which starts at the Central Railway Station. Some of the side streets leading from it are specialized; the lace shops are in the streets near the cathedral, and *Meir* has just about everything.

USEFUL ADDRESSES. *American Consulate,* 5 Nationale Straat (4th floor) (tel. 03–225 00 71); *British Consulate,* Lange Klarenstraat 24 (tel. 03–232 69 40); Tourist Office, opposite central station on Koningin Astridplein, and on Grote Markt 15 (tel. 03–232 0103). *American Express,* Frankrijklei 21 (tel. 03–232 59 20); *Wagons Lits,* Meir 11 (tel. 03–231 08 30).

Bruges

Bruges (Brugge) was ignored for centuries after the Zwin silted up and the port became a romantic Flemish backwater. This past misfortune is its present glory.

Little has changed in this city of interlaced canals, overhung with humped-back bridges and weeping willows.

Bruges has a large student population and this is reflected in the lively bars and summer concerts in the historic squares. The Burg, an intimate medieval square, is the inspiring setting for summer classical concerts. Even without a concert, Bruges is a very musical city: when the town belfry's 47 bells ring out, you expect the city to collapse like a house of cards.

There is no question of expense as far as taxis or guides are concerned in Bruges, for the only way to see and enjoy it is to walk. Most places are within a few minutes of each other. There you will find St. John's Hospital with its Memling collection and a delightful old pharmacy. Opposite is the Church of Our Lady (dating from 1230) with its priceless Michelangelo white marble Madonna and Child. From the church you can visit the quiet Béguinage, which belonged at one time to sisters and widows of knights killed in the crusades, and is now inhabited by nuns who still wear the black robes and white linen headdresses depicted by Memling. Then walk over an old bridge to the Minnewater—Lake of Love.

The main square has the beautiful belfry and in the neighboring square you will find the famous Basilica of the Holy Blood. Behind the altar is a small crystal phial said to contain a portion of blood-stained water washed from the body of Christ by Joseph of Arimathea. This is carried in a pageant on Ascension Day, one of the most important religious processions in Northern Europe.

Try to see Bruges in winter as well as spring or summer: the watery mists prompt unexpected reflections. Without people, the city retreats a few centuries. Besides, the Lake of Love, the inscrutable Memling paintings, and the crooked trees in the Béguinage are too good to share.

PRACTICAL INFORMATION FOR BRUGES

HOTELS. The city hotels are well above average in quality and choice but are reasonably priced: Moderate double rooms cost from 2,500 to 4,000 francs but all Inexpensive ones are under 2,000 francs. Many are converted merchants' houses in idyllic canalside locations.

Moderate

Bryghia, 4 Oosterlingenplein (tel. 050–33 80 59). Small and comfortable with 18 rooms; no restaurant.

Europ, 18 Augustijnenrei (tel. 050–33 79 75). 31 rooms, 28 with bath; pleasant, quiet atmosphere.

Pandhotel, 16 Pandreitje (tel. 050–34 06 66). 22 comfortable rooms with bath and TV. This is a new hotel within the shell of an old building.

Ter Brughe, 2 Oost-Gistelhof (tel. 050–34 03 34). 19 rooms in a wonderful 15th-century house.

Inexpensive

Fevery, 3 Collaert Mansionstraat (tel. 050–33 12 69). 11 rooms; pleasant.

Notre Dame, 3 Mariastraat (tel. 050–33 64 93). 8 rooms; close to museums.

Rembrandt-Rubens, 38 Walplein (tel. 050–33 64 39). 12 rooms; bar but no restaurant.

RESTAURANTS. There are many small, inexpensive restaurants and cafés in and around the main square, and you will see from the menus displayed outside that the majority of them serve special tourist menus. Just off the Markt (main square) is the Eiermarkt, where the restaurants are slightly less touristy: try *d'Eiermarkt* at 18 Eiermarkt (tel. 050–30 03 46). Moving slightly up-market try *'t Kluizeke,* 58 Sint-Jacobsstraat (tel. 050–34 12 24). In recent years Bruges has acquired a reputation among gourmets for its excellent new restaurants. If you feel like splurging, try *De Karmeliet,* 1 Jeruzalemstraat (tel. 050–33 82 59), *Vasquez,* 38 Zilverstraat (tel. 050–34 08 45) or *De Zilveren Pauw,* 41 Zilverstraat (tel. 050–33 55 66).

GETTING AROUND BRUGES. By Boat. Taking a short canal boat trip is an enjoyable way of seeing Bruges. There are several operators, and you never have to wait long at the landing. Equally enjoyable, but longer, is the excursion to Damme, 5 km. (3 miles) distant, on the *MS Zeehond* along the canal that connects Bruges with Sluis, a small Dutch border town. There are some five sailings a day each way during the summer. More than six centuries ago Damme was Bruges' crowded seaport and could accommodate 100 ships from all parts of the Western world. Now the sea has receded and Damme is a quiet village with some remarkable old buildings and a spacious square with a Gothic town hall. A 15th-century gabled house to the right of it is now the Jacob van Maerlant Museum. It was here that Charles the Bold and Margaret of York, sister of Edward IV, were married in 1468.

By Bicycle. These can be hired at the train station for 150 francs per day or with *Koffieboontje,* 4 Hallestraat, (tel. 050–33 80 27) for 250 francs per day.

WHAT TO SEE AND DO. Museums. Most museums are open 9.30–12, 2–5/6. Some close on Tuesdays. See the tourist office for details. Budget tip: a combined ticket lets you in to the major museums for only 200 francs.

Archers Guild of St Sebastian, Carmerstraat. A unique architectural complex that contains a remarkable collection of paintings and silverware.

Folklore Museum, converted from seven adjoining almshouses, is in the little street to the left of the Church of Jerusalem.

Groeninge Museum, on the Dijver canal, has an exemplary collection of work by Flemish painters, from some of the best-known masterpieces by Jan van Eyck, Van der Goes, Memling, Pourbus, Gerard David, and Hieronymus Bosch to work of the present day.

Gruuthuse Museum, close by, was originally the palace of the lords whose name it bears today, and it was King Edward IV's refuge in 1471 during his exile from England. It has lace, pottery, and gold.

Memling Museum, a one-time chapter room in St. John's Hospital's precincts, has a unique collection of the master's paintings. Interesting old furniture and household utensils can be seen on the cloister premises next to the medieval pharmacy.

Museum of the Holy Blood, alongside the cathedral, contains gold and silver reliquary made in 1617, wrought copperwork and paintings.

USEFUL ADDRESSES. *Tourist Office,* 11 Burg (tel. 050–44 86 86). Open Mon.–Fri. 9.30–6.30, weekends 10–12.30, 2–6.30.

Ghent

Ghent (Gent, Gand), capital of East Flanders, is 50 km. (32 miles) northwest of Brussels. Situated on the rivers Scheldt and Lys, it is intersected by canals like Bruges and has over 200 bridges. Although the outskirts are industrialized, the center retains much of its medieval character and the city is proud of the fact that it has more historic buildings than Bruges or Antwerp.

Between 1764 and 1767, the spinning jenny, which enabled 16 or more threads to be spun simultaneously by one person, was invented by James Hargreaves in England. By 1805 spinning and weaving equipment had been smuggled across the Channel to Ghent. The weaving of cotton has always flourished here and the local Cloth Hall, the meeting place of the drapers and wool merchants, is a splendid Gothic building. The cellar, happily for visitors, has been turned into an attractive café-restaurant but keeps its old world atmosphere.

Adjoining the Cloth Hall, the Belfry soars skyward for some 90 meters (300 feet). It is a square tower and on top of its cast-iron steeple a golden dragon acts as a weathervane. It is nearly 3.5 meters (12 feet) long and according to tradition, was brought from Constantinople by the Emperor Baldwin after the Crusades. Its carillon of 52 bells includes Roland, which is nearly 6 tons in weight.

Going for a walk in Ghent is a most rewarding experience. The buildings are floodlit from May to September and there is a famous view from St. Michael's Bridge in the center of the town. From here you can see the three great towers of Ghent ranged one behind the other. First, that of St. Nicholas's Church completed in 1250, then the belfry and, perhaps most impressive of all, that of St. Bavo's Cathedral.

PRACTICAL INFORMATION FOR GHENT

Hotels

Moderate

Arcade, 24–26 Nederkouter (tel. 091–25 07 07). 134 rooms, close to main shopping area.
Ascona, 105 Voskenslaan (tel. 091–21 27 56). 38 rooms; close to St. Peter's station.
Eden, 24 Zuidstationstraat (tel. 091–23 25 46). Close to historical sites.
Europahotel, 59 Gordunakaai (tel. 091–22 60 71). 39 rooms with bath.
Himatel, 2 Blankenbergestraat (tel. 091–20 15 15). 36 rooms, close to St. Peter's station.
Ibis Gent Centrum, 2 Limburgstraat (tel. 091–33 00 00). 120 rooms, next to St. Bavo's Cathedral.

Inexpensive

Castel, 9 Koningin Maria Hendrikaplein (tel. 091–20 23 54). Small, 12 rooms, handy for station.
De Ijzer, 117 Vlaanderenstraat (tel. 091–25 98 73). 16 rooms. Attractive; close to main sights.
University Housing, 6 Stalhof (tel. 091–22 09 11). Hostels and annexes with over 1,000 rooms during university vacation (mid-July to mid-Sept.).

Restaurants

Moderate

Carvery, 11 Kovenmarkt (tel. 091–24 28 21). An eat-as-much-as-you-can place in the city center.
Chantegrill, 32–34 Sint-Baafsplein (tel. 091–23 08 88). Restaurant and grill next to St. Bavo's Cathedral.
Graaf Van Egmond, Sint-Michielsbrug (tel. 091–25 07 27). Famous view of the towers of Ghent. French and Ghent specialties.
Raadskelder, 18 Botermarkt (tel. 091–25 43 34). In 14th-century vaults; good value *dagschotel.*

Inexpensive

De Warempel, 8 Zandberg (tel. 091–24 30 62). Good value selection of fish dishes and vegetarian food.
't Boontje, 6 Hoogpoort (tel. 091–25 56 00). Low cost snackery; open late.
Veneziana, 6 Geldmunt (tel. 091–25 92 45). Italian café opposite the Castle of the Courts—an institution.

WHAT TO SEE AND DO. Museums. Most museums open 10–5, closed for an hour at lunchtime. **Byloke Museum,** 2 Godshuizenlaan. Officially archeological, but by its contents more of a historical museum. Reproductions of late medieval Ghent homes, ironwork, weapons, costumes, etc.
Fine Arts Museum, in the citadel park. A fine collection of paintings by Breughel, Rubens, Jordaens, Pourbus, Tintoretto, Reynolds, etc.
Folklore Museum, 41 Kraanlei. Commemorates customs and traditions in the city. Interesting and entertaining.
St. Bavo Cathedral, has examples of late Gothic design in its 25 chapels. Among its many treasures is one of the world's great masterpieces, the famous painting by the Van Eyck brothers, *The Adoration of the Mystic Lamb.*

USEFUL ADDRESSES. The Tourist Office is in a crypt of the City Hall *(stadhuis),* tel. 091–24 15 55. It issues an excellent booklet that lists not only all the hotels and restaurants, but also university rooms and camp sites in Ghent and environs. Write to Belforstraat 9, B-9000 Ghent (tel. 091–25 36 41).

The Coast

Belgian coastal towns have the best budget prices. There are lots of bright cafés, variety shows, cinemas, shops open until late at night and many sports. Oostende, for instance, is a fine center for excursions even to Holland and France. Such jaunts can be inexpensive if you have your own car and buy picnic lunches. Aside from Knokke and Le Zoute, most of the coast is a resort for families on a limited budget.

The holiday season on the coast runs from mid-May to mid-September. You can combine a stay at one of the beaches with a trip to the nearby cities of art in Flanders. Oostende has over 200 hotels, many cafés and restaurants and the Wellington race course. It is flanked by several lesser resorts, each with individual appeal. De Haan has its 18-hole golf course, and sand-yachting is popular at De Panne near the French border. Caravan and camping sites are well run. Most visitors come primarily to laze about and enjoy the stretches of sand, swimming and sunbathing. Children love it. You can go along virtually the whole 64 km. (40 miles) of the coast by tram. Children may insist on the sandy coast near Blankenberge but parents may prefer Knokke, a more sophisticated resort.

There are so many hotels in all classifications along the coast that it would be impossible to list them all here. A comprehensive booklet by town, "Hotels in West Flanders," is available from the Tourist Office at 3 Wapenplein, Oostende (tel. 050–70 11 99). Here is a brief selection starting in the north.

PRACTICAL INFORMATION FOR THE COAST

Hotels

Blankenberge. *Marie José* (M), 2 Marie-Josélaan (tel. 050–41 16 39). 40 rooms, all with bath or shower. *Britannique* (I), 6 De Smet de Naeyerlaan (tel. 050–41 22 30). Only full- or half-board are available in this 12-room pension.

De Panne. *Teirlinck* (M), 175 Zeelaan (tel. 058–41 26 21). 52 rooms, 38 with bath; restaurant and bar. *Pavillon Bleu* (I), 69 Meeuwenlaan (tel. 058–41 12 82). 16 rooms; bar.

Knokke-Heist. *Prince's* (I), 171 Lippenslaan (tel. 050–60 11 11). 28 rooms; situated in the center of Knokke.

Oostende. *Burlington* (M), 90 Kapellestraat (tel. 059–70 15 52). 40 rooms; centrally located. *Glenmore* (I), 29 Hofstraat (tel. 059–70 20 22). 40 rooms, most with shower.

Bulgaria

Although Bulgaria may evoke images of rugged mountains, an equally rugged history and hardline communism, it is in fact a land of many contrasts. About the size of Tennessee, it contains forgotten valleys high in the Balkan, Rila and Rhodope mountain ranges; the broad flat Danube where industry alternates with countryside; the long and beautiful Valley of the Roses; and the Black Sea with its large sandy beaches and small picturesque villages perched defiantly on shaky cliffs. The Black Sea beaches have become the playground for tourists from both East and West Europe, and large modern hotel resorts have sprung up on the coast, though there are some smaller towns, passed over by the hordes, that retain their charm. The mountains to the south have ancient Thracian towns, small monasteries off the beaten track, and a way of life unchanged since the Middle Ages. Sofia, though largely rebuilt, retains architectural gems from its turbulent past and has one of the finest settings of any major European city. During her troubled history, Bulgaria has known three periods of independence: 681–1018, 1185–1396, and 1879 to the present. The first was followed by a period of Byzantine rule, and the second by half a millennium of Turkish domination, punctuated by many uprisings whose memorials pepper the landscape. Both influences are reflected in many aspects of Bulgarian culture and tradition. Following Soviet "liberation" from the Nazis in 1944, Moscow's influence was predominant. The overthrow of the Zhivkov regime in 1989 may herald a new era of independence although it is too early to say how far the present political changes will take Bulgaria toward democracy.

The independent and budget traveler will find that most of the official tourist areas are run for the package tourist who gets precedence in hotels, restaurants and theaters. However, many package arrangements offer quite a lot of flexibility; a system of prepaid vouchers overcomes many of the potential difficulties, while a sense of adventure can reveal facets of life, places and people denied the regular tourist. You can also book a freelance holiday with return flight and currency voucher that can be exchanged in Bulgaria, thus allowing maximum freedom of movement. It is very important, however, for individual travelers to be prepared to exercise patience and perseverance. It is also strongly recommended that you learn the Cyrillic alphabet, if only to know that a PECTOPAHT is a restaurant, identify museums and, in general, read road signs away from main roads and tourist centers. There is still very little tourist literature in English away from Sofia and the Black Sea resorts, and museum texts are very rarely in English. Special interest tours include various sports, art treasures, cookery and wine tasting.

PRACTICAL INFORMATION FOR BULGARIA

WHAT WILL IT COST. If you choose the more moderate Balkantourist hotels and restaurants, Bulgaria is very inexpensive. Even lower are the costs in hotels and restaurants run by municipal authorities and other bodies, but Balkantourist vouchers are not, of course, valid in these. Public transport is also extremely reasonable. Independent travelers must change $15 a day for the length of their stay ($10 if in transit). Package-tour operators usually include this amount as part of a package. If you want to stay longer than the length of your package tour, you can "pay" for the extra days at Balkantourist offices. Otherwise you will have to change the money at the border as you leave the country.

The monetary unit is the *lev* (plural *leva*) divided into 100 *stotinki*. The rate of exchange is approximately 1.35 leva to the pound sterling and 0.8 lev to the U.S. dollar. You may import any amount of foreign currency, including traveler's cheques, and exchange it at branches of the Bulgarian State Bank, Balkantourist hotels, airports and border posts. If possible, always exchange it through a Balkantourist office, which will add a currency bonus of 200%, providing you have prepaid a minimum of two nights' hotel accommodations. Always hang on to your official exchange slips. Avoid the active black market in foreign currency—there are heavy penalties, even imprisonment, for those caught in such illegal transactions (and anyway, you are likely to be cheated).

It is forbidden either to import or export Bulgarian currency. Unspent leva must be exchanged at frontier posts on departure, before going through passport control. You will need to present your official exchange slips to prove that the currency was legally purchased.

Sample Costs. Theater seat from 1.20–6.0 leva; museum entrance 0.20–0.90 leva; coffee in moderate restaurant 1–2 leva; bottle of wine from 4 leva; trip on a tram, trolley, or bus 6 stotinki. Because large price rises are likely during 1990, all prices quoted here and below can act only as a guide.

NATIONAL TOURIST OFFICE. Foreign tourist travel to Bulgaria is handled by *Balkantourist,* who operate a growing chain of hotels, run sightseeing excursions and longer tours (including special interest), maintain information offices, and are responsible for such matters as foreign exchange. A good system of meal vouchers enables holidaymakers to have the freedom to eat where they wish. A voucher document is obtained from the tour operator through whom they have booked and can be exchanged locally for vouchers that are valid in any Balkantourist restaurant throughout the country. In Sofia, there are information bureaus at 37 Dondukov Boulevard and at the Central Railway Station. In addition there are several other organizations catering to specific categories of visitor such as *Šipka* (for motorists), 5 Sveta Sofia St. (tel. 878801), *Pirin* (for hikers), 30 A. Stambolijski Blvd. (tel. 870687), *Cooptourist,* 33 A. Stambolijski Blvd. (tel. 8441), and *Orbita* (for youth), 45A Stambolijski St. (tel. 879552).

In the U.S.: Balkan Holidays, 161 East 86th St., New York, N.Y. 10028 (tel. 212–722–1110).

In the U.K.: Bulgarian National Tourist Office, 18 Princes St., London W1R 7RE (tel. 071–499 6988).

LANGUAGE. Bulgarian is a Slav language written in the Cyrillic alphabet. Spellings in English consequently vary considerably from one source to another. Most official maps use a system of accents, as in this chapter. However, many tourist publications employ phonetic spellings. The following may help in identifying (and pronouncing) places and names, spelled by this method: *Borovec*—Borovets; *Caravec*—Tsaravets; *Družba*—Drouzhba; *Nesebâr*—Nessebur; *Slânčev Brjag*—Slunchev Bryag; *Šipka*—Shipka; *Târnovo*—Turnovo; *Vitoša*—Vitosha; *Zlatni Pjasâci*—Zlatni Pyassutsi.

WHEN TO COME. The Black Sea coast season lasts from May to October; July and August are the warmest and most crowded months. Inland, March and April are wet, April/May are good months for fruit blossom, May/early June for the rose harvest, September for the fruit harvest, October for fall colors. The skiing season is mid-December through mid-April.

The climate is very warm (but not unpleasant) in summer, 2,240 hrs. of sunshine per year in coastal areas, nearly 30% more than southern England.

Average afternoon temperatures in degrees Fahrenheit and centigrade:

Sofia	Jan.	Feb.	Mar.	Apr.	May	June	July	Aug.	Sept.	Oct.	Nov.	Dec.
F°	34	39	51	62	70	76	82	82	74	63	50	37
C°	1	4	11	17	21	24	28	28	23	17	10	3

SPECIAL EVENTS. All the latest information can be obtained from Balkantourist.

Local traditional events are particularly lively along the Black Sea Coast throughout the summer and in the towns and villages around Christmas and New Year. The most important among them are Trifon Zaresan, the vinegrowers' festival, *February* 14; Martenitzas, the Festival of Spring, *March* 1; Lazaraouvane, Slavic festival of youth and of marriageable girls, taking place throughout the country, *April* 1; Labor Day, *May* 1; St. George's Day, May 6; and The Day of Bulgarian Culture, May 24. The International Sofia Weeks of Music run from *May* 24–*July* 1, and in the first half of *June* the Festival of Roses is celebrated with parades and carnivals at Karlovo and Kazanluk. The International Book Fair is held at the Lyudmila Zhivkova National Palace of Culture, 1 Bulgaria Sq., Sofia from June 2–7. The Golden Orpheus International Pop Festival (alternative years, even numbers) at Sunny Beach also falls in June.

From *June* 15–*July* 26 the Summer International Festival of Music is held in Varna and Golden Sands; the International Ballet Contest in Varna (every two years); and Song and Dance Festivals at Golden Sands. At Oreshak a range of craftwork from 40 countries can be seen at the International Exhibition of Arts and Crafts from *June* 15–*September* 15. In late *August* the International Folklore Festival flourishes at Bourgas and Sunny Beach. At Plovdiv the International Arts Festival is held from *September* through *October,* with theater, opera, ballet and concert performances at the Antique Theater, chamber concerts at Balbanov House, and exhibitions in the period houses in the old city. In May and September hotels here are filled with delegates attending the two International Trade Fairs. In *November* Pleven hosts the Katya Popova Laureate Days International Music Festival.

National Holidays. Jan. 1; Mar. 3 (Liberation from Turkish rule in 1877); May 1 & 2 (Labor); May 24 (Bulgarian Culture); Sept. 9 & 10; Nov. 7 (October Revolution).

VISAS. Tourists traveling on a package tour by charter flight or—in groups of 6 or more—by scheduled and independent transport, do not require a visa. Otherwise, nationals of almost all countries except Austria, Eastern bloc and Scandinavian countries require visas, which may be obtained from Bulgarian embassies for a small fee. Often the arrangements will be made by the tour operator. Visas are not issued at the border. They are renewable in Bulgaria. It is important to retain the yellow immigration card as it is required when leaving the country.

HEALTH CERTIFICATES. Not required for entry into Bulgaria from any country.

GETTING TO BULGARIA. By Plane. There are no direct flights from North America to Bulgaria but many western European capitals have direct or through flights to and from Sofia. From London, for example, *Balkan Air* (the Bulgarian National airline) have currently three flights weekly, and there is a daily service operated jointly by *Air France* and Balkan Air from Paris. Inclusive holiday charter flights—frequently at an amazingly low rate—operate from a number of west European countries including the U.K. in summer to Varna and Burgas for the Black Sea holiday resorts, and for winter sports holidays to Sofia and Plovdiv. Sofia airport is linked by bus nos. 84 or 284, both non-stop, to the city center, taking about 20 minutes for the six miles.

By Train. The most suitable way to go by rail from western Europe to Bulgaria is to take the *Istanbul Express* from Munich, traveling via Salzburg, Zagreb, Belgrade and Niš. First- and 2nd-class carriages and 2nd-class couchettes. No dining facilities, but the stop at Belgrade is about 30 minutes and at the Yugoslav-Bulgarian border just under an hour. It can be very crowded with Turks traveling to and from jobs in western Europe.

By Bus. There are no scheduled bus services from western Europe although you might use a service to Athens and change at Belgrade, going on from there by another (Bulgarian operated) service to Sofia. But be sure services are properly licensed.

CUSTOMS. Personal belongings including sports equipment, musical instruments, radios and cameras may be brought in duty free, but such valuable items should be recorded on the appropriate document on entry into Bulgaria in order to facilitate re-export. You may also import 250 gr. of tobacco or 200 cigarettes; 1 liter of spirits and 2 liters of wine; 100 gr. of perfume; gifts up to the value of 50 leva. Duty-free prices at *Corecom* shops are low. Foreign currency purchases may be freely exported, but only by showing the receipt of your purchase. Customs and currency inspection tend to be casual.

HOTELS. All accommodations for foreign tourists are handled by Balkantourist (groups and individuals), Šipka (motorists), Orbita (youth) or Pirin (hikers and mountaineers), catering mainly to groups. Hotels are also operated by municipal authorities, but of course Balkantourist vouchers are not valid in these. In any case hotels rarely accept people who have not been referred to them by the above agencies, so it is worth going directly to the centrally located offices. Preference is always given to organized groups (especially in Sofia), and as an individual you may find yourself at the whim of others. Independent travelers in any case are well advised to make prepaid arrangements through a travel agent as early as possible; the excellent system of vouchers also leaves them plenty of freedom of movement.

Hotels in Bulgaria are classified according to the international star system, which corresponds roughly to our own grading system of Moderate (M), the same as a 3-star hotel in Bulgaria, and Inexpensive (I), the same as a 2- or 1-star hotel in Bulgaria. Two people in a double room with half board in a Moderate hotel will pay from $46–56, and from $27–38 in an Inexpensive hotel. Prices outside Sofia are at the lower end of these ranges and there are reductions of 25–40% outside high season. The choice of private accommodations has increased enormously in recent years and can also be arranged through Balkantourist: double room with breakfast for two, from about $12 in Sofia, from $10 elsewhere. Ask for the *Rooms to Let* booklet from Balkantourist or the Bulgarian National Tourist Office.

If you arrive in Sofia without reservations go to Interhotels Central Office, 4 Sveta Sofia St. (Interhotels only); Balkantourist, 37 Dondukov Blvd.; Bureau of Tourist Information and Reservations, 35 Eksarh Josif St. (near Lenin Square) and at the Palace of Culture, 1 Bulgaria Sq. (off Vitoša Blvd.); at the Central Rail Station.

Hostels provide good, clean though basic accommodations. Privacy is hard to find, but they provide the chance to meet and talk with other travelers from abroad and also with many young Bulgarians from different areas of the country. Check with Orbita, 45A Stambolijski St. in Sofia.

Camping. There are now over 100 camping sites, 43 of them near Black Sea beaches and 63 inland, classified as three, two, and one star. Most have cabins for hire. A list with addresses and amenities is available at tourist information centers.

RESTAURANTS. Note the earlier comments on meal vouchers. An increasing number of traditional-style restaurants provide attractive settings for inexpensive meals. Service is often slow. Costs are lower still in cafeterias and restaurants, for example run by municipal authorities, but Balkantourist vouchers are not valid in these. Recently there has been a marked improvement in the standard of meals, which are often better in the smaller establishments than in the bigger tourist hotels. You should always ask for a written menu to see prices and check what is available on that day—the choice is unlikely to be more than three dishes. Our grading system runs—Inexpensive (I), 2–7 leva; Moderate (M), 7–15 leva; both for one person, three courses, no alcohol.

Food and Drink. A popular snack available everywhere is *kebapčeta,* tasty grilled small minced meat rolls, strongly spiced. Some good dishes to look out for are: *gjuveč,* a kind of hot pot of many vegetables, including potatoes and sometimes meat; *kavarma,* which is similar, with plenty of pork pieces; *pile paprikaš,* chicken in a rich sauce of tomatoes and peppers—another dish is fish with the same kind of garnish; *sarmi,* cabbage or vine leaves stuffed with meat, or peppers or aubergines treated in the same way. There are plenty of salads, a popular one being *šopska* salad composed of tomato, cucumber, sweet pepper, onion and topped with grated white goat's cheese. And, of course, this is the place for yogurt for Bulgaria is its original home (it's called *kisselo mleko* here). There is a great variety of fresh fruits and excellent pure fruit drinks, though the latter are not always easily available in restaurants which tend to go in more for mineral water, locally made Coca-Cola and similar beverages. The beer is tolerable, but specify you want the local brew or you'll pay heavily for imported brands. Plenty of wines, too, which as elsewhere are always much cheaper in the shops. Coffee is in thick, black Turkish style, though espresso is increasingly available, and more expensive, as is "Nes" (instant coffee in hot-water!).

TIPPING. Officially discouraged, but acceptable. 10% is safe.

MAIL. Letters and postcards cost 45 stotinki to the U.K., 60 to North America; but check before mailing.

CLOSING TIMES. Generally speaking, stores keep about the same hours as their counterparts in Britain and America. Most stores open between 8 and 10 and close between 5 and 7 Monday through Friday, or 12 to 2 on Saturday. Quite often though, smaller shops may close for several hours in the middle of the day, staying open late in the evening, especially in summer. In main centers, some stores are open all day. Museums are usually open 8–6.30, but are often closed on Monday or Tuesday. Check locally.

GETTING AROUND BULGARIA. Be prepared for delays. **By Plane.** *Balkan Bulgarian Airlines (Balkanair)* have frequent services from Sofia to Varna and Burgas on the Black Sea coast and a limited service to one or two other towns. Booking a ticket for an internal flight can take time. Your best bet is to try through Balkantourist organization first. Not really budget travel.

By Train. Buy tickets in advance at a railway ticket office—there is one in each of the major centers—and avoid long lines at the station. Trains are very busy—seat reservations are obligatory on expresses. All medium and long distance trains have 1st- and 2nd-class carriages and limited buffet services; overnight trains between Sofia and Black Sea resorts have 1st- and 2nd-class sleeping cars and bunk beds. From Sofia there are five main routes—to Varna and to Burgas on the Black Sea coast; to Plovdiv and on to the Turkish border; to Dragoman and the Yugoslav border; and to Kulata and the Greek border. Large sections of the main line are electrified—plans to electrify the rest are under way.

By Bus. There are a number of bus services but these are mainly linking with rail services to towns and districts not connected by train. Full information from tourist information bureaus. Buses are always very busy.

By Boat. Hydrofoils link main communities along the Bulgarian Danube and the Black Sea, and there are coastal excursions from some Black Sea resorts. A ferry from Vidin to Calafat links Bulgaria with Romania.

Sofia

The city sprawls on a high fertile plain in the lee of the Balkan Mountains, or Stara Planina, a high range running eastward to the Black Sea. Sofia is a fast-growing metropolis of one million, with wide, straight, fluorescent-lit, tree-shaded streets, 384 parks and grassy squares, and a rash of recent architecture, much of it inspired by Moscow and often described as Stalinist Gothic.

One of the most dominant features of Sofia is the glittering Alexander Nevski Memorial Cathedral in Pl. Al. Nevski (Alexander Nevski Square), erected to commemorate Bulgaria's liberation from the Turks in the Russo-Turkish war of 1877–78. Designed by a Russian architect, it was decorated jointly by Russian, Bulgarian

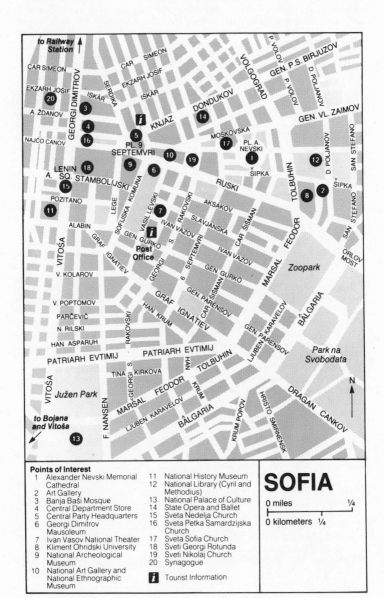

Points of Interest

1. Alexander Nevski Memorial Cathedral
2. Art Gallery
3. Banja Baši Mosque
4. Central Department Store
5. Central Party Headquarters
6. Georgi Dimitrov Mausoleum
7. Ivan Vasov National Theater
8. Kliment Ohridski University
9. National Archeological Museum
10. National Art Gallery and National Ethnographic Museum
11. National History Museum
12. National Library (Cyril and Methodius)
13. National Palace of Culture
14. State Opera and Ballet
15. Sveta Nedelja Church
16. Sveta Petka Samardzijska Church
17. Sveta Sofia Church
18. Sveti Georgi Rotunda
19. Sveti Nikolaj Church
20. Synagogue

i Tourist Information

SOFIA

0 miles   ¼

0 kilometers   ¼

and Czechoslovak artists with onyx, marble, alabaster and mosaics. Excellent icons are in the crypt. Just across the square from here is Sofia's most distinctive church, St. Sofia (Sveta Sofia)—from which the city took its name. This stately Byzantine basilica, with its cruciform cupola-topped structure, dates from the sixth century. A short jog south brings you to the large and pleasant Liberty Park *(Park na Svobodata)*, with its numerous leisure amenities.

The heart of Sofia is Pl. Lenin (Lenin Square) and just off it, the oldest of all the landmarks is the restored 5th-century church of Sv. Georgi, a charming building that crouches in the courtyard of the Sheraton Sofia-Hotel Balkan. Under restoration, the little church houses remnants of medieval frescoes and, along-side it, excavations have revealed even earlier foundations from the Roman period.

One block east and a thousand years later, the Turks built Sofia's largest mosque, the Bouyouk. Its nine cupolas today shelter Bulgaria's archeological museum. Around the corner is Pl. Deveti Septemvri (September Ninth Square), which does for Sofia what Red Square does for Moscow. Here the towering red star atop the semi-skyscraper of the former Bulgarian Communist Party headquarters dominates the skyline. An underpass from here takes you not only across the square, but almost, as it were, back to the Roman period in the shape of foundations of walls and a variety of artifacts. Nearby is the mausoleum of Georgi Dimitrov, a giant in the history of Bulgarian communism. But he may be supplanted by political changes—there is now talk of moving the mausoleum out of the way.

Back towards Lenin Square you will come to another charming little old church, sunk below ground level, and surrounded by shops and an open air café. This is Sveta Petka Samardzijska Church from the 14th century. Soaring beyond it is the other of Sofia's two mosques, Banja Basi, while across Georgi Dimitrov Street from this is the lively central market.

Also near Lenin Square is the outstanding new National History Museum on Vitoša Boulevard, a lively shopping street, which, in due course, passes the modern Palace of Culture as it heads towards the mountain dominating the capital. On the way to it you will also pass the fine, green acres of Južen Park. Rising to about 7,000 ft., Mt. Vitoša—now a national park and natural playground for the citizens in summer and winter—is served by chair lift and cable car. On its slopes about 10 km. from the city center, is the beautiful little medieval church of Bojana, a real showpiece, with 11th- to 13th-century frescoes. Long since closed for restoration, a replica has been built so that copies of the superb frescoes may be viewed without risk of damage to the originals.

PRACTICAL INFORMATION FOR SOFIA

HOTELS. If you haven't booked already, go to the Information Bureau at 37 Dondukov Blvd. (open 7 to 10.30) or the Central Railway Station. These offices also handle private accommodations.

Moderate

Bulgaria, Russky Blvd. 4 (tel. 871977). 72 rooms. Old-fashioned and quiet, though very central.

Hemus, Georgi Traikov Blvd. 31 (tel. 661415). Over 200 rooms. Less central.

Serdika, General Zaimov St. 2 (tel. 443411). 140 rooms, *Old Berlin* restaurant serving German specialties. Central.

Slavjanska Beseda, Rakovski St. 127 (tel. 883691). 110 rooms, no restaurant. Central.

Inexpensive

Orbita Student Hotel, Anton Ivanov 76. I.S.C.S. identity card required. Official student residence, modern amenities, well placed but some distance from the center.

Pliska, Lenin Blvd. 87 (tel. 71281). 210 rooms. Some distance from center, near Liberty Park.

Preslav, Trijadica St. 5 (tel. 876586). 90 rooms, restaurant, central.

Slavia, Sofijski Geroj St. 2 (tel. 525551). 75 rooms. Some distance from center to southwest.

Camping. Ivaniane, near Bankja spa, 17 km. (11 miles) west of city; Cernija Kos, (tel. 571129), 11 km. (7 miles) southwest of city on E-85; Vrana (tel. 781213), 10 km. (6 miles) southeast of city on E-80 to Plovdiv, pleasant setting, folk style restaurant and has the best facilities.

RESTAURANTS. In addition to the hotel restaurants, there is a growing number of eating places serving Bulgarian and other Eastern European specialties, often in attractive folkloric surroundings. Most of the following establishments qualify also as Inexpensive if you stick to basic dishes, but check before you order as menus in English are not readily available. In addition, there are plenty of workaday cafeterias and buffets where you can eat inexpensively.

Moderate

Berlin, V. Zaimov Blvd. 2. Bulgarian and German food. Can be expensive, so choose carefully. In Serdika Hotel.

Bojana, about 10 km. from center, near historic Bojana church. Folkloric program.

Cernata Kotka, about 13 km. southeast of city on E-80. Folk music.

Gorubljane, attached to motel about 10 km. southeast on E-80. Folk program.

Koprivštica, 3 Vitoša Blvd. Folk music.

Rubin, Lenin Sq. Eating complex in the city center, including a snack bar. Stick to the snack bar for budget eating.

Šumako, about 10 km. south of center on Simeonova-Bistrica road. Folk music.

Strandjata, 19 Lenin Square. Folk music.

Vodeničarski Mehani, (tel. 665088). Incorporating three old mills, at foot of Mount Vitoša above Dragalevci district. Folkloric show.

Zlatna Ribka, about 24 km. south of city on road to Borovec. Folk music.

GETTING AROUND SOFIA. Work has begun on a new **subway/underground** system, but for the moment you use **trams, buses** and **trolleys.** It's best to buy your tickets (6 stotinki each) in advance from special kiosks by the streetcar stop. The ticket must be punched in a machine after boarding the vehicle (watch how others do it).

ENTERTAINMENT. Cinema. Foreign films are shown in their original language.

Theaters. *Ivan Vazov National Theater,* 5 Vassillevski St., the largest; *National Folk Ensemble,* well worth going out of your way to see; *Central Puppet Theater,* 14 Gourko St., very popular and of high standard.

Opera. *State Opera House,* 1 Yanko Zaboulov St. Very high standard. Over the years the company has produced some international singers.

MUSEUMS. Entrance fees are very low, but buildings of interest are quite often closed for long periods (for restoration, or other reasons), so do check.

Alexander Nevski Memorial Church. Built in the early 20th-century in gratitude for Russian help in the struggle against the Turks. The crypt houses a stunning display of icons and other religious works. Try to hear the superb choir. Crypt open 10.30–6.30, closed Tues.

Bojana Church, about 10km. from the city center, has its superb medieval frescoes, but has long been closed for major restoration. Copies of the frescoes are displayed in a replica of the church.

Georgi Dimitrov Mausoleum, 9 Septemvri Sq. The guard is changed every hour. A museum devoted to the life of Dimitrov is at 66 Opâlčenska St. Hurry to catch these sites; political changes may soon sweep them away.

National Archeological Museum, 2 Alexander Stambolijski Blvd. Housed in a fine building, formerly a mosque. Open 10–12, 2–6, admission free.

National Art Gallery, 9 Septemvri Sq. Houses Bulgarian art from medieval times to the present, and a foreign art section, in part of the royal palace. Open 10.30–6.30, closed Tues.

National Ethnographical Museum, 6a Moskovska St. Folk art, particularly costumes, from every region; housed in another part of the former royal palace. Open 10.30–6.30, closed Tues.

National History Museum, 2 Vitoša Blvd. The best of its kind in the country. Exhibitions ranging from prehistory to 1878; finds from recent excavations include gold artifacts from up to 3600 B.C., the Pangjurište Gold Treasure from the 4th-3rd century B.C., Roman mosaics and early Bulgarian art. On no account miss this. Open Tues.–Thurs. and weekends 10.30–5.30, 2–5.30 on Fri., closed Mon.

SHOPPING. There is a network of *Corecom* shops in which goods—Bulgarian and imported—are sold at favorable prices for hard currency only. Good selection of arts and crafts at the shop of the *Union of Bulgarian Artists,* 6 Ruski Blvd., and a range of souvenirs at *Sredec,* 7 Lege St.; *Souvenir Store,* 7 Stambolijski Blvd.; *Prizma Store,* 2 Ruski Blvd. The *Central Market Hall,* 25 Georgi Dimitrov Blvd. is scheduled to be closed for renovations through 1991. The recently modernized *Central Department Store* is at 2 Georgi Dimitrov Blvd.

USEFUL ADDRESSES. *U.S. Embassy,* 1 Stambolijski Blvd. (tel. 884801/02/03); *British Embassy,* 65 Tolbuhin Blvd. (tel. 885361/878325); *Balkantourist,* 37 Dondukov Blvd. (tel. 884430), and Central Railway Station; *Orbita Youth Travel Bureau,* 45A Stambolijski St.; *American Express,* Balkantourist, 1 Vitoša Blvd.; *Wagons Lits Tourism,* 10 Lege St.; *Thomas Cook,* 1 Vitoša Blvd. (tel. 43331); *Emergency Medical Aid,* Pirogov Institute for Urgent Medical Aid, 21 Totleben Blvd; *Emergency,* motorists 146, ambulance 150, fire 160, police 166; 178 for information on all-night pharmacies.

Black Sea Beaches

The Black Sea coastline between Albena via Varna to Slânčev Brjag is a very popular resort area not only for Bulgarians but also for other Eastern bloc and, increasingly, Western visitors. Mostly they are huge, state-built tourist centers with large numbers of modern hotels overlooking wide beaches—rather clinical in atmosphere but with good amenities. Smaller picturesque towns have more charm, though accommodations are scarce in summer. Try lodgings in private houses, which are cheap and fun (bookings through Balkantourist). Nesebâr is a particularly attractive fishing village whose famous old churches draw hordes of sightseers. The fishing village of Sozopol in the south is another charming place with private accommodations. About 25 miles south of Burgas, the Primorsko International Youth Center has full amenities.

Perhaps the best place from which to explore the coast is the busy port of Varna, which is a hub of transport both by land and sea, has plenty of variety in the way of museums and entertainment and, as a large city, offers opportunities for more contact with the Bulgarian way of life than do the resorts.

PRACTICAL INFORMATION FOR THE BLACK SEA COAST

Hotels and Restaurants

There is a wide selection of accommodations in the Moderate and Inexpensive categories, including private accommodations, which offer excellent opportunities for getting to know the Bulgarians. If you have no reservations, you should go to Balkantourist, who have a branch in each center. Their main address in Varna is 1 Moussala St. (tel. 225524 or 238238).

Albena. *Dobrotica* (M), *Dorostor* (M) and *Orlov* (M) are near the beach. Restaurants include *Orehite* (M), open-air, situated in a walnut-tree grove, folk show; *Slavianski Kt* (M), specialty dishes, folk show; *Starobulgarski Stan* (M), game specialties, folk show.

Slânčev Brjag (Sunny Beach). The following are all by or near the beach: *Burgas* (M), 250 rooms, indoor and open-air pools; *Globus* (M), 100 rooms, many with a sea view, probably the best, indoor pool; *Kuban* (M), 210 rooms, in resort center; *Čaika* (I), 85 rooms; *Nesebâr* (I), 160 rooms. Folk restaurants include *Bčvata* (M), *Hanska Šatra* (M), about 5 km. up in the hills, *Picnic* (M), about 13 km. north, with fire dancing and barbecue, *Vjatrna Melnica* (M), above the resort, and *Čučura* (I). *Neptun* (I) and *Strandja* (I) are restaurants with taverns. *Ribarska Hiza* (I), by the beach, specializes in fish. *Rusalka* (I), is another beachside restaurant, plus disco.

Zlatni Pjasâci (Golden Sands). Among a wide selection are *Metropol* (M), 100 rooms, no restaurant but 10th-floor bar with good views; *Morsko Oko* (M), 90 rooms; *Diana* (I), no restaurant, wooded setting some distance from beach. A number of folk restaurants include *Košarata* (Sheepfold) on the outskirts, attractively set amidst the trees and with a lively folkloric show of good standards. Others, all (M), are *Mecha Poljana, Trifon Zarezan* and *Vodenicata.*

Museums

With its plethora of old churches, the whole of the little town of **Nesebâr,** 5 km. south of Slânčev Brjag, constitutes a museum. Otherwise most of the main museums of the coast are in **Varna,** including the fine *Archeological Museum,* 5 Šeinovo St.; *Ethnographical Museum,* 22 Panagjurište St.; *Museum of Art and History,* 41 Dimitar Blagoev Blvd., including some spectacular prehistoric artifacts; this is a "must". *Museum of Icons from the National Revival Period,* Church of St. Athanasius, 19 Graf Ignatiev St.; *Roman baths* (2nd century), Khan Krum St.; and the excellent *Aquarium* in the Maritime Park.

The Interior

The interior Balkan range of mountains gives the adventurous traveler the deepest and most satisfying picture of life in Bulgaria. They are not widely known tourist areas and rarely have the hotel and transportation services enjoyed by other areas. Patience with sluggish service will enable you to see the splendor and intact folk cultures of the Stara Planina range and the Rila and Rhodope mountains. Two main mountain resorts are Borovec in the Rila Mountains and Pamporovo in the Rhodopes, with accommodations of all categories. The Rila Monastery is the outstanding model of Bulgarian art with a fascinating history dating from its foundation by the hermit Ivan Rilski in the tenth century.

The Valley of Roses between the Stara Planina and Sredna Gora Mountains has much of historic interest and is a remarkable sight in June during the harvesting of millions of roses (for the famous attar of roses and other products). In the Sredna Gora mountains a few miles south of the head of the valley, the village of Koprivštica is a veritable living museum of traditional architecture, as well as a major historic site of revolutionary activity against the Turks. Tourist amenities are being developed here, and it will have special appeal for walkers, painters, and photographers.

Two recommended and highly contrasting centers are Plovdiv and Veliko Târnovo. Plovdiv, Bulgaria's second largest city, has a lot of industry and is the scene of major trade fairs, but it also has charming old districts with twisting cobbled streets hemmed in by 18th and 19th century houses in typical National Revival style, on the north bank of the Marica river. One of the hills is topped by the remains of walls from the old Thracian and subsequently Roman town, and another by the well-restored remains of a Roman amphitheater.

Veliko Târnovo is an amazing place. The city is stacked up against steep mountain slopes that hem the twisting course of the Jantra river. This setting is a natural fortress, to which Târnovo owes its role as the cradle of Bulgarian history. Indeed, during the 13th and 14th centuries, it was the capital of the country. It is today a museum city of marvelous church relics, works of art and fascinating panoramas.

PRACTICAL INFORMATION FOR THE INTERIOR

Hotels and Restaurants

Accommodations in both the Moderate and Inexpensive categories for Plovdiv and Veliko Târnovo are listed below. Private boarding houses are also available. Those without reservations should go to Balkantourist.

Plovdiv. *Bulgaria* (I), 78 rooms, central for old town. *Marica* (I), 170 rooms, modern, near fairgrounds; across river from city center.
Restaurants. *Alafrangues* (M), folk-style, in the old town. *Trakijski Stans* (M), also with traditional character.

Veliko Târnovo. *Yantra* (M), has stunning view across the river. *Etur* (I). 80 rooms, restaurant, and coffee shop. Folk restaurants include *Boljarska Izba* (M).

Museums

In **Plovdiv:** *Common Grave Memorial Center,* Malčika Blvd., powerful memorial to liberation from Turks; *Museum of National Revival,* 1 Starina St., housed in the beautiful National Revival style Georgiadi House; *National Archeological Museum,* 1 Suedinenije Square, includes a copy of the fabulous Panagjurište Gold Treasure from 4th century B.C.; *National Ethnographical Museum,* 2 Dr. Čomakov St., in another fine National Revival style building; *Nedkovič House;* Roman Amphitheater at south end of old town; *Roman forum,* some foundations and columns in Centralen Square. In **Veliko Târnovo:** the whole of the *Caravec* district, a fortified hill on which ruined palaces, churches, etc. are being restored; *Museum of National Revival,* 19 Rakovski St., housed in the splendid National Revival style Nikoli Han (former inn); the churches of *St. Dimitâr,* the *Forty Martyrs* and *Saints Peter* and *Paul,* all in the Asenova district of town.

USEFUL ADDRESSES. Addresses of *Balkantourist* are: **Plovdiv,** 34 Moskva Blvd. (tel. 53848). **Varna,** 1 Moussala St. (tel. 225524 or 238238). **Veliko Târnovo,** 1 Vasil Levski St. (tel. 21836). There are other branches in most centers.

Cyprus

The lovely but politically divided island of Cyprus, lying in the Eastern Mediterranean off the south coast of Turkey, has had a romantic yet troubled history. It is an island with a place in Greek legend—for Aphrodite, the Greek goddess of love and beauty, is said to have been born on the south coast of Cyprus near Paphos, where she rose naked and perfect from the sea. It is an island that knew the Romans, the Crusaders, and the Venetians, all of whom left behind architectural relics of their stay. And it is an island of religious contrasts: the Tekke of Hala Sultan, tomb of the Prophet Muhammed's foster-mother, on the shores of the great salt lake near Larnaca, is one of Islam's most important shrines; while there is said to be a piece of the True Cross in the Monastery of Stavrovouni. The Pillar of St. Paul at Paphos is where the apostle was tied and beaten for preaching Christianity.

But Roman mosaics, Venetian buildings, and Crusader castles are by no means the whole story. The island has a 400-mile coastline, with numerous glorious beaches that remain deserted for much of the summer; in the gentle countryside, spring produces an array of wild flowers that dazzle the eyes; autumn is simply an extension of summer. In winter the spectacular Troödos Mountains are ideal for skiing, a sport whose growth has given rise to the claim that in Cyprus you can ski in the morning and improve your suntan on the beach in the afternoon.

At the moment of writing, the island consists, politically, of two states. The southern two-thirds, inhabited mainly by Greek Cypriots, form the "Republic of Cyprus," the only part of the island to receive international recognition. The population of the northern third is now almost entirely Turkish Cypriot, plus a few families brought over from the Turkish mainland—and the often conspicuous Turkish military presence; this part of the island is recognized only by Turkey, under the name of the "Turkish Republic of Northern Cyprus." The two parts of the island are divided by the UN Green Line or "Attila Line." Nicosia, the capital, is itself similarly divided; each part of the city is of interest; the Greek half has the splendid museum and the Turkish half many picturesque ancient monuments.

Talks aimed at uniting the two communities in one bi-zonal federal state have been going on for years, lately under the auspices of the United Nations Secretary-General. Visitors should choose which part of Cyprus to visit and not expect to combine the two.

Most of the island is extremely beautiful; the weather is ideal and living is cheap; in addition, almost everyone the tourist is likely to come in contact with speaks English. In the following pages we shall try and give an objective picture of the amenities of both Greek and Turkish Cyprus.

PRACTICAL INFORMATION FOR CYPRUS

WHAT WILL IT COST. Life in both parts of Cyprus is inexpensive, whether you choose a hotel, a villa or a camping site. In the Republic of Cyprus the unit of currency is the Cyprus pound (C£), which is divided into 100 cents; rate of exchange at Easter 1990 was C£0.49 to the U.S. dollar and C£0.77 to the pound sterling. In North Cyprus a currency based on the Turkish Lira (TL) is used; this is subject to considerable inflation, but at the time of going to press was at the rate of about 1,900 TL to the dollar and 3,300 to the pound sterling. In order to simplify matters, we have quoted all rates in U.S. dollars unless stated otherwise. Prices tend to be slightly lower in North Cyprus than in the Republic of Cyprus, but standards are often lower, too.

Sample Costs. A moderate seat in a cinema—mostly outdoors in the warm weather—costs about $1.50. A cup of coffee or tea 30 cents; bottle of beer in a café 60 cents and up; bottle of local wine from $1–1.50. You should note that in North Cyprus drinks are imported from Turkey and may be slightly more expensive.

NATIONAL TOURIST OFFICES. The chief office of the Republic of Cyprus (Greek) tourist organization is at 18 Theodotou St., Nicosia; that of the North Cyprus (Turkish) tourist organization is in Mehmet Akif Ave., Nicosia. There are branches at all major resorts.

WHEN TO COME. Cyprus is an enjoyable vacation spot at almost any time of the year, though it is very hot in July and August. Along the coast the summer heat is often tempered by sea breezes. Although the tourist season is all the year round, prices are generally considerably lower from November through March.

Average afternoon temperature in degrees Fahrenheit and centigrade:

Nicosia	Jan.	Feb.	Mar.	Apr.	May	June	July	Aug.	Sept.	Oct.	Nov.	Dec.
F°	58	59	65	74	83	91	97	97	91	81	72	62
C°	14	15	18	23	28	33	36	36	33	27	22	17

National Holidays. These vary in the two zones; see separate sections.

VISAS. No visas are required by nationals of the USA, the U.K. and EC countries.

HEALTH CERTIFICATES. No certificates necessary to visit any part of Cyprus.

GETTING TO CYPRUS. See separate sections for Republic of Cyprus and North Cyprus.

CUSTOMS. Customs regulations are minimal, but the export of antiques and historical artifacts, whether gathered on land or during undersea explorations, is strictly forbidden unless a license is obtained from the Ministry of Tourism in Nicosia.

RESTAURANTS. The cost of a good meal at a Moderate (M) restaurant—you'll get three courses: *mezedes* (a variety of snacks), main dish and fruit—is usually up to $10 per person, excluding wine or beer. For around $15 or a little over, you should get a very good meal, including a bottle of wine. At Inexpensive (I) restaurants, such as a small *taverna* (in the Republic of Cyprus) or a *kebapçi* (in North Cyprus), you can often get a simple but tasty meal (a meat dish followed by fruit) for little more than $5 per person. Travelers in North Cyprus should look out for army-run *Mucahitler* restaurants—excellent value and open to the public. There's the *Otello* in Famagusta (opposite the Othello Tower), one at Gulsener outside Famagusta on the Salamis road, the *Istanbul* three miles outside Boğaz on the Boğaz road, and the *Alsancak* near Kyrenia down the turning after the road to Monte Mare.

Food and Drink. There is not a great deal of difference between Greek and Turkish cooking, though the Turks don't eat pork and are more sparing in their use of oil. The *tavernas*—their rough Turkish equivalent is a *kebabçi*—are often to be preferred to hotel-restaurants or other places designed to cater to the visitor; they are both less expensive and more fun. Hotel restaurants tend to serve their idea of "international" cooking, including French fries with practically everything. In the Greek and Turkish places you will get genuine Cypriot food—though it must be admitted that French fries are often served even in these—the result, no doubt, of the long British connection.

Meals usually start with a variety of *mezedes* (appetizers or *hors d'oeuvres),* which may include *kalamarakia* (fried baby squid), *melitsanasalata* (an eggplant-and-garlic dip), and *dolmades* vine or cabbage leaves stuffed with meat and rice), all of which are extremely popular. Other common dishes are *kebabs* (pieces of meat skewered and grilled over a charcoal fire) and different kinds of stew, consisting usually of meat, onions and various aromatic herbs and served with rice or *boulghouri* (boiled crushed wheat). One such stew is *tava,* which can be delicious. In some places, notably Paphos and Kyrenia, there are many kinds of superb fresh fish, including such delicacies as red mullet and swordfish. Fresh fruit, which normally ends the meal, is excellent and very cheap. Finally, one drinks a cup of Turkish coffee,—called Greek, or *elleniko,* coffee in the Republic of Cyprus—which is served sweet, semi-sweet or without sugar. You can also get delicious, but *very* sweet, pastries, such as *baklava.*

If there is no menu, the system is for the customer to go into the kitchen and make his choice there, or for the waiter to say what is available. The first of these two courses is to be recommended.

The Republic of Cyprus produces a wide range of good wines and also excellent spirits, including brandy and ouzo. *Mezedes* are usually served with a drink.

TIPPING. A service-charge is usually added to all bills, (in restaurants in the Republic of Cyprus there is a service charge of 10% and a tax of 3%) but a tip is unlikely to be refused.

ENTERTAINMENT. Cinemas are numerous. In the warm weather, performances are held after sunset in the open. Sitting at a village café (or "coffee-shop," as it is usually known) is perhaps the best entertainment of all. In a few minutes you may well have got to know lots of interesting—and often inquisitive—people; you must not be surprised by the intimacy of some of their questions.

There are many nightclubs, above all in Limassol, where the choice is enormous; they charge from $4 and up a drink. Discos abound, too; they are slightly less expensive. All tend to keep very late hours.

SPORTS. Cyprus offers superb bathing (including water-skiing, windsurfing and skin-diving), especially from mid-May through October. Among the most popular beaches are those around Larnaca, Limassol, Paphos and Ayia Napa in the Republic of Cyprus and around Kyrenia and north of Famagusta in North Cyprus. There are sailing-clubs in the larger resorts and you can ski on Mount Troödos from January to March. Horse-riding and tennis are available at all the main resorts.

SHOPPING. Handmade lace and embroidery, ceramics, copperware, filigree silver and leather goods, are particularly worth buying. Also, optical goods, including sunglasses, are a good buy. Wines and spirits are a major industry in Cyprus and are available at incredibly low prices. The usual shopping hours are 7.30 A.M. to around 1 P.M.; the afternoon hours vary according to the season. Many shops close on Wednesday and Saturday afternoons, although in the tourist centers, souvenir shops and supermarkets generally remain open until late at night and all day on Sunday.

The metric system of weight officially replaced the imperial system in 1987, although in some out-of-the-way places, you may still find the *oke* (= 2.8 lbs.) in use.

The Republic of Cyprus

Nicosia, the capital, is famous for its massive Venetian walls and for its splendid Museum, which pictures the history of Cyprus from the Neolithic Age. The town is divided into two by the so-called "Green Line" and many of the more interesting ancient monuments are in the northern, Turkish, sector. However, Nicosia is worth a day's exploration. Particularly interesting is the restored and expanding area, Laiki Yeitonia. Its traffic-free, traditional streets offer tree-shaded, open-air cafés and restaurants, craft and antique shops, and galleries. It is, at the time of writing, possible to take a day trip from the Greek to the Turkish sector, via the official checkpoint, returning by curfew. Visitors based in the Turkish sector cannot cross to the Greek sector.

Many visitors, however, will be content to confine themselves to the seaside resorts. Both Larnaca and Paphos, at one of which your plane will land, make excellent centers. Larnaca has fine beaches close at hand; Limassol adds to its seaside attractions a lively night life; Paphos, in the west of the island, is quietly beautiful and has much of historic interest, as well as superb seabathing. A new resort has grown up around Ayia Napa, east of Larnaca.

The Troödos Mts., north of Limassol, are sought in the summer for their shady coolness and in winter for their skiing. There are several comfortable hotels in the Hill Resorts, providing bases for skiers going to 6,406—foot-high Mount Olympus, with its four ski lifts. In summer the wooded slopes and bubbling streams are a welcome change from the heat of the beaches.

PRACTICAL INFORMATION FOR THE REPUBLIC OF CYPRUS

NATIONAL TOURIST OFFICE: Addresses of overseas offices of the Cyprus Tourist Office are:
In the U.S.: 13 East 40th St., New York, N.Y. 10016 (tel. 212–213–9100).
In the U.K.: 213 Regent St., London W1R 8DA (tel. 071–734 9822).

GETTING TO THE REPUBLIC. There are no direct flights from North America to Cyprus. You can fly by *Cyprus Airways* or *British Airways,* direct from London, Birmingham and Manchester to the airports at Larnaca and Paphos. *Alitalia* has a flight from Rome in summer, and *Cyprus Airways* operates from Frankfurt and Munich. Or you can travel by sea from Italian and Greek ports. An inclusive tour is the cheapest way to get to Cyprus.

GETTING AROUND THE REPUBLIC. By Bus. Buses are the cheapest form of transport, with intercity fares ranging from $1.15 to $3. Perhaps the most convenient way to travel is to book a seat in a fixed-departure "shared taxi," or "service taxi," which costs about double the bus fare. From Larnaca to Nicosia (32 miles) by such a cab is about $2.30, from Larnaca to Paphos (69 miles) about $4.00.

By Car. British and international driving licenses are acceptable. Roads are generally good, though often narrow and twisting. *You drive on the left.* Petrol (gasoline) costs around $2.40 a gallon.

Car hire prices start at about $30 a day with unlimited mileage. Rental firms have offices in all towns, as well as at Larnaca International Airport, all with English-speaking personnel.

NATIONAL HOLIDAYS. Jan. 1; Jan. 6 (Epiphany); Feb. 22; Mar. 25 (Independence); Apr. 5–8 (Greek Easter); May 27 (Pentecost Monday); Aug. 15 (Assumption); Oct. 28 (Oxi); Dec. 25, 26 (Christmas).

HOTELS. Hotels are marked (M) for Moderate and (I) for Inexpensive. (M) hotels in the Republic of Cyprus are in general very well run and provide every comfort, including in most cases full airconditioning.

A double room with bath and breakfast in an (M) hotel will cost about $45–$65. Many (I) hotels will not have full airconditioning, but will have private baths or showers; a double room with breakfast will cost between $35 and $45. There are also a number of so-called "guest-houses," where a double with breakfast—but without bath—will cost as little as $10 or so, but such accommodation will, of course, be very simple.

Ayia Napa. *Nissi Park* (M), tel. 037–21121. 80 rooms. Close to its big brother, the more expensive *Nissi Beach,* and near sandy Nissi Bay; bed and breakfast only. Pool. *Adam's Beach* (I), tel. 037–21275. 57 rooms, overlooking beach. Pool, tennis.

Restaurants. There is a choice of tavernas serving fresh fish around the harbor.

Larnaca. *Four Lanterns* (M), tel. 041–52011. 56 rooms, Traditional, friendly atmosphere. Also good restaurant and dancing. *Lordos Beach* (M), tel. 041–57444. 175 rooms. By the sea just outside town. Pool, tennis, dancing. *Cactus Hotel* (I), tel. 051–27400. 56 rooms. New, with pool and restaurant. 20 minutes from sea front and tavernas.
Restaurants. Several, including *Kellari* (I), tel. 041–5166.

Limassol. *Curium Palace* (M), tel. 051–63121. 63 rooms. Not on sea, but closest to the center of town and with excellent pool; also tennis. *Pavemar* (I), tel. 051–24535. 65 rooms. Recently refurbished hotel on sea front. Pool. *King Richard* (I), tel. 051–21330. 50 rooms. At the ancient site of Amathus, 5 miles east of Limassol, on beach. Pool.
Restaurants. Many tavernas (M-I).

Nicosia. *Churchill* (M), tel. 02–448858. 52 rooms. Central and good value; dancing. *Kennedy* (M), tel. 02–475131. 97 rooms. Very central. *Philoxenia* (M), tel. 02–499700. 35 rooms. Small but good; central. Pool, tennis.
Restaurants. *The Corner* (M), tel. 02–465735, *Plaka* (I), tel. 02–446498.

Paphos. *Aloe* (M), (tel. 061–34000); 113 airconditioned rooms, all with bath; close to sea. Pool, tennis, sea-sports facilities. *Cynthiana Beach* (M), tel. 061–33900. 200 rooms. Quiet location, with good swimming from improved beach area. Pool, tennis; further facilities planned for 1991. *Apollo* (I), (tel. 061–33909); 32 rooms, all with bath; airconditioning an optional extra. Recommended. *Pelican Inn* (tel. 061–32827); guest house near sea.
Restaurants. *Britannia* (M), tel. 061–36032, *Nautical Club* (M), tel. 061–33745. Many Moderate and Inexpensive fish restaurants.

PARALIMNI-PROTARAS. 9 miles from Ayia Napa, on Fig Tree Bay, the tiny village of Protaras is now a thriving resort area. *Vrissiana Beach* (M), tel. 031–31216. 138 rooms, all either overlooking the bay or the mountains. Constructed in the shape of a cruise liner and set among mimosa trees; recently renovated. Pool, tennis. *Pernera Beach* (I), tel. 031–31011. 92 rooms. Long-established hotel overlooking beach. Pool, tennis.

PISSOURI. *Columbia Pissouri Beach* (M), tel. 052–21201. 129 rooms. 25 km west of Limassol toward Paphos; splendidly isolated on lovely beach. Car essential. Pool, tennis, disco. *Bunch of Grapes Inn* (I) tel. 052–21275. 11 rooms with bath or shower. Comfortable small hotel in attractive village. 10 min. by car from Pissouri beach.

TROÖDOS HILL RESORTS. Pedhoulas. *Churchill Pinewood Valley* (M), tel. 0295–2211. 33 rooms. Comfortable hotel in charming hill village. Pool, tennis. *Jack's* (I), tel. 0296–2350. 10 rooms. Small and good value. **Platres.** The largest of the hill resorts. *Forest Park* (M), tel. 054–21751. 91 rooms. 1930s hotel, once the haunt of King Farouk of Egypt; idyllic site. Pool, tennis, dancing. *Pendeli* (I), tel. 054–21736. 35 rooms.

USEFUL ADDRESSES. *British High Commission:* Alexander Pallis St., Nicosia, tel. 02–473131. *U.S. Embassy:* Dossitheos St. and Therissos St., Nicosia, tel. 02–465151. *Thomas Cook:* 17 Evagoras Ave., Nicosia, tel. 21–443132.

MAIL Airmail postal rates (subject to change) to the U.S.: 10g. letter 26 Cyprus cents, postcard 18 Cyprus cents. To the U.K.: 19 and 16 Cyprus cents respectively.

North Cyprus

The Turkish half of Nicosia is the capital of North Cyprus; in addition to the vast Venetian walls already mentioned, it contains the Selimiye Mosque, formerly the church of St. Sophia and a fine example of Gothic architecture. There are several other interesting ancient monuments, including the former "Tekke" of the Whirling Dervishes, now a museum.

Of the coastal resorts, Kyrenia, situated around its picturesque semi-circular yacht-filled harbor, is the chief attraction. There are excellent bathing-beaches to the east and west of the town, which, if it is perhaps no longer the sparkling international "jewel" of former years, is acquiring a new lustre, with many English and other foreign residents. The ruins of the former abbey of Bellapais, a few miles out, should on no account be missed. Famagusta, North Cyprus's chief port, has fine Venetian walls and a splendid Gothic cathedral, now a mosque. Many of its hotels lie empty and desolate in a sort of "no-man's-land" between Greek and Turk, but several good hotels, most of them standing on superb beaches, are once again open. The medieval castles of St. Hilarion and Kantara, on the mountains lying behind Kyrenia, are interesting.

It is important to note that Turkish names—some of them the original ones—have been given to all towns and villages in North Cyprus; thus Nicosia is now officially *Lefkoşa*, Kyrenia has become *Girne* and Famagusta *Magosa*. These new names are those appearing on signposts—sometimes with the earlier version alongside. A useful map showing the new names is available free from travel offices.

PRACTICAL INFORMATION FOR NORTH CYPRUS

NATIONAL TOURIST OFFICE. Addresses of the tourist office of the Turkish Republic of North Cyprus overseas are:

In the U.S.: 821 U.N. Plaza, New York, N.Y. 10017 (tel. 212–687–2350).

In the U.K.: Office above Cyprus Turkish Airlines, 28 Cockspur St., London SW1 5BN (tel. 071–839 5530).

GETTING TO NORTH CYPRUS. By Air. By *Turkish Airlines, Cyprus Turkish Airlines,* and *Noble Air,* usually with a change of plane at Istanbul; but there are direct flights from Izmir. Aircraft land at Ercan airport, near Nicosia.

By Sea. There are ferries from Mersin and Taşucu in Turkey to Famagusta and Kyrenia respectively, but in both cases the journey is long and tiring.

GETTING AROUND NORTH CYPRUS. By Bus. Buses and shared taxis (known as *dolmus*) are the cheapest forms of transport. A bus from Nicosia to Kyrenia would cost around 40 cents and to Famagusta about 70 cents. A seat in a *dolmus* for the same journeys would cost about 90 cents and $1.70 respectively. Services are frequent on all main routes.

By Car. British and international driving licenses are acceptable. Petrol (gasoline) costs around $2.50 a gallon, subject to increase. *Drive on the left.*

Car hire prices range from $20 a day up; cheaper in the winter or for long periods.

NATIONAL HOLIDAYS. Jan. 1, Apr. 23, May 1, May 19, Aug. 30, Oct. 29, Nov. 15 and various Moslem religious holidays, which vary from year to year.

HOTELS. Hotels are marked (M) for Moderate and (I) for Inexpensive. Establishments in North Cyprus are generally comfortable enough, but poor management in some cases takes away from the warmth of the welcome. In all (M) hotels you will find airconditioning, full or partial, and all rooms will have a bath. In (I) hotels airconditioning is rare, but private baths are the rule. Prices tend to be lower than in the Republic of Cyprus and standards can reflect this. For a double room in an (M) hotel, with bath and breakfast, you will pay about $40; for a similar room in an (I) hotel, expect to pay around $35. There are no "guest-houses," but simple accommodation can be found in 1-star hotels, where you will pay around $15–$20 for a double room with breakfast but without bath.

Bogaz. *Bogaz* (M), (tel. 037–12459); on a fine sandy beach 16 miles north of Famagusta. 40 rooms, all with bath. The food is praised.

Famagusta. *Rebecca* (M), (tel. 036–65800); 6 miles north of town, 5 mins. from the beach and with swimming pool. 42 airconditioned rooms, all with bath. *Mimoza*

Beach (I), (tel. 036–65460), on the beach a few miles north of the town; 52 rooms, all with bath.

Restaurants. *Kemal's Fish Restaurant* (M); *Patek Pastanesi,* opposite sea gate, good patisserie for Turkish coffee and cake.

Kyrenia. *Dome* (M), (tel. 081–52453). On seafront in town. Pool, casino, popular disco. Restaurant has Turkish and international food. *Dorana* (M), (tel. 081–53521). 33 rooms, all with bath and airconditioning. 300 yards from sea. Recommended. *Rocks* (M), (tel. 081–52238); on sea front and with small, rocky beach and swimming pool. 50 rooms, all with bath. Public rooms are airconditioned, as is the rather noisy disco. *Ergenekon* (I), (tel. 081–52240), overlooking the harbor. 16 rooms, all airconditioned and all with bath.

Club Acapulco Village (tel. 081–53510), 6 miles to the east, has well-appointed bungalows on beach, restaurant, beach bar, and tennis court.

Restaurants. Many round harbor: *Harbor Bar* with quality French cooking. In town, *Kyrenia Tavern,* and in Çatakoy village 5 miles along Nicosia road, *Zia's* fish restaurant.

Nicosia. *Saray* (M), (tel. 020–71115); comfortable hotel in busy Atatürk Square; 72 rooms, some airconditioned and all with bath. Splendid view over town from 9th-floor restaurant, and a new casino. *Sabris Orient* (I), (tel. 020–72161); hotel on outskirts of town; restaurant. *Picnic* (I), (tel. 020–72122); small and comfortable hotel in suburbs; restaurant, casino, and popular disco.

USEFUL ADDRESSES. The British High Commissioner has an office in the Turkish section of Nicosia. The main tourist information office is at Mehmet Akif Ave., Nicosia. There are local offices at major resorts. *Emergencies:* Ambulance, fire brigade and police, tel. 199.

Czechoslovakia

One of the nearest and most accessible countries of the former Eastern bloc, Czechoslovakia provides a vivid contrast for the jaded Westerner. The independent traveler will find many contradictions, contrasts and complexities but, with a spirit of adventure, can meet with a fascinating experience. Czechoslovak tourism is best geared to prepaid services, which are available for independent travelers as well as groups; without these, you may run into varying degrees of bureaucratic frustration but, if you are prepared to take your chances, you may well end up with a unique experience of this extremely rich and varied country.

There are fine opportunities for all kinds of outdoor activities from climbing and hiking to canoeing and gliding, but as yet there is no machinery for the individual traveler to pre-arrange this kind of special interest holiday. Nevertheless, if you are a determined individual and can make contact with a local sports club, you're almost certain of a warm welcome. Walkers are well served by an excellent system of marked trails through most scenic areas. Art and music lovers will also find rich rewards. Entrance fees are low and tickets reasonable, especially if you are prepared to tackle the box office yourself; but you will need to check what's on and where on the spot. It is wise, too, to make sure that places of particular interest to you are open, for a major program of restoration can lead to unexpected closures for long periods.

Historically part of a loose alignment of Central European kingdoms, modern Czechoslovakia is a political union of three contrasting provinces. The Czechs, who are clever and rather serious, predominate in the western province of Bohemia, where wealthy burghers' houses still fill the narrow streets of old spa towns full of beguiling Central European charm. In contrast, the easygoing Slavs of Slovakia suggest the flavor of Eastern Europe in a natural setting of virgin forest, hidden lakes and craggy peaks of the Tatra mountain range, which gradually drops down to the Danubian plains. Moravia's gently undulating land, Renaissance towns and painted wooden villages link the two together.

Czechoslovakia is at the heart of Europe, an often unenviable position throughout its history. In 1968, Dubček's ill-fated attempt to combine Communist ideology with democratic rights brought Soviet tanks rumbling into the streets of Prague. Since the peaceful collapse of the Communist regime in November 1989 and the election of a new government under playwright-president Vaclav Havel, the country has regained a sense of vitality and hope that has long been missing.

PRACTICAL INFORMATION FOR
CZECHOSLOVAKIA

WHAT WILL IT COST. *Čedok,* the Czechoslovak Travel Bureau, are responsible for all practical matters connected with your visit. They (and the many travel agents accredited to them) also operate a varied range of package tours that provide the most hassle-free way of traveling, although not necessarily the cheapest. Some of the tours are quite flexible, covering a return flight from the U.K. and a currency voucher with which you can purchase whatever services you want. Traveling in Czechoslovakia is made easier with such prepaid services. If you prefer to go it alone, this can also have its rewards, but the bureaucratic machine may at times test your patience! The country's political changes should soon improve the situation for tourists.

U.S. and Canadian citizens are no longer required to exchange a minimum amount of currency each day. Those travelers who need a visa to enter the country (see *Visas,* below) must exchange the equivalent of 30 German Marks per day unless they have prepaid hotel arrangements. Any sum beyond this amount can be converted at the higher tourist exchange rate. The monetary unit is the crown or *koruna* (Kčs.) which is divided into 100 heller or *haler.* There are coins of 10, 20 and 50 haler and 1, 2, and 5 Kčs.; banknotes are of 10, 20, 50, 100, 500 and 1,000 Kčs. Czechoslovakia will probably have introduced internal convertibility of the koruna by 1991. This will mean that a single rate of exchange will be in effect; it will probably be around 24 Kčs. to the U.S. dollar and 41 Kčs. to the British pound.

At press time, the rate for obligatory exchange is 27.2 Kčs. to the pound sterling, 16.2 Kčs. to the U.S. dollar. The normal tourist exchange rate (applicable in all other cases) was 24.8 Kčs. to the U.S. dollar and 41.8 Kčs. to the pound at press time. Note that crowns acquired at this higher tourist rate cannot be reconverted when you leave, so do not exchange more money than you think you'll need. You can bring in any amount of foreign currency, but must declare it. The import and export of Czechoslovak currency is not permitted. All exchanges should be noted on your visa, as only surplus crowns from obligatory exchanges will be converted back to Western currency when you leave. Black market dealings not only carry heavy penalties but are also hardly profitable under the new system—so avoid tempting offers.

Sample costs. Cinema seat from 10 Kčs. (special shows up to 30 Kčs.); theater seat (Moderate) 40–60 Kčs.; museum entrance 2–5 Kčs.; coffee in snack bar 6 Kčs.; beer (half-liter in tavern) 6–10 Kčs., less for mild; carafe or bottle of wine in tavern from 40 Kčs., in Moderate restaurant from 60 Kčs.

NATIONAL TOURIST OFFICE. *Čedok* handle all the practical aspects of travel in Czechoslovakia. Their offices in Prague include: for information, exchange and travel tickets—Na příkopě 18, Prague 1; for accommodations—Panská 5 (just round the corner), Prague 1; for sightseeing, tours, theater tickets—Bílkova 6 (opposite Intercontinental Hotel), Prague 1. They arrange excursions and longer trips of many kinds but are not particularly budget-oriented. They can, however, book accommodations in all categories. See also "Hotels" below.

The *Czechoslovak Youth and Students Travel Bureau* (CKM), Žitná 12, Prague 2, caters to all kinds of youth travel.

As well as the many offices they have within Czechoslovakia, Čedok has a number of offices overseas. Their addresses are:

In the U.S.: 321 E. 75th St., New York, N.Y.10021 (tel. 212–988–8080).
In the U.K: 17–18 Old Bond St., London W1X 4RB (tel. 071–629 6058).

WHEN TO COME. The cultural sights can be enjoyed at any time, but note that some monuments, especially castles, are closed in winter. Spring and summer are generally best for sightseeing. May is particularly attractive—for fruit blossom and for the Prague Spring Music Festival. The forests are glorious in the fall. The winter sports season is mid-December until March.

Average afternoon temperatures in degrees Fahrenheit and centigrade:

Prague	Jan.	Feb.	Mar.	Apr.	May	June	July	Aug.	Sept.	Oct.	Nov.	Dec.
F°	34	38	45	55	65	72	74	73	65	54	41	34
C°	1	3	7	13	18	22	23	23	18	12	5	1

SPECIAL EVENTS. *May* Prague Spring Music Festival (tickets can be expensive); Dvořák Music Festival, Příbam; Summer Theater in Castle grounds, Karlštejn and Konopiště (through August); *June* Bratislava International Song Festival; Strážnice Folk Art Festival; Vychodná Folk Art Festival; Every five years (next in 1995), the Spartakiada is held; it is one of the world's greatest gymnastic events. *July* Brno Grand Prix Motor Rally; Karlovy Vary International Film Festival (biennial); *July–August* Bratislava Music Summer; *August* Chod Festival (folklore), Domažlice; *September* Dvořák Festival, Karlovy Vary; Znojmo Wine Festival; *September–October* Brno Music Festival, Bratislava International Music Festival.

National Holidays. Jan. 1 (New Year's Day); April 1 (Easter Mon.); May 9 (Liberation); June 5 (not Slovakia); July 5; October 28 (Independence), Dec. 24, 25, 26.

VISAS. Visa requirements are gradually being dismantled. U.S. and Canadian citizens no longer need visas for visits of under 30 days. At press time, British citizens still needed visas; call the consulate to find out if this has changed. In the U.K., Čedok will process you visa for £14 if you've booked an inclusive Čedok tour and for £23 if you haven't. The Czechoslovak consulate in London, 28 Kensington Palace Gardens, London W8 4QY (tel. 071–727–3966) charges £20. Apart from a passport valid for five months, you will need two passport-size photos; allow several weeks if applying by mail.

If you stay with relatives or friends, you must register with the local police authorities within 48 hours of your arrival. In Prague, the police station for foreigners is at Olšanská 1, Prague 3; open weekdays 8–4. This is also the place to go extend your visa.

The obligatory minimum daily expenditure in hard currency (see "What Will It Cost," above) will apply for the number of days for which the visa is valid. If you don't need a visa, you don't have to exchange money.

HEALTH CERTIFICATES. No vaccinations are required to enter Czechoslovakia from any country.

GETTING TO CZECHOSLOVAKIA. By Plane. There are regular (usually one or two per week) services by *ČSA* (Czechoslovakian Airlines) from New York and Montreal to Prague; and by *Pan Am* from New York to Prague via Frankfurt. From London and other west European capitals—including Paris and Brussels—there are also services (usually daily or five or six times weekly) to Prague. There are also flights from Vienna, Berlin (East), Copenhagen and all the Comecon capitals, plus Belgrade.

By Train. The best route is via the *Paris-Prague* through service known in Czechoslovakia as the *Zapadni Express.* This leaves Paris (Gare de L'Est) at 11 P.M. and arrives in Prague at about 5.50 P.M. the following day having traveled via Mainz, Frankfurt and Nurnberg. It carries 1st- and 2nd-class day carriages and 2nd-class couchettes. Buffet car from Frankfurt to Prague. There are also three trains a day from Vienna that go on to East Berlin. From Nurnberg there are also two other through services to Prague daily. There is also a direct route from Warsaw via Wroclaw. The best connection to Bratislava is from Vienna by bus.

CUSTOMS. Travelers may import 250 cigarettes or the equivalent in tobacco, 2 liters (3.4 pints) of wine and 1 liter (1.7 pints) of spirits. Jewelry and valuable objects should be entered on your customs declaration. Note that if you buy certain items (including cut glass, porcelain, and sporting goods) in local currency, they require an export license and may be subject to 100% duty when you leave.

HOTELS. Accommodations are now officially classified by the international one-to five-star system and, though standards may not always conform to equivalent categories in some Western countries, on the whole prices are also lower. Remember that most hotels have rooms in more than one category. Čedok run the largest group, known as Interhotels, in which approximate prices for two people in a double room without bath/shower but with half board are: 3-star, the equivalent of our Moderate (M), $25–$60; 2- or 1-star, the equivalent of our Inexpensive (I), $15–$40. Prices at the higher end of the scale apply to main cities and resorts in the high season; lowest prices apply in other centers or in the low season.

Accommodations in hotels operated by other groups and following a similar system of classification can be booked through Čedok and, as there is a shortage of accommodations in Czechoslovakia, it is wise to make advance reservations. Those without prebookings in Prague should go to Čedok, Panská 5, or Pragotur (for non-Čedok and often lower-priced hotels), U Obecního domu 2, both in the city center and both offering private accommodations. All hotels of 3 stars and above require payment in hard currency. Cheaper hotels may allow you to pay in crowns, but check first.

Youth Hostels. These do not exist in the western sense but, in summer, accommodation in various premises throughout the country is made available to youth organizations and a percentage of this is at the disposal of holders of International Youth Hostels Federation cards. It's best to check the latest situation with CKM, who run their own hotels, youth centers and camps, offering limited accommodations for independent travelers. Beds may also be available in student colleges in main cities in summer only (precise dates vary, so check); ask for *kolej* in Czech and *internat* in Slovak. Student organizations run an advisory office in summer at the main train station for young people looking for cheap accommodations.

Camping. A map marking and listing sites throughout the country is obtainable from Čedok. Some sites have small inexpensive cabins for hire. Note that CKM run their own camps.

RESTAURANTS. On group tours, *table d'hôte* meals are included in the price on a full or half board basis. In the case of Čedok's regular weekend and one-week breaks to Prague, and in all cases of independent hotel arrangements, meal coupons are provided. These can be used in all Čedok hotels and restaurants in the city or region where you are staying, but the value of unused coupons cannot be refunded. Otherwise, estimate the cost of restaurant meals, excluding drinks, to be: Moderate (M) 50–100 Kčs., and Inexpensive (I) 30–50 Kčs. (up to 50% less outside Prague). These rates apply to a wide selection of attractive restaurants, beer taverns and wine cellars; you will fare even better in self-service snack bars and workaday restaurants all over the country that may not look romantic but serve inexpensive, wholesome food.

Food and Drink. A square meal starts off with an assortment of cold meats—famous Prague ham, smoked tongue, Russian crab meat in mayonnaise—but good soups are much cheaper. Don't be taken in by tempting trays of hors d'oeuvres—you pay for each one. Meat is usually well-cooked, drowned in delicious thick gravy and often accompanied by large dough *knedliky*, the Czechoslovaks' beloved dumplings, and *zeli*, or spiced red cabbage. Desserts are rich. What is sadly lacking, however, is a variety of fresh vegetables and salads.

The beer is good—draft is the cheapest, but the many excellent bottled beers *(Urquell, Budvar)* are reasonably priced in popular taverns and restaurants. *Slivovice,* a strong plum brandy, *borovicka,* a pungent gin, and *becherovka,* an herb brandy, are the local spirits—imported ones cost the earth. There are plenty of pleasant wines, especially from Mělník, Moravia and the Bratislava region. Coffee is usually in so-called Turkish (unfiltered) style, served black.

TIPPING. In a popular restaurant, it is usual to round up a bill by a few Kčs. If in doubt, 10% is generous. Hotels and restaurants include a service charge of 10% in better places, 5% in others.

MAIL. An airmail letter costs 7 Kčs., a postcard 5 Kčs., to the U.S.; 4 Kčs. for letters to European countries, 3 Kčs. for postcards. But check before mailing.

CLOSING TIMES. Generally, opening hours are from 9 to 6 Monday through Friday (food shops 6 to 6), with stores often closing for lunch and early on Saturdays. Main stores open Thursdays to 8 P.M. Banks open 8 to 2 Monday through Friday.

GETTING AROUND CZECHOSLOVAKIA. Regular ČSA flights connect Prague with the rest of the country, but trains and buses are the best ways of getting about and services are very well integrated. For students, the Eastern Bloc IUS student ID card can officially help with discounts, but it is best to get your tickets via CKM rather than at the railway station where they may simply ignore your discount card. Otherwise there are no special tourist tickets, but costs are reasonable. Seat reservation is not absolutely necessary but advisable on long-distance journeys. Travel by train is usually slower and cheaper than by bus. Reservations for both are advised. Hitchhiking is accepted and lifts are not hard to come by; sporting your national flag and a certain respectability of dress can help.

If you're traveling by car, you must buy gasoline coupons in hard currency either at the border or, in advance, at the Zivnostenska Bank, 104–106 Leadenhall St., London EC3A 4AA. You need only your National Driving License and Green Card insurance. Traffic drives on the right, seat belts are compulsory and drinking and driving absolutely prohibited. Speed limits are 60 k.p.h. (37 m.p.h.) in built-up areas, 90 k.p.h. (50 m.p.h.) on the open road, 110 k.p.h. (68 m.p.h.) on motorways. On-the-spot fines are imposed for offenses and, if they are not paid, your license is liable to confiscation. You are advised to bring a spare parts kit. For 24-hour car repairs in Prague call 774455; for emergency road-service facilities call 154.

Prague

The best way to get acquainted with Prague is to start with a bird's eye view of it from the corner of Hradčanské náměstí (Castle Square). Hradčany (the Castle area) itself, once the seat of Bohemian kings and now the official residence of the President of the Republic, is over a thousand years old. It includes every style of architecture that Prague has known, from early Romanesque (St. George's Church) to Gothic and Baroque.

From the parapet overlooking the city you will see a magnificent panorama before you. A high point is the cupola of the Baroque St. Nicholas Church. All around it, between the Castle and the Vltava river, lies Malá Strana (Lesser Town) with the palaces and gardens built in the 17th and 18th centuries by the aristocracy, and the smaller but still beautiful houses constructed by burghers and artisans. To the right of the Lesser Town are a series of interlinked parks with promenades and the ruins of a medieval wall. Below you is the 14th-century Charles Bridge (pedestrians only) with its two watchtowers and Baroque statues. Across the river are Staré Město (Old Town), Nové Město (New Town, founded in the 14th century!) and much of modern Prague. The hub of the New Town is the famous Václavské náměstí (Wenceslas Square) which has restricted access for cars. To the right of the Old Town, just across the May 1st Bridge is the newly renovated National Theater; further down the embankment are the remains of Vyšehrad Castle perched on a rock, and in roughly the same area the ultramodern Palace of Culture.

Public transport in Prague is cheap and, once you get the hang of it, easy to use; but the Castle area, Lesser Town and Old Town are well worth some footwork and this is the only way to make your own discoveries amongst a host of charming details. Much restoration has been done, more is in progress, so be prepared for a good deal of scaffolding, and do check that sights of particular interest to you are open at the time of your visit.

From Prague, it is easy to visit the four corners of Bohemia: west for the famous spas (such as Karlovy Vary, Mariánské Lázně); south to where the Hussite movement was born amidst lakes and woods and a host of pretty towns; east to the medieval silver "capital" of Kutná Hora; and north to the Giant Mountains (Krkonoše).

PRACTICAL INFORMATION FOR PRAGUE

HOTELS. Some older Prague hostelries have been attractively renovated. Others are ultrafunctional and lack charm. If you haven't prebooked, go to Čedok, Panská 5, Prague 1, or Pragotur, U Obecního domu 2, Prague 1, near the Powder Tower. Both also offer limited private accommodations.

CKM will be able to advise on the latest situation for budget and student accommodations.

Moderate

Central, Rybná 8, Prague 1 (tel. 2324351). Very central Old Town location, next to Kotva department store. Over 100 rooms, some (I). Disco, popular local rendezvous; could be noisy.

Centrum, Na poříčí 31, Prague 1 (tel. 2310009). Fairly central, near Bila Labut department store. 60 rooms, some (I).

Europa, Václavské nám. 29, Prague 1 (tel. 2365274). Very central, recently renovated *art nouveau* style. Over 100 rooms, some (I).

Olympik II-Garni, Invalidovna, Prague 8 (tel. 830274). 275 rooms; guests use nearby Olympik's restaurant.

Paříž, U Obecního domu, Prague 1 (tel. 2322051). Very central Old Town location, near Powder Tower; newly and tastefully renovated in *art nouveau* style. Over 100 rooms.

Splendid, Ovenecká 33, Prague 7 (tel. 375451). Not central, but quiet location near Strahov Stadium and zoo. 45 rooms.

Zlata Husa, Václavské nám. 7, Prague 1 (tel. 221351). Very central, 87 rooms. Service erratic. Popular disco. Prices can be expensive in High Season.

Three "botels" anchored along the Vltava river are popular despite cramped quarters, all Moderate: **Amirál,** Hořejší nábřeží, Prague 5 (tel. 547445); **Albatros,** Nábřeží L. Svobody, Prague 1 (tel. 2316996); **Racek,** U Dvorecká louky, Prague 4 (tel. 425793).

Inexpensive

Adria, Václavské nám. 26, Prague 1 (tel. 2360472). Very central. 46 rooms without bath or shower. No restaurant.

Atlantic, Na poříčí 9, Prague 1 (tel. 2318512). Fairly central. 62 rooms, very few private baths. No restaurant.

Junior Hotel Praha, Žitná 12, Prague 2 (tel. 299941). Run by CKM, 60 rooms.

Merkur, Tešnov 9, Prague 1 (tel. 2316951). Fairly central, very few private baths.

Opera, Tešnov 13, Prague 1 (tel. 2315609). Fairly central. 75 rooms, some private baths.

Savoy, Keplerova 6, Prague 1 (tel. 537457). In the Hradčany (castle) area, near Loretto shrine. 27 rooms, without bath or shower.

There are several student houses and hostels, open only in July and August (but precise dates vary), for which reservations must be made either ahead or through Čedok, Panská 5, Prague 1: *Jarov,* Konevova 198, Prague 3. *Jarov II,* Pod lipami 33, Prague 3. *Kajetanka,* Radimova 6, Prague 6. *Strahov,* Spartakiadni 5, Prague 6, near the Strahov Sports Stadium.

RESTAURANTS. Eating for a reasonable price is not difficult in Prague. There are plenty of workers' restaurants, which may not be glamorous but offer filling, wholesome meals, and a growing number of quick self-service snack bars; a very central one is *Koruna* at the bottom of Václavské náměstí near the corner of Na příkopě. Other central ones are *Blaník* and *Družba* on Wenceslas Square, another next to the Alcron Hotel in Štěpánská, and the *Moskva* in Na příkopě. Many beer halls *(pivnice)* and wine cellars *(vinárny)* serve hot dishes or snacks and are usually the best value for a lively atmosphere. Restaurants in main department stores (Kotva, Bílá Labut, Družba) also offer good value. For slightly more expensive but better food, try the *Paris* snack bar, Jindřišská ul. 7. Many places close weekends or Mon., so check in advance. An all-night snack bar operates in the *Slovanský Dům* restaurant, Na příkopě 22.

Moderate

Klášterní Vinárna, Národní Trida 8, Old Town (tel. 294863). Ex-convent serving good food, but be selective to keep the cost down; near National Theater.

U Kalicha, Na bojišti 12, New Town (tel. 296017). Associations with the Good Soldier Svejk, Czech food.

U Pastýřky, Belehradska 12, Prague 4 (tel. 434093). Slovak setting, with open fire for spit roasts.

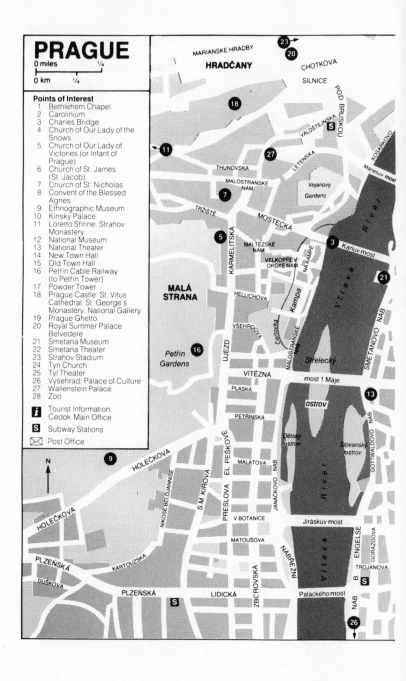

PRAGUE

0 miles ¼
0 km ¼

Points of Interest

1 Bethlehem Chapel
2 Carolinium
3 Charles Bridge
4 Church of Our Lady of the Snows
5 Church of Our Lady of Victories (or Infant of Prague)
6 Church of St. James (St. Jacob)
7 Church of St. Nicholas
8 Convent of the Blessed Agnes
9 Ethnographic Museum
10 Kinsky Palace
11 Loretto Shrine: Strahov Monastery
12 National Museum
13 National Theater
14 New Town Hall
15 Old Town Hall
16 Petřin Cable Railway (to Petřin Tower)
17 Powder Tower
18 Prague Castle: St. Vitus Cathedral. St. George's Monastery. National Gallery
19 Prague Ghetto
20 Royal Summer Palace Belvedere
21 Smetana Museum
22 Smetana Theater
23 Strahov Stadium
24 Tyn Church
25 Tyl Theater
26 Vyšehrad: Palace of Culture
27 Wallenstein Palace
28 Zoo

i Tourist Information: Čedok Main Office

S Subway Stations

✉ Post Office

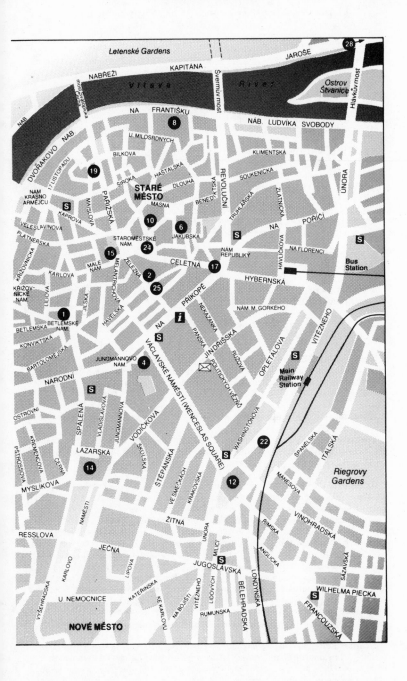

Vikárka, Hrad Vikářská 6, Prague 1 (tel. 535158). Very popular, may be crowded.

Inexpensive

U Bonaparta, Nerudova 29, Lesser Town (tel. 539780). A lively beer restaurant packed with young people.

U Medvídků, Na Perštýně 7, Old Town (tel. 2358904). Old alehouse serving South Bohemian food in jolly atmosphere.

U Pinkasů, Jungmannovo náměstí 15, Old Town (tel. 265770). The draught beer and the goulash are the attractions here.

U Zlatého tygra, Husova 17, Old Town 1 (tel. 265219). Good beer tavern.

GETTING AROUND PRAGUE. Tickets costing 2 Kčs. are valid for all forms of the city's public transport system; they must be bought in advance from newsstands, metro stations, tobacco shops, some stores, or hotels. A day ticket (16 Kčs.) valid for unlimited travel can be bought from "blue ticket" machines and some metro stations.

By Subway/Underground. Prague's sleek, modern network is easy to use. Most new maps of Prague mark the routes.

By Tram/Bus. Tickets should be punched in a machine after boarding the vehicle (watch how other people do it).

By Boat. In summer there are trips of varying duration on the Vltava river right through Prague. Check timetables locally.

By Taxi. These are marked with a broken white line. Charges are reasonable but they can be hard to get.

ENTERTAINMENT. Wine cellars and beer taverns. Known as *vinárny* and *pivnice,* these are the places to go for a lively atmosphere and to watch the Pragueites at one of their favorite occupations—talking. Most young Czechs gather in the considerable number of wine bars. Many restaurants feature dancing.

Cinema. Foreign films are quite often shown in their original language.

Discos. There is a growing number. Two central ones are *Astra* and at the *Zlata Husa Hotel,* both in Václavské náměstí. Also in the three botels, Admirál, Albatross and Racek.

Theaters. Czech opera is outstanding and the splendid *National Theater (Narodni Divadlo)* has been magnificently restored; the *Tyl Theater,* Železná 11, will be closed for restoration until 1992. Also notable is the *Smetana Theater,* Vitězneho února 8, near the National Museum. The *Laterna Magika,* Národní 40, (some performances in the new section of the National Theater), presents an extravaganza combining live actors, mime and advanced cine techniques, and this is very popular with foreign visitors. The *Theater on the Balustrade (Divadlo na Zabradlí),* Anenské nám. 5, is the home of the famous Black Theater (shadow ballet), which is often away on tour, and where the mime Fialka and the chanson singer Hegerova perform. Puppet theater is a high art form at the *Špejbl & Hurvínek Theater,* Římská 45. A monthly program of events is available from the Prague Information Service. Tickets are very cheap and should be bought at the theater box offices either a few days in advance or immediately before a performance.

Concerts. Regular venues include the *Palace of Culture, House of Artists (Dům Umělců), Smetanovo Sin,* the *National Museum, Strahov Library* and various historic palaces. There are regular Mozart concerts at the *villa Bertramka,* marvelous organ recitals in churches such as *St. James'* (Old Town), *U Křižovniků* (near Charles Bridge) and *St. Nicholas* (Lesser Town), and rousing military bands in the *Castle Gardens* in summer.

MUSEUMS. Prague has a large number of good ones. They are generally open from 9 or 10 to 4 or 5 and are closed Monday; entrance fees are usually low. Some of the more worthwhile ones are:

Amerika, Ke Karlovu 20, New Town. Former baroque summer palace, now Dvořák museum.

Bertramka, Mozartova 169. Delightful villa in which Mozart stayed when visiting Prague, now housing Mozart Museum.

Convent of the Blessed Agnes, Anežská ulice, Old Town. Built in the 13th century and recently restored to house 19th-century Czech art.

History Exhibition, in the Lobkovic Palace, Jiřska Street, Prague Castle. Fine new collection.

Jewish Museum. Spread over several buildings in the former ghetto in Old Town, including an old synagogue, ancient cemetery and many Jewish artifacts, and reflecting the tragic Nazi liquidation of nearly 80,000 Czech Jews in World War II.

National Gallery, Hradčanské nám. 15. Near the castle, with a wonderful collection of old and modern art, including paintings by Dürer, Bruegel, Cranach, Kokoschka, Schiele, and Klimt, as well as some superb woodcuts and carvings.

National Museum. A landmark dominating Václavské náměstí, built in the 1880s, with rather fusty historical, archeological and numismatic exhibits and a famous mineralogical collection.

Smetana Museum, Novotného lávka. Fine views of the river and city from the museum's windows as you listen to the composer's great works on tape.

St. George's Monastery. Ideal setting in Prague castle for national collection of old Czech art.

Strahov Library, Strahovské nádvoří 132. Beautifully preserved ancient manuscripts, including bibles from all over the world, exhibited in gorgeous rooms, but viewing restricted to prevent damage.

SHOPPING. *Tuzex,* the government chain, has a network of shops throughout the country where you can purchase quality goods of foreign and local production for Tuzex vouchers or directly in exchange for hard currency. For the latest information on their outlets, their information center is at Rytířská 11, Prague 1.

There are some local currency shops specializing in various wares. **Jewelry:** Na příkopě 12 and Staroměstské náměstí 6. **Glass and porcelain:** Malé náměstí 6 (modern Bor glass); Pařížská 2 (traditional Bohemian glass); Keramo, Melantrichova (traditional pottery). **Paintings, prints:** several Dilo shops including that at 28 Října 6. **Folk art:** Krásná jizba-ULUV, Národní 36. There are several UVA shops including that at Na příkopě 25. Probably the lowest prices are in the department stores: *Bílá Labut,* Na poříčí 23; *Družba,* Václavské nám.; *Kotva,* nám. Republiky 8, all Prague 1.

USEFUL ADDRESSES: *American Embassy,* Tržiště 15, Lesser Town (tel. 536641); *Canadian Embassy,* Mickiewiczova 6 (tel. 326941); *British Embassy,* Thunovská ulice 14, Lesser Town (tel. 533347); *Čedok, Thomas Cook,* Na příkopě 18, New Town (tel. 212711); *Čedok Accommodation Service,* Panská 5 (tel. 227004); *Pragotur,* U Obecního domu (near Powder Tower) (tel. 2317281); *Prague Information Service,* Na příkopě 20 (tel. 544444); *Main Post Office,* Jindřišská ulice 24, New Town; *Clinic for foreigners,* Fakultní poliklinika, Karlovo náměstí 32, Prague 2 (tel. 299381); *CKM Czechoslovak Youth and Students Travel Bureau,* Žitná 12, Prague 2. *Emergency telephones:* 155 (medical help), 158 (police).

Slovakia

Easternmost and most mountainous region of Czechoslovakia, Slovakia can claim to be the Switzerland of Central Europe, not only because it is similar in size, population and geography, but because, like Switzerland, it is really three countries in one. In the southwest is the vast, bountiful plain of the great Danube river bordering on Hungary and rising northward to the Carpathian foothills. Central Slovakia is composed of a number of fine mountain ranges; but the most famous part of all is the High Tatras in Eastern Slovakia, a spectacular cluster of peaks and valleys studded with winter and summer resorts. South and east of the mountains, the rolling countryside is dotted with exquisite little Gothic and Renaissance towns, of which Levoča and Kežmarok are outstanding examples. Beautiful old wooden churches are also a feature of eastern Slovakia—Bardejov and Prešov are good bases from which to visit these. Folk art and traditions also survive to a marked degree in the eastern regions.

Bratislava, capital of Slovakia and the region's main city, has little to offer the tourist. The majestic castle overlooking the Danube and dominating the old town, and the elegant, super-modern bridge with a restaurant perched on a high pylon, are the only sights. Otherwise, the city is rather dreary, a fine example of postwar East European town planning. Accommodations are often difficult to find and on the expensive side.

A regular bus service links Bratislava with Vienna. Trains link the main towns and a good network of bus services reaches all areas. There is marvelous hiking and a well developed system of marked trails in all the mountain areas.

PRACTICAL INFORMATION FOR SLOVAKIA

Hotels and Restaurants

Bratislava. *Bratislava* (M), Urxova 9 (tel. 238920). 344 rooms. Modern, on outskirts of town, nightclub. *Juniorhotel Sputnik* (M), Drieňova 14 (tel. 288084). 100 rooms. New, by the lake on outskirts of town. Wine cellar, sports complex. *Palace* (M), Poštová 1 (tel. 335656). 70 rooms, some (I), central. *Sporthotel* (I), Neruɖova 2 (tel. 23497). 27 rooms.

Restaurants. For inexpensive eating look out for self-service snack bars and workers' restaurants. More attractive and still reasonably priced are the taverns and small local-style restaurants *(koliba)*. *Bajkal* (M), Bajkalská 25, attractive rustic decor and Slovak specialties. *Kláštorná vináreň*, Pugačevova, in a 300-year-old monastery. *Stará Sladovňa*, Cintorínska 32, restored old malt-house specializing in beer, with several restaurants. *U Remeselníkov* (at the Artisans'), Beblavého 1, good snack bar in restored historic building housing museum of Artistic Crafts. *Vélki františkáni*, Diebrovo nám., spread over several rooms in medieval vaults, lively atmosphere.

The address of *Čedok* in Bratislava is Štúrova 13.

Smokovec. Really three resorts in one, linked together on the lower slopes of the High Tatras. Main center for shops and information is **Starý Smokovec**, with *Úderník* (I), 40 rooms, modern. In **Novy Smokovec:** *Park* (M), 96 rooms, modern, one of the best for value; *Tokajík* (M), 13 rooms; *Bystrina* (I), 44 rooms. In **Horný Smokovec:** *Šport* (I), 66 rooms, none with shower; modern. At **Hrebienok**, reached by funicular, there are several chalets with good, simple accommodations and restaurants.

Tatranská Lomnica. Near Smokovec. *Slovan* (M). 84 rooms. In resort center; modern, with nightclub.

Restaurants. *Tatranská kuria,* Slovak specialties, folk atmosphere. *Zbojnícka koliba,* Slovak specialties prepared on open fire, folk music.

The *Motel Eurocamp FICC* has chalets for hire, shops, restaurant, and stunning views of the High Tatras.

Denmark

The Danes have a glorious history behind them. At one time or another they've ruled vast areas of Norway and Sweden as well as parts of Germany, territories to the east of the Baltic, and most of England. Both the Faroe Islands, which lie between Scotland and Iceland, and the northern hemisphere's largest island, Greenland, come under the Danish Crown, though each has control over most of its internal affairs. At the height of their civilization the Vikings reached most of the then-known world and are said to have sailed to America long before Columbus. Parts of this history can be traced in Denmark through the runic stones and Viking remains that abound, and in the numerous exhibits in Danish museums.

Although Denmark is very small, it is full of charm and historical interest. The countryside, with its castles, manor houses and quaint half-timbered buildings, is remarkably unspoiled and still evokes the spirit that inspired Hans Christian Andersen to write his fairy tales.

Today, Denmark, in common with Norway and Sweden, has a reputation as an expensive country. True, the country can be pricey if you go determined to live it up, but then, what country wouldn't be? Copenhagen, the delightful capital of Denmark, has significantly higher prices than most other areas of the country, but no visit to Denmark would be complete without a day or two there. In some ways, it's the most appealing of the Scandinavian capitals. The real secret of getting the best out of a limited budget in Denmark is to get away from the cities and out into the flat, rolling countryside. Hire a bicycle—as thousands of Danes do—and strike out on your own. There are practically no hills in Denmark and the country is ideal for slow and easy peddling, stopping from time to time at one of the many *kros,* Denmark's traditional country inns. (And while on the subject, you'll find that inexpensive food and drink here is as good as, if not better than, anywhere in Europe). The country also has a veritable multitude of excellent sandy beaches, some 7,500 km. (4,600 miles) to be exact. They can be a little bracing at times, but when the summer weather is good, they can be hard to beat. Jutland, the only part of Denmark linked to the mainland of Europe, has the best of the beaches.

Travel in Denmark is easy, thanks to the efficient network of buses, trains and ferries connecting the various islands. To the east of Jutland, the island of Funen is linked by road and rail bridges to the mainland, allowing a painless excursion to the town of Odense, childhood home of Hans Christian Andersen. Zealand, the largest and most densely populated of islands and the site of Copenhagen, is reached by frequent ferries from both Funen and Germany. Daily ferries also ply the route from Copenhagen to the tiny Danish island of Bornholm, some 160 miles out in the Baltic between Sweden and Poland.

Various all-inclusive budget holidays are available in Denmark, and many hotels offer lower prices in the winter months. Enquire about youth or pensioner discounts, and off-peak rail and air fares.

PRACTICAL INFORMATION FOR DENMARK

WHAT WILL IT COST. Hotels cost less outside Copenhagen and North Zealand though prices are rising in the North Sea coastal resorts. The best-value areas are probably Funen and Jutland. A good bet for the budget traveler is a *kro* (country inn) or a farm. Both will be clean and comfortable, though not all rooms may have private bathrooms. Buy a book of inn vouchers to cover around 66 inns (198 kr. per person, per night, with bath) and the inn-keeper can phone ahead to book your next night's accommodations. Self-catering holidays have also become very popular, both for Danes and visitors, and accommodations are usually good.

The monetary unit in Denmark is the *krone* (kr.), which divides into 100 *ore*. The smallest coin is 25 øre, so that all prices are rounded to a multiple of 25. At the time of writing the exchange rate for the krone was 7.1 to the U.S. dollar and 11.4 to the pound sterling. These rates will almost certainly change before and during 1992.

Sample costs. Cinema ticket 40–60 kr.; theater ticket 60–280 kr.; museum entrance varies but is often free; cup of coffee 12–16 kr.; a beer about 15–25 kr.; a carafe of wine from 65–75 kr.

NATIONAL TOURIST OFFICE. The *Danish Tourist Board* will provide you with more ideas for a budget oriented vacation in Denmark, and to help you during your trip there are tourist information offices in most Danish cities. In the capital the address is H.C. Andersens Boulevard 22, DK-1553 Copenhagen V (tel. 31–111325).

Addresses of the main offices of the Danish Tourist Board overseas are:

In the U.S.: 655 Third Ave., New York, N.Y. 10017 (tel. 212–949–2333).

In Canada: Box 115, Station "N," Toronto, Ontario, M8V 3S4 (tel. 416–823–9620).

In the U.K.: 169–173 Regent St., London, W1R 8PY (tel. 071–734 2637).

WHEN TO COME. Most visitors arrive in July and August, but in May, June, or September there are fewer crowds and many hotels offer out-of-season discounts. Danish school holidays are mid-June to mid-August, when it is usually quieter in Copenhagen. However, the season for many big hotels throughout the country now lasts virtually all year.

Average afternoon temperature in degrees Fahrenheit and centigrade:

Copenhagen

	Jan.	Feb.	Mar.	Apr.	May	June	July	Aug.	Sept.	Oct.	Nov.	Dec.
F°	36	36	41	50	61	67	72	69	63	53	43	38
C°	2	2	5	10	16	19	22	21	17	12	6	3

SPECIAL EVENTS. Cultural policy in Denmark is progressive and supports a wide range of activities, from the Royal Theater with drama, opera, and ballet, to sports, exhibitions, and festivals of all kinds. Because of the Government's support, these events are normally cheap, and sometimes free. A small selection of annual events includes: *May* Ballet Festival at the Royal Theater, Copenhagen. Copenhagen Marathon. *June* Around Funen sailing event. Riverboat jazz festival, Silkeborg. Viking Festival with Viking Play at Frederikssund (also Jels in *July*). Skagen Folk Festival at Skagen harbor. Midsummer celebrations on June 23, with bonfires, all over Denmark. *June-July* Mid-Funen Festival—folk, rock and entertainment at Ringe. *June-September* Organ festival at Soro church. *July* Ten-day International Jazz Festival, Copenhagen. Fourth of July celebrations by Danish Americans at Rebild Park, Aalborg. Roskilde Festival—Northern Europe's largest rock music festival. *July* Veteran car rally around island of Bornholm. Hans Christian Andersen Festival, Odense. *July-September* Copenhagen Summer Festival, classical music. *August* Tønder Festival, South Jutland. *September* Århus Festival, biggest of its kind in Denmark—concerts, theater, exhibits, sporting events, etc. Medieval market in Old Town.

National Holidays. Jan. 1 (New Year's Day); March 29–April 1 (Easter); April 26 (Common Prayer); May 9 (Ascension); May 20 (Whit. Mon); June 5 (Constitution Day; shops close at noon); Dec. 24, 25, 26.

VISAS. Nationals of the U.S.A., Canada, Australia, New Zealand, EC countries and practically all other European countries do not require visas for entry into Denmark.

HEALTH CERTIFICATES. No vaccinations are required to enter Denmark.

GETTING TO DENMARK. By Plane. There are non-stop flights to Copenhagen from the following North American cities: New York, Boston, Chicago, Los Angeles, Seattle, and Miami. If you travel *SAS* and also intend to fly once in Scandinavia, ask about joint external and internal travel deals. There are services from most other European capitals, either non-stop or through flights. From the U.K., in addition to services from London, there are flights from Birmingham, Manchester, Humberside, Dundee, Dublin, Aberdeen and Glasgow. *Maersk Air* flies from London (Southend) to Billund in Jutland seven times a week and *SAS* and British Airways have service from London to Århus. Discounts are available on certain days; check when you book.

By Boat. The Danish shipping line *Scandinavian Seaways* operates car and passenger ferry services from Harwich to Esbjerg, three to four sailings a week, year–round (approx. 20 hours). Newcastle to Esbjerg, two sailings a week (approx. 18 hours). *Fred Olsen Lines* sails from New Castle to Christiansholm, Norway, to Hirtshals in Jutland once a week.

By Train. There are three choices of route from London to Copenhagen. One leaves London Victoria station for Dover and the crossing to Oostende (either by conventional ferry or the faster jetfoil), where it picks up the overnight *Nord Express* to Copenhagen. Another leaves Liverpool Street station for Harwich and the longer crossing to the Hook of Holland, where the *Holland-Scandinavian Express* runs overnight to Copenhagen. An alternative route from Harwich is by *Scandinavian Seaways* to Esbjerg to pick up the fast rail connection to the Danish capital.

CUSTOMS. Tax-free import and export of liquor, wine and tobacco vary according to itinerary, nationality and length of stay. Bank notes, traveler's cheques, and other legal tender, Danish or other, may be imported and exported freely.

HOTELS. Guide price for a double room with bath in a Moderate hotel in Copenhagen during high season is 670–900 kr. per night. Inexpensive hotels charge 325–670 with bath or shower. Outside Copenhagen prices are lower.

In the towns Mission Hotels provide clean, low-priced rooms while in the country local inns offer good food and reasonable rooms, often with private bathrooms. Many of the inns are ancient buildings full of character. *Dansk Kroferie* is an association of inns that offers vouchers for 198 kr. per person for overnight stay and breakfast; they are available from authorized travel agents or from Dansk Kroferie, Søndergade 31, DK-8700 Horsens, tel. 75–623544. Local tourist information offices often have details of rooms to rent in private houses.

The Danish Tourist Board is keen to promote holiday packages that emphasize active, outdoor family vacations in rural areas, and there are many variations on these holiday schemes. It should not be difficult to find the one that suits you. Though Danish accommodations are almost invariably good, to avoid disappointment, be sure to find out all details of a package—with or without bath, full or half board, self-catering, children's reductions, etc. Local tourist offices are helpful and will probably be able to provide detailed information.

Youth Hostels. Danish youth hostels are open to visitors of all ages at an overnight charge of between 40–60 kr. Non YHA members have to pay a guest fee of 18 kr. per night extra. Sleeping bags alone are not allowed; you can hire linen at some hostels but the best solution is to take a sheet, sleeping bag or duvet, and pillow cases. Many hostels provide reasonably priced meals with free use of the kitchens. Details from the tourist office.

Camping. There are over 500 camp sites in Denmark, many with huts and cabins for hire that must be booked in advance. You will need an international camping carnet or guest card. Most sites charge about 28 kr. per person (half for children). Details from the Danish Camping Council, Gammel Kongsvej 74D, DK–1850 Copenhagen.

Also available at reasonable cost are country cottages, farmhouse holidays and self-catering chalets. Details from Danish Tourist Board and travel agents.

RESTAURANTS. Danish food is of excellent quality as well as being beautifully presented most of the time. Be warned—liquor is expensive. The most popular drink is pilsner, a light beer such as Tuborg or Carlsberg; lager in Denmark is a darker, heavier brew.

The meal most typical of Denmark is the Cold Table *(det store kolde bord),* an extensive buffet of hot and cold meats, fish, shellfish, cheeses, salads and a variety of breads. Although not cheap, this is usually excellent value for money as customers can help themselves as often as they like to as much as they want; it also provides an opportunity to sample all kinds of local specialties. Available at lunch only.

Open sandwiches have reached an art form in Denmark and are available everywhere, in every variety and in take-out lunch boxes.

Look out for the small cafés that are especially popular in central Copenhagen. You can get a café au lait and an over–stuffed sandwich for about 35 kr.

Cheapest of all are the sausages and hamburgers from streetside sausage vans *(polsevogn).*

Food and Drink. The normal Danish breakfast or *morgen complet* consists of coffee or tea and an assortment of breads with cold meats, cheeses, jam and Danish pastries. For budget travelers, this is a marvelous arrangement because you can help yourself without limit.

Apart from beer, *Akvavit* is the national drink of Scandinavia; it is popularly known as *snaps.* Neither an aperitif, cocktail nor liqueur, it is meant to be drunk with food, preferably with a beer chaser. Akvavit is served ice-cold and should be drunk with cold food.

TIPPING. Hotels and restaurants quote fully inclusive prices: you should tip only for special personal help. Washroom attendants get 1 kr. Taxi fares include a tip. Do not tip cinema or theater ushers or in barbershops.

MAIL. Surface and airmail letters and aerogrammes to the United States cost 4.40 kr. for 20 grams, postcards 3.40 kr. Letters, aerogrammes and postcards to the United Kingdom and EC countries cost 3.20 kr. All go airmail.

CLOSING TIMES. Shops are open from 9 to 6, with the exception of Monday and Friday when they stay open until 7 or 8. On Saturday they close between noon and 2 P.M. Post offices open from 10 to 5 or 9 to 5.30. Bank hours are 9.30 to 4 on weekdays (Thursday to 6), but they are closed on Saturday. Hours do tend to vary outside Copenhagen.

GETTING AROUND DENMARK. By Plane. Denmark has an extensive domestic air service. A total of 11 routes bring you to every corner of the country in 30–55 minutes. Reductions on the off-peak "green departures" reduce fares to about half. Book ahead as flights are busy.

By Train. Although the country is made up of the peninsula of Jutland and many islands it has a good railway system. Bridges link several of the islands and between the island of Zealand (Copenhagen is on this) and Funen there is a train ferry system giving a high frequency of services. Apart from the Copenhagen suburban services (part of which form the city's Underground) the lines are not electrified, but diesel operated. Trains are clean and punctual.

Enquire at any DSB (Danish State Railways) station for information on discounts for young people or senior citizens, and on group discounts for three or more people traveling (Nordturist) together. There are substantial reductions if you travel on Tuesdays, Wednesdays, or Thursdays in summer, and every day but Friday and Sunday in winter.

Nordic Tourist Tickets provide unlimited travel by rail, and a reduction on some sea routes in Denmark, Sweden, and Finland. Valid for 21 days, they cost $218 for adult second class, $163 for those aged 12–25, children half-price. Available from travel agents or railroad stations.

By Bus. Bus routes radiate from main railway centers and they also operate on some routes in conjunction with the trains. As with trains they are clean and run very punctually. Full details from bus information points and all local tourist offices. As bus and rail stations are usually next door to each other, this simplifies travel connections, and carrying luggage.

By Bicycle. But why not go bicycling? In Denmark some railroad stations and many tourist offices rent bicycles. Planned holidays on wheels, including bike hire, accommodations, meals and a map of a pre-selected route, are operated from *Dansk Cykelferie,* c/o DVL-Rejser, Kultorvet 7, DK-1175 Copenhagen, tel. 33–132727. Further information on cycling is available from the *Danish Cyclists Association* (Dansk Cyclist Forbund), Kjeld Langes Gade 14, DK-1367, Copenhagen. The Danish Tourist Board produces a pamphlet on *Cycling Holidays in Denmark.*

Copenhagen

Copenhagen was founded in the 12th century when a small fishing village was fortified and named Kopmannaehafn or Merchant's Haven. However, the great growth of the city did not begin until the rule of King Christian IV (1588–1648) when Rosenborg Castle, the old Stock Exchange, the Round Tower of Trinity Church and the two-story yellow naval houses of Nyboder were built. Those interested in royalty will want to visit Amalienborg, home of the present royal family.

The place to start your first walking tour of Copenhagen is the City Hall Square (Rådhus Pladsen). Take a walk down Strøget as the Danes call it (in fact it consists of five different streets) to Kongens Nytorv. Strøget was one of the first pedestrian streets in the world, if not the first. Today the street is full of colorful life 24 hours a day, all year round, so your first walk in Copenhagen will not be a quiet one. Outside the posh displays of the fur and porcelain shops, the sidewalks have the festive aura of a street fair.

With Strøget as your landmark, you can make excursions into the old part of Copenhagen, to the old canals and cross one of the bridges to Amager and Christianshavn.

Tivoli, the well-known amusement park, is open May–Sept. and offers all kinds of diversions including one of the last pantomime theaters in Europe. There are firework displays twice a week.

To escape the crowds, take the "S" train to Klampenborg and hire a bicycle or walk to the wooded Deer Park where route markers indicate places of interest. The park has several open-air restaurants and is home to Bakken, a 400-year-old amusement park.

PRACTICAL INFORMATION FOR COPENHAGEN

HOTELS. You will generally find a high standard of hotels in Denmark. But in Copenhagen, it has to be said, some of the hotels in the red light district around Istedgade are in pretty bad shape. Choose carefully if this is the area you plan to stay in: many hotels are cheap and centrally located and that is all. But there are the mission hotels (see below).

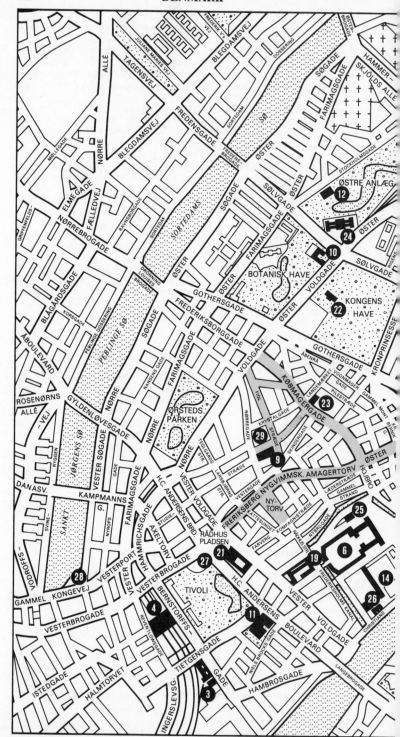

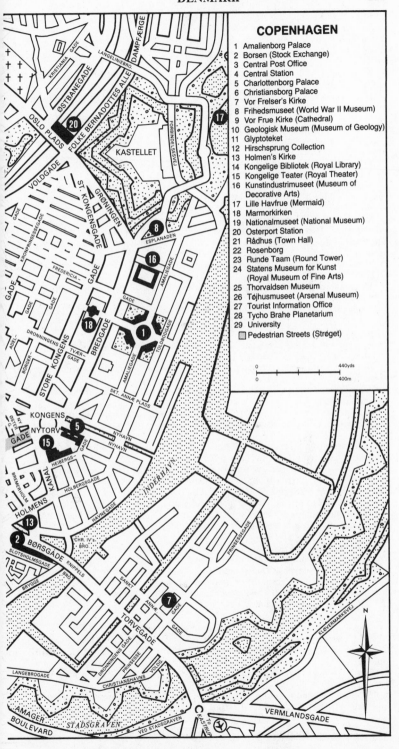

COPENHAGEN

1 Amalienborg Palace
2 Borsen (Stock Exchange)
3 Central Post Office
4 Central Station
5 Charlottenborg Palace
6 Christiansborg Palace
7 Vor Frelser's Kirke
8 Frihedsmuseet (World War II Museum)
9 Vor Frue Kirke (Cathedral)
10 Geologisk Museum (Museum of Geology)
11 Glyptoteket
12 Hirschsprung Collection
13 Holmen's Kirke
14 Kongelige Bibliotek (Royal Library)
15 Kongelige Teater (Royal Theater)
16 Kunstindustrimuseet (Museum of
   Decorative Arts)
17 Lille Havfrue (Mermaid)
18 Marmorkirken
19 Nationalmuseet (National Museum)
20 Osterport Station
21 Rådhus (Town Hall)
22 Rosenborg
23 Runde Taam (Round Tower)
24 Statens Museum for Kunst
   (Royal Museum of Fine Arts)
25 Thorvaldsen Museum
26 Tøjhusmuseet (Arsenal Museum)
27 Tourist Information Office
28 Tycho Brahe Planetarium
29 University
▨ Pedestrian Streets (Strøget)

0   440yds
0   400m

Prices for Moderate hotels (M) in the list are from 670–900 kr. for a double room with bath and for Inexpensive hotels (I) the prices are 325–670 kr. for a double room without bath.

Moderate

Ascot Hotel, Studiestraede 57 (tel. 33–126000). 70 rooms, all with shower. Centrally located.

Hotel Danmark, Vester Voldgade 89 (tel. 33–114806). 51 rooms, all with bath or shower.

Park, Jarmers Plads 3 (tel. 33–133000). 64 rooms, all with bath. Five minutes' walk from Town Hall Square.

Savoy, Vesterbrogade 34 (tel. 31–314073). 72 rooms with marble bath/shower rooms. Recently renovated.

Triton, Helgolandsgade 7–11 (tel. 31–313266) 123 rooms, all with bath or shower. Cool blue tones; superb breakfasts.

Webers, Vesterbrogade 11 (tel. 31–311432). 80 rooms, 40 with bath. Spacious and comfortable; recently redecorated.

Mission hotels. These unique hotels, found in several Danish cities, are between Moderate and Inexpensive. They are good value for money, and are clean and pleasant, but not all rooms have own bath, and they have no liquor license. Centrally located Copenhagen Mission Hotels include:

Missionhotellet Ansgar, Colbjørnsensgade 29, DK-1652 Copenhagen V (tel. 31–212196).

Missionhotellet Hebron, Helgolandsgade 4, DK-1653 Copenhagen V (tel. 31–316906).

Missionhotellet Nebo, Istedgade 6, DK-1650, Copenhagen V (tel. 31–211217).

Inexpensive

Absalon Hotel, Helgolandsgade 15 (tel. 31–242211). 260 rooms, 167 with bath or shower. Near Central Station.

Hotel Amager, Amagerbrogade 29 (tel. 31–544008). 26 rooms, 14 with bath. Restaurant (breakfast and lunch). Limited facilities.

Esplanaden, Bredgade 78 (tel. 33–132175). 50 rooms. Limited facilities, but near bus and underground. Overlooking Langelinie.

København, Vesterbrogade 41 (tel. 31–212166). 46 rooms, centrally located.

Saga Hotel, Colbjørnsensgade 20 (tel. 31–249967). 75 rooms, very limited facilities.

Skovriderkroen, Strandvejen 267 (tel. 31–626340). 20 rooms, all with bath. In wonderful surroundings on the edge of Charlottenlund woods, near the beach.

Skovshoved, Strandvejen 267 (tel. 31–640028). Five miles (eight km.) from town center. Old world charm, thoroughly modernized.

Hotel Viking, Bredgade 65 (tel. 33–124550). 90 rooms, 19 with private bath. Centrally located near old city ramparts and Kastellet (the Citadel).

An accommodation service is to be found at the Central Station, where Kiosk P books hotels and private rooms for personal callers.

RESTAURANTS. Copenhagen's 2,000 restaurants cater to every culinary taste. Many foreign restaurants offer specialties and small lunch restaurants offer open sandwiches and the typical Danish cold table. Most department stores have cafeterias. When you are in a rush, the city has many fast-food outlets, plus cheap, good hot dog stands on sidewalks and street corners. The free publication *Copenhagen This Week,* in large shops and hotels, gives a useful list.

Moderate

Bøf & Ost, Gråbrødretorv 13 (tel. 33–119911). "Beef & Cheese". Closed Sunday.

Copenhagen Corner, Rådhus Pladsen (tel. 33–914545). Great views of Town Hall Square, and terrific smørrebrød besides.

Faergekroen, in Tivoli, Vesterbrogade 3 (tel. 31–129412). Good inexpensive spot for lunch.

Hereford Beefstouw, Vesterbrogade 3 (tel. 33–127441). Also a smaller and quieter branch at Abenra 8 (tel. 33–119190). Open 11.30 A.M.–2 P.M. and 5–9 P.M. (Sat.

and Sun. 5 P.M.–9 P.M. only). Best steaks in town and good atmosphere. Serve-yourself salad bar.

Ida Davidsen, St. Kongensgade 70 (tel. 33–913655). A Copenhagen institution; synonomous with smørrebrød. A splurge, but worth it. Lunch only; closed at week-ends.

Mongolian Barbeque, Store Kongensgade 64–66 (tel. 33–146466), also at Storm-gade 35, Strandvejen 26. Newly popular Mongolian chain, with filling and inexpen-sive all-you-can-eat meals.

Royal Porcelain Shop Restaurant, on top floor of shop, Amagertorv 8 (tel. 33–137101). Elegant and stylish, with food served on famous porcelain. Mon. to Fri. 10–5; Sat. 10–1. Closed Sun. and evenings.

Victor's, Ny Ostergade 8 (tel. 33–133613). Smart, elegant; with bohemian atmo-sphere. Good food.

Inexpensive

Cafe Asbaek, Ny Adelgade 8–10 (tel. 33–122416). Modern restaurant in art gal-lery. Closed evenings and Sundays.

Cafeen i Nikolaj, Nikolaj Church (tel. 33–116313). Good Danish food in magnif-icent one-time church. Open daily noon–5.

Cafe Smukke Marie, Knabrostraede 19 (tel. 33–155644). Delicious stuffed crepes at this cinema cafe.

Chico's Cantina, Borgergade 2 (tel. 33–114108). Superb Mexican food at reason-able prices. Extremely popular so go either early or late. Open noon–3 P.M.; 5–midnight.

Green's, Gronnegade 12–14 (tel. 33–151690). Healthy vegetarian cuisine, with much emphasis on grains and natural sweeteners.

Krasnapolsky, Vestergade 10 (tel. 33–328800). Interesting and unusual food, sal-ads, snacks. Near the university; a brooding youth at every table. Open 11.30 A.M.–midnight. Sun. 3 P.M.–midnight.

Peppe's Pizza, Gothersgade 101 (tel. 33–132215). Open noon–midnight; Fri. and Sat. noon–3 A.M. Freshly made pizzas of all kinds; house wine excellent value. Good atmosphere.

GETTING AROUND COPENHAGEN. By Bus and Train. A joint fare system, with optional transfers, covers all buses and trains in the Copenhagen region. A one-hour ticket to cover three zones costs 8 kr., from bus drivers and railroad sta-tions. You can buy a packet of 10 of these basic tickets for 70 kr. This system covers an area that stops south of Køge, west of Roskilde, and includes these towns as well as Hillerød, Elsinore and Copenhagen.

Better value for visitors is the Copenhagen Card. This costs 90 kr. for one day, 140 kr. for two days, and 180 kr. for three days; children between 4 and 11 travel half-price. This provides unlimited travel by bus and train throughout the metropol-itan region including North Zealand. It also gives free admission to around 40 muse-ums, sights and attractions (including Tivoli), and 50% discount on crossings to Sweden. Available from hotels, travel agencies, main rail stations in the metropoli-tan region, Central Railway Accommodation Service at Central Station, and Tour-ist Information office opposite Copenhagen City Hall.

By Bicycle. Bicycles can be hired for 30–50 kr. per day (deposit 100–200 kr.). Try *Danwheel-Rent-a-Bike,* Colbjornsensgade 3, or *Urania Cycler,* Gammel Kongevej 1.
Avoid taxis: they are expensive.

ENTERTAINMENT. Cinema. Cinemas have varying prices for seats and the cheapest are in the front rows. Afternoon performances are cheaper than evening and films are usually shown with the original soundtrack and Danish subtitles. Cin-emas are cheaper outside Copenhagen.

Nightlife. Copenhagen goes to bed late, and a city that is lively by day can be even livelier by night, with jazz clubs, music taverns, and discotheques. The Tivoli Gardens are humming till after midnight, with entertainment and sideshows, and the evening march by the band of the Tivoli Boys Guard (the Royal Guard in miniature). The *Tivoli Concert Hall* is the stage for orchestral performances at 7.30 and 9 P.M. (sometimes free). There is also jazz in *Slukeftker* just beside the Tivoli's Vesterbrogade entrance. Other jazz and music clubs include: *Jazzhus Montmartre*, Nørregade 41 (tel. 33–114667) for excellent modern jazz. Open 8 P.M.–1 A.M. and to 4 A.M. Fri. and Sat. *Ben Webster's*, Vestergade 7 (tel. 33–938845) for local and international jazz acts. Open daily 6 P.M.–5 A.M. *De Tre Musketerer*, Nikolaj Plads 25 (tel. 33–112507), the home of traditional jazz. Open 8 P.M.–2 A.M., 3 A.M. Fri. and Sat. Closed Sun. *Musikcafeen* for folk music at Rådhusstraede 13 (tel. 33–112932). Open 9 P.M.–1 A.M. *The Purple Door*, Fiolstraede 28 (tel. 33–136628). Open Thurs. to Sat. 8.30 P.M.–1 A.M.

Discotheques include *Fellini Nightclub* (in SAS Royal Hotel) at Hammerichsgade 1 (tel. 33–141412). Open 10 P.M.–4.30 A.M. *New Daddy's/Cafe Rio* Aexeltorv 5 (tel. 33–116950). Open Wed. and Thurs. 10 P.M.–4 A.M., Fri. 11 P.M.–6 A.M., Sat. till 7 A.M. *Woodstock*, Vestergade 12 (tel. 33–112071). Open Sun. to Wed. 9 P.M.–2 A.M., Thurs. till 3 A.M., Fri. and Sat. till 5 A.M.

The *Vin & Olgod*, Skindergade 45 (tel. 33–132625), offers food, drinks, dancing and group singing. Viking dinners and a fanfare blown every night on genuine Viking "Lures". Open 8 P.M.–2 A.M. Closed Sun.

Theaters. The *Royal Theater* is Copenhagen's dramatic heart and outstanding ballet and opera performances play across its boards. Repertoire information, call 33–152220 (automatic answering). The least expensive seats at the *Old Stage* are *galleriet* (galleries) and *anden etage* (second upper circle). At the *New Stage* and other balconied theaters in the city, sit in the *anden etage*, the *forste etage* (first upper circle), the *forste etage siden* (first upper circle, side) and *parterre* (pit). In other theaters the rear seats are the cheapest. Matinees are cheaper than evening performances.

During June, July and August, most theaters are dark, yet Danish revues are often staged. For young people under 25 there are substantial reductions on seats. The Festival of Fools is staged each June, featuring plays, cabaret, ballet and street theater performed by visiting groups from all over the world.

Tivoli also stages theater attractions at different locations in the park.

MUSEUMS. This is a small selection from a large number in Copenhagen. Check opening times in the free booklet *Copenhagen This Week*. **Botanical Garden**, Gothersgade 28. Danish plants, also foreign mountain plants and a palm house with tropical and subtropical specimens.

Carlsberg Museum, Valby Langgade 1. 140 years of the history of the famous beer. Family museum.

Ny Carlsberg Glyptotek, Dantes Plads. Egyptian, Greek, Etruscan, Roman art; Impressionists and 19th-century Danish art. Winter garden.

Kastellet, Langelinie. 300-year-old military fortifications.

Kunstindustrimuseet, Bredgade 68. Museum of decorative art, European and Oriental, in rococo building.

Københavns Bymuseum, Vesterbrogade 59. 800 years of the city's past in pictures and other mementos. Kierkegaard relics.

Louisiana, Gammel Strandvej 13, Humlebaek. Warhols vie for space with Rauschenbergs at this world-class modern art collection; spectacular setting by the sea.

Nationalmuseet, Frederiksholms Kanal 12. From the Ice Age to the Vikings, Oriental, Classical, Numismatic, and Ethnographical collections. Closed Mon.

Open Air Museum, Kongevejen 100, Lyngby, on the northern edge of Copenhagen. Old rural houses and farm buildings show how Danes lived in the past.

Rosenborg Slot, Øster Voldgade 4A. Renaissance castle, crown jewels.

Rundetårn, Købmagergade. A 120-ft.-high round tower built in 1642 as an observatory.

Tycho Brahe Planetarium, Gammel Kongevej 10. Newly opened with changing astronomy exhibits and an Omnimax theater.

SHOPPING. Scandinavian design is world famous, and a stroll down Copenhagen's shopping heartland, the area around Strøget, will soon make clear the high quality (and correspondingly high prices) of Danish furs, glassware, silver, sweaters and children's toys. To get an idea of local goods and prices, browse first in department stores like *Daells Varehus,* which carries a reasonably priced assortment of Danish and foreign goods and only accepts cash. For Danish goods at lower than center city prices, try the stores and shopping centers outside Copenhagen.

In town, be sure to visit *Den Permanente,* Vesterbrogade 8, and *Illums Bolighus* for superb displays of Danish design and lay-out; browsers welcome. *Magasin* on Kongens Nytorv, and *Illum* on Strøget are big stores with huge selections. The famous Danish porcelain is on display at *The Royal Copenhagen Shop* and *Bing* and *Grondahl,* both on Strøget have "seconds" at reduced prices and offer tours of their factories free of charge.

The National Museum sells reproductions of Danish art objects.

If you do not want to go far from the city center, try *Vesterbro* and *Norrebro* for everything from shoes to meat. Prices are low. Look for the sign "Tax Free for Tourists" which offers savings of 18.2% for visitors from outside EC countries.

Flea markets are also popular. From May to Sept. at Israels Plads, Sat. 8 A.M.– 2 P.M.

USEFUL ADDRESSES. *American Embassy* Dag Hammarskjöldallé 24 (tel. 31– 423144); *British Embassy* Kastelsvej 36–40 (tel. 31–264600); *Canadian Embassy* Kristen Bernikowsgade 1 (tel. 33–122299); *Tourist Information* H.C. Andersens Boulevard 22 (opposite city hall) (tel. 33–111325).

The Danish Countryside

There are several good reasons for looking at Denmark outside Copenhagen. It is different—and it is cheaper. Copenhagen has lively entertainment and a fast lifestyle—like many European capitals—but lifestyles in the Danish countryside are unlike anywhere else.

The Danish farmer has always played a major role in the national economy. The Danes claim that being a small country has contributed to their relaxed way of life, which is especially prevalent in the countryside. Thousands of tourists, as well as the Danes themselves, enjoy the Danish countryside each year and the 7,500 km. (4,600 miles) of beaches.

Heavily laden orchards and rich farmland make Funen "the garden of Denmark", and it is also the area for castles and manor houses (many now turned into hotels). Its main city, Odense, which celebrated its 1,000th anniversary in 1988, is the birthplace of Hans Christian Andersen. Interesting city sights in Odense are Andersen's home, the open-air museum and the town cathedral. Also do not miss mid-island Egeskov Castle with its vintage car and aircraft museum. The city museums in Svendborg and nearby Fåborg have interesting collections. To the south, Funen has two small picturesque islands: Tåsinge with the town of Troense and its 17th-century Valdemar Slot (castle), and Aerø with the town of Aerøskøbing, which has a noted museum with bottled and model ships.

Near the lake district, Jutland's 1,000-year-old town of Århus is Denmark's second-largest seaport. The Old Town (Den gamle By) has an open-air museum, and the 13th-century Århus Cathedral is Scandinavia's longest church. Day tours (groups only) pass lakes and wooded hills, taking tourists to the museums of Silkeborg, to Skanderborg with its country views, and Øm Monastery.

Randers has a medieval character and visitors can walk the narrow streets and admire the old building which now houses the Tourist Information Office, where resident storks nest on the roof. Outside Randers are the manor houses of Clausholm and Rosenholm, and also the delightful market town of Mariager renowned for its rose-filled gardens. Ribe, 10 kms. from the ferry terminal at Esbjerg, is Denmark's oldest town and still retains a medieval atmosphere. From May to September a night-watchman tours the town singing traditional songs and giving details of history (in English) nightly at 10 P.M

PRACTICAL INFORMATION FOR ODENSE, ÅRHUS AND AALBORG

Hotels and Restaurants

Odense. *Missionshotellet Ansgar* (M), Østre Stationsvej 32, DK-5000 Odense (tel. 66–119693). Centrally located. Pleasant, clean rooms at reasonable prices. *Motel Odense* (M), Hunderupgade 2, DK-5230 Odense M (tel. 66–114213). An old farm converted into a popular motel with good facilities. Situated on the ringroad around Odense. *Ansgarhus Motel* (I), Kirkegårds Alle 17–19, DK-5000 Odense (tel. 66–128800). Only a few rooms with toilet and very limited facilities. *Hotel Fangelkro* (I), Fangelvej 55, Fangel, DK-5260 Odense S (tel. 65–961011). Small hotel situated a little outside the town, but very cheap and with reasonable facilities. *Kahema* (I), Dronningensgade 5, DK-5000 Odense (tel. 66–122821). Small hotel with limited facilities. *Ydes Hotel* (I), Hans Tausensgade 11, DK-5000 Odense (tel. 66–121131). Centrally located. Restaurant and sauna.

Restaurants. *Den gamle Kro* (M), Overgade 23. Cozy and old-fashioned. *Klods Hans* (M), Vindegade 76. Pub-like. *Sortebro Kro* (M), Den Fynske Landsby. Old-fashioned inn. *China House* (I), Vestergade 1. Chinese food. *Grand Café* (I), St. Gråbrødrestraede. Light snacks only. *Målet* (I), Jernbanegade 17. Sports club decor; hearty sausages.

Århus. *Ansgar Missions Hotel* (M), Banegårdspladsen 14, DK-8100 Århus (tel. 86–124122). Centrally located just opposite the railway station. Good value for money. *Hotel Ritz* (M), Banegårdspladsen 12 (tel. 86–134444). Next to the *Ansgar*. *Motel La Tour* (M), Randersvej 139, DK-8200 Århus N (tel. 86–167888). Situated a little north of Århus. All rooms have bath and toilet. Restaurant. *Eriksens Hotel* (I), Banegårdsgade 6–8, DK-8000 Århus C (tel. 86–136296). Centrally located. Restaurant. *Hotel Windsor* (I), Skolebakken 17 (tel. 86–122300). Restaurant, but few other facilities. *Park Hotel* (I), Sonder Alle 3, DK-8000 Århus C (tel. 86–123231). Small hotel with limited facilities.

Restaurants. *Borsen* (M), Mindebrogade 2. Excellent food at reasonable prices. *Den Gronne Gren* (M), Vestergade 7. Vegetarian; cool green decor. *Jacob's Bar B.Q.* (M), Vestergade 3. Open charcoal barbecue. *Raadhus Kafeen* (M), Sønderallé 3. Cozy place, Danish food. *Simonsens Have* (I), in the Old Town. Healthy food; cheerful atmosphere.

Aalborg. *Hotel Ansgar* (M), Prinsensgade 14, DK-9000 Aalborg (tel. 98–133733). Centrally located. Restaurant. *Missionshotellet Krogen* (M), Skibstedsvej 4, Hasseris, DK-9000 Aalborg (tel. 98–121705). Situated a little outside the center and rather small. *Hotel Scheelsminde* (M), Scheelsmindevej 35, DK-9100 Aalborg (tel. 98–183233). Popular hotel with own restaurant. All rooms have bath and toilet. *Missionshotellet Krogen* (I), Skibstedsvej 4, Hasseris, DK-9000 Aalborg (tel. 98–121705). A bit outside the center; small. *Turist-Hotel* (I), Prinsensgade 36, DK-9000 Aalborg (tel. 98–132200). 10 rooms with bath/shower.

Restaurants. *Den lille Kro* (M), Kastetvej 118. Danish food. *Fyrtojet* (M), Jomfru Ane Gade 19. *Stygge Krumpen* (M), Vesteraa 1. Old-fashioned cooking. *Glashuset* (I), Bispensgade 18. Cafeteria. *Rio Bravo* (I), Østeraagade 27. Western saloon.

Skagen

If you want a taste of real Danish summer holiday life, try Skagen at the top of Jutland. Skagen is the traditional holiday resort for a lot of Danes. At the turn of the century several Danish painters and other artists settled down in this little fishing hamlet. It is still an artists' colony and a rather fashionable resort.

PRACTICAL INFORMATION FOR SKAGEN

Hotels

Hotel Skage (M), Gl. Landevej 39 (tel. 98–442233) clean and comfortable. *Ruths Hotel* (M), Chr Ruthsvej, DK-9990 Skagen (tel. 98–441124). Open Mar. through Oct. *Badepension Marienlund* (I), Fabriciusvej 8, DK-9990 Skagen (tel. 98–441320). 23 rooms; simple. *Inger* (I), 17 Hulsigvej, DK-9990 Skagen. 190 rooms; closed Nov. *Somandshjem* (I), Østre Strandvej 2, DK-9990 Skagen (tel. 98–442110). *Strandly Skagen* (I), Østre Strandvej 35, DK-9990 Skagen (tel. 98–441131).

Finland

Among Finland's particular attributes are lovely scenery, pure air, fine architecture, an intelligent and creative people, an abundance of glorious space, and summer sunshine up to 24 hours long. If you hate forests and water, keep well away from it for there are nearly 200,000 lakes, thousands of islands, and over 70% of the land is covered by forests! It's mostly low-lying countryside, broken by lines of ridges formed in the last Ice Age, with higher ground increasing toward the north and reaching its highest point in the fells of Finnish Lapland—Haltia at 1,325 meters (4,350 feet).

About a third of the land lies north of the Arctic Circle. Most of the country's population of about 4,900,000 live in the southern half in towns where industry, mainly based on forest resources or metalworking, flourishes in idyllic rural settings. These are clean, modern towns with fine examples of that modern architecture for which Finland has earned world fame. The resorts are tucked away among the lakes and forests, too, or along the blessedly uncrowded coast where there is good bathing from smooth shoulders of Finland's bedrock granite or sandy beaches that reach enormous proportions in the little known west. It's marvelous country for outdoor activities such as swimming, boating, fishing, walking, canoeing, and one of the best ways of experiencing it is to rent one of the many cottages available for hire. The more sophisticated holiday villages can be expensive, but there are any number of simple cottages where you may have to draw water or hew your own wood, and where the setting will be every bit as lovely as that enjoyed by the grandest hotel. A lively cultural life is reflected in a series of festivals in different centers throughout summer.

You should also try that Finnish specialty, the sauna, which has now spread to many other countries but is rarely matched elsewhere. The small wooden sauna house by lake, sea or river shore is an intrinsic part of the Finnish scene and the interludes of relaxation overlooking the view, between and after sessions in the sauna, provide memorable moments.

The Finnish passion for freedom matches that of its great open spaces. Linked with Sweden for six and a half centuries and under Czarist Russia for a century, Finland proclaimed her independence in 1917. Conflicts with her giant eastern neighbor in World War II lost her valuable territory and left her with crippling war reparations that were paid off with dogged determination. Today, Finland has created for itself one of the highest standards of living in the world.

The Finns are basically reserved but will go to endless trouble if approached for help. Their attractive language is related to Estonian and Hungarian (Swedish is a second official language), but English is widely spoken.

PRACTICAL INFORMATION FOR FINLAND

WHAT WILL IT COST. The cost of living is high, but the less expensive facilities—camp sites, hostels, simple cottages for self-catering—are invariably situated in a setting every bit as lovely as the most luxurious hotel. You can eat at reasonable prices, if not cheaply, if you go to the right places, and there is a variety of special travel tickets that are particularly advantageous if you intend to travel widely.

The monetary unit is the *markka* (Fmk.) which is divided into 100 *penniä*. The rate of exchange at the time of writing was 6.62 Fmk. to the pound sterling, 4.10 Fmk. to the U.S. dollar. Banks give the best rate.

Sample Costs. Cinema seat from 25 Fmk.; theater seat (moderate) from 100 Fmk.; museum entrance 2–10 Fmk.; coffee in snack bar 5–6 Fmk.; beer (mild) in café 9 Fmk.; beer (medium) in Moderate restaurant 13.50 Fmk.; bottle of wine in Moderate restaurant from 90 Fmk.

NATIONAL TOURIST OFFICE. The *Finnish Tourist Board* dispenses information on all aspects of tourism through its offices overseas, which also issue lists of tour operators marketing holidays of all kinds in Finland. A reasonable percentage of these feature inexpensive accommodation, camping trips and outdoor activities. In Helsinki, information is available from the City Tourist Office, Pohjoisesplanadi 19; or (for all Finland) Tourist Information, Unioninkatu 26, or through travel agents. Students will find help from the Finnish Student Travel Service, Travela, Mannerheimintie 5. There is a tourist office in every town and tourist center.

Overseas addresses are:

In the U.S.: 655 Third Ave., New York, N.Y. 10017 (tel. 212–949–2333).

In Canada: 1200 Bay St., Suite 604, Toronto, Ontario M5R 2A5 (tel. 416–964–9159).

In the U.K.: 66–68 Haymarket, London SW1Y 4RF (tel. 071–839 4048).

WHEN TO COME. From mid-June to mid-August is the warmest period, with daylight up to 24 hours long in the far north. This is the period, too, when facilities for outdoor summer activities and regular boat services on the lake systems are in full swing. Spring is fresh and green; fall, from early September in the far north, produces fabulous coloring. There's good skiing throughout the winter, and this activity reaches its peak in March, when the days are longer and often sunny. Helsinki can be at its best in May. In recent years, following the worldwide trend, Finland has been enjoying much warmer temperatures in all seasons.

Average afternoon temperatures in degrees Fahrenheit and centigrade:

Helsinki	Jan.	Feb.	Mar.	Apr.	May	June	July	Aug.	Sept.	Oct.	Nov.	Dec.
F°	27	27	32	43	55	63	71	66	57	45	37	31
C°	-3	-3	0	6	13	17	22	19	14	7	3	-1

SPECIAL EVENTS. There are many annual events of interest (full details from the Finnish Tourist Board), of which the following are among the most important. *Vapunaatto* (Walpurgis Night) on *April 30* is a nationwide welcome to the return of spring, with an emphasis on student festivities, and is followed by *Vappu* (May Day) Labor Day celebrations on *May 1*. Midsummer Eve (Juhannus)is celebrated during the weekend closest to *June 24,* with bonfires throughout the country. In *June,* too, are held the Vaasa Summer, Kuopio Dance and Music Festival, the Naantali Music Festival. The Jyväskylä Arts Festival (different theme each year) begins end of *June.* The Savonlinna Opera Festival, Pori Jazz Festival, Kuhmo Chamber Music Festival and Kaustinen Folk Music Festival are all in *July.* They are followed in *August* by the Turku Music Festival, Lahti Organ Festival and Tampere Theater Summer. The Helsinki Festival, a major event offering two weeks of music and drama of all kinds, begins late *August.*

National Holidays. Jan. 1 (New Year's Day); Jan. 12 (Epiphany); Mar. 29–April 1 (Easter); Apr. 30 (May Day Eve); May 1 (May Day); May 9 (Ascension); May 18–19 (Pentecost); June 21, 22 (Midsummer's Eve and Day); Nov. 2 (All Saints'); Dec. 6 (Independence); Dec. 24–26 (Christmas).

VISAS. Nationals of the U.S., Canada, Australia, New Zealand, E.C. countries and almost all other European countries do not require visas for entry into Finland. However, they do require a valid passport.

HEALTH CERTIFICATES. Not required for entry into Finland from any country. There are strict rules governing the entry of pets into Scandinavia (including a four-month quarantine for most animals).

GETTING TO FINLAND. By Plane. *Finnair,* the national carrier, has direct flights from Helsinki to New York, Montreal, Seattle and Los Angeles. Otherwise you get there by flying to London and onwards by *British Airways* or Finnair; or to Copenhagen, Frankfurt, Amsterdam or Paris and thence by intra-European services.

From London both Finnair and British Airways fly daily.

By Train. From western Europe there is a choice, the best way being by rail to Travemünde (near Lübeck) in West Germany and thence by the fast *Finnjet* ferry to Helsinki. This takes approximately 23 hours in the summer (slower in winter). Train connections to Travemünde from Hamburg are excellent with eleven each way daily, taking about 75 minutes for the run. Hamburg is easily reached by rail from Hook of Holland, Amsterdam, Oostende and all main cities in Germany.

An alternative route (suitable for those holding the various runabout European rail passes) is as follows—from London (Liverpool St.) take the morning (dep. approx. 9.40 A.M.) boat train to Harwich, day boat to the Hook of Holland then the *Nord West Express* to Copenhagen, change trains (excellent connection) and on to Stockholm arriving there late afternoon of the following day. You can take the overnight ferry either direct to Helsinki or to Turku in western Finland arriving the following morning. Total traveling time from London about 48 hours. Another route is by *DFDS* Seaways Harwich–Gothenburg, then bus to Stockholm and *Silja Line* to Turku or Helsinki. An extensive network of modern ferries, all offering drive-on facilities, links Sweden and Finland. Unfortunately it is no longer possible to travel right through by passenger train to Finland. The cross border section from Haparanda to Kemi is now operated by bus. However the journey from Stockholm to Helsinki via northern Sweden can still be made by the intrepid traveller on foot or by plane, car, or bus.

CUSTOMS. All travelers entering the country may bring in up to 1,500 Fmk., which may include foodstuffs up to 15 kg. (33 lb.), inclusive of 5 kg. (11 lb.) of edible fats; however not more than 2.5 kg. (5.5 lb.) of butter. Also, 200 cigarettes or 250 grams (8.8 ounces) of other tobacco products (double for residents over age 16 of non-European countries), and, for travelers aged 20 years and over, 1 liter of spirits, 2 liters beer and 1 liter of other mild alcoholic drinks.

HOTELS. A free list of all hotels in Finland is available from the Finnish Tourist Board and this gives considerable detail of the amenities offered by each, as well as indicating those providing full board. There is no official hotel grading system, however, and the following is an indication of price range rather than of standards, which, generally speaking, are very high. A *Finncheque* system (150 Fmk. per person per day in a double room) is valid June through August in many hotels in three categories, in the lowest of which (equivalent to Moderate) covers accommodation, breakfast and a self-service or packed lunch.

For accommodations for two in a double room, approximate prices in Helsinki and main centers are: Moderate (M) 330–550 Fmk.; Inexpensive (I), under 330 Fmk. Elsewhere count 15–25% less. Note that many hotels have family rooms at lower rates per person, or will put in an extra bed at a moderate charge. A recently introduced form of bed and breakfast accommodations brings costs down to 80–140 Fmk. per person (details from Lomarengas, Museokatu, 3, Helsinki). For private rooms, local tourist offices can advise. Simple cottages for self catering are available, as opposed to the more sophisticated amenities of fully equipped holiday villages. A free Finnish Tourist Board leaflet lists booking centers. Another free leaflet details Farm Holidays with reasonable half or full board rates.

Youth and Family Hostels. These are open to all ages and to motorists. Many have self-service kitchens and some sell refreshments. They are divided into four categories, with overnight rates ranging from 30–150 Fmk. (Additional charge if you are not a member of your national youth hostel association.) It's advisable to carry your own washable sleeping sheet (sleeping bags may not be used), for they are quite expensive to hire. Ask for the map-brochure and "Finland for Hostellers" brochure from the Finnish Tourist Board.

Camping. The free *Camping* booklet from the Finnish Tourist Board lists many of the 350 camp sites that are classified into three grades with prices ranging from 25–60 Fmk. per night for two adults, children, car, tent or trailer. You can stay at Ratsila near Helsinki for 40 Fmk, for example (prices are according to number of stars given in Finland Camping Guide). If you don't hold an international camping card, you will need to buy a National Camping Card (10 Fmk.), valid for the whole year. Many sites offer inexpensive cottages for hire. Finncamping Checks, valid May 15 to Sept. 15, are accepted by over 200 sites belonging to the Finnish Travel Association, but are only available as part of a package (e.g. inc. transportation). Details from the Finnish Tourist Board.

RESTAURANTS. Taking into account Finland's cost of living and high standards, you can get a good meal at a reasonable price especially if you stick to *table d'hôte* menus served between fixed times, which are usually fairly early, particularly in more Moderate establishments. The number of pleasant snack bars for quick and inexpensive refreshments has increased enormously in recent years. In the restaurant listings in this chapter, the following approximate prices apply for *table d'hôte* meals, per person: Moderate (M) 50–80 Fmk.; Inexpensive (I) 25–50 Fmk.

Food and Drink. You will meet Swedish *smörsgåsbord* (Finnish *voileipäpöytä*) with local variations in many restaurants, usually at lunch time, and no one will be surprised if you return for two or three helpings. Thick, nourishing soups are popular, with pea soup *(hernekeitto)* and fish soup *(kalakeitto)* the most popular of all. There is a good variety of fish, from expensive salmon to the versatile perch-pike, with the Baltic herring and the succulent crayfish, for which there is a special two-month summer season, featuring prominently in innumerable forms. Among the leading meat dishes are Karelian hotpot *(karjalanpaisti)*, a mélange of different meats; mutton with dill sauce *(tillilammas)*, meat balls *(lihapyörykät)* served with cream sauce and lingonberry jam. There are also many reindeer meat and game dishes, but these tend to be more expensive. *Karjalanpiirakka*, a rice-filled pasty, makes a nourishing snack.

Spirits are expensive, imported ones extremely so. Imported wines bottled in Finland are more reasonable, but it is better to stick to the excellent beers, milk (very popular at lunch time) and the ever-available coffee, which is usually strong, black or with cream.

TIPPING. The hotel service charge of 15% takes care of everything. The 14% service charge in restaurants (15% at weekends and public holidays) is usually sufficient, though you may want to leave a few extra coins. 5 Fmk. fee per bag to railway porters (when you can find them); usually 5 Fmk. to restaurant doormen or cloak-room attendants who are by no means limited to the more expensive restaurants. Taxi drivers, theater ushers, hairdressers, are not tipped. A general guideline is that you can tip for good service, but it is not expected. When you do, 5 Fmk. is the norm.

MAIL. Airmail letters to the U.S. 3 Fmk.; to the U.K. and rest of Europe 2.50 Fmk.; postcards to the U.S., U.K. and rest of Europe 2.50 Fmk. (Lower rates within Scandinavia.) There will probably be a slight price increase by early 1991.

CLOSING TIMES. Shops open from 8.30 or 9 to 5 or 6 (in some cases to 8 on weekdays); Saturday they close at 1 or 2. In the subway by Helsinki rail station, shops of all kinds remain open until 10 P.M. including Sundays and, in summer, some other shops open for a few hours on Sundays. Banks open Monday through Friday, 9:15–4:15, and are closed Saturdays. Additional exchange facilities are available at Helsinki railway station and airport seven days a week.

GETTING AROUND FINLAND. By Plane. Finnair operates an excellent network of services including the far north of Lapland. Helsinki is the radiating point for most of these although many services link other cities, e.g. Turku to Rovaniemi in Lapland. Domestic fares are among the lowest in Europe. Reductions of 50% for young people (between 12 and 23) and pensioners (65 years and over) apply on most flights except on weekend and public holidays. The special Finnair Holiday Ticket giving unlimited travel for 15 days costs U.S. $250. For 12–23 year olds there is the Finnair Youth Holiday Ticket at $200. Watch for "red" summer days, when fares to many popular destinations drop enormously.

By Train. Although it is sparsely populated, Finland has a very good and extensive railway system reaching all main centers of the country. Tickets that combine rail, bus and ferry travel are available and offer a discount if you can plan your itinerary in advance. A *Finnrail Pass* gives unlimited travel for eight, 15 or 22 days, costing in 2nd class $90, $145, $181, respectively. Finland is also a partner in the *Nordtourist Ticket* scheme, valid 21 days for unlimited travel throughout Scandinavia. The *Eurail Youth Pass, Inter Rail Ticket* and *Rail Europe S-card* are valid on Finnish Railways; reductions on journeys of at least 76 km. also apply to over-65s who should buy a special card (50 Fmk.) from any railway station. The card entitles holders to a 50% discount.

By Car. The main road network is excellent, except for a few rough sections in the far north. Some secondary roads may be temporarily closed during the spring thaw. Seat belts for all car passengers, and crash helmets for motorcyclists, are compulsory, as is the use of headlights outside built-up areas, at all times regardless of weather conditions. Note the strict laws regarding drinking and driving; penalties are severe.

By Bus. Bus travel plays a leading role and in remoter areas, including nearly all Lapland, is the only means of public transport. Costs are slightly lower than by rail. A Coach Holiday Ticket (280 Fmk.) entitles you to 1,000 km. of travel within two weeks. "65 tickets," for those aged 65 years and over, are available at 25 Fmk. (photograph needed) from coach stations and give a 30% reduction on journeys over 75 km. Reductions also apply to family groups.

By Bicycle. This is becoming increasingly popular. Several regions, including the Helsinki area, have marked cycling routes and cycles available for hire. The Finnish Tourist Board or local tourist offices can give addresses. In Helsinki, bicycles can be rented from the youth hostel at the Olympic Stadium for 35 Fmk. per day.

By Boat. In summer, there are regular services through some of the lake systems on which you can travel for a few hours or two or three days, sleeping on board or in port and picking up another boat another day. Regular services, year round, also link Turku or Naantali in the southwest with the Åland Islands. Boats can be hired in many places.

Helsinki

The heart of the town is the dignified Senate Square, designed in the 1820s and 1830s by the German-born architect, Carl Ludvig Engel, and his Finnish partner Johan Albrekt Ehrenström. Between them, they replanned the town, which had been devastated by fire in 1808 and which then in 1812 became Finland's capital. Here stand the cathedral, the State Council building, and the University Library (Engel's masterpiece), a group of majestic buildings composed in a pure classic style that certainly presaged the well-known work of such later Finnish architects as Eliel Saarinen and Alvar Aalto. In one corner is one of the new shopping quarters, Senaatti Center.

Engel also designed the nearby Town Hall in the Market Square, down by the South Harbor. The best time to see the latter is before noon when the flower and fruit sellers are grouped around the fountain of Havis Amanda, the sea maiden who represents Helsinki rising from the waves. In summer the market reopens again at 3.30 P.M. and closes at 8; adjoining it is the renovated Kauppahalli (market hall) with dozens of fresh meat, cheese, and delicatessen stalls and a café (weekdays 8–5, Sat. 8–2). Notice the obelisk, known as the Empress Stone, which commemorates the 1833 visit to Helsinki of Czar Nicholas I and his consort Alexandra Feodorovna. The building along the edge of the square, facing the sea and patrolled by a sentry in field gray, is the President's Palace. Summer-through, the South Harbor buzzes with activity: yachts, sightseeing boats, ferries to the islands and the huge car ferries docking from Sweden and North Germany.

From this area, the parallel thoroughfares of Esplanadi and Aleksanterinkatu run west into the main shopping districts, leading to Mannerheimintie, Helsinki's main artery leading north. Just off Aleksanterinkatu and Mannerheimintie is Railway Square, with the imposing main railway station designed by Eliel Saarinen, the newly re-opened Ateneum Art Gallery with its collections of foreign and Finnish art including the sculptures of Wäinö Aaltonen, and the National Theater. The main Post Office is next to the station on the corner of Mannerheimintie and near there is the shopping precinct of Kaivopiha, linked with the railway station and the city's new metro (underground) network. It's only a short stroll up Mannerheimintie from the Post Office to the impressive, red granite Parliament building with its massive columns, and the National Museum with its church-like tower. Further north up Mannerheimintie you reach the Olympic Stadium, two kilometers (1 ⅓ miles) from the city center, from whose slender tower are fine views of the city.

Some good examples of Finland's famous modern architecture include the magnificent Finlandia House Concert Hall and Congress Center, designed by Alvar Aalto, near the National Museum (Finland's House will close for renovation in spring 1992, so try to see it in '91); the City Theater, Eläintarhantie; the extraordinary Dipoli Hall at the engineers' suburb of Otaniemi; and the whole of the satellite town of Tapiola. One of Europe's most unusual churches is that of Temppeliaukio, built into the subterranean rock in Töölö, one of the older residential districts of the city.

Three highly recommended outdoor attractions are the Botanical Gardens and their Water Tower, if you want another splendid panorama; Linnanmäki, close to the water tower, Helsinki's permanent amusement park; and the Open-air Museum of Seurasaari.

You will also enjoy the island fortress of Suomenlinna, which has been developed as a cultural and recreational center. Begun in 1748 this "Gibraltar of the North" was never taken by assault. The surrounding parks and gardens are lovely in spring and summer, and there is a summer café in an old sailing ship. Good bathing facilities and a sandy beach are here too. There is a frequent ferry service from the South Harbor marketplace.

Indeed, Helsinki's many islands offer a wealth of attractions, including the zoo (Korkeasaari), restaurants, sailing clubs and bathing beaches.

PRACTICAL INFORMATION FOR HELSINKI

HOTELS. The central accommodation booking service in the railway station is open mid–May to mid–Dec., Mon.-Fri. 9–9, Sat. 9–7, Sun. 10–6; the rest of the year Mon.-Fri. 9–6. The booking charge is 15 Fmk. Most hotels have saunas, and restaurants are licensed unless otherwise stated.

Moderate

Anna, Annankatu 1 (tel. 648011). 58 rooms, cafeteria. Small, nicely renovated, in center.

Haaga, Nuijamiestentie 10 (tel. 578311). 110 rooms, pool. Less central.

Helka, P.Rautatiekatu 23 (tel. 440581), 150 rooms.

Hospiz, Vuorikatu 17B (tel. 170481). 166 rooms, unlicensed restaurant.
Marttahotelli, Uudenmaankatu 24 (tel. 646211). 44 rooms, unlicensed restaurant.
Ursula, Paasivuorenkatu 1 (tel. 750311). 32 rooms, cafeteria only.

Inexpensive

Academica, Hietaniemenkatu 14 (tel. 4020206). 217 rooms, summer only, disco, pool.
Asuntohotelli Kongressikoti, Snellmaninkatu 15 (tel. 174839) 10 rooms, boarding house.
Clairet, It. Teatterikuja 3 (tel. 669707). 15 rooms, boarding house.
Dipoli Summer Hotel, Jamerantaival 1, Otaranta (tel. 435811). 244 rooms, disco, pool, sporting facilities. In Espoo district, out of town.
Erottajanpuisto, Uudenmaankatu 9 (tel. 642169). 15 rooms, boarding house.
Finn, Kalevankatu 3B (tel. 640904). 28 rooms, no restaurant.
Lönnrot, Lönnrotinkatu 16 (tel. 6932590). 26 rooms, boarding house.
Omapohja, It. Teatterikuja 3 (tel. 666211). 15 rooms, boarding house.
Pensionat Regina, Puistokatu 9 (tel. 656937). Boarding house.
Private Hotel Borg, Cygnaeuskatu 16 (tel. 499990). 4 rooms, boarding house.
Satakuntatalo, Lapinrinne 1 (tel. 6940311). 64 rooms, summer only.
Youth and Family Hostels. Olympic Stadium (year round) and Porthaninkatu 2 (summer only).
Camping. Rastila, 13 km. (8 miles) east of city center. Open May 15–Sept. 15.

RESTAURANTS. Note that fixed-price menus served between fixed hours reduce costs sharply. There is an increasing number of bright, attractive cafés *(kahvila, baari)* and snack bars for quick, inexpensive food, as well as a number of (more or less) English style pubs serving snacks.

Moderate

Kappeli, in the Esplanade gardens near South Harbor (tel. 179242). Several sections, including open-air summer restaurant.
Omenapuu, Keskuskatu 6 (tel. 630205). Family restaurant in heart of busy shopping center.
Ostrobotnia, Dagmarinkatu 2 (tel. 408602). Finnish specialties, good value.
Perho, Mechelininkatu 7 (tel. 493481). Run by Helsinki Hotel and Restaurant College, good value, recently renovated.
Robert's Bar and Saloon, Iso Roobertinkatu (tel. 6164247). Popular among the young.
Vanha Maestro, Fredrikinkatu 51–53 (tel. 644303). Popular afternoon dance restaurant.
Wellamo, Vyökatu 9 (tel. 663139). Small and intimate with rustic atmosphere; strong on garlic.

Inexpensive

Carrols, self-service hamburger restaurants at Mannerheimintie 19, in the City Passage, and at Keskuskatu 3.
Chez Marius, Mikonkatu 1 (tel. 669697). Good value French cooking. Beer and wine only.
Eliel, in the railway station (tel. 177900). Self-service.
Kellarikrouvi, P. Makasiininkatu 6 (tel. 655198). Cozy wine cellar atmosphere.
Kynsilaukka (Garlic), Fredrikinkatu 22 (tel. 651939). Their gourmet dishes are daringly dashed with garlic; rustic decor. Beer and wine only.
Rivoli, Albertinkatu 38 (tel. 643455). Italian food, good for quick lunch.
Wienerwald, Kaivokatu 6 (tel. 663589) and Lauttasaarentie 1 (tel. 677239). Part of the Austrian chain.

GETTING AROUND HELSINKI. An excellent buy is the Helsinki Card, available for 1, 2 and 3 days (65, 85, and 105 Fmk. respectively; around half price for children). It entitles you to free travel on all public transport and free entry to many museums, and reductions on sightseeing tours and in many shops, saunas, restaurants and cafés. Available from the Helsinki Tourist Office, the Hotel Booking Service in the rail station, and elsewhere.

By Subway. The first section of Helsinki's splendid new subway has recently opened; it goes from the main railway station northeast to Itäkeskus (same fare and transfer system as tram/bus below).

By Tram/Bus. A ride costs 6.50 Fmk. (58 Fmk. for 10-ride ticket), allowing transfers within a one-hour period. The 3T tram, with commentary in several languages in summer, follows a figure-eight circuit right around the city center.

By Boat. Regular ferries link the South and North Harbors with island sights, and there are sightseeing excursions by boat throughout summer.

On Foot. Ask the Helsinki City Tourist Office for its excellent free booklet, *See Helsinki on Foot.*

ENTERTAINMENT. In the summer, city dwellers tend to head for the countryside, but there is plenty of entertainment in the way of open-air theater and concert performances. The Helsinki City Tourist Office can tell you what's on and where. Alternatively, consult *Helsinki This Week* and *Helsinki Today,* both available free.

Cinema. Foreign films are shown in their original language. For information on showings of free tourist films, contact the Helsinki Tourist Office.

Discos. Young people who want to meet their Finnish counterparts can try one of the following: *Alibi,* Hietaniemenkatu 14; *The Underground,* Eerikinkatu 3; *Harald's,* Kasarmikatu 40; *Ky-Exit,* 2, Pohj. Rautatiekatu 21; *Tavastia-Klubi,* Urho Kekkosenkatu 4–6. Also check the tourist office's "Clubs and Music Bars" list, with a day-to-day breakdown, and the various Helsinki guides.

The *Foreign Student Club* (postal address PL 224, Helsinki 17) aims at bringing foreign and Finnish students into greater contact. The dates and times for local club evenings can be checked at the Foreign Students' Bulletin Board in Porthania, Hallituskatu 11–13. There is a small membership charge.

Theaters. These close in summer when open-air theaters come into their own with dramatic or folkloric performances, notably at Seurasaari and on the islands of Suomenlinna and Mustikkamaa. International variety shows are put on at the Peacock Variety Theater in Linnanmäki Amusement Park on Tivolitie-Helsinginkatu, which is a fun place to go anyway, with a moderate admission charge that includes some free open-air shows. If you are in Helsinki during the conventional theater season, the cheapest seats are in the *parvake* (balcony or back of circle).

Concerts. These are held in a number of attractive settings in summer, including the Cathedral, Temppeliaukio Church and the House of Nobility (Ritarihuone, at Ritarihuoneen puistikko); tickets at general ticket number, tel. 643043. Programs in Helsinki guides. There are open-air performances in several parks and on the island of Suomenlinna.

MUSEUMS. Opening hours vary considerably and some museums and art galleries close for one or more days each week, usually including Mondays. Entrance fees are normally between 2–10 Fmk.; some museums are free on certain days. The following are some of the more important or interesting sights.

Applied Arts Museum, Korkeavuorenkatu 23A. Finnish design—ceramics, architecture, textiles, furniture—is highlighted at this handsome museum in central Helsinki, the oldest of its kind in Scandinavia.

Ateneum Art Gallery, Kaivokatu 2–4. Foreign and Finnish paintings and sculptures. Has just undergone a massive five-year restoration.

Gallen Kallela Museum, Leppävaara, Tarvaspää, reached by tram No. 4 to Munkkiniemi, then a pleasant 2 km. (1 mile) walk. The home and works of one of Finland's greatest painters in charming surroundings.

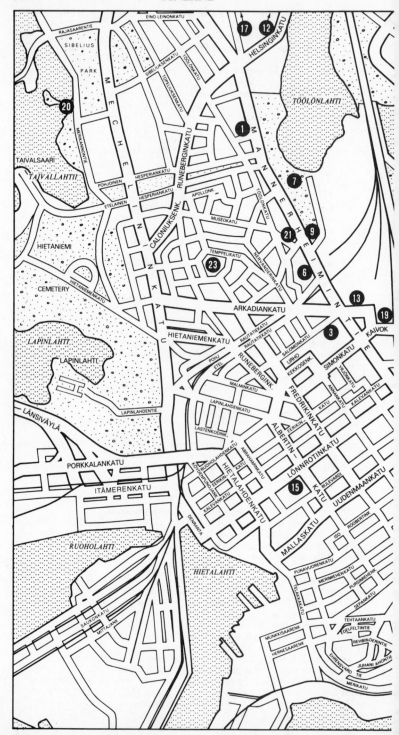

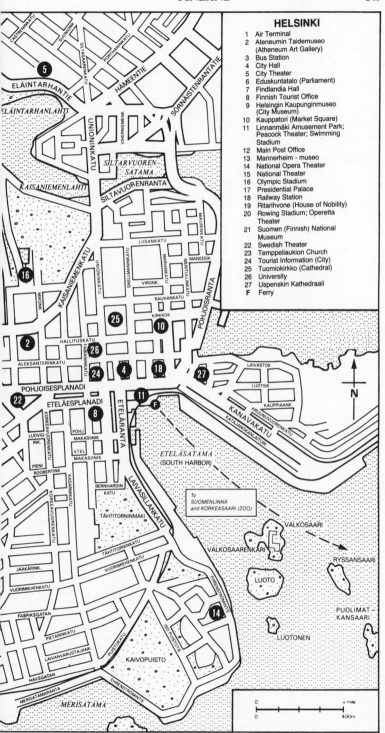

HELSINKI

1 Air Terminal
2 Ateneumin Taidemuseo (Atheneum Art Gallery)
3 Bus Station
4 City Hall
5 City Theater
6 Eduskuntatalo (Parliament)
7 Findlandia Hall
8 Finnish Tourist Office
9 Helsingin Kaupunginmuseo (City Museum)
10 Kauppatori (Market Square)
11 Linnanmäki Amusement Park; Peacock Theater; Swimming Stadium
12 Main Post Office
13 Mannerheim - museo
14 National Opera Theater
15 National Theater
16 Olympic Stadium
17 Presidential Palace
18 Railway Station
19 Ritarihvone (House of Nobility)
20 Rowing Stadium; Operetta Theater
21 Suomen (Finnish) National Museum
22 Swedish Theater
23 Temppeliaukion Church
24 Tourist Information (City)
25 Tuomiokirkko (Cathedral)
26 University
27 Uspenskin Kathedraali
F Ferry

Helsinki City Art Museum, Tamminiementie 6. Finnish and French paintings, and statuary.

Helsinki City Museum, Karamzininkatu 2, off Mannerheimintie. Illustrates the history of the city.

Heureka, at Tikkurila, Vantaa district. Brand new Finnish Science Center where science fiction becomes reality. High entrance fee, but worth it.

Korkeasaari Zoo, reached by ferry from South Harbor, or by footbridge from Mustikkamaa Island, which is accessible by road.

Mannerheim Museum, Kalliolinnantie 14, Kaivopuisto district. Home of Marshal Mannerheim, containing his collected trophies.

National Museum, Mannerheimintie 34. Three sections: prehistoric, historic, ethnographic.

Seurasaari, island linked by causeway to the city. A fine collection of old farms and manor buildings from various parts of the country.

Suomenlinna, frequent ferry service from South Harbor. Fortifications on series of islands, restored and developed into a multi-purpose center; Nordic Arts Center, museums, etc.

OUTDOOR ACTIVITIES. The tourist office can give you some good suggestions on where to ski, hike, fish, or just relax in the Helsinki area.

SHOPPING. Finland has won international fame for design of all kinds in glass, ceramics, enamelware, stainless steel, wood, jewelry, fashion goods. The huge department store of *Stockmann's* on Aleksanterinkatu sells a big selection, but look out for the many smaller specialty shops and boutiques. One large, basic department store, *Aleksi 13,* is on the corner of Aleksanterinkatu and Mikonkatu. *Hakaniemi Market Hall,* Hämeentie, with 50 shops above the covered food market, is varied and fun. So is *Hietalahti flea market,* open every morning Monday to Saturday at the southwest end of Bulevardi, a handsome wide street lined with many good stores. Remember that the shops in the subway near Helsinki railway station are open every evening until 10. Attractive new small shopping precincts are blossoming in various parts of the city—expensive but good for window shopping. The latest is Senaatti Center, near the Cathedral; another is the Forum Shopping Center on Mannerheimintie. There are now two pedestrian shopping streets, Iso Roobertinkatu (known as "Roba"), and Kluuvikatu, both worth a stroll. The shops on Esplanadi and in the Senaatti Center are open on Sundays in summer 12–4. Fredrikinkatu is a good place to find smaller stores and specialty boutiques with slightly lower prices.

USEFUL ADDRESSES. *American Embassy,* I. Puistotie 14A (tel. 171 931); *Canadian Embassy,* E. Pohjoisesplanadi 25B (tel. 171 141); *British Embassy,* Uudenmaankatu 16–20 (tel. 647 922); *Helsinki City Tourist Office,* Pohjoisesplanadi 19 (tel. 169 3757); *Tourist Information* (for all Finland), Unioninkatu 26; *Finnish Student Travel Service - Travela,* Mannerheimintie 5; *American Express,* Travek Travel Bureau, Katajanokan Pohjoisranta 9–13 (tel. 12511); *Thomas Cook,* 10A Kaivokatu (tel. 18261); *Main Post Office,.* Mannerheimintie 11 (tel. 1955 117); *Emergency hospital for foreigners,* Helsinki University Central Hospital, Haartmaninkatu 4 (tel. 4711).

Turku and the Southwest

Turku, Finland's oldest city, founded in the 13th century, and the Finnish capital until 1812, is situated on both banks of the Aura river. With a population of 165,000, it is the country's third-largest city and is sometimes called "the cradle of Finnish culture". Commercially its great importance lies in the fact that its harbor is the most easily kept open throughout the winter. In fact, the very word, *turku,* means trading post. It is also widely known for its shipyards. It has both Finnish and Swedish Universities, the new buildings of the Finnish one being well worth a visit.

Called Åbo by the Swedish-speaking Finns, Turku is the center of the southwest part of the country, whose land is fertile and winters are milder. With a cathedral over 700 years old, the city is still the seat of the Archbishop of Finland. Where the Aura river flows into the sea stands Turku Castle, the city's second most important monument. Once a prison, it has been attractively restored and now houses the Historical Museum. Turku's third major attraction is the Handicrafts Museum, a street of houses and shops that survived the 1827 fire. The comb-maker, weaver, potter and many others still ply their trades in summer, using equipment and techniques that date back a century and a half. Turku also offers some fine modern architecture and interesting museums that include those devoted to two famous Finns: Sibelius and the sculptor Wäinö Aaltonen.

Turku is a splendid launching point for some of the 30,000 islands scattered off Finland's coast. There are regular services to the delightful Åland Islands and many other nearer island and coastal destinations. The hinterland is rather rich in historical remains, especially medieval stone churches.

PRACTICAL INFORMATION FOR TURKU

Hotels and Restaurants

Most hotels have saunas and restaurants and are licensed unless otherwise stated. *Domus* (M), Piispankatu 10 (tel. 329470), cafeteria only. *Rantasipi Ikituuri Summer Hotel* (M), Pispalantie 7 (tel. 376111), pool, disco. *Turun Karina* (M), Itäinen Pitkäkatu 30b (tel. 336666), cafeteria only. *Aura* (I), Humalistonkatu 13 (tel. 311973). *Turku Youth and Family Hostel,* Linnankatu 39. There is a campsite at Saaronniemi, Ruissalo Island, 10 km. (6 miles) from city (accessible by road).

Restaurants. *Haarikka* (M), Eerikinkatu 19 (tel. 502912).*Hämeenportti* (M), Hämeenkatu 7 (tel. 315054). *Casa Mia Trattoria* (I), It. Pitkäkatu 12–14 (tel. 321243). *Foija Café* (I), Aurakatu 10 (tel. 518665). *Hiidenkolo* (I), Konstantsankatu 4 (tel. 390737). *Hiivari* (I), Käsityöläiskatu 5 (tel. 314008). *Nättinummi* (I), Ekmaninkatu 4 (tel. 484067).

Useful Addresses. *South-West Finland Travel Association,* Läntinen Rantakatu 13 (tel. 517333); *City Tourist Office,* Käsityöläiskatu 3 (tel. 336366); *Information Office,* Aurakatu 4 (tel. 315262), and *Silja Line* terminal at the harbor (tel. 303563).

The Lake Districts

Finland's nearly 200,000 lakes are scattered throughout the country, but the greatest concentration is in the center and especially the east, where Saimaa is a labyrinthine lake system through which you can travel for days without ever doubling on your tracks. It might be a good idea to adopt Savonlinna as your headquarters. It is an attractive lakeside resort also noted as a watering place and is the terminus of the Saimaa lake steamers. Some of the regular services have been trimmed recently, but those that remain, combined with the choice of lake excursions, still give plenty of opportunities for waterborne travel. The healing baths are to be found in the Casino Park. The latter is on one of the many islands, which, together with a cape jutting out into the lake, constitute the town of Savonlinna. Besides its location and its baths, Savonlinna's outstanding attraction is the fortress of Olavinlinna, Finland's finest medieval castle and one of the best-preserved historical monuments in Scandinavia.

A Danish-born knight built this fortress with the object of providing a bastion for the eastern frontier of the then kingdom of Sweden-Finland to assist in repulsing attacks and invasions from the east. During the numerous wars of the 18th century it changed hands repeatedly, but it lost its military significance when Finland became a Grand Duchy of Russia. An International Opera Festival is held here throughout July (when prices go up and accommodations are hard to find). Savonlinna has good sports facilities, too, including small boats for hire.

Near the Castle, a venerable steam schooner, the *Salama,* is part of a fascinating museum devoted to the history of lake traffic, including the floating timber trains that are still a common site on Finland's lake systems. About 20 miles away, the Retretti Art Center, partly gouged out of the living rock on Punkaharju Ridge, is well worth visiting both for its exhibitions and their setting.

Over towards the west is Finland's second city, Tampere. Almost every book, pamphlet, brochure, and guide will inform you that Tampere, the country's second-largest city, is Finland's Manchester. Many of these sources omit mention of the fact that this city combines industry with some very beautiful scenery. Artful location is the secret of Tampere's many factories. An isthmus less than 2 km. wide at its narrowest point separates the lakes Näsijärvi and Pyhäjärvi, and at one spot the Tammerkoski Rapids provide an outlet for the waters of one to cascade through to the other. Called the "Mother of Tampere", these rapids provide the power on which the town's livelihood depends. Their natural beauty has been preserved in spite of the factories on either bank, and the well-designed public buildings of the city grouped around them enhance their general effect. Also in the heart of town is Hämeensilta bridge with its four statues by the well-known sculptor Wäinö Aaltonen. An area of old warehouses near the bridge has recently been restored to provide an attractive complex of shops, studios and restaurants.

The high ridge of Pyynikki forms a natural park near the center of town, and on its top is an outlook tower commanding a view of the surrounding countryside. Not far away, the even higher, modern observation tower of Näsineula soars above the lake, forest and town, topped by a revolving restaurant. The same building houses the first planetarium in Scandinavia and a well-planned aquarium. From these towers you can fully appreciate the truly amazing contrasts between the industry humming at your feet and the quiet lakes stretching out to meet the horizon. At the foot of this Pyynikki Ridge is the Pyynikki Open-Air Theater with its revolving auditorium, which can be moved even with a full load of spectators to face any one of the sets, ready prepared by nature. The theater in Tampere is particularly lively, and there are also a number of interesting museums and some fine modern architecture and sculpture.

Two important lake routes meet at Tampere: the Silver Line motor vessels link the city to Hämeenlinna, Sibelius' birth place, to the south; and the Poet's Way leads north to Virrat.

PRACTICAL INFORMATION FOR THE LAKE DISTRICTS

Hotels and Restaurants

Savonlinna. *Pietari Kylliäinen* (M), Olavinkatu 15 (tel. 22901). *Malakias* (M), Pihlajavedenkuja 6 (tel. 23283), summer only. *Vuorinlinna Summer Hotel* (M), Kasinonsaari (tel. 24908). *Holiday Home Hirvasranta* (I), Nätki (tel. 57115). *Savonlinnan Hospits* (I), Linnankatu 20 (tel. 22443).

Camping Vuohimäki, 6 km. from town. Open summer only.

Restaurants. *Majakka* (M), Satamakatu 11 (tel. 21456). *Martina* (M), Pilkkakoskenkatu 2 (tel. 21227). *Restaurant Ship Hopeasalmi* (M), (tel. 21701). *San Martin* (M), Olavinkatu 46 (tel. 13004). *Musta Pässi* (I), Tulliportinkatu 2 (tel. 22228).

Useful Addresses. *City Tourist Office* and *Savonlinna Tourist Service Association,* Puistokatu 1 (tel. 13492).

Tampere. *Maisa* (M), Maisansalo (tel. 789700), sports resort 36 km. out of town. *Otavala* (M), Rautatienkatu 22 (tel. 38400), cafeteria only. *Domus* (I), Pellervonkatu 9 (tel. 550000), disco, pool, summer only. *Härmälä* (I), Nuolialantie 5 (tel. 650400), 4 km. from center, summer only, near camp site, sports facilities.

YWCA Youth Hostel, Tuomiokirkonkatu 12 (tel. 35900), summer only; *Uimahallin Youth and Family Hostel,* Pirkankatu 10–12 (tel. 229460). *Maisansalo Camping,* 36 km. from town; *Tampere-Camping,* Härmälä, 4 km. *Taulaniemi Camping,* Taulaniemi, 35 km.

Restaurants. *Kaijakka* (M), Laukontori 12 (tel. 123494). *Natalie* (M), Hallituskatu 19 (tel. 32040). *Oskarinhovi* (M), Itenäisyydenkatu 25 (tel. 555103). *Rapukka* (M–I), Tammelanpuistokatu (tel. 110086). *Salud* (M), Otavalankatu 10 (tel. 35996). *Silakka* (M–I), Vuolteenkatu 20 (tel. 149740). *Tillikka* (M), Hämeenkatu 16 (tel. 127209). *Antika* (I), Väinölänkatu 1 (tel. 111282). *Kantarelli* (I), Kalevanpuistotie 16 (tel. 554420). *Next Door* (I), Insinöörinkatu 23 (tel. 174436). *Pizzeria No. 1* (I), Aleksanterinkatu 31 (tel. 38887).

Useful Addresses. *City Tourist Office* and *Tampere Provincial Tourist Association,* Verkatehtaankatu 2 (tel. 126652).

Finnish Lapland

Lapland has been called Europe's last wilderness. Its horizons are huge and its silence likewise. Gradually the extensive forests of the south give way to marsh and tundra and bare-topped fells as you proceed northward from the Arctic Circle. Airplanes and trains bring you swiftly to this remote region and modern communities provide all the comforts most of us take for granted, yet you won't have to go very far to find yourself in an almost primordial solitude.

There are only some 2,500 pure Lapps still living in the province, the remainder of the population of 220,000 being Finns. A few words should be said about the Lapps (or *Same,* as they prefer to be known), a proud, sensitive, and intelligent people. Remember this is their country and they have an ancient culture, language and customs of their own. Modern influences have changed many aspects of their traditional way of life; for example, the attractive costumes are less frequently seen, except on festive occasions. The young especially have been affected by the changes, and many of them are far more interested in becoming teachers, lawyers or engineers than breeding reindeer or hunting from their remote homesteads. Yet others have found profit from selling souvenirs to the tourists.

Practically on the Arctic Circle is the "Gateway to Lapland", Rovaniemi, the administrative hub and communications center of the province where the Ounas and Kemi rivers meet. In the process of post-World War II rebuilding, Rovaniemi's population shot up from 8,000 to its present 33,000, so don't expect to arrive in a backwoods shanty town. This modern city on the edge of the wilderness comes as a surprise to most people with its excellent architecture and amenities—quite a lot of it, including the layout of the town—in the shape of a reindeer's head—the work of Alvar Aalto. Note especially Lappia Hall, the new concert and congress center that also houses the world's northernmost professional theater, and the Library, both beautifully designed by Aalto.

Quite a lot of light industry has come to Rovaniemi, too, and with all the varied amenities it has to offer, the city attracts visitors from all over the province on business or pleasure, for health or further education, or simply because it has the best selection of shops of anywhere on or north of the Arctic Circle. Among other places to visit here are the modern church with its impressive mural, and various museum collections devoted to the region.

From Rovaniemi, two main roads bore into the increasingly lonely wilderness: the Arctic Highway north to Ivalo, Inari and its huge lake and eventually the northern border with Norway, and the road heading into the northwest "arm" of Finland, where the fells are the highest and probably the loveliest. It takes time and preferably some sturdy footwork to get under the skin of Lapland, but many who go there find the lure to return irresistible. Though there are a number of long-distance marked trails, you should never set out into the wilderness alone unless you are experienced and properly equipped. Always follow local advice, tell someone in which direction you are going and when you expect to be back. Take some insect repellent; the mosquitoes in high summer can be diabolical. The inns in the area take full advantage of their settings. Many are made up of groupings of log cabins with huge picture windows and fireplaces. Their menus may include reindeer, elk, and many wild berry dishes.

An invaluable source of information on all aspects of travel in Finnish Lapland is Lapland Travel, Maakuntakatu 10, Rovaniemi.

PRACTICAL INFORMATION FOR LAPLAND

Hotels and Restaurants

Inari. Village by the large lake of Inari and an excellent center for excursions in north Lapland. *Kultahovi* (M), (tel. 51221), lovely riverside location. Many holiday cottages in the area.

Rovaniemi. *Aakenus* (M), Koskikatu 47 (tel. 22051). *Lapinportti* (M), Pohjolankatu 19 (tel. 22555), pool. *Oppipoika* (M), Korkalonkatu 33 (tel. 20321), pool, owned by Hotel School. *Ammattioppilaitoksen Kesähotelli* (I), Kairatie 75 (tel. 392651), also run by Hotel School, cafeteria only, summer only. *Rovaniemi* (I), Koskikatu 27 (tel. 22066).

City Youth and Family Hostel, Hallituskatu 16. There is camping at *Ounaskoski,* near town center; *Ounasvaara,* skiing stadium.

Restaurants. *Lapinpoika* (M), Ruokasenkatu 2 (tel. 16890), excellent cold table, intimate atmosphere. *Pinja* (M), Valtakatu 19 (tel. 14272). *Sampo* (M), Korkalonkatu 32 (tel. 312574). *Giovanni* (I), Valtakatu 34 (tel. 16406). *Lapinpaula* (I), Hallituskatu 24 (tel. 15838). *Oppipoika* (M), Korkalonkatu 33 (tel. 20321), home base of the gourmet Lappland À La Carte program. *Ristorante Martina Café* (I), Korkalonkatu 27 (tel. 313285).

Useful Addresses. *City Tourist Office,* Aallonkatu 1 (tel. 16270 or 322 2279) and at the Railway Station (summer only), tel. 22218.

Saariselkä. Hiking center for fabulous wilderness area near the Arctic Highway, with expanding accommodations and sports facilities. Hotels are mostly expensive, but have some lower-priced rooms, and there are cottages for hire.

France

Few visitors to Europe want to miss out on France. This fascinating country has so much to offer that is special, even in these days when instant communications and mass travel have ironed out national differences and made one city, one airport and one seaside resort much like another. For centuries France was the trendsetter of Europe, indeed of the world, her language spoken wherever civilized people met, her fashions copied, her writers revered; artists flocked to Paris for inspiration, intellectuals gathered to discuss the world's problems.

Things may have changed now. Yet one thing is the same. France is still a mecca for tourists the world over. She has retained her reputation as the gastronomic center of the world, and the individuality that is so much a part of the French character has survived to give a distinctive flavor that is recognized by all visitors. There is still an amazingly wide variety of different regions, so that traveling is bound to be a rewarding experience.

Though an expensive country in some respects, and, in Paris and the Riviera, with two of the most expensive regions of Europe to her name, France remains excellent value for money, even with a weakened dollar. But we have anyway included a wide range of tips to ensure that your visit is not spoiled by worries about dwindling funds. And you will find that the tourist authorities are increasingly aware that they must provide for those who want to camp or stay in modest family hotels; who will travel by public transport or bicycle rather than luxury coaches; who cannot afford three-star restaurants but still want to enjoy genuine French cuisine. This new attitude is a godsend for budgeteers. Of course you must still be careful, and above all you must plan ahead, especially if you are traveling in the crowded summer months, when budget accommodations are in demand from French families as well as foreign visitors.

What should you look out for that you will not find elsewhere in Europe? The way of life in country districts has changed remarkably little. You will find craftsmen still producing beautiful goods uninfluenced by mass consumer tastes. You will come across sleepy little hotels where service is still important. You will eat in modest restaurants where the food is prepared with loving care and artistry. The French do not like to hurry their meals. Eating, even at the most inexpensive level, is an experience to be savored. You will find that in country districts and small towns where the pace of life is slower the local people will be kind and welcoming. The nation's reputation for xenophobia has been earned by the harassed citizens of Paris with their big-city mentality, but as in other countries attitudes differ outside the large metropolitan areas.

You will also be delighted with the variety of scenery. You can stay in the mountains or by the sea; choose the dramatic granite cliffs of Brittany or the sun-soaked beaches of the south; and escape from city stresses in the lavender-covered hills of Provence, the lush pastureland of Normandy or the sleepy villages of the southwest. Last, but definitely not least, France offers a wealth of historic and art treasures, from imposing castles to remote Romanesque churches, from some of the world's finest museums to tiny local galleries with little-known works of art. Only Italy can rival France in this respect.

Having decided to visit France, how do you do it without spending a fortune? One solution is to buy an all-in package. Most British travel agents offer good-value French holidays including ferry or hovercraft crossing and accommodations in small hotels or self-catering apartments or cottages. The ferry companies, too, have a wide choice of package deals. Both of these can be combined with the lowest transatlantic air fares. Remember that by traveling out of the high season (July to mid-September) you can benefit from some really low bargain offers, including winter weekends where the all-in rate will turn out to be little more than the normal ferry costs. The *gîte* formula is now well-known and every region of France can provide lists of places where you can enjoy self-catering holidays. Gîtes vary a great deal in size and quality. If you have read about people who have stayed in a palatial wing of a château—and it can happen—you may be disappointed when your gîte turns out to be a modest cottage. As always with budget traveling it is crucial to plan ahead and see exactly what you are getting for your money. Incidentally, gîte owners normally supply a photograph.

France is now well endowed with tourist offices (2,880 throughout the country) and even the sleepiest towns and villages often have one. Look for the letters SI, standing for *Syndicat d'Initiative*, or OT, for *Office de Tourisme*; alternative names are *Maison de Tourisme* or *Pavillon de Tourisme*. The smaller ones are usually manned by helpful volunteers who know their area intimately but will not necessarily be able to help you with information concerning places or sights outside their immediate area. The larger ones are crammed with leaflets covering the whole region and can sometimes help you with plans for moving on to a different part of the country. Medium-sized towns or large villages near tourist centers usually have a card index of local families who are willing to put up guests on a bed-and-breakfast basis. The French refer to this system as *chambres d'hôte*. The accommodations will vary enormously, from a room in the local manor house to a remote farm cottage, but the prices will be reasonable and you will have a great opportunity to meet and talk to French families. Most people offering such rooms will have at least a smattering of English, but you will obviously find it more interesting if you can speak a little of their language.

Farm holidays are becoming increasingly popular and camping has, of course, long been a budget possibility. All tourist offices will now supply you with lists of local camp and trailer sites. But we cannot emphasize enough the need to steer clear of the peak summer period. In spite of attempts at government level to persuade the French to stagger their holidays, virtually the whole nation is on holiday between Bastille Day on July 14 and Assumption Day on August 15, and you will find camp and trailer sites bursting at the seams then. Trains and roads will also be unpleasantly overcrowded.

Whether you are traveling independently or on a package tour, the final golden rule is—do as the French do. Before selecting a restaurant linger a while to see where the locals are eating; it will be much better value than one frequented solely by foreign tourists. If you are self-catering, try out local products and local dishes rather than buying expensive imported goods. Do not complain about the plumbing in modest hotels: think French and concentrate instead on the excellent meals so many of them provide. Picnic or eat proper meals: do not waste your precious funds on indifferent snacks. That way you will discover that France really can be a budget vacationer's paradise.

PRACTICAL INFORMATION FOR FRANCE

WHAT WILL IT COST. France is one of the more expensive countries in Europe. However, it is such a varied country that you can spend a pleasant vacation here without breaking the bank if you plan carefully, and pick those areas and cities that have not become over-priced because of an influx of jetsetting tourists. Even in Paris you can manage on surprisingly little if you follow our budget hints and steer clear of the tourist traps. For the rest of the country, you would be well advised to stay either in large cities that offer a wide range of accommodations or in one of the picturesque villages that are one of France's delights. Although package holidays are usually good money-savers, try wherever possible to avoid guided tours with tourist buses. You can make huge savings by traveling as the locals do, by train or local bus, and you will have the added bonus of seeing something of the local people and their way of life.

The main unit of currency in France is the French franc, which is divided into 100 centimes. Bank notes in circulation are 500, 200, 100, 50 and 20 francs. Coins in use are 10, 5, 2 and 1 franc; and 50, 20, 10 and 5 centimes. At the time of writing there were about 9.50 francs to the pound sterling and about 5.70 francs to the U.S. dollar.

Sample Costs (in Paris). Cinema seat 30–40 francs (30% less on Mondays except hols.); theater seat 50–180 francs, but often more; museum entrance fee 10–30 francs; coffee in a bar or café: standing at the bar 4 francs, seated 6–10 francs; coffee in a restaurant 6–12 francs; beer in a café 8–10 francs, in a restaurant 12–15 francs; 50 centiliter carafe of wine in a café or Inexpensive restaurant 8–12 francs, in a Moderate restaurant 15–30 francs.

NATIONAL TOURIST OFFICE. This can be found at 127 av. des Champs-Elysées, 75008 Paris (Métro: George-V or Charles-de-Gaulle-Etoile) and is open Mon.–Sun. 9–8; closed Christmas and New Year's Day, (tel. 47–23–61–72). It has a wide range of information about both the capital and the rest of the country. The hostesses all speak English and can arrange your Paris hotel reservation for you in exchange for a small fee, which depends on the grade of hotel you pick. However, they can only make reservations on the same day, not in advance. They can give you brochures listing hotels all over the country, but cannot make hotel reservations outside Paris. There are branch offices at main rail stations often open longer hours. The Gare du Nord office (tel. 45–26–94–82) is open Easter through Oct., Mon.–Sat. 8–10, Sun. 1–8; Nov. to Easter Mon.–Sat. 8–8, Sun. 1–8. The Gare de l'Est (tel. 46–07–17–73) and the Gare de Lyon (tel. 43–43–33–24) have the same opening times from Easter through Oct., and from 8–1 and 5–8 for the rest of the year. The Gare d'Austerlitz (tel. 45–84–91–70) is open from Easter through Oct. 8–10, Nov. to Easter 8–3 only. The Eiffel Tower office (tel. 45–51–22–15) is open May to Sept., Mon.–Sun. 11–6. The Champs Elysées office also houses the main French Rail (SNCF) tourist office, which sells tickets and makes reservations or all-in holiday packages for the whole country, as well as booking couchettes. You will also find a travel agent and a theater ticket agency beside the tourist office.

Addresses of the French Government Tourist Office overseas are:

In the U.S.: 610 Fifth Ave., New York, N.Y. 10020 (tel. 212–757–1125); 9454 Wilshire Blvd., Beverly Hills, CA 90212 (tel. 213–271–6665); 645 N. Michigan Ave., Chicago, IL 60611 (tel. 312–337–6301); 1 Hallidie Plaza, Ste. 250, San Francisco, CA 94102 (tel. 415–986–4174); 2305 Cedar Springs Rd., Dallas, TX 75201 (tel. 214–720–4010).

In Canada: 1981 Ave. McGill College, Esso Tower, Suite 490, Montreal P.Q. H3A 2W9 (tel. 514–288–4264); 1 Dundas St. West, Suite 2405, Toronto, Ontario M5G 1Z3 (tel. 416–593–4723).

In the U.K.: 178 Piccadilly, London W1V 0AL (tel. 071–499 6911/071–491 7622).

WHEN TO COME. The main tourist season in France runs from Easter to the end of September. July and August, normally the warmest months, are both crowded and more expensive. June and September are better bets for budgeteers and usually have equally excellent weather. For list of resorts fully open then write to *Association Nationale des Maires des Stations Classées,* 41 Quai d'Orsay, 75007 Paris (tel. 45–51–49–36). Paris is particularly pleasant at Easter and in May, June and October; between mid-July and early September many shops and restaurants are closed and the weather can be sticky, but there is less traffic than during the rest of the year. A few Paris hotels offer lower rates in July and August. The winter sports season is from December to April; avoid Christmas and the school half-term period in February, when prices are high and all resorts are crowded.

Average afternoon temperatures in degrees Fahrenheit and centigrade:

Paris	Jan.	Feb.	Mar.	Apr.	May	June	July	Aug.	Sept.	Oct.	Nov.	Dec.
F°	42	45	52	60	67	73	76	75	69	59	49	43
C°	6	7	11	16	19	23	24	24	21	15	9	6

Nice												
F°	56	56	59	64	69	76	81	81	77	70	62	58
C°	13	13	15	18	21	24	27	27	25	21	17	14

SPECIAL EVENTS. *January* Monte Carlo Rally. *February/March* mid-Lenten carnivals and festivals in various cities; the best-known in Nice, which includes famous Battle of Flowers; Lemon Festival in Menton; Mimosa Festival in La Napoule. *Easter* Good Friday and Easter Sunday processions in various places; fashionable race meetings at Paris racecourses. *April* bullfights in Roman arena in Arles; Horse Show in Nice. *May* Cannes Film Festival; Joan of Arc celebrations in Orléans and Rouen; Gypsies Pilgrimage at Les Saintes-Maries-de-la-Mer; Monaco Grand Prix; International Tennis Championships at Paris' Roland-Garros stadium. *June* Prix de Diane at Chantilly's racecourse; Air Show at Le Bourget near Paris held every two years; Versailles Festival; Grand Fénétra Fair in Toulouse; Le Mans 24-hour motor race. *July* French Grand Prix; Tour de France cycle race; countrywide celebrations on Bastille Day (the 14th); Inter Celtic festivals in Brittany (Quimper and Lorient); Battle of Flowers in Nice. *August* celebrations and pilgrimages on Assumption Day (the 15th), the biggest being the pilgrimage to Lourdes; Musical Saturdays in Chartres (until October); bloodless bullfights in the southwest; famous *Pardon* in Perros-Guirec and other towns in Brittany. *September* Autumn Pilgrimage to Mont-St.-Michel. *October* Prix de l'Arc de Triomphe at Paris' Longchamp racecourse; Auto Show in Paris (even-numbered years only); grapeharvest festivals in all wine-producing regions; Rosary Pilgrimage to Lourdes. *November* Les Trois Glorieuses in Burgundy, with wine auction in Beaune; international Tour de Corse motor race in Corsica. *December* midnight masses on Christmas Eve all over France; special festivities for Christmas and New Year's Eve.

National Holidays. Jan. 1 (New Year's Day); April 1 (Easter Mon.); May 1 (Labor Day); May 8 (VE Day); May 9 (Ascension); May 20 (Whit Mon.); July 14 (Bastille Day); Aug. 15 (Assumption); Nov. 1 (All Saints); Nov. 11 (Armistice); Dec. 25.

VISAS. No visa is required to visit France for anyone from an EC member-state (including the U.K.). Nor is a visa required for U.S. or Canadian nationals.

HEALTH CERTIFICATES. No vaccinations are required to enter France from any country.

GETTING TO FRANCE. By Plane. Paris is one of the main air gateways to Europe with flights by *Air France* and also *TWA* and *Pan Am* as well as *Air Canada* from a number of North American cities, principally New York. Other cities are Chicago, Washington, Boston, Miami, Los Angeles, Houston, Dallas, Montreal and Toronto. Flights go to both Charles de Gaulle (Roissy) Airport and to Orly Airport. Be sure which one it is, especially if you are changing to an internal flight there. Also, check on departure whether your flight leaves from terminal 1 or 2 at Roissy/Charles-de-Gaulle, or from Orly Sud or Orly Ouest. Direct flights also New York–Lyon.

The route from London to Paris is the busiest in Europe with flights virtually on a shuttle basis—13 flights on Saturday, 15 on Sunday, and up to 17 on weekdays each way from Heathrow *(British Airways* and *Air France)* and four or five each way from Gatwick, all to Roissy/Charles de Gaulle. There are also regular flights to Paris, Charles-de-Gaulle, from Stanstead and the new London City Airport, and there are services from several regional airports in the U.K.—including Birmingham, Manchester, Glasgow and Southampton—to Paris. In addition flights go from London to Nice, Lyon, Bordeaux, Lille, Marseille, Clermont–Ferrand, Caen, Quimper, Nantes, Montpellier and Toulouse, as well as from Manchester to Nice. Third level airlines also link cities like Plymouth and Exeter with destinations in northern France. Additional services, such as London–Deauville, run summer only. For those on a strict budget, *Nouvelles Frontières,* 1–2 Hanover St., London W1R 9WB (tel. 071–629 7772) run scheduled charter flights from Gatwick from around £30 single, £55 return. If you want a short break in Paris book a bargain package. Check with *Paris Travel Service,* Bridge House, Ware SG12 9DF (tel. 0920 3922), or *Time Off Holidays,* Chester Close, London SW1X 7BQ (tel. 071–235 8070).

By Train. There are several routes from the U.K., but the quickest is using the hovercraft services of *Hoverspeed* between Dover and Boulogne. From the end of March through September there are four *CityLink* crossings a day (two in winter) from London Victoria station, by train to Dover, then hovercraft to Boulogne (about 35–45 minute crossing) and then by direct train from the Hoverport to Paris (Gare du Nord). Total journey time is about 5½ hours, more if the sea is rough. Note that if the weather is very bad you will be rerouted via one of the ferries, adding 2–3 hours to the journey.

There are several services a day from London Victoria to Paris via Dover Harbour station/Calais Maritime or Folkestone Harbour station/Boulogne Maritime where there are good connections between rail and ship. There is also a service via Newhaven/Dieppe. For overnight travel in comfort use the service from London Waterloo to Portsmouth for the P&O crossing to Le Havre. In the morning an express train from Le Havre will have you in Paris just after 10 A.M.

Paris is linked by through trains to all of western and central Europe as well as to Scandinavia. Overnight trains carry sleeping cars and in almost all cases couchettes also. For example, from Amsterdam to Paris it takes just over 5 hours by the best trains; from Köln about 6 hours; from Geneva around 3½ hours; from Milan about 9 hours; and from Brussels merely 2½ hours.

By Car. The fastest crossings are by Hoverspeed hovercraft from Dover to Calais and Boulogne taking 35–40 minutes, but these can be disrupted in bad weather. Frequent car ferry services run from Dover to Calais and Boulogne operated by *P&O European Ferries. Sealink* sails from Dover to Calais, and from Folkestone to Boulogne. The crossing time on these short sea routes varies from 75 minutes to 1 hour 50 minutes. There is also a crossing from the sleepy Sussex port of Newhaven to Dieppe, but the crossing is much longer at four hours. This route, however, has the a shorter driving distance between London and Paris, as does the Portsmouth–Caen crossing (5½ hrs) run by Brittany Ferries.

By Bus. Quickest service is Hoverspeed's *Citysprint,* which runs four crossings a day in summer. Buses depart from London's Victoria coach station and hovercraft are used for the Channel crossing before a second bus takes you close to the Gard du Nord in Paris. Journey time is around eight hours. From the U.K., several companies operate under the *National Express-Eurolines* banner to various French destinations. Details from *National Express-Eurolines,* 13 Regent St., London SW1Y 4LR (tel. 071–439 9368).

Eurolines services link Paris with Amsterdam, Brussels, London, Köln, Hamburg, Stockholm, and Barcelona directly and an indirect service runs to Frankfurt. There are other services also from Barcelona to Toulouse, Brussels to Lyon and the Côte d'Azur, and Antwerp to Le Havre.

CUSTOMS. Travelers from outside Europe may import 400 cigarettes or 100 cigars or 500 grams (17.6 ounces) of tobacco; 1 liter (1.7 pints) of spirits of more than 22° proof or 2 liters (3.4 pints) of spirits up to 22° proof and 2 liters of wine; 50 grams (1.7 ounces) of perfume and 0.25 liters (0.8 fluid ounces) of toilet water; other goods to the value of 300 francs (passengers under 15 years 150 francs).

Travelers from a country inside the EC may import 300 cigarettes or 150 cigarillos or 75 cigars or 400 grams (14 ounces) of tobacco; 1.5 liters of spirits over 22% vol. (38.8°) proof or 3 liters below 22% vol. or 3 liters of fortified or sparkling wine and 5 liters of still table wine; 75 grams (2.6 ounces) of perfume and 0.25 liters (0.8 fluid ounces) of toilet water; other goods to the value of 2,400 francs (passengers under 15 years 620 francs).

Travelers from non-EC countries within Europe may import 200 cigarettes or 50 cigars or 250 grams (8.8 ounces) of tobacco; 1 liter (1.7 pints) of spirits of more than 22° proof or 2 liters (3.4 pints) of spirits up to 22° proof and 2 liters of wine; 50 grams (1.7 ounces) of perfume and 0.25 liters (0.8 fluid ounces) of toilet water; other goods to the value of 300 francs (passengers under 15 years 150 francs).

HOTELS. France is so well endowed with hotels that you can find budget hotels all over the country. Even expensive resorts have some, although they will be in side streets or outlying areas and may be noisy. The official French classification is a star system ranging from 1-star for budget hotels to 4-star deluxe for luxury hotels. Recommended hotels below are graded into Moderate (M) and Inexpensive (I). These correspond roughly to 2 to 3-stars and 1 to 2-stars respectively. All hotels are required by law to have the room rate pinned up in the room itself and most also have a table showing rates in the reception area or, increasingly, pasted up on a door or window so that you can check rates before entering the hotel. Rates must, by law, include service charges and taxes. Breakfast is not normally included in the rate. It will cost from 20 francs in an Inexpensive hotel, 25 and 30 francs in a Moderate hotel and will consist of tea or coffee, small quantities of bread or rolls, butter and jam. You can, of course, save money by having a coffee and *croissant* in a café where at least you can be sure that the coffee will be hot!

Hotels with restaurants normally offer special rates if you stay three days or longer and take at least one meal. Half board *(demi-pension)* and full board *(pension)* rates are always advantageous. Some also have weekend rates outside the high summer season. An increasing number of hotels make only a small extra charge (about 30 francs) if an extra bed is included in a double room: a good bargain for couples traveling with a child, or for three adults traveling together. Rates vary considerably. Outside Paris a Moderate hotel will cost about 250–400 francs for two people, excluding breakfast. An Inexpensive hotel will cost about 100–250 francs for two. Hotel chains to look out for are the *Mercure, Campanile, Arcade* and *Ibis,* all of which are Moderate. Hotels belonging to the *Logis de France* association are almost always good value and particularly pleasant (a guide is available for 45 francs from bookshops or from 83 av. d'Italie, 75013 Paris, tel. 45–84–83–84).

BUDGET ACCOMMODATIONS. France is a good place for budget accommodations if you plan carefully. *Gîtes Ruraux* are the best-known example and they are very popular with foreign visitors. They are self-catering accommodations, generally small houses or apartments in rural areas, and can be rented by the week, the fortnight or the month. Gîtes range from very modest farm cottages to quite luxurious accommodations. Prices rise in July and August, for which you must reserve well ahead of time. The *Fédération Nationale des Gîtes Ruraux de France,* 35 rue Godot-de-Mauroy, 75009 Paris (tel. 47–42–25–43), will supply regional brochures, as will many tourist offices. A Gîtes de France booking service is available from the French National Tourist Office in London in return for a small membership fee, which entitles you to receive a fat brochure listing well over 1,000 gîtes set aside for British holidaymakers in particularly popular areas. Packages with reduced ferry rates are offered. *Vacances Franco-Britanniques,* Normandy House, 311 High St., Cheltenham, Glos., TL50 3HW (tel. 0242–526338), also specializes in gîte-type rentals.

Auberges de France now belong to the Logis de France association, but are not normally officially graded as tourist hotels. They are usually small, modest and in rural districts, but they must comply with minimum standards of comfort, cleanliness, amenities, and regional cuisine. The *Fédération Nationale des Logis et Auberges de France* 83 av. d'Italie, 75013 Paris, (tel. 45–84–83–84), will supply a list and so will government tourist offices.

Villages Vacances Familles (VVF) is the largest organization running vacation villages in holiday areas. They are good value, but you will feel more at home with the families who stay in them if you speak at least some French. Write to VVF at 38 blvd. Edgar-Quinet, 75014 Paris (tel. 43–22–88–88), for their brochure covering 100 villages all over the country. VVF also has an office for the Ile de France region at 42 blvd. Edgar-Quinet, 75014 Paris (tel. 43–22–57–04).

Most local tourist offices have lists of families with rooms to let for a night or more in their homes *(chambres d'hôte).* You will usually be offered bed-and-breakfast but you may sometimes be able to have main meals there too. Most départements also now have a brochure, usually called *Accueil à la Ferme,* listing farms where you can stay, put up a tent and eat nourishing local cuisine for very reasonable rates. The brochure is available from the Fédération Nationale des Gîtes Ruraux de France in each département. A complete list of the coordinating bodies in each département is supplied by the *Agriculture & Tourisme* organization, at Maison des Chambres d'Agriculture, 9 av. George-V, 75008 Paris. Ask for a *Bienvenue à la Ferme* brochure. Look out too for signs saying *Tourisme Vert:* these are a clue to farms participating in some type of farm holiday scheme.

Résidences hôtelières or *hôtels-résidences* (apartment hotels) are normally restricted to visitors staying a minimum of one week. They are a cross between a hotel and self-catering accommodation, leaving you free but giving you plenty of optional facilities such as cleaning, laundry, and childminding. They are rarely found outside seaside and winter resorts.

Youth Hostels. France has about 300 youth hostels where hikers and cyclists (not car drivers in most cases) can get modest but clean accommodations and adequate meals for very low rates. Lists of addresses are available from the *Fédération Unie des Auberges de Jeunesse,* 10 rue Notre Dame de Lorette, 75009 Paris (tel. 42–85–55–40) or for the Ile de France region, 9 rue Brantôme, 75003 Paris (tel. 48–04–70–30). Try the *Maison Internationale des Jeunes* pour la Culture et la Paix, 4 rue Titon, 75011 Paris, (tel. 43–71–99–21); ideal for groups, reservations necessary.

Camping. There are some splendid campsites in France and all over the country you will find burgeoning tent cities of varying degrees of comfort, but mostly well run. Each region publishes an annual list of campsites, giving details of facilities. Apply to regional tourist offices or to the government tourist office in your own country. There is, however, a real problem now on the south coast in July and August. Indifferent summers in northern Europe have encouraged hundreds of thousands of foreign tourists to converge on campsites there and the situation has become frankly unendurable. Many campsites now accept bookings and this is recommended as otherwise you are liable to find yourself precariously perched alongside a main road, constantly being moved on by polite but firm policemen, and with conditions of comfort, hygiene, and noise beyond belief. The French authorities are desperately trying to dissuade would-be campers from heading for the south coast during the main holiday months and we urge you most strongly to follow their advice and choose a less sought-after area.

RESTAURANTS. France richly deserves its reputation as a food-lover's paradise in spite of the recent invasion of fast-food chains and the microwave oven. You can now find fast-food restaurants all over the main cities, but you can eat just as inexpensively, enjoying genuine French specialties, if you follow our budget tips carefully.

First, always look for restaurants that have a fixed-price menu (known in French as simply a *menu*). In rural districts you will probably have only a choice of *menus,* two or three covering quite a wide price range. In towns and cities there will be a choice of dishes *à la carte,* too, but this will always work out to be more expensive than a *menu.* Even if you do not feel like a full meal, it is bound to be more expensive to have even a light omelette and salad. So do as the locals do, have the set meal, choosing the lightest dishes if necessary. The first course will almost always offer you the choice of *crudités* (attractively presented raw vegetables, diced, sliced or chopped and with an oil-and-vinegar dressing) or *hors-d'oeuvre variés,* whose contents will depend on the region and the time of year but will usually include tomatoes, carrots and other non-filling goodies. Unless you are in a hurry, avoid snacks, but you can often find good, well-priced sandwiches in a *boulangerie* (bakery).

Secondly, look for restaurants patronized by the local people; steer clear of those that seem to cater exclusively to tourists.

Thirdly, all restaurants are now obliged to state *service compris* or *prix nets* (service included). Both mean that there is no extra service charge to pay. It is then up to you. If you find the service particularly good, you can always leave the waiter a few coins. Cover charges, incidentally, are illegal in France, although restaurants are allowed to charge a modest sum for children accompanying adults and not having a meal.

Fourthly, see whether wine is included. It often is on tourist menus *(menus touristiques)*, but you can usually have beer or mineral water instead if you prefer. The wine will be a local one, perfectly drinkable but not the finest vintage. Otherwise the least expensive alternative is to ask for a *carafe* of red *(rouge)*, white *(blanc)* or rosé. A 25-centiliter carafe is the usual quantity for one person (the equivalent of two glasses), a 50-centiliter carafe is usual for two people, though of course a liter (bigger than a bottle) will be available too. Wine is rarely served by the glass in French restaurants (though it is in cafés or wine bars). You will have to spend a bit more if you pick something from the wine list, but you will find it offers wines at a wide variety of prices, and do not feel embarrassed at picking one of the least expensive—many French people do. The best-value wines will generally be local specialties.

Logis de France hotels usually have good restaurants with low prices and many regional dishes; and the famous *Relais Routiers* (a superior version of the transport café) are remarkably good value. You can buy a countrywide guide listing them (available all over France and at some London bookshops, or write to Relais Routiers, 354 Fulham Rd., London SW10 9UH).

Prices vary considerably from one part of the country to another. In country districts and small towns Inexpensive restaurant meals cost about 50–100 francs; Moderate meals about 100–200. In Paris and other large cities the equivalents are 80–150 and 150–250 francs. These prices apply to fixed-price *menus* and do *not* include wine. In our lists of restaurants, the price grading is based on the fixed-price menus; if you eat *à la carte* you must expect to pay more.

Buying Food and Drink. France is a good place for picnics and self-catering. The best buys are usually to be found in the picturesque street markets, which offer real value for money. Covered markets in towns or cities are a bit more expensive but again the standard of freshness is very high. Supermarkets are common in France and are good for packaged groceries and household products. They also sell low-priced wine, but the quality tends to be variable; small grocers are good bets for reasonably-priced local wines. Bottles of mineral water are always best bought in supermarkets; buy the biggest size for value. Do not order mineral water or soft drinks in your hotel if you are keen to save money. Avoid imported groceries such as cereals, which are invariably expensive. Stick instead to French specialties such as *charcuterie* (a huge range of cold pork products) and cheeses, choosing local varieties for best value.

French bread is world-famous. The traditional long loaf is called a *baguette;* a thinner version is a *ficelle* and a fatter one simply *un pain* (in Paris) or *un parisien* (outside Paris); a round loaf is known as a *boule* or *miche de pain. Pain de campagne* is country-style bread and comes in various shapes and sizes; it costs more than ordinary bread, and *pain de son* (made with bran) and *pain complet* (wholemeal bread) are even more expensive. All bread can be bought by the half loaf, ask for *une demi-baguette, un demi-pain,* etc. *Pain de mie* is the best type for toasting.

YOUTH PASS. A special Youth Pass *(Carte Jeune)* available from youth information centers, post offices, tourist offices, and city halls, or from the Crédit Mutuel and CIC banks, is for under-26s and valid for a year. Costing 75 frs it gives over 4,000 special reduced rates for some hotels, restaurants, theaters, state-owned museums, trains, some air services, and so on. You'll need to take your passport to prove your age.

TIPPING. Restaurants and cafés are obliged to state net prices, *(service compris, prix nets)* so you need not worry about the 15% service charge. Tipping in a café usually entails leaving the waiter the small change brought back to you, but in a restaurant it is considered a sign of appreciation of good service if you leave anything up to 10 francs (depending on the size of the bill). In hotels, if someone carries your baggage, tip around 5 francs per case. Tip the receptionist only if he or she performs a specific service (say 5 to 10 francs for making phone calls for you). Tip the chambermaid only if you stay more than 4 or 5 days; about 5–10 francs per day. Taxi drivers are given roughly 15% and so are hairdressers. Usherettes in cinemas, theaters or sports stadia expect at least 2 francs per person. There is a fixed rate for rail porters, pinned to their uniforms (currently about 10 francs per item).

MAIL. Letters to the U.S.A. and Canada cost 3.80 francs for 20 grams, 6.40 francs for 30 grams, 6.70 for 40 grams and 7 francs for 50 grams; to the U.K. 2.30 francs up to 20 grams (0.7 ounces); to other EC countries, and within France 2.30 francs; to other European countries 3.70 francs. Postcards cost 2.10 francs within France, to Canada and all EC countries (including Britain); 3.00 francs elsewhere.

TELEPHONES. For calls within France, all numbers now have eight digits. The system has conveniently been rationalized so that the country has been divided into just two zones: Paris and the Ile-de-France; and the rest of France. Thus, dialing from outside Paris merely dial the eight-digit number, even if you're dialing within the same area, for anywhere *except* Paris and the Ile-de-France; for Paris and the Ile-de-France only, dial 16, wait for a second tone, then dial 1 followed by the eight-digit number. If you're dialing from Paris or the Ile-de-France, to make a call within the same area, merely dial the eight-digit number; to dial anywhere else in France, dial 16, wait for a second tone, then dial the eight-digit number.

If you need to make regular calls from a public booth, buy a phone card *(Télé-carte)* from a post office, PTT agency, or some tobacconists. The price varies according to the number of units purchased.

CLOSING TIMES. Food shops open between 7.30 and 8, close between 12 or 12.30 and 4, then reopen till 7.30 or 8. Other shops open at 9 or 9.30 and close between 6.30 and 7.30; in provincial towns most of them close between 12 and 2, but in Paris this applies only to small boutiques or galleries. Department stores all over the country normally stay open all day, from 9.30 to 6.30 or 7, but some are closed on Monday mornings; in Paris some stay open late one night a week. In provincial cities and villages many shops and services (hairdressers and drycleaners, etc.) are closed all day Monday but open all day Saturday, and sometimes Sunday morning too. Hairdressers throughout the country usually close Mondays. Small food shops and street markets usually operate on Sunday mornings. The Paris drugstores stay open till about 1.30 A.M. seven days a week.

Banks are open from 9 to 4.30 or 5. In Paris and big cities they are open Monday to Friday only, whereas in towns and villages they are often closed Monday but open Saturday. Outside Paris most banks close for at least 1½ hours for lunchtime, but times vary greatly.

GETTING AROUND FRANCE. By Plane. France's dynamic domestic airline *Air Inter* covers most of the country and offers some good reductions (e.g. for couples, families of which at least three members travel together, students, men over 62 and women over 60). These apply only to certain flights, but the number seems to be increasing every year (called *vols bleus,* ask for timetables). Check with *Air France* or your travel agent for details of *Visit France* fares offered in conjunction with transatlantic flights between the U.S.A. and France. They may save you money. France also has several small airlines connecting mainland cities with each other and with Corsica, such as *TAT* or *Air Littoral.* Some services operate in the summer months only.

By Train. The French rail network (SNCF) is efficient, good value and comfortable. Always pick a *train corail* whenever possible; these streamlined, modern, air-conditioned trains are really excellent. At busy times of the day, some trains require payment of a supplement even in second class. Budgeteers should avoid these—they are clearly marked in timetables. The SNCF now runs the splendid TGV (*train à grande vitesse* or high-speed train), for which a supplement is payable only at certain peak periods of the week or year. It currently runs from Paris to Dijon, Lyon, Grenoble, Geneva (in Switzerland); and on to Valence, Avignon, Marseille, Nîmes, Montpellier and Nice. There is also a daily TGV service from Lille to Lyon, avoiding Paris. A new high-speed line (operating from Gare Montparnasse) now links Paris to Angers and Nantes, and a TGV Paris-Bordeaux link serving Poitiers and Angoulême opened in 1990.

Various reduced-fare passes are available: the *Carte Vermeil* for those over 60; the *Carte Jeune* and *Coupon Jeune* for those under 26; the *Carte Couple* for married

couples; and the *Carte Kiwi* for families. For most of these passes, you will need
to provide two passport-size photos and proof of age/status. Passes entitle you to
50% reductions during blue periods (most of the time); 20% during white periods
(most of the weekend); but no reduction during red periods (peak holiday times).
Once you have started your journey in the blue period you can continue even if
the latter part of the day is coded red or if you have to change trains and stations
in Paris. If you stick to blue periods you get a 25% reduction if you make a round
trip covering more than 1000 km. (620 miles) and stay away a minimum of 5 days
or part of a Sunday. These reductions also apply to the TGV. Children between
4 and 10 travel half-fare; infants under 4 travel free if they do not occupy seats.

Another good-value pass is the *France Vacances Special* ticket. This gives free
travel on all French railways on any four days out of 15, or nine days in any one-
month period. Cost is £64/$99, £108/$160 respectively in 2nd class. French railways have recently introduced a new package called *Liberté*, combining the *France
Vacances* runabout ticket with half board hotel accommodations on a go-as-you-
please basis throughout France. It is excellent value for money, starting at £299
for a four-day pass with 10 nights' accommodations. Other bargains to look out
for are special day rates to seaside resorts, Chantilly racecourse and so on, and winter weekend rates (October to Easter) for some Normandy routes. There are no
ordinary day return tickets in France. If you travel overnight you must either sit
up or pay 75 francs extra for a *couchette* or bunk (6 to a compartment in 2nd class).
A blanket and pillow are provided.

All SNCF tickets are valid for two months only, and it is essential that you have
your ticket punched in the bright orange machines at platform entrances. Put the
ticket into the slot and move it slightly to the left till you hear a loud click. *You
will be fined if you fail to comply with this regulation.* If you break your journey
on the same day you need not have the ticket repunched, but you must if you do
an overnight stop.

By Car. If you bring your own car you only require proof of third-party insurance. You can use your home driving license for up to a year in France. There is
a good motorway network but the tolls *(péages)* are high. Most other roads are
good. Speed limits are as follows: 130 k.p.h. (81 m.p.h.) on motorways; 110 k.p.h.
(68 m.p.h.) on dual carriageways and feeder roads; 90 k.p.h. (56 m.p.h.) on other
non-urban roads; and 60 k.p.h. (37 m.p.h.) or 50 k.p.h. (31 m.p.h.) in built-up areas.
When it is raining maximum speeds are lower: 110 k.p.h. on motorways, 80 k.p.h.
on other non-urban roads. Fines for speeding are heavy, and so are fines for not
wearing your seatbelt (compulsory at all times). The controversial law making
dipped headlights compulsory in towns has been rescinded, but many motorists still
do this, so beware of dazzle. A red warning triangle, a spare tyre and a spare set
of light bulbs are compulsory pieces of equipment to carry in the car. The most
important traffic rule to remember is that traffic coming from the right has priority
at all times, except if there is a STOP sign or if entering a traffic circle. Remember
also that children under 10 must travel in the back of the car by law. Parking in
cities is controlled by meters, or tickets that you must place inside your car, so have
some loose change ready. Check carefully before you leave your car, as there are
very heavy fines if it is clamped or taken away to a compound. Underground garages
are found in most towns. Car hire is expensive in France.

By Bus. Tourist buses are run by private agencies, by the SNCF and its subsidiary Europabus. *Wagons Lits* and *American Express* are quite expensive but offer
some less expensive circuits. Local buses divide into two groups: sightseeing buses,
usually operating at Easter and in the summer months only; and year-round scheduled bus routes. Local or regional tourist offices will give you details of the former;
for the latter, study the timetables posted up in the bus station *(gare routière)*, or
inquire at the ticket desk. You can get about quite successfully at much lower cost
than with tourist buses, but bear in mind that some ordinary buses do not operate
as frequently, or even at all, during school holidays.

By Boat. Barge holidays on France's canals and rivers are very popular: over
20 agencies offer packages in Burgundy alone. Some of these are gastronomic tours
unsuitable for budgeteers, but check with your French government tourist office
or local tourist offices for less luxurious offers.

By Bicycle. Biking is becoming increasingly common in ecology-conscious
France. The SNCF hires bicycles by the half-day or day from nearly 200 stations
in France (ask for a list in any SNCF office), and in many cases you can travel with
your bicycle on trains without paying any extra. Many seaside resorts have rent-a-
bike schemes during holiday periods and cycle shops in some provincial towns offer
this service too. Unless you have a credit card, you must put down a deposit, usually
200 francs, and show your passport. In Paris *Paris Vélo* at 4 rue du Fer-à-Moulin,
75005, rents out bikes, or look in the Yellow Pages of the telephone directory under
location de bicyclettes.

Paris

Ignore gloom-mongers who label Paris one of the world's most expensive cities.
It *can* be expensive—if you are in pursuit of *haute couture* or *cordon bleu* cooking—
but it can also be enjoyed on the cheap, providing you plan ahead and stick to a
few simple rules.

Snacks and soft-drinks are overpriced in Paris, so either rustle up a picnic (with
a baguette loaf and some cheese or ham), or schedule a proper three-course meal.
Restaurant prices vary dramatically, but you can consult the menu before venturing
in—so there's no excuse for inadvertent overspending. Keep away from tourist traps
(clue: beware of English translations) and head into the bustling, narrow streets
where the locals eat. Bar snacks in cafés are overpriced and so, too—despite their
picturesque appeal—are the pancakes sold on street-corners.

If you are in urgent need of a drink, pick a café that looks down-to-earth and
stand at the bar—saving you time and money. If you want to watch the world go
by, choose a café with sidewalk tables and a decent view. You'll pay up to twice
as much as you would at the bar but, to compensate, you'll have all the time in
the world.

Paris is relatively small, and you can get around for free: on foot. So bring comfortable shoes and, before stepping out each day, spend ten minutes planning a co-
herent route. Don't hesitate to take the cheap and efficient Metro. Don't buy tickets
one at a time: a carnet of ten works out twice as cheap.

Museum and monument admission prices can soon add up, so keep an eye open
for things to do for free or almost free. On Sundays, and sometimes Wednesdays,
many museums have half-price or free entry. Go then—early in the morning or
at lunchtime (1–2.30 P.M.) to avoid crowds.

The best place to start exploring Paris is on the islands: the Ile St-Louis—an
oasis of inner-city repose—and the larger Ile de la Cité, home to the mighty Notre-
Dame Cathedral, begun in 1163. Close by, beyond the sweet-smelling Flower Market, is the turreted Conciergerie, a one-time prison with a superb vaulted 14th-
century hall. Round the corner is the Sainte-Chapelle, whose walls consist of little
else but gorgeous 13th-century stained glass.

The southern side of the Seine is known as the Rive Gauche (Left Bank). Head
east as far as the Jardin des Plantes, attractive botanical gardens flanked by natural
science museums and, more surprisingly, the Paris mosque. Moslem culture re-
ceives a thorough overview inside the new Arab Institute beside the Seine.

The Left Bank heartland extends from the Pont St-Michel towards the Sorbonne,
Paris's ancient university. Students here used to listen to lectures in Latin, which
is why the area is known as the Quartier Latin. The Sorbonne's pompous 17th-
century buildings contrast with the bohemian charm of the surrounding narrow
streets with their bookshops and Greek restaurants.

The Musée de Cluny, close to the Sorbonne, contains artifacts from the late Middle Ages and Renaissance; don't miss the Lady with the Unicorn tapestries. The
Panthéon, with its huge dome and elegant colonnade, was intended to be a church,
but was swiftly earmarked as a hall of fame; its crypt contains the remains of such
national heroes as Zola, Voltaire and Rousseau. The tumbling Rue Mouffetard—
site of a colorful market and restaurants—lies beyond the Panthéon, which looks
down towards the Luxembourg Gardens, a joyous mixture of fountains, statues,
and tree-lined alleys.

Visible from the Gardens are the lopsided towers of the enormous 17th-century
church of St-Sulpice. Continue down towards the Boulevard St-Germain and the
sturdy pointed tower of St-Germain-des-Prés, the oldest church in Paris. The spirit

of writers Jean-Paul Sartre and Simone de Beauvoir lingers in the Café de Flore opposite.

Carry on westwards, through the Carré Rive Gauche and its many art dealers, towards the Musée d'Orsay, opened in 1986 and one of Paris's star tourist venues. The Impressionists head the French arts (1848–1914) displayed on three floors in this sumptuously transformed rail station.

A short walk along the Seine takes you to the Invalides, founded by Louis XIV in 1674 to house wounded war veterans. Today it contains the Army Museum and the Musée des Plans-Reliefs (17th-century scale models of French towns). The Invalides church possesses the city's most elegant dome as well as the tomb of Napoleon.

Close to the Invalides is the Musée Rodin, filled (like its superb rose-garden) with the sculptures of Auguste Rodin. To the west, at one end of the Champ de Mars, is the Eiffel Tower, built by Gustave Eiffel for the World Exhibition of 1889. Long lines for the elevator are inevitable, so save time and money by climbing the stairs to the second stage.

Across the Seine from the Eiffel Tower is the Palais de Chaillot, a 1930s culture-center containing an aquarium and museums devoted to the Cinema, Seafaring, Anthropology and Historic Monuments. From here you can head southwest to the Musée Marmottan (magnificent Monets) and the Bois de Boulogne (woods and lakes), or make straight for the Arc de Triomphe, a 164-foot high arch planned by Napoleon to celebrate his military successes. It has emerged resplendent from a recent face-lift.

The cosmopolitan pulse of Paris beats strongest on the gracefully sloping, 1¼-mile Champs-Elysées, originally laid out in the 1600s by André Le Nôtre. Place de la Concorde, at the far end, was home to the notorious Revolutionary guillotine that put paid to Louis XVI and Marie-Antoinette. It has been replaced by an obelisk—shipped in from Egypt in 1833.

The formal Tuileries gardens, with their Orangerie museum of early 20th-century French art, lead up to the Arc du Carrousel and the Louvre—originally a royal palace, today the world's largest museum. I.M. Pei's controversial glass pyramid, providing a breathtaking new entrance vestibule, is the highlight of a modernization program that has left the Louvre less cramped and better organized. Star attraction is undeniably Leonardo da Vinci's Mona Lisa, while three-dimensional marvels start with the soaring Victory of Samothrace (3rd century BC) and the Venus de Milo (end of 2nd century BC). Make sure to inspect the recently excavated 13th-century towers of the original Louvre.

Perrault's colonnaded eastern façade, facing the quaint Gothic church of St-Germain l'Auxerrois, is a formidable demonstration of disciplined Baroque. The Louvre looks south across the Pont des Arts footbridge at the bedomed Institut de France, home to the Académie Française; it also looks west across busy Rue de Rivoli at the Palais-Royal, whose enclosed garden, bordered by arcades and boutiques, is all too easily missed . . . unlike the forest of candy-striped modern pillars at its entrance.

East of the Palais-Royal are Les Halles—site of Paris's central market, until the much-loved glass and iron sheds were torn down in the late sixties. The area now combines children's garden, trendy shopping complex (Le Forum), restaurants, and cafés, including Café Beaubourg and Café Costes, renowned for their novel interior design. The bulky outline of St-Eustache church patrols the horizon.

Across Boulevard de Sébastopol is the futuristic funnel-topped Pompidou Center, home to a Museum of Modern Art, exhibitions, and a plethora of activities. Continue east from Beaubourg (another name for the Center) into the Marais, one of Paris's most historic quarters. The spacious affluence of its restored 17th-century mansions contrasts with winding streets full of shops and restaurants. Highlights range from the stylish Picasso Museum to the harmonious Place des Vosges, with its soft pink brick and cloister-like arcades. In one corner is the Maison de Victor Hugo, containing souvenirs of the great poet's life.

Place de la Bastille boasts a gilded statue of Liberty atop a soaring column, and the shining, curved facade of the new Bastille Opera. The broad, leafy Grands Boulevards run from Bastille to the original Paris Opera—a pompous jumble of styles, where you can visit the monumental foyer and admire the auditorium ceiling painted by Marc Chagall.

From rue de Rivoli, Rue de la Paix leads down to Place Vendôme, one of the world's most opulent squares with a central column made from the melted bronze of 1200 cannon captured at the Battle of Austerlitz in 1805. The nearby church of La Madeleine has columns of its own—rows and rows of them, giving it the feel of a Greek temple. The portico's majestic Corinthian colonnade supports a gigantic pediment with a sculptured frieze of the Last Judgment. Admire the vista down Rue Royale across the Seine, via the Concorde obelisk to the not dissimilar façade of the French parliament. Another vista leads up Boulevard Malesherbes to the dome of St-Augustin, a mid-19th century church notable for its innovative use of iron girders as structural support.

Place de la Madeleine is in the heart of Paris's prime shopping district; the famous Grands Magasins department stores of Printemps and Galeries Lafayette are in nearby Boulevard Haussmann.

Montmartre, in northern Paris, has not lost its traditional color or slightly sleazy character, typified by the quaint Place du Tertre, with its painters and cute (though overpriced) restaurants. The gleaming white Sacré Coeur basilica, built in a bombastic, mock-Byzantine style between 1876 and 1910, is a noted Paris landmark, and there is a magnificent view of the city from its dome.

PRACTICAL INFORMATION FOR PARIS

HOTELS. Paris has such a wide range of hotels that you can find budget accommodations in most areas. You can get a complete list of well over a thousand hotels in the capital from government tourist offices or the Paris tourist office. Most rooms in Moderate hotels have a shower or bath, but fewer do in the Inexpensive hotels. None of the hotels in the list below has a restaurant unless it is mentioned. Hotel reservations can be made for you at the tourist office at 127 av. des Champs-Elysées, 8e, or at Les Invalides air terminal, but only for immediate occupation—you cannot make advance reservations there. There is a small charge for this service, based on the hotel's star rating. Please bear in mind that although telephone numbers were accurate at the time of writing, they change with amazing frequency in Paris, so you may be answered by a recorded message in French giving you a new number to call.

Note that single rooms are often well below the standard of comfort of double rooms and are relatively expensive.

Moderate

Arcade, 7 rue de l'Arcade, 8e (tel. 42–65–43–85). Small hotel in a side street behind La Madeleine church. Very central and convenient for big stores, theaters, and sights. All rooms with TV.

Banville, 166 blvd. Berthier, 17e (tel. 42–67–70–16). Pretty rooms, all with TV; friendly staff. In a quiet area not far from the Porte Maillot, with good bus and metro services nearby.

Bellechasse, 8 rue de Bellechasse, 7e (tel. 45–51–52–36). Small, but very comfortable hotel on a quiet street near the Musée d'Orsay and the Seine.

Bretonnerie, 22 rue Ste.-Croix-de-la Bretonnerie, 4e (tel. 48–87–77–63). In a charming little street in the Marais, near the Pompidou Center. Some rooms are small, though many are furnished in Louis XIII style.

Choiseul-Opéra, 1 rue Daunou, 2e (tel. 42–61–70–41). Modern hotel on the same street as the famous Harry's Bar. Good rates for single travelers.

Collège de France, 7 rue Thénard, 5e (tel. 43–26–78–36). Small, quiet, and traditional, with pleasant decor, in the heart of the Latin Quarter.

Empereur, 2 rue Chevert, 7e (tel. 45–55–88–02). Recently renovated and close to Les Invalides. Also within walking distance of the Eiffel Tower.

Esméralda, 4 rue St.-Julien-le-Pauvre, 5e (tel. 43–54–19–20). In an attractive, 17th-century building on the Left Bank opposite Notre-Dame. Rooms are small, but well furnished, some with superb views over the cathedral.

Family, 35 rue Cambon, 1er (tel. 42–61–54–84). Excellent service and a friendly welcome. Renovated in 1988 and near La Madeleine, pl. de la Concorde, Tuileries Gardens, and the Louvre.

La Havane, 44 rue de Trévise, 9e (tel. 47–70–79–12). Comfortable rooms, each with its own "personalized" style. Near the Opéra.

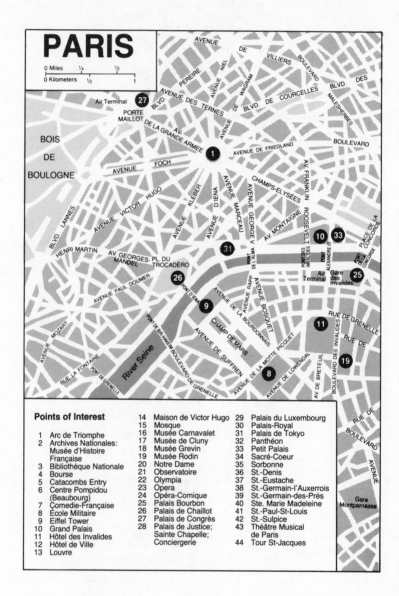

PARIS

0 Miles ¼ ½
0 Kilometers ½ 1

BOIS DE BOULOGNE

Air Terminal **27**

PORTE MAILLOT

AVENUE DE LA GRANDE ARMEE

AVENUE DES TERNES

AVENUE NIEL

AVENUE DE WAGRAM

BLVD. DE COURCELLES

BLVD. DES MALESHERBES

AVENUE DE VILLIERS

BOULEVARD

PEREIRE

1

AVENUE FOCH

AVENUE DE FRIEDLAND

BOULEVARD

AVENUE VICTOR HUGO

BLVD. LANNES

HENRI MARTIN

AV. GEORGES MANDEL

PL. DU TROCADÉRO

26

AVENUE PAUL DOUMER

KLEBER

AVENUE DIENA

AVENUE MARCEAU

AVENUE GEORGE V

CHAMPS-ELYSEES

AV. FRANKLIN ROOSEVELT

AV. MONTAIGNE

31

10 **33**

PLACE DE LA CONCORDE

PONT ALEXANDRE III

Air Terminal

Gare des Invalides

25

PONT D'IENA

9

AVENUE RAPP

AVENUE BOSQUET

AVENUE DE LA BOURDONNAIS

11

RUE DE GRENELLE

RUE DE

AVENUE MOZART

RUE LA FONTAINE

PONT DE GRENELLE

PONT DE BIR-HAKEIM

River Seine

BOULEVARD DE GRENELLE

CHAMP DE MARS

AVENUE DE SUFFREN

AVENUE DE LA MOTTE PICQUET

8

AVENUE DE LOWENDAL

AV DE BRETEUIL

BOULEVARD DES INVALIDES

19

RUE DE

BOULEVARD

AVENUE

Gare Montparnasse

Points of Interest

1 Arc de Triomphe
2 Archives Nationales: Musée d'Histoire Française
3 Bibliothèque Nationale
4 Bourse
5 Catacombs Entry
6 Centre Pompidou (Beaubourg)
7 Comedie-Française
8 École Militaire
9 Eiffel Tower
10 Grand Palais
11 Hôtel des Invalides
12 Hôtel de Ville
13 Louvre

14 Maison de Victor Hugo
15 Mosque
16 Musée Carnavalet
17 Musée de Cluny
18 Musée Grevin
19 Musée Rodin
20 Notre Dame
21 Observatoire
22 Olympia
23 Opera
24 Opéra-Comique
25 Palais Bourbon
26 Palais de Chaillot
27 Palais de Congrès
28 Palais de Justice; Sainte Chapelle; Conciergerie

29 Palais du Luxembourg
30 Palais-Royal
31 Palais de Tokyo
32 Panthéon
33 Petit Palais
34 Sacré-Coeur
35 Sorbonne
36 St.-Denis
37 St.-Eustache
38 St.-Germain-l'Auxerrois
39 St.-Germain-des-Prés
40 Ste. Marie Madeleine
41 St.-Paul-St-Louis
42 St.-Sulpice
43 Théâtre Musical de Paris
44 Tour St-Jacques

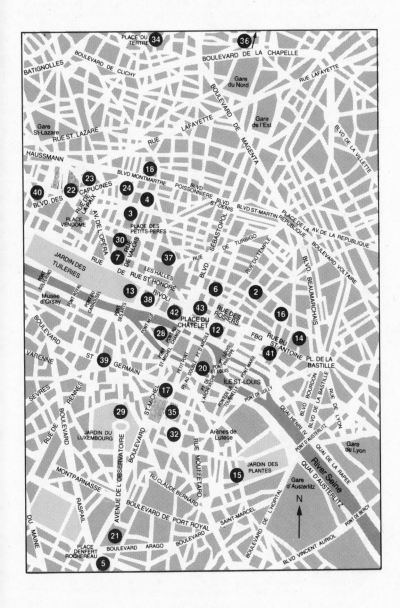

London Palace, 32 blvd. des Italiens, 9e (tel. 48–24–54–64). Comfortable and well run, with considerable reductions in July and Aug.

Londres-Stockholm, 13 rue St.-Roch, 1er (tel. 42–60–15–62). Popular with American tourists, comfortable and conveniently placed near Palais-Royal and the Tuileries Gardens.

Marronniers, 21 rue Jacob, 6e (tel. 43–25–30–60). Charming hotel with small, attractive garden in the heart of St.-Germain-des Prés. Pretty, but very tiny rooms.

Médéric, 4 rue Médéric, 17e (tel. 47–63–69–13). Considerable renovations and improved facilities have added to the charm of this small hotel near the Park Monceau. Expect a warm welcome.

Palais Bourbon, 49 rue de Bourgogne, 7e (tel. 47–05–29–26). Situated in a quiet area near Les Invalides and the Seine. Large, fully-equipped rooms; six with wash-bowl and bidet only. Rates include breakfast.

Place des Vosges, 12 rue de Birague, 4e (tel. 42–72–60–46). Tiny hotel, renovated in 1988, but still full of character. Pleasant service and some inexpensive rooms.

Poussin, 52 rue Poussin, 16e (tel. 46–51–30–46). In a chic district, not far from Auteuil race course and the Bois de Boulogne. A completely renovated classical building, decorated in pinks and pastels, with some superb views over the rooftops.

Queen's, 4 rue Bastien-Lepage, 16e (tel. 42–88–89–85). Small, attractive hotel with each of its 22 rooms decorated with paintings by a contemporary artist. Some inexpensive rooms and pleasant service.

Saint-Germain, 88 rue du Bac, 7e (tel. 45–48–62–92). Well run hotel; all its double rooms have bathrooms.

Saint-Louis, 75 rue St.-Louis-en l'Ile, 4e (tel. 46–34–04–80). Located in one of the prettiest areas in Paris, the island of St. Louis. Attractive double rooms, some with showers only.

Seine, 52 rue de Seine, 6e (tel. 46–34–22–80). Well placed and well run hotel in a delightful Left Bank street, lined with art galleries, and with a lively street market.

Sèvres-Vaneau, 86 rue Vaneau, 7e (tel. 45–48–73–11). Furnished in 1900s style and situated in a chic district.

Terminus-Lyon, 19 blvd. Diderot, 12e (tel. 43–43–24–03). Opposite the Gare du Lyon, this is a comfortable hotel for a stop-over. A bit impersonal for a longer stay and breakfast is pricey.

Verneuil-St.-Germain, 8 rue de Verneuil, 7e (tel. 42–60–24–16). On a quiet street in the St.-Germain quarter, full of character and carefully selected antique furniture. Most rooms have oak beams. All rooms are less expensive in July and Aug.

Inexpensive

Avenir, 52 rue Gay-Lussac, 5e (tel. 43–54–76–60). Very modest, but friendly hotel in the Latin Quarter, on six floors (no elevator). A good bet for those with unbreakably low budgets.

Bellevue, 46 rue Pasquier, 8e (tel. 43–87–50–68). Family-style hotel near St.-Lazare rail station. Very inexpensive rooms, all with showers.

Delambre, 35 rue Delambre, 14e (tel. 43–20–66–31). Close to the Tour Montparnasse and the trendy 6th district. Rates include breakfast.

Europe, 98 blvd. Magenta, 10e (tel. 40–37–71–15). Good value for money and pleasant service in this hotel close to both the Gare de l'Est and the Gare du Nord stations. Especially good rates for the single traveler.

Malar, 29 rue Malar, 7e (tel. 45–51–38–46). Charming little family hotel between Les Invalides and the Eiffel Tower. Rates include breakfast.

Palais, 2 quai de la Mégisserie, 1er (tel. 42–36–98–25). Very reasonably-priced, small hotel, opposite the Ile de la Cité and handy for the Sainte Chapelle and Notre-Dame. Most rooms have wash basin and bidet only.

Ranelagh, 56 rue de l'Assomption, 16e (tel. 42–88–31–63). A rarity in this chic part of Paris—a genuine, modest spot for budget travelers.

St. André des Arts, 66 rue St.-André-des-Arts, 6e (tel. 43–26–96–16). A hotel with character, situated in in a lively pedestrian precinct in the St.-Michel quarter. Reasonably-priced rates include breakfast.

Studio, 4 rue du Vieux-Colombier, 6e (tel. 45–48–31–81). Fully-equipped rooms in the heart of St.-Germain. Open all year round.

Victor Massé, 32 bis rue Victor-Massé, 9e (tel. 48–74–37–53). In the Pigalle area at the foot of Montmartre. Recommended for keen budgeteers.

Vieux Paris, 9 rue Gît-le-Coeur, 6e (tel. 43–54–41–66). Friendly, atmospheric, small hotel in a picturesque street in the St.-Michel area. Some rooms are more pricey, but singles are reasonable; all rates include breakfast.

Wilson, 10 rue de Stockholm, 8e (tel. 45–22–10–85). A no-nonsense establishment just behind the St.-Lazare station. Few rooms with own showers, but all rates include breakfast.

RESTAURANTS. Some Paris restaurants can be expensive, but you can still find plenty of moderate and inexpensive ones if you are careful. There are plenty of inexpensive restaurants serving Tunisian and Vietnamese cuisine, and pizza houses are springing up all over the city, but the lists below include restaurants that serve genuine French dishes. The best areas for finding a wide choice of low-priced restaurants with a pleasant atmosphere are the Latin Quarter, St.-Germain-des-Prés, Les Halles, Montparnasse and the new *quartier chinois* close by Place d'Italie along avenue de Choisy, 13e, but you will find places where the locals eat all over Paris—the French are great restaurant-goers. Do not be intimidated by the wine list. All Moderate and Inexpensive restaurants serve wine by the carafe. In wine bars, which are increasingly common in Paris, you can buy wine by the glass and eat good, light meals. Few Inexpensive restaurants are willing to take reservations, so you may have to wait for a table. Opening days sometimes change without warning, so check locally.

Moderate

Alsace, 39 av. des Champs-Elysées, 8e (tel. 43–59–44–24). Open 24 hours, year round. Large brasserie with lively ambiance. Excellent seafood and sauerkraut.

Au Pactole, 44 blvd. St.-Germain, 5e (tel. 46–33–31–31). Closed Sat. lunch and Sun. Imaginative *nouvelle* and classical cuisine. Discreet restaurant, now entirely redesigned. Good-value lunchtime *menu.*

Balzar, 49 rue des Ecoles, 5e (tel. 43–54–13–67). Closed Aug. and Christmas to New Year. Popular bistro in the Latin Quarter. 1930s decor and traditional cuisine—*pâtés, terrines,* pig's feet, garnished sauerkraut. Sawdust on the floor.

Barrière Poquelin, 17 rue Molière, 1er (tel. 42–96–22–19). Closed Sat. lunch, Sun., first fortnight in Aug. Booking essential. Intimate restaurant whose decor is inspired by Molière's plays. Some original fish dishes, a range of game, and an excellent-value *menu.*

Bofinger, 5 rue de la Bastille, 4e (tel. 42–72–87–82). Open to 1 A.M. daily. Open since 1864, this is one of the oldest and most typical brasseries in town. Wide variety of dishes, served by waiters in black jackets and white aprons.

Coconnas, 2 bis pl. des Vosges, 4e (tel. 42–78–58–16). Closed Mon. and Tues. Attractive decor and setting in this beautiful square in the old Marais quarter. Reputable, traditional *cuisine à l'ancienne* and good value *menus.*

Lipp, 151 blvd. St.-Germain, 6e (tel. 45–48–53–91). Closed first fortnight in Aug. A Paris institution, long a favorite haunt of politicians and intellectuals. Good, brasserie-style cooking. Tends to get very crowded.

Le Muniche, 27 rue de Buci, 6e (tel. 46–33–62–09). Open to 3 A.M. daily. Lively and popular brasserie serving typically French cuisine, with an accent on fish and seafood. Friendly service.

Le Petit Zinc, 25 rue de Buci, 6e (tel. 46–33–51–66). Open to 3 A.M. daily. Like Le Muniche next door, but more intimate. Excellent oysters. Booking essential.

Tourtour, 20 rue Quincampoix, 4e (tel. 48–04–85–10). Open to 1 A.M. daily. Near the Pompidou Center and decorated to look like the streets of old Paris. Good-value *menus;* simple, traditional French cuisine.

Vagenende, 142 blvd. St.-Germain, 6e (tel. 43–26–68–18). Open to 1 A.M. daily but often closed one week in Feb. Delightful *art nouveau* brasserie serving traditional but sophisticated cuisine. Try the home-made *fois gras.*

Inexpensive

Amanguier, 110 rue de Richelieu, 2e (tel. 42–96–37–79); 51 rue du Théâtre, 15e (tel. 45–77–04–01); 43 av. des Ternes, 17e (tel. 43–80–19–28); 12 av. de Madrid, Neuilly (tel. 47–45–79–73). Open to 12 A.M. daily. Four good-value restaurants, newly refurbished in leather and cane upholstery. Fresh, light cuisine, lots of salads, and superb desserts.

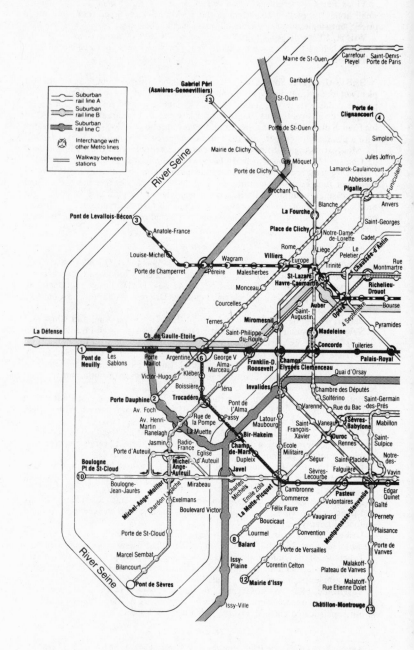

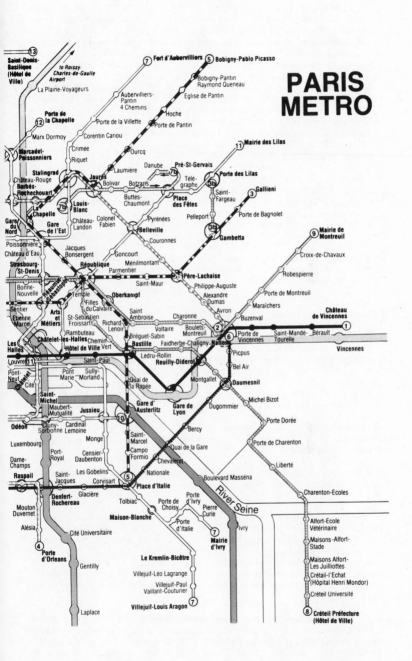

PARIS METRO

André Faure, 40 rue du Mont-Thabor, 1er (tel. 42–60–74–28). Closed Sun. and holidays. Cozy and intimate bistro. At lunchtime there's a *plat du jour* that changes daily, and in the evenings a very good value *menu.*

Bistro de la Gare, 30 rue St.-Denis, 1er (tel. 40–26–82–80); 59 blvd. du Montparnasse, 6e (tel. 45–48–38–01); 1 rue du Four, 6e (tel. 43–25–89–06). Open all year. Popular restaurants with fashionable and interesting interiors. "Formula" meals, reasonable wines, good choice of starters and main dishes.

Bistro Romain, 9 blvd. des Italiens, 2e (tel. 42–60–22–78); 103 blvd. du Montparnasse, 6e (tel. 43–25–25–25); 6 pl. Victor Hugo, 16e (tel. 45–00–65–03). Open daily, year round. Popular chain belonging to the owners of Bistro de la Gare and run on the same lines, though here you'll find an Italian flavor.

La Bonne Table, 5 rue Séveste, 18e (tel. 46–06–96–40). Closed Sun. evening. Authentic, good-value Montmartre bistro with well-priced *menus.*

Brasserie de l'Ile St.-Louis, 55 quai Bourbon, 4e (tel. 43–54–02–59). Closed Wed. and Thurs. lunch. Crowded brasserie in a lovely setting. The decor is Alsatian, but the cuisine is very French. Game in season and good *cassoulet.*

Charpentiers, 10 rue Mabillon, 6e (tel. 43–26–30–05). Closed Sun. Reliable country cooking in an unpretentious bistro, full of mementos of the time when it was the Carpenters' Guild.

Chartier, 7 rue du Faubourg Montmartre, 9e (tel. 47–70–86–29). Open all year. One of the best value restaurants in Paris. Always very crowded but also good fun.

Fontaine de Mars, 129 rue St.-Dominique, 7e (tel. 47–05–46–44). Closed Sat. evening, Sun., and Aug. Simple, family-style restaurant near the Eiffel Tower. The express *menu* at lunchtime has made it very popular with local residents.

Petit St.-Benoit, 4 rue St.-Benoit (no telephone reservations). Closed Sat. and Sun. Traditional French cuisine, at very reasonable prices in a popular and crowded St.-Germain bistro.

Petite Chaise, 36 rue de Grenelle, 7e (tel. 42–22–13–35). Open to 11 P.M. daily. Opened in 1680 and still going strong. An excellent value *menu* with a wide choice of dishes, plus a range of house specialties.

Polidor, 41 rue Monsieur-le-Prince, 6e (tel. 43–26–95–34). Genuine long-established bistro with literary associations—Joyce, Hemingway, Gide, and Verlaine all used to eat here. Good home-cooking in generous portions and at low prices.

Procope, 13 rue de l'Ancienne-Comédie, 6e (tel. 43–26–99–20). Open to 2 A.M. daily. Famous café-restaurant, said to be the oldest in Paris—Balzac and Voltaire knew it as a coffee house. Best to book.

Thoumieux, 79 rue St.-Dominique, 7e (tel. 47–05–49–75). Closed Mon. Large 20s-style restaurant, near the Eiffel Tower specializing in dishes from southwest France. Lots of duck dishes and a good value *menu.*

If you need to fuel up very inexpensively, look for the word SELF, which indicates one of the many cafeterias found all over Paris. The food will be adequate and the prices low.

GETTING AROUND PARIS. Getting around in Paris is easy. Buy a *Plan de Paris* at any newspaper stand. It is one of the best city guides there is, with an alphabetical street directory and clear maps of all 20 *arrondissements,* métro (subway), express métro (RER) and bus lines. At presstime, there were eight "SITU" machines, in or near main métro and RER stations. These are the latest idea to speed travelers and tourists on their way. You feed in the name of the street, museum or tourist sight you want and a card emerges telling you the best method of getting there.

By Métro. The quickest way to get about in Paris is by métro. Every station has a big map showing all the lines and stations, and you can make as many transfers (*correspondances*) as you want on a single ticket. It is best to keep to second-class travel if you are on a tight budget. Ticket prices for both the métro and the buses are uniform. Single tickets at 5 francs are much more expensive than a *carnet* (book) of 10 (31.20 francs), or a day's season ticket (21 francs). The métro runs from 5.30 A.M. to 1.15 A.M. The express métro will take you out into the suburbs, but the central stretch between the Etoile, the Opéra, Les Halles/Châtelet and Luxembourg is also extremely useful within town as it cuts traveling time dramatically. There are clear maps in all RER stations, too. Within the city you can use your ordinary métro ticket; if you are going further out you will need to get a special ticket from one of the slot machines.

By Bicycle. Cycling in Paris' fast and chaotic traffic is not recommended, but you can hire bicycles in the Bois de Boulogne (near Les Sablons métro station) and the Bois de Vincennes if you feel like exploring on the edges of Paris.

By Bus. Buses have only one class and you use the same tickets as for the métro (prices are the same—see above). You may, however, need two tickets, depending on the distance; study the plan at the bus stop. Buses run from 6 A.M. until about 9 or 10 P.M. and there are all-night buses running from Châtelet. Buses are marked with their destination in front, and with the major points they pass along the side. Most do not run on Sundays.

The RATP (Paris Public Transportation System) offers a touring ticket (*Paris-Visite*) which is valid for three or five consecutive days, and entitles you to unlimited travel on the métro, the city buses (and some in the suburbs) and the RER. You can buy the ticket from any métro station. A monthly pass *(Carte orange)* is a good buy if you are staying for some time, but you will need to produce a passport-sized photograph.

ENTERTAINMENT. Probably the most characteristic way of enjoying yourself in Paris for the minimum outlay is joining the café society. You will find cafés with sidewalk tables all over the city and you will never tire of watching the world go by. The traditional places for this form of people-watching are the Champs-Elysées, Saint-Germain-des-Prés, Montparnasse, Les Grands Boulevards, Quartier Latin and the Palais-Royal area. Round the Pompidou/Beaubourg Center you will find plenty of places for observing the avant-garde at work or play. If you feel like more structured entertainment, you should buy one of the weekly What's on in Paris publications, *L'Officiel des Spectacles,* or *Pariscope,* both of which come out on Wednesdays, the day movie programs change. You can also call a special number at the Paris Tourist Office, 47–20–88–98, for a recorded rundown in English of what's on during that particular week. It covers concerts, ballet, *son-et-lumière* times at Les Invalides, exhibitions, parades and special events of all kinds.

Cinema. Paris has hundreds of cinemas, some huge and palatial, some tiny. Parisians are great cinema-goers and the latest films, both foreign and French, are widely discussed. The letters *v.o. (version originale)* beside a foreign film in a newspaper or magazine listing mean that it is showing in the original language; the letters v.f. *(version française)* mean it has been dubbed in French. British or American films with subtitles are usually to be found on the Champs-Elysées or in the small Left Bank cinemas. Paris has two cinémathèques, showing classics from all over the world; one in the Pompidou/Beaubourg Center, the other at the Palais de Chaillot in the pl. du Trocadéro.

Discos. Paris is full of discos these days, and many a little bar or club that used to offer live music now throbs to the sound of the latest discs, generally accompanied by strobe lighting. They usually open about 10 and stay on the boil till around dawn. Most are closed Monday but very few close in the summer; check locally to be safe, however. Prices usually start at around 40 francs entrance fee and first drink.

Les Bains, 7 rue du Bourg-l'Abbé, 3e. Once public baths, now an "in" disco deliberately designed in appalling taste—it's been described as "opulent tacky" and that just about sums it up. Often hard to get in.

Balajo, 9 rue de Lappe, 11e. Lively, crowded and lots of fun. Often plays nostalgic '60s records.

Caveau de la Huchette, 5 rue de la Huchette, 5e. Dixieland in a hectic, smoke-filled atmosphere. Open to 3.30 A.M. Fri. and 4 A.M. Sat.

Gibus, 18 rue du Faubourg du Temple, 11e. Popular spot for the young and trendy. Distinctly cosmopolitan feel—anything goes.

Mambo Club, 20 rue Cujas, 5e. There's a brash, pseudo-tropical feel to this recent Left Bank newcomer near the Sorbonne. Open 11 P.M. until dawn. Closed Mon. and Tues.

Whisky à Gogo, 57 rue de Seine, 6e. Pleasantly old-fashioned, in spite of the inevitable use of dazzling laser beams, and somehow nostalgic. Very popular.

Zed Club, 2 rue des Anglais, 5e. Purely disco these days, with plenty of dancing. Wed. is rock-and-roll night. Closed Mon., Tues., and Aug.

Theaters. There are three types of theater in Paris: national (i.e. state-subsidized) theaters, commercial or boulevard theaters, and experimental theaters. The best-known state theaters are:

Comédie Française, pl. du Théâtre Francais, 1er. One of the world's best-known theaters, specializing in elaborate performances of the great 17th-century dramatists Corneille, Molière and Racine, but also staging the work of modern dramatists from all over the world. Cheap tickets are sold 45 minutes before any performance, but get there early.

Odéon, pl. de l'Odéon, 6e. Used mainly as an overspill for the Comédie Française, but also houses many visiting foreign and provincial companies. Cheap tickets are sold 45 minutes before any performance.

Théâtre de Chaillot, pl. du Trocadéro, 16e. Stages experimental productions of plays from all over the world.

Théâtre de la Colline, 15 rue Malte-Brun, 20e. Opened in 1988, with a program of classics.

Théâtre de la Ville, pl. du Châtelet, 4e. Offers a major international theater festival, plus opera and ballet at times.

For the many commercial theaters you will need to study one of the *What's on in Paris* publications. Most of these theaters are in the Opéra and Montparnasse areas and stage a mixture of translations of international hits (often British or American), and plays by well-known modern French dramatists. Most of the experimental theaters are on the Left Bank, around the Pompidou/Beaubourg Center or on the outskirts of Paris. The *Cartoucherie* in the Bois de Vincennes and the *Lucernaire* in Saint-Germain-des-Prés, 53 rue Notre-Dame des Camps, usually have something good on. Prices vary, but you can usually get a seat up in the rafters from about 50 francs.

Concerts. Paris is a good place for contemporary music, thanks partly to the influence of Pierre Boulez, France's greatest living composer-conductor, who now heads the contemporary music section at the *Pompidou/Beaubourg Center,* where interesting concerts are frequently given. You can also attend concerts at the *Salle Gaveau,* 45 rue La Boétie, 8e; the *Salle Pleyel,* 252 rue du Faubourg St.-Honoré, 8e; the *Salle Wagram,* 39 av. Wagram, 17e; the new *Opéra-Bastille* on Place de la Bastille, 12e; and the *Théâtre des Champs-Elysées,* 15 av. Montaigne, 8e. However, try to attend a concert in one of the city's magnificent historic churches and thus combine sightseeing with listening to music. Have a look to see if there is a concert being performed in *Notre-Dame* (free organ recitals on Sundays at 5 P.M.), *Saint-Louis-des-Invalides, St.-Germain-l'Auxerrois, St.-Merri* or the *Sainte-Chapelle.* The candlelit concerts in the Gothic Sainte-Chapelle are spellbinding. In the summer months you will also find a wealth of interesting music being performed all over the city and the Ile de France during the *Ile de France Festival,* the *Festival Estival* (Summer Festival), and the *Marais Festival.* You can even attend concerts on the sightseeing *bateaux-mouches* that ply the Seine (usually on Saturdays).

MUSEUMS. For details of exact opening times (which change frequently) and special exhibits showing see *L'Officiel des Spectacles* or *Pariscope.* National (i.e. state-owned) museums, marked N in the list below, close on Tuesday all day, and charge only half the normal fee on Sunday or are free, as at the Louvre. City of Paris museums, marked CP in the list, close on Mondays and are free on Sundays. Many museums are closed on all or some public holidays (check locally). Opening times vary considerably but you are usually safe between 10 and 5, though some museums still close for lunch. If museums have unusual opening times they are noted below.

Children, students, teachers, men over 62 and women over 60 get reductions at all times. In CP museums senior citizens are admitted free of charge at all times, (take your passport to prove your age!).

Arts Décoratifs, 107 rue de Rivoli, 1er. Applied arts and furniture in the opposite wing of the Louvre Palace from the Louvre Museum. Has been extensively modernized to give excellent presentation of exhibits. Has good boutique and bookshop. Open Wed. to Sat. 12.30–6, Sun. 11–6.

Archives Nationales, 60 rue des Francs-Bourgeois, 3e. The history of France illustrated by documents and exhibits, set in the lovely old Hôtel Soubise.

Art Moderne de la Ville de Paris, 11 av. du Président-Wilson, 16e. 20th-century art plus good temporary shows. Open to 8.30 Wed. CP.

Arts et Traditions Populaires, 6 route du Mahatma-Gandhi, Bois de Boulogne (Sablons entrance), 16e. Astounding variety of objects related to rural activities in pre-industrial environments. Half price on Sun. N.

Balzac's House, 47 rue Raynouard, 16e. Mementos of the writer in delightful setting; good temporary exhibits related to his life and times. CP.

Carnavalet, 23 rue de Sévigné, 3e. Costumes through the ages, china, history of Paris. Mementos of Mme. de Sévigné; 17th- and 18th-century French furniture. CP.

Centre Beaubourg or **Centre National d'Art et de Culture Georges Pompidou,** rue St.-Martin, 4e. Open noon to 10 P.M. weekdays, except Tues.; weekends 10–10. Huge futuristic cultural center, including the *National Museum of Modern Art,* industrial design, temporary exhibits, library, theatrical activities, experimental music. No admission charge to the Centre itself, but you pay to visit the National Museum of Modern Art. N.

Cluny, 6 pl. Paul-Painlevé, 5e. Medieval museum in a delightful 15th-century abbey, with remnants of Roman baths. Do not miss *La Dame à la Licorne* tapestry in rooms built into the Gallo-Roman foundations or the recently discovered fragments of sculptures from Notre-Dame.

Conciergerie, 1 quai de l'Horloge, 1er. Relics of the French Revolution, Marie Antoinette's cell. Superb 14th-century vaulted hall.

Delacroix Studio, 6 pl. de Fürstemberg, 6e. In a charming old square, the Romantic artist's studio has been preserved as he left it. N.

Histoire Naturelle, Jardin des Plantes, 57 rue Cuvier, 5e. Zoological, mineralogical, and paleontological exhibits open 10–5, hothouses 1–5, insects 2–5. Closed Tues. Also has menagerie (open 9–5 in winter, 9–7 in summer).

Invalides and **Musée de l'Armée,** Esplanade des Invalides, 7e. Napoleon's Tomb, military museum, weapons, armor, battle flags. Sound and Light program (including English version) nightly in summer.

Louvre, rue de Rivoli, 1er. The world's largest museum in the world's largest palace. Has six main sections: Greek and Roman; Oriental; Egyptian; sculpture; paintings and drawings; furniture and *objets d'art* from the Middle Ages to the 19th cent. Plus of course the *Mona Lisa.* Lecture tours in English and French at frequent intervals. N.

Marine, Palais de Chaillot, pl. du Trocadéro, 16e. Ship models and seafaring objects.

Marmottan, 2 rue Louis-Boilly, 16e. Magnificent collection of Monet's works and some remarkable illuminated manuscripts.

Musée de l'Homme, Palais de Chaillot, pl. du Trocadéro, 16e. Fine anthropological museum, with excellent modern presentation. Documentary films shown daily.

Musée d'Orsay, 1 rue de Bellechasse, 7e. French arts from 1848 to 1914 in a converted rail station. Interior designed by Gae Aulenti. Open to 9.45 P.M. on Thurs; closed Mon.

Musée Picasso, Hôtel Salé, 5 rue de Thorigny, 3e. Converted historic mansion in the Marais. Open weekdays 9.15–5.15 and till 10 Wed., closed Tues. Free for under 18s.

Orangerie. Museum of modern art in the Tuileries, across from the now-neglected Jeu de Paume. Renoir and Monet (including his waterlilies) top the bill. Open 9.45–5.15; closed Tues.

Palais de la Découverte, 1 av. Franklin-Roosevelt, 8e. Scientific and technical exhibits, working models, planetarium.

Rodin, 77 rue de Varenne, 7e. A delightful house and garden where Rodin once lived and worked and which he filled with his sculpture. N.

Victor Hugo's House, 6 pl. des Vosges, 4e. The great writer once lived in this fine house, which is now full of exhibits connected with him. CP.

PARKS AND GARDENS. The center of Paris has few real parks, but there are several delightful formal gardens that are ideal for strolling or enjoying a picnic lunch. Do remember, however, that in France "Don't walk on the grass" is very much the order of the day—you will soon be called to order by a uniformed park keeper if you try it.

The most central garden is the *Jardin des Tuileries*, running between the pl. de la Concorde and the Louvre, and originally designed by the great landscape artist Le Nôtre. Acting as a foil to it you will find the *Jardin des Champs-Elysées*, on the other side of the pl. de la Concorde and running parallel to the eastern end of the Champs-Elysées. Also central is the *Jardin du Palais-Royal*, which forms an oasis of peace beside the Comédie Française.

On the other side of the Seine near the Austerlitz station the *Jardin des Plantes* or Botanical Garden is little known to tourists but is popular with Parisians. It has a good display of flowers and is well worth a visit if you are going to see the Natural History Museum. Along the Seine, close to the Jardin des Plantes, is a new garden filled with modern sculpture and known as the Musée des Sculptures en Plein Air. Further north in the Latin Quarter do try to head for the delights of the *Jardin du Luxembourg*, with its leafy avenues, elegant statues and boat-sailing children; puppet shows are held there most of the year, usually around 3 P.M. The *Jardin des Invalides*, laid out on the Esplanade des Invalides, is a great improvement on the dusty carpark that used to disfigure the magnificent panorama sweeping from the Seine to the Hôtel des Invalides. Not far from there is one of Paris' most pleasant gardens, the *Jardin du Musée Rodin*, full of roses and sculptures by Rodin himself and by other sculptors. And on the southeastern edge of the city you will find the little-known *Parc Montsouris*, close to the Cité Universitaire and surrounded by charming little streets that seem to have survived from an age when Paris was a series of villages rather than a bustling metropolis.

On the northern edge of Paris you have a choice of the *Parc Monceau* off the blvd. Courcelles, popular with old-established families living in the grand apartments of the 17th arrondissement, and the *Parc des Buttes-Chaumont* (in the 19th), perched high above the city and offering splendid views.

Many of these parks have refreshment booths where you can get inexpensive snacks. The woodland areas on the very edge of Paris—the *Bois de Boulogne* on the far west and the *Bois de Vincennes* on the far east—are wilder as you venture into the heart of them. Do not do so at night, however, as they are full of undesirable characters as soon as dusk falls. Both Bois do have their formal aspect too—lakes, a Shakespeare Garden, the Bagatelle flower gardens (which you must pay to enter), a children's zoo, two racecourses and even a cricket ground in the Bois de Boulogne; and a zoo, a trotting racecourse, museum, and several lakes in the Bois de Vincennes.

Near the Bois de Boulogne are the *Jardins Kahn*, full of trees and flowers from all over the world. Further south is the *Parc de St.-Cloud*, ideal for a Sunday afternoon stroll or dinner on a summer evening (before 9 P.M.).

SHOPPING. Paris's tempting window displays often show alarmingly high prices and you may well feel that window shopping is the closest you will get to making a purchase. But you can come away with a little something without emptying your wallet if you take some simple precautions. Have a look at the smart little boutiques in Saint-Germain-des-Prés or in and around the Forum des Halles, selling fashions, jewelry, antiques, prints and so on. Also pop into the chic department stores, *Galeries Lafayette* or *Printemps*, just north of the Opéra, and the elegant shopping arcades leading off the Champs-Elysées. But then head for the less expensive areas to make your actual purchases, in the places where ordinary Parisians, as opposed to the rich cosmopolitan set, do their shopping. Try the rue St.-Antoine, between the Bastille and St.-Paul métro stations, the boutiques round St.-Lazare station or up the blvd. St.-Michel, and the side streets in the 15th arrondissement. You might well find a bargain in one of the street markets that are all over Paris with stalls selling excellent bargains in clothes and accessories—but you are more likely to find a trinket to take home at the *Marché d'Aligre* (behind the Bastille at weekends). The famous flea market *(Marché aux Puces)* at the Porte de Clignancourt on the northern edge of the city might come as a disappointment though, as clothes and antiques are now easily as expensive as in the shops.

Look out for the chainstores called *Monoprix* and *Prisunic*. They are good places for stylish children's clothes, fun accessories, and attractive stationery. The down-market department stores close to the Seine on the rue de Rivoli have reasonably priced goods; try the *Bazar de l'Hôtel-de-Ville* and the *Samaritaine.*

For souvenirs of your visit the best place is the rue de Rivoli, the stretch between the Concorde and the Palais-Royal. Here you will find miniature copies of Limoges porcelain, charms of the Eiffel Tower and other monuments for a charm bracelet, corny but attractive scarves with views of Paris, little busts of Napoleon and so on—plenty of choice and reasonable prices. If you are good at dressmaking, you may feel like visiting the amazing *Dreyfus* at 2 rue Charles-Nodier, 18e, part of the Marché St.-Pierre, at the foot of the Butte Montmartre, where you can acquire a leftover couture fabric for remarkably little and fashion yourself a Paris outfit. Lastly, if you are keen to take home an edible souvenir, avoid the grand stores around the pl. de la Madeleine and buy your goodies in any ordinary little grocer's or *charcuterie* (delicatessen). Discount perfume shops are becoming more common and give reductions of at least 20 per cent; keep your eyes peeled.

USEFUL ADDRESSES. *U.S. Embassy,* 2 av. Gabriel, 8e (tel. 42–96–12–02); *Canadian Embassy,* 35 av. Montaigne, 8e (tel. 47–23–01–01); *British Embassy,* 35 Faubourg St.-Honoré, 8e (tel. 42–66–91–42); *Paris Tourist Office,* 127 av. des Champs-Elysées, 8e (tel. 47–23–61–72); *American Express,* 11 rue Scribe, 9e (tel. 42–66–09–99); *Wagon Lits* 106 rue Danton, Le Vallois-perret (tel. 42–68–24–00); *Thomas Cook,* 9 blvd. Malesherbes (tel. 42–66–91–46); *Main post office* (open 24 hours a day), 52 rue du Louvre, 1er; *American Hospital,* 63 blvd. Victor-Hugo, Neuilly (tel. 47–47–53–00); *British Hospital,* 48 rue de Villiers, Levallois-Perret (tel. 47–58–13–12).

Ile de France

The Ile de France is the name given to the large area surrounding and including Paris that was once a separate province and was the base from which France's earliest kings gradually spread their authority until they ruled over the whole kingdom. It contains a wealth of treasure that no visitor should miss, and can be explored from Paris in a series of one- or two-day excursions. Avoid the comfortable but expensive tourist buses and coaches and opt for a more leisurely voyage of discovery by public transport. The RER (express métro) will take you out cheaply and quickly to enjoy the wonders of the Palace of Versailles; charming Malmaison where Josephine was at first so happy and then so tragically alone; the castle of St.-Germain-en-Laye with its excellent museum devoted to the prehistoric period, the Gallo-Roman period and the Merovingians, and a new museum in an attractive old priory once lived in by Nabis painter Maurice Denis; the gardens and Ile de France Museum in Sceaux; or the fascinating château de Breteuil, which has been lived in by the same family since it was built in the early 17th century. Easy train journeys will allow you to travel further afield to the wonderful Gothic cathedral at Chartres with its breathtaking stained glass; to the twin châteaux at Chantilly, surrounded by lovely grounds; to Fontainebleau with its palace and forest and the nearby artists' village of Barbizon; Compiègne where the 1918 armistice was signed; and the splendid but unfinished cathedral at Beauvais.

The ordinary métro now goes as far as the town of Saint-Denis with its basilica where all but three of France's kings were buried and where you can see magnificent medieval and Renaissance sculpture. There is also a Museum of History and Art in a former monastery, about ten minutes away. From Saint-Denis bus 268C traveling to Ezanville will drop you off at Ecouen, where the beautiful château now houses an excellent Museum of the Renaissance. The Château de Vincennes to the east of Paris can also be reached by métro; there you will see the royal pavilion where Louis XIV spent his honeymoon and the keep where Henry V of England, the victor at Agincourt and Shakespeare's Prince Hal, died in 1422.

But if you have time for only one excursion the obvious "must" is the Palace of Versailles, which can also be reached by train from the Gare St.-Lazare, or by RER from the Invalides or St.-Michel stations. You can visit the state apartments, the celebrated Galerie des Glaces or Hall of Mirrors, and the royal bedrooms, all of them now splendidly furnished and full of magnificent paintings and furniture. In the huge and beautiful grounds you will find a palace in miniature, the Grand Trianon, again full of works of art, and the Petit Trianon where Queen Marie-

Antoinette liked to escape the rigors of court etiquette. Nearby is the Hameau or
Hamlet in which she and her companions, dressed as shepherdesses, frolicked round
the thatched cottages, the dairy and the mill. Allow yourself time to stroll round
the town of Versailles, which has some beautiful houses and gardens.

PRACTICAL INFORMATION FOR THE ILE DE FRANCE

Hotels and Restaurants

Ile-de-France restaurants are crowded on Sundays so it is advisable to reserve,
though Inexpensive restaurants will not always accept reservations. Hotels do not
have restaurants unless they are mentioned. Closing days sometimes change without warning so check first.

Barbizon. *La Clé d'Or* (M), 73 Grande-Rue (tel. 60–66–28–50). Small and central Logis de France with garden. *Auberge des Alouettes* (I), 4 rue Antoine-Barye
(tel. 60–66–41–98). Another Logis de France, with garden and tennis courts. Both
hotels have restaurants.
Restaurants. *Relais de Barbizon* (M), 2 av. Charles-de-Gaulle (tel. 60–66–40–28).
Traditional French dishes served in the garden in fine weather. Good value *menu.*
Broche de Barbizon (I), 86 Grande Rue (tel. 60–66–40–76). On edge of forest, rustic
décor, good grills.

Beauvais. *Chenal* (M), 62 blvd. Général-de-Gaulle (tel. 44–45–03–55). Small,
with bar; close to station. *Mercure* (M), 1 av. Montaigne (tel. 44–02–03–36). On
edge of town; modern with pool and light meals.
Restaurants. *Crémaillère* (M), 1 rue Gui-Patin (tel. 44–45–03–13). Closed Wed.
all year and Tues. eve. in winter. Good regional cuisine. *Marignan* (I), 1 rue Mal-
herbe (tel. 44–48–15–15). Closed Sun. eve., Mon., and Feb. Close to cathedral and
tourist office. Offers a range of inexpensive *menus.*

Breteuil. On Sundays from Easter until October you can eat pleasantly in the
crêperie (I) in the grounds of the château. *Auberge du Moulin* (M), in nearby
Chevreuse (tel. 30–52–16–45). Attractive. Closed Tues. and mid-Aug. to mid-Sept.

Chantilly. *Campanile* (M), Les Huit Curés, rte. Creil, Gouvieux (tel. 44–57–39–
24). Modern motel; quiet and well-run, with restaurant.
Restaurants. *Relais Condé* (M), 42 av. Joffre (tel. 44–57–05–75). Closed Mon.
and Tues. Traditional and modern fare. *Capitainerie du Château* (I), tel. 44–57–15–
89. Closed Mon. and Tues. Help-yourself buffet available non-stop 10.30–6.30.

Chartres. *Grand Monarque* (M), 22 pl. des Epars (tel. 37–21–00–72). Good mix-
ture of classical and more modern cuisine in this pleasant converted coaching inn.
Mercure-Châtelet (M), 6 av. Jehan-de-Beauce (tel. 37–21–78–00). Central, modern
and well run, with restaurant.
Restaurant. *Buisson Ardent* (M), 10 rue au Lait (tel. 37–34–04–66). Closed Sun.,
Tues. eve., Wed., and Aug. Imaginative cuisine, good-value menus.

Compiègne. *France* (I), 17 rue Eugène-Floquet (tel. 44–40–02–74). 17th-
century inn, with restaurant (M).
Restaurant. At Choisy-au-Bac (825 rue Vineux) 2 miles northeast, *Auberge des
Etangs du Buissonnet* (M), tel. 44–40–17–41. Closed Sun. and Mon. Good classical
cuisine including some regional dishes. *Le Picotin* (I), 22 pl. de l'Hôtel de Ville (tel.
44–40–04–06). Closed Tues. eve. and Wed. Near the château.

Fontainebleau. *Ile de France* (M), 128 rue de France (tel. 64–22–21–17). Delightful typically French house with flowery garden and, oddly enough, Chinese
cuisine in the restaurant. Very reasonably priced.
Restaurants. *Dauphin* (M), 24 rue Grande (tel. 64–22–27–04). Reader-
recommended; closed Tues. eve. and Wed. *Filet de Sole* (M), 5 rue Coq-Gris (tel.
64–22–25–05). Closed Tues., Wed., and July. Exquisite fish dishes.

Malmaison. Restaurants. *Auberge des Tilleuls* (M), 2 quai Conti (tel. 39–69–00–97), slightly further west at Louveciennes. Closed Mon. and Tues. *Pavillon des Guides* (M), 193 av. Napoléon-Bonaparte, Rueil-Malmaison (tel. 47–51–82–83). Lunch only, closed Sat. Well-prepared, traditional cuisine. Lovely terrace overlooking the Seine. *Relais de St.-Cucufa* (M), 114 rue Général-de-Miribel (tel. 47–49–79–05). Closed Sun., Mon. eve., and second fortnight in Aug. Good fish dishes and Italian specialties.

Saint-Germain-En-Laye. Restaurants. *Petite Auberge* (M), 119 bis rue Léon-Désoyer (tel. 34–51–03–99). Closed Tues. eve., Wed., and July. Nice atmosphere, traditional homestyle dishes, game in season, wine from the barrel. *Coches* (M), 7 rue des Coches (tel. 39–73–66–40). Closed Sun. eve., Mon., and Aug. Fashionable, with good food.

Versailles. *Versailles* (M), 5 rue Ste.-Anne (tel. 39–50–64–65). Modern, near château; no restaurant. *Richaud* (I), 16 rue Richaud (tel. 39–50–10–42). Convenient for station. No restaurant.

Restaurant. *Quai No1* (M), 1 av. de St-Cloud (tel. 39–50–42–26). Closed Sun. eve. and Mon. A salty backdrop of barometers and sails for shipshape fish and seafood.

Normandy

William the Conqueror and Joan of Arc, the Bayeux Tapestry and Norman architecture, the Canadian Jubilee Raid and the D-Day landings—Normandy probably has more associations for English-speaking visitors than any other part of France. Easily reached from Paris, and from Britain, it offers varied scenery ranging from the wild granite cliffs in the west to the long sandy beaches along the Channel coast; from the wooded valleys of the south to the lush green meadows and apple orchards in the heart of the region. These produce the rich butter, cheese (Camembert, Livarot, Pont-l'Evêque) and cream, the cider and calvados (apple brandy) that have made this one of the best-known gastronomic regions in a country famed for fine eating. Normandy's historic cities have been restored and rebuilt after wartime bombing and offer a wealth of fine buildings and museums, while the mighty abbeys are of endless interest. Mont St.-Michel, that glorious Gothic abbey perched on top of a rocky sea-girt mound, is one of the country's major tourist sights.

You will certainly want to set aside a day to visit the Mount and do not be put off by the hordes of tourists and souvenir sellers. It has been a popular pilgrimage center since the first chapel was built here in the 8th century and medieval pilgrims were as eager for souvenirs as today's more secular tourists. Conducted tours of the abbey take place in English at frequent intervals and you should leave enough time to walk round the ramparts with their glorious views of the bay. But do be careful if you plan to walk around the Mount—the tide comes in with breathtaking speed and there are patches of quicksand too.

Moving northwards from Mont St.-Michel, the Cotentin Peninsula is a good place for budget holidays, with a good choice of *gîtes ruraux* and farm accommodations as well as modest little resorts on the west coast such as Barneville-Carteret or Granville. The wild stretch of coast on the northwestern edge of the peninsula ending in the granite promontory of the Nez de Jobourg and the Cap de la Hague is well worth exploring.

Normandy's other points of interest are less spectacular. Caen is a good center for exploring the long sandy beaches where so many young Allied soldiers lost their lives during the dramatic days of June 1944. Do not miss the excellent museum devoted to the D-Day landings on the seafront at Arromanches, or the impressive American Cemetery to the west beyond the charming little fishing harbor of Port-en-Bessin. Caen itself has been successfully restored and is now a lively modern city with some splendid tourist attractions—William the Conqueror's castle, the richly carved Gothic church of St.-Pierre, and the wonderful twin abbeys, the Abbaye aux Dames and Abbaye aux Hommes, built by William and his wife Matilda. There are also two good museums.

From Caen you can visit little seaside resorts such as Courseulles, famous for its oyster beds, and historic Bayeux, with its magnificent tapestry (in fact an embroidered scroll) illustrating in lively detail the dramatic story of the Norman Conquest. East of Caen along the coast you will find the picturesque fishing harbor of Honfleur, and the chic resorts of Deauville and Trouville—fun to visit but you had better stay in one of the less expensive resorts such as Houlgate. Inland from here is the Pays d'Auge, cheese-cider-and-calvados country with picturesque lanes and with many opportunities for farm holidays and meals in inexpensive inns. Lisieux, where St. Thérèse lived and died, is the largest town in this area.

On the other side of the Seine estuary lies busy Le Havre, rebuilt in a rather uninspired fashion but with a good museum of modern art. Eastwards stretches the Alabaster Coast with its tall white cliffs and friendly little resorts—Etretat, Fécamp, and further on St.-Valéry-en-Caux and Veulette-sur-Mer. The biggest town on this coast is busy Dieppe, a mecca for the budget tourist with its many cafés and inexpensive restaurants around the harbor.

The best center for visiting the meandering valley of the Seine, famous for its abbeys, including the mighty ruins of Jumièges, is Rouen, which is only an hour by train from Paris. Rouen is an invigorating blend of old and new, with its wonderful Gothic cathedral (painted by Monet), its magnificent churches and beautifully restored old streets and houses contrasting with the startlingly modern church and memorial dedicated to France's patron saint, Joan of Arc, in the ancient marketplace where she was burnt at the stake in 1431.

PRACTICAL INFORMATION FOR NORMANDY

Hotels and Restaurants

Arromanches. *Marine* (I), 1 quai Canada, right on seafront (tel. 31–22–34–19). Closed mid-Nov. through Feb. Good views and restaurant.

Barneville-Carteret. *Isles* (M), blvd. Maritime, Barneville (tel. 33–04–90–76). Garden, sea views and good restaurant. *Marine* (M), 2 rue de Paris, Carteret (tel. 33–53–83–31). Complicated opening, check locally. Good views and pleasant restaurant.

Bayeux. *Lion d'Or* (M), 71 rue St.-Jean (tel. 31–92–06–90). Closed Dec. 20th to Jan. 20th. Exceptionally pleasant and comfortable, good restaurant.
Restaurant. *Gourmets* (I), 3 rue du Dr-Guillet (tel. 31–92–02–02). Closed Wed. eve., Thurs., second fortnight in Oct., mid-Feb. to early Mar.

Cabourg. *Paris* (M), 39 av. de la Mer (tel. 31–91–31–34). Small, close to sea. No restaurant. *L'Oie Qui Fume* (I), 18 av. Brèche-Buhot (tel. 31–91–27–79). Closed Jan. Overlooking harbor.

Caen. *Relais des Gourmets* (M), 15 rue de Geôle (tel. 31–86–06–01). Just by castle, a bit staid, but comfortable and good value, with good restaurant. *Moderne* (M), 116 blvd. Maréchal-Leclerc (tel. 31–86–04–23). Central but quiet; good restaurant. *Univers* (I), 12 quai Vendeuvre (tel. 31–85–46–14). Central, overlooking Bassin St.-Pierre; no restaurant.
Restaurant. *Dauphin* (M), 29 rue Gémare (tel. 31–86–22–26). Closed Sat., Feb., and mid-July to mid-Aug. Good mixture of classical and new cuisine, also has a few rooms.

Deauville. *Marie-Anne* (M), 142 av. République (tel. 31–88–35–32). Closed Jan., last 3 weeks in Nov. Converted private house with garden; no restaurant. *Patio* (I), 180 av. République (tel. 31–88–25–07). Pleasant rooms, garden, no restaurant.
Restaurants. *Spinaker* (M), 52 rue Mirabeau (tel. 31–88–24–40). Closed Wed., Thurs. in winter, mid-Nov. to mid-Dec. Highly original cuisine. *Les Vapeurs* (I), 160 blvd. F. Moureaux (tel. 31–88–15–24). In Trouville. Open all year. Popular and lively, with 50s decor. Serves excellent seafood.

Dieppe. *Windsor* (M), 18 blvd. de Verdun (tel. 35–84–15–23). Traditional hotel overlooking sea, comfortable, with restaurant.

Restaurants. *Marmite Dieppoise* (M), 8 rue St.-Jean (tel. 35–84–24–26). Closed last week in Jun. and first week in July, Sun. eve., Mon., and mid-Dec. to mid-Jan. Good regional cooking, nice atmosphere. *Port* (I), 99 quai Henri-IV (tel. 35–84–36–64). Closed Thurs. and mid-Jan. to mid-Feb. Quayside restaurant with good fish cooked in the classic manner. *Sully* (I), 97 quai Henri-IV (tel. 35–84–23–13). Closed mid-Nov. to mid-Dec., Tues. eve., and Wed. Attractive quayside restaurant, opposite car ferry terminal.

Etretat. *Falaises* (M), 1 av. René-Coty (tel. 35–27–02–77). Open all year. Not far from casino and beach; no restaurant. *Escale* (I), pl. Maréchal-Foch (tel. 35–27–03–69). Closed Dec and Jan. Restaurant closed Tues. eve. and Wed. Pleasant rooms and good-value restaurant.

Restaurant. *Roches Blanches* (I), rue Abbé-Cochet (tel. 35–27–07–34). Complicated opening, check locally. On seafront, a friendly, family restaurant serving lots of Normandy specialties.

Fécamp. *Angleterre* (M), 91 rue de la Plage (tel. 35–28–01–60). Comfortable, 250 yards from the beach. No restaurant.

Restaurants. *Escalier* (M), 101 quai Bérigny (tel. 35–28–26–79). Closed Mon. and beginning Nov. Good seafood. *Martin* (I), 18 pl. St.-Etienne (tel. 35–28–23–82). Closed Sun. eve., Mon., first half of Mar. and first half of Sept. Good-value Normandy cooking, with particularly good fish. Also has 7 rooms.

Honfleur. *Lechat* (M), 3 pl. Ste.-Catherine (tel. 31–89–23–85). Open all year. Just behind harbor in pretty square. Good restaurant and service. *Pélerins* (I), 6 rue Capucins (tel. 31–89–19–61). Unpretentious; some (M) rooms, comfortable.

Restaurants. There is a wide choice of eating places in Honfleur, the most picturesque ones being around the harbor. *Absinthe* (M), 10 quai Quarantaine (tel. 31–89–39–00). Closed Mon. eve., Tues. (except in summer). Mixture of traditional and *nouvelle cuisine. Ancrage* (M), 16 rue Montpensier (tel. 31–89–00–70). Closed Tues. eve. out of season, Wed., and Jan. Overlooking the *Vieux Bassin,* full of yachts in summer. Vast seafood platters and good choice of fish dishes.

Houlgate. *Lieu Marot* (M), 21 rte. Vallée (outside town via D24), tel. 31–91–19–44. Peaceful setting among apple trees; pleasant rooms, homestyle cooking. *Hostellerie Normande* (M), 11 rue Emile-Deschanel (tel. 31–91–22–36). Closed Jan. Restaurant (closed Tues.) serves Normandy cuisine.

Lisieux. *Place* (M), 67 rue Henry-Chéron (tel. 31–31–17–44). Close to cathedral, with large, well-appointed rooms; no restaurant. *Maris-Stella* (I), 56 bis rue Orbec (tel. 31–62–01–05). Hotel closed Christmas; restaurant closed Sat. lunch and Sun. eve. in winter. Not far from basilica.

Restaurant. *Auberge du Pêcheur* (M), 2 bis rue de Verdun (tel. 31–31–16–85). Excellent fish and shellfish. Closed Mon. and Tues.

Mont-St.-Michel. *St.-Aubert* (M), on D976 on mainland (tel. 33–60–08–74). Modern hotel, large well-decorated rooms. No restaurant.

Restaurant. *Terrasses Poulard* (M), Grande-Rue, tel. 33–60–14–09. Marvelous view; meals served outside in good weather; good traditional cooking. Closed Jan.

Rouen. *Cathedrale* (M), 12 rue St.-Romain (tel. 35–71–57–95). Open all year. In pedestrian street near cathedral; a bit old-fashioned but charming, with tiny flower-filled garden. No restaurant. *Normandie* (M), 19 rue Bec (tel. 35–71–55–77). Quiet, in pedestrian street in old town. Also no restaurant.

Restaurants. *Beffroy* (M), 15 rue Beffroy (tel. 35–71–55–27). Closed Aug. and part of Feb. Attractive, deliciously light cuisine. *La Couronne* (M), 31 pl. du Vieux Marché (tel. 35–71–40–90). Closed Sun. eve. Good traditional cooking in the "oldest inn in France" (1345). *Dufour* (M), 67 rue St.-Nicolas (tel. 35–71–90–62). Closed Sun. eve., Mon., and mid-July to mid-Aug. Genuine Norman atmosphere; good fish dishes.

Yvetot. *Havre* (I), 2 rue Guy-de-Maupassant (tel. 35–95–16–77). Central and modern; good seafood restaurant.

Brittany

The old province of Brittany jutting into the sea at France's northwestern tip has long been a favorite of budget tourists. It offers varied scenery, architecture unlike anything you will see elsewhere and a number of colorful customs and ceremonies. Although it has smart resorts along its 1,200 km. (750 miles) of jagged coastline, you will have no trouble in finding charming little family resorts, with inexpensive accommodation and really good-value eating. Inland you can explore tiny villages with their strange-looking granite churches, puzzle over prehistoric megaliths and dolmens, and camp or stay on the many farms dotting the green countryside.

Many British travel agents offer good-value all-in holidays, generally based on small seaside resorts. The ferry companies, too, have good packages. If you want a self-catering holiday, the region is well supplied with gîtes, holiday villages and the like. The tourist authorities are well organized to deal with budget tourists and publish a series of annual lists of holiday rentals, including vacation villages, of camp and caravan sites, youth hostels, and of hotels. Ask too for the *Destination Bretagne* brochure, giving details of around 60 hotel-restaurants offering reasonable prices all over the region.

Many visitors start their Brittany holiday with picturesque St.-Malo, surrounded by medieval ramparts and full of nice little restaurants. It makes a good base for exploring the eastern corner of Brittany, which boasts several Renaissance châteaux. Close to St.-Malo is chic Dinard in a picturesque setting, and all along the coast westwards you will find granite cliffs alternating with small sandy beaches and coves. The most popular resorts lie in the center of the Channel coast, clustered around lively Perros-Guirec—Trébeurden, Trégastel, and Ploumanach are all good bets. Among dozens of family resorts on the Atlantic coast, particular favorites are Concarneau, much frequented by painters, Bénodet, and Beg-Meil, while Tréboul and the nearby fishing and canning center of Douarnenez are larger but no less attractive.

If you prefer to base yourself in a town and travel out from there, you might like to pick Quimper, a lively cathedral town near Douarnenez, and the center of an area in which Breton traditions are still very much alive. From here you can make bus excursions to various seaside resorts, to the curious parish enclosure at Pleyben, and to the little towns of Pont-Aven and Le Pouldu, made famous by the painter Paul Gauguin. Another good base in southern Brittany is Vannes, the best place from which to attend the famous *Pardon,* Brittany's best known religious festival, at Sainte-Anne-d'Auray. This takes place in July and gives you a chance to see the traditional costumes and intricate lace headdresses that few women now wear except on special occasions. From Vannes you can also visit the splendid château at Josselin, and the strange seaside village of Carnac with over 3000 prehistoric megaliths, including the amazing rows of standing stones that even the experts cannot fully explain. The long peninsula of Quiberon is worth a visit for magnificent seascapes and beautiful grottoes; ferries leave from here to the lovely Belle-Ile—a real gem of an island that is a particularly good place to be on Bastille day with the harbor packed, fireworks, and the little square with its pavement restaurants full to bursting point.

Brittany's largest town and capital is Rennes, on the eastern edge of the region. It is a pleasant, dignified city with a good art museum and an attractive Old Town round the cathedral. You might like to use it as a base for visiting interesting Vitré, a small town that is still essentially medieval in appearance, and Fougères with its multi-towered castle and its Balzac associations.

PRACTICAL INFORMATION FOR BRITTANY

Hotels and Restaurants

Bear in mind that Brittany is a very popular holiday destination for French families as well as foreign visitors, so you must make reservations well ahead if you are planning a vacation in July or August. You will find seaside resorts less crowded, and prices often lower, in June or September. Inexpensive hotels are clean and friendly but rarely have the modern amenities you find in more prosperous areas. Restaurants are good value, with wonderfully fresh seafood. Many hotels and restaurants are closed from October to Easter.

Bénodet. *Kastel-Moor* (M), av. Plage (tel. 98–57–05–01). Closed late Oct. to Easter. Near sea, modern with own restaurant. Swimming pool, tennis courts.
Restaurant. *Jeanne d'Arc* (M), 52 rue Plage, at Sainte Marine over the river (tel. 98–56–32–70). Good mixture of Burgundian and Breton cuisine.

Cancale. *Continental* (M), quai Administrateur-Thomas (tel. 98–89–60–16). Traditional hotel on harbor's edge, restaurant. A couple of miles north, is yet another good Logis de France. *Pointe du Grouin* (M), (tel. 99–89–60–55). Open Apr. to end Sept., closed Tues. except mid-July through Aug. Charming and quiet with views to Mont St.-Michel.
Restaurant. *Cancalais* (M), 12 quai Gambetta (tel. 99–89–61–93). Closed second half of both Nov. and Jan. Lovely views; also has 8 (I) rooms.

Carnac. *Genêts* (M), 45 av. Kermario (tel. 97–52–11–01). Closed Oct. through May, except for Easter hols. Set among pine trees not far from beach.

Combourg. *Château et Voyageurs* (M), 1 pl. Chateaubriand (tel. 99–73–00–38). Closed mid-Dec. to Jan. 20. Garden and restaurant.
Restaurant. *Lac* (I), 2 pl. Chateaubriand (tel. 99–73–05–65). Closed Nov., Fri., and Sun. eve. in winter. Large and good value; also has 30 rooms (M).

Concarneau. *Sables Blancs* (M), plage des Sables Blancs (tel. 98–97–01–39). Quiet hotel near beach; some rooms with sea view. *Jockey* (I), 11 av. P.-Guéguin (tel. 98–97–31–52). Small traditional hotel near harbor; no restaurant.
Restaurant. *Coquille* (M), 1 rue Moros, tel. 98–97–08–52. Closed first half Jan., second half May, Sun. eve. (except July and Aug.) and Mon. By harbor. Reasonably priced, traditional *menus*.

Dinan. *Marguérite* (I), 29 pl. Du-Guesclin (tel. 96–39–47–65). Closed Jan. Highly regarded, traditional hotel with restaurant (I) serving regional dishes.

Dinard. *Printania* (M), 5 av. George-V (tel. 99–46–13–07). Marvelous views, restaurant. *Altaïr* (I), 18 blvd Féart (tel. 99–46–13–58). Closed Sun. eve. Hotel with 21 rooms and well known for its restaurant. Good *nouvelle cuisine;* inventive fish dishes.

Fougères. *Voyageurs* (M), 10 pl. Gambetta (tel. 99–99–08–20). Closed Christmas and New Year. Close to castle. Also has restaurant serving regional dishes (tel. 99–99–14–17). Closed second fortnight in Aug., Sun. eve. and Sat. (except July and Aug.).

Josselin. *Château* (M), 1 rue Général-de-Gaulle (tel. 97–22–20–11). Closed Feb., Sun. eve. and Mon. in winter. Lovely views of château. Restaurant (I).

Perros-Guirec. *St. Yves* (I), 11 blvd. Aristide Briand (tel. 96–23–21–31). Closed Nov. Close to Trestraou beach.

Pont-Aven. Restaurant. *Bois d'Amour* (I), 11 rue E.-Bernard (tel. 98–06–00–53). Closed Oct. and Wed. Friendly, good value.

Quimper. *Tour d'Auvergne* (M), 13 rue Réguaires (tel. 98–95–08–70). Closed Christmas and New Year. Traditional hotel with good regional cooking. *Terminus* (I), 15 av. Gare (tel. 98–90–00–63). Just by the station. No restaurant.
Restaurants. *Capucin Gourmand* (M), 29 rue Réguaires (tel. 98–95–43–12). Closed mid-July to mid-Aug., Sat. and Sun. Good traditional cuisine in elegant setting. *Buffet de la Gare* (I), pl. Louis-Armand (tel. 98–90–01–03). at the station. *Ambroisie* (I), 49 rue Fréron (tel. 98–95–00–02). Closed Mon. out of season and part of Oct. Cozy modern decor; á la carte can be pricey.

Rennes. *Du Guesclin* (M), 5 pl. Gare (tel. 99–31–47–47). Open all year. Traditional hotel near station, with restaurant *Goéland. Angélina* (I), 1 quai Lamennais (tel. 99–79–29–66). Close to old part of city; no restaurant.

Restaurants. *Corsaire* (M), 52 rue d'Antrain (tel. 99–36–33–69). Inventive yet reasonable *menu. Le Piré* (M), 18 rue Maréchal-Joffre (tel. 99–79–31–41). Closed Christmas, Sat. lunch, and Sun. High-standard nouvelle cuisine; delightful garden for outdoor meals. *Ti-Koz* (M), 3 rue St.-Guillaume (tel. 99–79–33–89). Closed Sun. and holidays. Classical cuisine served in beautiful 16th-century house near the cathedral.

Ste.-Anne-d'Auray. Restaurant. *Auberge* (I), 56 rue de Vannes (tel. 97–57–61–55). Closed 2½ weeks in both Feb. and Oct., Tues. eve., and Wed. Good value. Has 7 rooms.

St.-Brieuc. *Le Théâtre* (M), 17 pl. Poste (tel. 96–33–23–18). Open all year. Small, very central, overlooking market square; no restaurant. *Ker Izel* (I), 20 rue Gouët (tel. 96–33–46–29). Open all year. Quiet and comfortable.

St.-Malo. *Elizabeth* (M), 2 rue Cordiers (tel. 99–56–24–98). In 16th-century building intra-muros, no restaurant.

Restaurants. *Duchesse Anne* (M), 5 pl. Guy la Chambre (tel. 99–40–85–33). Closed Dec. and Jan. Smart; excellent seafood. *Atre* (I), 7 Esplanade Cdt.-Menguy, Port Solidor (tel. 99–81–68–39). Closed mid-Dec. to mid-Feb. Modest little spot right by the sea at nearby Saint-Servan.

St.-Quay-Portrieux. *Bretagne* (I), 36 quai de la République (tel. 96–70–40–91). Overlooking the harbor. Closed Jan. Friendly little family hotel with good seafood.

Trébeurden. Restaurant. *Glann Ar Mor* (M), 12 rue Kerariou (tel. 96–23–50–81). Closed Wed. and first half Oct. Good-value, traditional cuisine. *Ti al Lannec* (M), allée de Mézo-Guen (tel. 96–23–57–26). Delicious seafood among the Breton specialties.

Trégastel. *Belle Vue* (M), 20 rue Calculots (tel. 96–23–88–18). Charming atmosphere, with views and garden, yet reasonable prices. *Beau Séjour* (I), plage Coz Pors (tel. 96–23–88–02). Closed end Sept. to Easter. Pleasant family hotel overlooking sea, with lovely view from restaurant.

Vannes. *Image Ste.-Anne* (M), 8 pl. de la Libération (tel. 97–63–27–36). Nice atmosphere, good restaurant for seafood. *Marébaudière* (M), 4 rue Aristide-Briand (tel. 97–47–34–29). Excellent service and good restaurant.

Restaurant. *Le Lys* (M), 51 rue Maréchal-Leclerc (tel. 97–47–29–30). Excellent nouvelle cuisine with good use of fresh produce. Closed Sun. eve. out of season, Mon., and mid-Nov. to mid-Dec.

The Riviera

There are few places to rival France's Riviera, the azure coast that stretches from Cassis, east of Marseille, to Menton on the Italian border. The constant temperatures of the Mediterranean contribute to the exceptionally clement climate by cooling the coast in summer and warming it in winter. At the turn of the century, the Côte d'Azur, as it is also known, was a popular winter resort that attracted the European aristocracy and wealthy Americans, who were to give it the name of the Riviera.

Today the coast is popular all year round—almost unbearably so in the height of summer when the traffic around the major resorts is worse than in Paris and tacky roadside campsites crowd the entrances to most towns.

The best times to visit are spring and fall: May and September are perfect. The vegetation of the valleys and hills of the Riviera and Upper Provence is unlike any you will find elsewhere in France. Over 60 varieties of olive tree flourish here at altitudes of up to 2,000 feet. Flower-growing has been an important industry in the region for over a century and fragrances fill the air from Bandol to Menton.

At Grasse, the world capital of the perfume industry, there are guided tours that show how the essence of these flowers is transformed into perfume.

The Riviera is an area of contrasts; while the coastal resorts seem to live exclusively for the tourist—Cannes, Nice, and St.-Tropez all have more than their fair share of yachts, deluxe hotels, and expensive restaurants—the hinterland remains almost untouched. Exquisite little villages, perched high up on the hills, hidden behind their medieval ramparts, often look as though they don't belong to the 20th century. Gourdon, Eze, Utelle, and Peille, among others, bear witness to the ancient way of life of Provence.

Artists have played an important role in the development of the Côte d'Azur and their contribution is reflected in the number of modern art museums: the Musée Picasso at Antibes, the Musée Renoir at Cagnes-sur-Mer, and the Musée Jean Cocteau at Menton. Vence has the added attraction of the Maeght Foundation of Modern Art, and St.-Paul-de-Vence the Chapelle Matisse, entirely designed and decorated by the famous painter. Cimiez, once a Roman town, on the heights above Nice, offers the perfect setting for the modern Chagall Museum, designed especially to house the artist's paintings, sculptures, and mosaics. The ruins at Cimiez are a reminder of the once-powerful Roman presence along the Riviera. You can visit the arena and the remains of the Roman port at Fréjus and the Trophée des Alpes, a huge tower erected to the glory of Augustus Caesar and reconstructed in the '30s thanks to American philanthropy.

PRACTICAL INFORMATION FOR THE RIVIERA

Hotels and Restaurants

Antibes. *Auberge Provençale* (M), 61 pl. Nationale (tel. 93–34–13–24). In the old town, near harbor. Restaurant with modern-style cuisine. *Le Caméo* (I), pl. Nationale (tel. 93–34–24–17). Closed Jan. Small and central, with popular restaurant.

Restaurants. *L'Auberge du Jarrier* (M), at Biot, 30 pass. de la Bourgade (tel. 93–65–11–68). Closed Dec., Tues., and Wed. lunch. Original dishes made from fresh regional produce, served in a magnificent garden. *Oursin* (I), 16 rue de la République (tel. 93–34–13–46). Closed Aug., Sun. eve. and Mon. Good-value fish.

Cagnes-Sur-Mer. *Horizon* (M), 111 blvd. de la Plage (tel. 93–31–09–95). Closed Nov. to mid-Dec. Modern, with pleasant countryside views.

Restaurants. *Josy-Jo* (M), 2 pl. du Planestel, at Haut-de-Cagnes (tel. 93–20–68–76). Closed mid-Dec. to mid-Jan., and Sun. Good regional cuisine. *Peintres* (I), 71 Montée Bourgade (tel. 93–20–83–08). Closed Dec. and Wed. Superb views, good-value menus.

Cannes. *Le Modern* (M), 11 rue des Serbes (tel. 93–39–09–87). Closed Nov. to Christmas. Just behind the Croisette. *Le Cheval Blanc* (I), 3 rue Guy-de-Maupassant (tel. 93–39–88–60). Closed Nov. Pleasant hotel in quiet area. *Les Roches Fleuries* (I), 92 rue Georges-Clemenceau (tel. 93–39–28–78). Closed mid-Nov. to end Dec. Near the Old Port, with garden and sea-view.

Restaurants. *La Mirabelle* (M), 24 rue Saint-Antoine (tel. 93–38–72–75). Closed first fortnight in Mar., Dec., and Tues. Inventive cuisine, excellent wine list. *Le Ragtime* (M), 1 blvd. de la Croisette (tel. 93–68–47–10). Closed Sun. out of season. Piano-bar style restaurant with terrace. *Le Grill d'Attila* (I), 6 rue Florian (tel. 93–38–45–95). Closed Mon. and lunch out of season. Lavish, serve-yourself starters and mixed meat grills; very good value. *La Flaméche* (I), 22 rue Cousin (tel. 93–38–27–17). Recommended for typical Provençal cuisine.

Eze. *Hermitage du Col d'Eze* (M), on D46 (tel. 93–41–00–68) Small and pleasant. *Soleil* (I), av. de la Liberté (tel. 93–01–51–46), Near beach on Basse Corniche. Closed mid-Nov. to mid-Dec. Friendly, with good-value restaurant.

Restaurants. *Bergerie* (M), in village on Grande Corniche (tel. 93–41–03–67). Closed mid-Oct. to mid-Jan. and Wed. Charcoal-grilled meats and local specialties. *Nid-d'Aigle* (M), rue Château (tel. 93–41–19–08). Good Provençal cuisine.

Grasse. *Ibis* (M), rue Martine-Carol (tel. 93–70–70–70). New Ibis hotel; full waiter service, swimming pool, and tennis court. *Panorama* (M), 2 pl. du Cours (tel. 93–36–80–80). Modern, comfortable, good views. *Patti* (M), pl. du Patti (tel. 93–36–01–00). Brand new hotel, with own brasserie and *Salon de Thé*.

Restaurants. *Lou Pignatoun* (I), 13 rue de l'Oratoire (tel. 93–36–11–80). Closed Sun., lunches only. Excellent traditional cooking in a lunchtime favorite with the locals. *La Serre* (I), 20 rue Félix-Raybaud at St. Jacques, a mile from Grasse, (tel. 93–70–80–89). Closed Feb., Sun. eve., and Mon. Attractive decor, inventive cuisine. *Vieux Bistrot* (I), 5 rue des Moulinets (tel. 93–36–87–84). Little restaurant offering original dishes, including an occasional Indian curry.

Menton. *L'Ermitage* (M), 30 av. Carnot (tel. 93–35–77–23). Wonderful sea-views and excellent restaurant. *Princess et Richmond* (M), 52 av. Gén.-de-Gaulle (tel. 93–35–80–20). Closed Nov. 5–Dec. 20. Comfortable, with terrace and solarium; no restaurant. *Céline-Rose* (I), 57 av. de Sospel (tel. 93–28–28–38). Closed Dec. Family hotel with garden.

Restaurant. *Francine* (M), 1 quai Bonaparte (tel. 93–35–80–67). Closed Dec. and Mon. eve. Good fish specialties.

Nice. *Hôtel Alfa* (M), 30 rue Masséna (tel. 93–87–88–63). Simple, comfortable, and central. *Hôtel Gounod* (M), 3 rue Gounod (tel. 93–88–26–20). Swimming pool and garden. *Hôtel Napoléon* (M), 6 rue Grimaldi (tel. 93–87–70–07). Peace and quiet guaranteed here.

Restaurants. *Le Grand Pavois* (M), 11 rue Meyerbeer (tel. 93–88–77–42). Closed July and Mon. Recommended for fish and seafood, also the famous *bouillabaisse*. *Le Bistrot d'Antoine* (I), 26 blvd. Victor Hugo (tel. 93–82–09–05). Closed Sun., Sat. lunch, Christmas and New Year. Exceptionally good value regional cooking; warm and welcoming.

St. Raphaël. *Le Sol e Mar* (M), at Le Dramont, 4 miles west of St. Raphaël on N98 (tel. 94–95–25–60). Closed mid-Oct. to Easter. Many rooms with sea view, garden, swimming pool, and restaurant. Half-board compulsory.

Restaurant. *Le Voile d'Or* (M) 1 blvd. du Général de Gaulle (tel. 94–95–17–04). Closed Dec., Tues. eve., and Wed. First-rate service and some excellent specialties.

St. Tropez. *Ermitage* (M), av. Paul Signac (tel. 94–97–52–33). Open all year. Central, with own garden and family atmosphere. At the top end of our price bracket. *La Méditerranée* (M), 21 blvd. Louis Blanc (tel. 94–97–00–44). Pleasant and peaceful, with restaurant. Half-board compulsory. *Hélios* (I), Port Pilon (tel. 94–97–00–64). Closed Nov. through Jan. Inexpensive for St. Tropez.

Restaurants. *La Ramade* (M), rue du Temple (tel. 94–97–00–15). Delicious, good-value regional specialties. *Lou Revelen* (I), 4 rue des Remparts (tel. 94–97–06–34). Closed Jan. through Mar., and Sun. eve. out of peak period. Lots of regional dishes and excellent *bouillabaisse*.

Vence and St. Paul de Vence. *Floréal* (M), 440 av. Rhin-et-Danube (tel. 93–58–64–40). Modern hotel; most rooms overlook pool and garden. *Miramar* (M), Plateau St.-Michel (tel. 93–58–01–32). Well-equipped, with views over sea and the Alps. Good bar; no restaurant. *Roseraie* (I), av. H. Giraud (tel. 93–58–02–20). Closed Jan. Charming private house, with restaurant serving excellent cuisine from the Périgord.

Restaurants. *Le Château des Arômes* (M), 2618 rte. de Grasse (tel. 93–58–70–24). Subtle cuisine full of flavor. *Farigoule* (I), 15 rue Henri-Isnard (tel. 93–58–01–27). Closed mid-Nov. to mid-Dec., and Fri. Good-value Provençal cuisine.

Germany

Within days of the collapse of the Berlin Wall in November 1989 West Germany and East Germany began earnestly looking for ways to reconcile the economic, political, and social differences that had separated them since the end of World War II. As soon as the borders were opened politicians and citizens from both sides began working for reunification. Plans to reintegrate the two societies moved along at an astonishingly swift pace, and a concrete program aimed at complete social and political unity was soon in place. At press-time, the two Germanys had agreed on the details of monetary reform (in July 1990 East Germans began using West German Deutsch Marks) and had laid the ground work for the election of an all-German parliament in December 1990.

Although the barbed wire is gone and Wall has fallen, it will still take some time to achieve full integration in the economic and social spheres. The two 'halves' of Germany are in many ways still distinct from each other and present travelers—and in particular, budget travelers—with different kinds of opportunities and conditions. Because of this we have chosen to provide separate background information on traveling in East Germany beginning on page 228. The first section of the chapter covers travel in West Germany.

Over the course of the last two decades, **West Germany** has become one of the richest countries in the world, and its citizens enjoy the highest standards of living. Consequently, prices are high for foreign visitors. But, with care, it is possible to enjoy a memorable holiday here without going bankrupt.

Germany offers a variety of scenery ranging from coastal resorts to high mountains; forests, lakes, moors, islands, valleys, romantic villages, Medieval townships and startling modernity. There are historical and artistic associations that cover thousands of years. You will see Roman mosaics, Romanesque and Gothic cathedrals, Renaissance townhalls, Baroque palaces, sensational Rococo churches, galleries bursting with masterpieces from all periods plus examples of highly sophisticated modern architecture and technical know-how.

Bavaria, especially Munich, and the Rhineland are particularly popular. But there is also enormous charm and interest in the Eifel region near the frontiers with Belgium, Luxembourg and France, and in the southern regions around the Black Forest and around the shores of Lake Constance, basking in sub-tropical summer sunshine and gazing toward the Swiss Alps. There is also much to enjoy in northern Bavaria and among the curious shapes of the sandstone territory known as Franconian Switzerland near Bayreuth. The shoreline of the great river Rhine has charmed visitors for centuries, as has the Neckar valley with its castles and fortresses.

Berlin should be high on the list of any visitor, especially since the divided city has virtually become one again with the breaching of the notorious Wall in November 1989. Since the beginning of the process of reunification of the two Germanies, Berlin is again being talked about as a future capital city. Only diplomats take Bonn seriously as West Germany's capital. Regionalism is strong and each region has its own identity and self-respect, born of centuries of separatism. Don't be afraid to use your German. Unlike the French, the Germans won't refuse to understand if you don't pronounce their language correctly.

189

Hospitality has a long and honorable tradition in Germany, going back to the Roman *taberna,* the lodgings reserved for the nobility on their travels, the hostels and the hospices of the Middle Ages, the inns of later centuries and down to the modern hotel. Today the visitor can find a range of interior decoration from simple country-style to pompous elegance.

The variety of holidays to be had is numerous. There are facilities for every taste ranging from air trips to individual centers and city tours; for the motorist, touring the country by car on the extensive, 4,600 mile-long Autobahn network—you can drive from Hamburg to Munich in eight hours—served by motorway facilities and motels adapted to meet the motorists' requirements; farmhouse holidays; holidays in castles, mansions and historic hostelries; health cures; beauty farms; wine-tasting tours; river cruises, camping holidays and much, much more.

Despite the monetary and political union of the two Germanys, the **East Germany** remains for the most part an unexplored treasure trove for the budget traveler. Since the monetary reform of the summer of 1990, prices in the major East German cities have gone up and may even with those in the western part of the country. But if you're willing to put up with the confusions of a one-time communist country undergoing transition to a democracy, then the eastern part of Germany can be a fascinating place to visit right now.

East German territory is scenically appealing; with a few exceptions, no traces remain of the devastation of World War II. Many buildings, squares—in fact, whole towns—have been skillfully and lovingly restored despite limited resources. You'll find splendid museums, concert halls and theaters quite the equal of those in the western part of the country. With the renaissance of private enterprise, secondhand bookstores, cafés and bier kellers have blossomed.

Your first destination will probably be Berlin, still the most accessible city in the east. The 750th anniversary of Berlin's founding in 1987 gave officials in the eastern sector reason to rebuild whole sections of the city, and the general effect remains fresh and attractive, even if the style falls a bit short of recapturing the original. Dresden, too, has been largely rebuilt from the ashes of WWII, and the result is overwhelming, when you compare photos from 1945 with the city of today.

As a budget traveler, your best approach is to plan and organize the trip in advance, using a travel agency that knows and specializes in the eastern part of Germany. During the transition period of reunion, many agencies have sprung up advertising their skills, but be careful; the opening of the east has spawned many opportunists in the west, and you can all too easily find yourself sold a bill of goods that will end up costing far more than the budget trip you have in mind.

Our information is being compiled at a time when many uncertainties still remain regarding the union of the two Germanies. To what extent organizations such as the *Reisebüro der DDR* (the former government's travel agency) will continue to function, is unclear at press time. We have given addresses, telephone numbers and other logistical details based on best available information, but please understand that changes are taking place at such a pace that no publication can keep up. On the other hand, East Germans are friendly and helpful and eager for contact with Westerners (contact was formerly discouraged), so should you have problems, don't fail to turn for assistance to whomever may be at hand.

One of the problems of the past for budget travelers was that you were effectively forced to stay in state-run hotels, the cheapest of which were at best in the upper-budget categories when compared with western prices. The eastern region of the country still lacks accommodation in the middle to lower price brackets, but now that the doors are open to western visitors, you can find quite satisfactory accommodation in the smaller hotels and in private homes, possibilities which barely existed a little over a year ago.

Prices for the former super-bargains—food, drink, local transportation—have risen since monetary union, but even so, these still represent good value and are well within the budget considerations.

PRACTICAL INFORMATION FOR WEST GERMANY

WHAT WILL IT COST. West Germany has one of the world's lowest inflation rates—less than 3%. At the time of writing, the US dollar remained low against the deutschemark, but Germany as a holiday land is not necessarily as expensive as might be imagined, especially in comparison with other European countries whose price increases have lately been much more alarming.

A vacation in West Germany can work out less expensively than one in either the U.S. or Britain. But needless to say, if you visit one of the lesser-known resorts or towns, your vacation costs will run to considerably less than in one of the major tourist centers or cities. Try for instance the Harz mountains in Lower Saxony for summer *and* particularly reasonable winter sports holidays; the Eifel region of the Rhineland-Palatinate, the Palatinate Forest *(Pfälzer Wald)* Nature Park in the southern part of the hyphenated state and the Southern German Wine Road for lovers of wine and romantic scenery from Neustadt southwards to Schweigen on the Swiss border. The Allgäu, too, offers charming resorts (avoid the main centers like Oberstdorf) such as Kleinwalsertal, while East Bavaria and the Bavarian Forest offer excellent quality at very reasonable prices for summer and winter holidays.

There are also many extremely favorable package deals in Germany, such as an inclusive-term holiday *(Pauschalarrangements),* of which there is a wide choice. Seven-day packages are arranged by the German Reservation system of Frankfurt (ADZ), while special all-inclusive rates are offered by most holiday resorts upon enquiry at the local tourist office *(Fremdenverkehrsamt).* The *Verkehrsamt* of Lindau on Lake Constance, for example, offers from May 1 onwards through the summer, seven days' bed-and-breakfast in a choice of hotels and inns in various categories of comfort ranging from DM 220 per person for a double room in a private pension to DM 380 per person for a room with shower in a middle-class hotel. German Railways (DB) also offer a similar arrangement for three to six days including rail travel. Both arrangements include sightseeing trips and other extras.

Special weekend rates are becoming a popular feature throughout Germany and usually include sightseeing and some form of entertainment. Munich's *Weekend Key* offers one to six nights' bed and breakfast (single) from DM 91 in standard hotels (without bath) to DM 742 for more comfort, including city and countryside tours, museum, restaurant and theater ticket reductions, or you can combine the package with one of German Rail's City Tours (Städtetouren) from Berlin, Frankfurt, Köln or Hamburg. Second class from Köln plus two nights in a comfortable hotel would cost around DM 350, and in a pension, DM 270. These prices are even cheaper between Nov. and Jan., and in April. Other large cities such as Hamburg, Stuttgart, and resorts like Garmisch-Partenkirchen or Aachen offer similar reduced weekend rates.

Also, in all these areas, self-catering holidays in new and comfortable apartments, and houses are available. The basic price per week naturally varies according to location, season and facilities, but a Category III (moderate comfort) studio apartment for two people would cost about 200 marks per week and a holiday flat for four to six persons around 500 marks. The German Automobile Club, *ADAC,* offers selected "family" self-catering holidays in holiday apartments *(Ferienwohnungen),* bungalows and farmhouses at a wide range of prices in lesser-known resorts. Details from the German Tourist Department or write to ADAC-REISEN, Am Westpark 8, 8000 Munich 70.

When reserving a holiday apartment or bungalow don't forget to add on the price for *Nebenkosten* (utilities such as electricity, warm water, heating etc. and sometimes fresh bed linen) before deciding whether the offer is good value.

The West German monetary unit is the mark (DM), which is divided into 100 pfennigs. Coins are issued in denominations of 1, 2 and 5 mark pieces, 1, 2, 5, 10 and 50 pfennig pieces, and there are 10, 20, 50, 100, 500, and 1,000 mark notes.

At the time of writing, the exchange rate for the mark was 1.78 to the dollar and 2.79 to the pound sterling.

Sample Costs. Cinema, moderate seat DM 10; theater, moderate seat DM 30; museum, DM 2.50 to 8.00; coffee, in stand-up coffee shop DM 2.00, in café DM 3.00; beer, in Gasthof or café DM 3 (per half liter), in moderate restaurant DM 3.50 (per half liter); carafe wine (per quarter liter) in Gasthof DM 5, in moderate restaurant DM 8.

NATIONAL TOURIST OFFICE. The German National Tourist Office is an immensely helpful and endlessly useful source of information for all vacationers planning to visit West Germany (see below for addresses) and can supply much useful information at no charge.

In Germany itself, there are Tourist Information Offices in all cities, most towns and many villages. These are called *Verkehrsamt* or in spa resorts, *Kurverein,* and can supply information on local places of interest as well as providing lists of accommodations. It is well to write in advance; addresses are in the following pages. They usually also have lists of houses with rooms to rent, and which they will have inspected.

The addresses of the German National Tourist Office overseas are:

In the U.S.: 747 Third Ave., New York, N.Y. 10017 (tel. 212–308–3300); 444 S. Flower St., Los Angeles, CA 90071 (tel. 213–688–7332).

In Canada: 175 Bloor St. E., North Tower, Suite 604, Toronto, Ont. M4W 3R8 (tel. 514–844–9166).

In the U.K.: 65 Curzon St., London W1Y 7PE (tel. 071–495–3990).

WHEN TO COME. The climate is temperate, but sometimes winters can be very cold, with the temperature dropping many degrees below freezing. In winter the German mountains are thickly covered in snow. Winter sports are possible at heights from 1,600 ft. upwards. Average temperature in January (the coldest month of the year) is around 0°C; in the mountains it is approximately minus 10°C. The winter lasts from December till March, and in the Alps can continue till May.

In April skiing is still possible in the high Alps, while the fruit trees are already in blossom on the Bergstrasse, in the Palatinate and around the Black Forest and Lake Constance.

In summer, average temperatures in the valleys and plains are around 20°C. The best time for swimming is between June and August.

Average afternoon temperatures in degrees Fahrenheit and centigrade:

Munich	Jan.	Feb.	Mar.	Apr.	May	June	July	Aug.	Sept.	Oct.	Nov.	Dec.
F°	33	37	45	54	63	69	72	71	64	53	42	36
C°	1	3	7	12	17	21	22	22	18	12	6	2

Note: in the south of Germany, temperatures are a couple of degrees higher.

SPECIAL EVENTS. Fasching (Carnival) is held in various parts of the country from December 31 through Shrove Tuesday. It is celebrated with particular vigor in Aachen, Köln, Düsseldorf, Mainz, Augsburg and Munich, reaching its peak in mid-February or early *March. January* is International Winter Sports Week at Garmisch-Partenkirchen in the Alps and towards the end of the month Berlin's famous Green Week gets under way. *March* sees Munich's International Fashion Week and the Starkbier (Strong Beer) Festival at the Nockherberg. In early *April* the Leonhardi Ritt equestrian procession takes place in Furth in Wald in the Bavarian Forest. Walpurgis Night festivities are the attraction in the Harz mountains. *May* sees the Wiesbaden International Festival, one of the leaders in the long list of year-round musical and theatrical events, but there is also the Berlin Theater Festival, the summer theater in Stuttgart lasting until the end of *October* and the traditional Meister Trunk play in Rothenburg-on-Tauber has its first performance of the year in *June.* Also in June, the Kiel Week sailing regatta and in Landshut, Bavaria, the Landshuter Hochzeit (Wedding 1475) open-air historic pageant. Mid-*July* to mid-*August* sees the Munich Opera Festival (horribly expensive tickets, if you can get them), the Bayreuth Wagner Festival (also expensive), the Berlin Bach Festival and the Schleissheim Palace summer concerts near Munich. These are also the months of the wine festivals along the Rhine and the Moselle with the famous Rhine in Flames (floodlight and fireworks display) around the 14th of August. *September* (through to *October*) hosts the Munich Oktoberfest, which begins on the third Saturday of the month and is the biggest festival of its kind in the world. The beginning of the month sees the wine festivals in Bad Kreuznach, Bernkastel Kues, Saarburg, Boppard and the famous Dürkheim "Sausage Fair" Wine Festival in Bad Dürkheim. Major car races are held every month at the Hockenheim Ring near Mannheim, but the principal events take place in *May, August* (the German Grand Prix) and September. In *November* there are St. Martin's Day parades and festivals in Heidelberg and other towns in the Rhineland and North Baden. In *December,* from the beginning of the month, Christkindl Markts (Christmas Markets) are held all over Germany, especially in Nürnberg and Munich.

There are numerous folklore events and trade fairs throughout the year. The German Tourists' Center (DZT) in Frankfurt can supply full details in English.

National Holidays. Jan. 1; March 29, April 1 (Easter); May 1 (May Day); May 9 (Ascension); May 20 (Whit Monday); May 30 (Corpus Christi, S. Germany only); June 17 (German Unity Day); August 15 (Assumption Day, Bavaria and Saarland only); Nov. 1 (All Saints); Nov. 20 (Day of Prayer and Repentance); Dec. 25, 26.

VISAS. Nationals of the United States, Canada, Australia, New Zealand, EC countries and practically all other European countries do not require visas to enter West Germany. You must of course have a valid passport.

HEALTH CERTIFICATES. These are not required to enter West Germany from any country.

GETTING TO GERMANY. By Plane. There are direct flights from New York, Boston, Washington, Chicago, Los Angeles, Miami, Houston, San Francisco, St. Louis, Montreal and Toronto to Germany with Frankfurt and Munich being the main arrival points, and some services also go to Düsseldorf, Köln–Bonn, and Hamburg. *Lufthansa* is the national carrier but *Pan Am* and *TWA* fly from the U.S. and *Air Canada* from Canada.

From London every major German city is served by direct flights by *Air Europe, British Airways* and *Lufthansa* (not to Berlin). Flights also operate from Manchester, Birmingham and Glasgow to Düsseldorf; from Manchester and Birmingham to Frankfurt; from Manchester and Glasgow to Berlin. There are also charter flights from Gatwick and Luton to Düsseldorf for around £100 return, and to Munich.

West Germany has excellent air links with the rest of Europe. West Berlin, however, is served only by *British Airways, Pan Am, Air France* and some charter lines. *Lufthansa* does not fly to Berlin.

By Train. From London there are three main routes. The quickest is via Dover and the Jetfoil to Oostende, there to pick up an EC or IC express to Köln, a center in the German Inter-City network. Köln can be reached by 4.30 P.M., Stuttgart, Hannover, Wurzburg and Bremen by 9, Hamburg before 9.30 and Munich just after 11—all with a 7.45 A.M. start from London. You must book in advance for the Jetfoil (a £7 supplement on the ferry fare).

A slower route is via Harwich and the Hook of Holland, but is best taken overnight. Departs London on the *EuroCity* "Benjamin Britten" at 7.45 P.M., arriving Köln 10.45 the following morning. Advance reservations essential.

Finally, the boat train leaves London Liverpool Street station for Harwich, connecting with the *Danish Seaways* sailings every other day to Hamburg. The journey takes 24 hours. It is a pleasant, leisurely route in summer, but the North Sea crossing can be rough in winter.

Several bargain fares are available for second-class travel, by day to the Hook, and overnight to Oostende. For short breaks of about four nights, ask about European savers.

By Boat. There is one direct route from the U.K. to Germany. This is operated by *Danish Seaways* and sails 3/4 times weekly in each direction from Harwich to Hamburg. The connecting boat train leaves London Liverpool Street station at 1.15

P.M. and arrives at Harwich Parkstone Quay at 2.38 P.M. The boat sails at 3.30 P.M. (4.30 in winter), and arrives at Hamburg at 1.30 P.M. the following day.

By Bus. There is a twice-weekly *Eurolines* bus to Travemünde on the Baltic that calls at Leer, Oldenburg, Bremen and Hamburg en route. This service operates on Wednesdays and Fridays, leaving London (Victoria Coach Station) in the late evening and reaching Hamburg Central Bus Station (Z.O.B.) mid-evening on the following day. Round trip is about £90. International Express runs a daily service to Köln and Munich during the summer. The run to Köln is overnight, reaching the city at 9.45 A.M.; Munich is reached at around 7 P.M. In addition, *Transline* have services to Düsseldorf, Dortmund and Hannover.

Details of *Europabus* services within Germany are available from the *Deutsche Touring GmbH,* Am Römerhof 17, Postfach 900244, D-6000, Frankfurt am Main.

CUSTOMS. There are three levels of duty-free allowance for goods imported into Germany. Travelers coming from a European country outside the EC may bring in 200 cigarettes or 50 cigars or 250gr. of tobacco; 1 liter of spirits more than 22% proof or 2 liters of spirits less than 22% proof and 2 liters of wine; 50gr. of perfume; other goods to the value of DM 115. Travelers coming from an EC country may bring in 300 cigarettes (200 if bought in a duty-free shop) or 75 cigars or 400gr. of tobacco; 5 liters of wine and 1.5 liters of spirits (1 liter if bought in a duty-free shop) more than 22% proof or 3 liters of spirits or sparkling wine up to 22% proof; 75gr. of perfume and 0.375 liters of toilet water; other goods to the value of DM 780. Travelers coming from outside Europe may bring in 400 cigarettes or 100 cigars or 500gr. of tobacco; spirits and perfume limits are the same as those for non-EC countries; other goods to the value of DM 115.

You may bring into and take out of Germany any amount of foreign and German currency.

HOTELS. Leaving aside student hostels and youth hotels, accommodations can be found in the following order of cost: hotel, *Gasthof* or *Gasthaus* (inns really, with some rooms for travelers and often particularly cosy with lots of local atmosphere); *Fremdenheim* (a pension or boarding house); Pension; and, often displayed by a sign on private houses, *Zimmer* (room), sometimes with the word *frei* (free) or *zu vermieten* (to let) on a green sign. A red sign *besetzt* indicates there are no vacancies. If a hotel has the word *garni* it means there is no restaurant but breakfast is available.

The standard of hotels and pensions in the economy category in West Germany is good. You are more likely to get better value for money in the suburbs than in the city center, although small hotels in the areas around the main stations are usually cheaper but should be looked over more carefully before making reservations. Check that breakfast is included in room price. It can be up to DM15 extra. There is no official rating system of hotels in Germany, but roughly speaking they fall into five categories, from hotels and inns with modest facilities (i.e. with wash basin only in room) through those with fair comfort (WC or shower), hotels with middle-ranged comfort and hotels with a high degree of comfort or luxury establishments. In the following sections we have grouped accommodations into just two categories; (I) for Inexpensive (hotels, pensions and inns offering modest to fair comfort) and costing between DM 40–DM 70 for a double room, and (M) for Moderate, costing between DM 75–DM 150 for a double room.

You'll find that many of even the smallest villages have an accommodations office *(Zimmernachweis)* of some sort, but if you can't find anything that answers to that description, ask anyone who looks local—a railway porter, a policeman, newspaper seller or café waitress—for a *Zimmer zu vermieten* (room to rent) or a *Gasthof.* People genuinely appreciate this sort of question and will usually come up with an answer that should prove suitable. But make it clear you want a room in a house and not in a hotel.

Self–Catering. For families or groups there are numerous possibilities for self-catering holidays, in bungalows or apartments for from two to six or more persons. Write to the local tourist offices for details of *Ferienwohnungen* or contact the German Automobile Association *ADAC* for their catalogue of *Familien-Ferien* where not only holiday flats are offered but also family holidays on farms *(Urlaub am Bauernhof)*, in holiday centers or Alpine huts. For further information about the increasingly popular farmhouse holidays, the *D.L.G.* (German Agricultural Society) issues a brochure of quality-controlled farms in Germany, including holiday flats and even whole farmhouses for rent at reasonable rates. Write to *D.L.G. Reisedienst,* Rusterstr. 13, 6000 Frankfurt 1.

Camping. German National Tourist Offices (addresses, see below) publish a folder giving details about camp sites. There are also over 400 winter camping sites and facilities are generally excellent. Every weekend in high season VHF services of several regional broadcasting stations give details of availability on various camp sites. The *German Camping Club* is at Mandelstrasse 28, Munich 40 and has comprehensive information including a handbook that covers the whole of Europe— DM 10 to members, DM 21 to others—including sites where caravans and mobile homes can be rented. The ADAC issues a brochure and map of campsites near Autobahn exits entitled *Campingplätze im Bereich der Bundesautobahnen.* The YHA also offer inclusive packages with 7 nights' hostel accommodations and the return air flight to several European resorts.

Youth Hostels. The age ceiling in Bavaria is 27 but this does not apply elsewhere in Germany. There are over 600 hostels and they are among the best in the world. The Youth Hostel Association in Britain, 14 Southampton St., London W.C.2 has details as do the American (P.O. Box 37613, Washington D.C. 20013– 7613) and the Canadian, 1600 James Naismith Drive, Suite 608, Gloucester, Ont. K1B 5N4. Most comprehensive is the German one, *Deutsches Jugendherbergswerk Hauptverband,* Bismarckstr. 8, D4930 Detmold.

RESTAURANTS. In general, there are many ways to save food costs while enjoying Germany's specialties. It is always wise to try to select the set menu of the day *(Tageskarte)* rather than eating *à la carte,* where each course offered is priced separately. Main meals are likely to be at midday for Germans, consequently *table d'hôte* menus appear then. They usually include soup and a main course with side salad. Expect to pay a minimum of DM 10 and don't be surprised if the cheapest is DM 15 in large towns. Forget coffee after a meal; the Germans seldom drink it then, but wait until late in the afternoon and go to a café where it is better and cheaper. It is cheapest drunk standing up in one of the numerous coffee houses such as *Tschibo* or *Eduscho.* To quench your thirst, buy a bottle of pure natural fruit juice *(Saft)* or mineral water from a supermarket—that is if you don't like beer, which is always available at any street corner kiosk, grocer's store, or even some newsstands.

For lunch, the restaurants at local department stores are recommended because their meals are wholesome, appetizing and inexpensive. Cafeterias in some of the bigger museums offer good-value meals. Or try local butcher's shops, like *Vinzenz-Murr* in Munich, the *Nordsee* fish shops for good-value fish lunches, or the stalls in the open markets for warm snacks, usually served with a roll. And throughout Germany you will come across the *Imbiss* or snack bar (often on wheels), serving *Wurst* (sausages) of every shape and size, rolls filled with cheese, cold meat or fish, or the proverbial hamburger, known as *Bulette* in the north and *Fleischpflanzl* in the south.

For evening meals try the local inns or *Gaststätten,* which are not only restaurants, but also places where people just meet in the evening to drink beer or play cards. Almost every street has a Gaststätte "just around the corner", though those in the suburbs or out in the countryside are naturally cheaper than in the city centers. The menu of every Gaststätte is posted in a little glass box outside the door with prices, which are usually reasonable. Service is always included, but you usually round up the bill to the next mark or half mark. A dinner of soup and a main course can be had here for about DM 15–DM 20. Prices for beer and wine are also reasonable.

Three reliable, inexpensive restaurant chains, which also operate elsewhere in Europe, are *Wienerwald, McDonald's,* and *Pizza Hut.* The food is pretty much standardized, but with something of a local flavor nonetheless and the settings are perfectly acceptable. Wienerwald sometimes also has accommodations.

In the restaurant lists that follow, we have divided restaurants into two categories, (M) Moderate, where a set main meal for one person costs between DM 18 and DM 25, and (I) Inexpensive, where a menu for one person costs between DM 10 and DM 18.

Food and Drink. German food leans unmistakably towards the rich and the wholesome. Germans love sausages, pork, veal and game. Butter is used in many dishes and starch is practically the national dish—potatoes in the north, dumplings *(Knödel)* or *Spätzle* (a species of noodle) in the south.

The south Germans are very fond of dipping into a little *Brotzeit* (a snack of bread, sausage and beer). Follow suit and you'll find that this is the moment to sample those tempting regional sausages. Frankfurters, for example, of which the American version is no more than an imitation; Regensburger, a heavily-spiced pork sausage; Weisswurst, a white sausage made of veal, calves' brains and spleen and seasoned with fresh herbs; Bratwurst, the grilled pork sausage of Nürnberg after which the famous *Bratwurststube* restaurants all over Germany are named.

Other outstanding German specialties: *Leberkäs,* a delicious meat loaf, *Rindsrouladen* (beef olives), *Schweinebraten* or *Schweinshax'n* (roast pork or roast knuckle of pork), *Eisbein mit Sauerkraut* (boiled leg of pork served with pickled cabbage), *Sauerbraten* (a joint of beef marinated in herbs and wine, then roasted) and, of course, *Schnitzel,* pork, beef or veal escalopes fried in batter or served plain. Schwetzingen is famous for its asparagus, as is Schrobenhausen; and the alpine lakes provide wonderfully fresh *Renke* (salmon trout). The gamut of mouth-watering sweets includes: *Käsekuchen,* delicious cheesecake, *Schwarzwälder Kirschtorte,* a Black Forest cherry cake, liberally soaked in *Kirschwasser* (cherry Schnaps); spicey *Apfelkuchen* (apple-tart) or, in Southern Germany, juicy plum-tart known as *Zwetschgen-Datschi* and *Lebkuchen* (gingerbread).

The beer is good. Say *Helles* (in the south) or *Export* if you want light, *Dunkles* if you want dark beer. In Bavaria, try the beer brewed from wheat, *Weissbier.*

Germany produces a lot of wine, much of it of superlative quality. Generally speaking, you will probably be happy with the house wine in most restaurants, or with one of those earthenware pitchers of cold Mosel that are usually available. These are refreshing and inexpensive. From the southernmost end of the Rhine wine region, a number of fruity white wines are produced. The best include *Forst, Deidesheim, Wachenheim, Ruppertsberge* and *Schwarzer Herrgott.*

The Rhine Hesse region, beginning at Worms, produces the world-famous *Liebfraumilch.* A little further north you will find two very fine wines indeed, the best of this region: *Niersteiner* and *Oppenheimer.* Other top wines in this region are *Nackenheimer* and *Bodenheimer.* The Nahe valley, which joins the Rhine at Bingen, produces the smooth white *Monzinger, Kreuznacher* and *Huffelsheimer,* and in Franconia you will find the famous squat, bulbous-shaped bottles of first-class dry white wine known as *Bocksbeutel.* Try a *Würzburger Stein,* an *Eschendorfer Lump* or splash out on a *Neusässer Glatze.*

TIPPING. The service charges on hotel bills suffice, but if for any reason you wish to tip (the porter who brings in your bags might be one example), quite small amounts are acceptable. Whether you tip the hotel concierge depends on whether he has given you any special service. Although restaurant bills include 10% for service, it is customary, as is also the case with taxi drivers, to round up the price to the next half mark or full mark, but not by more than 5%. Station porters (available only in resorts and small towns) get 2 marks for one bag, 1 mark for each additional bag; add 40–50 pfennigs as a tip. It is also customary to tip hairdressers 10% of the bill. Hotel doormen are given 1 or 2 marks for small services such as calling a cab. Theater ushers and barmen do not expect a tip.

MAIL. Current rates for airmail letters up to 50 grams: to the U.S. DM1.60; to the UK DM1. Postcards: to the U.S. 80 pfennigs; to the UK 60 pfennigs.

CLOSING TIMES. In general, shops are open from 8.30 or 9 to 6 or 6.30 and close Sat. afternoons, except for the first Sat. in each month. Late night shopping on Thursdays until 8.30 P.M. Hairdressers generally close Mon. Banking hours vary from state to state and city to city, but are generally between 8.30–3.30 (with an hour for lunch) Mon. to Fri. (8.30–5.30 Thurs.).

GETTING AROUND GERMANY. By Plane. *Lufthansa* operates an intensive network of flights within the Federal Republic. The cities served are Frankfurt, Düsseldorf, Hamburg, Bremen, Münster, Köln-Bonn, Stuttgart, Hannover, Nürnberg, Munich, Saarbrucken and Westerland on the island of Sylt. Check out the special Lufthansa "Flieg and Spar" reduced rates on selected inland flights. They are 30%–40% cheaper than full round trip fares. *German Wings* competes with Lufthansa on domestic routes.

By Train. With a really fine and well-operated network of trains *German Railways* or *Deutsche Bundesbahn* (usually known as DB) offer excellent services all over the country. The *Euro-City* and *Inter-City* services are fast and frequent, with time-saving (mostly hourly) connections where, at the relay points of Dortmund, Hannover, Köln, Mannheim and Würzburg, necessary changes of train can be made by crossing the platform. Euro-City trains connect German cities with other European centers; Inter-City services operate only within West Germany. All Euro-City, Inter-City, Express (D-Züge), semi-fast (E-Züge) and local trains carry 1st- and 2nd-class carriages, suburban services usually one class only. Complementing the Inter-City network are the Fern Express (FD) trains, providing fast, daily connections between the densely populated industrial areas of northern Germany around the Ruhr and Hamburg with the major tourist regions of the south and Austria. In addition an East–West route links Frankfurt with Vienna and Paris. On overnight trains 1st- and 2nd-class sleepers and 2nd-class bunk beds are carried. There are dining, buffet or refreshment car services on all long and many medium distance daytime trains. Standards of comfort and cleanliness are high. While fares are also relatively high there are many reduced-rate tickets that give anything from 10% to 50% off the standard fares. They include Senior Citizens tickets, under-26s, students, 12–17 year olds, group and family travel tickets, with reductions based on the distance traveled. Details of these cheap tickets are available at all railway stations and ticket agencies; get the brochure (in English) by German Railways (entitled *Welcome to the Federal Republic of Germany and its Railroad System*) from the German National Tourist Office. The Tourist Card issued by DB for visitors gives unlimited travel on all rail routes, some Rhine steamers and certain bus routes (the Romantic Road or Rhine–Moselle routes). On the rail route through East Germany into Berlin the Tourist Card gives a reduction on the basic fare. And it gives free entry to the railway museum at Nürnberg. The Tourist Card is issued for 4, 9, and 16 days. At the time of writing, prices were $100, $150, and $200 2nd class. Half price for children. The cards are available only to non-Europeans and must be purchased in your home country. Half-fare for children 4–12.

Interesting also are the all-inclusive special offers, e.g. city tours (Städte-Touren) in and outside the Federal Republic. Included in the price are rail costs and bed and breakfast and evening meals (half pension). Inquire at Federal Railway Stations (DB-offices), Ameropa (the official DB tour operator) and DER travel offices.

By Boat. During the summer (usually April to October) there are steamer or boat services on Germany's main rivers—the Danube, the Elbe, the Main, the Weser, the Neckar, the Moselle, the Inn and, above all, the Rhine. In addition there are also services on various lakes including the Bodensee (Lake Constance), Ammersee, Chiemsee, Starnbergersee and Königsee. The Rhine and the Mosel have by far the best service operated by the *KD Line* whose 18 vessels and a hydrofoil sail between Düsseldorf and Mainz (and also to Frankfurt), Köln, Koblenz and Trier.

By Bus. Urban services exist either as local buses or trams. Fares are about DM 2 for town journeys and in some places—Munich for example—it is cheaper to buy a strip-ticket for several journeys. Germany is also well covered by intercity bus services, most of them using coaches of the latest design, with adjustable seats, sliding and glass roofs for maximum visibility, loudspeakers, radio—even with bars, buffets and stewardesses in some. For about 10 marks you can buy a timetable giving the schedules of all buses operated by the Federal Railways or the post office. The latter operates a number of special long distance services in summer, while all year round its buses penetrate into some of the remote mountain regions where there are no railroads. In isolated rural areas especially in Bavaria there are Post Bus services that operate all year.

By Bicycle. Facilities for bike hire exist between April and October at more than 280 railroad stations. For rail travelers the daily charge is DM 5. Otherwise the cost is DM 10. Most stations operate hire-it-here, leave-it-there. Full details in the pamphlet *Fahrrad am Bahnhof,* obtainable from most larger railroad station ticket offices. Your own bike can be brought in without restriction. Helpful addresses are the German cycling organization: *Bund Deutscher Radfahrer,* Otto-Fleck-Scheise 4, 6000 Frankfurt 71, and the British one: *Cyclists' Touring Club,* 69 Meadrow, Godalming, Surrey. Contact the German National Tourist Office for information on bicycle tours organized by German tour operators.

Hiking and Walking Tours. Regional tourist offices are responding to the increasing popularity of walking holidays. They now offer a variety of planned hiking routes combined with inexpensive accommodations in farmhouses, for example, for as little as DM 20 bed and breakfast. There are various arrangements for hikers' luggage to be sent on ahead *(Wandern ohne Gepäck).* Also on offer are combined rail and mountain walking tours.

Some railroad stations in Alpine areas and the Black Forest now rent cross-country skiing equipment (Langlauf) on a daily basis. Inquire at major train stations.

Munich

Capital of the free state of Bavaria (Bayern) and the third largest city in the Federal Republic, Munich is an intellectual, entertaining and earthy meeting place that attracts the young much as does the West Coast in the U.S. or the Riviera in France. The city has about it an air of permissiveness that contrasts sharply with what the Bavarians regard as the puritanical uprightness of the Prussians in the north. The people of Munich are goodnatured and easygoing and possess an almost infinite capacity for fun and laughter. This bonhomie reaches its peak during Fasching, the carnival that runs from Epiphany on January 6 to Mardi Gras (Shrove Tuesday), and which encompasses some 2,000 masked balls of every imaginable kind.

Real Fasching enthusiasts end these wild nights only the next morning with a *Weisswurst* breakfast (Munich white sausage) before going straight to work. It's not unusual to see costumed crowds walking the streets in the early morning, especially on Shrove Tuesday (Fasching-Dienstag) when the shops close early and throngs of costumed revelers fill the city to ring out the carnival period in style.

Munich is a city bursting with atmosphere; it's exciting and easy to explore and is plentifully supplied with accommodations. Plus, it falls well within the budget bracket. Even though terribly ravaged by the war, its revival has been remarkable. With its operas and theaters, galleries and old buildings, parks and squares, splendid countryside within easy reach and wide variety of nightlife, Munich is too good for the budget vacationer to miss.

Munich has many major museums, but the most important are the Alte and Neue Pinakotheks (Old and New Picture Galleries), located opposite each other in central Barerstrasse, offering collections that have been growing since the 16th century. The Alte Pinakothek is bursting at the seams with works by Memling, Holbein, Dürer, the Breughels, Rubens, Rembrandt, El Greco, Botticelli and Giotto, to mention only a few. The Neue Pinakothek, so called because it was intended to house contemporary works, was originally founded in 1846, but was so badly bombed in the war that it had to be demolished. It was not until 1975 that work began on the *new* Neue Pinakothek. This was finally opened in March 1981 on the site of its predecessor at the corner of Barer and Theresienstrasse. It starts where the Alte Pinakothek leaves off and consequently houses a considerable collection of 18th- and 19th-century works. Strong points are the French Impressionists, English 18th-century works, Goya and many examples of the 19th-century Munich School. The collection was formerly housed in the Haus der Kunst in the Prinzregentstrasse, where today you will find the Staatsgalerie Moderner Kunst, a splendid collection of 20th-century works. In addition, important modern art exhibitions are held here from June through September, as well as annual antique and book fairs. The Bavarian National Museum has one of the most complete displays of crafts in the world, including the best tapestries and wood carvings in Germany, and the unique Krippenschau collection of Christmas cribs. The famous Deutsches Museum, replete with planetarium and hundreds of fascinating exhibits from alchemy to zymurgy is one of the most impressive science museums in the world.

To explore the city, you should take your time. Munich's motto is *Gemütlichkeit.* It can't be translated exactly, but roughly speaking it means something like easygoing and relaxed. And that's exactly the approach you should adopt. Try sitting in one of the beer gardens or strolling through the pedestrian streets.

The heart of the old city, which was largely rebuilt after bomb damage incurred during World War II, is the medieval square known as Marienplatz where the Gothic town hall (Altes Rathaus) is situated. Pedestrianized streets fan out from this square to permit leisurely exploration.

From Marienplatz you can reach all the main monuments and the leading shopping streets of Maximilianstrasse (if only to window gaze!) and Sendlingerstrasse, where the spectacularly lavish late-Baroque church the Asamkirche is to be found.

But we begin our tour close to the main railroad station (Hauptbahnhof) at Karlsplatz, also known locally as Stachus. Karlsplatz is a busy car and streetcar junction. Below ground level there is a maze of shopping passages, subway entrances, an information office, and a clutter of inexpensive stand-up snack bars.

The Karlsplatz entrance to the pedestrianized area is marked by one of the old city gates, the Karlstor. Walk through this big arch to enter Neuhauserstrasse. On your left as you walk down the mall you come to the first of three architecturally important churches, the Bürgersaal. Wedged between big department stores, this Baroque place of worship, built in 1710, offers a momentary cool and quiet escape from the hustle and bustle outside. A series of paintings illustrate ancient places of pilgrimage in Bavaria. Continuing down the mall you come next to the 16th-century Michaelskirche, which offers a stark contrast to the Bürgersaal. In the crypt lie the royal remains of numerous Wittelbachs—including the eccentric, dreamy, 19th-century King Ludwig II. The Wittelbachs ruled Bavaria for seven centuries before the monarchy abdicated at the end of World War I. The north transept houses the tomb of Napoleon's stepson, Eugene de Beauharnais, who died in Munich in 1824.

For a complete change, the building next door to the Michaelskirche is a hunting and fishing museum—housing the biggest collection of fish hooks in the world.

Turn left into Augustinerstrasse to reach Munich's cathedral, known as the Frauenkirche. Its 300-foot-high, twin onion-shaped domes tower above the surrounding buildings. They survived the World War II air raids mainly intact, but large sections of the rest of the mid–15th-century structure were ruined and had to be rebuilt.

Markets were held in Marienplatz in medieval times and the square is lined with arcaded streets. On one side is the neo-Gothic town hall (Neues Rathaus), in whose tower is the endearing Glockenspiel. When this sounds (daily at 11 A.M. plus 5 P.M. in summer), two levels of performing figures—knights on horseback and folk-dancers—revolve to the music of this giant musical box 280 feet above the Marien-platz. Across from the Rathaus is the Gothic St. Peter's Church, whose 300-foot tower is fondly called Der Alte Peter. It is Munich's oldest church, and dates back to the 12th century. Climb the tower if a white sign is outside the entrance door—it means the view is clear all the way to the Alps.

Behind St. Peter's is the Viktualienmarkt, a colorful outdoor market of stalls offering a huge range of fresh fruit, vegetables, spices and herbs, cheeses, and fine wines. Burly country women in traditional dress compete to sell dried posies and other seasonal decorations. The focal point of the market is a small, boisterous beer garden surrounded by food stalls offering a variety of inexpensive any-time-of-the-day snacks (Brotzeiten). Buy a bite to eat and sit at one of the uncovered wooden beer tables. The famous Munich comedian, Karl Valentin, has his memorial fountain and statue on the Viktualienmarkt.

Retrace your steps to Marienplatz and turn right to enter a broad street known as Tal, which leads to another old city gate—Isartor—and, if you continue straight on, the River Isar and Deutsches Museum. Isartor is adorned with a fresco showing the victorious return of Ludwig of Bavaria in 1322 after his victory at Ampfing. The tower of the gate contains a curious museum, dedicated to Karl Valentin and bearing his name: the Valentin Museum. There's a handy and attractive coffee bar on the top floor. Continue down Zweibrückenstrasse and the river is ahead. The Isar is crossed here by the Ludwigsbrücke. On the big island in the middle of the river is the colossal Deutsches Museum of Science and Technology. Continue onward from the museum island into Rosenheimer Strasse, where you will see the new concert hall/cultural center, "Gasteig" Kulturzentrum, completed towards the end of 1985. Return to the Isar and walk northward through a riverside park to the next bridge and the Maximilianeum, built just over a century ago and now the seat of the Bavarian State Parliament and Senate. Crossing back over the river by the Maximiliansbrücke you enter the Maximiliansstrasse, a wide avenue leading into the center again, and, together with the Theatinerstrasse, one of Munich's most elegant shopping streets.

In the center of the street is the large monument to Emperor Maximilian, the Max II Denkmal, opposite which is the small comedy theater, Kleine Komödie am Max II Denkmal. Farther along the street, on the left opposite the opulent Vier Jahres Zeiten Hotel, a tiny street called Am Kosttor takes you into Platzl, where you'll find the Hofbräuhaus. It was founded in 1589 by Duke Wilhelm V to supply beer to the royal household. Today the brewery is owned by the state and has moved to another part of town, but still supplies this most famous of beer halls. The huge tap room is an absolute must, but don't be shocked by the rowdy atmosphere. It wouldn't be half as much fun if it wasn't noisy. You won't be able to drink anything other than a liter mug of beer downstairs, but in the gallery above there's a quiet restaurant. Close by, is the Alter Hof, the medieval residence of the Bavarian Dukes and later of the Emperor Ludwig.

Back on Maximilianstrasse turn left to reach Max-Joseph-Platz. Here, you are faced by the Residenz on one side and the National Theater with the Bavarian State Opera on the other. A large complex of buildings, the Residenz has been the home of the dukes, princes and kings of the House of Wittelsbach for over 650 years. Built on from the 16th to the 19th centuries, it was almost totally destroyed in the last war. But enough of the rich furnishings were saved to enable a successful restoration to take place. The Residenz is divided into four sections: the Alte Residenz and central sections of the palace, which include the Cuvilliés Theater, the one-time court theater and a delightful specimen of Rococo architecture; the Königsbau, which houses the Schatzkammer or Treasury of the Wittelsbachs; the Residenz Museum itself, a vast complex brimming with paintings and tapestries; and the Festsaalbau, which includes the Herkules Saal concert hall, and, behind the palace, the Hofgarten, framed by arcades and full of flowers.

Leading away from the far corner of the Hofgarten (at Odeonsplatz) is Ludwigstrasse with the beautiful Theatiner Church on the opposite side of the square. It begins at the equestrian statue of Ludwig I. In this vast, planned boulevard is the State Library (State Library), the University and the church of St. Ludwig and other imposing buildings. Ludwigstrasse ends at the Siegestor, the Arch of Victory, and beyond this there is the district of Schwabing.

What Greenwich Village is to Manhattan, Schwabing is to Munich. The main artery through Schwabing is the Leopoldstrasse, a shopping street, which in summer takes on a south-European air, with many of the ice cream parlors, coffee shops, and bars spilling on to the pavement with tables and chairs. Schwabing, once an artist student quarter, is now noted for its nightlife and jazz bars.

Lying along the east side of Schwabing is the English Garden. It's Munich's most famous park and the largest city-park in Europe. It was established by royal commission as long ago as 1789 by the American-Briton, Sir Benjamin Thompson, later Count Rumford, and last year the city celebrated its 200th anniversary with open-air parties and concerts. The Garden covers a huge area and includes a Chinese pagoda (Chinesischer Turm), the Monopteros (a small Greek temple with a fine view over the city), a boating lake with a pleasant café/restaurant and endless walks. There is no better (or cheaper) way of experiencing a true Munich summer evening than to buy your own picnic supper *(Brotzeit)* from a butcher or supermarket and bear it off to the beer garden at the Chinese pagoda. After buying your mug of beer from the Ausschank, take a seat at one of the long wooden trestle tables, and enjoy your supper. There are no formalities with everyone pressed together, and it won't be long before one or more locals pluck up courage to practice their English. Apart from "Grüss Gott," the friendly term of greeting (which literally means "God's Greeting"), you will probably find the Bavarian dialect impenetrable.

One final attraction: Schloss Nymphenburg, far out in the northwest part of the city. Summer residence of the kings of Bavaria, Schloss Nymphenburg is an exceptionally harmonious Baroque palace. Its showpiece is the great Festival Hall, where concerts are given in the summer. Ludwig I's Gallery of Beauties is worth a passing glance, too, with its portraits of 24 ladies who took the king's eye, including the notorious Lola Montez. If you like porcelain, don't overlook the exhibition in the northern wing of the Schloss, or the showrooms of the famous Nymphenburger Porzellan Manufaktur, which are also here. The park around Schloss Nymphenburg is even more beautiful than the palace. In May and June its rhododendrons are in full bloom, but this excursion is worthwhile any time.

PRACTICAL INFORMATION FOR MUNICH

GETTING INTO TOWN FROM THE AIRPORT. A regular bus line operates between the airport and the main railroad station (Hauptbahnhof), up to four times an hour in both directions, from early morning until 9 P.M. The fare is DM 5 one-way.

Tourist information offices are at the airport, Hauptbahnhof, and Sendlingerstr. 1, near Marienplatz.

HOTELS. At any time of the year, it's a good idea to make reservations in advance for Munich, particularly during the Oktoberfest beer festival in the last week of September and first week of October, and in the fashion weeks *(Mode Wochen)* in March and October. In general hotels are expensive, and it is advisable to seek out either accommodations outside the city center or hotel-pensions or private guest houses.

Moderate

Adria, Liebigstr. 8a (tel. 293081). Between Prinzregenten and Maximilianstr. Garni. 71 beds. Closed Dec. 23–Jan. 7.

Dachs, Amalienstr. 12, in Schwabing (tel. 282086). 85 beds. Comfortable if perhaps a bit loud. Garni.

Gästehaus Englischer Garten, Liebergesellstr. 8 (tel. 392034). 34 beds. Right on the edge of the Englischer Garten. Quiet and ivy-clad. Garni.

Haberstock, Schillerstr. 4 (tel. 557855). Centrally located hotel, 116 beds with shower or bath.

Lettl, Amalienstr. 53 (tel. 283026). 55 beds, with shower or bath, centrally located. Garni. Closed Dec. 16–Jan. 6.

Müller, Fliegenstr. 4 (tel. 266063). 70 beds, mostly shower or batch. Closed Dec. 23–31.

Nikolai, Am Nikolaiplatz (tel. 397056). Apartment hotel in Schwabing between the English Garden and Leopoldstr.

Parkhotel Neuhofen, Plinganserstr. 102 (tel. 7231086) in Mittersendling section. 60 beds, mostly double rooms. S-Bahn to city center.

Pension Monopteros, Oettingenstr. 35 (tel. 292348). Small, centrally located at southern end of English Garden with good streetcar connection to city center. Friendly and personal.

Stachus, Bayerstr. 7 (tel. 592881). Near Main Station, 110 beds. Garni.

Uhland, Uhlandstr. 1 (tel. 539277). 50 beds, with shower or bath, centrally located. Garni.

Inexpensive, Pensions, Guest Houses

Agah, Hohenzollernstr. 97, Schwabing (tel. 2717844). 20 beds. Garni.

Blauer Bock, Sebastiansplatz 9 (tel. 2608043). 115 beds, with shower or bath, centrally located not far from Viktualienmarkt food market. Garni.

Grunwald, Altostr. 38 (tel. 875226). Located west of Nymphenberg on S-bahn 4 (Aubing). 60 beds, good value. Breakfast buffet.

Pension Beck, Thierschstr. 36 (tel. 225768). A handsome, well-located art nouveau building with 50 comfortable rooms, some multi-bedded.

Pension Kriemhild, Guntherstr. 16 (tel. 170077). Very quiet house near Nymphenburg Palace. 32 beds. Garni. Buffet breakfast.

Utzelmann, Pettenkoferstr. 6 (tel. 594889). Good value but only 19 beds.

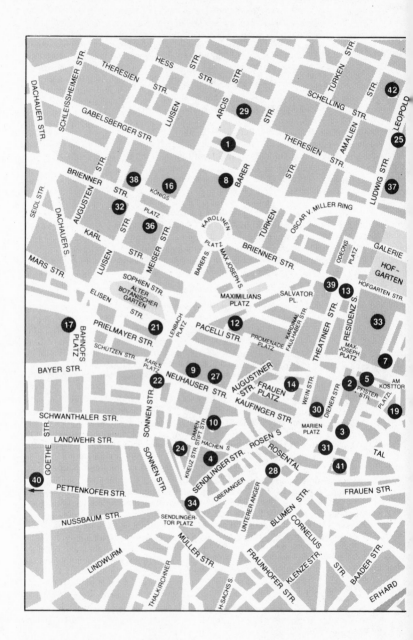

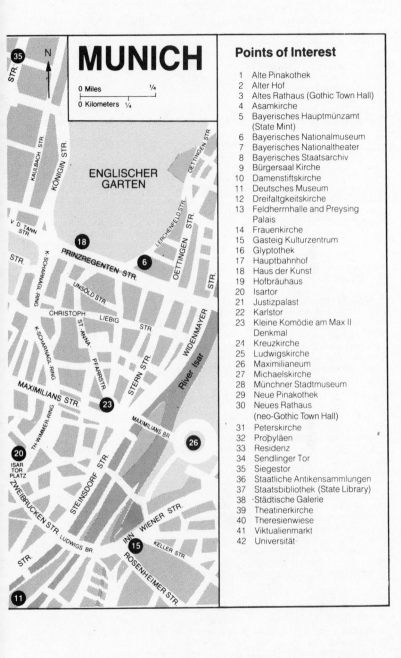

MUNICH

0 Miles ¼

0 Kilometers ¼

ENGLISCHER GARTEN

River Isar

Points of Interest

1 Alte Pinakothek
2 Alter Hof
3 Altes Rathaus (Gothic Town Hall)
4 Asamkirche
5 Bayerisches Hauptmünzamt (State Mint)
6 Bayerisches Nationalmuseum
7 Bayerisches Nationaltheater
8 Bayerisches Staatsarchiv
9 Bürgersaal Kirche
10 Damenstiftskirche
11 Deutsches Museum
12 Dreifaltgkeitskirche
13 Feldherrnhalle and Preysing Palais
14 Frauenkirche
15 Gasteig Kulturzentrum
16 Glyptothek
17 Hauptbahnhof
18 Haus der Kunst
19 Hofbräuhaus
20 Isartor
21 Justizpalast
22 Karlstor
23 Kleine Komödie am Max II Denkmal
24 Kreuzkirche
25 Ludwigskirche
26 Maximilianeum
27 Michaelskirche
28 Münchner Stadtmuseum
29 Neue Pinakothek
30 Neues Rathaus (neo-Gothic Town Hall)
31 Peterskirche
32 Propyläen
33 Residenz
34 Sendlinger Tor
35 Siegestor
36 Staatliche Antikensammlungen
37 Staatsbibliothek (State Library)
38 Städtische Galerie
39 Theatinerkirche
40 Theresienwiese
41 Viktualienmarkt
42 Universität

Youth Hostels, Student Accommodations and Camping

DJH Jugendherberge, Wendl-Dietrich Str. 20 (tel. 131156). 535 beds, bed and breakfast.

DJH Jugendherberge Burg Schwaneck, Burgweg 4–6, 8023 Pullach bei-München (tel. 7930643). About 8 miles outside town and easily reached by S-Bahn. Picturesquely located in renovated castle on hill over river Isar. Sportsground and bowling alley. Bed and breakfast. Evening meals extra.

DJH Jugengästehaus, Miesingstr. 4 (tel. 7236560). 344 beds, bed and breakfast; day rooms and disco.

Haus International, Elisabethstr. 87 (tel. 120060). 480 beds, swimming pool.

Jugendhotel Marienherberge, Goethestr. 9 (tel. 555891). Girls only, age limit 25.

Kolping-Haus, Adolf-Kolpingstr. 1 (tel. 594852). Youth hostel card required, curfew at 11, forced wake up at 7.

YMCA (CVJM), Landwehrstr. 13 (tel. 555941). Only a few hundred yards from Main Station. Men and women. 80 beds.

There are also a number of camping sites around the city. One of the best is *München-Obermenzing* at the beginning of the autobahn to Stuttgart (tel. 8112235). Another is *München-Thalkirchen,* near Hellabrunn Zoo, Zentralländstr. 49 (tel. 7231707); open mid-March to end Oct. There is also a site at Langwieder See, near the Munich end of the Stuttgart autobahn, at Eschenriederstr. 119 (tel. 8141566); open April to Oct. and a huge communal sleeping tent "Kapuzinerhölzl" at Franz-Schrank Str. 8 (tel. 1414300), opposite the main entrance to the Nymphenberg Botanic Gardens (Streetcar No. 12), open June through August, price DM 5 including blankets and air mattress.

RESTAURANTS. Munich is full of Moderate and Inexpensive restaurants, and those we list here constitute only a small fraction of the total. So you will find it well worth while to take a little time off to explore a few of the eating areas. Apart from ordinary restaurants, the city also has an almost equally large number of beer halls, beer restaurants, wine taverns and cafés, most of which also serve inexpensive food (though those in the immediate vicinity of the Marienplatz are higher priced). They are listed separately under Entertainment, below. *Wienerwald, Pizza Hut* and *McDonald's* all over town.

Moderate

Asia, Einsteinstr. 133 (tel. 472124). Chinese food with special midday menu at reduced rates.

Augustiner Gaststätten, Neuhauser Str. 16 (tel. 5519901). You will be pleased with the big platefuls in this bustling and ornate beer restaurant. Zither music occasionally.

Biermuseum, Burgstr. 12 (tel. 224315). Centrally located near Marienplatz. Six different beers from the barrel. Good-value Munich specialties.

Feldherrnkeller, under the Feldherrnhalle with entrance from both Residenzstrasse and Theatinerstrasse (tel. 296565). Good food and wines in cozy wood-panelled surroundings; music in the evening.

Ochs'n Wirt (in *Schwabinger Bräu*), Leopoldstr. 82 (tel. 332032). Munich specialties and good steaks.

Straubinger Hof, Blumenstr. 5 (tel. 2608444). Excellent range of Bavarian dishes. Be there before noon to find a table. Closed Sun.

Wurstkuchl, Amalienstr. 87 (tel. 281577). Oldest sausage restaurant in the world.

Inexpensive

Augustiner Keller, Arnulfstr. 52 (tel. 594393). Local specialties.

Bella Italia, Hohenzollernplatz 8, Sendlingerstr. 66, Türkenstr. 50, Passing Bahnhofsplatz, Herzog-Wilhelmstr. 8. A group of five low-priced Italian restaurants; even the beer is cheap.

Java, Hessstr. 51 (tel. 522221). An Indonesian-food self-service restaurant. Very budget-minded.

Mensa Technische Hochschule, Arcisstr. 17. Student snack bar (only with student card).

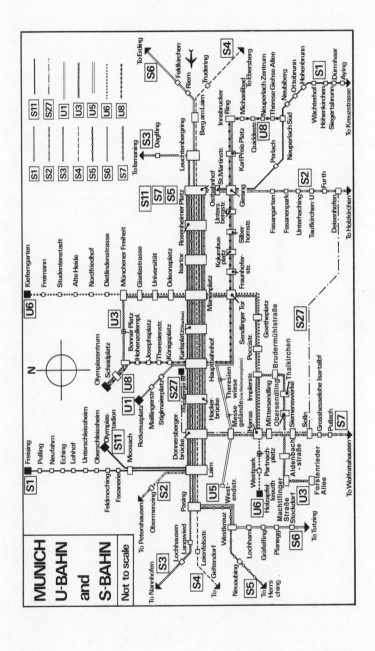

MUNICH
U-BAHN
and
S-BAHN
Not to scale

Murr-Imbiss. Snack bar for warm meals (self-service) run by the Vinzenz-Murr butcheries throughout town. Excellent soups and roasts.

Pizza-Hut, Zweibrückenstr. 1, Leopoldstr. 60, Bayerstr. 13. Even local Italians praise its pizzas.

Schnellimbisse, Marienplatz and Karlsplatz below-ground concourses, and Viktualienmarkt (closed Sun.). Stand-up snack bars with mainly sausage selections, but look for more filling Leberkäs.

Department stores Hertie, Kaufhof, and Karstadt offer excellent-value late breakfasts and lunches.

GETTING AROUND MUNICH. By Metro-Bus-Tram. Public transport in Munich is excellent.

There is a comprehensive and efficient metro (U-Bahn) and an equally reliable suburban train service (S-Bahn) which serves 134 stations in the town and surrounding areas and is still being extended. Trains, buses and trams run from about 5 A.M. to after 1 A.M. The heart of the train system is the Hauptbahnhof (Main Station) in the Bahnhofsplatz. The city is also well served by buses and trams, the network extending well into the suburbs. A city map is available showing all tram and bus lines and stops.

The same fares apply to both the U-Bahn and S-Bahn and all bus and tram services, allowing travel on all or any of these services with the same ticket. Break your journey as often as you like, for up to two hours. Red strip tickets are for children only; cancel one strip per journey. Blue strip tickets for adults cost DM 9.50 (10 strips) or DM 15 (16 strips). For the inner zone all journeys require cancellation of two strips. If you're making a longer journey across more than one zone, check the fare lists at stations before starting your journey. An honor system operates, but there are frequent checks by plain-clothes inspectors. The fine for traveling without a ticket, or with an incorrect ticket, is DM 60—and there are no exceptions for foreign tourists. Two alternatives to the strip tickets: single-journey tickets (inner zone), which cost DM 2.40 per ride; or 24-hour tickets, which allow unlimited travel and cost DM 7 for inner zone, DM 12.50 for the entire network.

By Bicycle. Bicycle hire (see below for details) is widely available in Munich,

and the city and environs can be delightfully explored on two wheels as bicycle tracks total around 450 miles. The Tourist Office has a brochure (50 pfennigs) for cyclists giving four routes, where to hire bicycles and how to transport them on the local train network or subway.

The most pleasant routes are those through the English Garden, where you can cycle the full length of the park from the Haus der Kunst in the Prinzregenten Str. northwards along the Isar to the suburb of Ismaning right out in the country. If you feel brave enough to cross the city center on two wheels, a long stretch of track runs southwards along the banks of the Isar (past the Deutsches Museum) out towards Thalkirchen and Hellabrunn Zoo. If you continue in this direction you will find lovely picnic and sunbathing areas along the riverside, and further southwards still you can reach the pretty towns of Pullach, Grünwald and the road to the old market town of Wolfratshausen.

The area north of the center, out towards Olympic Park, is again well served with cycle tracks, as is Munich West, near the Hirschgarten Park and Nymphenburg Palace. Once in the west of town, it's worth proceeding towards the Garmisch Autobahn (starting at Luise-Kiesselbach-Platz), where a long stretch of cycle track follows the old main road next to the motorway all the way out to Starnberg Lake. It's a very enjoyable day's trip, and one that can be combined with bicycle hire at the S-Bahn stations, because if you don't feel like the trek back to town, you can always leave your bike at Starnberg S-Bahn station and take the electric train back into the city center.

Bicycles can be hired in the English Garden on the corner of Königin and Veterinärstr. Open May-Oct., Saturday and Sunday and holidays (in good weather) (tel. 397016). Hire fees: 1 hr.: DM 5; 2 hrs: DM 8; a whole day costs DM 18. Reduced rates for groups. Bike tours of the city—including bike hire—are organized by City Hopper Touren (tel. 2721131).

Bicycles can also be hired at 17 S-Bahn stations and 54 other stations in Upper Bavaria. Rental costs are DM 5 per day if you use Munich public transport (MVV), the railway or connecting buses to reach the station with bicycles for hire. Otherwise the cost is DM 10. A brochure, *Fahrrad am Bahnhof*, can be obtained from ticket offices of the Deutsches Bundesbahn.

ENTERTAINMENT. Beer Halls. Beer drinking and all its attendant mythology are taken very seriously here in this easy going city, as the large number of beer halls, restaurants and gardens makes only too clear.

In the biggest beer halls, such as Hofbrauhaus, and the big beer gardens, such as the Chinese Tower, the minimum quantity you can order is a *Mass*, a 1-liter mug (a bit over a U.S. quart); elsewhere *ein Halbes* (half liter) is the standard serve. You order *Helles* (light) if you like the regular or *Dunkles* (dark) if you prefer a heavier and sweeter type. Among the several seasonal types of beer, all of them stronger than the "regular," are: *Wiesenbier*, brewed for Oktoberfest, which takes place on the *Wiesen* (meadows), hence the name; various kinds of *Starkbier* (strong beer) produced during the Lent season, the best known of which is *Salvator; Maibock*, brewed and drunk in May. If none of these is available and you want a strong beer, ask for *Bock* (light or dark). Alternatively, try the sour but refreshing *Weissbier* (wheat beer), which you will see served in tall glasses shaped like flower vases.

The beer halls are mostly owned by large breweries and are enormous in size. The liveliest activity is concentrated in the large main hall (in summer usually in a vast garden) where a brass band plays folk tunes. There is usually dancing on weekends. Prices are low.

Augustiner Keller, Arnulfstr. 52.

Hofbräuhaus, Platzl Square. Always crowded—but often with tourists.

Salvator-Keller, at Hochstr. 77 on Nockherberg, is particularly lively in March when the strong Salvator is on draft for a few weeks.

Pschorr-Keller at Theresienhöhe, near the exhibition grounds and the statue of Bavaria, serves Pschorr beer.

Hacker Keller, Theresienhöhe 4. Near the above.

Beer Restaurants. These are usually sponsored, if not owned, by large breweries. They're intended primarily for eating and serve mainly Bavarian fare and the sponsor's beer, although some wine can be had in most of them.

Spöckmeier, Rosenstr. 9, is among the oldest in this category.

Spatenhaus, Residenzstr. 12, opposite the Opera, is famous for good food.

Franziskaner und Fuchsenstuben, Perusastr., close by and similar.

Peterhof on Marienplatz offers an attractive cellar and a fine view of the Rathaus from upstairs windows.

Haxnbauer, Münzstr. 2, near Platzl, a small, original rustic tavern, serves Kalbshaxen and Schweinshaxen from open fireplace.

Beer Gardens. Am Chinesischen Turm in the English Garden. Seating for 6,000, self-service from snack stands. Very cosmopolitan; usually crowded and loud.

Hirschgarten, near Nymphenburg Palace, Hirschgartenallee 1. Seating for 6,500, self-service—but you have to wait in line for a long time for half-a-chicken on warm summer evenings. Better take your own picnic. Children's playground; deer and game enclosures.

Two small gardens:

Max-Emanuel-Brauerei, Adalbertstr. 33 near the University. Also good-value restaurant.

Osterwaldgarten, Keferstr. 12, in Schwabing, on the edge of the English Garden.

Wine Taverns. Munich has a type of genuine wine tavern where drinking rather than eating is the thing. In addition to the long lists of bottled wines, they usually offer some two dozen types of open wine, sold by the ¼-liter glass, prices ranging according to quality. Long tables get you acquainted with your drinking partners.

Ratskeller-Schoppenstuben, beneath the Rathaus on Marienplatz. "Schoppen" means a glass of wine.

Pfälzer Weinprobierstube, in the Residenz Palace, entrance at Residenzstr. 1, also specializes in Palatinate wines.

Weinkrüger, Maximilianstr. 21. Good-value food. Favorite of opera and theatergoers.

Weinstadl, Burgstr. 5. Historical wine tavern in the Burghof in the heart of the old city.

Cafés. It is more expensive to drink coffee sitting down in a café (although more comfortable) than at a stand-up coffee-shop such as *Tschibo* or *Eduscho,* where freshly ground coffee is sold and you can drink a cup for DM 1.50. Here, it is perfectly acceptable to bring your own pastry too.

Ander Uni, Ludwigstr. 24. Young crowd, mostly from nearby university. Mugs of coffee, good pastries.

Café Glockenspiel, top floor of Marienplatz 28. Offers fine pastries and an excellent view of the Rathaus; it's also a very good place to watch the Glockenspiel.

Café Munchener Freiheit, Schwabing. Popular with the trendy young. Also sells some of the best ice cream (to take out) in Munich, plus marzipan delicacies in unusual shapes.

Feldherrnhalle, Theatinerstr. 38. Among the best spots for pastries.

Hag, Residenzstr. 26. Another excellent pastry-lover's haunt.

Clubs, Bars and Discos. These are all expensive, though you can pass an evening in a regular bar without spending too much. Clubs and discos are as expensive as anywhere else and a Scotch can cost DM 10–12. Some spots that won't break the bank:

Alter Simpl, Türkenstr. 57. Once a literary café and still frequented by the Schwabing crowd.

Crash, Lindwurmstr. (an extension of the Sendlingerstrasse). Lively, loud disco. Admission charge entitles you to a drink. Good DJs. Younger public.

Doktor Flotte, Occamstr. 8, Schwabing. Offers loud disco music, occasionally live.

Domicile (Jazz club), Leopoldstr. 19. Good jazz here. Best nights are Friday, Saturday and Sunday. No admission charge, but drinks are expensive.

Drugstore, on the corner of Feilitzschstr. and Siegesstr. in the heart of Schwabing. Part of a trendy craze, this place combines a bar, boutiques and a restaurant. Drinks are reasonable and you can eat fairly cheaply, too.

East Side, Rosenheimerstr. 30. Very chic night spot, room for over 600; selective admittance maintains the tone.

Fregatte, Sonnenstr. 17. Live bands of international fame. Open until 4.00 A.M. Mixed and slightly older crowd here.

Jenny's Place in the Blue Note, Moosacherstr. 24. Offers popular jazz nightly except Sun. Some theaters are closed July–Aug.

Rumpelkammer, Trautenwolfstr. 1. Disco with canned music in a funky Victorian attic atmosphere.

Tabarin, Thierschstr. 19. American blacks and students from Africa and the Near East are here in impressive numbers. The best sounds come from the first band of the month (1st week), as well as every Wednesday and weekends.

West Side, Wendl-Dietrich-Str. 11 (near the Youth Hostel). Good disco, mainly younger clientele.

Theater and Opera. Munich has always been a great theatrical city. Get the monthly brochure "Monatsprogramm" (DM 1.50) for the best summary of what's happening while you're in town.

Tickets for the opera can be purchased at the opera house itself. The advance sales office is on Maximiliansstr., behind the opera house. It's open Mon.-Fri. 10–1 and 3.30–5.30 P.M., Sat. 10–12.30 P.M. Standing room tickets can cost as little as DM 5.50. Other ticket agencies are *ABR-Theaterkasse,* Neuhauserstr. 9; *Max Hieber,* Liebfrauenstr. 1 (at the Cathedral) and the *Otto Bauer* music-shop at the back of the Rathaus.

As befits a city that was host to four world premières of Wagner's operas, Munich has a fine opera company in the Bavarian State Opera, which performs in the *Bavarian National Theater* at Max-Joseph-Platz. The State Opera Company's former home, the *Prinzregententheater,* which fell into disuse after the war, was reopened in 1988 after extensive restoration work.

Other principal theaters include the *Staatstheater am Gärtnerplatz,* at Gärtnerplatz 3, where operettas and light opera are performed, while for plays there are the *Münchner Kammerspiele* in the Schauspielhaus at Maximiliansstr. 26, and the *Bayerisches Staatsschauspiel* in the Residenztheater, Max-Joseph-Platz 1 where classical and contemporary plays are performed. The Rococo *Altes Residenztheater*, better known under the name Cuvilliés-Theater, is where Baroque-period operas, Richard Strauss and Molière are performed. *Theater in der Briennerstrasse*, at no. 50 in the street of the same name, and *Theater am Marstall*, Marstallplatz, are mainly for drama. Among the several smaller theaters, giving mainly comedies, are *Intimes Theater* in Künstlerhaus Lenbachplatz 8; *Die Kleine Freiheit*, Maximiliansstr. 31; and *Kleine Komödie* with two halls, at Promenadeplatz Passage (Bayerischer Hof) and at Max II Denkmal. There is also the ultra-modern *Deutsches Theater* in Schwanthalerstr for variety shows, concerts and musicals.

Munich has a puppet theater, the *Marionettentheater*, at Blumenstr. 29a, and two theaters devoted exclusively to productions for children and young people, the *Theater der Jugend*, at Franz-Josef-Str. 47, and the *Münchner Theater für Kinder*, Dachauerstr. 46.

Concerts. The big concert halls of Munich are the *Herkules Saal in der Residenz*, the *Kongress Saal* of the Deutsches Museum, on its island in the middle of the Isar and the new, super-modern *"Gasteig" Cultural Center*, home of the Munich Philharmonic, with library, conservatory and monumental concert hall, just up the hill from the Deutsche Museum. Soloists and chamber music groups appear in the *Sophiensaal*, Sophienstr. 6, where there is a fine organ; the *Festsaal of Künstlerhaus*, Lenbachplatz 8; *Galerie im Lenbachhaus*, Luisenstr. 33; *Hochschule für Musik*, Arcisstr. 12 and the new *Carl-Orff-Saal* in the Gasteig Kulturzentrum. Munich has three symphony orchestras—the Munich Philharmonic, the Bavarian State Orchestra and the Bavarian Radio Orchestra. There are several choral societies, including the famous Bach Choir, the Münchner Motettenchor and the Musica Viva, the latter for contemporary music.

The best church music is provided by the choirs of St. Michael's (Neuhauserstr.), St. Matthews (Matthäuskirche, Sendlinger-Tor-Platz), and the Cathedral Choir (Domchor), which sings sometimes in the *Frauenkirche* and sometimes in the *Dreifaltigkeitskirche*, (Holy Trinity Church). Much church music can be enjoyed free of charge.

Pop and/or rock concerts are often given in the *Circus Krone*, Marstrasse 43, where you can also see the circus between December 25 and March 31, in the *Kongress Saal* of the Deutsches Museum and the *Olympiahalle*, Olympic Park.

Cinema. Apart from an outstanding film festival in June, Munich has nearly 50 cinemas showing the latest international and German films all over the city and suburbs. Some of the most central are: *Leopold*, Leopoldstr. 80 (tel. 347441). *Mathäser* Filmpalast, Bayerstr. (tel. 595363). Several small cinemas each showing a different film. *Marmorhaus*, Leopoldstr. 35 (tel. 344046). Five different cinemas. *Neues Arri*, Türkenstr. 91 (tel. 38190450). *Stachus Kinocenter*, Sonnenstr. 6 (tel. 594275). *Theatiner Filmkunst*, Theatinerstr. 32 (tel. 223183). *Türkendolch*, Türkenstr. 74 (tel. 2718844).

Films in English are shown at the *Europa-Fremdsprachenkino*, in the Atlantik-Palast, Schwantalerstr. 2–6 (tel. 555670), the *Museum-Lichtspiele*, Ludwigsbrucke (tel. 482403), *Cinema*, Nymphenburgerstr. 31 (tel. 555255), and *Filmmuseum*, in the Stadtmuseum, St. Jakobsplatz 1.

MUSEUMS AND ART GALLERIES. Most of these are open Tues. to Sat., 9.30 or 10 to 4.30; Sun. 10–1. Nearly all of them are closed on Mondays. As opening times vary, it's best to check them with the Tourist Office or in the monthly Official Program. Most places charge for admission, between DM 2 and DM 5. However, there are reductions and sometimes free entry for students and all the museums are free on Sundays and holidays.

Alte Pinakothek, Barerstr. 27. European paintings from the 14th to 17th century. Among the chief treasures of this museum are works by most of the Continent's greatest names. One of Europe's greatest galleries.

Bayerisches Nationalmuseum (National Museum of Bavaria), Prinzregentenstr. 3. Contains a remarkable collection of medieval art and sculpture, miniature art, arts and crafts, folk art, applied art, etc. Among its more notable exhibits are the largest collection of early German sculpture in the country, the best tapestries in Germany, a fine group of woodcarvings by Tilman Riemenschneider, 16th-century armor and the unique *Krippenschau,* Christmas crib collection.

Bayerisches Staatsbiblothek (Bavarian State Library), Ludwigstr. 23. This great library lost 500,000 of its 2,000,000 books (the collection has now grown to over 3,000,000) in World War II air raids, but saved all of its 16,000 incunabula and its priceless medieval books, including the Bible of Emperor Otto III, with its Reichenau illuminations and its ivory binding inset with gems.

BMW Museum, Petuelring 130, opposite Olympic Park. Vintage cars and motorcycles displayed using the latest and most dazzling audio visual techniques.

Deutsches Museum (German Museum of Science and Technology), Museum Island. First-rate scientific museum covers just above everything in its realm. See the mining exhibit, showing just how mines are and were worked and the 16th-century alchemists' workshops. A planetarium capable of projecting some 4,500 stars inside its semi-circular dome is one of the many attractions. Open daily.

Deutsches Jagdmuseum (German Museum of Hunting and Fishing), Neuhauserstr. 53. Housed in the former Augustinian church. Among exhibits are 3,000 hunting trophies, historic hunting weapons, 200 stuffed animals in dioramas representing their natural surroundings.

Glyptothek und Antikensammlung (Museum of Antiquities), Königsplatz 1–3. Collection of Egyptian, Etruscan, Greek and Roman sculpture and art.

Haus der Kunst, Prinzregentenstr. 1. Antique fairs and book exhibitions are held year-round. *Staatsgalerie Moderner Kunst* is housed in the west wing, with over 400 20th-century paintings and sculptures. One of the surviving examples of Nazi-era architecture.

Münchner Stadtmuseum (City Historical Museum), St-Jakobs-Platz 1. The history of Munich. The museum also houses collections of musical instruments, photography, beer making and puppet-theaters; and has recently opened the largest collection of historical fairground exhibits in the world.

Museum für Völkerkunde (Museum of Ethnology), Maximiliansstr. 42. Fine collections from the Far East and South America.

Neue Pinakothek, Barerstr. 29. Magnificent modern building houses some of the best works by 19th-century artists and sculptors, particularly German and French impressionists. A superb gallery.

Prähistorische Staatssammlung (State Prehistoric Collection), Lerchenfeldstr. 2. Prehistoric finds from all over Bavaria, and regular exhibitions of international interest.

Residenzmuseum, Max-Joseph-Platz 3. State rooms and princely suites in Renaissance, Rococo and neo-classic styles, porcelain, silverware. Schatzkammer (Treasury) in the same building features masterpieces in gold and precious stones from the last ten centuries. In the same group of buildings is the Alte Residenztheater (Cuvilliés Theater). A unique example of the Rococo style. In the summer, many concerts are held here.

Schackgalerie, Prinzregentenstr. 9. Late–19th-century German painters, such as Böcklin, Feuerbach, Schwind.

Staatliche Graphische Sammlung (State Collection of the Graphic Arts), Meiserstr. 10. Drawings and prints from the late Gothic period until the present.

Städtische Galerie im Lenbachhaus (Municipal Gallery), Luisenstr. 33. The works of Lenbach and other prominent Munich artists such as Rottmann and Spitzweg as well as a noted collection of the *Blaue Reiter* (Blue Rider) school—Kandinsky, Marc, Macke—and Paul Klee.

Theatermuseum, Galeriestr. 4a. Collection still has its 40,000 volume library, portraits of actors, designs for stage sets, etc.

Valentin-Museum, in the tower gate of Isartor. Museum of curiosities and nonsense dedicated to the German comedian. Has good café.

Zoologische Staatssammlung, Münchhauserstr. in suburb of Obermenzing. Largest zoological collection of its kind in the country, housed in a new building opened in 1985.

SHOPPING. Munich, boasting a variety of shopping streets, is generally considered one of Germany's best shopping towns. Of the many pedestrian shopping areas, the largest runs from Karlstor to Marienplatz and is home to the department stores

Karstadt and *Kaufhof.* Both have a considerable variety of goods as well as many souvenirs such as Bavarian wood carvings, pewter, elaborate wax candles and ceramics. Another good department store is *Hertie's* at the main railway station. There is a smaller branch in the heart of Schwabing, at Münchener Freiheit.

If you're after traditional Bavarian clothes, such as *dirndls* and knickerbockers *(Kniebundhosen)*—excellent for hiking—try *Dirndl Ecke,* am Platzl 4. Be warned, though, a genuine *dirndl* is costly.

There are many sports shops, though they are a little expensive. However, all these stores have a good selection of special offers *(Sonderangebote)* from time to time, particularly during the winter sales, in January.

You can also pick up a worthwhile souvenir from one of the several flea-markets that take place in the summer. The most well known is the Auer Dult Market on Maria-Hilfplatz. This is a combination of an antique fair and a white-elephant bazaar and takes place in the spring (April-May) and autumn (September-Oct.). The variety of objets d'art and contents of grandmother's attic is enormous. True flea-markets also take place every Saturday and Sunday at Dachauerstr. 128 (near the Olympic Park) and at the Dingolfinger Strasse, in Haidhausen.

For window-shopping stroll down the Theatiner or Maffeistrasse in the pedestrian area between Marienplatz and Odeonsplatz or the Maximilianstrasse near the Opera and admire the elegant boutiques. In the same way have a look around the super-luxurious food stores *Dallmayr,* Dienerstrasse 14, with the best selection of fresh-roasted coffee in town, and *Käfer,* Prinzregentenstr. 73, where you can get just about any delicacy from any part of the world—at a price!

USEFUL ADDRESSES. *"ASTA",* Amalienstr. 73. *Internationales Student Foyer,* Adelheidstr. 15. *Verkehrsamt,* (Tourist Office), Sendlingerstr. 1, airport and at train station. *Studentenschnelldienst,* Veterinärstr. 1. *Fremdenverkehrsverband München-Oberbayern,* (Bavarian Tourist Association), 8 München 15, Sonnenstr. 10 (tel. 597347). *America House,* Karolinenplatz 3; or *Federation of German-American Clubs,* Birnauerstr. 6 (Meet the Germans). *Youth Information Center,* Paul Heysestr. 22. *Transalpino,* Budget Youth Travel, Sonnenstr. 8 and Dachauerstr. 149. *German Camping Club,* Mandlstr. 28 (tel. 334021).

U.S. Consulate General, Königinstr. 5–7 (tel. 23011). *British Consulate,* Amalienstr. 62 (tel. 394015). *ABR* (Official Bavarian Travel Office), with branches in the main railroad station, at Promenadeplatz 12, Sendlinger Str. 70, Münchner Freiheit 6, Stachus, Arabellapark, Pasing, Tegernseer Landstr. 11 and the airport (central tel. no. 23911). *American Express,* Promenadeplatz 6. *Thomas Cook,* 1m Hauptbahnhof (tel. 12041). For cheap charter flights within Europe try *Travel Overland,* Barerstr. 73 or Wörthstr. 49.

The Bavarian Forest

To the east of Munich there is an area of perfect budget terrain that is well worth exploring. Here is the Bayerischer Wald, the Bavarian Forest. Running north east/south west along the Czechoslovak border and covering over 300 square miles of unspoiled wildlife reserve, it is the largest stretch of unbroken mountainous forestland in Central Europe. It was also the first German National Park.

There are three rail lines; the main route running east to Vienna, the new Munich–Passau–Bayerisch–Eisenstein express route; the local line that threads its way to Bodenmais through tiny towns and villages; and finally, the special direct FD–Alpen Express route from June to September between Dortmund, Frankfurt, Nürnberg, Regen, Zwiesel and Bodenmais. There is much to see. Cham, for example, is idyllically situated on the river Regen, with its splendid old Rathaus, 13th-century Biertor gate and towers and boisterous folk festival at the end of July. There's also Fürth-im-Wald, closer to the Czech border and famed for its bizarre Dragon Slaying pageant in August in which a fearsome model dragon is done to death. Viechtach, a quiet resort and delightful in both summer and winter. Regen, with the nearby Pfahl ridge of rocky towers and the ruins of Weissenstein castle, whose one-time owner, the aptly-named Count Hund (meaning Dog), had his wife walled up alive after she drowned their child having heard a terrible prophecy concerning its fate; it seems she got the wrong end of the stick. Lallinger Winkel is a pretty, unspoiled 7-mile-wide "triangle" at the southern tip of the Bavarian Forest, and has recently opened its doors to tourism as a cure and holiday resort.

This area centers on the Arber, a 5,000 ft. mountain surrounded by skiing and hiking country and with several delightful winter and summer resorts, such as Bayerisch-Eisenstein, Bodenmais (famous for its crystal and former salt mines) and St. Englmar, the highest village in the Bavarian Forest.

In fact, the winter sports possibilities in this part of Bavaria are not to be ignored. Although not considered a particularly important winter sports region, there are nonetheless many excellent facilities for both downhill and cross country skiing and the resorts have something to offer every winter sports enthusiast. The season here in the Bavarian Forest lasts from December to March. The most important centers are Bayerisch-Eisenstein, Bodenmais, St. Englmar and Schönsee, but Arrach, Lam, Lohberg, Kötzting, Falkenstein, Grafenwiesen, Eschlkam and Waldmünchen are also not to be sneered at.

PRACTICAL INFORMATION FOR THE BAVARIAN FOREST

Hotels and Restaurants

Bayerisch Eisenstein. *Area code: 09925.* Neuwaldhaus (M), Hauptstr. 5 (tel. 444). 32 rooms. *Pension am Regen* (M), Anton-Pech-Weg 21 (tel. 464). Breakfast only. Closed Oct. 20–Dec. 15. *Pension Arberblick) (I)*, Bahnhofstr. 15 (tel. 307). Beds as low-priced as DM 17 with breakfast. 15 beds.
Restaurant. *Gasthof Arberseehaus* (I), (tel. 276). On the shores of the Grosser Arbersee lake, panoramic view from terrace.

Bodenmais. *Area code: 09924.* Good-value, 7-day package arrangements for winter, spring and fall, including half board, in all the following hotels. *Bayerwald-Hotel Hofbräuhaus* (M), Marktplatz 5 (tel. 7021). Hotel with tradition and atmosphere, very comfortably-furnished rooms, sun-terrace and garden, sauna, indoor pool and cosy fireside room with bar. Closed beginning of Nov.–mid-Dec. *Hubertus* (M), Amselweg 2 (tel. 7026). Pool and sauna; quiet with a fine view and within a few minutes of lovely forestland. All rooms furnished in rustic style with bath or shower. Own pool with sauna and solarium, restaurant, *Jägerstüberl* café and rustic *Jägerhütt'n* tavern with open fireplace. Closed Nov. 7–Dec 15. *Neue Post* (I), Kötzinger Str. 25 (tel. 7077). Special 6-day tennis-week holidays on own courts. Good-value menu.
Restaurant. *Franzl's Pils und Weinstube* (M), Bahnhofstr. 68 (tel. 1831). As the name implies, a beer and wine tavern; good-value local dishes.

Cham. *Area code: 09971.* In addition to a wide selection of good value hotels, pensions and holiday flats, Cham offers several opportunities for family holidays on the farm. Write for a full catalogue of farm addresses to *Landratsamt Cham*, Postfach 1432, 8490 Cham, asking for details of "Ferienwohnungen und Urlaub auf dem Bauernhof". *Hotel-Restaurant Ratskeller* (M), Am Kirchplatz (tel. 1441). Good restaurant. Closed Jan. 6–30. *Randsberger Hof* (M), Randsbergerhofstr. 15 (tel. 1266). 89 rooms. *Gästeheim am Stadtpark* (I), Tilsiter Str. 3 (tel. 2253). Fine view. *Ödenturm* (I), Am Ödenturm 11 (tel. 3880). Quiet.
Farmhouse-Pensions. *Gasthof-Pension Steif* (I) in nearby Obertraubenbach (tel. 09461–235). *Hotel Sonnenhof* (I), Am Fuchsbuhl 14 (tel. 30398). In Schlondorf.

Fürth Im Wald. *Area code: 09973.* Hohenbogen (M), Bahnhofstr. 25 (tel. 1509). 32 rooms, restaurant and café with dancing. Kitchen specializes in diet meals. *Zur Post* (I), Stadtplatz 12 (tel. 1506). 36 beds. Good-value restaurant. Closed mid-Nov.–mid-Dec.

St. Englmar. *Area code: 09965.* One of the most popular winter and summer resorts, with correspondingly higher prices. However, there is a good selection of special package arrangements for edge-of-season winter holidays, family holidays and 7-day arrangements for senior citizens. *Apart-Hotel Predigstuhl* (M), tel. 81. Situated at the famous Predigstuhl peak, famous for its ski-runs, this is an apartment hotel with 424 holiday apartments for 1–5 persons between DM 350–686 per week. Well-equipped, with indoor and outdoor pools, sauna, solarium, tennis, bowling, restaurant and café. *Berggasthof Bernardshöhe* (M), in nearby Kolmberg, Kolmberg 5 (tel. 258). On a hill with a wonderful view. Very quiet, with pool, solarium, terrace, tennis and good-value restaurant. Closed Nov.–Dec. 20. *Beim Simmerl* (I), in Maibrunn (tel. 590). 56 beds. Quiet house.

Restaurant. *Unterwirt* (I), Bayerweg 35 (tel. 225). Also has a few rooms.

Hamburg

After Berlin, Hamburg is Germany's largest city, with a population well on the way to the two million mark. And though more than 60 from the sea, it is one of the world's major ports, being linked to the North Sea by the Lower Elbe, which has constantly to be dredged deeper and deeper to accommodate the ever increasing draught of ships. The largest ships are able to ride into Hamburg only by taking advantage of the tide. The size of the port itself is about that of a medium-sized city. It is united by a network of ferries and launches. Not only is this a paradise for anyone who loves boats, it is also a relaxed and animated city to visit, perhaps not for a full holiday but certainly for a few days.

Hamburg was one of the worst bombed cities in Germany in the war and as a result is now a showpiece of modern architecture. Her tremendous new office buildings, underwater tunnel, bridges (especially the fine and fairly recent Köhlbrandbrücke suspension bridge down by the port), apartment blocks and so on, are not only splendid examples of modern construction, but in a real way carry on the traditions of the city's great medieval builders.

The true city of Hamburg, the Alt-Stadt, can be seen on foot in a day. The actual walls no longer exist, but where they once stood the streets are called "wall" *(Wallanlagen),* so you can easily trace the old boundaries.

To explore the city, begin at the rail station (Hauptbahnhof). Head out towards the Glockengiesserwall, a rather monstrous street heavy with traffic. On the right is the monolithic domed Art Hall (Kunsthalle), which is well worth a visit especially for the 20th-century German works.

When you emerge, cross the Alster by the Lombard Bridge (Lombardsbrücke) and press on along the Esplanade, leaving the ultramodern Opera House to your left. The first opera house in Germany was built here in 1677 on the site of the old Gänsemarkt (goose market) and Hamburg has been closely linked with the opera ever since. Straight ahead of you are the Botanical Gardens. They were laid out in 1821 on the site of the original Hamburg fortress. The Palmenhaus (Palm House) and the Victoriahaus with its water lilies from the Amazon are particularly interesting. Beyond the Botanical Gardens and bordering Jungiusstrasse is the most famous park in Hamburg, the Planten un Blomen. The masses of tulips in spring are followed by marvelous displays of flowers in the summer. On summer nights, there is a water ballet played out by special fountains and accompanied by colored lights and music.

Beyond the park is the Fairground (Messe), with congress halls and exhibition grounds and a year round program of trade fairs. To the north of the railway (the line that runs from the Hauptbahnhof to Dammtor and beyond) is the University.

But following the wall, the next place you come to is Karl-Muck Platz, with Hamburg's premier concert hall (Musikhalle). Continuing along the Holstenwall, with parkland to the right, the next important stop is the Hamburg Historical Museum (Museum für Hamburgische Geschichte). It has a splendid collection of marine models, and for a modest fee American visitors can trace in its archives any ancestors who set out for the New World from Hamburg.

Swinging southwest towards the river, you enter the infamous St. Pauli district. At night it is a lurid buzz of neon lights, music and street life of every sort, but by day it's rather quiet. Follow the Reeperbahn (which *really* comes to life at night) as it runs parallel to the river. At the crossing with Davidstrasse, where Hamburg's most famous police station stands, turn left and walk towards the river.

Now the ground slopes down towards the Elbe. The old riverside buildings are gone and a new complex of offices, shops and apartments is under construction. Walk down to the waterfront. On the left are the St. Pauli piers (Landungsbrücken), where local passenger ships and excursion boats tie up. It's well worth taking one of the tours around the port.

To the right, the road leads to Altona, with its fascinating Sunday morning fish market and, above it, the graceful town hall and State Museum. It's worth exploring this area in more detail. This is best done by heading west along the river shore to Övelgönne, a narrow, riverside way with the beautiful old houses of captains and river-pilots.

Near the St. Pauli piers you can see the dome above the old Elbe tunnel, built in 1911. The new one, further west, was opened in 1975.

To get back to the city center, turn away from the river and go up Helgoländer Allee towards the Bismarck memorial. East of it, you'll see the tower of St. Michael's church. You can take the elevator up to its greenish cupola for a great view out over the town. But be sure to take in the interior of the church as well. Hard by St. Michael's, in little streets that have not changed that much since the Middle Ages, is a group of beautiful old buildings, the Krameramtswohnungen, which a grateful municipality thoughtfully provided for the widows of its officials in the late 17th century.

Continue east on Ost-Weststrasse and at Herrengraben you run into a fascinating section of narrow canals called the Fleete. This is a place to wander around, trying whatever sidetrack takes your fancy. If you eventually come to the Stadthaus Brücke, you can take Neuer Wall, parallel to the last part of which are the lovely Alster Arcades. They offer attractive views of the old town, including the Rathaus. If you can visit only one building in Hamburg, it should be the Rathaus. It has a fine festival hall, vaulted ceiling and marvelous elaborate doorways among many other interesting features. Nearby on Adolphsplatz is the Stock Exchange (Börse). It was originally founded in 1558.

On the other side of the main station from that at which this tour began, is the Schauspielhaus, the best theater in Hamburg; and the biggest in West Germany, reopened at the end of 1984 after nearly three years of extensive renovation. It now has a British manager-director. The Applied Arts Museum is south of the station, with many treasures.

PRACTICAL INFORMATION FOR HAMBURG

HOTELS. Hamburg has something of a shortage of budget accommodations, so it's a good idea to stick to the cheaper pensions and guest houses. Most of these are near Dammtor station at Stephansplatz in Harvesthude and on the other side of the Alster lake. Bear in mind too the special short-stay arrangements offered by the larger chain hotels such as *Novotel* and *Intercontinental,* as well as the ready-made discount city package stay entitled "Happy Hamburg Days," organized by the Tourist Office and offering reduced rates for any number of nights in over 70 hotels in four different categories. The price includes bed and breakfast and a "city pass" (free travel for three days on Hamburg's entire transport system; free city tours, harbor cruise, museum visits, etc.). There is a hotel accommodation office at both the airport and the main station. Details from Tourist Information Hamburg, Postfach 102249, Hamburg 1. Most of the large hotels in town, especially in the center, are expensive.

Moderate

Aachener-Hof, St. Georgstrasse 10 (tel. 241313). Pleasant hotel-pension just outside the center. 63 beds. Garni.

Bellevue, An der Alster 14 (tel. 248011). A popular hotel with splendid view of the Alster Lake and modernized rooms. 100 beds, restaurant. Newly-decorated.

Graf Moltke, Steindamm 1 (tel. 2801154). Rather more expensive hotel-pension near the station. 150 beds. Garni, but snacks are available in the coffee shop. Generous breakfast buffet.

Hotel Schmidt, Reventlowstr. 60 (tel. 882831). 60 beds. Garni.

Metro-Merkur, Bremer Reihe 12–14 (tel. 247266). 200 beds. Newly-renovated. Bar. Garni.

Rex, Kieler Str. 385 (tel. 544813). Small hotel in the suburb of Stellingen. 49 beds. Garni.

Royal, Holzdamm 51 (tel. 243753). 44 beds. Between Aussenalster and the station. Small breakfast-only hotel.

Wedina, Gurlittstr. 23 (tel. 243011). 37 beds, sauna and swimming-pool, garden, sun-terrace. Rather pleasant if small. Garni.

Inexpensive

Alameda, Colonnaden 45 (tel. 344290). Centrally located with basic but comfortable rooms, all with TV/radio. Garni.

Elite, Binderstr. 24 (tel. 454627). In suburb of Rotherbaum, 24 beds. Garni.

Forsthaus, Reinbeker Weg 77 (tel. 7213084). Small and quiet in the southern suburb of Bergedorf. Restaurant with terrace.

Gasthaus zum Wattkorn, Tangstedter Landstr. 230 (tel. 5203797). In Langenhorn not far from Fühlsbüttel airport. Small inn/café, with home-made cakes and small snacks. 13 rooms. Garden with wild-bird enclosure and pond.

Youth Hostels and Camping

Auf dem Stintfang, Alfred-Wegener-Weg 5 (tel. 313488). YHA members only. 350 beds. In a good location near the St. Pauli Landing Stages.

Hamburger Jugendpark Langenhorn, Jugendparkweg 60 (tel. 5313050). For groups only. Near airport.

Horner Rennbahn, Rennbahnstr. 100 (tel. 6511671). 204 beds. Outside the center near the Horn Race Course and U-Bahn station. YHA members only.

Horner Rennbahn Gästehaus, Rennbahnstr. 100 (tel. 6511671). Annexe to Horner Rennbahn hostel. 102 beds.

Groups of young people or school parties of between 10 and 20 persons can get very cheap accommodations (albeit simple dormitories) in the Hamburg YMCA (C.V.J.M.) in Eppendorf, Carl-Cohn-Str. 89 in the summer between 20 June and 20 August. Cooking facilities.

The principal camp sites in Hamburg are: *Campingplatz Buchholz,* Kieler Str. 374 (tel. 5404532); *Campingplatz Ramcke,* Kieler Str. 620 (tel. 5705121); *Camping Anders,* Kieler Str. 650 (tel. 5704498); *Camping Brünning,* Kronsaalweg 86 (tel. 5404994).

RESTAURANTS. In addition to the countless restaurants serving foreign food from all parts of the world (of which Indonesian and Chinese are perhaps the best value), there are a number of very good inexpensive eating places in Hamburg. The *Wienerwald* and *Block-House* chains, both of which have many outlets in the city, are also good and inexpensive spots to sample Hamburg specialties. Apart from Hamburger steak, which of course comes from here, there are many excellent seafood specialties to be had. You might also want to try the famous Hamburg *Aalsuppe* (eel-soup), which contains at least five different kinds of vegetable as well as herbs, fruit, ham and eel. In fact, most of the Hamburg soups are good, especially *Arfensuppe mit Snuten un poten,* a thick pea soup made with pig's feet, and *Hamburger Frische Suppe,* which is made of beef, veal meat balls and vegetables in season. Other Hamburg specialties are *Stubenküken* (spring chicken), *Vierländer Mastente* (duck), *Birnen, Bohnen und Speck* or *Gröne Hein* (pears, beans and bacon), and the sailor's favorite, *Labskaus* (herring, minced meat, cucumber, bacon and onions minced together and served with hard boiled eggs).

Moderate

Alt-Hamburger Bürgerhaus, Deichstr. 37 (tel. 373633). An old Hamburg-style restaurant near the Nikolai Fleet. Not altogether budget, but good value.

Landungsbrücken Restaurant, at the St. Pauli Landing Stages (tel. 314527). Fish restaurant with view over Elbe. Quick-service bar.

Nikolaikeller, Cremon 36 (tel. 366113). In one of Hamburg's most picturesque parts. Try one of the 25 ways Matjes (white herring) is prepared. Closed Sun.

Ratsweinkeller, in the Rathaus (tel. 364153). This beautifully-vaulted cellar restaurant in the town hall has been in existence since 1892 and still serves marvelous food and fine wines. Closed Sun.

Inexpensive

Alt-Poseldorfer Bierstuben, Milchstr. 7 (tel. 444383). Beer is the basic fare in this lively haunt in fashionable Poseldorf (get there from central Hamburg on an Alster ferry), and the food is wholesome and inexpensive.

Bei Tante Anni, Wexstr. 34 (tel. 352408). Near the Grossneumarkt in the new part of the city. Hearty home-cooking and good-sized portions at very reasonable prices.

Fischerhaus, St. Pauli Fisch Markt 14 (tel. 314053). Lots of local atmosphere and particularly praiseworthy cuisine; extremely good value for money. Open daily 11 A.M.–11 P.M.

Jever Krog, Besenbinderhof 57 (tel. 2803481). Rustic spot with good food. Closed Sun.

At Nali, Rutschbahn 11 (tel. 4103810). Turkish, very friendly, and very good value.

Vegetärische Gaststätte, Alsterarkaden (tel. 344703). Above the Alster Arcades on Neuer Wall 13. The oldest vegetarian restaurant of its kind in the world. Light meals and a terrace-café.

Zum Ochsenwirt am Schlachhof, Sternstr. 96 (tel. 433545). Its location close to Hamburg's slaughterhouse guarantees good quality and enormous portions. Open from 3 A.M.

GETTING AROUND HAMBURG. By Metro and Train. Hamburg has an excellent public transport system incorporating a metro (U-Bahn), suburban trains (S-Bahn), buses and ferries. The entire system is interlinked and tickets and fares are uniform, as well as being valid for the whole system. A single ticket for the central city zone costs DM 2, for the whole metropolitan area DM 3.10. There are no reduced-cost strip tickets, as in many other German cities, but the local transport authority offers various special tickets, some of which are particularly good value for families. A one-day family ticket, for instance, is valied for up to four adults and three children to the age of 12 and costs DM 10.50. Tickets are available at all U-Bahn and S-Bahn stations, on buses and boats, and from automatic machines. The tickets are valid for travel on the Elbe River ferries run by the HADAG company, but not on Alster Lake and canal boats. There are 13 different U-Bahn and S-Bahn lines, 9 of which cover the city itself. The U-Bahn and S-Bahn are the fastest and easiest way of getting around.

By Bus. 192 excellent bus routes augment the railway system. They include the more expensive express buses (nos. 21–49). There are also night buses, which run *all* night, departing hourly from the Rathausmarkt and the main station (nos. 600–640).

By Boat. There are 13 regular Alster and Elbe ferry and water-taxi routes running from Apr. to Oct. All are linked to the rail and bus services. Alster taxis leave from the Jungfernstieg pier for points along the lake and canals. There is also a 50-minute Alster cruise and 2-hour canal cruise from the same pier. Both have regular sailings. Inquiries can be made by phone (tel. 341141–45). For harbor trips (from St. Pauli; commentary in English) check the timetable of the *HADAG* company (tel. 3768000). A round trip lasts about one hour and costs DM 11.

ENTERTAINMENT. Clubs. Most of the hottest spots are, as one would imagine, concentrated around the Reeperbahn, mainly in a little side street called Grosse Freiheit (Great Freedom). The shows themselves are expensive, but to walk through this area is an experience in itself and you can soak in the atmosphere without spending anything. The best idea, however, is to join in one of the organized night tours of St. Pauli and the Reeperbahn arranged by the Hamburg Tourist Office. These depart nightly from Easter through October (Friday and Saturday only in winter) at 8 P.M. from the square in front of the Main Station (Hachmannplatz) and stop at the hotels Reichshof, Atlantic, Vier Jahreszeiten, CP Hamburg Plaza and Inter-Continental. The tour takes in several pubs and clubs and ends with an explicit sex show, and the DM 80 fare includes a drink at each stop.

Nightlife need not, however, be entirely identified with St. Pauli. You will also find a variety of restaurants, pubs and entertainment in Eppendorf, Pöseldorf, Winterhude, St. Georg and Blankenese.

If you prefer to visit the clubs independently, take care to bring along no more than the amount of money you want to spend, and no checks. Check the menu and wine-list before every order and pay immediately to avoid any unpleasant surprises at the end of the evening. The following are a small selection of the clubs, discos and jazz bars. All are open until very late.

Blauer Satellit, Hotel Plaza, Marseillerstr. 2. Good disco.

Blockhütte, Grosse Freiheit 64. Country and western music from live bands.

Café Keese, Reeperbahn 19–21. Respectable dancing spot with no shortage of partners.

Cotton Club, Alter Steinweg 27–31. Almost legendary spot on the Hamburg nightlife scene. Dixieland and traditional jazz in cozy, smokey surroundings.

Fabrik, Barnerstr. 36. Jazz, rock, pop, folk and blues. Theater rebuilt after being burnt down. A Hamburg tradition.

Grünspan, Grosse Freiheit 58. Wild dancing spot.

La Paloma, Gerhardstr. 12. Artist's haunt in St. Pauli; normally packed by midnight.

"Pöseldorf" Beer Village, Mittelweg 141 in Pöseldorf section. 7 pubs under one roof. Bands frequently play on the "village" square. Disco twice weekly.

Pulverfass, Pulverteich 12. Spicey drag show.

Safari, Grosse Freiheit 24–8. Good non-stop strip program.

Salambo, Grosse Freiheit 11. Shocking mixture of sex and revue.

Top Ten, Reeperbahn 136. Hard rock music from live bands. Open till 5 on Sunday mornings.

Theaters. Hamburg, with almost 30 theaters, has much to offer as an international cultural center. Consult the monthly *Hamburg Vorschau* for details of what's on and when. Tickets for both the theater and opera can be obtained in advance from *Theaterkasse Altona,* Neue Grosse Bergstr. Pavillon 5a (tel. 386264); *Theaterkasse Central,* in the Hamburg Tip center, Gerhart Hauptmann Platz (tel. 324312); *Konzertkasse Gerdes,* Rothenbaumchaussee 77 (tel. 453326).

Altonaer Theater, Museumstr. 17 (tel. 391545). Mixed program. Mainly classical. Hamburg's most popular theater.

Deutsches Schauspielhaus, Kirchenallee 39 (tel. 248713). One of Europe's leading theaters and Germany's largest, magnificently renovated and now directed by an Englishman. During restoration, valuable ceiling frescoes were discovered beneath centuries-old coats of paint. Its allied workshop company is located in the Kampnagel Fabrik building in the Jarrestr.

The English Theater, Lerchenfeld 14 (tel. 225543). Plays in English.

Ernst Deutsch Theater, Mundsburger Damm 60 (tel. 2270142). Young and progressive private theater. Mainly classical plays.

Hamburger Kammerspiele, Hartungstr. 9–11 (tel. 445162). Acclaimed international productions; offers lighter fare.

Hamburgische Staatsoper, Dammtorstr. 28 (tel. 351721). World famous opera and ballet company. Its workshop, the *Opera Stabile,* is at Studio an der Büschstr.

Hansa Theater, Steindamm 17 (tel. 241414). Germany's last original variety theater.

Kleine Komödie, Neuer Wall 54 (tel. 367340). Boulevard comedies.

Neue Flora Theater, Stresemann-Str., Ecke Alsenstr. The latest addition to the Hamburg theater scene. It opened with "Phantom of the Opera" in July 1990.

Ohnsorg Theater, Grosse Bleichen 25 (tel. 35080321). Local dialect *(Plattdeutsch)* productions.

Operettenhaus, Spielbudenplatz 1 (tel. 311176). "Cats" has been playing here for the past four years, and there's still no end of the run in sight.

Das Schiff, An der Deichstr, Holzbrücke 2 (tel. 364765). A theater on a ship moored at the Holzbrücke. Famous for Hamburg cabaret and variety shows.

Thalia Theater, Alstertor (tel. 322666). Comedy, as well as classical and modern drama. Has a great tradition.

Concerts. Hamburg has three major orchestras: the Hamburg Philharmonic, the most traditional, and well-known for its guest performances, internationally-acclaimed conductors and tours abroad; the Norddeutsche Rundfunk Radio Symphony Orchestra (NDR) and the Hamburg Symphony Orchestra. Focal point of all orchestral concerts is the large Baroque *Musikhalle* Concert Hall on Karl-Muck-Platz (tel. 346920).

MUSEUMS. Many museums have one day a week when entry is free. Most also close on Mondays. But as opening times vary, it's best to check both these and entrance charges with the local tourist office, or consult their official monthly program.

Altonaer Museum/Norddeutsches Landesmuseum (North German Regional Museum), Museumstr. 23 (tel. 3807–483) in the suburb of Altona. Contains a wealth of interesting exhibits on the culture and life of North Germany. At the time of writing, it was only partially open as a result of fire damage.

The Kunsthalle, Glockengiesserwall 1 (tel. 24861). This is Hamburg's principal art gallery and contains some of the best works of art in northern Germany. The collections include paintings from late Middle Ages to modern.

Museum für Hamburgische Geschichte (Hamburg Historical Museum), Holstenwall 24 (tel. 3491–22360). Apart from the displays concerning Hamburg's history, the most interesting items concern the development of the port and seafaring in general. Now also houses the new and fascinating *Historic Emigration Office*, the first of its kind in Germany, where you can trace ancestors who emigrated via Hamburg (mostly to the U.S.A., Canada and Australia).

Museum für Kunst und Gewerbe (Museum of Decorative Arts and Crafts), Steintorplatz 1 (tel. 24862630). The collections cover centuries of developments in the applied arts. Among them is some remarkable medieval gold and silver work, Renaissance furniture, 18th-century porcelain and art nouveau.

Museum für Völkerkunde (Ethnology Museum), Rothenbaumchaussee 64 (tel. 4419–5524). Particularly good African and South American collections.

Övelgönne Museumshafen (Harbor Museum), Övelgönne. Literally a floating museum in the harbor at Ovelgönne; with old sailing boats, original and restored freighters from the turn of the century, fire-ships, etc. Open until the Elbe freezes over in winter.

Övelgönner Seekiste, Övelgönne 63 (tel. 8809327). Captain Lührs will conduct you round this fascinating collection of maritime nostalgia. Open Sat. and Sun. 2–6 P.M.

SHOPPING. The shops along the Jungfernstieg, Grosse Bleichen, Neuer Wall and Dammtorstrasse are excellent but expensive. The glass-roofed arcades in the Colonnaden, Gänsemarkt, Poststr., Grosse Bleichen and Jungfernstieg are particularly enticing. The *Galleria im Zentrum* is good for window-shopping. Mönckebergstrasse and its side streets are crowded with less expensive department stores and shops.

USEFUL ADDRESSES. *Tourist information:* near Main Station: Bieberhaus, Hachmannplatz (tel. 30051244); at the airport: Arrival Hall (tel. 30051240); St. Pauli Piers (tel. 30051200); the Hanseviertel shopping arcade (tel. 51220). *Hotel reservations:* at Main Station (tel. 30051230); at the airport: Arrival Hall (tel. 30051240). *Consulates:* American: Alsterufer 27 (tel. 411710); British: Harvesterhude Weg 8a (tel. 446071). *Thomas Cook:* Ballindamm 39 (tel. 40309080).

There is a *Post Office* (open 24 hours a day) in the lobby of the Main Station.

The Neckar Valley

The Valley of the river Neckar runs through a large area in the south west of Germany known as Neckarland-Schwaben, in the state of Baden-Württemburg. With its diversity and richness of scenery and landscape, it is both impressive and appealing as a holiday land. The total area of the Neckarland-Schwaben stretches from the Rhine plateau in the north west all the way to the Danube valley in the south east. It incorporates the delightful and dramatic Tauber, Jagst and Kocher rivers, still suitable for swimming, the Neckar itself, which is not recommended for bathing, as well as the peaceful rolling hills of Odenwald to the east of Mannheim and the romantic Swabian mountains down in the south western corner of

Germany. Between the Neckar and Rhine rivers, there are abundant and fertile vineyards as well as such busy industrial centers as Stuttgart, Esslingen and Sindelfingen.

But the area we concentrate on here is that part of the Neckar valley to the north west of Stuttgart. It is in fact the first part of a scenic holiday route that is in all 300 km. (195 miles) long and that eventually runs all the way to Nürnberg. It's known as the Burgenstrasse (Castle Road).

Join the road on the outskirts of Heidelberg, the old capital of the Kurpfalz that, with its castle rising above the town and the river, might almost be a stage set for an operetta. The castle is a ruin today, but is still well worth visiting. It can be reached by foot, by car or cable railway. Heidelberg is, of course, famous for its University. It was founded in 1386, and even today about one-sixth of the population are students. Apart from anything else, this means that the town has a great many reasonably-priced eating houses.

Following the road along the north bank of the Neckar, where the valley forms a gorge between high wooded hills, Neckargemünd is the next place of interest, rising calmly on the south bank with its church steeple dominating the old houses. Beyond it is Neckarsteinach, with four castles, while across the river is the walled fortress of Dilsberg, surrounded on three sides by the river. Further up-river is Hirschhorn, where the knights of Hirschhorn built their fortress in 1200.

At the narrowest point of the Neckar valley lies Eberbach in the Neckar-Odenwald nature park. It dates back to 1196, and its buildings are clustered thickly about the ancient river-bridge. Thence on to Stolzeneck, whose castle, Burg Stolzeneck, rises proudly on the forested left bank of the Neckar, and Zwingenberg, where there's another castle, possibly the most impressive and best preserved on the whole Burgenstrasse.

The countryside around Mosbach, with its riverside section of Neckarelz now begins to change character, and forests give way to meadows and orchards. The remains of an ancient Roman settlement, the Villa Rustica, are here as well as many lovely old buildings and churches. The recorded history of Mosbach can be traced back to 736. It is a wonderful town with whole streets of half-timbered houses. Moving on, Neckarzimmern is the site of Hornberg Castle where Götz von Berlichingen, the outlaw knight with the iron hand and hero of Goethe's play of the same name, spent the last years of his life. Across the river are the castles of Guttenberg and Ehrenberg.

Bad Friedrichshall is a small spa located at the junction of the Neckar and the Kocher. A little above the town, another river, the relatively unpolluted Jagst, joins the Neckar and is suitable for swimming. It's worth following it to Jagsthausen, where there are three castles, all of which belong to the Berlichingen family. It was in the oldest that Götz von Berlichingen was born. There is open-air theater in Götzenburg castle from mid-June to mid-August.

Back on the Neckar, you come next to Bad Wimpfen on the south bank. It is an old imperial free town and has a tight cluster of houses round its so-called Blue Town; well worth visiting. This brings us to Heilbronn and the end of that section of the Burgenstrasse through the Neckar valley. Another imperial town, and world-famous as the scene of Heinrich von Kleist's play *Das Käthchen von Heilbronn,* Heilbronn is today a flourishing community and the largest wine center of the Neckar valley with a huge annual wine festival at the beginning of September. There are many interesting buildings, some restored to their former state.

PRACTICAL INFORMATION FOR THE NECKAR VALLEY

Hotels and Restaurants

Bad Friedrichshall. *Area code:* 07136. *Gasthof Sonne* (M), Deutschordenstr. 16 (tel. 4063). 23 beds, all rooms with own bathroom or shower. Fine view from terrace; reasonably-priced menu. *Gasthof Schöne Aussicht* (I), Deutschordenstr. 2 (tel. 6057). 26 beds. Panoramic view. Café with good-value menu. Terrace with panoramic views.

Bad Wimpfen. *Area code:* 07063. *Blauer Turm* (M), Burgviertel 5 (tel. 225). Hotel in quiet location with lovely terrace. 38 beds, almost all rooms with bath or shower. Good-value menu. *Gasthaus Traube* (M), Hauptstr. 1 (tel. 266). 17 beds. Good budget-value restaurant with garden. Closed on Wednesdays in summer. *Hotel Neckarblick* (I), Erich-Sailer-Str. 48 (tel. 8548). Renovated house with view of the Neckar. 27 beds.

Eberbach. *Krone-Post* (M), Hauptstr. 1 (tel. 2310). 85 beds. Has a splendid view from the terrace and a modern restaurant.

Heilbronn. *Area code:* 07131. Special 2–7-day packages, Käthchen Pass, available through the Tourist Office. *Kronprinz* (M), Bahnhofstr. 29 (tel. 83941). 48 beds. Reasonably-priced menu with good Swabian specialties. *Beck* (I), Bahnhofstr. 31, near station (tel. 81589). 44 beds. *Gasthof Rutsch* (I), Deutschhofstr. 37 (tel. 82862). 17 beds in this small inn centrally located near the Historical Museum and St. Kilian's Church. Good budget menu. *Grüner Kranz* (I), Lohtorstr. 9 (tel. 85633). Near the Rathaus. Good value.

Restaurants. *Wirtshaus Am Götzenturm* (M), Allerheiligenstr. 1 (tel. 80534). Excellent food, not particularly cheap but worth the extra marks. Interior in traditional local style. *Ratskeller* (M), in the Rathaus at Markt Platz 7 (tel. 84628). Superb food and has good wines. Own garden. *Festhalle Harmonie,* (M), Friedrich-Weber-Allee 28 (tel. 86890). Near the Stadtgarten Park, with lovely garden terrace.

Hirschhorn. *Area code:* 06272. Schlosshotel auf Burg Hirschhorn (M) (tel. 1373). On a section of the castle above the town (on road no. B37), a modernized castle hotel retaining its medieval appearance. Moderate restaurant and a splendid view from the terrace over the Neckar. *Forelle* (I), Langenthalerstr. 2 (tel. 2272). 28 beds, terrace and skittles in house.

Jagsthausen. *Area code:* 07131. Burghotel Götzenburg (M) (tel. 2222). Standing in own park and open from 1 April until 15 Oct., the feudal castle of the famous knight, Götz von Berlichingen. 27 beds, interior decorated in true medieval style. Particularly comfortable restaurant in fitting style, reasonably priced.

Mosbach (riverside section is Neckarelz). *Area code:* 06261. *Lindenhof* (M), Am Markt (tel. 7148). In Neckarelz. 22 rooms, all with bath. Skittles, restaurant. Restaurant with moderate prices. *Goldener Hirsch* (I), Hauptstr. 13 (tel. 2307). 26 beds; restaurant with reasonably-priced menu.

Neckarsteinach. *Area code:* 06229. Vierburgeneck (M), Heiterswiesenweg 11 (tel. 542). 32 beds, riverside terrace, garden restaurant and café. *Zum Schiff* (M), Neckargemunder Str. 2 (tel. 324). 40 beds, over half with own bathroom and WC; riverside terrace.

Neckarzimmern. *Area code:* 06261. Burghotel Hornberg (M) (tel. 40645). 50 beds. Castle dating from 1040 and located on a hill with 1 km. long driveway. A spectacular view, good restaurant and their own very good wines. Accommodations also available in nearby guest house, slightly cheaper.

Campsites

The attractive scenery of the Neckar Valley is particularly appealing to campers. Most sites also have riverside recreational facilities like boating, and swimming (heated indoor and outdoor pools).

Eberbach. *Campingplatz Eberbach,* tel. 06271–1071. Riverside.

Hirschhorn. *Odenwald Camping,* tel. 06272–809. Forestland site.

Jagsthausen. *Campingplatz der Heilbronner Campingclub,* tel. 07131–54198. Riverside site. Swimming in the Jagst.

Neckarzimmern. *Campingplatz Cimbria,* tel. 06261–2562. Riverside site with private beach.

West Berlin

Throughout the winter of 1989/90, Berlin—both East and West—was the focal point of dramatic changes in Europe. As communist regimes the length of the Iron Curtain collapsed in the wake of massive street demonstrations, all eyes turned to this former capital of Germany. Since August 1961 the ugly, gray, concrete Berlin Wall had been the stark symbol of a politically divided Europe. It had even become a tourist attraction for westerners, who could climb wooden platforms to look over the Wall from the western side into the sombre eastern sector. Suddenly, in November 1989, all this started to change, and by mid-January 1990 the Wall was being dismantled. The Brandenburg Gate, that huge architectural symbol of German unity, came out of the no-man's land to which it had been consigned since the Wall was built. An enormous New Year's Eve party of hundreds of thousands of people—Berliners, not West Berliners or East Berliners—was held under the Gate's arch. Today, the physical division of this city has been virtually dispatched into history, although political divisions remain real enough for the time being. But the changes mean that tourists can now travel with ease about the whole of Berlin, indeed the whole of East Germany. Traveling by air is the quickest way to reach West Berlin, but with the old land-travel restrictions erased it will be increasingly more attractive to drive, bus, or train through East Germany from West Germany. There are regular flights into West Berlin's Tegel Airport from Hamburg (the closest city), Frankfurt, Munich, Düsseldorf, Bremen, Hannover, Köln, Saarbrücken, Stuttgart, and Nürnberg. Entry into East Germany (and East Berlin) still requires a visa, but this is a formality, obtainable at the increasing number of border points. It's no longer necessary to stick to the old "transit" roads through East Germany, but strict driving rules still apply: There is a speed limit of 62 miles (100 kms) an hour, and safety belts must be worn, as in West Germany.

East and West Berlin are a third the size of Luxembourg, and a third of Berlin consists of water, trees and fields. It has large woods, lakes and much agricultural land and a number of independent villages, besides the huge industrial compounds and the pulsating center of the western sector—the Kurfürstendamm, which by itself has tended to give Berlin the reputation of being one large den of conspicuous nightclubs and bars. In addition to the forests of Grunewald, Glienicke, Spandau and Tegel, there are large areas of unspoiled countryside under the protection of national trusts with over 450 miles of foot-paths and bicycle tracks throughout the state. Among the numerous lakes dotted all over the city's environs, Wannsee is the most appealing. It has the largest lakeside bathing-beach in Europe. Pleasure cruisers run regular services on both the Wannsee and the adjoining Havelsee, taking in the city's canal network and the River Spree.

Returning to the city itself, a sightseeing tour of West Berlin should begin in its most famous shopping street, the Kurfürstendamm (Ku-damm), the heart of the city by day and night. Along its 2-mile stretch and in the neighboring side-streets, you will find over 1,100 shops, boutiques, department stores, and antiques galleries—something indeed for every taste. After dark, the Ku-damm is transformed into the throbbing heart of Berlin nightlife. This is theaterland: the Komödie on Kurfürstendamm itself, the Schiller Theater nearby and the Opera just a block away. And there are a score or more of film palaces.

Other highpoints of West Berlin are: the Zoo (Zoologischer Garten), one of the best in Europe with its new Aquarium in Budapesterstr, both in the Tiergarten district; the Siegessäule or Victory Column (it commemorates the Franco-Prussian war) on the square called Grosser Stern, and from the 210 ft. top of which you will have a sweeping view of Berlin; the English Garden, opened by Anthony Eden (hence known to Berliners as The Garden of Eden), which is in the vast stretch of parkland called Tiergarten, in the suburb of the same name; east of the English Garden is Schloss Bellevue, the restored official residence of the President of West Germany and open to the public in summer months. Beyond it to the southeast is the concert hall of the Berlin Philharmonic Orchestra (Philharmonie), the New National Gallery, the Museum of Applied Art, and the Staatsbibliothek, the largest archive of its kind in the world. The Hansa Viertel, a district around the Tiergarten of delightfully painted, fancifully-balconied apartment houses, includes the work of leading architects from a dozen nations; the Reichstagsgebäude (the Parliament building) at the Platz der Republik in Tiergarten was built between 1884 and 1894 and reconstructed after the war. A little further east, at the end of the Strasse des 17 Juni, and on the border of the eastern sector is the Brandenburg Gate (Brandenburger Tor), through which you can now stroll. It was built in 1789 to celebrate Prussian military victories. In the vicinity you may still see remnants of the Berlin Wall. Rathaus Schönberg at John F. Kennedy Platz, is the seat of Berlin's House of Representatives and Senate. It has a replica of the Liberty Bell on top of its 215 ft. tower that rings out at noon every day. Deutschlandhalle on Messedamm at Charlottenburg is Germany's largest sports and entertainment hall, seating over 11,000 people. Finally, there is the nearby Messegelände or Fair Grounds, a whole city of exhibition buildings grouped around the 490-ft. Funkturm radio tower. An elevator takes you to the top for an extensive view of the surroundings, which include the Olympic Stadium to the West and the new International Congress Center (ICC), one of the foremost congress centers in Europe.

PRACTICAL INFORMATION FOR WEST BERLIN

GETTING INTO TOWN FROM THE AIRPORT. From the West Berlin airport (Tegel) there is an express bus service (No. 9, taking about 40 minutes) to the Zoo Station in the center, one of the main transport hubs of the city. Operated by BVG it runs every 10 to 20 minutes from 5 A.M. to 11 P.M., and costs DM 2.70.

HOTELS. Berlin is plentifully supplied with hotels, pensions and youth hostels, so except for those periods when the important trade fairs and exhibitions are held it's always possible to get in somewhere. And you'll find that standards of comfort, cleanliness and hygiene are uniformly high, so you can approach even the most inexpensive places with confidence. Hotel prices in general are very high.

The official tourist office (Verkehrsamt Berlin) publishes a complete list of all hotels, pensions etc. in the city, as well as other queries. It is located in the Europa Center (entrance on Budapester Str.); tel. 2626031. Another information office is at the main train station (Hauptbahnhof), open 8 A.M.–11 P.M.

Moderate

Alpina, Trabener Str. 3 (tel. 8913517). Delightful little villa with terrace and garden very near S-Bahn station Grunewald.

Berlin Mark Hotel, Meinekestr. 18–19 (tel. 88002–0). Opened in 1986. Modern, comfortable and very central.

Dom Hotel, Hohenzollerndamm 33 (tel. 879780). Simple but adequate. Restaurant.

Econotel, Sommeringstr. 24 (tel. 344001). Families are particularly at home in this friendly hotel near Charlottenburg Palace.

Hotel Franke, Albrecht-Achilles-Str. 57 (tel. 8921097). Comfortable and clean hotel in a quiet side street off the Kurfürstendamm. Restaurant.

Hotel Frühling am Zoo, Kurfürstendamm 17 (tel. 8818083). Near the zoo, with 110 beds; some rooms with bath.

Hotel Hospiz Friedenau, Fregestr. 68 (tel. 8519017). Small, quiet and very good value; no restaurant.

Kardell, Gervinusstr. 24 (tel. 3241066). A 33-room hotel with restaurant in the Charlottenburg district.

Pension Seeblick, Neue Kantstr. 14 (tel. 3213072). Small and central, though quiet; close to the fairgrounds.

Pichler's Viktoriagarten, Leonorenstr. 18–22 (tel. 7716088). Small, good value hotel with restaurant; closed for four weeks in July/Aug.

Inexpensive

Atrium, Motzstr. 87 (tel. 244057).
Central, Kurfürstendamm 185 (tel. 8816343).
Elton, Pariserstr. 9 (tel. 8836155).
Engelberger, Mommsenstr. 6 (tel. 8815536).
Flora, Uhlandstr. 184 (tel. 8811617).
Gribnitz, Kaiserdamm 82 (tel. 3025529).
Molthan, Lietzenburger Str. 76 (tel. 8814717).

Pension Havelhaus, Imchenallee 35 (tel. 3655800). In the suburb of Kladow on the banks of the river Havel with own bathing beach and boats for hire. Quiet and good value; restaurant next door.

Viola, Kantstr. 146 (tel. 316457). Near the zoo.

Youth Hostels and Camping

Foreign guests in German youth hostels must buy a membership card, costing DM 20 for one year; or you can buy a nightly stamp for DM 4.

Studentenhotel Berlin, Meiningerstr. 10 (tel. 7846720). Good hostel with sauna, pub and food.

YMCA (CVJM), Einemstr. 10 (tel. 2613791).

Youth Guest House, Kluckstr. 3, Tiergarten (tel. 2611097).

Youth Guest House am Wannsee, Kronprinzessinweg 27 (tel. 8032034). Also specially equipped for the handicapped.

Youth Hostel, Bayernallee 36 (tel. 2623024).

Youth Hostel "Ernst Reuter", Hermsdorfer Damm 48/50 (tel. 4041610). Book well in advance for the youth guest houses and hostels at "Deutsches Jugendherbergswerk", Geschäftsstelle, Bayernallee 35, 1000 Berlin 19 (tel. 2623024).

Details on camping in Berlin are available from the *Deutscher Camping Club,* Geisbergstr. 11, 1000 Berlin 30 (tel. 246071). Some principal camp sites are:

Dreilinden, Albrechts-Teerofen (Wannsee) (tel. 8051201). Open year-round. Bus No. 18.

Zeltplatz in Kladow, Krampnitzer Weg 111, Berlin 22 (tel. 3652797). Space for approximately 400 tents/caravans. Open all year round. Buses 35 and 37.

Campingplatz Haselhorst, Pulvermühlenweg, Berlin 20 (tel. 3345955). Open all year round. Subway station Haselhorst.

RESTAURANTS. Berlin is replete with Moderate and Inexpensive eating houses of all kinds where you can enjoy some of the delicious Berlin specialties such as *Bockwurst* (a chubby frankfurter); yellow pea soup with Bockwurst and/or a slice of bacon; and *Eisbein* (pig hock) with sauerkraut. You'll find that Bockwurst stands are as common as the ubiquitous hot dog stand in the States. The *Berliner Kindl* chain, which has restaurants all over town, is a sure bet for Eisbein. Generous portions are the norm in Berlin.

Two excellent spots for lunch are the *Alt-Berliner Weissbierstube* in the Berlin Museum, which serves typical Berlin food as well as Berlin's favorite beer, *Berlinerweisse* (flavored with raspberry juice, believe it or not), and the restaurant in the Dahlem Museum, which has a wide variety of dishes at low prices. The *Silberterrasse* restaurant in the super department store, *Ka-De-We,* at Wittenbergplatz is also well worth investigating.

One other characteristic budget eating option are the *Imbiss-Stände,* stand up snack bars. These are dotted around the city and specialize in curry wurst with french fries (which really isn't as horrible as it sounds) and *Buletten* with *Kartoffelsalat* (meat balls with potato salad). Numerous breakfast bars, *Frühstückskneipen,* are particularly "in" for brunch between 10 A.M. and 2 P.M. and they are relatively economical.

Moderate

Alter Krug, Königin-Luise-Str. 52 (tel. 8325089). Close to the Dahlem Museums; open-air dining in summer.

Alt Nürnberg, Europa Center (tel. 2614397). Food from southern Germany; spicy and very tasty. Open late but worth a visit any time.

Berliner Kindl Bräu, Bismarckstr. 66 and many other locations. One of the chain that features beer and *Eisbein.* Full meals at fixed prices are also good.

Grunewaldturm, Havelchaussee 61 (tel. 3041203). Right in the famous Grunewald. A good meal and a totally different view of Berlin.

Hardtke Senior, Meinekestr. 27 (tel. 8819827). Perhaps the most typical of all Berlin restaurants. They do a "special lunch" at lower prices.

Hecker's Deele, Grolmannstr. 35 (tel. 8890–1). Westphalian specialties; also has some rooms.

Joe am Ku-Damm, Kurfürstendamm 225. North German specialties in Empire-style building and very good value; dancing in the evening. On Sundays in summer concerts from 11 A.M.

Pichlers Victoriagarten, Leonorenstr. 18, (tel. 7716088). Excellent-value German menu, plus accommodation.

Ratskeller Schonberg, Schonberg Rathaus (tel. 7828326). Always a good set menu at Berlin's town-hall cellar restaurant.

Savoia, Windscheidstr. 31 (tel. 3241807). First-rate Italian food, good value. Home-baked bread.

Schultheiss-Bräuhaus, Kurfürstendamm 220 (tel. 8817059). Very central and popular eating spot serving all Berlin's specialties. The meal of the day is always a good deal.

Silberterrassen, Tauentzienstr. 21–24 (tel. 2134030). In the Ka-De-We department store; fresh and varied food. Self-service restaurant **Zille-Stuben** is adjacent.

Inexpensive

Berlin Pavillon, Strasse des 17. Juni (at the Tiergarten S-bahn stop). Old Berlin Kneipe with breakfast buffet.

Club Culinar im Wertheim, Kufürstendamm 231 (tel. 8833647). In the basement of the Wertheim department store.

Essen & Trinken, Leibnizstr. 35, near Kantstr. (tel. 3128335). Open daily, except Sundays, 10 A.M.–11 P.M. As the name implies, honest and simple Berlin cooking, and at honest and simple prices.

Kalkutta, Bleibtreustr. 17 (tel. 8836293). Open daily from 6 P.M. to 2 A.M. Specialties from India and Pakistan.

Lützower Lampe, Behaimstr. 21 (tel. 3426145). Vegetarian restaurant; close to Schloss Charlottenburg.

Pizzeria Piccolo Taormina, Uhlandstr. 29 (tel. 8814710). Italian self-service spot just off Ku-damm; very good value.

Zum Ambrosius, Bergmannstr. 11 (tel. 6927182), in the Kreuzberg area. Hearty home-cooking at good-value prices.

The American chain **Burger King** can be found all over town, particularly at: Kurfürstendamm 202 and 224; Wilmersdorferstr. 50; im Forum Steglitz; Karl-Marx-Str. 100.

GETTING AROUND BERLIN. By Metro and Train. Berlin is a vast city and, except for the center, cannot be comfortably explored on foot. But thanks to the excellent public transport system no one really needs a car or taxi. The metro (U-Bahn) and suburban train system (S-Bahn) represent the best way to get around. The S-Bahn extends into all the more outlying areas.

By Bike. Fahrrad Krause, Mariendorfer Damm 24, hires bicycles by the day (DM 10) or the week (DM 50).

By Bus. Buses run to the remotest areas of West Berlin and provide an effective supplement to the train services. Special night buses have an "N" next to the number.

Tickets are the same for all public transport. Single journey tickets cost DM 2.70 (children under 14, DM 1.50). Multiple journey tickets, good for up to five trips, cost DM 11.50 (children under 14 DM 6.50). Both types of ticket are good for all public transport. Generally speaking, the multiple journey tickets represent the best value. They are available from vending machines at many bus stops and at U-Bahn ticket offices. You must cancel your ticket yourself in one of the red machines. There is also a good range of discount tickets for individuals and groups. Public-transport information office, tel. 2561.

ENTERTAINMENT. Kneipen. Berlin has around 5,000 pubs, bars, dives and the like, all of which come under the general heading of *Kneipen*—the local spot on the corner where you call in for a beer, a snack, a discussion and perhaps a dance. The Kneipen round Olivaer Platz, Savignyplatz, Ludwigkirchplatz and Lehniner Platz are particular hunting grounds of the young, as also are those in the Kreuzberg area, Berlin is also a major jazz center, and every fall there's a big international festival. Check the tourist office for details.

Cour Carree, Savignyplatz 5. Open daily from midday to 2.00 A.M. Art nouveau style with French food and garden.

Dicke Wirtin, Carmerstr. 9 (on Savignyplatz). Open from midday to 6.00 A.M. Very lively with lots of nostalgia; a Berlin original.

Leydicke, Mansteinstr. 4. A must for every tourist; they distill their own liqueurs and wines. Open from midday, Tues. and Thurs. from 4 P.M., and Sun. from 5 P.M.

Schiller Klause, Schillerstr. 10. Open Mon.-Fri. 4.00 P.M. to 2.00 A.M., Sat. from 9.00 P.M. Closed Sun. Traditional theatergoers' pub next door to the Schiller Theater, with an atmosphere of its own and people of all ages.

Sperlingsgasse, Lietzenburgerstr. 82–84. 13 different pubs and beer gardens here just off the Ku-damm; open from 7 P.M.

Spree-Athen, Leibnizstr. 60 (entrance on Mommsenstr.). Lots of Berlin atmosphere and specialties; open from 6 P.M. Closed Sun.

Zwiebelfisch, Savignyplatz 7. Meeting-place of literary folk of all ages; good atmosphere for getting to know people. Small menu.

Nightclubs and Discos. As in any major city, nightclubs are expensive. It's therefore always a good bet to tag along with one of the nightclub tours organized by the large Berlin tour operators, which include dinner and three or four nightclub stops for drinks. The cost is between DM 95 and DM 119. Call 8831015 for information.

One of the best nightclubs/cabarets in town that will not cost you the earth is *New Eden,* Kurfürstendamm 71, with dancing to live bands, strip show, and reasonably-priced drinks. Others include:

Big Eden, Kurfürstendamm 202. For the younger tourist, open from 4.00 P.M. Dance-bar, reasonably priced with plenty of space.

Chez Nous, Marburgerstr. 14. The best drag shows in Berlin. Not cheap, but fun—and central, near the Europa Center.

Eierschale, Podbielskialle 50, for the best jazz nightly after 8.30 P.M.

Empire, Hauptstr. 30 (tel. 7848565). Discos, videos, live music on three floors; in Schöneberg. Open from 8 P.M.

Metropol, Nollendorfplatz 5 (tel. 2164122). Wed.–Sun. from 9 P.M. Disco with all the latest technical gags; also live bands.

Quartier Latin, Potsdamer Str. 96. Jazz, rock, folk, blues, pop. Admission fee according to program.

Riverboat, Hohenzollerndamm 174. Dancehall and very popular with students. Mississippi riverboat decor. Closed Mon.

Cinema. Film fans will certainly not want to miss the annual Berlin Film Festival in February. Otherwise Berlin is well provided with cinemas. Most are located round the Memorial Church (Gedächtniskirche), Ku'damm, Zoo area and along the Tauentzienstrasse. Here you can see the usual international and German productions. For something a bit different try one of the *Off-Kinos;* so called because they are situated off the Ku'damm and the center and are cheaper than other cinemas. Here you can enjoy classics of film history, trial runs of the latest German films and much else besides. Local papers give full details of programs; and one other bonus is that the Off-Kinos are often next door to cafés and Kneipen. Film buffs might also try *Filmbühne am Steinplatz,* Hardenbergstr. 12, which presents a constantly changing program of film classics.

Europa Center. Near the Zoo station, the Europa Center is full of entertainment possibilities. There are a couple of movie theaters, a regular theater, many student-type cafés, restaurants and bars and all sorts of shops. You can have a good time here both by day and at night, but at night it's best not to be on your own.

For a refreshing break, go for a swim in the *Thermen am Europa Center,* Nürnberger Str. 7 (tel. 2616031). Thermal bath, sauna, fitness room, plus restaurant and cafeteria.

Theaters. Except for operetta and musicals, theater in Berlin is mostly for those who understand German well. The *Schiller Theater,* Bismarckstr. 110, has been rebuilt in modern style and specializes, as before the war, in heavy fare—classical plays and Goethe, for example—while its *Workshop* presents modern plays and folk dramas. The *Theater am Kurfürstendamm,* Kurfürstendamm 206, specializes in comedies. So does a small house, the *Schlosspark Theater,* Schlossstr. 48. *Schaubüh-*

ne am Lehniner Platz is one of the greatest and most talked of dramatic theaters today.

The *Renaissance Theater,* Hardenbergstr. 6, and the *Komödie,* Kurfürstendamm 206, prefer comedy, and often present foreign actors. Summer pop or classical concerts in the outdoor *Waldbühne,* which seats 24,000. Among the experimental and small intimate theaters is the *Tribüne,* Otto-Suhr-Allee 18–20, a youthful enterprise, and the *Hansa-Theater,* Alt Moabit 48.

There are also some cabaret-theaters: *Bügelbrett* in the Steinplatz-Kino, Hardenbergstr. 12; *Die Stachelschweine* in Europa Center, *Die Wühlmäuse,* Lietzenburgerstrasse, specializing in satiric commentaries on the affairs of the day. For children try the *Grips Theater,* Altonaer Str. 22.

Concerts. Berlin is a great music center. The *Berlin Philharmonic* is the focus of musical activity. There is also the *Radio Symphony Orchestra.* Internationally famous soloists and ensembles appear in Berlin. Among the best musical events in the former capital are the summer concerts given outdoors in the courtyard of the Jagdschloss Grunewald. There are two principal concert halls in West Berlin, the *Philharmonic Concert Hall* at Kemperplatz in the Tiergarten quarter and the *Konzertsaal am Steinplatz* on Hardenbergstrasse, in the Charlottenburg quarter. The Philharmonic Concert Hall, home of the Berlin Philharmonic Orchestra, rebuilt and reopened in 1963, 20 years after its destruction during the war, is one of the most modern buildings of its kind in Europe, and the concert hall boasts an admirable architectural and acoustical design.

The *Deutsche Oper Berlin,* newly built and opened in the fall of 1961, is in Bismarckstr., Charlottenburg, and stands on the site of the prewar Opera House. There are daily performances of the standard operatic repertoire. Light opera and musicals are performed at the beautifully-restored *Theater des Westens,* Kantstr. 12 (tel. 3121022). Twice-weekly concerts are given in the glass-sheathed Memorial Church *(Gedächtniskirche)* and Bell Tower next to the old Kaiser Wilhelm Memorial church. Ticket agencies: *Theaterkasse Sasse,* Ku'damm 24; *Theaterkasse Centrum,* Meinekestr. 25.

MUSEUMS AND GALLERIES. West Berlin has three important museum centers: those in the Charlottenburg Palace; the cluster of museums, institutes and archives in the Dahlem district, known as the Dahlem's Museums; and the cultural center, Kulturzentrum, at the Tiergarten. There are also a handful of other museums dotted around the city. All are open daily except Monday; most have an entrance charge ranging from DM 1.50 to DM 6.

Charlottenburg Palace, Luisenplatz. Former summer residence of the Prussian kings, the central building of which was originally built in 1695–99 for Sophie Charlotte, wife of Frederick I, though many extensions were subsequently added. The interior represents decor from almost two centuries, from Baroque to Biedermeier. Gutted from bombing in 1943, it has now been renovated. Don't miss the Knobelsdorff wing and the Galerie der Romantik. Here you can also find:

Ägyptisches Museum (Egyptian Museum) in front of the palace. Important Egyptian cultural history. The main exhibits to see are finds from excavations at Tell-El-Amarna, including the most famous portrait bust in the world, that of Nefertiti, Queen of Aken-Aton the Heretic.

Antikenmuseum und Schatzkammer (Museum of Antiquities and Treasury) next door to Egyptian Museum. Greek and Roman treasures upstairs; glittering silver and gold from the past 3,000 years, including the Hildesheim Hoard of Roman silver vessels, downstairs in the Schatzkammer.

Museum für Vor- und Frühgeschichte, in West Wing (Langhansbau). Archeological finds from prehistoric times to early Middle Ages.

Dahlem's Museums, Dahlem-Dorf, Konigin-Luise-strasse 48. Gemälde Galerie entrance on Arnim Allee 23. One of the great collections of paintings, ranging from the 13th to 18th centuries, includes no less than 25 Rembrandts (the authenticity of a 26th, *Man with Golden Helmet,* is now in doubt), 14 Rubens, and other well-known masters from Giotto to the Impressionists.

Kupferstichkabinett (Etchings Gallery), Arnimallee 23, open 9–5. Important collection of drawings, printed graphics and illustrated books of the 15th to 20th centuries. Of particular interest are the drawings by Rembrandt and the etchings by Dürer, Holbein, Cranach.

Museum für Deutsche Volkskunde (German Folklore Museum), Im Winkel 6.

Museum für Islamische, Indische und Ostasiatische Kunst, (Museum for Islamic, Indian and East-Asian Art), Lansstrasse 8. Fine collections.

Museum für Völkerkunde (Ethnological Museum), Lansstrasse 8. A marvelous collection of ethnic works from all over the world. Five sections are devoted to Ancient America, Africa, the South Seas and South and East Asia. Includes Mayan carvings, masks from the South Seas, Benin bronzes, etc. The settings are particularly impressive, as are the nautical and South Seas sections.

Sculpture Gallery. European sculpture from antiquity to the 18th century. Outstanding German medieval and Italian Renaissance pieces.

Kulturzentrum Tiergarten. On the edge of the zoological garden a row of buildings housing Prussian cultural possessions is in the process of being expanded to form a new cultural center on Kemperplatz.

Kunstgewerbemuseum (Museum of Applied Arts), Matthäikirchplatz 10. A wonderful collection of European craftsmanship from the early Middle Ages to the 20th century. The highlight is the Guelph Treasure, but there is also priceless gold- and silver-smiths' work, carpets, glass, porcelain, ivory and technical instruments.

Museum of Musical Instruments (Musikinstrumentenmuseum), Tiergartenstr. 1. Fascinating for anyone with a taste for musical history (it includes Frederick the Great's flute among other instruments of the famous).

Neue Nationalgalerie, Tiergarten, Potsdamerstr. 50. 19th- and 20th-century art, and the most important museum in the Kulturzentrum.

Other Important Museums. Bauhaus Archives and Museum, Klingelhöferstr. 13–14. The still faddish '20s school of architecture founded by Walter Gropius.

Berlin Museum, Lindenstrasse 14. Three hundred years of Berlin as seen through its art and culture. Also has a moderately priced restaurant with local fare.

Reichstag (former German parliament), Platz der Republik, has new significance amid the calls for reunification of the two Germanies. Houses an exhibition of German history since 1800. Entry free.

Deutsches Rundfunk Museum, foot of Berlin Radio Tower. Covers the development of radio technology from 1923.

Haus am Checkpoint Charlie, Friedrichstr. 44. Documentation about the Berlin Wall, escape attempts and the border situation. Open daily until 10 P.M.

State Museum's Art Library (Kunstbibliothek), Jebenstrasse 2. Architectural drawings, poster collection, library of costumes, etchings, etc.

Zoological Garden, Budapesterstr. Very popular with Berliners and a delightful place to wander in; the animals are excellently housed and imaginatively displayed. Has Europe's largest aviary. Eat at the handy restaurant.

SHOPPING. The principal shopping street in Berlin is the Tauentzienstrasse between the Gedächtniskirche and Wittenbergplatz. At the latter square, you'll find *Ka-De-We,* the largest department store in Europe. It's a must and the food department has to be seen to be believed.

Another good shopping area, where shops of all kinds jostle one another, is the Kurfürstendamm itself, and its side streets as far as Olivaer Platz.

Antiques abound in Berlin. The best areas are in the Eisenacher Strasse/Motzstrasse district and the area around Keithstrasse, as well as along the Ku'damm. But prices are high and most of the shops rather specialized. So for lower prices and more variety, head for the numerous *Trödelgeschäfte,* second hand and junk shops. They have everything under the sun and, with a bit of luck, there's a good chance of stumbling across a really interesting souvenir. The best *Trödel* areas are in the Kreuzberg around the Bergmannstr. and in Neukölln near the Flughafenstrasse. There are also a number scattered round Schöneberg and Charlottenburg. Keep your eyes open.

You might also try one of the famous flea markets; unfortunately not so cheap as they once were. A good one is *Ku'damm-Karree* at Ku'damm 207 (open daily except Tues. 3–10 P.M.). But check out the *Flohmarkt,* Nollendorfplatz as well, where all the shops are old railway carriages. Open daily (except Tues.) from 11 A.M. to 7 P.M. Live music Sun.

USEFUL ADDRESSES. *American Mission,* Clay-Allee 170, Dahlem (tel. 832 4087); *Canadian Consulate,* in the Europa Center; *British Consul,* Uhlandstr. 7 (tel. 309 5292). *Berlin Tourist Information Office,* in the Europa Center (tel. 262 6031), and at Tegel Airport (tel. 41013145), both are open daily from 8 A.M. to 10.30 P.M. *American Express,* in the U.S. Army post exchange across the street from Clay-Allee 170, and at Kurfürstendamm 11. *Thomas Cook,* Kurfürstendamm 195 (tel. 884 2830). *Post Office* (day and night service), Bahnhof Zoo, where a bank is open daily 8 A.M.–9 P.M. for changing money.

PRACTICAL INFORMATION FOR EAST GERMANY

WHAT IT WILL COST. Eastern Germany is definitely still in the budget bracket, except when it comes to accommodations. Under the former regime, the newer hotels were all in the expensive to luxury categories, meaning that acceptable budget hotel accommodations—at least in Berlin—were hard to find. This is unfortunately pretty much still the case, so finding accommodations in a private home may be the best answer for the budget traveler. Overall, costs in eastern Germany are now going up at a staggering rate, as earlier socialist subsidies for services such as transportation are cut back or eliminated. You can still find enough bargains to make the effort worthwhile, however Berlin, as you might expect, is still the most expensive city, followed by Dresden and Leipzig. Once you wander off the beaten path, however, you'll find many prices still not too much higher than those of the pre-unification days; by any measure, those were indeed bargains.

Sample Costs. As subsidies continue to be withdrawn, prices will undoubtedly rise. At press-time (Summer 1990), you could get a ticket for the theater for between 5 and 15 marks; a coffee for 3 marks; beer in a café for 3 marks, in a Bierstube for under 2 marks; and museum entry for 1 mark.

HOW TO GO. To take advantage of the best offers under very fluid conditions, your best bet is probably to make arrangements with a travel agency that knows eastern Germany. Now that border formalities have been dispensed with, if you decide at the last minute to include the eastern districts in your travels, there are no problems with a visa. Nevertheless, because accommodations are limited, it's to plan ahead and book in advance.

NATIONAL TOURIST OFFICE. The experts on travel in eastern Germany are at the *Reisebüro der D.D.R.,* which at press time still had offices in a number of western countries as well as in both halves of Berlin. In the U.K., the authorized representatives are *Berolina Travel, Ltd.,* 22 Conduit St., London W1R 9TB (tel. 071–629–1664). In the U.S., specialists in travel in the eastern provinces include *Koch,* 157 E. 86th St., New York, NY 10028 (tel. 212–369–3800); *Cal Simmons Travel,* 1631 Washington Plaza, Reston, VA 22090 (tel. 703–471–1900); and *Maupintours,* 1515 St. Andrews Dr., Lawrence, KS 66046 (tel. 800–255–4266). These agencies can book package tours that include the highlights and offer good value if you have the time to spend in Eastern Germany; unfortunately, few of the packages are in the budget category.

WHEN TO COME. The main tourist season in the eastern provinces runs from late May to the end of August, and the bulk of organized tours are scheduled for this period. There is little advantage for budget travelers to visit outside of the summer since prices vary little from one season to another. The "shoulder" seasons of April–May and September–October are particularly enjoyable. Winter, on the other hand, can be bitterly cold, and summer, at least in Berlin, sometimes hot and humid.

Average afternoon temperatures in degrees Fahrenheit and centigrade:

Berlin	Jan.	Feb.	Mar.	Apr.	May	June	July	Aug.	Sept.	Oct.	Nov.	Dec.
F°	35	38	46	55	65	70	74	72	66	55	43	37
C°	2	3	8	13	18	21	23	22	19	13	6	3

SPECIAL EVENTS. The Leipzig Trade Fair, one of the major general fairs in Europe and formerly among the most significant of the East—West trade events, is held twice a year, in the first weeks of *March* and *September.* The fair is fascinating, as it gives an overview of international industrial production, but all accommodations in Leipzig and environs—and indeed even as far away as Berlin—are reserved for business visitors, and prices rise accordingly. The Weimar Shakespeare Festival takes place in *April.* In *May* Dresden mounts its Music Festival, an event gaining in international reputation. *June* sees the Handel festival in Halle, honoring its native son, the composer Georg Friedrich Handel. In *July* the Haneastic cities of Rostock and Straslund stage a week of festivities, the Ostseewoche. *September* and *October* see the Berlin Music and Drama Festival.

National Holidays. Jan. 1 (New Year's Day); Mar. 29 (Good Friday); April 1 (Easter Monday); May 1 (Labor Day); (Whit Monday); Oct 7 (Republic Day); Dec. 25, 26 (Christmas).

GETTING TO EAST GERMANY. By Plane. There are no direct connections from North America to any of the cities of the eastern Germany, but a growing number of airlines in addition to *Interflug* (formerly the East German national carrier) offer regular flights to Berlin/Schönefeld, Leipzig and Dresden from key European cities. The airport is about 15 miles from the center of Berlin, 50 minutes by bus, 45 minutes with the *S-Bahn* city train, which runs directly from a station near the airport. A number of international airlines serve the western sector of Berlin.

By Train. From the U.K., the most convenient route is via Harwich and the Hook of Holland or via Dover and Oostende. From both of these points, there are through coaches to Berlin (Ost. Station). (Before reunification, Eastern officials had renamed the station as the *Hauptbahnhof,* or main station; this could now revert to its former designation as *Ostbahnhof,* or East station, to avoid confusion with stations in the western sector of the city). The trip from London, including the sea crossing, takes about 23 hours. These trains also stop at the *Friedrichstrasse* station, the former dividing or transfer point between the east and west sectors of the city.

Within Germany itself, you can get trains from Hamburg, Nürnberg and Munich. Ferry services from Rodby in Denmark connect to trains at Warnemünde on the Baltic, and from Trelleborg in Sweden at Sassnitz. Daily rail service runs from Vienna via Prague and Dresden.

CUSTOMS. You now enter the eastern districts just as you do the western parts of the country, so the same rules apply as to what you may or not bring in without duty (see Practical Information for West Germany).

HOTELS. Formerly you had little choice but to book into one of the hotels run by the government's *Interhotel* chain. In the upper (expensive and luxury) categories, these were the equivalent in comfort and value to anything you might find in the West. Unfortunately, the available budget (moderate) hotels in the *Interhotel* chain were often used to house government groups and guests; since their stays were often gratis, neither guests nor management were particular about housekeeping or maintenance. It's expected that this rather unhappy condition will now change. There are far too few of them to handle the onrush, but the hotels in the "H-O" group, run by the local trade organizations (which might also disappear in the course of reunification) and the Mitropa hotels run by the Mitropa restaurant and sleeping car organization offer good budget accommodations. For a real bargain, the seven hostels run by the Evangelical (Lutheran) Church are the best deal, clean and comfortable, if modest.

Our hotel listings are divided into two categories, Moderate (M) and Inexpensive (I). Two people in a double room in a Moderate hotel can expect to pay about DM70–90 per night; in an Inexpensive room, this will come to about DM40–70. These rates are for lodging and breakfast. Occasionally a Moderate hotel at the upper end of the range will include a bath or shower, but most budget rooms have only hot water. Please note that our price ratings are based on conditions that prevailed at press time; these could change considerably by the time you get to Germany; we advise you check in advance.

Youth Hostels. You'll find an extensive network of Youth Hostels throughout eastern Germany in or near major cities. Accommodations are good, but with the opening of the region and the rise in the number of tourists from the west, you'll need to book well in advance. Check with *Jugendtourist* (Alexanderplatz 5, 1026 Berlin, tel. 2150) or one of the authorized tourist offices abroad, such as Berolina in the U.K. Rates are extremely reasonable. The age limit is 30.

Camping. The eastern region offers over 30 *Intercamp* sites, most with good facilities, open May 1 to Sept. 30. These too are in great demand, so you will need to book your campsite before arriving (details are available from the *Reisebüro*, Alexanderplatz 5, 1026 Berlin).

RESTAURANTS. In Berlin, at least, dining is no longer the indifferent affair it used to be. The "face lift" that accompanied Berlins's 750th anniversary brought with it a number of new cafés and restaurants, and the union has brought further competition and upgrading, both in quantity and quality.

The one remaining problem that many of the restaurants are really tiny, so reservations are needed, but we've noted this in our listings. Finding a place at one of the moderate or inexpensive restaurants at noon on a workday can be a challenge; if you see a line outside a restaurant, it is probably both good *and* inexpensive! Old habits die slowly, so if all tables seem to be booked (a standard response given in the "old days" when staff got paid the same whether they worked or not), a small tip to the headwaiter (DM2 or 3, depending on the locale) will usually get you a favored spot. With some exceptions (which we note below) budget tourists will do best by avoiding the hotel restaurants and seeking out the smaller *Stuben* and *Kellern*, where you'll meet local residents rather than other tourists. Waiters will be helpful when you come to order. Prices are going up, but in the smaller restaurants, prices are still so low that you can hardly overspend. Look for the daily fixed menu specials; these are usually posted outside and represent excellent value.

A full meal in a Moderate restaurant will cost DM20–30, DM10–20 in an Inexpensive restaurant. These prices are for one person and include a small beer. In many places you can have the daily menu of soup, a main dish, and a beer for under DM7.

Food and Drink. Dishes on East German menus in cities are heavily influenced by Eastern European cuisine. Explanations are usually given in several languages, including English, and generally speaking regional specialties manage to make themselves known. In Berlin, for instance, you will find the famous *Eisbein mit Sauerkraut* (knuckle of pork with pickled cabbage), *Rouladen* (rolled stuffed beef), *Spanferkel* (suckling pig), *Berliner Schüsselsülze* (potted meat in aspic), *Schlachteplatte* (mixed grill), *Bürgermeister-Suppe* (thick soup), *Hackepeter* (minced meat), and *Kartoffelpuffer* (potato pancake).

Just outside Berlin, in the haven and tranquility of Spreewald (the Spree woods) and their "streets" of waterways (much of this district has no roads, so boats are the only means of transport), freshwater fish specialties abound, as well as the familiar sausages peculiar to every spot of Germany, East or West. Good ones to try are *Spreewälder Wurstplatte mit Meerrettich* and *Quark mit Leinöl* (various types of sausage with horseradish; and cream cheese with oil dressing). *Fisch in Spreewaldsosse* (fish in season with a local sauce) or *Aal mit Gurkensalat* (eel and cucumber salad) number among the best fish dishes. There are seafood restaurants throughout East Germany, many of them called *Gastmahl des Meeres*.

Thuringia specializes in venison, poultry and fish. *Röstbrätl* (pot-roast), *Thüringer Sauerbraten mit Klössen* (pickled roast meat and dumplings), *Bärenschinken* (ham) are typical, and *Thüringer Kesselfleisch, Würzfleisch, Schlachteplatte, Thüringer Wurstplatte* are all local sausage dishes.

In the Harz Mountains, you may come across *Halberstädter Käsesuppe* (cheese soup), or *Harzer Köhlerteller mit Röstkartoffeln* (meat cooked over a charcoal grill and served with roast potatoes).

Wines and spirits tend to come from eastern rather than western climes; the Bulgarian wines and Polish and Russian vodkas in particular are worth sampling. A local throat-scorcher found around the Harz Mountains is *Schierker Feuerstein*.

TIPPING. Under the communist regime, tipping was officially abolished, but certainly accepted. Tip a bit less than you would in western Germany. DM1 or 2 is sufficient in most cases.

MAIL. Postal rates and stamps are the same as in West Germany.

CLOSING TIMES. Stores are mostly open from 9 to 6 outside Berlin, 10 to 7 (8 on Thurs.) in Berlin. Only department and larger stores are open Sat. morning. Most banks are open from 8 to 11.30 Mon. to Fri. Most museums are open from 10 to 6, Sun. included, and are closed Mon. or Tues.

GETTING AROUND EASTERN GERMANY.
The country is relatively small so there are virtually no internal flights. Rail is the preferred means of travel and services are frequent and cheap. Bus services are also widespread, but not as comfortable as rail. The system of highways is constantly being improved, but roads other than major routes are often in poor condition.

By Train. The East German railway system, known as *Deutsche Reichsbahn,* is being absorbed into the West German *Deutsche Bundesbahn* (DB) system. During the period of transition, you may experience a few inconveniences, but generally the service is good. Travelers can choose from three types of trains: Express, the fastest, shown as "Ex" in timetables, fast, shown as "D", and semi-fast, shown as "E". All have varying degrees of supplementary fare, which local trains do not. Rail travel is still cheap, but fares are rising as subsidies are reduced. Most long- and medium-distance trains have both 1st and 2nd class and many have either dining or buffet cars or refreshment services. Under the DB management, these services may be somewhat more regular than in the past and variety should be greatly improved. Many overnight trains include 1st and 2nd class sleeping cars and 2nd class bunk beds. As rail travel is popular, trains are usually very full, so have your travel agent book in advance.

By Bus. Apart from coaches used on all-inclusive package trips, there are no long distance coaches. However, all towns and cities are well-served by tram and bus services; in cities operating both tram and bus services, tickets are generally interchangeable and transfers permitted.

By Car. As the two Germanys are brought together, many adjustments between practices in the two countries must be reconciled. One of these is the East German road-use tax, charged according to distance driven. Unless you're in a group, traveling by car is not the budget way to see eastern Germany, although this could change as well. Many of the former rules of the road will continue to apply, at least for the time being. Drinking and driving is totally forbidden, and fines are heavy for violators. Speed limits are 100 km (63 mph) on the Autobahn, 80 km (55 mph) on other roads, 50 km (30 mph) in towns. In the past, gasoline has been hard to find in some areas, but increasingly you will find the familiar signs of filling stations you know.

By Bicycle. Getting around is easy enough, particularly in the flatter lands north of Berlin, but if you're taking your own bicycle, be sure to take the essential spare parts with you. Bicycle rentals will most certainly be among the early private enterprises to spring up.

East Berlin

A good starting point for a tour of East Berlin is the mighty Brandenburg Gate. It was here on Pariser Platz on Dec. 22, 1989, that crowds from both halves of the city joyously celebrated the collapse of the Berlin Wall. Crowning the gate is the restored Quadriga, the two-wheeled chariot drawn by four stallions. In addition to the fine shops, the current version of Unter den Linden, once Berlin's most fashionable avenue, is graced with a number of ministries and embassies, including that of the U.K. The block-long complex on the right-hand side as you look east toward the television tower Unter den Linden is the Soviet embassy. Humboldt University founded in 1810 by Wilhelm von Humboldt, is at its lower end. The German State Library with over 4 million volumes is here, also the Museum of German History in whose courtyard concerts are held in summer, the German State Opera, the Opera Café (once the Princesses' Palace), the former Royal Library, used today by the University, St. Hedwig's Cathedral, and the National Gallery.

In a moment you arrive at a great open expanse, and if you knew Berlin before the 1939–45 war, you will gaze at it in bewilderment. This was the heart of the city in those days, where stood the great museums, the cathedrals, and the massive buildings of the old Imperial Palace. Begun in 1538, the palace, thanks to the genius of Andreas Schlüter, has been one of Berlin's most prized architectural monuments for four centuries. It was severely damaged during the war, but not to such an extent that it could not have been restored. In 1951 it was razed and every trace of its existence obliterated, to make way for the bare desolation of the Marx-Engels-Platz, the Red Square of Berlin and somewhat calling to mind Munich's Königsplatz.

Passing East Berlin's red brick city hall and the nearby 14th-century Marienkirche, you come next to Alexanderplatz, or "Alex" as the East Berliners know it, dominated by the 365-meter high (1,200 ft.) television mast, East Berlin's landmark. Around the square are a number of shops and restaurants and the eastern sector's largest department store, Centrum.

Whether or not it's on your tour route, take time to explore the narrow streets, bridges and canal backwaters of the Fischerinsel district, a few blocks south of Alexanderplatz. This charming area is in part original Berlin, in part beautifully restored. Adjacent is the Nikolai quarter, restored with affection and taste, with shops and restaurants as well as small park areas. It is a heartening contrast to the often ugly modern post-War buildings of Karl Marx Allee or the Leipziger Str.

If you take a city tour, this may include the Soviet cemetery at Treptow, another monolithic construction built with marble taken from Hitler's Reich Chancellery, among other places. On either side of a broad avenue leading to a massive figure of a Russian soldier are bas-reliefs in white stone portraying episodes of World War II and interpreted by commentaries in Russian and German.

PRACTICAL INFORMATION FOR EAST BERLIN

HOTELS. East Berlin is well supplied with hotels, many, especially the newer and larger ones, built with the Western visitor very much in mind. Though it is best to make reservations in advance, it is possible to make them on the spot through the accommodations office *(Zimmernachweis)* at Alexanderplatz 5 (tel. 215–5233 or 215–4324). Most Moderate hotels have private showers or baths and though Inexpensive hotels do not for the most part they are always clean. Interhotels, accustomed to and equipped for Western tourists, are more expensive. If there really is no other choice than the Interhotels, then try for the 4-star category, although those are outside our normal budget range. Best choices are *Unter den Linden,* Unter den Linden 14, corner Friedrichstrasse (tel. 220–0311). What the hotel lacks in class, it makes up for in location. *Berolina,* Karl-Marx-Allee 31 (tel. 210–9541). Less central but satisfactory. *Stadt Berlin,* Alexanderplatz (tel. 2190). The city's largest, and includes some bargain dining in the cafeteria and bier-stube. Of the inexpensive accommodations, the Evangelical hostels are the best bets.

The Grünau Youth Hostel is at Dahmestrasse 6, on one of the lakes in the suburb of Grünau out toward the airport, reachable by S-Bahn railway; central information on all hostels (tel. 635–4030); closer to the center is the Youth Tourist Hotel Egon Schultz, Franz-Mett-Str. 7 (tel. 525–6218) opposite the zoo. Camping sites are at Krossinsee and Müggelsee, both on lakes and both reserved for foreign tourists.

Moderate

Adria, Friedrichstrasse 134 (tel. 282–5451). H–O group. Fairly convenient location, but few rooms with bath. Popular and inexpensive restaurant.

Newa, Invalidenstrasse 115 (tel. 282–5461). H–O group. 10 minutes by streetcar from center. Older hotel; few rooms with bath. Inexpensive and fairly good restaurant.

Inexpensive

Berliner Hof, Friedrichstrasse 113A (tel. 282–7478). Private.
Broeschke, Friedrichstrasse 124 (tel. 282–3620). Private.
Hospiz Augustrasse, Augustrasse 82 (tel. 282–5321). Evangelical church hostel. 10 minutes to center by streetcar. 66 rooms, some with bath. Breakfast only.
Hospiz am Bahnhof Friedrichstrasse, Albrechtstrasse 8 (tel. 282–5396). Evangelical church hostel. Close to Friedrichstrasse rail station. 110 rooms, some with bath. Inexpensive and popular restaurant.
Merkur, Wilhelm Pieck–Strasse 156 (tel. 282–8297). Private.

RESTAURANTS. We note in the listings where reservations are necessary. If restaurants are all full at midday, most cafés serve light dishes at noon in addition to the usual coffee and cake.

Moderate

Berlin-Esprit, Alexanderplatz, in Hotel Stadt Berlin (tel. 2190). Among top choices for Berlin specialties. Reservations recommended.
Brecht-Keller, Chausseestrasse 125, in Bertolt Brecht house (tel. 282–3843). Intimate cellar restaurant serving Viennese cuisine, weekdays only from 7.30 P.M. Reservations essential.
Café Flair, Am Marstall (ground floor), Rathaustrasse at Marx-Engels-Forum (tel. 212–4569). New, excellent and justifiably very popular. Slightly limited but good choice of food, service fine. Tables outside for nice days. Reservations recommended.
Gastmahl des Meeres, Spandauer Strasse 4 (tel. 212–3300). International fish specialties.
Ganymed, Schiffbauerdamm 5 (tel. 282–9540). Top of the Moderate category, but recommended for particularly attractive rooms, piano in the evening. Wide choice of excellent dishes from cold plates to cordon bleu, mixed grill, even Indonesian. Closed Monday noon. Reservations advisable, particularly for evenings.
Historische Weinstuben, Poststrasse 23 (tel. 212–4122). Intimate wine restaurant, Berlin's oldest. Limited menu. Reservations essential.
Linden-Corso, Unter den Linden 17 (tel. 220–2461). Restaurant, concert café, dancing evenings; Havanna bar open to 4 A.M.
Operncafé, Unter den Linden 5 (tel. 200–0256). Elegant rooms in one-time palace. Restaurant, popular café and wine tavern. Reservations advisable for restaurant.
Ratskeller, Rathausstrasse 14, in basement of huge brick City Hall (tel. 212–4464; 212–5301). Atmospheric and highly popular wine and beer cellars (entrances at opposite ends of the building). Reservations recommended.
Stammhaus-Bierclub, Friedrichstrasse, in Grand Hotel. New. Wide range of beers and lighter dishes and snacks.
Wernesgrüner Bierstube, Karl-Liebknecht-Strasse 4 (tel. 282–4268). Pleasant beer cellar serving Berlin food. No-smoking room at noon. Reservations advisable, particularly at noon.

Inexpensive

Alex Grill, Alexanderplatz, in Hotel Stadt Berlin (tel. 2190). Cafeteria, with no-smoking section. Popular at noon.
Alt-Cöllner Schankstuben, Friedrichsgracht 50 (tel. 212–5972). Friendly and charming. Café and beer restaurant. Tables outside overlooking canal on pleasant days.
Arkade, Französische Strasse 25 (tel. 208–0273). Café-restaurant in art deco style, tables outside in good weather. Grill counter in back. No reservations.
Newa, Invalidenstrasse 115, in Hotel Newa (tel. 282–5461). Short on charm but a fairly extensive menu, even a limited salad bar.
Quick, Karl-Liebknecht-Strasse 5, in Palast Hotel. Self-service cafeteria, good variety and quality. Packed at noon. Open to 8 P.M.

Raabe Diele, Märkisches Ufer 10–12, basement of Ermeler House (tel. 279–4036). Beer cellar with excellent service, good food. House was moved in 1969 to present location, so cellar is new and less atmospheric than famous upstairs (and more expensive) rooms. Canned music may be distressing.

Rathauspassagen, Rathausstrasse 5. Restaurants range from the *Bierhaus "zur Haxn"* inside the complex and specializing in Eisbein (knuckle of pork) from 8 A.M. to midnight, to the *Wurstchen Bar* on the street offering various frankfurters and sausages. Also includes the *Café Rendezvous* upstairs and the *Alex Treff,* a self-service restaurant and dance café.

Zenner, Alt-Treptow 14–17, in Treptower Park outside the center, reachable by streetcars. One of the city's oldest beer gardens, tables outside on banks of the Spree river in summer.

Zillestube, Alexanderplatz, in Hotel Stadt Berlin (tel. 2190). Typical and popular beer cellar/restaurant serving Berlin specialties.

Zum Paddenwirt, Poststrasse 17 (tel. 212–5067). Small but charming beer restaurant. Limited variety of hot and cold foods. Live music on Sundays at 10 A.M. No reservations.

Zur letzten Instanz, Waisenstrasse 14–16 ("U"-Bahn Klosterstrasse) (tel. 212–5528). Original (established 1525) and utterly charming. Limited food choice but genuine Berlin and good. Friendly service. Highly recommended. Reservations essential, noon and night.

Zur Rippe, Poststrasse 17 (tel. 212–4932). Minuscule but delightful, specializing in spare ribs. Excellent service. Reservations advisable.

GETTING AROUND EAST BERLIN. By Metro (U-Bahn). With the integration of the eastern and western parts of the city, transportation links are changing as well. Check on availability, but before reunification, a system ticket for 2 East German marks would give you unlimited travel for a full day on all public transport in the eastern part of the city. Get tickets and information at the tourist office, Alexanderplaltz 5, or any main rail station. You can get as many of these tickets as you want, but they should be separately stamped with the date of the day you want to use them. The metro is fairly extensive; route maps and fare details are available from the Alexanderplatz city rail station and from the tourist office. Maps are posted in all stations, and a system route map is included in the *"Wohin in Berlin"* booklet. Some of the routes are now being reconnected to those in the western part of the city; otherwise transfer at Jannowitzbrücke or Friedrichstrasse. There is also an S-Bahn (suburban railway) which serves the more outlying areas, including Schönefeld airport. Get tickets for the S-Bahn from coin-operated dispensers or ticket windows in the stations.

By Bus/Tram. Tickets are very inexpensive, but buses can be rather uncomfortable and crowded, and hot in summer. Tram routes are displayed on all tram stops *(Halt).*

On Foot. This is certainly the best way to get to know central East Berlin. Get a map from your hotel or from the information center at the base of the TV tower at Alexanderplatz. Some newsstands may also sell maps. Cross streets at intersections; jaywalking is forbidden.

ENTERTAINMENT. Bier Kellers. There are a number of enjoyable and attractive bier kellers throughout the city; most are inexpensive and do serve food, even if only snacks. The majority close at midnight, but some stay open till 4 A.M. Among them are: *Altberliner Bierstuben,* 17 Saarbrückestrasse; *Berliner Weinstuben,* Rathaus-Passagen, an exclusive wine tavern; *Historische Weinstuben,* Poststrasse 23, in the Nikolai quarter, a charming setting with much atmosphere.

Discos. Most of the bigger hotels have discos which you can usually get into for a modest entry fee. Among them are: *Hotel Stadt Berlin, Palast, Berolina* and the *Metropol.* Some restaurants and bars also have disco nights (see above for addresses).

Theaters and Concerts. Berlin has about 14 theaters, many of which also have concerts, but unless you speak German, only those listed below will have much appeal. Information about programs and advance tickets can be had from all box offices daily from 12 to 6. There is a central theater ticket agency selling tickets for all cultural, sporting, and theater events in the Palast Hotel. Check also the booklet *Wohin in Berlin?* (What's On in Berlin).

Deutsche Staatsoper, Unter den Linden (tel. 200–0491), a magnificently restored 18th-century theater with first-class opera productions; *Komische Oper,* Behrenstrasse 55–57 (tel. 229–2555), the house that under Walter Felsenstein reestablished Berlin's postwar theater reputation—repertoire now includes opera, operetta, musicals; *Metropol Theater,* Friedrichstrasse 101 (tel. 207–1739), mainly musicals; *Berliner Ensemble,* Berthold-Brecht-Platz (tel. 282–3160), dedicated to maintaining Brecht's works and reputation; *Distel,* Friedrichstrasse 100 (tel. 287–1226), plays various locations with as biting a satirical cabaret as possible. Pop concerts, modern music, and other varied entertainments take place in the *Palast der Republik,* Marx-Engels-Platz (tel. 238–2352); classical music in the *Schauspielhaus,* Platz der Akademie (tel. 227–2156), a beautifully restored gem of a house.

MUSEUMS. Arts and Crafts Museum (Köpenick Palace). Lovely setting for European arts and crafts of four centuries and special exhibitions. Open Mon. to Sat. 9–5, Sun. 10–6.

Berlin Zoo (Tierpark). A gem of a zoo, easily reached on the U-Bahn. Wide variety of animals, lovely setting with many pleasant cafés.

Bodemuseum, Am Kupfergraben. Egyptian, early Christian and Byzantine collections, plus Italian masters from the 13th to 18th centuries. Open Wed. to Sun. 10–6.

Markisches Museum, 5 Am Köllnischen Park. East Berlin's museum of city and cultural history, with changing exhibits. Permanent exhibition on Berlin's theater history. Open Wed. and Sun. 9–6, Thurs. and Sat. 9–5, Fri. 9–4.

Museum of German History, Unter den Linden. Western visitors may be surprised at this interpretation of East German history, but it is impressively done. Open Mon. to Thurs. 9–7, Sat. and Sun. 10–5.

National Gallery, Bodestrasse. 19th- and 20th-century German paintings and sculptures. Open Wed. to Sun. 9–6, Fri. 10–6.

Pergamon Museum, Am Kupfergraben. One of the world's great museums, so allow plenty of time. The greatest treasure is the Pergamon Altar, which dates from 180 B.C. and was one of the Seven Wonders of the World. The street from Babylon is equally impressive. The Egyptian collections are on a par with those in the Louvre and the British Museum. Open Wed. to Sun. 9–6, Fri. 10–6 (Pergamon Altar also open on Mon. and Tues.).

SHOPPING. A number of good shops can be found along Unter den Linden and the Alexanderplatz. The huge *Centrum* department store on Alexanderplatz is Berlin's largest and prices are very reasonable for most items a tourist would want to buy. A series of new shops and shopping arcades have opened in the upper and lower Friedrichstrasse. But don't expect to find bargains in Meissen porcelain, East German-made optical goods or other specialties; these are mainly to order only. Look for handwork, lace, glasswork, wood carvings and such, either at Centrum or at smaller specialty shops.

USEFUL ADDRESSES. *U.S. Embassy,* Neustädtische Kirchstr. 4–5 (tel. 200–2741); *British Embassy,* Unter den Linden 32–34 (tel. 220–2431); there is no Canadian Embassy in East Berlin; *Main Post Office,* corner of Ostbahnhof and Strasse der Pariser Kommune; *Reisebüro.* (National Tourist Office), Alexanderplatz 5 (tel. 215–4402). Open Mon.–Fri. 8–8 and Sat./Sun. 9–6.

Dresden

Splendidly situated on the banks of the river Elbe, Dresden was the capital of Saxony as early as the 15th century. However, the city's chief claim to fame is its 18th-century architecture which includes some of the finest Baroque and Rococo buildings in Europe (the majority renovated after World War II). The most outstanding are the Zwinger Palace, the Opera House, the cathedral and the National Gallery, home to a superb collection of pictures. However, the Zwinger Palace also has an excellent collection—but see the note below under "Museums"—which includes Raphael's *Sistine Madonna* as well as 12 Rembrandts, 16 Rubens and 5 Tintorettos. The city has some 18 further museums. The Semper Opera House, entirely destroyed in the war and reopened in 1985 after decades of careful reconstruction, is an achievement of which the East Germans can be justly proud.

A short trip down the Elbe brings you to Meissen, famed for its exquisite porcelain. The town also boasts a castle and a fine late-Gothic cathedral which has an excellent Cranach. Halfway between Meissen and Dresden, and a few miles inland from the Elbe, is the Baroque Moritzburg Castle, a former hunting lodge for the Saxon kings.

PRACTICAL INFORMATION FOR DRESDEN

Hotels

Moderate

Astoria, Ernst-Thälmann-Platz (tel. 475–5851). Interhotel. About 1 km. from city center, near zoo. Simple but comfortable. Two restaurants.

Gewandhaus, Ringstrasse 1 (tel. 49–6286). H–O group. Central location and good café. Some rooms with bath.

Interhotel Prager Strasse, Prager Strasse (tel. 48–560). Interhotel. Consists of two hotels combined, **Königstein** and **Lilienstein,** each with 300 rooms with bath. Near the main railroad station. Restaurants, shops.

Inexpensive

Parkhotel Weisser Hirsch, Bautzner Landstrasse 7 (tel. 36–851). Considerable distance from city center. 50 rooms in pleasant surroundings, although facilities are simple. Restaurant, café, dancing.

Restaurants

Moderate

Café Pöppelmann, Grosse Meissner G. 15, (tel. 56–620). Part of the Hotel Bellevue complex. Baroque atmosphere in a restored old city house.

Café Prag, Altmarkt. Long-established and reliable spot.

Kulturpalast Dresden, Ernst-Thälmannstrasse. In the museum itself and both very good value and convenient.

Luisenhof, Bergbahnstrasse 8. Superb location, reached by cable car, overlooking the city and the Elbe.

Ratskeller, Dr. Külz-Ring. Wide variety of dishes; as good and as popular as Ratskellers throughout the country.

Szeged, Ernst-Thälmannstrasse 6. Well-known and good Hungarian restaurant.

Inexpensive

Aberlausitzer Töppl, Strasse der Befreiung. Probably the best bet in Dresden for value. Specialties from the Sorb region south of Dresden; the fish is particularly popular.

Am Gewandhaus, Gewandhausstrasse 3. Open for breakfast. Non-smoking area.

Pirnaisches Tor, Pirnaischer Platz. Choice of fish grill, restaurant proper, terrace café and coffee bar.

Schillergarten, Schillerplatz 8. Good; in quiet location.

WHAT TO SEE AND DO. Museums. Albertinum, Brühlsche Terrasse. Houses the picture gallery of New Masters, the famous Green Vault displaying royal jewels from the 16th to 18th centuries and the coin and sculpture collections. Open Tues. to Sun. 9–5.

Jägerhof, Köpkestr. 1. 16th-century Renaissance building that now houses a Museum of Folk Art.

Schloss Pillnitz. Hillside and riverside palaces on the Elbe river. Museum of Arts and Crafts. The Schloss is a harmonious blend of Baroque and Chinese architecture. Open May–Oct., Tues. to Sun. 9.30–4.

Zwinger, Julian-Grimm Allee. Dresden's famous Baroque building, comprising the Gallery of Old Masters, and the historical museum. See also the porcelain collection and the mathematical and physical sciences salon. Open Tues. to Sun. 9–5.

Theaters. Since its reopening in 1985, the *Semper Opera House* has regained its reputation as one of the top two houses in the country and a leading house in Europe as well. Seats are hard to get, although not expensive. For operetta and lighter fare there is the *Staatsoperette,* Landstrasse 131. There are also two excellent *puppet theaters* at Leipzigerstrasse 220 and in the Grosser Garten (summer only). Central ticket office in Schinkelwache, between the opera and Zwinger palace. Tel. 48–420.

Leipzig

Leipzig first grew to prominence in the Middle Ages when it was an important trade center, a role it has reaffirmed for itself today as the center of the East European printing and book trades and as the home of the twice-yearly Leipzig Trade Fair which has brought together exhibitors and traders from all over the world for more than 50 years. The Fair now constitutes the single most important meeting point for East-West trade. In the Napoleonic era, Leipzig was the site of an important battle between the French and the Prussians in 1813, and in the same year Richard Wagner was born here. In fact the city boasts a long and rich musical tradition which includes the Gewandhaus Orchestra, founded in 1781, and the St. Thomas Church Boys' Choir, once closely associated with J.S. Bach. Halle, only 22 miles from Leipzig, was the birthplace of Handel. Today, an annual Handel festival is held there. Sadly, little is left of old Leipzig following considerable destruction in World War II.

PRACTICAL INFORMATION FOR LEIPZIG

Hotels

Moderate

International, Tröndlinring 8 (tel. 71880). In pleasant neighborhood. Interhotel.
Zum Löwen, Rudolf Breitscheidstrasse (tel. 7751). Facilities are just adequate but the staff is helpful. Interhotel.

Inexpensive

Bayerischer Hof, Wintergartenstrasse 13 (tel. 209251). Adequate.
Park-Hotel, Richard Wagnerstrasse 7 (tel. 7821). Good and helpful service.
Vier Jahreszeiten, Rudolph Breitscheidstrasse 23 (tel. 291604). Old style and popular hotel; name means Four Seasons.

Restaurants

Moderate

Auerbachs Keller, Grimmaische Str. 2–4 (tel. 209131). Not exactly budget but, as one of the country's most famous restaurants, worth it nonetheless, especially for the historic setting. Book ahead.
Barthels Hof, Marktstr. 8. A different motif in each of its three halls.
Burgkeller, Naschmarkt 1. Romanian specialties. Good restaurant; small cocktail bar.
Gastmahl des Meeres, Dr. Kurt Fischerstrasse 1. An excellent fish spot. (The name is widely used for fish restaurants throughout the country.)
Paulaner, Klostergasse 3. Attractive and quiet, by Dominican abbey.

Inexpensive

Kaffeebaum, Klaus Fleischergasse 4, (tel. 20–452). Allegedly the oldest café in the country, in a Burgerhaus well over 450 years old. Worth visiting.

Regina, Hainstrasse 14. Cozy wine restaurant, book ahead (tel. 28–2052).

Panorama Café, Karl-Marx-Platz, atop the university building, (tel. 7466).

Stadt Kiew, Petersstrasse, Messehaus am Markt. Ukrainian specialties.

WHAT TO SEE AND DO. Wine Taverns. Leipzig boasts a number of these and they can be very pleasant spots to while away a little time inexpensively. Among the best are: *Bachstüb'l,* Thomaskirchhof, close by Bach's church and suitably atmospheric. *Csarda,* Schulstrasse 2, Hungarian, offers a lively time. *Falstaff,* Georgring 9, historic and popular spot. *Freyburger Weinstube,* Dr. Kurt Fischerstrasse 20, one of the best in a street full of good spots.

Theaters and Concerts. The controversial and monolithic new Leipzig *Gewandhaus* contains several concert halls and is the center of the city's outstanding musical life. Otherwise, the *Musikalische Komödie,* Dreilindenstrasse 30, and *Neues Opernhaus,* Karl-Marx Platz, for operetta and opera respectively, are the only places where you will not need to speak German to enjoy yourself. The principal drama theaters are the *Schauspielhaus,* Bösestrasse 1, the *Kammerspiele,* Gottschedstrasse 16, and the *Kellertheater im Neuen Opernhaus,* Karl-Marx Platz. There is a central theater box office at Sachsenplatz 1 (tel. 79590).

MUSEUMS. *Altes Rathaus* (Old Town Hall), Markt, houses the museum of city history. *Gohliser Schlösschen* (Gohliser House), Menckestrasse 23, houses the Bach archive. *Grassimuseum,* Johannesplatz 5–11, is a complex including the Museum of Arts and Crafts, Geographical Museum, and Musical Instruments Museum in a beautiful setting. *Georgi Dimitrov Museum,* Georgi-Dimitroff-Platz 1, houses the city's impressive art collection. *Exhibition Pavilion,* Leninstrasse 210, includes the vast diorama portraying the Battle of Leipzig in 1813; the nearby memorial commemorates the battle. *Schloss Dölitz,* Helenstrasse 24, shows historic tin soldiers, but is open only on Sunday mornings.

Three further places of interest are the St. Nikolai Church, Nikolaikirchhof, which dates from the 12th century; St. Thomas Church, Dittrichring, dating from the 13th century and where Bach, who is buried here, once worked; it is also the home of the renowned St. Thomas Choir; and the Zoo, Dr. Kurt Fischerstrasse.

Harz Mountains

The Harz is the best known of the mountain districts of central Germany. Apart from the splendid natural scenery, the area also has a number of extremely attractive towns, of which perhaps the best to visit is the delightful medieval town of Wernigerode, dominated by a marvelous castle. But Magdeburg, the largest town in the region, runs it a close second. Among its attractions is Germany's first Gothic cathedral, some fine Baroque houses and several theaters, including a puppet theater. Quedlinburg is also worth visiting and has some charming half-timbered houses among its winding lanes, and a fine cathedral. You should also visit the timber-framed houses of Halberstadt and Thale, whose immediate surroundings include the beautiful Bode Valley, the aptly-named Witches' Dancing Place (Hexentanzplatz) and the Harz mountain theater, which is reached by cable car.

In the southern Harz are Rübeland, which has a number of stalactite caves, and Stolberg, which boasts some fine Renaissance houses and a Baroque castle.

Accommodations throughout the area are very limited and you may well find it best to stay in Magdeburg and Wernigerode.

PRACTICAL INFORMATION FOR THE HARZ MOUNTAINS

Hotels and Restaurants

Magdeburg. *International,* an Interhotel—above the budget category.

Restaurants. Ample budget restaurants in (M) and (I) categories, such as *Bötelstube,* Alter Markt, good if basic, and *Rathauskeller,* Alter Markt 13, charming setting with a good variety of dishes and wines.

Wernigerode. *Weisser Hirsch* (I), Markt 5 (tel. 2434). H–O group. No rooms with bath, but pleasant. *Hotel zur Post* (I), Marktstrasse 17 (tel. 2436). Charming setting and inexpensive. *Zur Tanne* (I), Breitestrasse 59 (tel. 2554).

Restaurants. *Rathauskeller* (M), Markt 1. Probably the best place in town. *Eselskrug* (I), An der Malzmühle, *Harzland* (I), Schreiberstrasse 19, or *Zur bunten Stadt* (I), Breitestrasse 49.

Great Britain

Britain's standing as a budget vacationland changes from one year to the next, indeed from one month to the next. The dollar/pound rate of exchange has swung from $2 to $1 in the last few years, with every stop in between, which makes budgeting a trip in advance very tricky. But, whatever the financial problems, the mere facts that the natives speak English and that signs are fully comprehensible make life for the American visitor a lot simpler and keep Britain's popularity steady, however the pound in your pocket may gyrate.

Being able to speak the language without difficulty—in spite of the school of thought that says "English is a common language that divides us"—means that it is even easier to take advantage of the multitude of budget possibilities that Britain offers. Some simple rules might be of help. Visit mainline rail stations when the booking-hall staff isn't too busy and ask about the dozens of special offers they have—British Rail is legendary for complicating the cost of travel. Before you leave the United States, be sure to find out about Britrail Passes. You pay a fixed price for one, two, or three weeks or one month and, if you really like trains, you can cover 150 or 200 miles a day easily at a bargain price.

Use country buses when you are outside London. The fares have gone up in a way that seems diabolic to the British, but—as most of the buses are double-deckers—it is a magnificent way of seeing the rich countryside.

Sometimes it will be almost impossible to do without a car, but you will find that rental costs and gas prices are high compared with the United States. If you do have a car, though, you can save by sampling country inns and guesthouses.

Mix and match your lodgings. Vary nights in B&Bs with nights in moderate hotels. Your wallet will be content and you will see a lot more of local life that way. If you manage to wander outside London to enjoy the delights of the countryside, be prepared for a marked change in two things. Hotels will be less impersonal and more friendly, and prices will take a gentle nosedive. If you are lucky enough to find yourself in an oak-beamed bedroom that has a lumpy mattress, heating pipes that gurgle in the night, an asthmatic owl in a nearby tree, and ghostly creaks in the corridor, just tell yourself it's atmosphere. But be warned. Find out where the bathroom is before you go to bed. Many budget lodgings don't have them *en suite*.

Whether or not you are a hearty eater, try out all the alternative places to feed—especially pubs, where lunchtime meals are great value and don't need to be heavy. The landlord hopes you will buy drinks, so he keeps the price of the food down as a loss leader.

One thing we cannot stress too strongly is the budget advantage of visiting parts of Britain other than London. It's easy to get out of the city for a day or a weekend less expensive regions. Fast trains will speed you to the university cities of Oxford and Cambridge; to see the cathedrals of Canterbury, Winchester, and Salisbury; or even farther afield to York. Bath is just an hour distant from the capital.

Britain has become much more tourist conscious in the last few years. Many cities—York is a leading example—have gone out of their way to make it easy and interesting to visit them. They have dynamic, well-informed tourist offices, ever ready to help the passing guest with such things as accommodations, what to see, budget travel tips, where to eat, etc. There are tourist information centers virtually all over the country, and the highly recommended publications (often budget-oriented) of the national tourist boards for England, Scotland and Wales are on sale at these centers and in bookshops everywhere.

The further you go from London, the cheaper the lodging prices will be, and the same is true, though not to quite the same extent, with the cost of food. The southeast corner of England is the country's priciest area, though it does have the most extensive network of public transport and positively oozes historic sites. Besides, no visitor to Britain should miss the wild and spectacular scenery of Wales and Scotland, nor the warm hospitality of the Welsh and Scots.

PRACTICAL INFORMATION FOR GREAT BRITAIN

WHAT WILL IT COST. London now ranks with Tokyo as one of the world's most expensive hotel capitals. The cost of food in the shops and of meals in restaurants has risen considerably and public transport fares too take annual leaps. Add to this the current unfavorable exchange rate, and you'll see how quickly your money might trickle away. But with a bit of careful planning you should be able to stretch your budget a little further.

As we say, if you have enough time to play with, divide it between London and the rest of the country. The gulf between prices in London and outside the capital is very wide. Anyone visiting London would be well advised to shop around for a hotel—there are still some at reasonable prices, though few are in the dead center of town—and to check out a restaurant before going in, to be sure it lies within the scope of one's pocket.

A major factor of all vacations these days is the travel component—and in Britain this takes a front seat. Getting around is expensive in comparison with other countries. With this in mind you would be well advised to take full advantage of the many good-value reductions available, whether on train or coach, bus or subway. Always ask about possible cheap fares when buying your ticket. The various transit authorities are constantly coming up with new schemes, many of which will last for only a couple of months. And don't forget that some of the best budget tickets, such as BritRail Pass, can be purchased only outside Britain and will need a little planning before you leave home.

Travelers on a budget will be relieved to hear that most state-owned museums (in London, the vast majority) are free to visit. So are almost all churches and cathedrals although the cost of maintaining these magnificent buildings is nowadays so phenomenal, that you are often asked to leave a donation.

The cost of dining out in even moderate restaurants has risen exorbitantly but this has fortunately been balanced by the ever increasing number of fast food places, wine bars, and pubs with excellent food tables, which have sprung up around the country. And of course the ubiquitous Chinese and Indian restaurants are still hard to beat for satisfying meals and sheer value for money.

The monetary unit is the pound sterling, approximately $1.95 at the current rate of exchange. It is divided into 100 new pence often abbreviated to "p". There are banknotes of £50, £20, £10 and £5. Coins are £1, 50p, 20p, 10p and 5p, all cupro-nickel (jokingly called silver), and 2p and 1p, both copper. The old two-shilling and one-shilling pieces are still in use and are identical in size and equivalent in value to 10p and 5p pieces.

Sample costs (London). A cinema seat for one £4.50; moderate seat in a theater £9 (much higher for musicals); visit to a monument or stately home from £2 (remember that many museums are free); coffee 70p; beer—1 pint in a pub £1.15, glass in a moderate restaurant £1.25; house wine—by the glass in a pub £1.20, by the bottle (or carafe) in a moderate restaurant £6.50.

NATIONAL TOURIST OFFICE. The *London Tourist Board* (LTB) at Victoria Station in London has a large selection of brochures, booklets and general information on all aspects of tourism in London and the rest of England. Be warned that it can be very crowded. Many of their leaflets are free whilst their booklets are reasonably priced, usually ranging from around £1 to £4.95. While planning your trip, much helpful information on Britain is available from the *British Tourist Authority* at the British Travel Center, 12 Regent St., London SW1Y 4PQ. This provides a full information and reservation service for all parts of Britain, and has a useful bookshop that carries lots of practical guides to Britian, a souvenir shop and bureau de change. Information is also available from BTA offices in the U.S. and Canada (see below for details).

There are many accommodation guides published by the British Tourist Authority and by the English, Scottish and Welsh national tourist boards. Those published by the BTA are available by mail order in your own country (ask your local BTA office for details); those from the national tourist boards are available from the Victoria Tourist Information Center (for England) and the British Travel Center (for England, Scotland and Wales), as well as from individual tourist information centers throughout Britain. They give details of all possible types of accommodations, including hotels, guest houses, farmhouses, holiday cottages, hostels, caravan sites and campsites. Particularly useful for visitors on a budget is the publication *Let's Go,* which gives details of bargain two- and three-day breaks in hotels in the quieter seasons.

Every sizeable town and city of tourist interest has its own local information center. These centers display a sign saying 'Tourist Information' with a distinctive "i", and are usually open Mon.-Fri., 9–5. Some smaller centers are open only in the summer months, others, especially in seaside resorts or places of outstanding interest, are also open on Saturdays in summer. Many information centers also provide an accommodation reservation service.

Scotland and Wales have their own tourist boards and both publish similar literature on all aspects of tourism in their respective countries. For information on Wales write to the *Wales Tourist Board,* Brunel House, 2 Fitzalan Rd., Cardiff CF2 1UX. The London office of the Wales Tourist Board is at 34 Piccadilly, W1V 9PB. The *Scottish Tourist Board* is at 23 Ravelston Terrace, Edinburgh EH4 3EU, also 19 Cockspur St., London SW1Y 5BL.

The overseas addresses of the British Tourist Authority are:

In the U.S.: 40 West 57th St., New York, N.Y. 10019–4001 (tel. 212–581–4700); World Trade Center, 350 S. Figueroa St., Suite 450, Los Angeles, CA 90071 (tel. 213–628–3525); Suite 210, Cedar Maple Plaza, 2305 Cedar Springs Rd., Dallas, TX 75201 (tel. 214–720–4040); Suite 3320, John Hancock Center, 875 N. Michigan Ave., Chicago, IL 60611 (tel. 312–787–0490).

In Canada: 94 Cumberland St., Suite 600, Toronto, Ontario, M5R 3N3 (tel. 416–925–6326).

WHEN TO COME. Britain's weather is weird and wonderful. Folk memory has it that winters are rarely very cold and summers rarely very hot, but the last few years have seen long, hot summers, and muddled winter weather. Even in summer you should make sure you have some warm and thoroughly waterproof clothing with you. Rain is frequent in all seasons.

The traditional tourist season runs from mid-April to mid-October. Spring is the time to see the countryside at its freshest and most beautiful, and the fall colors can also be striking. In September and October the northern moorlands and Scottish highlands are at their best. May and June are probably the best holiday months, July and August being when most British families take their annual vacation; accommodations in many resorts are at a premium then, and Channel ferries to the Continent can well be booked solid. Theater and other entertainments are, by and large, year round, with almost every town holding a festival, which could fall at any time from Easter to September.

The off-season, late October through March, is in many ways an ideal time to come for budget vacationers. Many hotels throughout the country offer special packages for winter weekend breaks, often with 2 or 3 nights' accommodation for the price of one. Many concessionary fares are available on the rail and coach network throughout the country to promote travel in winter. Even if you do not take advantage of these special off-season reductions, you will still benefit from the greater choice of hotels with vacancies, especially in London where finding budget accommodations during July and August can be very difficult indeed. Remember that some hotels in seaside resorts and remoter country areas may close for the winter months.

Average afternoon temperatures in degrees Fahrenheit and centigrade:

London	Jan.	Feb.	Mar.	Apr.	May	June	July	Aug.	Sept.	Oct.	Nov.	Dec.
F°	43	45	49	55	62	68	71	70	65	56	49	45
C°	6	7	9	13	17	20	22	21	18	13	9	7
Edinburgh												
F°	43	43	47	50	55	62	65	64	60	53	47	44
C°	6	6	8	10	13	17	18	18	16	12	8	7

SPECIAL EVENTS. *January,* Burns night celebrations throughout Scotland on 25th. *February,* Cruft's Dog Show in London; pancake races throughout the country on Shrove Tuesday. *March,* in London the Ideal Home Exhibition at Earl's Court and the Oxford and Cambridge Universities' Boat Race on the Thames; Grand National Steeplechase at Liverpool; Easter Parade at London's Battersea Park. (The last three events can occur in early April, depending on when Easter falls.) *April,* Shakespeare's Birthday Celebrations at Stratford-upon-Avon on 23rd; Pitlochry Music and Drama Festival opens in Perthshire, Scotland (until end of Sept.).

May, Royal Horse Show at Windsor; Chelsea Flower Show in London; International Music Festival in Bath; Chichester Drama Festival (through Oct.). *June,* Glyndebourne Opera Season in Sussex (through Aug.) though tickets are way beyond the budget range; the Oaks and Derby horse races at Epsom, Surrey; international motorcycle races on the Isle of Man; Trooping the Colour in London for the Queen's birthday; Royal Ascot Race Meeting, 3rd week in June; Aldeburgh Music Festival in Suffolk; Lawn Tennis Championships at Wimbledon, London.

July, Royal Regatta at Henley-on-Thames, Oxfordshire; British Open Golf Championships, often held in Scotland; opening of Albert Hall Promenade Concerts in London (through Sept.); Tynwald Ceremony and Peel Viking Festival, Isle of Man, 1st week of July; Royal Welsh Agricultural Show at Builth Wells, 3rd week of July; Battle of Flowers at St Helier on the Isle of Jersey, last Thurs. in month; Royal International Horse Show at the National Exhibition Center, Birmingham. *August,* Edinburgh Music and Drama Festival, also the spectacular military tattoo; military tattoo in Colchester, Essex; Cowes Week, Isle of Wight, a big yachting event; Coracle Regatta at Cilgerran in Wales; Eisteddfod poetry and music festival in Wales; Highland games and gatherings all over Scotland.

September, Royal Highland gathering at Braemar in Scotland; St. Leger horse race at Doncaster, Yorkshire; "Last Night of the Proms", a traditional English institution at the Albert Hall, London. *October,* Nottingham Goose Fair (a huge fun fair) on first Thurs., Fri. and Sat.

November, Lord Mayor's Show in the City of London on second Sat.; London to Brighton Veteran Car Rally; on 5th, Guy Fawkes' Day celebrations all over the country, bonfires and firework displays; the Queen performs the State Opening of Parliament; laying of wreaths at the Cenotaph, Whitehall in London on Remembrance Sunday. *December,* celebrations for Christmas, including the Festivals of Carols at Ely cathedral, King's College, Cambridge, and St Martin's-in-the-Fields, Trafalgar Sq., London; Xmas lights in London's Regent St.; New Year's Eve Hogmanay celebrations in Scotland, and revelries in Trafalgar Sq., London.

National Holidays. *England and Wales:* Jan. 1; Mar. 29 (Good Friday); Apr. 1 (Easter Monday); May 6 (May Day Holiday); May 27 (Spring Bank Hol.); Aug. 26 (Summer Bank Hol.); Dec. 25, 26. *Scotland:* Jan. 1, 2; Mar. 29; May 6; May 27; Aug. 5; Dec. 25, 26.

VISAS. Not required for entry into Britain by American citizens, nationals of the British Commonwealth (except India, Pakistan, Bangladesh, Sri Lanka and some West African countries), and most European and South American countries.

HEALTH CERTIFICATES. Not required for entry to Britain.

There are *extremely rigid* controls on the importation of animals into Britain, caused by the rapid spread of rabies on the Continent. If you are likely to be taking animals into Britain (from the Continent or elsewhere), make very sure you have checked on the quarantine (*always* 6 months) and other regulations.

GETTING TO BRITAIN. By Plane. London's Heathrow Airport is the busiest international airport in the world—and Gatwick the fourth busiest. This means that London is one of the easiest places to reach by air. From North America there are currently 15 airlines (mainly scheduled) that operate into London flying from 16 U.S. cities and 8 in Canada, either on non-stop or through-flight routes. *Air Canada* flies into Prestwick (Glasgow) from Montreal, Toronto, Halifax, Winnipeg, Calgary and Vancouver.

About the best bargains going at the time of writing (Easter 1990) were the *Virgin Atlantic* flights from New York (Newark) to London (Gatwick). But check on all fares and services before booking.

Getting from U.K. Airports to City and Town Centers. There are good reliable bus services from all international and almost all regional airports into town. These services operate throughout the day, but with varying frequencies according to flights. They are inexpensive and are *always* much cheaper than taxis.

In London, Heathrow is linked to the city center by the Piccadilly Line of the Underground (subway) taking about 40 to 45 minutes, with trains every five to 15 minutes according to day and time of day. London Regional Transport runs an Airbus express bus service into Central London. Fares are double those on the Underground. Buses leave from each terminal and take about an hour to reach their destinations: A1 goes to Victoria Rail Station, A2 to Euston, calling at several stops en route convenient to all London's main hotel areas. Airbus and Underground cease after about midnight, but L.R.T.'s N97 Night Bus runs hourly 12 to 5 A.M. from Heathrow into Central London.

From Gatwick airport there is a direct British Rail train link with London's Victoria Station, four trains an hour between 5.20 A.M. and midnight and one every hour through the night. The trip takes 30 minutes, but be warned that long lines form at the ticket counter, so either be prepared to wait or purchase your ticket through British Rail offices in the U.S. before you leave home.

By Boat. The U.K. is linked to Europe by a network of ferries owned by *Sealink-British Ferries, P&O European Ferries, Danish Seaways, Brittany Ferries, Olau Line, Sally Viking Line* and *North Sea Ferries.* They operate from 15 ports. In addition the hovercraft services of *Hoverspeed* operate from Dover to Calais and Boulogne, plus the passenger only *Jetfoil* service from Dover to Oostende. The ferry routes serve 20 ports on the Continent. To the Republic of Ireland there are several ferry routes operating across the Irish Sea.

CUSTOMS. There are two levels of duty-free allowance for people entering the U.K.; one, for goods bought outside the EC or for goods bought in a duty-free shop within the EC; two, for goods bought in an EC country but not in a duty-free shop.

In the first category you may import duty free: 200 cigarettes or 100 cigarillos or 50 cigars or 250 grams of tobacco plus one liter of alcoholic drinks over 22% vol. (38.8° proof) or two liters of alcoholic drinks not over 22% vol. or fortified or sparkling wine; plus two liters of still table wine; plus 50 grams of perfume; plus nine fluid ounces of toilet water; plus other goods to the value of £32.

In the second category you may import duty free: 300 cigarettes or 150 cigarillos or 75 cigars or 400 grams of tobacco; plus 1½ liters of alcoholic drinks over 22% vol. (38.8° proof) or three liters of alcoholic drinks not over 22% vol. or fortified or sparkling wine; plus five liters of still table wine; plus 75 grams of perfume; plus 13 fluid ounces of toilet water; plus other goods to the value of £250 (*Note* though it is not classified as an alcoholic drink by EC countries for Customs' purposes and is thus considered part of the "other goods" allowance, you may not import more than 50 liters of beer).

In addition, no animals or pets of any kind may be brought into the U.K. The penalties for doing so are severe and are strictly enforced; there are *no* exceptions. Similarly, fresh meats, plants and vegetables, controlled drugs and firearms and ammunition may not be brought into the U.K. There are no restrictions on the import or export of British and foreign currencies.

HOTELS. Nightly rates may be quoted either per person to include bed and breakfast, or on a room basis with breakfast charged extra for each occupant. Traditionally British hotel prices should include breakfast but some hotels now offer room-only rates, and even more hotels, particularly in London, now serve only Continental breakfast instead of the traditional English breakfast. Be sure to clarify this when you check in. A hotel that includes English breakfast in its rates is usually a good budget bet: a substantial breakfast means you need only buy a light lunch, and you will find that unlike the U.S. not many cafés or restaurants serve breakfast.

British hotels with at least four bedrooms or eight beds are obliged to display on the reception desk an explanation of their rates. Study it carefully. Remember also that rates in June, July and August can be as much as 30% higher than in other seasons. Rooms without private bath, and there are many of these in the older hotels, are obviously much cheaper. If a service charge is included with the price of your room this must be clearly stated. Most budget hotels are in older buildings and you may well find that your room does not have a private bathroom, though there should always be a wash basin. The nearest shower or bathtub and the toilet will usually be just down the hall, but check on this before you take the room, there are some hotels that send you on a marathon before you locate their facilities!

Our hotel suggestions in this book fall into two categories, *Moderate* (M) and *Inexpensive* (I). In the *Moderate* category, expect to pay between £35 and £50 and in *Inexpensive,* up to £35. These prices are for two people sharing a double room, and include breakfast. They apply to hotels in the provinces only. Hotel prices in London are substantially higher—our (M) category covers the £40–£60 range, with (I) at under £40. Some hotels also add a service charge to your bill; where this is the case, they must say so when the offer of accommodation is made.

Remember that just because you are staying in a hotel does not mean you always have to eat there, in fact many of our (I) selections are B&B establishments that serve only breakfast. Sometimes it will be more convenient—and certainly cheaper—to pick up a snack of fish and chips, a pizza or a Chinese meal elsewhere.

Remember too, that during the off-season many good hotels offer bargain two or three-day package deals. Terms are usually for full or half board only. These are an excellent way of staying in some of Britain's better hotels and beauty spots at a not too exorbitant price. For details see the British Tourist Authority's publication *Let's Go,* available free from BTA offices overseas.

Guest Houses and Bed-and-Breakfast. These are where Britain really scores for the budget traveler. Whereas hotel prices tend to be high, these offer some excellent value accommodations and at the same time afford the foreign visitor a good glimpse of the British way of life. These budget accommodations are generally small and family run. They are often without private bathrooms and dining facilities other than for breakfast. Guest houses are the larger of the two, and may well have a comfortable lounge with television, but usually no bar; bed and breakfast places are almost always in private homes where accommodation is offered for the night in spare bedrooms with a shared bathroom and dining room. With guest houses you can book your stay in advance and often choose whether or not to have an evening meal. With bed and breakfast it is more common simply to drop in when you arrive. A "B&B" sign is displayed in the house window or on a board at the garden gate.

Booking Services. Many of the 700 Tourist Information Centers in Britain offer a local accommodations service for a fee of around £1 (in England; free in Scotland, Wales and Northern Ireland). Many also participate in the "Book-A-Bed-Ahead" scheme where, for a small fee, they will reserve accommodations for you in any town with a center participating in the scheme.

Holiday Homes. These can be rented in all parts of Britain and vary from quaint old cottages or cleverly-converted farm buildings to modern houses and apartments, situated in town or countryside. The BTA publishes two booklets, *Holiday Homes,* which lists properties for rental throughout Britain, and *Apartments in London* for accommodations in the capital. Both are available free from your local BTA office. The national tourist boards for England, Scotland and Wales also produce books listing properties, and these can be purchased from bookshops and tourist information centers throughout Britain. For parties and families visiting Britain, holiday-home rental is by far the best value-for-money accommodation, though bear in mind that you can be tied down to one location for a week. Prices range from about £100 to £350 per week, depending on location and time of year, but remember that this is the cost for the whole party, not per person, with only food to pay for on top. Great savings can be made by renting between October and March, as much as 50 per cent, particularly if you book for two nights or more.

Staying on a Farm. Farmhouses offering accommodations with breakfast and sometimes an evening meal are listed in the NTB's *Where to Stay* books. Prices range from around £80 per person per week for bed, breakfast and evening meal. *The Farm Holiday Bureau,* National Agricultural Center, Stoneleigh, Kenilworth, Warwickshire CV8 2LZ (tel. 0203–696909), working in conjunction with the national tourist boards, provides information on farm holidays throughout the country and can book your farm holiday for you. Ask your BTA office for the free leaflet *Farmhouse Vacations,* which gives full details. *Stay on a Farm* published by the BTA also lists farms where you can go for a working holiday. The Wales Tourist Board runs a special Farmhouse Award scheme. Awards are made only to farms meeting the Board's high standards.

Youth Hostels. There are approximately 350 Youth Hostels throughout England, Wales and Scotland. Some are very basic, some very good indeed; many are located in remote areas of great natural beauty. Despite their name there is no restriction on age of visitors. Their accommodation is cheap and reliable, and usually they provide meals or catering facilities. For further details contact the *YHA Headquarters.* Trevelyan House, 8 St Stephen's Hill, St Albans, Herts AL1 2DY (tel. 0727–55215) for England and Wales, and the Scottish Youth Hostel Association, 7 Glebe Crescent, Stirling, FK8 2JA (tel. 0786–51181), for places north of the border. The *Campus Travel Service,* 14 Southampton St, London WC2E 7HY (tel. 071–836 8541) can also provide information for those under 26 only. Prices are very low. Even the London rate is under £7 a night, less if you are under 21.

Student Halls of Residence. Accommodation is often available for groups and individuals during vacations, usually in smart, well equipped single or double rooms on various university campuses around the country. Cost per night is from around £12 per person. For details write to *British Universities Accommodation Consortium,* Box 486, University Park, Nottingham NG7 2RD (tel. 0602–504571).

Camping. If you have your own tent, obviously it is cheaper to bring it with you, but you can also hire one once in Britain. Britain has many camping sites ranging from large, well-equipped ones often attached to caravan sites, to small fields with primitive facilities belonging to the local farmer. The BTA in your own country will provide details, or else contact the *Camping and Caravan Club,* 11 Lower Grosvenor Place, London SW1W OEY (tel. 071–828 1012). Camp and caravan sites are also listed in the English, Scottish and Welsh tourist boards' camping and caravan booklets.

RESTAURANTS. Britain now offers a wide range of international restaurants with an exciting choice of dining—much of it in the budget area. Unfortunately, restaurants serving traditional British fare are few and far between, and where such places exist they tend to be rather pricey.

Most restaurants display their menu in the window and it is vital to check their prices before you go in. Remember to make sure whether or not VAT (Value Added Tax) is included in the listed price; this should always be stated on the menu. Many restaurants make a service charge of between 10 and 15%. Another point to bear in mind for budget considerations is that a lot of restaurants add a cover charge on top of service and VAT. This is a flat charge of around 80p to £1.20 per person.

Wine served in restaurants is much more expensive than that bought from a store, but as very few restaurants allow you to bring your own bottle, you won't have much choice in the matter. Remember that house wine is cheaper than listed wines and can often be bought by the glass. Always remember that liquor inflates a check enormously, and if you are trying to stick to a tight budget, go easy on the drinks.

The sort of restaurants to look for in the budget range are French or Italian bistros, often with their menus written up on a blackboard; Greek, or possibly Israeli or Lebanese, kebab houses; Indian curry houses and Chinese restaurants. These latter two can be found in even the smallest town and are extremely good value for money. Their prices are generally lower than European restaurants and as you will probably prefer to drink lager beer with your curry or jasmin tea with your chop suey, you will not be paying for expensive bottles of wine to send your bill rocketing. Cheaper Chinese restaurants tend to serve Cantonese; the Peking-style restaurants are usually more expensive. Many offer good-value 3-course business lunches and fixed price menus in general are becoming more widespread. Both offer a good filling meal at affordable prices.

As a general guide, a 3-course dinner in the sort of restaurant mentioned above, should work out, per person (excluding drinks), at £8–£15 in the Moderate (M) category, and under £8 in Inexpensive (I). In London prices will be higher (see page 257). If this seems a bit expensive for your everyday budget, try some of the suggestions below.

Wine Bars. These are now popular throughout the country and are open at lunchtime and in the evening. You are not obliged to eat there but they usually offer a selection of cold dishes and hot savory snacks; good cheese board and selection of pâtés, chile con carne, vegetable hotpot, and a wide variety of salads.

Pubs. Here is your chance to try something typically British. Most pubs now provide food as well as drink, especially at lunchtime. Prices are competitive as the publican expects you to drink as well as eat, and this is where he makes his money.

Pub lunches can be had for £1.50 to £3. Try a ploughman's lunch (crusty bread, Cheddar cheese, pickled onion or sweet pickle); veal and ham pie; steak and kidney pie; or bangers (long meaty sausages) and mash.

Quick Food. Cheapest of all are the take-away sandwich bars open at lunchtime in every town. Many also serve hot meat pies and sausage rolls. *McDonalds, Burger King* and *Wendys* will be familiar to Americans. McDonalds are the best established, with hundreds of branches throughout the country. Greek doner kebab houses and Chinese take-outs are also plentiful and provide good light inexpensive meals though possibly somewhat tricky to eat outside your hotel room.

There are plenty of pizza houses all over Britain. They have the advantage of offering cheap meals (a pizza costs £2.50–£4) in a restaurant atmosphere. They are mostly licensed. Of the London chains *Pizza Express* is probably best for décor, *Pizza Hut* for variety and *Pizzaland* for real budget bargains.

Fish and Chips. No visit to Britain would be complete without your tasting this greatest of all English traditions: fish deep fried in batter and good solid English chips, no fancy French fries. It costs from £1.25 upwards depending on the kind of fish you choose, quite a lot more in London. Fish and chip shops are usually found in the suburbs and side streets rather than in the city center. They are open at lunchtime and again in the evening from around 5 P.M. to 11 P.M. Closed on Sundays.

Transport Cafés. For a real glimpse of traditional British life and food, try a visit to a transport café where truckers eat. Elegant they aren't, but they are cheap and lots of fun. Ideal for such traditional delights as steak and kidney pud, toad-in-the-hole (a baked sausage-and-egg dish), and bangers and mash.

Motorway cafeterias have improved slighty in recent years, though in terms of value for money you'll still do better if you take sandwiches or look for a country pub off an exit road.

Food and Drink. Many of Britain's traditional specialties like fish and chips, steak and kidney pudding; and bangers and mash have been mentioned above and there is no doubt that these sort of things are usually best in pubs. A few other traditional dishes should still be mentioned. If you want roast beef and Yorkshire pudding with horseradish sauce (or even roast lamb and mint sauce), best find a family to ask you to lunch on Sunday. Failing that, try your hotel or look for some of the *Carveries* that offer fixed price menus. Beef prices are now so high, that roast beef is no longer the traditional Sunday staple it once was; it can still be found, but avoid restaurants that serve it too cheaply; the quality is likely to be poor.

For a good English breakfast you'll do better outside London, and the best are often those served in simple guest houses. You should try porridge—a Scottish cereal of oats served hot with milk and sugar—and kippers—a smoked herring that is a traditional breakfast food. Marmalade made from Seville oranges is still a real British tradition at breakfast time.

Cockles, winkles and jellied eels are a Cockney specialty and can be bought in pubs or off stalls in the East End of London. Around Petticoat Lane market on a Sunday morning is a good time to find them.

As with the traditional Sunday roast, typical puddings like jam roly-poly and custard, rhubarb crumble, rice pudding or treacle tart, are probably best found in hotels (or else transport cafés). Restaurants serving these at budget prices cannot always be recommended though you will find superb British food in the few upmarket traditional British restaurants, inn diningrooms and some small establishments outside London.

As for drinks, the first thing we should stress is that ice is still not used as commonly as in the United States. If you like your beer cold, you'll have to ask for it specifically. The beer from the pumps can be lukewarm. Beer is generally dark in color, warm and much stronger than American beer. There's bitter, mild, brown ale, light ale, stout and Guinness. If you want a lighter, more American-type beer, try lager. Many pubs now stock a British version of American brands like Budweiser. Cider (the alcoholic kind), shandy (beer and lemonade) and lager-and-lime are other typical drinks. American-type cocktails are found in hotel and cocktail bars but not in many pubs.

The liquor laws have been changed, and now allow restaurants to serve alcohol with food throughout the afternoon. Pubs, too, are now allowed to stay open throughout the afternoon, though not all of them take advantage of this. At present, hours vary from region to region; at the longest they are open Mon. to Sat. 11–11, and Sun. 12–2 and 7–10.30. The legal age for drinking alcohol is 18; in England and Wales young people between 14 and 17 are allowed in pubs as long as they stick to soft drinks; in Scotland no one under 18 is allowed in a bar, but most Scottish pubs are open all day from 11 A.M. to 11 P.M.

TIPPING. Some hotels add a service charge to the bill, though this is not common in the budget range. Otherwise tipping for a short stay in a budget hotel is not really necessary. Tip bellboys and doormen calling you a cab, about 50p, more if you have a lot of luggage. In guest houses and bed and breakfast it is not normal to tip. Most restaurants will add a service charge of between 10 and 15% to the bill. If they don't, leave 10%. In cafés or tearooms, 40p will usually do. Don't tip for coffees or when drinking in a pub; if the barman has been particularly friendly, offer to buy him a drink. Tip taxi drivers about 10%, barbers about 50 p, hairdressers 50p–£1 (more in London). Unlike most European countries restroom attendants in Britain rarely expect a tip (those that do set out a saucer for your 10p.) Nor do cinema or theater ushers or gas station attendants (unless they check your water, oil and tires). Railroad porters get about 50p per bag, though they are rarely available. Be prepared to help yourself to a luggage cart at both rail stations and airports.

MAIL. Current rates for airmail letters up to 10 grams to the U.S. and Canada, 34p; postcards 29p, aerogrammes 30p. Letters and postcards to Europe not over 20 grams, 24p (20p to EC member countries). Letters within U.K., first class, 20p; second class and postcards, 15p. These rates will increase by early 1991.

TELEPHONES. Please note that the new London codes—071 and 081—came into use in May 1990, and they have to be used *within* London. If you are calling an 071 number from within that zone, then you do not dial the code, and the same for 081. But you will have to dial 081 from an 071 phone and vice versa.

CLOSING TIMES. Shops do not usually close for lunch, except in small country towns or villages, and are open from 9 to 5.30. They close at about 1 P.M. on one weekday (Early Closing Day) that varies from town to town. Most shops in central London stay open all day, 6 days a week, with one late evening, usually Wednesday or Thursday, till 7.30 or 8. All large stores and most small shops are closed on Sunday.

Banks are generally open from 9.30 to 3.30, Monday to Friday, closed Sunday, with slight variations in Scotland. A few branches now open (with restricted service) from 9.30 to 12 on Saturdays. The automated teller machine (ATM) has revolutionized the way Britian Banks.

GETTING AROUND BRITAIN. By Train. British Rail have their own information offices in New York, Los Angeles, Chicago, Vancouver and Toronto. If you intend to do a lot of traveling the *BritRail Pass* or the *BritRail Youth Pass* is a good budget bet giving you unlimited travel on Britain's railroads (and some bus and ferry routes) for periods of 8, 15, 22 days or one month. The *Silver Pass* (standard class) costs $189, $285, $359, and $415 respectively. There is also a *Flexipass* valid for any 4 days out of 8, 8 out of 15, and 15 out of a month at $159, $229, and $329 respectively. There are Senior Citizen (over 60s) and Youth (16–25) versions of all these tickets at lower cost. They *must* be obtained before you leave the U.S.

In London information can be obtained from British Rail Travel Center at 14 Kingsgate Parade, Victoria St., SW1E 6SH, from major stations and from the British Travel Centre, 12 Regent St., SW1Y 4PQ. Ask at the Travel Centers or Information windows at stations to see what the latest offers are. Always ask about special deals *before* you buy your ticket. Bargains can often be had by purchasing your ticket up to 24 hours in advance. One good budget tip worth bearing in mind is that if you travel outside the rush hours, you can often find a means of doing so at reduced cost. Although British Rail has made a number of attempts at simplifying its fare system, it remains fairly complex. The best advice is to check carefully at any station or travel agency before buying your ticket to make sure you are getting the best deal.

By Bus. This is the most economical form of public transport, fares being about half the price of rail travel, and the network is extensive, radiating outwards from Victoria Coach Station in London. *National Express* is the main carrier in England and Wales and *Scottish Omnibuses* in Scotland. Following government deregulation, there are considerable, and increasing, numbers of private bus operators offering competitively-priced services throughout Britain.

The best runabout ticket for overseas visitors is the *BritExpress Card,* which entitles you to up to one-third off standard fares for any number of journeys made during 30 consecutive days on all National Express services in England and Wales, selected services to and within Scotland, and some other services by associated companies. Buy it in advance from travel agents in your own country or on presentation of your passport, from Victoria Coach Station, Buckingham Palace Rd., London SW1 9TP, or from the *Scottish Coach Travel Centre,* 298 Regent St., W1R 6LE, or from *Campus Travel at YHA,* 14 Southampton St., WC2E 7HY. It can also be purchased from main bus stations in Glasgow and Edinburgh and from *YHA Travel* offices in Birmingham, Cambridge, Cardiff and Manchester.

Holders of international student cards (ISIC) are entitled to discounts of around a third on all long-distance fares.

Note that in England and Wales, the word "coach" is used for long-distance buses. Local bargain fares on buses and coaches include *Explorer* round trip tickets and *Runabout/Rover* tickets. Further information is available from National Express Information Office, Victoria Coach Station, Buckingham Palace Rd., London SW1 9TP, or for Scotland, from *Scottish Omnibuses Ltd.,* Buchanan Bus Station, Killermont St., Glasgow; or contact any local bus or coach station. Many of these have travel centers that can advise on tours, excursions and package holidays by coach.

By Bicycle. Cycling is now popular again and you won't have any trouble finding places to rent a bike in most towns, including London. Any cycle shop or Tourist Information Center will direct you to the nearest rental firm, or look in Yellow

Pages. Cost is from £8 to £10 a day (plus a fairly hefty deposit). If you are planning a cycle tour, and can arrange things well ahead, contact the British Tourist Authority in your own country—they can give you details of cycling holidays and rental firms. Good news for budgeteers, British Rail will carry bicycles free of charge (except on InterCity 125 trains and certain trains into London) so you can get to your chosen region at the cost of only the fare (and a reduced one at that!).

By Boat. There are over 1500 miles of navigable rivers and canals in Britain and the BTA in your own country or the English Tourist Board can help with details of holidays on these inland waterways such as hiring a motor launch on the Norfolk Broads or a barge for a canal trip on the Grand Union Canal. Or you can contact the *British Waterways Board,* Melbury House, Melbury Terr., London NW1 6JX (tel. 071–262 6711).

On Foot. Many organizations run group walking holidays during the summer months and these are especially popular in the Welsh mountains and other beauty spots such as the Lake District and Exmoor and Dartmoor. Luggage is usually transferred from camp to camp by Land Rover or pack horse. Details from the British Tourist Authority who will send you a free booklet.

HISTORIC MONUMENTS. Many historic houses, gardens and monuments throughout Britain give free entry to holders of *Great British Heritage* tickets. These are especially designed for overseas visitors and give entry to over 600 attractions, and can be bought from your travel agent or British rail agent, or at the British Travel Centre, 12 Regent Street, London SW1Y 4PQ, on production of a non-British passport. Cost for a month £24, £16 for 15 days (no reduction for children).

London

London is one of the most fascinating cities in the world, a conglomeration of villages that have brought nearly 7 million souls together in a vast metropolis. Discovering London becomes more exciting and rewarding in exact ratio to the amount of time you can put into researching the city. There's historical fascination hidden at every street corner, in the pub and road names, in the carved facades, in the luxuriant parks, in the galleries and museums.

Piccadilly Circus is the hub of London, ablaze with lights; it is the Times Square of London and shares a few of Times Square's more sordid characteristics. Eastward, along Coventry Street, you'll come to Leicester Square, now a pedestrian precinct. In the center of the square is a marble William Shakespeare, and, to the western side, an appealing statue of Charlie Chaplin and a booth selling half-price theater tickets for that day's performance only.

Westwards from Piccadilly Circus is Piccadilly itself, home of airline offices, hotels and expensive shops such as Simpson's and Fortnum and Mason's. Wren's Church of St. James and the Royal Academy, home of many prestigious art exhibitions, are other landmarks. The Burlington Arcade, a fascinating covered arcade of luxury shops, leads off to the north and a little further on is Bond Street(Old and New), one of London's most exclusive shopping streets.

Leading from Piccadilly on the south side is St. James's Street, a special world of men's clubs and shops. Don't miss the William IV street lamps in Little St. James's Street and the great houses bordering St. James's Park, a perfect place for strolling on a spring or summer's day. Near Horse Guards Parade the bunker from which Churchill commanded World War II operations is open to visitors. At the other end of the Park is Buckingham Palace dominated at the front by an elaborate memorial to Queen Victoria. The wide sweep of the forecourt in front of the Palace is the scene of the spectacular Changing of the Guard held every morning from May to July and every other day during the rest of the year. So long as you can fight your way through the crowds and contrive to see over the heads of those taller than yourself, this traditional pageant provides an excellent opportunity for budget—free!—sightseeing.

Houses of Parliament and Westminster Abbey

At the far end of St. James's Park from Buckingham Palace lies Westminster, encompassing one of London's major tourist sights, Westminster Abbey, and the Houses of Parliament and Whitehall, administrative center of Britain. Westminster Abbey, founded in 1050, is where all but two of England's kings and queens have been crowned since Saxon Harold in 1066. Many of them are also buried here. Don't miss Poets' Corner, memorial area of poets from Chaucer to Kipling, nor the monuments to great statesmen like Disraeli and Gladstone and scientists Newton and Darwin. Be sure to see the Henry VIII chapel, a gem of Tudor architecture, and the Coronation Chair of Edward I.

Across the square lie the impressive Houses of Parliament built between 1840 and 1860 in imposing Victorian Gothic style. London's most popular landmark, the 320-foot clock tower known affectionately as Big Ben, dominates the Palace of Westminster. For millions all over the world the chimes of Big Ben speak with the very voice of Britain. A visit to the Strangers' Gallery of either the House of Commons or the House of Lords is recommended for an insight into the workings of British parliamentary democracy. Tickets are available from your embassy.

Whitehall is the wide avenue that runs from Parliament Square up to Trafalgar Square. It is lined with pompous government buildings and in the center, the Cenotaph commemorates the dead of two world wars. Downing Street, with the Prime Minister's house at no. 10, stands unobtrusively off to the left; notice the Horse Guards a little higher up, and further up on the right is the Banqueting Hall where King Charles I was beheaded in 1649. His statue stands at the top of Whitehall looking towards the place where he died.

Trafalgar Square

Trafalgar Square, commemorating Nelson's defeat of the French fleet at the Battle of Trafalgar in 1805, is dominated by a statue of that naval hero, three times life-size, on the top of a column 185 feet high. There are as many pigeons here as there are in St. Mark's Square in Venice, and they're just as photogenic and even dirtier.

The National Gallery, on the north side, is one of the world's great art collections, while tucked into its right-hand side, opposite the beautiful church of St. Martin in the Fields, is the National Portrait Gallery, unbeatable for an insight into the British character.

Above St. Martin's in the Fields comes St. Martin's Lane, where the Coliseum, home of the English National Opera stands, close to a series of little alleyways, crowded with fascinating secondhand bookshops.

To the west is the Charing Cross Road, good for bookshops, and beyond that lies Soho, full of sex shops, porno movie houses, delicatessens, restaurants and pubs, altogether a sleazy, vibrant atmosphere, which finally erupts in the maelstrom of Piccadilly Circus.

Covent Garden and the Strand

To the east of St. Martin's Lane you will come into a labyrinth of small streets full of trendy shops and eating places, that lead eventually to the old Covent Garden Market, once the central fruit and vegetable market for London. It has sprung back to life after years of neglect and is one of London's most fascinating areas to explore. The *My Fair Lady* church of St. Paul's stands on one side of the market buildings and Covent Garden Opera House on another. It is a neighborhood that repays the hours spent wandering around its narrow streets. Craft shops and wine bars rub shoulders with up-market boutiques open till late in the evening and the whole place is alive with musicians, mime shows, Punch and Judy and the like. Below the Opera House are the London Transport Museum—great for the kids—and the Theatre Museum.

In the Strand, you might drop in at Somerset House, which has recently become the home of the Courtauld Institute's collection of art, especially worth seeing for

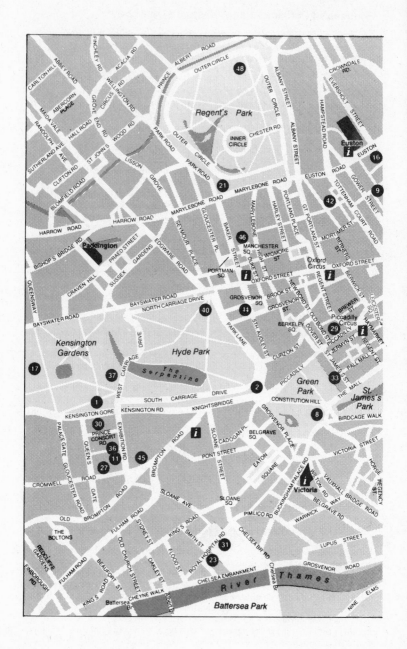

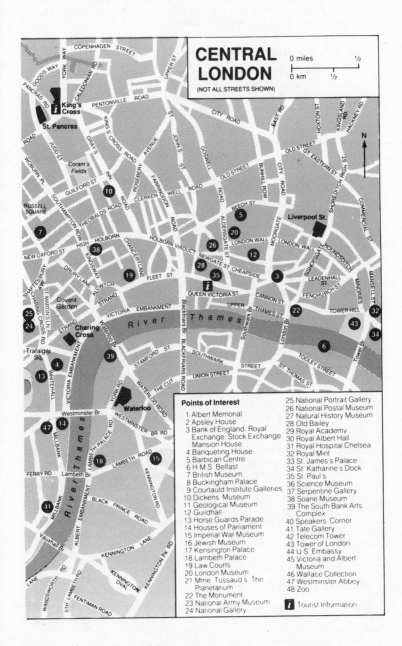

CENTRAL LONDON

(NOT ALL STREETS SHOWN)

0 miles ½
0 km ½

Points of Interest

1 Albert Memorial
2 Apsley House
3 Bank of England; Royal Exchange; Stock Exchange; Mansion House
4 Banqueting House
5 Barbican Centre
6 H M S Belfast
7 British Museum
8 Buckingham Palace
9 Courtauld Institute Galleries
10 Dickens Museum
11 Geological Museum
12 Guildhall
13 Horse Guards Parade
14 Houses of Parliament
15 Imperial War Museum
16 Jewish Museum
17 Kensington Palace
18 Lambeth Palace
19 Law Courts
20 London Museum
21 Mme Tussaud's The Planetarium
22 The Monument
23 National Army Museum
24 National Gallery

25 National Portrait Gallery
26 National Postal Museum
27 Natural History Museum
28 Old Bailey
29 Royal Academy
30 Royal Albert Hall
31 Royal Hospital Chelsea
32 Royal Mint
33 St James's Palace
34 St Katharine's Dock
35 St Paul's
36 Science Museum
37 Serpentine Gallery
38 Soane Museum
39 The South Bank Arts Complex
40 Speakers' Corner
41 Tate Gallery
42 Telecom Tower
43 Tower of London
44 U.S. Embassy
45 Victoria and Albert Museum
46 Wallace Collection
47 Westminster Abbey
48 Zoo

i Tourist Information

its Impressionist works. At the Fleet Street end of the Strand are the Law Courts, and slightly to the east lie the Inns of Court, Gray's and Lincoln's, and the Middle and Inner Temple, havens of medieval peace.

The City and St. Paul's Cathedral

The City, underneath which lies the original Roman London, can be entered in the west at Temple Bar in the Strand. The City of London, the financial district similar to New York's Wall Street, covers exactly one square mile and its limits are marked everywhere by a statue of a griffin. Fleet Street was once the headquarters of some of Britain's newspapers (though they have all moved now to other parts of London), and journalists being a thirsty lot, there are several good wine bars and pubs here, notably El Vino's, The Cock, and Ye Olde Cheshire Cheese. Up Ludgate Hill looms the imposing edifice of St. Paul's Cathedral, surrounded by modern office blocks that have risen from the ashes of the most bomb-devastated area in the City. St. Paul's is the second largest church in the world after St. Peter's in Rome. This ambitious Baroque structure (365 feet high, 515 feet long, with a nave 125 feet wide) was completed in 1711 when its architect Christopher Wren was nearly 90. Scene of the Royal Wedding, in 1981, it contains an effigy of the poet John Donne, the tombs of the Duke of Wellington, Nelson and Christopher Wren, an impressive whispering gallery and an American Memorial Chapel.

Just to the north of St. Paul's is the vast Barbican redevelopment with its attractive modern Museum of London illustrating 2,000 years of London's history, and its splendid arts complex—the Barbican Centre—opened in 1982.

The narrow streets of the City and Cheapside, Cornhill and Leadenhall Street, are somber with great banking houses, insurance companies, shipping offices, the Stock Exchange, the Bank of England, the Royal Exchange and Lloyds. Don't miss the Monument commemorating the Great Fire of London, which broke out in Pudding Lane in 1666. There is a breathtaking view from the top if you can manage all those dark spiral stairs.

The Tower of London

Started about 1078 under William the Conqueror, the White Tower or central keep of the Tower of London is one of the oldest buildings in the capital. Once a palace, this fortress-like Norman building became a prison, its history one of imprisonment, execution and murder. Among the scores of famous people who were beheaded here were Sir Thomas More, two of Henry VIII's wives (Anne Boleyn and Catherine Howard) and that versatile favorite of Queen Elizabeth, the Earl of Essex. Elizabeth herself was imprisoned here by Bloody Mary (her sister), and Sir Walter Raleigh spent 13 years in the Tower, working on his *History of the World.* The axe that severed so many distinguished heads can still be seen but you will probably prefer the dazzling splendor of the Crown Jewels and the Yeomen Warders of the Tower ("Beefeaters"), resplendent in their Tudor-style uniforms.

After visiting the Tower make a short stop at the nearby St. Katharine's Dock, a delightful renovated dock complete with tourist shops, boats and the atmospheric Dickens Inn. The latest attraction in this area is the Tower Bridge walkway; a museum and walkway high over the world-famous Tower Bridge.

Bloomsbury and Oxford Street

Bloomsbury is London's student quarter, dominated by the white pile of the University of London building on Malet Street. It is a district of neat squares—Russell, Bedford, Woburn and Bloomsbury—with their towering trees. The focal point is the British Museum, housing one of the world's truly great collections.

Crossing westward over busy Tottenham Court Road, you will come to Oxford Street with its great department stores, Selfridges, John Lewis and others, and its multitude of clothes shops including such budget favorites as Marks and Spencer and C&A.

Hyde Park, Kensington and Chelsea

At the far end of Oxford Street you come to Marble Arch and Hyde Park, which offers 361 acres of grass, fine trees and flowers; Rotten Row where the elite ride; and the Serpentine where you can go rowing. Speakers' Corner near Marble Arch is a London institution. Here on Sundays, orators on soap boxes hold forth on every subject under the sun. Beyond Hyde Park lie Kensington Gardens in one corner of which is Kensington Palace, home of the Prince and Princess of Wales and Princess Margaret. To the west of the palace lie the shopping areas of Kensington High Street and the antique shops of Kensington Church Street. On the south side of the park are the ornate Albert Memorial and the great dome of the Royal Albert Hall. South of them are the Science Museum, Museum of Natural History and, above all, the Victoria and Albert Museum, with its vast collections of furniture, jewelry, musical instruments, costumes and much, much more.

Not far away is elegant Knightsbridge, London's most exclusive shopping district, with, of course, that most famous of all stores, Harrods. Chelsea lies a little to the south alongside the river Thames. Once an artists' colony, the area is now given over to boutiques and wine bars, but there are some pleasant streets, notably Cheyne Row and Cheyne Walk. Try to visit the Chelsea Hospital, built by Christopher Wren as a home for disabled warriors, who are known as Chelsea pensioners. The King's Road is the main thoroughfare, lined with dress shops and antique galleries, and playing host to a bizarre throng of the latest way-out styles on weekends.

London Villages—Greenwich, Hampstead and Richmond

If you have time, some interesting half-day excursions can be made to Greenwich in the southeast to see the Maritime Museum, the Cutty Sark tea clipper and the Royal Observatory close to which the Greenwich Meridian passes. Nearby Blackheath also has some delightful houses and streets.

In the north picturesque Hampstead village lies close to the vast area of green, Hampstead Heath, which affords some wonderful views over London. Here you can visit Keats' House or attend an open-air summer concert at Kenwood Lakeside on the Heath.

Richmond in the southwest is attractively situated alongside the Thames. It has many beautiful houses, squares and shops and you can take a boat trip from Richmond Bridge up river to visit the Tudor splendors of Hampton Court Palace and its lovely gardens.

PRACTICAL INFORMATION FOR LONDON

HOTELS. Rooms in London are hardest to find in June, July and August, though there may also be a shortage of vacant rooms when a special exhibition or conference is taking place, such as the Ideal Home Exhibition. If you are having trouble finding a room apply *in person* to the London Tourist Board accommodation service at Victoria Station or Heathrow Central Underground Station. They will ask for a returnable deposit (deducted from your final hotel bill) and a small service charge if they make a reservation for you. There are several other hotel agencies at Victoria Station who will also reserve rooms for you for fees of up to £5. For advance bookings of two nights or more, write to the *London Tourist Board* at 26 Grosvenor Gardens, SW1W 0ET, at least six weeks before your intended arrival date. The leaflet *London Value Hotels* is most useful (available free from BTA offices), or you can buy a copy of the London Visitor and Convention Bureau's *Where to Stay* guide at tourist information centers in London. Both list budget accommodations.

Rates are often quoted per person rather than per room but single rooms are nevertheless considerably more expensive than doubles. In the categories below bed and breakfast for two people sharing a room will cost approximately £40–£65 in *Moderate* and up to £40 in *Inexpensive*.

One word of warning—it is much cheaper to make a phone call from a pay phone than to call from your room. Hotels levy exorbitant charges for this service.

Moderate

Amsterdam, 7 Trebovir Rd., SW5 9LS (tel. 071–370 2814). 20 rooms, all with bath. The accommodations are modern and clean in this hotel, close to Earl's Court tube.

Annandale, 39 Sloane Gdns., SW1W 8EB (tel. 071–730 5051). 12 rooms, 10 with bath. Excellent value for money; visitors keep on making return visits.

Camelot, 45 Norfolk Sq., W2 1RX (tel. 071–723 9118). 34 rooms, 28 with bath. Top marks to this affordable hotel; the rooms are beautifully decorated.

Claverley, 13 Beaufort Gdns., SW3 1PS (tel. 071–589 8541). 32 rooms, 20 with bath. This gracious hotel is also close to Harrods and won London's top B&B award in 1988.

Clearlake, 19 Prince of Wales Terr., W8 5PQ (tel. 071–937 3274). 17 rooms, all with shower. The hotel nestles in a quiet Victorian street, a block from Hyde Park. It's self catering, and rooms have refrigerators and ample storage space.

Crichton, 36 Bedford Pl., WC1B 5JH (tel. 071–637 3955). 62 rooms, 39 with shower. Parts of the hotel are over 225 years old, though the interior is quite modern.

Henley House, 30 Barkston Gdns., SW5 0EN (tel. 071–370 4111). 20 rooms, 8 with bath or shower. The location is the attraction here, as the hotel's very close to Earl's Court tube.

Knightsbridge, 10 Beaufort Gdns., SW3 1PT (tel. 071–589 9271). 20 rooms, 13 with bath or shower. The decor is pleasant and the hotel is right in Knightsbridge.

Morgan, 24 Bloomsbury St., WC1B 3QJ (tel. 071–636 3735). This Georgian terrace hotel is family-run with charm and panache.

Observatory House, Observatory Gdns, W8 7NS (tel. 071–937 1577). 26 rooms in an old house built on the site of a former observatory. Three blocks north of Kensington High Street.

Parkwood, 4 Stanhope Pl., W2 2HB (tel. 071–402 2241). 18 rooms, 12 with bath. This is in a serene block of Victorian and Edwardian town houses.

Prince, 6 Sumner Pl., SW7 3EE (tel. 071–589 6488). 20 rooms, 19 with bath or shower. The Prince is unashamedly upmarket, yet the rates are quite reasonable for what you get.

Ruskin, 23 Montague St., WC1B 5BN (tel. 071–636 7388). 35 rooms, 7 with shower. It's just opposite the British Museum; rooms are clean though nondescript.

Sir Gâr House, 131 Ebury St., SW1 9QU (tel. 071–730 9378). 11 rooms, 3 with bath or shower. The rooms are small, though perfectly adequate. Guests can sit in a pretty brickwalled garden full of flowers.

Tria, 35–37 Stephen's Gdns., W2 5NA (tel. 071–221 0450). 42 rooms, all with bath. Just the thing for the antiques maven, as the Tria is in the center of the Portobello area.

Vicarage, 10 Vicarage Gate, W8 4AG (tel. 071–229 4030). 19 rooms, none with private bath. This is a splendid hotel. The Vicarage is beautifully decorated, and sits in a quiet location overlooking a magnificent garden square.

Wansbeck, 6 Bedford Pl., WC1B 5JD (tel. 071–636 6232). The Wansbeck is made up of three stately, terraced Georgian houses.

Woodville House, 107 Ebury St., SW1W 9QU (tel. 071–730 1048). 13 rooms, none with bath. The rooms are well decorated, though rather small.

Inexpensive

Abbey House, 11 Vicarage Gate, W8 4AG (tel. 071–727 2594). 15 rooms, none with bath. This is close to Kensington Palace and Gardens.

Andrews House, 12 Westbourne St., W2 2TZ (tel. 071–723 5365). Family-run B&B, near the Lancaster Gate tube and the Oxford Street shops.

Ashley, 15 Norfolk Sq., W2 1RU (tel. 071–723 3375). 52 rooms, 18 with shower. The Ashley is three handsome Italianate houses overlooking Norfolk Square.

Beverley House, 142 Sussex Gdns., W2 1UB (tel. 071–723 4615). 20 rooms, 15 with shower. Modest hotel overlooking leafy Sussex Gardens.

Chesham House, 64 Ebury St., SW1W 9QD (tel. 071–730 8513). 22 rooms, none with bath. Modest and clean, with reasonably sized rooms, with washbasin and TV.

Garden Court, 30 Kensington Gardens Sq., W2 4BG (tel. 071–727 8304). 36 rooms, 10 with shower or bath. In a Bayswater Square just north of Kensington Gardens.

Gower House, 57 Gower St., WC1E 6HJ (tel. 071–636 4685). 14 rooms, none with bath. The hotel is generally in good shape with small, though clean, rooms.

Maree, 25 Gower St., WC1E 6HG (tel. 071–636 4868). 31 rooms, 3 with shower. This place has low prices and adequate accommodations.

Oakley House, 71 Oakley St., SW3 5HF (tel. 071–352 7610). 24 rooms, 1 with bath. The rooms, while small, are attractive and have Indian bedspreads. The public showers are clean and gigantic.

Ridgemount, 65 Gower St., WC1E 6HJ (tel. 071–636 1141). 15 rooms, none with bath. The public areas, especially the breakfast room, have a pleasantly cluttered Victorian feel.

Youth Hostels. Among the London Youth Hostels are: 36 Carter Lane, EC4V 5AD (tel. 071–236 4965); 38 Bolton Gdns., Earls Court, SW5 0AQ (tel. 071–373 7083); 84 Highgate West Hill, Highgate, N6 6LU (tel. 081–340 1831); 4 Wellgarth Rd., Hampstead, NW11 7HR (tel. 081–458 9054); King George VI Memorial Youth Hostel, Holland House, Holland Walk, Kensington, W8 7QU (tel. 071–937 0748).

Staying with a British Family. This is an ideal way of finding out about the British way of life and is a real budget bonus. Ask your BTA for a copy of the booklet *Stay with a British Family.*

RESTAURANTS. London is loaded with foreign restaurants almost all of them serving tasty dishes at reasonable prices. What you may have to look for a bit is good English food as opposed to French, Italian, Greek, Indian or Chinese. Don't forget that wine bars and pubs also serve inexpensive meals, ideal for those on a budget, especially at lunchtime.

One thing to remember is that many restaurants are closed on Sunday and that getting a meal much after 11 P.M. is not often easy. Chinese and Indian restaurants tend to be an exception to the Sunday closing rule, but always check with your chosen restaurant beforehand to avoid a wasted journey. Drinks push up the cost of a meal considerably, so go easy on the wine list. See also the points in the Restaurant section in *Practical Information for Britain.*

In the establishments below, expect the check for a three-course dinner for two, including house wine, to come to around £32 in an *Inexpensive* restaurant, and about £35–£45 in a *Moderate* one.

One useful phone number to know is 081–888 8080, which is the number of the *Restaurant Switchboard.* They take calls Mon.–Sat., 9 A.M.–8 P.M. and will answer all kinds of inquiries to do with dining out and make suggestions and recommendations for you.

Moderate

Bertorelli's, 44A Floral St., WC2E 9DA (tel. 071–836 3969). Business is always brisk at this restaurant. It's across the road from the Royal Opera House stage door. Closed Sun.

Borscht'n'Tears, 45 Beauchamp Pl., SW3 1NX (tel. 071–589 5003). People come here for the atmosphere more than the food.

Café des Amis du Vin, 11–14 Hanover Pl., WC2E 9JP (tel. 071–379 3444). Reservations are always necessary here as it's right next to the Royal Opera House. The cold platters are often better than the hot dishes. Closed Sun.

Café Pelican, 45 St. Martin's Lane, WC2N 4EJ (tel. 071–379 0309). Plenty of traditional bistro atmosphere, but the food can be chancy. Handy to the theaters.

Costa's Grill, 14 Hillgate St., W8 7SP (tel. 071–229 3794). This is the spot for eccentric service and Greek food at low prices. Eat outdoors in summer.

Grill St. Quentin, 136 Brompton Rd., SW3 1HY (tel. 071–581 8377). Snack on a French sandwich or feast on a barbecue grill with *pommes allumettes* in this huge and stylish basement.

Joe Allen, 13 Exeter St., WC2E 7DS (tel. 071–836 0651). This famous American basement eatery is open for lunch and pre- and post-theater meals. It's a great place to spot well-known actors and other show-business folk.

Luba's Bistro, 6 Yeoman's Row, SW3 2AH (tel. 071–589 2950). This Russian bistrovich has a long-established reputation for atmosphere and generous portions. Bring your own wine. Closed Sun.

Mon Plaisir, 21 Monmouth St., WC2H 9DD (tel. 071–836 7243). There's a truly French feel to this small, bistro-style haunt. Reservations are essential. Closed Sat. lunch and Sun.

Poons, 4 Leicester St., WC2H 7LB (tel. 071–437 1528). There are often lines for this popular Chinese restaurant whose Cantonese cooking is something out of the ordinary; famous for its wind-dried specialties. Good value set lunch. Closed Sun.

Inexpensive

Bistro Vino, 1 Old Brompton Rd., SW7 3HZ (tel. 071–589 3888) French cuisine. A long-established London budget tradition.

Bloom's, 90 Whitechapel High St., E1 7RA (tel. 071 247 6001). Just like mother used to make, if she was Jewish. Noisy, crowded, friendly, huge servings. Closed Fri. evening and Sat., but ideal for that Sunday East End excursion.

Café Pacífico, 5 Langley St., Covent Garden, WC2H 9JA (tel. 071–379 7728). Good value Mexican food and cocktails with a dash of tequila and mescal. A combination plate lets you try a bit of everything.

The Carvery, branches at the Cumberland Hotel, Marble Arch; Charing Cross Hotel, Strand; Regent Palace Hotel, Piccadilly Circus; Hotel Russell, Russell Sq.; Strand Palace Hotel, Strand, W.C.2. Eat all you want from huge joints of beef, pork or lamb, or three-course set dinners for around £11.50 per person.

Chicago Pizza Pie Factory, 17 Hanover Sq., W1R 9AJ (tel. 071–629 2669). Hectic and crowded, purveying deep-dish pizza.

Chuen Cheng Ku, 17 Wardour St., Soho, W1V 3HD (tel. 071–734 3281). Excellent Cantonese food in what is supposed to be Europe's largest Chinese restaurant. *Dim sum* dishes are the best budget bets and pots of free tea come with your meal.

Cosmas Taverna, 29 Goodge St., W1P 1FD (tel. 071–636 1877). Welcoming Greek restaurant serving all your favorite dishes.

Cranks, 8 Marshall St., Soho, W1V 1LQ (tel. 071–437 9431). One of the original vegetarian, health food restaurants. Wide range of salads and hot dishes, delicious desserts and wonderful fruit juices and yogurt drinks. Also good for breakfasts. Many other branches including 9–11 Tottenham St.and Unit 11, Central Ave., Covent Garden Market. Closed Sun.

Dumpling Inn, 15A Gerrard St., W1V 7LA (tel. 071–437 2567). Bare décor and shared trestle tables make this one of London's most lively budget Chinese diners. Famous for its dumplings and bean dishes.

Fatso's Pasta Joint, 13 Old Compton St., W1V 5PH (tel. 071–437 1503). Fill yourself up with generous portions of pasta at this informal eatery.

Food For Thought, 31 Neal St., WC2H 9PR (tel. 071–836 0239). Popular vegetarian and wholefood spot in Covent Garden. Mon.–Fri. and Sat. lunch only.

Fortnum & Mason's Fountain Restaurant, 184 Piccadilly, W1A 1ER (tel. 071–734 8040). Treat yourself to elegance and nostalgia in London's top food store. Ice cream sodas, pastries, light snacks or full scale meals; a good place to go for traditional teas.

Fox and Anchor, 115 Charterhouse St., EC1M 6AA (tel. 071–253 4838). Victorian pub near the Barbican noted for its hearty British breakfasts and lunches. No food at weekends.

Gallery Rendezvous, 55 Beak St., W1R 3LF (tel. 071–437 4446). Honorable Peking food served in fine oriental atmosphere.

Garfunkel's. A reliable, basic chain, with sensible hamburger/chicken/salad menus, located on nearly every street in the West End, especially in the theater district.

Geale's, 2 Farmer St., W8 7SN (tel. 071–727 7969). Hearty fish-and-chip joint in Notting Hill. Always crowded.

Hard Rock Café, 150 Old Park Lane, W1Y 3LN (tel. 071–629 0382). A loud-rocking favorite, with burgers and juke box. The address is misleading—it's really on Piccadilly, near Hyde Park Corner.

Jimmy's, 23 Frith St., W1V 5TS (tel. 071–437 9521). A real Soho tradition. Crowded, basic, Greek restaurant. Closed Sun.

Kebab and Houmus, 95 Charlotte St., W1P 1LB (tel. 071–636 3144). Popular Greek Cypriot diner, well frequented by students in this lively street packed with Greek restaurants.

Neal's Yard Bakery and Tea Room, 6 Neal's Yard, WC2H 9DP (tel. 071–836 5199). Small upstairs tearoom above a bakery. Delicious wholefoods, and hot savories. Very popular, with long lines forming outside.

Porters English Restaurant, 17 Henrietta St., WC2E 8QH (tel. 071–836 6466). Traditional English pies from goose and gooseberry, chestnut and turkey to lamb and apricots, fish and potato, and of course, steak and kidney.

Raw Deal, 65 York St., W1H 1PQ (tel. 071–262 4841). Very inexpensive serve-yourself vegetarian restaurant. Bring your own wine.

Ruby in the Dust, 102 Camden High St., NW1 OLU (tel. 071–485 2744). Multi-ethnic restaurant with the aura of a Mexican canteena—eat Guacamole, pasta, satay or chicken Kiev among hanging plants.

Sea Shell, 49 Lisson Grove, NW1 6UH (tel. 071–723 8703). One of London's best fish and chip bars. Be prepared for lines, but the food is worth the wait.

Spaghetti House. Another good, basic chain of eateries at a number of central locations, including one beside the Coliseum for hungry operagoers.

Standard, 21 Westbourne Grove, W2 4UA (tel. 071–727 4818). Very popular, above average Indian restaurant. Plain décor but unusual dishes all at reasonable prices. Very crowded, best to book.

Wine Bars. Wine bars in their dozens have opened all over London in the past few years. You can go in just to drink wine, or to eat, or both. Most serve house wine alongside their better vintages and their food counters offer appetizing selections of hot and cold dishes ranging from bread and cheese or pâté to various hot savories and casseroles. If you treat them as inexpensive restaurants and go there to eat with just one glass of house wine you won't overstep your budget. They are open much the same time as pubs, often closed on Sundays. Many offer live entertainment in the form of jazz, piano or guitar music. The following are just a few of the many possibilities:

Blakes, 34 Wellington St., WC2E 7BD (tel. 071–836 5298). Popular Covent Garden wine bar with Victorian-Edwardian décor serving pies, stews and an appetizing cold buffet.

Brahms and Liszt, 16 Russell St., Covent Garden, WC2B 5HP (tel. 071–240 3661). Very good value food supported by funky décor and very loud music. The odd name is Cockney slang for drunk.

Cork and Bottle, 44 Cranbourn St., WC2H 7AN (tel. 071–734 6592). Downstairs cellar just off Leicester Square with excellent selection of food. Cheeseboard and pâtés are especially good.

Le Metro, 28 Basil St., SW3 1AS (tel. 071–589 6286). Art Nouveau décor and out-of-the-ordinary food make this elegant Knightsbridge wine bar a cut above the average. Handy for Harrods and the swanky shops. Closed Sun.

Shampers, 4 Kingly St., W1R 5LF (tel. 071–437 1692). A relative of the Cork and Bottle with similar food and wide ranging wine list.

El Vino, 47 Fleet St., EC4Y 1BJ (tel. 071–353 6786). Something of a London institution; once the haunt of journalists, men must wear jacket and tie, women *not* permitted in trousers. Open for lunch only; sandwiches available in the ground floor bar and traditional English pies and roast beef salad in the downstairs restaurant where a minimum charge is enforced.

Pubs. Even if you're a teetotaler, you will find it mandatory to go to at least one British pub for steak and kidney pie and conversation that belies the British reputation for being reserved. There are at least 4,000 pubs in London, ranging from the shabby to the magnificent. New licensing laws mean that pubs can serve alcohol from 11 A.M. to 11 P.M., on weekdays, with slight local differences of half an hour, though many still close between 3 P.M. and 5.30 P.M., Sundays noon to 2 P.M. and 7 to 10.30. The bartender or barmaid will warn you when it's "time"—meaning time to order the last one and drink up.

Admiral Codrington, 17 Mossop St., SW3. Country pub atmosphere with buffet.

Anchor, Bankside, SE1. The original pub, near the site of Shakespeare's Globe Theater, was destroyed in the Great Fire. Excellent restaurant and seven different bars.

Angel, Rotherhithe St., SE16. Pepys came here to sit overlooking the river.

City Barge, 27 Strand-on-the-Green, Chiswick, W4. Old Thameside pub.

Cock Tavern, Fleet St., EC4. Dickens, Thackeray and Pepys drank here.

Dickens Inn, St. Katharine's Way, E1. Charming old converted warehouse with bars and two restaurants. Set in a growing marina near the Tower of London.

King's Head, 115 Upper Street, Islington, N1. One of London's best live fringe theaters.

Jack Straw's Castle, North End Way, NW3. Right in the middle of Hampstead Heath. Highwayman Dick Turpin and Charles Dickens were among its regulars.

Mayflower, Rotherhithe Street, SE16. The Pilgrim fathers are supposed to have hung around here while waiting for their ship to leave for the New World. The original pub was blitzed during the war, so the current one is a replica.

Nag's Head, James St., Covent Garden, WC2. Next to the opera house. Where ballerinas and stage hands mingle.

Old Coffee House, 49 Beak St., W1. A coffee house in the 18th century, this has for many years been an agreeable pub, wood-panelled and popular.

Prospect of Whitby, 57 Wapping Wall, E1. On the riverside and named after a sailing ship. The Earl of Sandwich was said to have made his great invention here, and Pepys and Whistler were habitués. Today it's jammed.

Punch Tavern, 99 Fleet St., EC4. Traditional pub with cartoons and cuttings from the famous British magazine *Punch*.

The Salisbury, St. Martin's Lane, WC2. Fine Edwardian decor.

Sherlock Holmes, 10 Northumberland St., Strand, WC2. Used to be the Northumberland Arms, mentioned in The Hound of the Baskervilles. Replica of Holmes' study upstairs.

Ye Olde Cheshire Cheese, Wine Office Court, off Fleet St. EC4. Dr. Johnson practiced his lexicography here while Boswell admired. Now a tourist favorite and for good reason. Steak and kidney pie a specialty.

GETTING AROUND LONDON. From Airport to City Center. Tourist Information Centers are located at both Heathrow (in the Underground Station) and Gatwick airports and will be able to help with any queries. For details of transport into Central London, see page 244.

By Underground. The underground, or tube, is probably the quickest and most efficient method of getting around London but several fares a day can prove a little pricey so look out for inclusive tickets (details below). The tube system is divided into five concentric zones. Flat fares are in operation within each zone, and fares increase if you cross from one zone to another. Buy your tickets at ticket booths or from automatic machines and make sure you keep them to the end of your ride. Clear maps of the system are on display in all ticket halls and platforms or you can obtain a free tube map from any of London Regional Transport's (LRT) information centers at Heathrow Central, Piccadilly and Oxford Circus, Victoria, St. James', Euston or King's Cross.

At presstime the minimum tube fare was 60p and the maximum, for journeys within Greater London, £1.90. Flat fares for the Central Zone cost 60p.

A *Visitor's Travelcard,* if bought before you arrive in Britain, is available for three, four, or seven days, for $15, $21, or $35, respectively. Only the seven-day ticket is available in Britain. The card can be used on the bus and the tube in all zones, and includes the *Airbus* between Heathrow and Central London.

An alternative is the *one-day Travelcard,* available for bus and tube journeys after 9.30 A.M. Mon. to Fri. and all day on weekends (but not valid on the *Airbus*); cost: £2.30. *Travelcards* are also valid weekly, but you need to have a passport photo.

By Bus. Bus travel can be slow and crowded but it's a good way of seeing London and is slightly cheaper than the tubes (for very short journeys), minimum fare at presstime being 40p. Tell the conductor, or sometimes the driver, where you want to go and pay the appropriate fare. Route numbers and destinations are listed on bus stops and a route map is available from the LRT centers listed above. The system is divided into five zones.

See above for details of the *Visitor's Travelcard,* or *Travelcard* combined bus and tube tickets.

By Boat. Water buses operate on the Thames from April to October, downstream as far as the Thames Flood Barrier at Woolwich and upstream to Richmond

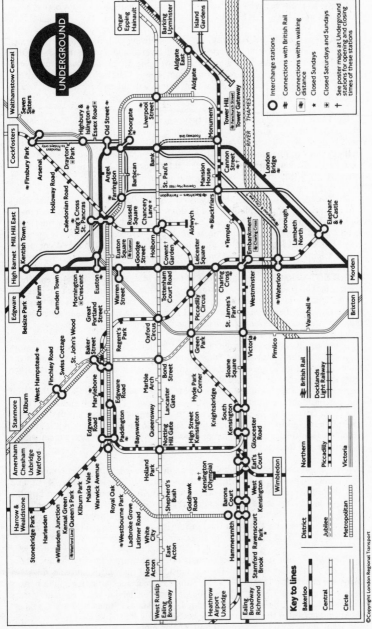

and Hampton Court. There are also year-round services to the Tower of London and Greenwich. You can join the water buses at Tower Pier, Charing Cross Pier, Westminster Pier, or at any floating landing-stage on the central section of the river. For River Boat Information, call 071–730 4812 (Mon.–Fri., 9–5.30). The Thames-line Riverbus runs between Chelsea and Greenwich, with seven stops between. Information at 081–897 0311.

By Docklands Light Railway. The light railway, with its computer-operated trains, opened in 1988 and is the best way to travel to and around the Isle of Dogs in the East End, an area once dominated by working docks and now featuring new business developments. The route runs from Tower Gateway to Island Gardens, at the southernmost point, where a foot tunnel will take you under the river to Greenwich. Information on 071–222 1234.

By Taxi. Taxis are not cheap but they will take up to four people, so if several share, the fare may be no more than separate tube fares. Even so, this is definitely not a budget way of getting around. There are additional charges for luggage carried in the driver's compartment and extra passengers, and an expensive charge for night fares between 8 P.M. and 6 A.M. and weekend fares between 8 P.M. Fridays and 6 A.M. Mondays. Tip the driver at least 10% but never less than 30p.

On Foot. The Silver Jubilee Walkway covers 10 miles of London's historic sights and is marked by metal plaques in the sidewalks. It is best begun in Parliament Square. Group guided walks to such places as Dickens' London or Jack the Ripper haunts are also popular, usually meeting at a pub or tube station, mostly on weekends. For details look in *Time Out,* listen to Capital Radio (95.8 FM) or phone *London Walks* at 081–441 8906 or *Discovering London* at 0277 213704.

ENTERTAINMENT. London is one of the world's greatest centers for entertainment whether traditional or avant-garde theater, cinema, jazz, rock or classical music, dance or just plain drink appeal to you. For news of what's on in town look in the evening paper *Evening Standard* or in any of the weekly publications, *Time Out, City Limits,* or *What's On in London.*

Cinema. There is no shortage of cinemas in London though American visitors may well find that many of the "new" films showing in town were around in the States anything up to two years before. In general West End cinemas cost rather more than suburban ones, probably £3.50–£7 as against £3–£4, and it is often necessary to book or stand in line for a long time to see a popular film. Some West End cinemas have cheaper seats all day Mondays (about £2) and for matinées Tues.–Fri. To see what movies are showing, look in the evening papers or any of the weekly entertainment guides. The National Film Theater in the South Bank Arts Complex near Waterloo Bridge shows different films each day and a temporary membership is available for foreign visitors—take your passport.

Discos. So long as you don't go wild on drinks this is a fairly economical way of spending an evening. Some discos make an entrance charge, usually £4–£5, and give you a ticket for your first drink, others have free entrance and you buy the drinks. Some discos serve beer, which is the best budget bet, but many don't and mixed drinks will start at around £2.50, depending on the disco. As a general rule London discos are packed with foreign tourists or else young Londoners mostly under 23 or so. You have to be 18 to get into most discos.

Theater. A visit to a London show is of course a must for any visitor. There are about 50 theaters staging plays and musicals all the year round and the standards are high. Most theaters have a matinée twice a week and an evening performance beginning at 7.30 or 8. Prices for seats vary widely; unreserved gallery seats can be had for as little as £4 but you may have to stand in line for hours. Cheapest reserved seats are in the upper circle, next come rear stalls, followed by dress circle and front stalls. Top prices are around £20 or more.

The West End tends to be the home of light comedy, mystery drama and musicals, with only an occasional stab at serious plays. Most West End theaters are within walking distance of each other. *Theatre Royal*, Drury Lane, is the oldest working theater; it was opened in 1663 but has been reconstructed several times. The *Haymarket* is another lovely, historic theater with a fine interior.

Head and shoulders above most other London drama is the work of the state-subsidized theaters, the *National* on the South Bank, and the London home of the *Royal Shakespeare Company* in the exciting new *Barbican Arts Complex.*

Of the experimental theaters, the *Royal Court* in Sloane Square is perhaps one of the best, often putting on controversial productions. The *Riverside Studios* in Hammersmith have also achieved wide acclaim for their exciting, off-beat plays. Look in *Time Out* for details.

So long as you don't mind standing in line, it is better to buy your tickets from the theater booking office as many agents charge up to 30% commission. Best time to buy from a theater is around 10 A.M. when they open. Tickets for previews are always cheaper as are matinées at most theaters. There is a very popular ticket booth in Leicester Square, open Monday to Saturday 12–2 for matinées and 2.30–6.30 for evening performances, which sells tickets normally costing £5 or over, at half price, plus a £1 service charge, for that day's performances only.

Opera and Ballet. The *Royal Opera House*, Covent Garden, WC2E 7GA (tel. 071–240 1066), and The English National Opera at the *Coliseum*, St. Martin's Lane, WC2N 4ES (tel. 071–836 3161), are the two major opera houses, with international stars at Covent Garden—and at international prices—and with native talent singing in English at the Coliseum. Prices at the Coliseum are less than half of those at Covent Garden though the latter's "Prom" performances are a good budget bargain. The Royal Ballet stages regular performances at Covent Garden and there are seasons of visiting companies at the Coliseum, especially in the summer, and at Sadler's Wells Theater (tel. 071–278 8916), where the Royal Ballet's second company has its home base.

Concerts. The *Royal Festival Hall* on the South Bank has three auditoria and the lion's share of music performances. (Box office, 071–928 3191, information 071–928 3002).

The *Royal Albert Hall*, Kensington Gore, SW7 2AP (tel. 071–589 8212) is the home of the annual Promenade Concerts, which have to be experienced to be believed. Some tickets are very reasonable indeed. The "last night of the Proms" is an institution in itself but has to be booked long in advance. *St. John's*, Smith Sq., SW1P 3HA (tel. 071–222 1061) is a delightfully converted church, now a concert hall, often with lunch time recitals. The *Wigmore Hall*, Wigmore St., W1H 3DF (tel. 071–935 2141) is a small auditorium famous for debuts and chamber work.

The *Barbican Centre* (Box office tel. 071–638 8891, information tel. 071–628 2295), home of the London Symphony Orchestra, is worth a visit, not only for the music, but to see one of Europe's newest arts complexes.

Jazz. Top of the jazz scene is *Ronnie Scott's Club*, 47 Frith St., W1V 5TE (tel. 071–439 0747). This is the place for international jazz at its very best. Another venue is the *100 Club*, 100 Oxford St., W1N 9FB (tel. 071–636 0933). Some pubs also feature jazz, look in *Time Out*.

Rock. Top concert venues are Wembley Stadium; Hammersmith Odeon; Fairfield Hall, Croydon; Earl's Court and the Dominion Theatre, Tottenham Court Rd. For details, see the daily or evening papers. Tickets are usually bought in advance by mail but the touts abound on concert night.

MUSEUMS. London is one of the two or three most important cultural centers in Europe, and many of the museums are incomparable in their scope, variety and imaginative presentation. Here is a brief selection of the more specialized collections. Admission is mostly free. Bank Holiday closings vary greatly from museum to museum so check first.

British Museum, Great Russell St., WC1B 3DG. The single most important institution of its kind in the world. It is an immense library as well as a treasurehouse of antiquities. Among the various departments are prints and drawings; coins and medals; Egyptian and Assyrian relics; Greek, including the famous Elgin marbles,

Roman, British, medieval and Oriental artifacts. Open Mon.–Sat. 10–5; Sun. 2.30–6.

Cabinet War Rooms, Clive Steps, King Charles St., SW1A 2AQ. Churchill's wartime bunker; provides fascinating glimpse of WWII. Daily 10–5.50. Admission charge.

Courtauld Institute Galleries, Somerset House, The Strand, WC2R 1LP. Italian paintings from the 14th to 16th century, Princes Gate collection of Old Masters and the best collection of French Impressionists and post-Impressionists in the country. Recently moved to these premises; opening times under review. Admission charge.

Dickens' House, 48 Doughty St., WC1N 2LF. Weekdays 10–5, closed Sun. and Bank Holidays. Occupied by the author from 1837 to 1839. On display are portraits, letters, first editions, furniture and autographs. Admission charge.

Geological Museum, Exhibition Rd., SW7 2DE. Large collection of gemstones and The Story of the Earth: 5,000 million years of the history of our planet. Open Mon.–Sat. 10–6; Sun. 1–6. Admission charge (free after 5).

Hayward Gallery, South Bank, behind Royal Festival Hall. Major art exhibitions. Mon.–Wed. 10–8, Thurs.–Sat. 10–6, Sun. 12–6. Varied admission charge.

Imperial War Museum, Lambeth Rd., SE1 6HZ. Comprehensive collection on Britain and the Commonwealth during two world wars, including an art collection and a library of films, photographs and books. Mon.–Sat. 10–5.50, Sun 2–5.50. Admission charge, free on Fri.

Jewish Museum, Woburn House, Upper Woburn Pl., WC1H OEP. Fine collection of Jewish antiquities. Tues.–Thurs. (and Fri. in summer) 10–4, Sun. (and Fri. in winter) 10–12.45.

London Dungeon, 28–34 Tooley St., SE1 2SZ. Authentic exhibitions of the Great Plague, Tyburn hangings and other gruesome aspects of British history. Daily 10–5.30, Oct.–March 10–4.30. Admission charge.

London Transport Museum, Covent Garden, WC2E 7BB. Two centuries of London Transport in the old flower market. Drive a tube train simulator. Open daily 10–5.15. Admission charge.

Madame Tussaud's, Marylebone Rd., NW1 5LR. World's best known waxworks of the famous and infamous. Open daily 10–5.30. Admission charges. Next door are the *Planetarium* and *Laserium*. For times of shows, call 071–486 1121.

Museum of London, London Wall, EC2Y 5HN. 2,000 years of London's history, including the Lord Mayor's Coach and "Fire of London" exhibition. Tues.–Sat. 10–6, Sun. 2–6.

Museum of Mankind, Burlington Gdns., W1X 2EX. (behind Royal Academy). Exhibits of tribal life and culture throughout the world, excitingly displayed. Open Mon.–Sat. 10–5; Sun. 2.30–6.

Museum of the Moving Image (MOMI), South Bank, SE1 8XT. The history of the moving image, from Chinese shadow plays through motion pictures to satellite TV. Could be your only chance to operate a movie camera. Allow plenty of time; there are always long lines. Open Tue.–Sat. 10–8, Sun. 10–6.

National Gallery, on Trafalgar Sq., WC2N 5DN. Weekdays 10–6, Sun. 2–6. Magnificent collection of Italian, Dutch, Flemish, Spanish, German and French paintings up to 1900, plus British painters from Hogarth to Turner. While extension building goes on the collection is always being moved around, with some rooms closed.

National Maritime Museum, Romney Rd., Greenwich, SE1O 9NF. Superlative collection of ship models, navigational instruments, charts, uniforms, medals, portraits and paintings of naval scenes. Open Mon.–Sat. 10–6 (5 in winter); Sun. 2–6 (5 in winter). Admission charge.

National Portrait Gallery, at St. Martin's Pl., Trafalgar Sq., WC2H OEH. Paintings, drawings, busts of famous British men and women over the last 450 years, and also of George Washington and Benjamin Franklin, who were British before 1776. Open Mon.–Fri. 10–5, Sat. 10–6, Sun. 2–6.

Natural History Museum, Cromwell Rd., SW7 5BD. Animals, plants, minerals, fossils and insects (nearly 15,000 specimens). Daily 10–6, Sun. 1–6. Admission charge.

Queen's Gallery, adjoining Buckingham Palace. Selection of paintings and other masterpieces from the Royal Collection. Tues.–Sat. 11–5, Sun. 2–5. Admission charge.

Royal Academy of Arts, Burlington House, Piccadilly, W1V ODS. Founded in 1768, and home of some of London's best temporary exhibitions, as well as the annual Summer Exhibition (May–August) for works of living artists. Open daily 10–6. Admission charge; cheaper on Sunday mornings.

Royal Britain, Aldersgate St., Barbican, EC2Y 8UH. Imaginatively displayed story of Britain's monarchy. Opposite the Barbican tube. Open daily 9–5.30. Admission charge.

Science Museum, Exhibition Rd., SW7 2DD. Illustrates the development of mathematics, physics, chemistry, engineering, transport, mining, communications (an operating radio station) and industry, as a whole. Originals of famous locomotives, aircraft and cars. Many working displays. Daily 10–6, Sun. 11–6. Admission charge.

Tate Gallery, Millbank, SW1P 4RG. Primarily dedicated to British artists, especially Turner, Blake and the pre-Raphaelites. Also modern and foreign painting and sculpture. Daily 10–5.50, Sun. 2–5.50.

Theatre Museum, Russell St., W.C.2. Famous theatrical costumes, scenery, photographs, props—also its own small theater and a box office selling tickets for all West End theaters. Open Tue.–Sun. 11–7. Admission charge.

Tower of London, Tower Hill, EC3N 4AB. London's number one monument, dating back to Norman times. Scene of the imprisonment and execution of many of England's famous. On show in the Jewel House are the Crown Jewels, including the 530-carat Great Star of Africa and the Koh-i-Noor diamonds, St. Edward's Crown, the Imperial Crown of State (set with 3,093 precious jewels) and other treasures. Very crowded, long lines at most times of the year. Open Mon–Sat. 9.30–5 (4 in Nov.–Feb.); Sun. 2–5 (closed Nov.–Feb.). High admission charge, extra for Crown Jewels. **Ceremony of the Keys** takes place nightly at 9.35 P.M. For passes to the 900-year-old ceremony, send S.A.E. to the Resident Governor, H.M. Tower of London, E.C.3 well in advance.

Victoria and Albert Museum, Cromwell Rd., SW7 2RL. Illustrates fine and applied arts of all countries and styles, British, European and Oriental; a magnificent collection. Daily 10–5.50, Sun. 2.30–5.50. Closed on Fridays. Voluntary admission charge.

Wallace Collection, in Hertford House, Manchester Sq., W1M 6BN. Fine works of Dutch, Flemish, French, Spanish, Italian and British painters, together with sculpture, furniture, china, armor and work in gold. Daily 10–5, Sun. 2–5.

SHOPPING. Shopping is exciting in London. Apart from the concessions available to visitors from overseas (goods are tax-free for purchases over a certain amount so long as you make arrangements at the shop to declare the goods on your way out of the country), the new spirit abroad in the past decade has been reflected in the opening of many adventurous young shops alongside the old, traditional establishments.

The serious shopper might first of all call at the *Design Centre,* 28 Haymarket, S.W.1. Here there is a constantly changing exhibition of consumer goods that have reached a high standard of design—furniture, textiles, glass, cutlery, china, pottery and so on. Once you have scouted out the territory, start walking. The London street without at least one interesting shop is rare, but the main shopping areas are concentrated in the west part of the downtown. Oxford Street, Regent Street, Bond Street and Piccadilly are the boundaries for an area of high-class, often very exclusive shops. Further west, there are Kensington High Street, Knightsbridge, Brompton Road, Beauchamp Place and Sloane Street. Chelsea has its good shops, too. King's Road is the boutique district.

London shops are generally open Monday to Saturday from 9 to 5.30 though a few stores, especially in Bond St., close Saturday afternoons. In the West End (Oxford Street) late night shopping is on Thursdays when stores stay open till 7.30, and in Knightsbridge, Sloane Square and Kings Road on Wed. till 7.

Prices vary from area to area. The more exclusive the area, the higher the price. There is little from anywhere in the world that is unobtainable in London, and nothing from the British Isles that is not sold. But you should be warned that London is no longer the budget shoppers' paradise it once was. You may be appalled by some of the prices you see, but don't despair. Shopping around is certain to bring bargains to light.

The most famous department store in London is *Harrod's,* Knightsbridge, S.W.1. Anything bought here has the expected cachet of being the best, and almost anything can be bought here. To avoid the crowds, shop here first thing in the morning, or on Wednesday, late afternoon. Not budget—just for fun.

The traditional store for the gourmet is *Fortnum & Mason,* Piccadilly, W.1. Look for the best English foods—marmalade, honey, cheese—and treat yourself to a traditional tea in its celebrated tearoom.

Every area has its department store—in Knightsbridge, after *Harrod's,* it's *Harvey Nichols,* with a good fashion section; in Sloane Square, it's *Peter Jones,* for household equipment and a wonderful selection of yard goods. *Selfridges* is the best Oxford Street department store. *Liberty's* in Regent Street is a treasure cave of attractive goodies, and you will have to be budget-obsessed not to yield to one of their beautiful ties or headscarves.

Inexpensive clothing and shoe stores line the whole length of Oxford Street—it boasts well over 50 shoe shops! This is the mecca of chain store and mass production, a quick sale often being more important than high quality. But one particular institution deserves a mention, *Marks & Spencer* at 458 and 173 Oxford Street. Value for money at "Marks & Sparks" is legendary, especially for sweaters and underwear.

The old fruit and vegetable market in Covent Garden has been lovingly restored and now houses some beautiful boutiques selling clothes, crafts, gifts, toiletries, etc., as does the whole surrounding area, which is also well supplied with trendy wine bars and eating houses. Well worth a visit but it's not cheap.

Street Markets. Camden Lock, Chalk Farm Rd., NW1. Saturdays and Sundays. Trendy, colorful junk, crafts and clothes stalls. Not cheap.

Camden Passage, Islington, N1. Shops open daily, antique market Wed. and Sat. Fascinating antiques, good silverware and some over-priced junk.

Leather Lane, EC1. A lively lunchtime market selling a bit of everything; close to Hatton Garden, home of London's jewelers and diamond trade.

New Caledonian, Tower Bridge Rd., SE1. The dealers' antique market. Fridays only from 7 A.M. till 12 P.M. Best bargains are early in the morning.

Petticoat Lane, Middlesex St., E1. Famous Sunday morning street market in the East End: pets, clothes, fabrics and curios of all description. Watch your wallets!

Portobello Road, off Notting Hill, W11. Best day is Saturday. Antique and junk stalls but no bargains. Can be a rip-off and tourist trap for antiques. But atmosphere is fun and there are lots of cheap clothes and food stalls.

USEFUL ADDRESSES. *U.S. Embassy,* Grosvenor Sq., W1A 1AE (tel. 071–499 9000). *Canadian High Commission,* 1 Cockspur St., Trafalgar Sq., SW1Y 5BY (tel. 071–629 9492). *London Tourist Board:* 26 Grosvenor Gdns., SW1W ODH; or the National Tourist Information Center and shop at Victoria Station, also in Selfridges and Harrod's department stores. The *British Travel Center,* 12 Regent St., SW1Y 4PQ, provides a full information and reservation service covering all parts of Britain (open Mon.–Sat., 9–6.30, Sun. 10–4); tel. 071–730 3400. *American Express,* 6 Haymarket, SW1Y 4BS (tel. 071–930 4411). *Thomas Cook,* 45 Berkeley St., W1A 1EB (tel. 071–499 4000). *Main Post Office,* William IV St., just off Trafalgar Sq.

Days Out from London

Distances in Britain being small and public bus and train services very good, you will find there are many pleasant and interesting day trips that you can make from London should you wish to keep your base there. In case you fancy an overnight stop away from the hurly burly of the big city we have included a few hotel suggestions as well as restaurants where you can go for lunch.

Hampton Court, Runnymede, Windsor and Eton

This most popular of all excursions from London will take a full day if you intend visiting all of these places at once, or you could break it into two half-day excursions, one to Hampton Court and one to Windsor. Hampton Court lies just outside

London's southwestern suburbs and can be reached by British Rail from Waterloo, by Green Line 718 from Eccleston Bridge, or by tube to Wimbledon, then bus 131, or by river boat from Westminster Pier or Richmond (summer only). This beautiful Tudor palace was built over 400 years ago by Cardinal Wolsey, Chancellor to Henry VIII, who was forced to give it to his royal master. The State Apartments, Great Hall and Great Kitchen are all open to the public and you can also see the famous maze, orangery and the Great Vine with a branch over 100 feet long. Later additions by Wren make parts of the palace a masterpiece of English architecture.

On the way to Windsor from Hampton Court you will pass by the island of Runnymede where the Magna Carta was signed in 1215. Nearby are three acres of land given to the U.S. by the people of Britain as a memorial to John F. Kennedy.

Windsor is a delightful small town on the banks of the Thames famous for its castle begun in the time of William the Conqueror. It is still a favorite residence of the Royal Family. You can visit the State Apartments when the Queen is not in official residence, and the Queen Mary's Doll House. In the castle complex is St. George's Chapel, home of the famous order of the Knights of the Garter and burial place of eight English kings. Also worth visiting is Madame Tussaud's Royalty and Empire Exhibition. Across the river lies the twin town of Eton, home of England's most élite public (private) school for boys founded in 1440 by Henry VI. For tourist information on Windsor Castle, phone (0753) 868286, and for St. George's Chapel, (0753) 865538, Mon.–Fri. 9 A.M.–5 P.M. To reach Windsor, take a train from Waterloo Station or Green Line coach nos. 701 or 718 from Eccleston Bridge, Victoria. For Green Line information, call 081–668 7261.

PRACTICAL INFORMATION FOR WINDSOR

Hotels

Clarence (M), 9 Clarence Rd., Windsor, tel. (0753) 864436. 21 rooms, 19 with bath or shower, some singles.

Arfers (I), 48 Clarence Rd., Windsor, tel. (0753) 855062. 3 rooms in a pleasant Victorian house, run by two ladies and named Arfers because it's " 'alf 'ers and 'alf mine"!

Restaurants

Bensons (M), 4 Church Lane, tel. (0753) 858331. Attractive, central wine bar, close to Guildhall. Friendly service. Eat in the downstairs brasserie, not the more expensive restaurant upstairs.

Charley's Horse (I), 4 Goswell Hill, tel. (0753) 858090. This Mexican restaurant is located in one of the arches at Windsor train station.

Dôme, (I), 5 Thames St., tel. (0753) 864405. French specialties, ranging from *croque-monsieur* to delicious steaks and charcuterie.

Canterbury

This beautiful city, 80 miles to the southeast of London, in the heart of Kent, centers on the magnificent Gothic cathedral, seat of the Primate of All England. The cathedral dates from 1070 and contains the site of the shrine of St. Thomas à Becket who was murdered in 1170. It was to his shrine that the pilgrims of Chaucer's *Canterbury Tales* made their way, and about his martyrdom that T.S. Eliot wrote his play *Murder in the Cathedral.* Much of the ancient city wall is still intact and there are interesting Saxon churches, a Roman mosaic pavement, and sections of the city wall. To reach Canterbury take a train from Charing Cross or Victoria Station or a coach from Victoria Coach Station.

PRACTICAL INFORMATION FOR CANTERBURY

Hotels

Ann's (M), 63 London Rd., tel. (0227) 68767. 19 rooms, 12 with bath or shower. Comfortable Victorian guest house convenient for city center.

Magnolia House (M), 36 St. Dunstan's Terr., tel. (0227) 65121. 6 rooms. Peaceful Georgian house on pleasant central street.

Guildford Lodge (I), 42 Nunnery Fields, tel. (0227) 462284. 21 rooms, 4 with bath. Small family-run guest house off the Old Dover Rd; 15 mins. walk from cathedral.

Kingsbridge Villa (I), 15 Best Lane, tel. (0227) 66415. 12 rooms. It's right in the city center; some rooms have views of the cathedral.

Restaurants

Waterfield's (M), 5A Best Lane, tel. (0227) 450276. *Nouvelle cuisine*-influenced dishes. Dinner may be pricey, but fixed-price lunches good value. Closed Sun. and lunch Mon.

Alberry's (M), 38 St. Margaret's St., tel. (0227) 452378. Busy wine bar with good food. Added attractions are a Roman pavement in the basement bar and free jazz and rock in the evenings.

Crotchets (I), 59 Northgate, tel. (0227) 458857. Wine bar serving tasty home-cooked food. Jazz most nights; garden in summer.

Winchester, Salisbury and Stonehenge

About 65 miles southwest of London, Winchester is one of Britain's most historic cities. Once a Roman town and capital of England under the Saxons, Danes and Normans, this is the city of Alfred the Great. The legendary Round Table of King Arthur can be seen in the Great Hall, and Winchester College is the country's oldest public school. The magnificent cathedral is the longest Gothic church in Europe.

Salisbury, 24 miles further west, is another ancient town whose origins date back to Roman times. Its soaring cathedral is immortalized by the paintings of Constable. Unusually for a Gothic cathedral, it took only 38 years to build and was finished in 1258. The famous 404-foot spire is the highest in England and the cathedral close one of the loveliest.

Eight miles to the north on Salisbury Plain stands Britain's most famous prehistoric circle, Stonehenge, whose impressive monoliths may date back as far as 2,000 years B.C. Trains from London to both Winchester and Salisbury leave from Waterloo Station.

PRACTICAL INFORMATION FOR SALISBURY AND WINCHESTER

Hotels

Byways House (I), 31 Fowlers Rd., Salisbury, tel. (0722) 28364. 17 rooms, 10 with bath. Victorian house close to city center; parking.

Harestock Lodge (M), Harestock Rd., Winchester, tel. (0962) 881870. 20 rooms, all with bath or shower. On northern side of city, built in 1885.

Holmhurst (I), Downton Rd., Salisbury, tel. (0722) 23164. 8 rooms, 5 with bath. Attractive townhouse, 10-minute walk from cathedral.

Stratford Lodge (I), 4 Park La., Castle Rd., Salisbury, tel. (0722) 25177. 4 rooms, all with bath. Great value—attractive rooms and creative cooking.

Stratton House (I), Stratton Rd., Winchester, tel. (0962) 63919. 6 rooms, 2 with bath, 2 with shower. Victorian house in large grounds on St. Giles Hill.

The Hollies (I), 58 St. Cross Rd., Winchester, tel. (0962) 60815. 3 rooms, 1 with bath. Bed-and-breakfast in a former Victorian rectory.

Restaurants

Harpers (M), 7 Ox Row, Market Square, Salisbury, tel. (0722) 333118. Ideal for light lunches and evening meals. Closed Sun.

Haunch of Venison (M), Minster St., Salisbury, tel. (0722) 22024. Traditional English cooking such as game and pies. Open daily; in summer Sun. evenings as well.

Michael Snell (I), 8 St. Thomas Sq., Salisbury, tel. (0722) 336037. Friendly place with high standards and delicious food. Ideal for lunch or tea.

Old Chesil Rectory (M), 1 Chesil St., Winchester, tel. (0962) 53177. The 15th-century rectory, one of the oldest houses in Winchester, serves genuine old English food. Closed Sun. and Mon. evening and Sat. lunch.

Mr. Pitkin's (I), 4 Jewry St., Winchester, tel. (0962) 69360. A friendly wine bar full of plants, serving a wide selection of hot and cold food.

Richoux (I), 101 High St., Winchester, tel. (0962) 841790. This magnificent Tudor building houses a coffee shop-cum-restaurant that also sells confectionery and specialty teas.

Oxford

This lovely golden-stoned city, home of one of the most famous universities in the world, is a delight to visit. Wander down the High Street among the colleges, quadrangles, spires and bridges. University, Balliol and Merton are the oldest colleges, founded in 1249, 1263 and 1264 respectively; St. John's, All Souls and Magdalen probably the most rewarding for the tourist. Christ Church chapel is Oxford's cathedral. Be sure to see the Botanic Gardens, off the High Street, the Radcliffe Camera, Sheldonian Theatre—built by Wren—and the Bodleian Library, one of the most important libraries in the world. The Ashmolean Museum has one of the best art collections outside London.

Eight miles north in Woodstock is the magnificent Blenheim Palace, home of the Duke of Marlborough, and birthplace of Sir Winston Churchill, who is buried in the churchyard of nearby Bladon.

PRACTICAL INFORMATION FOR OXFORD

Hotels

Pickwicks Guest House (M), 17 London Rd., Headington, tel (0865) 750487. 9 rooms, 7 with bath. 1 ½ miles from center; recently renovated.

River (M), 17 Botley Rd., tel. (0865) 243475. 24 rooms, 19 with bath or shower. Some rooms overlook the Thames. Not far from the station.

Acorn (I), 260 Iffley Rd., tel. (0865) 247998. 6 rooms. This comfortable, modern guest house is east of the city center.

Gables (I), 6 Cumnor Hill, tel. (0865) 862153. 5 rooms, 2 with bath. Modern guest house, 2 miles from city center. Comfortable and hospitable; reader-recommended.

Walton (I), 169 Walton St., tel. (0865) 52137. 7 rooms. Close to bus and train stations.

Restaurants

Browns (M), 5–9 Woodstock Rd., tel. (0865) 511995. Lively restaurant; something of an Oxford tradition especially with students.

Munchy Munchy (I), 6 Park End St., tel. (0865) 245710. Between rail station and city center, this simple spot serves delicious Indonesian and Malaysian food. Closed Sun. and Mon.

Cambridge

Fifty-four miles north of London and reached by train from Liverpool Street Station lies Cambridge, England's other world-famous university city. Cambridge is smaller and usually more popular with tourists than Oxford. The university atmosphere pervades the whole town and the "Backs", a tranquil stretch of the River Cam bordered by colleges and smooth lawns, will delight you as you stroll around. King's College chapel is one of the most splendid examples of ecclesiastical architecture in existence. See Trinity College gateway and Great Court, St. John's College (1511); Magdalene with its 17th-century library given by Samuel Pepys; Jesus College and Christ's College. Don't miss the Church of the Holy Sepulchre, oldest of the four round crusader churches in England.

PRACTICAL INFORMATION FOR CAMBRIDGE

Hotels

Arundel House (M), 53 Chesterton Rd., tel. (0223) 67701. 90 rooms, 71 with bath. Great setting overlooking the river.

Sorrento (M), 190–196 Cherry Hinton Rd., tel. (0223) 243533. 22 rooms, 19 with bath. Quiet family hotel within easy walking distance of city center.

Ellensleigh (I), 37 Tenison Rd., tel. (0223) 64888. 7 rooms. Open during student vacations only. A real budget find—inexpensive, friendly and with huge, hot breakfasts.

Six Steps Guest House (I), 93 Tenison Rd., tel. (0223) 353968. 19 rooms, 16 with bath or shower. Close to station. Bed and breakfast only.

Restaurants

Varsity (M), 35 St. Andrews St., tel. (0223) 356060. Large, popular; in historic building on one of the main streets. Cosmopolitan cooking.

Arts Theater Roof Garden (I), 6 St. Edward's Passage, tel. (0223) 355246. Everything from snacks to theater suppers; outdoor dining on roof in summer. Adjoining **Pentagon (I)** has a cold buffet and special value 2-course lunch.

Crusts (I), Northampton St., tel. (0223) 353110. Informal restaurant and bars in an 18th-century building—open fires for winter, tables outside for summer.

Fort St. George (I), Midsummer Common, tel. (0223) 354327. This is one of the best pubs in the city, with lots of atmosphere and reasonable food. It's right on the river, set among the university boat houses, and is a delightful place to while away a summer's evening.

Free Press (I), Prospect Row, tel. (0223) 68337. Tiny, well-run pub serving good food at lunchtime.

Bath

The beautiful city of Bath with its honey-colored stone and stately terraces is one of the showpieces of the west of England. The streets and squares are supreme examples of English 18th-century architecture, but Bath's special glory are the Roman Baths—some of the most striking Roman relics in Europe. See also the adjoining Pump Room, the Abbey, the Circus, the Royal Crescent, the Assembly Rooms and Holburne Museum and Craft Study Center. The Bath International Festival of Music and the Arts attracts thousands of visitors each summer (details in the U.S. available from Edwards and Edwards, 1 Times Square, New York, N.Y. 10036, toll free tel. 800–223–6108). Just outside the city is Claverton Manor, a delightful American Museum, complete with colonial goodies in its cafeteria.

PRACTICAL INFORMATION FOR BATH

Hotels

Carfax (M), Great Pulteney St., tel. (0225) 462089. 36 rooms, 31 with own bath or shower. In fine Georgian Street overlooking Henrietta Park at rear.

Eagle House (M), Church St., Bathford, tel. (0225) 859946. 7 rooms, all with bath. The hospitality is marvelous here. It's recommended for its tasty cooking.

Kennard (M), 11 Henrietta St., tel. (0225) 310472. 12 rooms, 9 with shower. Georgian house close to Henrietta Park and within walking distance of center.

The Tasburgh (M), Warminster Rd., tel (0225) 25096. 13 rooms, most with bath or shower. Bed and breakfast in an Edwardian country house hotel set in large gardens with wide views.

Avon Guest House (I), 160 Newbridge Rd., tel. (0225) 23866. 4 rooms, none with bath. Attractively sited guesthouse, 1 ½ miles from city center. Excellent food.

Lynwood (I), 6–7 Pulteney Gdns., tel. (0225) 26410. 14 rooms, all with shower. Bed and breakfast only. It's on a road leading to the charming Kennet and Avon canal.

Pulteney (I), 14 Pulteney Rd., tel. (0225) 60991. 15 rooms, 6 with bath or shower. Georgian house with garden.

Restaurants

Claret's (M), 7A Kingsmead Sq., tel. (0225) 66688. Pleasant basement restaurant and wine bar.

Moon and Sixpence (M), 6A Broad St., tel. (0225) 60962. Lively restaurant and wine bar in courtyard setting. Wide choice, very popular.

Canary (I), 3 Queen St., tel. (0225) 24846. A pretty restaurant serving lunches and teas. Open till 5.30 P.M.

Number Five (I), 5 Argyle St., tel. (0225) 444499. Attractive spot close to Pulteney Bridge. Open 10 to 10, with fixed-price menu in the evening.

Stratford-upon-Avon

This small market town in the very heart of England with its half-timbered houses and slow-flowing river Avon is a joy to visit. The whole town is virtually a shrine to one man, William Shakespeare. You can see his birthplace in Henley Street, his baptismal record and burial place in Holy Trinity Church, the thatched cottage at Shottery where he lived with Anne Hathaway, and his mother, Mary Arden's, home at Wilmcote. Nash House, New Place and the old grammar school all have links with the famous man. You can buy less expensive all-inclusive tickets for five main Shakespearean properties; just ask at the first one you visit. You will most probably want to attend an RSC performance at the Memorial Theatre, which was built in 1932 with generous donations from many Americans. Inquire about Shakespeare Stopovers, a budget bargain including theater ticket, meal at the River Terrace Restaurant and guest house accommodations. Also of interest to Americans is the lovely timbered Harvard House in the High Street, built in 1596 by the grandfather of John Harvard, who gave his name to the university.

PRACTICAL INFORMATION FOR STRATFORD-UPON-AVON

Hotels

Eastnor House (M), Shipston Road, tel. (0789) 68115. 6 rooms, 5 with bath. Attractive interior, with oak paneling. Short distance from theater.

Hardwick House (M), 1 Avenue Rd., tel. (0789) 204307. 14 rooms, 5 with bath. A family-run Victorian guest house a short walk from center.

Twelfth Night (M), Evesham Pl., tel. (0789) 414595. 7 rooms, 6 with bath or shower. Central Victorian villa, well renovated; nonsmokers only.

Woodburn House (M), 89 Shipston Rd., tel. (0789) 204453. 8 rooms, 4 with shower. Comfortable, small; close to town center.

Caterham House (I), 58 Rother St., tel. (0789) 67309. 11 rooms, 2 with bath. Well-appointed bed and breakfast accommodations. It's a Georgian building full of antique furniture.

Payton (I), 6 John St., tel. (0789) 66442. 5 rooms, 2 with shower. Georgian house close to center; specializes in personal attention.

Salamander (I), 40 Grove Rd., tel. (0789) 205728. 7 rooms. Welcoming and good value.

Restaurants

Box Tree (M), Waterside, tel. (0789) 293226. Enjoy fine cooking in the Memorial Theatre's relaxed main restaurant, which overlooks the river. Top of this price range, but well worth it.

Dirty Duck (M), Waterside, tel. (0789) 297312. Really the *Black Swan,* this pub is ideal for an after-dinner drink or for dinner before or after you visit the theater. Also serves snacks at the bar and good-value lunches.

Bobby Brown's (I), 12 Sheep St., tel. (0789) 292554. An olde worlde café on the first floor in one of Stratford's oldest houses. Ideal for morning coffee, afternoon tea or light meals. Full Sunday lunches but closed Sun. evening.

Riverside (I), Royal Shakespeare Theatre, tel. (0789) 295623. Self-service theater cafeteria right by the river. Open all day until after the evening show.

Slug and Lettuce (I), 38 Guild St., tel. (0789) 299700. If the name doesn't put you off, this attractive pub serves original hot dishes and cold snacks.

Vintner Wine Bar (I), 5 Sheep St., tel. (0789) 297259. Near theater; good food, copious helpings; desserts especially tasty.

York

York is the joy of the north and one of Europe's finest medieval cities. With its ancient city walls and gates and the care that has been taken in preserving the atmosphere of the old cobbled streets and overhanging timbered gables, your visit here will be one of the highlights of your trip to Britain. Walk on the medieval walls, visit the magnificent Minster with its priceless stained glass, and explore the exceptional Castle Folk Museum, the imaginative new Jorvik Viking Center or the National Railway Museum. The narrow medieval streets are packed with fascinating shops.

PRACTICAL INFORMATION FOR YORK

Hotels

Bootham Bar (M), 4 High Petergate, tel. (0904) 658516. 10 rooms, all with bath. Attractive 18th-century house, right next to one of York's fortified gateways and near to Minster.

Jorvik (M), Marygate, Bootham, tel. (0904) 653511. 18 rooms, 16 with bath. Delightful Victorian house, attractively decorated, close to Bootham Bar. Highly recommended.

The Bentley (I), 25 Grosvenor Terrace, Bootham, tel. (0904) 644313. 6 rooms, 2 with bath. Comfortable, family-run hotel close to Minster and city center.

Briar Lea (I), 8 Longfield Terr., Bootham, tel. (0904) 35061. 6 rooms. One of several good guest houses on this street.

Farthings (I), 5 Nunthorpe Ave., tel. (0904) 53545. 7 rooms, 1 with bath. Updated Victorian house in quiet cul-de-sac, 10 minutes' walk from city center.

Greenside (I), 124 Clifton, tel. (0904) 623631. 8 rooms, 2 with bath. Friendly, spotlessly clean bed-and-breakfast overlooking Clifton Green; good food.

Restaurants

Ristorante Bari (M), 15 The Shambles, tel. (0904) 33807. Right in the picturesque Shambles and open daily for lunch and dinner.

Russells (M), 34 Stonegate, tel. (0904) 641432. Stylish carvery on picturesque main street. Good-value traditional English cooking.

Betty's (I), 6 St. Helen's Sq., tel. (0904) 659142. Stylish tearoom and restaurant with turn-of-century decor. Excellent Ploughman's lunches and good Yorkshire cakes and lemon-curd tart. Daytime only.

Oat Cuisine (I), 13A High Housegate, tel. (0904) 672929. Excellent spot for a light but delicious meal—try the club sandwich. Closed Sun.

Plunkets (I), 9 High Petergate, tel. (0904) 37722. Choose from a varied, interesting menu (everything from tacos to vegetarian). Small, friendly; near Minster. Mon. to Sat. 12–11, Sun. 12–10.30.

St. William's (I), 3 College St., tel. (0904) 34830. Coffee, light lunches and teas in outstanding timbered house behind Minster. Mon. to Sat. 10–5, Sun. 12–5.

Scotland

When you cross the Tweed and enter Scotland you will sense immediately a different feeling, for though there are no border formalities or change of language, the Scots have a personality, friendliness and national spirit all of their own. They will greet you with a warm welcome and make you feel instantly at home.

But here is where your BritRail Pass or Brit-Express Travelcard (valid for Edinburgh, Glasgow, Perth and Aberdeen) comes in useful. Many other bargain tickets are available in Scotland—the Highlands and Islands Travelpass, and the Freedom of Scotland tickets, for example—as are budget-oriented holidays and a wealth of helpful literature. For details of all of these write to The Scottish Tourist Board, P.O. Box 15, Edinburgh EH1 1UY.

Edinburgh

Edinburgh is one of Europe's great and beautiful cities, "the Athens of the North." Few visitors to Scotland's capital could fail to respond to the broad, handsome sweep of Princes Street with its gardens and thrilling vista of Castle Rock, dominated by the ramparts of historic Edinburgh Castle.

Edinburgh is virtually two cities: the New Town north of Princes Street is a rare example of 18th-century town planning and boasts many noble squares and streets. To the south lies the Old Town, a fascinating labyrinth of narrow streets and ancient houses over which towers the dark brooding bulk of the Castle, steeped in Scottish history. From its ramparts you can get a panoramic view of the city and the Firth of Forth. Inside you can see a magnificent display of Scottish regalia and visit the apartment where Mary Stuart's son, James VI of Scotland and I of England, was born. A military tattoo on the Castle Esplanade is a highlight of the Edinburgh Festival.

The route from the Castle to Holyrood Palace is known as the Royal Mile and passes many famous landmarks: St. Giles's Cathedral, Parliament House, John Knox's House. Holyrood Palace is rich in memories of the turbulent life of Mary Queen of Scots, not least the room in which her husband, Lord Darnley, murdered her favorite, Rizzio. The Palace is still used as a royal residence when the Royal Family visits Scotland.

On Princes Street is the monument to Sir Walter Scott, a conspicuous Gothic spire 200 feet high. If you have the energy to climb its 287 steps, you will be rewarded with another fine view of the city.

Edinburgh's annual International Festival of Music and Drama takes place for two weeks at the end of August and early in September. Tourists in their thousands flock to the city at this time and if you are one of them make sure you have reserved accommodations long in advance.

To help you get around the city, call in at the Transport Information Center at North Bridge or contact Lothian Transport Head Office, 14 Queen St. tel. (031) 554 4494 and enquire about the *Touristcard* and *Edinburgh Freedom Ticket.*

PRACTICAL INFORMATION FOR EDINBURGH

HOTELS. There are hundreds of hotels and guest houses all around Edinburgh so only a small selection can be given here. You can obtain a free copy of the *Edinburgh Accommodation Register* listing most available hotels and guest houses by writing to the City of Edinburgh Tourist Accommodation Service, Waverley Market, 3 Princes St., Edinburgh EH2 2QP. Or on arrival you can call in person at this address, which is also the local Tourist Information Center, conveniently situated beside Waverley Station, tel. (031) 557 1700. *Homebased Holidays,* 1 Durham Terr., Edinburgh, tel. (031) 669 3115, is a friendly organization specializing in family-type accommodations for the elderly or single traveler.

Albany (M), 39 Albany St., tel. (031) 556 0397. 20 rooms, all with bath or shower. Three Georgian houses converted into attractive, simple hotel; garden; in New Town, close to city center.

Maitland (M), 33 Shandwick Pl., tel. (031) 229 1467. 27 rooms, 10 with bath. Former town house of the Earl of Maitland; located at the west end of Princes St.

Osbourne (M), 53–59 York Pl., tel. (031) 556 5746. 32 rooms, 27 with bath. Restaurant and coffee shop. In city center close to bus station.

Castle Guest House (I), 38 Castle St., tel. (031) 225 1975. 8 rooms with TV. Cooked breakfast. Unfussy and agreeable and only yards from Princes St.

Counan (I), 6 Minto St., tel. (031) 667 4454. 4 rooms all with shower and TV; sleeping up to 12 guests. Full breakfast. Friendly welcome.

Galloway (I), 22 Dean Park Cres., tel. (031) 332 3672. 10 rooms, 5 with bath. Good value, family-run, handsome Victorian guest house.

Youth Hostels: Edinburgh has three hostels: at 7 Bruntsfield Cres., tel. (031) 447 2994, at 18 Eglinton Cres., tel. (031) 337 1120, and the High Street Youth Hostel in Blackfriars St., tel. (031) 557 3984.

Restaurants

Chez Julie (M), 110 Raeburn Place, tel. (031) 332 2827. Attractive bistro with good value and service.

Jackson's (M), 2 Jackson Close, High St., tel. (031) 225 1793. A summer-only, atmospheric spot, modeled on an old-time tavern. Good Scottish fare.

Shamiana (M), 14 Brougham St., tel. (031) 228 2265. Small restaurant specializing in Kashmiri and other north Indian dishes.

Edinburgh Wine Bar (I), 110 Hanover St., tel. (031) 220 1208. Popular atmospheric wine bar open till late daily. Beer as well as wine, light lunches (good vegetable soups) and early evening dinners.

Hendersons (I), 94 Hanover St., tel. (031) 225 2131. Informal restaurant and wine bar with an enormous selection of vegetarian dishes.

Kalpna (I), 2 St. Patrick Sq., tel. (031) 667 9890. Indian vegetarian restaurant where set meals *(thalis)* are excellent value.

La Lanterna (I), 83 Hanover St., tel. (031) 226 3090. No-nonsense, good-value, Italian home cooking.

Lilligs Weinstübe (I), 30 Victoria St., tel. (031) 225 7635. German-style café in the Old Town just off the Grassmarket serving hearty meals and bottled German beer. Open daily 11–11.

MUSEUMS, GALLERIES AND GARDENS. During the Festival many museums are open longer hours.

Canongate Tolbooth, 163 Canongate. Exhibition of local life and work in old courthouse/jail. Mon.–Sat. 10–5 (10–6, June–Sept.).

City Art Center, 2 Market St. Works by 19th- and 20th-century Scottish artists. Temporary exhibitions. Mon.–Sat. 10–5 (10–6, June–Sept.).

Edinburgh Castle. Apr.–Sept. weekdays 9.30–5.50, Sun. 11–5.50; Oct.–Mar. weekdays 9.30–5.05, Sun. 12.30–4.20.

Georgian House, 7 Charlotte Sq. Furnished in the style of its period. Apr.–Oct. Mon.–Sat. 10–5, Sun. 2–5; Nov. Sat. 10–4.30, Sun. 2–4.30. Admission charge.

Gladstone's Land, 483 Lawnmarket. Typical Old Town house built in 1620. Apr.–Oct., Mon.–Sat. 10–5, Sun. 2–5; Nov. Sat. 10–4.30, Sun. 2–4.30. Admission charge.

Huntly House (City Museum), 142 Canongate. Local city history with an old-fashioned Scots kitchen. Weekdays 10–5 (10–6, June–Sept.).

Lady Stair's House, Lawnmarket. Relics of Burns, Scott and R.L. Stevenson. Mon.–Sat. 10–5 (10–6, June–Sept.).

National Gallery of Scotland, The Mound. European and Scottish artists 1300–1900. Weekdays 10–5, Sun. 2–5.

Palace of Holyroodhouse. Official residence of Royal Family in Scotland. Relics of Mary Queen of Scots. Closed during Royal visits (usually late May, early June). To check opening hours, call (031) 556 7371.

Royal Botanic Garden, Inverleith Row. Garden open all year, Mon.–Sat. 9 to sunset, Sun. 11 to sunset (closes one hour before sunset Apr.–Oct.).

Royal Museum of Scotland, Chambers St. Largest overall collection in Britain. Outstanding scale models in Technology Dept. Mon.–Sat. 10–5, Sun. 2–5. Also at Queen St. (east end), Celtic and Roman finds. Weekdays 10–5, Sun. 2–5.

Scotch Whisky Heritage Centre, 358 Castlehill. The story of Scotland's vital fluid; close to the castle. Apr.–Oct., daily 9–6.30; Nov.–Mar. daily 10–5.

Scottish National Gallery of Modern Art, Belford Rd. 20th-century collection including Picasso, Matisse, Giacometti and modern Scottish paintings, in the Royal Botanic Garden. Mon.–Sat. 10–5, Sun. 2–5.

Scottish National Portrait Gallery, Queen St. (east end). Portraits of prominent Scots from 16th century to present day, and a major photographic collection. Weekdays 10–5, Sun. 2–5.

USEFUL ADDRESSES. *Tourist Information Center,* Waverley Market, 3 Princes St., tel. (031) 557 2727. *British Rail,* Waverley Station, tel. (031) 556 2451. *Bus Station,* St. Andrew's Sq., tel. (031) 556 8464. *Post Office,* Waterloo Pl. *U.S. Consul,* 3 Regent Terr., tel. (031) 556 8315. *Thomas Cook,* 79A Princes St., tel. (041) 221 4424. *American Express,* 139 Princes St., tel. (031) 225 7881.

Wales

Wales is the most romantic and mystic part of Britain, the place in whose mountain fastness the Britons sought refuge from conquering Romans, Saxons and Normans. Here they preserve poetic legends of kings and princes, their sense of Celtic individuality and their language.

Wales is a holiday paradise for those who love the outdoor life. It provides ample opportunity for walking, mountain climbing, fishing or pony-trekking. It is an ideal place to rent a country cottage or to stay on a farm, and holidays of this kind can be enjoyed at very moderate prices. An ideal free publication to arm yourself with is the Wales Tourist Board's *Wales Holidays* brochures, which detail the main attractions, as well as extensive accommodations listings, much of them in inexpensive bed-and-breakfasts and farmhouses.

The transport system in Wales is well developed. Inquire about local excursion and budget tickets from any British Rail station, and remember that there are numerous bus services, including the north–south *Traws Cambria,* and many excellent-value day or half-day coach tours to places of tourist interest. Welsh bus companies offer several bargain tickets for their own regions. One such is the *Pass Cambria,* giving unlimited travel on most public transport in Mid Wales.

Wales's greatest appeal stems from its magnificent rugged mountain scenery and its stunning coastline. For a popular seaside resort try Llandudno in the north. A visit inland from there to the Snowdonia National Park is a must; be sure to see the woods and waterfalls of Betws-y-Coed. A mountain railway runs right to the top of Snowdon, the highest peak in England and Wales. This is one of no less than ten colorful narrow-gauge railways that operate in Wales. For full details contact the Tourist Board. If castles intrigue you, then be sure to visit Caernarfon, Conwy and Harlech high above Tremadog Bay. St. David's Cathedral in southwest Wales is another great attraction, as is the rugged Pembrokeshire Coast National Park. Cardiff, the capital, is an interesting cosmopolitan seaport and university town with a splendid civic center, huge castle and fascinating National Museum of Wales.

Wales's heritage has given rise to many museums and festivals. Potteries, woolen mills, woodcarvers and flourmills proliferate. Old slate quarries and coal mines have been converted into unique visitor centers offering underground tours. A spectacle never to be forgotten is the National Eisteddfod, a poetry and musical festival conducted entirely in Welsh and presided over by white-robed Druids. In 1991 it will be held in Mold, Clwyd, during the first week of August.Another spectacle is the Llangollen International Eisteddfod, which attracts artists and performers from all over the world. It is held every year in early July.

PRACTICAL INFORMATION FOR WALES

HOTELS AND RESTAURANTS. Wales Tourist Information Services operate a free Book-A-Bed-Ahead scheme, and a bed and breakfast booking scheme. In conjunction with other operators, they also offer a *Welcome to Wales* service giving discounts at selected hotels, and a Book-A-Pub-Ahead scheme. Ask also about farmhouse holidays. For details contact the *Wales Tourist Board,* 34 Piccadilly, London W.1, tel. 071–409 0969, the *Cardiff Tourist Information Center* at Brunel House, 2 Fitzalan Rd., Cardiff CF2 1UY, tel. (0222) 227281 or, before leaving the U.S., call *Reservations Wales* in New York on Freephone 800–444–9988.

Bala (Gwynedd). A good center for Snowdonia National Park. *Plas Coch* (M), High St., tel. (0678) 520309. 10 rooms with bath or shower.

Betws-Y-Coed (Gwynedd). *Henllys* (M), tel. (06902) 534. 10 rooms, 8 with bath or shower, in a delightful old courthouse. *Ty'n-y-Celyn* (I), Llanrwst Rd., tel. (06902) 202. 8 rooms, all with bath. Big Victorian guest house with lovely views.

Caernarfon (Gwynedd). *Black Boy Inn* (M), Northgate St., tel. (0286) 3604. 12 rooms, 6 with bath. Friendly hotel in 16th-century building inside the castle walls. *Menai Bank* (I), North Rd., tel. (0286) 673297. 15 rooms, 9 with bath.
Restaurant. *Bakestone* (I), 26 Hole in the Wall St., tel. (0286) 5846. Tiny crêperie-cum-restaurant. Interesting food, good fish dishes. Closed in winter.

Cardiff. *Ferriers* (M), 130–132 Cathedral Rd., tel. (0222) 383413. 26 rooms, 4 with bath. Newly renovated Victorian house, close to city center. *Wynford* (M), Clare St., Riverside, tel. (0222) 371983. 30 rooms, 22 with bath. A few minutes' walk from city center; privately-owned and prides itself on personal service and good facilities. *Acorn Lodge Guest House* (I), 182 Cathedral Rd., tel. (0222) 221273. Victorian house with 10 rooms. A few minutes' walk from city center; full Welsh breakfast and high teas.
Restaurants. *Blas ar Gymru* (M), 48 Crwys Rd., tel. (0222) 382132. Traditional Welsh food; try salt duck with onion sauce or lamb with ginger and honey. Closed Sun. *Gibsons* (M), Romilly Cres., tel. (0222) 341264. Imaginative cooking in a simple restaurant, away from the city center.

Cardigan (Dyfed). *Penbontbren Farm* (M), at Glynarthen, tel. (0239) 810248. 10 rooms, all with bath. Dinner available as well as breakfast. Well worth searching out this unusual new hotel in converted farm buildings.

Conwy (Gwynedd). *Berthlwyd Hall* (M), Llechwedd, tel. (0492) 592409. Newly refurbished Victorian manor, fine food, and panoramic views over Snowdonia National Park. *Sunnybanks Guest House* (I), Woodlands, Llanrwst Rd., tel. (0492) 593845. Attractive guest house with personal attention and lovely gardens. 7 rooms.

Harlech (Gwynedd). *Castle Cottage* (M) tel. (0766) 780479. 6 rooms, 4 with bath. Also a delightful restaurant in this 16th-century beamed cottage close to Harlech castle.

Llandogo (Gwent). *Sloop Inn* (M), tel. (0594) 530291. 4 rooms, all with bath. Award-winning inn located in the lovely Wye Valley near Monmouth.

Llandudno (Gwynedd). A popular holiday resort with hundreds of large hotels and guesthouses. *Bryn y Bia Lodge* (M), Craigside, tel. (0492) 49644. 14 rooms,

13 with bath. Set in its own grounds overlooking the town. Spacious and gracious. *Loretta Hotel* (M), Deganwy Ave., tel. (0492) 82797. 55 rooms, 52 with bath. Centrally located between the resort's two beaches. *Winston* (I), 5 Church Walks, tel. (0492) 76144. 7 rooms, 2 with bath. Central guest house with good food.

Restaurants. *King's Head* (I), Old Rd., tel. (0492) 77993. Llandudno's oldest pub; excellent range of bar meals and a good restaurant. *Number 1* (I), London House, Old Rd., tel. (0492) 75424. Bistro-style food in this restaurant-cum-wine bar. Closed Sun.

St. David's (Dyfed). *Warpool Court* (M), tel. (0437) 720300. 25 rooms, all with bath. Gardens, pool, coastal walks, great food. More expensive rooms also available. *Redcliffe House* (I), 17 New St., tel. (0437) 720389. 6 rooms. In the city center.

Restaurants. *St. Non's Hotel* (I), tel. (0437) 720239. Good bar snacks, and lunches on Sun. Popular with locals. A few miles up the coast, at tiny Porthgain harbor, is the *Harbour Lights* (M), tel. (03483) 549. Charming restaurant, superb salads and main meals.

Swansea (W. Glamorgan). *Tides Reach* (I), 388 Mumbles Rd., Mumbles, tel. (0792) 404877. Exceptionally comfortable and well-furnished guesthouse. 7 rooms, 1 with shower. Some rooms overlook the sea and most have T.V.

Restaurant. *Heritage* (M), 2 Prospect Pl., tel. (0792) 473886. Everything from steak and fish to vegetarian meals.

Trecastle (Powys). *Castle* (M), tel. (087482) 354. Old coaching inn with 7 tastefully appointed rooms, 4 with bath or shower, 2 with fourposter beds. The hotel also has a restaurant.

Youth Hostels

There are around 50 Youth Hostels in Wales, often in places of great beauty. For further information contact *YHA Regional Office,* 1 Cathedral Rd., Cardiff CF1 9HA tel. (0222) 396766.

Greece

Greece, a mountainous peninsula extending south of the Balkans into the Mediterranean, covers, together with some 1,500 surrounding islands, 51,137 square miles and is inhabited by nearly 10 million people. Landscapes and seascapes, archeological treasures and low prices make Greece particularly attractive to tourists, and the annual number of visitors exceeds three quarters of the population. With an enormously long coastline, Greece has established itself as a leading center of nautical sports. Mountaineers and skiers also find pleasure in the mainland's mighty mountain chains, the fabled Mt. Olympus rising to 9,574 feet. The home of the gods of Antiquity lures lovers not only of nature, but of mythology, history and art who have long been drawn to the birthplace of Western civilization, however weakened it may be after 2,500 years of wear and tear. The millenia of Antiquity and the Middle Ages are represented by a stately cavalcade of classical temples, Hellenistic palaces, Byzantine churches, Crusader castles and an occasional Turkish mosque, all in equally varied settings.

Having invented and tried out all possible and several quite impossible regimes, Greece returned to democracy in 1974 after seven years of military rule, with the veteran conservative statesman Karamanlis as premier. He was elevated to President of the Republic in 1980, and negotiated Greece's entry as a full member into the EC. The Socialist government of Andreas Papandreou ousted Karamanlis in 1985 and remained in power for four years until corruption and disarray hastened its demise in November 1989. Issues of considerable controversy—Papandreou's affair with 35-year-old Dimitra Liani (now his wife), scandals involving government officials in fraud and embezzlement, and the treatment of middle-Eastern terrorists—caused political crisis for Papandreou. Two elections in 1989 failed to bring forward a majority government and, at press time, it seems unlikely that the forthcoming 1990 election will conclusively settle matters. The political future of Greece remains uncertain.

Besides the capital, Athens, there are several main tourist areas, including the islands of Corfu, Crete, Mykonos and Rhodes, the splendid ruins of Delphi and Olympia, the beaches of the Halkidiki peninsula in northern Greece, all with a large number of modern hotels in all price categories. At the other end of the scale are some still relatively unspoiled villages, whose alluring pictures seem the very stuff of which travel agents' dreams are made but where the accommodations—modern if simple—are so restricted that it is almost impossible to find a room in high season, unless you have booked well in advance. Unfortunately, individual booking letters are not always answered and agencies usually do not deal with moderate and inexpensively-priced hotels. You'll also find that Greek families on holiday fill those rooms for rent in private houses in these once out-of-the-way places. So on the coast, venturing off the beaten track can be chancy. But this does not apply to the off season, when rates are also much lower. However, in the big resorts you are more likely to find rooms in moderate and inexpensive hotels.

Language presents no difficulties. Even in the smallest place someone has returned from the U.S. or Australia, and in the unlikely event that nobody working in your hotel or restaurant speaks English, a guest will always be willing to help.

In the countryside the people are still helpful and hospitable, though in Athens and the main tourist centers manners can range from the indifferent to the outright rude.

As the sad side effects of mass tourism take effect in the main centers, it increasingly makes sense to strike out along the lovely coast and venture to the smaller islands. Except for accommodations, there is little difficulty in doing this as there is a good choice of ferry boats, hydrofoils, planes and buses. But those staying for a short period only should still concentrate on the classical sites and the coast. The mountain areas, though lacking nothing in natural beauty, are at best a second choice and can be viewed from afar.

PRACTICAL INFORMATION FOR GREECE

WHAT WILL IT COST. Devaluations have failed to keep pace with increasing inflation. Hotel prices still equal those of Greece's main competitors in tourism around the Mediterranean, but meals are expensive for the quality offered. Greece is no longer the outstanding buy of yesteryear. Rates are 15–20% lower Apr. 15–May 31 and Sept. 15–Oct. 31, and up to 40% lower in the few seaside hotels that stay open from Nov. 1 to Apr. 15. During the Christmas and Easter holidays high-season prices are charged. Rhodes and Corfu are more expensive than elsewhere, but in general there are no regional price differences and therefore no special budget areas.

The monetary unit in Greece is the *drachma* (dr.). There are coins of 1, 2, 5, 10, 20 and 50 drachmas and notes of 50, 100, 500, 1,000 and 5,000 drachmas.

At the time of writing, the exchange rate for the drachma was 153 to the U.S. dollar and 256 to the pound sterling. These rates are adjusted daily. Check them carefully both before and during your trip.

Sample Costs. An *ouzo* costs from 100–240 dr., a small bottle of beer 100–300 dr., a bottle of local wine from 300–1000 dr., half a liter of retsina 120–200 dr., Turkish (now called Greek) coffee 80–150 dr., American coffee 180–300 dr.

Most cinemas have a uniform price, 300–500 dr., open-air cinemas in the provinces are cheaper. The only theater of interest to non-Greek speakers would be the numerous festivals of ancient drama, 750–3,200 dr. per seat, depending on the performance. A moderate seat for an opera or concert at the Athens Festival would be in the middle of this range. Museums and archeological sites cost 200–600 dr.

NATIONAL TOURIST OFFICE. *The National Tourist Office of Greece* is occasionally a useful source of information on holidays in Greece. They are particularly active in promoting winter tourism, especially to Rhodes and Crete. They will supply lists of tour operators who organize package holidays at amazingly low rates with accommodations in otherwise expensive hotels.

Their addresses overseas are:

In the U.S.: 645 Fifth Ave., Olympic Tower, New York, N.Y. 10022 (tel. 212–421–5777); 611 West 6th St., Los Angeles, CA 90017 (tel. 213–626–6696); 168 North Michigan Ave., Chicago, IL 60601 (tel. 312–782–1084).

In Canada: 1233 rue de la Montagne, Suite 101, Montreal, P.Q. H3G 1Z2 (tel. 514–871–1535); 1300 Bay St., Toronto, Ontario M5R 3K8 (tel. 416–968–2220).

In the U.K.: 4 Conduit Street, London, W1R ODJ (tel. 071–734 5997).

WHEN TO COME. The main tourist season in Greece lasts from around the middle of June to the middle of September when the weather is at its best—guaranteed hot, and rarely humid, except on the west coast. This is also the most expensive period, however, so the budget-conscious traveler might well want to consider May or late September, when prices are down on the high season and the beaches are beautifully empty. Though bear in mind that the sea can still be fairly chilly in May; in the early fall, however, it is at its warmest.

From the end of October to early May temperatures differ considerably between the northern and southern regions, with the islands remaining the warmest but rainiest. But even on the mainland rains can be torrential and can last for up to a week. Christmas can be drier than Easter, but this is entirely a matter of luck. The mountainous and sometimes snowbound interior can be very cold in winter; winter sports are restricted to a very few places. Outside Athens and Thessaloniki there is very little entertainment, though of course the main archeological sites remain open.

Average afternoon temperatures in degrees Fahrenheit and centigrade:

Athens	Jan.	Feb.	Mar.	Apr.	May	June	July	Aug.	Sept.	Oct.	Nov.	Dec.
F°	54	55	60	67	77	85	90	90	83	74	64	57
C°	12	13	16	19	25	29	32	32	28	23	18	14

SPECIAL EVENTS. The least expensive of all international artistic events, the Athens Festival, lasts from *June* well into *September.* The ancient Herodes Atticus open-air theater on the slopes of the Acropolis is the setting for classical Greek tragedies and comedies as well as for operas, ballets, and concerts with renowned conductors and soloists. This is complemented by the Epidaurus Festival, ancient drama performed by the Greek National Theater Company in the splendid 4th-century B.C. open-air theater seating 14,000 spectators; *July–August.* Classical drama is performed throughout the summer in ancient theaters all over the country.

Greek folkdances take place from *May* to *September* on the Philopappos Hill opposite the Acropolis; at the Old Venetian Castle, Corfu; and the Rodini Theatre, Rhodes. Prices range from 300 dr. (in Corfu) to 1200 dr. (in Rhodes). Sound and light performances are also presented from *April* to *October* on the Pnyx Hill, opposite the Acropolis in Athens, at the Old Venetian Castle in Corfu, and at the Palace of the Knights in Rhodes. Prices of these tickets run from 100 dr. to 500 dr.

The International Fair of Thessaloniki is held in *September* in the capital of northern Greece. This important commercial event, which attracts a large number of visitors, is complemented by the Greek Film Festival and the Light Song Festival. It is followed in *October* by the *Dimitria,* a Byzantine Arts Festival dating back to the 13th century. Events include ballet, music concerts, and art exhibitions.

From *July* to *early September,* a Wine Festival is held, near the medieval monastery of Daphni, 7 miles from Athens. The entrance fee is 600 dr. and wines from all over Greece are offered. Similar wine festivals are held at Thessaloniki and Alexandroupoli (northern Greece), Rethymnon (Crete), and on Rhodes and Evvia. In *February,* Carnival is celebrated everywhere, culminating in parades with floats and dancing in the streets in Athens, Piraeus and Patra.

The most famous of the many Greek Orthodox Holy Day celebrations is that of the Epitaph on *Good Friday* when candle-bearing worshippers follow a flower-decked bier representing the body of Christ solemnly through the streets, with gorgeously-robed clergy, and bands and choirs singing ancient Byzantine hymns.

National Holidays. Jan. 1 (New Year's Day); Jan. 6 (Epiphany); Mar. 13; Mar. 25 (Independence); Apr. 5 (Greek Orthodox Good Friday); April 8 (Easter Monday); May 27 (Pentecost Monday); Aug. 15 (Assumption); Oct. 28 (Ochi); Dec. 25, 26.

VISAS. Not required. Nationals of the U.S. and most American countries have to apply for a residence permit after a stay of two months; British subjects and Europeans, after three months.

HEALTH CERTIFICATE. Not required for entry into Greece.

GETTING TO GREECE. By Plane. Athens is served direct from North America (New York, Los Angeles, San Francisco and Montreal) by *Olympic Airways,* the Greek national carrier, and charter *TWA.* Some flights are non-stop; others make an additional call en route. From the U.K. there are direct non-stop flights by Olympic and *British Airways* to Athens, Thessaloniki, and Corfu. In addition from the U.K. (London and several regional airports) there are direct charter flights in connection with inclusive holidays to many Greek destinations including some of the smaller islands such as Kos and Kefalonia. The Greek authorities have tightened up on these charters and they require evidence that at least nominal accommodation be reserved in connection with these flights. All good travel agents will be able to give you the latest position. The charter flights are substantially cheaper.

By Boat. There are no direct sailings from North America to Greece. From the U.K. there are only cruise ships (May to October) to Athens and the islands. However Greece is linked to Italy and Yugoslavia by a number of ferry routes, some all year round, others summer only. Trieste and Venice to Patra; Brindisi to Corfu, Igoumenitsa, Patra; Ancona to Corfu and Patra; Bari to Corfu, Igoumenitsa and Patra; Rijeka to Corfu, Igoumenitsa and Patra; Venice to Piraeus. From Patra and Igoumenitsa there are direct bus links to and from Athens. Full details of services from travel agents.

By Train. There are no through trains from the Channel ports or Paris to Greece now. But there are daily services from Köln (Cologne) and Venice. With the last you leave Venice in the late afternoon and—traveling via Zagreb, Belgrade, Skopje and Thessaloniki—arrive in Athens at breakfast time two days later. The total traveling time is about 38 hours. The train carries 2nd-class bunk beds and both 1st- and 2nd-class day carriages all the way. Buffet or restaurant car services part of the way. The train is called the *Venezia Express*.

From Köln, the *Attika Express* leaves after lunch and runs through Stuttgart to München (Munich), which is reached in the early evening, then overnight to Zagreb in Yugoslvaia, via Salzburg. The following day is spent traveling through Yugoslavia, and the train finally arrives in Athens at 6.30 A.M. the next day. The train offers 2nd-class bunk beds and day carriages and buffet or refreshment services part of the way.

By Bus. The best services are those operated by *National Express-Eurolines,* which has two routes to Greece. One is an "express" service to Thessaloniki and Athens, taking three and a half days, which leaves London at 7.30 P.M. on the evening of day one, arriving in Athens at around 10 A.M. on the morning of day four. This service runs via Belgium, Germany, Austria and Yugoslavia, with a change of vehicles in Munich; the bus only runs in the summer, twice a week. Round trip fare for 1991 should be around £150. The other service runs twice weekly down through France and Italy, then by ferry from Brindisi to Patra via Corfu. The final leg from Patra to Athens is again by bus. To give an idea of the journey time, the Monday departure—which runs year-round—reaches Athens mid-evening on Thursday. The round trip fare is around £160, including a reclining seat on the ferry.

CUSTOMS. There are two levels of duty-free allowances for goods imported into Greece. Travelers arriving from an EC country may bring in 300 cigarettes or 75 cigars or 150 cigarillos or 400 grams of pipe tobacco; plus 1.50 liters of alcoholic beverages or 5 liters of wine; plus 75 grams of perfume and 0.375 liters of toilet water. You may also import gifts up to a value of 55,000 dr.

Travelers arriving from any other countries may bring in 200 cigarettes or 50 cigars or 100 cigarillos or 250 grams of pipe tobacco; plus 1 liter of alcoholic beverage or 2 liters of wine; plus 50 grams of perfume and 0.25 liters of toilet water. You may also import gifts up to a value of 7,000 dr.

Whatever country you arrive from, you may import any amount of foreign currency, but cash in excess of $1,000 should be declared for re-export. You may not import or export more than 20,000 dr. plus foreign currency to the value of $1,000.

HOTELS. Greek hotels are officially classified as L (deluxe), A (first class), B (moderate) and C and D (inexpensive). We have selected only B, C and D hotels for our lists. These correspond largely to our gradings of Moderate (M), and Inexpensive (I). Two people in a double room, breakfast, tax and service charges included, can expect to pay 5,500–8,000 dr. in a Moderate hotel; in an Inexpensive hotel, a double room, breakfast, tax and service charges included, would run 3,000–5,000 dr. for two people. Prices are prominently displayed in all rooms.

Many B hotels are airconditioned, while C and D hotels in main tourist centers are adequate and all have private showers. But though they offer the expected modern comforts, most Greek hotels are of a strictly utilitarian sameness and lack any individual features. Pricewise they are in the middle range of Mediterranean countries. Since most Moderate hotels have restaurants, we have only indicated the absence of these. Inexpensive hotels, on the other hand, only have restaurants where specifically stated. Moderate hotels by the sea usually insist on half board, which is in any case advantageous budget-wise. However, hotel food is generally uninteresting, to say the least, though the service possesses all the variety the food lacks.

Youth Hostels. The *Greek Youth Hostels Association,* Dragatsaniou 4, Athens, is affiliated to the *International Youth Hostel Federation* and members are admitted to its 16 hostels throughout the country. The fee for joining in Greece is 1,200 dr. Members may stay at a hostel for three consecutive nights, but this rule is not rigid; bed 450–600 dr., sheets extra.

More comfortable are the *Y.W.C.A,* Amerikis 11, Athens; and (summer only) Agias Sofias 11, Thessaloniki, women only! The *Y.M.C.A.,* Omiron 28, Athens, is less inspiring.

Camping. There are more than 100 camps at key points throughout the country, about one-half are fully equipped; the best are those run by the Greek National Tourist Organization, which provides lists of all camp sites. Fees are 330–600 dr. per person, plus about 100 dr. for the car, 700 dr. for a tent, and 800 dr. for a caravan.

Houses. On all the islands and in several mountain villages simple accommodations are available in private houses. The charges range from 1,500–3,000 dr. for a double room.

RESTAURANTS. Greek restaurants have the same grading as hotels. The official B equals our Moderate (M), 1,200 to 2,500 dr., and the official C and D our Inexpensive (I), 800–1,200 dr. These prices are for one person only and do not include drink. The classification is prominently displayed on all restaurants, though sometimes only in Greek.

By far the most economical, but also most indifferent meals, are the set menus offered by most hotels. These are available hardly anywhere else.

All restaurant menus quote two prices: with and without tip. The latter applies if the food is not consumed on the premises but taken out, and this only applies in Inexpensive restaurants. Wine is, of course, considerably cheaper if bought in a shop, but it would cause a riot to bring it into a restaurant and you would probably not be served. Snack restaurants and fast-food places of many kinds are increasingly common and sometimes very good. In the evening you might try a taverna, a restaurant with or without music staying open till late, and where it is customary to walk into the kitchen to point out what takes your fancy. Seafood restaurants and tavernas by the sea are usually good but in a higher price range. Don't be deceived by the simple appearance!

Food and Drink. Greek food can be very good, and should be preferred to the indifferent international fare.

Hotel breakfasts are continental style, consisting of instant coffee ("Nes") or tea with bread and butter, jam or honey. Eggs are available for a small extra charge.

Arni is lamb, *moschari* veal, *hirino* pork, all served with generous helpings of vegetables and salads in season, but unfortunately in the cheaper tavernas all too often drenched in lukewarm oily tomato sauce. *Dolmades* are stuffed vine leaves; *moussaka* is minced meat with eggplant; *pastitsio,* minced meat with macaroni; *youvarlakia* are sautéed meat balls in a lemon sauce; *keftedakia,* fried meat balls. *Souvlaki* is shish kebab, not only of the customary meats but also of swordfish, which can be highly recommended. Seafood is perhaps the best part of the Greek cuisine, but also the most expensive, except for *marides,* fried whitebait, and *kalamarakia,* fried squid which, when small, are delicious but grow rubbery with size; try also *oktapodi,* octopus, particularly good when cooked with onions in a wine sauce. *Mydia,* mussels, are excellent in a *mydia saganaki,* when they are served with a spicy, cheesy sauce in a dish straight from the oven. Fresh fish of all the Mediterranean varieties is usually served fried or grilled, often with oil added; sauces are practically unknown, but *avgolemono,* the Greek egg-lemon fish soup, is quite famous. *Pitta* is pie, *tyropitta* cheese pie being the most popular, but *spanakopitta,* spinach pie, the most original. There is a whole gamut of exceedingly sweet pie and honey pastries, the most common being *baklava* and *kataïfi.*

Porto Carras,—white, rosé *(kokkineli)* and red—is the outstanding table wine. It is expensive by Greek standards at 800 dr. a bottle or more in a restaurant, but cheaper than anything comparable elsewhere in Europe. Of lower-priced wines the best are *Apelia, Elisar,* and *Tsantali* (white), *Boutari (Naoussa), Castel Danieli* (red); *Demestica* red and white is a good low-priced wine. Sweet dessert wines are *Mavrodaphni* and *Samos.* Since ancient times, the Greeks have been adding resin to their wines, the result being called *retsina.* Try by all means—its strong taste can be mellowed by adding soda—but more likely than not you will return to *aretsinato,* meaning no resin. *Ouzo* with an aniseed flavor is the national apéritif, *tsipouro* its stronger country cousin, but vermouth and brandy are also made locally. Greek beer costs about the same as retsina, and the light lagers are refreshing. Soft drinks are often too sweet, as also the liqueurs, and can be more pleasing to the eye than the palate.

TIPPING. Hotels include a 15% service charge, but a little extra is expected. Restaurants also add 12 to 15%, rising to 20% round Christmas and Easter, but the waiter's assistant depends on your tip. Round off the charge on the taxi meter to the next 50 dr., 50 dr. extra per bag for luggage; at Christmas drivers expect a 70 dr. "gift" on top of this. Hotel porters expect 50 dr. a bag; theater and cinema ushers, 20–30 dr. Washroom attendants receive 20 to 50 dr.

MAIL. Airmail letter within Europe, 60 dr. for 20 grams; postcards 50 dr. To U.S.A. and Canada: 70 dr.; postcards 60 dr. (Increases expected.)

CLOSING TIMES. The NTOG supplies a list of banks that remain open afternoons and Sundays. Business hours, an eternal subject of parliamentary debate, vary from season to season and from district to district; thus, Athens summer hours are as follows:

banks.................	8 A.M. to 2 P.M. (Mon.–Fri.)
travel agencies	8.30 or 9 A.M. to 4.30 or 5 P.M. (closed Sat. afternoons)
restaurants	noon to 3.30 P.M. and 7.30 P.M. to midnight
cafés.................	8 A.M. to well after midnight
nightclubs	9 P.M. to 5 A.M.
cinemas	5 P.M. to midnight (open-air, 8 to midnight.)

PLACE AND STREET NAMES. Except for very familiar names like Athens, these are given in Latin characters, according to the modern Greek pronunciation. *Odós* (street) is omitted, but not necessarily *Leofóros* (avenue) or *Platia* (square), while the name is in the possessive case; thus Agios Pavlos (Street) becomes Agiou Pavlou. Governments frequently indulge in renaming streets, the principal result of which is considerable confusion. You may also encounter alternative spellings for many place and street names in Greece.

GETTING AROUND GREECE. By Plane. *Olympic Airways* operate an extensive network of internal routes between Athens and most towns and islands. Thessaloniki is linked with the main islands and by at least eight flights daily with Athens. There are also inter-island flights connecting Crete, Rhodes, and various other islands. All flights are heavily booked in summer.

By Train. Greek Railways are limited and little used. There is a main line from Athens to Thessaloniki, where it splits, one route going north to Yugoslavia, the other east to Turkey, with a branch into Bulgaria. There is also a secondary line running west from Thessaloniki. In the Peloponnese there is a narrow gauge system that operates from Athens via Corinth to Patra and Kalamata. Speeds are not high but there are four daytime and four overnight expresses daily between Athens and Thessaloniki, taking about 7 hours for the 320 mile journey and costing 3,040 dr. for a 2nd-class return trip. Day trains carry refreshment services or a restaurant car; overnight trains have sleepers and 2nd-class bunk beds. The Peloponnese route is very scenic but not fast, a leisurely way to see much of rural southern Greece. Diesel trains on these lines have either a dining car or a refreshment service. Call the Athens office of the OSE (Greek Railways), tel. 01/362 4402, for tickets and information.

There is a runabout ticket called the *Greek Tourist Card* issued for 10, 20 and 30 days in 2nd class only. This allows unlimited rail travel throughout the country and also on the extensive bus routes operated by the railway. It is excellent value, especially if you are staying a full month in Greece. The ticket is only available from within Greece; check with the tourist office for details.

By Bus. In addition to the wide variety of bus tours (from half-a-day to a week) operated from Athens by numerous companies, there is a wide network of scheduled coach services reaching to even the smallest village. Some are owned and operated by the railway; others by private companies. Full details from many travel agents in Greece and also from tourist information offices. Travel by bus in Greece is cheap, always crowded, sometimes a bit trying on the nerves, but by far the most popular way to get about.

By Boat. With such a wide scattering of islands especially in the Aegean there is, not surprisingly, a large network of ferries operating from Piraeus (the port of Athens) to the islands and also linking the islands with each other. The small ports of Agia Marina, Lavrio and Rafina, on the coast east of Athens, are less crowded points of departure for southern Euboea and the Cyclades, and closer to them. Schedules are constantly changing. Most ships have at least two classes, plus the cheapest of all—deck class. Overnight services provide berths in cabins or in dormitories at small additional cost. Like the buses, the ferries are always busy. Wherever possible get your tickets beforehand, but for shorter trips this is not necessary. If you require sleeping berths these should certainly be reserved as far ahead as possible.

Always check departure and arrival times. The printed timetables are often changed without notice.

Athens

The historical origins of Athens are lost in the mists of mythology. Poseidon and Athena, two of the most powerful gods on Olympus, contended for the patronage of the city. Poseidon, to prove the justice of his claim, struck the earth with his trident causing a magnificent horse to spring forth. But the astute Athena merely produced an olive tree from the ground, explaining that it represented peace and prosperity, which would serve mankind better than the arts of war personified by Poseidon's steed. The council of gods decided in her favor, and the city was named for the goddess of wisdom. In the age of recorded history, Pisistratus, a 6th century B.C. tyrant who was nonetheless a sound economist and administrator, raised Athens from the status of country town to a city of international importance. Athens attained its Golden Age under Pericles, to whom it is indebted for the architectural splendor that remains. It was during this period of Athenian democracy that the Parthenon, the Erechtheion and the Propylaea of the Acropolis were built, and that Aeschylus, Sophocles and Euripides, Phidias and Myron, Herodotus, Thucydides and Xenophon and—above all—Socrates and Plato made Athens the cultural capital of antiquity.

Today Athens is a large and bustling capital of over four million inhabitants. White marble apartment blocks sprawl from the port of Piraeus to the foot of Mount Hymettus for more than 150 square miles. Most of the ancient monuments are centered around the Acropolis, which rises like a massive sentinel, squat and impregnable, out of the center of the city. Sightseeing is therefore confined to a fairly limited area and is not likely to prove too tiring.

Having survived 2,500 years of sieges, occupations, desecrations and bombardments, the sacred rock is today threatened by a new enemy, air pollution. Though several salvage operations have been undertaken to preserve what remains of the glory that was Greece, no permanent solution has yet been found.

The first ancient monument along Dionysiou Areopagitou Ave. on the Acropolis, is the theater of Dionysus, where the great ancient plays were first performed. The theater of Herodes Atticus built in the 2nd century A.D. is the scene of each summer's Athens Festival of Music and Drama. A drive winds up the hill to the Propylaea, the magnificent gateway to the "upper city." To one side is the temple of Nike Apteros (Wingless Victory), built to commemorate the Greek victories over the Persians in the 5th century B.C. Passing through one of the five gates of the Propylaea onto a rocky plateau, one is confronted with a staggering view of the western front of the Parthenon, its honey-colored columns of Pentelic marble rising from a massive limestone base extending across the highest part of the Acropolis. The Sacred Way from the gate to the Parthenon was once lined with statues covering every inch of the once again barren rock. The Parthenon (Virgin's Chamber) was dedicated to the worship of the virgin goddess Athena. Designed by Ictinus, with sculptural decoration by the great Phidias, the Parthenon has eight fluted columns at either end and 17 on each side. Built on the "golden rectangle" concept, the Parthenon does not, however, contain any straight line—the shafts of the columns incline inward, bulge slightly, and both the stylobate (base) and the entablature rise gradually to a point higher in the middle than at either end.

The exterior sculptural decorations were of a fabulous quality and richness. Phidias and his pupils executed 92 sculptured metopes, 44 statues ornamenting the gables, and a frieze 523 feet long. Most of the sculpture that escaped the Venetian bombardment of 1687 was collected in the 19th century by Lord Elgin and shipped to the British Museum.

As outstanding in the Ionic style as the Parthenon is in the Doric, though considerably smaller, the Erechtheion cannot be matched by any other monument of antiquity, for sheer elegance and refinement of design and execution. The northern portico is famous for its doorway and six slender columns, the southern portico is that of the Caryatids, six maidens in long draperies supporting a two-ton roof of Pentelic marble. The originals, badly damaged by acid rain, are in the Acropolis museum and the British Museum, London; casts have taken their place in the restoration carried out with EC assistance and completed, after eight years' work, in 1988.

The Acropolis is open from 8 A.M. to 7 P.M. during the week and from 6.30 A.M. to 3 P.M. on weekends and holidays; the museum is closed on Monday morning. The hill opposite is the Pnyx, where every evening from April to October the Sound and Light performance is presented.

Other highlights of ancient Athens are the Monument of Lysicrates, the Arch of Hadrian, the Temple of Olympian Zeus, the Olympic Stadium and the wrongly-named Theseion (really the Hephaestion), the best preserved temple in Greece. Though designed by the same architect who built the Parthenon, it lacks sophistication and barely rises above the ancient Agora, the central market place and civic center and a sprawling confusion of stones, slabs and foundations dominated by the restored Stoa of Attalus. Of other eras in Athens' long history, little remains. A few churches are the meager remnants of a thousand years of Byzantine rule, and the tortuous lanes of the Plaka are all that is left of the 19th-century Athens that Byron knew—though he would have difficulty recognizing the few remaining old houses, mostly occupied by tavernas, in this pedestrian zone on the northern slope of the Acropolis.

The center of modern Athens is Syntagma (Constitution) Square. It is built on an incline, bordered with hotels and travel agencies, brightened by orange trees, a fountain and cafés that stay open until late at night. From this square run the two chief thoroughfares of the city, Stadiou Street, the main shopping street, and Panepistimiou Avenue, with the neoclassic Academy, Library and University. Both terminate in Omonia Square, the teeming center of downtown Athens. Returning to Syntagma Square, Vassilissis (Queen) Sofias Avenue, a broad avenue lined with embassies leads north to the hill suburb of Kifissia. Amalias Avenue runs east to the Arch of Hadrian past Parliament House and the National Gardens, beyond which lies the Olympic Stadium, restored in 1896 for the revival of the Olympic Games. The Greeks deeply desire the selection of Greece as the venue for the Centenary Games of 1996. Irodou Attikou Street separates the National Gardens from the presidential palace. Kolonaki, the most fashionable residential quarter is situated on the slope of Mt. Lycabettus. Three times the height of the Acropolis, Lycabettus can be reached by funicular railway, and from the summit you see all of Athens and the plain of Attica, the islands of Aegina and Salamis and the distant mountains of the Peloponnese to the south, pollution permitting.

Piraeus, connected with Athens by six miles of suburbs, is the main port and industrial center of Greece. Though it contains little of interest to the sightseer, it is one of the busiest ports on the Mediterranean. From here, numerous ships depart every day for the islands of the Aegean and Ionian Seas.

PRACTICAL INFORMATION FOR ATHENS

GETTING INTO TOWN FROM THE AIRPORT. Elliniko Airport has two terminals: the East Terminal, which is for international flights; and the West Terminal, for domestic flights and all Olympic Airways flights. A new blue-and-yellow coach service connects the two air terminals, Syntagma Square, and bus and train stations with Piraeus. They run every 15 minutes from 6 A.M. to midnight (fare: 100 dr.) and every 90 minutes from midnight to 6 A.M. (fare: 150 dr.). Taxis are about 600 dr. to the town center, though tourists may be stung for five times as much.

Because there are two terminals at the airport, fairly far apart, be sure you are on the right bus!

HOTELS. Prices of Athens hotels are well within reach of the budget traveler. And even in inexpensive hotels you will usually get basic comfort and cleanliness. But, as is the case throughout the country, most hotels are of a utilitarian sameness and there is little, if anything, to distinguish one from another, except location. The Greek word for hotel is *xenodochion,* "a container for strangers", and that is exactly what they are; good for a rest (though avoid rooms fronting the street) and a wash, but not to spend any time in. When there are any public rooms, which is rare, they are dark and forbidding. Some Moderate and Inexpensive hotels have no restaurant.

Moderate (All airconditioned)

Near Omonia Square—**Athens Center,** Sofokleous 26 (tel. 524 8511). 136 rooms, pool, roofgarden.
Candia, Deliyanni 40 (tel. 524 6112). 142 rooms, pool, roofgarden.
Dorian Inn, Pireos 15 (tel. 523 9782). 146 rooms, pool, roofgarden.
Grand, Veranzerou 10 (tel. 524 3156). 99 rooms, above average food.
Ionis, Halkokondyli 41 (tel. 523 2311). 102 rooms.
La Mirage, M. Kotopouli 3 (tel. 523 4071/3). 208 rooms, new, partly sound-proofed.
Titania, Panepistimiou Ave. 52 (tel. 360 9611). 398 rooms, roofgarden.

Beyond Omonia Square—**Anastasia,** Platia Viktorias 7 (tel. 883 4511). 61 rooms, in residential district.
Crystal, Achilleos 4 (tel. 523 1083). 84 rooms.
Oscar, Samou 25 (tel. 883 4215). 124 rooms, roofgarden; near the railway station.
Plaza, Acharnon 78 (tel. 822 5111). 126 rooms, roofgarden, recently redecorated. Good value.
Stanley, Odysseos 1 (tel. 524 1611). 395 rooms, pool, roofgarden.
Xenophon, Acharnon 340 (tel. 202 0310). 186 rooms, roofgarden.

Closer to Syntagma Square—**Arethousa,** Mitropoleos 6 (tel. 322 9431). 87 rooms.
Athens Gate, Syngrou Ave. 10 (tel. 923 8302). 106 rooms, close to Acropolis.
Lycabette, Valaoritou 6 (tel. 363 3514). 39 rooms, in a quiet pedestrian zone. Well furnished.
Minerva, Stadiou 3 (tel. 323 0915). 50 rooms, on top floors of office block.
Pan, Mitropoleos 11 (tel. 323 7817). 48 rooms, near the Plaka district.

Beyond Syntagma Square—**Austria,** Mouson 7 (tel. 923 5151). 40 rooms, no restaurant, fairly new. On Philopappos hill.
Christina, Petmeza 15 (tel. 921 5353). 93 rooms, quiet.
Clare's House, Sorvolou 24 (tel. 922 2288). 20 rooms, spotless pension in quiet location; excellent value.
Damon, Syngrou Ave. 142 (tel. 923 2171). 97 rooms, roofgarden.

Beyond the Hilton—**Alexandros,** Timoliontos Vassou 8 (tel. 643 0464). 96 rooms, near the U.S. Embassy.

Athinais, Vassilissis Sofias Ave. 99 (tel. 643 6442). 84 rooms, also close to U.S. Embassy.

Ilissia, Mihalakopoulou 25 (tel. 724 4051). 90 rooms. Good location.

Inexpensive

Near Omonia—**Alkistis,** Platia Theatrou 18 (tel. 321 9811). 120 rooms, roof-garden.

Aristides, Sokratous 50 (tel. 522 3881). 90 rooms.

Aristoteles, Aharnon 15 (tel. 522 8126/7). 60 rooms, restaurant.

Athens Connection Hostel, Ioulianou 20 (tel. 821 3940). Hostel type, with single and double rooms as well as four-bed dorms.

Attalos, Athinas 29 (tel. 321 2801). 80 rooms, roofgarden, restaurant.

Capri, Psaromilingou 6 (tel. 325 2085). 44 rooms, roofgarden, airconditioned, restaurant.

Omonia, Platia Omonias 4 (tel. 523 7210). 260 rooms, large bar overlooking the busy square.

Paradise, Mezonos 28 (tel. 522 0084). 12 family rooms; near railway station.

Near Syntagma—**Aphroditi,** Apollonos 21 (tel. 323 4357). 84 rooms, airconditioned, roofgarden.

Acropolis House, Kodhrou 6 (tel. 322 2344). 19 rooms, good situation and good value.

Hermes, Apollonos 19 (tel. 323 5514). 45 rooms, some (M), roofgarden. Modern facade, plain rooms.

Myrto, Nikis 40 (tel. 322 7237). 12 rooms, good for the price, with small bar.

At Piraeus

Overlooking the Saronic Gulf—**Cavo D'Oro** (M), Vassileos Pavlou Ave. 19 (tel. 411 3742). 74 rooms, airconditioned, disco, roofgarden.

Arion (I), Vassileos Pavlou Ave. 109 (tel. 412 1425). 36 rooms, no restaurant.

Leriotis (I), Akti Themistokleous 294 (tel. 451 6640). 45 rooms, quiet for a longer stay.

Near the main harbor—All (M) and airconditioned are:

Homeridion, Harilaou Trikoupi 32 (tel. 451 9811). 59 rooms, disco, roofgarden.

Park, Kolokotroni 103 (tel. 452 4611). 80 rooms, disco, roofgarden.

Savoy, Iroon Politehniou 93 (tel. 413 1102). 71 rooms, roofgarden.

Both (I)—**Anemoni,** Evripidou 65 (tel. 411 1768). 45 rooms.

Anita, Notara 25 (tel. 412 1024). 26 rooms.

Beach Resort Hotels

The southeast coast of Attica, from Faliro to Sounio, is studded with hotels. Most insist on half board. Distances in miles from Athens are shown in parentheses.

Anavissos (31). *Kalypso Motel* (M), tel. 53 154/7. 47 rooms, on beach, disco. *Silver Beach* (I), tel. 36 203. 28 rooms, 100 yds. from beach, restaurant. *Eden Beach* (I), tel. 52 761/5. 286 rooms, pool, minigolf, disco, restaurant.

Glifada (11). *Emmantina* (M), tel. 898 0683/5. 80 rooms, roofgarden, disco, pool. *Fenix* (M), tel. 894 7229. 139 rooms, pool, disco, roofgarden. *Four Seasons* (M), tel. 894 2211/3. 78 rooms, roofgarden. *Regina Maris* (M), tel. 894 0468. 72 rooms, pool, minigolf nearby. *Sea View* (M), tel. 894 7681. 74 rooms, tennis and pool nearby. All airconditioned and all 100–200 yds from beach. *Avra* (I), tel. 894 7185. 43 rooms, small pool. *Beau Rivage* (I), tel. 894 9292. 82 rooms, airconditioned, roofgarden, tennis nearby. *Glyfada* (I), tel. 894 1137. 52 rooms, small pool, tennis. *Oceanis* (I), tel. 894 4038. 73 rooms, small pool. All near beach and all with restaurants.

Kalamaki (8). Very near airport, sea polluted. *Albatross* (M), tel. 982 4981/4. 80 rooms, airconditioned, 50 yds. from beach. *Hellinikon* (M), tel. 981 7227. 52 rooms, airconditioned, beach across the road, minigolf. *Tropical* (M), tel. 981 3993/4. 46 rooms, some (I), garden, minigolf. *Galaxy* (I), tel. 981 8603/4. 44 rooms, airconditioned, beach across the road, restaurant.

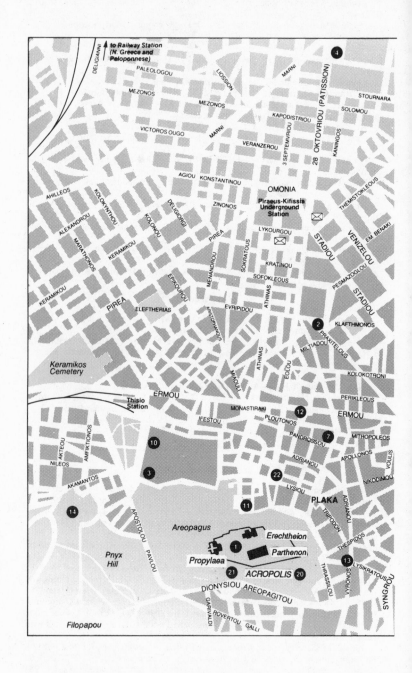

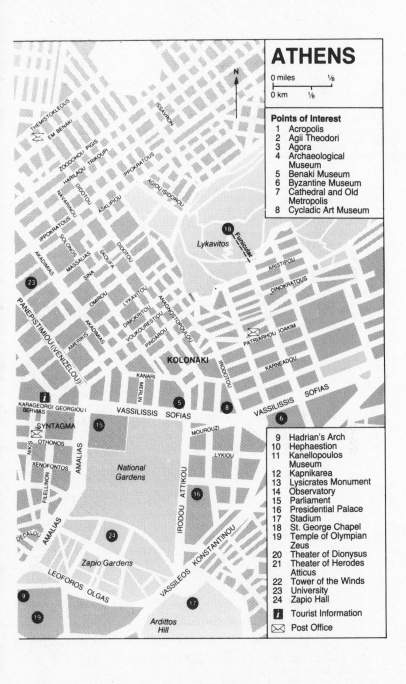

ATHENS

0 miles   ⅛
0 km   ⅛

N

Points of Interest

1 Acropolis
2 Agii Theodori
3 Agora
4 Archaeological Museum
5 Benaki Museum
6 Byzantine Museum
7 Cathedral and Old Metropolis
8 Cycladic Art Museum

9 Hadrian's Arch
10 Hephaestion
11 Kanellopoulos Museum
12 Kapnikarea
13 Lysicrates Monument
14 Observatory
15 Parliament
16 Presidential Palace
17 Stadium
18 St. George Chapel
19 Temple of Olympian Zeus
20 Theater of Dionysus
21 Theater of Herodes Atticus
22 Tower of the Winds
23 University
24 Zapio Hall

i Tourist Information
✉ Post Office

Lykavitos

KOLONAKI

National Gardens

SYNTAGMA

Zapio Gardens

Ardittos Hill

Kavouri (14). *Pine Hill* (M), tel. 896 0871/2. 83 rooms, airconditioned, beach across the road, tennis, roofgarden, pool.

Paleo Faliro (5). Polluted sea. *Possidon* (M), tel. 982 2086. 90 rooms, airconditioned, pool, beach across the road. *Avra* (I), tel. 981 4064/5. 39 rooms, beach across the road.

Sounio (44). *Surf Beach Club* (M). tel. 22 363/4. 265 rooms in hotel and bungalows, pool, tennis, disco. *Saron* (I), tel. 39 144. 28 rooms, beach 120 yds., restaurant.

Varkiza (19). Best beach along the coast. *Varkiza* (M), tel. 897 0927/9. 30 rooms, roofgarden, beach 200 yds. *Holidays* (I), tel. 897 0915/7. 34 rooms, beach 500 yds.

Voula (13). *Castello Beach* (M), tel. 895 8985. 34 rooms, tennis nearby. *Rondo* (I), tel. 895 8605. 44 rooms, beach 100 yds. Both with restaurants.

Vouliagmeni (16). Quieter than Glifada and slightly more chic. *Paradise* (M), tel. 896 2298. 58 airconditioned rooms, roofgarden, pool. *Strand* (M), tel. 896 0705/7. 72 rooms, airconditioned, disco. Both have beach across the road.

RESTAURANTS. Hotel dining rooms are probably the budgeteer's best bet as they alone offer set menus, but, alas, all too often nothing else. One set-menu meal a day is probably enough for most people, and it's easy to get something lighter. You could try one of the several *Psistaria* (grillrooms) in the pedestrian zone at Omonia Square. No, you won't get a steak—which in any case is hardly ever worth the money in Greece—but try *doner kebab* or *gyros:* slices are cut from a huge hunk of pressed seasoned meat turning on a spit outside. Also available, and cooked *inside,* are chicken, *souvlakia, keftedakia,* salad and *tiri feta* (goat's cheese) which is tasty but salty. Prices for psistaria are in the lower Moderate range. They are so alike that listing one rather than another is unjustifiable. This applies also to the numerous pizzerias, and also to the dozens of snack bars of various kinds, some of them good, such as the one at Venizelou 52. There are hundreds of these inexpensive shops selling take-away cheese or spinach pies (*tiropites* and *spanakopites*) and *tosts,* toasted bread with every imaginable filling. *Koulouria,* sesame-seed–covered bread rings, can be bought from barrows on street-corners to ease pangs of hunger. Fruit is plentiful and cheap.

Moderate

Delphi, Nikis 13. Near Constitution Square. Popular, often crowded. Good lunchtime spot.

Diros, Xenofontos 10. Good food, friendly service, reasonably priced.

Drugstore, Stoa (Passage) Koraï. Restaurant and *ouzerie* downstairs, very pleasant café above.

Hermion, Pandrossos 15. Delightful courtyard. Fixed-priced menus.

Ideal, Panepistimiou 46. Exceptionally large menu; good service. Open 11 A.M. to 2 A.M.

Kostoyannis, Zaimi 37. Near National Archeological Museum. Excellent and popular; very wide range including the best Greek dishes.

Psarra, Erotokritou and Erechtheou, Plaka. Good fresh swordfish and *souvlaki;* guitarist. Closed Wed.

Taverna Xinos, Angelou Vlachou 4. Large taverna for evening dining, (unresinated) wine and guitar music. Very popular with Athenians. In the Plaka. Closed Sun.

Vassilaina, Etolikou 72, in Piraeus (to the right of the main harbor). The only fish restaurant that can be recommended in this category—fresh fish is decidedly expensive, so beware the string of inviting establishments lining picturesque Mikrolimano—and astonishingly good value at 1300 dr. for the vast set menu (up to 24 different courses). Set in renovated grocery store.

Inexpensive

American Restaurant, Karageorgi Servias 1. Real breakfasts; good range of main meal dishes. Closed Sun.

Eden, Flessa 3, Plaka. Pleasant vegetarian restaurant serving imaginative dishes. Rooftop terrace.

Floca, Emmanuel Benaki 16. Large range of hot and cold dishes, self-service, well run and spotless. Closed Sat. eve., and Sun.

Kentrikon, Kolokontroni 3. Good standard. Spacious, modern and clean. Closed every eve., Sat. and Sun.

Nea Olympia, Emmanuel Benaki 3. Very popular for lunch. Closed Sat. eve. and Sun.

Sidrivani, Filellinon 5. Old-established and reliable, tables in the courtyard.

GETTING AROUND ATHENS. By Bus/Trolley Bus. Plentiful, when not on strike, and cheap (only 30 drs. standard fare), but they operate only until midnight and are very crowded during rush hours. From the city center, the suburbs and the beaches of the southern coast can be reached by bus.

For buses to other parts of Greece, there are terminals at Kifissou 100 and Liossion 260 (latter for buses to Euboea and Eastern Central Greece). Buses to destinations within Attica leave from various fairly central locations. Ask your hotel porter or at the tourist office for details.

By Electric Train. The summer resort of Kifissia and the port of Piraeus are connected by electric trains that run via the underground (subway) stations of Omonia, Monastiraki, and Theseion.

By Taxi. Taxis are numerous but, being cheap, not always easy to get. Go by the meter—some drivers try to overcharge strangers grossly. Don't expect detailed knowledge of the city.

ENTERTAINMENT. Cinema. Cinemas showing the latest foreign pictures are plentiful and English-language films are listed in the daily *Athens News* (60 dr.). The *Athenian* (325 dr.), an English-language monthly magazine, also lists screenings, as well as exhibitions, concerts, and lectures. There are also open-air cinemas, mostly in the suburbs, in summer. There is an open-air cinema in the Zapio Gardens in the center of town.

Tavernas. A part of the Plaka district below the Acropolis is given over to tavernas with music, usually guitars, or with full programs. The latter are veritable tourist traps and are best visited on an *Athens by Night* tour. The former, though, present genuinely traditional entertainment, and at moderate prices, but in the summer are entirely taken over by tourists. If you don't mind braving the chaotic traffic, you might, as the Athenians do, try the numerous open-air tavernas and nightclubs that stretch along the coast from Faliro to Sounio. These are really accessible only by car, however, for the buses in the evening are infrequent and very crowded.

Among those in the Plaka are:

Klimataria, Klepsidras 5. Lively, noisy. Sometimes closed Mon.

Loukas, Prytanion 18. Guitar music and dancing.

Palia Taverna Stamatopoulou, Lysiou 26. Not so geared to tourists as some tavernas.

Theophilos, Vakhou 1a. Good wine; closed Sun.

Then there are the bouzoukia taverns, where the noise of the large mandolin-like instruments is amplified to levels comparable to a Concorde take off. Food is sinfully expensive, at least 2,500 dr. per person, and don't imagine you get away with less by just ordering fruit or a drink—it's better to get a bottle of whiskey.

Athina, Syngrou Ave. 165.

Lido, Zoodohov Pigis 3 and Akadamias (in center of town).

Discos and Clubs. There is a large concentration in the Kolonaki district and on Syngrou Ave. The question of membership never arises and dancing continues till 2 A.M. They are all much of a muchness, however, so to single out any particular ones rather stretches the credibility gap; strangely enough, it would be easier to list those to avoid, as the expensive variety last, while the moderate and inexpensive ones wax and wane.

THEATERS AND CONCERTS. The *Athens Festival of Music and Drama,* held each year from June to September, attracts many visitors to the theater of Herodes Atticus, the ocher-colored Roman building that glows in a brilliant floodlit scene that includes the Acropolis, the monument of Philopappus and the Temple of

Olympian Zeus. The purpose of the festival is to provide a series of artistic events in a setting recalling the Dionysian Festivals of antiquity. The programs include symphony concerts by the Athens State Orchestra, as well as by various foreign orchestras. There are also performances of opera and ballet by Greek and foreign companies.

One of the highlights of the festival is the cycle of ancient Greek tragedies and Attic comedies put on by the National Theater. The performances are all in modern Greek. Ancient drama and concerts are also presented at the Lycabettus Theater, while the Philoppapos Theater is given over to folk dancing. Tickets for the festival should be obtained in advance from the ticket office in the passage at Stadiou 4.

MUSEUMS. Opening hours for the most part 8.30 A.M.–3 P.M.; closed on national holidays and Monday, unless otherwise stated. Archeological sites are generally open from 8 A.M. in summer to sunset. In winter they close earlier. The Acropolis is open in summer from 8 A.M. to 7 P.M. during the week and 8.30 A.M. to 3 P.M. on weekends and holidays.

The Acropolis Museum, closed Mon. mornings. Full of sculptures from the Acropolis. Among the main exhibits are the Caryatids of the Erechtheion, brought indoors to save them from further pollution.

Benaki Museum, Koumbari 1 and Vassilissis Sofias Ave. 17, open 8.30 A.M. to 2 P.M., closed Tues.Exhibits range from ancient sculpture, through Byzantine pieces, Ottoman ceramics and Chinese jade to modern pictures. Stunning collection of Greek national costumes.

Byzantine Museum, Vassilissis Sofias Ave. 22, open 8 A.M. to 7 P.M. In attractive 19th-century building with modern additions. Huge collection of icons, and some lovely embroidery, especially the 14th-century *Epitaphios of Thessaloniki.*

Museum of Cycladic and Ancient Greek Art, Neofytou Douka 4, open 10 A.M. to 4 P.M. Closed Tues. and Sun. Spans 5,000 years, with special emphasis on the Cycladic civilization 3,000–2,000 B.C.

Museum of Greek Folk Art, Kydathineon 17, open 10 A.M. to 2 P.M. Traditional folk art, a collection of Rhodian pottery, clerical robes, costumes and embroideries.

The Kanellopoulos Museum, open 8.45 A.M. to 3 P.M. Small, excellent, and over-looked, at junction of Theorias and Panos Streets, below the Acropolis. Traditional arts, Byzantine jewelry, icons etc. Worth a visit.

The Keramikos Museum, Ermou 148, finds from the ancient cemetery.

National Archeological Museum, Tossitsa 1, open 8 A.M. to 7 P.M.; 8.30 A.M. to 3 P.M. on weekends and holidays. Closed Mon. morning. One good reason for visiting Athens. Staggering collection of treasures beginning with Schliemann's now slightly controversial finds from Mycenae. Exhibits not always well labelled, but they speak for themselves. This is a must for anyone wanting to get oriented to Greek classical art and history, before setting off on a tour of sites elsewhere in Greece.

National Gallery, Vassileos Konstantinou 50, open 9 A.M. to 3 P.M.; 10 A.M. to 2 P.M. on Sun. and holidays. Opposite the Hilton, contains some El Grecos, but mainly 19th-century paintings.

Naval Museum, Freatis, Piraeus, open 9 A.M. to 12.30 P.M.; 10 A.M. to 1 P.M. and 5 P.M. to 8 P.M. on Sun. and holidays. Model ships and naval memorabilia.

Piraeus Archeological Museum, Harilaou Trikoupi 31, includes two very fine bronze statues.

Stoa of Attalos Museum at the ancient Agora, near Thission Square, shows finds of the American School of Classical Studies, worth visiting while seeing the Agora itself.

SHOPPING. Even in Athens, though less than in other principal cities of Europe, browsing will pay off. You will find numbers of small shops and bazaars full of attractive things: embroideries, unusual handwoven materials, traditional jewelry and silverware, pottery from Rhodes and Skyros, Byzantine icons, rugs, and lots of brass and copperware.

Shopping hours are liable to constant changes, not only from one season, but even from one day to the next. Enquire of your hotel porter, specifying the kind of shop you want. A word about prices. The larger stores and smart shops have fixed prices, but the further you get away from Constitution Square and into the

Monastiraki area, the more you can bargain, particularly for handicrafts and antiques.

For Greek **handicrafts** there are many souvenir shops in the Syntagma area. Be sure to see the *National Fund's Handicraft Shops,* at Voukourestiou 24 and Ypatias 6 (near the Cathedral), which have authentic peasant craft and folk art. The *Greek Women's Institute,* at Kolokotroni 3 (in the courtyard), has laces and embroideries. At *EOMMEX,* Mitropoleos 9 (first floor), there are handicrafts from the villages, and at Pandrossou 36 (upstairs) you'll find a wide selection, and a good café snack bar.

Greek rugs, those handwoven, brilliantly colored, long tufted, all-wool ones called *flokates,* can be found in two shops in Mitropoleos, on the corner of Pentelis and at no. 27; both shops have other handmade rugs. The *National Fund* and *EOMMEX* also have rugs and carpets. Pandrossou Street has, among many souvenir shops, some **antiques** dealers, who spread to the area of Syntagma Square. When buying antiques, note that there are Greco-Roman and Byzantine antiquities, and relics of the Turkish domination. There is a bewildering variety of icons, coins, pottery and votive offerings with a high proportion of modern fakes. The genuine stuff is certainly not cheap, and requires an export permit.

The Athens **flea market** is at the end of Ifestou Street, just off Monastiraki Square, in the same general area as antiques. It is held on Sunday mornings when all the wares are spread out on the ground. Here you'll find including old furniture, clothes, shoes, records, second-hand books, used motorbikes, brass knick-knacks, and mirrors. Ifestou Street itself is most interesting for there are copper and blacksmith shops here, as well as antiques dealers.

USEFUL ADDRESSES. *U.S. Consulate,* Vassilissis Sofias 91, tel. 721 2951; *Canadian Consulate,* Ioannou Genadiou 4, tel. 723 9511; *British Consulate,* Plutarchou 1, tel. 723 6211; *American Express,* Ermou 2, Syntagma, tel. 324 4975; *Thomas Cook,* 7 Stadiou St., tel. 923 5358; *Wagons Lits/Tourisme,* Stadiou 5, tel 324 2281; *Post Offices,* Syntagma Square, Eolou 100, and Omonia Underground Station; *National Tourist Information Office,* in the bank at Karageorgi Servias 2, Syntagma, tel. 322 2545; *Tourist Police,* Leoforos Syngrou 7, tel. 171; *Emergency first aid,* tel. 166.

Delphi

The "Parnassus Country" is a term frequently applied to the mountainous area between the Boeotian plains and the sparsely populated Gulf of Corinth. Most of this highland region is rich in mythological and historical allusion. The rugged slopes of Mt. Kithairon are associated with the haunts of Pan, the god of shepherds, and his satyrs. The sacred grove where the nine muses dwelled lay in a secluded valley of Mt. Helicon. The caves and crevices of Parnassus itself were the scene of bacchanalian revels and nocturnal dances. Delphi, the most celebrated oracle of antiquity, rose terrace-by-terrace above what the ancients called the "navel of the earth."

After the Acropolis in Athens, the site of Delphi is the one most likely to make a lasting and powerful impression on the visitor. In the sanctuary, with its ruined temples, treasuries and the foundations of various monuments, uncovered by French excavations beginning in 1892, only the treasury of the Athenians and a few temple columns have been re-erected. But it is not impossible to conjure up a vision of what the scene must have been like when Delphi was the holiest place in all Greece. Of the great temple of Apollo, the seat of the oracle in the very center of the sanctuary, little remains but the podium and peristyle, though several Doric columns have been replaced in their original positions.

It was from a subterranean fissure here that the mysterious exhalations came. Before each prophecy, the priestess (always a woman over the age of 50) was purified with water from the adjacent Kastalian spring, then she would sit upon a tripod above the crevasse. An animal was sacrified and the entrails carefully examined. Questions relating to the fate of a war, colonization, marriage or business enterprise would be put to the priestess, who in a trance would make incoherent utterances interpreted by a prophet. Most of the oracle's pronouncements were indeed ambiguous, but they nonetheless had their effect on history.

Above the temple rises the 4th century B.C. theater, covered with marble during the Roman epoch. Higher up on the cliff are the well-preserved ruins of the Stadium, where the Pythian games were held. Below the Kastalian spring is the Marmaria, the term applied to a group of ruins, including the two temples of Athena, the much-depicted Tholos, a mysterious circular sanctuary, the Gymnasium and other traces of the marbled past. The museum contains some outstanding Greek and Roman antiquities and the superb 5th-century B.C. *Chariotter,* one of the few surviving bronze statutes from that time.

PRACTICAL INFORMATION FOR DELPHI

Hotels and Restaurants

Telephone area code: 0265.

Europa (M), next to the European Cultural Center, tel. 82 353/4. 46 rooms. *Kastalia* (M), tel. 82 205/7. 26 rooms. Both half board only. *Hermes* (I), tel. 82 318. 24 rooms. *Iniohos* (I), tel. 82 316. 15 rooms. *Pan* (I), tel. 82 294. 14 rooms. Peaceful location at quiet end of town. *Parnassos* (I), tel. 82 321. 23 rooms. *Pythia* (I), tel. 82 328. 27 rooms. Most have restaurants and all are in the village main street.

Two cheap pensions offer excellent value: *Manatis* (I), tel. 82 134, 7 rooms; *Odysseus* (I), tel. 82235, 8 rooms.

Restaurants. Except for the *Chalet Maniati* (M), *Taverna Asteras* (I), and *Taverna Vakhos* (I)—all serving fairly cheap and tasty meals—meals on restaurant terraces rely on the magnificent view down to the sea in compensation for the very indifferent food. The large purple Amfissa olives produced here are among the best in the country.

The Peloponnese

Shortly after the last houses of the sprawling Athenian conglomeration on the way to the Peloponnese, is the 6th-century monastery of Daphni, rebuilt some seven hundred years later by Cistercian monks as the burial place of Athens' Frankish dukes. It contains superb mosaics. Facing the island of Salamis across the narrow straits where Xerxes' Persian fleet was decisively defeated in 480 B.C., the ruins of Eleusis, site of antiquity's most important mystery celebrations since time immemorial, are today sadly polluted by the surrounding factories.

Old Corinth, 58 miles by the motorway and across the spectacular Corinth Canal, opened in 1893, was a Roman town founded by Julius Caesar on the site of the destroyed Greek city, of which only the sixth-century B.C. temple of Apollo remains. You can drive up to the huge Crusader castle of Acro-Corinth, once crowned by a sanctuary to Aphrodite, where a thousand sacred prostitutes earning their dowry while working for the goddess.

Even if you are not in Greece for the annual Epidaurus Festival in summer, you should visit Epidaurus, only 18 miles from Nafplio, another shrine of ancient Greece, the sanctuary of Aesculapius, God of Healing. See the foundations of the temples and hospitals, but especially the incomparable open-air theater, whose acoustics you can test yourself. You can actually hear a stage whisper from the top row of this theater, which still seats 14,000 spectators at the summer festival.

Mycenae, 80 miles from Athens, was a fortified town, destroyed in 468 B.C. and totally forgotten until 1874, when the German archeologist Schliemann unearthed this fabulous stronghold of the 13th-century B.C. Achaean kings. This was the seat of the doomed house of Atreus, of Agamemnon and his wife, the vengeful Clytemnestra, sister of Helen of Troy. When the now somewhat discredited Schliemann uncovered the six shaft graves of the royal circle he felt sure that among these were the tombs of Agamemnon and Clytemnestra. The gold masks and crowns, the daggers, jewelry and other treasures found in the tombs of Mycenae are now in the National Archeological Museum in Athens. The astounding bee-hive tombs cut into the hills outside the reconstructed walls, the Lion Gate and castle ruins crowning their barren hill are the shell of the first great civilization of continental Europe. Further south, beyond Argos, Europe's oldest continuously inhabited town, and the cyclopean ramparts of Tiryns, is Nafplio, a beautifully situated, picturesque little town protected by huge Venetian fortifications.

Matching Delphi's majestic grandeur with idyllic serenity, Olympia lies 200 miles southwest of Athens, by the motorway via Patra, capital of the Peloponnese. The first Olympic Games were held in 776 B.C. and were celebrated quadrennially until A.D. 393, when the Christian Roman Emperor Theodosius I banned these "pagan rites." Excavations are still uncovering statues and votive offerings among the olive groves and pine trees surrounding the Olympic stadium and the imposing ruins of the temples of Zeus and Hera in the sacred precinct. Outstanding among the two museums' many treasures is one of the most perfect pieces of sculpture in existence—the *Hermes* by Praxiteles.

PRACTICAL INFORMATION FOR THE PELOPONNESE

Corinth. *Ephira* (I), tel. 0741–22 434. 45 rooms, roofgarden.

Epidaurus (Palea). 12 miles from the ruins, on the sea. *Apollon* (I), tel. 0753–41 295. 38 rooms. *Saronis* (I), tel. 0753–41 514. 39 rooms, good site, poor beach.

Mycenae. *La Petite Planete* (I), tel. 0751–66 240. 29 rooms, with garden restaurant.

Nafplio. Telephone area code: 0752. *Amphitryon* (M), tel. 27 366/7. 48 rooms, pool. *Agamemnon* (I), tel. 28 021/2. 40 rooms, with pool and roofgarden. *Dioscouri* (I), tel. 28 550. 51 rooms. *Park* (I), tel. 27 428. 70 rooms, airconditioned. *Rex* (I), tel. 28 094. 51 rooms. *Victoria* (M), tel. 27 420. 36 rooms, airconditioned. All with restaurants.

Olympia. Telephone area code: 0624. *Antonios* (M), tel. 22 348/9. 65 rooms, roofgarden. *Apollon* (M), tel. 22 522. 110 rooms, roofgarden, pool. *Ilis* (I), tel. 22 547. 57 rooms, roofgarden. *Kronion* (I), tel. 22 502. 23 rooms. All with restaurants.

Patra. Telephone area code: 061. *Galaxy* (M), Agiou Nikolaou 9, tel. 27 5981/3. 53 rooms, airconditioned. *Moreas* (M), Iroon Polytehniou 40, tel. 42 5494. 105 rooms, restaurant. *Adonis* (I), Kapsali 9, tel. 22 4213. 56 rooms. *Delfini* (I), Iroon Polytehniou 102, tel. 42 1001/5. 71 rooms, airconditioned, restaurant, pool, but less central, half a mile from both town and beach.

At **Paralia Proastiou:** 2 miles, on beach; *Achaia Beach* (M), tel. 99 1801/4. 87 rooms, pool, tennis, disco. *Tzaki* (M), tel. 42 8303. 38 rooms, restaurant.

The Greek Islands

There are about 1,500 islands in the Aegean and Ionian Seas, and one of them is just right for you. The Aegean is the heart of the Greek world. In ancient times, its center was in the sanctuary of Apollo on the sacred island of Delos. Grouped round this small island are the Cyclades. These link up, intermingle sometimes, with the islands in the other groups—the Sporades, the Dodecanese and the offshore islands—to form stepping stones from east to west. Both yesterday and today in mountainous Greece, it is the land that separates, the sea that unites. The islands are delightful for sailing, swimming, sunning and fishing. Even if you leave your swimming and scuba gear behind, however, there is enough history in these islands to fill a library. Even those who have "small Latin and less Greek" never fail to respond to the beauty of the place names, and the age-old romance of the islands. From any island that you visit, views of its neighbors will attract you to endless exploration. All the summers of a lifetime could be spent among them, from Crete, the largest, to all those of historic or scenic importance—Ydra, Spetses, Mykonos, Delos, Thira, Rhodes, Patmos, Corfu, Skiathos. Nearly all island capitals bear the island's name.

PRACTICAL INFORMATION FOR THE GREEK ISLANDS

GETTING TO THE GREEK ISLANDS. By Boat. Athens' main port, Piraeus, is supplemented by the Attic ports Agia Marina, Lavrio, and Rafina. Days and hours of island boats are subject to change. By far the easiest and quickest to reach are the offshore islands of Aegina, Poros, Ydra and Spetses, numerous daily ferries being complemented by hydrofoil from Zea Harbor, Piraeus.

The main Cyclades islands of Tinos, Mykonos, Syros, Paros, Naxos, Ios, and Thira are served at least twice daily; the smaller islands of Serifos, Sifnos, Milos, and others have ferries most days. There are daily car ferries to Hios, Lesbos, and Samos, and one or two a day to Hania and Iraklio in Crete.

The Sporades, including Skyros, Skiathos, and Skopelos are best reached from Agios Constantinos or Volos, by car ferry or hydrofoil. There is also a service from Thessaloniki. Thasos is reached by frequent car ferries from Kavala or Keramoti in Macedonia. Ferries for Samothraki leave from Alexandropoulis.

The Dodecanese, including Kos and Rhodes, are served daily by car ferry. The Ionian islands are connected to Patra and other west coast ports.

To spread the tourist dollar more evenly, transport by boat from the more to the less popular islands is free from May through Sept.

By Plane. The more important islands are connected with Athens by at least three flights daily. Some also have flights from Thessaloniki. Many other islands have at least one flight daily, and there are flights between islands.

HOTELS AND RESTAURANTS. Despite the large number of hotels on all major islands, it is essential to book well in advance in season. In most smaller beach resorts private accommodation is available, usually a few rooms with showers in a separate building. It is wise to take a look at the lodgings, almost exclusively shoe-stringers' delights, before accepting. You can always check with the tourist police, or the tourist office, if there is one, to find accommodations.

You will not find famous eating places catering to gourmets on the Greek islands. Restaurants are often run by families with mama in the kitchen and papa acting as maitre-d'. You go in, look around, see what's good and point to it. Fish is just as expensive and harder to come by than in Athens, to which most of the catch is sent.

The Saronic Isles

Aegina. Largest of the islands in the Saronic Gulf and with the most varied scenery. The town, also Aegina, is on the site of an ancient Greek city, but the islands' best preserved temple rises above the beach resort of Agia Marina.

Telephone area code: 0297.

Hotels. In town: *Danae* (M), tel. 22 424/5. 52 rooms, pool, 50 yds. from the rather poor town beach. *Avra* (I), tel. 22 303. 33 rooms, half board, disco, beach across the road. *Klonos* (I), tel. 22 640. 46 rooms, beach 50 yds. *Nafsika* (I), tel. 22 333. 34 rooms, half board, bungalows, on beach. All with restaurants.

At **Agia Marina:** *Apollo* (M), tel. 32 271/4. 107 rooms, pool. *Argo* (M), tel. 32 471/3. 60 rooms, half board. Both on beach and both with tennis. *Pantelaros* (M), tel. 32 431/2. 55 rooms. *Aphaea* (I), tel. 32 227. 18 rooms. *Galini* (I), tel. 32 203. 35 rooms, half board. *Marina* (I), tel. 32 301. 29 rooms, half board. All close to beach. All, except *Pantelaros,* with restaurants.

At **Perdika,** 5 miles south: *Aegina Maris* (M), tel. 25 130. 164 rooms, airconditioned, beach, pool, disco, tennis.

Poros. This island is so close to the Peloponnese that the steamer just manages to squeeze by. In *The Colossus of Maroussi,* Henry Miller said it made him feel as if he were sailing among houses. The thickly-wooded hillside is nice for hiking while longer excursions will take you to remains of the ancient temple of Poseidon, or on the mainland to the beautifully situated ruins of ancient Troezen, scene of the tragedy of Phaedra. The beaches on Poros are not as good as those on neighboring Aegina and Ydra.

Telephone area code: 0298.

Hotels. At **Galata,** on the Peloponnese opposite: *Galatia* (I), tel. 22 227. 30 rooms, restaurant. *Papasotiriou* (I), tel. 22 841. 33 rooms, 100 yds. from beach.

On the island—*Sirene* (M), tel. 22 741/5. 120 rooms, half board, pool, disco, roofgarden; on its own beach two miles from Poros town. Nearer town: *Neon Aegli* (M), tel. 22 372. 72 rooms. On pine-fringed Askeli beach. *Poros* (I), tel. 22 216/8. 91 rooms, disco, roofgarden. Both on beach. In the town: *Latsi* (M), tel. 22 392. 39 rooms, some without showers; on the waterfront and noisy. All with restaurants.

Restaurants. The numerous seaside tavernas get very crowded in the summer and the food and service are both erratic. However, *Caravella* (I), on the waterfront, is good value. The *Garden of the Hesperides* (M) near Canalia beach, *Galaxy* (I) on Monastiri beach, and *Panorama* (I) at Askeli, are all worth trying.

Spetses. This pine-clad island is less arty-crafty than Idra and more for those who prefer the pastoral scene.

Telephone area code: 0298.

Hotels. *Ilios* (M), tel. 72 488. 27 rooms, airconditioned, with roofgarden; on the waterfront. *Possidonion* (M), tel. 72 208, 55 rooms, pleasantly Edwardian and old-fashioned; not all the rooms with private facilities. The author John Fowles used it as a setting in his novel *The Magus.Faros* (I), tel. 72 613. 47 rooms, bed and breakfast only; on the central square. *Myrtoon* (I), tel. 72 555. 39 rooms; restaurant, roofgarden. *Roumanis* (I), tel. 72 244. 35 rooms. *Star* (I), tel. 72 214. 37 rooms, airconditioned, with roofgarden and restaurant.

The Peloponnese offers a wider choice of accommodations, if not a better one. Telephone area code: 0754. At **Kosta:** *Cap d'Or* (M), tel. 51 360/3. 147 rooms, pool, minigolf, tennis, disco. *Lido* (M), tel. 51 393. 40 rooms. Both on beach.

At **Porto Heli:** *Apollo Beach* (M), tel. 51 431. 151 rooms in bungalows; disco. *Galaxy* (M), tel. 51 271/6. 171 rooms, airconditioned; garden. *Giouli* (M), tel. 51 217/8. 163 rooms, airconditioned. *Ververoda Holiday Resort* (M), tel. 51 343/5. 244 rooms in main building and bungalows; disco. All these are on or near the beach and have pools, restaurants and tennis. *Alcyon* (I), tel. 51 479. 89 rooms, airconditioned, restaurant, disco; 300 yds. from the beach.

Restaurants. Among those on the harbor side are *Soulias* (M) and the *Pizzeria* (I). There are also several cheaper tavernas.

Ydra. This barren, mountainous island has been chosen by many artists and writers, the genuine article outnumbered by the would-be's. The town is picturesque, with quaint old buildings.

Telephone area code: 0298.

Hotels. Accommodations in town are not satisfactory. *Hydroussa* (M), tel. 52 217. 36 rooms in converted mansion, restaurant. *Leto* (I), tel. 52 280. 39 rooms, half with showers, no restaurant. *Miranda* (M), tel. 52 230. 14 rooms in coverted 18th-century mansion. Top of the (M) range. *Mistral* (M), tel. 52 509. 18 rooms, rather forbidding-looking pension, recently built.

At **Mandraki Beach,** one mile outside town: *Miramare* (M), tel. 52 300/1. 28 rooms, restaurant.

At **Petrothalassa** (Ermioni) on the Peloponnese opposite the island the accommodations and amenities are far superior. *Aquarius* (M), tel. 0754–31 430/4. 415 rooms, pool. *Lena-Mary* (M), tel. 0754–31 450/1. 120 rooms, airconditioned. Both are half board and have disco, minigolf, and tennis.

Restaurants. *Drouskos* (Xeri Elia) (M), in the square, is good. *Yacht Club* (M) features entertainment plus drinks and food. *Loulou's* (I), adequate but pretty basic.

The Cyclades

Delos. Delos is the legendary birthplace of the sun god Apollo. In classical times, Delos was a center of religious worship and under the Romans a thriving emporium. Largely abandoned for over a thousand years, it served as a quarry for the surrounding islands. Among the ruins the five Naxian marble lions dating from the 7th century B.C. are the best known. There are also some fine temples to Apollo and an assortment of Greek, Roman, Egyptian and Syrian gods, plus sumptuous houses with mosaic floors, reminders of their days of splendor. There is currently no accommodation on the island. Visitors must stay on nearby Mykonos and travel to and fro by boat.

Mykonos. People used to merely stop over on Mykonos on their way to Delos, However, But over the last 20 years, Mykonos has become one of the most popular and expensive islands in the Aegean, with a reputation as a good-time resort. Despite the crowds, the town is still strikingly beautiful, with dazzling white houses around the harbour and hundreds of tiny chapels and churches, all typical of the architecture of the Cyclades. The beaches, too, are idyllic, despite or because of a nudist reserve, while the horizon is enlivened by the round, white, thatched windmills characteristic of the island.

Telephone area code: 0289.

Hotels. *Alkistis* (M), tel. 22 332. 102 beach bungalows, on Aghios Stefanos beach, one mile from town. *Panorama* (I), tel. 22 337. 27 rooms, disco, minigolf, tennis. *Paralos Beach* (I), tel. 22 600. 40 rooms. All with restaurants. **In town** or nearby: *Despotiko* (M), tel. 22 009. 36 rooms, airconditioned, pool, no restaurant. *Korali* (M), tel. 22 929. 28 rooms; on outskirts. *Kouneni* (M), tel. 22 301. 19 rooms. *Mykonos Beach* (M), tel. 22 572. 27 bungalows; disco. *Rohari* (M), tel. 23 107. 53 rooms. *Theoxenia* (M), tel. 22 230. 57 rooms. Inexpensive accommodations are best found in private houses.

Restaurants. *Antonini's* (M), in the square where the bus leaves, *Fouskis* (M) and *Zani's* (M), on the waterfront, are all good. *Nikos* (I), behind the O.T.E., is excellent for lunches.

Among the many bars, mostly catering to the young, are *Nine Muses* and *Remezzo* and, for something a little different, *Piero's* and *Nefeli*—all (M). Discos include *La Mer, Rainbow,* and *The Yacht Club.*

Paros. You'll find architecture here similar to that at Mykonos and varied terrain with much greenery. The church of Ekatontapyliani is the best known and most historic church in the Aegean. The marble—brilliantly white—that was much used at Delos in more ancient times was quarried here.

Telephone area code: 0284.

Hotels. In town: *Argo* (I), tel. 21 367. 44 rooms. **On nearby beaches:** *Apollon* (M), tel. 22 364. 23 rooms. *Paros Bay* (M), tel. 21 140. 65 rooms. *Polos* (M), tel. 22 173. 21 rooms. *Nicolas* (I), tel. 22 259. 43 rooms, on a clifftop overlooking the beach. **At Naoussa.** *Atlantis* (M), tel. 51 209. 28 rooms. *Ippokambos* (M), tel. 51 223. 49 rooms in bungalows. *Calypso* (I), tel. 51 488. 24 rooms, restaurant. *Minoa* (I), tel. 51 309. 26 rooms, restaurant.

Restaurants. The *Barbarigou* (I), near the shore, and the *Pantheon* (I), are both reasonably good.

Thira. This spectacular island, also called Santorini, has been identified with legendary Atlantis, ever since a highly sophisticated Bronze Age town was discovered on the rim of a crater that was forged by a shattering volcanic explosion in about 1450 B.C. Eruptions and earthquakes have continued throughout the centuries, the last, in 1956, toppling the Venetian capital high up on the crater's ridge.

Telephone area code: 0286.

Hotels. Small hotels scattered over the island. **In town.** *Kallisti Thira* (M), tel. 22 317. 33 rooms. *Panorama* (M), tel. 22 481. 20 rooms, disco; restaurant. **At Kamari Beach:** *Kamari* (M), tel. 31 243. 55 rooms, pool, tennis, disco, roofgarden. *Pelican* (M), tel. 23 113. 18 rooms, next to bus station. *Santorini* (I), tel. 22 593. 24 rooms.

Restaurant. *Zorba's* (M) and *Camille Stefani*, (M), both have good reputations, but owners (and even names) change most seasons.

The Dodecanese

Kos. After a devastating earthquake in 1933, Kos was rebuilt with low, white buildings designed to withstand future tremors. The birthplace of Hippocrates, the Father of Medicine, Kos is rich in antique, medieval and Turkish remains. Its lush vegetation inspired the pastoral poetry of Theocritus.

Telephone area code: 0242.

Hotels. *Atlanta Beach* (M), tel. 28 889. 44 rooms. *Kos* (M), tel. 22 480. 137 rooms, pool. *Theoxenia* (M), tel. 22 310. 42 rooms. All back on to the pebbly town beach. In the town: *Alexandra* (M), tel. 28 301. 88 rooms, disco, roofgarden. *Anastasia* (I), tel. 28 598. 43 rooms. *Elli* (I), tel. 28 401. 78 rooms, roofgarden. *Elma* (I), tel. 22 920. 49 rooms; in the picturesque port. *Maritina* (I), tel. 23 241. 68 rooms. *Oscar* (I), tel. 28 090. 160 rooms, small roofgarden; the only hotel in this category with a restaurant.

Rhodes. On this lovely island stood the Colossus of Rhodes, one of the seven wonders of the ancient world. Rhodes, with its fine walled town, is Greece's biggest and most cosmopolitan resort, with some 22,000 beds in hotels of all categories. The sights of the main town are the medieval walls, the Palace of the Grand Masters, and the houses of the Knights Hospitallers.

More remarkable is the ancient town of Lindos, on the east shore, with its colonnaded acropolis on a high headland. In the interior of the island is the famous Valley of Butterflies—a long, wooded gorge where butterflies fill the air with a shower of reddish gold.

Telephone area code: 0241.

Hotels. Hotels fill the entire northern promontory outside the walled town. Prices tend to be higher than elsewhere and there are fewer (I) hotels. Most listed are within easy walking distance from the sandy, crowded and slightly polluted town beach; a very few remain, unpredictably, open in winter. The long Ixia beach, some miles west (frequent buses) has better bathing.

Acandia (M), tel. 22 251/4. 82 rooms. *Alexia* (M), tel. 24 061/3. 135 rooms, roofgarden, beach across road. *Cactus* (M), tel. 26 100. 177 rooms, roofgarden, beach across road. *Constantinos* (M), tel. 22 971. 133 rooms. *Corali* (M), tel. 24 911. 115 rooms, no restaurant. *Esperia* (M), tel. 23 941. 191 rooms, half board. *Manoussos* (M), tel. 22 741/5. 124 rooms, roofgarden, pool. *Plaza* (M), tel. 22 501/5. 128 rooms, pool. *Solemar* (M), tel. 22 941. 102 rooms, pool; at Ixia. *Spartalis* (M), tel. 24 371/2. 79 rooms; at the port.

Amaryllis (I), tel. 24 522. 39 rooms. *Astron* (I), tel. 24 651. 43 rooms. *Congo* (I), tel. 24 023. 36 rooms. *Diana* (I), tel. 24 677. 42 rooms. *Elite* (I), tel. 22 391. 45 rooms. *El Greco* (I), tel. 24 071. 75 rooms. *Majestic* (I), tel. 22 031. 79 rooms. *Parthenon* (I), tel. 22 351. 79 rooms, roofgarden.

Restaurants. Except for the fish restaurants around the old port, food is on the whole rather disappointing in the moderate open-air restaurants along the seafront of the new town. Generally the hotel restaurants, where most tourists eat anyway, offer the better food. Recommended restaurants are the *Kabo n' Toro* (M), corner of Ormilou and Parado Sts., one of the smallest and best in Rhodes, and *Neorion* (M), Platia Neorion, a café-restaurant. The hotels also have a monopoly on the nightlife.

Crete

Crete is a paradise for the amateur archeologist. For 400 years before 1450 B.C.—while Europe was still barbaric—one of the most brilliant and amazing civilizations the world has ever known flourished on this 160-mile-long island. This was the Minoan civilization, and its fascinating remains—including the stupendous Palace of Knossos—are among the most impressive sights of the entire Mediterranean. Knossos, the island's largest palace, was built about 2000 B.C., destroyed 300 years later and then replaced by a more magnificent group of buildings. They were discovered by the German archeologist Heinrich Schliemann, but it was Sir Arthur Evans who excavated Knossos, beginning in 1899. Guarding practically all the Minoan treasures brought to light is the Archeological Museum in Iraklio. The Venetian ramparts withstood a 24-year siege before final surrender to the Turks in 1669.

Hotels. Iraklio. Telephone are code: 081. Largest town, 3 miles from the next beach. *Atlantis* (M), tel. 22 9103. 164 rooms. *Atrion* (M), tel. 24 2830. 65 airconditioned rooms. *Mediterranean* (M), tel. 28 9331/5. 55 rooms, half board, partially airconditioned, roofgarden. *Petra* (M), tel. 22 9912. 30 rooms, no restaurant.

Apollon (I), tel. 25 0025. 50 rooms. *Asterion* (I), tel. 22 7913. 60 rooms, restaurant, roofgarden. *Daedalos* (I), tel. 22 4391. 60 rooms, airconditioned. *Grabelles*

(I), tel. 24 1205. 42 rooms, airconditioned, restaurant. *Olympic* (I), tel. 28 8861/4. 73 rooms, roofgarden.

Restaurants. *Maxim Fish Tavern* (M) and *Ta Psaria* (M), both opposite the sea fortress on the rather forbidding waterfront, have fresh fish. *Caprice* (I) and *Knossos* (I), both in the pedestrian zone round the pretty Morosini fountain on central Venizelou Square and both open-air spots, offer undistinguished food. *Dedalou* (I), also open air, has more of the same; just off the square.

There are numerous discos on and near the huge Platia (Square) Eleftherias, as well as many handicraft shops.

One beach resort follows another to the east. Distances (in miles) from Iraklio in parentheses. The following six resorts have the telephone area code: 0897.

Karteros (5). *Amnissos* (I), tel. 22 3008. 54 double rooms in bungalows, half board, pool. *Motel Xenia* (I), tel. 28 1841/3. 42 rooms, restaurant.

Hani Kokkini (7). *Kamari* (I), tel. 76 1340. 36 rooms, pool.

Gouves (10). *Aphrodite* (M), tel. 41 102. 234 rooms. *Mon Repos* (I), tel. 41 280. 37 rooms, restaurant.

Limenas Hersonissou (16). *Glaros* (M), tel. 22 140. 141 rooms, pool. *Nora* (M), tel. 22 271/5. 181 rooms, half board, pool, roofgarden, disco. *Eva* (I), tel. 22 090/2. 33 rooms, airconditioned, disco, restaurant. *Palmera Beach* (I), tel. 22 481/3. 72 rooms, restaurant.

Stalida (20). *Blue Sea* (M), tel. 31 371/4. 197 rooms in bungalows, half board, pool, disco. *Heliotrope* (I), tel. 31 515. 81 rooms, pool.

Malia (22). Below another Minoan palace ruin, but most of the large holiday complexes on the finest beach are well beyond the budget limits. *Malia Beach* (M), tel. 31 210. 185 rooms, pool. *Phaedra Beach* (M), tel. 31 560. 71 rooms, minigolf. *Florella* (I), tel. 31 614. 31 rooms. *Malia Holidays* (I), tel. 31 206. 81 rooms. Last two have no restaurants.

Agios Nikolaos (39). A pretty fishing village grown into Crete's largest beach resort. Telephone area code: 0841. *Coral* (M), tel. 28 363/7. 170 rooms, roofgarden, pool. *Miramare* (M), tel. 22 962. 53 rooms, pool. *Rhea* (M), tel. 28 321/3. 118 rooms, roofgarden, disco. *Akratos* (I), tel. 22 721. 31 rooms, roofgarden and restaurant. *Almyros Beach* (I), tel. 22 865. 47 rooms. *Ariadni Beach* (I), tel. 22 741/4. 76 rooms in bungalows, restaurant. *Cronos* (I), tel. 28 761. 38 rooms. *Du Lac* (I), tel. 22 711. 40 rooms; on the small lagoon connected by a canal with the sea. *Sgouros* (I), tel. 28 931. 28 rooms, airconditioned, restaurant.

Sitia (82). Telephone area code: 0843. *Alice* (I), tel. 28 450. 36 rooms, roofgarden, disco. *Crystal* (I), tel. 22 284. 41 rooms. *Itanos* (I), tel. 22 146. 72 airconditioned rooms, the only one with restaurant. *Vaï* (I), tel. 22 288. 44 rooms; close to the fine sandy beach.

To the west of Iraklio are the following resorts.

Rethymno (49). Lies on an excellent beach fronting a small town below the Venetian fortifications. Telephone area code: 0831. *Braskos* (M), tel. 23 721/3. 82 rooms, disco, roofgarden. *Jo-an* (M), tel. 24 241/4. 50 rooms, airconditioned, roofgarden, no restaurant. *Xenia* (M), tel. 29 111/2. 25 rooms, directly on beach. *Ideon* (I), tel. 28 667/9. 71 rooms, restaurant. *Olympic* (I), tel. 24 761/4. 59 rooms, airconditioned, roofgarden. On nearby beaches: *Adele Beach Bungalows* (M), tel. 71 047. 50 rooms, roofgarden, pool, tennis. *Golden Beach* (M), tel. 71 012. 72 rooms, pool, tennis, minigolf. *Orion* (M), tel. 71 471. 73 rooms, pool, roofgarden.

Astali (I), tel. 24 721. 36 rooms. *Steris Beach* (I), tel. 28 303. 45 rooms, restaurant. *Valari* (I), tel. 22 236. 29 rooms, roofgarden. There are several restaurants and tavernas along the waterfront, but they are more pleasing for their situation than for their food.

Hania (85). The capital, and, though smaller, it is more attractive than Iraklio. A maze of lanes surrounds the picturesque Venetian port where most of the restaurants are concentrated. Unfortunately, once again, the settings tend to be better than the food. Telephone area code: 0821.

Kriti (M), tel. 21 881/5. 98 rooms, pool, roofgarden; the only one without a restaurant in this category. *Porto del Colombo* (M), tel. 50 975. 6 rooms. A well-restored Turkish house in traffic-free quarter, near waterfront; roofgarden. *Porto Veneziano* (M), tel. 29 311/3. 63 rooms, airconditioned; in a converted 18th-century house in the port. *Xenia* (M), tel. 24 561/2. 44 rooms, half board, small pool, beach nearby; inside the Venetian fortress. *Canea* (I), tel. 24 673/5. 49 rooms, pool. *Dik-*

tynna (I), tel. 21 101/3. 35 rooms. Less than two miles east: *Aptera Beach* (I), tel. 22 636. 46 rooms in bungalows, restaurant.

The most interesting taverna and café is *Aposperida,* near the old port in a 17th-century soap factory; close to several discos.

Corfu

Corfu, less than an hour by air from Athens, is not in the Aegean but the Ionian Sea. This strikingly beautiful island is as popular with tourists as Rhodes. Part of the same island group is Ithaca, whose king was Odysseus. The unrivalled beauty of the island is enhanced by the inhabitants' famed courteousness, the happy result of centuries of unbroken civilization. Corfu is the only part of modern Greece never to have experienced Ottoman rule. Though later controlled by France and Britain, Corfu still bears the influence of Venetian rule in its tall 18th-century buildings on arcaded streets. British colonization left its mark, too—cricket is still played on the Esplanade. The island has many sights, among them Kanoni, one of the world's famous beauty spots, and the lovely bay of Paleokastritsa. There are frequent car ferries from Igoumenitsa on the mainland, and many from Italian ports.

Telephone area code: 0661.

Hotels. (Corfu Town). *Astron* (M), tel. 39 505. 33 rooms, by the old harbor. *Olympic* (M), tel. 30 532. 50 rooms. *Arcadion* (I), tel. 37 671. 55 rooms, very central. On the Esplanade. *Atlantis* (I), tel. 35 560. 58 rooms, airconditioned; at the port. *Ionion* (I), tel. 39 915. 89 rooms, half board. Also at the port.

Restaurants. *Aegli* (M) offers the widest choice of dishes among the café-restaurants under the arcades on the Esplanade. For local specialties, try the *Taverna Kostas* (I), Platia Taxiarhon, in the old town.

On the southeast coast, distances (miles) from Corfu Town in brackets: **Kanoni** (3). *Salvos* (M), tel. 37 889. 92 rooms. *Royal* (I), tel. 37 512. 114 rooms. Both half board with small pool, roofgarden, disco.

Perama (5), *Aeolos Beach* (M), tel. 33 132/4. 324 rooms in bungalows, minigolf, pool. *Akti* (M), tel. 39 445. 55 rooms, motel, pool. *Oasis* (M), tel. 38 190. 66 rooms, roofgarden, pool, disco. *Pontikonissi* (I), tel. 36 871. 49 rooms, roofgarden.

Benitses (7). *Corfu Maris* (I), tel. 92 381. 31 rooms. *Potomaki* (I), tel. 30 889. 149 rooms, pool, disco, roofgarden.

Cavos Lefkimis (28). *Cavos* (I), tel. 22 107. 21 rooms.

Moraitika (13). *Margarita* (I), tel. 55 267. 35 rooms. *Sea Bird* (I), tel. 92 348. 16 rooms.

Messongi (14). *Messongi Beach* (M), tel. 38 684/6. 828 rooms, pool, disco, minigolf, tennis. *Melissa Beach* (I), tel. 55 229. 32 rooms, restaurant, pool. *Rossis* (I), tel. 55 352. 30 rooms, airconditioned, restaurant.

On the northeast coast: **Alykes** (2). *Sunset* (M), tel. 31 203. 53 rooms, airconditioned, pool. *Salina* (I), tel. 36 782. 16 rooms, roofgarden, restaurant.

Gouvia (5). *Park* (M), tel. 91 310. 196 rooms, half board. *Pheakion* (I), tel. 91 497. 36 rooms. *The Village,* just a mile inland, recreates traditional lifestyles in a small museum, handicraft shops and a variety of moderately-priced open-air tavernas and nightspots.

Dassia (9). *Paloma Bianca* (I), tel. 93 575. 36 rooms, airconditioned, pool, beach, restaurant, tennis. *Dassia* (I), tel. 93 224. 54 rooms, beach, restaurant.

On the west coast: **Arillas** (28). *Arilla Beach* (I), tel. 31 401. 32 rooms. **Paleokastritsa** (14). *Oceanis* (M), tel. 41 229. 71 rooms, with good views; half board, pool, beach. *Apollon* (I), tel. 41 211. 23 rooms. *Odysseus* (I), tel. 41 209. 36 rooms. *Paleokastritsa* (I), tel. 41 207. 163 rooms, disco, pool. All of these have restaurants and are within 200 yds. of beach.

Holland

The Netherlands offer far more than windmills and tulips. Every region has its season. Delft is luminous after a wintry storm. In April, the lush polders (lowlands reclaimed from the sea) and wild flowers entice cyclists through a landscape of windmills and waterways. In May, Gelderland's cherry orchards are in blossom, while Flevoland is covered with a brilliant yellow blanket of rape seed. In summer, the island of Texel draws hardy walkers across the Wadden Sea mudflats in a sport akin to horizontal mountain climbing. In September, the red deer wander through a mass of purple heathland in the Veluwe nature reserve. Fall in the Utrecht countryside can be as dramatic as in New England. After a quiet December, Amsterdam explodes in firework displays and street dancing to celebrate New Year.

Yet historical towns such as Delft, Leiden and Utrecht have not been prettified out of existence. Their gables, canals, and paintings remain a tribute to Holland's Golden Age of architecture, trade, and art. But the gabled houses are not trapped in a 17th-century timewarp: the Dutch have sensitively converted many into hotels, restaurants, or exhibition halls. Amsterdam's Nieuwe Kerk, both a church and a cultural center, embodies the Dutch spirit of practicality and social responsibility.

This venture is also a sign of Amsterdam's cultural prominence: the city is now as famous for its jazz, modern art, and ballet as it is for the magnificent Rembrandts and Van Goghs. Holland's most misunderstood painter, Van Gogh, has a posthumous chance to put the record straight in 1990: the centenary of his death is marked by exhibitions of his work all over Holland. His genius, both tormented and celebratory, can be seen in exhibitions in Amsterdam, Dordrecht, Groningen, Rotterdam, and Den Haag (The Hague).

The Hague, sedate and refined, presents a contrast to Amsterdam's vitality and progressiveness. Diplomacy and ceremony color the lives of all residents, from Queen Beatrix, ambassadors, and parliamentarians, downwards. Even the local herring seller will have a view on the role of the monarchy, probably favorable.

Holland is not as flat as it seems. Certainly low-lying Zeeland lives with the sea and on the sea—its oysters and mussels are world famous. Yet versatile northern Holland is not restricted to sand dunes and melancholy seascapes. Just inland from Bergen-aan-Zee, deep woods and moorland encircle the village of Bergen, once an artists' enclave. In southern Holland, bulb fields and windmills abound, but so do nature reserves, inland lakes, lush polders and rolling hills.

If people are the main attraction of a country for you, you will appreciate the dignified Dutch way of life, in which tolerance, friendship and hospitality play a major part. Moreover, a large proportion of the population speaks English well enough for you not to have any language worries.

PRACTICAL INFORMATION FOR HOLLAND

WHAT WILL IT COST. Holland is a prosperous country with a high standard of living so the minimum you can expect to pay is similar to that in other Northern European countries. But tourism is of major importance to the Dutch, so there are many savings possible for the careful traveler. Amsterdam is 10–20% more expensive than smaller towns. Overnight costs can be minimized by staying in the high-standard youth hostels and other accommodations specially designed for the budget traveler. Bear in mind that as distances in Holland are never great, traveling costs can be kept correspondingly modest. Moreover, Dutch railways and buses offer a variety of reduced fares (see *Getting Around Holland,* below).

The monetary unit in Holland is the *gulden* (guilder or florin), written as f., fl., Hfl., or Dfl. Notes are in denominations of 1,000, 100, 50, 25, 10 and 5 guilders. Coins are 5 guilders, 2.5 guilders, 1 guilder, 25, 10, and 5 cents. Dutch bank notes have a code of dots that can be felt. This is for the convenience of the blind.

At the time of writing, the exchange rate for the guilder was fl. 1.90 to the U.S. dollar and fl. 3.61 to the pound sterling. Banks open working days 9 to 4. You can also change money at *GWK bureaux de change,* which are open Mon. through Sat., 8–8, Sun. 10–4. *GWK* offices in major cities or at border checkpoints open 24 hours a day.

Sample Costs. Half day city tour fl. 33; one day bicycle hire fl. 8 (plus deposit, at least fl. 50); half liter of wine fl. 12; beer or coffee fl. 2.50; museum entrance fl. 3.50–8.

Budget Tips. The Museum Card. The Museumkart, which can be bought either from local information offices (VVV) or from museums, gives a year's free or reduced admission to 350 museums. It costs fl. 15 if under 18, fl. 40 if older. Take along a photo and a passport.

Leisure Card. This discount card provides significant reductions on rail travel, car rental, hotels, tours, entertainment and shopping. Valid for a year, it costs fl. 25 from the NBT (in the US or Holland) or from main train stations and VVV offices.

NATIONAL TOURIST OFFICE. The head office of the Netherlands Board of Tourism (NBT) is at Vlietweg 15, 2266 KA, Leidschendam (tel. 070–705705). They also operate helpful and efficient offices in New York, San Francisco, Chicago, Toronto, London and most European capitals (see below for addresses). Offices of the national airline, *KLM,* are also well supplied with general information to help you plan your trip. General information about particular aspects of tourism can be obtained from the NBT, including details on water sports, cycling, camping, as well as bungalow guides, tourist maps and lists of all sorts.

The *VVV* is a network of 450 local tourist information offices often located in or near rail stations or tourist centers. VVVs also have an accommodations booking service, for a small fee, but only over the counter and on the day you want the accommodations. So if you are in Haarlem and would like accommodations that night in Groningen, the VVV in Haarlem will phone the Groningen VVV for you and arrange it.

Addresses of the Netherlands Board of Tourism overseas include:

In the U.S.: 355 Lexington Ave., New York, N.Y. 10017 (tel. 212–370–7367); 90 New Montgomery St., San Francisco, CA 94105 (tel. 415–543–6772); 225 N. Michigan Ave., Suite 326, Chicago, IL 60601 (tel. 312–819–0300).

In Canada: 25 Adelaide St. East, Suite 710, Toronto, Ont., M5C 1Y2 (tel. 416–363–1577).

In the U.K.: 25–28 Buckingham Gate, London SW1E 6LD (tel. 071–630 0451).

WHEN TO COME. The prime tourist season runs from mid-April through mid-October but peaks during school vacation periods (Easter, plus July and August) when hotels may impose a 20% surcharge. Dutch bulb fields bloom from early April to mid-May, as do room rates in the local hotels. June is an ideal time to catch the warm weather but miss the crowds. The summer is generally warm but beware of sudden rains and sharp coastal winds. Winters are cold and wet but not without clear days. It was the watery quality of light after a cloudburst that inspired Vermeer and other great Dutch painters.

Average afternoon temperatures in degrees Fahrenheit and centigrade:

Amsterdam

	Jan.	Feb.	Mar.	Apr.	May	June	July	Aug.	Sept.	Oct.	Nov.	Dec.
F°	41	41	46	52	60	65	69	68	64	56	47	41
C°	5	5	8	11	16	18	21	20	18	13	8	5

SPECIAL EVENTS. Southern Holland celebrates Carnival seven weeks before Easter (usually late *Feb.* or early *Mar.*). Late *March* Keukenhof opens its famous flower gardens at Lisse to the public. From *April* there are weekly cheese markets, at Gouda on Thursdays and at Alkmaar on Fridays. Queen's Day is celebrated on *April 30* with festivities throughout the country. *May 5* is Liberation Day. In *June* the Thursday cheese market at Purmerend starts and the Annual Holland Festival of music, ballet and drama takes place with events in all major Dutch cities. The 19 windmills near Kinderdijk (near Rotterdam) are all in full swing on each Sunday afternoon in *July.* Flower processions take place at Aalsmeer in *September.* On the third Tuesday in *September* Queen Beatrix rides in her golden coach drawn by eight horses to open parliament in Den Haag. The centenary of Van Gogh's death will be celebrated all over Holland.

The NBT produces a free booklet called "Holland Major Events", listing all major festivals, fairs, cultural and sporting events throughout the year.

National Holidays. Jan. 1 (New Year's Day); March 29–April 1 (Easter); Apr. 30 (Queen's Day) (shops open unless falls on Sun.); May 5 (Liberation); May 9 (Ascension); May 19; Dec. 5 (Sinterklass); Dec. 25, 26 (Christmas).

VISAS. Visas are not required for visits of less than 3 months, but of course valid passports are. For a British citizen a British Visitor's Passport is enough.

HEALTH CERTIFICATES. No vaccinations are required.

GETTING TO HOLLAND. By Plane. From the US there are frequent flights run by *Northwest, Delta, TWA,* and *PanAm* (the last via London). KLM, Royal Dutch Airlines, operate nonstop flights between 13 US cities and Holland. From the UK, *British Airways* and *KLM* fly from London (Heathrow) to Amsterdam (£103 and £79). *Miracle Bus* operate the cheapest flights (£80 return). For cheap packages from the UK, try *Thompson* (tel. 071–387 6534), *Travelscene* (tel. 071–935 1025) or *Time Off* (071–235 8070).

By Boat. From the UK, Sealink operate a day and night sailing from Harwich to the Hoek van Holland. Travelers from Hull can take an overnight North Sea Ferries service to Rotterdam. Road connections from both ports are good.

By Bus. The following services are part of *National Express-Eurolines.* Hoverspeed's *CitySprint* runs at least two buses a day from London (Victoria coach station) to Amsterdam, calling at Den Haag and Rotterdam. The 10 A.M. departure arrives at 9.15 P.M. Excellent value and not much slower than the train. *Grey-Green/Wallace Arnold* run two overnight services on the same route, calling at Breda, Rotterdam and Den Haag. Twice a week the bus continues to Hengelo. Transfers to and from the ferry are made in the middle of the night. From London, *Miracle Bus* (tel. 071–379 6055) currently run the cheapest service (£40 for the round trip).

By Train. There are two routes from the U.K. One is via Harwich and the Hoek van Holland (sea crossing takes 7–9 hours) with both day and night sailings. Daytime you leave London (Liverpool St. Station) about 9.40 A.M. and reach Amsterdam about 9.30 P.M. that day. With the night crossing you leave London at around 7.50 P.M. and reach Amsterdam at 9 A.M.

The other route is from London (Victoria) to Dover, Jetfoil to Oostende, for the train to Brussels where a change is made for the express to Rotterdam and Amsterdam. Leaving London at 7.45 A.M. you are in Rotterdam just after 4 P.M. and in Amsterdam just over an hour later. Supplements are payable on Express trains. The round trip costs about £60 but overnight sailings cost less. Travel by ferry takes so much longer that you are better off ferrying via the Hoek van Holland as trains and ferries are so much better on this route.

From neighboring countries there are excellent train services to Amsterdam, Rotterdam, Den Haag and Utrecht. For example it is around 6 hours from Paris or Frankfurt to Amsterdam, less to Rotterdam. From Köln to Amsterdam is about 3½ hours; from Hamburg it is 6 hours. Brussels the train takes only 3 hours. If planning to travel extensively in Europe, take advantage of the cost-saving Eurailpass (see Facts at Your Fingertips, below).

CUSTOMS. Travelers from outside Europe can bring in 400 cigarettes or 100 cigars or 500 grams of tobacco, 1 liter of spirits of 2 liters of non-sparkling wine; 4 liters of non-sparkling wine; or 2 liters of non-sparkling wine plus 2 liters of sparkling wine/liqueurs. 50 grams of perfume, ¼ liter eau de cologne and goods to the value of fl. 125. Travelers from EC countries may import 300 cigarettes or 75 cigars or 400 grams of tobacco; 5 liters of non-sparkling wine plus 1½ liters of spirits/sparkling wines; or 8 liters of non-sparkling wine; or 5 liters of non-sparkling wine plus 3 liters of liqueurs/sparkling wine. In addition, you can import 75 grams of perfume, ⅜ liter of eau de cologne and goods worth fl. 890. Travelers from non-EC countries within Europe may import 200 cigarettes or 50 cigars or 250 grams of tobacco. The drink allowance is 2 liters of non-sparkling wine plus 2 liters of liqueurs/sparkling wine; or 4 liters of non-sparkling wine. In addition, 50 grams of perfume, ¼ liter of eau de cologne, and goods to the value of fl. 125 are permitted.

HOTELS. For the budget traveler, Holland offers a wide range of accommodations, at efficient city hotels, traditional small town hotels and family-run guest houses. In Amsterdam, Moderate hotels cost between fl. 150–200 for a double room while Inexpensive hotels charge fl. 90–150. Outside the capital, prices are about 10–20% lower and rooms are easier to find. Remember that these prices include service charges, VAT and a huge Dutch breakfast. To book hotels in advance, use the free National Reservation Centre, PO Box 404, 2260 KA Leidsechendam (tel. 070–202500). Alternatively, for a small fee, VVV offices can usually make reservations at short notice. Bookings must be made in person, however. Budget travelers may prefer to stay in friendly bed-and-breakfast establishments. These are in short supply and need to be booked on the spot at local VVV offices. The cost of a double room averages fl. 50 per person per night. (fl. 75 in major cities). Dormitory arrangements are available for around fl. 25.

Youth Hostels. The Dutch Youth Hostel Association (NJHC, Prof. Tulpplein 4, Amsterdam, tel. 020–264433) has over 50 youth hostels all over Holland, for members only. Those aged between 14 and 35 years can join at any hostel (not necessary for IYHF members). Bed and breakfast costs from fl. 30 per person, including breakfast. Note that hostels in the bigger cities are usually full during high season; best book ahead.

Camping. There are over 2,000 official campsites in Holland. Costs are from fl. 20 to 30 for 4 persons. A list of campsites can be obtained from the NBT, VVV offices or from the NTKC, Daendelstraat 11, Den Haag. Camping in parks and on beaches is actively discouraged.

Self-Catering. Bungalows and self-catering summer houses are increasingly springing up all over the Netherlands and begin at fl. 500 per week in spring, fl. 700 in summer. It is strongly advisable to book these several months in advance, and this can be done through the NBT or any of the local VVV tourist information centers.

RESTAURANTS. Holland offers a great variety of restaurants, with a good choice for every taste and purse. Many restaurants offer a tourist menu (indicated outside) consisting of 3 courses for about fl. 20 including service and tax. In the six university towns of Holland you will find small restaurants to suit a student's pocket. Good food at low prices can be enjoyed in many of the Chinese/Indonesian restaurants where you can eat a filling and delicious *bahmi* or *nasi goreng* (fried noodles or rice) for about fl. 18. The cheap hamburger franchises have also found their way to Holland. Note, however, that the more expensive Dutch restaurants tend to be full, so it is a good idea to book in advance. They often also close early, around 9 P.M.

Our grading system is as follows: Moderate restaurant fl. 30–40 per person, drinks excluded; Inexpensive restaurant under fl. 30 per person, drinks excluded.

Food and Drink. Of the many earthly pleasures the Dutch enjoy, eating probably heads the list, with the appetite sharpened by the national institution of the *borreltje,* a little nip of gin at five o'clock usually taken with a little snack like the tasty *bitter-ballen*—fried meat balls. You'd better take something to stimulate your appetite in this hearty land. Your breakfast, replete with several varieties of bread, cheese, cooked ham or meat, possibly a boiled egg, butter, jam and steaming coffee or tea, is a far and welcome cry from the usual Continental *petit déjeuner.* It will sustain you until the Dutch ritual of eleven o'clock coffee, just as the *Koffietafel,* a "light" lunch of bread, cold cuts, soup and cheese, or particularly an *uitsmijter,* slices of bread topped with cold meat or ham and fried eggs, will fend off starvation until dinner, usually taken very early, around 6 P.M.

Typical Dutch dishes appear in season (mostly in winter). Some of the best Dutch specialties are: *Erwtensoep,* a rich and delicious thick pea soup with bits of sausage or pig's knuckles, a meal in itself, as is *Hutspot,* a meat, carrot and potato stew. *Haring* is particularly popular, especially the "new herring" caught between May and September and served brined, garnished with onions; also, *Rodekool met Rolpens,* red cabbage and rolled spiced meat with sliced apple. Other specialties include *Pannekoeken* and *Flensjes,* pancakes, in various varieties, shapes and sizes, all of them delectable and often eaten in special pancake restaurants. *Koeken* and *Koekjes,* cakes and cookies, are usually on the sweet and rich side.

As for cheeses, the two famous classifications are *Gouda* and *Edam,* both mild in comparison with French and Italian cheeses. Try the spicier *Leidse* cheese with cumin or *Friese* cheese with cloves for a change. Seafood is abundant and well-prepared; most shellfish is rather expensive, except for the delicious mussels from the province of Zeeland.

If run-of-the-mill Dutch fare begins to pall, try an Indonesian restaurant (the best are in Amsterdam and Den Haag) where the specialties of Holland's former colony are served. The chief dish here is *rijsttafel,* a heaped bowl of perfectly steamed rice together with 20 or more side dishes like *saté babi,* bite-size morsels of pork skewered on a wooden spit and cooked in a mouthwatering sauce. The best beverage to accompany an Indonesian *rijsttafel* is beer, of which there are several excellent varieties, both Dutch and foreign.

The indigenous Dutch liqueur is *jenever* (gin), a potent and warming spirit. It comes in many varieties depending on the spices used, but most popular are the *jonge* (young) and the *oude* (old). Neither has the remotest similarity to dry gin, being both sweeter and oilier. Jenever is drunk neat and chilled.

TIPPING. Hotel prices now include a 15% service charge and VAT, as do most restaurant checks, and nightclub charges. Tip porters fl. 1 per bag or per service. Taxi fares generally include 15% service charge (when indicated on meter), but it is usual to give the driver any small change. Hairdressers' and barbers' charges include service.

MAIL AND PHONE. Airmail letters to the U.S. and Canada, up to 10 grams, cost fl. 1.50, postcards 75 cents, aerograms fl. 1. To the U.K. and rest of Europe, letters up to 20 grams are 75 cents, postcards 55 cents, aerograms 65 cents. Direct dialed international phone calls can be made from most public phone booths or at main post offices. To call the USA direct, dial 06–022–9111 for an operator.

CLOSING TIMES. Shops are open in general from 8.30 or 9 A.M. to 5.30 or 6 P.M. weekdays and Saturdays, but close at midday once a week; days vary locally. On Mondays department stores and most shops, especially in shopping precincts (Den Haag, Amsterdam) do not open till 1 P.M. and many others close on Wednesday afternoons. Late night shopping is usually Thursday or Friday, but varies locally. Only central post offices in the large cities are open on Saturday, until noon.

GETTING AROUND HOLLAND

By Train. Holland is blessed with a frequent and reliable railway network. There is an express intercity network, and trains run every 30 minutes to the major cities and local trains run at least once an hour to the smaller towns. If you are traveling through Belgium and Luxembourg, the five-day *Benelux Tourrail* card is the best bet. It allows for unlimited travel and is valid for any five days within a period of 17 consecutive days. Cost is about fl. 154, or fl. 108 for those under 26. Some weekend round-trips offer a 25% reduction. *Dagtochtkaartjes* are tickets combining train, boat, or bus, plus an exhibition. Using the Leisure Card is another option.

By Bus. Holland has an excellent bus network between and within towns. Bus excursions can be booked on the spot and at local VVV offices. In the major cities the best buy is a *strippenkaart* multi-ticket (fl. 8.85), valid on all bus, tram and metro services. A *strippenkaart* with 45 strips is available for fl. 25.35. Alternatively, buy a *Dagkaart* ticket for unlimited travel for 1 and 2 days. Costs are fl. 8.85 and fl. 11.80.

By Bicycle. Holland is a 'cyclist friendly' country with specially designated cycle paths, signposts and picnic areas. Bikes can be rented in most cities and towns, often at train stations. Rental costs around fl. 7.50 per day or from fl. 28 per week, plus a deposit of fl. 100–200. Advice on renting and routes is available at local VVV offices; cycling packages can be booked at the larger offices. For a brochure detailing more than 60 cycling routes, write to NRTU, Postbus 326 3900AH Veendaal.

By Boat. There are ferry connections to the five islands in the Waddenzee and from the west to the east coast of the Ijsselmeer (leaving Enkhuizen for Staveren and Urk). Cars are not permitted on the islands of Vlieland and Schiermonnikoog.

Hitchhiking. Though not prohibited in Holland, hitchhiking is not encouraged. It is *not* allowed on main roads, motorways or their approaches.

Amsterdam

From the Central Station, walk to the Oude Kerk, the city's oldest church. Built in the 14th century but badly damaged by iconoclasts after the Reformation, the church still maintains its original belltower and a few remarkable stained glass windows. From the tower, there is a typical view of old Amsterdam stretching from St. Nicolaaskerk to Medieval gables.

This area bordered by two canals (Oude Zijds Voorburgwal and Oude Zijds Achterburgwal) is the heart of the rosse buurt, the red-light district. Between Amsterdam's oldest canals, traditional gables vye with this equally traditional leisure industry. In the windows at canal level, lumpish, naked women slouch, stare or do their nails. Drawn red curtains above suggest a brisker trade. The area is generally safe but midnight walks down dark sidestreets to explore unusual gables are not advisable. The timid can view the area by boat since many of the cruises pass this way.

Leaving the red-light district, walk to the Dam, the broadest square in the old section of town. It was here that the fishermen used to come to sell their catch; today it is busy with shops, people and traffic. It is also a popular young center for outdoor concerts. To the right of the square is the Nieuwe Kerk (New Church). The once Gothic church was gutted by fire in 1645 and then reconstructed in an imposing Renaissance style, as interpreted by strict Calvinists. As befits Holland's national church, it is now the site of all coronations, including the crowning of Queen Beatrix in 1980. But in democratic Dutch spirit, the church is also used as a meeting place, an indoor extension of Dam Square.

From Dam Square, walk west to Westermarkt and the Westerkerk (West Church). Built in 1631, the church has a fine carillon and the highest tower in the city. Rembrandt and his son Titus are buried in the church. During the summer, you can climb to the top of the tower for a fine view over the city.

From the Dam, turn down Kalverstraat, an attractive shopping street. You will notice a striking Renaissance gate (1581) which guards a series of tranquil inner courtyards originally a nunnery, then an orphanage, and now part of the Amsterdam Historical Museum. In Medieval times, this whole area was an island devoted to piety. Although the bordering canals are now filled in, the spot remains a place apart.

The museum traces the city's history from its humble origins as a fishing village on the sandbanks through the 17th century Golden Age of material and artistic wealth to the decline of the trading empire in the 18th century.

A small passageway and courtyard link the museum with the Begijnhof, an enchanting, enclosed square of almshouses founded in 1346. The "beguines" were women who chose to lead a partial form of convent life, often taking the vow of chastity. The last beguine died in 1974 and her house, number 26, has been preserved as she left it. Number 34, dating from the 15th century, is the oldest and the only one to keep its wooden Gothic facade.

In the center of the square is a church given to Amsterdam's English and Scottish Presbyterians over 300 years ago. On the church wall are tributes to the Pilgrim Fathers who sailed from Delfthaven to New York in 1620. Opposite the church is another of the city's "secret" Catholic chapels, built in 1671. The spiritual atmosphere hushes even the most agnostic visitors.

Once back in Kalverstraat, you soon come to Spui, a lively square in the heart of the university area. It was a center for student rallies in revolutionary 1968. Now it is a center for boat trips and bars, including the cozy "brown cafes". A right turn and then a left turn over the bridge brings you to the floating flower market on the Singel Canal.

From the Singel, take Leidsestraat to the Herengracht, the city's most prestigious Gentlemen's Canal. The stretch of canal from here to Huidenstraat is named "The Golden Bend" for its sumptuous patrician houses with double staircases and grand entrances. 17th century merchants moved here from the Amstel River to escape the disadvantages of their wealth: the noisy warehouses; the unpleasant smells from the breweries; and the risk of fire in the sugar refineries. These houses display the full range of Amsterdam facades: "neck", "bell" and "step" gables next door to grander Louis XIV style houses with elaborate cornices and frescoed ceilings.

Take the Museumboat from one of its many landing stages to Waterlooplein, the heart of the old Jewish quarter. From there, walk along Jodenbreestraat to the Museum Het Rembrandhuis. Once the painter's home, the house is filled with Rembrandt's etchings, engravings and presence.

Catch the Museumboat from Blauwbrug on Waterlooplein to the Central Station. If you feel like a breath of fresh air after seeing Rembrandt's house or the intense Jewish Museum, stroll along Nieuwe Herengracht, once known as the Jewish Gentlemen's Canal. In Rembrandt's day, there were views of distant windjammers sailing into port but today the canal is oddly deserted.

PRACTICAL INFORMATION FOR AMSTERDAM

GETTING INTO TOWN FROM THE AIRPORT. Taxis from Amsterdam's Schiphol airport to the city center are expensive—around fl. 50. The direct train link to Central Station is easy and cheap, fl. 4.40 for the 30 min. trip, trains arrive every 10–15 min. Some airlines have a plane-train arrangement that includes fare from the airport to town.

HOTELS. Accommodations are tight from Easter to summer so early booking is advisable. The other snag is parking. Amsterdam is a pedestrian's paradise but a driver's nightmare. Since few hotels have car parks, cars are best abandoned in a multi-storey car park for the duration of your stay. Most tourists prefer to stay inside the concentric ring of canals. Within this, the quiet museum quarter is a convenient choice for the Rijksmuseum yet is near enough to the Vondelpark for light jogging. More atmospheric is the historic canalside neighborhood with its gabled merchants' houses. Note that many hotels offer rooms at different prices and rates within the same hotel and that room prices at smaller hotels often include breakfast.

Moderate

Ambassade, Herengracht 341 (tel. 020–262333). Only five minutes from the tranquil *Begijnhof* (almshouses), the hotel is equally out of touch with the present. Canalside location, Louis XV decoration and Oriental carpets. Service is gracious and old-fashioned. No restaurant, but these abound on the Herengracht. 11 rooms with bath.

Atlas. van Eeghenstraat 64 (tel. 020–766336). Well-situated for the major museums. Modern but intimate, this hotel includes a cozy bar and restaurant. Ask for a room overlooking Vondelpark.

Cok Budget (Tourist Class), Koninginnweg 34 (tel. 020–6646111 for 3 adjoining hotels in different price categories). Located near the museum district and Vondelpark. This sprawling, impersonal hotel is popular with groups. 70 rooms (190 beds). (The (I) 'Student Class' hotel includes many multi-bedded rooms).

Het Canal House, Keizergracht 148 (tel. 020–225182). Antiques take precedence over television sets in the rooms of this gracious, American-owned hotel. Spacious rooms overlook the canal or the illuminated garden. 20 rooms with bath.

Inexpensive

Agora, Singel 462 (tel. 020–272200). Set beside the Singel flower market, this small hotel is light and spacious. Ask for a room overlooking the canal. The recently refurbished 18th-century house has a summery dining room. Considerate staff and a relaxed neighborhood. 14 rooms with bath.

Centralpark West, Roemer Visscherstraat 27 (tel. 020–852285). Located near the museum district and Vondelpark, slightly outside the center. Rooms are comfortable, spacious and good value.

De Gouden Kettingh, Keisersgracht 270 (tel. 020–248287). This 17th-century merchant's house is decorated in Old Dutch style. The knowledgeable Australian manager encourages guests to take Amsterdam seriously as a dynamic arts capital. Breakfasts are delicious. 24 rooms, 20 with bath.

Engeland, Roemer Visscherstraat 30A, (tel. 020–180862). Located near the museum district, this hotel is also convenient for the major museums. The staff are welcoming and helpful. 28 rooms, many with bath.

Weichmann, Prinsengracht 328–330 (tel. 020–263321). On the edge of the lively Jordaan area, this unpretentious hotel is popular for its warmth and reasonable prices. Bedrooms are modern but the reception rooms are attractively old. Some rooms have just been converted and the tiered prices have risen. Family rooms are available. 35 rooms, most with bath.

Restaurants. Amsterdammers are less creatures of habit than the Dutch in general. Even so, set menus and early dinners are preferred by these health-conscious citizens. The 'Tourist Menu' sign guarantees an economical yet imaginative set menu created by the head chef. For traditionalists, the *'Nederlands Dis'* soup tureen sign is a promise of regional recipes and seasonal ingredients. "You can eat in any language" is the city's proud boast, so when the Dutch restaurants are closed, Indonesian, Chinese, or Japanese restaurants are often open. Between meals, you can follow your nose to the nearest herring cart or drop into a cozy 'brown cafe' for a coffee and an apple tart.

A Moderate meal costs fl. 35–55 and an Inexpensive meal costs under fl. 35, slightly higher than elsewhere. (Prices are per person including service and VAT but not drinks). Look for the blue and white 'Tourist Menu' sign. The menu is available at an officially controlled price, currently about fl. 20.

Moderate

De Orient, Van Baerlestraat 21 (tel. 020–734958). A popular Indonesian restaurant. A safe choice is always the *rijsttafel,* rice and a myriad of side dishes.

De Roode Leeuw, Damrak 93–4 (tel. 020–249683). Traditional Dutch cuisine at its best. Varied regional dishes and seasonal menus. Try the smoked eel, Zeeland mussels or asparagus wrapped in ham.

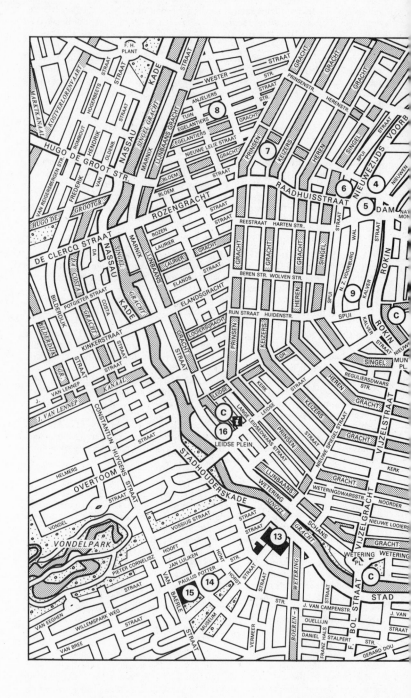

AMSTERDAM

1 Central Station
2 St. Nicolaaskerk
3 Oude Kerk (Old Church)
4 Nieuwe Kerk (New Church)
5 Koninklijk Paleis (Royal Palace)
6 Telecom Huis (Main
   Telecommunications Center)
7 Anne Frank Huis
8 Joordan District
9 Amsterdam Historisch Museum
10 Zuiderkerk (South Church)
11 Museum het Rembrandthuis
12 Zoological Gardens
13 Rijksmuseum
14 Rijksmuseum Vincent Van Gogh
15 Stedelijk Museum (Municipal Museum)
16 Stadsschouwburg (Theater)
17 Joods Museum
18 Muziek Theatre
19 Main Post Office
Ⓒ Canal Trips - starting points
🛈 VVV Tourist Information Offices

SCALE |———|———|———|———|———| 440yds
       |———|———|———|———|———| 400m

Intermezzo, Herenstraat 28 (tel. 020–260167). An intriguing French-Dutch hybrid, both in character and cuisine. The fish is particularly good.

Oesterbar, Leidseplein 10 (tel. 020–362463). The Oyster Bar specializes in seafood. The ground floor bistro offers budget dining, while upstairs, presentation and price are higher.

Rosa's Cantina, Reguliersdwarsstraat 38 (tel. 020–259797). This American-owned restaurant provides delicious Mexican dishes. Crowds are drawn to the exotic dishes, margaritas, friendly atmosphere and low prices.

Sea Palace, Oosterdokskade 8, (tel. 020–264777). This is a huge, floating Chinese pavilion. The Cantonese menu is only of modest quality, but the surroundings make up for it.

Sluizer, Utrechtsestraat 45 (tel. 020–263557). One section serves mainly meat while the other concentrates on fish. An arty crowd is drawn to the fish restaurant, the decor, and the reasonable prices. A lively yet relaxed atmosphere.

Inexpensive

Bojo, Lange Leidsedwarsstraat 51 (tel. 020–227434). As the best value Indonesian restaurant in town, Bojo is worth the wait for a table. Try their snacks (*sate* or *pangsit*) or a full meal. Open until 4 A.M.

Egg Cream, St. Jacobstraat 19 (tel. 020–230575). Considered the best vegetarian restaurant in town despite its name, Egg Cream offers an imaginative menu, fresh ingredients and a lively atmosphere. Closes at 8 P.M.

Frappe, Tuindwarsstraat 12 (tel. 020–236854). One of the best pizzerias in town. The Italian starters are good and the prices are very reasonable.

Oud Holland, NZ Voorburgwal 105 (tel. 020–246848). Not far from the Leidseplein. One of the few Amsterdam restaurants to offer the excellent 'Tourist Menu'.

Pancake Bakery, Prinsengracht 191 (tel. 020–251233). A chance to try a traditional Dutch way of keeping costs down. The name of the game is pancakes—for every course including dessert, for which the toppings can be ice cream, fruit or liqueur. A friendly, busy atmosphere.

Speciaal, Nieuwe Leliestraat 14 (tel. 020–249706). Although set in the picturesque Jordaan area, this Indonesian restaurant looks deceptively unspecial. The copious *rijsttafel,* chicken, fish and egg dishes provide tasty variants on a sweet and sour theme. Last orders at 11.

GETTING AROUND AMSTERDAM. By Bus/Tram/Metro. Public transportation is good. A zonal fare system applies with tickets purchased from automatic dispensers or from the driver on buses and trams. But it is less expensive to buy *strippenkaart* (strip tickets) which are good for several journeys, or the Amsterdam *dagkaart* covering all city routes (one-day card, fl. 8.85; two-day card, fl. 11.80). You can get them from the main VVV office, along with route maps of the public transportation system. Most drivers speak English.

By Taxi. These are expensive. They are not usually hailed in the street but from ranks near stations and at key road intersections.

By Bicycle. For the adventurous and fit, bicycles can be hired by the day or week near the central station, though central Amsterdam is probably better attempted by bike only if you're a seasoned cyclist. Prices from around fl. 7.50 for the day or fl. 28 a week. A deposit of fl. 50–200 is usually charged.

On Foot. Small, concentrated Amsterdam is an excellent city for walking around, but you *must* use a map. The concentric circles of the canals are very confusing and you can easily find yourself walking in exactly the wrong direction. The VVV issues guides to seven walking tours around the center.

By Boat. Boat trips can be booked through the VVV, ranging from a 1½-hour canal tour (fl. 8–fl. 12) to a wine and cheese tour (fl. 30) to a candlelight dinner tour (fl. 60). You can design your own pedal-boat tour through *Canal-Bike* (tel. 020–265574); prices begin at fl. 18 per hour. The same company operates a waterborne canal bus from 10 A.M. to 6 P.M. daily; fl. 12.50 for a one-day pass, fl. 20 for two days. From April to September a special Museum Boat ferries passengers between cultural landmarks. Tickets (fl. 8 adults, fl. 6 children) include a discount on museum admission. Book through the VVV.

ENTERTAINMENT. Cafés. The most characteristic, and also the cheapest form of entertainment, is to spend time in one of the famous *bruine kroegen* (the Dutch version of the pub). These cafés stay open until 2 A.M., sometimes till even later in the morning. Of course, every café has its own atmosphere, its own clientèle. It is worth having a beer at any café around the Leidseplein, which is transformed into a terrace during the summer. The café in the middle of the Vondelpark is very pleasantly crowded in summer.

Café Americain, Leidskade 97. Crowded around 5 P.M. for the aperitif.

Café Gollum, Raamsteeg 4. For beer lovers: has more than 50 varieties.

Café Hoppe, Spui 18, across from the Atheneum bookstore. Crowded around 5 P.M. for the aperitif.

Het Koetshuis, Spuistraat 245. Stays open very late.

Café Nol, Westerstraat 109. The heart of the Jordaan, authentically decorated, recommended, and a must during the Jordaan Festival in the third week of September.

Music and Theater. Events can be booked in person through the VVV from 10–4. Classical music is performed at the renowned *Concertgebouw,* van Baerlestraat 98 (tel. 020–718345). Chamber music, recitals, jam sessions, opera and ballet are also staged here. While ticket prices for international orchestras are high, Wednesday lunchtime concerts are free. The box office is open 9.30–7 for personal callers; lines for telephone bookings are open 10–3. *Stalhouderij Theater* 1e Bloemdwarsstraat, (tel. 020–262282). A former stable sets the scene for English-language plays by an international cast of young performers. For experimental theater and colorful cabaret in Dutch, try the *Shaffeytheater,* Keizersgracht 324 (tel. 020–231311). Most cinemas are in the Leidseplein district. All movies are shown in their original language and subtitled in Dutch.

Jazz Clubs. *BIMhuis,* Oude Schans 173–7 (tel. 020–233373). Set in a converted warehouse, this is currently the most fashionable jazz club. Ticket holders can sit in the adjoining BIMcafe and enjoy a magical view across Oude Schans to the port. Open Thurs.–Sat. from 9 P.M. For jazz and singing, try the discreet *Cab Kaye's* Jazz Piano Bar, Beulingstraat 9 (tel. 020–233594). Open Tues.–Sat. until 3 A.M. If you long for good Dixieland jazz, go to *Joseph Lam Jazz Club,* Van Diemenstrat 8 (tel. 020–228086). Only open at weekends.

Bars and Discos. The *Bamboo Bar* in Lange Leidsewarsstraat 64 is informal, expensive, relaxing and typically international. It boasts good jazz and blues around the longest bar in Amsterdam. Discos are hidden in cellars around the Leidseplein. The young discos only fill up after midnight. *Club La Mer,* in Korte Leidsedwarstraat 73 draws a trendy, young crowd to dance to motown and soul. *Zorba The Buddha,* in OZ Voorburgwal, is run by the religious Baghwan sect in the heart of the red-light district. *Mazzo,* in Rosozengracht 114, uses dramatic lighting and slick videos to attract student poseurs, would-be musicians and artists.

Nightlife. Amsterdam has a wide variety of night clubs, bars and cabarets ranging from the respectable to the outright bizarre. The areas around Rembrandtsplein and Thorbekeplein have the best live shows (very expensive), as well as plenty of less obviously sex-oriented shows. This is also the gay bar center.

MUSEUMS. Holland is a feast for art lovers. Amsterdam is rich in museums of all kinds, with a total of over 40. Remember that there is an admission charge. For anyone planning to visit many museums, buy the Museum Card, available through VVV offices. Cost fl. 15 for those under 18; fl. 40 for those to age 65; fl 25 for those older. The card allows you to visit over 350 museums and galleries throughout the country at no extra charge.

Anne FrankHuis, Prinsengracht 263. The house in which the young Jewish girl Anne Frank, author of the famous diary, hid from Nazi agents during World War II has been chosen as the seat of an International Youth Center with club and lecture rooms. The rooms where the family was hidden are open to visitors. Tues.–Sat. 10 to 5, Sun. 1–5. Admission fl. 5.

The Joods Historisch Museum, Jonas Daniel Meijerplein 204. Set in a complex of three ancient synagogues. These once served a population of 100,000 Jews, shrunk to under 10,000 after 1945. The museum, founded by American and Dutch Jews, displays religious treasures in a clear cultural and historical context. Since the synagogues lost most of their treasures in the War, their architecture and history are more compelling than individual exhibits. Open daily 11–5. Admission fl. 8.

The Rijksmuseum, Stadhouderskade 42. Its fame rests on its unrivalled collection of 16th- and 17th-century Dutch masters. Of Rembrandt's masterpieces, make a point to see The *Nightwatch*, concealed during World War Two in caves in Maastricht. Also see Jan Steen's family portraits, Frans Hal's drunken scenes, van Ruysdael's romantic but menacing landscapes, and Vermeer's glimpses of everyday life. Open Tues.–Sat. 10–5, Sun. 1–5. Admission fl. 7.

The Rijksmuseum Vincent Van Gogh. Paulus Potterstraat 7. This modern museum contains the world's largest collection of the artist's works. Windswept wheatfields gradually give way to overblown cypresses and twisted olive trees as the painter's life becomes more tormented. The dramatic colors of the south of France inspire his later work; beside these, his watery Dutch landscapes pale into insignificance. To mark the centenary of van Gogh's tragic death in 1890, there are exhibitions of his work all over Holland but especially here. Open Tues.–Sat. 10–5, Sun. 1–5. Admission fl. 7.

The Stedelijk Museum, Paulus Potterstraat 13. This Municipal Museum has a stimulating collection of modern art and ever-changing displays of contemporary art. Before viewing the works of Cezanne, Chagall, Kandinsky, and Mondrian, check the list of temporary exhibitions in Room 1. Museum policy is to trace the development of the artist rather than merely to show a few masterpieces. Do not forget the museum's artistic restaurant overlooking a garden filled with modern sculptures. Open 11–5, Sun. 1–5. Admission fl. 8.

SHOPPING. Serious shoppers should buy the VVV's four excellent shopping guides to markets, art and antique shops, boutiques and department stores (fl. 10). Twenty percent sales tax rebates are available to all visitors from non-EC countries on purchases costing over $150 (fl. 300). Ask the store for your tax rebate check and collect refunds by mail or from "cashpoints" at Schipol Airport or main border crossings.

If you want to (window) shop for diamonds, try *Van Moppes Diamonds,* Albert Cuypstraat 2–6. It is conveniently situated beside the city's best market so if you fail to buy a diamond, cheaper consolation is at hand. Both the shop and market are open Mon.–Sat. 9–5. Porcelain is a less pricey purchase. The Dutch have been producing Delft, Makkum, and other fine porcelain for centuries. Focke and Meltzer stores have been selling it since 1823. The price range varies from affordable, newly-painted tiles (fl. 8) to expensive Delft blue and white pitchers. One store is situated near the Rijksmuseum, 65–67 P.C. Hoofstraat. As for markets, there is a lively open-air flea market on Waterlooplein (Mon.–Sat. 11–4). The floating flower market on the Singel is open Mon.–Sat. 10–5. If you are interested in old books, head for the book market at Oudemanhuispoort, held Monday through Saturday. In summer, art lovers can buy etchings, drawings and watercolors at the Sunday art market on Thorbeckeplein.

USEFUL ADDRESSES. *U.S. Consulate,* Museumplein 19 (tel. 020–790321); *British Consulate,* Koningslaan 44 (tel. 020–764343); *American Express,* Damrak 66 (tel. 020–262042); *Thomas Cook, Victoria Hotel, Damrak 1–5 (tel. 020–234255); Wagons Lits,* Dam 19 (tel. 020–247310); *Principal Post Office,* Oosterdokkade 15, (tel. 020–555 8911); *VVV offices,* Stationsplein opposite Central Station (tel. 020–266444), and Leidsestraat 106.

The Hague (Den Haag)

In the 17th-century The Hague was known as the "whispering gallery of Europe" because it was thought to be the secret manipulator of European politics. Although the Golden Age is over, Den Haag is still a dignified diplomatic capital, quietly boastful of its royal connections.

The heart is the Ridderzaal (Knight's Hall), the center of a government complex, by the peaceful lake. This 13th-century great hall is now mainly used for ceremonies: every year the Queen's gilded carriage brings her to open Parliament. The two chambers sit separately in buildings on either side of the Ridderzaal and can be visited when Parliament is not in session.

Keeping the Ridderzaal on your right, pass through two narrow arches and emerge on the far side of the Binnenhof, the former Inner Court of the castle. The small, well-proportioned Dutch Renaissance building on your left is the Mauritshuis, one of the greatest small art museums in the world. This superb 17th-century palace contains a feast of art from the same period, including 15 Rembrandts. Of the Rembrandts, the most powerful is *The Anatomy Lessons of Dr. Tulp*, a theatrical work depicting a gruesome dissection of the lower arm. By contrast, Rembrandt's self-portrait, painted in the year of his death, reflects both symbolism and narrative in a somber appreciation of old age. Vermeer's celebrated *Girl Wearing A Turban* and his glistening *View of Delft* are other masterpieces in the collection.

Outside the Mauritshuis, follow the Korte Vijverberg past the lake. The lake is bordered by patrician houses with revamped 18th- and 19th-century facades. Turn right at Lange Vijverberg and walk until you come to Lange Voorhout, a large L-shaped avenue. In the last century, horse-drawn carriages clattered along the cobbles and deposited dignitaries outside the various palaces. Apart from the trams, not much has changed. Diplomats still eat in the historic Hotel des Indes while Queen Beatrix and her staff work in the 16th-century Noordeinde Palace. The small streets leading off Lange Voorhout were once part of a busy canal network that was filled in last century. This is now the city's trendiest neighborhood. The few remaining canals are surprisingly peaceful, given the number of boutiques and bars. This is the place for a quick Dutch pea soup, pancake, or Indonesian snack. The locals often prefer the cart in Maliestraat.

A longer walk around the outskirts of the city could take in the Panorama Mesdag, a huge painting-in-the-round showing Schevingen as it looked in 1880. Nearby is Rijksmuseum H. W. Mesdag, one of the finest collections of Impressionist paintings outside France. Not far away is the Vredespaleis (Peace Palace), partly founded by Andrew Carnegie, and now the Court of European Justice.

Scheveningen

Scheveningen is an old fishing village to the north of The Hague. Since the last century it has become an increasingly popular resort, thanks to its magnificent pier and to the success of the Kurhaus Hotel and casino. But in spirit, Scheveningen is still a traditional fishing village, wary of cosmopolitan Den Haag. Many elderly women dress entirely in black in winter. On Sunday, the blackness is covered by a gray cape, but an elaborate headdress peeps out of a lace bonnet.

The beach itself is fronted by a high promenade that protects the village from fierce winter storms. It is possible to cycle for miles along the fine, sandy beaches. On summer evenings, the beach and pier are illuminated by a dramatic fireworks display.

PRACTICAL INFORMATION FOR DEN HAAG AND SCHEVENINGEN

Hotels

Moderate

Badhotel, Gevers Deynootweg 15, Scheveningen (tel. 070–3512221). 78 double and 18 single rooms with bath/shower.

Bali, Badhuisweg 1, Scheveningen (tel. 070–3502434). Small, with excellent Indonesian restaurant.

Carlton Beach, Gevers Deynootweg 201, Scheveningen (tel. 070–3541414).

Esquire, van Aerssenstraat 59, Den Haag (tel. 070–3522341).

Petit, Groot Hertoginnenlaan 42, Den Haag (tel. 070–3465500). 40 beds, 12 rooms with shower.
Savion, Prinsestraat 86 (tel. 070–3462560). Small and reasonable.

Inexpensive

Aristo, Stationsweg 166, Den Haag (tel. 070–3890847).
Enak, Keizerstraat 53, Scheveningen (tel. 070–3556169).
Excelsior, Stationsweg 133, Den Haag (tel. 070–3882415). 64 beds, only 6 rooms with bath/shower.
Meerbeek, Dirk Hoogeirraadstraat 212 Scheveningen, (tel. 070–3550884). 11 rooms, all with shower. 3 minutes from beach.
Neuf, Rijswijkseweg 119, Den Haag (tel. 070–3900748).
't Seehuis, Zeekant 45, Scheveningen (tel. 070–3559585). Youth hostel.

Restaurants

Moderate

Chalet Suisse, Noordeinde 123 (tel. 070–3463185). Swiss food; crowded.
't Goude Hooft, Groenmarket 13, Den Haag (tel. 070–3469713). Large building near Grote Kerk. Old Dutch atmosphere. Terrace in summer.
Raden Ajoe, Lange Poten 31, Den Haag (tel. 070–3644592). Indonesian foods.
Wilhelm Tell, Laan van Meerdervoort 324 (tel. 070–3605609). Closed Wed.

Inexpensive

Buffeterie, Palace Promenade. Cheap.
Camel Club, Strandpaviljoen 53, Scheveningen (tel. 070–3540111). Open during summer, right on the beach.
Klein Seinpost, Deltaplein 600 (tel. 070–3681388). For pancakes.
Promenade, Strandweg 105, Scheveningen (tel. 070–3540880).

WHAT TO SEE AND DO. Museums. Haags Gemeentemuseum (Municipal Museum), 41 Stadhouderslaan. Art, ceramics, silver, glass collections and fine period rooms. Open Tues.–Sat. 10–5, Sun. 1–5. Admission fl. 4.
Madurodam, Haringkade 175. Holland in miniature; lovingly-detailed model of Dutch towns and countryside. Open Mar.–June, 9 A.M.–10 P.M., June–Aug. 9 A.M.–10.30 P.M. Sept. 9–9, Oct.–Jan. 9–6. Admission fl. 8.20.
Mauritshuis, Kneuterdijk 6. Lovely Dutch Renaissance building; magnificent picture collection. Open Tues.–Sat. 10–5, Sun. 11–5. Admission fl. 6.50.
Panorama Mesdag, Zeestraat 65b. Largest panoramic painting in the world, 1700 sq. m., depicting Scheveningen in 19th century. Open Mon.–Sat. 10–5, Sun. 12–5. fl. 3.
Ridderzaal, Binnenhof 8a. Open Mon.–Sat. 10–4. Tours fl. 4.40.
Rijksmuseum H.W. Mesdag, Laan van Meerdervoort 7f. Paintings of the Hague School and Impressionist paintings by Corot, Courbet and Rousseau. Open Tues.–Sat. 10–5, Sun. 1–5. Admission fl. 4.
Scheveningen Museum, Neptunustraat 92. An interesting collection of local costumes and fishing traditions. Open Tues.–Sat. Admission fl. 3.
Vredespaleis, Carnegieplein 2. Open Mon.–Fri. 10–12, 2–4. Adm. fl. 3.
Other places of interest and entertainment are the *Fleamarket* at Herman Coster-straat (weekdays 8–6); and *Omniversum* (planetarium), President Kennedylaan 5.

GUIDED TOURS. By Boat. Day trips and candlelit dinner cruises can be booked at The Hague VVV. Scheveningen offers fishing boat tours around the Dutch coast. Contract Sportsviscentrum, Scheveningen (tel. 070–3541122).

By Bus. City sightseeing tours can be booked by the VVV office next to the Central Station. The size and diversity of The Hague makes a bus tour a logical choice. Fom May through September, the Royal Bus Tour is a special treat. It leaves the main VVV office at 1.30 every day except Sunday and costs fl. 20 for a 3-hour trip.

USEFUL ADDRESSES. *U.S. Embassy,* Lange Voorhout 102 (tel. 070–362–4911); *Canadian Embassy,* Sophialaan 7 (tel. 070–3614111); *British Embassy,* Lange

Voorhout 10 (tel. 070–3645800); *American Express,* Venestraat 20 (tel. 070–3469515); *Wagons Lits,* Buitenhof 46 (tel. 070–3656850); *VVV,* (in Babylon Center beside main station) tel. 070–3546200; *VVV,* Corner Scheveningseslag and Gevers Deynootweg, (tel. 070–3546200).

Hungary

Hungary offers travelers the combined benefit of a central location in the heart of Europe along with the opportunity to experience a unique blend of language, culture, food, and people. This small country, bordered by the USSR, Romania, Yugoslavia, Austria and Czechoslovakia, and with a population of 10.7 million, has been able to retain its identity through 11 centuries by withstanding invasions and turbulence from all sides. Hungary still has traces of ancient Roman ruins from as early as 100 A.D., relics from 150 years of Turkish occupation in the 16th and 17th centuries, and architecture in Western Hungarian towns that reflects the 500 years' association with the Habsburg dynasty. This pleasant mixture of old world charm is coupled with the extensive effort to offer visitors every modern comfort.

Even though Hungarians may complain about their current economic difficulties, such as rising yearly inflation of 20% and the highest per capita foreign debt in Eastern Europe, they spare visitors much of the bureaucracy associated with the region. Foreigners are allowed to travel freely and are not required to exchange a specified amount of currency.

Although a landlocked nation, Hungary is dominated by two rivers, the Danube and the Tisza, and the largest lake in Central Europe, Lake Balaton. The Danube (Duna) flows from the western frontier of Hungary, turns south near the town of Vác, and bisects Budapest along its path to the southern border with Yugoslavia. The smaller Tisza flows from the northeast of Hungary, dividing the Nagyalföld (the Great Plain), and likewise enters Yugoslavia, south of the city of Szeged. The splendor of Lake Balaton lies in its many contrasts. Its shores and surrounding areas include internationally known spas (including Hévíz and Balatonfüred), wonderfully preserved Baroque villages, magnificent vineyards on the northern shore, and inexpensive restaurants dishing up the catch of the day.

The other regions of Hungary offer a wide selection of towns and cities rich in history and culture. Pécs, in the southwest region, is surrounded by the Mecsek hills and is known for its Mediterranean climate and a vast spectrum of architectural wonders. Sopron, near the northwestern border with Austria, displays medieval and baroque buildings from the Habsburg era. In the Nagyalföld of central and eastern Hungary, one experiences the folklore and customs of the Magyars (what Hungarians call themselves and their language).

Budapest, home to more than two million, has an unrivaled location on both banks of the Danube. Buda, with its relaxing, rolling hills and historic districts, contrasts with the closely packed hotels, cafes, restaurants, and shops of Pest. The city offers an outstanding selection of opera, theater, music, and art. In addition to its many elegant hotels, Budapest offers inexpensive accommodations including a network of private guesthouses.

The Hungarians are friendly and outspoken people who are proud to show their hospitality. They enjoy meeting foreigners, especially those who show an interest in the country. There's a feeling of anticipation and anxiety as they cope with political and economic reforms, including a new multi-party system, a less centralized bureaucracy, and an increase in trade with the West. Increasing openness pursued by each new leadership eases the way for tourists as well.

PRACTICAL INFORMATION FOR HUNGARY

WHAT WILL IT COST. An enjoyable vacation in Hungary with the appropriate Western standards is still relatively inexpensive, even with the recent introduction of VAT (value-added tax) and the removal of certain price controls. Inflation is set to rise by 20%, but this shouldn't inconvenience the traveler as much as the local consumer, since Western currencies will adjust accordingly. The unit of currency is the *forint* (Ft.) divided into 100 *fillér* (f). There are coins of 10, 20, and 50 fillér and 1, 2, 5, 10 and 20 forints; bank notes circulate in denominations of 20, 50, 100, 500 and 1,000 forints. At press time, the U.S. dollar was worth 64 Ft., while the pound sterling was valued around 100 Ft. Official exchange rates are adjusted every Tuesday morning.

Major credit cards are accepted in most hotels, first class restaurants, downtown shops and gas stations. Holders of Eurocheque cards can cash personal checks in all banks and in many hotels.

Sample Costs. Cinema (moderate seat) 40 Ft.; theater or concert (moderate seat) 200 Ft.; museum entrance fee 10 Ft.; cup of coffee 35 Ft.; beer in a pub 40–60 Ft.; beer in a moderate restaurant 50–75 Ft.; half liter of wine in a restaurant 100–125 Ft. These prices are approximate. Note that only top-grade restaurants and cafés have menus in English, so make sure you know what you are ordering and, to avoid an unpleasant surprise, what it will cost.

NATIONAL TOURIST OFFICE. *Tourinform* (Hungarian Tourist Board), Sütő utca 2, Budapest V., in the inner city, near Deák tér metro station. Open daily 8–8, tel. 1179–800. *IBUSZ* (the main tourist organization), Budapest VI., Tanács körút 3/c, tel. 1423–140. The *IBUSZ* office at Petőfi tér 3 (behind the Inter-Continental Hotel) specializes in finding accommodations to match your budget; it is open 24 hours every day (tel. 1211–000).

Their addresses overseas are:

In the U.S.: *IBUSZ Hungarian Travel Company,* 1 Parker Plaza, Fort Lee, NJ 07024 (tel. 201–592–8585).

In the U.K.: Danube Travel, 6 Conduit St., London W1R 9TG (tel. 071–493 0263).

WHEN TO COME. From May through September is the best time. July and August are hot in Budapest, but can be quite enjoyable (if you don't mind the crowds) at Lake Balaton resorts. Spring and fall are often delightful, with numerous fairs and festivals and less congestion. Winters, everywhere, are very cold.

Average maximum daily temperatures in degrees Fahrenheit and centigrade:

Budapest

	Jan.	Feb.	Mar.	Apr.	May	June	July	Aug.	Sept.	Oct.	Nov.	Dec.
F°	34	39	50	63	72	79	82	81	73	61	46	39
C°	1	4	10	17	22	26	28	27	23	16	8	4

SPECIAL EVENTS. *February;* Film Festival, Budapest. *March;* Spring Festival Week, Budapest. *May;* International Trade Fair, Budapest. *June;* Historical Pageants and Tournaments, Visegrad. *June-July;* Summer Theater Festival, Pecs. *June-August;* Beethoven Memorial Concerts, Martonvásár; Festival Weeks, Sopron. *July;* International Equestrian Days, Hortobagy. *July-August;* Haydn and Mozart Concerts in the Castle at Fertöd; Open-air Festival, Szeged; Days of Music and Art, Szentendre. *August;* Formula One motor races, Mogyoród; National Flower Festival, Debrecen; Horse Show, Bugac Puszta. *September;* International Trade Fair, Budapest; Budapest Art and Music Weeks; Vintage Days, Sopron. *October;* Limestone Caves, Concerts, Aggtelek.

National Holidays. Jan. 1 (New Year's Day); March 15 (Anniversary of 1848 War of Independence); Apr. 7–8 (Easter); May 1 (Labor Day); Aug. 20 (St. Stephen's and Constitution Day); Oct. 23 (1956 Revolution Day); Dec. 25, 26.

VISAS. It is advisable to obtain a visa beforehand from a Hungarian embassy or through an *IBUSZ* representative. The completed application form must be accompanied by two recent photographs and the passport must be valid for six months after the date for which the visa is requested. The fee is $15 or £10 (often included in package-tour charges) and the visa is valid for a stay of up to thirty days. Travelers by air or private car can obtain visas on arrival, but this may cause lengthy delays. Travelers by train, bus or hydrofoil *must* obtain their visas in advance.

HEALTH CERTIFICATES. No vaccinations are necessary to enter Hungary.

GETTING TO HUNGARY. By Plane. Pan Am (in a joint venture with the Hungarian airline MALÉV) flies daily from New York to Budapest, sometimes nonstop, otherwise one-stop (Vienna or Frankfurt). MALÉV and other national airlines fly non-stop from most European capitals. In London, shop around for the most competitive fares; they start from £100 one way. There are also many charter flights in the summer.

By Train. From western Europe the best-known train into Hungary is the *Orient Express* (yes, it still runs, although shorn long since of any pretensions to glamor) which leaves Paris (Gare de l'Est) nightly at 11.15 P.M., traveling via Munich, Salzburg and Vienna arriving in Budapest at 8.10 P.M. the next day. It has through 2nd-class day cars to Budapest and 2nd-class sleeping cars and bunk beds as far as Salzburg or Vienna. There are through 1st- and 2nd-class sleeping cars from Paris to Salzburg or Vienna. Restaurant car from Stuttgart to Budapest. The *Wiener Walzer* leaves Basel, Switzerland, at 8.27 P.M. and Zürich at 9.34 P.M., with through 2nd-class day cars to Budapest, which it reaches at about 1.20 P.M. the next day; it also has 2nd-class sleeping cars and 2nd-class bunk beds as far as Vienna and a restaurant car from Salzburg onwards. From the U.K., the best route is via Dover and Oostende and the *Oostende–Vienna Express* has through sleeping cars, 2nd-class bunk beds and 2nd-class day cars to Vienna, where it connects with the Wiener Walzer. You leave London around noon, arriving in Budapest at 1.20 P.M. the next day. The fastest train from Vienna is the *Lehár*, a EuroCity express (the $4 surcharge includes a seat reservation). It leaves at 7.45 A.M. and arrives at 10.33 A.M., almost an hour faster than any other train on the route.

By Bus. There are two deluxe buses daily from Vienna, one leaving at 7 A.M. and arriving in Budapest at 11.10 A.M.; the other at 5 P.M., arriving 9.30 P.M. There is an especially good reduction on round-trip tickets; the departure times from Budapest are the same as from Vienna. Reservations are required. They can be made in Vienna through the Blaguss Travel Agency (tel. 50180–110) and in Budapest at Blaguss-Volánbusz at Erzsébet (Engels) tér bus station (tel. 1177–777).

By Boat. An unusual, pleasant and relatively quick way from Vienna to Budapest is by hydrofoil. From June to early September there are two daily departures from Vienna at 8 A.M. and 2.30 P.M. arriving in Budapest at 12.30 P.M. and 7 P.M. respectively. Return journeys leave Budapest at 8 A.M. and 1.30 P.M. arriving in Vienna at 1.30 P.M. and 7 P.M. respectively. During April, and from late September to early October, there are daily departures from both Vienna and Budapest at 8 A.M. arriving in Budapest at 12.30 P.M. and in Vienna at 1.30 P.M. Bookings can be made through IBUSZ in Vienna (tel. 512–29–57) and Budapest (tel. 1211–007). No winter service.

CUSTOMS. Personal belongings and 250 cigarettes or 50 cigars or 250 gr. tobacco and one liter of spirits and two liters of wine and 250 gr. of perfume may be brought into Hungary. Valuable gifts for people in Hungary should be declared. There is a 30% customs charge on gifts valued over 10,000 Ft. Gifts of a noncommercial nature that have been bought for hard currency (or legally exchanged forints) may be freely exported, but you must keep the bills or receipts. Only enough food for a three-day journey may be taken out of Hungary. On leaving Hungary, any extra forints (up to 50% of the officially exchanged sum, and not in excess of $100), can be re-exchanged for Western currency on showing the appropriate receipts and passport.

HOTELS. Most Moderate and Inexpensive hotels in Hungary, whether in Budapest or in the provinces, are well-run, clean and comfortable. Many double rooms have private baths, but comparatively few single ones do. The hotels are graded by stars, 5-star being De Luxe and 1-star downright simple. We have, in general, listed 3-star hotels in the Moderate (M) category and 2- and 1-star hotels in the Inexpensive (I) category. There is also very inexpensive dormitory accommodation in so-called "Tourist Hotels."

A good way to meet Hungarians is to stay in a privately-run guest house. These are inexpensive, usually centrally located and provide a "family" atmosphere. Details from IBUSZ.

We give below what cannot be more than *approximate* prices for the various kinds of accommodations. In Budapest, in a Moderate hotel expect to pay around $55–$90 for a double room with bath and breakfast, about $45–$50 without bath. In an Inexpensive hotel expect to pay around $35–$50 for a double with bath or shower and breakfast, from $30–$35 without bath or shower. Breakfast is usually substantial—fruit juice, ham and eggs to order, butter and preserves, with tea or coffee, or else a buffet that often includes spicy supper leftovers. Single rooms usually cost about three quarters the price of a double. In the provinces (with the exception of Lake Balaton) rooms usually cost at least 30% less than in Budapest. At hotels on Lake Balaton full board is generally compulsory and a 3-star hotel might charge, for a double room with bath, from $65–$90 a day, according to the season. A 2-star hotel would charge, for a room with shower, from $50 a day up. July and August are the most expensive months, May and September are slightly less expensive; most Balaton hotels are closed in winter. Single rooms are not easy to come by.

Self-Catering. Villas, bungalows and accommodations in private houses are widely available. The villas are mainly situated on the shores of Lake Balaton and are very comfortable. There are bungalows in Budapest, at Lake Balaton, and also in a large number of popular resorts throughout the country. They usually have two rooms and are simple, but well equipped. Full details and rates can be obtained from tourist offices in Hungary and abroad and they can also arrange bookings.

Accommodations in private houses are available almost everywhere. A double room in a private house costs from about $15–$20 up, including heating in the cold season and use of the bathroom, but usually no meals are provided. All such accommodations can be booked through the official Hungarian travel bureau *IBUSZ* or simply by looking out for the sign "szoba kiadó" (room to let) in Hungarian or, even more frequently, "Zimmer frei" in German. If you book a room direct through the landlady, you will have to register with the local police station; if you book through an agency, it takes care of this.

Camping. There are over 140 camping sites in Hungary, found mainly in the country's chief beauty spots; most of them cater only to campers bringing their own equipment, but a few provide tents. Information about bookings can be obtained from the *Hungarian Camping and Caravanners' Club*, Üllői út 6, Budapest VIII (tel. 1336–536), or through travel agencies. Camping is forbidden except in the specially designated areas.

Youth Hostels. The *Express Travel Bureau*, Szabadság tér 16, Budapest V., can arrange cheap accommodations in hostels and, in summer, converted dormitories. There are no age limits in Hungarian hostels.

RESTAURANTS. One of the pleasures of a holiday in Hungary is eating. Budget-minded travelers are particularly advised to look out for a restaurant advertising on the price-list outside its door a so-called *Menü*—served only at midday, a no frills, two- or three-course table d'hôte meal at a very reasonable price. You can find such a meal for as little as 60 Ft., though you may pay a good deal more at a fashionable place. Otherwise, for a very good 3-course meal expect to pay from 350–425 Ft. a head in an (M) restaurant and up to 250 Ft. in an (I) restaurant. In neither case is wine or beer included in the prices mentioned. There are also many inexpensive self-service restaurants *(önkiszol-gáló étterem)*, snack-bars *(bisztró* or *ételbár)* and buffets *(büfé)*.

Food and Drink. Hungary takes great pride in its cuisine and the variety it offers. Although it is often only identified with paprika and goulash, there are many other stews, and fish and game dishes to choose from, as well as quality breads, spicy salads and desserts.

Paprika dishes vary from mild to burning hot. Among the most common are *gulyás* (a soup with cubed beef or pork), *pörkölt* (outside Hungary known as goulash), a rich meat stew of meat or chicken in which onions play an important role, *paprikás* (meat or bird served with a sauce of onions, sour cream and red pepper) and *halászlé*, a fish soup that is Hungary's sharp reply to *bouillabaisse*—it can be fiery indeed!

Desserts include the popular *rétes*—strudel—its crisp leaves of pastry filled with cherries, apple, walnuts, almonds or cream-cheese.

Hungary has been blessed with many fine wine-producing regions. The volcanic hills of the northern shore of Lake Balaton produce some of the best known white wines, while the Villanyi region in the southwest yields many good reds. The most famous red wine, "Bull's Blood" (*Bikavér*), comes from Eger and is dry and strong, while *Tokaji Aszu* (Tokay) is renowned as a sweet dessert wine.

TIPPING. Tips are generally expected, in addition to any service charge. Hotel staff—don't forget the head porter!—waiters and barbers should be given at least 10%, taxi-drivers up to 15% of the fare.

MAIL. Airmail letter to U.S. (5 grams), 18 Ft., postcard 12 Ft. Surface mail to Europe is as fast as airmail and costs 15 Ft. for a letter and 10 Ft. for a postcard.

CLOSING TIMES. Most stores open at 10 and close at 6. They are closed on Saturday afternoons. Banks: 8 to 1; offices: 8 to 5 (closed Saturdays).

PHOTOGRAPHY. Do not photograph military installations or railways.

GETTING AROUND HUNGARY. By Train. The railway network, especially the express train network (*gyors vonat*) is easy to use. It is usually worth traveling 1st Class on longer journeys, especially during peak weekends in the summer. Although "Run Around" tickets, giving unlimited travel, are available, they do not always represent a saving. Snacks and drinks are available on all express trains but these tend to be poorly stocked, so pack a lunch just in case. All students with a valid I.D. pay half price. For more information in Budapest about rail travel contact *MÁV Passenger Service,* Budapest VI, Népköztársaság útja 35 (tel. 1228–049, 1228–056). You must reserve seats on long-distance expresses. Inter-Rail cards, allowing free rail travel to those under 26, are valid in Hungary. "Rail Europ Senior" tickets, available in many European countries, including the United Kingdom, for senior citizens, grant a reduction of 30% on Hungarian railways.

By Bus. There is an extensive bus network. Seat reservations are advisable on long distance routes. Information and tickets are available at the Erzsébet tér bus station, next to Deák tér (tel. 1172–966, 1172–318).

Car Hire. This is not cheap and is best done through the IBUSZ/Avis Rent-a-Car office at Martinelli tér 8, Budapest V (tel. 1184–158, 1184–240). The cheapest car (a Lada, made in Eastern Europe) costs about $15 a day, plus 15 cents a kilometer; in addition, a returnable deposit of $150 or its equivalent in other "hard" currencies, must be made. Petrol (gasoline) costs around 100 Ft. a gallon, but this is, of course, liable to change.

Bicycles. These can be hired from some of the larger railway stations around Lake Balaton. For guided bicycle tours contact *Huntours,* Budapest II, Retek u. 34 (tel. 1152–403, 1363–916).

Hitchhiking, though not expressly forbidden, is frowned on and is not recommended.

Budapest

Whatever their politics, Budapest's two million inhabitants are unanimous on one point: their city is the loveliest in the world. Its situation is certainly magnificent, located as it is on both sides of the wide river Danube. Buda dominates the scene with its many rounded hills and bluffs rising from the curved arms of the river; Pest is young and growing and stretches flatly eastwards across the plain. The lovely Margaret Island (Margit-sziget) is a 112-acre paradise of flowers, trees and medicinal baths. If all of Budapest's 526 parks and oases were rolled into one, the resulting area would cover 1,500 acres, nearly twice the size of New York's Central Park or London's Hampstead Heath. The city boasts 123 mineral hot springs, Celtic and Roman ruins, an 80,000-fan sports stadium, the second oldest subway (underground railway) in the world (built in 1896), as well as two of the world's most modern.

For a perfect first glimpse of Budapest, get out of downtown, climb a hill, and admire the view. The hike from Gellért tér (square) on the Buda side, 770 feet up to the top of the Gellérthegy (Mount Gellért) is rewarded by a panorama of all the Danube bridges, Parliament and Pest to the east, Buda Castle and the blue mountains to the north. Mount Gellért is crowned by a stone fort and topped by a towering memorial to the liberation of Budapest by Soviet troops in 1945. During the 14-week winter siege, 33,000 buildings were totally destroyed and every bridge was demolished. However, the city was almost completely restored within about twenty years. Bullet holes are still visible in some of the older buildings in Budapest.

Two other hills rise up from the Danube on the Buda side—Castle Hill (Várhegy) and the Hill of Roses (Rózsadomb). Behind these scenic summits curves a range of higher hills, of which the loftiest is the conical Jánoshegy, 1,435 feet in height, and topped by a lookout tower. The hills are easily reached from Buda by a cogwheel railway (terminus at Városmajor, opposite the Hotel Budapest) or by a chairlift (terminus at Zugligeti út). The cogwheel railway connects at its upper end with the famous Pioneer Railway, whose eight miles of narrow-gauge track and snappy red-and-white passenger cars are owned and operated by the children of Hungary. Except for the engineer (driver), no employee of the Pioneer Railway is over 15 years of age.

After drinking in the Budapest panorama from the hills, it is time to get acquainted with the city itself. Before leaving the Buda side, ramble around Castle Hill, with its many Gothic landmarks. This oldest section of the city suffered the most damage during World War II. Bombardments destroyed a great deal of Renaissance architecture, revealing many older walls and arches, some medieval. The post-war governments rebuilt much of the district following its original town plan. The reconstructed former Royal Palace, now a museum and cultural center, covers the south end of Castle Hill; farther north is the Fishermen's Bastion, a round neo-Romanesque lookout tower and wall built in the last century.

Close to the Bastion stands the 13th-century Coronation Church, where the last two kings of Hungary were crowned. Here in 1456 the Pope's edict was proclaimed ordering all churches in Christendom to ring their bells at noon in honor of János Hunyadi's victory over the Turks at Belgrade. (The Angelus of modern church bells still recalls this event.) Next to the church stands the tastefully integrated Hilton Hotel, a miracle of architectural imagination and restraint.

Now walk down to the Danube and cross the river over the impressive Chain Bridge to Pest, the commercial section of the city, where you will find the main banks, department stores and theaters. Behind several impressive new hotels lies the so-called Inner City, with Budapest's most chic shops—and most stylish customers—on Váci utca, part of a pedestrian zone.

PRACTICAL INFORMATION FOR BUDAPEST

HOTELS. Budapest has accommodations of every kind, from the De Luxe suite to the simple dormitory bed. Although several new hotels have been built in recent years, it is still often difficult to find a room, especially from May through September. If you have any difficulty, go to the *IBUSZ* office at Petőfi tér 3 for help.

Here is our selection of budget hotels, hostels and restaurants. The Roman figures in Budapest addresses (e.g. V.) denote the district of the city.

Moderate

Erzsébet, V., Károlyi Mihály utca 11–15 (tel. 1382–111). Traditional hotel in Inner City, completely modernized. 123 rooms with shower, TV and minibar. Public rooms airconditioned. Restaurant and popular beer-hall with folkloric décor.
Európa, II., Hárshegyi utca 5–7 (tel. 1767–122). 13-story hotel in Buda woods area with fine views. 160 rooms with bath. Restaurant, folkloric shows.
Nemzeti, VII, József krt. 4 (tel. 1339–160). Located in the heart of Pest, the hotel was renovated in 1987. 72 double rooms with bath, and turn-of-the-century style. Restaurant and brasserie.
Vörös Csillag, XII., Rege út 21 (tel. 1750–522). Alpine style hotel on Széchenyi Hill, with fine views. 41 rooms, some with bath. Restaurant, pool. Also bungalows in wooded grounds—residents share hotel's amenities. At the terminus of the cogwheel railway.

Inexpensive

Citadella, XI., Gellérthegy (tel. 1665–794). In the former fortress, with fine views over city. 20 rooms, each with 2–4 beds; showers in corridors; popular and inexpensive restaurant. Primarily intended for young people.
Metropol, VII., Rákóczi út 58 (tel. 1421–175). Shabby but comfortable hotel on main shopping street. 102 rooms, some doubles and singles with bath. Restaurant. Recommended for value, not services.
Volga, XIII., Dózsa György út 65 (tel. 1290–200). North of the city center, but with direct metro connection. 308 rooms with bath or shower, all with 2 or more beds.
Wien, XI., Budaörsi út 90 (tel. 1665–400). In southwestern outskirts, near junction of Vienna and Lake Balaton motorways. 100 double rooms, many with bath. Car repair shop and filling-station. Recommended only for those traveling by car.
Hostels. *Express,* XII., Beethoven utca 7–9 (tel. 1752–528). Silence imposed after 10 P.M. *Strand,* III., Pusztakúti út 3 (tel. 1671–999). Both of these are some way out from the center; for beds, apply to *IBUSZ* tourist bureau. *Academia* and *Universitas,* two student hostels, open to young people in July and August; apply well in advance to *Express Travel Bureau,* Szabadság tér 16, Budapest V.

RESTAURANTS

Moderate

Apostolok, V., Kigyó utca 4–6 (tel. 1183–704). Famous beer-hall and restaurant which serves a reasonably priced midday *menü.* Located in the Inner City pedestrian district.
Duna-Corso, V., Vigadó tér 3 (tel. 1186–362). On the Danube bank in Pest, with a Hungarian clientele and good food. Open all day, music in the evening.
Kisbuda, II., Frankel L. utca 34 (tel. 1152–244). Near the west end of Margaret Bridge. With a garden terrace in summer and music in the evening, their specialty is fish. Ask waiter for unlisted daily specials. Closed Sun. eve.
Kispipa, VII., Akacfa utca 38 (tel. 1422–587). Very popular restaurant in the heart of Pest; open all day with piano music in the evening. Booking advisable.
Opera, VI., Népköztársaság útja 44 (tel. 1328–586). In theater district and popular for a meal after the show. Gypsy music in the evenings.
Pest-Buda, I., Fortuna utca 3 (tel. 1569–849). Delightful little restaurant on Castle Hill, with friendly service. Open evenings only, when old-time music is played.
Tabáni Kakas, I., Attila út 27 (tel. 1757–165). Delightful small restaurant west of Castle Hill. Famous for its goose dishes. A pianist plays and sings.

Inexpensive

Bástya, VII., Rákóczi út 29 (tel. 1183–464). Popular restaurant in the city's main shopping street. Quick and friendly service. Open all day; no music.
Csarnok, V., Hold út. 11 (tel. 1122–016). Popular restaurant near the U.S. Embassy. Excellent food and Hungarian draught beer. Closed on weekends.

Kaltenberg, IX., Kinizsi út 30–36 (tel. 1189–792). Beer hall in brewery. Basic food, excellent raspberry strudel. Music in evening.

Lucullus, VII., Erzsébet körút 7 (tel. 1223–001). Extremely simple, but cheap and good food.

Muskétás, I., Dísz tér 8 (tel. 1161–283). On Castle Hill. Part restaurant, part snack bar. Unpretentious and inexpensive.

PASTRY SHOPS AND CAFÉS. Among many are: *Gerbeaud,* Vörösmarty tér in Inner City, a stylish landmark since 1857; also in the inner city is the elegant, newly renovated *Gourmand Café,* Semmelweis utca 2; *Ruszwurm,* Szentháromság utca 7 on Castle Hill, a bakery since the 16th century. All are famous for coffee and desserts. There are cafés *(eszpresszó)* on nearly every street.

GETTING AROUND BUDAPEST. By Bus. There is an extensive network. Tickets costs 6 Ft. and, like those for all city transport, must be bought in advance from tobacconists or metro stations, and self-canceled on the bus. The fine for traveling without a properly-canceled ticket or pass is 250 Ft.

By Tram and Trolleybus. Tickets cost 5 Ft. and must also be canceled in the tram or trolley.

By Metro (subway). This is efficient and quick. Tickets, bought in advance, must be canceled in special machines at the entrance to each station. They cost 5 Ft. A day pass for use on all forms of transport within the city costs 48 Ft. If you intend staying in Budapest for more than a week it might be practical to purchase a monthly pass for 280 Ft. Inquire at any metro station.

There is a bus service to the airport that leaves from Erzsébet tér, platform 1, every 30 minutes from 5 A.M.–9 P.M. The trip takes 30–40 minutes and costs either 30 or 40 Ft., depending on which terminal you are going to.

ENTERTAINMENT. Hungary has a lively night life. A useful monthly "Programme" in English and German is available free at hotels and travel offices and contains details of a variety of entertainments—from classical to pop concerts, from puppet to mime to folk dance shows. Prices are very reasonable and tickets can be obtained from the Central Booking Agency (Vörösmarty tér 1. Open 11–6 weekdays).

You'll find young people, students, drink, dancing, and rock music at the Youth Leisure Center (Petőfi Csarnok) in the City Park and at the Casino on Margaret Island. Pleasure boats cruise along the Danube 3 times a day, starting from the quay in front of the Duna Inter-Continental Hotel; on summer evenings there is dancing on board.

The best discos are attached to the University colleges—ask a student which are the "in" spots.

There's an excellent circus, a large amusement park, and a zoo in the City Park.

Theater and Cinema. In addition to Hungarian films that occasionally interest foreigners, cinemas in Budapest usually show several foreign films (many in English and German) in the original language. There are some 20 theaters in Budapest, but many are closed between June and September.

MUSEUMS. National Museum, Múzeum körút 14–16. Hungarian history from the Dark Ages to the present day. In the Hall of Honor is the Holy Crown of St. Stephen, as well as other coronation regalia, returned by the United States in 1978.

National Gallery, in the former Royal Castle on Castle Hill. It contains an admirable collection of Hungarian painting and sculpture.

Fine Arts Museum, Dózsa György út 41, at the entrance to the City Park. It contains an impressive collection of painting and sculpture. It is particularly rich in Dutch, Flemish and Spanish old masters.

Budapest History Museum, in the former Royal Palace. It illustrates the 1,000-year-old history of the city.

Most museums are open daily except Monday from 10 to 6; admission is usually free on Saturdays, with discounts for students the rest of the week.

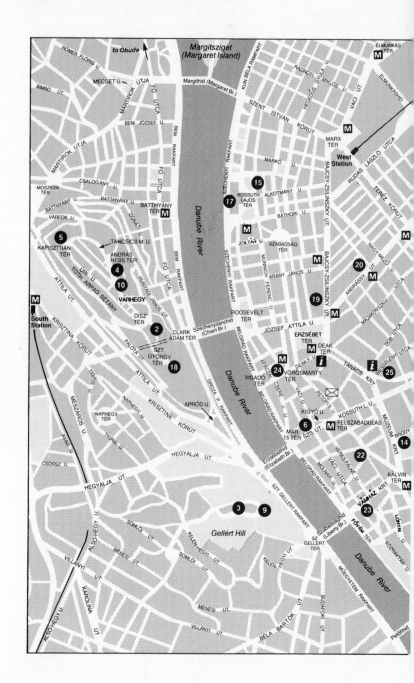

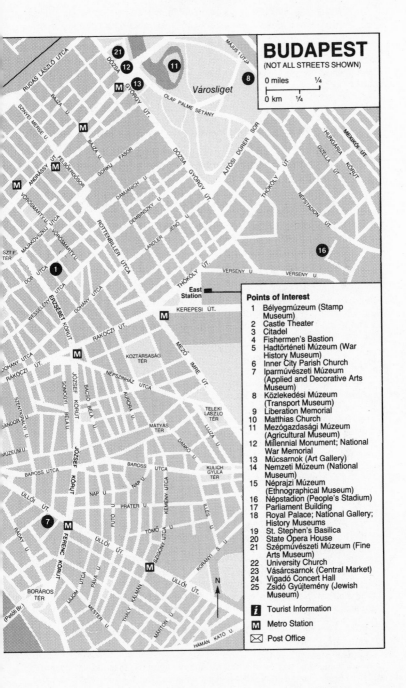

BUDAPEST
(NOT ALL STREETS SHOWN)

0 miles ¼

0 km ¼

Városliget

East Station

Points of Interest

1   Bélyegmúzeum (Stamp Museum)
2   Castle Theater
3   Citadel
4   Fishermen's Bastion
5   Hadtörténeti Múzeum (War History Museum)
6   Inner City Parish Church
7   Iparművészeti Múzeum (Applied and Decorative Arts Museum)
8   Közlekedési Múzeum (Transport Museum)
9   Liberation Memorial
10 Matthias Church
11 Mezőgazdasági Múzeum (Agricultural Museum)
12 Millennial Monument; National War Memorial
13 Múcsarnok (Art Gallery)
14 Nemzeti Múzeum (National Museum)
15 Néprajzi Múzeum (Ethnographical Museum)
16 Népstadion (People's Stadium)
17 Parliament Building
18 Royal Palace; National Gallery; History Museums
19 St. Stephen's Basilica
20 State Opera House
21 Szépművészeti Múzeum (Fine Arts Museum)
22 University Church
23 Vásárcsarnok (Central Market)
24 Vigadó Concert Hall
25 Zsidó Gyűjtemény (Jewish Museum)

i   Tourist Information

M   Metro Station

✉   Post Office

SHOPPING. Shopping is best done in the morning after 10 A.M., as shops tend to be crowded in the afternoon. The main shopping streets are Váci utca (a pedestrian precinct) and the adjoining Kossuth Lajos utca, both in the Inner City. Perhaps the finest selection of items is to be found at the *Intertourist* and *Konsumtourist* shops, which only accept Western currency and credit cards. But the store at Váci utca 14, which accepts Hungarian money, has a wide range of folk art, and a small shop in Kigyó utca, in the same area, sells the beautiful Herend and Zsolnay porcelain for forints. Other good buys include classical, as well as "pop," music records, of which there is an enormous selection at very reasonable prices, high quality yet inexpensive art, and travel books. If you like browsing in department stores, try those in Rákóczi út, or the *Skála-Metro,* opposite the West Station. The big central indoor market on Tolbuhin Körút 1–3 is well worth a visit, as is the Flea Market (Ecseri Piac) on Nagykőrösi út 156, XIX. Take Bus 158 from Boráros tér.

USEFUL ADDRESSES. *U.S. Embassy,* V., Szabadság tér 12 (tel. 1126–450). *British Embassy,* V., Harmincad utca 6 (tel. 1182–888). *Canadian Embassy,* XII., Budakeszi út 32 (tel. 1767–711). *IBUSZ* main office VII., Tanács körút 3/c (tel. 1211–007). *Express Student Travel,* V., Szabadság tér 16 (tel. 1317–777). *Budapest Tourist,* V., Roosevelt tér 5 (tel. 1173–555). *Wagons-Lits/Cook,* V., Dorottya utca 3 (tel. 1182–788). *Thomas Cook, 5 Felszabadulas tér (tel. 186–866).*

Lake Balaton

Lake Balaton, largest in Central Europe, is about 50 miles long and varies in width from one to eight miles. The northern shore is marked by a chain of long-extinct volcanoes, while the southern shore is generally flat with long, sandy beaches. The water is very shallow and is often lukewarm. In places you can walk for almost a mile before the water deepens, so the lake is ideal for children.

The Hungarian government has heavily promoted Lake Balaton to the point where tourists from all over Europe are flocking to it in droves. While the area has much to recommend it, the crowds do get a bit like Blackpool or Coney Island during the intense part of the season. This is especially true of the southern shore; the northern one is somewhat less hectic.

Water sports are naturally popular throughout the villages lining the 120-mile shoreline along the lake. Swimming, sailing, waterskiing, windsurfing and fishing are major pursuits. (There is a closed season on fishing from April 25 to May 25.)

Siófok is the largest community along the southern shore. The long, golden beach here is the main attraction and Siófok is also a fine center for excursions to the surrounding countryside.

With special permission from the National Office of Nature Protection (Országos Természetvédelmi Hivatal), Költo utca 21–23, Budapest XII, it is possible to visit a 6,000-acre wildlife preserve at Kis-Balaton. There are herons, black ibises and many rare migratory species of birds.

The northern shore of Balaton, with smaller villages and less intense tourist development, may be a better bet during the busy season. The beaches are less sandy but the scenery is even more picturesque and the water is still inviting.

Balatonfüred is known as a health resort. The waters of volcanic springs, with a strong carbonic content, have for a long time attracted pilgrims seeking cures. There is a big cardiac hospital, 11 medicinal springs and scenic vineyards.

The ancient village of Tihany is reached by bus or ferry. Here, many of the houses are thatched and boast curved, colonnaded porches as their finest feature. There is an open-air museum that consists of some ancient houses preserved in their original form plus folk art and craft collections. There is also a remarkable Baroque church in the village.

On the western side of the lake is the culturally rich town of Keszthely, which features the magnificent Festetics Palace. Summer concerts, an ethnographic museum and library, parks and beaches make it an attractive and lively town that also draws a fair tourist crowd. Near Keszthely lies Hévíz, a beautifully built spa, which also has quality accommodations and a casino.

PRACTICAL INFORMATION FOR LAKE BALATON

Hotels and Restaurants

Balatonfüred. *Annabella, Margaréta* and *Marina* are all (M) and on lake shore. *Arany Csillag* (I), in town center. Bungalows; first-class camping site.
Restaurants. *Balaton, Halászkert* (fish specialties). Also the *Kedves* pastry shop. All (M).

Heviz. *Gyöngyvirág* (I). *Piroska Guest House* (I).
Restaurants. *Kulacs, Piroska,* both (I).

Keszthely. *Helikon* (M); *Phoenix* (I). Bungalows. Camping site.
Restaurant. *Halászcsárda* (M). Fish specialties.

Siófok. *Európa, Balaton, Lido* and *Hungária* are all (M) and on lake shore. *Napfény* (I), near lake. Motel. Bungalows. Camping site.
Restaurants. *Fogas* (M). *Borharapó* has local wines.

Tihany. *Kistihany* (M), recently refurbished. Paying-guest accommodations and camp site.
Restaurants. *Fogas* (M), *Sport* (I).

The Rest of Hungary

Longhorn cattle, fast range ponies, cowboys in broad-brimmed hats—Hungary's Far West lies 100 miles due east of Budapest. Its quarter million acres of treeless rangeland is called the Hortobágy Puszta. Actually, the puszta is more of a marsh (like the French Camargue) than a prairie, and is the country's first national park. There are various historic inns where you can eat or stay over, and the horse shows are quite remarkable. Another fascinating and less known puszta region is Bugac, part of the Kiskunság National Park, 80 miles southeast of Budapest, where sand dunes alternate with marshes and various types of forest, and a chain of small lakes yields rich bird life.

Hungary has many old and picturesque towns. Eger is an historic town in the northeast of the country; Debrecen, the "capital" of Hungarian Protestantism, and Szeged, are two interesting university cities in the eastern half of the country.

In southwestern Hungary, Pécs, with the backdrop of the Mecsek hills, has a magnificent cathedral and a Turkish mosque, while Sopron in the upper northwestern corner is an eclectic mix of Gothic, Renaissance and Baroque. All are only a few hours' train journey from Budapest. Szentendre, which can be reached by the HÉV train from Batthany tér, for 20 Ft., is an almost perfect Baroque town on the Danube, with a thriving arts community.

PRACTICAL INFORMATION FOR THE REST OF HUNGARY

Hotels and Restaurants

Debrecen. *Arany Bika* (M), good food. *Fönix* and *Sport,* both (I). Camping site.
Restaurants. *Hungária, Szabadság,* both (M).

Eger. *Eger* and *Park,* both (M). *Unicornis* (I). Camping site.
Restaurants. *Fehér Szarvas* (M), game. *Kazamata* and *Mecset,* both (I), and many good wine-tasting bars.

Hortobágy. *Csárda* (I), a restaurant with rooms. *Fogadó* (I).

Pécs. *Fönix, Palatinus,* and *Pannonia,* all (M), in town; *Hunyor* (M) and *Dömörkapu* (I),on hills above town.

Restaurants. *Dom, Minaret,* and *Elefántos Ház,*in town, *Vadásztanya,* game specialties, in hills above town, all (M).

Sopron. *Sopron,* new, *Lövér* and *Palatinus,* all (M); *Pannonia* (I). Camping site.
Restaurants. *Gambrinus* and *Deák,* both (M). *Cézár* (wine and cold cuts) (I).

Szeged. *Hungária, Royal* and *Tisza,* all (M). Motel. Camping site.
Restaurants. *Hági, Szeged* and *Halászcsárda* (fish restaurant), all (M).

Szentendre. *Party* and *Danubius,* both (M) and both on banks of the Danube.
Restaurants. *Arany Sárkány* and *Görög Kancsó,* both (M).

Iceland

The second largest island in Europe, Iceland has a great deal more to offer than you might think at first, particularly for the lover of the great outdoors. Its scenery includes geysers, boiling mud pools, glaciers, live volcanoes and fantastic waterfalls, surprisingly green valleys and ruggedly dramatic coastlines, all set within a lunar landscape, all very different from the grey and white image garnered from its name. The name of its capital Reykjavik too, taken from the Norse "smoke" and "bay," belies the words. Thanks to the limitless supplies of near-boiling natural water from hot springs, heating systems of houses, hotels and industries in this modern city are clean, so that Reykjavik, along with the rest of Iceland is almost entirely free from pollution, and Icelanders aim to keep it that way. Piped-in water is also used to heat greenhouses where bananas, vegetables and flowers are grown, but as almost all supplies are imported, costs are very high for the visitor and there is really no such thing as an inexpensive holiday. However, Iceland's horrific rate of inflation is balanced by the fluctuating rate of exchange, which recently more than doubled in the visitor's favor. In any case, the sheer spectacle of Iceland makes a trip memorable.

Keflavik airport is one of the largest in the world, but it also has one of the highest airport taxes, so allow for this in your budgeting. Air travel is one of the main methods of transport within Iceland since the terrain is so difficult, and the roads are poor, so the island is well served with landing fields. Alternative methods of ground travel include the stout Iceland pony. Specially constructed buses penetrate even the remote interior.

Icelanders are thought to be reserved, but widespread knowledge of the English language makes it easy to establish contact. You may have to take the first step in meeting an Icelander, but the reward is natural warmth and exceptional hospitality, as well as an unexpectedly dry sense of humor.

An increasing number of visitors tour the circumference of Iceland since the last gap in the road circling the whole country was filled in 1974, and a very spectacular, if at times rough, road it is too. Motor campers, the use of "wild" camp sites, hostels and private accommodation are the cheapest ways to travel, outside organized tours, but it should be clearly understood that there is little budget travel as such. Also, if you want to explore the interior, unless you are highly experienced, you should join a walking or safari trip in the interest of safety. The extra cost involved is more than justified.

PRACTICAL INFORMATION FOR ICELAND

WHAT WILL IT COST. As has already been said, the cost (and standard) of living is high in Iceland and the only way to minimize it is by camping or staying in hostels or private accommodations.

The monetary unit is the *krona* (plural *kronur*), divided into 100 *aurar*. The rate of exchange is 100 Ikr. to the pound sterling, 61 Ikr. to the U.S. dollar, but as this is reviewed frequently in order to counteract the effects of inflation, it is subject to constant change. It is wise, therefore, not to convert your money into *kronur* until you need to.

Sample Costs. Cinema 400 Ikr.; theater seat 1,500 Ikr.; coffee in snack bar 75 Ikr.; beer in snack bar or in Moderate restaurant 150–200 Ikr.; bottle of wine in Moderate restaurant. 1,300 Ikr.

NATIONAL TOURIST OFFICE. *The Iceland Tourist Board* dispenses information on all aspects of tourism through its overseas offices. Its address in Reykjavik is Ingólfsstraeti 5 (tel. 623045).

Addresses of the Iceland Tourist Board overseas are:

In the U.S.: 655 Third Ave., New York, N.Y. 10017 (tel. 212–949–2333).

In the U.K.: 3rd Floor, 172 Tottenham Court Rd., London W1P 9LG (tel. 071–388 5346).

WHEN TO COME. Mid-June to the beginning of September is the best time to visit. In June and July there is perpetual daylight and, of course, the famous Midnight Sun. In the fall the colorful Northern Lights (Aurora Borealis) begin to appear. Iceland has modest winter sports facilities, mainly centered near Akureyri.

The climate is basically temperate with cool summers, though the south of the island can be rainy.

Average afternoon temperatures in degrees Fahrenheit and centigrade:

Reykjavik

	Jan.	Feb.	Mar.	Apr.	May	June	July	Aug.	Sept.	Oct.	Nov.	Dec.
F°	36	37	39	43	40	55	58	57	51	44	39	38
C°	2	3	4	6	10	13	14	14	11	7	4	3

National Holidays. Mar. 29–Apr 1 (Easter), April 25 (first day of summer), May 1 (Labor Day), May 9 (Ascension), May 19–20 (Pentecost), June 17 (National Day), August 5 (public holiday), December 25–26 (Christmas).

VISAS. Visas are not needed by citizens of the U.S., U.K. or Canada.

HEALTH CERTIFICATES. No vaccinations are required to enter Iceland from any country.

GETTING TO ICELAND. By Plane. *Icelandair* offers service from New York, Baltimore, and Orlando. "Winter Breakaway" and "City Breakaway" week and weekend packages September to May can save money. *SAS, Lufthansa,* and *Eagle Air* fly from some major cities in Europe. *Greenland Air* and *Helgi Jónsson Air* fly from Kulusuk, Nuuk, and Narssarssuaq in Greenland.

By Boat. From late May to early September, *Smyril Line* sail weekly from the Shetlands, Norway, Denmark and Faroe, to Seydisfjördur (East coast of Iceland). Details from *P&O Ferries,* P.O. Box 5, Jamieson's Quay, Aberdeen AB9 8DL (tel. 0224 572615). *Smyril Line* offer fly-cruise options at attractive prices.

CUSTOMS. The import of 200 cigarettes or 250 gr. of tobacco, 1 liter of alcohol and 1 liter of wine is allowed. Icelandic beer is not recommended. You may buy duty-free spirits and tobacco on entering as well as leaving through Keflavik.

HOTELS. There is no official classification, but standards are high. Your best bet is to use the Edda summer hotels, open from mid-June to late August (student accommodations or schools the rest of the year) or private accommodations. In Reykjavik, the following approximate prices apply per night for a double room for two: Moderate (M) Ikr. 4,000–6,600. Inexpensive (I) Ikr. 2,300–4,000. Count on up to about 25% less outside Reykjavik. Farmhouse accommodations, usually with full board, come into the (I) category. Farm holiday brochures available from tour operators.

Youth Hostels. Several in Reykjavik and Akureyri, plus a score of other places where inexpensive accommodations are available for those with their own sleeping bag. The Youth Hostel Association (Bandalag Íslenskra Farfugla, Laufásvegur 41, Reykjavik) operates reasonably-priced tours for bird-watching and hiking, and it can also issue tickets for *Omnibus* and *Circle-pass* long-distance buses.

Camping. You will find registered sites near main centers and places of tourist interest, costing around 300 Ikr. per night or less. Elsewhere camping is generally free, but in farming country permission should be obtained from the landowner. Camping is not always permitted in the National Parks. Camping equipment and ski-rental in winter from Tjaldleigan, Hringbraut (bus terminal), tel. 13072.

RESTAURANTS. There have been some welcome additions recently to the selection of eating places in Reykjavik and there is now a small but attractive choice of restaurants catering to all pockets. One advantage in many places is that you get your coffee cup re-filled free. Clean and reasonably priced snack bars can be found attached to gasoline stations. Self-caterers are advised to take a supply of dehydrated packaged foods, though you should try some of the very tasty preserved fish items in which Iceland specializes. Our price grading, for two people is as follows—(M) $30–$60, (I) $15–$30.

Food and Drink. Specialties include *hangikjöt* (smoked lamb), *saltfiskur* (salted cod), *hardfiskur* (dried fish), many seabird platters, and *skyr* (made from curdled milk, creamy and delicious). Local beer is very mild, spirits, very expensive. Don't miss Iceland's cold schnapps, especially the local *Brennivin*, known as Black Death! You can buy duty-free items on entering as well as leaving Iceland through Keflavik.

TIPPING. No tipping. Your bill includes 26% VAT.

MAIL. At time of going to press: airmail letters to the U.S. 40 Ikr., to the U.K. 24 Ikr., postcards to the U.S. 24 Ikr., to the U.K. 21 Ikr.; prices will increase by 1991.

CLOSING TIMES. Shops are open on weekdays from 9 to 6, Saturdays from 9–12 during summer, 9–4 during winter. Many shops are closed on Saturdays during the summer. Banks are open weekdays 9.15 to 4; Thurs. 5–6; Saturdays closed.

GETTING AROUND ICELAND. By Plane. *Icelandair* and *Eagle Air* serve around 50 towns and villages. There is a good *Air Rover* ticket that offers advantageous discounts, as well as a combined *Air/Bus Rover* ticket that is good for both air and bus travel. There are several day excursions from Reykjavik.

By Bus. There are no railways in Iceland, so the comprehensive bus network is the best way to get around the country inexpensively. Though the roads may seem rough, they take you through superb scenery. Apart from the Air/Bus Rover ticket (see above), there is also a special holiday ticket called the *Omnibus Passport,* which is valid for unlimited travel on scheduled bus services, and the *Full Circle Passport,* which is valid for a circular trip by bus around Iceland with no time limit. *BSÍ Travel,* Vatnsmýrarveg 10 (tel. 91–223000), offers tours from Reykjavik with scheduled buses.

Reykjavik

The Icelandic capital, located mid-way between New York and Moscow, is frequently, if somewhat ambitiously, referred to as "the Capital of the North." It has several good museums and art galleries, especially if you are interested in the fascinating culture of the early settlers and the sagas that they contributed to the world's

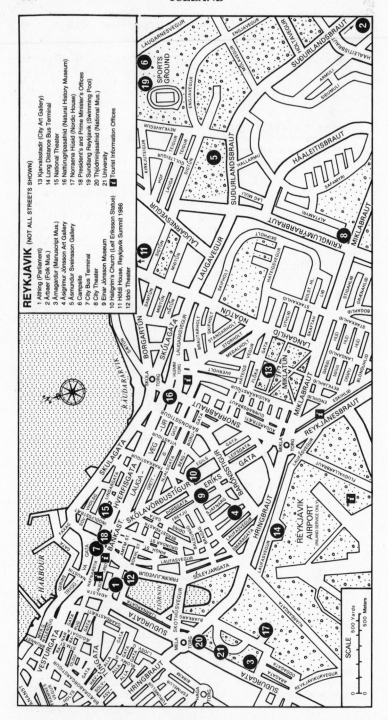

REYKJAVIK (NOT ALL STREETS SHOWN)

1 Althing (Parliament)
2 Arbaer (Folk Mus.)
3 Arnagardur (Manuscript Mus.)
4 Asgrimur Jónsson Art Gallery
5 Asmundur Sveinsson Gallery
6 Campsite
7 City Bus Terminal
8 City Theater
9 Einar Jónsson Museum
10 Hallgrim's Church (Leif Eriksson Statue)
11 Höfdi House, Reykjavik Summit 1986
12 Idno Theater
13 Kjarvalsstadir (City Art Gallery)
14 Long Distance Bus Terminal
15 National Theater
16 Natturugripasafnid (Natural History Museum)
17 Norraena Húsid (Nordic House)
18 President's and Prime Minister's Offices
19 Sundlaug Reykjavik (Swimming Pool)
20 Thjódminjasafnid (National Mus.)
21 University
i Tourist Information Offices

literature, or if you like modern art and sculpture at which the Icelanders excel. But a day or two will be enough to do the city sights.

The most important buildings are the Parliament, the Cathedral, National Library, National Theater, University, Navigation School, Nordic House, and the Hallgrims, Church which dominates the rocky plateau above the harbor, along with a statue of Leif Erickson, presented to the people of Iceland by the United States on the one thousandth anniversary of the Althing, the Icelandic Parliament, in 1930. Right in town, Lake Tjörnin is a delightful oasis for strollers and bird-spotters.

PRACTICAL INFORMATION FOR REYKJAVIK

HOTELS. There is no such thing as a really inexpensive hotel. Guest houses, hostels, and private accommodation are the lowest. The Tourist Information Center in Ingólfsstraeti (tel. 623045) can help with reservations.

Moderate

Hotel Borg, Pósthússtraeti 11 (tel. 11440). 46 rooms, very central.
Hotel City, Ránargata 4a (tel. 18650). 31 rooms, central.
Gardur, Hringbraut (tel. 15656). 44 rooms. Open summer only.
Odinsvé, Odinstorg (tel. 25224). 20 rooms, 2 restaurants.
Geysir, Skipholt 27 (tel. 26210). 23 rooms.

Inexpensive

Guesthouse, Brautarholt 22 (tel. 20986). 24 rooms. Open summer only.
Guesthouse, Flókagata 5 (tel. 19828). 11 rooms, central.
Guesthouse, Snorrabraut 52 (tel. 16522). 18 rooms. Comfortable.
Hotel Jörd, Skólavördustíg 13a (tel. 621739). 8 rooms, central.
Salvation Army Guesthouse, Kirkjustraeti 2 (tel. 13203). 24 rooms.
Viking Guesthouse, Ránargata 12 (tel. 19367). 11 rooms.
Youth Hostel, Laufásvegur 41. Short walk from the center.

RESTAURANTS. Many restaurants are licensed and have an international cuisine with table d'hôte and à la carte dishes. However, there is 24% state tax included in your bill.

Moderate

Gaukur á Stöng, Tryggvagata 22 (tel. 11556). Bar-restaurant and live music Sun. to Wed.
Hard Rock Café, Kringlan (tel. 689888).
Hornid Restaurant, Hafnarstraeti 15 (tel. 20366). Attractive atmosphere and very central. Famous Icelandic lamb among the specialties.
Laugavegur 22, Laugavegur 22 (tel. 13628). Very popular.
Potturinn og pannan, Brautarholt 22 (tel. 11690). Excellent food in a pleasant setting. American salads.
Náttúran, Laugavegur 20b (tel. 28410). Vegetarian. Reasonably priced.
Punktur og pasta, Amtmannsstígur 1 (tel. 13303). Icelandic specialties in charming 19th century atmosphere.

Inexpensive

Café Hressó, Austurtraeti 20 (tel. 14353). Very popular meeting place.
El Sombrero, Laugavegur 73 (tel. 23866). Spanish food and pizzas.
Lauga-ás, Laugarásvegur 1 (tel. 31620). Popular dishes at sensible prices. Near the Reykjavík campsite.
Múlakaffi, Hallarmúli (tel. 37737). Typical Icelandic fare.
Pítuhornid, Bergthórugata 21 (tel. 12400). Pitas, soups, and salads. Good value for money.
Saelkerinn, Austurstraeti 22 (tel. 11633). Central. Italian dishes.

GETTING AROUND REYKJAVIK. The best method in this small metropolis is on foot. Otherwise, by taxi. The sign "laus" means that the taxi is available. Public transport is by bus; reasonably priced and frequent services. Tickets bought by the sheet are less expensive.

ENTERTAINMENT. An Icelandic specialty are the naturally warm water **swimming pools,** including some open-air pools.

Spectator sports include soccer, handball and basketball. There are some golf courses; horse riding and pony trekking are very popular. Trout and salmon fishing is plentiful, but expensive. Travel agents and tour organizers will give you full details.

Cinema. There are eight movie theaters; foreign films are shown in their original language. Films on Iceland itself are shown daily in the Osvaldur Knudsen Film Studio by the Hotel Holt.

Discos. These include *Hollywood,* Ármúli 5; Keisarinn, Laugaveg 116, Austurvöllur and *Thórskaffi,* Brautarholt 20; *Tunglid,* Laekjargötu; *Hotel Island,* Armuli; *Glaesibaer,* Alfheimar 74.

Theaters. These are closed during July/August. An attractive show in English called "Light Nights" provides an introduction to traditional Icelandic stories and folk songs. The Society of Icelandic Solo Singers also gives recitals of Icelandic poetry and songs every week in July and August.

MUSEUMS. Normally open 1.30–4. Closed Mondays. In some cases entrance is free.

Árbaer, on the outskirts of town. A charming collection illustrating Iceland's past way of life, housed in an old farmhouse.

Ásgrimur Jónsson's Gallery, Bergstadastraeti 74. The home and works of this well known Icelandic artist.

Ásmundur Sveinsson Gallery, Sigtún. A collection of original sculptures.

Einar Jónsson Museum, Njardargata/Skólavörduholt (tel. 13797). Displays the works of this well-known Icelandic sculptor.

Gallery Borg, Pósthússtraeti 9. Work by contemporary artists.

Hallgrimskirkjuturn, Skólavörduholt (Observation Platform in Steeple).

Museum of Natural History, Hverfisgata. Open Sat., Sun., Tues., and Thurs.

National Art Gallery, Frikirkjuvegi. Very attractive building, once a fish-processing plant.

National Museum, Hringbraut. Historic, ethnographic.

Nordic House, near Hringbraut and the University. Library. Exhibition on occasions. Coffee room.

Reykjavik Art Gallery (Kjarvalsstadir), Miklatún. Includes the works of famous artist Johannes S. Kjarval, and Erro, an artist known in the U.S.

SHOPPING. Iceland produces top-quality hand knitted goods that will certainly be cheaper than at home. Recommended are: *Álafoss Store,* Vesturgata 2; *Framtidin,* Laugavegur 45; *The Hand-knitting Association of Iceland,* Skólavördustig 19; *Hilda,* Borgartún 22; *The Icelandic Handicrafts' Center,* Hafnarstraeti 3; *Kúnst,* Laugavegur 40; *Rammagerdin,* Hafnarstraeti 19. Lava ceramics and silver make unusual buys. Bookshops are excellent and plentiful. The *Central Bookstore* of *S. Eymundsson,* Austurstraeti 18, has a good selection of books in English. In food stores you can buy specially packed samples of Icelandic food to take home or send away. The smoked salmon, herring and shrimps are to be recommended.

USEFUL ADDRESSES. (All in Reykjavik.) *U.S. Embassy,* Laufásvegur 21 (tel. 29100); *British Embassy,* Laufásvegur 49 (tel. 15883). *Iceland Tourist Board,* Ingólfsstraeti 5 (tel. 623044); *American Express, Útsyn Travel Bureau,* Austurstraeti 17 (tel. 26611); *Thomas Cook,* Samvinn Travel, Austurstraeti 12 (tel. 27077); *Main Post Office,* corner Austurstraeti & Pósthússtraeti; *National Union of Students* (Studentarad Islands), Hringbraut (same building as Hotel Gardur); *Hospital* casualty (tel. 91–696600), counseling (91–622280).

Outside Reykjavik

Recommended sights include the Great Geysir area, where Strokkur performs at regular intervals; Gullfoss waterfall; and Thingvellir, site of the first Parliament. Mount Hekla and Thjórsárdalur require more time, so does the magnificent area of Southeast Iceland, which takes in the glacial tongues of Vatnajökull, Skaftafell nature reserve and Svartifoss. Never attempt the glacier without proper equipment and guidance. A good range of half- or full-day excursions, as well as longer trips, is available from Reykjavik.

Northern Iceland, reached either quickly by plane, or more laboriously by car, camper or bus, has Akureyri as starting point for famous lake Mývatn, a paradise for ornithologists, set in an extraordinary volcanic landscape that includes the twisted scenery of Dimmuborgir and sulfur fields vivid with bubbling colored mud pools. Other northern sights are Godafoss, (the waterfall of the Gods, and splendid it is too!), Dettifoss (Europe's largest waterfall) and the fascinating national park of Ásbyrgi.

The southwestern part of Iceland is comparatively easily accessible from Reykjavik. The long peninsula of Snaefellsnes, with the mountain glacier of Snaefellsjökull, has magnificent scenery, with basalt rocks jutting into the sea. Further north the terrain becomes still more rugged. This is the land of the Western Fjords (Vestfirdir), where only occasional villages dot the firths and fjords, and the intervening landscape makes every traveler feel that he is an explorer of uncharted territory. However, civilization reaches even these parts by way of the airstrips at Patreksfjördur and Ísafjördur. Ferries to the smaller fishing villages operate across the fjords.

Finally there are the beautiful Westmann Islands off the south coast, reached by plane or by boat. Since the eruption of Helgafell in 1973, the islands are back to normal, but it is eerie to walk on the volcanic dust knowing that many of the houses of the little town of Heimaey are beneath your feet. The cliff scenery is spectacular and so is the bird life.

PRACTICAL INFORMATION FOR THE REGIONS

HOTELS AND RESTAURANTS. Particularly good value are the Edda Hotels that are operated by Iceland Tourist Bureau. Mostly, these are modern boarding schools that have been adapted into summer hotels. Many have swimming pools and sauna. In country districts, restaurants are limited to those in hotels, or snack bars at gas stations.

The North

Akureyri. *Nordurland* (M), tel. 96–22600. 24 rooms. *Edda* (I), 68 rooms without bath; open summer only.

Blönduós. *Edda* (M), tel. 95–4126. 30 rooms with bath/shower.

Húnavellir. *Edda Svinavatn* (M), tel. 95–4370. 23 rooms. Swimming pool and sauna.

Húsavik. *Húsavik* (M), tel. 96–41220. 34 rooms with bath or shower.

Mývatn. *Reykjahlíd* (M), 12 rooms without bath; summer only. *Reynihlíd* (M), tel. 96–44170. 44 rooms. Swimming pool. U.S. astronauts were trained in the surrounding lunar-like landscape.

Raufarhöfn. *Nordurljós* (I), tel. 96–51233. 8 rooms.

Saudarkrókur. *Maelifell* (M), tel. 96–5265, 7 rooms.

Siglufjördur. *Höfn* (I), tel. 95–71514. 14 rooms, without bath.

Skagafjördur. *Varmahlid* (I), tel. 95–6170. 17 rooms, without bath.

The East

Breiddalsvik. *Edda Stadarborg* (I), tel. 97–5683. 9 rooms without bath.

Eidar. *Edda* (I), tel. 97–13803. 60 rooms without bath; summer only.

Egilsstadir. *Valaskjálf* (M), tel. 97–11500. 24 rooms with bath/shower. *Egilsstadir* (I), 15 rooms with bath; open summer only.

Hallormsstadir. *Edda* (I), tel. 97–11705. 22 rooms without bath; summer only.

Hornafjördur. *Höfn* (M), tel. 97–81240. 40 rooms. *Edda* (I), tel. 97–8470. 30 rooms, shower available. Open summer only.

Neskaupstadur. *Egilsbúd* (I), tel. 97–71323. 5 rooms without bath.

Raufarhofn. Nordurljós (I), tel. 96–51233. 8 rooms.

Seydisfjördur. *Snaefell* (M), tel. 97–21460. 10 rooms.

The South

Flúdir. *Summermotel Flúdir* (M), tel. 99–66710. 27 rooms.

Hveragerdi. *Ljósbrá* (I), tel. 99–34588. 7 rooms without bath.

Hvolsvöllur. *Hvolsvöllur* (M), tel. 99–78187. 20 rooms.

Kirkjubaejarklaustur. *Edda* (M), tel. 99–74799. 32 rooms with bath/shower.

Laugarvatn. *New Edda* (M), tel. 99–61154. 27 rooms; open summer only. *Edda* (I), 88 rooms with bath/shower; summer only.

Selfoss. *Thóristún* (M), tel. 99–21633. 17 rooms.

Skógar. *Edda* (I), tel. 99–78870. 37 rooms; summer only.

Thingvellir. *Valhöll* (M), tel. 99–22622. 37 rooms; summer only.

Westmann Islands. *Hótel Gestgjafinn* (M), tel. 98–12577. 14 rooms with bath/shower. *Guesthouse Heimir* (I), tel. 98–11515. 22 rooms without bath.

The West

Akranes. *Akranes* (I), tel. 93–12020. 11 rooms without bath.

Borgarfjördur. *Hótel Bifröst* (M), tel. 93–50000. 31 rooms.

Borgarnes. *Hótel Borgarnes* (M), tel. 93–71119. 35 rooms with bath/shower.

Isafjördur. *Mánakaffi* (I), 15 rooms without bath. *Salvation Army Hostel* (I), 17 rooms without bath.

Kroksfjördur. *Edda Bjarklalundur* (I), tel. 93–47762. 12 rooms, showers available.

Ólafsvik. *Hotel Nes* (I), tel. 93–61300. 18 rooms.

Reykholt. *Edda* (I), tel. 93–51260. 64 rooms, showers; open summer only. Swimming pool.

Snaefellsnes. *Búdir* (I), tel. 93–56700. 20 rooms without bath; summer only. *Stykkishólmur* (M), tel. 93–8330. 26 rooms.

Vatnsfjördur. *Edda* (I), tel. 94–2011. *Flókalundur,* 14 rooms without bath; summer only.

Ireland

Visitors who arrive in Ireland by air are always impressed by the greenness of the land beneath them. Unfortunately a small price must be paid for this beautiful natural phenomenon. Seldom do more than three days pass without a shower of rain, which can vary from the finest light mist to a torrential downpour. But the rain, in this outdoor-loving country, is never allowed to spoil an excursion. A raincoat or umbrella and a good pair of boots will allow you to venture forth in "soft weather," as it is called.

The vagaries of the Irish climate make it a popular year-round destination. It can be gloriously sunny in the summer months, but the countryside is even more delightful in the spring when daffodils and wild primroses bloom, and in the fall with its russet shades. Off-season visitors will also find that hotel prices are considerably reduced at this time of year (October-April).

Ireland is an excellent budget vacation choice. British and American visitors enjoy a favorable rate of exchange and will find that prices in Dublin, which is rather more expensive than the rest of the country, compare well with other European capitals. Outside Dublin we strongly recommend farmhouse accommodations, not only because they are economical, but also because you will meet people in their home environment.

The Irish way of life is unpretentious, with the best amusements inexpensive and often free. Theater tickets can be had for around IR£5.50, and a day at the races can cost as little as the IR£2 entrance fee. Friendly bars form the center of Irish social life and a convivial evening of good music and conversation need cost no more than the price of a "pint". In summer the famous Puck Fair in Killorglin, County Kerry, is among the many local festivals offering a wide variety of free entertainment. In winter the slow pace of life is savored at its best, and in the evening your hosts will usually provide a glowing open fire.

The Lakes of Killarney are justifiably the country's most famous beauty spot—romantic, boulder-strewn mountains strung with a chain of deep-blue lakes. The Ring of Kerry provides a day-long tour through coastal vegetation lush because of the Gulf Stream. Northward, on the coast of Clare, the Cliffs of Moher—vertical rocks up to 700 ft. high—are pounded by Atlantic breakers. Offshore are the Aran Islands where old customs are still adhered to, while inland, in the eerie limestone desert called The Burren, rare flowers from the Arctic and the Mediterranean bloom side by side. The blue hills of Connemara remain the inspiration of many famous paintings, and you will find the Shannon peppered with numerous historic castles.

Ireland is not a wealthy country, and visitors should adjust their expectations accordingly. Most roads, for example, are narrow and winding, and are not designed for speed. While there are many excellent international-class luxury hotels, some of the more modest establishments can be a little shabby, and you are unlikely to find an *en suite* bathroom in the lower price ranges. But appearances are not everything, and the genuinely courteous service that you will encounter almost everywhere makes up for a lot.

The Irish are proud of their literary heritage, and the visitor can seek out places made famous by W.B. Yeats, J.M. Synge, Somerville and Ross and many other well-loved writers. But you will also find something of the literary tradition surviving in the everyday language of the Irish people. Take time out for a leisurely chat as often as possible, for it is the warmth of the people of Ireland, just as much as its scenery and its literary and artistic heritage, that will make your visit a memorable one.

PRACTICAL INFORMATION FOR IRELAND

WHAT WILL IT COST. The cost of living in Ireland is high, but there are nonetheless many ways of keeping holiday costs within reasonable bounds, especially for American visitors who currently enjoy a very favorable rate of exchange with Ireland. Try staying at a guest house, of which tourist offices have extensive lists, rather than in an hotel. In guest houses you'll find comfort and friendliness at extremely reasonable rates, though not all serve evening meals. But the traditional "hearty Irish breakfast" should set you up for much of the day. Some restaurants offer tourist menus with three-course meals from IR£5.75 to IR£12. Get a free booklet listing these spots, together with details of many other budget bargains, from the Irish Tourist Board (addresses, see below). Best bet is to have a snack lunch and take your main meals at night.

You can cut costs further by staying in "Bed and Breakfast" accommodations (B&B). The Irish Tourist Board list approved establishments in their booklet *Farmhouses, Town and Country Homes* (IR£1).

The monetary unit in Ireland is the pound or *punt* (pronounced *poont*) and written as IR£, although in Ireland the letters IR are often omitted. The British pound is referred to as the "pound sterling". At the time of writing the exchange rate was IR.50 to the U.S. dollar and IR£1.08 to the pound sterling.

Sample Costs. The price of a moderate seat at the theater is IR£5.50, at the cinema it is IR£3.50. Admission to most museums and art galleries is free, but the charge for some famous historic houses and spots like Blarney Castle varies between 50p and IR£2.50. Coffee in a café costs about 50p. Beer (dark beer is called stout) is the national drink and varies from about IR£1.70 a pint in an ordinary bar to IR£1.90 in city lounges and hotels, plus a tip (10p) if you are served at a table. Drinking is more fun in bars than in hotels—you meet more people. Prices are generally around 10% lower away from Dublin.

NATIONAL TOURIST OFFICE. The Irish Tourist Board *(Bord Failte)* has its headquarters at Baggot Street Bridge, Dublin, tel.(01) 765871, and is well informed on budget type packages and special interest holidays. A new program pays special attention to the smaller hotels (40 rooms and less) which are usually in the budget price bracket. The Board has a Central Reservations Service at 14 Upper O'Connell Street, Dublin 1, tel.(01) 747733, which will handle reservations for all types of registered and approved accommodations.

Addresses of the Irish Tourist Board overseas are:

In the U.S.: 757 Third Ave., New York, N.Y. 10017 (tel. 212–418–0800).
In Canada: 10 King St. E., Toronto, Ontario M5C 1C3 (tel. 416–364–1301).
In the U.K.: 150 New Bond St., London W1Y OAQ (tel. 071–493 3201).

WHEN TO COME. Avoid July and August if you are really on a budget. It is the peak of the season and prices likewise. The Irish like to believe the season starts with St. Patrick's Day (March 17th) and many Americans arrive for the traditional celebrations in Dublin and elsewhere in the country that take place during the week. Winters are mild and prices are at rock bottom, but for the budget traveler the best choices are the May/June (the sunniest months) and September/October periods. Some seasonal hotels may be closed in the early and late periods, but there is enough good accommodation everywhere at all times.

Average afternoon temperatures in degrees Fahrenheit and centigrade:

Dublin	Jan.	Feb.	Mar.	Apr.	May	June	July	Aug.	Sept.	Oct.	Nov.	Dec.
F°	47	47	51	54	59	65	67	67	63	57	51	47
C°	8	8	11	12	15	18	19	19	17	14	11	8

SPECIAL EVENTS. *January;* Horse racing in eight centers including Leopardstown, 8 km. (5 miles) out from the center of Dublin. In *February* there's at least one Rugby Union international, and if you think American football is tough, watch these unpadded warriors. On St. Valentine's Day (14th) the saint is formally honored in the Carmelite Church, Whitefriars St., Dublin, where his body is entombed; Irish singing and dancing are at their best in Limerick at Féile Luimni. *March* sees St. Patrick's Week (of course); Gaelic Football and Hurling finals are held at Croke Park, but try to get tickets early. In *April* Cork City hosts an International Choral and Folk Dance Festival. The Irish Grand National is run at Fairyhouse, Co. Meath on Easter Monday.

The Royal Dublin Society's Spring Show at Ballsbridge, Dublin, in *May* is worth a visit, although it is expensive (about IR£4–5). James Joyce's great novel, *Ulysses,* is celebrated in Dublin in *June,* (16th) with literary pilgrimages and street carnival; contemporary literature is a strong point during the Kinsale Arts Week in Co. Cork. The Irish Derby is run at the Curragh, 48 km. (30 miles) from Dublin. On the last Sunday of *July,* thousands of pilgrims climb the slopes of Croagh Patrick (85 m., 2,510 ft.) in Co. Mayo to honor St. Patrick. The country's biggest International Golf Championship is held on the Royal Dublin course. The Dublin Horse Show follows in *August,* about IR£8 for both the show and the international show jumping. The annual Puck Fair in Killorglin, Co. Kerry, takes place over the Bank Holiday weekend. At the Festival of Kerry in Tralee in *September,* the year's "Rose of Tralee" is chosen from among international contestants of Irish descent. In Galway an Oyster Festival opens the oyster season, an event that can be moderate to expensive, depending on your enthusiasm. Waterford stages an International Festival of Light Opera.

October sees the Dublin Theater Festival (tickets are the same price as at other times of year) and the Wexford Opera Festival (expensive, but worth saving for). The Dublin Marathon (28th) attracts around 9,000 runners.

The International Jazz Festival in Cork is the biggest event of its kind in the year and takes place in several spots around Cork city at the start of *November. December;* Christmas Day may be quiet, but horse racing starts after a short break at Leopardstown (Dublin) on the 26th.

National Holidays. Jan. 1; Mar. 17 (St. Patrick's Day); March 29 (Good Friday); April 1 (Easter Monday); June 3, Aug. 5, Oct. 28, Dec. 25–26 (Christmas). If you're planning a visit at Easter remember that theaters and cinemas are closed for the last three days of the preceding week.

VISAS. Nationals of the U.S. and U.K. do not require visas to enter Ireland.

HEALTH CERTIFICATES. Not required for entry into Ireland from any country.

GETTING TO IRELAND. By Plane. From North America: *Aer Lingus,* the Irish national carrier, have direct flights (daily in summer) from New York and Chicago and Boston to Shannon and Dublin. Shannon is also served by *Pan Am* from New York, by *Delta* from Atlanta, GA, and by a variety of charter services from many U.S. cities between May and September.

From the U.K. there are frequent flights by Aer Lingus and *British Airways* from London (Heathrow and *Dan Air* from Gatwick) to Dublin and also to Shannon and Cork, Ireland's two other international airports. Aer Lingus also connects Dublin with a number of European cities including Paris, Brussels, Amsterdam, and Dusseldorf; the national airlines of these countries have similar services. From the U.K. there are flights by Aer Lingus and various U.K. airlines including British Airways and *Dan Air* from regional airports such as Glasgow, Edinburgh, Newcastle, Liverpool, Manchester, Leeds-Bradford, Birmingham and Cardiff to Ireland, mainly Dublin but also several to Cork. *Ryan Air* flies direct from Luton to Dublin, Waterford, Knock, Shannon, Kerry, Waterford, and Cork from £84 return. For reservations in the U.S. and Canada call Toronto Toll Free on 1–800–268–6755; in the U.K. call 071–435 7101. *Aer Lingus* has a special late saver to Cork for around £95. Flight time London–Dublin, 55 minutes. *Virgin* has also entered the fray offering a one way ticket to Dublin from Luton (London) for £35. In the U.S. call Toll Free 1–800–862–8621 for reservations; in the U.K. call 0293–38222. There is fierce competition for your custom on the Irish routes, check with the airlines for the best offers.

By Boat. The shortest route to the Republic of Ireland is Holyhead–Dun Laoghaire, which takes about 3½ hours. Daily services are operated by the British-based *Sealink* using modern drive-on, drive-off ferries. Sealink run a daily service between Fishguard and Rosslare, and *B & I Line* sail daily from Pembroke to Rosslare. *Swansea Cork Ferries* have up to five sailings a week from Swansea to Cork between late March and early January, a 12-hour sea-crossing. *B&I Line* sail from Holyhead to Dun Laoghaire, with a bus link (30 mins.) to Dublin. There are services to Northern Ireland with *Sealink* sailing from Stranraer (in southwest Scotland) to Larne near Belfast (about 2¼ hours) and by *P & O European Ferries* from Cairnryan near Stranraer also to Larne in more or less the same time. From Liverpool to Belfast there is an overnight service taking about 8 hours, operated by *Belfast Car Ferries. Irish Continental Lines* operate from Le Havre to Rosslare and Cork, and from Cherbourg to Rosslare. *Brittany Ferries* operate from Roscoff, northern France, into Cork; they have large, drive-on drive-off ferries with adequate cabins on this route; sailing time is about 19 hours. The future of *Swansea Cork Ferries* depends on their profits in 1990; their 1991 operation is not assured.

By Train. Most of the ferry routes mentioned above have connecting train services with through trains from London to Holyhead, Fishguard and Stranraer. For Liverpool there is the regular InterCity service with connecting bus to the dock. For example, using the Holyhead-Dun Laoghaire route you leave London (Euston) at 9.20 A.M. (earlier on Sundays) and arrive in Dublin at around 7.30 P.M. Overnight service leaves Euston at 9.45 P.M., reaching Dublin by 7.45 A.M. Reserve ahead of time at peak weekends and in summer. Return fare to Dublin from £50.

By Bus. The cheapest way to travel from the U.K. to Ireland is by bus. Under the International Express banner, *Supabus* run daytime and overnight to Dublin from London Victoria coach station. The daytime departure is at 8.15 A.M., arriving 11.30 P.M.; overnight it's 9.30 P.M., arriving 11 A.M. Return from £45. *Supabus* also run from London to Londonderry and from Birmingham and Bristol to Belfast; from London to Ballina, Dublin, Galway, Limerick, Tralee, and Cork. Also services by *Slattery's,* 162 Kentish Town Rd., London N.W.5 (tel. 071–485 2778) and 43 North Wharf Rd., London W.2. (Terminal) (tel. 071–724 0741).

Note. From Northern Ireland there is a direct rail link from Belfast to Dublin (it takes about 2 hours with four buffet-restaurant expresses each way daily), as well as various bus services from Belfast to Dublin, Galway and intermediate points, plus a route from Derry to Galway and Dublin.

CUSTOMS. Only verbal declaration necessary. Coming from North American countries you may bring in duty-free 200 cigarettes or 250 grams (approximately 9 ozs.) of tobacco, 1 liter bottle of spirits, 2 liter bottles of wine, and other dutiable goods to the value of IR£31. If you buy goods in any of the EC countries and pay duty or tax on them at the time of purchase keep the receipts to show the Customs on arrival to ensure no additional duty is charged. There is a new system that permits visitors who make purchases in Ireland and pay Value Added Tax on them to recover the tax before leaving the country. There are duty-free shops on the ferries between Britain and Continental Europe and Ireland, and similar facilities at the major airports.

HOTELS. Ireland has a grading sytem, operated by *Bord Failte* (Irish Tourist Board) for its hotels and guest houses. This is admirable up to a point, but prices vary widely within a single grade. For the budget-minded we recommend the B and C grades as Moderate (M) hotels, which, in Dublin, range from about IR£60 to IR£80 per night for two persons in a double room.

There are comparatively few hotels in the cities that might be rated as Inexpensive (I) and we find it preferable to extend the recommendation to guest houses, which are generally quieter; a number have licenses to sell wine but not beer or "hard" liquor. Many have en suite bathrooms, all are inspected and registered by the Irish Tourist Board. A double room for two in Dublin should cost up to IR£45 and provide good comfort.

Service standards vary, but hotels and guest houses on the lists given below have good reputations.

Away from Dublin prices are usually about 10 to 20% cheaper.

If you have a problem about accommodations a local Tourist Information Office—designated with the symbol I—will help by making a reservation for 50p. A reservation for another area costs about IR£1.50, plus a 10% deposit, deductible from your bill. If you do use a Tourist Information Office for reservations, specify the price range you want. The advice of cab drivers is not always the best.

Private Homes. These cater to visitors in many parts of the country; most have about three or four rooms available at a price less than half that of a hotel. Farmhouses, too, cater to visitors in most districts, charging a bed-and-breakfast rate of about IR£24 for two people with a dinner price of IR£10; a high tea (invariably with a meat dish) is about IR£7.50, and very good value. Farmhouses usually have three or four bedrooms for letting. See also Self-Catering.

Self-Catering. There is a wide variety of self-catering accommodations available from the Rent-an-Irish-Cottage scheme, which has a U.S. base at Shannon Development Company, 757 Third Ave., New York, N.Y. 10017. This project offers 100 "traditional" cottages in 11 areas in the counties of Clare, Limerick and Tipperary. A cottage sleeping eight persons is available in a price range from IR£150 a week in the October-April period up to a peak of around IR£340 a week. There are similar cottages in County Mayo, contact *Louisburgh Holiday Cottages,* Louisburgh; in Connemara at Renvyle, contact *Connemara West Centre;* at Letterfrack, Co. Galway, and Carraroe, contact *Hotel Carraroe,* which manages the cottages; and in Donegal, at Cruit Island, Dungloe, contact *Conor and Mary Ward* at Rosses Point, Co. Sligo. Prices vary with season and area. In Connemara the range is from about IR£100 to IR£260, in Donegal from IR£105 to IR£280.

The Irish Tourist Board publishes *Self Catering* (IR£2; available in U.S. from I.T.B. at 757 Third Ave., New York, N.Y. 10017) which provides full information, including pictures and prices, on holiday cottages, castles, houses, bungalows, chalets, flats and apartments in all parts of the country. Rates vary with location and season but are around IR£130 a week.

Youth Hostels. There are 43 youth hostels (three in Dublin, the rest in attractive rural/seaside areas) operated by *An Oige.* Holders of a Youth Hostel Card issued by American Youth Hostels, P.O. Box 37613, Washington, D.C. 20013–7613, or Canadian Youth Hostel Association, 1600 James Naismith Dr., Suite 608, Gloucester, Ont. K1B 5N4, can stay for around IR£6.50 in Dublin and IR£4 in other hostels at the peak of the season. All hostels are self-catering.

The YWCA has hostels at Dublin and Tramore, Co. Waterford with prices at IR£10 for bed and breakfast. *The Young Traveller,* St. Mary's Place, Dublin, provides bed and breakfast for around IR£9 per night. *Dublin Tourist Hotel* (not operated by *An Oige*), formerly I.S.A.A.C., in Frenchman's Lane, has 22 rooms and four dormitories with a rate around IR£3.75 per night. *Kinlay House,* Lord Edward St., Dublin, offers bed and breakfast from £6.50 per night in four-bed units, twin rooms from IR£10.50. The *Independent Hostel Owner's Association* lists 65 independent hostels around the country that have no curfew or membership and offer bunkbeds at IR£3.50 to IR£4.50 per night and some private rooms. For a list of their hostels write to Patrick O'Donnell, Dooey Hostel, Glencolumcille, Co. Donegal, tel. 073–30130.

RESTAURANTS. Restaurants in Ireland are generally not expensive and the food, while not always of gourmet standard, is plentiful and filling. Most hotels have restaurants, but in many country towns the meals can lack a little in imagination. In these cases you may do better to search out the small country restaurants where standards can be surprisingly high and where home-made dishes and local specialties are the norm.

You should be able to get a reasonable meal for around IR£12 at an Inexpensive restaurant, less if you pick carefully from the menu. Portions are generally larger than in other countries—the Irish are hearty eaters and especially fond of their excellent meat. Look out for places advertising "Special Value Tourist Menus", a scheme approved by the Irish Tourist Board. A three-course meal will cost you a maximum of IR£5.75 to IR£12.

Wine is expensive. A glass of house wine (a matter of luck) costs about IR£1.50, a bottle of drinkable but unremarkable wine in a restaurant is about IR£12.

A service charge is made in most restaurants, usually around 12%, so a tip is not necessary unless you are feeling generous.

We have rated restaurants as Moderate (M), around IR£14 and up, and Inexpensive (I), under IR£10. These prices are for one person, and do not include wine or beer.

Food and Drink. The Irish may not have a national style of cooking but they do have some special dishes that you will find particularly flavorsome. Boiled bacon and cabbage is not often on hotel menus in the city, but guest houses and farmhouses will serve it. Irish stew sometimes appears on restaurant menus and whenever it is listed, try it—you eat it with a spoon. There is also plenty of good beef, lamb, pork and fresh vegetables, and a special vegetable dish called *champ* consisting of mashed potatoes, peas, chives, parsley, onions and other ingredients; sometimes it's called *colcannon.* It's tasty and inexpensive.

Galway oysters, eaten only when there is an "R" in the month (in other words from September to April), are expensive, but spoil yourself; and enjoy them with a glass of Guinness (preferably draught). Ireland is very good for seafood with Dublin Bay prawns at the top of the list, but they are likely to be expensive so make that meal a special occasion. Mussels, usually from the beds off Wexford, are great—they often feature as *moules marinières* on the menu; as the Irish say "there's eatin' and drinkin' " in the dish.

Salmon, trout, and plaice are widely available. Lobster, scallops, crab, oysters and prawns are plentiful in seaports and need not be expensive if eaten as "bar food". Many pubs serve interesting lunchtime snacks at around IR£4.50. Smoked fish—salmon, trout, mackerel—make good starters, especially if eaten with local brown wholemeal bread, which is always excellent.

To slake your thirst, there's Guinness, and if you want something lighter, there's lager or light beer. Irish whiskey is not just a constituent of Irish coffee; it's potent and pleasant, but remember that Irish spirit measures are bigger than you'll get in Britain.

TIPPING. The standard tip and service charge in Ireland is 12½ percent. Most hotels include this service charge on the bill; guest houses don't. In more elegant establishments, a small extra tip is expected. It's common practice to tip porters, car park attendants, taxi drivers, barbers, and waiters or waitresses, but not bar staff.

MAIL. Letters to Ireland and continental Europe (including the U.K.) cost 30p for the first 20 grams; postcards are 26p, and automatically go by air. Airmail to the U.S., Canada and other countries outside Europe costs 50p for the first 10 grams; airletters are 45p and postcards 32p. These rates may rise in 1991.

CLOSING TIMES. Most shops open at 9 and close at 5.30 or 6, six days a week in Dublin and Cork, but in other places they shut for half-days (about 1 P.M.) either Wednesday, Thursday or Saturday, depending on the locality. Banks open weekdays 10 to 12.30 and 1.30 to 3 (5 on one selected weekday), but they are closed on Saturdays. Post Offices open 9 to 5.30 weekdays, 9–5 Saturdays. There is a 24-hour service at Shannon Airport. Pubs open every day 10.30 to 11.30, open Sundays, 12.30 to 2 and 4 to 11. From October to May, pubs close at 11 P.M. Mondays to Saturdays. Although it is no longer obligatory, some city pubs close for an hour or two on weekday afternoons.

GETTING AROUND IRELAND. By Plane. Though this is not a particularly cheap way to get around, it can be useful if you are in a hurry. *Aer Lingus* have internal services from Dublin to Shannon, Cork, Galway, Knock, Kerry, and Sligo. *Aer Arann* operates from Galway to the Aran Islands. The latter costs around IR£45 return; the same company operates between Dublin and Shannon. There are also services between Donegal and Derry.

By Train. The state-owned *Córas Iompair Eireann* (National Transport Company of Ireland) is the holding company for Irish Rail (*Iarnrod Eireann*) and Irish Bus (*Bus Eireann*). It is usually referred to by its initials CIE. Services are generally good and frequent. The railway network, although much cut back in the last 25 years, is still quite extensive. All trains are diesel, and the main expresses have very comfortable airconditioned carriages. There is a combined Rail/Road Rambler ticket for unlimited travel by rail and bus costing about IR£62 for 7/8 days out of 15. There are also 15-day tickets valid within a 30-day period, IR£95.

There is also an All Ireland *Overlander Ticket* issued jointly by Irish Rail, Northern Ireland Railways and Ulsterbus. Issued for 15 days, in 2nd (Standard) class it costs about IR£115. Children under 16 (under 15 for the Overlander pass) travel at half price. Available only within Ireland.

By Bus. The combined Rail/Road *Rambler* ticket (see above) is well worth investigating, as is the bus-only *Rambler Pass.* Irish Bus have an Expressway coach service to all major centers with interchange points enabling you to switch your route without returning to your point of departure.

By Bicycle. Though a little hilly in places, and wet, Ireland is a fine country to bike around. There is a specially designed bicycle, known as a Tourer, available for hire from about 50 Rent-a-Bike concessionaires throughout the country. Cost is about IR£22 per week with IR£30 deposit. Contact the Irish Tourist Office for details. See Dublin Practical Information for addresses.

Dublin

Dublin is an easy place to get about in, and the old heart of the city, developed around the river Liffey, can be comfortably explored on foot. There is a well-marked tourist trail (the numbered indicators are on lamp standards above eye level) which takes in the special points of interest and you can get a booklet detailing the route from the Dublin Tourist Office at 14 Upper O'Connell Street. For the less energetic, CIE runs city tours; check with the office in O'Connell Street opposite the Dublin Tourist Office; Dublin City Tours, Wilton Place, near Baggot Street Bridge, also operate similar trips.

Start in statue-filled O'Connell Street, which is marked at each end by impressive monuments to Irish statesmen of the last century, Charles Stewart Parnell at the north end and Daniel O'Connell (by John Henry Foley), Dublin's Lord Mayor in 1829, at the south end. About halfway down is the General Post Office, the best piece of architecture in the street and historic as the center of the Irish Rising in 1916. There is a fine bronze statue of the legendary Irish hero Cuchulainn inside, and the Philatelic Office can provide interesting sets of Irish commemorative stamps, which make good souvenirs.

Crossing O'Connell Bridge over the Liffey, particularly at dusk in the evening, look westwards towards Phoenix Park; a slight mistiness blurs the outlines of distant buildings, conjuring up images of the Dublin of a century or more ago. Looking east, a railway bridge cuts across the view of one of the city's most famous buildings, the Customs House on the north bank of the Liffey; it was designed by the great architect James Gandon and built almost two centuries ago. Gandon also designed the Four Courts, the seat of civil justice, which is westwards up the river, but is best seen from the south bank.

Dublin's most distinguished public building, the 18th-century Parliament House, is now the Bank of Ireland (recently cleaned, and now all the more imposing). A visit to the building to see the imposing Parliament Chamber is worth the diversion. Across the road is Trinity College, founded back in the 16th century by the first Queen Elizabeth of England. Two of its most famous alumni, the poet and dramatist

Oliver Goldsmith and orator/statesman Edmund Burke, dominate the entrance in statues, again by John Henry Foley.

Through the entrance there's a different cobblestoned world. The students bustle around, as students everywhere, but the buildings give an impression of quiet and contemplation while the city roars by outside. In the Examination Hall on the right there are frequent music recitals; check the notice board in passing. Visit the Long Room in the Library to see its fabulous collection of manuscripts, including the world famous Book of Kells dating from the 8th century and considered by some the most beautiful illuminated manuscript in existence. In the new Arts Block, close by, the Douglas Hyde Gallery has frequent interesting art exhibitions (admission free). On a pleasant day a rest in the quadrangle or by the cricket field (perhaps with a sandwich) is a help for further touring. Go out through the Lincoln Place gate and you are close to Merrion Square, which still preserves its beautiful 18th-century mansions where Oscar Wilde, Daniel O'Connell, the writer George Moore and the Duke of Wellington once lived. Today most of the houses are occupied by offices but the character is delightfully preserved. Merrion Square itself is a public park, noted for its floral displays. One side of the Square is dominated by the National Gallery of Ireland, don't miss it, and take a look at the bronze statue near the entrance—it's George Bernard Shaw, whose bequest of part of the royalties on his work has done much to help the acquisition of outstanding works of art in recent years.

Walking up the Square past the gardens of Leinster House, once the Duke of Leinster's home and now the seat of the Oireachtas (Irish Parliament—Dail and Senate), there are the National Natural History Museum, and the impressive group of Government Buildings. This route leads on to St. Stephen's Green, another oasis and the open-air lunchtime spot for many Dubliners in fine weather. Just off "The Green"—Dubliners never call it anything else—the new National Concert Hall is on Earlsfort Terrace; it features many kinds of music from symphonic to pop; average admission is about IR£5. Just off Stephen's Green in Dawson Street there is the ornate if uninspiring Mansion House—the home of the city's Lord Mayor—and beyond it St. Ann's Church where Thursday lunchtime concerts (free or about IR£1) are popular.

Parallel to Dawson Street is Grafton Street, for window shopping only, unfortunately, if you are on a budget. But it's better to take the Kildare Street route, which passes the National Museum, (with its fine collection of gold ornaments), the entrance to the Parliament Building (Leinster House) and the National Library.

Dame Street, which runs from the front of Trinity College up to Christ Church Cathedral, includes one modern building of distinction, the Central Bank, on the right a little before Dublin Castle, itself almost hidden behind the City Hall. Dublin Castle dates from the 13th century and while it now houses part of the civil service the sumptuous State Apartments can be visited with an official guide when they are not in use. It was here that then-President Reagan was entertained on his 1984 visit. Between Dame Street and the Liffey is Temple Bar, a fashionable district worth investigating for its inexpensive but original restaurants and shops, and its lively art galleries.

Christ Church Cathedral is a hundred yards up the hill. It was founded by King Sitric the Dane in 1038 and has recently been restored to protect the fabric and its great nave. Between the cathedral and the river Liffey new civic buildings have been built on Wood Quay, to the annoyance of many conservationists as important remains of early Viking settlements were discovered on the site. To the west of Wood Quay and Christchurch Cathedral is St. James's Gate, headquarters of the Guinness Brewery. The Visitors' Center will explain the brewing process and offer you a sample.

Visit nearby St. Patrick's Cathedral, which was founded in 1130. Here the great Jonathan Swift, author of *Gulliver's Travels,* was Dean for over 30 years in the 18th century, and near the doorway is his tomb and the bitter epitaph he wrote for himself. Next door is Marsh's Library (1707), the oldest library in Ireland still to have chained books and the cages into which students were once locked to stop them stealing books.

Take a bus from the city center (Nos. 10, 14 in O'Connell Street or 25, 26 on Aston Quay) to the Phoenix Park (1,760 acres) and visit its zoological gardens. All sports played there (including polo) can be watched for free. The official residences of the President of Ireland and the United States Ambassador are in the Park.

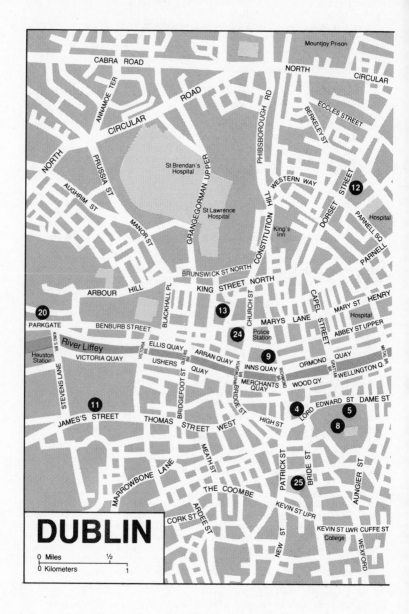

CABRA ROAD

NORTH   CIRCULAR

Mountjoy Prison

ANNAMOE TER

ROAD

PHIBSBOROUGH RD

ECCLES STREET

BERKELEY ST

CIRCULAR

PRUSSIA ST

NORTH

AUGHRIM ST

MANOR ST

GRANGEGORMAN UPPER

St Brendan's Hospital

St Lawrence Hospital

WESTERN WAY

DORSET STREET

12

CONSTITUTION HILL

King's Inn

Hospital

PARNELL SQ

PARNELL

BRUNSWICK ST NORTH

KING STREET NORTH

CHURCH ST

MARYS LANE

CAPEL STREET

MARY ST   HENRY

ARBOUR   HILL

BLACKHALL PL

13

24

Hospital

ABBEY ST UPPER

20

PARKGATE

BENBURB STREET

Police Station

ORMOND   QUAY

WELLINGTON Q.

River Liffey

Heuston Station

VICTORIA QUAY

ELLIS QUAY

VICTORIA BR

Q BR

ARRAN QUAY

USHERS   QUAY

BRIDGEFOOT ST

QUEENS BR

WHITWORTH BR

BRIDGE ST

INNS QUAY

O'DONOVAN

9

MERCHANTS QUAY

WOOD QY

GRATTAN BR

METAL BR

11

JAMES'S   STREET

THOMAS

STREET   WEST

HIGH ST

LORD EDWARD ST   DAME ST

4

5

8

STEVENS LANE

MARROWBONE   LANE

MEATH ST

PATRICK ST

BRIDE ST

AUNGIER ST

ARDEE ST

THE   COOMBE

KEVIN ST UPR

25

CORK ST

NEW ST

KEVIN ST LWR   CUFFE ST

College

WEXFORD

DUBLIN

0 Miles .... ½
0 Kilometers 1

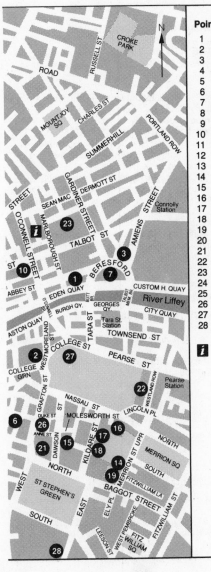

Points of Interest

1 Abbey Theater
2 Bank of Ireland
3 Central Bus Station
4 Christ Church Cathedral
5 City Hall
6 Civic Museum
7 Customs House
8 Dublin Castle
9 Four Courts
10 General Post Office (GPO)
11 Guinness' Brewery
12 Hugh Lane Gallery of Modern Art
13 Irish Whiskey Corner
14 Leinster House
15 Mansion House
16 National Gallery
17 National Library
18 National Museum
19 Natural History Museum
20 Phoenix Park
21 Royal Irish Academy
22 Royal Irish Academy of Music
23 St. Mary's Catholic Pro-Cathedral
24 St. Michans
25 St. Patrick's Cathedral
26 St. Theresa's
27 Trinity College
28 University College
   (National Concert Hall)

i Tourist Information Office

The National Botanic Garden at Glasnevin is another bus ride away (Nos. 13, 19). It has a fine collection of shrubs and trees.

Dubliners are a friendly people so don't hesitate to ask directions.

PRACTICAL INFORMATION FOR DUBLIN

GETTING INTO TOWN FROM THE AIRPORT. There is a bus shuttle every 20 minutes—7.30 A.M. to 11.30 P.M.—operated by CIE. Fare IR£2.50. Taxis are inclined to be expensive.

HOTELS. There are comparatively few hotels in Dublin in the moderate price bracket, but the deficiency is made up by the range of guest houses under IR£45 per night for two people in a double room. Both hotels and guest houses conform to the standards of the Irish Tourist Board, and there is also a considerable volume of registered accommodations in private homes that have been visited and approved by the Irish Tourist Board as meeting the minimum requirements for tourists. The average rate is about IR£26 per night for two persons.

If you have not booked in advance the best bet is to check with the Dublin Regional Tourism Office's desk at Dublin Airport or 14 Upper O'Connell Street, Dublin. Unless pre-booked, visitors may be asked by hotels and guest houses to make a one-night payment on arrival.

Many hotels and some guest houses charge a room rate with breakfast as an add-on. In private house accommodations—officially known as town houses and usually about a 60p bus ride from the city center—the overnight charge includes breakfast.

The Irish Tourist Board's *Guest Accommodation* (IR£2) and *Town and Country Homes* (IR£1) give maximum prices for approved establishments throughout the country.

Moderate

Ariel, 52 Lansdowne Rd. (tel. 685512). 16 rooms with bath. Comfortable and well-run, near bus and train services.

Clarence, Wellington Quay, close to city center (tel. 776178). 67 rooms with bath. Overlooks river Liffey.

Deer Park, Howth (tel. 322624). 30 rooms with bath. Golf. On the north side of Dublin Bay, 20 minutes by DART or bus from center.

Harcourt, 60 Harcourt St. (tel. 783677). 20 rooms, 6 with bath. Central location.

Ormond, in the city on the riverside (tel. 721811). 49 rooms, most with bath. Recently refurbished. Popular with visitors from the country.

Russell Court, 21–23 Harcourt St. (tel. 784991). 22 rooms with bath. New, centrally located hotel.

St. Aiden's, 32 Brighton Rd. (tel. 902011). 12 rooms. Inner suburban guest house.

Wynn's, Lr. Abbey St. (tel. 745131). 65 rooms with bath. Central.

Inexpensive

Abrae Court, 9 Zion Rd. (tel. 979944). 14 rooms with bath. Inner suburban location.

Beddington, 181 Rathgar Rd. (tel. 978047). 16 rooms, some with bath.

Carrick Hall, 69 Orwell Rd. (tel. 960444). 9 rooms with bath. Good facilities in a quiet southside suburb.

Egan's, 7–9 Iona Park (tel. 303611). 23 rooms with bath. On the north side of the city.

Iona House, 5 Iona Park (tel. 306217). 14 rooms, most with bath. Quiet location.

Kilronan House, 70 Adelaide Rd. (tel. 755266). 11 rooms with bath. Convenient spot on the south side of town.

Maples, 81 Iona Rd. (tel. 303049). 21 rooms with bath. Midway between airport and center.

Mount Herbert, Lansdowne Rd. (tel. 648321). 88 rooms, most with bath. Inner suburban location, popular with regular visitors.

Parkview House, North Circular Rd. (tel. 743697). 14 rooms with bath. By Phoenix Park.

St. Jude's, Pembroke Park, Ballsbridge (tel. 680928). 8 rooms. Another of the small guest houses in pleasant quiet area.

Youth Hostels. The *YWCA* has a hostel at Radcliff Hall, St. John's Rd., Sandymount (tel. 694521) with 58 single rooms; around IR£10 per night. The *Dublin Tourist Hotel,* 2–4 Frenchman's Lane (tel. 749321), has a rate of around IR£4 per night; while *Kinlay House,* Lord Edward St. (tel. 796644), has 38 twin and four-bedded rooms from IR£6.50 per night. Dormitory accommodation and 6 double rooms at IR£3.50 and IR£5 per night are available at *Dunsinea House,* Castleknock (tel. 383252); similar accommodation can be found at *The North Strand,* 49 North Strand Rd. (tel. 364716).

RESTAURANTS. A sample listing of Dublin restaurants is given below. Most close quite early. Where it is advisable to book, telephone numbers are given. Food in Dublin tends to be hearty and filling, but there are some gourmet spots with prices to match. If you're serious about the budget get the Special Value Tourist Menu brochure (free) from the Irish Tourist Board.

Moderate

Bad Ass Café, 9 Crown Alley, off Dame St. Great pizzas, cook your own steak. Loud and lively.

Barry Fitzgerald's, 90 Marlborough St. Pub lunches and early dinners in upstairs bar.

Beefeaters, 99–100 Lr. Baggot St. Prime Irish beef served in 15 different ways.

Coffer's, 6 Cope St. Emphasis on fresh wholesome food and good value. Behind Temple Bar.

Conway's, Parnell St., opposite the famous Rotunda Hospital. A cheerful Dublin pub serving a wide variety of meals.

Hugh Lane Gallery of Modern Art, Charlemont House, Parnell Sq., has a pleasant restaurant in the basement—the old kitchen of Lord Charlemont's House. Lunches and snacks.

Kitty O'Shea's, 23–25 Grand Canal St. Well known pub-restaurant with old Dublin charm.

National Gallery, Merrion Square. A pleasant spot for lunch or a snack. Open till 8 P.M. on Thursdays.

Nico's, 53 Dame St. (tel. 773062). Top quality plus a little atmosphere in this Italian-Irish place.

Old Stand, 37 Exchequer St. Famous eating pub just off Grafton St.

Periwinkle, Powerscourt Center. Dublin's first seafood bar. If you haven't met a periwinkle, it's extracted (by the eater) with the aid of a toothpick from its blackish shell; small but succulent.

Rudyard's, 15–16 Crown Alley. Small and informal with wholesome menu.

Waterfall, Irish Life Center, Lower Abbey St. Extensive menu and striking modern decor.

Inexpensive

Beshoff's, Westmoreland St. and O'Connell St. Superior fish and chips in Victorian surroundings.

Bewley's, 78 Grafton St.; 10 Westmoreland St.; 13 South Great George's St. They close at 5.30, and so are for lunches and teas only; really an Irish version of a Continental *pâtisserie,* cakes in profusion.

Captain America's, Grafton Court, Grafton St. Lively spot with good burgers and Tex-Mex.

Casper & Giumbini's, Wicklow St. Choice of pub food in the bar or a separate restaurant.

Davy Byrne's, 21 Duke St. (off Grafton St.). Elegant bar with lunchtime and early evening "specials" and salads.

Da Vicenza, 133 Leeson St. Upper (tel. 609906). Lively pizzeria also serving pasta, fish, and steak.

Flanagan's, 61 Upper O'Connell St. Central steak house with excellent basement pizzeria.

Little Lisbon, 2 Upper Fownes St. (off Dame St.) (tel. 711274). Portuguese and Brazilian seafood.

Mary Rose, Powerscourt Center. Pleasant for snacks, coffee or lunch; real home-made soup and apple tart.

McDonald's have seven spots, among them one in Grafton St., and another in O'Connell St.

Pasta Pasta, 27 Exchequer St. Lotsa pasta and a few Italian specials.

Stag's Head, Dame Court. This is *the* place at lunchtime for the traditional Irish dish of corned (salt) beef and cabbage; good spot.

GETTING AROUND DUBLIN. By Bus. It's very easy to get around Dublin by bus; many of the buses start out from the center of the city in O'Connell Street, near the General Post Office building. Buses marked *An Lar* (The Center) have their terminal here and go right across town by many routes. Other bus terminals are on quays adjoining O'Connell Bridge, or D'Olier Street, College Street, and on North Earl Street. Fares start at 45p.

CIE runs coach tours in and around Dublin at reasonable prices; details from CIE at 59 Upper O'Connell Street; *Dublin City Tours,* 3 Wilton Place, also run similar tours.

By Train. CIE has recently electrified a main suburban rail line from Howth on the north arm of Dublin Bay, passing though the city center, to Bray, an outer seaside suburb in County Wicklow. Known as the DART (Dublin Area Rapid Transport), it is primarily a commuter line, but useful for tourists.

By Taxi. Taxis don't cruise the streets, but are based on stands near main hotels, rail termini and other strategic points. They can be called by phone, but charge 70p per mile to the pick-up point. Fare for one person is 85p plus 80p per mile, with a minimum charge of IR£1.80; 40p for each additional passenger and each piece of baggage. There is a supplementary charge of 50p for hiring between 8 P.M. and 8 A.M. and on Sunday; on public holidays, 60p. If you hire a taxi at Dublin Airport there's another supplement of 70p. These prices are likely to rise before 1991.If you plan to travel some distance, say 12 miles or so, it is best to check the approximate fare with the driver first.

By Bicycle. You can hire a bike at *Dawson's,* 316 North Circular Rd.; *Ryan's,* 115 Upper Dorset St.; and *USIT Rent-a-Bike,* 58 Lower Gardiner St. Rate is about IR£4.50 a day, £22 a week plus IR£30 deposit.

ENTERTAINMENT. Bars. *Bowes,* Fleet St., meeting place for journalists and the literati. *The Oval* on Middle Abbey St.has a similar clietele. *Davy Byrne's,* Duke St., typically Irish and very popular. *The Bailey,* Duke St., is on a site that has been a hostelry since the seventeenth century. James Joyce mentions its forerunner in *Ulysses* and Oliver St. John Gogarty in *As I Was Going Down Sackville Street.* The celebrated front door from *Ulysses* is part of the furnishings.

Sinnott's, in the basement of the new Stephen's Green Shopping Center, is a likely place to meet actors, or they may be around the corner in *Neary's* of Chatham St., a good pub in the traditional style. There is another meeting place for theater folk across the road from the Abbey Theatre, *The Plough.*

Madigan's in Moore St., *Madigan's* in Earl St. and *Mooney's* in Abbey St. are spots city center workers favor.

Mulligans in Poolbeg St. has the "best pint" in Dublin. See the Long Hall for splendid old fittings.

Doheny & Nesbitt's, Waterloo House and *Searson's* are all on Baggot St. and popular meeting places for the young. In Ballsbridge, a short distance away, the *Horse Show House* and *Crowe's* are always bustling—and more so on Saturday nights.

The *Stag's Head,* in Dame Court off Dame St. is one of Dublin's oldest pubs; the *Long Hall,* not far away in South Great George's St. is another.

Scruffy Murphy's just off Lower Mount St., and *Kitty O'Shea's* beside the Grand Canal Bridge in Shelbourne Rd. are both "in" places to be.

Singing Pubs. A television set in the corner of a bar is not a good sign of conver-sation to come, but in the Singing Pubs (also known as Ballad Pubs), there is some lively entertainment around the city. Some places have a cover charge of IR£2, but the majority do not. But if you do pay a cover charge, the entertainment is likely to be top quality. Then there are others that depend on local minstrels. Most likely you will be asked to join in the singing. Ballads are the main attraction, although some pubs also offer other forms of entertainment.

Around the city center, *Abbey Inn,* Mary's Abbey, off Capel St; *Baggott Inn,* Baggott St.; *Brazen Head,* 20 Lower Bridge St; *Slattery's,* Capel St.; and *O'Meara's,* Aston Quay, right beside O'Connell Bridge are representative. *O'Donoghue's* in Merrion Row is one of the best near the city center; and on the north side of town *Clontarf Castle,* Clontarf, is a good spot where you can get something to eat.

As some of the pubs don't present shows every night it is worth checking the notices in the evening newspapers, or taking the advice of the hotel porter who will certainly know the current top spots.

Cinema. Cinemas are mostly located around the city center. Most seats cost about IR£3.50. There is a fairly wide selection of the latest American films, as well as British and Continental fare, on offer.

Discos. Dublin has a number of discos, many of them short-lived, however. *Annabel's,* behind the Burlington Hotel, and *Flamingo's* at Parke's Hotel, Stillorgan, are the smartest and most expensive. *Rumours Night Club,* beside the Gresham Hotel on O'Connell St. and *Chiki's,* at the Harcourt Hotel, 60 Gt. Harcourt St., are both newer spots. Prices vary with the location from about IR£5 up. Some are licensed to serve wine.

Theaters. The famous *Abbey Theatre* has an impressive modern building on Marlborough St. Company performs mainly Irish plays (in English) and the repertoire includes works by Yeats, Synge and O'Casey as well as works by new writers. Nearly all the great Irish players from Sara Allgood and Barry Fitzgerald to the late Siobhan McKenna, and Cyril Cusack have acted here. Closed Sun. and for three days preceding Easter. The *Peacock Theatre* in the same building is used for experimental works, many of considerable interest. There is also a 30-minute lunchtime theater.

Other Dublin theaters include the *Gaiety,* South King St., for grand opera, ballet and musical comedy as well as drama; the *Gate Theatre,* Parnell Sq., for modern drama, revue and Irish works (in English); the *Olympia,* Dame St., for ballet, musical comedy and modern drama; the *Project Arts Centre,* East Essex St., and *Focus,* Pembroke Pl., are pocket theaters that frequently present plays of off-beat interest. Check the evening papers to see what's playing.

The *Dublin International Theatre Festival* (October) is the occasion for a heavy concentration of talent and new plays by Irish and foreign writers lasting for two action-packed weeks.

Concerts. There are many musical groups in Dublin: the *Dublin Festival Singers, Guinness Choral Society, Consort of St. Sepulchre* (medieval music), *Palestrina Choir* of the Pro-Cathedral and other groups present concerts along with soloists and orchestra. Opera seasons are in spring and winter. The National Concert Hall, Earlsfort Terrace, features the *Radio Telefis Eireann Symphony Orchestra,* and often accommodates visiting orchestras and soloists.

Soloists and small ensembles sometimes present concerts at the National Gallery. Pop concerts are usually staged at the National Stadium or at the Royal Dublin Society's premises in Ballsbridge. Concert-going is reasonable, costing between IR£3.50 and IR£10 a seat; but about double that for an international pop star. There are occasional noon-time concerts (free) in the Hugh Lane Gallery of Modern Art, on Sundays.

MUSEUMS. Unless otherwise stated, admission is free. For further details of the museums listed here, see the *Directory of Local Museums and Local Societies in Ireland.* This is available at a small cost from tourist information offices, the National Gallery of Ireland and some bookshops.

Aviation Museum, Dublin Airport. A good way of whiling away the time if you're waiting for a plane; or if you're an aircraft buff. Admission 50p.

Chester Beatty Library, Shrewsbury Rd. Has a fine collection of Oriental and medieval manuscripts, including the oldest manuscript of the New Testament. Open Tues. to Fri., 10 to 5, Sat. 2 to 5.

Civic Museum, South William St. Fine museum full of interesting sidelights on old Dublin. Open 10 to 6, Sun., 11 to 2; closed Mon.

Dublin Castle (signposted from Dame St.). It was from here that the Irish Crown Jewels were stolen, just before a royal visit in 1907. Open weekdays 10 to 12.15 and 2 to 5, Sat. & Sun. 2 to 5; guided tours of State Apartments every half hour (when not in use). Adults IR£1.50, children 75p.

Guinness Museum, James's St. Industrial museum with good exhibits on the ancient craft of coopering (making wooden barrels) and brewing business; 30-minute video plus free sample of the brew at the Visitors' Center.

Hugh Lane Gallery of Modern Art, Parnell Sq. Open 9.30 to 6, Sun., 11 to 2; closed Mon.

Joyce Museum, Sandycove. Has a collection of material associated with writer James Joyce, who once lived in this old Martello Tower. Open daily in summer, 11 to 4.

Kilmainham Jail, Kilmainham. Exhibits associated with the Irish fight for independence. Open on Sun., 2 to 6.

Marsh's Library (near St. Patrick's Cathedral). Founded in 1707 and has an important collection of old books of theology and medicine, with Hebrew, Syriac, Greek and Latin literature. Open Mon., Wed., Thurs. and Fri. from 2 to 4 and on Sat. from 10.30 to 12.30.

Museum of Childhood, Palmerston Park. A fine collection of dolls and a 12-ft. 20-room crystal palace. Open afternoons 2 to 6.

National Gallery, Merrion Sq. Open Mon. to Sat. 10 to 6, Sun. 2 to 5; late night viewing on Thurs. till 9.

National Library of Ireland, Kildare St. Open weekdays 10 to 10, and Sat. 10 to 1; closed for three weeks in July and Aug.

National Museum of Irish Antiquities, Kildare St. Art, Industrial and Natural History sections. See the Torques from Tara, the Tara brooch, the famed Ardagh chalice and the Cross of Cong. New discoveries unearthed in 1980 at Killenaule, Co. Tipperary, include wonderful examples of 8th- and 9th-century work. Open 10 to 5, Sun. 2 to 5; closed Mon.

National Natural History Museum, Merrion Square. Open 10 to 5, Sun. 2 to 5. Beside the government buildings.

National Portrait Gallery, Malahide Castle, a few miles north of the city. Frequent guided tours (IR£1.50). Open 10 to 5 Mon. to Fri., 10 to 1 Sat., 2 to 5 Sun.; late night viewing on Thurs. till 9.

National Wax Museum, Granby Row. Life-size figures of Irish personalities, past and present. Open daily (about IR£1) 10.30 to 5.

Royal Hospital, Kilmainham. One of Dublin's most beautiful buildings. Fully restored interior representing several decorative styles of the 17th, 18th and 19th centuries. Open Sun. 11 to 6 for guided tours; exhibitions only Tues. to Sat. 2 to 5. Tours: Adults IR£1, children 50p.

Royal Irish Academy Library. Open 9.30 to 5.30 weekdays, 9.30 to 1 Sat.; closed last three weeks in Aug.

Trinity College Library. Exhibits include the famous *Book of Kells,* considered one of the most beautifully illustrated Gospels in the world. Open Mon. to Fri. 9.30 to 4.45, Sat. 9.30 to 12.45.

SHOPPING. Irish linen, tweeds and woolens, handknit sweaters, hats and scarves, Irish whiskey and handmade jewelry are all reasonably priced and justly famous native products and can all be found in Dublin.

Handwoven tweeds are always good value—*Kevin and Howlin,* in Nassau St. beside Trinity College, specializes with a wide range and also features all styles of tweed hats. Also in Nassau St. is the *Kilkenny Design Centre,* which markets Irish craft goods of all types and runs right through the price scale. Handweaves and handknits (hats and scarves are "in") also at *The Woollen Mills,* Ormond Quay, and the major department stores.

Traditional shopping streets are Grafton (expensive), O'Connell, Henry and Mary Streets, but new shopping centers have broadened the choice. The *Powers-*

court Centre is in Clarendon St. and is worth at least a window-shopping visit; the *ILAC Centre* is another good (and bigger) under-cover shopping area, and beside it you'll find a range of the traditional Dublin street-traders in action. Also in the city center, off Abbey St. is the *Irish Life Centre,* a similar type of operation. A IR£50 million glass-and-steel shopping center is a new feature on the Grafton Street corner of Stephen's Green.

Cleo in Kildare St. is a good place for women's clothes, and *Pia Bang* in the Powerscourt Center has all the latest younger styles.

Big department stores are *Switzer's, Brown Thomas* and *Arnott's,* all in Grafton St.; *Clery's,* O'Connell St. are good in the middle bracket; and in the lower price range *Dunne's, Penney's, Roche's, Marks and Spencer* and *BHS* (all in the city center).

USEFUL ADDRESSES. *American Express,* 116 Grafton St. (tel. 772874); *Thomas Cook,* 118 Grafton St. (tel. 771721); *United States Embassy,* 42 Elgin Road, Ballsbridge (tel. 688777); *Canadian Embassy,* 65 St. Stephen's Green (tel. 781988); *British Embassy,* Merrion Rd. (tel. 695211); *CIE,* 35 Lower Abbey St. (tel. 302222); *Aer Lingus,* Upper O'Connell St. (tel. 370191); *British Airways,* 112 Grafton St., opposite Trinity College, near American Express and Cooks (tel. 686666); *Air Canada,* 4 Westmoreland St. (tel. 771488); *Automobile Association,* 23 Suffolk St. (tel. 779481). Passenger enquiries: *City bus services* (tel. 734222); *Irish Bus* (provincial services) (tel. 366111); *Irish Rail* (tel. 366222).

The Southeast

The Irish like to put labels on areas—the counties of Wexford, Waterford, Kilkenny and Carlow are known as the "sunny southeast" and there is justification for the tag because the weather station on the coast at Rosslare reports that it gets more hours of sunshine than anywhere else in the country.

Kilkenny is reputedly famous for its fighting cats, but that must have been a long time ago. If you are around in August there is an excellent arts festival at which the events and exhibitions are reasonably priced. See Rothe House, a well-preserved medieval merchant's house that is now, in part, a museum. Much of the craft work of Kilkenny Design Center, beside Kilkenny Castle, is on display (free) at the Center; modern Irish silverware isn't expensive. Kyteler's Inn was once the home of a famous witch, Dame Alice Kyteler, who escaped the penalties for her sorcery; the inn is still a hostelry.

The country around historic Wexford—part of the town's ancient walls still remain—has many links with America. Commodore John Barry, founder of the American Navy, is honored by a statue (presented by the U.S.) on the quayside, near a good maritime museum in an old lightship. The forbears of John F. Kennedy came from nearby Dunganstown and there is now a J.F.K. Memorial Park with an international 270-acre arboretum and 140-acre forest garden on the mountainside at Slieve Coilte, near Wexford town. Even if you're not keen on trees, it's worth driving to the top for the view.

Wexford's big event of the year is the fall Opera Festival, which brings international singers, directors and conductors to the tiny Georgian Theatre Royal, where little-known operas are the specialty. Seats are expensive and must be booked well in advance, but there is a lot of other entertainment around.

The first Normans to land in Ireland, away back in the 12th century, landed in County Wexford; the first Vikings had established themselves in Waterford a century earlier—the city's name is a corruption of an old Norse name. Reginald's Tower is now a museum, and for something more modern you can visit the factory where the famous (and sadly expensive) Waterford Glass is made. The Irish enjoy music at all times and the International Festival of Light Opera in the fall brings songsters from the U.S. as well as Britain and Continental Europe.

PRACTICAL INFORMATION FOR THE SOUTHEAST

Hotels and Restaurants

Kilkenny. *Springhill Court* (M), tel. (056) 21122. 47 rooms, most with bath. *Lacken House* (I), tel. (056) 65611. 8 rooms with bath.

Rosslare Harbor. At the ferry port. *Hotel Rosslare* (M), tel. (053) 33110. 22 rooms with bath. *Tuskar House* (M), tel. (053) 33363. 20 rooms with bath. *Coral Gables* (I), tel. (053) 31213. 12 rooms with bath.

Waterford. *Diamond Hill* (I), tel. (051) 32855. 8 rooms, half with bath. *Dooley's* (I) tel. (051) 73531. 37 rooms, most with bath. *Maryland House* (I), tel. (051) 76162. 20 rooms with bath. *Portree* (I), tel. (051) 74574. 15 rooms.

Wexford. *County* (I), tel. (053) 24377. 13 rooms. *Faythe House* (I), tel. (053) 22249. 10 rooms. *St. Aidan's Mews* (I), John St, tel. (053) 22691. 11 rooms. *Whitford House* (I), tel. (053) 43444. 25 rooms with bath or shower.

The South and Southwest

Cork is the official capital of the South and Southwest, but for visitors Killarney is the heart of the territory. Nonetheless, Cork is a good touring base; you can play the famous bells of Shandon in the steeple of a church in the city center, or take a trip out to Blarney Castle to kiss the Blarney Stone and earn yourself the gift of eloquence. Off Kinsale there is exciting deep sea fishing, and along the coast at Baltimore an international sailing school has its Irish headquarters.

Cork is a musical city and plays host to an international choral and folk dance festival in the spring and a Jazz International in the fall.

Along the coast of Cork—about 50 miles west of the city—there's the former home of the Earls of Bantry, Bantry House, built in 1750 and wonderfully furnished. Offshore at Glengarriff there is a wonderful Italianate garden on Garnish Island (also known as Ilnacullin).

Inland, about 8 miles east of Mitchelstown, lie the Mitchelstown Caves; of the four the Mitchelstown New Cave is the most interesting. The excursion is worthwhile because it is in spectacular country between the Galtee Mountains and the Knockmealdown Mountains.

Ballyporeen in Tipperary, near Clogheen, is where former President Ronald Reagan's paternal great-grandfather was born and RR made a visit here in 1984. You'll hear the saga in the Ronald Reagan Lounge in the village.

Moving westwards into Kerry, a good route is over the dramatic Healy Pass into what is known as "The Kingdom"—County Kerry—and, of course, the target of visitors for more than a hundred years—Killarney. The town is not interesting itself, but the Lakes of Killarney and Muckross Park, officially Killarney National Park, all 19,995 acres of it, demand attention. There are well-signposted nature trails (admission is free, and you can hire a bicycle in Killarney), and take in Muckross House itself, not least because it houses the Kerry Folklife Centre. It is a good museum with a blacksmith, weaver, basketmaker and potter demonstrating their skills.

Tralee, further west, is famous for its "Rose of Tralee" Festival in the fall, which brings Irish beauties from home and abroad, and for its National Folk Theatre, which features traditional folk theater in "Siamsa". There's rambunctious entertainment in Killorglin for three days in August when a goat is crowned King Puck.

PRACTICAL INFORMATION FOR THE SOUTH AND SOUTHWEST

Hotels and Restaurants

Cork. *John Barleycorn* (M), tel. (021) 821499. 16 rooms with bath. *Gabriel House* (I), Summerhill, tel. (021) 500333. 20 rooms with bath.*Lotamore House* (I), tel. (021) 822344. 20 rooms with bath. *Victoria Lodge* (I), tel. (021) 542233. 32 rooms with bath.

Restaurants. All hotels in the Cork region have restaurants. A "high tea", which always includes a meat or egg dish, is a good budget bet. *Chew Chews* (I), Phoenix St.; *Gallery Cafe* (I), Crawford Gallery, Emmet Place; *Halpin's* (I), Cork St.; *Mary Rose* (I), Savoy Center. All four are good bargain spots.

Killarney. There are plenty of accommodations in Killarney except in high season when prices strongly reflect demand. *Arbutus* (M), tel. (064) 31037. 35 rooms with bath. *Dromhall* (M), tel. (064) 31894. 58 rooms with bath. *Lake* (M), tel. (064) 31035. 65 rooms with bath. *Kathleen's Country House* (I), tel. (064) 32810. 10 rooms with bath *Linden House* (I), tel. (064) 31379. 20 rooms with bath.

Restaurants. Like most high concentration tourist areas Killarney has a lot of restaurants, most of them in the Inexpensive range. Among them are the*Foley's Seafood & Steak* (M), 23 High St.; *Gaby's Seafood Restaurant* (M), High St.; *Brewery Grill/Coffee Shop* (I) in the International Hotel; and *Kiely's* (I), College St.; *Linden House* (I), New Road; and *Sheila's* (I), High St.; *Sugan Kitchen* (I), in town center, has entertainment.

Shannonside

Shannon Airport is the key to the whole of the southwest and west of Ireland for visitors from America, and the tag, Shannonside, embraces a wide area of spectacular scenery as well as many things to do and see. The lordly river Shannon flows past the airport, and just up the road Bunratty Castle, restored to its medieval splendor, welcomes guests each night to banquets as in days of old, with colleens in 15th-century costumes, music and song and much, much laughter. This is something to save up for; it costs around IR£25 per person. Dunguaire and Knappogue are other nearby castles with special medieval entertainments.

Be sure to visit Bunratty Folk Park where there is a recreation of a village of 100 years ago complete with shops doing business, and sample some soda bread and scones made in the farm kitchen.

Limerick, the city of the Shannonside region, has preserved a number of old buildings that are worth taking time to see. King John's Castle beside Thomond Bridge is a good example of 13th-century architecture, and St. Mary's Cathedral in Bridge Street dates from the 12th century. Dunraven Castle at Adare, a few miles southwest of Limerick, is a stately manor in a village of outstanding beauty.

While hereabouts visit Lough Gur, just south of Limerick. An interpretive center is located in buildings modeled on dwellings of the Neolithic period (about 3,000 B.C.) and features many replicas of artifacts found around here, a spot first settled some 5,000 years ago. The Craggaunowen Project at Quin in County Clare should also be visited because there is a full-scale model of a lake dwelling of the Bronze Age, a reconstructed ring fort from the early Christian period, and in a castle nearby is part of the Hunt collection of medieval art; the rest of the collection can be seen in the National Institute of Higher Education in Limerick, which also houses a collection of self-portraits of Irish artists. The Craggaunowen Project is open April-October. The Belltable Theatre in Limerick is worth a visit for its productions, and there's usually an art show as well.

Also in this storied area see the Cliffs of Moher on the Clare coast, rising some 700 ft. up out of the Atlantic, and the intriguing limestone desert called The Burren where plants from the Mediterranean and the Arctic grow side by side, and where there are also strange caves. Visit the Ailwee Cave in one of the most impressive parts of The Burren for a guided tour through nearly a mile of a mysterious underworld of the past. It's open March-October.

There is a forest park with nature trails of over 600 acres at Curraghchase, about 14 miles south of Limerick, and there's real Irish pub fun in Durty Nellie's, just beside Bunratty Castle; then there's Becky Kelly's at Ruan in County Clare, reputedly Ireland's oldest pub; why not drink an egg flip at Fanny O'Dea's between Ennis and Kilrush and hear why a judge ordained it the traditional drink of the house?

PRACTICAL INFORMATION FOR LIMERICK

Hotels and Restaurants

Glentworth (M), tel. (061) 43822. 55 rooms, 50 with bath. *Royal George* (M), tel. (061) 44566. 58 rooms with bath. *Woodfield House* (M), tel. (061) 53023. 22 rooms, most with bath. *Alexandra House* (I), tel. (061) 318472. 8 rooms, 2 with bath. *Railway* (I), tel. (061) 43653. 20 rooms, 13 with bath.

But best bet with a family or small group is to rent one of the traditional cottages in the area through *Rent-an-Irish-Cottage Ltd.,* Shannon Airport, for around IR£250 for eight people. But book early.

Restaurants. *Jonathan's* (M), O'Connell Street; Jury's Hotel *Coffee Dock* (M); *Le Rendezvous* (M), O'Connell St., *Jasmine Garden* (M), also in O'Connell St. and the *Royal George Hotel* (I). *Baker's Kitchen* (I), O'Connell St.; *Hanratty's Hotel* (I), Glentworth St.; *The Upper Krust* (I), William St.

Galway and the West

The West starts where the river Shannon cuts from North to South, and if you are traveling from Dublin the difference is felt soon after the Shannon has been crossed. More stone walls, lonely roads, spectacular scenery building up on the horizon—it can be an exciting journey. Officially, the West embraces Galway, Mayo, Sligo, Leitrim and Rosscommon, but we bring in Donegal up in the north-west because it's the same sort of place. People are warm and friendly, you'll hear Irish being spoken and feel a special warmth that seems to heighten the Irish welcome.

Galway is the capital of the West and gateway to the area embracing the beauties of Connemara and the Aran Islands off the entrance to Galway Bay. Galway is an ancient city that had strong links with Spain in the Middle Ages—there's still a Spanish Arch in the city; and Columbus is said to have prayed in the Church of St. Nicholas before setting out on one of his voyages. There's a tiny theater where the plays are staged in Irish, *Taibhdhearc* (pronounce it *Ty-vark*), which has nurtured many players who have become famous on the world stage, among them the late Siobhan McKenna. If there's a play at the Druid Theatre don't miss it, the company is outstanding.

From Galway make a trip to the Aran Islands either by the ferry or, if you don't fancy the Atlantic rollers, there's an air service from the local airport. Here you'll find the traditional handknits, Aran style hats for men (a present for your favorite golfer), traditional shoes known as pampooties and tweed trousers and skirts made to keep out the wind. Despite their increased contact with the mainland the lives of the people are still hard: fishing from currachs—still made from hides—remains a way of life. You'll learn something of real peace on the islands. J.M. Synge caught their atmosphere in his plays *Riders to the Sea* and *The Playboy of the Western World,* and in the cinema Robert Flaherty's classic *Man of Aran* is still outstandingly evocative. Painters like Paul Henry, Maurice McGonigal and many others have also captured the atmosphere of the West; its remoteness (though it is only three hours from Dublin), timelessness and spectacular mountain and lake scenery.

Coole Park at Gort was once the home of Lady Augusta Gregory, a founder of the Abbey Theatre, who played hostess to all the great playwrights of her time—they left their autographs on a tree in the grounds—George Bernard Shaw's among them. The house no longer stands, but admission to the park is free.

The Mayo coast is famous for its deep sea angling and international competitions are usually based on Westport. Inland, visit Ballintubber Abbey; it has been in continuous use for 750 years. At Lough Key, a lake on the upper reaches of the Shannon, there is an impressive forest park that has well-equipped caravan and camping facilities (boats for hire) and a bog garden—an unusual garden with many strange plants and impressive rhododendrons; also see the Cypress grove and the deer enclosures in the park.

Another western park, the 1,400-acre Portumna Forest Park on the shores of Lough Derg in County Galway has a wildlife sanctuary. Elsewhere, blinds for bird-watching have been set up. Knock in Mayo has a basilica and is a famous pilgrimage site.

Sligo is the country of the poet William Butler Yeats, although you can see one of his homes at Thoor Ballylee, a castle at Gort in County Galway. Each August students from many countries come to study the works of the poet who helped create the Abbey Theatre and to visit his Lake Isle of Innisfree in Lough Gill. His grave is at Drumcliff, under Ben Bulben, and a short drive brings you to Lissadell, still the home of the Gore-Booth family, whose daughter Constance Markiewicz captivated the poet. It is now open to the public and contains many mementoes of Yeats and Constance.

The appeal of Donegal lies in its marvelously dramatic coastline and the spectacular Donegal Highlands, but visit Gweedore where they make handwoven tweeds and Foxford where a special type of rug is made that bears the town's name—and keeps a lot of people warm. The Ards Forest Park on the shore of Sheep Haven Bay has a wide diversity of trees, plants, rocks and links with Ireland's prehistory. Donegal's Lough Derg has an island known as Station Island visited by some 30,000 penitents a year between June and mid-August who stay fasting and praying for three days.

There is a great National Park in the heart of the Donegal Highlands, Glenveagh, which covers about 25,000 acres and includes lakes (one, three miles long), a castle, and the fine Derek Hill art collection and museum. At New Mills a corn and flax mill of long ago is being restored. This area has only been recently opened up. It's worth discovering.

PRACTICAL INFORMATION FOR GALWAY AND THE WEST

Hotels and Restaurants

Achill Island. Hotels are mostly open May-Sept. *Achill Head* (I), tel. (098) 43180. 23 rooms. *Achill Sound Hotel* (I), tel. (098) 45245. 36 rooms with bath. *Atlantic* (I), tel. (098) 43113. 10 rooms, some with bath. *Gray's* (I), tel. (098) 43244. 15 rooms with bath. *Slievemore* (I), tel. (098) 43254. 18 rooms, 2 with bath.

Aran Islands. *Johnston Hernon's* (I), tel. (099) 61218. 8 rooms. On Inishmore, largest of the islands. Open May to Sept.

Ballinrobe (Co. Mayo). There are 9 attractive cottage homes at Creagh on the shores of Lough Mask; each accommodates 8 people. Around IR£280 per week at the peak season. Contact Mrs. Nellie Keady, Lough Mask, Ballinrobe, tel. (092) 41671.

Cruit Island (Co. Donegal). Away from it all: Thatched cottages at IR£105–IR£280 (depending on the season). Contact Conor and Mary Ward, Rosses' Point, Sligo tel. (071) 77197.

Galway. *Anno Santo* (M), tel. (091) 22110. 14 rooms with bath. *Imperial* (M), tel. (091) 63033. 52 rooms with bath. *Skeffington Arms* (M), tel. (091) 63173. 21 rooms with bath. *Atlanta* (I), tel. (091) 62241. 19 rooms, 4 with bath. *Sacré Coeur* (I), tel. (091) 23635. 41 rooms, 24 with bath.

Restaurants. All hotels have restaurants. Try also *The Brasserie* (I), Middle St.; *Conlon & Son* (I), Eglinton St.; *Fat Freddie's* (I), The Halls, Quay St.; *Galleon Grill* (I), Salthill; *Tigh Noctan* (I), High St.

Paddy Burke's and *Moran's of the Wier* are the places for oysters; just outside town at Clarinbridge.

Gortahork (Co. Donegal). *McFadden's* (M), tel. (074) 35267. 19 rooms, 10 with bath.

Letterkenny. *Gallagher's* (I), tel. (074) 22066. 27 rooms with bath.
Restaurant. *Rumpoles* (I), Bright, modern restaurant.

Louisbourgh (Co. Mayo). 10 traditional-style cottages, each sleeping 7/9 people. Around IR£250 a week in mid-summer. Great location for touring Connemara or relaxing. Contact: *Tourist Office,* Galway, tel. (091) 63081.

Sligo. *The Southern* (M), tel. (071) 62101. 50 rooms with bath. *Clarence* (I), tel. (071) 42211. 15 rooms, 5 with bath. *Bonne Chere* (I), tel. (071) 42014. 18 rooms, 13 with bath. *Ocean View* (I), Strand Hill tel. (071) 68115. 11 rooms, some with bath.
Restaurants. *Bonne Chere* (M), High St. *The Italian Warehouse* (I), Hyde Bridge. *Kate's Kitchen* (I), Market St.

Westport (Co. Mayo). *Castle Court* (M), tel. (098) 25920. 40 rooms with bath. *Clew Bay* (I), tel. (098) 25438. 27 rooms with bath. *Grand Central* (I), tel. (098) 25027. 18 rooms, 6 with bath.
Restaurant. *The Asgard* (I), just outside town on the Quay, has choice of either pub grub or a restaurant, both of exceptional quality.

Italy

With its relatively strong economy and decreasing rate of inflation, Italy is no longer the happy haven for budget-minded tourists that it was just a few years ago. Also, the U.S. dollar is weaker, and travelers are finding that meals and accommodations cost them much more than before. However, Italy still offers good value to the tourist who plans his or her vacation well and puts our budget tips to work.

Its trio of tourist cities—Rome, Florence and Venice—are essential stops on any tour. The first two offer a wide choice of reasonable accommodations and eating places, while Venice is frankly expensive and a real challenge to the cost-conscious traveler, but with the right information at hand it's possible to sleep and eat relatively cheaply even there.

To appreciate fully the variety that makes Italy a wonderful place to visit, you've got to see the big cities *and* the countryside. That's why we suggest two other budget destinations, each typical of a different facet of Italian life. The Sorrento peninsula embodies all the clichés used to characterize Italy—resplendent sun, spectacular scenery, and omnipresent pizza—yet it manages to present them to you in a totally fresh and personal manner. In contrast, Assisi stirs you in a subtler way, steeping you in an atmosphere of medieval mysticism.

Package tours offer one of the best ways to get the most for your money in Italy; look for one that allows some degree of flexibility in terms of free time, a feature that will permit you to do some wandering about on your own, whether just to get the feel of a place or to go back to some of the sights or museums that you liked especially. When selecting a tour, figure out what the cost-per-day is and compare it with our budget guidelines. Check on the location of the hotels that your tour uses. Budget tours often use economical hotels on the outskirts of town, which means that you'll be faced with the problem of using public transportation to the center if you want to do anything on your own. Beware of brochures boasting that a hotel is "five minutes from St. Peter's"; you can be sure that a crow might make it in five minutes, but that it will take a wingless tourist two bus connections and at least half an hour in the best of traffic conditions.

Independent travel can be much more fun. It makes for more direct contact with the people and gives you more leeway to do as you please. It's also more likely to involve you in those curious situations, inevitable in exuberant Italy, that make the best travel stories when you get back home. Independent budget travel in Italy requires good though not necessarily rigid planning and a degree of adaptability to varying hotel standards. Your travel agent can help you map out your itinerary and make your bookings; then, with the help of a phrase book and a lot of gestures, you'll be on your way.

Whether you're traveling with a group or independently, you should time your trip to take advantage of low-season rates. Blessed with an enviably mild climate, Italy's a good place to visit all year round, excepting perhaps the relatively cold months of January and February. By avoiding high season you'll not only save money but you'll also avoid the mobs of tourists jostling for a better view of the Sistine Chapel or Michelangelo's *David*.

In any case, don't come to Italy in August, main vacation month for the Italians themselves, when coastal resorts burst at the seams, highways and public transportation resemble conveyor belts in a sardine factory, and city restaurants and shops are shuttered and abandoned.

Whenever you decide to make your trip to Italy, try to acquire the Italians' fail-safe philosophy of life, by means of which they uncannily manage to discern something good—or at least acceptable—in even the most disastrous circumstances. The more cynical among them retort that their ancestors perforce had to develop this capacity under the domination of mad emperors, poison-happy Renaissance princes and imperious dictators, and that it's presently being further refined in the presence of bureaucratic bungles and political scandals. Cynic or not, the Italian is staunchly proud of his heritage and very conscious of its historic and artistic consequence. So you'll do well on your travels through Italy to imitate this attitude. Accept the frustrations of erratic timetables and faulty plumbing, and enjoy all the extraordinary things that Italy offers you.

Italy's strategic situation has made it a Mediterranean crossroads throughout the centuries. Explorers and invaders landed on its shores to look around or to plunder, and some of them stayed on. First to come were probably the Phoenicians, though they may have been preceded by the Etruscans, a mysterious people who created a highly developed civilization in Central Italy several centuries before Christ. Colonists from Greece established the splendid cities of Magna Graecia. Later invaders came and went, like the barbarians from the North and the Saracens from the East.

All left their mark on the land and its people. The great diversity of the landscape—the peaks of the Alps and Dolomites, the rolling, cypress-dotted hills of Tuscany, the magnificent coasts of the South—corresponds to striking differences in the inhabitants and the way they express themselves in dialect, folklore and art.

There are, nevertheless, some constants in Italian life that you will readily discover, even on a brief visit. The first, and it's overwhelming, is art—great, minor, secular, religious, ancient, modern—art that is a vital element in daily life in Italy. Italians live with art. Walk down practically any street in the center of Rome, Florence or Venice. In the distance you will see one of the city's great monuments, an integral part of the urban panorama. Over there is a 15th-century palace, perhaps built over some Roman ruins; now it's divided into apartments, and women with shopping bags pass under its beautifully carved stone portals. A few steps away is an artisan's workshop, where an old man in a long gray apron is working iron into delicate floral shapes that will form a handsome gateway for a villa. Across the street, in a church with an elegant Baroque façade, the faithful kneel on a centuries-old pavement and raise their eyes to images of the saints depicted by Rubens, or Caravaggio, or Tintoretto. Shop windows along the street are decorated with great flair, and the owner of the trattoria on the corner is arranging fruit and vegetables into a gastronomic still life to delight the senses of his patrons. No matter where you look, you are surrounded by art.

Another constant on the Italian scene is the enthusiasm of the inhabitants, a vivacious, voracious approach to life that engenders a third constant: noise. Public and private activities, carried on with enthusiasm or, at the very least, a respectable degree of intensity, tend to make noise. Italians don't seem to mind it; you may, so forewarned is forearmed.

Then there are the immutable attractions of authentic Italian cuisine, as varied as the country itself but as consistently good, based on fresh ingredients prepared with imagination and respect for nature's seasonal bounty. Be sure to try the local specialties wherever you go. Ask for local wines, too, easy on both palate and pocketbook.

Ideally, your visit to Italy will combine these certainties with the unforeseen pleasures of a sunny, lazy hour or two at a sidewalk café, or the chance discovery of some curious corner of the city, perhaps a little piazza, that will give you a better insight into Italy than any tour guide ever can.

PRACTICAL INFORMATION FOR ITALY

WHAT WILL IT COST. Italy can still be a travel bargain, comparatively speaking; the inflation rate is fairly low, and prices tend to remain stable. To get the most for your money, inquire about package tours that generally give good value and also about money-saving tickets for air and rail travel within Italy. Off-season travel can mean lower hotel rates in such places as Venice and Sorrento, where local tourist offices and hotel associations also promote off-season packages offering discounts on restaurants, excursions, and entertainment as well as special rates for room and meals at your hotel. Florence also offers winter packages.

The Italian monetary unit is the *lira*. Coins are worth 10, 20, 50, 100, 200, 500, and 1,000 lire; bills are issued in denominations of 1,000, 2,000, 5,000, 10,000, 50,000, 100,000, and 500,000 lire. You can change money in Italy at banks and exchange offices. Exchange offices usually give better rates than banks, and are much faster. At presstime the exchange rate was about 1,354 lire to the U.S. dollar and about 2,440 to the pound sterling.

Sample Costs. Half a liter of carafe wine in a Moderate restaurant costs around 5,000 lire, while a beer is about 2,000 lire standing at a café bar, 3,000 in a Moderate restaurant. Coffee standing in the café comes to 800 lire, 3,000 if you prefer to sit at a table.

At the cinema it's 8,000 lire for new films with Italian soundtrack; English-language versions are about 5,000 lire in Rome. A moderate seat at the theater or opera comes to around 20,000 lire. Entrance to a museum, about 2,000–5,000 lire. Half-day guided bus tour, about 30,000 lire.

NATIONAL TOURIST OFFICE. The *Italian National Tourist Office* (ENIT), Via Marghera 2, Rome (tel. 49711) can supply information and brochures on all of Italy. More specific budget-oriented information is available at local tourist information offices, designated *Ente Provinciale Turismo* (EPT), *Azienda Promozione Turismo* (APT) or *Azienda Autonoma Turismo* (AAT). In addition to giving advice on special-interest excursions and low-cost hotels and restaurants, they will also help you find a room if you're without reservations.

Addresses of the Italian National Tourist Office overseas are:

In the U.S.: 630 Fifth Ave., Suite 1565, New York, N.Y. 10111 (tel. 212–245–4822); 500 N. Michigan Ave., Chicago, IL 60611 (tel. 312–644–0990); 360 Post St., Suite 801, San Francisco, CA 94108 (tel. 415–392–6206).

In Canada: 3 Place Ville Marie, Montreal, P.Q. H3B 2E3 (tel. 514–866–7667).

In the U.K.: 1 Princes St., London W1R 8AY (tel. 071–408 1254).

WHEN TO COME. The main tourist season starts at Easter in Rome, May elsewhere, and runs through the end of September, though in places where the Italians themselves vacation, July and August are high season. You would do well to avoid all resorts in July and August and even better not to travel at all in Italy during August. In large cities many restaurants and shops close during August. Though the traffic is pleasantly diminished, and it's easier to get around, it may be hard to find a place to eat, especially around the mid-August holiday, *Ferragosto*. Shoulder seasons (April–May–June and September–October) are fine at both cities and resorts. Ski resorts are most expensive in December and February; the so-called "White Weeks," when hotels offer lower rates, inclusive of meals, ski pass and often also of ski lessons, begin after the Epiphany (Jan. 6) and continue through the month, to be offered again in February and March.

Low-season travel is worthwhile throughout Italy; outside the main tourist cities you'll find lower hotel rates and easier access to less expensive eating-places, in addition to attractive off-season packages.

Average afternoon temperatures in degrees Fahrenheit and centigrade:

Rome	Jan.	Feb.	Mar.	Apr.	May	June	July	Aug.	Sept.	Oct.	Nov.	Dec.
F°	54	56	62	68	74	82	88	88	83	73	63	56
C°	12	13	17	20	23	28	31	31	28	23	17	13

Milan												
F°	40	47	56	66	72	80	84	82	76	64	51	42
C°	4	8	13	19	22	27	29	28	24	18	11	6

SPECIAL EVENTS. *January,* Epiphany Fair at Piazza Navona, Rome; Greek Catholic rites at Piana degli Albanesi, near Palermo. *February,* pre-Lenten carnivals (continuing in March), particularly those of Viareggio and Venice; Almond Blossom Festival at the Valley of the Temples, Agrigento; the Saint Agatha Festival at Catania; the Flower Show at San Remo. *March* nationwide mid-Lent festivals and popular feasts, usually on St. Joseph's Day, March 19th. *April,* International Handicrafts Fair, Florence; "Spring in Merano" events; International Horse Competition, Rome; Florence's Scoppio del Carro (on Easter Sunday). *May,* Feast of Sant'Efisio, Cagliari; Festa dei Ceri, Gubbio; Sardinian Costume Cavalcade, Sassari; Maggio Musicale, Florence. *June,* Tournament of the Bridge, Pisa; Festival of Two Worlds, Spoleto; Corpus Domini religious pageant, Orvieto.

July, the Palio, Siena (repeated in August); the Feast of the Redeemer, Venice; Giostra dell'Orso, medieval tourney, Pistoia. *August,* conclusion of the Palio, Siena; Tournament of the Quintana, Ascoli Piceno; International Film Festival, Venice; Feast of the Redeemer, Nuoro (Sardinia); nationwide celebrations of Ferragosto, August 15. *September,* The Joust of the Saracen, Arezzo; Historic Regatta, Venice; Joust of the Quintana, Foligno. *October,* celebrations in honor of Columbus, Genoa; Festival of Tyrolean brass bands, Merano. *November,* Feast of the Madonna della Salute, Venice. *December,* traditional Christmas celebrations throughout the country; opera season openings at Milan's La Scala and at other major opera houses (through April).

National Holidays. Jan. 1 (New Year's Day); Jan 6 (Epiphany); Mar. 31, Apr. 1 (Easter Sun. and Mon.); Apr. 25 (Liberation); May 1 (May Day); June 2 (Republic); Aug. 15 (Assumption); Nov. 1 (All Saints); Dec. 8 (Immaculate Conception); Dec. 25, 26.

VISAS. Not required by nationals of the United States, Canada, Australia, New Zealand, EC countries, and practically all other European countries. However, you must of course have a valid passport.

HEALTH CERTIFICATE. Not required for entry into Italy.

GETTING TO ITALY. By Plane. There are direct flights from New York, Boston, Chicago, Toronto, and Montreal to Milan and Rome, mainly by *Alitalia* but also by other airlines including *TWA, PanAm,* and *Canadian Airlines International.* From London, *Alitalia* and *British Airways* fly to Milan, Rome, Turin, Venice, Naples, Pisa (for Florence), Genoa, and Catania (Alitalia only).

In summer there are many charter flights from various British regional airports including Luton, Gatwick, Birmingham, Manchester, Glasgow, Edinburgh and Newcastle to a number of Italian airports—including all those mentioned plus Rimini, Bologna and Palermo.

By Train. The 10:20 A.M. leaves London (Victoria Station) and crosses to Basel via Dover and Calais. The "Italia Express" leaves Basel at 1:50 A.M.and passes through Milan (7A.M.), Bologna (9:06 A.M.), and Florence (10:27 A.M.), before reaching Rome at 12:58 P.M.

There are excellent rail services from neighboring countries, with no fewer than eight main crossing points. From Paris the best train is the EuroCity sleeper, the *Palatino,* which leaves the French capital nightly at 6.47 P.M. and arrives in Rome at 9.35 A.M. the next day. The train carries 2nd-class sleeping cars and 2nd-class bunk beds to all Italian destinations; buffet and refreshment services most of the way.

By Bus. There are express bus services from London (Victoria Coach Station) to various destinations in Italy—including Milan, Florence and Rome—operated by *Eurolines,* part of the National Express network. In summer three coaches a week travel to Rome, departing London in the evening of day one and reaching Rome mid-morning on day three. *Europabus* operate from Antwerp (and Brussels) to Milan, Bologna, Rimini and Cattolica. With one overnight stop the journey takes about 18 to 19 hours. There are also other bus services from Germany, France, Switzerland and Austria into Italy.

CUSTOMS. Travelers arriving from a country within the EC may bring into Italy 300 cigarettes or 75 cigars or 150 cigarillos or 400 grams of tobacco; plus 1.5 liters of spirits over 22° proof or 3 liters of light wine of less than 14° proof and 3 liters of wine or beverage of no more than 22° proof; plus 75 grams of perfume and 0.375 liters of toilet water; plus 750 grams of coffee or 300 grams of coffee extract, and 150 grams of tea or 60 grams of tea extract. You may also import other goods up to the value of 75,000 lire.

Travelers arriving from a European country outside of the EC may bring in 200 cigarettes or 50 cigars or 100 cigarillos or 250 grams of tobacco; plus 1 liter of spirits over 22° proof or 2 liters of any beverage of no more than 22° proof; plus 50 grams of perfume and 0.25 liters of toilet water; plus 500 grams of coffee or 200 grams of coffee extract, and 100 grams of tea or 40 grams of tea extract. Other goods may be brought into the country up to the value of 15,000 lire.

Travelers from outside Europe may bring in 400 cigarettes or 100 cigars or 200 cigarillos or 500 grams of tobacco; plus 1 liter of spirits of more than 22° proof or 2 liters of any beverage under 22° proof; plus 50 grams of perfume and 0.25 liters of toilet water; plus 500 grams of coffee or 200 grams of coffee extract, and 100 grams of tea or 40 grams of tea extract. In addition, other goods up to a value of 15,000 lire.

HOTELS. Budget hotels are generally good in Italy, and there are plenty of them in the main tourist cities. They give fair value for your money, sometimes much more in terms of friendly interest and helpfulness. Officially, hotels are classified as deluxe or 5-star, 1st or 4-star, down to 1-star, which includes small, basic pensions and guest houses. Official ratings are not necessarily indicative of the quality of the establishment but provide guidelines for their prices.

Our Moderate (M) range includes selected 3- and 2-star hotels, while Inexpensive (I) accommodations include less expensive 2-star establishments as well as 1-star pensions and religious institutes. A very nice place may charge as little (or as much) as an inferior one. Our selections take into account location, rates and abundance of bathrooms, either private or shared.

Third-class hotels and some 2nd-class pensions approximate to our Moderate (M) range; while Inexpensive (I) accommodations include inns, pensions and religious institutes. In a Moderate hotel you'll pay from 85,000–125,000 lire for two people in a double room with bath, from 10,000–15,000 less without bath. An Inexpensive room costs about 70,000 for two people in a double without bath, about 50,000 for two in a religious institute. Moderate hotels usually offer simply furnished rooms and few frills, but you'll probably find decent public rooms and a private bath if you desire. Inexpensive hotels tend to be very basic if not downright spartan, and you'll have to share the bath. Most hotels quote breakfast charges in inclusive room rate, thus adding 8,000–12,000 lire per person to your bill, which you can save by having a stand-up breakfast of *cappuccino* and *brioches* at a nearby café. If you choose to do so, make it clear when checking in that you do not want breakfast at the hotel. Hotels listed as Garni have no restaurant. The official approved room rate is always posted inside the door of your room; never pay more, except for optionals such as airconditioning.

Budget Accommodations. Religious institutes provide about the cheapest accommodations, sometimes dormitory-style, usually posting a curfew. If you're eligible for a youth hostel or student digs you'll pay even less. There are about 155 hostels in Italy, some in such beautiful settings as medieval castles; rates are about 15,000 lire per person per night. Headquarters in Italy is the *Associazione Italiana Alberghi per la Gioventù,* Piazza Civiltà del Lavoro, Quadrato della Concordia, 00144 Rome, a member of the International Youth Hostels Federation. Students should obtain the "Guide for Foreign Students" from the Ministry of Education, Viale Trastevere, Rome. It gives detailed information on student hotels and other facilities.

Camping. Camp sites are plentiful, many beautifully situated in wooded areas near the large cities or near lakes, mountains and the seashore. Rates for two persons with tent are about 20,000 a day. Information and the official guidebook can be obtained from the Federazione Italiana del Campeggio, Casella Postale 649, 50100 Florence. Camping grounds in seashore and other resort areas are jammed with Italian vacationers during July and August.

Self-Catering. ENIT, local EPT offices and your travel agent can furnish information on self-catering apartments or cottages, ideal for families and for long stays. For information on a country holiday in accommodations with a farm family, write to *Agriturist,* Corso Vittorio Emanuele 101, Rome, or to the AAST in the locality that interests you.

Vacation villages feature attractive off-season rates; ask your travel agent about Club Med., Valtur and Forte Village packages.

RESTAURANTS. Eating in restaurants is becoming more expensive than in the past, though it's still possible to get a good meal at a reasonable price. Always check the menu that's on display in the window to get an idea of what your meal will cost. In all but the simplest places there's always a cover charge (*pane e coperto*) and usually a service charge (*servizio*); these will increase your bill by 15–20%. Many restaurants in tourist cities feature a *menu turistico,* a fixed-price, limited choice menu, usually good value, though quality varies. A *ristorante* can be anything from deluxe to just another *trattoria,* which is generally a simple, family-run place where the emphasis is on food rather than service.

A full meal (first and second courses, salad or vegetable and fruit) in a Moderate (M) restaurant costs 35,000–40,000 lire per person with house wine; in an Inexpensive (I) restaurant you'll pay from 20,000–27,000, but you can save on this by eliminating one of the courses and the fruit. Carafe wine is much cheaper than bottled wine. Order tap water (*aqua semplice*) instead of mineral water to keep your check down. At a *rosticceria* or *tavola calda* you can get snacks or meals at the counter; some items are priced by the portion, others by weight.

If you're really pinching pennies go into a food store and ask for a *panino* (roll) *con salame* (with salami), *prosciutto cotto* (boiled ham), or *formaggio* (cheese), and the man behind the counter will whip up a sandwich to take out. Pick up some of your favorite beverage, and have a picnic. If you like pizza, there are countless ready-to-go pizza places.

TIPPING. Charges for service are included in most hotel bills and restaurant checks. In restaurants in large cities and resorts it's customary to leave a few hundred lire for the waiter; inexpensive restaurants often don't make a service charge, so you may want to increase your tip accordingly. Budgeteers aren't expected to be big tippers, but you could leave a few hundred lire a day for the chambermaid in your hotel, say 4,000 per week for a double room. Give 1,000 to the bellboy. At a café, tip 100 lire for a stand-up drink, 300–500 at a table. Checkroom attendants expect about 500 lire, washroom attendants 200–300 lire; taxi drivers 5–10% for short rides, a little less for long ones. Railway porters charge a fixed fee per bag. Tour guides expect about 2,000 lire per person, more on all-day tours.

Tipping practices vary depending on where you are. Our guidelines apply to major cities. In smaller cities and towns, Italians tip less. Tips may not be expected at all for many services in northern Italy.

MAIL. Postal rates are subject to increases; check with the tobacconist or postal clerk who sells you stamps, or with your hotel concierge.

CLOSING TIMES. In Rome and southern Italy shops are usually open from 9 to 1, closed from 1 to 3.30, and then open again until 7.30 or 8. In the northern cities this siesta is either not observed or considerably abbreviated. Some shop hours in Rome have become much more elastic to accommodate both tourists and residents, and in any event there are bound to be individual variations. Banking hours are from 8.30 to 1.30 or 2, and from 3 to 4 in the afternoon, closed Saturday. Exchange *(cambio)* offices, however, have store hours. Museum hours vary greatly, and it's best to check locally. All are open at least in the morning; some close Monday. Vatican Museums close Sundays and religious holidays. Rome shops close Saturday afternoons from June through Sept., Monday mornings in other months. Churches keep their own mysterious hours, usually close for two or three hours at noon.

GETTING AROUND ITALY. By Plane. National lines are *Alitalia, ATI* and *AerMed,* which are affiliates, and *Aliblu,* among others. Bookings for all domestic flights can be made at any travel agency; inquire about special discounts offered on flights in non-peak hours and on weekends. Airport buses provide fast and cheap transportation between airports and town terminals.

By Train. The state-owned *Ferrovie dello Stato* (FS) runs trains having first- and second-class cars and some deluxe class EC (Eurocity) trains. The fastest long- and medium-distance trains are *Intercity* (IC), which charge a supplement; many require seat reservations. Other types of train are: *espresso,* fast long-distance expresses; *diretto,* medium-fast, making more stops than an *espresso;* and *locale,* the slowest. Second-class travel is comfortable except during peak travel periods around holidays and during the August *Ferragosto* period, when it's impossible. Most long-distance trains have at least buffet-car service, but it's a good idea to take along some food and drink (no potable water on tap on trains). We strongly advise reserving seats for all trips, either at stations or travel agencies.

For the independent traveler anxious to see a lot, we recommend the *Travel at Will* ticket, which gives you unlimited travel on all FS trains including Rapidos (with first-class tickets) without additional charge. It's also valid on FS ferries to Sicily. Issued for 8, 15, 21, and 30 days, second-class tickets cost approximately £65, £79, £92 and £112 respectively, though these will almost certainly have increased by summer 1991. Children under 12 travel half-fare. This type of ticket should be purchased *before* entering Italy. In the U.K. they can be purchased from C.I.T., 50 Conduit Street, London W.1. (tel. 071–434 3844). Another good buy is the *kilometrico* ticket on sale at railway ticket offices and travel agencies; it's valid for 3,000 kms. for 30 days. For travelers outside Europe the Eurailpass is better value for money. Students should buy an Inter Rail card.

By Bus. There is a good network of bus services operated by CIAT, part of the *Europabus* consortium. Local EPT offices can tell you about bus excursions and special-interest tours in the vicinity of the main tourist cities.

By Bicycle. Your hotel or the local tourist office can tell you where to rent a bicycle. In Rome and Florence you'll find several bike-rental agencies. Some also rent mopeds and provide the mandatory helmet.

Rome

Like its very beginnings with Romulus and Remus, Rome is a fascinating combination of legend and reality. Each of its great sights has a story connected with it, for in everything the Romans do—talking, eating, living and loving—they love to embellish reality, embroidering on it, making it bigger than life.

Thus an ancient sewer cover becomes La Bocca della Verità, and will punish liars; a coin tossed into the Trevi Fountain will ensure your return to Rome; and every year on the Ides of March a mysterious hand will lay some flowers at the feet of Caesar's statue at the Forum. Relax and enjoy this refreshing atmosphere of make-believe.

Beset by political and administrative problems, Rome can still treat tourists well, mainly by offering its magnificent sights to all comers. You'll want to see the Colos-

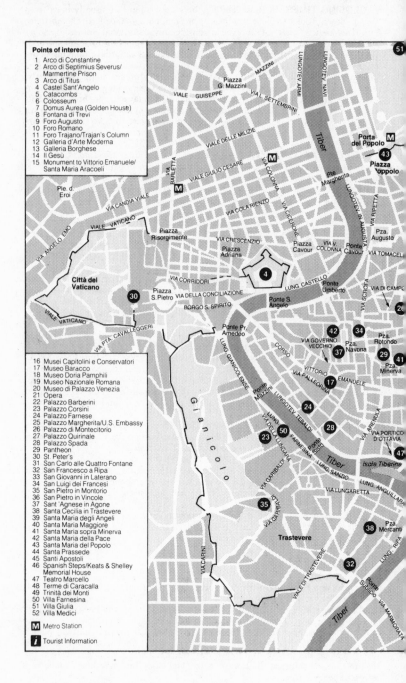

Points of interest

1 Arco di Constantine
2 Arco di Septimius Severus/
  Marmertine Prison
3 Arco di Titus
4 Castel Sant'Angelo
5 Catacombs
6 Colosseum
7 Domus Aurea (Golden House)
8 Fontana di Trevi
9 Foro Augusto
10 Foro Romano
11 Foro Trajano/Trajan's Column
12 Galleria d'Arte Moderna
13 Galleria Borghese
14 Il Gesù
15 Monument to Vittorio Emanuele/
   Santa Maria Aracoeli

16 Musei Capitolini e Conservatori
17 Museo Baracco
18 Museo Doria Pamphili
19 Museo Nazionale Romana
20 Museo di Palazzo Venezia
21 Opera
22 Palazzo Barberini
23 Palazzo Corsini
24 Palazzo Farnese
25 Palazzo Margherita/U.S. Embassy
26 Palazzo di Montecitorio
27 Palazzo Quirinale
28 Palazzo Spada
29 Pantheon
30 St. Peter's
31 San Carlo alle Quattro Fontane
32 San Francesco a Ripa
33 San Giovanni in Laterano
34 San Luigi dei Francesi
35 San Pietro in Montorio
36 San Pietro in Vincole
37 Sant 'Agnese in Agone
38 Santa Cecilia in Trastevere
39 Santa Maria degli Angeli
40 Santa Maria Maggiore
41 Santa Maria sopra Minerva
42 Santa Maria della Pace
43 Santa Maria del Popolo
44 Santa Prassede
45 Santi Apostoli
46 Spanish Steps/Keats & Shelley
   Memorial House
47 Teatro Marcello
48 Terme di Caracalla
49 Trinità dei Monti
50 Villa Farnesina
51 Villa Giulia
52 Villa Medici

M Metro Station

i Tourist Information

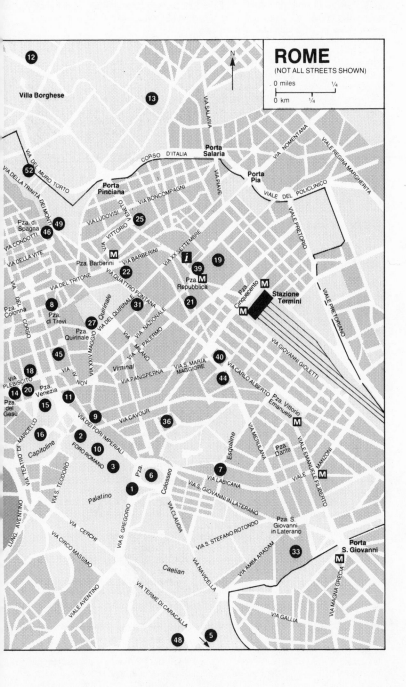

ROME
(NOT ALL STREETS SHOWN)

0 miles   ¼

0 km   ¼

seum and the Forum, of course, then the Pantheon and the Baths of Caracalla, along with Trajan's Column and other monuments (some covered for restoration, as are many historic buildings and fountains).

The earliest relics of the Christian era are the catacombs along the cypress-lined Via Appia and the oldest of the 450 or so churches in Rome. By far the most famous of these is St. Peter's, in which religious ideals and artistic genius combined to create one of the world's greatest buildings, but you should also visit Santa Maria Maggiore and San Giovanni in Laterano, both impressive.

During the Renaissance and Baroque ages Rome's churches and palaces were decorated by the masters of the time; Michelangelo, Raphael, Bramante, Donatello and Bernini are the best known authors of the city's artistic splendors. Although many of their works are in the city's museums, especially the Vatican Museum, Sistine Chapel, Borghese Gallery and National Gallery at Palazzo Barberini, you'll find many others under the brilliant Roman sky—in the piazzas, parks and palaces that these artists designed and that are still a functional part of the urban structure. Take a good look at Piazza San Pietro, a vast auditorium; Piazza Navona and Piazza di Spagna, Baroque stage sets; and Piazza del Campidoglio, worthy site of the government that once ruled an empire.

Modern Rome is a sprawling city that extends way beyond the original Seven Hills, but its heart remains in the historic center of town and in the vibrant Latin spirit of its inhabitants.

Exploring Rome

Since walking is the cheapest and most satisfying way to see Rome, you can organize your sightseeing in several itineraries that will take in the highlights while giving you glimpses of the Rome that bus tours never touch.

You might as well begin in the Piazza Venezia. You can't avoid the huge white Victor Emmanuel Monument, known to the Italians as the "Altare della Patria" (the Country's Altar), also nicknamed "The Wedding Cake." The unknown soldier is buried here, and all official ceremonies take place in this square. Behind, Michelangelo's stairs lead you to the Campidoglio, Rome's City Hall.

Part of a trio of fine buildings here, the Capitoline Museums offer another perspective on Roman history, with their collections of classical sculptures and important Renaissance paintings. Behind the Campidoglio lie Rome's greatest archeological treasures—the ruins of the Imperial Fora and the Roman Forum.

Highly recommended from here is the half-mile walk down the Via dei Fori Imperiali to the most stupendous monument of ancient Rome—the Colosseum. Originally known as the Flavian Amphitheater, this colossal structure was built in A.D. 72. It was the chief circus of the Roman Empire, scene of gladiatorial battles, the martyrdom of Christians and other cruel glories of the capital. Used as a fortress in the 12th century and as a quarry for Renaissance building material, it was finally saved by the popes, who declared it a sacred relic because of the countless Christians who lost their lives inside it. See it at dawn, at sunset, and at night with the spotlights illuminating the old stone. And walk to the top for an impression of the real size of this stadium, which used to seat 50,000 persons.

Outside the Colosseum, you will pass near the Arch of Constantine on your way to the Baths of Caracalla, the grandest of Rome's ruined public baths.

Once you've seen these imposing monuments of ancient Rome, you can choose among several other itineraries. The first might start at Piazza del Popolo, just below the panoramic terraces of the Pincio, Rome's original public gardens. Head for Piazza di Spagna, with its lovely Bernini fountain and famous Spanish Steps, which ascend past Babington's Tea Room and the house in which Keats died, to the Church of Trinità dei Monti. Then windowshop your way past the elegant emporia of Via Condotti and head down Via del Corso, for Piazza Colonna and Trevi Fountain, where a coin tossed into the huge basin guarantees your return to toss another one. Then turn off the Corso toward the Tiber, into Renaissance Rome, the part of the city that the popes built. You'll see the Pantheon, a pagan temple rebuilt by Hadrian and the best-preserved monument of Imperial Rome; Piazza Navona, much as it was in the 17th century, with Bernini's great Fountain of the Rivers; and many other interesting palaces, churches, marketplaces and shops.

Another walk starts at bustling Piazza Barberini, with its Fountain of the Triton, designed by Bernini in 1640, and takes you up Via Veneto, past the macabre crypt of the Capuchin Church (Santa Maria della Concezione), elaborately decorated with skeletons and assorted bones. At Porta Pinciana you enter Villa Borghese, a lovely park, where you stroll to the right to the Casina Borghese, a charming small-ish museum containing such treasures as Canova's reclining nude statue of Pauline Borghese, Napoleon's sister, and some breathtaking Bernini sculptures. The fine paintings by Titian, Raphael and Caravaggio in the upstairs art gallery won't be visible until structural restorations are completed. You might then head for the handsome 16th-century Villa Giulia, where there's a world-famous collection of Etruscan art.

As an alternative to city sightseeing on a good day, pack a picnic lunch and take a bus out to the Via Appia Antica to see the catacombs, the ruins of the Circus of Maxentius, the Tomb of Cecilia Metella and the hauntingly evocative scenery along this "Queen of Roads."

Back in town, you should visit the beautiful basilicas of Santa Maria Maggiore, resplendent with gilt mosaics and woodwork, and San Giovanni in Laterano, the cathedral of Rome. Try to fit in visits to the Church of San Pietro in Vincoli to see Michelangelo's *Moses,* to the Church of Santa Maria della Vittoria to see Berni-ni's St. Theresa, and to the spectacular Piazza del Quirinale.

Explore the colorful quarter of Trastevere, where true Romans and foreign bohe-mians mix in the pretty piazza of Santa Maria in Trastevere. Nearby, on Via della Lungara, you can see Raphael's fresco decorations at the Villa Farnesina, more paintings at the National Gallery at Palazzo Corsini and the Botanical Garden, nearby.

The National Gallery houses well-known works by Raphael, Holbein, and many others. The important Museo delle Terme, housed in what were once the Baths of Diocletian, opened a new section in 1990 in Palazzo Massimo, across the avenue, to accommodate part of its impressive collection of ancient Roman and Greek works.

And on your way to the Vatican, stop off at Castel Sant'Angelo—part museum, part fortress—built as his tomb by the Emperor Hadrian in A.D. 135 and used by the popes as a refuge from hostile invasions.

Vatican City

Since the Lateran Treaty of 1929 between the Holy See and the Mussolini Gov-ernment, the Vatican City has been an independent and sovereign state. When you step into the great square before St. Peter's, you are on Vatican territory. You can enter the basilica, the Borgia apartments, the Sistine Chapel, and the museums, but not if wearing shorts. Apply to the information office for Vatican garden tours and directions to the Prefettura Vaticana for audience tickets, which you can also obtain free through Santa Susanna church or the North American College office at Via dell'Umiltà 30.

San Pietro in Vaticano—better known as St. Peter's (it is not a cathedral)—is the largest church in the world and a fitting climax to Rome, no matter what your religion. The enormous Piazza San Pietro, which took Bernini 10 years to build, has held as many as 400,000 people within the confines of its quadruple colonnade. It is one of the world's most beautiful squares. The church had its beginnings about 326, when the Emperor Constantine built a basilica here over the tomb of St. Peter, but it was not until 1626 that St. Peter's stood as we know it today—a masterpiece of Renaissance architecture and art. Bramante, Raphael, Michelangelo, Peruzzi and Antonio Sangallo were all busy beautifying this church at the time of their deaths. Note the mosaic by Giotto in the portico; Michelangelo's *Pietà* in the first chapel; the reliquary of St. Peter's Chair by Bernini and the Confessional Altar. Visit the Treasury and ascend to the roof: the climb on foot to the lantern, 308 feet above, is very taxing. Save the Vatican Crypt for last, as the exit takes you outdoors again.

PRACTICAL INFORMATION FOR ROME

HOTELS. Well-equipped budget hotels abound in Rome, but it's always advis-able to book ahead. The EPT tourist office operates information desks at Termini railway station, Fiumicino airport and at the autostrada exit. They will help you find accommodation. Rock-bottom rates are offered by religious institutes and by the Youth Hostel. Camping grounds handiest to the city are *Flaminio,* Via Flaminia Nuova (tel. 3279006), and *Nomentano,* Via Nomentana (tel. 6100296); both are between 8 and 12 km. from the city and all have bus connections. *Capitol,* Via Castelfusano 45 (tel. 5650621), is near the beach at Ostia, connected to Rome by Metro.

Moderate

Astoria Garden, Via Bachelet 8 (tel. 4940409). Garni. Near station, small and quiet, all doubles with bath or shower; nice garden for relaxing.

Aventino, Via San Domenico 10 (tel. 5755231). Garni. In the quiet Aventine district, near public transport. Smallish villa hotel, reasonable and comfortable.

Campo de' Fiori, Via Biscione 6 (tel. 6540865). in Old Rome, near Piazza Navona. 27 rooms, half with bath or shower, some of them tiny but all attractively decorated.

Dinesen, Via Porta Pinciana 18 (tel. 460932). Garni. Fine location just off Via Veneto, overlooking Borghese gardens; immaculate Nordic air. Old-fashioned furnishings with lots of chintz and oriental rugs in the lounges, bedrooms being starker.

Domus Maximi, Via Santa Prisca 11B (tel. 5778565). In Aventine district, quiet, basic, with pretty garden. A long walk to public transport.

Homs, Via della Vite 71 (tel. 6792976). Located in the shopping district, handy to most sights and to transport. Clean, simply furnished rooms and a pleasant roof terrace.

Ivanhoe, Via dei Ciancaleoni (tel. 486813). Tucked away in one of Rome's most interesting old districts near the Forum. Modern though basic comforts and plenty of atmosphere.

Margutta, Via Laurina 34 (tel. 6798440). Near Spanish Steps; bright and cheerful, and all rooms have a shower.

Portoghesi, Via dei Portoghesi (tel. 6564231). Garni. Near Piazza di Spagna, this small, historic hotel is reliable.

Santa Prisca, Largo Gelsomini 25 (tel. 571917). 45 rooms, all with shower. In Aventine district; pleasant garden.

Suisse, Via Gregoriana 56 (tel. 6783649). Garni. Near Spanish Steps; well-kept pension in good location.

Villa San Pio, Via Sant'Anselmo 19 (tel. 5781325). 60 rooms with bath. Garni. In quiet Aventine district, an attractive old villa with pleasant lounges and garden. Rates vary, some rooms are in more expensive range.

Inexpensive

Ausonia, Piazza di Spagna 35 (tel. 6795745). Near Spanish Steps; intimate, cordial atmosphere.

Brotzky, Via del Corso 509 (tel. 3612339). Very central, 13-room hotel, handy for shops and sights.

Smeraldo, Via dei Chiodaroli 11 (tel. 6875929). In Old Rome, near Pantheon. Functional furnishings and good room-to-bath ratio.

Erdarelli, Via Due Macelli 28 (tel. 6791265). Near Piazza di Spagna, basic, cheerful rooms, friendly staff.

Fiorella, Via Babuino 196 (tel. 3610597). Near Spanish Steps. Small, student-type pension.

Lancelot, Via Capo d'Africa 47 (tel. 735266). Near Colosseum; clean, spacious and reasonable rooms.

Marcus, Via Clementino 94 (tel. 6873679). Near Spanish Steps and shopping district. Small, basic hotel popular with American students for clean accommodations and friendly staff. All doubles with shower.

Ostello (Hostel), Via delle Olimpiadi at Foro Italico (tel. 3964709). 350 beds, AIG or IYHF cards only. For booking, write to AIG, Via Carlo Poma 2, 00195, Rome.

Seven Hills, Via Firenze 47 (tel. 4742107). Garni. Central, smallish pension.

Della Lunetta, Piazza del Paradiso 68 (tel. 6861080). Near Campo de Fiori Piazza Navona, handy to everything. Comfortable rooms, good value.

Tefi, Via San Basilio 53 (tel. 461283). Near Piazza Barberini; small, friendly and well-run, and nicely furnished. Good value.

Trinità dei Monti, Via Sistina 91 (tel. 6797206). Garni. Well-located for shopping, sightseeing; plenty of baths and showers.

RESTAURANTS. Romans love to eat out, and their city has everything from deluxe restaurants to earthy trattorias. Even on the budget level, food and service can be a pleasant surprise, for Roman hosts take great pride. Remember to check the menu on display at the entrance in order to get an idea of what your meal will cost. Usually, the cheaper the trattoria the bigger the portions of pasta it serves; this means that with the addition of a salad or vegetable and a carafe of wine you can put together a very satisfying meal inexpensively.

As the pace of Roman life quickens, more fast-food places are opening, offering a wider choice of light meals and snacks. You'll find well-stocked snack counters in many bars, too. In good weather it's pleasant to pick up simple provisions along the way and picnic discreetly among the ruins of the Colosseum, Forum and Palatine or more freely along the Via Appia Antica or in Villa Borghese. In Roman *osterias,* neighborhood wineshops, no one minds if you bring along your lunch; some can provide a simple sandwich to go with your carafe of Frascati.

Moderate

Abruzzi, Via del Vaccaro 1 (tel. 6793897). Closed Sat. Near Piazza Venezia, a classic trattoria serving hearty pastas.

Archimede, Piazza dei Caprettari 63 (tel. 6875216). Closed Sunday. Near the Pantheon. Classic Roman restaurant. Try *carciofi* (artichokes) or fried *zucchine* flowers.

Barroccio, Via dei Pastini 13 (tel. 6793797). Closed Monday. Near the Pantheon. This is the quieter part of a double-barrelled enterprise that includes the *Fagiolaro,* across the street, which serves pizzas and beans.

Buca di Ripetta, Via Ripetta 36 (tel. 6789578). A few steps from Piazza del Popolo, a tiny, popular place. Get there early to find a table.

Campana, Vicolo della Campana 18 (tel. 655273). Closed Monday. From Via Condotti, straight on toward the Tiber; a no-frills Roman trattoria.

Colline Emiliane, Via degli Avignonesi 22 (tel. 4757538). Closed Friday. Just off the Piazza Barberini, a haven of home-made pastas and Bolognese cuisine.

Fiammetta, Piazza Fiammetta, off Via Zanardelli (tel. 655777). Near Piazza Navona, a Tuscan trattoria serving pizza.

Ai Fori, Largo Corrado Ricci 2 (tel. 6786133). Closed Tuesday. Close to the Roman Forum, this popular place offers pizzas or a full menu at reasonable prices.

Gioia Mia, Via Avignonesi 34 (tel. 462884). Near Piazza Barberini, a trattoria popular with Romans and tourists alike.

Hostaria del Belli, Piazza Sant'Apollonia 9 (tel. 5803782). Closed Monday. In Trastevere, this is a friendly place with good food and outdoor tables.

Luigi, Piazza Sforza Cesarini. Closed Monday. Short walk from Piazza Navona. Good trattoria, outdoors in summer.

Le Maschere, Via Monte della Farina 29 (tel. 6879444). Closed Tuesday. Behind Teatro Argentina. Evenings only. Piquant Calabrian specialties and pizza in downstairs locale.

Orso 80, Via dell'Orso 33 (tel. 6564904). Closed Monday. In Old Rome fairly near Piazza Navona; cheerful, and ample antipastos.

Otello alla Concordia, Via della Croce 81 (tel. 6791178). Closed Sunday. In the shopping district, it's a favorite with tourists for a pleasant respite; shady summer courtyard.

Polese, Piazza Sforza Cesarini (tel. 6861709). Closed Tuesday. Off Corso Vittorio, near Piazza Navona. Straightforward cuisine.

La Rampa, Piazza Mignanelli (tel. 6782621). Closed Sunday. Near Piazza di Spagna, behind American Express, rustic atmosphere, vast menu.

Tavernetta, Via del Nazzareno 3 (tel. 6793124). Closed Monday. Located between Spanish Steps and Trevi Fountain. Tasty specialties and good value tourist menu.

Inexpensive

Baffetto, Via del Governo Vecchio 114 (tel. 6861617). Near Piazza Navona. Very popular for tasty and inexpensive pizzas. Evenings only.

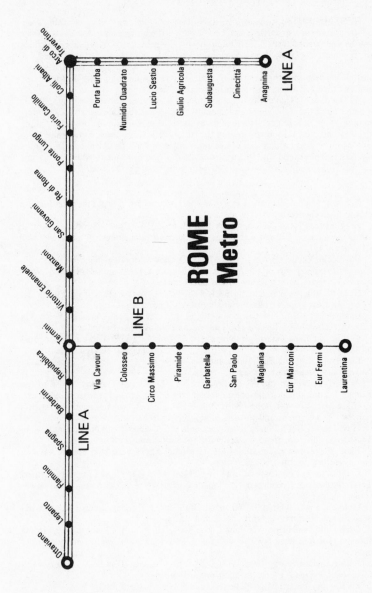

Birreria Dreher, Piazza Santi Apostoli, near Piazza Venezia. Lively beer-house.

Birreria Tempera, Via San Marcello 9, (tel. 6786203). Closed Sun. Convivial beer hall serving light lunch or supper.

La Casareccia, Borgo Pio (tel. 6861016). Closed Thursday. Near St. Peter's. No-frills trattoria serving pizza, too.

Da Catena ai Due Scalini, Via Morgagni (tel. 363819). Closed Sunday. Near the university, a typical Roman trattoria, good for pizza.

Delfino, Corso Vittorio at Largo Argentina. One of Rome's most famous *rosticcerie.*

Da Enzo, Vicolo dello Scavolino 72 (tel. 6790974). Closed Sunday. Near Trevi Fountain; rock-bottom prices, hearty food.

Hostaria Farnese, Via Baullari 109 (tel. 6541595). Closed Tuesday. Near Piazza Navona. Tiny, busy, homey.

Italy & Italy, Via Barberini 16. Italian-style fast food.

Matricianella, Via del Leone 4 (tel. 6783870). Closed Sunday. Simple trattoria off Via del Corso. Ample portions.

Mozzicone, Borgo Pio, near St. Peter's. Good lunch stop.

Nazzareno, Via Magenta 35 (tel. 4957782). Closed Wednesday. In the railway station area; large, attractive restaurant.

Primavera, Via Gracchi 90 (tel. 351113). Closed Sunday. Near the Vatican, a straightforward Roman eating place.

Al Picchio, Via del Lavoratore 40, near Piazza Venezia. Pizza and snacks.

Pizzeria Moroni, Viale Trastevere 50. Cheap and popular, with outdoor tables.

Risorgimento, Piazza Risorgimento 8 (tel. 317345). Closed Mon. Near St. Peter's; boasting "the best pasta in the world."

La Sagrestia, Via del Seminario 89 (tel. 6797581). Near the Pantheon, good atmosphere and pizzas.

Tulipano Nero, Via Roma Libera 15, Piazza San Cosimato (tel. 5818309). Closed Wednesday. In Trastevere, attracts a young crowd for pastas, pizzas and salads.

Da Umberto, Piazza San Giovanni della Malva (tel. 5816646). Closed Wednesday. In Trastevere, behind Piazza Trilussa. A *simpatico* trattoria.

GETTING AROUND ROME. By Metro. Line A of the *Metropolitana* is the newer and is the one that will take you to most of the sights. It runs in two directions from Termini Station, one toward San Giovanni in Laterano and beyond, another westward with stops at Piazza di Spagna and Piazzale Flaminio (Piazza del Popolo), ending at Via Ottaviano, near the Vatican Museums and St. Peter's. The original line, Line B, runs from Termini, with stops at Via Cavour, Colosseum, Circus Maximus, Pyramid and San Paolo (St. Paul's outside the walls) to the new EUR district. At Ostiense station you can catch a train to Ostia Antica. On lines A and B fares are 700 lire; tickets at change booths at main stations, or above ground at tobacconists or newsstands. *B.I.G.* ticket is a good buy, valid for one day on all metro and bus routes. Book of ten tickets sold at discount. The metro closes from 11.30 P.M. to 5.30 A.M.

By Bus. Rome has an extensive bus network, running from about 6 A.M. to 12 P.M., with skeleton (*notturno*) services on main lines during the night. Fares are 700 lire. On most routes you must buy your tickets beforehand at a machine or at newsstands or tobacconists. At the ATAC (Surface Transport Agency) booths in front of Termini Station, at St. Peter's and main piazzas, buy weekly tourist tickets or discount books of ten, as well as the official route map (also available from newsstands). For 1,000 lire you can buy a *biglietto orario,* good for unlimited travel from 6 A.M. to 2 P.M. or 2 P.M. to midnight. You can also book for the three-hour ATAC sightseeing tour of the city, which costs much less than those run by private agencies. There's no running commentary, but you're given a printed guide with which you can easily identify the sights.

By Bicycle. Rome's traffic will probably discourage cyclists more than its seven hills; rental bicycles are available at shops in Via del Pellegrino 82, near Campo dei Fiori, at Piazza Navona 69, next to Bar Navona, and at stands in Piazza del Popolo, Largo Argentina, Piazza di Spagna (next to Metro station) and Villa Borghese. Mopeds, on the other hand, are a great way to get around. Try *Scoot-a-Long,*

Via Cavour 302, or *Scooters For Rent,* Via della Purificazione 66, near Piazza Barberini.

On Foot. Undoubtedly the best way to see Rome, walking has a few disadvantages. Don't be lulled into a false sense of security in the so-called pedestrian islands; watch out for delivery vans, buses, taxis and police cars. Wear comfortable, low-heeled shoes to cushion your impact with the cobblestones, and keep an eye on your belongings.

ENTERTAINMENT. Much of what you see and do during a visit to Rome constitutes impromptu entertainment. For the price of a cup of coffee you can sit at a sidewalk café on one of Rome's beautiful piazzas and watch the world go by. Get off the beaten track and stroll down sidestreets and into out-of-the-way piazzas, looking for the entertaining minutiae of daily life in Rome. Except during the coldest months of January and February, you'll find free art shows, handicraft fairs and band concerts held outdoors. From June through September the pace quickens with city-sponsored street fairs, games, festivals, and dancing under the stars. The traditional festivals of San Giovanni (June) and the Christmas-Epiphany fair at Piazza Navona are always fun and don't cost a lira. Free concerts are held frequently in Rome's churches. All events are announced in the posters you'll see throughout the city (church concerts posted outside churches). The daily papers carry the main events, but there are usually lots more if you can find them.

Café-sitting is a fine art in Rome, and though you pay more if you sit down, it's worth it to watch the action from the tables of *Tre Scalini* at Piazza Navona, *Doney* or the *Café de Paris* on Via Veneto, *Rosati* on Piazza del Popolo, the cafés on Piazza della Rotonda in front of the Pantheon, or any other that strikes your fancy. For the best ice cream in Rome, go to Giolitti, Via Uffici del Vicario, near the Pantheon.

Cinema. The English-language cinema in Rome is the *Pasquino,* Vicolo del Piede (tel. 5803622), just off Piazza Santa Maria in Trastevere. Film clubs sometimes present films in the original English version.

Discos. While Rome has never been a great city for nightlife, the disco scene is lively. Clubs are open until about 3 A.M.; most close in August. Prices at such as *Bella Blu, Jackie O'* and *Cabala* are out of budget range. Others cost about 20,000–25,000 lire.

Hysteria, Via Giovannelli 3 (tel. 864587). Upwardly-mobile crowd and the latest disco music.

Piper 80, Via Tagliamento 9 (tel. 854459), in Salario district. Vast, frenetic and very popular, with lots of special events, live concerts.

Scarabocchio, Piazza dei Ponziani 8 (tel. 5800495). In Trastevere. A reliable, longtime favorite, high on decibels and big on videos.

Uonna, Via Cassia 871 (at Tomba di Nerone, on outskirts). Hard rock and new wave attract a punk crowd.

Veleno, Via Sardegna 27 (tel. 493583). Sport and show biz celebs and the under-30 crowd like the funky music here.

Vicolo delle Stelle, Via Beccaria 22 (tel. 3611240). Features soul, funk, and rap.

Jazz and Folk Clubs. Alexanderplatz, Via Ostia 9 (tel. 3599398). Near the Vatican. Talented Italian jazzmen play nightly (except Sun.).

Big Mama, Vicolo San Francesco a Ripa 18 (tel. 582551). In Trastevere. A *simpatico* place for good jazz.

Music Inn, Largo dei Fiorentini 3 (tel. 6544934). A Roman institution, where visiting jazzmen often drop in.

St. Louis Music City, Via Cardello 13a (tel. 4745076), just off the Via Cavour. A favorite for great contemporary jazz.

Concerts. Rome has a number of concert series, most by subscription; tickets for single performances are hard to come by, but your concierge may be able to help out. Prices range from about 7,000 up to 20,000 for the better seats. Student or youth ID cards get you a discount.

Accademia di Santa Cecilia, Via dei Greci (tel. 6541044). Prestigious concert series; tickets rarely available.

Accademia Filarmonica, Teatro Olimpico, Piazza Gentile da Fabriano 17 (tel. 3962635). An innovative concert program; excellent visiting ballet companies.

Associazione Musicale Romana (tel. 6568441). Organizes music festivals and concerts in churches throughout the year.

' **Gonfalone,** Via del Gonfalone 32 (tel. 68759527). The best of Baroque music.

Instituzione Universitaria dei Concerti, San Leone Magno auditorium, Via Bolzano 38 (tel. 853216). Subscribers have the monopoly on this fine series finely balanced between classical and contemporary music.

Opera, Teatro dell'Opera, Via del Viminale (tel. 67595725 for information in English; tel. 67595721 to book tickets in English). Season November–May. Tickets go on sale two days before performance; box office open from 10–1 and 5–7 P.M. Prices range from 8,000 to 44,000 lire, more for first nights. The summer season (July–early August) is held at the Baths of Caracalla (take a warm wrap). Tickets at Teatro dell'Opera or at Caracalla box office from 8–9 P.M. on performance nights.

MUSEUMS. Part of Rome's enormous artistic heritage is preserved in its monuments and museums. Such places of interest as the Colosseum and the Forum are generally open from 9 until one hour before sunset but close early some days; the Pantheon opens 9–2; Castel Sant'Angelo 9–2. A few major museums open 9–7, others 9–2. Early closing is on Sunday. Also, most museums and some monuments close Monday, but some close Tuesday. It's essential to check current hours with Rome EPT office or your hotel concierge. A free student or tourist group pass can be obtained from the Ministero dei Beni Culturali, Piazza del Popolo 18, tel. 6797787, and must be requested by school headmaster or tour organizer.

Galleria Borghese, Via Pinciana, Villa Borghese. Canova's famous statue of Pauline Borghese, and lots of Bernini sculptures. Major renovation work proceeds slowly, so upstairs picture gallery is still closed. During work, entrance from Via Raimondi.

Galleria Colonna, Via della Pilotta 17. A private collection of masterpieces displayed in sumptuous salons. Sat. only.

Galleria Doria Pamphili, Piazza del Collegio Romano 1A. Another extraordinary private collection in a princely residence. Tue., Fri., Sat., Sun. only.

Galleria Nazionale dell'Arte Antica, Palazzo Barberini, Via Quattro Fontane 13. In a beautiful Baroque palace, a rich collection of 13th- to 16th-century paintings, including Raphael's *Fornarina.* Additional sections of the collection are at Palazzo Corsini, Via della Lungara 10.

Galleria Nazionale di Arte Moderna, Viale delle Belle Arti 131. A vast and important collection of modern art, with some sections newly opened.

Keats-Shelley Memorial House, Piazza di Spagna 26. Keatsiana and a good library of Romantic works in the house where the two poets lived.

Musei Capitolini, Piazza del Campidoglio 1. In two elegant palaces designed by Michelangelo, an extraordinary collection of Greek and Roman antiquities and some Renaissance paintings.

Museo di Palazzo Venezia, Via del Plebiscito 118. In Pope Paul II's 15th-century palace, a fascinating collection of Renaissance arts and crafts.

Museo Nazionale di Villa Giulia, Piazza di Villa Giulia 9, Villa Borghese. One of the world's great Etruscan collections, beautifully displayed.

Museo Nazionale Romano, Via delle Terme di Diocleziano. Housed in a monastery adapted from part of the Baths of Diocletian, a vast collection of archeological material, also in Palazzo Massimi annex opened in 1990.

Musei Vaticani, Viale Vaticano. Among incredible artistic riches, the most important is the Sistine Chapel, with Michelangelo's frescoes. The Borgia apartments, Raphael's *Stanze* and Loggia and the Chapel frescoed by Fra Angelico along with the Picture Gallery and rooms full of Greek, Roman and Egyptian antiquities, are on some of the four color-coded itineraries that guide your visit according to the time at your disposition. All give at least a glimpse of the Vatican Library, a treasurehouse of incunabula. Closed Sun. and religious hols., except last Sun. of month when entrance free.

CHURCHES. As center of the Christian world, Rome is full of churches of every type, size and age. Opening times are erratic, generally from about 7 to noon and from 3 to 7. Bear in mind that they are places of worship and appropriate dress and behavior are required.

You might also want to visit the catacombs, which are not strictly churches, though underground basilicas were added to some of these early Christian burial grounds. Check hours with EPT. On the Via Appia Antica, *Catacomb of San Callisto,* at no. 110, closed Wednesday, and *Catacomb of San Sebastiano,* at no. 132, closed Thursday. At Via delle Sette Chiese 282, *Catacomb of Domitilla,* closed Tuesday. At Via Nomentana 349, *Catacomb of Sant'Agnese,* open every day. At Via Salaria 430, *Catacomb of Priscilla,* open every day.

Il Gesù, Piazza del Gesù. Jesuit church designed by Vignola in 16th century, magnificently decorated.

San Giovanni in Laterano, Piazza San Giovanni. The cathedral of Rome, with ancient Baptistry and Holy Stairs nearby.

Santa Maria degli Angeli, Piazza della Repubblica. Originally the Baths of Diocletian, transformed into an enormous church by Michelangelo.

Santa Maria del Popolo, Piazza del Popolo. Designed mainly by Bramante, it contains important paintings by Caravaggio and some Bernini sculptures.

Santa Maria della Vittoria, Via Venti Settembre, at Largo Santa Susanna, it holds Bernini's famous *St. Theresa in Ecstasy.*

Santa Maria Maggiore, Piazza Santa Maria Maggiore. Magnificent interior gleaming with 5th- and 13th-century mosaics; gilt wood ceiling.

San Paolo fuori le Mura (St. Paul's Outside the Walls), Via Ostiense. One of the first Christian churches in Rome, destroyed by fire in 1823 and rebuilt. The cloisters escaped damage and are exquisite.

San Pietro in Vincoli (St. Peter in Chains), Piazza San Pietro in Vincoli, off Via Cavour. The interior dates to the 5th century; it contains Michelangelo's *Moses* and a very obtrusive souvenir shop.

SHOPPING. Such famous names as Gucci, Bulgari and Valentino are not for the budget-minded, but that shouldn't stop you from window-shopping along the Via Condotti, lined with elegant purveyors of Italian style and quality. The entire Piazza di Spagna area is full of shops, some geared to tourists' budgets. Prices and goods are competitive along the Via del Corso, where the Romans themselves shop, and Via Ottaviano, near the Vatican, offers a wide range of reasonably priced merchandise. Throughout Rome, the *UPIM* and *Standa* chains can provide minor necessities and sometimes attractive and inexpensive souvenir items as well. *Croff,* with several stores in Rome, specializes in **housewares.**

On Sunday morning the **flea market** at Porta Portese occupies one fringe of Trastevere, offering mainly new and secondhand clothing, in addition to some old furniture and curiosities. Here and at other street stalls you can and should bargain; everywhere else, fixed prices are the rule.

At Piazza Fontanella Borghese there's a permanent **street market** specializing in old prints that make nice souvenirs.

USEFUL ADDRESSES. *U.S. Embassy,* Via Veneto 119, tel. 46741; *U.S. Consulate,* Via Veneto 121, tel. 46741; *Canadian Embassy,* Via G. B. De Rossi 27, tel. 8415341; *Canadian Consulate,* Via Zara 30, tel. 4403028; *British Embassy and Consulate,* Via Venti Settembre 80A, tel. 4825441; *American Express,* Piazza di Spagna 38, tel. 67641; *Wagon Lits,* Via Buoncompagni 25, tel. 4817545; *Thomas Cook,* Via Paolo Mercuri 6, tel. 6868941; *Main Post Office,* Piazza San Silvestro; *ENIT* (National Tourist Office), Via Marghera 2, tel. 4971282; *EPT* (Regional Tourist Office) for specific Rome-area information, Via Parigi 5, tel. 463748, and Termini Station; *International hospital,* Salvator Mundi, Viale delle Mura Gianicolense 67, tel. 586041. Telephone service bureau for assisted long-distance calls, Piazza San Silvestro, Termini Station and Fiumicino Airport, also in post office on Via Porta Angelica near St. Peter's and at Villa Borghese exit of Piazza di Spagna Metro station.

Florence

One of the world's great art cities, Florence would seem to be just one big museum if it weren't for the bustle of daily life that goes on in and around such stupendous monuments as the cathedral, with its Baptistery and bell tower, the Palazzo

Vecchio, still the town hall, and the many other historic buildings. The museums themselves are almost always humming with groups of visitors, duly impressed by the seemingly endless ranks of Botticellis, Michelangelos and Leonardos. The Uffizi alone houses one of the most important art collections in the world; add the Pitti Palace, the Bargello, the Accademia, San Marco and even more and you're in danger of becoming culturally saturated. The secret of survival is to take Florence in easy installments, alternating museums and churches with excursions into the suburbs—Fiesole, for example—and beyond into the Tuscan countryside. Florence offers some good-value budget accommodations, but book ahead as it's a year-round attraction.

Best place to begin a survey of the staggering riches of Florence is in the Piazza del Duomo. The lofty cathedral (Santa Maria del Fiore) is the largest church in the world after St. Peter's in Rome. Its exterior, faced with white, green and red marble, may take some getting used to, but inside, the church is a stupendous example of Tuscan Gothic architecture. The giant dome, designed by Brunelleschi, is decorated by an immense fresco, *The Last Judgment*, now hidden while the dome undergoes structural repairs. Look for the famous frescoes on the left wall by Paolo Uccello and Andrea Del Castagno, and visit the cathedral museum to see a Michelangelo Pietà and other exceptional sculptures that once decorated the church.

Next to the cathedral, Giotto's 14th-century Campanile rises to a height of 292 feet. It has been called the most beautiful bell tower in the world. Luca della Robbia created the first row of exterior bas-reliefs with Andrea Pisano. Climb 414 steps for a superb view of Florence.

In front of the cathedral, you will find the famous Baptistery of San Giovanni, for which Ghiberti sculpted the East Door or "Gate of Paradise". (Some panels have been removed for restoration and can now be seen in the Duomo museum.) It took the artist 27 years—1425 to 1452—to complete this matchless work in bronze. The North Door, representing the Life of Christ and the Evangelists, is also Ghiberti's work. Andrea Pisano sculpted the South Door.

From the Piazza del Duomo take the Via Calzaioli, and you will come to the Piazza della Signoria, in whose center Savonarola was executed. The square is dominated by the Palazzo della Signoria, better known as the Palazzo Vecchio (The Old Palace). Built between 1298 and 1314, it is now the city hall. The Michelangelo *David* in front of it is a copy; the original is in the Academy Gallery, safe from the ravages of weather. Like many other outdoor statues, Donatello's bronze *Judith,* now inside the Palazzo, also has been replaced by a copy.

Next to the Palazzo Vecchio is the 14th-century Loggia della Signoria, with famous sculptures by Giambologna, Benvenuto Cellini and others. It, too, is undergoing restoration. Nearby is the Palazzo degli Uffizi (Uffizi Palace), which houses what may be the most important collection of paintings in the world. Don't try to see it in less than half a day.

Here are other selected highlights of Florence—the Mercato Nuovo (New Market), covered by an arcade; the Ponte Vecchio (Old Bridge) across the Arno, spared by the Germans but hit hard by the 1966 flood, and lined on both sides with shops of goldsmiths, silversmiths and Florence's best jewelers; the Palazzo Pitti (Pitti Palace), a massive 15th-century building full of vast halls and salons, which in turn are full of tapestries, portraits, sculpture and an important collection of 16th- and 17th-century paintings, together with a silver museum; the finely planned Palazzo Strozzi, outstanding Renaissance palace and stately courtyard marred by a modern iron staircase; Church of Santa Trinità, Florence's most beautiful Gothic church, with frescoes by Ghirlandaio and Luca della Robbia's marble tomb of Federighi; Church of Santi Apostoli, built in the 11th century, one of Italy's oldest Romanesque buildings; Church of Santo Spirito, one of Brunelleschi's best creations; Church of Santa Maria del Carmine, whose Brancacci Chapel contains a celebrated series of frescoes by Masaccio; Church of Santa Maria Novella (Ghirlandaio and Masaccio); Church of Ognissanti, with Botticelli frescoes and, in the adjoining convent, Ghirlandaio's *The Last Supper*.

Then there are the following—the Medici-Riccardi Palace, built by Michelozzo, with a handsome courtyard and a tiny gem of a chapel frescoed by Gozzoli; Brunelleschi's Church of San Lorenzo, with the adjoining New Sacristy by Michelangelo with its famous tombs of Giuliano and Lorenzo, Duke of Urbino; and the Church of San Marco, with its museum containing the most important works of Fra Angelico. *The Annunciation* of Fra Angelico is here, and we recommend this particular visit even if it means giving up something else. Also try to see the majestic Church of Santa Croce, with Giotto's frescoes.

Take the Viale dei Colli to Piazzale Michelangelo for a picture-postcard view of Florence and the high peaks of the Apennines. At the top of the hill stands the Romanesque Church of San Miniato al Monte, built in 1013, and one of the most beautiful and famous churches in Florence. Visit Siena to see its stunningly decorated Gothic cathedral, and the Piazza del Campo, as well as its lovely churches and palaces. Nearby San Gimignano has a delightfully-preserved medieval atmosphere and is well worth the trip.

PRACTICAL INFORMATION FOR FLORENCE

GETTING AROUND FLORENCE. By Bus. There's an extensive network of city buses, but you'll find that Florence is mainly a town to walk in. The fare is 600 lire for one ride, 700 lire for a ticket valid for 70 minutes on all lines. Purchase tickets from tobacconists before boarding. Suburban buses charge according to distance. AAST and EPT tourist offices can provide route maps and information on villa and wine-country tours in the surrounding area. You'll probably find it cheaper to do the outlying villas on your own, but check villa opening hours.

On Foot. The center of the city is relatively small and traffic is limited but nevertheless intense during rush hours. When walking in so-called pedestrian zones, watch out for mopeds, buses, taxis and police cars.

HOTELS. There's an official tourist and hotel information office (ITA) at the main railway station (open 8.20 A.M. to 9 P.M.), but it's always advisable to have your booking before you get into town.

Moderate

Annalena, Via Romana 34 (tel. 222402). Near Palazzo Pitti. Spacious rooms, good atmosphere in small pension.

Aprile, Via della Scala 6 (tel. 216237). Garni. Well-located, this historic town house is a comfortable hotel with bar, garden.

Loggiato dei Serviti, Piazza Santissima Annunziata 3 (tel. 219165). Central, exceptional location in historic loggia; tastefully decorated.

Mario's, Via Faenza 89 (tel. 212039). Near the station. Small, attractively furnished in Florentine style. Good atmosphere.

Martelli, Via Panzani 8 (tel. 217151). Garni. Central, attractive medium-size hotel, all rooms with bath or shower.

Morandi alla Crocetta, Via Laura 50 (tel. 2344747). In a central and historic palazzo. Charming, private-home atmosphere; comfortable, well-furnished rooms.

Pendini, Via Strozzi 2 (tel. 211170). Central, medium-size pension, well decorated. Book ahead for nicest rooms on the piazza.

Porta Rossa, Via Porta Rossa 19 (tel. 287551). Garni. Conveniently located hotel with faded turn-of-century decor, spacious rooms, comfortable lounge.

La Residenza, Via Tornabuoni 8 (tel. 284197). 24 rooms. Well-located pension in refurbished palazzo. Rooms nicely furnished.

Royal, Via delle Ruote 52 (tel. 483287). Near San Marco museum. Small, all rooms with bath. Parking.

Silla, Via dei Renai 5 (tel. 234288). Across the Arno from Santa Croce. Clean and friendly pension.

Inexpensive

Bandini, Piazza Santo Spirito 9 (tel. 215308). Rooms with fireplaces and frescoes; loggia overlooking historic square.

Donatello, Via Alfieri 9 (tel. 245870). A 10-minute walk from sights. Small, clean and friendly hotel, popular with students.

Liana, Via Alfieri 8 (tel. 245303). Garni. Just outside historic center, quiet and pleasant villa with garden.

Maria Luisa de' Medici, Via del Corso 1 (tel. 280048). Central, charming, but two flights up and no lift. Large rooms, generous breakfast; book in advance.

Medici, Via Medici 6 (tel. 284818). 24 rooms, all with bath. Central, comfortable, small hotel.

Palazzo Vecchio, Via Cennini 4 (tel. 212182). Near the station. Minimal decor; parking.

Panorama Angelico, Via Cavour 60 (tel. 214243). Fairly central, comfortable, and friendly.

Villa Camerata, Viale Righi 2 (tel. 601451). Youth hostel on outskirts; if it's full try *Santa Monaca,* Via Santa Monaca 6 (tel. 268338). Information from ITA Tourist Office at station.

Camping. At Viale Michelangelo 80 (tel. 6811977), there's a well-located ground with a fine view of the city, while that at Villa Camerata, Viale Righi (tel. 610300), is next to the youth hostel.

RESTAURANTS. Dining hours in Florence are earlier than those in Rome, starting at 12.30 for the midday meal and at 7.30 for dinner. Budget restaurants are usually small and always crowded, so get there early and be prepared to share a table. For an Inexpensive meal, try one of Florence's many old wineshops, where you can get great Chiantis and hot or cold snacks for a few thousand lire. Many restaurants close in August.

Moderate

Antico Fattore, Via Lambertesca 1 (tel. 261215). Closed Sunday, Monday. Local specialties and a good house wine.

Borgo Antico, Piazza Santo Spirito 6r. (tel. 210437). Closed Sunday. Good pizzeria-trattoria, outdoors in summer.

Cantinetta Antinori, in Palazzo Antinori (tel. 292234). Closed Saturday evening, Sunday. Attractive wine-cellar offering snacks and full meals along with the famous wines of the house.

Casa del Vin Santo, Via Porta Rossa 15r (tel. 216995). Good for full meals, snacks and pizzas. Closed Tuesday evening and Wednesday.

Il Cavallino, Via delle Farine 6 (tel. 215818). Closed Tuesday evening, Wednesday. In beautiful setting at Palazzo Vecchio, a fine restaurant, one of Florence's oldest and most reliable.

Croce al Trebbio, Via delle Belle Donne 49 (tel. 287089). Busy trattoria serving copious portions.

Dino, Via Ghibellina 51 (tel. 241452). Closed Sunday evening, Monday. Near Santa Croce, this pleasant place specializes in wines and fine cheeses.

Fagioli, Corso Tintori 47 (tel. 244285). Closed weekends. An excellent trattoria offering Tuscan specialties.

Natalino, Borgo degli Albizi 17 (tel. 263404). Closed Sunday. Rustic atmosphere and country-style cooking.

Il Profeta, Via Borgo Ognissanti 93 (tel. 212265). Closed Sunday. Relaxed atmosphere, good menu.

I Rosso, Via Borgognissanti 1 (tel. 284897). Closed Sunday, Monday noon. Reserve for supper in this small "buca," popular with locals and tourists.

Sasso di Dante, Piazza delle Pallottole 6 (tel. 282113). Americans like this place for its substantial portions at a fixed price.

Trattoria il Teatro, Via degli Alfani 47r (tel. 2479327). Closed Sunday. Central, small, and attractive; varied menu.

Inexpensive

Acqua al Due, Via dell Acqua 2r (tel. 284170). Near Bargello. Pasta dishes and young crowd. Evenings only; closed Monday.

Angiolino, Via Santo Spirito 36r (tel. 298976). On the Pitti side of the Arno, charming atmosphere, tasty food.

Anita, Via Parlascio 2 (tel. 218698). Closed Sunday. Family-style trattoria, local dishes.

Bargello, Borgo dei Greci 37 (tel. 218605). Closed Friday evening, Saturday. Reasonably priced, satisfying meals.

Benvenuto, Via dei Neri at Via Mosca (tel. 214883). Closed Wednesday and Sunday evening. Family-style.

Buca Nicolini, Via Ricasoli 3. Good local dishes in this tiny, central spot.

Cantinone del Gallo Nero, Via Santo Spirito 6 (tel. 218898). Closed Monday. A brick-vaulted wine-cellar serving typical dishes, fine Chiantis. Popular, so book for evening meal.

Che c'è C'è, Via Magalotti 11 (tel. 262867). Closed Monday. Near Santa Croce. Spicy dishes and *risotto alle rose.*

Il Latini, Via Palchetti 6r (tel. 210916). Closed Monday. Unlimited portions at fixed prices; popular and crowded.

Mario, Via Alfani 60. A small trattoria that's good and very inexpensive.

Mossacce, Via del Proconsolo 55 (tel. 294361). Closed weekends. Tiny, busy; fast service and good food.

Nuti, Borgo San Lorenzo 39r (tel. 210410). Postmodern decor, paper placemats, good pizza, pasta, and salads.

L'Orologio, Piazza Ferrucci 5 (tel. 6811729). Closed Sunday. A good place for steak.

Pinocchio, Via della Scala 28r (tel. 218418). Closed Sunday. Near Santa Maria Novella. Unpretentious. Popular with locals.

San Niccolò, Via San Niccolò 60 (tel. 282836). Closed Sunday. Lively student trattoria; good house wine.

Tarocchi, Via Renai 12 (tel. 217850). Popular for pizza. Evenings only.

Za-Za, Piazza Mercato Centrale 26r (tel. 215411). Closed Sunday. Share a table in simple, wood-paneled trattoria with typical cooking.

Wineshops. Atmospheric little wineshops where you'll find hot or cold snacks to go with your Chianti: *Fiaschetteria,* Via dei Neri 17r; *Borzoli,* Piazza dell'Olio 15; *Fratellini,* Via dei Cimatori 38. *Niccolino,* Volto Dei Mercanti, is a favorite for stand-up snacks. *Granduca,* Via dei Calzaioli, and *Vivoli,* Via Isola delle Stinche 7, are famous for their ice cream. Wineshops are usually open from noon to 3, and 5.30 to midnight.

Lunch Stops. Siena. *Nello* (M), Via Porrione 28 (tel. 289043). *Tre Campane* (M), Piazzetta Bonelli (tel. 286091). **San Gimignano.** *Bel Soggiorno* (M), Via San Giovanni (tel. 940375). *Le Terrazze* (M), Piazza Cisterna (tel. 940328).

WHAT TO SEE AND DO. Concerts. Music lovers will find a full schedule of concerts and operas, with both summer and winter seasons, plus the prestigious *Maggio Musicale* in May and June. For information and tickets, write Teatro Comunale, Corso Italia 16, 50123 Florence (tel. 2779313), or book through *Globus,* Piazza Santa Trinita 2r (tel. 214992), or try on arrival at *Universalturismo,* Via Speziale 7r (tel. 217241).

Folklore events worth remembering include the *Scoppio del carro* on Easter Sunday in Piazza del Duomo, and the 16th-century football games—part competition, part pageant—held in May and June. The International Crafts Fair takes place in April and there are flower shows in April and May.

Museums. Below we list some of the most outstanding museums and galleries in Florence. National museums close Mondays, and are usually open 9–2, 9–1 on Sunday. The Uffizi is open 9–7, 9–1 on Sunday. Check museum hours with the local tourist office.

Accademia Gallery, Via Ricasoli 60. Michelangelo's *David* is here, along with some other works of his.

Archeological Museum, Via della Colonna 36. Important Etruscan collections, Greek and Roman sculpture.

Casa Guidi, the home of Robert and Elizabeth Barrett Browning, is open to visitors, Piazza San Felice 8, opposite southern wing of Pitti Palace.

Davanzati Palace (Museum of the Old Florentine House), Piazza Davanzati. Home furnished as it would have been in the 14th–17th centuries.

Fra Angelico Museum (Museum of San Marco), Piazza San Marco. Large number of works of Beato Angelico.

Medici Chapels (Church of San Lorenzo), Piazza Madonna degli Aldobrandini. Tombs by Michelangelo.

Museo di Santa Maria del Fiore (Duomo), Piazza Duomo 9. Collection of outstanding works from Duomo, Baptistery and Campanile.

National Museum (Bargello), Via del Proconsolo 4. Sculptures by Donatello, Cellini, Verrocchio, and other decorative arts.

Pitti Palace, with *Galleria Palatina, Galleria d'Arta Moderna* and *Museo degli Argenti,* on Piazza Pitti. Some of the most famous galleries in Italy. Site also of Boboli Gardens.

Uffizi Gallery (Uffizi Palace), Piazza della Signoria. One of the world's great collections, particularly rich in Italian and Flemish paintings.

Churches. These are usually open all day until sunset, apart from closing for an hour or two at midday.

Cathedral of Santa Maria del Fiore, Piazza del Duomo. Crowned by Brunelleschi's magnificent dome, it contains important works by Paolo Uccello and others, and its baptistery and bell tower are world-famous.

Orsanmichele, Via dei Calzaioli. Gothic building erected as a grain storehouse, transformed into a church in 1380. The statues on the exterior of the patron saints of craft guilds exemplify Florentine Renaissance sculpture. Many are copies.

San Lorenzo, Piazza San Lorenzo. Designed by Brunelleschi, it contains two pulpits by Donatello and an Annunciation by Filippo Lippi.

Santa Croce, Piazza Santa Croce. A 13th-century Gothic masterpiece (façade and bell tower are 19th-century additions). Inside, important sculptures and Giotto frescoes.

Santa Maria del Carmine, Piazza del Carmine. Famous for the Brancacci Chapel, with frescoes by Masaccio, recently restored.

Santa Maria Novella, Via degli Avelli. Gothic church with frescoes by Filippo Lippi, Ghirlandaio and Masaccio, and a Giotto crucifix. Visit the Gothic cloister at Piazza Santa Maria Novella 19.

Santa Trinita, Via del Parione. Baroque façade and lovely Gothic interior. The Sassetti Chapel is decorated with a noteworthy series of frescoes by Ghirlandaio.

USEFUL ADDRESSES. *U.S. Consulate,* Lungarno Vespucci 38; *British Consulate,* Lungarno Corsini 2; *American Express,* Via Guicciardini 49r (tel. 278751); *Thomas Cook,* Lungarno Acciaiuoli (tel. 295271); *Wagons Lits,* Via del Giglio 27r (tel. 218851); *Central Post Office,* Via Pietrapiana 53; *City Tourist Offices,* AAST, Via Tornabuoni 15 (tel. 216544), and the rail station; *APT Provincial Tourist Office,* Via Manzoni 16 (tel. 2478141).

Venice

Venice is one of the world's most anachronistic cities. Far from the problems of urban renewal, burgeoning skyscrapers, and main boulevard drag racing, it seems to continue eternally, moving in slow motion to a tempo all its own.

Founded on marshes by the inhabitants of the Byzantine duchy of Tre Venezie escaping from the barbarians, it became the most powerful and wealthy of the Italian city-republics during the Middle Ages. Merchant princes called Doges fought for control of world trade routes and schemed for power with Machiavellian cunning and ferocity. As commerce declined, after the 16th century, the art and culture of Venice dwindled but there was a resurgence of interest in the 18th century when such painters as Tiepolo, Ricci, and Piazzetta were at the height of their dazzling powers.

The most famous of Venetian Renaissance masters were Titian, Giorgione, Tintoretto, Veronese, Carpaccio, and the Bellinis.

Other than its artists, the most famous Venetians were adventurers. Marco Polo, the 13th-century traveler, was a son of the adventurous Venetian spirit. Casanova, an explorer of another type, also claimed Venice as his birthplace.

Today the center of Venice is fabulous Piazza San Marco, more Levantine than Renaissance, and a focal point for tourists, the local populace and 5,000 or so pigeons. Along with St. Mark's, the Doges' Palace, and the Bridge of Sighs, we recommend a stroll through the Castello and Cannaregio districts, which are much less crowded.

The museum with the finest collection is the Accademia, containing seminal works by Carpaccio, Titian, Mantegna and others. Many other works of art are displayed in churches or palaces where they can be seen in appropriate settings.

A half-day's walk away from tourist-clogged San Marco and Lista di Spagna will give you a chance to savor Venice's unique atmosphere of apparent decadence; take a good map. A trip to the islands, especially Burano and Torcello, is well worth the 40-minute vaporetto ride. Murano is less than 10 minutes from Venice. Do the islands on your own. Organized island tours are very commercial, pressuring you to buy glass or lace.

PRACTICAL INFORMATION FOR VENICE

NOTE. Venice is very, very expensive, so it's a real challenge to the budget-conscious. Also, *acqua alta,* or partial flooding, occurs ever more frequently during the winter months.

GETTING AROUND VENICE. By Boat. If you come into Venice by train you'll walk out of the station right onto steps leading down into the Grand Canal. You can get a vaporetto (water bus) to the landing nearest your hotel, then walk. It may be some distance, so have a folding luggage cart along for your bags. It is essential that you know how to get to your hotel before you arrive.

If you arrive by air, you can take the airport bus (about 4,000 lire) to Piazzale Roma (parking terminal) and then proceed as above. Or you can take the *Cooperativa San Marco* motorboat (about 11,000 lire per person, incl. bags) to the San Marco landing and continue on from there. Water taxis to and from the airport are prohibitively expensive.

The motorist reaches Venice by causeway and must park his car in one of the multi-story garages at Piazzale Roma, or on the adjacent Tronchetto parking island or in the more distant terminals of Fusina or San Giuliano; all handy for vaporetto lines. Consider leaving your car in Padua or Mestre.

Porter's charges are complicated: between any two points within the center of town (bounded by the railway station and Piazzale Roma) you pay 7,000 lire for one or two bags, more for additional bags or night service.

Gondolas are expensive, but it's an experience you shouldn't miss. Late afternoon, early evening hours are best, with less boat traffic on Grand Canal. Agree on terms with the gondolier before you start out. The current minimum is about 90,000–110,000 lire for 40 minutes for up to five people, more after 9 P.M.

Water taxis are expensive, have a complicated fare system, and are best avoided.

Vaporetto Line 1 is a local, passing all sights on the Grand Canal and along the lagoon. Line 4 takes in the same sights, makes limited stops. Vaporetto fare is 1,700 lire up. You can buy a tourist ticket for about 9,000 lire, valid 24 hours. If you're staying a few days, the *Carta Venezia* is a good buy (have extra passport photo handy). After 10 P.M. a supplement of 25% is applied to all public transport, including gondolas.

For island-hopping trips to Murano, Burano and Torcello, use the regular vaporetto service; it's cheap and you won't be pressured to buy by the diehards who run the guided island tours. For Murano take Line 5 steamer, which leaves every 15 minutes or so from Riva degli Schiavoni. For Burano and Torcello, Line 12 steamers leave every hour from Fondamente Nuove. Remember that most everything on the islands closes from noon to about 3 P.M., so plan your day accordingly. Frequent vaporetto service between the islands allows flexibility.

On Foot. Venice has more than 150 canals forming 115 little islands linked together by minuscule arched bridges, humped to allow boat traffic through. Most of your sightseeing will be done on foot, and going up and down all those bridges can be tiring. Another problem is that the names of streets and canals appear on signs in Venetian dialect, which can be confusing. Buy a map on which all streets are named. Use *traghetto* (350 lire) to cross the Grand Canal. The best view of Venice is from the bell tower of San Giorgio Maggiore.

HOTELS. Hotel rates are above average in Venice, so you'll have to accept a lower grade of creature comfort in order to stay within your budget. Hotels and pensions having restaurants insist that you take half-pension terms in high season (March 16–November 4 and December 19–January 1), so you must be selective. Since restaurants are expensive, this may work out to be an economical solution to your meal problem, but be warned that half-pension rates at some hotels and pensions are very high. Choose carefully. Book well in advance if possible and to save money ask for a room without a private bath or a view of the Grand Canal. The AVA hotel association desks at the rail station, airport and at the city garage on Piazzale Roma will find you a room to suit your budget. The 20,000-lire deposit is discounted from your hotel bill. AVA desks are open daily 9–9.

Moderate

Agli Alboretti, Rio Terrà Sant'Agnese 882 (tel. 5230058). Near Accademia. Small, friendly, family-run. Bright and compact decor, tiny garden.

Alla Fava, Castello 5525 (tel. 5229224). Garni. Near the Rialto. Fairly small, good atmosphere, friendly staff.

Casa Frollo, Giudecca island (tel. 522723). Garni. Exceptional ambience in villa hotel. Book ahead. Location necessitates constant use of vaporetto.

Iris, San Tomà 2910 (tel. 5222822). In the San Polo district, near Frari church. Clean, bright rooms over popular inexpensive trattoria.

Madonna dell'Orto, Cannaregio, next to church of same name (tel. 719955). Excellent value, atmosphere. Few private baths. Out-of-the-way but handy to vaporetto line 5.

Paganelli, Riva degli Schiavoni (tel. 524324). Basic furnishings but fine location and pleasant restaurant. Front rooms have lagoon view but are expensive.

La Residenza, Campo Bandiera e Moro 3608 (tel. 5285315). Near San Zaccaria. In a gorgeous Gothic palace; solid comfort and dignified atmosphere. Closes part of November and January.

San Fantin, San Marco 1930 (tel. 5231401). Garni. Clean, pleasant small hotel near La Fenice theater.

San Stefano, Campo Santo Stefano (tel. 5200166). Central, a 14-room gem. Very good value. Book ahead.

Seguso, Zattere 779 (tel. 5222340). Comforts and atmosphere of a Venetian home; mandatory half-pension terms.

Inexpensive

Casa di Stefani, San Barnaba 2786 (tel. 5223337). Central, small, no frills but low rates.

Da Cici alla Salute, Dorsoduro 222 (tel. 522271). Large pension in centuries-old palazzo. Rooms without bath within budget range.

Dalla Mora, Salizzada San Pantalon 42 (tel. 5235703). Near Frari church. Simple rooms, most of them with bath.

Domus Cavanis, Dorsoduro 899 (tel. 87374). Religious institute offering basic accommodations.

Eden, Cannaregio 2357 (tel. 720228). Garni. Quiet, fairly central.

Galleria, Accademia 878/a (tel. 5204172. Sharing the Accademia Gallery square, it offers simple accomodations, friendly welcome, and some rooms with Grand Canal view.

Hostel, Giudecca at Fondamenta Zitelle (tel. 5238211).

Minerva e Nettuno, Cannaregio 230 (tel. 715968). Near the station, not luxurious but good modest accommodations.

Sturion, Calle Sturion 679 (tel. 5236243). Near Rialto market, overlooking Grand Canal. Exceptional ambience and value. 12 rooms furnished in Venetian style, a few with private bath.

Tintoretto, Santa Fosca 2316 (tel. 721522). Interesting location halfway between station and San Marco. Good trattorias nearby. Low off-season rates.

Camping. Summer only. At Fusina, good for quick connections to Venice, but in heavily polluted industrial zone. Others at Cavallino are fine, boat connections to Venice fairly costly.

RESTAURANTS. It's not impossible to eat cheaply in Venice, but it's not easy to eat well there, either. The cheapest places are the *tavole calde, rosticcerie* and *osterie* or *enoteche* (wineshops). In general, you'll have to add another 10,000–15,000 lire over our budget guidelines for meals in Venice, or make do with the usually dreary *menu turistico.*

Moderate

Antica Besseta, Calle Salvio 1395 (tel. 5221687). Closed Tuesday. In Santa Croce district, a non-touristy trattoria, very popular with locals.

Ai Cugnai, Calle Nuova Sant' Agnese (tel. 5289238). Near the Accademia. Reasonably priced and good.

Al Conte Pescaor, Piscina San Zulian 544 (tel. 5221483). Closed Tuesday. Near San Marco; popular place for Venetian specialties, good service.

Ai Coristi, near La Fenice (tel. 26677). Closed Wednesday. Lively, friendly place, good local dishes.

Da Ignazio, Calle dei Saoneri 2749 (tel. 5234852). Near Rialto market. Closed Saturday. Smallish; agreeable dining on classic Venetian dishes.

Due Foscari, Calle della Regina 2331 (tel. 89276). Closed Monday in winter. Neapolitan specialties, including pizza.

Fiore, Calle del Scaleter (tel. 5237208). Near Campo San Polo. Favorite with Venetians for fish. Closed Sunday, Monday.

Gazebo, Rio Terrà San Leonardo 1333a (Strada Nuova), (tel. 5216380). Closed Thursday. Near rail station. Courteous service, good food and pizza.

Ai Gondolieri, Ponte del Formagher. Popular with students and tourists for food, atmosphere.

Montin, Fondamenta Eremite 1147 (tel. 5227151). A Venetian institution. Unexceptional but good food; lots of paintings on walls, nice garden.

Inexpensive

Agli Amici, Calle dei Botteri 1544 (tel. 87631). Closed Sunday. Busy wineshop; tasty meals at counter or table.

Altanella, Calle dell'Erbe (tel. 27780). On Giudecca, family-run trattoria. Very popular, book ahead. Closed in fall and winter.

Antica Adelaide, Calle Priuli, off Strada Nuova (tel. 5203451). Closed Sunday. Good food; garden courtyard.

Antica Mola, Fondamenta degli Ormesini. In Cannaregio near the Ghetto. (Tel. 717492). Closed Saturday. Inconspicuous family-run trattoria with garden. Mainly for lunch; closes early in evening.

Antiche Carampane, S. Polo Carampane 1911 (tel. 35165). Closed Sunday. Modest place, very popular with students.

Burchiello, Campo Santa Maria Formosa (tel. 28989). Good for a simple meal or pizza.

Le Chat qui rit, near American Express. Bustling *rosticceria* where cafeteria service is your best bet.

Alle Colonne, Campiello del Piovan, just behind San Giacomo dell'Orio (tel. 89481). Closed Tuesday. Good, courteous, very reasonable.

Giardinetto, Calle del Cristo 2908, in San Tomà district (tel. 5222882). Closed Monday, Near the Frari. Typical Venetian dishes or pizza in wood-paneled dining room or vine-shaded courtyard.

Da Mario, Campiello dei Sansoni 900 (tel. 704818). Closed Monday. A simple, popular place with reasonable prices.

Al Mascaron, Calle Lunga Santa Maria Formosa. Closed Sunday. Old-fashioned wineshop, snacks, some hot dishes.

Il Milion, San Giovanni Crisostomo 5841 (tel. 5229302). Closed Wednesday. Typical *osteria* where you can eat cheaply and well.

Sacrestia, Castello 4442. Seafood and other specialties in a modest place with informal service.

Al Vagon, Calle Dolfin 5597. Fixed price menu in a quiet area away from the madding crowd.

La Zucca, Ponte del Megio, near San Giacomo dell'Orio (tel. 700462). Trendy atmosphere with good pasta and wine.

WHAT TO SEE AND DO. Though many insist that the entire city of Venice is itself the finest museum, you will not want to miss the special pleasures of the following outstanding collections of art.

Accademia delle Belle Arti, in Convent and Church of Santa Maria della Carità, on Grand Canal. Venetian paintings, 14th–18th century.

Correr Museum, entrance under Portico dell'Ascensione, on west side of Piazza San Marco. History of Venice.

Franchetti Gallery, Ca d'Oro. Renaissance paintings and bronzes in splendid Gothic palace on Grand Canal.

Guggenheim Collection, Palazzo Venier dei Leoni on the Grand Canal. The late American heiress's exceptional collection of modern art.

Jewish Museum, Campo del Ghetto Nuovo. A fascinating chapter in Venetian history, in one of the city's quaintest districts.

Naval History Museum, Campo San Biagio. Near the Arsenal entrance, a variety of exhibits illustrating Venice's maritime history.

Museo Vetrario, Murano. The famed glass museum, glass objects from Roman times onward.

Querini-Stampalia Palace, near Church of Santa Maria Formosa. Art gallery and library.

Rezzonico Palace, left bank of Grand Canal. Decorative arts, paintings by Guardi, Longhi, Tiepolo.

Scuola di San Rocco, opposite Santa Maria Gloriosa dei Frari. 40 major works by Tintoretto restored in a 3½-year project financed by U.S.-based Kaufman Foundation.

Palaces and Churches. Ca d'Oro, on Grand Canal, fanciful 15th-century example of Venetian Gothic architecture. Renaissance art collection.

Palazzo Ducale, airily magnificent palace built for the Doges in the 14th century. See the Porta della Carta, the courtyard and Scala dei Giganti and Scala d'Oro. Dimly lit, it's best seen on a bright day.

San Giorgio Maggiore, on the island of San Giorgio. Its harmonious forms are a symbol of Venice; it contains works by Tintoretto and Carpaccio. Bell tower (reached by elevator) affords superb view of Venice and lagoon.

San Marco, St. Mark's Basilica, one of the world's most famous churches, mostly Byzantine in style, with brilliant mosaics. See the Pala d'Oro (gold altarpiece), the Treasury and upstairs gallery with marvelous view of the interior. Bell tower has elevator to top. At its base, the Loggetta (1540) by Sansovino.

Santa Maria Gloriosa dei Frari, near San Polo. Venetian Gothic church; contains beautifully carved choir and Titian's masterful *Assumption.*

Santi Giovanni e Paolo, in Castello district. Gothic church containing noteworthy works of the Venetian school.

Entertainment. The cheapest form of entertainment in Venice is wandering about, getting the feel of this unique city. The regular concerts at Piazza San Marco are free to all listeners, though intended for the patrons of Florian's and Quadri's. Free musical and theatrical events enliven the Carnival season in February–March. Throughout the year, check with local tourist office for concerts (many are free) and other events. La Fenice opera has a winter season. Folklore spectacles include the Feast of the Redeemer in July and the Historical Regatta in September. Island-hopping around the lagoon costs only your steamer fare; aside from Murano, Burano and Torcello, there are a number of other fascinating islets to visit, such as San Francesco del Deserto and San Lazzaro degli Armeni.

USEFUL ADDRESSES. *British Consulate,* Campo Santa Maria della Carità 1051 (tel. 5227207); *American Express,* San Moise 1474 (tel. 5200844); *Thomas Cook,* Rialto 5126 (tel. 5287358); *AAST,* Ascensione 71c, under portico at end of Piazza San Marco, opposite basilica (tel. 5226356); also at Santa Lucia railway station and at Piazzale Roma 540d (summer only) (tel. 5227402).

Sorrento

The Sorrento peninsula has spectacular natural beauty, southern Italian charm, and is still a good budget buy. The town of Sorrento has spread out in recent years along the crest of its cliffs, as many of its fabled orange groves have been sacrificed to highrise apartment buildings. Noisy and frankly touristy, Sorrento can't be recommended during its peak season of July–August; rather, we suggest scheduling your visit for spring or fall—even during the balmy winter—when things calm down a bit. The sometimes tawdry appurtenances of modern mass tourism can never dim the delights of a marvelous climate and a stupendous view of the Bay of Naples, with Vesuvius looming on the right and Capri rising out of the sea on the left.

Use Sorrento as your base for excursions to some of the most beautiful spots in the world. Capri is an island paradise, legendary site of the orgies of Tiberius, a very popular resort and so expensive that a day's excursion is all your budget can stand. On the Amalfi side of the peninsula, much less touristy, you'll find small towns like Positano, Amalfi and Ravello, each with a beauty and character of its own. You should consider spending a night or two in one of these towns; budget accommodations are plentiful, and you'll have more time to explore quiet, white-washed byways and discover breathtaking panoramas. You'll make another excursion to Pompeii, the Roman city buried under volcanic ash from Vesuvius nearly 2,000 years ago. Extensively excavated, the ruins give an idea of how the ancients lived and died. Naples, glimmering in the distance across the bay from Sorrento, is known for chaotic traffic and pervading shabbiness, but you should go there to see such attractions as the National Museum, with its priceless collection of antiquities, and Capodimonte Museum, a veritable treasurehouse. It's a long bus ride from Sorrento, but if you're interested in archeology you should see Paestum, famous for its majestic and well-preserved Greek temples and for an important small museum.

Getting about in the area is no problem. Organized excursions abound, but it's much cheaper to travel about independently, using public transport. Sorrento is the hub of a transportation network that includes the Circumvesuviana Railway, which provides a fast link to Pompeii and Naples. The town is starting point for SITA buses to all points on the peninsula as far as Salerno, and steamers for Capri and Naples put in at its small port. For local jaunts, though the terrain's hilly, you can rent a bicycle or moped in Sorrento at the moped shop on Via Sant'Antonio.

PRACTICAL INFORMATION FOR SORRENTO AND PENINSULA

Hotels and Restaurants

Generally, higher-category hotels in this area remain within budget-rate guidelines. Hotels in Sorrento can be noisy if on heavily-trafficked streets; ask for a quiet room. Budget hotels in Amalfi and Positano may be located on steep stairways that double as streets. Half-pension terms are mandatory during high season. A number of well-equipped camping grounds are located in the immediate vicinity of Sorrento.

Amalfi. Low season rates (from October 1 through June 1, except Christmas and Easter) keep fine higher-category hotels such as *La Bussola, Dei Cavalieri, Miramalfi,* within Moderate range.
Centrale (M), tel. 871243. Garni. Small, simple hotel in picturesque center. *Dei Cavalieri Annex* (M), tel. 871333. Garni. Small villa just outside town. *Marina Riviera* (M), tel. 871104. Garni. Oldish but comfortable hotel in town. *Amalfi* (I), tel. 872440. Small pension, all rooms with bath or shower. *Il Nido* (I), tel. 871148. Just outside town on busy main road, small pension, some rooms with view.
Restaurants. *Caravella* (M), tel. 871029. On main road near arch, family-run, good pastas, cheese crêpes. *Maria* (M), on main street through town. Fish expensive, otherwise fine. *Sant'Andrea* (M), at foot of Cathedral steps, small, good for pastas, pizzas. *La Barcaccia* (I), off Piazza dei Dogi. On a picturesque square; informal place for tasty food. *La Vinicola* (I), Piazza Marini, up main street from Cathedral; good local wines. *Lemon Garden* (I). Follow the signs, worth the walk. Outdoors only, open June–Sept.

Positano. Low season rates (October through May, except Christmas and Easter) are advantageous. Book well in advance. Many hotels close November–February. There are many guest houses; the local AAST tourist office (closed in winter) will help you find a room.
California (M), Via Colombo (tel. 875382), on main street through town, good-size rooms with bath, terraces with view. *Casa Albertina* (M), Via della Tavolozza (tel. 875143), smallish hotel, attractive well-decorated rooms with bath, balcony,

view. *Margherita* (M), Via Marconi (tel. 875188), on main road overlooking town, villa-type, simple rooms with spectacular views. *La Tavolozza* (M), Via Colombo (tel. 875040). Attractive guest house in the heart of town. *Il Gabbiano* (I), Viale Pasitea (tel. 875306). Uphill from piazza, pretty guest house. *Casa Buonocore* (I), Via Colombo (tel. 870885). Central, comfortable guest house. *Villa Cosenza* (I), Via Trara Genoino (tel. 875063). Cordial, family-run guest house with spectacular terrace. *La Fenice* (I), Via Nazionale (tel. 875513). Hillside villa on edge of town.

Restaurants. *Capurale* (M), tel. 875374, near beach, upstairs in winter, on slanting sidewalk in summer, good food. *Taverna del Leone* (M), on road toward Praiano, a few bus stops outside town. Some of the best and cheapest pizzas on the coast, lots of other specialties. *Tre Sorelle* (M), on beach; fish is expensive, but pastas and pizzas make good budget fare. *Vincenzo* (M), Curva San Martino; simple local dishes. *Grottino Azzurro* (M). At Chiesa Madre bus stop. *San Gennaro* (I), in Vettica, 5 km (3 mi) toward Amalfi. Budget paradise with a view; good food, low prices.

Ravello. Generally lower rates in all categories (especially in low season, October through May, except Christmas and Easter) make this lovely town an ideal spot for budgeteers.

Parsifal (M), tel. 857144. Medium-size hotel, attractive rooms, terraces with view. *Toro* (M), tel. 857211. Small, villa-type, with garden. *Villa Amore* (M), tel. 857135. Smallish hotel in beautiful position, quiet, comfortable. *Bonadies* (I), tel. 857137. 7 rooms, all with bath. *Villa Maria* (I), tel. 857170. Small pension, recommended, pretty villa with garden, good food.

Restaurants. *Compa Cosimo* (M), tel. 857156. Closed Monday in winter. Unpretentious, reasonable. *Garden* (M), near Villa Rufolo, terrific view. *Villa Maria* (M), on Villa Cimbrone path, *pensione* restaurant.

Sorrento. *Eden* (M), Via Correale 25 (tel. 8781909). Medium-size, central, fairly quiet; friendly and well-decorated, with large garden and pool, has small annex (I) sharing its amenities. Open March–Oct. *Minerva* (M), Via Capo 30 (tel. 8781011). Medium-size hotel with annexes (I), on busy road high above sea, on outskirts of town. A bit old-fashioned but pleasant, with garden, pool, terraces. Open April–Sept. *Regina* (M), Via Marina Grande (tel. 8782721). Smallish hotel, fairly central; simply furnished rooms, all with bath or shower, lots of balconies, garden. Open April–Sept. *Rota* (M), Via Rota (tel. 8782904). Central, modern and well-equipped hotel. *Villa di Sorrento* (M), Via Fuorimura 4 (tel. 8781068). Garni. Very central, small, comfortable, just off noisy main piazza. All rooms with bath or shower, open all year.

Ascot (I), Via Capo 6 (tel. 8783032). Near center, on busy main street, modern, anonymous but comfortable; open April–Sept. *Dania* (I), Via Calata Puolo 2 (tel. 8781097). On outskirts near beach, family-run pension on hillside; open April–Sept. *Del Mare* (I), Via del Mare 30 (tel. 8783310). Small, overlooking sea, simple, clean and cordial. *Girasole* (I), Corso Italia 302 (tel. 8781371). Central, friendly, on noisy main road; bright bedrooms, nice garden. *Loreley et Londres,* (I), Via Califano 2 (tel. 8781508). Near cliffs and belvedere, small old hotel with garden. Open March–Sept.

Restaurants. *Antica Trattoria* (M), Via Giuliani 33. Located in center of town; courteous service, fine local cooking. *Gigino* (M), Via Nicotera 10 (tel. 8789426). Popular and busy, variety of antipasto and dessert offerings, inexpensive pizza. *Cavallino Bianco* (M), Via Correale. Typical local cooking. *Parrucchiano* (M), Corso Italia. Traditional, interesting atmosphere, good food. *Vecchie Arcate* (M), Via Sant'Antonino 12. Bright, centrally located restaurant-pizzeria. *Zi 'Ntonio* (M), Via de Maio 11, a friendly place with tables on patio.

Umbria: Assisi, Gubbio, Spoleto, Todi

Near Perugia, Assisi hugs the slopes of Mount Subasio. The town's pink and white stone buildings strike a surprisingly bright note against the green hill. As you approach, you'll see the massive monastery and Basilica of St. Francis, built to honor the saint only two years after his death. Once inside the town's medieval walls, you'll be struck by its serenity. Assisi suffers from none of the overemphatic kitsch of so many sanctuaries and shrines throughout the world. Here all is peace, harmony and quiet, if you are wise enough to come off-season and on weekdays, avoiding the big religious holidays and the pilgrimage month of August. The town has carefully preserved its medieval aspect, softened by the delightful rose color of the stone from Mount Subasio's quarries.

The Basilica of St. Francis, Assisi's principal monument, was built on two levels. The lower church, dark and vaulted, was covered with frescoes in the early 14th century by Cimabue, Giotto and Simone Martini. In contrast, the upper church is light and airy, famous for Giotto's important cycle of frescoes depicting the life of St. Francis.

From Assisi you can visit some of the interesting Umbrian towns in the vicinity. Perugia, university city of Etruscan origins and medieval importance, has the magnificent Palazzo dei Priori, which houses the noteworthy collections of the National Gallery of Umbria. A little farther off are Gubbio, one of the best-preserved medieval centers in Italy; Todi, with an attractive piazza dating to the Middle Ages; and Spoleto, where Roman, Medieval and Renaissance monuments blend to create enchanting views. There are scheduled bus and train connections between these towns, and the ride offers fine views of the bluish-green Umbrian countryside.

PRACTICAL INFORMATION FOR UMBRIA

Hotels and Restaurants

Assisi. You get very good value in Assisi's hotels, where higher-category accommodations are available at budget rates. *Dei Priori* (M), tel. 812237. Central, smallish and pleasant. *San Francesco* (M), tel. 812281. Good-size hotel next to basilica. *Umbra* (M), tel. 812240. Smallish; an excellent choice. All foregoing have some rooms without bath at very reasonable rates. *Roma* (I), tel. 812390. Garni. Older, comfortable hotel. *San Pietro* (I), tel. 812452. Near basilica, modern, medium size. *St. Anthony's Guest House* (I), Viale Galeazzo Alessi 10, in medieval palace. Gardens, view, full pension at reasonable rates.

Restaurants. *Buca di San Francesco* (M), Via Brizi. Local specialties; crowded on Sundays, holidays. *La Fontana* (M), Via San Francesco, country cooking in wine cellar. *Taverna dell'Arco* (M), Via San Gregorio. Another popular place. *Cecco* (M) and *Carletto* (M) are good, family-style trattorias. *Del Carro* (M), reader-recommended for pizzas.

Gubbio. Restaurants. *Taverna del Lupo* (M), Via Ansidei (tel. 9271269). Hearty local specialties. *Porta Tessenaca* (M), Via Baldassini (tel. 9272765). Atmosphere, good dining. *Grotta dell'Angelo* (I), Via Gioia (tel. 9271747). Modest place, fine pastas.

Perugia. Restaurants. *Falchetto* (M), Via Bartolo (tel. 61875). Good choice. *La Lanterna* (M), Via Rocchi (tel. 66064). Local dishes.

Spoleto. Restaurants. *La Barcaccia* (M), Piazza Fratelli Bandiera 3 (tel. 21171). Pleasant trattoria with outdoor tables on tiny square. *Del Festival* (M), Via Brignone (tel. 32198). Central, rustic decor, very good food and house wine. *Panciolle* (M), Largo Clemente near Duomo (tel. 45598). Local dishes. Go early for a table outdoors in good weather. *Trattoria del Mercato* (I), Piazza del Mercato 29. Closed Sunday. Modest place serving satisfying food at low prices.

Todi. Restaurant. *Jacopo* (M), Piazza Jacopone (tel. 882366). Atmosphere, rustic dishes. *Cavour* (I), Corso Cavour 23 (tel. 882491). Closed Thursday. Typical provincial trattoria.

Luxembourg

The Grand Duchy of Luxembourg, a thriving, Rhode-Island-sized land, offers travelers one of the better tourist bargains of Europe. There are castles and museums enough for the most ardent seekers of history or atmosphere. The Duchy has abundant campsites, hostels, well-marked footpaths, majestic landscapes, trout or white-water streams, and cliffs for nature lovers to scale, as well as nightclubs, discothèques and gourmet food for sophisticates, and sports for everyone. Prices are 15–20% lower than in neighboring Belgium.

French and German are widely spoken, as is English, which is convenient for the English-speaking traveler, as only those from Luxembourg can manage the vernacular language, Letzeburgesch. Luxembourg's food combines German heartiness with French delicacy. Luxembourg's dry white wines, beers, and fruity liqueurs are renowned.

The seat of government is Luxembourg City, once a fortress of solid rock called the Gibraltar of the North, now the banking center of the European Community, with over 160 international banks. Visit the city's turreted ramparts and the *casemates,* a honeycomb of underground fortifications. Place d'Armes is a traditional square that is often the scene of open-air concerts.

The highlight of Luxembourg City is not usually one specified building, but it is rather the overall impression of the quaint, medieval city. At night, the floodlit skyline of castles, turrets, bridges, spires, and ramparts is stunning.

The smaller centers and villages outside Luxembourg City sit in areas little changed by 20th-century development. Echternach, for example, lies along the meandering Sûre river and marks the beginning of a vast natural park that stretches into Germany. The imposing ruins of Bourscheid castle tower above the river in a landscape of wooded glens, ravines, and mysterious rock formations. Echternach, with its 7th-century Benedictine abbey, is also a convenient center for visiting the Moellerdall, Luxembourg's pocket Switzerland.

By contrast, Wiltz offers a trip through Luxembourg's history, from the Counts' Medieval château and Renaissance altar to a museum recalling the Battle of the Ardennes in World War Two.

Other local centers are Vianden, site of the beautifully restored ancestral castle of the Orange-Nassau dynasty; Clervaux, noted for its 12th-century castle and Benedictine abbey; Esh-sur-Sûre, a moated town dominated by crags and castle; Diekirch, a sports center and home to a World War Two museum; and Grevenmacher, heart of the wine country.

PRACTICAL INFORMATION FOR LUXEMBOURG

WHAT WILL IT COST. Luxembourg City is an international banking, business, and political center, so prices tend to be slightly higher than in the countryside.

Since information on the rest of Luxembourg is more readily available in the capital, the first-time visitor would do well to be based there. An efficient and inexpensive public transport system means that no town is further than a few hours away.

In Luxembourg, as in Belgium, the unit of currency is the franc. Luxembourg issues its own currency in bills of 100, 500, and 1,000 francs and coins of 1, 5, 20, and 50 francs. Belgian currency can be used freely in Luxembourg and both currencies have exactly the same value. However, Luxembourg currency is not valid in Belgium. At press time (fall 1989) the exchange rate was 38 fr.L to the dollar and 60 fr.L to the pound.

Sample Costs. Cinema ticket 150 fr.L.; theater ticket 40 fr.L.; museum entrance fees from 6 to 150 fr.L., but the best are free. Coffee 35 fr.L.; a *demi* of beer in a café 35 fr.L., in a restaurant 50 fr.L.; a ¼-liter carafe of wine in a café 60 fr.L., in a restaurant 80 fr.L.

NATIONAL TOURIST OFFICE. There is an *Office National du Tourisme* (National Tourist Office) at the airport and at the Place de la Gare. For the least expensive tour of Luxembourg City pick up the free pink leaflet available from either of these addresses. For local information on Luxembourg City, go to the *Syndicat d'Initiative,* (City Tourist Office), Place d'Armes (tel. 22–80–9), open 9–1 and 2–6. It shows various routes around the capital and describes what you see along the way. Walking tours are scheduled each weekend and holidays, and information can be obtained from the ONT or the *Fédération Luxembourgeoise des Marches Populaires,* P.O. Box 1157, L–1010 Luxembourg. There is a nominal fee for these walks, but they are a great way to meet people. H. Sales, 26 rue du Cure (tel. 46–18–18) offers daily tours of Luxembourg City all year and, in season, half- or full-day tours for between 300 and 600 fr.L. These visit the Ardennes, "Little Switzerland," and the Moselle Valley. In summer, *minitrain tours* (200 fr.L.) of the Old Town and the Petrusse Valley start from the Place de Bruxelles. *Circuits Trains-Pédestres* shows you how to get around most efficiently by train to a spot where the walking is rewarding, and there are many such places in Luxembourg. *Circuits Auto-Pédestres* describes similar tours by car. Both are available at newsstands and book stores. For bikers, a new booklet called *Cycling Tracks* is available from the ONT, P.O. Box 1001, L–1010 Luxembourg.

Addresses of the Luxembourg National Tourist Office (ONT) overseas are:

In the U.S.: 801 Second Ave., New York, N.Y. 10017 (tel. 212–370–9850).

In the U.K.: 36 Piccadilly, London W1V 9PA (tel. 071–434 2800). This office is scheduled to move to another address; details not available at press time.

WHEN TO COME. The tourist season runs from around Easter until mid-September. Although summer is the best time to come numerous off-season attractions and price reductions are worth checking out before you make any decisions. Write the ONT, P.O. Box 1001, L–1010 Luxembourg, for details.

The climate is temperate, with summer tending to be cool though winters are not severe. Rain is fairly frequent.

Average afternoon temperatures in Fahrenheit and centigrade:

Luxembourg

	Jan.	Feb.	Mar.	Apr.	May	June	July	Aug.	Sept.	Oct.	Nov.	Dec.
F°	36	40	49	58	65	71	74	73	65	56	45	39
C°	2	4	9	15	18	22	23	23	18	13	7	4

SPECIAL EVENTS. Many ancient traditions, neglected elsewhere, persist in Luxembourg. Carnival is thoroughly celebrated with processions and balls. Other ceremonies include Candlemas, Wintersend, May Day and Harvest Home. Eimaischen is a folklore fair held in Luxembourg City's Marché-Aux-Poissons on Easter Monday. On the third Sunday after Easter there is a great pilgrimage procession to Our Lady of Luxembourg; on Whit Tuesday the famous dancing procession of Echternach, which bears a remarkable resemblance to the legend of the Pied Piper of Hamlin. There is also the Springprozession in honor of St. Willibrord; and Wiltz

Genzefest; a unique broomflower festival with parades, pageants and dancing. In *May–June,* the Spring Music Festival (classical and modern) is held in the capital, followed soon after by the international vintage car tour. In *June–July,* the International Festival of Classical Music is held at Echternach. *July* marks the start of the open-air theater and music festival at Wiltz. The second week of *September* signals the Wine Festival and Folklore Parade at Grevenmacher. There are many wine festivals and tasting days along the Moselle from May onwards. Bikers appreciate the almost monthly cross-country races, many of them international or world events. The Christmas market in the capital's Place d'Armes is a time to browse for traditional gifts or simply to eat potato cakes and drink mulled wine. Ask the ONT office for the "Calendrier des manifestations," the complete list of events.

National Holidays. Jan. 1; Feb. 26 (carnival); April 1 (Easter Monday); May 1 (May Day); May 9 (Ascension); May 20 (Pentecost Monday); June 23 (National Day); August 15 (Assumption); November 1 (All Saints Day); Nov. 2 (All Souls Day); Dec. 15, 25 and 26. *In Luxembourg City:* Feb. 6 (Carnival Mon.); Nov. 2 (All Souls).

VISAS. Nationals of the United States, Canada, Australia, New Zealand, Japan, EC countries and practically all other European countries do not require a visa for entry into Luxembourg.

HEALTH CERTIFICATE. No vaccinations are required from any country.

GETTING TO LUXEMBOURG. By Plane. *Icelandair's* budget flights via Reykjavik link New York and Orlando with Findel airport. Service from Washington is expected to start early in 1990. The Grand Duchy can also be reached by changing at London, Paris, Amsterdam, Copenhagen, or Frankfurt where *Luxair* and other carriers have daily flights. Check with your travel agents for the many short-break holidays available.

By Train. From the U.K. the quickest route is from London via Dover and the *Jetfoil* service to Oostende, then by train via Brussels Gare du Midi to Luxembourg. The fastest journey time is 9 hours. There are frequent trains from Paris (4 hours), Amsterdam (6 hours), and Brussels (3 hours). These include the *Iris EC* (Brussels to Chur) and the *Edelweiss* (Amsterdam to Zürich) which have 2nd-class sections. There are good train connections with most German cities via Koblenz.

By Bus. There are no through buses from London to Luxembourg, so take the excellent CitySprint service to Brussels and catch the train to Luxembourg. Buses run from adjacent areas of Belgium, France and Germany. The city of Luxembourg is a favorite over-night stop on bus tours.

CUSTOMS. Travelers arriving from non-EC countries may bring in 200 cigarettes or 50 cigars or 100 cigarillos or 250 grams (8.75 ounces) of tobacco; 1 liter of spirits over 22% proof or 2 liters of sparkling wine plus 2 liters of other wine; 50 grams (1.7 ounces) of perfume and 0.25 liters of toilet water; other goods to the value of 2,000 fr.L.

Travelers arriving from a country within the EC may import 300 cigarettes or 75 cigars or 150 cigarillos or 400 grams (14 ounces) of tobacco; 1.5 liters of spirits over 22% proof or 3 liters of sparkling wine plus 5 liters of other wine; 75 grams (2.6 ounces) of perfume and ⅜ liter of toilet water; other goods to the value of 15,800 fr.L.

HOTELS. In the capital, most hotels in the Moderate and Inexpensive range are rather characterless. Outside the capital, hotels are more likely to be in tranquil countryside settings. Ask the *ONT* at the airport or in station square, stating clearly your limits, or get their free hotel guide. This indicates such amenities as whether bath or shower, or breakfast, are included in the price. The Moderate hotels listed here cost from 2,000 fr.L to 3,000 fr.L for two people in a double room and the Inexpensive from under 2,000 fr.L. You can still find a Moderate or Inexpensive hotel in the tourist centers of Bourscheid, Clervaux, Diekirch, Echternach, Esch-sur-Sûr, Ettelbruck, Grevenmacher, Remich, Vianden or Wiltz in season. In nearby villages, modest but comfortable lodgings can be found in both categories. Many hotels, especially in the capital, welcome the handicapped.

Ask for the *Bargain Rates* booklet, listing special fares available October to June, at the ONT; proposals are made for weekends or longer stays at package prices, including fringe benefits such as guided tours, use of bicycles or a bottle of wine to take home. A number of hotels offer a Gourmet Weekend package—four main meals and accommodation for prices ranging from 2000 fr.L. to 7,000 fr.L. depending on the hotel, for the two-day vacation. Some offer 5 days at 4,600 fr.L. to 8,000 fr.L. Month-long deals are very rare, particularly during the tourist season. Many offer free lodging for children staying in the same room as their parents, but ask at the ONT for guidance to places and events that have reduced prices for pre-teens.

Budget Accommodations. There is no point in Luxembourg where you are more than a couple of hours' walk from a youth hostel or camp site. Hostels cost 135 fr.L. a night for everyone under 26 provided you buy at least one meal on the premises, and 150 fr.L. if you don't. For those over 26 add 40 fr.L. to the cost. For hostels in Luxembourg City add another 20 fr.L. Breakfast and dinner cost 80 fr.L and 195 fr.L respectively. Try Hollenfels hostel, in a 9th-century castle. The *Luxembourg Youth Hostels Association,* 18 Pl. d'Armes, Luxembourg City (tel. 2–55–88), gives information. Equally good are the hostels at Echternach, Grevenmacher, Vianden, and Wiltz. For terms or the brochures, films and slides designed to help plan your stay in these ask the ONT. Your prime source of information on campsites, vacation homes, special train fares, group travel, youth theater, youth musical events and other bargains is the ONT. For advance planning, write to them at P.O. Box 1001, Luxembourg City. The Syndicat d'Initiative in all main towns gives great on the spot help. For special youth events or study programs write the *Service National de la Jeunesse,* 1 rue de la Poste, Luxembourg City (tel. 47–88–38). The *Gîtes d'Etape Luxembourgeois,* 23 blvd. Prince Henri, Luxembourg City (tel. 2–36–98), have rest houses and vacation homes. Luxembourg is probably the best country in Europe for campsites. Sites are clean and well organized. Ask the ONT for their "Camping '90" brochure or write to the *Federation Luxembourgeiose de Camping et Caravaning,* 174 Rue de Soleure, Belvaux.

RESTAURANTS. The *Syndicat d'Initiative* publishes a good free guide to city restaurants. It mentions restaurants providing Luxembourgish specialties, vegetarian cuisine and even diet meals. Most restaurants offer a cheaper, set 'Tourist Menu' and more expensive *à la carte* menu. Do not be surprised to see menus written in French or German; many are written in three languages, including English. Dishes like *quenelles de foie de veau* (a tasty dish of minced liver balls) and *Judd mat Gardelbounen* (smoked pork with broad beans in a creamy sauce) are best accompanied by a fine yet fruity *Rivaner* or the drier more refined *Elbling,* both excellent local wines. Local fish and game are also excellent, especially *truite* (trout) and *Marcassin* (wild boar). A meal in a Moderate restaurant costs from 900–1,500 fr.L.; in an Inexpensive one from 450–900 fr.L without drinks.

The cafés in Luxembourg are too numerous to mention. In most of them you can get a sandwich or snack, perhaps Ardennes ham, cheese toasted Swiss-style, or mussels in tomato sauce. Check the menus, usually posted outside, and choose your price range in advance.

TIPPING. In all Luxembourg restaurants and hotels, the bottom line of your bill is the price you pay. All taxes and service charges are included. This frees everyone from complexes about tipping. Tips are valued as clear appreciation of attention beyond the call of duty. A smile and a kind word are also welcome. Taxi drivers expect a 15% tip and hairdressers appreciate the same.

MAIL. Current rates for airmail letters up to 20 grams: to the U.S., 26 fr.L; to the U.K. and Western Europe, 12 fr.L.

CLOSING TIMES. Shops are open from 8 until noon, and from 2 to 6, except on Monday when most do not open before 2 P.M. Banks open from 8 until noon, and 1 to 4.30, Monday to Friday. Both shops and banks close on public holidays.

Change windows at the airport and railway station are open every day from 8 A.M. until 9 P.M.

GETTING AROUND LUXEMBOURG. By Train.

Luxembourg Railways (CFL) has regular services to Belgium, France, and Germany. Within Luxembourg, excellent deals include half-price weekend travel to key tourist destinations and half-price travel to anyone over 65. One-, two-, three-, and five-day runaround tickets are issued in conjunction with bus services. The five-day ticket (fr.L. 658) and the one-day ticket (fr.L. 217) are particularly popular. In Luxembourg City, book at the train station or tel. 49–24–24 between 7 A.M. and 8 P.M.

By Bus. There is a network of buses reaching all parts of the Grand Duchy—most link with train services. In Luxembourg City there are about 20 city bus routes most of which radiate from the railway station: 35 fr.L., or 200 fr.L. for a 10-trip card, available at the railway ticket window. Popular destinations from the city are the Eisch Valley and Echternach.

Route 9 links with the airport taking about 25 minutes for the four-mile trip. Services are about every 20 minutes from both the airport main terminal and the railway station from 6 A.M. to about 11 P.M. A taxi downtown will cost you about 450 fr.L.

By Taxi. Most taxis have a pickup charge of 90 fr.L., and then a rate of 26 fr.L. per kilometer, but ask first: there are so-called luxury taxis circulating that charge much more. There are taxi stands at the Gare Centrale (train station) and by the main post office.

By Boat. From spring through fall, regular boat service between Schengen and Wasserbillig, and on into Germany, gives a scenic tour on the Moselle. There are bus connections to the capital.

By Bicycle. Special cycle trails exist in the Diekirch-Echternach and Vianden-Reisdorf areas; ask at the ONT or Syndicat d'Initiative offices. To rent a bike, you need to travel 48 km (30 miles) from Luxembourg City to Reisdorf, where the Syndicat d'Initiative, at the railway station (tel. 86778 or 86698), will help you. Bicycles are carried free on trains. They are not accepted as baggage on buses. Hitchhiking is legal. For discount student and youth travel, contact *Sotour,* 15 pl. du Theatre, Luxembourg (tel. 46 15 14).

Luxembourg City

Luxembourg City is rewarding to explore on foot. A walk along the ramparts and visit to the *casemates* invoke a past when this fortress was called the Gibraltar of the North. The model of the citadel, rue du Curé near the Place d'Armes, can help to orient you. Don't miss the National Museums in the oldest part of town, the splendid late Gothic cathedral of Notre Dame, nor the Chapel of St. Quirinus, partially cut into the rock at the foot of the Montée de la Pétrusse. Above the old Three Acorns bastion you see the European Community buildings on the Kirchberg, for this millenial city is now the banking center of the EC. You can ramble around the city happily and not be afraid to ask your way: English is widely spoken.

PRACTICAL INFORMATION FOR LUXEMBOURG CITY

Hotels

Moderate

Air Field, 6 rte. de Trèves (tel. 43–19–34). 10 rooms. At Findel Airport.

Alfa, 16 pl. de la Gare (tel. 48–65–65). 100 rooms. Reliable, ever since the days when General Eisenhower stayed here.

Bristol, 11 rue de Strasbourg (tel. 48–58–29). 30 rooms. An old fashioned yet comfortable hotel. Hunting and fishing trips can be organized from here.

Central Molitor, 28 av. de la Liberté (tel. 48–99–11). 36 rooms. A formal hotel with traditional, elegant restaurant. Set near the banking area.

Cheminée de Paris, 10 rue d'Anvers (tel. 49–29–31). 24 rooms. Terrace.

City, 1 rue de Strasbourg (tel. 48–46–08). 30 rooms. Near the station area.

Dauphin, 42 av. de la Gare (tel. 48–82–82). 35 rooms. Welcomes young people.

Delta, 74–76 rue Adolphe Fischer (tel. 49–30–96) 24 rooms. Garage.

Empire, 34 pl. de la Gare (tel. 48–52–52). 45 rooms. Excellent restaurant.

Fort Reinsheim, 41 route d'Esch (tel. 44–14–36). 26 rooms. Parking.

Français, 14 pl. d'Armes (tel. 47–45–34). 26 rooms. Quiet, bright, and comfortable hotel with a good Franco-Italian restaurant that produces Luxembourgish specialties on request.

Italia, 15–17 rue d'Anvers (tel. 48–66–26). 20 rooms. This central hotel has a good Italian restaurant.

San Remo, 10 pl. Guillaume (tel. 47–25–68). 13 rooms. Terrace.

Schintgen, 6 rue Notre-Dame (tel. 2–28–44). 35 rooms. A modest hotel near the banking area.

Walsheim, 28 pl. de la Gare (tel. 48–47–98). 19 rooms. Opposite the train station.

Inexpensive

Century, 6 rue Joseph Junck (tel. 48–94–37). 26 rooms.

Chemin de Fer, 4 rue Joseph Junck (tel. 49–35–28). 25 rooms. Modest, friendly.

Dauphin, 42 av. de la Gare (tel. 48–82–82). 35 rooms. Welcomes young people.

Mertens, 16 rue de Hollerich (tel. 48–26–38). 8 rooms. Parking.

Le Parisien, 46 rue Zithe (tel. 49–23–97). 9 rooms, all with TV.

Sporting, 15 rue de Strasbourg (tel. 48–43–32). 15 rooms. Near the station.

Touring, 4 rue de Strasbourg (tel. 48–46–29). 15 rooms. Near the station.

Zürich, 36 rue Joseph Junck (tel. 49–13–50). 14 rooms.

Restaurants

Moderate

Caesar, 18 av. Monterey (tel. 47–09–25). Franco-Italian cuisine. Closed Sun.

Club 5, 5 rue Chimay (tel. 46–17–63). Good salads. Terrace. Closed Sun.

Kamakura, rue Munster 24 (tel. 47–06–04). Japanese specialties including sushi and tempura preparations.

Mister Grill, 15 pl. d'Armes (tel. 2–75–37). Irish beer and lots of salad.

Osteria del Teatro, 21–25 Allée Scheffer (tel. 2–88–11). Franco-Italian. Vegetarian dishes a specialty.

Peffermillen, 61 av. de la Gare (tel. 48–01–42). Home cooking including local specialties. Closed Mon.

Poele d'Or, 20 rue Marche-aux-Herbes (tel. 47–06–04). A classic French menu in a former chapel. Closed Mon. and Jan.

The President, 32 pl. de la Gare (tel. 48–61–61). Vegetarians food offered. Closed Sun.

Stones Steakhouse, 8 av. Pasteur (tel. 2–48–15). Steaks or diet meals available.

Taverne du Passage, 18 rue du Curé, 14 pl. Guillaume (tel. 4–06–63). Closed Tues. *Raclette* and other Swiss dishes.

Um Bock, 4–8 rue de la Loge (tel. 47–53–08). Italian cuisine in a lively atmosphere.

Inexpensive

Ancre d'Or, 23 rue du Fossé (tel. 47–29–73). Luxembourgish cuisine. A friendly restaurant serving local dishes, including pork with beans. Closed Sun.

Le Calao, 47 av. de la Gare (tel. 49–49–71). Substantial portions.

Maison des Brasseurs, 48 Grand 'rue (tel. 47–13–71). Luxembourg grills. Closed weekends.

la Marée, 37 av. de la Liberté (tel. 49–08–99). Seafood. Closed Mon.

l'Orangerie, 15 pl. d'Armes (tel. 2–75–61). Vegetarians dishes.

Peking Garden, 31 rue Philippe II (tel. 47–55–51). Chinese specialties.

Pôle Nord, 2 pl. de Bruxelles (tel. 47–23–23). French style with German portions. Closed Jan-Feb.

Quick Hamburger, 9–12 pl. d'Armes (tel. 2–41–25).
Rigoletto, 2a rue des Capucins (tel. 47–45–12). Italian and local cuisine.
San Remo, 10 pl. Guillaume (tel. 47–25–68). International menu.
La Taverne, 5 av. Marie Therese (tel. 4–32–16). Luxembourgish cuisine.
Taverne Nobilis, 47 av. de la Gare (tel. 49–49–71). Parking.
Um Dierfgen, 6 côte d'Eisch (tel. 2–61–41). Steaks (horse or beef).
Welle Mann, 12 rue Wilthein (tel. 47–17–83). Light snacks in a cosy rustic atmosphere with wonderful views across the Alzette Valley. Open 10–7. Closed Mon.

ENTERTAINMENT. To have a good time—take your time. Luxembourgers do: on terraces, in cafés, at meals, over tea or under the trees in the square on a long summer afternoon with a cool drink in hand, friends about and a band playing in the background. On rainy days you can ask any café owner for a deck of cards. Sports are a good way to meet people. You will find Luxembourgers very friendly where there are common interests.

While nightclubs are hardly budget diversions, in Luxembourg the prices are not excessive and the floor shows are fair. By law all clubs must close by 3 A.M. The Casino at Mondorf-les-Bains offers roulette, black-jack and slot machines with an international program of variety and dance.

Plan your entertainment before coming or upon arrival with the ONT or Syndicat d'Initiative, which can give you the time, place and price of events.

Cinema. Watch café and store windows for posters that give the week's cinema offerings. Some are sure to be in English. VO means "original version," which, if the company is British or American, can mean English.

Discos. There are many, especially in the capital city, such as *Byblos,* 10 av. Monterey (tel. 2–32–29), *Club Wall Street 5,* 5 rue du Mur (tel. 48–33–77), *Royal Bugatti,* rue des Bains (tel. 4–12–41) or *Metropolis,* 56 rue du Fort Neipperg (tel. 48 22 11), which features three floors of laser disco. Most others are upgraded cafés or former night clubs where you pay the maximum for drinks. Occasionally a minimum is set or an entrance fee charged, usually entitling you to drinks. "In" people go out to *Cafe am Häffchen* with its wonderful terrace, which is located in the "Bissorwee" (lower old town); open from 5 P.M. daily except Mon.

Theaters. All major towns and many smaller ones have a theater season. Open-air events in summer are especially enjoyable, often in a castle setting such as the château de Wiltz. In the capital there is *Théatre Municipal,* Rond Point Robert Schuman (tel. 47–08–95/96), or *Théatre des Casemates* (tel. 4–08–32), actually inside the ancient fortifications. The *Théatre Municipal,* pl. du Brill at Esch-sur-Alzette (tel. 54–03–87) frequently has programs worth the ride. Although a few plays are in English, most are in French or German. It may be worth going to a German play in the Bock *casemates* simply to absorb the strange atmosphere.

Concerts. These are also in the municipal theaters as a rule and larger events, such as jazz festivals, in sports centers. In summer either might be outdoors. Events are varied, from chamber music to grand opera, and in all modes from classical through blues and hard rock to avant-garde experiments. Most are at quite affordable prices and band concerts are free. Don't forget that useful student ID card for reductions.

MUSEUMS. Museums and archeological or historical sites to visit are not lacking in Luxembourg. Trips to the Cathedral in Luxembourg City and the Basilica in Echternach are high on the list. Admissions range from 200 fr.L. About 30% are free. Check with the ONT. The best in the capital are:

Historical Model of Luxembourg's Citadel, rue du Curé (tel. 2–28–09). Adults 40 fr.L. Open in season 10 to 12.30, 2 to 6. Closed Tuesday 2 to 6.

Pescatore Museum, Villa Vauban, rte. d'Arlon. Adults 20 fr.L. Open daily, except Tuesday, from 1 to 6, Saturday and Sunday 9 to 12 and 3 to 7.

Post and Telephone Museum, 19 rue de Reims (tel. 476–52–45). Admission free. Open Tuesday, Thursday and Saturday, 10 to 12, 2 to 5.

State Museums, Marché aux Poissons (tel. 47–87–10). Admission free. Open daily, except Monday, 10 to 12, 1 to 5. Rich collections of painting, sculpture, natural history, history and archeology. It also houses the outstanding Bentinck-Thyssen collection of 15th- to 19th-century art, including work by Breughel, Rembrandt, and other masters.

In the regions, there are the following museums of note:

Bech Kleinmacher. *A Possen,* Sandtegass (tel. 69–82–33). Adults 50 fr.L. Open daily in season except Monday, 2 to 7. Folklore.

Clervaux. *Abbey of St. Maurice and St. Maur* (tel. 9–10–27). Exhibitions on the monastic life. *Castle of Clervaux* (tel. 9–10–48). Adults fr.L. 40 each exhibit. Open 10 to 5 in season. "The Family of Man" photographs by Edward Steichen and 22 models of Luxembourg's castles. Museum of the Battle of the Bulge.

Diekirch. *Museum of the Battle of the Ardennes.* Adults 80 fr.L. Open daily, 10–12, 2–6.

Ehnen (Wormeldange area). *Wine Museum* (tel. 7–60–26). Adults 60 fr.L. (includes drink). Open in season daily except Monday, 9.30 to 11.30, 2 to 5.

Mersch. *Roman Museum,* rue des Romains. Admission free. Ask for the key at 1A rue des Romains (Mme. Bettendorf), or at the town hall. There are picturesque walks from Mersch through the woods and valleys and some prehistoric caves.

Rumelange. Situated in a rocky red valley, the mining museum is carved into a former mine. Follow the signs. Adults 60 fr.L. Open daily in season 2 to 6, or tel. 56–54–71 for reservations.

Vianden. *Victor Hugo House,* Grand'rue (tel. 8–42–57). Adults 20 fr.L. Open daily except Wed. in season 9.30 to 12, 2 to 6. Dwelling where Victor Hugo lived in exile in Luxembourg. *Museum of Rustic Art,* 98 Grand'rue (tel. 8–45–91). Adults 40 fr.L. Open daily 10 to 12, 2 to 6.

To the many other castles, admission is 20–80 fr.L. There are wine cellars to visit all along the Moselle. Admission costs 35–50 fr.L., including wine tasting.

SHOPPING. A popular stopping point is Luxembourg's *Villeroy and Boch* china factory outlet where you can buy from the full range of top quality dishes or take what they have in seconds and thirds at cut-rate prices. At 330 rue de Rollingergrund. Or visit the new first-choice Villeroy and Boch shop in town, on the corner of rue du Fosse and rue du Cure. Hi-fi equipment can be bought in the station area at prices considerably lower than in neighboring countries.

Purchase of goods for export often qualify for a sales tax refund (TVA) of 12%. Ask the store to fill out a refund form. You must then have it stamped by the customs officials on leaving the Benelux.

USEFUL ADDRESSES. *American Embassy* 22 blvd. Emmanuel Servais (tel. 40–123); *British Embassy* 28 blvd. Royal (tel. 29–864); *Wagons Lits Tourisme* 6 rue Aldringen (tel. 46–03–15); *Thomas Cook* 15 rue Notre Dame (tel. 22–931); *Tourist Office* Air Terminal, Pl. de la Gare (tel. 48–11–99) and Pl. d'Armes (tel. 2–28–09).

PRACTICAL INFORMATION FOR THE REGIONS

Hotels and Restaurants

Beaufort. This "Little Switzerland" scenery is one of tumbledown castles and hilly paths. *Binsfeld* (M), 1 Montée du Château (tel. 8–60–13). *Rustique* (M), 55 rue du Château (tel. 8–60–86). 7 rooms, all without shower or bath. *St. Jean* (M), 59 Grand'rue (tel. 8–60–46).

Berdorf. Central location for walking, including to high viewpoints. Forests. Rock climbing. *Le Chat Botté* (M), 36 route d'Echternach (tel. 7–91–86). *Herber* (M), 91 rte. de Echternach (tel. 7–91–88). *Pittoresque* (I), 115A Um Wues (tel. 7–95–97).

Bourscheid. Castle being restored. *St. Laurent* (I), 27 rue Principale (tel. 9–00–10).

Clervaux. Castle, abbey, walks, fishing. *Koener* (M), 14 Grand'Rue (tel. 9–10–02). *Du Parc* (I), 2 rue du Parc (tel. 9–10–68).

Diekirch. Comfort, tradition and diversity. *Du Parc* (M), 28 av. de la Gare (tel. 80–34–72). *Au Beau Séjour* (I), 12 Esplanade (tel. 80–34–03). *Aveirense* (I), 33 av. de la Gare (tel. 80–33–24).

Echternach. *de l'Abbaye* (I), 2 rue des Merciers (tel. 72–91–84). *Aigle Noir* (I), 54 rue de la Gare (tel. 7–23–83). Terrace. *Bon Accueil* (I), 3 rue des Merciers (tel. 7–20–52). Terrace. *Etoile d'Or* (I), 39 rue de la Gare (tel. 7–20–95). Free garage. *Petite Suisse* (I), 56 rue A. Duchscher (tel. 7–21–78). *Au Soleil* (I), 20 rue des Remparts (tel. 7–20–33). Children's playground.
Restaurants. *La Petite Marquise* (M), 18 pl. du Marché. *du Pont* (I), 34 rue du Pont (tel. 7–20–26).

Ehnen. Heart of Moselle wine country. *Bamberg's* (M), 131 rte. du Vin (tel. 7–60–22).

Esch-Sur-Sûre. *du Moulin* (I), 6 rue du Moulin (tel. 8–91–07). *de la Sûre* (I), 1 rue du Pont (tel. 8–91–10).

Ettelbruck. Busy market. *Cames* (M), 45 rue Prince Henri (tel. 8–21–80). *Central* (M), 25 rue de Bastogne (tel. 8–21–16). *de Luxembourg* (M), 7–9 rue Prince Henri (tel. 8–22–57). *Hotel du Marché* (I), 5 rue de Bastogne (tel. 8–22–44).

Grevenmacher. Wine center. *Le Roi Dagobert* (M), 32 rue de Treves (tel. 7–57–17). *Govers* (I), 15 Grand'rue (tel. 7–51–37).
Restaurants. *Princess Marie-Astrid* (I), 32 route de Thionville (tel. 75–82–75). Dining aboard a river boat.

Mersch. At entrance to Valley of the Seven Castles. *Au Bon Accueil* (I), 34 rte. de Luxembourg (tel. 3–22–76).

Mondorf-les-Bains. Traditional spa, with casino. *International* (M), 58 av. Fr. Clement (tel. 6–70–33).

Remich. On the Moselle. *Beau-Sejour* (M), 30 quai de la Moselle (tel. 69–81–26). *de la Poste* (I), 16 pl. du Marché (tel. 69–81–33).

Vianden. Castle of Orange-Nassau dynasty. Chairlift. *Du Château* (M), 74–78 Grand'rue (tel. 8–48–78). Terrace. *Oranienburg* (M), 126 Grand'rue (tel. 8–41–53). *Clees* (I), 8 rue de la Gare (tel. 8–44–74). *Le Petit Palais* (I), 13 rue de la Frontière (tel. 8–41–57). *Réunion* (I), 66 Grand'rue (tel. 8–41–55).
Restaurant. *Veiner Stiffchen* (M), 26 rue de la Gare (tel. 8–41–74).

Wiltz. *Du Vieux Château* (M), 1 Grand'Rue (tel. 9–60–18). *Auberge Michel Rodange* (I), 11 rue M. Rodange (tel. 95–82–35). *Beau Séjour* (I), 21 rue du X Septembre (tel. 95–82–50).

Malta

Malta may be a small island (only 17 miles long and 9 miles wide) but its strategic position in the center of the Mediterranean has given it a stirring history. Sightseeing is not only fascinating but also offers much that is unusual—neolithic temples, artifacts of the Crusades and a strange cave where archeologists have found skeletons of pygmy elephants and hippopotami that were about the size of large dogs.

The Maltese people are famous for their warm hospitality. As far back as A.D. 60 when St. Paul was shipwrecked on Malta, St. Luke wrote—"The inhabitants showed us no small courtesy". Add to this reasonable prices, warm blue water for swimming and skin diving and the fact that the people of Malta and her sister islands, Gozo and Comino, speak English. What more could you want?

The capital, Valletta, lies between two natural harbors. It is festooned with ramparts and fortifications left by the Knights of St. John of Jerusalem, which not only have beauty of design but give an impression of indomitable strength. When in 1522 the Turks drove the Knights from Rhodes, King Charles V of Spain gave them Malta and Gozo. A romantic flavor was added to the agreement by the stipulation of an annual tribute of one falcon from the Knights to King Charles to acknowledge the sovereignty of Spain. This explains why the falcon is often associated with Malta. In 1565 the Knights then withstood almost the entire might of the Turks during the famous Siege of Malta, one of the most romantic, and bloody, chapters in the long history of this little Mediterranean island. In World War II, the Maltese endured another equally grim siege, this time against the might of the Nazi war machine. Their gallant defense led to the granting of the George Cross to the islanders by King George VI. The cross appears on the island's flag.

Apart from agriculture, many people are employed in private industry, offices, workshops, factories and the docks. In recent years tourism has come to the fore and is now a major employer. Farming families work from dawn till dusk in Malta and Gozo and stick to the maxim "Early to bed and early to rise" but they enjoy their relaxation. The men gather in the evening to talk, play cards or drink beer or wine and many of the bars have TV. Many radio and TV programs are in English.

All kinds of fish from giant rays to anchovies and sardines swarm close to the islands: mackerel, tunny, dolphin, sea bream and lobsters to mention a few. Deep sea fishing expeditions can easily be arranged. For the skin diver there are shoals of tiny Mediterranean fish of exquisite coloring to watch and photograph. Then there is the amazing Blue Grotto reminiscent of the one in Capri.

The Maltese are Roman Catholics but there are also churches belonging to various other denominations. St. Paul's cathedral in Valletta and Holy Trinity in Sliema are Anglican.

PRACTICAL INFORMATION FOR MALTA

WHAT WILL IT COST. With Malta's rapid tourist development, prices are inevitably rising, though less than in most countries. The Maltese lira (LM) divides into 100 cents, and 1 cent is comprised of 10 mils. There are LM10 and LM5 bills and 1,2,5,10, 50 cents, and LM1 coins in silver and bronze. At the time of writing, there were around $3.30 and £1.79 to the Maltese lira.

You can take into the country any amount in travelers checks and other currency, but only up to LM50. You may take out of the country currencies up to the amount imported and declared to Customs on arrival, also Maltese currency up to LM25.

Sample Costs. Cinema, 40 cents each; Theater, LM1.50 each; Museum, 25 cents each; Coffee, 25 cents a cup; Beer, 25 cents a bottle; Carafe of wine, 75 cents; Bottle of vermouth, LM2. Bottle of wine, about LM 1.50.

NATIONAL TOURIST OFFICE. The head office of the *Malta National Tourist Organization* is in Harper Lane, Floriana (tel. 224444). There is also an office at the airport. Tourists are advised to visit the office situated under the arcades adjacent to City Gate (tel. 227747) for information. They have free maps and leaflets, the addresses of hotels and restaurants and particulars of sightseeing trips.

Addresses of the Malta National Tourist Organization overseas are:

In the U.S.: c/o Maltese Consulate, 249 East 35th St., New York, N.Y. 10016 (tel. 212–725–2345).

In the U.K.: Suite 207, College House, Wrights Lane, Kensington, London W8 5 SH (tel. 071–938 2668).

WHEN TO COME. The Mediterranean climate in Malta is more or less predictable being divided into two seasons. Summer lasts from May to October and winter from November to April. July and August are the hottest months; although sea breezes cool the islands and may give some relief, you're advised not to come in August. In September you may get a little rain. During October and November you often get what the Maltese call St. Martin's summer with clear skies, temperatures in the sixties and some rain. The average yearly rainfall is about 21 inches.

Average afternoon temperatures in degrees Fahrenheit and centigrade:

Malta	Jan.	Feb.	Mar.	Apr.	May	June	July	Aug.	Sept.	Oct.	Nov.	Dec.
F°	59	59	62	66	71	79	84	85	81	76	68	62
C°	15	15	17	19	22	26	29	29	27	24	20	17

SPECIAL EVENTS. On Good Friday solemn but colorful processions are held in several towns and villages. There is a carnival in Valletta during the weekend before Lent begins. The "Mnarja" (folk festival) takes place on the weekend nearest to 28th *June* and is an all-night traditional festa with folk music, dancing and singing. Several other festivals are held throughout the islands between *May* and *October*, the dates changing annually. There is a water carnival on the Sunday nearest *September* 8th when boat races and band marches commemorate the Great Siege of 1565 and the lifting of the more recent one of 1940–43.

National Holidays. Jan. 1 (New Year's Day); Feb. 10 (St. Paul's shipwreck); March 19 (St. Joseph's Day); March 31 (Freedom Day); Mar. 29 (Good Friday); Mar. 31 (Easter); May 1 (St. Joseph the Worker); June 29 (Sts. Peter and Paul); August 15 (Assumption, or Santa Marija); September 8 (Our Lady of Victories); September 21 (Independence Day); December 8 (Immaculate Conception); December 13 (Republic Day); December 25 (Christmas).

VISAS. Nationals of the United States, EC and many other European countries do not require visas for entry into Malta. However, you must of course have a valid passport.

HEALTH CERTIFICATES. These are not required to enter Malta.

GETTING TO MALTA. By Plane. Malta's international airport of Luqa has air services with various European destinations by direct or through flights, but there are no direct flights from the U.S. Fly from London, Manchester, Paris, Frankfurt, Zurich, Rome, Catania, Palermo, Tunis and Tripoli. *Air Malta* is the national carrier but *British Island Airways, Alitalia, KLM, Libyan Airlines, Lufthansa, Swissair* and *Tunis Air* fly into and out of the island. Flying time from London is about 3 hours. There is a local bus service from Luqa, with a stop just outside the airport, to Valletta, every 20 minutes from 6 A.M. to 11 P.M. The fare is about 7 cents.

By Ferry. The *Gozo Channel Co.* (tel. 603964), operates weekly from Syracuse in Sicily (summer only). The *Tirrenia Line* (U.K. agents: Serena Holidays, 40–42 Kenway Rd., London SW5 ORA, tel. 071–248 8422), operates throughout the year from Naples via Reggio Calabria (once weekly) to Catania and Syracuse (three times weekly). This crossing includes a call at Syracuse. Both ferries carry cars and offer refreshment facilities.

By Package Tour. The bulk of Malta's holiday visitors come on a package holiday of one kind or another. These are run by many operators, with the U.K. in the vanguard of this business. Accommodation is in hotels or self-catering apartments. The holidays are for one week to one month. Charter flights, such as those by *Britannia Airways,* augment the scheduled services for these holidays. Leading U.K. operators include *Cosmos, Thomson, Cadogan, Intasun,* and *Belle Air,* and *Medallion,* the latter two part of the Air Malta Group.

CUSTOMS. You may bring into the country 200 cigarettes or 250 gr. of tobacco; spirits or cordials or liqueurs up to 1 full bottle and 1 bottle of wine; perfumery and/or toilet water. You may bring in up to LM50 in Maltese currency.

HOTELS. Moderate (M) hotel prices run from about LM12 to 20 for two people sharing a double room and breakfast; Inexpensive (I) runs from LM8 to 12 for two people in a double room. There are many reasonably priced guest houses. There is also a limited self-catering sector at varying prices. There is a *Youth Hostel Association* at 17 Tal Borg St., Paola (tel. 229361). There are no camping sites.

RESTAURANTS. Prices range upwards from about LM2. Cafés are cheaper and fairly plentiful as are bars. A cup of tea or coffee and a ham sandwich is about 60 cents, steak and chips about LM1.50. One or two fast food chains have appeared.

TIPPING. It is customary to leave a tip of 10% when a service charge is not included in the bill.

MAIL. Airmail letters to North America cost 14c, postcards 10c. Letters to the rest of Europe 9c, postcards 8c.

CLOSING TIMES. Shops are open from 9 to 7, Mon. to Sat. There is usually a lunchhour closing for around three hours. Banking hours are from 8.30 to noon Mon. to Fri.; 8.30 to 11.30 on Sat. (closed a half hour later in winter).

GETTING AROUND MALTA. By Bus. Buses radiate from Valletta and the various routes are numbered. Always packed to capacity they are very cheap indeed, fares being on the distance traveled; you can cover the whole island for about 12 cents. There are timetables but they are not always adhered to, so check. There is no railway on Malta.

By Car. Cars can be hired for a modest price. Road conditions are good. Driving is on the left-hand side of the road. Speed limits are 40 kph (25 mph) in towns, 80 kph (50 mph) elsewhere. International driving licenses are acceptable.

By Ferry. Malta is linked to its neighboring island of Gozo by a drive-on, drive-off car ferry from Cirkewwa and Pieta on Malta to Mġarr on Gozo, taking about 25 minutes from Cirkewwa, with service every hour. There are motor launch services from the northwest end of Malta to the tiny island of Comino, which lies between Malta and Gozo. The round trip LM1 for adults and 50 cents for children.

Valletta

On your way into Valletta, capital of Malta, you pass through a drab 1960s city gate that replaced the Baroque gate of the Knights, destroyed by bombs in World War II. It opens onto an undistinguished but vast square flanked by modern arcades.

Republic Street, the main thoroughfare, acts as the spine of the city. Other streets are laid out in a grid pattern across it sloping down precipitously at each end to the water. Many are stepped and lined with old buildings decorated with overhanging enclosed balconies. The ornate palaces and museums, though not all that big in fact, seem enormous in this mini-city where everything is within easy walking distance.

PRACTICAL INFORMATION FOR VALLETTA

HOTELS. While there are some hotels in Valletta, the majority, and there are many, are spread around the island; some inland and some on the coast. As the whole area is so small, it is impractical to list them by districts, and that which follows is an island-wide sample. As has been mentioned a comprehensive list of all types of accommodations is obtainable from the Tourist Office.

Moderate

British, St. Ursula Street 267, Valletta (tel. 226019). Its restaurant has a lovely view over the Harbor.

Castille, St. Paul's St., Valletta (tel. 623677). A converted castle with a panoramic view over the Grand Harbor and facing a piazza.

Osborne, South St. 50, Valletta (tel. 623656). Centrally located, with spacious rooms but undistinguished decor. The rooftop lounge has wonderful views.

Inexpensive

Angela, Antonio Sciortino St., Msida (tel. 339541).
Crown, 166 Tower Road, Sliema, (tel. 331094).
Helena, Marina St., 192 Pieta (tel. 336417).
Regina, Tower Rd., Sliema 107 (tel. 330721).

RESTAURANTS. Many restaurants will serve the kind of food you are used to at home but this is not always so in seaside cafés or country inns. If you are unadventurous in your eating habits remember that pork is the islands' best meat and that the fish is excellent, especially cooked fresh from the sea.

Moderate

Luzzu Lido, Qawra Rd., Qawra, St. Paul's Bay (tel. 473925).
Tunny Net, Mellieha Bay (tel. 474338/9).

Inexpensive

Coxswain's Cabin, Marsaskala.
Buck's Head Tavern, Birzebugga.
There are several inexpensive cafés in Republic St. in Valletta and in South St. Also many in Sliema, which is the largest town in Malta and, these days, is practically a suburb of Valletta.

THEATERS. The *Manoel Theatre,* in Valletta, with its beautiful pencil-thin pillars, is said to be the oldest in Europe. It was built by Grand Master Antonio Manoel de Vilhena of the Knights of St. John in 1731. Today it stages concerts, plays and even opera.

MUSEUMS. All those in the city are within comfortable walking distance of one another. The *National Museum of Archeology* has prehistoric pottery, statuettes and Punic and Roman remains. The *National Museum of Fine Arts,* containing paintings by such artists as Mattia Preti and Tintoretto, is housed in a magnificent 18th-century palace. *St. Johns Co-Cathedral* and museum, which contains Caravaggio's masterpiece *The Beheading of St. John,* is close to the Grand Master's Palace, with its State Apartments and Armory of the Knights.

SHOPPING. Malta is well known for fine jewelry with intricate filigree work and for lace. Also briar pipes and handsome brass door knockers. There is a *Government Craft Center* in St. John's Square, Valetta Valletta. Watches and French perfume are often cheaper than elsewhere in Europe. Local wine sells at about 70 cents a bottle and is amazingly good. Best known are Lachryma Vitis and Marsovin.

USEFUL ADDRESSES. The head office of the *Malta National Tourist Organization* is in Harper Lane, Floriana (tel. 224444). Tourists are advised to visit either the office at the airport or the one under the arcades adjacent to City Gate (1 City Arcade, Valletta; tel. 227727) for information or advice. *Thomas Cook,* 20 Republic St. (tel. 233629).

The British High Commission Office is at 7 St. Anne Street, Floriana (tel. 233134); the *U.S. Embassy* is at Development House, also on St. Anne Street (tel. 620424).

Luqa Airport, (tel. 229915).

The Rest of Malta

The Hypogeum (an ancient underground chamber) at Paola is unique and was found by accident while workmen were digging an underground water storage cistern. The only indication above ground is a plaque on a house in Burial St. In the hall are displayed jewelry and pottery found during the excavations. Then you descend steps taking you three stories below ground into chambers with decorated ceilings where once an oracle made his fateful pronouncements.

Nearby are the Hal Tarxien temples, four in all, built of huge blocks of stone along the lines of Stonehenge. Some are carved and cut with great precision. The animal carvings are forceful and beautiful.

Mdina, the old walled capital of Malta, stands on rising ground in the center of the island and, if you are lucky enough to see it floodlit at night, seems almost to float in the sky. Also called the Silent City, it is well worth walking through it to admire the architecture and absorb the atmosphere. Outside the walls there is a Roman villa containing some mosaics, and there are catacombs not far away.

Gozo and Comino

One of the best budget areas is Malta's sister island, Gozo. (The return ferry trip per person costs LM1.50, cars LM5.) It is a peaceful place famous for its lace work. Victoria is its capital. If you are not in an organized party you can obtain advice on arrival at Mġarr Harbor from the Gozo Tourist Office there (tel. 553343).

Gozo is only 9 miles by 4½ with a population of 25,000. It has flat topped hills and quite deep valleys with streams so that agriculture is easier than in Malta. Gozitans make the best of their island with intensive cultivation, artificial irrigation and terracing. The island produces many fruits and vegetables. There is an open-air market daily in Victoria, still known locally by its pre-British name, Rabat.

It is claimed that the local prison has never been used and this may be a pointer to a wonderful place to get away from it all. You can go anywhere by bus for 14 cents. Apartments and villas are inexpensive; an all day bus tour costs about LM6 including lunch; the beaches are unspoiled and there is a citadel, temple and some caves to be visited. Small wonder that Ulysses is said to have dallied here with Calypso.

Comino is so small that it was originally kept by the Knights of Malta as a private game reserve. Today there is only the Comino Hotel complex here, a two-storied building with some family suites overlooking St. Nicholas Bay. The water is incredibly clear and very suitable for scuba diving; the Blue Lagoon lives up to its name and is one of the loveliest havens on the island.

There are fewer than 50 permanent inhabitants, one policeman and one postman. There are no proper roads and no cars so it is safe for even the smallest children. You need to be a little self-contained and resourceful to enjoy a holiday here to the full. If you are, it is well worth a visit.

PRACTICAL INFORMATION FOR GOZO

Hotels and Restaurants

Calypso (M), Marsalforn (tel. 556131). Delightful position overlooking a partially enclosed fishing harbor. *Cornucopia Hotel* (M), 10 Gnien Imrik St., Xaghra (tel. 556486). A converted farmhouse. *Duke of Edinburgh* (M), 85–89 Republic St., Victoria (tel. 556468). Near the main square It Tokk.

Restaurants. *Gesther* (I), Xaghra (tel. 76621). Delicious fish and local wine. *Il-Kenur* (I), (tel. 551583). Perched on top of Xlendi valley; magnificent view. *It Tokk* (I), It Tokk Square, Victoria (tel. 556292). *Triton's Bar and Restaurant* (I), Rabat St., Marsalforn (tel. 556152).

Norway

Norway is Europe's last frontier. Its elongated, spiny shape arches over the tops of Sweden and Finland to touch the Soviet border by the freezing Barents Sea. Drive its length and you will have covered more than 2,000 difficult road miles, mostly through rough, uninhabited territory ruled by mountains, lakes, rivers, glaciers and forest. In the winter, the northern half of Norway is a place of perpetual darkness and many of the roads remain impassable for months on end.

Outside the cities, where most of Norway's 4½ million people live, lies the remote beauty of the fjords. These were formed during the Ice Age a million years ago. The ice cap was fairly thin near the coast but very thick farther inland, and its weight assumed enormous proportions. Thus, where rivers had already dug valleys, the ice burrowed deeper and deeper. Since the ice pressure was lower at the coast, most fjords' entrances are shallow, about 500 ft. below the sea floor's level, while the depth of the fjord may reach 4,000 ft. Although there are fjords all along the coast—Oslo is at the head of a fjord—the most dramatic ones lie within "Fjord Country," where long fingers of sea indent the high coastal terrain between Stavanger and Trondheim. Summer travelers might also be enticed north to the Lofoten Islands, or the Land of the Midnight Sun.

Unfortunately, Norway is enormously expensive—even by Scandinavian standards. Although prices plummet outside cities, long-distance transportation brings higher costs. Finding affordable meals, alcohol and accommodations in the cities is a challenge. Norwegian oil is one of the reasons prices are so high here, and goes some way to explaining why Norwegians enjoy Europe's highest standard of living. Yet by taking cost-cutting measures like longer stays in simple accommodations, and devoting days to outdoor pursuits—fjord-gazing, hiking, fishing, berry-gathering, skiing, or whatever you choose—you too can afford to spend your leisure-time in much the same way as would a Norwegian.

PRACTICAL INFORMATION FOR NORWAY

WHAT WILL IT COST. The cost of living is high in Norway, but budget travelers should find many ways of stretching their dollars and pounds. When you compare prices in the hotel list published annually by the Norwegian Tourist Board, always check whether breakfast is included in the room rate. Also remember that most country hotels offer lower rates (pension terms) when you stay 3 or 5 days or longer at the same hotel. Some hotels offer reduced terms before and after the peak season. Advantage can also be obtained by using the Inter-Nor hotel check system, called Bonus Passport, which gives discounts of 15–40% at hotels in more than 30 towns and resorts between June 15 and Aug. 20, as well as from the *Fjord Pass,* offering a discount of up to 20 or 30% in 170 hotels. Other chains' discount schemes are covered in the all-Norway Accommodation Guide, available from tourist offices. The guide is free outside Norway, within the country it costs NOK 5. Both cards are sold by travel agents. And the *Nordturist* rail ticket can mean a considerable saving if you intend to travel by train in Scandinavia. In towns, always look at the local guide to ascertain on which days there is free admission to museums and other sights.

The unit of currency in Norway is the krone, written as NOK and divided into 100 ore. You may import unlimited amounts of Norwegian and foreign currency, but you cannot take out more than NOK 2,000, and no banknotes may have denomination over NOK 100. The current rate of exchange (mid-1990) is approximately NOK 6.7 to the U.S. dollar, and NOK 10.7 to the pound sterling.

A good deal in restaurants and cafés is the *Dagens rett* (dish of the day), usually consisting of a main course and coffee for NOK 40–80 including service charge and tax. Since breakfast is often included in the room rate, you might pay only NOK 45 for lunch—and a bit more for dinner—perhaps having an occasional 3-course meal if the menu is priced to suit your purse.

Sample Costs. In moderate restaurants a carafe of table wine costs NOK 150, a bottle of beer NOK 35. A bottle of beer in a pub costs NOK 35, a coffee in a snack bar NOK 9. A moderate seat in a cinema costs NOK 35, in a theater NOK 75–200. Special events NOK 200–500. Museum admission varies between NOK 5 and 10, though many museums are free.

NATIONAL TOURIST OFFICE. *The Norwegian Tourist Board,* Nordtra Post Box 499, Sentrum, N–0105, Oslo 1 (Havnelagene), has a great number of useful publications. First of all, the annual hotel price list gives lots of valuable information in addition to current prices and gives a list of discount hotels. Then, the Tourist Time Tables contain schedules and fares for boat services to and in Norway, rail services, domestic air travel, ferry and bus services, sketch maps for the various regions, also a list of names and addresses of transportation companies. Another folder gives information about campsites and youth hostels. These publications are free but for postage.

Addresses of the Norwegian National Tourist Office overseas are:
In the U.S.: 655 Third Ave., New York, N.Y. 10017 (tel. 212–949–2333).
In the U.K.: 5–11 Lower Regent Street, London, SW1Y (tel. 071–839 6255).

WHEN TO COME. The summer season extends from May through September, with the peak season in June-July-August. Many hotels offer reduced rates before and after the peak season (see special offers for Oslo and other hotels, below), and the coastal express steamers also have attractive off-season rates.

Winter extends from Christmas until well after Easter, with the peak winter sports season in February and March. Some hotels offer lower rates during January. High mountain skiing is possible through May.

It is much warmer in Norway than one would expect. Thanks to the Gulf Stream the climate is mild and, and not unduly damp. In recent years Norway has shown signs of warming, with very warm summers (nearly 100°F reached in summer 1989) and milder winters than ever before.

There is never any real darkness in Norway from the end of April to early August. At midsummer (June 24), the maximum hours of daylight are 24 hours in Hammerfest, 20½ hours in Trondheim, 19 hours in Bergen and 18½ hours in Oslo and Stavanger. Norway is certainly more solar than polar! The Midnight Sun is one of Norway's outstanding tourist attractions. The sun does not sink below the horizon at North Cape between May 14 and July 30. Of course, the opposite is true in winter. The sun never rises in the extreme north, while in Oslo the days are relatively short; at winter solstice (Dec. 21) there will only be about seven hours of daylight.

Average afternoon temperature in degrees Fahrenheit and centigrade:

Oslo	Jan.	Feb.	Mar.	Apr.	May	June	July	Aug.	Sept.	Oct.	Nov.	Dec.
F°	30	32	40	50	62	69	73	69	60	49	37	31
C°	-1	0	4	10	17	21	23	21	16	9	3	-1

SPECIAL EVENTS. *January,* Monolith Ski Race in the Vigeland Park, Oslo. *February,* international fur auctions in Oslo—Saga mink and blue fox. *March,* Holmenkollen Ski Festival in Oslo, international skiing competitions. *April* (Easter), Sami (Lapp) festivals in Karasjok and Kautokeino, reindeer races on ice-covered river. *May,* the Midnight Sun season begins on May 14, at North Cape; Bergen International Festival of music, drama, and folklore, held annually since 1952 in Bergen, Edvard Greig's city, 20–31. *June,* Midnight Cup Golf Tournament in Trondheim, commencing at 10 P.M.; North Sea Fishing Festival in Haugesund and North Norway Festival of Music and The Arts in Harstad. *July,* International Yacht Races in Oslo fjord; Viking Festival at Stiklestad near Trondheim; Bislett Games, International athletics. *July,* International Jazz Festival in Molde, with top players from U.S. *September,* Norway Cup, International Youth Football Tournament in Oslo. World's biggest soccer tournament. Gløgerne kommer (Oslo area), an international performing arts festival. *October,* ceremonial opening of Parliament by King Olav V, in Oslo. *December,* presentation of the Nobel Peace Prize in Oslo.

National Holidays. Jan. 1; March 29–April 1 (Easter); May 1 (May Day); May 9 (Ascension Day); May 17 (Constitution Day); May 18–19 (Whitsun); Dec. 25, 26.

VISAS. American, British and Canadian visitors do not require visas to enter Norway. You must of course have a valid passport; most tourists are allowed a three–month stay in Scandinavia.

HEALTH CERTIFICATES. These are not required to visit Norway.

GETTING TO NORWAY. By Plane. There are direct flights from New York to Bergen and Oslo by *SAS;* from New York via London by *Pan Am* and *TWA;* and from New York via Reykjavik to Oslo by *Icelandair.* Otherwise, there are good connecting services to Oslo, Bergen and Stavanger from Copenhagen, which in turn has direct flights to New York, Chicago, Los Angeles, and Seattle by SAS.

In the U.K., there are direct flights from London Heathrow to Oslo and Stavanger and from Gatwick to Bergen. Charter flights sometimes leave from Stansted and arrive at Gardermoen, about 50 km. (30 miles) north of Oslo. There are also good services from Manchester and Aberdeen.

Most European capitals and major cities are linked with Oslo by air, either direct or via Copenhagen, and land at Fornebu 9 km. (6 miles) from Oslo.

By Boat. There are no direct sailings from North America to Norway by liners, although there are one or two passenger-carrying freighters. From the U.K. *Fred Olsen Line* run weekly from Harwich to Oslo via Hirtshals. Leaving late afternoon, the "Braemar" reaches Oslo in the early morning two days later. Summer sees a weekly service Harwich to Kristiansand. *Norway Line* sail three times a week to Bergen from Newcastle from May to September; twice weekly the rest of the year. *Scandinavian Seaways* DFDS operate a service from Harwich and Newcastle to Norway via Denmark.

By Train. The most practical way from the U.K. is to take the train from London (Kings Cross) to Newcastle, where there is a direct bus connection to the ferry quay for the crossings to Bergen and Stavanger. Total traveling time is between 25 and 33 hours.

If you prefer to travel mostly by train leave London (Liverpool St.) at 9.40 A.M. and proceed via Harwich, day boat to the Hoek van Holland, and then the *Nord-West Express* (day carriages and 2nd-class couchettes) to Copenhagen. There you change to a through express to Oslo arriving at about 5 P.M. on the day after departing London.

CUSTOMS. One liter of spirits and one liter of wine, or two liters wine, and 200 cigarettes may be brought in duty free by Europeans over 16 (non-European visitors 400 cigarettes or 500 grams other tobacco goods by anyone over 20). Very strict rules are in force for the import of cats, dogs and other pets so leave them at home!

HOTELS. All hotels in Norway are subject to strict regulations and inspections. Resort hotels offering superior accommodations are called "tourist" or "mountain" hotels (*høyfjellhotell* in Norwegian)—the latter are situated at least 2,500 ft. above sea level. Town hotels are generally more expensive than country hotels. The grading system used in this book includes two grades—moderate and inexpensive, since no expensive hotels are listed. The cost of a double room with breakfast for two persons in Oslo varies from NOK 600 and upwards in a Moderate hotel, to between NOK 350 and NOK 600 in an Inexpensive hotel. Remember there is a significant price drop in summer and on weekends. Special rates for weekends and public holidays. (See also p. 410).

Summer Hotels. There are several large hotels in the principal cities, available during the summer season only, because they are used by students during the rest of the year. They are generally modern and well equipped, also fairly inexpensive.

Youth Hostels. There are some 100 youth hostels spread all over Norway. They are among the best in Europe. Sheet sleeping bags are obligatory, so bring your own or hire one at the hostel. If you are not a member of YHA in your country, you can buy an international membership card at most youth hostels. There is no age limit. The charge for a bed is generally NOK 100 per night in the best hostels, or NOK 65–82 in more modest hostels. There is a reduction of NOK 20 for members of any YHA. A useful list is available from the *Norske Ungdomsherberger,* Dronningensgate 26, Oslo 1.

Cabin and Farmhouse Accommodations. Hundred of cabins are available to rent through travel agents. When renting a cabin or cottage, bear in mind that facilities vary considerably, and prices vary accordingly. Farmhouse accommodations are also available. An unusual and inexpensive alternative is to rent a primitive wooden dwelling or *rorbu* in the northerly Lofoten islands in the Midnight Sun country. Contact Norske Hytte Formidlingen, Kierschowsgt 7, Oslo 4, tel 02/356710, or tourist boards for brochure and information.

Camping. There are over 1,400 authorized campsites in Norway, classified according to standard and amenities. Ask the Norwegian Tourist Board for details; cost approximately NOK 100 per night, although shared cabins are cheaper.

RESTAURANTS. It generally pays to eat where the locals do. Look for the sign that says *Dagens rett* (dish or menu of the day), where a main course with coffee usually costs NOK 50–120. Don't be afraid of entering luxury hotels, because they usually also have inexpensive cafeterias or coffee shops, in addition to top-grade restaurants. Two chains, *Dickens* (pub-style) and *Peppe's* (pizza), can be found in many towns and are reasonably priced but very wholesome places to eat.

Restaurants listed in this chapter are graded moderate (M) or inexpensive (I). Lunch at a moderate restaurant will cost between NOK 50–120, dinner from NOK 90 and up. Inexpensive restaurants will charge NOK 50–100 for lunch or dinner, but youth hostels may provide lunch or dinner (supper) for as little as NOK 30–50. Needless to say, all prices exclude beer and wine.

Food and Drink. Breakfasts at mountain or resort hotels are often enormous with a variety of fish, meats, cheese and fine bread, served from the cold buffet along with coffee and boiled or fried eggs. When breakfast is included in the room rate, it usually is "Continental breakfast" with bread, rolls, butter, jam and coffee or tea. A national institution is the *koldtbord* (cold table), which will often be in evidence at lunch time, featuring smoked salmon, shrimps and other seafood, also assorted meats, salads, cheeses and desserts etc. However, remember to check the price list before you dig in, because the koldtbord tends to be expensive. Many restaurants and stores in summer have special offers for this buffet so eat as much as you can for an inclusive price. The sandwiches (*smorebrod*) are a meal in their own right.

Liquor and wine are sold only by *Vinmonopolet* (State-run monopoly), and licensing laws are rather severe. You can't drink at a bar before 1 P.M. in resort hotels and before 3 P.M. in town restaurants, and bars are closed on Sunday, but if you can afford it, you can stock up at the Vinmonopolet stores (closed Saturdays at 1

P.M. and all day Sundays). Hard liquor is scarce in outlying regions. However, most hotels and restaurants are licensed to sell beer and wine at any time. Hours in Oslo are gradually being liberalized. You can now drink beer or wine into the wee hours, an unheard possibility until very recently.

TIPPING. Norway is not accustomed to much tipping, particularly outside the cities. Service charge and VAT (value-added tax) are always added to the bill in hotels, restaurants and bars. Round out the bill to the nearest krone if you wish, and of course tip for special service. Porters—if found—are usually tipped NOK 5 per bag. At the hairdressers, simply round off the amount on the bill. Taxi drivers don't expect tips either, but if in doubt, add a small amount. It is usual to tip sightseeing guides if you feel they've been helpful.

MAIL. Current rates for letters up to 50 grams to Europe, NOK 4; outside Europe NOK 5; up to 50 grams NOK 10; postcards NOK 5. No extra charge for airmail within Europe.

CLOSING TIMES. Shops open from 9 to 5 (4 in summer). On Saturdays they may close as early as 2, especially in summer. Banking hours are 8.30 to 3.30, Monday through Friday, but closed on Saturdays. Museums are usually open until 6 during the peak summer season.

GETTING AROUND NORWAY. By Plane. Most towns in Norway are reached easily by air, and when you consider the cost of gas, meals, and accommodation along the way, flying is a good deal. It takes only 40 minutes to fly from Oslo to Bergen, or 4 hours from Oslo to Kirkenes near the Russian border. There are discounts for family travel and youth travel, and special bonus rates at different seasons; ask your travel agent. Inquire about "Visit Norway" passes, relatively cheap packages of domestic flight coupons (usually only good for summer travel). Details from *SAS*, SAS Building, Ruseløkkveien 6, Oslo 2 (tel. 02/429970); *Braathens SAFE AS*, Ruseløkkveien 26, Oslo 2 (tel, 02/411020); *NorskAir* (Gardermoen Airport, Akershus, tel. 06/978220); and *Wideroes Flyveselskap AS*, Mustadsveien 1, Oslo 2 (tel. 02/555960).

By Train. The railroads in Norway are well run, punctual and very clean. Because of the mountainous terrain, overall speeds are not high. Several routes are very scenic—particularly the Oslo–Bergen railroad and the Oslo–Trondheim–Bodø route, which takes you across the Arctic Circle. The *Eurailpass* is valid in Norway as is the *Nordturist* pass, which offers unlimited rail travel for 21 days and discounts on ferries and hotel chains in Scandinavia. Interail pass for youth up to 26 valid here too.

By Bus. Many bus services connect with rail and ferry services. One of the longest bus journeys in Europe is found beyond the Arctic Circle—from Fauske on the Nordland railroad to Kirkenes near the Russian border, a trip of 4 days each way. Bus fares are generally very reasonable.

By Bicycle. Many resort areas have bicycles for hire. The official hotel price list contains a special sign for hotels that have bikes for hire. In Oslo, bicycles can be rented; details are available from Oslo tourist offices. Try Den Rustne Eike ("The Rusty Spoke") behind the Royal Palace at Oscarsgt 32, Oslo, tel. 02/441880. Charges: NOK 60/day, NOK 300/week, NOK 500 security deposit).

By Boat. Perhaps the most spectacular boat trip in Europe is to go by coastal express steamer from Bergen to Kirkenes near the Russian frontier. It is a journey of 2,500 scenic miles, a round trip of 11 days, calling at 33 ports. There are attractive fare reductions when you travel out of peak season. This is a mailboat and you can join it for a day or two at any of its ports of call. Otherwise, there are many delightful boat trips from Bergen and Stavanger into the Fjord Country. You may also travel the entire length of Lake Mjøsa—largest in Norway—on board the world's oldest paddle steamer. Information on boat trips is available from *Landslaget for Reiselivet i Norge* (Norwegian Travel Association), Langkai 1, Oslo 1 (tel. 02/427044).

Oslo

Situated at the top of the 80-mile-long Oslofjord and the only world capital that is also a ski resort, Oslo is a perfect place to stay before exploring any of the rest of this spectacular country. The main street, Karl Johansgate, leads from the Central Station uphill to the Royal Palace (Slottet). Halfway between is a small green park where you'll find Stortingsgata (Parliament Street) and then, the National Theater with its entrance flanked by the statues of two of Norway's famous sons, Henrik Ibsen and Bjornstjerne Bjørnson. Behind the theater is the entrance to an underground station, departure point for excursions to Holmenkollen and some of Oslo's suburbs. Oslo City Hall (Rådhuset) facing the harbor is a twin-towered building that contains striking murals by leading Norwegian artists. In immense contrast are the romantic spires and ramparts of Akershus fortress, dating from about 1300. The occupying Nazis used it as their military H.Q. between 1940 and 1945, and a stone monument honors the memory of the Norwegian patriots who were executed within its walls. Next to the monument is the Resistance Museum (Norsk Hjemmefrontsmuseum), very well worth seeing for its factual, completely unembittered presentation of the often terrible events of the occupation of Norway. Frogner Park, known as Vigeland Park, on Kirkeveien, in the northwest section of the city, contains the world famous statues created by Gustav Vigeland, which depict the cycle of life in a graphic, sometimes tormented way. Another collection that you certainly should see is the works of Edvard Munch in the Munch Museum in Tøyen.

The best view of Oslo is from the terrace of the Merchant Marine Academy, Sjømannsskolen. Best seen during the Holmenkollen Week in March, when all Oslo climbs the hills to watch the international skijumping events; summer also brings marvelous views from the top of the jump. The most rewarding of all Oslo's many excursions is to Bygdøy. Reached either by bus or by the boat (summer only) from the quay marked "Bygdøy" in front of the City Hall, you can see *Fram*, the sturdy little ship used by Nansen and Amundsen, on their polar journeys, Thor Heyerdahl's frail balsa raft, *Kon Tiki,* which crossed the Pacific Ocean with the loss of only the parrot, and the papyrus boat *Ra II,* which crossed the Atlantic in 1970. By far the most impressive are the Viking ships, *Oseberg, Tune* and *Gogstad,* found in areas along Oslofjord with many relics from that era in Norway's past. The Maritime Museum and the Folk Museum are also in Bygdøy. Among the many fine examples of old Norwegian houses, don't miss the Gol Stavkirke, the wooden church built around A.D. 1200 and still in use. There are many good, organized city tours, and among the most highly recommended are the Oslo Highlights and Morning & Afternoon Tours. Excursions by sightseeing boats depart from Pier C, facing the City Hall (reduced schedule in cold months). Ski trails and alpine hills can be reached by public transport within half an hour from the city center and details of both winter and summer safaris in the Oslo forests by Landrover can be obtained from the Tourist Information at City Hall, Oslo 1, as can most information regarding the tours and sites listed above.

PRACTICAL INFORMATION FOR OSLO

HOTELS. Oslo has a great choice of hotels in all price ranges. The standard is very high throughout, and most hotels have good restaurants. The Oslo Guide includes a very comprehensive list of hotels and restaurants. It is available from Oslo Tourist Information. They also run an accommodations center at the Central Station for reservations in hotels, pensions and private homes. You must apply in person, and no advance bookings are accepted. The booking fee is NOK 10 per adult, NOK 5 for children. In addition, you must pay 10 per cent of the room rate, but this will be refunded when you check in. Hotels in Oslo do not offer pension terms, but 23 of them offer special reduced-rate packages valid from the end of June until the beginning of August, all weekends year-round and on public holidays. Details from Tourist Information or in the Oslo Card brochure. These packages cannot be booked more than three days in advance.

A double room in Oslo—with or without breakfast—will cost from NOK 500–600 in a Moderate hotel, or from NOK 350–500 in an Inexpensive hotel.

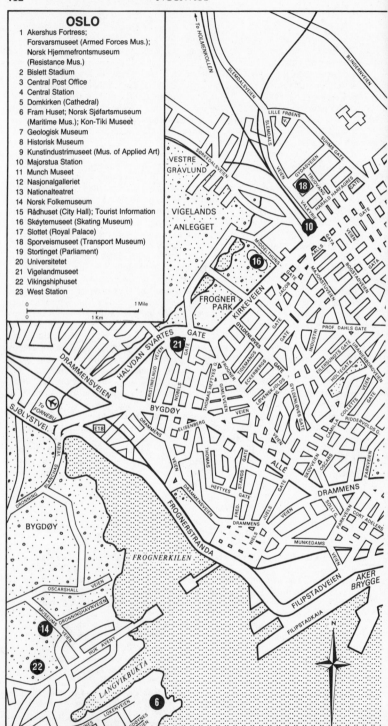

OSLO

1 Akershus Fortress;
  Forsvarsmuseet (Armed Forces Mus.);
  Norsk Hjemmefrontsmuseum
  (Resistance Mus.)
2 Bislett Stadium
3 Central Post Office
4 Central Station
5 Domkirken (Cathedral)
6 Fram Huset; Norsk Sjøfartsmuseum
  (Maritime Mus.); Kon-Tiki Museet
7 Geologisk Museum
8 Historisk Museum
9 Kunstindustrimuseet (Mus. of Applied Art)
10 Majorstua Station
11 Munch Museet
12 Nasjonalgalleriet
13 Nationalteatret
14 Norsk Folkemuseum
15 Rådhuset (City Hall); Tourist Information
16 Skøytemuseet (Skating Museum)
17 Slottet (Royal Palace)
18 Sporveismuseet (Transport Museum)
19 Stortinget (Parliament)
20 Universitetet
21 Vigelandmuseet
22 Vikingshiphuset
23 West Station

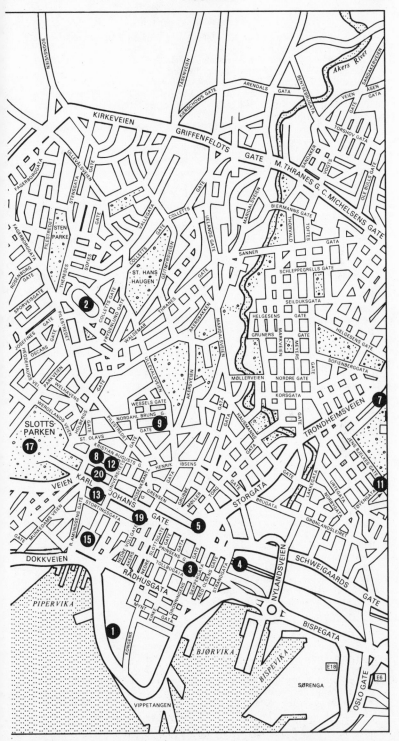

Moderate

Akershus, Akershuskaien (tel. 02/428660). 144 beds on floating hotel by the Akershus Fortress; restaurant.

Astoria Hotel (Mullerhotell), Akersgate 21 (tel. 02/426900). 99 beds, all rooms with facilities. Restaurant. In town center by Parliament.

Europa, St. Olavsgate 31 (tel. 02/209990). 280 beds; no restaurant.

Mullerhotel Europa, situated 6 km. E. of Oslo. (tel. 02/807500). 235 rooms, plus family accommodations with 3–4 beds. Opened in 1982; restaurant, bar, indoor swimming pool, trim room.

Mullerhotel West, Skovveien 15 (tel. 02/562995). 75 beds, most rooms with bath. Coq d'Or grill, popular eating place, also bar.

Norum, Bydgøy Alle 53 (tel. 02/447990). 90 beds, most rooms with facilities. Bistro with good food.

Ritz, Fr.Stangsgate 3 (tel. 02/443960). 68 beds. Hotel and pension. Restaurant. Quiet street 5 mins. by tram from center.

Saga, Eilert Sundtsgate 39 (tel. 02/427480). 65 beds, all rooms with facilities.

Sara Hotel, B. Gunnerusgt. 3 (tel. 02/429410). Right by Central Station. 464 beds; restaurants, bar, parking, all facilities.

Stefanhotellet, Rosenkrantzgate 1 (tel. 02/336290). 200 beds, all rooms with facilities. Good restaurant with lunch buffet. Very central; no liquor license.

Inexpensive

Anker, Storgata 55 (tel. 02/114005). 500 beds. Summer hotel only (June–Aug.); many rooms with 4 beds, also cooking facilities and small refrigerator; restaurant, cafeteria, supermarket.

Ansgar, Møllergata 26 (tel. 02/204735). 80 beds. Mission hotel, unlicensed.

Bondeheimen, Rosenkrantzgate 8 (tel. 02/429530). 100 beds. Unlicensed.

Det Nye City, Skippergaten 19 (tel. 02/413610). 95 beds. Probably cheapest hotel in Oslo.

Fjellhaug, Sinsenveien 15 (tel. 02/377090). 190 beds. Summer hotel only (June–Aug.); no alcohol.

Fønix, Dronningensgate 19 (tel. 02/425957). 94 beds.

Gyldenløve, Bogstadveien 20 (tel. 02/601090). 330 beds. Bed & breakfast only; no alcohol.

Haraldsheim, Haraldsheimvei 4 (tel. 02/218359). 270 beds, 6 in each room. One of the finest youth hostels in Scandinavia, truly international atmosphere. Showers in corridors, sauna, cafeteria.

IMI, Staffeldtsgate 4 (tel. 02/205330). 110 beds. Mission hotel, no alcohol.

Norrøna, Grensen 19 (tel. 02/426400). 65 beds. Cafeteria, no alcohol.

Panorama, Sognsveien 218 (tel. 02/187080). 770 beds. Summer hotel only (June–Aug.). Most rooms with facilities; restaurant, cafeteria.

Standard, Pilestredet 27 (tel. 02/203555). 72 beds. Restaurant.

Triangel, Holbergs plass 1 (tel. 02/208855). 200 beds; restaurant, no alcohol.

Camping. There are campsites within the city boundary, and they are of high standard with all facilities. The best is *Bogstad Camping,* Oslo 7, (tel. 02/507680), facing lake Bogstad, near Bogstad golf course, 9 km. from City Hall, operated by the Norwegian Automobile Assoc. (Postboks 494, Sentrum, N–0105 Oslo 1); NOK 85 per night; space for 1,200 tents, also 20 log cabins for hire, restaurant, shop, laundromat, kitchen, post office, bank, gas station, toilets (facilities for handicapped persons); open all the year round. Bus 41 Søkedalen from the National Theater. Camping Norway guide is available free outside Norway (NOK 5 in Norway) from tourist offices.

RESTAURANTS. It is difficult to pinpoint whether a restaurant is moderate or inexpensive since you can have an inexpensive meal even in expensive restaurants if you order a smallish bistro-style meal like soup, bread, and salad.

There are three restaurants, classified as expensive, which would be worth visiting, simply because they are outstanding in their own right–and you should be able to get away with it at reasonable cost, if you study the menu carefully. They are the famous *Frognerseter* restaurant on the hilltop overlooking city and fjord, the bustling *Theater Café* of the Continental Hotel, visited by artists, actors and journalists, and *Blom,* at Karl Johansgt. 41, a traditional artists' restaurant for nearly a century with a wine and food bar called "Fru Blom".

Details of all restaurants in Oslo including opening times are found in the Oslo Guide, available from Oslo Travel Association, City Hall. In addition to restaurants in the various hotels, here is a short list of other restaurants:

Moderate

Café Sjakk Matt, Haakon VII's gt. 5 (tel. 02/423227). Trendy, popular with the younger set.

Charley's Wine & Food Bar, St. Olavsgate 33 (tel. 02/113000). In same building as SAS Hotel. International cuisine in pleasant, intimate surroundings.

Den Lille Fondue, President Harbitzgate 18 (tel. 02/441960). Oslo's only fondue restaurant, small and intimate, taped music.

Frascati's Lille Kjøkken, Stortingsgaten 20 (tel. 02/111228). Light meals and a multitude of sandwiches; near the City Hall.

Gallagher's Steak House, Karl Johansgate 10 (tel. 02/336346). Pizza pub, American style steaks and pancakes, light music in evenings.

Gamle Raadhus (Old Town Hall), Nedre Slottsgt. 1 (tel. 02/420107). Oldest restaurant dating from 1640. Specializes in fish.

Herregardskroen, Frogner park (tel. 02/553424). Small inn in City Museum, also open-air summer restaurant, serving good sandwiches.

Holmenkollen Cafeteria, Holmenkollvn. 119 (tel. 02/146226). Opposite Holmenkollen station, with magnificent views of the city. Restaurant luncheon buffet a bit more expensive.

Mamma Rosa, Øvre Slottsgate 12 (tel. 02/420130). Pleasant atmosphere, guitar music in evening.

La Mer, Pilestredet 31 (tel. 02/203445). Fish and shellfish specialties. Expensive but good.

Peking House, St. Olavsgate 23 (tel. 02/114878). Good—and quickly served—Chinese cuisine. Very pleasant surroundings and friendly service.

Peppe's Pizza, Stortingsgate 6 (tel. 02/412251). Attractive wooden decor and small, intimate rooms make good setting for reasonable Italian specialties; close to the Parliament building.

Inexpensive

Baron and Baroness, Stortingsgate 10 (tel. 02/412857). Intimate restaurant, inexpensive lunch table, bar and disco. A young clientele.

Bella Napoli, Storgt. 26 (tel. 02/410052). Italian food, very popular.

Café Frølich, Drammensvn 20 (tel. 02/443737). Oslo's first music café in old-fashioned style. 6 or 7 instruments including grand piano used by young music students and any visitor who can play—everything from classical to rock. Varied menu, ice cream specialties.

Dampen, Torggata 8 (tel. 02/331783). Good cafeteria, liberal helpings.

Den Runde Tønne, Pløensgate 4 (tel. 02/337305). Beer house, unusual interiors, accordion music.

Grillstova and **Kaffistova.** Chain of inexpensive coffee shops, generous helpings. Check phone book for addresses.

Vegeta, Munkedamsvn. 3B (tel. 02/428557). Vegetarian meals, salads. Good value: eat as much as you like at fixed prices. Entertainment.

GETTING AROUND OSLO. The *Oslo Card* (from hotels, travel agents and Tourist Information) gives the tourist free transport in the city, rebates on sightseeing and restaurants, 50% discount on NSB travel to and from Oslo and within Norway and free parking in all municipal parking lots in Oslo. Valid for 1, 2, or 3 days at an adult cost of NOK 80, 120, 150, respectively (children half).

By Metro/Underground. All western suburban lines now radiate from the National Theater underground station, and all eastern suburban lines radiate from the Jernbanetorg underground station. A single ticket costs NOK 13, but it does not allow you to transfer except between subway lines.

By Bus/Tram. Streetcar and bus fares are NOK 13, but if you travel often, buy a *Maxikort* for 12 trips at NOK 135. A *minikort* (mini-card) costs NOK 60 and gives you four coupons plus transfers. There's also a good value Tourist Card for unlimited travel for 24 hours; cost NOK 35.

By Taxi. Taxi stands are found at many points, but you can phone 348 or 02/388090 (phone-requested taxis may take up to an hour to arrive) for a taxi at any time during day or night—or ask your hotel porter to help you. There are many taxi stands in Oslo, especially near hotels and major transport points. If you have to make a train during rush hours, order your cab at least one hour in advance. But beware—taxis here will strain your budget. The meter starts NOK 15 daytime, higher in the nighttime, NOK 33 if phone-ordered.

On Foot. Oslo's many pedestrian-only precincts make it a pleasure to explore on foot. A series of walking charts is available from the tourist office.

ENTERTAINMENT. Pubs. Visitors will enjoy doing a round of the pubs on Oslo's central streets, where beer is more reasonable than in restaurants and the entertainment—usually in the form of music—is as lively as it is varied. See the Oslo Guide for details.

Discos. Discos and youth clubs abound in Oslo, and they provide inexpensive enjoyment for young visitors throughout the year. The Oslo Guide contains up-to-date information on all current places, including hours and details of special entertainment. Always bring your passport, because you may then pay lower admission fees. Minimum age is anywhere from 18 to 26 for men; between 18 and 24 for women.

Cinema. Cinemas show American and British films in the original with Norwegian sub-titles. Wall posters on current films are displayed outside Stortingsgate 30. Shows begin at fixed hours (see newspapers for current times), usually at 5 and 7 and 9. No late-comers are admitted, ticket or not. No smoking. Compared with prices in other capitals, cinemas in Oslo are reasonably cheap, NOK 30–35.

Theaters and Concerts. Oslo has several theaters, though most are closed during July and August. Foremost is the *National Theater,* in Studenterlunden, rich in tradition from the times of Bjørnson and Ibsen and still serving as guardian of classic drama and as sponsor of modern plays by Western authors. Performances are in Norwegian, of course, but the opportunity of seeing an Ibsen drama presented here might still tempt you.

Other theaters are *The Oslo New* and *The Norwegian.* The Norwegian Theater, now housed in a brand-new building opened in 1985—the most modern and technically advanced theater in Europe—specializes in musicals, classics and works by contemporary playwrights who use the "new" Norwegian language as their medium. An interesting puppet theater provides good entertainment for children and adults alike. It is located in Oslo City Museum at Frognerveien 67.

The concert season extends from September to May, and the *Concert Hall,* Munkedamsveien 14, is the most modern of its kind in Europe. (Folk dancing is also staged here on Monday and Thursday evenings in July and August, 9 PM). Concerts are given during the summer in Akershus Castle, the courtyard of the Vigeland Museum, the Cathedral and the Munch Museum. See daily press and Oslo Guide for details. The *Norwegian Opera* with resident ballet company (Storgaten 23) has regular performances from October to May.

MUSEUMS. Oslo has a number of unique tourist sights such as the famous Viking ships, the great sculpture park created by Gustav Vigeland and the astounding display of Edvard Munch's paintings. There is free admission to several museums, or the fee is negligible. Consult the Oslo Guide for opening times.

Akershus Castle and Fortress, near City Hall built nearly 700 years ago, its banqueting halls are still used on official occasions. The fortress also contains the *Armed Forces Museum* and the *Norwegian Resistance Museum* with interesting exhibits from the Nazi occupation 1940–45.

Artists Association, Kjeld Stubsgate 3. Contemporary Norwegian art, also hand-icrafts.

Artists' Center (Kunstnernes Hus), Wergelandsveien 17. Alternating exhibitions of Norwegian and foreign paintings, sculpture and prints.

Bazaar Arcade, behind Oslo Cathedral. Center for applied art, which is for sale.

Bogstad Manor, Sørkedalen, 10 km. from City Hall by bus 41. Patrician manor from 1760, once owned by prime minister Peder Anker, rich art treasures. Open end-June to mid-Aug., Wed. and Sun.

Fram Museum, Bygdøynes. Polar ship used by Fridtjof Nansen and Roald Amundsen. Closed winter. Open Apr. to Nov.

Henie-Onstad Art Center, Høvikodden. Modern art collections donated by film star Sonja Henie and shipowner husband Niels Onstad; situated 13 km. W. of City Hall. Changing exhibitions of contemporary art.

Historical Museum, Frederiksgate 2. Ethnographical museum, collection of antiquities, numismatic collection.

Kon Tiki Museum, Bygdøynes. The balsa raft used by Thor Heyerdahl to cross the Pacific in 1947, also the papyrus boat Ra II in which he sailed across the Atlantic in 1970.

Munch Museum, Tøyengate 53. Over 20,000 works bequeathed to Oslo City by Europe's greatest expressionist painter, Edvard Munch (1863–1944).

Museum of Applied Art, St Olavsgate 1. Norwegian and foreign applied art from the Middle Ages to the present day. Top exhibit is the famous Baldishol tapestry from 1180.

National Gallery, Universitetsgate 13. Paintings by famous Norwegian and foreign artists. Contemporary art now at Bankplassen museum.

Natural History Museums, Tøyen. Botanical gardens, conservatories, mineralogical, geological, paleontological and zoological museums.

Norwegian Folk Museum, Museumsvei 10. Stave church dating from 1200, medieval farm buildings, Sami section, altogether 170 wooden buildings.

Norwegian Maritime Museum, Bygdøynes. Collections illustrate Norwegian maritime traditions through the ages; also polar ship "Gjøa" on waterfront.

Norwegian Museum of Science and Industry, Kjelsåsvn. 141, Oslo 4. 8,000 square meters of exhibition halls. Industrial and technical development right into the space age, and including demonstration models of, for example, telecommunications. Cafeteria, picnic area, good parking.

Old Aker Church, Akersbakken 26. Built around 1100, oldest stone church in Scandinavia still in use as parish church.

Oscarshall, Bygdøy. Pleasure palace built in 1847–52 by King Oscar I of Norway and Sweden. Open Sundays only June to Sept.

Oslo Art Association, Radhusgate 19. Situated in residence from 1626, exhibitions of paintings, sculpture, prints and etchings.

Oslo Cathedral, Stortorvet. Built in 1694–97 and restored in 1849 and 1939.

Oslo City Hall, City Hall Square. Built in 1931–50, lavishly decorated by leading painters and sculptors.

Oslo City Museum, Frognerveien 67. In Frogner manor, built in 1790, ancient interiors. New section shows development of Oslo.

Oslo Concert Hall, Munkedamsveien 14. Built in 1977, most modern of its kind in Europe, 1633 seats; plus a chamber music hall with 300 seats.

Postal Museum, Dronningensgate 15. Three centuries of postal history, interesting stamp displays.

Skating Museum, Frogner Stadium (beside Vigeland Park). Focuses on Norway's many speed skating champions.

Ski Museum, Holmenkollen. World's oldest ski museum located beside the Holmenkollen ski tower, overlooking city and fjord.

Theater Museum, Nedre Slottsgt. 1, on 2nd floor above Gamle Rådhus restaurant in 17th-century building. Oslo's theater history from the beginning of the 19th century to today.

Transport Museum, Vognhall 5, Slemdalsvn. 1–3 Norway's only collection of old tramcars and buses. History of public transport in pictures.

University Aula, Karl Johansgate 47. Festival hall with murals by Munch.

Vigeland Museum, Nobelsgate 32. Studio and home of Gustav Vigeland (1869–1943), displays of 1,600 sculptures, 12,000 sketches and 423 woodcuts.

Vigeland Park, Frogner. 192 sculpture groups comprising 650 sculptures, capped by the famous Vigeland monolith, all created by Gustav Vigeland.

Viking Ship Museum, Huk Aveny 35. Three Viking ships—the Oseberg, Gokstad and Tune—from around 800 or 900, together with collections of household articles from the Viking Age.

SHOPPING. One of the many delights when visiting Oslo is to go window shopping. Best buys are Norwegian handicrafts, crystal and glass, pewter, knitwear including sweaters and dolls in regional costume, also famous enamel on silver or gold. Ask for tax-free purchase form at shops and collect your refund at departure airport or port. There are many new shopping malls in Oslo. For lower prices, shop along Grensen. At the back of the Domkirke you'll find Basarhallene flea market.

USEFUL ADDRESSES. *U.S. Embassy,* Drammensveien 18 (tel. 02/448550); *Canadian Embassy,* Oscarsgate 20 (tel. 02/466955); *British Embassy,* Ths Heftyesgate 8 (tel 02/563890); *American Express,* c/o Winge, Karl Johansgate 33 (tel. 02/429150); *Thomas Cook,* Arbinsgate 3 (tel. 02/551901); *Central Post Office,* Dronningensgate 15, *Central Telegraph Office,* Kongensgate 21; *Norwegian Tourist Board,* H Heyerdahlsgate 1; *Oslo Tourist Information Office,* City Hall (tel. 02/427170), or in Central Station (tel. 02/416221).

Telemark and the South Coast

The highlights of Telemark (Norway's largest southern province) include several lakes and waterfalls, the majestic Mount Gausta (6,177 ft.), and ancient wooden stave churches at Heddal and Eidsborg. Skien, Henrik Ibsen's birthplace, has a modern cultural center, Ibsen House, and a memorial to the great writer five kilometers out of town. You can explore the interior from Skien via the Bandak Canal on a ten-hour boat trip that runs daily in summer. Details from the Oslo Tourist Office.

Norway's southern holiday coast is a marked contrast to the great mountains, deep valleys and glaciers of the fjord country. On the small islands and rocky coast, the water is warmed by the Gulf Stream and is as clear and clean as one could wish. This is the land of the small boat enthusiast, the fisherman, the camper and the out-of-door families. Bamble, Brevik, Kragerø and the island of Jomfruland are popular resorts. A daily boat service from Oslo runs along this coast in summer. Inland, the road to the Telemark mountains lies along valleys that, until the beginning of this century, were seldom visited even by other Norwegians, and therefore have retained their old legends and many of their old ways. In Setesdal one still sees many national costumes in everyday use. Although there are regular trains from Kristiansand to Oslo and Stavanger, the motorist has the advantage in being able to find his own spots in which to camp and enjoy the magnificent scenery.

PRACTICAL INFORMATION FOR KRISTIANSAND

Hotels

Nearly all hotels in Kristiansand have low-price summer offers. Ask the tourist office for details.

Moderate

Norge, Dronningensgate 5 (tel. 042/23320). 130 beds, all rooms with facilities. Restaurant, cafeteria.

Rica Fregatten, Dronningensgate 66 (tel. 042/21500). 110 beds, many rooms with facilities. Restaurant, bar.

Savoy Hotell, Kristian IV's gt. 1 (tel. 042/24175). 40 beds. Next to harbor, bus and train termini, fun pub.

Inexpensive

Bondeheimen, Kirkegaten 15 (tel. 042/24440). 47 beds. Cafeteria, unlicensed.
Metropole, Dronningensgate 8 (tel. 042/21465). 21 beds. Restaurant.

Roligheten, Marvikveien 100 (tel. 042/94947). 135 beds. Youth hostel.

Restaurants

All hotels have reasonable restaurants, while local tourist offices can also recommend other good spots. In addition, try:

Lazy, V. Strandgt. 23 (tel. 042/25700). Popular café open day and night.

Restaurant Sjøhuset, Ø. Strandgate 12a (tel. 042/26260). Popular seafood restaurant on the waterfront; large open-air section in summer.

Telford's Pub (M), Caledonien Hotel, Vestre Strandgate 7 (tel. 042/29100), and the adjoining *Tartan Room* are popular among the younger set.

Vestre-Mad & Vinhus and **Pavarotti,** Vestre Torr, V. Strandgt. 32 (tel. 042/23660). Pasta meals.

Stavanger

Stavanger, founded in the eighth century, is an interesting city on whose old streets historic houses stand side by side with modern buildings. It is Norway's fourth largest city, and used to be the fish-canning capital of Europe. Now a booming oil city, it serves as a base for the oil rigs in the North Sea. The city's pride is the Anglo-Norman cathedral of the late 11th century. Ledaal is a fine patrician mansion, where the King resides when he visits Stavanger, and is part of the Stavanger Museum, which displays relics from the area and includes a maritime section. An ultra-modern concert hall and arts center opened here in the mid-1980s. Viste Cave outside Stavanger is said to be 6,000 years old. Ullandhaug is an Iron Age farm, reconstructed from the Migration period. When it comes to excursions, there is nothing to beat the dramatic Lysefjord.

PRACTICAL INFORMATION FOR STAVANGER

Hotels

Moderate

Alstor, Tjensvoll 31 (tel. 04/527020). 144 beds, all rooms with facilities. Restaurant, bar, dancing in the evening.

Grand, Klubbgate 3 (tel. 04/533020). 110 beds, most rooms with facilities. Bed and breakfast.

KNA Hotel, Lagaardsvn. 61 (tel. 04/528500). 400 beds, most rooms with facilities. Reasonable summer rates. Restaurant.

Scandic Hotel, 4040 Madla (04/526500). 10 km. W. of city center. 270 beds, all rooms with facilities. *Scandic* piano bar, grill and bar.

Sola Strand, Axel Lunds v. 27, 4050 Sola (tel. 04/650222). 15 km. from city center. 100 beds, 23 rooms with bath/shower. Restaurant, bar. Near airport.

Inexpensive

Bergeland, Vikedalsgate 1A (tel. 04/534110). 49 beds. Pension.

City Gjestehuset, Madlaveien 18/20 (tel. 04/520437). 45 beds, some rooms with facilities.

Commandør, Valberggate 9 (tel. 04/528000). 71 beds, most rooms with bath or shower; restaurant, pub.

Havly, Valberggt. 1 (tel. 04/533114). 46 beds, all rooms with facilities.

Mosvangen Turistsenter, Henrik Ibsensgt 21, Tjensvoll (tel. 04/527560). 120 beds. Popular youth hostel 3 km. from station. Open June to Sept.

Rogalandsheimen Gjestiveri, Musegate 18 (tel. 04/520188). 20 beds.

Restaurants

Moderate

Elisabeth Restaurant, French cuisine and intimate atmosphere.

Jan's Mat & Vinhaus, Breitorget (tel. 524502), French food of high standard in attractive ambience.

Skagen, Skagenkaien (tel. 04/526190).

Straen, N. Strandgt. 15. Fish specialties.

Viking, Jernbanen (tel. 04/528747).

Inexpensive

Korvetten, Torget 8 (tel. 04/521111). Opposite flower market. On three floors; *Vinstuen* is an intimate wine cellar, where good food is served to the accompaniment of light music; *Korvetten* is a standard restaurant; the *Pub* on the top floor serves drinks only.

La Gondola, Nytorget 8 (tel. 04/534235). Italian food.

Mikado, Østervåg 9 (tel. 04/561681). Japanese.

Moon House, Sølvberggt. 9 (tel. 04/534340). Chinese.

Bergen

Founded in A.D. 1070, Bergen is the second largest city in Norway, as well as the ancient capital. Today it calls itself the "Fjord Capital" and is, for many travelers, a favorite city. There is Scandinavian folk culture everywhere, from the Fish Market to Bryggen Tracteursted (the 1708 complex created by a Hanseatic trust, where members of the commercial guilds had their meals and where a restaurant still exists today). Old Bergen is an outdoor museum, which recreates a 19th-century village. St. Mary's Church is the oldest building in Bergen, while the Harriet Backer Collection at the Rasmus Meyer Museum is one of the most revealing and exciting displays of turn-of-the-century Norwegian art.

The Fantoft Stave Church, dating from the 12th century, is worth seeing. Nearby is Edvard Grieg's manor house, now a museum. The Funicular to Fløien gives you a spectacular view of the city and harbor below, and is a marvelous starting point for hikes. The Hanseatic Museum (with its really fine guided tours) offers one of the most unusual depictions of Norwegian history and mentality. It is one of the best-preserved buildings along Bryggen, and one of the last remaining structures of archaic Bergen.

Bergen is also the doorway to two of Norway's most famous fjords: Hardanger and Sognefjord. The least expensive way to travel the Hardangerfjord (and get a glimpse of the Folgenfonn glacier) is to take a round trip by bus from the Central Bus station.

The Bergen-Oslo railway was opened in 1909. It is one of the most scenically impressive runs in all of Europe. During the long journey, you pass forests, lakes, waterfalls, fjords, glaciers and, near Finse, the highest point traversed by any European railroad, (4,267 feet), which at these latitudes is a land of perpetual ice, even in August! The railroad serves a number of fine tourist resorts that are very popular all year round. Voss and Geilo are the best-known, catering to both cross-country and alpine skiers and Finse has skiing until June. Hemsedal, near Gol, is Scandinavia's best alpine center with accommodation in all price categories.

Bergen is the starting-point for the famous coastal express steamers to North Cape and beyond, a round trip of 11 days. There are also boat trips to Hardangerfjord, Sognefjord, and Nordfjord. Special express boats connect southwards with Stavanger.

PRACTICAL INFORMATION FOR BERGEN

Hotels

Moderate

Strand, Strandkaien 2/4 (tel. 05/310815). 100 beds, some rooms with facilities. Breakfast only.

Toms, C Sundtsgate 52 (tel. 05/232325). 78 beds, all rooms with facilities inc. refrigerators. Dining room.

Victoria, Kong Oscarsgt. 29 (tel. 05/315030). 83 beds. Bed and breakfast. *Valente* Italian restaurant on 1st floor in same building.

Inexpensive

Augustin, C Sundtsgate 24 (tel. 05/230025). 65 beds. Popular family hotel, all rooms with facilities. Breakfast à la carte.

Bergen Apartment, Hakonsgate 2 (tel. 05/233962). 59 beds, all rooms with facilities, unlicensed.

Fantoft, 5036 Fantoft (tel. 05/282910). 668 beds. Summer only (June–Aug.), all rooms with facilities, restaurant, cafeteria.

Hordaheimen, C Sundtsgate 18 (tel. 05/232320). 122 beds, some rooms with facilities. Unlicensed.

Montana, Johan Blydtsvei 30 (tel. 05/292900). Modern youth hostel, 250 beds, 5 in each room, all with H & C water, showers in corridors.

Restaurants

Many of the leading hotels have inexpensive coffee shops or cafeterias.

Moderate

Bryggen Tracteursted, Bryggestredet (tel. 05/314046). In Hanseatic surroundings. You may buy live fish at the fish market and ask the chef to cook it any way you want it.

Chianti, Strømgate 8 (tel. 05/326430). Popular place for good food with orchestra and dancing.

Excellent, Torggaten la (tel. 05/327735). Dance restaurant, also grill, cafe, bar and pub.

Grand Café, Olav Kyrresgate 11 (tel. 05/317732). Specialty Chinese food, also pavement café in summer.

Inexpensive

Bryggestuen, Bryggen 6 (tel. 05/310630). Popular for morning coffee and light lunch.

Holbergstuen, Torgalmenning 6 (tel. 05/318015). Popular meeting place, good seafood.

Wesselstuen, Engen 14 (Ole Bulls place) (tel. 05/322900). Favorite haunt for the Bergensers, busy any time of day.

The Fjord Country, Central and Eastern Valleys

No tour guide can do justice to the soaring peaks and deep, narrow fjords of Norway's Fjord Country. Whether it might be on the banks of one of the fjord's famous salmon or trout streams, or rowing in the shadow of a thousand-foot rock face, or relaxing with a pot of good coffee and pleasant company on some fjord farm, there will always be that element of tranquil calm. There are good tourist centers along most fjords, such as Eidsfjord, Godøysund, Kinsarvik, Norheimsund, Odda, Øystese, Ulvik and Utne on the Hardangerfjord; Aurland, Balestrand, Fjerland, Flam, Laerdal, Leikanger, Marifjøra, Skjolden and Sogndal on the Sognefjord; Førde, Jølster, Loen and Olden on the Nordfjord; and in the villages of Andalsnes, Geiranger, Hellesylt and Stranda, and the towns of Alesund, Kristiansund and Molde in the county of Møre and Romsdal.

East of Bergen lie two scenic valleys, Gubrandsdalen and Østerdalen. (For car travelers beginning and ending their trip in Oslo, this might be a way to round off a tour of the south, i.e. Oslo through Telemark to Bergen, then east to the valleys and south again to Oslo). Gubrandsdalen, the longest valley, is a rich farming area offering good cross-country skiing and a boat trip on Lake Mjøsa at its southern end; alpine skiing at resorts like Lillehammer and Oppdal. The eastern valley of Østerdalen has a wilder landscape and here the old 17th-century town of Roros is a focal point.

Trondheim

Founded in A.D. 997, Trondheim is Norway's third largest city—with many outstanding tourist attractions. The Nidaros cathedral, first completed in 1320 and restored several times since, is Scandinavia's largest medieval building and the pride of Norway. Also impressive is Stiftsgarden from 1774, a magnificent rococo structure, the second largest domestic wooden building in Scandinavia (the largest is a student hostel, also in Trondheim). The Bishop's Palace is a fine relic of Trondheim's medieval glory. Kristiansten fortress built in 1682 by General Cicignon, and Trondheim open-air folk museum and the Resistance Museum and the unique Music Museum at Ringve should be seen by every visitor. The whole city has an atmosphere worthy of its historic role as the coronation place of Norway's kings.

PRACTICAL INFORMATION FOR TRONDHEIM

Hotels

Moderate

Augustin, Kongensgate 26 (tel. 07/528348). Mission hotel, dining room, cafeteria, unlicensed. All rooms with facilities.
Scandic Hotel, Brøsetveien 186 (tel. 07/939500). 250 beds, all rooms with facilities. Restaurant, bar, sauna, car park.

Inexpensive

Norrøna, Ths Angellsgate 20 (tel. 07/532020). 35 beds. Mission hotel, daily prayer meeting, cafeteria, unlicensed.
Residence, Munkegate 26 (tel. 07/528380). 120 beds, all rooms with facilities, restaurant, bar, open-air café in summer.
Singsaker, Rogersgate 1 (tel. 07/520092). 200 beds. Summer hotel only (June 15 to Aug. 15), restaurant, bodega, billiards, sauna.
Trønderheimen, Kongensgate 15 (tel. 07/527030). 77 beds, some rooms with bath/shower, dining room, cafeteria.
Trondheim Youth Hostel, Weidemannsvei 41 (tel. 07/530490). 200 beds, cafeteria.

Restaurants

Moderate

Bajazzo Rica, Søndregate 15 (tel. 07/525686). Grill, disco, night club.
Benito, Var Fruegate 4 (tel. 07/526422). Italian food, wine lodge.
Cavalero, Kongensgate 3 (tel. 07/523303). Restaurant, grill, bar, dancing.
Daniel, Tinghusplass 1 (tel. 07/525160). Steakhouse and grill.
Grenaderen, Kongsgården (tel. 07/520540). Behind the cathedral, in old forge from 1780, music, dancing, also open-air café in summer.
Kunstnerkroen, Prinsensgate 38 (tel. 07/520719). Intimate artistic restaurant with music, dancing, bar.
Naustloftet, Prinsensgate 42 (tel. 07/521880). In old boathouse, popular place for seafood.

Inexpensive

Brasseriet, Nordregate 11 (tel. 07/524730). Pizzeria, grill, disco, dancing, open-air café in summer.
China House, Søndregate 17 (tel. 07/525220). Chinese food.
Dickens, Kjøpmannsgt. 56 (tel. 07/515750). Pub, pizzas.
Erichsen, Kongensgate 3 (tel. 07/533303). Coffee house, lunch and dinner.
Landlord, Prinsensgate 40 (tel. 07/522515). English pub, draft beer.
Peppe's Pizza Pub, Kjøpmannsgate 25 (tel. 07/532920). American pizza parlor in old warehouse.

North Norway

The northernmost part of Norway encompassing the regions of Nordland, Troms, and Finnmark, is very different from the rest of the country. There are many short and narrow fjords, steep and elegant mountains of miniature alpine appearance, lakes and rivers, glaciers and vast areas of tundra with nomadic Lapps and reindeer herds. And to cap it all, there is Midnight Sun from mid-May to the end of July.

Distances in North Norway are enormous, and long-distance trips can be costly, though there are special inland rates in summer for those under 26. You can fly from Oslo to Kirkenes near the Russian frontier in 4 hours in summer; there are special reductions on all domestic flights. Or you can take the coastal express steamer from Bergen to Kirkenes and back in 11 days. This journey is available at greatly reduced cost out of peak season. You can travel by train from Trondheim to Bodø—a trip covering almost one-third of Norway's tremendous length—in one day, and continue by the Polar Express bus service from Fauske to Kirkenes in 4 days. There is also a rail service between Stockholm and Narvik. If you travel by car, the distance from Oslo to North Cape is 2,233 km. (1,383 miles).

PRACTICAL INFORMATION FOR NORTH NORWAY

Hotels and Restaurants

Alta. Finnmark, a war-ruined former Finnish and Sami (Lapp) settlement; the Hjemmeluft rock carvings are the main interest; salmon fishing in river Alta. *Alta Sommerhotel* (M), Løkkevn 2 (tel. 084/35000). 210 beds. Fully licensed.

Bardu. Troms. *Bardu Motor Hotel* (M), Setermoen, (tel. 089/81022). 78 beds. All rooms with facilities.

Berlevag. Finnmark; fishing village. *Ishavs Hotel* (M) (tel. 085/81415). 32 beds. All rooms with facilities. Fully licensed.

Bodø. Nordland, unusual cathedral built in 1956; Nordland county museum, Saltstraumen maelstrom 33 km from town.
Central Hotel (M), Prof. Schyttesqt. 7 (tel. 081/23585). 74 beds, all facilities. *Norton Grand Hotel* (M), Storgaten 3 (tel. 081/20000). 70 beds. All facilities. *Norrona* (M), Storgaten 4B (tel. 081/25550). 170 beds, all rooms with facilities. Restaurant. *Flatvold* (I), Rønvik-krysset (tel. 081/21240). 132 beds. Popular youth hostel.

Hammerfest. Finnmark, world's northernmost town, first town in Europe with electric street lighting.
Rica Hotel (M), Sørøygt. 15 (tel. 084/11333). 117 beds, all rooms with facilities. Restaurant. *Brassica* (I), Storgt 9–11 (tel. 084/11822). 38 beds, some rooms with shower. Restaurant. *Hammerfest Motel* (M), (tel. 084/11126). 192 beds in apartments for 2–4 persons. A la carte restaurant. *Hammerfest Youth Hostel* (I), (tel. 084/12247). 56 beds.

Harstad. Troms, Trondenes church from 1250, restored in 1950; annual arts festival in June; international sea fishing festival in July.
Grand Nordic (M) in summer, more expensive in winter. Strandgt. 2 (tel. 082/62170). 129 beds. *Viking Nordic* (M), Fjordgate 2 (tel. 082/64080). 160 beds, all rooms with facilities; swimming, sauna. Restaurant. *Stangnes* (I), Plassenvei 27 (tel. 082/73820). 80 beds. Popular youth hostel.

Honnigsvåg. Finnmark, 22 miles from North Cape, road open June–Sept. only; North Cape Hall is a cafeteria and souvenir shop, open June–Sept.
SAS Nordkapp Hotell (M), Nordkappgt 2–4 (tel. 084/72333). 266 beds, some rooms with facilities. Fully licensed. *Nordkapp Youth Hostel* (I), Skipsfjorden (tel. 084/75113). 40 beds. Also campsite.

Karasjok. Karasjok and Kautokeino are Sami (Lapp) centers.
Karasjok SAS Turist Hotel (M), Storgaten 12A (tel. 084/66203). 140 beds. Pizza tavern, sauna. *Karasjok Turistsenter* (M), (tel. 084/66446). 65 beds, café, sauna. *Karakroa Motel and Campinghytter* (I), Kautokeinov. 9 (tel. 084/66446). 60 beds. All rooms and cabins with facilities.

Kautokeino. *Kautokeino Turist Hotel* (M), (tel. 084/56205). 114 beds, some rooms with facilities. Restaurant, café. *Kautokeino* Youth Hostel (I), (tel. 084/56016). 35 beds.

Narvik. Nordland, world's largest port installations for iron ore exports; spectacular railroad to Sweden and Stockholm; cableway to top of Fagernesfjell mountain; 4000 years old rock carvings at Brennholtet; WWII museum.
Grand Royal (M), Kongensgt 64 (tel. 082/41500). 210 beds, all rooms with facilities. Breakfast only, fully licensed. *Victoria Royal* (M), Dronningensgt 58 (tel. 082/41584). 78 beds. Some rooms with facilities, restaurant. *Nordkalotten* (I), Havnegt 3 (tel. 082/42598). 110 beds. 7 km from station, popular youth hostel.

Svolvaer. Most important tourist center in Lofoten Islands and artists' center. In winter main port for Norway's cod fishing season.
Norton Hotell Lofoten (M), Siv Nilsensgt (tel. 088/71200). 96 beds. All facilities; restaurant, bar. *Havly* (I), (tel. 088/70344). 90 beds. *Vita-Nova Motel* (M), Damskipkaien (tel. 088/70544). 100 beds. Apartments; all facilities. *Lofoten Motel & Veikro* (I), Vesteralsvn. (tel. 088/70777). 100 beds. All facilities.

Tromsø. Troms, starting point for many attempts to reach the North Pole; Tromsø museum in Folkeparken; Tromsø town museum at Skansen; Tromsdal church with one of Europe's largest stained glass paintings; cableway to top of Storsteinen mountain.
Polar Hotel (M), Grønnegt 45 (tel. 083/86480). 88 beds, all rooms with facilities. Fully licensed. *Saga* (M), Richard Withspl. 2 (tel. 083/81180). 100 beds, all rooms with facilities, restaurant. *Tromso Hotel* (M), Grønnegt 50 (tel. 083/87520). 70 beds, all rooms with facilities. Breakfast only. *Tromso Youth Hostel* (I), (tel. 083/85735). 64 beds.

Poland

A country with no natural defensible borders, for the past 200 years Poland has been a regular victim of invasions, partitions and occupations. Roughly the size of New Mexico, Poland has a population of 37 million people, consisting predominantly of Polish-speaking Roman Catholics. Due to the loss of some six million people in World War II (half of them Jews), followed by an extended baby boom, over half the population today is under 30, making Poland one of the most youthful countries in Europe.

Poland has an outstanding variety of landscapes, ranging from the beaches and picturesque ports of the Baltic coast to the Tatra Mountains in the south, while inland there are innumerable lakes, rivers and woods. Steam trains are still to be found puffing majestically through the countryside in certain regions and horses continue to be worked in the fields. Of the main cities, only beautiful Cracow and manufacturing Lodz were not destroyed by the war. The others, including the industrial centers of Poznań, Gdańsk and Wrocław have been lovingly restored.

Poland does not fit easily into preconceptions of a state that for 45 years was under Communist rule: Over 80% of the land is in private hands, and the country's population has remained profoundly Catholic. Moreover, Polish culture both past and present is strongly Western-oriented, and continues to flourish with or without government approval. The pride and independence of mind of the Poles was dramatically demonstrated by the formation in 1980 of Solidarity (Solidarność), the first independent trade union in the Soviet bloc, which enveloped the hopes and aspirations of many Poles. The movement's popularity and enthusiasm for democratic change, however, proved unacceptable to Poland's Communist rulers, and martial law was imposed in December 1981. Though martial law was lifted in 1983, and a semblance of normality restored, continuing discontent led to negotiations between Communists and the Solidarity-led opposition; there were relatively free elections in June 1989, and Poland now has a government led by the first non-Communist prime minister in the Soviet bloc.

Of all the Soviet satellites, Poland has the most to offer the independent "budget traveler". Constant devaluations of the local currency have made the country a comparatively cheap place for the Western visitor, especially if one avoids the beaten tourist track. However, the country's economic difficulties have given rise to shortages of foods, many basic goods and services, though for the most part the visitor remains unaffected by them.

Yet, for all its problems, the warmth, friendliness and charm of its people will ensure that any visit to Poland will be hugely rewarding.

PRACTICAL INFORMATION FOR POLAND

WHAT WILL IT COST. Group and individual tours to Poland are best arranged by *Orbis,* the official Polish travel bureau, which operates all the best hotels and pensions, and accredited travel agents. They will make all necessary arrangements including visas, accommodations and pre-payment. They can organize many different types of package holiday as well as specially tailored holidays for individuals, fly-drive holidays and special budget holidays for young people.

In the **U.K.** travel agents specializing in trips to Poland include:

Magic of Poland, 100 Dean St., London W1V 6AQ (tel. 071–734 5101).

Polorbis Travel, 82 Mortimer St., London W1N 7DE (tel. 071–637 4972).

Tazab Travel, 273 Old Brompton Rd., London SW5 9JB (tel. 071–373 1186).

In the **U.S.:**

Orbis Polish Travel Bureau, 500 Fifth Ave., New York, N.Y. 10110 (tel. 212–391–0844).

Polish National Tourist Office, 333 N. Michigan Ave., Suite 228, Chicago, IL 60601 (tel. 312–236–9013).

The monetary unit in Poland is the *złoty,* which is divided into 100 *groszy* (rarely seen). There are notes of 10, 20, 50, 100, 200, 500, 1,000, 2,000 5,000, 10,000, 20,000, 50,000, 200,000 and 400,000 złoty and coins of 1, 2, 5, 10 and 20 złoty.

At the time of writing, the official National Bank exchange rate for the złoty was 9,500 to the U.S. dollar, 15,200 to the pound sterling. Compulsory conversion of foreign currency by tourists ended in January 1990, but to pay hotel bills you must exchange hard currency at Orbis cash desks at this official rate. It is also possible to buy złoty at a free-market rate in privately operated bureaux de change (kantor wymiany walut), but the rate here is currently slightly below the bank rate. Many Poles, however, still prefer to be paid in dollars and this certainly includes waitresses, porters, taxi drivers etc.—so it is not necessary to change more than the minimum amount of foreign currency for złoty. Keep your currency in small denominations (e.g. one or five dollar notes—Poles prefer dollars).

Sample Costs (all in U.S. dollars). Moderate seat in a cinema 25 cents; a moderate theater seat, 50 cents; museum entry, under 25 cents; a cup of coffee, 50 cents–$1; a beer in a café or moderate restaurant $1.50–$2.00; a carafe of wine $2.50.

WHEN TO COME. Spring and summer, frequently very warm though the spring can be windy, are the best periods for sightseeing. Fall sees most of the major cultural events, which generally take place in the cities. The Tatra mountains are at their best in the fall, which can be long and sunny. The winter sports season lasts from December to March.

Summer, being the high season, is the most expensive time to visit, especially the seaside resorts of Gdańsk, Gdynia and Sopot. The mountain resorts, as might be expected, are most expensive in winter. You will also find that hotel prices in particular go up when special events take place, such as the Poznań International Fair in June. However, in Warsaw and Cracow hotel prices remain fixed all year long.

Average afternoon temperatures in Fahrenheit and centigrade:

Warsaw	Jan.	Feb.	Mar.	Apr.	May	June	July	Aug.	Sept.	Oct.	Nov.	Dec.
F°	30	32	41	54	67	72	75	73	65	54	40	32
C°	-1	0	5	12	19	22	24	23	18	12	4	0

SPECIAL EVENTS. *May,* International Chamber Music Festival, Łancut; Festival of Contemporary Polish Plays, Wrocław; International Book Fair, Warsaw. *May-December,* Symphonic and chamber music concerts in Wawel Castle courtyard (Cracow). *June,* International Trade Fair, Poznań; Organ Music Festival, Frombork; Polish Song Festival, Opole; Midsummer "wianki" celebrations on June 23 throughout Poland. *June-September,* Chopin recitals at composer's birthplace, Żelazowa Wola near Warsaw; International Song Festival, Sopot. *August,* Chopin Festival at Duszniki Zdrój; Festival of Folklore Troupes, Sosnowiec. *September,* Oratorio and Cantata Festival, Wrocław; International Festival of Song and Dance Ensembles, Zielona Góra. *October,* Jazz Jamboree, Warsaw; "Warsaw Autumn" festival of contemporary music, Warsaw. *November-December,* Presentation of year's most outstanding dramas, Warsaw. *December,* Competition for the best Christmas crib, Cracow.

Prices for these events are mostly moderate. It is advisable to check if a particular event is to take place and to book in advance. Orbis will make bookings for you.

National Holidays. Jan. 1 (New Year's Day); Mar. 31, Apr. 1 (Easter); May 1 (Labor Day); May 30 (Corpus Christi); July 22 (National Day); Nov. 1 (Remembrance); Nov. 11 (Polish independence, 1918); Dec. 25, 26.

VISAS. These are required for all western citizens hoping to visit Poland. You may apply for a visa from any Orbis office or any Polish embassy. Travel agents can also advise you on getting a visa. You must provide two photographs, and each potential visitor must complete three application forms. Allow around two weeks for applications to be processed. A visa costs $35, or the equivalent in any other currency. These regulations were accurate at the time of writing, but may well change during 1990.

Visas are issued for a period of 90 days, but when applying specify how many days you intend to spend in Poland. A visa remains valid for entry for six months from the date of issue.

HEALTH CERTIFICATES. Not required for entry into Poland.

GETTING TO POLAND. By Plane. The Polish national airline *LOT* flies direct from Montreal, New York, and Chicago to Warsaw. Otherwise, the quickest way is to fly to London, Paris, Frankfurt or Brussels and go on from there to Warsaw. LOT also flies London to Cracow and Gdansk in summer. *Pan Am* provides a daily service between New York or Chicago and Warsaw in the summer switching to three times a week in the winter.

By Train. The best route leaves London Liverpool Street station for Harwich and the ferry crossing to the Hook of Holland where you board the *Hoek-Warszawa Express* for the run to Warsaw, which is reached at 3.40 P.M. on the day after leaving London. Alternatively, take the train from London Victoria station to Dover for the ferry or jetfoil to Oostende. From Oostende catch the *Ost-West Express*, which arrives in Warsaw at 5.10 P.M. on the day after leaving London. Reservations are obligatory on both trains.

By Bus. A cheap but less comfortable bus service runs from Manchester through Birmingham and London to Poznań and Warsaw from May to the end of September. Contact *Fregata Travel*, 117A Withington Rd., Manchester (tel. 061–226 7227).

CUSTOMS. Persons over 17 may import duty free into Poland 250 cigarettes or 50 cigars or 250 grams of tobacco; plus 1 liter of wine and 1 liter of other alcoholic beverage; plus other articles for personal use. You may also import duty-free goods to the value of $200. Any amount of foreign currency may be imported but must be declared on arrival.

Articles not exceeding $100 in value may be taken out of Poland duty free, but certain items such as jewelry, ambers and leatherware are restricted, so *check with Orbis about the latest regulations since they are subject to change.*

HOTELS. Accommodations for foreign visitors are handled by *Orbis,* which runs all the best hotels in Poland. However, there are also a number of other hotels, hostels and student hostels at less expensive rates, though the Orbis hotels are not expensive by Western standards. These latter include *Municipal Hotels,* which are frequently rather old but which normally have a few rooms with bath or shower, and *PTTK* hotels, which are run by the Polish Tourist Association and are usually called *Dom Turysty.*

There is a significant price difference between hotels in the big cities and those elsewhere in the country. In high season prices everywhere are about 25% higher.

American Express, Eurocard, Carte Blanche, Diner's Club, Visa and other major credit cards are accepted in most hotels (as well as in most restaurants, nightclubs and for all Orbis services).

We have graded hotels in our listings as Moderate (M) and Inexpensive (I). Two people in a double room with bath can expect to pay from $36–$80 in a Moderate hotel depending on location and season. Two people in a double room (without bath and breakfast) can expect to pay from $15–$35 in an Inexpensive hotel.

Youth Hostels. The *Polish Youth Hostels Association* operates around 1,500 hostels. They are open to all and provide basic accommodations; they are clean, warm and dry but be warned that some lack even the most basic facilities such as cold water showers. A list of the best 200 hostels can be found in the IYHF Handbook. Prices vary according to category but are all inexpensive. Early reservations recommended (send your reservation card direct to the hostel). Tourists with IYHF membership pay 25% less. Maximum stay is 3–4 nights in one hostel. The address of the Polish Youth Hostels Association is ul. Chocimska 28, 00–719 Warszawa (tel. 49 83 54).

Camping. There are about 240 campsites in Poland. Facilities usually include washrooms, canteens and nearby restaurants and food kiosks. About 75% have power points (220 volts AC). Facilities are primitive by West European standards. Information can be obtained from Orbis offices abroad and reservations made through Polorbis in the U.K. and the Orbis Polish Travel Bureau in the U.S. (see page 426 for addresses). Information inside Poland can be obtained from the Polish Camping and Caravanning Federation, Królewska 27, Warsaw (tel. 26 80 89).

Other Budget Accommodations. During July and August *Almatur* have a number of modern student hostels open for general tourists' use. They have 2- to 3-bedded rooms, though with no private facilities, and accept visitors up to the age of 35. One day with full board costs students $8 and non-students $12. Full board is not, however, compulsory and the difference is refundable. For details contact *Almatur Travel Office,* Ordynacka 9, Warsaw (tel. 26 84 04). Student hostels operate on a voucher basis only (these are obtainable through Orbis and Polorbis). These guarantee reservations.

Self-catering accommodations are on the increase in Poland, but can only be arranged in Poland. Your best bet is to contact the national tourist office in the town in which you want to stay. *Orbis* can arrange lodging in advance, but this is more expensive.

RESTAURANTS. The selection of restaurants in Poland is wide, but, as a result of food shortages, the quality of their cuisine can vary from one day to the next. Consequently you may well find that it is advisable to eat in the more expensive hotels as they get the most reliable food supplies as well as having the best ingredients.

We have graded restaurants as Moderate (M) and Inexpensive (I). A meal in a Moderate restaurant should cost around 10,000–25,000 złoty, and a meal in an Inexpensive restaurant should cost around 5,000–10,000 złoty. These prices are for one person and do not include beer or wine.

Roadside inns *(zajazdy)* are less expensive and normally serve traditional Polish food. Even less expensive are milk bars, *(bary mleczne)*; self-service snack bars and coffee bars. Cafés *(kawiarnia),* a way of life in Poland, normally serve delicious pastries although supplies can be irregular. Note that many restaurants close as early as 9 P.M.

Food and Drink. Polish food is basically Slavic with Baltic overtones, giving rise to an interesting variety of soups and meats (with the emphasis on pork) as well as fresh water fish. Much use is made of cream, which is inexpensive, and pastries are rich and delectable.

Some of the best typically Polish meals are, in normal times, to be found in the villages and market towns where delicious *barszcz* (clear beetroot soup) is served in large helpings along with sausage, cabbage, potatoes, sour cream, *czarny chleb* (coarse rye bread) and beer. Other dishes are: *Pierogi* (a kind of ravioli), which can be stuffed with various savory fillings; *Gołąbki,* cabbage leaves stuffed with minced beef; *Zrazy Zawijane,* a kind of beef rissole; *Flaki,* a very select dish of tripe, served boiled or fried; *Bigos,* sauerkraut with meat and mushrooms; *Kołduny,* a kind of ravioli with lamb meat filling.

Bottled *Żywiec* (beer) is delicious. Western drinks (whiskey, gin, brandy) can be had at most bars, but are very expensive. *Vodka,* of course, is a Polish specialty, and is often drunk before, with and after meals. Try *Wyborowa* (plain), *Żytnia* (rye vodka), *Jarzębiak* (rowan vodka) and *Żubrówka* (bison brand, a buffalo grass-flavored vodka). You might also try a Polish mead, a honey wine.

TIPPING. A service charge is usually added to restaurant bills; if not, add 10%. Tipping is not obligatory, but readily accepted. Cab drivers get 10%.

MAIL. Current rates for airmail letters up to 5 grams: to the U.S., 1,500 złoty; to the U.K. and the rest of Europe 1,200 złoty; postcards are 1,050 and 750 złoty respectively. These will increase in 1990. Post Offices are open 8 A.M. to 8 P.M.

CLOSING TIMES. Food shops are open from 6 or 7 A.M. to 7 P.M. on weekdays, 9 A.M. to 1 P.M. Saturday. Banks 8 A.M. to 3 or 6 P.M. Department stores are open 11 A.M. to 7 P.M. on weekdays, 9 A.M. to 1 P.M. Saturday; and "Ruch" newspaper kiosks from 8 A.M. to 6 P.M. Offices are generally open from 9 A.M. to 4 P.M. Local tourist information centers can advise on opening times of historic monuments and museums.

PHOTOGRAPHY. You may not take photographs from the air, nor of industrial or transport installations.

GETTING AROUND POLAND. By Plane. *LOT* has daily flights linking 11 main cities. Warsaw's Okęcie airport handles both international and domestic flights. Fares begin from about $80 round trip. Be sure to book well in advance, especially during the summer season.

By Train. Internal rail travel in Poland is cheap, so trains are always crowded, especially in summer. It is advisable to travel first class if possible and always get to the station well in advance of the advertised departure time. Recently services have deteriorated significantly and trains are frequently late. Reservations are obligatory on certain express services such as those linking Warsaw with Katowice. On overnight trains there are first- and second-class sleeping cars and second-class bunk beds. Most long distance trains carry buffet cars, but to avoid disappointment or a possible upset stomach, bring your own food. There is a runabout ticket called *Polrailpass,* which, at the time of writing, cost around $72 for eight days; this is worth buying for the convenience, but it is much cheaper to simply buy your tickets for złoty in Poland.

By Bus. Bus routes radiate from main cities into rural areas and there are also long distance buses, particularly in the southern mountainous region. They are usually very crowded.

By Bicycle. Contact the bicycle section of the *PTTK,* 4–6 Krakowskie Przedmieście, Warsaw (tel. 26 30 11). Larger campsites throughout the country can probably also advise on bicycle hire.

Hitchhiking. Hitchhiking is both popular and even encouraged in Poland. Hitchhikers can buy special books of coupons at tourist information centers and, on obtaining a lift, should give the driver the appropriate coupon covering the distance they ride. Drivers who collect the most coupons during the year then receive prizes. There is also a system of inexpensive accommodations for hitchhikers. Details obtainable from the Hitchhiking Committee *(Komitet Autostopu),* Narbutta 27a, Warsaw.

Warsaw

In January 1945 Warsaw—Poland's capital since the 17th century—was a desert of ruin and rubble, a victim of systematic Nazi destruction. But Warsaw's survivors, determined to rebuild their city, set about the task so energetically that today the new Warsaw of a million-plus inhabitants amazes its visitors.

The historic districts have been painstakingly reconstructed following old prints and paintings. The result is remarkable; and the atmosphere is enhanced by the fact that the Old Town is closed to traffic. Here you can visit the living replica of the city's old marketplace, the cobblestoned Rynek Starego Miasta where open-air exhibitions of modern paintings by local artists are held. All over the Old Town, churches, palaces and lovely burghers' houses have been beautifully rebuilt, the most recently-completed and largest being the Royal Palace, which houses a museum. In front of it rises the King Sigismund Column, symbol of Warsaw.

The busy main thoroughfares, Krakowskie Przedmieście and Nowy Świat lead to the city's grandest open space, Łazienki Park, where the Polish kings built their "out-of-town" summer palaces in the 17th and 18th centuries, Belvedere and Łazienki. Near the Łazienki Palace is the charming 18th-century Theater on the Isle, and it is only a short stroll from here to the Chopin monument, beside which concerts are held in summer on Sundays.

With ironic humor, Poles say the best place for a view of the city is from the top of the 37-story Palace of Culture and Science, a wedding-cake skyscraper and personal gift from Stalin. Why? It's the only place in Warsaw where you can't see the Palace itself. From its pinnacle there is a remarkable view of the whole city and out across the river.

PRACTICAL INFORMATION FOR WARSAW

GETTING INTO TOWN FROM THE AIRPORT. Although *Lot Polish Airlines* operates a regular bus service into Warsaw, it is much cheaper to take an ordinary bus. The 175 bus takes you from the international airport to the center of town, and the 114 bus does the same from the domestic airport. Taxis are also available.

HOTELS. Warsaw is relatively well supplied with hotels, but it is advisable to book accommodations in all price categories well in advance as they may be difficult to arrange on the spot. This is particularly true of the more inexpensive accommodations in summer and during special events.

However, if you do not already have accommodations booked before arriving in Warsaw, there is an accommodations bureau that may be able to help. The service is free. Their address is: *Syrena,* Krucza 16–22 (tel. 25 72 03). They should also be able to arrange private accommodations.

The head office for Youth Hostels in Warsaw, as well as the most central hostel, is at Smolna 30 (tel. 27 89 52).

All Moderate hotels listed below have rooms with bath and restaurant and snack bar. Inexpensive hotels generally have rooms without bath, though with hot running water, and either a restaurant or a snack bar.

Moderate

Hotel Solec, Zagorna 1 (tel. 29 79 04). 147 rooms.

Novotel, ul. 1-go Sierpnia 1 (tel. 46 40 51). All rooms with bath. Restaurant and outdoor pool.

Nowa Praga, B. Brechta 7 (tel. 19 82 35). 143 rooms. Restaurant and bar.

Saski, Pl. Dzierżyńskiego 7 (tel. 20 46 11/2/3/4). 106 rooms. Central location and comfortable rooms.

Syrena, Syreny 23 (tel. 32 12 56). 148 rooms.

Vera, ul. Wery Kostrzewy 16 (tel. 22 74 21).

Inexpensive

Druh, Drom Wycieczkowy, Niemcewicza (tel. 22 48 68/9). 70 rooms.

Dom Nauczyciela, Wybrzeze Kościuszkowskie 31 (tel. 27 92 11, 26 26 00). 216 rooms. Comfortable.

Dom Turysty, Krakowskie Przedmieście 4–6 (tel. 26 26 25). 63 rooms. Friendly hotel right in town.

International Student Hotel Almatur, Żwirki i Wigury 95–97. Located away from city center on way to the International airport (bus number 175). Large and well equipped. Summer only.

Riwiera, ul. Warynskiego 12. Almatur-run student house centrally located. Two, three and four bedded rooms all with shower/bath. Restaurant, coffee bar and other amenities. Unless you have pre-paid Almatur vouchers you may be refused accommodation in the high season. Summer only.

If all else fails, a room can be rented from one of the landladies that hang around the front of the Polonia and Metropol hotels. They charge $15–$20 a night.

RESTAURANTS. Warsaw has a number of good restaurants but as a result of the current food shortages only the top hotels have guaranteed supplies and, though these establishments are relatively expensive, many visitors may find it is more convenient to eat in them. Rynek Starego Miasta (the Old Town Market) has a number of good restaurants and cafés. Orbis (see p. 432 for address) should be able to advise you of the best places to try.

Moderate

Ambassador, Ul. Matejki 2.
Cristal-Budapest, Marszałkowska 21–25. Hungarian cuisine.
Fukier, Rynek Starego Miasta 27. Popular wine-cellar cum coffee-house.
Kameralna, Foksal 16.
Kamienne Schodki, Rynek Starego Miasta 26. Intimate, candle-lit atmosphere in stone built restaurant. Duck in wine the house specialty.
Pod Samsonem, ul. Freta 4. Typical Warsaw atmosphere and menu.
Rarytas, Marszałkowska 15. With floorshow.
Rycerska, Szeroki Dunaj 9–11. Old peasant-style restaurant in the Old Town.
Staropolska, Krakowskie Przedmieście 8. The name means "Old Polish", and large portions of typical Polish fare are served until 11 P.M. Often packed at lunchtime.
Suwalska, Spokojna 4.
Zalipie, Filtrowa 83.
Żywiecka, Marszałkowska 66.

Inexpensive

A lot of self-service and espresso bars have very good cheap snacks and are liberally dotted over the city. Recommended:
Europejski Expresbar, Plac Zwycięstwa.
Bar Mleczny. Part of a chain of milk bars all over the city. Good dairy and egg dishes at very low cost. Recommended is the **Uniwersytecki Bar Mleczny** at Krakowskie Przedmieście 19.
Gruba Kaśka, al Świerczewskiego 68.
Oaza, ul. Targowa 42.
Praha, al. Jerozolimskie 11–19.
Bar Kawowy Murzynek, ul. Nowomiejska 3.

GETTING AROUND WARSAW. By Bus and Tram. Tickets for trams (240 złoty) and buses (240 złoty, 480 złoty for express buses) must be bought in advance from "Ruch" newsstands. You punch your ticket into the machine on the bus or tram, which automatically cancels it. After 11 P.M. night buses operate, charging double fares.

Orbis runs sightseeing bus tours of the city all year long, though with more frequent trips in summer when they also have trips into the surrounding countryside. Half-day trips from 15,000 złoty, full-day trips from 25,000 złoty. This includes meals and some form of traditional entertainment.

By Taxi. Finding a taxi in Warsaw can be quite a headache. Fares have gone up so frequently that meters no longer reflect the price of a journey. Allow for at least 100 times the meter charge. There are also a few horse-drawn cabs. Negotiate the fare yourself with the driver (usually around $5 per hour). You can enjoy a number of inexpensive sightseeing tours by cab. They are organized by the *Warsaw Tourist Services Office,* Syrena, ul. Krucza 16–22.

By Boat. There are trips by pleasure boat on the river Vistula in the summer. Details from the *Warsaw Navigation Agency,* Dworzec Wodny, or from Orbis.

ENTERTAINMENT. Cafés. Outdoor cafés and the indoor *Winiarnie* (wine bars) are a feature of Polish nightlife. Recommended are: *Fukier* and *Murzynek* in Rynek Starego Miasta and, in particular, *U Hopfera* at Krakowskie Przedmieście

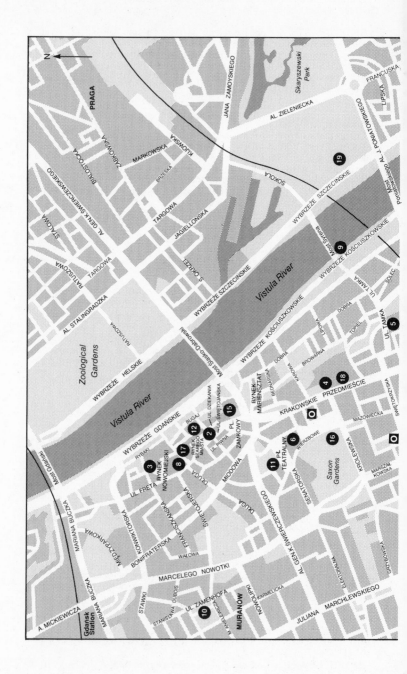

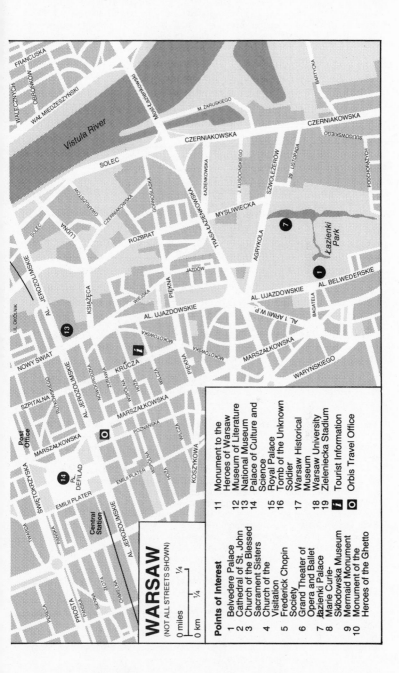

WARSAW

(NOT ALL STREETS SHOWN)

0 miles ¼
0 km ¼

Points of Interest

1 Belvedere Palace
2 Cathedral of St. John
3 Church of the Blessed
  Sacrament Sisters
4 Church of the
  Visitation
5 Frederick Chopin
  Society
6 Grand Theater of
  Opera and Ballet
7 Łazienki Palace
8 Marie Curie-
  Skłodowska Museum
9 Mermaid Monument
10 Monument of the
  Heroes of the Ghetto
11 Monument to the
  Heroes of Warsaw
12 Museum of Literature
13 National Museum
14 Palace of Culture and
  Science
15 Royal Palace
16 Tomb of the Unknown
  Soldier
17 Warsaw Historical
  Museum
18 Warsaw University
19 Zeleniecka Stadium
i Tourist Information
◉ Orbis Travel Office

53. Others worth trying are: *Krokodyl,* Rynek Starego Miasta 19; *Gong,* al. Jerozolimskie 42, marvelous selection of imported teas; *Alhambra,* al. Jerozolimskie 32, very good for Turkish coffee; *Teatralna,* Corazziego 12; *Telimena,* Krakowskie Przedmieście; *Trou Madame,* Łazienki Park, in a beautiful setting; *Gwiazdeczka,* ul. Piwna 40a, a student hangout; *Bombonierka,* Rynek Nowego Miasta 1, elegant decor and tranquil, excellent ice cream; *Le Petit Trianon,* Piwna 42, tiny 18th-century French style.

Cinema. Poles rarely dub Western films, but check before you buy your ticket. Check *Warszawski Informator Kulturalny* (WIK), the bi-weekly guide to what's on in Warsaw, or *Życie Warsawy,* the city's daily paper, for details. Both are on sale at Ruch kiosks.

Discos and Clubs. Discos are not Warsaw's strong point so for this kind of fun it is best to stick to the nightclubs in the better hotels. Otherwise, the best discos are *Hybrydy,* ul. Koniewskiego 7–8 and *Stodoła,* ul. Batorego 2.

Music clubs (prices can go to 5,000 złoty per person) include: *Akwarium,* Emilii Plater St, an interesting jazz club; *Amfora,* on the East Wall, an intimate and romantic spot with good music and good food; *Wanda Warska's Modern Music Club,* Stare Miasto, a very popular, candle-lit jazz club; book ahead. Warsaw's most famous cabaret is *Pod Egidą* on Nowy Swiat, renowned for its political satire.

Theaters and Concerts. Warsaw currently boasts some 17 theaters, many of them with excellent and highly imaginative productions and first rate acting. However, unless you speak Polish their appeal is likely to be limited. Ticket prices are 1,000–2,000 złoty.

Among the leading theaters are: *Teatr Wielki,* for grand opera and ballet; *Teatr Dramatyczny* and *Teatr Studio,* both in the Palace of Culture and Science and both producing contemporary works; *Ateneum,* ul. Stefana Jaracza, for both traditional and contemporary works; *Wspólczesny,* ul. Mokotowska 13 (contemporary).

The *National Philharmonic Hall,* ul. Sienkiewicza 12, is the leading venue for concerts, many of them of a very high standard. On Sundays from June to September, there are free open-air piano recitals next to the Chopin monument in Łazienki Park. (There are Sunday concerts from June to September at Żelazowa Wola, Chopin's birth place, 50 km. (30 miles) from Warsaw; also free.) Orbis will supply details of performance by the ever popular Polish folk dance troupes *Mazowsze* and *Sląsk.*

MUSEUMS AND CHURCHES. The most important church in Warsaw is the late 14th-century *Cathedral of St. John,* on the right of ul. Swiętojanska, now extensively and lovingly rebuilt and restored. The crypt contains the tombs of many famous Poles. Two other remarkable churches are the Baroque church and convent of the *Blessed Sacrament Sisters* in the Rynek Nowomiejski, which dates from 1688, and the Gothic church of the *Visitation,* the oldest church in the New Town and situated on an embankment overlooking the Vistula.

Warsaw has around two dozen museums. They are open all week except Mondays. Except for Sunday, which is free, there is a nominal entry fee (50% discount for students). Among the more interesting are:

Archeological Museum, ul. Długa 52. Arsenal. Many remnants of the old Slavonic tribes, especially the Biskupin (550–440 B.C.) collection. Closed Sat.

Chopin Museum, ul. Okólnik 1. Many pieces, pianos and scores from Chopin's life assembled here.

Łazienki Park. Contains several former royal summer residences including that of Poland's last king, Stanislaus Augustus Poniatowski. It dates from the 18th century and today is an attractive museum.

National Museum, al. Jerozolimskie 3. The principal Warsaw museum; it contains a fine collection of works by contemporary Polish painters as well as collections of ancient art and of European paintings, principally Flemish. Much of the collection was removed during the Nazi occupation but has been restored to its rightful place and is being added to constantly.

Pawiak Prison Museum, ul. Dzielna 22–26. Situated on the outskirts of the former ghetto; this was the main place of imprisonment, torture and execution of members of Poland's resistance movement by the Nazis.

Museum of Resistance and Martyrdom, al. Armii Wojska Polskiego 25. A grim reminder of World War II, these former Gestapo headquarters remain much as they were; they include the interrogation center.

Marie Skłodowska-Curie Museum, ul. Freta 16. A collection devoted to the life and work of Marie Curie; located, appropriately, in her former house.

Wilanów Palace, 10 km. (6 miles) out of town. Former royal summer residence built by King Jan III Sobieski; as well as the many beautiful pieces of furniture in the collection, there is also a permanent exhibition of modern posters.

Zachęta, pl. Małachowskiego 3. Warsaw's art gallery.

Zamek Królewski, Plac Zamkowy. The Royal Palace, recently rebuilt in its former splendor after wartime destruction. Well worth enduring the crowds and bustle to visit this national symbol.

SHOPPING. Stores are generally open 11 A.M. to 7 P.M. on weekdays, 9 A.M. to 1 P.M. Saturdays. Two mega-stores worth visiting are *Centrum* and *Junior,* on Marszałkowska, opposite the Palace of Culture. Nowy Swiat and Krakowskie Przedmieście are the best shopping streets for chic boutiques. *CEPELIA* stores are outlets for craftsmen's **folk art.** These accept local and foreign currency. *PEWEX* shops sell mainly imported items. If you want a glimpse of Poland's booming "second economy", visit the Bazar Różyckiego (ul. Targowa) and the flea market at the *Skra* sports stadium (al. Żwirki i Wigury) on Sundays. But prepare for some tough haggling if you want to buy anything.

USEFUL ADDRESSES. *U.S. Embassy,* al Ujazdowskie 29–31 (tel. 38 30 40/9); *Canadian Embassy,* ul. Matejki 1–5 (tel. 29 80 51); *British Embassy,* al. Róż 1 (tel. 28 10 01); *British Consulate,* ul. Wawelska 14 (tel. 25 30 31); *Polish Travel Office* (Orbis), ul. Bracka 16 & ul. Stawki 2 (tel. 26 02 71); *PTTK* (Polish Tourist Association), Swietokrzyska 36; *Thomas Cook,* ul. Stawki 2 (tel. 27 35 26); *Central Post Office,* ul. Swietokrzyska 21–23 (open 24 hours a day, 7 days a week).

Cracow, Zakopane and the Southern Mountains

Medieval Cracow, ancient seat of the Polish kings and Poland's oldest academic institution, the Jagiellonian University, is one of the few major cities in the country that escaped devastation during the war. Today, its fine ramparts, towers, dungeons and churches, spanning seven centuries of Polish architecture, as well as its theatrical and musical life, conspire to make the city one of Poland's major tourist attractions.

Cracow's principal showcase is the well preserved 16th-century castle Wawel. Wawel cathedral, close by, shelters the delicately-carved sarcophagi of many kings while the building itself is a remarkable example of different architectural styles, the earliest dating from the 10th century. Below Wawel hill, in the heart of the city, you can wander through Cracow's medieval Town Square, the largest in Europe, with its famous Cloth Hall, which today houses a number of folk art shops.

Scattered through the town are some 67 Romanesque, Gothic and Baroque churches. Don't miss the 12th-century church of St. Mary's (Mariacki) which has a 15th-century triptych, a masterful example of Gothic woodcarving.

Zakopane is about 110 km (70 miles) south of Cracow, 3,000 ft. high in the dramatic Tatra mountains along the Czechoslovak border. It is the country's most popular health and holiday resort. It is also the center of Poland's winter sports resorts.

PRACTICAL INFORMATION FOR CRACOW AND ZAKOPANE

GETTING AROUND CRACOW. There are trams and buses in Cracow, but it is perfectly possible, and indeed desirable, to visit the Old Town on foot. Zakopane is some two hours from Cracow by bus.

Hotels and Restaurants

Cracow. There is a Youth Hostel at ul. Oleandry 4 (tel. 33 89 20). Private accommodations through *Wawel Tourist,* Rynek Główny (tel. 22 08 52).

Francuski (M), ul. Pijarska 13 (tel. 22 51 22). In the center of town with good café and restaurant. *Olimp Międzynarodowy Hotel Studencki* (M), Nawojki 23 (tel. 37 00 11), summer only. *Polonia* (M), Basztowa 24 (tel. 22 12 33). In the town center. *Krakowianka* (I), Żywiecka boczna (tel. 66 41 91). Three-person rooms only. *Dom Turysty PTTK* (I), Westerplatte 15–16 (tel. 22 57 19). Very central and reasonably priced.

Restaurants. *Wierzynek,* Rynek Główny 16, in beautiful historic buildings, very popular; *Balaton,* Grodzka 37 (Polish and Hungarian food); *U Wentzla,* Rynek Główny 18, quite elegant; *Dniepr,* 18 Stycznia 55; *Staropolska,* Sienna 4; *Kurza Stopka;* all (M).

Zakopane. There are Youth Hostels at al. Przewodników Tatrzanskich 3 (tel. 35 37) and Nowatorska 45 (tel. 42 03). Private accommodations are available through the office at ul. Kościuszki 23a.

Dom Turysty PTTK (M), Zaruskiego 5 (tel. 32 81/2/3/4). Attractive chalet-type building; also has some less expensive rooms. *Gazda* (M), Zaruskiego 5 (tel. 50 11/16), *Giewont* (M), ul. Kościuszki 1 (tel. 20 11). 52 rooms. *Warszawianka* (I), Jagiellonska 7 (tel. 32 61/2/3).

Restaurants. *Jedrus, U Wnuka* (regional), *Gubałówka, Kasprowy Wierch, Watra,* and *Wierchy,* all (M). *Kmicic* is a pleasant café. *Siedem Kotów* and *Obrochtowka* have good local atmosphere, both (I).

Museums

Czartoryski Museum (Collection of the Princes Czartoryski) Pijarska 9. Canvases by old European masters, including some fine Rembrandts and a beautiful Leonardo. **Ethnographical Museum,** Pl. Wolnica. An excellent folk museum. **National Gallery of Polish Painting** (Cloth Hall), Rynek Główny. Interesting collection of Polish canvases. **Wawel Castle Museum.** 71 rooms of treasures including superb Flemish tapestries and lovely furnishings.

USEFUL ADDRESSES. *Orbis* (Cracow), Rynek Główny 41 (tel. 22 30 44). *Tourist Information Office,* Ul. Pawia 8 (tel. 22 04 71). *Orbis* (Zakopane), Ul. Krupowki 22 (tel. 48 12). *U.S. Consulate,* ul. Stolarska 9 (tel. 22 97 64).

Poznań

A sedate and quiet town, Poznań is very conscious of its role as the cradle of the Polish state. However, its chief attraction to the tourist lies in its varied and interesting architecture, which runs the whole gamut of styles from the Romanesque through the Renaissance and Baroque to neo-Classicism. Indeed, the whole city has a strange mixture of Germanic, Slavic and Italian architectural and cultural flavors to it.

The important International Trade Fair is held here every year (and has been since 1922) and as a result Poznań has become a major trading center between the Communist and Western worlds.

Near Poznań is Biskupin, a restored prehistoric fort—the "Polish Pompeii"—and Romanesque Gniezno, former capital of Poland and legendary birthplace of the Polish state.

PRACTICAL INFORMATION FOR POZNAŃ

GETTING AROUND POZNAŃ. As elsewhere in Poland there is a full bus and tram network. Prices are the same as Warsaw. To hire a bicycle, try the Tourist Information Center (see below for address).

Hotels and Restaurants

Note that hotels in Poznań tend to be heavily booked during the Trade Fair, and up to 40% more expensive. There are Youth Hostels at Stalingradzka 32–40 and Berwinskiego 2–3 (tel. 66 36 80).

Poznański (M), Marcinkowskiego 22 (tel. 52 81 21). 110 rooms. *Dom Turysty PPTK* (I), Stary Rynek 91 (tel. 52 88 93), 41 rooms. *Dom Wycieczkowy* (I), Chwiałkowskiego 34 (tel. 33 24 44). 40 rooms.

Restaurants. *Magnolia,* Głogowska 40 (dancing); *Adria,* Głogowska 14; *Arkadia,* Pl. Wolności 11; *Smakosz,* 27 Grudnia 8; *U Dylla,* Stary Rynek 37–39. All (M).

MUSEUMS (Closed Mon.). **Archeological Museum,** Wodna 27 (Gorki Palace). Many interesting artifacts on display here from this part of Poland's past.

Arts and Crafts Museum, Góra Przemyśla 1. Splendid Chinese vases and a good collection of Italian majolicas.

Museum of the History of the Town of Poznań, Stary Rynek (Market Square). Located in the Town Hall.

Museum of Musical Instruments, Stary Rynek 45 (Market Square). A wide collection of folk instruments from all over Europe as well as the East.

National Museum, Marcinkowskiego 9. Large number of Polish paintings, plus pictures from many other parts of Europe.

USEFUL ADDRESS. *Poznań Tourist Information Center,* Stary Rynek 77 (tel. 52 61 56). *U.S. Consulate,* ul. Chopina 4 (tel. 52 95 86).

Gdańsk

Gdańsk, formerly the "Free City" of Danzig, is another of Poland's beautifully restored towns displaying a rich heritage of Gothic and Renaissance architecture. This is where the first shots of World War II were fired, and also where the free trade union Solidarity was born. Visit the delightful handicraft boutiques on Długa street and make sure you also see the Solidarity monument, standing outside the Lenin shipyards. The city's old town is a beautiful assembly of Renaissance and Baroque townhouses and narrow streets. Nearby Sopot is Poland's most popular seaside resort.

PRACTICAL INFORMATION FOR GDAŃSK

Hotels and Restaurants

Orbis Hewelius (M), ul Heweliusza 22. 250 rooms. *Orbis Marina* (M), ul. Jelitkowska 20. 193 rooms. *Orbis Novotel* (M), Ul Pszenna 1. 154 rooms. *Orbis-Monopol* (M), ul. Gorskiego 1. 125 rooms opposite the railway station.

Restaurants. There are plenty of good and well-stocked restaurants, cafés and nightclubs. *Gedania* (M), ul. Długa 75. *Kristal,* ul. Grunwaldzka 105. *Marysieńka,* ul. Szeroka 29. *Olimp* (M), Grunwaldska 92.

MUSEUMS. Museum of the History of Gdańsk, ul. Długa 46. **National Museum of Gdańsk,** ul. Toruńska 1.

USEFUL ADDRESSES. *Orbis* (Gdańsk), Pl. Gorkiego 1 (tel. 314 944). *Tourist Information Office,* ul. Heweliusza 8 (tel. 310 338).

Portugal

Portugal is a haven of quiet and traditional living, where politeness and an easy relaxation are the norm. It is a country largely avoided by those who prefer the so-called high life, for there is little in the way of international night life and other diversions, except in the package tour paradise of the Algarve. Prices tend accordingly to be low. The charm of the people and the natural beauty of the country, combined with this inexpensiveness, make Portugal an irresistible destination for the budget vacationer.

Lisbon, the capital, with a population of around a million, stretches along the north bank of the Tagus river in a broad semi-circle, spanned by the great American-designed suspension bridge. The wide, lovely river makes Lisbon one of the most beautiful capital cities in Europe. Only round the periphery have highrise buildings been allowed and the center of the town is still largely 18th century in appearance with, oddly enough, some exciting manifestations of art nouveau.

Portugal became a great Colonial power through the imagination and foresight of Prince Henry the Navigator (1394–1460), who inspired the dynasty of ocean voyagers such as Vasco da Gama, who discovered the sea route to the Indies round Africa, and Pedro Alvares Cabral, the first European to land in Brazil. The tiny caravels that made these epic voyages sailed from Belem just outside Lisbon, and for centuries the country was so enamored of her past glories that she preferred to remain apart from modern European trends. This aloofness was encouraged by the late Dr. Salazar who, having rescued the country from complete financial ruin in the late 1920s, remained in power, a dictatorial, patriarchal figure, until 1968. His successor, Marcelo Caetano, was unable to bring the country into line with modern Europe as fast as the people wished, largely owing to years of Colonial war in Africa. Thus it was that on April 25, 1974, a military coup overthrew the Government and a bloodless revolution ensued. Since then there have been frequent elections but in 1987 for the first time since the revolution an overall majority was gained in a general election. The Prime Minister, Cavaco Silva, a Social Democrat, is a man of the people and is generally respected and admired. Portugal is fast becoming a successful and up-to-date country, well able to compete in the modern world, and is now an EC member.

But two things that haven't changed are the fact that Portugal is still astonishingly cheap, in spite of the inflation that prevails here much as it does elsewhere in Europe, and the welcome that Portugal extends to visitors. This is a country that has budget possibilities scattered throughout the length and breadth of the land; it only needs a little searching and, presto, you have a holiday with a difference . . . for a song. And that song may well be *fado,* a style of singing that must come straight from the heart to be authentic. Portugal is the home of *fado,* a melancholy, haunting wail—a lament that signifies not only individual longing and torment, but a common feeling of the Portuguese people as a whole, memories of past greatness. You may not think that is a good symbol for an enjoyable holiday, but believe us (and many previous generations of travelers who have fallen in love with the country), it is.

PRACTICAL INFORMATION FOR PORTUGAL

WHAT WILL IT COST. The cost of a holiday in Portugal, as indeed anywhere, will very much depend on the traveler. The cheapest way of seeing the country is by rail and local buses, sleeping in pensions or rooms recommended by a café, and eating in the small restaurants. This way, it should not cost you more than Esc. 8,000$00 a day—well under $100 or £20 sterling. Also, many of the good hotels charge very moderate low-season prices for room and breakfast.

The monetary unit in Portugal is the escudo (Esc.), which is divided into 100 centavos. The symbol for the escudo is the $ sign; thus 50 escudos is written Esc. 50$00, while 50 centavos is $50. At the time of writing, the exchange rate for the escudo was 143$00 to the U.S. dollar and 263$00 to the pound sterling, but do check as these rates will almost certainly change before 1991. Since Portugal joined the EEC, VAT is charged on certain goods and services.

Sample Costs. A carafe of house wine in a café or Moderate restaurant is about 300$00, 200$00 for a half; a beer is 100$00, and a coffee 60$00. A Moderate seat in the cinema is around 500$00, at the theater 1,000$00. Entrance to a museum, approximately 350$00 to 500$00.

NATIONAL TOURIST OFFICE. There are three branches of the *Portuguese Tourist Office* in Lisbon. They are staffed by very helpful and pleasant young women who are multi-lingual. You can obtain details of organized sightseeing trips, as well as leaflets on places of interest and lists of accommodations. Addresses: Palácio Foz, Praça dos Restauradores; Ave. António Augusto Aguiar, 86; and at the airport.

Their addresses overseas are:
In the U.S.: 590 Fifth Ave., New York, N.Y. 10036 (tel. 212–354–4403).
In Canada: 2180 Yonge St., Toronto, Ontario M4S 2B9 (tel. 416–487–3300).
In the U.K.: 1–5 New Bond St., London W1Y 0NP (tel. 071–493 3873).

WHEN TO COME. Portugal, having such a long coastline, is fortunate in not having extremes of heat and cold. It very rarely snows except in the high mountains of the Estrela, and there are only a few frosts in winter. Rain is rare between May and October, but it never gets insufferably hot—although the Algarve, on the southern coast, is definitely warmer than Lisbon and the northern parts of the country.

Average afternoon temperatures in degrees Fahrenheit and centigrade:

Lisbon	Jan.	Feb.	Mar.	Apr.	May	June	July	Aug.	Sept.	Oct.	Nov.	Dec.
F°	56	58	61	64	69	75	79	80	76	69	62	57
C°	13	14	16	18	21	24	26	27	24	21	17	14

Algarve												
F°	61	61	63	67	73	77	83	84	80	73	66	62
C°	16	16	17	19	23	25	28	29	27	23	19	17

SPECIAL EVENTS. Market days are an attraction anywhere, and Portugal's are well worth experiencing. The bargains in pottery, kitchen utensils, leather goods, basket work, fruit and vegetables are outstanding. Every town in the country has its market day, usually either once a week or once a month. Among the best known are those at Cascais, near Lisbon (every Wednesday and Saturday—the latter day fruit and vegetables only); at Carcavelos (Thursdays); at S. Pedro de Sintra (second and fourth Sundays every month); at Azeitão (first Sunday); at the Thieves Market, behind the Church of S. Vicente de Fora in Lisbon (Tuesdays and Saturdays); in the Algarve: at Albufeira (third Sunday of the month); at Lagos (first Saturday of the month); at Loulé (every Saturday, junk on first and second Sundays); at Portimão (first Monday of the month); at S. Brás de Alportel (every Saturday); and at Silves and Tavira (both the third Monday of the month). In the north, at Barcelos, there is an enormous fair every Thursday, and every Saturday at Estremoz in the Alentejo.

National Holidays. Jan. 1 (New Year's Day); Feb. 12 (Carnival, Shrove Tues.); March 29 (Good Friday); Apr. 25 (Anniversary of Revolution); May 1 (Labor Day); May 30 (Corpus Christi); Jun. 10 (National Day); Aug. 15 (Assumption); Oct. 5 (Day of the Republic); Nov. 1 (All Saints); Dec. 1 (Independence Day); Dec. 8 (Immaculate Conception); Dec. 25 (Christmas Day).

VISAS. Nationals of the EC and the U.S. do not require visas. Visas are required by Australians, and citizens of some African and Asian countires. Up to date information from Portuguese consulates.

HEALTH CERTIFICATES. These are not required to visit Portugal.

GETTING TO PORTUGAL. By Plane. The best services to Portugal are by *Air Portugal (TAP)* and also by *TWA,* both of whom fly from New York to Lisbon. Air Portugal call at Terceira in the Azores en route on certain flights. *Canadian Airlines International* flies from Montreal and Toronto in conjunction with Air Portugal.

Lisbon has services from most west European capitals as well as from Africa and South America. From London, *British Airways* and *Air Portugal* fly daily to Lisbon, several times weekly to Oporto and also to Faro in the Algarve. There are regular charter flights from several British airports to Lisbon and Faro with one or two also to Oporto. Charters from London operate from Gatwick as do some British Airways flights to Portugal.

By Boat. There are no direct passenger sailings from North America to Portugal, nor any from the U.K. or European ports. *Brittany Ferries* will take you and your car from Plymouth (England) to Santander (Spain), from where it is a two-day drive into Portugal. Lisbon is a popular cruise port for several lines.

By Train. There are no through services from the Channel ports to Portugal. But from Paris the long-established *Sud Express* has through 2nd-class couchettes to both Lisbon and Oporto. The train leaves Paris (Gare Austerlitz) at 7.51 A.M. and the Franco-Spanish border at Hendaye at about 3 P.M. There the wheels of the through carriages are changed (the gauge of both Spanish and Portuguese railways is wider than in the rest of western Europe) and it proceeds into Spain. The Portuguese sections divide at Pampilhosa, north of Coimbra, one section going to Lisbon, the other to Oporto, arriving respectively at 8.39 A.M. and 9.15 A.M. Roughly a 24-hour trip from Paris. Buffet or dining car most of the way. Also sleeping cars (1st class) and 2nd-class couchettes from Hendaye to Lisbon. *Wasteels-Expresso,* Ave. Antonio Augusto Aguiar 88, 1000 Lisbon (tel. 579655), is good for sleeper and couchette reservations.

There are also two expresses daily (one overnight with 1st-class sleepers and 2nd-class couchettes) between Madrid and Lisbon (about nine hours). The time changes one hour at the Portuguese frontiers.

By Bus. There are regular long-distance bus services from France to Portugal, and buses from Madrid and other Spanish cities into the country. From April through September, *Eurolines/SEAFEP,* part of International Express, run twice weekly services from London via Paris (where you change buses) to Coimbra, Lisbon and Lagos.

CUSTOMS. Duty-free allowances for travelers entering Portugal are 200 cigarettes or 100 cigarillos or 50 cigars or 250 grams of tobacco (double the quantity for residents of countries outside Europe); plus 1 liter of alcoholic beverage over 22° proof or 2 liters up to 22° proof and up to 2 liters of wine; plus 100 ml of perfume and 0.25 liters of toilet water. No limit for foreign currency. Computerized customs services make random and often thorough checks on arrival, less so on departure.

HOTELS. Prices of accommodations in Portugal are no longer controlled, but tourists will find rates moderate in general—though Lisbon does tend to be a bit more expensive than outlying places. However, despite the construction of new hotels and the modernization of existing establishments, accommodations are limited and reservations are a must in high season.

Moderate (M) accommodations in Lisbon come at about 9,000$00–10,000$00 a night, Inexpensive (I) from 8,000$00. Pensions, depending on the category, may run from 5,000$00. All prices are for a double room with bath and breakfast, except in the case of the really cheap pensions, which rarely have private baths, though facilities are usually clean and well-run. *Residências* (breakfast only) are more modern than pensions and slightly more expensive as a result.

Youth Hostels. These are open all year to young travelers of all nationalities who have valid membership cards bearing the current year's stamp of a Youth Hostel Association belonging to the International Federation of Youth Hostels. There are hostels in Areia Branca (Lourinhã), Arganil, Braga, Catalazete (Oeiras), Coimbra, Évora, Gerês Nature Reserve (Vilarinho das Furnas), Leiria, Lisbon, Mira, Oporto, Penhas de Saúde, Portalegre, Portimão, Sagres, São Martinho, São Pedro de Moel Vila Nova de Cerveira, and Vila Real de Sto. António. There's an official limit of three days in any one hostel, but this can be extended on a space-available basis. Contact Lisbon Hostel, Rua Andrade Corvo 46, 1000 Lisbon (tel. 532696) for further information.

Camping. In Portugal, camp sites are graded and inexpensive, and many good camping sites are available all over the country. One of the largest is the *Monsanto Parque Florestal* site, run by the Lisbon Municipality, about five minutes from the city center, with every facility, sports, pool, tennis, and a mini-market. For information, contact the Tourist Office or the *Federacão Portuguesa de Campismo,* Rua Voz do Operario 1, 1100 Lisbon (tel. 862350); Ave. 5 de Outubro 15–3, 1000 Lisbon (tel. 522715). The camping guide book, *Roteiro Campista,* can be obtained from the Portuguese Travel Office in your home country. In general camping is not restricted.

Roadside Inns. In and outside many towns, but easily accessible, are government-controlled *pousadas,* and also private *estalagems*—the latter both attractive and cheap. Standards of comfort and service are usually excellent. Country-house owners all over the country receive visitors in their homes for bed and breakfast (and sometimes dinner on request). Details from Turismo de Habitação, Avenida Antonio Augusto d'Aguiar 83–3, 1000 Lisbon, (tel. 575091).

RESTAURANTS. It's almost worth making a special trip to Portugal for the cuisine alone. The principal influence is Italian. Nowadays, the regional dishes are very tasty indeed, and, in smaller places, relatively inexpensive. However, you may wish to memorize the phrases *sem azeite,* which means "without olive oil," and *sem alho* "without garlic." All restaurants have their price list displayed outside. Only the 5-star and luxury restaurants will reserve tables.

A meal at a Moderate (M) restaurant could come to about 3,000$00, depending on which wine you drink; at an Inexpensive (I) establishment reckon on around 2,500$00. These prices are both per person. Your best bet to keep the cost down is to ask for *vinho da casa* to drink. This is the house wine of a *vin ordinaire* type; it is reasonably priced and sometimes surprisingly good. Wines in Portugal differ from region to region and some of the best don't travel, so always try to choose from the local ones.

Food and Drink. Small restaurants, called *tascas* and identified by their tables being covered with paper tablecloths, all serve well-cooked fresh food at about 2,000$00 a meal. Vegetables and fruit are those in season as frozen food is so expensive in Portugal that few residents buy it, let alone popular restaurants. The best dishes are those made with chicken or pork, as beef and mutton are both apt to be very tough. Fresh fish is excellent, but not cheap. The house wine *(vinho da casa),* either red or white, is always good and costs around 200$00 for half a bottle or 300$00 for a whole bottle. In the country areas this is served in earthenware jugs, the wine drawn straight from the barrel.

As for sweets, or puddings, there is almost always caramel custard *(pudim flan)* or baked apples *(maças assadas)* and a variety of small local cheeses, which have gone up surprisingly in price in the last few years, but at least they are interesting and fresh, unlike the segments of factory-made cheese in silver paper.

Those in self-catering accommodations will find fruit always available—oranges, tangerines and delicious sweet *Clementinas,* a small and almost tomato-red variety of orange, and very sweet *peros,* a kind of tender apple, in the winter. With late spring there come plums *(ameixas),* damsons, apricots *(alperches),* peaches *(peçegos)* and nectarines or bald peaches *(peçegos carecas),* and in late June the delicious small green figs of St. John. In August, the larger blue figs with red flesh come on sale as do greengages *(Rainha Claudia).* Cherries and strawberries can be bought in June and July, wild blackberries in August, when the many varieties of grapes appear in the shops and markets. The muscatel are the sweetest. Melons of all kinds, cantaloupe, honey-dew, yellow-skinned and the water variety with great black seeds, go on from late September right into the winter. Incidentally, storekeepers and market vendors allow their customers to feel and inspect the fruit or vegetables on sale, and will proffer a plastic bag for the purchaser to fill at their choice.

Fresh vegetables include broad beans, peas, spinach, turnip tops, cabbages of all types, tomatoes, eggplants, cucumbers, courgettes, lettuces of all varieties and herbs. Coriander is especially good with broad beans. Potatoes, onions, carrots and turnips are available all year round.

There is a huge choice of locally-caught fresh fish, though it is often rather more expensive than in other countries. But it is fun to try out varieties that you might not have seen or eaten before, such as conger eel, which can be excellent cooked in red wine, or *lampreia* (lamprey), a kind of large bluntheaded eel from the northern rivers. But you might also try *espadarte* (swordfish), particularly good smoked, *peixe galo* (John Dory), *raia* (skate), *savel* (shad), *choco* (cuttlefish), *lula* (squid), *polvo* (octopus)—the last three normally stewed in olive oil and red wine—and fresh *sardinhas* (sardines) grilled, fried or filleted and rolled in oatmeal—perfect for a light lunch.

TIPPING. Hotel service charges cover everything. But give 200$00 per bag to whoever brings your luggage up. 100$00 is sufficient for those who perform minor services for you—the doorman, for instance, who calls you a cab, and washroom attendants. Taxi drivers should get 15–20%. Service charge is included in restaurant bills, but a 5–10% tip is welcomed. At hairdressers, around 20% is the custom; at barbershops, 25%. Service station attendants should get 10$00 for pumping gas, 20$00–50$00 for checking oil and tires.

MAIL. Postal rates, both domestic and foreign, increase frequently. For the current rates, ask at your hotel reception or post office.

CLOSING TIMES. Shops open at 9 and shut at 7, with a closure during the day between 1 and 3. Many shopping malls and supermarkets stay open later and all day Saturday and Sunday. Banking hours are 8.30 to 3; they do not open on Saturdays. Main post offices in towns stay open all day to 6; country post offices close for lunch and open again until 6.

GETTING AROUND PORTUGAL. By Plane. The internal air services of Air Portugal (TAP) connect (Praça Marques Pombal 3, 1200 Lisbon, tel. 01/575020). Lisbon, Oporto, Faro, Funchal (Madeira), Porto Santo, the Azores, Viseu, Vila Real, and Bragança.

By Train. In Portugal the rolling stock is good, but services are not frequent. Northern Portugal is linked to Lisbon (Santa Apolónia Station) via Coimbra and Oporto by several fast trains a day, each way. Between Sintra and Lisbon (Rossio Station), trains are frequent and comfortable. From Lisbon (Cais do Sodré Station), very frequent electric trains take you to Estoril, Cascais, and along the "Sunny Coast." Both these local lines are very full at rush hours, which are from 8 to 10 in the morning, and from 5 to 7.30 P.M. South-bound passengers do the first lap of their journey in a ferry boat from the Sul e Sueste Station on the Praça do Comércio, to get to the train that leaves from the quay at Barreiro on the opposite bank of the Tagus. The express to the Algarve is called the *Sotavento,* leaving daily just after lunch. There is usually no difference in train times between weekdays and Sundays, except on suburban lines.

To cover the country by rail, the best system is to take the train to central points and make excursions from there. Your stops might be—for the north, Coimbra, from which you can go to Viseu; or, if you want to see mountain scenery, you can entrain for Guarda, and return by the line going through Castelo Branco and Santarém along the banks of the Tagus, and Oporto, a jumping-off point for either Viana do Castelo and the northern frontier with Spain at Valença do Minho, or Vila Real and Braganza. For the center, there is a direct line to Evora and Elvas over the frontier into Spain, and for the south to Lagos, Faro and Vila Real de S. António, also a frontier post, with a ferry over the river Guadiana to Ayamonte in Spain. A bridge is being planned.

Don't forget that Portugal is not a big country and you can cover a lot of ground cheaply by train. It may take a little time, but it will be fun while you're doing it. If you intend traveling around by train consider buying the *Bilhete Touristico,* which gives unlimited second class travel for 7, 14, or 21 days and costs 11,475$00, 18,300$00, and 26,140$00, respectively. This can either be bought at TAP airline offices outside Portugal or on arrival. Passengers over 65 years of age can get a 50% reduction on the rail ticket price with a RailEurop Senior card. On suburban lines only outside of rush hours and weekends. Don't attempt to buy tickets on the train as there's a huge surcharge if you do so.

By Bus. Most of the bus companies in Portugal have been nationalized under the general name of *Rodoviaria Nacional,* whose main passenger terminals in Lisbon are at 18 Avenida Casal Ribeiro (tel. 577715). *Mundial Turismo* of Avenida Antonio Augusto de Augiar 90-A. (tel. 523713) and *Novo Mundo,* Rua Augusto Santos 9 (tel. 575908) run luxury bus services daily to and from the Algarve and Oporto and all over the country. *Sol Expresso,* Rua Entrecampos 1 (tel. 773748), go to the Algarve, Estremadura, and Alentejo; *Capristanos,* Ave. Duque de Loulé 47 (tel. 543580), has organized bus tours. All the above firms are in Lisbon.

Lisbon

Driving in from the airport, the capital can be seen in its most modern aspect, with new apartments and wide avenues along which dash rapid autobuses and the green-roofed taxis. The airport is only twenty minutes away from the center of the city. The Avenida da Liberdade, the Champs Elysées of Lisbon, goes up from the Restauradores square (with the main tourist office in the Palácio Foz), to the Eduardo VII park in which are Lisbon's famous coolhouse or *Estufa Fria,* and hothouse, *Estufa Quente,* covering several acres of trees, plants and ferns. The old parts of the city, around the banks of the river Tagus, delight the eye, with colored glazed tiles, some with patterns or forming large scenes, adorning 17th- and 18th-century buildings. Cobbled streets wind their way uphill to the thousand-year-old honey-colored walls of the Castelo de S. Jorge, which tower high above the river. These walls are surrounded by elegantly kept public gardens with stone seats and tables for picnickers. The view over Lisbon and the Tagus is magnificent, as is the view from the terrace of the *miradouro* or belvedere of Santa Luzia, which you pass on your way up.

The famous Praça do Rossio, buzzing with crowds and traffic, is the very heart of Lisbon, a fascinating, animated forum, in perpetual motion over the stylish black-and-white inlaid pavement. The entire Baixa, or Lower Town, is a hive of business activity. As geometrical as New York, it was planned by the great Marquis of Pombal after the earthquake of 1755. The architectural gem of this reconstruction known to foreigners as Black Horse Square, is the Praça do Comércio (or Terreiro do Paço), which opens onto the river, the other three sides flanked by elegant, color-washed, arcaded buildings.

Some of the smart shops in and around the Rua Garrett or Chiado, as it is usually called, were destroyed by a disastrous fire in 1988. The sector is now being reconstructed.

Cafés abound in this city, and are crowded from morn till night. The Lisboans, gossips and gourmands by nature, enjoy nothing more than talking, talking, talking, while consuming endless tiny cups of black coffee, *bicas,* and those special egg-yolk-whipped-cream cakes.

Far removed from this atmosphere of quiet secretiveness is the surging animation of the so-called *bairros populares,* the oldest parts of the city around St. George's Castle or the quarter of Madragoa.

Away from the center of town is Belém, with its old riverside Torre de Belém and the Jeronimos Monastery. This is one of the masterpieces of that unique and wholly Portuguese style of late Gothic architecture called Manueline. There are many churches and castles throughout the country ornamented with this strange decoration, mostly taken from sea motifs, coral, seaweed, ropes and sails, but Jeronimos is the finest example.

PRACTICAL INFORMATION FOR LISBON

GETTING INTO TOWN FROM THE AIRPORT. By taxi cab, the fare from the airport works out at about 1,000$00, and takes around 20 minutes.

HOTELS. Lisbon is bursting at the seams with quite cheap pensions (*pensões*). They are clustered in several areas, but in particular on the Avenida da Liberdade and the streets just off it, and on the Avenida da República. It is prudent to call first at the National Tourist Office on the Praça dos Restauradores and get a list of the one- and two-star establishments, together with a recommendation from the staff. There are plenty—so be choosy.

Moderate

Hotel Apartamentos Impala, Rua Filipe Folque 49 (tel. 528914). 26 apartments for up to 4 people, with bath and kitchenette.

Hotel Dom Carlos, Avenida Duque de Loulé 121 (tel. 539071). 73 rooms with bath. Breakfast only.

Hotel Flamingo, Rua Castilho 41 (tel. 532191). 39 rooms with bath. Friendly staff. Restaurant.

Hotel Presidente, Rua Alexandre Herculano 13 (tel. 539501). 59 rooms with bath. Just off Avenida da Liberdade. Only breakfast.

Hotel Principe, Avenida Duque d'Avila 201 (tel. 536151). 67 rooms with bath. Restaurant.

Hotel Reno, Avenida Duque d'Avila 195 (tel. 548181). 56 rooms with bath. Breakfast only. Private parking.

Hotel Roma, Avenida de Roma 33 (tel. 767761). 264 rooms with bath. Pool. Restaurant and snack bar. Good value. Not in center.

York House, Rua das Janelas Verdes 32 (tel. 3962435). 27 rooms, most with bath. In old convent with garden, up long flight of steps. Annex at no. 47 in same street. Restaurant. No parking.

Inexpensive

Hotel Borges, Rua Garrett 108 (tel. 3461951). 100 rooms with bath. Central, somewhat old-fashioned but very pleasant. Restaurant. No parking.

Hotel Lis, Avenida da Liberdade 180 (tel. 563434). 62 rooms with bath. Reasonable. Breakfast only. Central.

Hotel Miraparque, Avenida Sidónio Pais 12 (tel. 578070). 101 rooms with bath. Overlooking Park Eduardo VII. Mediocre restaurant.

Hotel Senhora do Monte, Calçada do Monte 39 (tel. 862846). 27 rooms with bath. Somewhat away from center in old part of town near St. George's Castle. Stunning view over city.

Pensão Casa de S. Francisco, Avenida da República 48 (tel. 766600). 24 rooms. Very reasonable in price.

Pensão Mansão Santa Rita, Avenida António Augusto de Aguiar 21 (tel. 547109). 15 rooms.

Pensão Ninho das Aguias, Costa do Castelo 74 (tel. 860391). 16 rooms. Under castle walls. Good view. No parking.

Residência America, Rua Tomás Ribeiro 47 (tel. 531178). 56 rooms. Restaurant.

Residência Canada, Avenida Defensores de Chaves 35 (tel. 538159). 40 rooms.

Residência Horizonte, Avenida António Augusto Aguiar 42 (tel. 539526). 52 rooms.

Residência Imperador, Avenida 5 de Outubro 55 (tel. 574884). 45 rooms.

These *residências* and pensions are central, modern, and good value. Rooms with bath; breakfast only served.

Residencial Avenida Alameda, Avenida Sidónio Pais 4 (tel. 532186). 28 rooms. Very reasonable.

Residencial Avenida Parque, Avenida Sidónio Pais 6 (tel. 532181). 40 rooms. Very reasonable.

RESTAURANTS. There are reasonably priced restaurants to be found over the length and breadth of Lisbon. Menus together with prices should be on display outside—so beware if this is not the case. Except in expensive establishments, don't expect to book a table: if the restaurant is full, you simply wait until a place becomes free. Most restaurants in the capital shut on Sunday, but cafés serving snacks are open.

Moderate

A Quinta, top of Santa Justa lift, off Largo do Carmo (tel. 3465588). Amusing country decor. Fine view. No parking. Closed Sat. evening and Sun.

Antonio, Rua Tomás Ribeiro 63 (tel. 538780). Very popular at lunchtime.

Charme e Mesa, Travessa da Cara 20–22 (tel. 3469359). Small, but very tasteful decor. Try their *fondue.* Closed Sat. lunch and Sun.

Colina, Rua Filipe Folque 46 (tel. 560209). Very good food and pleasant atmosphere. Open until midnight.

Delfim, Rua Nova de S. Mamede 23, (tel. 690532). Portuguese specialties. Closed Sat.

La Trattoria, Rua Artilharia Um 79–85 (tel. 650209). Very smart premises. Italian food at reasonable rates.

O Alexandre, Rua Vieira Portuense 84 (tel. 3634454). Near Coach Museum. Closed Sat.

O Forno da Brites, Rua Tomás Ribeiro 73–75 (tel. 542724). Quiet, efficient service, well adapted for tourists, and also popular with the locals. Closed Sat.

O Paco, Avenida Berna 44B (tel. 7970642). Opposite the Gulbenkian Museum, pleasant folkloric set-up, nice, fairly reasonable. Closed Mon.

Toni das Bifes (*bife* meaning steak), Avenida Praia da Vitoria 50 (tel. 536080). Small, cozy, good. Closed Sun.

Inexpensive

A Carruagem, Rua Filipe Folque 49-A (tel. 561333). Beneath Hotel Apartamentos Impala. Snack-Bar and restaurant. Always open.

A Primavera, Travessa da Espera 34 (tel. 320477). Super fish in the Bairro Alto district. Closed Sun.

Aldeia do Moinho, Feira Popular (tel. 732310). Good country food; grilled sardines. Closed Sat. evening and Sun.

Bonjardim (tel. 324389) and **Arameiro** (tel. 3467185), both on Travessa Santo Antão, at side of General Post Office. Parking underneath Restauradores. Each is inexpensive and always crowded (go early or late); main specialty of both: chicken on the spit or roast suckling pig. Always open.

Bota Alta, Travessa Queimada 35 (tel. 327959). Excellent food at reasonable prices. Very popular. Closed Sat. lunch and Sun.

Ceuta, Avenida da República 20C (tel. 531305). Serves meals as well as delicious cakes. Snack bar. Closed Sun.

China, Rua Andrade Corvo 7B (tel. 549455), closed Tues., and **Xangai,** Avenida Duque de Loulé 20B (tel. 557378). Closed Tues. Both have good Chinese cooking and are near U.S. Library.

Colombo, Avenida da República 10 (tel. 549225). Serves lunches and dinners as well as teas. Huge variety of good cakes. Always open till 10 P.M.

The Great American Disaster, Praça Marquês de Pombal 1 (tel. 521266). Amusing place serving excellent American-style steaks, hamburgers, fries, salads and ice cream. Good cold beer as well as the usual wines. Music. Always open.

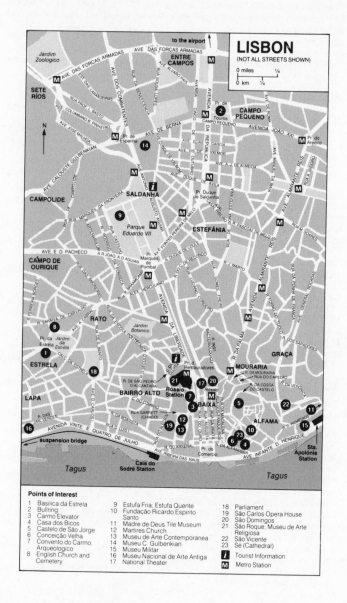

LISBON
(NOT ALL STREETS SHOWN)

Points of Interest

1   Basilica da Estrela
2   Bullring
3   Carmo Elevator
4   Casa dos Bicos
5   Castelo de São Jorge
6   Conceição Velha
7   Convento do Carmo:
    Arqueologico
8   English Church and
    Cemetery
9   Estufa Fria; Estufa Quente
10 Fundação Ricardo Espirito
    Santo
11 Madre de Deus Tile Museum
12 Martires Church
13 Museu de Arte Contemporanea
14 Museu C. Gulbenkian
15 Museu Militar
16 Museu Nacional de Arte Antiga
17 National Theater
18 Parliament
19 São Carlos Opera House
20 São Domingos
21 São Roque; Museu de Arte
    Religiosa
22 São Vicente
23 Sé (Cathedral)
i Tourist Information
M   Metro Station

Ladeira, Avenida Marques de Tomar 33 (tel. 7972520). Serves half portions as well as whole, which two persons can share. Closed Fri. evening and all day Sat.

Laurentina, Avenida Conde Valbom 71A (tel. 760260). Run by Mozambicans, so good, somewhat exotic food. Closed Sun.

Lira de Ouro, Rua Nova de São Mamede 10 (tel. 3963306). Closed Sun.

Mimo, Avenida Duque d'Avila 6 A-B (tel. 570072). Well-cooked, reasonably priced dishes served by active and attentive waiters. Closed Sun.

O Guardanapo, Rua Padre António Vieira 4A (tel. 691016). Near Ritz Hotel. Small and cheerful. Very reasonable. Closed Sat. and Sun.

O Manel, Pq. Mayer (tel. 3463167). Off Avenida Liberdade. Portuguese cooking at its simple best. Closed Sun.

O Rafael, Rua de Belém 106 (tel. 3637420). Located between Jeronimos and Coach Museum, with a pretty patio for outdoor eating. Closed Mon.

Pap'Açorda, Rua da Atalaia 57 (tel. 3464811). Good Portuguese food and specialties.

Porto de Abrigo, Rua de Remolares 18 (tel. 3460873). Very full for lunch. More room at dinner. Excellent value. Try their crab or duck with olives. Closed Sun.

Telheiro, Rua Latino Coelho (tel. 534007). Good Portuguese cooking.

Cervejarias. The so-called *Cervejarias* (*cerveja* meaning beer) and snack bars are very easy on the budget. At the latter, however, do not expect to get what you would at home; the name is somewhat misleading. Snack bars, *Pastelarias* and cafés are all over town. Among the best-known are the following:

Moderate

Cervejaria Ribadouro, Rua do Salitre 2 (tel. 549411). Popular with the locals, mounds of seafood, excellent. Always open.

Inexpensive

Cervejaria Trindade, Rua Nova da Trindade 20-C (tel. 323506). One of the very best in this category. Patio. Always open.

Pastelaria Ritz, Rua Rodrigo da Fonseca 129. (tel. 681661). Good cakes and very reasonable meals. Closed Sat.

Snack Bar Imperial, Avenida António Augusto Aguiar 27C (tel. 547108). You can eat at a counter or at tables. Closed Sun.

Snack Bar Self-Service Buzina, Rua Rodrigo da Fonseca 204 (tel. 681434). Pleasant roomy atmosphere. Closed Sun and Sat. evening.

Casas de Fado. Restaurants where you can hear the *fado* are apt to be expensive and it is wise to find out the *consumo minimo*—minimum charge—beforehand. The singing never starts before around 11 P.M.

Luso, Travessa Queimada 10 (tel. 322281). Closed Sun.

Machado, Rua do Norte 91 (tel. 3460095). Closed Mon.

Mesquita, Rua Diário de Noticías 107 (tel. 3462077). Closed Sun.

O Faia, Rua da Barroca, 54 (tel. 326742). Closed Sun.

O Forcado, Rua da Rosa, 219 (tel. 3468579). Closed Wed.

Senhor Vinho, Rua do Meio à Lapa 18 (tel. 672681). Closed Sun.

GETTING AROUND LISBON. By Subway/Train. Subways, called *Metropolitano,* connect the Rossio with the Zoological Gardens at Sete Rios and with Campo Grande, Entrecampos (site of the bull ring), also with Alvalade. Fare 50$00 to any point; book of ten tickets 400$00. Beware of pickpockets. Cable cars link some of the high and low areas of the city. Frequent and excellent one-class electric trains leave from Cais do Sodré Station, traveling along the Costa do Sol and terminating at Cascais, beyond Estoril. Trains for Sintra start from Rossio Station. Buy your tickets at the booking office because there is a huge surcharge if you get them on the train.

By Bus and Tram. *Citirama,* of Avenida Praia da Vitória 12B (tel. 575564) operate daily sightseeing tours, with taped commentary in several languages, picking up passengers at the leading hotels. The Portuguese Tourist Office at Palácio Foz, Praça dos Restauradores, has particulars of these and other tours. In Cascais,

TIP Tours, Rua Costa Pinto 91-A (tel. 283821), also run tours and hire out bicycles. Buses 52, 53 and 54 cross the Tagus Bridge.

The tram service is one of the best in Europe, and is still cheap. Tourist one-week season tickets cost 1,500$00—4-day tickets 1,000$00—and provide unlimited travel on both buses and trams; these and books of 20 tickets with 20% discount can be bought at Cais do Sodré and other terminals. Try routes 18, 24, 28, 29 and 30 for an unusual tour of the city, on one of the world's oldest, and steepest, tram networks. The bus service is very good and reaches every part of the city.

By Boat. Ferry boats for Barreiro and Montijo leave from Estação do Sul e Sueste, alongside the Praço do Comércio; for Cacilhas from Cais do Sodré and the Praça do Comércio; and for Trafaria and Porto Brandão from the Estação Fluvial de Belém. The ferries from Cais do Sodré take cars. No pedestrians are allowed on the Tagus bridge.

By Taxi. Taxis are plentiful and fairly cheap. Cabs, identified by their green roofs, start at 100$00, with a passenger limit of four people. There is a 50% increase for baggage weighing over 66 pounds; and a 20% increase in fares between 10 P.M. and 6 A.M. For trips out of Lisbon, the driver is entitled to the fare both ways, even if you don't return with him, and he has the privilege of quoting you a flat rate or running the meter. This makes it about 4,000$00 to Estoril or Cascais. Tip about 15%. For the panoramic view, it's worth taking a trip over the majestic Tagus bridge (toll 80$00 out, return free).

ENTERTAINMENT. Nightlife. Lisbon nightclubs in general don't rank international class. New ones open, fairly new ones fold; it's unpredictable. In general, they can be expensive.

Ad Lib, Rua Barata Salgueiro 28-7. Respectable and smart.

Alcantara-Mar, Rua da Cozinha Economica 11, (tel. 636432) Newest "in" place.

Banana Power, Rua de Cascais 51, Alcantara. Smart and very exclusive.

Monaco, Estrada Marginal-Caxias. Restaurant just outside Lisbon on coast road, with live band and dancing.

Stones, Rua do Olival 1. Smart, respectable.

MUSEUMS. Open from 10 to 5, but close Mondays and public holidays and often for lunch. Palaces close on different days. Entrance approximately 250$00–500$00, though Sundays are usually free.

Ajuda Palace, Largo da Ajuda. Splendid 19th-century rooms, good furniture, paintings, etc. (Buses: 14, 40, 42.) Closed Wed.

Ancient Art, Rua das Janelas Verdes. A fine collection of paintings, ceramics, jewelry, tapestries, silver etc. Portuguese primitives (don't miss the famous 15th-century polyptych by Nuno Gonçalves, *Triumph of St. Vincent*) and work by Hieronymus Bosch, Zurbarán, Frans Hals, Holbein, Durer, and many other Dutch, Spanish, and Italian painters. Be sure to see the Germain brothers' silver table service. Snack bar. (Buses: 27, 40, 49, 54.) Closed 1–2.30.

Aquarium, Dafundo. Open Mon.–Sat., 10–5.30, Sun. 10–6. Wed. free. (Bus: 29.)

Botanical Gardens, in Parque Eduardo VII. A vast cool house *(Estufa Fria)* and hot house *(Estufa Quente)* filled with rare specimens. Entrance 100$00. Open 9 A.M. to sunset. (Buses: 2, 3, 4.)

City of Lisbon, Palácio do Pimenta, Campo Grande. In a beautiful 18th-century house. Closed 1 to 2. (Buses: 1, 7, 33, 36, 50.)

Coach, Praça Afonso de Albuquerque, Belém. Finest collection of royal coaches and carriages in the world. (Buses: 12, 27, 28, 29, 43, 49.) Closed 1–2.30.

Contemporary Art, Rua Serpa Pinto. Portuguese painting and sculpture. Closed 12.30 to 2. (Tram: 28.)

Costume, Largo S. João Baptista, Lumiar. Costumes, materials, dolls. Set in lovely gardens. Closed 1 to 2.30. Restaurant (E). (Buses: 1, 7, 7B, 36.)

Ethnological, Praça do Imperio, Belém. Prehistoric, Greek and Roman remains. (Buses: 29, 43.)

Folk Art, Avenida Brasília, Belém. A rich and eloquent showing of provincial arts and lore. (Buses: 12, 29, 43.) Closed 12.30–2.

Gulbenkian Foundation, Avenida Berna. The collection here includes items bought from Leningrad's Hermitage Museum in 1929–30. This is one of the world's most impressive galleries, with rare coins, Persian carpets and artifacts, superb French furniture, 18th-century sculpture, Lalique jewelry, and several Rembrandts all set in custom-designed rooms, looking out over lovely gardens. Snack bar. Open 10–5. Sundays free. The Modern Gallery in the park has a good self-service restaurant. (Buses: 30, 41, 46, 56.)

Marionette, Largo Rodrigo Freitas 19-A. Lisbon's newest museum. (Bus: 37.) Open 11–1 and 3–5.

Maritime, Praça do Império, Belém. Model ships, paintings, maps, etc. Superbly arranged. Wednesdays free. (Buses: 29, 43.) Next to Planetarium.

Military, Largo dos Caminhos de Ferro. Weapons, uniforms, models. Open 10–4. (Buses: 9A, 13, 17, 35.)

Planetarium, Praça do Império, Belém. Next to the Maritime Museum. (Buses: 29, 43.) Times of shows vary. See notice board.

Ricardo Espirito Santo Foundation, in an old palace at Largo das Portas do Sol. Part museum, part training center for craftsmen, here you can see some of the best rugs, silver, furniture and lamps made in Portugal. Antiques are sent here for repair from all over the world. Open Mon. to Sat. 10–1 and 2:30–5. Closed 1–2.30. (Bus: 37.)

Theater, Estrada do Lumiar 10, near Costume Museum. Closed 1 to 2.30. (Buses: 1, 7, 7B, 36.)

Tile, Madre de Deus Convent, Rua da Madre de Deus. Tiles, many in pictorial panels, from Moorish times to the present day. (Buses: 6, 18.)

Zoological Gardens, Parque das Larangeiras. Very fine collection of animals in a large park. Restaurants. Open daily, winter 9 to 6, summer 9 to 8. Admission 300$00, children 3 to 8, 175$00. (Buses: 15, 16, 26, 31, 34, 41, 46.)

SHOPPING. Main centers are the Chiado and Rua Garrett for silks, woolens, linen etc.; Vista Alegre for porcelain; and the Baixa between the Rossio and the Praça do Comercio. Good buys are shoes (all over town); antique and modern silver, jewelry, at António da Silva, Praça Luís de Camões 40; azulejos and pottery at Viuva Lamego, Largo do Intendente 25; baskets at entrance to the Praça da Ribeira near Cais do Sodré Station; and embroideries at Tito Cunha, Rua do Ouro 179. Arts and crafts at Centro de Turismo Artesanato, Rua Castilho 61, who will also dispatch all goods abroad.

Stores are generally shut from 1 to 3 but stay open till 7 in the evening. They close at 1 P.M. on Saturdays and are closed all day Sunday. There are now shopping malls in many parts of the city. The huge Amoreiras Shopping Complex, Ave. Duarte Pacheco, with dozens of shops and restaurants, and parking, is the latest. These are often open till midnight, and some are even open on Sunday.

USEFUL ADDRESSES. *U.S. Embassy and Consulate,* Ave. das Forcas Armadas (tel. 726600); *British Embassy and Consulate,* Avenida da Liberdade 144–3 (tel. 347892); *Canadian Embassy and Consulate, American Express, Star,* Ave. Sidónio Pais 4 (tel. 539871); *Automobile Club,* Rua Rosa Aráujo 24 (tel. 563931); English bank: *Lloyds Bank International,* Ave. da Liberdade 222 (tel. 535171), Rua do Ouro 40 (tel. 3461211), with branches in Monte Estoril, Carcavelos, Faro, Oporto and Braga. *Rodoviaria Nacional,* Ave. Casal Ribeiro 18 (tel. 545439) have buses all over the country. *Portuguese Tourist Office,* Palácio Foz, Praça dos Restauradores (tel. 363314), Avenida António Augusto Aguiar 86 (tel. 575086), and at airport; *British Hospital* (English-speaking staff, in- and out-patients), Rua Saraiva de Carvalho 49 (tel. 602020, night 603785). Consult notice on door of any pharmacy for address of nearest one open after hours.

The Environs of Lisbon

The principal places of interest to visit near Lisbon are Estoril, Cascais, Sintra and Mafra, all to the west of the capital and easily reached by train from Cais do Sodré station in the case of the first two and from Rossio station in the case of Sintra. There are also road connections along the Estrada Marginal by the estuary of the Tagus from Lisbon to Estoril and Cascais (and the splendid Guincho beach past Cascais; bathing dangerous in bad weather) and to Sintra and Mafra by bus.

Estoril is a pleasantly old-fashioned seaside town with a sandy beach, beautifully-kept public gardens, an 18-hole golf course with pool and restaurant open to the public, and the Casino, where there is a restaurant, nightclub, theater and art gallery, as well of course as the gaming rooms. There's an admission charge to the gaming rooms, but the rest of the Casino is open free. In the summer the Gulbenkian Foundation subsidizes a music and ballet festival in the Casino theater, while an Arts and Crafts Fair is held in a wood nearby.

Cascais, the end of the rail line from Lisbon, is much more up-to-date than Estoril and boasts a considerable number of restaurants in all price ranges as well as many good shops. There are long sandy beaches and a fisherman's beach right in the center of town where the catch is landed before being taken for auction at the fish market.

Sintra is a few miles north of Cascais. If you are traveling via the inland road from Lisbon, you'll pass near Queluz palace, a charming pink 18th-century building with delightful interiors and formal gardens. It's open to the public, but shut on Tuesday.

Rising from a plain, the hills of Sintra are covered with a mass of rare vegetation and trees amid rocky outcrops. In the town center, you'll find the Palácio de Vila (closed Wed.) whose architecture comprises examples from every period of Portuguese history, from Gothic and Manueline to the high Victorian and Edwardian of the last Kings of Portugal. Look up from the square in front of the palace to the ruined Moorish castle and the Pena Palace (closed Mon.), built in 1840 on one of the highest points of the Serra da Sintra. It's a splendid architectural fantasy. In the huge park there are superb trees and shrubs such as camellias, bamboos, arbutus, tree ferns and exotic flowering plants. The famous gardens of Monserrate three miles along the upper Colares road past the Hotel Palácio de Seteais, are open from 9 until 6. A big country fair is held at S. Pedro de Sintra on the second and fourth Sundays of every month.

Mafra, 12 miles to the north, is a huge, early 18th-century palace/monastery with a famous library (closed Tues.).

PRACTICAL INFORMATION FOR THE ENVIRONS OF LISBON

Hotels and Restaurants

Cascais. *Albergaria Valbom* (M), Avenida Valbom 14 (tel. 2865801). 40 rooms with bath. Bar; breakfast only. *Hotel Baia* (M), Avenida Marginal (tel. 281033). 87 rooms with bath. Café-restaurant on terrace overlooking fishermen's beach. *Hotel-Apartamento Equador* (I), Alto da Pampilheira (tel. 2840524). 120 service apartments with bath. Pool, restaurant, supermarket, etc., and very good value. Not in center. *Hotel Nau* (I), Rua Dra, Iracy Doyle (tel. 282861). 56 rooms with bath. Restaurant.

Restaurants. *Alho Porro* (M), Rua Alexandre Herculano 13. Closed Mon. Good food and service. *Gil Vicente* (M), Rua das Navegantes 22. Closed Mon. *The Beefeater* (M), Rua Visconde da Luz 1A. An English-style pub, as is the *Duke of Wellington* (I), Rua Frederico Arouca 32. *Os Galegos* (I), Avenida Valbom 1. A real *tasca* with grilled chicken, and wine from the barrel. Open every day. *Pigalo* (I), Tr. Frederico Arouca 12. Intimate, with excellent service. Very good value. Closed Wed. *Victor* (I), Rua Visconde de Luz 43-A. Serves half portions. Very good value. Closed Wed.

Estoril. Casino. *Alvorada* (M), tel. 2680070. 50 rooms with bath. Breakfast only. Opposite Casino. Very good value. *Paris* (M), Estrada Marginal (tel. 2680018). 78 rooms with bath. Rooftop restaurant. Pool. *Lido* (M), Rua do Alentejo 12 (tel. 2684098). 62 rooms with bath. Pool. Quiet, but not near beach. *Inglaterra* (I), Rua do Porto 2 (tel. 2684461). 45 rooms, most with bath. Pool. Good family hotel. Reasonable. *Pensão Chic* (I), Ave. Marginal 60 (tel. 2680393). 14 rooms, most with bath. Excellent restaurant. *Residencial Smart* (I), Rua José Viana 3 (tel. 2682164). 14 rooms, half with bath. Breakfast only. English-run.

Restaurants. There are cafés and restaurants in the western arcade at the side of the gardens going down from the Casino to the Estrada Marginal and in the Avenida Biarritz.

Monte Estoril. *Grande* (M), Avenida Saboia (tel. 2684609). 71 rooms with bath. Pool. Good value. *Aparthotel Touring* (I), Rua do Viveiro (tel. 2683385). 99 apartments with bath, kitchenette. Pool. Some way from beach. *Londres* (I), Avenida Fausto Figueiredo 17 (tel. 2684245). 90 rooms with bath. Pool. *Zenith* (I), Rua Belmonte 1 (tel. 2680202). 48 rooms with bath. Shallow pool.

Restaurants. There are a number on Rua do Viveiro. *Adega do Monte* (M), Rua do Lago 1. New, roomy; good Portuguese food. Closed Sun. *Casa Pizza* (I), Rua do Viveiro 2-E, very good value. Italian food. *Cozinha do Mar* (I), Ave. São Pedro 9. Nice food, friendly. Two can share a dish. Closed Tues. *O Sinaleiro* (I), Avenida Saboia 35 (tel. 2685439). Excellent food and house wine. Very popular with locals. Closed Mon. There are also several bars in Avenida S. Pedro.

Sintra. *Central* (M), (tel. 9230063). 11 rooms with bath. On the Palace Square. Sit and eat on the wide terrace to watch the world go by. *Pensão Nova Sintra* (I), 11 rooms. Largo Afonso Albuquerque 25 (tel. 9230220). Lovely terrace up flight of steps. Small, very reasonable, friendly.

Restaurants. Among recommended restaurants and *tascas* is *O Cantinho* (M), by São Pedro da Sintra market. Exceptional cooking and good wine. Closed Mon. *Apeadeiro* (I), Ave. Miguel Bombarda 3. Nice, old-fashioned *tasca*. Closed Thurs. *Tulhas Bar* (I), Rua Gil Vicente 4. Excellent food and house wine. Closed Wed.

The Setubal Peninsula

The Setubal peninsula is directly south of Lisbon and lies between the river Tagus, to the north, and the estuary of the river Sado, to the south. It is easily reached by bus and car from Lisbon over the great suspension bridge, or by the passenger ferries that ply the Tagus from near Cais do Sodré station and from the Praça do Comércio to Cacilhas. From here there are buses to many parts of the peninsula, including Costa da Caparica, a popular resort with a long sandy beach and five camping grounds with almost 10,000 places.

A good place to begin an exploration is right down on the Sado estuary at the fishing village of Sesimbra. There is a fine castle, but unfortunately much of the town has been spoiled, uncharacteristically for Portugal, by highrise developments. Alternatively, you might like to start at the long, sickle-shaped beach of Portinho da Arrábida, which has a number of reasonably-priced restaurants. The bathing here is exceptionally good, and the water remarkably clear, if a little cold.

Running along the whole of this southern shore is the great limestone ridge of the Serra da Arrábida. It is thickly-forrested, and in places the northern slopes are almost impenetrable. Along the southern side there are two roads leading east to Setubal itself. The upper one winds far above the broad estuary, while the lower road follows the shores.

Setubal is a big fishing and canning town, but also has a good museum and the earliest Manueline building in the country, the Church of Jesus. There are many pleasant, small restaurants. Try some of the delicious Setubal wine, which is made with Muscatel grapes. Car ferries cross the Sado to Troia, recently developed and with an 18-hole golf course.

Just north of the town is Palmela, with narrow, twisting streets leading up to the enormous Templar castle crowning its hilltop, part of which is now a luxury *pousada.*

On the road back to Lisbon from Palmela is Bacalhoa, one of the earliest inhabited houses in Portugal. The gardens are filled with the scent of orange trees and lead to a large water tank supplying a pavilion with the earliest dated tile panel in the country—1565. You can view the gardens from 1 to 5 except Sundays and holidays. (Tip 200$00–300$00.)

PRACTICAL INFORMATION FOR THE SETUBAL PENINSULA

Hotels and Restaurants

Azeitão. *Estalagem Quinta das Torres* (M), tel. 2080001. 11 rooms with bath; 2 cottages in grounds. Restaurant open to visitors. In lovely country.

Cacilhas. Restaurants. Several restaurants on river wall. Get a table in a window and see the lights of Lisbon come up over the Tagus as you dine, or the porpoises playing in the river in rough weather, though the food could be better.

Costa Da Caparica. *Praia Sol* (I), Rua dos Pescadores 12 (tel. 2900012). 54 rooms with bath. Breakfast only.
Restaurants. *Bento* (I). Next to beach. *Carolina de Aires* (I), Ave. General Humberto Delgado. Good for fish. Very large and always open. Esplanade.

Sesimbra. *Espadarte* (I), Avenida 25 de Abril (tel. 2233189). 80 rooms with bath. Restaurant. On the esplanade by the sea.

Setubal. *Esperança* (M), Avenida Luisa Todi 220 (tel. 065 25152). 76 rooms with bath. Restaurant. *Pensão Bocage* (M), Rua S. Cristovão 14 (tel. 065 21809). 20 rooms with bath, 14 in annex. Breakfast only. *Mar e Sol* (I), Ave. Luisa Todi 606 (tel. 065 33016). 31 rooms with bath. Breakfast only.
Restaurants. *Bocage* (M), off Praça do Bocage. Excellent regional food and Setubal wines. Closed Tues. *O Tunel* (I), Praça do Bocage 52.

Troia. *Aparthotel Tulipamar* (M), Torre T03, tel. 065 44151. 184 self-service apartments. Restaurant, pool, golf. All facilities.

Estremadura

The province of Estremadura lies to the north of the capital and runs along the coast. From the Rossio station in Lisbon, there is a good train service that heads through fertile country to Torres Vedras, some 30 miles away and famous for the Lines built by Wellington to defend Lisbon against Napoleon during the Peninsular War. It then passes Bombarral, a great wine center, and continues on to Obidos where the *automotora,* or rail car, comes to a halt in a tiny station under the castle at one end of the beautiful old walled town. Climb up steep steps to a postern gate, past the *pousada* installed in the restored 15th-century castle, to the narrow streets winding past 17th- and 18th-century houses and early churches filled with the work of Josefa of Obidos, a late 17th-century woman painter. Bright flowers hang from every balcony and a walk along the wide top of the ramparts gives a marvelous view. There is also a charming museum.

Caldas da Rainha, a few miles further north and also on the railway, is a noted spa and pottery center specializing in glazed earthenware figures in human, animal and vegetable form.

Continuing north a further 14 miles brings you to Alcobaça, famous for the great 12th-century Cistercian church and monastery. It is not on the railway but is easily reached by bus. The abbey church, with its breathtaking interior, is the largest in Portugal and the tombs of King Pedro I and his adored Inez de Castro are memorable examples of Gothic sculpture. Alcobaça is a charming town, and, with its very reasonably-priced accommodations, makes a good base for exploring Nazaré, a famous fishing port and beach to the north west, and Batalha, some 10 miles to the north east. The splendid Abbey of Santa Maria de Vitoria is here. It was built in the 14th and 15th centuries to commemorate the victory in 1385 over the Spanish at Aljubarrota, which confirmed Portuguese independence. It's the finest example of decorated Gothic in the country and contains the Founders' Chapel with the tombs of King John I and his English Queen, Philippa of Lancaster. In the Chapter House, off the flamboyant Gothic double cloister, are the tombs of Portugal's two Unknown Soldiers from World War I; one for Europe and one for Africa. Behind the chancel of the abbey church, and only to be reached from outside the main building, are the extraordinary Unfinished Chapels dating from the early 16th-century and started by King Manuel I but only half completed when the King became engrossed in the building of Jeronimos at Belém, on the outskirts of Lisbon; these *Capelas Imperfeitas* remain open to the winds and the rain, their lace-like carvings rivaling in richness the temples of India.

About 12 miles east of Batalha is Fatima, one of the most famous European Shrines. On May 13 1917, the Virgin Mary is believed to have appeared here to three shepherds. On the 12th and 13th of each month, from May to October, huge crowds of pilgrims travel to the Shrine. The vast majority pray all night in the open air.

Tomar, 20 miles to the east, is noted for a marvelous Templar's Castle with seven cloisters of all periods from the 13th century and the original circular sanctuary, the *Charola.*

PRACTICAL INFORMATION FOR ESTREMADURA

Hotels and Restaurants

Alcobaça. *Pensão Corações Unidos* (I), Rua Frei António Brandão 39 (tel. 062 42142). 16 rooms. Good restaurant. *Santa Maria* (I), Rua Dr Zagalo (tel. 062 43295). Opposite the great abbey. 31 rooms with bath. Breakfast only.

Batalha. *Motel São Jorge* (M), on road to Fatima (tel. 044 96210). 10 bungalows for 4 persons with kitchenette and bath. Restaurant. Pool. Snack bars and restaurants near the abbey.

Caldas Da Rainha. Spa. *Malhoa* (M), Rua António Sergio 31 (tel. 062 35011). 113 rooms with bath. Restaurant. Pool. *Pensão Portugal* (I), Rua Almirante Cândido dos Reis (tel. 062 34280). 24 rooms, half with bath. Several pleasant restaurants.

Fatima. *Fatima* (M), Rua João Paulo II (tel. 049 52351). 76 rooms with bath. *Pax* (I), Rua Franciso Marto 52, tel. 049 51912. 78 rooms with bath. Near sanctuary; restaurant, elevator. *Regina* (I), Rua Conego Manuel Formigão (tel. 049 52303). 88 rooms with bath. Almost all the religious houses accept guests. They include *Beato Nuno* (Carmelite Friars), tel. 049 52199. 100 rooms, all with bath. *Exercito Azul* (Blue Army), tel. 049 51020. 106 rooms with bath. American foundation. *Irmas Dominicanas* (Dominican nuns), tel. 049 52317. 60 rooms, most with bath. Several café-restaurants.

Nazaré. *Nazaré* (M), Largo Afonso Zuquete (tel. 044 51311). 52 rooms with bath. Modern, comfortable. *Praia* (M), Avenida Vieira Guimarães 39 (tel. 044 51423). 40 rooms with bath. Breakfast only. *Dom Fuas* (I), Ave. Manuel Remigio (tel. 044 51351). Recommended. 32 rooms with bath. Open June through Oct. Dozens of restaurants.

Tomar. *Pensão Nuno Alvares* (I), Avenida D. Nuno Alvares Pereira 3 (tel. 049 32873). 12 rooms. Good country food and local wine. Several other pensions and restaurants, including the *Bela Vista* (M) by the bridge. Closed Tues.

Torres Vedras. *Pensão Moderna* (M), Avenida Tenente Valadim 18 (tel. 061 23146). 30 rooms, most with bath. Breakfast only. Several restaurants and snack bars.

The Douro

The Douro's capital is Oporto, and Oporto's capital is port. The whole province, away in the north of the country, owes its wealth to that wonderful wine, made from the grapes that ripen all along the scorching, terraced slopes of the river Douro. Try to visit the area at the end of September when the grape harvest takes place; it's an intoxicating experience. Watch the "must" poured into enormous casks and loaded onto trucks.

Oporto, so old it claims to have been founded by Noah, is a thriving bourgeois city, grown rich on the grape and its natural harbor. The chief ornaments are its gardens, filled with roses and camellias, and the river itself, with its golden green water speckled with white sails and spanned by three splendid bridges. Of these, the most interesting is the two-level Dom Luis Bridge. The Dona Maria Railway Bridge, a filigree of steel, was built by Eiffel; the impressive Ponte da Arrábida was opened in 1964.

Also worth visiting here is the Romanesque church of São Martinho da Cedofeita, one of the oldest in Portugal, and the Church of the Clerigos, which dominates the city with its many-storied tower. São Francisco's fantastic gilded baroque woodcarvings should be seen, also those in Santa Clara.

The wine lodges are across the river at Vila Nova de Gaia, on the slopes of which Wellington assembled his troops for the attack on Oporto in the Peninsular War. Warre, Sandeman and Ferreira are among the port wine firms that can be visited without appointment.

Boat trips on the Douro are organized from May to October by Port Ferreira, Rua da Carvalhosa 19, Vila Nova da Gaia, leaving on the hour every day except Saturday afternoon and Sunday.

Popular beach resorts in the environs of Oporto include Foz do Douro at the mouth of the river, Póvoa de Varzim, a picturesque fishing village, Espinho and Miramar.

PRACTICAL INFORMATION FOR THE DOURO

Hotels and Restaurants

Espinho. *Mar Azul* (I), Avenida 8, No. 676 (tel. 02 720824). 18 rooms with bath. Breakfast only. A number of other hotels and pensions; also two golf courses, pool, casino.

Oporto. *Grande Hotel do Porto* (M), Rua Sta. Catarina 197 (tel. 02 28176). 100 rooms with bath. *Imperio* (M), Praça da Batalha 127 (tel. 02 26861). 95 rooms with bath. *Tuela* (M), Rua Marquês da Silva 180 (tel. 02 667161). 197 rooms with bath. *Internacional* (I), Rua do Almada 131 (tel. 02 25032). 35 rooms. *Malaposta* (I), Rua da Conceição 80 (tel. 02 26278). 37 rooms with bath. Breakfast only. *Nave* (I), Avenida Fernão de Magalhaes 247 (tel. 02 576131). 48 rooms with bath. *Peninsular* (I), Rua Sá da Bandeira 21 (tel. 02 23013). 39 rooms with bath. Large number of *residências* and pensions.

Restaurants. Oporto is filled with reasonably priced eating houses. *Acquário Marisqueiro* (M), Rua Rodrigues Sampaio 163–179. Mainly seafood. Several amusing restaurants on the Cais da Ribeira with good food and wine. Fascinating street market on quays outside. *Neptuno* (I), Rua Rodrigues Sampaio 133. For good cheap seafood.

Praia De Miramar. *Mirasol* (M), Avenida Vasco da Gama (tel. 02 7622665). 25 rooms with bath. Golf.

Póvoa De Varzim. *Grande* (M), Passeio Alegre (tel. 052 622061). 101 rooms with bath. On the sea. Casino in town. Also, several restaurants.

The Beiras, Minho and Trás-os-Montes

These three provinces to the north of the country contain several fascinating towns. The Beiras, south of Oporto, stretch from the sea to the Spanish frontier, Minho is north of Oporto, and Trás-os-Montes is in the remote northeast.

Aveiro, in the Beiras, is a lovely watery place surrounded by sea lagoons. In the same province, Coimbra on the Mondego is famous for its university, founded in 1290; while Lamego and Viseu are two baroque cities well worth a visit.

Braga, Guimarães, and Viana do Castelo, all in the Minho, can boast splendid edifices and interesting museums. Trás-os-Montes ("Over-the-Hills") is wild and beautiful. The towns—notably Braganza and Miranda do Douro—have good museums and are still relatively unspoiled.

PRACTICAL INFORMATION FOR
THE BEIRAS, MINHO AND TRÁS-OS-MONTES

Hotels and Restaurants

Aveiro *Imperial* (M), Rua Dr. Nascimento Leitão (tel. 034 22141). 107 rooms with bath. *Arcada* (I), Rua Viana do Castelo 4 (tel. 034 23001). 45 rooms with bath. Breakfast only. Several good restaurants.

Braga *João XXI* (M), Avenida João XXI, 849 (tel. 053 22146). 28 rooms with bath. *Francfort* (I), Avenida Central 1 (tel. 053 22648). 15 rooms. Old fashioned. Easy parking. Central. Both with restaurants.
Restaurants. *Inacio,* Campo das Hortas; *Peninsular,* Largo S. Francisco; *A Toca,* Rua do Souto 127. All (I).

Braganza *Bragança* (M), tel. 073 22579. 42 rooms with bath. Restaurant.
Restaurants. *Arca de Noé,* Ave. do Savor. Closed Friday; *Manel,* Praça Camões 29. Closed Sunday. Both (I).

Coimbra *Avenida* (M), Avenida Emidio Navarro 37 (tel. 039 22156). 25 rooms with bath. *Mondego* (I), Largo das Ameias 4 (tel. 039 29087). 44 rooms, half with bath. Several *residências* and pensions.
Restaurants. *D. Pedro* (M), Ave. Emidio Navarro 58. *Piscinas* (M), Calhabé. Both closed Mon. *Santa Cruz* (M), Praça 8 de Maio.

Guimarães *Toural* (I), Largo do Toural 15 (tel. 053 411250). 38 rooms. Breakfast only. *Pensão Imperial* (I), Alameda Dr. Sá Carneiro 111 (tel. 053 415163). 29 rooms.
Restaurants. *Jordão* (M), Ave. D. Afonso Henriques 55. Closed Tues. *Dois Arcos* (I), Rua Paio Galvão 62.

Lamego *Parque* (I), tel. 054 62105. 32 rooms with bath. Near N.S. dos Remedios. *Pensão Solar* (I), Largo da Sé (tel. 054 62060). 25 rooms with bath. Breakfast only.
Restaurant. *Avenida*(I), Ave. Combatentes da Grande Guerra. Easy parking. Closed Mon.

Miranda Do Douro *Pensão Planalto* (M), Rua 1 de Maio (tel. 073 42362). 42 rooms with bath.

Viana Do Castelo *Rali* (I), Ave. Afonso III 180 (tel. 051 22176). 39 rooms with bath. *Aliança* (I), Avenida dos Combatantes da Grande Guerra (tel. 051 23001). 29 rooms, most with bath. Both breakfast only.
Restaurant. *Laranjeira* (I), Rua Manuel Espregueira 24. Good Portuguese cooking. Closed Sat.

Viseu *Avenida* (I), Avenida Alberto Sampaio 1 (tel. 032 23432). 40 rooms with bath. Several pensions and good restaurants.

The Alentejo

This is the largest province in the country and stretches from the sea coast south of Lisbon to the Spanish frontier. It is the granary of Portugal and the great cork-oak forests and olive groves are of major importance to the agricultural economy.

Evora, the capital, is a beautiful, unspoiled city, with a Roman temple alongside the battlemented cathedral. The old fortified town of Elvas on the frontier and the high keeps of Beja and Estremoz tower over the countryside as do many of the smaller towns situated on hill tops and snug inside their surrounding walls.

PRACTICAL INFORMATION FOR THE ALENTEJO

Hotels and Restaurants

Beja. *Pensão Bejense* (M), Rua Capitão Francisco de Sousa 57 (tel. 084 25001). 24 rooms with bath. *Pensão Coelho* (I), Praça da República 15 (tel. 084 24031). 26 rooms with bath. Both breakfast only. Several restaurants and cafés.

Elvas. *D. Luís* (M), Ave. de Badajoz (tel. 068 62756). 61 rooms with bath. **Restaurant.** *Aqueduto* (I), near great 15th-century aqueduct.

Estremoz. *Alentejano* (I), Rossio 50 (tel. 068 22717). 22 rooms. Breakfast only. Situated on huge main square with Saturday market. *Pensão Carvalho* (I), Largo da República 27 (tel. 068 22712). 15 rooms, most with bath. Breakfast only.
Restaurants. *Aguias de Ouro* (M), on main square. Delicious country food and wine.

Evora. *Planicie* (M), Rua Miguel Bombarda 40 (tel. 066 24026). 33 rooms with bath. Restaurant. *Santa Clara* (I), Trav. da Milheira 19 (tel. 066 24141). 30 rooms with bath. Recommended.
Restaurants. *Gião* (M), Rua da República. *Diana* (I), in the lovely oval Praça do Geraldo, and *Cozinha Altejana,* nearby.

The Algarve

The brilliantly-tinted, exotic and aromatic Algarve is Portugal's southernmost province. It has been indelibly marked by centuries of Arab rule, as the white houses with their flat roofs, orange and lemon groves and crouching fig trees with their delicious fruit make clear. Early February, when the almond blossom is out, is a particularly delightful time to visit. The white and pink blossoms are like powder puffs against the distant hills.

The capital of the Algarve is Faro. There's an international airport here, and indeed the majority of visitors to Portugal fly here rather than to Lisbon as the Algarve, with three casinos—at Alvor, Monte Gordo, and Vilamoura—and seven famous golf courses, all with generally low green fees, and miles and miles of hot, sandy beaches, has become a Mecca for those who yearn for lazy holidays in the sun. But although there are many luxury hotels, moderate accommodations can be found in most towns and villages. The Province is now one of Europe's leading areas for self-catering accommodations.

Faro is roughly in the center of the Algarve coastline, which stretches 100 miles from Sagres in the west to the Spanish frontier at Vila Real de Santo António on the river Guadiana. Faro is a city with interesting museums, lovely old churches and a yacht basin jutting into the main square. Other places of interest around Faro are the 18th-century palace of Estoi, near the extensive Roman remains of Milreu; Tavira on the river Sequa, which is crossed by a Roman bridge and filled with fine old houses; and Olhão, somewhat reminiscent of North Africa.

The area to the west of Faro is called the Barlavento. It is highly picturesque and ranges from golden beaches to the jagged cliffs and roaring waves of Sagres. Albufeira is here; still charming despite having become the most popular resort on the Algarve. Further west you come to Portimão on the estuary of the Arade and famous for its grilled sardines. A couple of miles away is Praia da Rocha with strange rock formations on the wide sandy beach; while 14 miles to the west lies Lagos, on a huge bay not unlike an estuary.

After Lagos the country changes and becomes desolate and wild until Sagres and Cape St. Vincent, on the extreme southwestern corner, come into view. It was at Sagres, in the fortress that still exists, that Henry the Navigator plotted and planned the sea journeys taken by all the early Portuguese explorers in the 15th century down the then unknown western shores of Africa. A curious tunnel-like entrance leads into the fortress.

Inland, the Algarve rises up into low hills. The principal spot here is Monchique, a small spa town surrounded by an amazing variety of semi-tropical trees. There are water pleasure parks at Alcantarilha, Almansil, and Estombar with amusements, restaurants, and snack bars; entrance costs 2,000$00 for adults, half price for children.

PRACTICAL INFORMATION FOR THE ALGARVE

Hotels and Restaurants

Albufeira. *Aldeia* (M), Areias de São João, tel. 089 55031. 99 rooms; pool, nightclub, etc. *Rocamar* (M), tel. 089 52611. 91 rooms with bath. *Pifaro,* Areias de S. João (tel. 53232). 40 rooms with bath. Pool, bar. Breakfast only. *Baltum* (I), Avenida 25 de Abril (tel. 089 52106). 26 rooms with bath, plus 23 rooms in annex. Near beach. There are dozens of other pensions, apartments, holiday complexes, restaurants, *Sir Harry's Bar* (M), an English pub, and *Fernando's* (I), on main square.

Faro. *Casa Lumena* (M), Praça Alexandre Herculano 27 (tel. 089 22028). 12 rooms with bath. English owners. *Faro* (M), Praça D. Francisco Gomes 2 (tel. 089 22076). 52 rooms with bath. Situated in fine central square with yacht basin. *Santa Maria* (I), Rua de Portugal 17 (tel. 089 24064). 30 rooms with bath.
Restaurants. *Dois Irmãos* (I) and *Fim do Mundo* (I), both in Largo Terreiro do Bispo 20.

Lagoa. *Motel Parque Algarvio* (M), Estrada Nacional 125 (tel. 082 52268). 22 units with bath, kitchenette, pool.

Lagos. *Meia Praia* (M), tel. 082 62001. 65 rooms with bath; pool, tennis. On beach, but some distance from town. *Motel Ancora* (M), Estrada do Porto de Mós (tel. 082 62033). 60 units with bath, kitchenette, pool. *Rio Mar* (M), Rua Cândido dos Reis 81 (tel. 082 63091). 40 rooms with bath. Modern, in center of town. Breakfast only. *São Cristovão* (M), Rossio de São João (tel. 082 63051). 77 rooms with bath. Good value. *Pensão Caravela* (I), Rua 25 de Abril 14 (tel. 082 63331). 17 rooms.
Restaurants. *Caçarola* (M), Praça Luís de Camões 13. *Jotta 13* (I), Rua 25 de Abril 58.

Loulé. *Pensão Dom Payo* (M), Rua Projectada à Antero de Quental (tel. 089 64422) 26 rooms with bath. Breakfast only.

Monchique. Restaurants. *Rampa* (M). Excellent piri-piri chicken. *Teresinha* (I). Good value. Country cooking. Terrace with stunning view. Closed Mon. Both in Estrada da Fóia.

Monte Gordo. Casino. *Navegadores* (M), Rua Gonçalo Velho (tel. 081 42490). 344 rooms with bath. Pool. *Residencia Catavento* (M), Rua Projectada (tel. 081 42490). 63 rooms with bath. Breakfast only. *Monte Sol* (I), Rua de Ceuta (tel. 081 42136). 37 self-service apartments.

Olhão. *Ria Sol* (I), Rua General Humberto Delgado 37 (tel. 089 72167). 53 rooms with bath. Breakfast only.
Restaurant. *Ilidio* (I), Clube Naval, Bairro dos Pescadores. Good fresh fish.

Portimão. *Globo* (M), Rua 5 de Outubro 26 (tel. 082 22151). 68 rooms with bath. In town center. *Pensão Baltazar* (I), Largo Engenheiro Sarrea Prado 1 (tel. 082 24280). 27 rooms. Dozens of pensions and restaurants. Attractive *tascas* on the quay serving fresh grilled sardines.

Praia Do Alvor. Casino. *Torralta Holiday Club* (I), tel. 082 20511. 644 self-service apartments. Pool, shopping center, nightclub etc. Very good value.

Praia de Galé. *Aparthotel Vila Galé* (M), (tel. 089 53724). 220 units with kitchenette, bath. Pool.

Praia da Quarteira. *Dom José* (M), Avenida Infante de Sagres 145 (tel. 089 33512). 134 rooms with bath. *Zodiaco* (I), Estrada Nacional (tel. 089 32858). 60 rooms with bath. Pool. Breakfast only.

Praia Da Rocha. *Rocha* (M), tel. 082 24081. 76 rooms plus 71 in annex, all with bath. *Pensão Sol* (M), tel. 082 24071. 32 rooms with bath. Breakfast only. *Solar Pinguim* (M), tel. 082 24309. 13 rooms with bath, above beach. English run. All these are on Avenida Tomás Cabreira.
Restaurant. *Fortaleza de Santa Catarina* (I). On esplanade, in old fort with picture windows onto sea. There are also several snack bars.

Praia Dos Três Irmãos. *Aldeamento Prainha* (M), tel. 082 20561. 39 service bungalows with finest pool in Algarve.

Sagres. *Baleeira* (M), tel. 082 64212. 108 rooms with bath. Pool. Lovely situation above beach. There are a number of pensions and restaurants.
Restaurant. *Carlos* (I). Delicious fish from the sea below.

Santa Luizia. *Pedras da Rainha* (I), tel. 081 22181. 350 villas and apartments. Pools, tennis, discos, restaurants. *Pedras d'El Rei* (I), tel. 081 22176. 691 apartments and villas with similar amenities.

Tavira. *Eurotel* (M), Quinta das Oliveiras (tel. 081 22041). 80 rooms and apartments. Pool. Out of town. *Pensão do Castelo* (I), Rua da Liberdade 4 (tel. 081 23942). 21 rooms with bath. *Pensão Lagoas* (I), Rua Almirante Cândido dos Reis 24 (tel. 081 22252). 17 rooms, most with bath. Both breakfast only. There are excellent *tascas* over the bridge alongside the river. Try chicken with clams.

Vilamoura. Casino. Two 18-hole golf courses. *Motel Vilamoura* (M), tel. 089 32321. 52 rooms with bath. Several service apartments, all with pools.

Vila Real De Santo Antonio. Car ferry over the river Guadiana to Ayamonte in Spain. *Apolo* (I), tel. 081 44448. 42 rooms with bath. Breakfast only.
Restaurants. *Caves do Guadiana* (M), Ave. República 90. Good food and wine in pleasant surroundings on riverside avenue. Closed Thurs. *Joaquim Gomes* (I), Rua 5 de Outubro. Closed Wed. in winter. *Pombalina* (I), Rua José Barão 1. Nice local cooking. Closed Mon.

Romania

Romania is a "Latin island" in Eastern Europe. The Romans named the country "Dacia" and colonized it during the latter years of the Empire. The language spoken today is clearly derived from Latin. An attractive Black Sea coast, the splendid Carpathian mountain ranges, pretty medieval towns, a uniquely preserved folk culture, and a miscellany of monuments from all periods are strong incentives to explore this country despite the current economic difficulties. Roman domination, intermittent or partial Hapsburg rule, and bitter struggles against the Turks have all left their marks and the frantic attempt of the late dictator, Nicolae Ceausescu, to pay off the entire foreign debt by exporting almost everything the country produced has left Romania the second poorest country in Europe after Albania. The new government's policy of rebuilding the country means that, although tourists are desperately needed as a source of hard currency, the exchange rate remains extremely unfavorable. The intrepid traveler who is free to stray off the beaten track into the remotest rural areas, will experience an extraordinary and often agreeable sensation of stepping back a couple of centuries. However, all available resources have been channeled into developing Bucharest, the Black Sea coast and the Carpathian skiing resorts as main tourist centers where, for those with prepaid arrangements, facilities are better geared and less expensive than elsewhere. The variety of package holidays has broadened considerably in recent years. For those who have not pre-booked, tours are available from Bucharest or from the Black Sea or mountain resorts, covering such outstanding destinations as the unique painted churches of Moldavia, the real and fictional sites associated with Count Dracula, the magnificent watery wilderness of the Danube delta, or the lovely old towns of Braşov or Sibiu.

At press time (early summer 1990) the U.S. State Department had issued a warning advising U.S. citizens to exercise caution when visiting Romania and to avoid any areas street demonstrations that are in progress. This was in response to violent civic disturbances following the spring elections. Check with the State Department or British Foreign Office before making traveling plans.

PRACTICAL INFORMATION FOR ROMANIA

WHAT WILL IT COST. Travelers are no longer required to exchange a minimum amount of currency per day. Gasoline must be paid for with vouchers purchased in hard currency from hotel reception desks, banks, and border stations.

The monetary unit is the *leu* (plural *lei*), divided into 100 *bani*. The rate of exchange is approximately 16.50 lei to the pound sterling, 10 lei to the U.S. dollar. It's best to take plenty of dollars in small bills; it is by far the most covenient currency. An unofficial exchange rate exists on the black market, but the risk of penalties and general unpleasantness resulting from being caught make any involvement highly undesirable.

Sample Costs. Cinema seat from 15 lei; theater seat (moderate) from 25 lei; museum entrance 4–12 lei; coffee in snack bar 10 lei; bottle of wine in moderate restaurant from 60 lei, in a shop from 30 lei.

NATIONAL TOURIST OFFICE. Information on all aspects of tourism is available from the *Romanian National Tourist Offices* overseas, who can also provide a list of travel firms marketing tours to their country. In Bucharest, information and reservations (for youth accommodations also) are handled by *Carpaţi National Tourist Office (ONT)*, 7 Magheru Blvd., who also have a network of offices throughout the country. ONT offices in the larger hotels can also be very helpful.

The addresses of the Romanian National Tourist Office overseas are:
In the U.S.: 573 Third Ave., New York, N.Y. 10016. (tel. 212–697–6971).
In the U.K.: 17, Nottingham Street, London W1M 3RD, (tel. 071/224–3692).

WHEN TO COME. Bucharest, like Paris, should be visited in the spring as the humid heat can be unbearable in July and August. The Black Sea coast season is from June to September, when all facilities are in full swing, but it can be very pleasant (and less expensive) earlier and later. A skiing holiday in the Carpathians is best taken January through March, a walking holiday in summer.

Average maximum daily temperatures in Fahrenheit and centigrade:

Bucharest

	Jan.	Feb.	Mar.	Apr.	May	June	July	Aug.	Sept.	Oct.	Nov.	Dec.
F°	34	39	50	64	73	81	86	86	77	64	50	39
C°	1	4	10	18	23	27	30	30	25	18	10	4

SPECIAL EVENTS. *March,* the Kiss Fair, Arad. *May,* Week of the Lads, Braşov. *July,* Young Girl's Fair, Mount Gaina. *August,* Celebrations at Mount Ceahlău, Bukovina (popular festival). *September,* Folklore Festival, Bucharest.

National Holidays. Jan. 1 (New Year's Day); Jan 2; May 1 (Labor Day); May 2; Aug. 23 (Liberation); Aug. 24.

VISAS. Visitors from the U.S. and the U.K. can obtain tourist visas from diplomatic missions and consular offices of the Romanian Socialist Republic, or on arrival at any entry point in Romania destined for international traffic; however, potential delay can be avoided by obtaining a visa in advance. At presstime the cost of a tourist visa for British subjects was £20 (except in the case of prepaid arrangements when it is included in the price); for other nationals $30. At the border, visas cost $39. If you have hotel vouchers, ask for a $10 visa.

Visa extension can be difficult so don't underestimate the length of your stay.

HEALTH CERTIFICATES are not required.

GETTING TO ROMANIA. By Plane. *Pan Am, SAS,* and the national airline *TAROM* currently operate flights from New York to Bucharest. Otherwise the most convenient way is to fly to London (or several other west European cities) and go on by connecting services. TAROM fly from London and also from several other west European capitals and cities including Paris, Brussels, Vienna and Amsterdam. They fly from all east European capitals. Otopeni International airport is 16 km. from the center of Bucharest. TAROM operates a direct bus service, operating hourly from 5 A.M. to 9 P.M. between the airport and the TAROM office in Strada Brezoianu, in the center of the city. The taxi fare is about 100 lei; be wary of private taxi drivers, who will charge about $100.

By Train. There are no through trains from Channel ports. The most convenient route is by the still-existing (but in name only) *Orient Express* from Paris via Munich, Vienna and Budapest to Bucharest, leaving the French capital at about 11.15 P.M. and arriving two days later at around 12.36 P.M. in Bucharest; through bunk beds to Salzburg and also from Budapest to Bucharest; through carriages to Budapest and then from there to Bucharest; buffet and dining car services much of the way. You can buy a ticket to Bucharest in hard currency at the foreign ticket desk in Budapest Keleti station for $7 first class, but the desk closes at 5 P.M. There are also through services from Switzerland, East Berlin, Prague, Warsaw and Moscow.

By Bus. There are currently no through bus services from western Europe, although there are from Hungary.

By Boat. Several companies operate cruises down the Danube from Passau or Vienna to the Danube delta throughout the summer. Those on the Romanian *Danube Line* run from Vienna to Cernavoda and are featured in a number of package arrangements.

CUSTOMS. Personal belongings, including jewelry, may be brought in duty free. Tape recorders and radio equipment must be declared at the border. You can also bring in duty free 200 cigarettes, 2 liters of liquor and 5 liters of wine, plus gifts up to a value of 2,000 lei. Purchases up to 1,000 lei in value may be exported duty free as can items bought with officially-exchanged currency, so keep your receipts. The export of works of art requires special authorization.

HOTELS. In due course, Romania will change to the international star system of hotel classification, but for the moment you are most likely to encounter the old system of Deluxe A and B, 1st category A and B, 2nd category, etc. This is misleading for most western visitors whose expectations of 1st category will certainly rarely be met, and we have therefore graded hotels in our lists with the following equivalents: 1st category A, 3-star (M); and 1st category B, 2-star (I). Prices for two people in a double room with bath or shower and including breakfast are as follows: (M) $30–50; (I) $20–30.

Standards are rarely comparable to those in the West. Plumbing in particular can be erratic and, at the time of writing, economies also mean that hot water may only be available between certain hours. These should be posted up at reception or in the room; if not, make inquiries.

Camping. There are well over 100 camp sites in Romania. All main towns and resorts have them. The best appointed are those at Brasov; Sibiu, *Padura Dumbrava* (Dumbrava Forest) and *Calea Dumbravii,* which offers showers with hot water and clean toilets; Suceava, *Strada Ilie Pintilie,* with limited showers and toilets, but clean; and at Cluj.

RESTAURANTS. Check prices and availability first as menus are rarely available in less expensive places. Service can be very slow. Though deep-fried food still dominates too many menus, there has been some improvement; in restaurants look for national and regional dishes, with attractive displays so that you can see what you are ordering. For one person, figure 70–90 lei for a Moderate (M) restaurant, and 40–70 lei for an Inexpensive (I) one. Restaurants open from 7–9 P.M. outside the main resorts, but you are unlikely to be served if you arrive after 8 P.M.

You can get cheap food in a *bufet expres* or *lacto vegetarian* self-service snack bar, but the quality is pretty low. Rich cakes and sometimes ice cream available at *cofetaria* establishments (which don't sell coffee!).

Food and Drink. Although there are some regional differences between the provinces, there is nonetheless a pronounced national culinary tradition, highlighted by such dishes as *ciorba de perisoare,* a soup with meatballs, *ciorba taraneasca* with meat and lots of vegetables, giblet soup, and richly varied fish soups. Sour cream or eggs are often added to soups.

The Romanians' all-purpose staple is *mamaliga,* a highly versatile cornmeal mush that can be served in countless ways. *Tocana* is a stew made with pork, beef or mutton, seasoned abundantly with onions, and served with mamaliga. *Ghiveci* is a preparation of over twenty vegetables cooked in oil and served cold or hot. Another typical dish is Moldavian *pirjoale*—flat meat patties, highly spiced, served with a wide variety of garnishes. Another dish greatly in demand is *sarmale*—pork balls wrapped in cabbage leaves.

One great speciality of Romania is charcoal-grilled meat, often in the form of sausages. Among the countless varieties are *mititei,* highly seasoned mincemeat grilled to order in cafés and restaurants, and *patricienti* resembling frankfurters.

When it comes to desserts, native to Romania are *placinta cu brinza* (cheese pie) and Moldavian *cozonac* (brioche). Of Turkish or Oriental origin are *baclava* and *cataif cu Frisca* (crisp pastry soaked in syrup with a whipped cream filling). Fruit, such as grapes, peaches and apples, is available at the markets, and is inexpensive, though not always easy to get in restaurants.

Tsuica is the traditional national strong drink, a powerful plum brandy whose strength, dryness and aroma all vary according to locality. There are some quite reasonable beers and plenty of wine—always much cheaper, of course, in the shops. The most famous wines come from the Murfatlar vineyards near the Black Sea, but there are good ones from several regions, including Moldavia. The availability of coffee is erratic, and the Romanians can't make good tea!

TIPPING. A 12% service charge is added to meals in most restaurants. Leave something extra (about 10%) if the service has been exceptionally good. Porters and taxi drivers should be given 5–10 lei. Instead of currency, a packet of American cigarettes will often speed up service, smooth out any difficulties, and achieve the "impossible".

MAIL. Airmail rate to the U.S. is 16 lei for a letter, 13 lei for a postcard; to Britain 11 lei for a letter, 8 for a postcard, but check before mailing.

CLOSING TIMES. Shops usually open from 9 or 10 to 6 or 8; food shops much earlier but close for some hours in the middle of the day. Most are open Saturday mornings and some also Sunday mornings. Supermarkets open daily 8 to 8.

GETTING AROUND ROMANIA. By Plane. *Tarom* maintains regular services between Bucharest and most major towns and resorts. Fares are reasonable, but be prepared for delays.

By Train. The railway system radiates from Bucharest. Romania is affiliated to the international systems *RIT* (Rail Inclusive Tour, incorporating accommodations and other services), and *Eurailtariff* (for tourists originating from outside Europe). Getting tickets other than for local trains is a time-consuming process, involving waiting in line for an hour or more at Bucharest's Gara de Nord (main railway station). It is better to buy a ticket and make a seat reservation at least a day in advance, but to do this you have to go to the Reservations Office in Strada Brezoianu 10; you will have to show your currency exchange slips to be able to pay in lei. There are *rapid, accelerat,* and *personal* trains—the latter very slow. Prices are moderate. Dining car or refreshments services on some trains; but always check. Romania is one of the countries covered by the Inter Rail Card (see page 32) and there are also reductions for senior citizens.

By Bus. There are both local and long distance bus services, again always very full. You can make reservations (recommended) on the long distance routes. Always check schedules.

By Boat. Regular passenger boats operate on much of the Danube, especially from Braila or Tulcea via the middle or southern arms of the river, through the delta, to the Black Sea.

Bucharest

With a population of over 1,800,000, Bucharest can boast of being one of Europe's larger cities. Although it was inhabited more than 1,000 years ago, the hamlet of Bucharest in the vast Danube plain only began to take shape in the 14th century. From that time on, it grew rapidly. Today its 19th-century houses share the metropolis along with great modern blocks of apartment buildings, and new suburbs are springing up all the time. From beside the cathedral on the city's one low hill you have a fine view of the city and of the Dimbovita River, which divides the town.

A blue-green chain of park-rimmed lakes dotted with tiny islands borders the city on the northeast.

Busiest part of town is the area around the Calea Victoriei, with its big governmental buildings, museums, shopping centers and modern apartments, liberally landscaped with gardens and courtyards. Stroll north up this main thoroughfare from Piata Natiunile Unite and you will come to several landmarks, such as the National History Museum; the charming little Cretulescu Church; Grigore Antipa the former headquarters of the Central Committee of the Romanian Communist Party; and the Palace of the Republic (formerly the Royal Palace), built in 1933 and housing, apart from government offices, the National Art Museum. This was the area of some of the fiercest fighting during the overthrow of the Ceausescu regime in December 1989, and the scars are still highly visible. At the top of the square is the Romanian Antheneum, Romania's finest concert hall.

For a complete contrast, turn off Calea Victoriei and into the old core of the city in the Lipiscani district, where you will find narrow shopping streets around the substantial remains of the Old Princely Court (15th century onwards), old churches, and some attractive restaurants adapted from the cellars of long ago. To the left along this southern section of Calea Victoriei you pass Blvd. Kogal Niceanu, from which you enter the attractive Cismigiu Gardens with their lakes and fountains.

More or less parallel with Calea Victoriei is the main artery formed by Blvds. 1848, Balcescu and Magheru, with their shops, hotels, and National Theater and the main Tourist Office. The northern end of Calea Victoriei comes into spacious Piata Victoriei, from which Kiseleff Avenue continues on to the distinctive Triumphal Arch and, beyond it, the extensive green spaces of Herăstrău Park. In this municipal paradise on the shores of Lake Herăstrău, you can go boating, swimming, fishing, or watch the world go by from pleasant lakeside restaurants. Here, too, is one of the oldest and most charming of Europe's village museums.

PRACTICAL INFORMATION FOR BUCHAREST

HOTELS. Those without reservations should go to the *Carpati Tourist Office,* 7 Magheru Blvd., or directly to hotels.

Moderate

Astoria, Dinicu Golescu 27 (tel. 49–52–10). 170 rooms. Near railroad station (de Nord), a little out of center.
Capitol, Calea Victoriei 29 (tel. 14 09 26). 80 rooms. Central.
Majestic, Str. Academiei 13 (tel. 16–21–74). 85 rooms. Central.
Minerva, Str. Lt. Lemnea 2 (tel. 50–60–10). 80 rooms. Central.
Negoiu, Str. 13 Decembrie 16 (tel. 15–52–50). 93 rooms. Central.
Parc, Blvd. Poligrafiei 3 (tel. 50–60–81). 275 rooms, pool. Near Herăstrău Park.
Union, Str. 13 Decembrie 11 (tel. 13–26–40). 221 rooms. Central.

Inexpensive

Banat, Piata Rosetti 5 (tel. 13–10–57). 34 rooms. Central.
Cismigiu, Bd. Gh. Gheorghiu-Dej 18 (tel. 14–74–10). 110 rooms. Central, near Cismigiu Gardens.
Dimbovita, Bd. Schitu Magureanu 6 (tel. 16–20–29). 40 rooms. By Dimbovita river and near Cismigiu Gardens.
Dunarea, Calea Grivitei 140 (tel. 17–32–20). 60 rooms. Near railroad (de Nord).
Muntenia, Str. Academiei 21 (tel. 14–60–10). 123 rooms. Central.
Opera, Brezoianu 37 (tel. 14–80–98). 63 rooms. Near Cismigiu Gardens, central.
Tranzit, Str. Militiei 4 (tel. 31–02–20). 107 rooms. Fairly central.

RESTAURANTS. In addition to hotel restaurants there is quite a wide selection, mostly at reasonable prices. In many cases there *is* no visible menu, so check prices before you order. Other establishments to look out for: *cofetaria* (for mouthwatering cream cakes and soft drinks), such as the one at the *Hotel Bucuresti* (side entrance), and *Calea Victoriei, bufet expres* or *lacto vegetarian* (self-service snack bars).

The following may be *Moderate* or *Inexpensive* depending on your choice of dish.

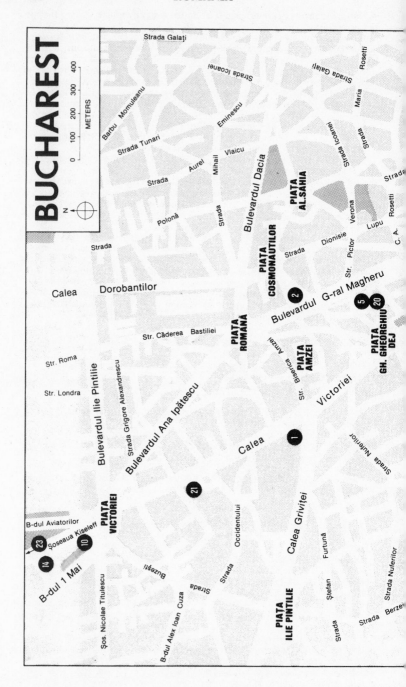

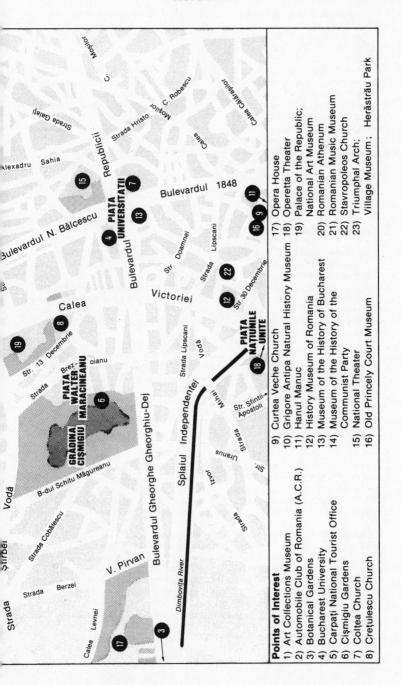

Points of Interest

1) Art Collections Museum
2) Automobile Club of Romania (A.C.R.)
3) Botanical Gardens
4) Bucharest University
5) Carpaţi National Tourist Office
6) Cişmigiu Gardens
7) Coltea Church
8) Creţulescu Church
9) Curtea Veche Church
10) Grigore Antipa Natural History Museum
11) Hanul Manuc
12) History Museum of Romania
13) Museum of the History of Bucharest
14) Museum of the History of the Communist Party
15) National Theater
16) Old Princely Court Museum
17) Opera House
18) Operetta Theater
19) Palace of the Republic;
     National Art Museum
20) Romanian Athenum
21) Romanian Music Museum
22) Stavropoleos Church
23) Triumphal Arch;
     Village Museum; Herăstrău Park

Carul cu Bere (Beer House), Str. Stavropoleos 5. Traditional late 19th-century beer house, lots of atmosphere; ground floor tavern and cellar restaurant.

Crama Domneasca, Selari St. 13. Attractive setting in ancient cellars adjoining Old Princely Court; traditional food.

Doina, Soseaua Kiseleff 4. Romanian food.

Hanul Manuc (Manuc's Inn), Str. 30 Decembrie 62. Romanian food. Opposite the Old Princely Court. Built round courtyard, one of the most attractive hostelries in town, dating from the early 19th century.

La doi cocosi, Șoseaua Străulești 6. Romanian food. About 15 km. from town.

Marul de Aur, Calea Victoriei 163. Reached through a courtyard, a little less central.

Monte Carlo, Cismigiu Gardens. Attractive location.

Padurea Baneasa, Baneasa Forest. Romanian food, folkloric entertainment.

Rapsodia, Str. Selari 2. Romanian food. Another attractive cellar restaurant near Old Princely Court, decorated with old folk masks.

GETTING AROUND BUCHAREST. By Metro/Underground. Generally less crowded than trams, buses and trolley buses. Three lines of the subway system are now in operation. Cost is 2 lei for any distance (1 leu from Piata Unirii); insert coins into a machine to open the barrier.

By Bus/Tram/Taxi. Trams cost 1 leu, buses 1.75 lei, and trolley buses 1.50 lei for any distance. Tickets for all three can be bought at kiosks near most stops and must be stamped in a machine as soon as you board the vehicle. As these are extremely crowded at most times, it is worth taking a taxi, although there are insufficient numbers of them in Bucharest. A packet of cigarettes is sometimes needed to persuade the driver to take you. Keep an eye on the indicator facing you in the taxi to gauge the fare—a trip within the city center should not cost more than 50 lei.

ENTERTAINMENT. Cafés. Parisian-type cafés and brasseries are always animated. Among the more widely patronized in the evenings are the *Tosca, Tic-Tac, Ciresica* and *Tomis* on Blvd. Kogal Niceanu, the *Turist* on Magheru, the *Unic* on Balcescu and the *Corso* at the Hotel Intercontinental.

Cafés and restaurants are obliged by law to shut at 10 P.M. and most do so by 8.30 P.M.

Cinema. The *Cinema Eforie,* Str. Eforie 5, runs a daily program of old, undubbed American and British films.

Theaters and Concerts. Opera at the *Romanian Opera House,* Blvd. Gheorghiu-Dej 70. Folkloric shows of high quality at the *Rapsodia Romana Artistic Ensemble,* Str. Lipscani 53. No language problem either at the *Tandarica Puppet Theater,* Cala Victoriei 50. The magnificent *Romanian Athenaeum,* Str. Franklin 1, plays host to two distinguished Romanian symphony orchestras.

MUSEUMS. Museums are generally open Tues. to Sun., 10 A.M.–6 P.M. Entrance fees are usually about 10 lei. **Art Museum** of S.R.R., 1 Stirbei Voda Str. In part of the former royal palace. A fabulous and relatively unknown collection of Bruegels, among other greats, as well as a good cross-section of Romanian painting.

Muzeul Colectilor de Arta (Art Collections Museum), Calea Victoriei 111. Combines several fine private collections of art treasures, including a number of excellent icons painted on glass.

Muzeul de Istorie al R.S.R. (History Museum of S.R.R.), Calea Victoriei 12. In the former Central Post Office building, has beautiful displays illustrating Romanian life and history, from neolithic to modern times. The collection of gold objects and precious stones (which can be visited separately) is quite stunning. *Note:* The building was damaged in the fighting in spring 1990 and could be closed for restoration.

Curtea Veche (Princely Court), Str. 30 Decembrie 31. Fascinating ruined complex of the First Princely Court in Bucharest, part of a very extensive site dating from the 15th century onwards.

Muzeul Satului (Village and Folk Art Museum), Soseaua Kiseleff 28–30. Outstanding of its kind, this is a major collection of genuine peasant houses and other buildings from all parts of the country, set on the edge of Herăstrău Park.

SHOPPING. *Comturist* is the foreign trade agency for the sale of Romanian products and imported goods for hard currency only; it has over a dozen outlets in Bucharest, most of them in hotels. The traditional shopping area of Lipscani has varied shops within walking distance of central hotels. Some addresses are: **Department stores:** *Unirea,* Piata Unirii 1; *Cocor,* Blvd. 1843 33; *Bucur-Obor,* Soseaua Colentina 2 and Bd. Republicii 14; *Romarta,* Calea Victoriei 60–68; *Victoria,* Calea Victoriei 17; *Bucuresti,* Baratiei 2; *Tineretului,* Calea Dorobanti 10. **Foreign books:** *Dacia Bookshop,* Calea Victoriei 45; *M. Sadoveanu,* Magheru 6. **Handicrafts:** *Artizanat,* Str. Academei 25; *Arta Populara,* Calea Victoriei 118; *Sateanca,* Calea Victoriei 91; *Hermes,* Sepcari 16; *Mesteri Faurari,* Strada Gabroveni 6. **Stamps:** *Filatelia,* 13 Decembrie 25. **Records and music:** *Muzica,* Calea Victoriei 41.

Look out for *Galerie de Arta* shops run by the Union of Plastic Artists *(Fondul Plastic).* Markets provide the only venue for private enterprise. The main one is at Piata Uniiri, selling fresh fruit, vegetables and flowers, as well as handicrafts. Open seven days a week, but best visited in the morning.

USEFUL ADDRESSES. *U.S. Embassy,* Tudor Arghezi 7–9 (tel. 12 40 40); *Canadian Embassy,* Nicolae Iorga 36 (tel. 50 63 30); *British Embassy,* Str. Jules Michelet 24 (tel. 11 16 34); *Main Post Office,* Calea Victoriei 37; *Carpati National Tourist Office,* Magheru Blvd. 7 (tel. 14 51 60); *Thomas Cook,* Magheru Blvd. 7 (tel. 14 51 60); *ACR (Romanian Automobile Club),* Str. Cihovschi 2 (tel. 110408).

The Black Sea and Danube Delta

Romanians can be justly proud of their splendid beaches, with their gentle surf and fine sands. Most of the resorts offer the choice of both lake and sea. Most popular seaside resort is Mamaia, its four-mile stretch of shore lined with villas and hotels, well-equipped with sports facilities. As it caters mainly to group tours, you can get extremely good value here, at low cost. Constanza is a busy Black Sea port built on the ruins of the old Greek colony, Tomis, where Ovid spent his last years. Today, its narrow streets and five mosques add Oriental charm and color to an otherwise modern town. Don't miss the superb Archeological Museum or the impressive Roman complex, which includes a fabulous mosaic. Eforie, 14 km. from Constanza, has hotels of all categories, minigolf, tennis and other sports, with motorboat trips on Lake Techirghiol. Neptun, close to Comorova Forest, has a wide beach with dozens of modern hotels, good water skiing, tennis, etc.; and is quieter than other seaside resorts. In Jupiter there are several new highrise hotels standing right on the beach. The newest resort is Venus, 43 kilometers from Constanza. Farther south, Mangalia (called Callatis in ancient times) is a town, port and resort. Greek and Roman remains up to 2,600 years old and old houses with wooden balconies stand next to modern hotels. Excursions are arranged to the archeological sites and the famous Murfatlar vineyards.

Another of the region's attractions is the Danube delta, Europe's leading wildlife sanctuary. This mighty European river divides into three main arms on this final stage of its journey to the Black Sea, and the fascinating and primeval wilderness created by its waters plays host to over 300 species of birds, plus a wide variety of fish, crustaceans, mammals, and plant life. There are regular passenger boat services and sightseeing trips. The Museum of the Danube Delta at Tulcea gives a splendid introduction to the region.

PRACTICAL INFORMATION FOR
THE BLACK SEA AND DANUBE DELTA

Hotels and Restaurants

There is a wide selection of accommodations in the Moderate and Inexpensive categories, but it is no use trying to book in unless you have a reservation or vouchers. You should instead go to the *Litoral National Tourist Office* at the Hotel Bucharest, Mamaia, or its branches in other resorts, who handle reservations and information for the Black Sea Coast or, in the case of the Delta, to the local tourist office at 1 Isaccea Str., Tulcea.

Constanța. *Continental* (M), 139 rooms. *Casa cu Lei* (House with Lions) is a restaurant in a charming converted old town house. The *Casino* (M), in ornate early 20th-century style with night bar, is by the sea.

Mamaia. *Ambassador* (M), *Lido* (M) and *Savoy* (M), grouped around open-air pools near beach in north of resort. Next door, with similar layout, are *Admiral* (M), *Comandor* (M), and *Orfeu* (M). *Bucuresti* (M), 60 rooms, open-air pool, is in resort center. *Dacia* (M), 370 rooms, near open-air pool and beach is in south of resort. Nearby is highrise *Parc* (M), 210 rooms, indoor pool. Restaurants include rustic-style *Insula Ovidiu* on island on Lake Mamaia; *Miorita,* Romanian food and attractive setting on lake shore; *Cherhana,* fish specialties served in Danube-delta style building on lake shore; *Satul de Vacanta* (Holiday Village), traditional Romanian architecture featuring numerous small restaurants serving local specialties; and *Vatra,* garden restaurant in resort center.

The Romanian Interior

The famed Bucovina painted monasteries are located in the northeast near the Russian border, and are most easily reached from Suceava, the regional capital. Built in the 15th and 16th centuries, the main monasteries, painted with frescoes inside and outside are: Voronet, Humor, Arbore, Sucevita and Moldovita. They are each different and all enchanting, but the most exquisite is the Voronet church, with an outside wall entirely dedicated to the depiction of *The Last Judgment.* Wind and rain have slightly eroded some of the frescoes on the northern walls, but the majority retain their vivid colors. Moldovita has undergone the most restoration and is still used as a small convent today. Well worth going for the Sunday morning Orthodox Liturgy, when many people come from the surrounding villages, some in their traditional costumes.

You should also consider the area northwest from Piatra Neamt. Here, the upper Bistritsa valley leads deep into the Carpathians and, especially above the man-made Bicaz Lake, brings you into a wild and lovely region full of folkloric interest.

Transylvania, with the Carpathian amphitheater as a natural barrier, was less subject to Tartar and Turkish invasions from the east and south than were other parts of Romania. At the same time its western section—flat country—was open to late Hungarian infiltration, and ethnic Hungarians are today a sizeable minority. Transylvania's principal communities are Cluj-Napoca, a cultural and university center, and Brașov, an ancient city now heavily industrialized, though its ancient core is still intact and includes the very impressive Black Church. Brașov is the gateway to the splendidly scenic Carpathian resort sector. Two medieval jewels are Sighisoara, where the historical Dracula was reputedly born, and Sibiu, site of the magnificent Brukenthal museum.

Though the smallest of Romania's traditional regions, Maramures in the northwest has made impressive contributions to industry, folklore, and tourism. Its largest city, Satu Mare, is a center for machine tools, textiles, furniture and lumber. Baia Mare, second in population, is Romania's mining capital. The region is especially famous for its truly beautiful 18th-century wooden churches and villages where folk costumes, handicrafts and traditions are part of everyday life. Another of its better-known attractions is the merry cemetery of Sapinta, its graves enlivened by cheerful, brightly painted designs, each depicting the profession, trade and character of the occupant.

Finally, in the southwest, the southern region of the Carpathians features magnificent scenery and the spectacular Iron Gate sector of the Danube. Fascinating Roman remains, including traces of a mighty bridge across the Danube, can be seen at nearby Turnu Severin. If you are traveling independently you will attract a lot of attention and a foreign car should never be left unattended in the smaller towns less frequented by tourists. You may receive offers of hospitality from Romanians in the villages, but it is against the law for them to put up foreigners in their houses for the night and they could be punished for it.

PRACTICAL INFORMATION FOR THE INTERIOR

Hotels and Restaurants

If you have not prebooked, you should go to the tourist office available in most towns, which handles accommodation bookings of all kinds and will be able to advise on local tours or transport. Some addresses are given below.

Baia Mare. *Bucuresti* (M), 74 rooms, in modern center of town, very good food; *Carpati* (M), 114 rooms, by river; *Minerul* (M), 48 rooms; turn-of-century building on main square of old town.

Braşov. *Parc* (M), 38 rooms, short stroll from center; *Postavarul* (M), 167 rooms, restored late 19th-century building near center. Restaurants include popular cellar restaurant *Cerbul Carpatin* (M) (if you choose the right dishes), in 17th-century merchant's house, with excellent folk show; *Cetatuia* fortress houses a restaurant complex.

Cluj. *Belvedere,* 150 rooms of which some (M), located among 18th-century fortifications on hill, linked by steps to center. *Napoca* 160 rooms, some (M), fairly modern, but not central. *Continental* (M), 50 rooms, old-fashioned but central. Restaurant *Transilvania* (M) serves specialties.

Sibiu. Hotels in town are fairly expensive but out of town near the camp site is *Padurea Dumbrava* (M), 65 rooms, in oakwood setting. Restaurants in the old town include the charming *Butoiul de Aur* (Golden Barrel), *Sibiul Vechi* (Old Sibiu) in Romanian folk style, and *Bufnita,* all tavern-type and (M); and *Dunarea* and *Unicum,* both (I).

Sighisoara. There is only one hotel in town, right in the center and about a 10-minute walk from the station. *Steaua* (M), 54 rooms.

Suceava. *Bucovina,* 130 rooms, some (M). *Arcasul,* 100 rooms, some (M).

Turnu Severin. *Trajan,* the latest, has some (M) rooms. *Parc* (M), is near banks of Danube.

USEFUL ADDRESSES. Most towns have tourist offices that will book accommodations and advise on local tours or transport. *Baia Mare,* 1 Culturii St.; *Braşov,* 74 Gh. Gheorghiu-Dej Blvd.; *Cluj,* 2 Gheorghe Sincai St.; *Sibiu,* 4 Unirii Sq.; *Suceava,* N. Balcescu St., Block 2A.

Spain

Spain means crisp white beaches to many travelers, castles and knights-errant to others. It means that and much more: an almost endless treasure trove of art and architecture ranging from the Romanesque churches in the verdant, rainy northern provinces, to glorious Gothic in Castile, and Roman and Moorish architecture in the south. It means drinking wine and sangría till the wee hours, nibbling on delicious shellfish, tortilla and olives, delighting in paella along the coast from Barcelona to Alicante. It means seeing a bullfight or a religious procession during Holy Week. Above all, it means being in a country where the sun often shines and whose inhabitants are both friendly and vivacious.

One of the advantages of Spain is the enormous variety of terrain and climates offered. Cultural and ethnic characteristics change from region to region, and even the languages spoken are different in Catalonia, the Basque Provinces and Galicia. Then there are the attractions come can be found nowhere else in Europe—the Holy Week processions, the bullfights, the jai alai (pelota) games, the festivals and folklore; and, of course, such unforgettable sights as the Alhambra in Granada, the mosque in Córdoba, the Prado in Madrid, the 2,000-year-old Roman aqueduct in Segovia, the architecture of Gaudí in Barcelona and the cathedrals of Burgos, Toledo and Seville. The feria of Seville is a unique sight and the running of the bulls in Pamplona is an experience that will never be forgotten.

In the '60s and early '70s Spain was one of Europe's major holiday destinations, particularly for the British tourist. A holiday in Spain was an automatically guaranteed budget vacation: prices were low, hotels and restaurants plentiful with willing high standards of service, shops bulged with inexpensive souvenirs, you could eat and drink for a fraction of the price back home, and a bargain was to be had round every corner. Then with the late '70s came democracy, and with democracy fast-soaring prices and the inevitable labor disputes. Wages, particularly those in the hotel and catering industries, rose steeply to come closer to those of Spain's neighbors to the north, and inflation was rampant. Spain's entry into the EC at the beginning of 1986 brought with it the inevitable levying of a value-added tax (IVA) of 6% (more in some cases) on all commodities including hotel and restaurant rates, and the country experienced an overall rise in the cost of living. But by presstime inflation had been brought down to 6%, and though periodic strikes or go-slows on public transport may still at times adversely affect the visitor, hotel rates no longer increase by leaps and bounds each year, and Spain has regained her popularity as a budget vacation destination. One black cloud that should be mentioned is that Spain has now joined ranks with those other European countries where declining standards of service and street crime—especially purse snatching—are distressingly common.

A tourist's main expenses, namely accommodations, eating out, transport, drinks and souvenirs, are still competitively priced compared to most other European countries. The sheer number and range of hotels in Spain is unbeatable. In even the remotest places you will most likely find a simple hostel where you can spend the night in reasonable comfort at real budget prices. In larger cities you have the choice of inexpensive hostel or moderate hotel: one good way of keeping down costs is to alternate moderate hotels with modest pensions; do without a private bath from time to time, and you will make enormous savings. In this guide, we have deliberately selected hotels at the lower end of the price range; all our Moderate suggestions have some, if not all, rooms with private bath, as do most, but not all, of those in the Inexpensive category. You should not, however, always expect to find the same standards of comfort as you would back home, especially if you are accustomed to staying in the chain-type motel so common in the United States. A sincere effort has been made to recommend clean, comfortable accommodations. As economy is uppermost in mind, you will find that the greater part of our suggestions are old hotels in the center of town, rather than the modern, often somewhat aseptic buildings that have sprung up in such places as the highly developed coastal areas. We hope that you will appreciate the atmosphere, charm and good location of these hotels as well as their sheer value for money.

One final thing we should mention is that the literally hundreds of rock-bottom pensions to be found all over Spain, have not been included among our suggestions. While not forgetting economy for one minute, we are writing not so much for the penniless student or shoestring traveler, as for the budget vacationer who is seeking a moderately priced vacation with basic comforts and enough money left over to enjoy perhaps the occasional splurge meal or a little evening entertainment. Certainly if you don't mind putting up with spartan conditions for the odd night or so, then some of the many one-star hostels or pensions that line the old streets of most Spanish cities may well fit the bill.

Where restaurants are concerned, it is becoming harder and harder to recommend really inexpensive eating places; but moderate ones abound and their standard of cuisine and value for money are amazingly good. One thing to remember is that in Spain lunch is the main meal, not dinner. As almost everything closes down during siesta time, it is worth following the Spanish custom of a large leisurely lunch; make your economies in the evening, perhaps by snacking in a couple of bars as you go tapas-hopping. Though alcohol prices were due to rise at presstime (Spring '90), many drinks—beer, wine, sangria and liqueurs, though not cocktails—are still moderately priced if you drink at the counter rather than in expensive sidewalk cafés. If the thought of a little indulgence in any of the above appeals, then Spain is definitely good news!

To many people a holiday in Spain conjures up the thought of hours of lazy basking on a beach soaking up the Mediterranean sun and perfecting a suntan. If this is the sort of holiday you're after, then we advise you to opt for an organized package tour. Simply as holidays in the sun, there is no better value for money and you will be offered the chance of a little local sightseeing as well. The Costa Brava, Costa Blanca and Costa del Sol are all highly developed beach resorts and the vast majority of their hotels deal almost exclusively with tour operators; bookings by the independent traveler, although feasible, are extremely rare and will cost much more.

We are assuming that as you are using this book you will be visiting several European countries and that your main interest will therefore be sightseeing. For this reason we have chosen to cover the principal showpieces of Spain. We are not claiming that these are the cheapest areas to tour, but feel that as your time in Spain is probably limited, they will be of prime importance. By all means, if you feel like branching out and exploring more off-the-beaten-track areas, then do so. The lesser-known villages of Castile, Extremadura, Galicia, Aragon and Andalusia offer many delights and little-known treasures, and their prices will undoubtedly be lower than the major tourist centers. Similarly, if you feel like a day or two at the beach, then go ahead; if you are patient and don't mind searching hard for budget accommodations, you can usually find a room somewhere, particularly if you avoid fiesta weekends and the months of July and August.

Whichever part of Spain you choose to visit, we hope that our recommendations will help you to appreciate and enjoy this exotic land, the charm and vitality of its people, the sheer beauty of its museums and cities and the richness and variety of the local customs, and all at a price that won't stretch your purse strings too far.

PRACTICAL INFORMATION FOR SPAIN

WHAT WILL IT COST. Spain's entry into the EC in 1986, coming as it did on top of a decade of fast rising prices, did not spell good news for the budget traveler. Though Common Market entry has not greatly increased Spain's cost of living (due to removal of previous purchase taxes) it has, with the levying of its 6% IVA tax on most hotel and restaurant bills and 12% four- and five-star hotels as well as on car hire, dealt a severe blow to the purse strings of the independent foreign visitor.

Spain has long been the mecca of the all-inclusive tour. Majorca, and numerous resorts along the Costa Brava, Costa Blanca and Costa del Sol are easily available to those who are happy with package holidays. Conversely, if you're one of those people who dislike package holidays, these are the places to avoid.

Basic tourist costs are now on a par with most European countries. Points in Spain's favor are its sheer number of hotels and restaurants, and, where hotels are concerned, their very wide range of prices. Public transport provides an extensive coverage of even the remoter places and is constantly being improved. Considerable savings can be made if you are willing to forgo just a few of the more luxurious aspects of travel; budget travel is very much a state of mind. Use buses and the metro instead of taxis; and use trains and buses instead of rented cars (gasoline prices are high by American standards, on a par with those of Britain, but public transport fares compare very favorably). In a restaurant, go for the menu of the day rather than eating à la carte; remember to ask at the local tourist office for free or reduced days at museums or concerts; alternate reasonable hotels with moderate pensions; in the bigger cities special combined tickets may well save you money on public transport.

A little careful planning will go a long way. Of course you will want to see the major attractions but exploring remote country areas will save your dollars and pounds and prove surprisingly rewarding too. When planning a day's sightseeing in a city, visit those locations that are close together on the same day; you will find that most of them are within walking distance of each other, only rarely will you have to pay for transport. Madrid is the most expensive city, followed closely by Barcelona and the showpieces of Andalusia, Seville, Granada and Córdoba. But lesser-known places such as Cáceres, Cuenca or Pontevedra, offer little-known delights and a chance to savor some of the old Spain that is now fast disappearing— and all at a much lower price. For a beach holiday, the Costa Blanca south of Alicante and the Costa de la Luz from Tarifa to the Portuguese border, are less developed than, say, Majorca or the Costa Brava; the same is true of the part of the Costa del Sol east of Málaga as opposed to the Torremolinos–Estepona section.

In shopping, avoid the obvious tourist-trap shops where the bus parties stop. There's usually more for your money in department stores such as the *Corte Ingles* and *Galerias Preciados,* which have branches in most major cities.

The monetary unit in Spain is the *peseta.* There are coins of 1, 5, 25, 50, 100, 200 and 500 ptas., and bills of 200, 500, 1,000, 2,000, 5,000 and 10,000 ptas. The exchange rate is often better at banks than at hotels, but most banks now take such a huge commission charge that your hotel exchange rate may not work out so very much lower. The exchange rate at the time of writing was approximately 115 ptas. to the U.S. dollar and 200 ptas. to the pound sterling. You may take any amount of foreign money and pesetas into Spain, but when you leave Spain, you may take out only up to 100,000 ptas. in Spanish currency and the equivalent of 500,000 ptas. in foreign money. Any amount of uncashed travelers' checks may be exported.

Sample Costs. A bottled beer costs around 150 ptas. in a café, a draught beer *(una caña)* about 80 ptas; carafe wine is 90 ptas. per glass in a bar, 700 ptas. a bottle in a moderate restaurant. A black coffee *(café solo)* is about 70 ptas. and a white coffee *(café con leche)* 110 ptas.

A seat at the cinema will set you back 300–450 ptas., at the theater 850. Entry to museums, about 250 ptas.

NATIONAL TOURIST OFFICE. Much useful information and advice is available from the *Spanish Tourist Office* in your own country (see below for addresses). They can supply you with details of tour operators organizing budget holidays to Spain as well as special interest tours (although the latter may well exceed budget price levels). Free road maps and information brochures on each province are also available, as are pamphlets on camping, sport, hunting etc. In Spain itself there is a tourist office centrally located in each provincial capital and town of tourist interest. Ask for a brochure *(folleto)* which contains a city plan and details, in English, of all monuments of interest. They can also help with bus and train schedules, museum opening hours etc. Although tourist offices do not provide an accommodations booking service, a list of all hotels, pensions and restaurants is available for your perusal and, often, the tourist office will make the telephone call to determine whether rooms are available. Offices are usually open Monday to Friday 9.30 to 1 and 4.30 to 7, Saturdays 9.30 to 1, though some now work an 8.30 to 3 day.

Addresses of the Spanish National Tourist Office overseas are:

In the U.S.: 665 Fifth Ave., New York, N.Y. 10022 (tel. 212–759–8822); 1221 Brikell Ave., Ste. 1850, Miami, FL 33131 (tel. 305–358–1992). 845 N. Michigan Ave., Chicago, IL 60611 (tel. 312–644–1992); San Vicente Plaza Bldg., 8383 Wilshire Blvd., Ste. 960, Beverly Hills, CA 90211 (tel. 213–658–7188).

In Canada: 102 Bloor St. W., Suite 1400, Toronto, Ont. M5S 1M8. (tel. 416–961–3131).

In the U.K.: 57 St. James's St., London SW1A 1LD (tel. 071–834 6667).

WHEN TO COME. The tourist season in Spain runs from April through October. Summer, except in the north, is hot and mainly dry—the peak vacation months of July and August can be too hot for comfort in some places, notably Córdoba, Seville and, in some years, Madrid. Hotel prices are highest mid-June through mid-September and the two weeks around Easter. Winters are moderate, except in Madrid and on the central plateau where it can be bitterly cold. Many hotels in seaside resorts and large cities offer special winter budget concessions. If winter sports fall within your budget, Spanish ski resorts are economical compared to those in France, Switzerland and Austria.

Average afternoon temperature in Fahrenheit and centigrade:

Madrid	Jan.	Feb.	Mar.	Apr.	May	June	July	Aug.	Sept.	Oct.	Nov.	Dec.
F°	47	51	57	64	71	80	87	86	77	66	54	48
C°	8	11	14	18	22	27	31	30	25	19	12	9

Barcelona												
F°	56	57	61	64	71	77	81	82	78	71	62	57
C°	13	14	16	18	22	25	27	28	26	22	17	14

SPECIAL EVENTS. In *January,* Granada's liberation from the Moors in 1492 is commemorated (on the 2nd); Three Kings parades everywhere on 5th and 6th. *March* sees the Fallas of San José in Valencia (12th–19th), with floats, bonfires, fireworks. Book hotels long in advance; prices rise during Fallas. At *Easter* there are Holy Week processions in Seville, Málaga, Cuenca, Granada, Valladolid, Zamora and many other cities. Again, book hotels long in advance and expect high prices—Seville is especially crowded and expensive. Ten to 14 days after Easter is the Seville fair: horse parades, bullfights, fireworks. In *April* the Burial of the Sardine takes place in Murcia, while in Alcoy (Alicante) Moor and Christian street battles are reenacted (23rd–24th). *May* has the Festival of Decorated Patios in Córdoba from the 1st to the 12th; the Feria de Jerez de la Frontera, with horse parades, a livestock fair and bullfights; and the Feast of San Isidro in Madrid with top bullfighting. At *Whitsun* there is the famous Romería (religious pilgrimage) of the Virgen del Rocío at Almonte (Huelva). On *Corpus Christi* (Thurs. after Trinity Sunday) spectacular processions in Toledo and Sitges, where the streets are carpeted with flowers.

June, there's the Granada International Music Festival in the Alhambra and Generalife gardens (through July). And from the 21st to 30th, the Hogueras de

San Juan in Alicante, with bonfires of effigies, cavalcades, fireworks. In *July,* San Fermines in Pamplona (6th–14th), running of bulls through the streets, bullfights, fireworks. Hotel accommodations are virtually impossible to find, restaurant, café and hotel prices all rise for two weeks. In Santiago on the 25th, the St. James festival, in front of the cathedral; pilgrimage to the tomb of the apostle, great pomp. *August* sees the Mystery Play of the Assumption on the 15th at Elche (Alicante), and the Feast of the Assumption celebration at La Alberca (Salamanca). *September* is the month of San Sebastián International Film Festival. Also, the Grape Harvest Festival at Jerez de la Frontera, with carnival queens, processions, much sherry drinking. *October:* Fiestas del Pilar, Zaragoza, around the 12th, floats, parades, jota dancing; shellfish festival in El Grove (Pontevedra); saffron festival in Consuegra (Toledo). *December* means Christmas celebrations, which last from the 24th through to the 6th January. Gifts are given on Jan 6th—the Day of the Kings. There are New Year's Eve celebrations in Puerta del Sol, Madrid, where people gather to eat a grape at each stroke of midnight.

National Holidays. Jan. 1 (New Year's Day); Jan. 6 (Epiphany); Holy Thurs., Good Fri. and Easter Mon. (varies from city to city); May 1 (May Day); Corpus Christi (second Thurs. after Whitsun); Jul. 25; Aug. 15 (Assumption); Oct. 12 (National Day); Nov. 1 (All Saints); Dec. 6 (Constitution Day); Dec. 8 (Immaculate Conception); Dec. 24 (P.M. only), 25. Other major holidays are Mar. 19 (Valencia region and often elsewhere) and May 2 (Madrid province); in addition each village or town has its own local fiesta.

VISAS. Not required for U.S. nationals or British subjects for visits up to 90 days.

HEALTH CERTIFICATES. Not required for entry into Spain.

GETTING TO SPAIN. By Plane. Flights from North America are operated by *Iberia* (the Spanish national airline) and *TWA* flying from New York to Madrid and Barcelona; Iberia also flies from Chicago, Los Angeles, Miami, and Montreal to Madrid, and from New York to Malaga and Barcelona.

Spain is linked to every west European country by both scheduled and charter flights. From London, *British Airways* flies from Gatwick to Madrid, Barcelona, Bilbao, Gibraltar, and Málaga. Iberia serves all of these, plus Alicante, Seville, Santiago de Compostela, Palma and Valencia. Flights leave from Heathrow. Some *BA* flights to Madrid and Barcelona also leave from Heathrow. There are also charter flights to many Spanish destinations from 12 regional U.K. airports.

By Train. Apart from special tourist trains for inclusive holidays by rail, the most convenient way from London by rail to Spain is via Paris. From here (from the Gare d'Austerlitz) there are through trains to Madrid (via San Sebastián and Burgos) and to Barcelona. With the former you leave the French capital at 8 P.M. and arrive in Madrid about 9 A.M. the next day. The train called the *Paris-Madrid Talgo* has 1st and 2nd class and special tourist class sleeping cars and both a dining car and buffet. With the latter you leave Paris at 9 P.M. and arrive in Barcelona at 9 A.M. next day. Again it has 1st and 2nd class and tourist sleepers, dining car and refreshment services. This is the *Barcelona Talgo.*

The only other through train from Paris to Madrid is the *Puerta del Sol,* with 2nd-class couchettes and a buffet car, which leaves Paris around 6 P.M. and arrives in Madrid at 10 A.M. next day. Like the Talgo, its wheels are changed at the border (the Spanish gauge is wider than the French) whilst you sleep. On all other rail services you will have to change trains at Irun.

The *Catalan Talgo* is a day train from Geneva via Valence, Avignon, Nimes, Narbonne and Port Bou to Barcelona, leaving Switzerland at about 11.30 A.M. and arriving in Barcelona at about 9 P.M. 1st and 2nd class with dining car.

By Bus. The main bus lines operating between England and Spain are under the International Express banner and are run by both British and Spanish bus companies out of London's Victoria Coach Station. Their main routes are to Gerona, Barcelona, Valencia and Alicante, and to San Sebastian, Burgos, Madrid and Algeciras and all intermediate destinations. For reservations and information contact the Travel Center at Victoria Coach Station (tel. 071–730 0202) or any International Express or *National Express* agent. *SSS International,* 138 Eversholt St., London NW1 1BL (tel. 071–388 1732), runs buses to northern Spain calling at Bilbao, Santander, Oviedo, Lugo, La Coruña and Santiago. Bus fares are not that competitive compared with last-minute flight deals. An adult return to Barcelona is about £100.

CUSTOMS. Visitors from outside Europe may import 400 cigarettes, 100 cigars or 500 grams of tobacco; 1 liter of liquor over 22° proof or 2 liters of liquor under 22° proof and 2 liters of wine; 50 grams of perfume and 0.25 liters of toilet water.

Visitors from a country within the EC may import 300 cigarettes or 75 cigars or 400 grams of tobacco; 1.5 liters of liquor over 22° proof or 2 liters of liquor under 22° proof, and 3 liters of wine; 75 grams of perfume and 0.25 liters of toilet water.

Visitors from non-EC countries within Europe may import 200 cigarettes, 50 cigars or 250 grams of tobacco; 1 liter of liquor over 22° proof or 2 liters of liquor under 22° proof, and 2 liters of wine; 50 grams of perfume and 0.25 liters of toilet water.

HOTELS. Spain is exceptionally well provided with hotels for all tastes and pocketbooks thanks to the 50 million tourists that invade the country each year. Room prices must by law be displayed at reception and are per room and not per person, though supplements are chargeable for extra beds. Single occupancy of a double room is charged at 80% of the usual rate.

Hotels are officially graded from 5-star to 1-star, and hostels and pensions from 3-star to 1-star. Prices have risen considerably, but nonetheless rates still compare favorably with many European countries. As a general rule, our Moderate (M) rating corresponds to a 2- or 3-star hotel or 3-star hostel, and our Inexpensive (I) to a 1- or 2-star hotel or 2-star hostel. In a Moderate hotel, expect to pay roughly between 5,000–6,500 ptas. for two people sharing a double room, and in the Inexpensive category, between 3,000–5,000 ptas. These rates do not include breakfast, for which there is usually an extra charge. Spanish hotels do not levy a service charge but a 6% value-added tax (IVA) will be added onto your bill at the end of your stay (on four- and five-star hotels, IVA is 12%). If you want something really cheap then try a pension, though more often than not you'll have to take at least one meal there as well; you may find some for as little as 2,000 ptas.

Always check whether or not you will be expected to take breakfast or even half board terms; some hotels insist upon this and you may be charged whether or not you have eaten there. Should you not have to take breakfast at your hotel, we recommend you try a local café for your morning *café con leche;* this will most likely be cheaper and few Spanish hotel breakfasts are very palatable to American and British tastes. On the other hand, half board or even full board terms at your hotel will usually work out more economically than dining out in restaurants. In any case, you may well find that many hotels insist on at least half board during the high season (June–Sept.), for the two weeks over Easter, and during periods of particular tourist interest, such as the Seville Fair or Pamplona San Fermines. If you want a room only, look for a *Hotel Residencia,* symbolized by HR or HsR.

For the most part, Spanish budget hotels are clean and good value, though possibly a little spartan for some American tastes. The golden rule is always to see your room before you take it. A few hostels in the Inexpensive category will not have private baths, only a wash basin.

Remember that the low season, generally October through March, means lower rates at most hotels, though Christmas and the New Year may sometimes prove an exception to this rule. When two prices appear on the price list, *estación alta* is high season and *estación baja* low season.

Self-Catering Villas. There are plenty of these in the popular coastal resorts such as the Costa del Sol, Costa Brava and the Costa Blanca. They are usually bookable through package tour operators and villa agencies (the Spanish National Tourist Office will provide a list), and prices normally include charter air fare. As a general rule a villa holiday will only save you money if at least four people share a villa and you stick strictly to cooking your meals at home. A few country cottages and farmhouses can be rented in inland regions such as the mountains of Andalusia, Asturias and Cantabria.

Youth Hostels. Due to the abundance of shoestring pensions, youth hosteling has never been as popular in Spain as it has in some other European countries. Many of the hostels are located in rather remote areas and cannot be reached on public transport. Spain has approximately 40 Youth Hostels, open to anyone with an international Y.H.A. card. The headquarters of the *Spanish Y.H.A.* is at Jose Ortega y Gasset, 71, 3a, 28006 Madrid. Open mornings only.

Camping. There are over 530 sites in Spain, most of them with food supplies available. Many sites are open year round, others April through October. Camping carnets are no longer needed. Information from the Spanish Tourist Office in your own country or from the Camping and Caravan Club Ltd., 11 Grosvenor Place, London SW1X 7HH or from Federación Española de Empresarios de Campings, Gran Vía 88, Grupo 3–10°–8, Madrid. It is advisable to reserve ahead for high season.

RESTAURANTS. Meals are eaten later in Spain than in any other European country. It is hard to find lunch before 1.30 and 3 P.M. is more common, especially on Sundays. Dinner before 8.30 is almost unheard of and 10 P.M. is the usual hour. Madrid keeps later hours than other parts of the country.

Spanish restaurants are officially graded by the government from 5-fork down to 1-fork. When dining on a budget, stick mainly to the 2-fork establishments, though from time to time you may come across a 3-fork restaurant with moderate prices. Most restaurants display their menu in the window so you should get an idea of how much you are letting yourself in for before you go in. In most places the 6% IVA should now be included in menu prices, but check to make sure. If not, the menu should state *IVA non incluído.*

A three-course meal for two with a bottle of house wine in a Moderate (M) restaurant will cost around 4,500–6,000 ptas.; in an Inexpensive (I) restaurant around 2,500–4,500 ptas. If you want to eat really cheaply head for the *restaurante económico,* recognized usually by its tiled walls, plastic tables, television set and youthful waiters.

Budget Tips. The *menu del día* or tourist menu offered by many restaurants is undoubtedly the most economical way to eat, if a little unexciting. It will comprise a soup or appetizer, main course, dessert and bread. Always ask for *vino de la casa* (house wine); if you don't, many restaurants will bring you Rioja, which is more expensive.

With ever rising prices it is becoming increasingly difficult to recommend many inexpensive eating places other than those serving good-value *menus del día.* However, in cities, if instead of dining in a restaurant you are prepared to opt for the *platos combinados* or toasted sandwiches offered by many cafeterias, or alternatively to venture into the bars and *mesones* for snacks and tapas, you may succeed in keeping your prices down. A *plato combinado* usually consists of something like a fried egg, French fries, sausage, potato salad or croquette, squid rings, and lettuce and tomato salad. But beware, *cafeterías* (cafés) can be expensive and high bills can be run up easily if you succumb to their mouthwatering pastries. Safer are the self-service establishments that are beginning to spring up around the country. Hamburger joints, similar to ones in the U.S., such as *Burger King, Wendy's* and *McDonalds,* have blossomed forth in larger cities, as have *Kentucky Fried Chicken* and *Pizza Hut.*

In a café or bar, it is cheaper to eat and drink at the counter than to have waiter service at a table. But do not buy your drink at the bar and carry it yourself to a table as this will offend.

Food and Drink. Olive oil is at the base of Spanish cookery and contrary to expectation, Spanish cooking is not generally fiery and peppery like Mexican cuisine. Don't hesitate to order seafood anywhere, even inland at Madrid. A fast service brings the fresh catch daily to the market, and the crabs, shrimp, crayfish and other crustaceans are all excellent.

Here are some special dishes to look for: *gazpacho,* a cold soup of tomatoes, garlic, bread crumbs, cucumber, green pepper and croutons, which is delicious and refreshing on a hot day. *Paella* delights most visitors, and is now so widely known outside Spain as to be thought of as the country's national dish. Try *jamón serrano,* sun-cured mountain ham, dark red in color and served in thin, translucent slices; or *tortilla,* a chunky potato omelet often served cold and cut in wedges. The Basques are great eaters, and some of their specialties are *Bacalao a la Vizcaina,* salt codfish cooked in a tomato sauce; *angulas,* tiny eels cooked whole in olive oil with garlic, and *merluza a la vasca,* white fish with clams, asparagus and hard boiled eggs. Other specialties include: *almejas marinera,* steamed clams in garlic and wine sauce, and *calamares,* squid rings fried in batter with lemon wedges. In the Basque Country or Galicia, order *centollo,* a huge crab cooked in its shell with a spicy sauce. If all this sounds too exotic you can always have grilled meat by asking for *a la parrilla.*

Sherry is the most characteristic of Spanish drinks. There are the finos, pale, dry, and drunk widely as an aperitif; amontillados, medium dry, same purpose; olorosos, dark, sweet and heavy, and generally drunk as a dessert wine. Manzanilla, not technically a sherry, is popular and very dry; it has a higher alcoholic content than any other sherry. The principal table wines are Rioja, Navarra, Penedés, Jumilla and Valdepeñas, named for the regions where they are produced. Rioja from the north is now well thought of internationally. Beer is of the light, lager type and Spanish beer *(cerveza española)* is cheaper than imported makes *(extranjera).* Cheaper still is *una caña,* a small draught beer. In summer you might try an *horchata,* a white, sweet drink, served chilled, in ice cream parlors. It looks like milk, but is made from nuts and has a delicious almond flavor. *Granizados de limón* or *de café* are another specialty: iced lemon or coffee on crushed ice.

TIPPING. As you are on a budget vacation you are unlikely to be staying anywhere where much tipping is required. If someone carries your bag to your room for you, then 50 ptas. is a normal tip. If you are eating in a hotel for, say, the best part of a week, then you might give the head waiter 500 ptas.; if your stay is short, only tip if you have some special service.

In a restaurant it is customary to leave about 10% (no more) even when service is said to be included. Tipping in cafés and bars is now dying out, but if you have spent a long time in a particular bar and the barman has been friendly, then 25–50 ptas. would not go amiss. The one thing you should be prepared for is washroom attendants, they always expect 5 or 10 ptas.

Station porters operate on a fixed rate, usually 60 ptas. a bag. Tip a taxi driver 10% of the fare if he uses the meter, otherwise nothing. Theater and movie ushers get 10 ptas. though this too is dying out. At a flamenco show, give the doorman 100 ptas., the coat check girl, 25 ptas.

MAIL. Airmail rates to the U.S., letters up to 15 grams cost 70 ptas., postcards 65 ptas.; to the U.K. and other EC countries, letters up to 20 grams cost 45 ptas.; and to non-EC countries 48 ptas.; postcards to Europe 40 ptas. If you wish to speed your overseas airmail letters, add 80 ptas. and mark the envelope "Urgente." At press time, increases in postal charges were expected. Stamps *(sellos)* can be purchased from post offices *(correos)* or tobacco shops *(estancos)* displaying a red and yellow *tabacos* sign. When addressing a letter, USA is E.E.U.U. in Spanish and England *Inglaterra.* Mail boxes are yellow and red and the slot marked *extranjero* is the one for abroad.

CLOSING TIMES. Shops in Spain open and close at different times, according to the nature of their business and the time of year. But basically you can expect shops to be open between 9.30 and 1.30 and 4.30 (maybe 5 in summer) and 7.30 or 8 P.M. A few big stores such as the *Corte Inglés* and *Galerías Preciados* now stay open during siesta hours. Some shops work a full day on Saturday though many close in the afternoon. Museum and church hours vary enormously, so check locally. Banks are open Mon. to Fri. 8.30–2, Sat. 8.30–1 (often 12 in the summer). At presstime the situation regarding Saturday banking hours was uncertain with some banks opening Saturday mornings while others were closed. Be sure to check.

GETTING AROUND SPAIN. By Plane. This is hardly budget travel, but if your time is short it may pay you to fly, and Spanish domestic flights are moderately priced. *Iberia,* the national airline, and *Aviaco* its subsidiary, link all the main cities. At holiday periods flights are very heavily booked, so reserve long in advance and turn up early. There is an hourly shuttle between Madrid and Barcelona. Children under 2 pay 10% of the regular fare, and from 2–12, 50%.

Iberia offers a "Visit Spain Airpass," for $249, which permits travel between 30 destinations in mainland Spain, the Ballearic Islands, and Spanish Morocco within a maximum of a 60-day period. For an additional $50, the Canary Islands are included. The ticket must be purchased in the United States prior to departure and in conjunction with a roundtrip ticket to Spain with at least the eastbound transatlantic portion of the ticket on Iberia Airlines.

By Train. The first thing to understand about Spanish rail fares is that they are determined by the kind of train you travel on and not the distance traveled. Thus if you travel on a *Talgo, Intercity, Electrotrén, Corail* or *TER,* all of which levy considerable supplements, you will pay much more than if you go on ordinary trains confusingly known as *rápidos* or *expresos.* So always compare the fares for the different trains traveling to your destination; this way you can make considerable savings.

Seat reservations and tickets are available from RENFE offices in town as well as at stations. Advance reservation is often advisable. Travel agencies displaying the blue and yellow *RENFE* sign also sell tickets at no extra charge. RENFE has a nationwide computer that enables you to buy a ticket even if you are not in the town where you will board your train.

Ask for a Blue Days *(Días Azules)* leaflet from any station or RENFE office. There are approximately 270 "blue days" each year when special discounts are available on such things as roundtrip fares or Madrid–Barcelona trips. Note that some of the Blue Day bargains, such as the pensioners' 50% discount or reduced rates for family groups, apply only to Spaniards or foreigners who live in Spain and have held a *residencia* permit for at least 6 months. On local (suburban) trips a 50% discount is available on roundtrip fares if the return journey is made on the same day and the day of travel is not a Sunday or holiday. (Useful for Madrid satellites.)

The RENFE Tourist Card is an unlimited kilometer pass available to anyone who lives outside Spain. It is valid for all RENFE lines and for any time of year. Cards can be bought for first- or second-class travel, and for eight, 15 or 22 days. At press time, the second class pass cost 10,000 ptas. for eight days, 16,000 ptas. for 15 days, and 21,000 ptas. for 22 days. It can be purchased from RENFE's representative in Europe, 3 Av. Marceau, 75116 Paris, France (tel. 47 23 52 00), from selected travel agencies, and main rail stations in Europe, and within Spain, at RENFE travel offices and the stations of Madrid, Barcelona, Port Bou, and Irún. In Britain it can be bought from *Wasteels,* 121 Wilton Rd., London SW1 1JZ (tel. 071–834 7066).

At any main station or RENFE office you can buy a special kilometric card known as a *Chequetrén.* This book of coupons allows you 25,000 ptas.' worth of rail travel but you pay only 21,250 ptas., or 35,000 ptas.' worth of travel for which you pay only 29,750 ptas. It can be used in 1st and 2nd class, on any train, and by up to six people. In Spring 1992 a high speed train, the TAV (Tren Alto Velocidad), is scheduled to commence service between Madrid and Seville, reducing travel time from six to three hours.

By Boat. There are daily sailings to the Balearics from Barcelona; also twice or thrice weekly in summer from Valencia and Alicante. For Tangiers and Ceuta, there are daily ferries and hydrofoils from Algeciras.

By Bus. Bus travel is a good, possibly the best, bet for the budget traveler. The network is extensive and enables you to reach smaller out-of-the-way places not served by the railroad. Except for luxury express buses, fares are usually lower than on trains. Bus terminals, where they exist (not in every city), tend to be more centrally located than train stations, and they usually provide left-luggage facilities—a service no longer found at rail stations.

Madrid

Of all the major cities of Europe, Madrid has been the one in which the greatest number of drastic changes have occurred over the past few years. By now it's not news that Spain is a healthy tourist center, a remarkable transformation from its prior isolation from the coming and going of American and European travelers.

But other changes have continued to be news. The previously static capital has turned rapidly into a high-energy metropolis with all of its attendant glitter and excitement. The population has increased to almost four million. In just five years, Madrid's surface area doubled, and its swarm of motorized vehicles multiplied over three times. Its pollution, unfortunately, has also increased markedly.

The impressive expanse of the Paseo de la Castellana cuts the city in two. It is flanked by luxury hotels, and the excellent Prado Museum is located in the section named Paseo del Prado. Formerly a promenade, it now has six lanes of bumper-to-bumper traffic in an endless procession.

As a result of such rapid change, hotels, restaurants, nightclubs, bars, and cafés have opened in huge numbers. With them have come the traditional neon marquees of commerce. Exactly like any other city in the throes of transition, Madrid has become a scene of contradictions. Near the Puerta del Sol, in the center of town, you need only fend your way through the mad traffic across the square to find yourself surrounded by narrow little back streets, where a car can hardly pass. With the narrow lanes come the authentic old restaurants straight out of Spain's romantic past, steeped in the austerity and the unhurried dignity of ancient Castile.

The major sight in Madrid is undoubtedly the Prado Museum, a storehouse containing not only the great Spanish painters, such as Goya, Velázquez, Zurbarán, Murillo, Ribera and El Greco, but also boasting a magnificent collection of Flemish and Italian works of art, most notably some world-famous Boschs.

Other major tourist attractions of the capital are the Royal Palace (Palacio Real), which includes a carriage museum, a pharmaceutical museum, a library and endless rooms of state; the Madrid Flea Market, the Rastro, in Plaza del Cascorro, a must on Sunday mornings (beware of pickpockets); and, located just to the east of Campo del Moro, the Plaza Mayor, a 17th-century, arcaded square closed to traffic and brimming with cafés and restaurants; some of the best flamenco restaurants in Spain, delightful parks and, in season, fine folkloric theater.

But perhaps some of Madrid's major attractions are its old streets and countless bars and restaurants, many located around the Plaza Mayor, where, to the sound of strumming guitars and the nasal intonations of flamenco, you can munch shrimp or mushrooms and drift into easy conversation with others who have come to relax and wander tavern to tavern.

PRACTICAL INFORMATION FOR MADRID

GETTING INTO TOWN FROM THE AIRPORT. The cheapest method of getting to Madrid city center (Plaza Colón) from the Barajas national and international terminals is by the yellow airport bus, which runs every 15 minutes between 5.15 A.M. and 12.45 A.M. The journey takes around 20 minutes and costs 200 ptas. The same journey by taxi would cost around 1,500 ptas.

HOTELS. Probably no other European capital can boast such a wealth of moderately priced hotels and pensions as Madrid. Furthermore, most of them are centrally located and within walking distance of the principal sights. But hotel rooms in Madrid are at a premium, particularly at Easter and all through the summer. For many of our Moderate suggestions, it is therefore advisable, though not always essential, to book in advance. At the lower end of the scale, few hostels or pensions take bookings; it's more a question of turning up at the right time—usually around midday.

The Tourist Office in the Plaza de España will provide lists of hotels as will its desk at Barajas Airport; however, it does not run an accommodations service. Privately run accommodations bureaus can be found at the airport and at Chamartin station. These only deal with certain hotels and they charge for their service, but are still worth using.

Moderate

Cliper, Chinchilla 6 (tel. 231 1700). Good functional accommodations and central location in a side street just off Gran Vía.
Francisco I, Arenal 15 (tel. 248 0204). Old fashioned hotel between Sol and Opera. Retains a certain old world style; top floor restaurant.

Inglés, Echegaray 10 (tel. 429 6551). Slightly more expensive and a well-recommended, smallish 3-star hotel, in the old Latin quarter, just off Puerta del Sol.

Moderno, Arenal 2 (tel. 231 1090). Traditional old style hotel right off Puerta del Sol; one of the most expensive.

Paris, Alcalá 2 (tel. 221 6496). This is the most expensive in this category (5,800 ptas.). A delightful hotel, full of elegant, old world charm, right on Puerta del Sol.

Negresco, Mesonero Romanos 12 (tel. 222 6530). Good budget hostel with 18 rooms in center, close to main shopping streets.

Ramón de la Cruz, Don Ramón de la Cruz 94 (tel. 401 7200). A quiet modern hotel situated in smart Salamanca district near Plaza Roma; this location is reflected in the slightly higher tariff.

Inexpensive

Americano, Puerta del Sol 11 (tel. 522 2822). Attractive hostel right in the heart of Madrid between Preciados and Carmen.

Andorra, Gran Vía 33 (tel. 232 3116). Friendly hostel, centrally located near Callao. Rates drop during low season.

Jamic, Plaza de las Cortés 4 (tel. 429 0068). Smallish 7th-floor—there's an elevator—hostel opposite Palace Hotel. Convenient for Prado.

Lisboa, Ventura de la Vega 17 (tel. 429 9894). Recently redecorated hostel in the heart of budget restaurant land; very popular with cost-conscious visitors.

Mendoza, Chinchilla 4 (tel. 521 6455). Small hostel next door to Hotel Cliper near Callao; all rooms with bath and phone; a good bargain.

Metropol, Montera 47 (tel. 521 2935). Delightful hostel overlooking the Red San Luis; one of Madrid's best budget accommodations.

Monaco, Barbieri 5 (tel. 222 4630). Simple older hotel in Chueca area, close to several good restaurants and in an interesting part of town, and slightly higher-priced than others in this category.

Mora, Paseo del Prado 32 (tel. 239 7404). Renovated older hotel convenient to Prado and Atocha Station.

Nuevo Gaos, Mesonero Romanos 14 (tel. 232 7106). Next door to Negresco and convenient for Callao shops and Gran Vía.

Roma, Travesía de Trujillos 1 (tel. 231 1906). Colorful, friendly hostel overlooking Plaza San Martín; long recognized as one of Madrid's best budget bets, low rates.

Youth Accommodations. The headquarters of the *Spanish Youth Hostel Association* (REAJ) is at Ortega y Gasset 71, tel. 401 1300. Open mornings only. There are two youth hostels in Madrid itself: *Richard Schirrmann* in the Casa del Campo park, tel. 463 56 99. 120 beds; open all year; nearest Metro: Lago. *Santa Cruz de Marcenado* is at no. 28 in the street of the same name, tel. 247 4532. 178 beds; open all year; bed and breakfast only. Nearest Metros: Argüelles, San Bernardo, Ventura Rodriguez.

RESTAURANTS. Madrid is plentifully supplied with good value restaurants; simply exploring the narrow streets of the old quarters where every other house seems to be an economical taverna, is a budgeteer's delight in itself. Remember that meal times in Madrid tend to be even later than elsewhere in Spain: lunch begins around 2.30–3 P.M. and dinner not much before 10 P.M. Bear in mind that lunch, not dinner, is the main meal here; everything closes down in the early afternoon so you might as well spend the siesta hours as the Spaniards do, enjoying a leisurely but economical lunch.

Maxims to bear in mind for budgeteers: always check the menu in the window first and check whether the 6% IVA tax is included in the menu prices; a spartan-looking restaurant may produce excellent fare; the *menu del día* is undoubtedly the cheapest way of eating; wine is cheaper than Coke; restaurant dining offers better value than eating in cafeterias.

Moderate

Good areas to try are: 1) in Old Madrid between Calle Mayor and Calle Segovia; 2) in the Plaza de Chueca area, Barbieri, Libertad, Agustín Figueroa.

La Argentina, Válgame Dios 8 (tel. 221 3763). Unpretentious setting with simple and hearty food. Go early to avoid the crowds.

La Bola, Bola 5 (tel. 247 6930). Old world charm; local specialties.

El Callejón, Ternera 6 on corner of Preciados (tel. 222 5401). An old standby, once frequented by Hemingway, serving superb seafood.

Carmencita, Libertad 16 (tel. 231 6612). A long standing Madrid tradition with delightful old-world atmosphere and excellent food. Good for an intimate, relatively expensive dinner.

Casa Ciriaco, Mayor 84 (tel. 248 0620). Atmospheric; an old stand-by.

La Colorada, Santa Engracia 49 (tel. 445 0145). Tiny tavern with only eight tables hides behind a bright red facade. Decorated with bullfight paraphernalia.

El Cuchi, Cuchilleros 3 (tel. 266 4424). Colorful, eccentric restaurant just below Plaza Mayor; a strong hint of Mexico and lots of fun.

Luarqués, Ventura de la Vega 16 (tel. 429 6174). Asturian restaurant known for good food and excellent value.

Terra a Nosa, Cava San Miguel 3 (tel. 247 1175) just off Plaza Mayor. Atmospheric bistro specializing in dishes from Galicia.

Inexpensive

For real bargain eating, search around these areas: 1) around Plaza Santa Ana, bound in the north by San Jerónimo, in the west by Carretas, and in the south and east by Calle del Prado. Ventura de la Vega and Echegaray are packed with economical diners; 2) north of Gran Vía, around Calle del Barco, though this is a red-light district.

Casa Marcelino, Toledo 10. Typical, colorful tavern just south of Plaza Mayor, serving good value *menus del día.*

Casa Mingo, Paseo de la Florida 2. Asturian ciderhouse well known for roast chicken.

La Caserola, Echegaray 3. A well known budget bargain offering *bocadillos* and *platos combinados* as well as a regular menu.

El Granero de Lavapies, Argumosa 10, near Lavapies metro station. Popular vegetarian restaurant open for lunch only and closed Mondays.

Goyamar, Ventura de la Vega 11. Pleasant decor, friendly service, and amazingly reasonable prices.

El Huevo, Pza. San Miguel 5. This well known *económico* behind the San Miguel market has been going strong for years; unbeatable value.

Hylogui, Ventura de la Vega 3. One of the best bargains on this street, offering a good choice of very affordable tasty dishes.

Lazaro, Zorilla 9. Simple lunch spot well patronized by regulars, behind Congress and convenient to Prado.

Pagasarri, Barco 7. The traditional budgeteer's delight—witness the lines forming outside well before 1 P.M.

Cafeterias. These are better for breakfast or coffee than for full meals, but one of their *platos combinados* or toasted sandwiches makes a good quick snack. Remember it is cheaper to sit at the counter than at a table. Reliable chains are *California, Kenya, Manila,* and *Morrison.*

American Food. *VIPS* and *Bobs* cafeterias have several branches all over town serving club sandwiches, hamburgers, and ice cream sundaes. *Foster's Hollywood* is one of Madrid's best known hamburger restaurants and also serves spare ribs, kebabs and American salads. Branches at Magallanes 1 near Gta. de Quevedo, Tamayo y Baus 1 opposite María Guerrero Theater, and Valázquez 80. *Pizza Hut* is at Orense 11 and Pza. Santa Bárbara 8, and *Pizza King* at Orense 12, Gaztambide 39 and Fuencarral 121. You will find branches of *McDonalds, Burger King* and *Wendys* all over town, but beware of pickpockets here.

GETTING AROUND MADRID. By Metro. This is the cheapest and easiest way of getting around Madrid. At presstime fares were 65 ptas. whatever distance you travel. After 10 P.M. many ticket offices are closed so you need change for the ticket machines, or you can buy a *taco* of ten tickets during the day. Buying a *taco* for 410 ptas. will save you money as will the *Metrotour* tourist card available for three

MADRID

0 Miles   ¼
0 Kilometers   ¼

Points of Interest

1   Atheneum
2   Biblioteca Nacional
3   Casa Cisneros
4   Casa de Lope de Vega
5   Casa de la Villa (City Hall)
6   Casón del Buen Retiró
7   Centro de Arte Reina Sofía
      (Queen Sofia Arts Center)
8   Fuente de la Cibeles
      (Cibeles Fountain)
9   Monasterio de la Descalzas Reales
10 Monasterio de la Encarnación
11 Municipal Museum
12 Museo Arqueológico
13 Museo de Artes Decorativas
14 Museo de Carruajes (Coach Museum)
15 Museo de Cera (Wax Museum)
16 Museo Cerralbo
17 Museo del Ejército (Army Museum)
18 Museo Etnológico
19 Museo Lázaro Galdiano
20 Museo Naval
21 Museo del Prado
22 Museo Romántico
23 Museo Sorolla
24 Palacio de Liria
25 Palacio Real (Royal Palace)
26 Puerta de Alcalá
27 Puerta del Sol
28 Real Academia de Bellas Artes de
      San Fernando
29 Real Fábrica de Tapices (Royal
      Tapestry Workshops)
30 San Antonio de la Florida
31 San Francisco el Grande
32 San Ginés
33 San Jerónimo el Real
34 San José
35 Teatro Español
36 Teatro Real
37 Teatro Zarzuela
38 Templo de Debod
39 Torre de Lujanes
40 Torre de Madrid

i   Information
✉   Post Office
Ⓜ   Metro Station

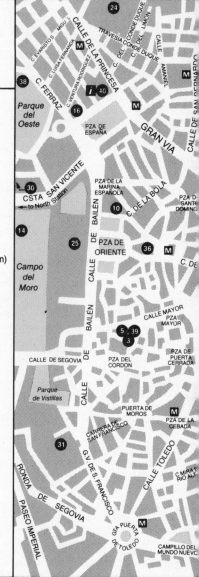

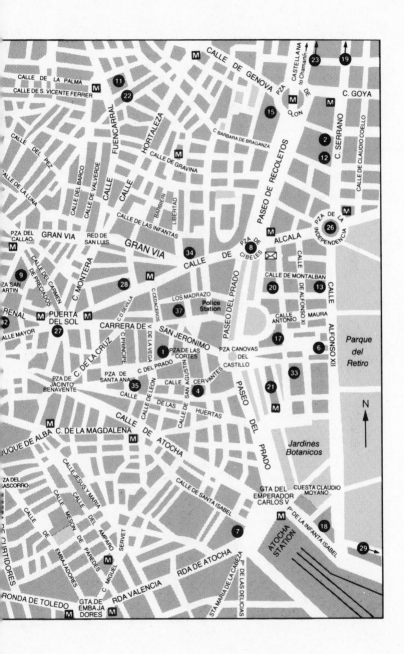

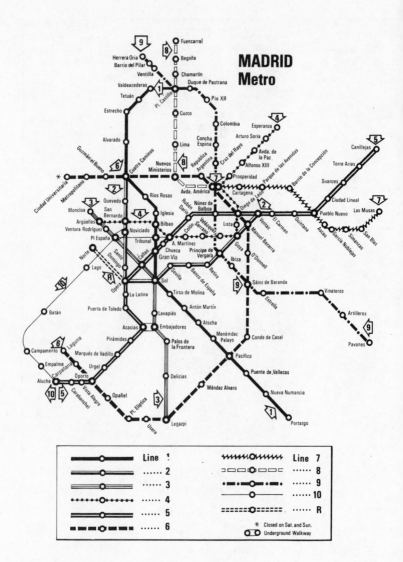

MADRID Metro

or five days' unlimited metro travel. Metro maps are available from hotels or the information office in Sol Metro station, best reached by the entrance between Montera and Carmen. The metro runs from 6 A.M. to around 1.30 A.M.

By Bus. City buses are red and run from 6 A.M. to around midnight (though check as some stop earlier). Fares at presstime were 65 ptas. for any distance. The smaller yellow microbuses also cost 65 ptas. Plans of the route followed are displayed at bus stops, and a map of all city bus routes is obtainable free from the EMT kiosk in Plaza Cibeles.

A *bono-bus,* good for ten bus rides, can be bought from EMT kiosks (e.g. at Cibeles, Sol or Callao) at a reduced cost of 410 ptas.

By Taxi. This may not be real budget transport, but compared to U.S. and U.K. taxis Spanish cab fares are still quite a bargain; the average city ride is unlikely to be more than 450 ptas. Up to four people can ride in a cab, so sharing the fare may not work out much more than a bus ride. At presstime the meter started at 100 ptas. and the rate was 42 ptas. per km. Supplements were 50 ptas. on Sundays and holidays, 50 ptas. between 11 P.M. and 6 A.M., 50 ptas. to or from railroad or bus stations, 50 ptas. to or from bullrings or soccer stadiums, and 25 ptas. per suitcase. There is a 150-ptas. supplement to or from the airport. When free for hire taxis display a *Libre* sign in daytime and a green light at night. They cruise the streets and there are cab ranks. Always check the driver puts his meter on when you start your ride.

ENTERTAINMENT. Cafés and Bars. A good way to savor the true flavor of Spain is to do as the locals do and sit in a sidewalk café sipping a *vermut* (vermouth) or *cuba libre* (rum and coke) and watch the world go by; or alternatively, you can do the rounds of the *mesones* off the Plaza Mayor, where, for the price of a glass of wine or beer, you may be able to hear spontaneous flamenco and strike up a conversation with one of the local residents.

Zarzuela. This is a kind of musical revue that you can enjoy without knowing Spanish. To see it, try the *Teatro Lirico Nacional de la Zarzuela* at Jovellanos 4, or the *Teatro Calderón,* Atocha 18.

Flamenco. Madrid has some of the best flamenco in Spain, but be warned: it is expensive. Should you also be visiting Seville you can expect prices there to be lower. Dining is vastly over-priced so opt for a drink *(consumicion)* only, which costs from 1,800–2,500 ptas.; you are not obliged to buy more than one drink. Though shows tend to be aimed at the tourist market, flamenco is a uniquely Spanish spectacle and is usually worth the extra outlay. Places to try are: *Arco de Cuchilleros,* Cuchilleros 7. Small and very good value. *Café de Chinitas.* Torija 7. Good and professional, tends to be expensive. *Los Canasteros,* Barbieri 10 in Chueca area. *Corral de la Morería,* Morería 17. Recommended *Corral de la Pacheca,* Juan Ramón Jiménez 26. A bit touristy but fun; folk dancing and *sevillanas* as well as flamenco. *Torres Bermejas,* Mesonero Romanos 11. Quality varies but can be good. *Venta del Gato* is 7 km out to the north on road to Burgos. Authentic flamenco, well recommended; advisable to reserve.

If these shows are beyond your budget, don't forget the *mesones* on a Friday or Saturday night; you may be lucky and come across spontaneous guitar playing, singing and dancing. Should the *mesones* insist you eat as well as drink, stick to a plate of cheese or tortilla.

Bullfights. Should you want to brave a bullfight while in Spain, Madrid has some of the best. There are two rings: the largest with 25,000 seats is at *Ventas,* and the smaller one, *Vista Alegre,* is in Carabanchel in the south of the city. Fights are held most Sundays between Easter and October and starting times vary from 5 to 7 P.M. The best matadors fight in Easter week and during the San Isidro festival in May.

The cheapest way to buy tickets is from the rings themselves. But be sure to go to the window and not the huts outside the ring as they levy a 20% surcharge. In the center of town, the official ticket office is at Calle Victoria 3, just off Puerta del Sol. There are many other *taquillas* in this street but they all levy a 20% surcharge. For the least expensive tickets, ask for *sol* (sun), and in the middle range, *sol y sombra* (sun and shade). Take sunglasses with you and a cushion if possible. Metros: Ventas and Vista Alegre.

Cinema. About half-a-dozen cinemas show films in their original language. See the weekly leisure guide *Guía del Ocío* or the daily *El País,* where they are listed under V.O. *(Versión Original).* In other movie theaters, films are always dubbed into Spanish. The official *Filmoteca* showing different films each day, and in their original language, is in the Cine Torre in the Torre de España Princesa 1 just off Plaza de España. A good cinema to try for films in English is the *Alphaville* with four screens, entrance on Martín de los Heros, also just off Plaza de España.

Discos. These are mammothly popular in Spain and stay open until 3 or 4 in the morning. They have a *tarde* session, early evening until around 10 P.M., and a *noche* session, approximately 11 P.M. onwards. *Tarde* sessions are often cheaper than *noche.* Entrances vary, and often cost more for men than women. Be prepared for some extremely licentious goings-on in many of them. You can expect to pay anything between 1,000 and 5,000 ptas; price usually includes the first drink. Some you might try are: *Joy Eslava,* Arenal 11, all the latest in lasers and electronics in the converted Eslava theater; *Keeper,* Juan Bravo 39, three floors with all the latest equipment; *Macumba,* serves crêpes and pizzas at Chamartín Station; *Zona Madrid,* Barceló 11, in former theater now decorated like New York's *Studio 54.*

Theaters. If your Spanish isn't too good, then the theater may prove a problem. But if you're curious to see a Spanish play, the *Teatro Español* at Príncipe 25 in Plaza Santa Ana, shows Spanish classics. Another highly reputed theater is the *María Guerrero,* Tamayo y Baus 4, home of the Centro Dramático Nacional. You might also investigate the *Centro Cultural de la Villa,* the experimental theater in the underground Plaza Colón development; language may not prove a problem here. Small, popular fringe theaters are the *Teatro Olimpia,* the *Teatro Lavapies* and the *Sala del Mirador,* all in the Lavapies area.

Most theaters have two curtains, at 7 and 10.30. They close once a week, usually Mondays. Tickets can sometimes be bought for as little as 500 ptas., and 700–1,200 ptas. is a good average. They are often available on the night itself.

Concerts. The *Auditorio Nacional de Madrid* on Príncipe de Vergara 136 (metro: Prosperidad) is the capital's newest concert hall. The second most important venue is the *Teatro Real* on Plaza del Oriente opposite the Royal Palace. Tickets from 800 ptas. *Teatro Lirico Nacional de la Zarzuela,* Jovellanos 4, has some concerts, ballet and opera; tickets 500–1,000 ptas. Other concerts (often free) at *Fundación March,* Castelló 77, and *Sala Fenix.* Paseo de la Castellana 37. Check the local papers or *Guia del Ocio* for programs and times; *El País* has the best listings.

Many of the foreign institutes also run concerts and these are often free. The *German Institute,* Zurbarán 21, is especially good. Try also the *British Institute,* Almagro 5, or the *French Institute* on Marqués de Enseñada. The *Washington Irving Center,* run by the U.S. government often puts on lectures, concerts and films at San Bernardo 107.

MUSEUMS. Although most museums are now free for Spaniards, foreigners still have to pay a moderate entrance fee (*note* the Prado and Royal Palace are much more expensive). Students with ISIC cards get in free to those belonging to the *Patrimonio Nacional.* Opening times change frequently and from summer to winter. For opening hours and admission charges, try checking with the Tourist Offices at Plaza Mayor 3, Señores de Luzón 10, the Plaza de España or at Barajas airport, who can usually supply details. As a general rule most museums are open the same time as shops, 9.30–1 or 1.30, then close for the siesta, and some open again in the later afternoon. Most museums close one day a week, usually Mondays, and many close in August too.

Archeological Museum, Serrano 13. Good collection of Greek vases and Roman artifacts. Home of the famous Dama de Elche and a replica of the Altamira Caves (the real ones are now only open for very limited visits).

Casón del Buen Retiro, Felipe IV 13. Spanish 19th-century paintings and the Picasso legacy including the famous *Guernica.*

Cerralbo Museum, Ventural Rodríguez 17. Aristocratic turn-of-the-century villa with tapestries, paintings and lovely porcelain.

Contemporary Art Museum, Avda. Juan de Herrera in the University City. Set in pleasant gardens with sculptures and paintings by Picasso and Miró.

Convent of Descalzas Reales, Plaza de las Descalzas Reales. A 16th-century convent with an interesting collection of medieval paintings.

Fine Arts Museum, also known as the *Royal Academy of San Fernando,* Alcalá 13. Paintings by Goya, Zurbarán, Murillo, Ribera and Rubens.

Goya Pantheon, in the Hermitage of San Antonio off Paseo de la Florida. Here you can see the frescoes Goya painted of respectable court officials hobnobbing with some less respectable ladies. Goya's headless body is buried here.

Lazaro Galdiano Foundation, Serrano 122. This is a "must." Housed in an old aristocratic mansion, it boasts the best collection of ivory and enamel in Europe, as well as works by El Greco, Zurbarán, Velázquez and Goya.

El Prado, Paseo del Prado. Madrid's number one sight, it ranks among the top four art galleries of the world. With emphasis on Spanish art, the Prado is also rich in works of the Italian and Flemish masters. Of major importance are the works of El Greco, Velázquez, Murillo and Goya; also Zurbarán and Ribera. But don't miss the marvelous pictures by Bosch. If your time is limited, bypass the ground floor and make for the first floor, which houses the greatest treasures.

Railroad Museum, located in the refurbished old Delicias station in Calle del Ferrocarril. Modest but well arranged display of lamps, models and switches, with one full-size old locomotive.

Reina Sofia Art Center, Santa Isabel 52, off Plaza de Atocha. Exciting art center that shows leading temporary exhibitions with plans to have its own permanent collection.

Royal Palace, Plaza de Oriente. Madrid's number two sight. Combination ticket includes entrance to library, palace and chapel, pharmaceutical museum and armory. A much cheaper ticket is available for the Palace only. Especially notable are the 800 tapestries and the Tiepolo ceiling of the throne room.

Royal Tapestry Factory, Fuenterrabía 2. Here you can see the actual weaving of many exquisite tapestries, many of them based on the sketches of Goya. Open mornings only Mon.–Fri.

SHOPPING. Madrid is no longer a budgeteer's paradise where shopping is concerned, but many a fascinating hour can be spent browsing around the hundreds of small shops in the narrow streets near the Plaza Mayor where age-old crafts are still lovingly practised. Avoid the obvious tourist shops near the major sights where prices are often marked-up, and look instead in the big department stores such as the *Corte Inglés* and *Galerías Preciados.*

Undoubtedly the best area to shop is the central part of town along the Gran Vía, the pedestrian streets of Preciados and Carmen, and the Puerta del Sol. Here you will find the big department stores and scores of smaller shops as well. The second, and more elegant—and naturally more expensive—area is the Salamanca district bounded by Serrano, Goya and Conde de Peñalver. Another area is the Azca shopping center between Orense and the Castellana, and the latest in vogue shopping mall is *La Vaguada* or *Madrid 2* way out in the northern suburbs in the Barrio del Pilar. Above all do not neglect the narrow side streets south of the Puerta del Sol and Calle Mayor; here you can wander happily in the Spain of 50 years ago and you might just still find a bargain!

Don't forget the Rastro, Madrid's famous flea market, which takes place on Sunday mornings around the Ribera de Curtidores. Here you can buy anything from antiques to bicycle tires. But beware the pickpockets; be on your guard at all times. There is a stamp and coin market every Sunday morning in the Plaza Mayor and secondhand books are on sale all year round on the Cuesta Claudio Moyano near Atocha station.

USEFUL ADDRESSES. *U.S. Embassy,* Serrano 75 (tel. 276 3600); *Canadian Embassy,* Núñez de Balboa 35 (tel. 431 4300); *British Embassy,* Fernando el Santo 16 (tel. 419 1528); *American Express,* Plaza de las Cortes 2 (tel. 429 5775); *Main* post office, Plaza de Cibeles; *Main Tourist Office*, in the Plaza de España; *City Tourist Office*, Plaza Mayor 3; *Telephone Exchange*, Gran Vía 30 on corner of Valverde; *Iberia*, Canovas del Castillo (tel. 429 7443); *TWA*, Plaza Colón 2 (tel. 410 6012); *British Airways*, Avda. Palma de Mallorca 43 (tel. 431 7575) and at Princesa 1 in the Torre de Madrid (tel. 248 7544); *Police Station* (to report lost passports, muggings), Los Madrazo 9 (tel. 221 9350).

DAYS OUT FROM MADRID

Madrid is particularly privileged in that it is surrounded by many towns and attractions that are just as interesting as the capital itself. Thus in any trip to Madrid, you should plan another three or four days for seeing the surrounding sights of Toledo, El Escorial, Ávila and Segovia.

Toledo

Toledo is the top tourist draw, a virtual museum in itself, lying only 70 kilometers from Madrid. You can go by train from Atocha Station or take a bus from the Estación del Sur; if you go by train a bus runs from Toledo Station to the Plaza Zocodover, the main square. Alternatively, you can go on one of the day trips organized by travel agencies. Of outstanding interest is the 13th-century cathedral, see of the Cardinal Primate of Spain. Other treasures you should not miss are the synagogues of El Tránsito and, if open again, Santa María la Blanca; the Hospital de Tavera; the museum of Santa Cruz; the church of San Juan de los Reyes; the chapel of Santo Tomé with El Greco's *Burial of the Count of Orgaz*, and lastly the house of El Greco himself. The view over Toledo from the other side of the Tagus on the Carretera de Circunvalación is breathtaking.

PRACTICAL INFORMATION FOR TOLEDO

Hotels and Restaurants

Most people make Toledo a day trip from Madrid but should you want to stay overnight, you will find the city transformed once the sightseers have headed back to the capital. *Imperio* (I), Cadenas 7, tel. 22 76 50. Simple, pleasant hotel with spacious rooms; central. *Maravilla* (I), Barrio Rey 5–7, tel. 23 33 04. Plain old-fashioned hotel with a good-value dining room just off Plaza Zocodover. *Sol* (I), Azacanes 15, tel. 21 61 59. Small, new modern hotel with garage close to Puerta del Sol; comfortable rooms, no meals.

If you have a car, you could try the *Almazara* (M), Ctra Toledo Argues y Guerba, Km 3,400 tel. 22 38 66. Two miles out of town, in a charming setting with splendid views. Old world charm, friendly service and highly recommended. *Los Cigarrales* (I), Ctra Circunvalación 12, tel. 22 00 53. Country house in pleasant location across the Tagus.

Restaurants. There is no shortage of good restaurants to try for lunch; your problem will be locating them in Toledo's maze of narrow streets. Many of them are well hidden so best ask for help. *Asador Adolfo* (M), La Granada 6, tel. 22 73 21. Very central, not far from cathedral. Good food but a little pricey. *Casa Aurelio* (M), Sinagoga 6, tel. 22 20 97. A popular restaurant near the cathedral. Toledo's specialties of partridge and quail are good here. *Los Cuatro Tiempos* (M), Sixto Ramon Parro, tel. 22 37 82. Very popular; well recommended. *Emperador* (M), Ctra de Circunvalación, tel. 22 46 91. Just out of town. Atmospheric tavern where you can enjoy the view of Toledo above the Tagus. *Marcial y Pablo* (M), Núñez de Arce 11, tel. 22 07 00. Good dining and great views over the Tagus to the north of town. *Venta de Cervantes* (M), Circo Romano 15, tel. 21 28 62. Pleasant inn on edge of town with garden; very good value.

El Aljibe (I), Plaza Padre Juan de Mariana. Bargain set menus. *Los Arcos* (I), Cordonerías 11, tel. 21 00 51. Inexpensive dining in pleasant surroundings right in center; excellent value. *Casa Paco* (I), Pozo Amargo 1. Typical and popular, an ideal budget diner just below Plaza Ayuntamiento. *El Patio* (I), Plaza San Vicente 4. Tourist oriented budget meals but attractive decor and patio. For lowest prices, explore the Barrio Rey behind the Plaza Zocodover, where you'll find a whole cluster of very inexpensive restaurants as well as the excellent restaurant of the *Maravilla* hotel.

Ávila

Ávila, 4,000 feet above sea level, is Spain's highest provincial capital. Famous for its splendid medieval walls (largely restored) dating back to 1090 with their many towers, turrets and storks' nests, it was also the birthplace of Saint Teresa, and today you can visit her shrine on the site of the house in which she was born. To reach Ávila from Madrid, take a train from Mediodía or Chamartín or else a bus from Paseo de la Florida 11.

PRACTICAL INFORMATION FOR ÁVILA

Hotels and Restaurants

Don Carmelo (M), Don Carmelo 30, tel. 22 80 50. Modern hotel, close to train station. *Continental* (I), Plaza de la Catedral 4, tel. 21 15 02. Across the square from the cathedral, an old-world hotel now a good budgeteer's hostel. No meals. *El Rastro* (I), Plaza del Rastro 1, tel. 21 12 19. Built right into the city walls, this old inn serves excellent low-price meals.

Restaurants. *Cuatro Postes* (M), on the road to Salamanca, just outside town. Rather aseptic décor, but the food is excellent (though watch those prices). Good view of walled city. *El Fogón de Santa Teresa* (M), Alemania 3. Typical Castilian restaurant serving local specialties, close to Rey Niño hotel. *Las Cancelas* (I), Cruz Vieja 6. Bright and cheerful, especially popular for Sunday lunch. *El Rincon* (I), Plaza de Zurraquín 6. Close to the market, serving regional Castilian dishes and a value-for-money *menu del día*.

Segovia

This beautiful golden-stoned city is one of the loveliest in Castile. Famed for its dramatically perched Alcázar (which inspired Disney's Cinderella's Castle), its 16th-century cathedral, wealth of medieval churches, and above all its 2,000-year-old Roman aqueduct, this is a place no one should miss. It can be reached by train from Mediodía or Chamartín stations or by bus from Paseo de la Florida 11.

PRACTICAL INFORMATION FOR SEGOVIA

Hotels and Restaurants

Acueducto (M), Padre Claret 10, tel. 42 48 00. Renovated hotel with good views over aqueduct and city walls. Quite expensive. *Las Sirenas* (M), Juan Bravo 30, tel. 43 40 11. A good, luxury hostel right in the center of town. *Plaza* (I), Cronista Lecea 11, tel. 43 12 28. Central hostel just off the main square. *Sol Cristina* (I), Obispo Quesada 40, tel. 42 75 13. Opposite rail station. No private bathrooms, but inexpensive and with clean, modern facilities.

Restaurants. Segovia's specialties are suckling pig, roast veal or lamb, and Castilian soup. *Mesón de Cándido,* Plaza del Azoguejo 5 by the aqueduct, and *Casa Duque,* Cervantes 12, are both rather pricey but worth a splurge for atmosphere and traditional Segovian fare. *Mesón El Cordero* (M), El Carmen 4, tel. 43 41 80. Good food in an imaginatively converted mansion; follow signs from aqueduct. *La Oficina* (M), Cronista Lecea 10, tel. 43 16 43. Typical and with two delightful dining rooms. Opposite at no. 11 is the good *Mesón Don José María* serving roasts and regional specialties. *La Taurina* (M), Plaza Mayor 8. Friendly, colorful restaurant on main square. *El Abuelo* (I), Alhóndiga 1 is a typical cellar-like tavern with a good range of set menus. *La Cocina de San Millán* (I), San Millán 3. Typical old Segovian house below city walls; hard to find but lunch menu is amazing value.

La Criolla (I), Ruiz de Alda 4. Simple, inexpensive tavern alongside Mesón de Cándido by the aqueduct.

El Escorial and the Valley of the Fallen

San Lorenzo de El Escorial is a small mountainside town about forty minutes' drive from the capital. It was here that Philip II chose to build his huge monastery-church-mausoleum, where Spanish kings from Charles V onwards now lie buried. Within the "sawed-off" skyscraper, as Le Corbusier called it, is a magnificent library, paintings, Philip II's living quarters, the mausoleum and endless historic relics. A combination entrance ticket (500 ptas.) allows you to visit the different parts of the monastery (closed on Mondays) in the order you choose, though most visitors opt for the *visita reducida* ticket (300 ptas.). You may, however, wander around the many patios and the stately gardens with their magnificent views for free. Buses from Madrid to El Escorial leave from Paseo Moret 7, and trains leave from Mediodía and Chamartín stations about every hour.

Should you have your own transport or have opted for a conducted tour, you will also be able to visit the Valley of the Fallen only a few kilometers away. Set high up on a mountain, this austere basilica surmounted by a gigantic cross was built by General Franco as a monument to those who died in the Civil War of 1936–39. José Antonio, founder of the Falangist Party, and Franco himself are both buried here with their plaques facing each other before the altar. While far from beautiful the architecture is undoubtedly impressive and the location superb, commanding a magnificent view across the foothills to the Guadarrama mountains. There is a modest admission fee for cars and motorcycles. If you don't have your own transport and wish to visit the Valley, you could try negotiating a price with the many taxis that ply for hire near the monastery coach park. But be sure to agree on a price first to cover round trip and waiting time, and make sure it is understood whether or not the fare includes the entrance to the Valley—it's a very long, steep walk from the gates up to the basilica.

PRACTICAL INFORMATION FOR EL ESCORIAL

Hotels and Restaurants

Miranda Suizo (M), Floridablanca 20, tel. 890 4711. Pleasant old hotel in center; its restaurant is good value. *Cristina* (I), Juan Toledo 6, tel. 890 1961. Delightful hostel with garden. *Escorial* (I), Arias Montano 10, tel. 890 1462. Well recommended.

Restaurants. In the summer evenings and at weekends, many *Madrileños* fleeing the heat of the capital drive up to El Escorial for dinner. As a result there are an inordinate number of restaurants for a town this size, some of which are naturally beyond our budget price limits. *Alaska* (M), Plaza San Lorenzo, tel. 890 4365. Castilian décor and outdoor dining on a pleasant terrace. *Castilla* (M), Plaza Constitución 2, tel. 890 5219. Good value, also some (I) dishes; tables outdoors in the square. *Mesón Serrano* (M), Floridablanca 4, tel. 890 1704. Good Spanish food either indoors or outdoors in the garden at the back. *Cafetería del Arte* (M–I), Floridablanca 14. Good range of snacks and traditional Spanish dishes. *Hostal Vasco* (I), Plaza Santiago. One of the few places where you can dine at affordable prices. Very economical *menu del día,* and Basque specialties for just a little more. *Madrid-Sevilla* (I), San Antón 2. Excellent value 4-course *menu del día* including wine. Just round the corner is *Bar La Cueva* belonging to the famous restaurant. This atmospheric mesón offers good *tapas* and *raciones* for those who can't afford La Cueva itself!

THE REST OF SPAIN

Salamanca

Salamanca, 212 kilometers from Madrid, is an ancient and lovely city, and your first glimpse of it is bound to be unforgettable. Beside you flows the Tormes river and beyond it rise the old houses of the city, topped by the golden walls, turrets, domes and spires of the Plateresque cathedral. The name Plateresque comes from *Plata* (silver) and implies that the soft stone is chiseled and engraved like that metal. Salamanca's cathedral and university buildings are among the finest examples of this style in existence. Besides having two cathedrals, three universities and the most beautiful Plaza Mayor in Spain, the streets of Salamanca are a veritable museum in themselves, lined as they are with colleges, convents and Romanesque churches. Be sure to see the House of Shells, the Las Dueñas Convent and the San Esteban Monastery.

PRACTICAL INFORMATION FOR SALAMANCA

Hotels

Moderate

Castellano II, Pedro Mendoza 36 (tel. 242812). In modern section on way to station. Dullish location but only short walk from center.
Condal, Santa Eulalia 3 (tel. 218400). Central and strongly recommended.

Inexpensive

Ceylán, Plaza del Peso 5 (tel. 212603). Smallish 2-star hotel, centrally located just off Plaza Mayor.
Clavero, Consuelo 21 (tel. 218108). Renovated old hotel in center; good budget bet.
Emperatriz, Compañía 44 (tel. 219200). Old-world hotel with lots of charm, if a little elderly; in an historic building near La Clerecía and university area.
Los Infantes, Paseo de la Estación 125 (tel. 252844). Bright modern hostel right opposite rail station.
Milan, Plaza del Angel 5 (tel. 217779). Central, just behind the market.

Restaurants

Moderate

El Candil, Ruiz Aguilera 10 (tel. 217239). A popular, atmospheric bodega dedicated to good eating. One of the best on this street with an excellent tapas bar.
El Mesón, Plaza Poeta Iglesias 10 (tel. 217222). Typical Castilian food and atmosphere, next to the famous Gran Hotel.
Río Plata, Plaza del Peso 1 (tel. 219005). Small and atmospheric, a little expensive. Closed July.

Inexpensive

El Bardo, Compañía 8 (tel. 219089). Popular with students and teachers from the university; very inexpensive with good value *menus del día*.
King Long, Plaza Libertad 7 (tel. 213456). Good value Chinese food.
Roma, Ruiz Aguilera 12. Old-fashioned budgeteer's delight, popular with tourists.
Valencia, Concejo 9. Traditional; sidewalk dining in summer.
For really low-priced meals you might try **El Clavel** or **La Camelia,** both in Clavel just off Pozo Amarillo, or any of the bars in and around Plaza Mercado at the back of the Plaza Mayor, or the student bars in Meléndez that offer economical *platos combinados* and menus.

Santiago de Compostela

Santiago de Compostela in northwestern Spain is the uncontested showpiece of Galicia. Like Salamanca it has a famous university and an even more famous cathedral. It was one of the great centers of medieval pilgrimage: the pilgrims' route through France and across northern Spain can still be traced to this shrine, which is believed to house the remains of St. James the Apostle. St. James (Santiago) is the patron saint of Spain and every year on St. James's day, July 25, great celebrations of pomp and splendor, pilgrimage and fireworks, take place in the small golden-stoned city. The festivities last for a week beginning on July 24 and accommodations are very hard to find if you haven't booked long in advance. You will be able to sample the atmosphere of this delightful city, one of Spain's greatest treasures, simply by standing in the magnificent Plaza del Obradoiro by the west door of the cathedral and framed by the Hostal del los Reyes Católicos, the San Jeronimo College and the Ayuntamiento (City Hall). Then take a stroll down the nearby Calle del Franco with its street vendors, bars and plentiful restaurants; in any of the narrow flag-stoned streets and squares at nighttime you may well come across the *tuna,* the traditional music group of Spanish universities, dressed in their black cloaks and ribbons, who will entertain you with their typical songs and music.

PRACTICAL INFORMATION FOR SANTIAGO DE COMPOSTELA

Hotels

Moderate

Rey Fernando, Fernando III el Santo 30 (tel. 593550). Recently built 2-star hotel with 24 rooms and very reasonable rates, not far from station.

Universal, Plaza Galicia 2 (tel. 585800). Simple hotel in convenient location on edge of old town.

Windsor, República de El Salvador 16 (tel. 592939). Good 3-star hostel about 5 mins. walk from old town.

Inexpensive

Alameda, San Clemente 32 (tel. 588100). Pleasant old-fashioned hostel close to the park and several budget bars and eating places.

Fornos, Gral Franco 7 (tel. 585130). Pleasant, clean, family hostel in the Plaza de Galicia.

Maycar, Dr. Teijeiro 15 (tel. 563444). 40 rooms. Modern hostel within walking distance of center.

México, República Argentina 33 (tel. 598000). Clean and well recommended; possibly a little far out.

Restaurants

Moderate

Camilo, Raiña 24 (tel. 581568). Pleasant family restaurant serving good Galician home cooking and well known for local Ribeiro wines.

El Caserío, Bautizados 13 (tel. 585980). Serves good Galician dishes, as does its neighbor **Victoria,** just a couple of doors down.

San Clemente, San Clemente 6 (tel. 580882). A pleasant restaurant overlooking the old town, some tables on sidewalk. Excellent display of shellfish. Next door is **Trinidad** (tel. 583392), also good.

If you walk down the Calle del Franco or the adjoining Raina, you will find literally hundreds of economical eating places.

Inexpensive

El Asesino, Plaza de la Universidad 16. A real Santiago tradition for over 100 years. Unbeatable for atmosphere and rock-bottom prices.

Extradense, Hórreo 17. Traditional diner known for its *empanadas* and simple, good-value fare.

Santiago also has many delightful **cafés** where you can eat at budget prices:

Alameda (M), Puerta Fajera 15. Has tables on the sidewalk and is very popular in the early evening. Upstairs is (M) restaurant.

Derby (M), on the corner of Plaza Galicia. Delightful old world café with charm and good service.

Fonseca (I), in Plaza Fonseca at top of Calle del Franco. Tables in the square and the free tapas with your drinks are so plentiful and generous, you won't need to eat afterwards. **Dakar** (I), a couple of doors down, has good budget snacks.

Barcelona

Barcelona, capital of the province and ancient capital of the kingdom of Catalonia, is Spain's second largest city (nearly two million inhabitants), a flourishing Mediterranean port, and a great tourist center. Expect the city to be in the midst of a construction boom as it prepares for the 1992 Summer Olympics. It commands a glorious position, similar to that of Naples, with a beautifully carved-out gulf and harbor. It enjoys a climate milder than that of Naples or Rome, and is only rarely oppressive in summer. A lively, sophisticated city, it takes great pride in asserting its Catalan character and individuality. Barcelona is not only the gateway to the Mediterranean, it is also a center of tourist excursions to the Monastery of the Holy Grail at Montserrat, to the ski resorts of the Pyrenees, to Roman Tarragona and the castle towns of Catalonia, and to that 145-kilometer stretch of summer playground known as the Costa Brava.

To absorb the atmosphere of Barcelona take a stroll down the Ramblas, those wide promenades which in 1860 replaced the city walls that once encircled the old town. The Ramblas are alive until the wee hours of the morning and hum with the incessant murmur of voices. Sunday morning is the time to see the Ramblas at their best: just before lunch it seems that every family in Barcelona is thronging the central promenade, strolling leisurely arm-in-arm past the hundreds of flower stalls, bookstands, fish tanks and bird cages that line the way. But take care, purse-snatching is common in Barcelona, and at its worst in the Ramblas and narrow streets of the Gothic Quarter.

In the more conventional sightseeing department, the cathedral has the place of honor, dominating the old town, or Gothic Quarter, which stretches from the Plaça de Catalunya to the Porta de la Pau. Known to the locals as La Seu, it is a splendid creation of Catalan Gothic, at once strong and exquisite. The cloisters are among the best in Spain. Other buildings in the Gothic Quarter share the same noble character: the Episcopal Palace, the Palau de la Generalitat, seat of the ancient parliament of Catalonia, and opposite it the magnificent Ajuntament with its famous Saló de Cent. On the nearby Plaça del Rei and in the Carrer del Rec, the 14th- and 15th-century palaces have a grace and elegance reminiscent of Florence. The beautiful Plaça Reial with its porticos and palm trees is best seen on a Sunday morning when the crowds gather to peruse the wares of stamp and coin vendors and listen to the numerous orators who set up their soap boxes here. Other Barcelona landmarks are the excellent Picasso Museum and the nearby Gothic church of Santa María del Mar.

If you are interested in Spain's regional architecture, visit the Poble Espanyol (Spanish Village), with buildings characteristic of each province in Spain. Built for the Fair of 1929, it is now a tourist trap, though it retains something of its original inspiration. When in the Montjuïc area, you might also like to visit the excellent Museum of Catalan Art, and the recently enlarged Miró Foundation, and admire the view from the top over the roofs of the city to the distant mountain of Tibidabo, which itself offers a spectacular panorama of the city and Mediterranean as well as on a clear day far away to Montserrat and the distant Pyrenees. Always popular is the cablecar ride from Miramar on Montjuïc to La Barceloneta, which affords a thrilling view of the city and harbor.

Finally, no visit to Barcelona would be complete until you have experienced for yourself some of the fantastic architectural vagrancies of the incomparable architect, Antonio Gaudí, who was tragically run-over by a tram in 1926. His most notable work, the fantasmagorical stalactite-stalagmite Church of the Sagrada Familia, begun in 1881 was still unfinished at his death, and it's still unfinished today, though work on it is now going ahead. Gaudí's strange buildings are dotted all around Barcelona; others well worth a visit are the Palau Güell, in Carrer Nou de la Rambla, just off Ramblas; two houses on Passeig de Gracià, Casa Milá and Casa Batlló; and finally the Parc Güell in the north of the city, a kind of art-nouveau extravaganza, best visited on Sunday afternoons. Fans of *modernista* architecture should also not miss a visit to the Palau de la Música concert hall.

PRACTICAL INFORMATION FOR BARCELONA

GETTING INTO TOWN FROM THE AIRPORT. The least expensive way to travel into town is to take the airport train to Sants-Central Station. This train runs every 30 mins. from 6.30 A.M. to around 11 P.M. and late at night buses connect the airport with the city. It is a long walk from the arrivals hall to the airport station so arm yourself with a luggage trolley that will go up escalators. At presstime no luggage-check facilities were available at either the airport or Sants Station. If you can't manage your luggage, best take a taxi, which will cost around 1,500 ptas. to the city center.

HOTELS. Hotels and hostels are plentiful in Barcelona, especially in the old part of town around the Gothic Quarter, and are reasonably priced. Many of the accommodations in the budget range tend to be old compared to those in many other Spanish cities, some of them may not provide exactly the facilities you would expect back home, but for a city of this size and importance they are moderately priced. To avoid disappointment always inspect your room before you take it and check on the situation with meals, especially breakfast—is it available, will you be charged whether or not you eat it? In the summer months, mid-June through mid-September, many hotels will be full and you may search for quite a while before finding a room. During the 1992 Summer Olympics (end of July and first 10 days of August) hotel rooms will be at a premium. At the lower end of the scale the streets of the Gothic Quarter are a good place to look but stay clear of the lower reaches from the Plaça Reial to the port.

Branches of the city tourist office will provide lists of hotels and hostels but they do not make reservations for you. Privately run agencies at the airport and at Sants-Central and Terminal stations will find you a room for a reasonable fee.

Moderate

Cataluña, Santa Anna 22 (tel. 301 9150). Good budget hotel centrally located in lively shopping street between Ramblas and Porta de l'Angel.

Continental, Ramblas 138 (tel. 301 2508). Excellent hostel at top of Ramblas. Friendly service, perfect location; one of the best budget bets.

Cortés, Santa Anna 25 (tel. 317 9212). Neighboring hotel to **Cataluña** and under same management.

International, Ramblas 78 (tel. 302 2566). Pleasant old hotel right across from Liceu.

Moderno, Hospital 11 (tel. 301 4154). Well maintained hotel just off Ramblas between Liceo and central market; quite expensive.

Monegal, Pelai 62 (tel. 302 6566). Third-floor hostel with just 12 rooms overlooking Ramblas and Plaça de Catalunya and slightly more expensive than others in this category.

Rubí, Via Laietana 42 (tel. 319 9500). Well maintained, clean, comfortable hostel but in very noisy position. Ask for a room at the back.

Urbis, Passeig de Gracià 23 (tel. 231 6904). In an excellent position close to Gran Vía but standards of rooms can vary, so check first.

Inexpensive

El Casal, Tapinería 10 (tel. 319 7800). Three-star hostel round corner from cathedral in pedestrian street off Via Laietana.

Cisneros, Aribau 54 (tel. 254 1800). Pleasant, very inexpensive, hostel on corner of Aragó, near budget restaurants.

Condestable, Ronda Universitat 1 (tel. 318 6268). Reliable hostel long patronized by budgeteers, close to university.

Inglés, Boquería 17 (tel. 317 3770). In colorful, narrow street off Ramblas with its own restaurant. Long a budgeteer's tradition; a good bet.

Lleo, Pelai 24 (tel. 318 1312). Oldish hotel on 2nd floor on busy street between Plaça de Catalunya and university.

Nouvel, Santa Anna 18 (tel. 301 8274). Simple old-world hotel in charming house with touches of modernista architecture; close to **Cataluña** and **Cortés.**

Paseo de Gracia, Passeig de Gracia 102 (tel. 215 5824). Comfortable hostel in same block as Gaudi's famous *La Pedrera* apartment building.

Villa de Madrid, Placa Vila de Madrid 3 (tel. 317 4916). Elderly but pleasant hotel overlooking small central square between Ramblas and Porta de l'Angel.

Youth Accommodations. *Barcelona Youth Hostel* is located near the Ciutadella Park at Passeig de Pujades 29 (tel. 300 3104). There is a second hostel, the *Albergue Pere Tarres,* Numancia 149 (tel. 230 1606) not far from Sants-Central station. The *BCN Youth Hostel* run by Xatrac Cooperative is at Pelai 62, 2nd floor.

RESTAURANTS. Barcelona offers a vast selection of restaurants and in the Moderate category you should have no difficulty finding an atmospheric restaurant serving the usual satisfying Catalan helpings. However, you will have to look around a bit and be prepared to brave some of the more typical areas such as the fishermen's quarter of Barceloneta. It is unsalubrious, scruffy and unrefined but it offers some marvelous taverns and restaurants.

Remember to study the menu in the window first and that the *menu del día* is nearly always cheapest. Many restaurants are closed on Sunday and some also close Saturday nights. Many also close for a month in July or August. Always check first.

Moderate

El Caballito Blanco, Mallorca 196 (tel. 253 1033). Old Barcelona stand-by; popular with locals. Wide selection of seafood and good cheeses.

Can Culleretes, Quintana 5 (tel. 317 6485). In narrow street sandwiched between Boquería and Ferran, just off Ramblas. This is a real find, superbly atmospheric and with real Catalan cooking. Very popular for lunch on Sat. and Sun.

Can Sole, Sant Carlos 4 (tel. 319 5012). Famous seafood restaurant; very atmospheric and located in Barceloneta.

Los Caracoles, Escudellers 14 (tel. 301 2041). One of the most popular old-time restaurants in town. Décor is superb; specialties are snails and paella.

Gargantua i Pantagruel, Aragó 214, corner of Aribau (tel. 253 2020). Attractive restaurant with several small diningrooms, specializing in grilled meat.

La Morera, Plaça Sant Agusti 1 (tel. 318 7555). Smart décor and very good value, just off the Ramblas between the Liceu and Boquería market.

Siete Puertas, Passeig Isabel II 14 (tel. 319 3033). Near the harbor with lots of old-world charm; a long-standing favorite.

Sopeta Una, Verdaguer i Callis 6 (tel. 319 6131). Delightful small restaurant near Palau de la Música, specializing in Catalan cuisine.

El Tunel, Ample 33 (tel. 315 2759). An old Barcelona tradition, much praised for good food and service.

Inexpensive

Agut, Gignàs 16 (tel. 315 1709). An old Catalan favorite deep in the Gothic Quarter.

Aquarium, Cardenal Casañas 15. Small bistro just off the Rambla de las Flores.

Del Teatre, Montseny 47. Located in the Teatre Lliure in Barrio de Gracià area. Simple food, friendly service and good value *menu del día.*

Egipte, Jerusalem 12 (tel. 317 7480). Small and friendly, hidden behind Boquería market; good home cooking and huge desserts.

Flash Flash, La Granada 25 (tel. 228 5567). Over 101 choices of omelet; fashionable black and white décor.

La Ponsa, Enric Granados 89 (tel. 253 1037). Family-run restaurant serving Catalan food at very moderate prices; excellent budget find.

Rey de la Gamba 1, 2 and 3, Passeig Nacional in Barceloneta. Unpretentious but the locals come here for fish, seafood and *pan tomate.*

Sandoval, Comtal 28 (tel. 302 2187). Popular budget diner with very inexpensive *menu del día,* between Porta de l'Angel and Vía Laietana.

Self Naturista, Santa Anna 13. Popular self-service vegetarian-wholefood café; very cheap with long lines at lunchtime.

Via Napoleone, Pelai 5. Pizzeria that serves other dishes too. Décor is ordinary but it's hugely popular with locals, very crowded, and incredible value.

GETTING AROUND BARCELONA. By Metro. This is the cheapest form of public transport. You pay a flat fare no matter how far you ride. A *multiviaje* ticket good for ten rides can be bought at a reduced cost from the transport kiosk in Plaça Catalunya or from metro ticket offices. Catalunya is the best connecting station for lines in all directions.

By Bus. Most of the bus routes pass through the Plaça de Catalunya. Again there is a flat-fare system. Bus rides cost a little more than the metro, and a bit extra on Sundays and holidays. A *multiviaje* ticket good for ten rides can be bought at a reduced cost from the transport kiosk in Plaça de Catalunya (opposite the Banco de Bilbao sign). To get to the beach at Castelldefels, take the UC from near the University.

To go up Mount Tibidabo, take a bus or metro from Plaça de Catalunya to Avda. de Tibidabo, from which a special tram *(tramvia blau)* runs to the funicular station. To reach the Parc Guell, take the metro to Lesseps, or even better, bus 24.

By Taxi. Most distances between places of interest are not that great so a cab may not be too expensive. Taxis available for hire show a *Libre* sign in the daytime and a green light at night. When you begin your ride a standard charge of around 200 ptas. will be shown on the meter. Further supplements are: 40 ptas. for each suitcase, 70 ptas. for night fares (10 P.M. to 6 A.M.) and for Sundays and holidays, 55 ptas. for rides to or from a station or port, and 150 ptas. to the airport. Make sure your driver turns down the flag when you start your ride.

On Foot. Modern Barcelona, north of the Plaça de Catalunya, is largely built on a grid system, though without the helpful numbering system of the U.S. However, the old town, on either side of the Ramblas, is straight out of the Middle Ages with its narrow meandering streets. This is an area that can only be explored on foot, so before you plunge into this fascinating labyrinth, best arm yourself with a street map, available free from branches of the City Tourist Office. We advise you not to carry purses in this area.

ENTERTAINMENT. For information on everything that's on in Barcelona you can buy the weekly *Guía del Ocio* for around 70 ptas. at newsstands all over town. It runs from Fri.–Thurs. and lists theaters, movies, art exhibitions, restaurants, concerts, discos and much more but you will need a knowledge of Spanish for it to be much use. The daily newspaper *El País* and *La Vanguardia* also have listings.

Bullfights. Corridas take place mostly on Sundays from Easter till October. There are two rings: *Monumental* in the north of the city, on the corner of Gran Vía and Carles I; and *Las Arenas* in the south, near the Plaça de Espanya though the latter is rarely used now. It's cheapest to buy your tickets at the ring on the day, or else in advance from the official ticket office on Muntaner 24. Elsewhere you will most likely have to pay a 20% surcharge.

Flamenco. Catalans often consider this Andalusian spectacle as anti-Catalan so Barcelona is not richly endowed with flamenco houses, and those that there are cater to the tourist. So if you are visiting other parts of Spain, particularly Madrid or Andalusia, best wait till you get there. However, Barcelona's large Andalusian community from which many of the performers come, should offer a touch of authenticity. The two main places to try are: *El Cordobés*, Ramblas 35 (tel. 317 6653) and *El Patio Andaluz*, Aribau 242 (tel. 209 3378). Entrance including one drink starts at around 2,000 ptas.

Cinema. Most international movies are dubbed into Spanish but there are a few movie theaters that show films in their original language (often English). These are all listed in the *Guía del Ocio* or in *El País* under *Versión Original (V.O.)*. The official *Filmoteca* at Travessera de Gracià 63 shows three films a day in their original language.

Discos. Barcelona has a large number of fashionable discos. Admission, usually including one drink, starts at around 850 ptas. but may well be as high as 2,000 ptas.; many are run as private clubs for members only. Some good ones are: *Duetto,* Consell de Cent 294; *Muntaner,* Muntaner 4; *Studio 54,* Paral-lel 54; *Trauma,* Consell de Cent 228; *Up and Down,* Numancia 179. The *tarde* sessions (approx. 6.30–10.30) may well be cheaper than the *noche* ones from 11 onwards.

Theaters. Much of the best theater is in Catalan or is silent. Mime is very popular and *Els Joglars* are an internationally-known Catalan troup. Leading theaters are the *Teatre Lliure,* Leopoldo Alas 2, *Poliorama,* Ramblas 115, and *Romea,* Hospital 51.

The *Gran Teatre del Liceu* in the Ramblas is one of the world's finest opera houses. Prices begin at around 2,000 ptas. for the 4th and 5th floors though standing room only is available at around 500 ptas. The advance box office is at Sant Pau 1, open mornings only; tickets on the day from the Ramblas entrance. Concerts are held regularly at the *Palau de la Música,* Amadeu Vives 1, just off Via Laietana. Its Sunday morning concerts are a Barcelona institution and are cheaper than weekday concerts. In the summer, concerts are given in the patio of the *Hospital de la Santa Creu.* The *International Theater Festival* is held in the Teatre Grec on Montjuïc in July and August.

MUSEUMS. Barcelona has a number of fine museums, notably the Museum of Catalan Art, the Picasso Museum and the Miró Foundation. Many of the best museums are now free, others have a free day on either Sunday or Wednesdays, and holders of ISIC cards and, in some cases, senior citizens, are often entitled to free entrance. Most museums close on Mondays.

Archeological Museum, in Montjuïc Park. Roman mosaics and a display of finds from Ampurias.

Costume Museum, Montcada 12. Costumes from 16th–20th centuries housed in lovely old palace near Picasso Museum.

Frederic Marés Museum, Comtes de Barcelona 10. Just around corner from cathedral; religious carvings and an outstanding collection of personal *bric-à-brac;* a fascinating museum.

Gaudí Museum, in the Parc Güell. Display of the architect's sketches, photos and documents in his house in this charming park. Open Sun. only.

Joan Miró Foundation, in Montjuïc Park. Works by Miró and young Catalan artists. Also many good temporary exhibits.

Maritime Museum in Reales Atarazanas in Porta de la Pau. Outstanding ship collection includes a gallery from the Battle of Lepanto, the first submarine and a nautical map by Amerigo Vespucci.

Military Museum, in Montjuïc Castle. Well arranged collection of historic weapons, miniature soldiers, and model Catalan castles.

Museum of Catalan Art, Palau Nacional on Montjuïc. One of the prides of Barcelona, this is a "must." Houses the greatest collection of medieval Catalan art in the world, as well as an interesting collection of ceramics. (Only partially open at presstime due to renovations).

Museum of the History of Barcelona, in Casa Padellás in Plaça del Rei.

Museum of Modern Art, in Ciutadella Park. Paintings from 18th to early 20th centuries. Many canvases evoke the era when Picasso lived in Barcelona.

Performing Arts Museum, Nou de la Rambla 3. History of Barcelona's theater, cinema and dance housed in Gaudí's **Palau Güell.**

Picasso Museum, Montcada 15. Good collection of the artist's work in an interesting old house. This is another of Barcelona's "musts."

Science Museum, Teodoro Roviralta 55. The first of its kind in Spain. Includes a planetarium.

MARKETS. Apart from the stalls on the Ramblas, Barcelona has two **flea markets** (known as *Els Encants*): *Belle Caire,* Plaça Glories Catalanes, open every day except Tuesday and Thursday; and *San Antonio,* in the old market building on the corner of Urgell and Tamarit, open all week but particularly good for secondhand books on Sundays. **Antique market** on Thursday mornings in the cathedral square; **stamp and coin market** in the Plaça Reial on Sunday mornings.

USEFUL ADDRESSES. *U.S. Consulate,* Via Laietana 33 (tel. 319 9550); *British Consulate,* Diagonal 477 (tel. 322 2151); *Train Stations,* Sants-Central at end of

Avda de Roma, *Terminal,* Avda Marqués de l'Argentera; *Bus station* (most destinations), Estació Vilanova, Avda Vilanova; *Post Office,* Plaça Antoní López; *Tourist Offices:* Gran Vía 648, Sants Central station, Terminal station, at the airport and in Columbus monument. *Hospital of the Foreign Colonies,* Alegre de Dalt 87 (tel. 219 7100). *American Express,* Rosselló 257 corner of Passeig de Gracià (tel. 217 0070). *Police,* Vía Laietana 49 (tel. 301 6666 for lost passports, etc.).

Andalusia—Córdoba

This is a town of the past. Córdoba was once one of the great cities of Europe, nourished by its river, its philosophers and its artists. It was the capital of Roman and Moorish Spain, and an important fortress under the Visigoths. For almost 500 years, until the Christian reconquest, it flourished. Today only the beautiful mosque, the *mezquita,* remains of all the monumental buildings of Islam. But in her dusty squares and narrow whitewashed streets, Córdoba remains a town as captivating, delightful and folkloric as Seville.

The beautiful red and white arched mosque will be the highlight of your visit but you should also see the synagogue, the only remaining one in Andalusia; the colorful bullfighting museum; the Alcázar; the Roman bridge and old Arab water wheel on the Guadalquivir; the now dilapidated Plaza de la Corredera where a market is held every morning; the Plaza de los Dolores; and the Plaza del Potro, site of an inn of the same name (*potro* means colt) mentioned by Cervantes in Don Quixote. Just off this square are the Fine Arts Museum and the charming museum of the Cordoban artist, Julio Romero de Torres.

But just as fascinating as any of the monuments is a stroll along the narrow winding streets with their wrought iron grilles, plant-filled patios and flower-strewn balconies. If you are here in early May Córdoba holds a patio fiesta where many families open their patios to the public and a prize is awarded for the best floral displays; a donation of 50 or 100 ptas. is all you need leave.

PRACTICAL INFORMATION FOR CÓRDOBA

Hotels

Moderate

Marisa, Cardenal Herrero 6 (tel. 473142). 28 rooms. In an attractive old Cordoban house on north side of mosque. A little expensive, but full of charm.

Selu, Eduardo Dato 7 (tel. 476500). Moderate hotel in center much patronized by tour groups but comfortable and well maintained.

Inexpensive

Andalucía, Jose Zorilla 3 (tel. 476000). Central, simple and basic, with a real budget restaurant that is open to non-residents.

Colón, Alhaken II 4 (tel. 470017). Good, functional hotel quite close to station and only a short walk from downtown.

Riviera, Plaza de Aladreros 7 (tel. 473000). Rather functional, but adequate, right in city center.

Serrano, B. Pérez Galdós 6 (tel. 470142). Simple but clean, friendly hotel off Avda Gran Capitán; plenty of Andalusian atmosphere.

El Triunfo, Cardenal González 87 (tel. 475500). Bright, modern hotel just south of mosque, with own restaurant. An ideal budget find, and highly recommended.

Restaurants

Moderate

Almudaina, Plaza Santos Mártires 1 (tel. 474342). Atmospheric location in old school overlooking Alcázar at entrance to Judería.

El Blasón, José Zorrilla 11 (tel. 480625). Under same management as famous Caballo Rojo, charming Cordoban decor and delicious food.

El Cardenal, Cardenal Herrero 14 (tel.480346). Elegant, stylish restaurant on north side of mosque near **Marisa** hotel.

El Churrasco, Romero 16 (tel. 290819). Popular with the Cordobeses for succulent grilled meats.

Mesón del Bandolero, Torrijos 8 (tel. 476491). Beautifully decorated meson in an old Cordoban mansion on the site of the philosopher Averröes' birthplace. Popular with tourists.

Inexpensive

El Aguila, Conde y Luque. Good low price meals and *platos combinados* in attractive patio.

Café Judás Levi, Plaza Judás Levi. Attractive setting with typical Andalusian patio. Economical set menus.

Mesón La Fragua, Tomás Conde behind Almudaina restaurant, and **Mesón de la Luna,** Calleja de la Luna, are both good economical *mesones* serving inexpensive snacks and light meals.

Los Patios, Cardenal Herrero 16. Self-service cafeteria near mosque; outdoor dining on beautiful, flower-decked patio.

The restaurants of the **Andalucía** and **El Triunfo** hotels are good budget bets.

Granada

About 144 kilometers from the coast lies the Moorish city of Granada, site of the Alhambra. This magnificent complex of buildings is the Moors' greatest legacy in Spain. You will find towers, arcades, quiet pools, marble baths, and lacelike carvings in the Alhambra, while the nearby Generalife gardens are cool and subtle perfection.

The modern city is not particularly beautiful but does have some interesting sites and streets. The Renaissance cathedral adjoins the Royal Chapel, which houses the tombs of Ferdinand and Isabella. The narrow streets of the nearby Alcaicería (the old silk exchange) have a charm of their own and are packed with souvenir shops. La Cartuja, a Carthusian monastery on the edge of town, revels in its over-ornate Baroque splendor. Both the house of the composer Manuel de Falla, and that of the poet and dramatist Federico García Lorca, are open to visitors.

Don't miss a visit to the Albaicín, the old Arab quarter. Here narrow cobbled streets wind up the hill among ancient houses and inexpensive and characteristic bars. Go to the balcony in front of San Nicolás church for the best view of the Alhambra. Dotted over the Sacromonte mountain are the gypsy caves for which Granada is so famous. A nighttime trip up here to watch flamenco and see the inside of these mansion-type dwellings could be a worthwhile experience but it isn't likely to be a budget one! At all costs, watch those gypsy children, they are excellent pickpockets.

PRACTICAL INFORMATION FOR GRANADA

Hotels

Moderate

Carlos V, Plaza de los Campos 4 (tel. 221587). 3-star hostel in old house in picturesque but run-down part of town.

Inglaterra, Cetti Meriem 8 (tel. 221559). Delightful old-fashioned hotel with style and charm, if a little aging.

Kenia. Molinas 65 (tel. 227506) Slightly expensive, but the warm welcome, comfort, and small garden make this a choice hotel.

Macia, Plaza Nueva 4 (tel. 227536). Functional, in pleasant central location.

Montecarlo, José Antonio 44 (tel. 257900). Good older hotel, close to center.

Rallye, Paseo de Ronda 107 (tel. 272800). Modern, functional, tour-group hotel in dull street far from center, but comfortable.

Sudán, José Antonio 60 (tel. 258400). Old-world hotel, charming if a bit faded, very central.

Inexpensive

Niza, Navas 16 (tel. 225430). Older hotel, renovated, but central and good.

Los Tilos, Plaza de Bib-Rambla 4 (tel. 266712). In old house in delightful central square with lots of cafés. Good value.

Victoriano, Navas 24 (tel. 225490). A real budget find. Charming but old-fashioned dining room with wide range of cheap menus.

Restaurants

Moderate

Altamura, Avda Andaluces 2 (tel. 272908). Excellent home-made pasta, pizzas, and good Italian meat dishes; close to rail station.

Columbia, Antequeruela Baja 1 (tel. 227433). Magnificently located on Alhambra hill with great views; dining to live guitar music. A little touristy and pricey, but fun.

Los Manueles, Zaragoza 2 (tel. 223415). Atmospheric, with ceramic tiles, and smoked hams hanging from ceiling. Famous since 1917.

Sevilla, Oficios 14 (tel. 221223). Small and picturesque with typical Granadino décor; in the Alcaicería beside cathedral.

Inexpensive

Abenhamar, Abenhamar 6, with a touch of the Moors and economical *menus del día.*

Mesón Andaluz, corner of Cetti Meriem and Elvira. Wide choice of menu and attentive service. Rather geared to tourists but friendly.

Nuevo Restaurante, Navas 25, opposite Victoriano Hotel. Another budgeteer's regular with several very cheap set menus; gets very crowded.

Pizzería Verona, Calle Elvira. Traditional Italian pizzeria, a definite favorite with the locals.

El Polinario, Real de la Alhambra. Situated within Alhambra precincts; garden dining in summer. Geared to tourists but convenient when visiting Alhambra.

Seville

Andalusia is the heart of all that is most mysterious in Spain, and the closest you can come to that heart is Seville, Andalusia's capital. Seville is the city of Carmen and Don Juan, and with its beautiful buildings, whitewashed houses and ancient streets and squares lined with orange trees, its exotic gardens, pavilions and patios, it is a place that cannot fail to enchant, though theft is rampant in this city and can tarnish your visit.

The first place you will want to visit is the superlative Gothic cathedral, the largest in Spain (and the largest Gothic building in the world) and the world's third-largest cathedral. It is the highest, and the richest in decoration and great works of art; Christopher Columbus lies enshrined within its walls. The cathedral tower, Seville's famous Giralda, is a Moorish minaret, a relic of the Arab mosque the Sevillians destroyed to build the cathedral. A climb to the top affords a breathtaking view over the city's rooftops. Nearby the cathedral is the sumptuous Alcázar built in the 14th century by Pedro the Cruel in Mudéjar style; its beauty is surpassed only by Granada's Alhambra. From here you can stroll through the picturesque streets of the Barrio Santa Cruz, with their flower-decked patios, iron grilles, sleepy squares fragrant with orange blossom and lazy fountains.

Other places you shouldn't miss are the Casa de Pilatos, the ornate Moorish palace of the Dukes of Medinacelli; the beautiful Baroque Alms House of La Caridad within whose walls Miguel Mañara, the original Don Juan, breathed his last; the Golden Tower on the banks of the Guadalquivir; the Archives of the Indies, home of all the documents and maps relating to Spain's discovery and conquest of the New World; and finally the beautiful gardens of María Luisa Park, especially the Plaza de España and the Plaza de América.

Should you be in Seville at Easter time you will see a spectacle you will never forget, for Seville's Holy Week processions are the most memorable in all Spain.

Following close on Holy Week comes the April Fair at the end of the month with spectacular horse parades, firework displays and overall fun and laughter late into the small hours. But remember, prices are at a maximum in this month and hotel accommodations are extremely hard to find if not booked well in advance.

PRACTICAL INFORMATION FOR SEVILLE

Hotels

Moderate

Ducal, Plaza de la Encarnación 19 (tel. 215107). Large, old-fashioned, comfortable rooms in central location.

Internacional, Aguilas 17 (tel. 213207). Charming old-world hotel in ancient house in a tangle of narrow streets near Casa de Pilatos.

Montecarlo, Gravina 51 (tel. 217503). An old hotel just off Reyes Católicos with a diningroom and plenty of old-world style and 19th-century touches.

Murillo, Lope de Rueda 7 (tel. 216095). Picturesque, clean and quiet, right in the Barrio Santa Cruz. Highly recommended; but can only be reached on foot.

Niza, Reyes Católicos 5 (tel. 215401). Old-fashioned friendly hotel though some rooms are now rather shabby and a lot of tour groups stay here. As with *Montecarlo* you will most likely be obliged to take half board terms in high season.

La Rabida, Castelar 24 (tel. 220960). Charming old hotel in picturesque Sevillian house in center of town; with restaurant.

Sevilla, Daoiz 5 (tel. 384161). A very pretty Andalusian house in the center near shops and cafés.

Inexpensive

Goya, Mateos Gago 31 (tel. 211170). Clean and comfortable, five minutes from cathedral on edge of Barrio Santo Cruz; one of Seville's most popular budget accommodations.

Londres, San Pedro Mártir 1 (tel. 212896). Pleasant hostel in narrow street near Fine Arts Museum.

Madrid, San Pedro Mártir 22 (tel. 214306). Good hostel quite convenient for railroad station; in narrow street off Gravina. Rates are quite high.

Monreal, Rodrigo Caro 8 (tel. 214166). This is a Sevillian tradition, especially with young foreigners. Charming but basic lodgings in a picturesque Seville house with patio and foliage, just behind cathedral in Barrio Santa Cruz. Rates during Holy Week and April Fair are exorbitant.

El Paraíso, Gravina 27 (tel. 217919). Another reasonable hostel near the Londres and the Madrid, and all convenient to Córdoba station. Rates are quite high.

Sierpes, Corral del Rey 22 (tel. 224948). Picturesque old house in the tangle of narrow streets in the center; recently renovated throughout.

Simón, García de Vinuesa 19 (tel. 226660). Charming 18th-century house built around a patio. As rooms are rather old-fashioned and basic, best inspect them first. Better suited to those who prefer old-world charm to creature comforts.

Restaurants

Moderate

El Bacalao, Plaza Ponce de León 15 (tel.21667). Good fish restaurant near Santa Catalina church, specializes in cod dishes.

Bodegón Torre del Oro, Santander 15 (tel. 213169). Rustic atmosphere, good food and popular with locals and tourists.

El Giraldillo, Virgen de los Reyes 2 (tel. 214525). Typical, colorful mesón, opposite entrance to cathedral. Popular with tourists and locals.

La Isla, Arfe 25 (tel. 215376). Nothing special about the décor but the cooking is excellent, especially the seafood.

La Judería, Cano y Cueto 13 (tel. 412052). Bright, modern restaurant serving good fish, and roast meat dishes from Avila. Very good value.

El Mero, Betis 1–3 (tel. 334252). Well known fish restaurant in the "sailors" district of La Triana. Décor is simple but quite elegant.

Inexpensive

La Cueva del Pez Espada, Rodrigo Caro 18. Colorful tavern in Barrio Santa Cruz, between Plaza Doña Elvira and Alianza. Friendly service.

El Escorial, Javier Lasso de la Vega 3. A pleasant family-run restaurant close to the Sevilla hotel and Plaza Duque shopping area. Specializes in Castilian home cooking and the owners recommend the *cordero asado* (roast lamb).

El Mesón, Dos de Mayo 26 (tel. 213075). Typical Sevillian bodega, close to La Caridad Convent. James Michener immortalized it in *Iberia.*

Mesón Castellano, Jovellanos 6 (tel. 214128). Ideal place for lunch just off Sierpes opposite church of San José. Specializes in Castilian roasts.

Modesto, Cano y Cueto 5 (tel. 416811). Good-value *menu del día* and Sevillian specialities in typical Andalusian house decorated with colorful tiles.

La Posada, in Plaza Alianza in Barrio Santa Cruz. Offers *gazpacho* and *paella* tourist-geared menus. The food and service are not good and prices high for the quality, but the location is a delight with outdoor dining in the square when weather permits.

For shoestring eating there are numerous cheap restaurants around the cathedral in Alemanes, Alvarez Quintero, Conteros and all along Mateus Gago. Many of them look attractive from the outside but often the food and hygiene leave much to be desired.

Sweden

Larger than California, nearly twice the size of the British Isles, Sweden is the biggest and richest of the Scandinavian nations. Its 450,000 square km. (173,000 square miles) stretch from the sunny, fertile plains of the south to the frozen tundra of the Arctic Circle. It is a land of stunning contrasts. From the cobbled streets of Stockholm's old town you can look across the water to modern apartments equipped with individual yacht basins; not far from the medieval Riddarholm Church where Sweden's kings are buried, there is a modern hospital with a heliport on its roof. And in the far north, where Lapps still herd their reindeer as they have done for a thousand years (now with radios and helicopters), the city of Luleå has a civic center whose sidewalks are centrally heated.

The main sights to see are: the beautiful capital Stockholm; the medieval cities of Visby, Uppsala and Sigtuna; the chateau country of Skåne; folkloric Dalarna province; Gripsholm and Skokloster castles near Stockholm. If you have more time, Midnight Sun excursions to the far north, and along the Göta Canal, which runs the breadth of the country, are also worthwhile. But Sweden is also a land where the great outdoors reigns supreme, and anyone who values wide open spaces, marvelous wooded landscapes and seemingly endless areas of still untamed land, will find Sweden very much to their liking.

Sweden today has long since cast off its reputation as a socialist paradise, where permissiveness and social experiment were allowed free rein and the country stood for all that was daring and modern. Though still one of the most tightly regulated countries in the world—the Swedish parliament has been happily passing legislation at an average rate of one new law every eight hours, or 1,000 a year, for a good many years now—Sweden has settled into civilized affluence. The standard of living is one of the highest of all Western countries, while politically Sweden is nothing if not stable, though maintaining doggedly her traditional neutrality.

In keeping with their well-deserved reputation for thoroughness, the Swedes have gone out of their way to make life easy for visitors, with a host of good-value hotel, restaurant and travel bargains. And you can be sure that hotels and restaurants, to name but two of the essential elements of any vacation, will operate to a high standard. While for those bent on outdoor activities, you'll find that camping, sporting, hiking, climbing and a whole range of other activities are all available. And in the same, all-important vein, you'll also find that the Swedes are a genuinely courteous and welcoming people, and English—the lingua franca of the modern world—is spoken widely and fluently.

PRACTICAL INFORMATION FOR SWEDEN

WHAT WILL IT COST. Sweden's reputation as an expensive country is by no means entirely justified, even though living standards are very high. As in any coun-

503

try, hotel and restaurant costs in larger cities can be on the high side, but the price of gasoline is among the lowest in Europe, and visitors can take advantage of hotel discount schemes during the summer. Low fares are available on all domestic flights during the summer peak season, and the level of rail fares has been held down in recent years. Many restaurants offer a reduced-price "dish of the day," and all major cities have budget transportation schemes that are often linked to discounted admission charges at visitor attractions. In some areas it will pay you to buy a *länskort,* which entitles you to unlimited travel for one month.

The monetary unit in Sweden is the *Krona* (abbreviated as SEK), which is divided into 100 *öre.* Silver coins come in denominations of 10 and 50 öre, 1 and 5 kronor. Familiarize yourself with the 1- and 5-kronor coins; they are very similar. Paper currency is in denominations of 10, 50, 100, 500, 1,000 and 10,000 kronor.

At the time of writing the exchange rate for the krona is 6.19 to the U.S. dollar, and 9.98 to the pound sterling. These rates are likely to change both before and during 1991.

Sample Costs. A beer will cost from SEK 30 – 40 (there are three different strengths); a cup of coffee about SEK 10–15; and a Coca-Cola 12–15. Museum charges vary from SEK 5 – 15, but in the main cities you can visit most museums free of charge if you buy one of the special discount sightseeing cards. A cinema seat will cost from SEK 45 and a theater seat anything from SEK 50 – 200 depending on whether it is subsidized.

NATIONAL TOURIST OFFICE. *The Swedish Tourist Board* is at Sweden House, Kungsträdgården, Stockholm. There are Swedish National Tourist Offices in New York and London. There are more than 350 local tourist information offices *(Turistbyrå)* in most towns and holiday centers in Sweden. These offices bear the international "i" sign, a guarantee of good service by personnel speaking foreign languages. Some are open only during the summer season. Attached to the tourist office is often a hotel booking service, *Rumsförmedling* or *Hotellcentral,* with a fee of SEK 25–35. Tourist offices have information on places worth seeing, events, suggestions for excursions, where to hire a bicycle, canoe or cottage.

Addresses of the Swedish Tourist Board overseas are:

In the U.S.: 655 Third Ave., New York, N.Y. 10017 (tel. 212–949–2333).

In the U.K.: 29–31 Oxford St., London W1 (tel. 071–437 5816).

WHEN TO COME. Swedes have 5 weeks of annual vacation, and they usually take off from the end of June to the beginning of August. Because there is very little business travel during these months, the hotels in the big cities and towns have plenty of vacancies and prices are low. Schools also have a winter holiday in February or March, when the mountain resorts are quite busy. At other times, especially in the summer, low package rates at these resorts are available.

Summer cottages are usually sold out, but May and August or September are the best months to look for bargains. A four-bed cottage can be had for from SEK 850–1,750.

The climate varies according to latitude, the north being generally colder and drier, with of course the longest skiing season. Much of the country has plenty of snow for 4–5 months; winter is dry and often fairly sunny. Spring arrives as early as March in the south. Summer can be long, with real heat waves in June, July and August. An average June day in Stockholm has 19 hours of daylight. Beyond the Arctic Circle the Midnight Sun reigns: from mid-May to mid-July the sun never sets. The Swedish autumn offers clear, fine days well into October, days that are mild because of all the summer's heat stored in the waters around Sweden.

Average afternoon temperatures in Fahrenheit and centigrade:

Stockholm

	Jan.	Feb.	Mar.	Apr.	May	June	July	Aug.	Sept.	Oct.	Nov.	Dec.
F°	31	31	37	45	57	65	70	66	58	48	38	33
C°	−1	−1	3	7	14	18	21	19	14	9	3	1

SPECIAL EVENTS. In *February* the Great Lapp Winter Fair takes place at Jokkmokk; in *March* there is the Vasa Ski Race, 55 miles cross-country from Sälen to Mora. On *April 30* the Walpurgis Night Festival is celebrated all over Sweden. In *June* there are folklore festivals all over the country to mark the arrival of midsummer. In *July* the Swedish Open tennis championship takes place in Båstad, and in Visby there are the traditional performances of the medieval mystery play *Petrus de Dacia* in the ruined cathedral. In *August* there are the annual celebrations of Sweden-America Day in Skansen Park, Stockholm, and Minnesota Day in Växjö in southern Sweden. On *December 13* St. Lucia Day is celebrated throughout Sweden, and also in this month the Nobel Prize ceremonies (by invitation only) take place in Stockholm.

National Holidays. Jan. 1 (New Year's Day); Mar. 29 (Good Friday); Apr. 1 (Easter Monday); May 1 (Labor Day); May 9 (Ascension Day); May 20 (Pentecost Monday); June 22 (Midsummer's Day); Nov. 2 (All Saints' Day); Dec. 25 (Christmas Day); Dec. 26 (St. Stephen's Day).

VISAS. Not required for British subjects, Canadian or U.S. nationals for stays of up to three months.

HEALTH CERTIFICATE. No vaccination required.

GETTING TO SWEDEN. By Plane. Across the North Atlantic there are direct flights during the summer from New York, Chicago, and Toronto to Stockholm. One-stop flights are available from many U.S. cities via the *Continental Airlines/SAS* hub at New York (Newark). There is also a wide range of services to Copenhagen, from which you can continue to destinations in Sweden by air or rail. Copenhagen is the best gateway if you are heading for southern Sweden, and there is a connecting hovercraft service to Malmö direct from Copenhagen Airport. From London (Heathrow or Gatwick) *British Airways* and *SAS* run up to 14 flights a day between them to Gothenburg, Malmö and Stockholm. BA also runs a scheduled service from Manchester to Stockholm via Copenhagen, while *Air Europe* operates from Gatwick to Stockholm. There are also regular charters from London (Stansted) to Stockholm operated by Star Tour of Scandinavia.

By Boat. There are no direct sailings from North America to Sweden by passenger liners although one or two freighters do carry a limited number (12 maximum) of passengers. These are always booked very far in advance.

From England *Scandinavian Seaways* operates from Harwich to Gothenburg. Sailings vary according to the time of year but there are always at least two round trips weekly, four at peak periods. The crossing takes about 24 hours. There are train connections from London (Liverpool Street Station) to Harwich, as well as train links at the other end from Stockholm and Oslo. Also, there are bus routes from London to Harwich; coaches to and from Stockholm connect at the Gothenburg quayside terminal with all the Harwich sailings. There is also a *Scandinavian Seaways* route from Newcastle upon Tyne to Gothenburg that takes about 23 hours and operates only during the summer (July and August) once weekly. From Denmark there is a shuttle ferry service from Copenhagen to Malmö (plus hydrofoil) and also from Helsingør (north of Copenhagen) to Helsingborg in Sweden.

By Train. The most convenient way to go by train to Sweden from the U.K. is to leave London (Liverpool St. Station) at 9.45 A.M. and travel via Harwich and the day ferry to the Hoek van Holland, arriving there at 7 P.M. with immediate rail connection on the *Nord-West Express* to Copenhagen, arriving at 8.10 the next morning (one hour later in winter). There is an immediate connection by train to Stockholm, arriving there at about 4.50 P.M. during the summer and 6.50 P.M. during the rest of the year. There are also convenient rail connections to Gothenburg and by ferry to Malmö from Copenhagen. Basic rail fare to Stockholm is about £255 roundtrip. Eurotrain for the under 26s from £165 roundtrip.

By Bus. International express services run once-weekly year-round (four in summer) from London to Malmö, Gothenburg and Stockholm by *Eurolines* in conjunction with *GDG Continentbus*. It is routed across the Channel from Dover to Oostende, then through Belgium, the Netherlands and Germany to Travemünde on the Baltic, where you board the ferry to the Swedish port of Trelleborg. Leaving London in the evening you arrive in Stockholm at the same time three days on. One night on the ferry and two on the bus. Roundtrip fare to Stockholm is about £145.

CUSTOMS European residents may bring in 200 cigarettes (or equivalent), 1 liter spirits, 1 liter wine (2 liters if no spirits brought in) and 2 liters beer. Non-European residents may bring in 400 cigarettes, and the liquor allowance is the same as for Europeans. Both may bring in a reasonable amount of perfume and gifts to the value of SEK 600. Only people of 20 years or older may import alcohol, and no one may import alcoholic beverages of over 60% (120° proof). There are now no limits on the amount of Swedish or foreign currency that can be imported or exported.

HOTELS. Budget travelers are recommended to take advantage of one of the money-saving hotel schemes described below.

The hotels we list are graded as Moderate (M) or Inexpensive (I). A single room in an (M) category hotel will cost from SEK 400–600 and in an (I) category hotel from SEK 250–450. Expect to pay SEK 725 for an (M) double room and SEK 650 for an (I) double room. The classification is based on minimum prices in the hotels. An (I) indicates that a hotel contains some rooms in (I) category, but is almost certain to contain more expensive rooms as well.

Many hotels offer discounted rates during the summer and some chains offer special deals that can be booked through travel agencies in advance. The SARA group, for example, offers the Scandinavian BonusPass, which costs about $25 and entitles the holder to discounts ranging between 15% and 40% from June 1 through August 31. The Scandic Hotel check scheme enables you to pay for your accommodations in advance, valid every weekend from January through mid-May and from early September to the year-end, and every day between mid-May and early September. The 1990 price was $29–$35 per person per night, including breakfast, but supplements are payable at some city-center hotels.

The Sweden Hotels group, Kammakargatan 48, S-111 60 Stockholm, has introduced a Hotel Pass program that offers 50% discounts on normal room rates at more than 100 hotels throughout Sweden between mid-May and mid-September. The Pass costs SEK 170 and is valid for an unlimited number of nights.

Most city hotels have special weekend rates during the winter months and lower rates throughout the week during the summer.

Youth Hostels. 280 comfortable hostels known as *vandrarhem* are operated by the Swedish Touring Club (STF). Almost all have 4 to 6 bed family rooms. Eighty of them have running hot and cold water in the rooms. Most are self service. Some offer full meal service. Linen may be rented. These hostels are open to anyone irrespective of age. Prices are about SEK 60 a night for members of STF or national youth hostel organizations affiliated with the International Youth Hostel Federation. For non-members there is an extra charge of SEK 25 a night. A youth hostel handbook is published annually by STF and by IYHF. Advance booking is recommended at hostels during the summer.

Holders of ISI cards are entitled to discounts or free admission to some museums, theaters (not movies), student hotels and some student restaurants.

Camping. There are about 750 camping sites all over the country. They are usually open from June 1 to September 1. Some are open all year round. The authorized sign for a campsite is a white C with a black tent silhouetted on a green ground. There are three classifications. All have satisfactory sanitation arrangements. Charges vary from SEK 35–100 per car and tent or caravan. Many sites have lower charges for cyclists and hikers.

An international camping carnet is often required, or you buy a Swedish camping card at the first site you visit. The charge is SEK 22. Some camp sites have 2 or 4 bed bungalows at SEK 100–250 per night. Most camping sites can be reached by bus or train.

An abbreviated list of camp sites is published annually with explanatory text in English. Ask for it at any Swedish tourist office.

Farm Vacations. Many farms throughout Sweden offer accommodations, either in the main farmhouse or in an adjoining cottage. Accommodations are usually on a bed-and-breakfast basis, with self-catering facilities for cooking other meals. Typical price is SEK 85–175 per person per day. A list of farm accommodations is available from Land-Resor, Vasagatan 12, 105 33 Stockholm.

RESTAURANTS. Many restaurants offer a special dish of the day (*dagens rätt* in Swedish) which costs about SEK 45 and usually includes a main dish, salad, light beer or milk, bread and butter, and coffee. The 13% service charge is included in menu prices in Sweden.

In our grading system restaurants in which you can buy a meal for SEK 200 or less for one are Moderate (M), and those where you can buy a meal for SEK 120 or less are Inexpensive (I). These prices are without drinks.

All sorts of fast food restaurants have established themselves lately, as have restaurants serving foreign food (Chinese, Japanese, Greek). Salad bars are a novelty. BAR on a sign means a place to eat with self service but no alcoholic drinks. Alcoholic beverages are expensive and are available only at *Systembolaget,* the government-run liquor stores. These stores are closed on Saturdays and Sundays. The minimum age limit for buying alcoholic beverages is 20 years.

Food and Drink. The Scandinavian cold table, in Sweden called *smörgåsbord,* is often abused in spelling, in pronunciation and in preparation. To enjoy it you have to eat the dishes in the traditional order—that is, you start with the herring and other fish dishes. Then you attack the cold meat, pâté, smoked reindeer. Try some of the hot dishes and finish with cheese or fruit salad. A slightly less lavish cold table is provided at breakfast time in all Swedish hotels and is often included in the room price. Do justice to a Swedish breakfast and you'll probably find that you can save money by skipping lunch!

Beer comes in a variety of light and dark qualities and in three strengths, Class I being the weakest and Class III the strongest. Export beer is expensive. Iced water may be charged for in some restaurants.

TIPPING. In hotels, restaurants and bars the service charge is included in the price, and no additional tip is considered necessary. It is usual to round off a restaurant bill to the nearest krona or 5 kronor depending on the amount of the bill. There is no need to leave any tips on the table in coffee shops or self-service bars. Wine stewards are not tipped.

Bellhops, baggage porters and chambermaids can be given SEK 3–5 for special services. Some hotels add the baggage service on the bill. If you always ask the porter to add his services to the bill, then you will not have to pay twice. Many hotels do not have porters. Ask the reception clerk for help.

Doormen who call taxis expect SEK 5. Hall porters should be given SEK 10–15 for special help. Cloakroom attendants should get SEK 8 per coat.

The only obligatory tip is 10% on taxi fares. The drivers pay tax on the tip whether they get it or not.

MAIL. Airmail letters and postcards to the United States and Canada weighing less than 20 grams cost SEK 3.90. Postcards and letters within Europe cost SEK 3.30. For philatelists there is a special shop opposite the main post office at Vasagatan 28, Stockholm.

CLOSING TIMES. Shops usually open 9–6 Mon. through Fri. On Sat. and the day before a holiday, closing time varies between 1 and 4. Department stores and many other shops in the larger cities stay open until 8 or 10 one evening in the week (usually Mon. or Fri.), but not in June or July, and some stores open on Sun. Banks are open 9.30–3 Mon.–Fri.; many also open in the evening between 4.30 and 6. In many larger cities the banks are open for business from 9.30 to 5.30. The bank at Stockholm's Arlanda International Airport is open daily from 7 A.M. through 10 P.M. There is also a bank at Gothenburg's Landvetter Airport, which is open daily from 8 A.M. to 8 P.M.

GETTING AROUND SWEDEN. By Plane. Sweden has an efficient domestic air network, operated mostly by SAS and Linjeflyg. Fares are discounted for offpeak travel year-round, and during peak tourist season (end-June to mid-August) these fares are valid on all flights. There are also reduced-rate family fares; if one adult pays full fare, an accompanying spouse and children qualify for big reductions, but all must travel together. Young people under 26 can use a standby fare that is set at a flat-rate SEK 150 or SEK 200 according to distance. Special bookable one-way fares for senior citizens of 65 or over cost SEK 200 or 300, depending on distance. There are usually special offers on domestic fares between the end of June and early August, so it is worth checking nearer the date of travel.

By Train. Rail travel in Sweden is comfortable, clean, and reliable, with excellent express services linking main cities. Most trains have both 1st and 2nd class; the latter is extremely good. Dining or self-service cars are carried on all long-distance trains. These are fairly expensive, but snacks are available at all main stations. Non-smoking is strictly observed in designated carriages and dining cars. R in timetables means that reservations are required.

On certain trains now listed as "Low price" or "Red" departures, fares are reduced by 50%, so careful planning is needed to take advantage of the lower price. Passengers traveling on the low fares cannot make any stopovers. There is a flat-rate maximum fare for all journeys of 550 miles (881 kilometers) or more. You can also buy a go-as-you-please ticket on the scenic *Inlandsbanan* (Inland Railway) line, which runs for more than 800 miles down the backbone of Sweden. A special card costing about SEK 450 gives you unrestricted travel over the line for 14 days as well as discounts on overnight accommodations, restaurant meals and sightseeing. Cards valid for 21 days are also available. Sweden is a partner in the Nordic Railpass scheme, which gives 21 days' unlimited travel within Sweden, Norway, Denmark and Finland and costs about SEK 1,355 for second class travel.

By Bus. Swedish Railways (SJ), Linjebuss and GDG operate a network of bus services all over Sweden. In addition to this regular traffic, there is a summer service of express coaches over longer distances. Some companies also operate special weekend-only services at bargain prices.

By Bicycle. With its uncrowded roads, Sweden is ideal for a cycling holiday, and cycles can be hired easily in most places if you inquire at the local tourist office. Typical hire costs are about SEK 50 per day or SEK 200 per week. The Swedish Touring Club (STF), Box 25, S-101 20 Stockholm, can give you information about cycling packages that include overnight accommodations, meals and cycle hire. Other useful sources of information on cycling holidays are *Cykelfrämjandet,* Box 6027, 102 31 Stockholm and *Svenska Cykelsällskapet,* Box 6006, 164 06 Kista. Enclose an international stamp coupon for airmail delivery.

Stockholm

Stockholm was founded in the 13th century but its growth is a relatively recent phenomenon. The summer beauty of the city, its islands and waterways, and the extensive parks make it a real Viking Venice.

Stockholm has a reputation for being high-priced, but this is only partially deserved. Cheap goods, accommodations and eatables are hard to find; however, those in the moderate-priced category have a uniformly high standard of value.

The Swedes are accomplished promotionalists and know how to combine their sophistication with their rural origins. The result is a city in the idiom of the North, with splendid atmosphere, which still retains its naiveté. Water is everywhere. Combined with this seaside grandeur is an animated social life.

Since Stockholm nimbly jumps from island to island, it has been called the Venice of the North, but so has every other northern city with a bed of water. But Stockholm is far more than a Venice lookalike; it's a city of unique character and beauty that has been guarded by the civic leaders since the 13th century.

Wherever you walk, you'll find parks and tree-lined squares and major boulevards, playgrounds, wading pools, and other fine urban features. The building codes are extremely strict. There is even a municipal "Beauty Council" that passes on the aesthetic qualifications of proposed buildings.

Stockholm's island geography may pose some communications problems, but for the tourist with a map, it has the advantage of dividing the city into neat parcels for exploration. First, there's the city between the bridges, Gamla Stan (Old Town), site of the Kungliga Slottet (Royal Palace), and its adjoining islands, Riddarholmen (Isle of Knights) and Helgeandsholmen (Island of the Holy Spirit). This section is essentially the heart of the capital and the nation. Södermalm is the southern section, across the bridge leading from the Old Town. Norrmalm, north of the Old Town, is the business and financial district of Stockholm; Kungsholmen, a large island west of Norrmalm, is the site of the famous Stadshuset (City Hall). Östermalm, east of Norrmalm, is mostly residential. Finally, there is Djurgården, a huge island, projecting east toward the Baltic. Here is the marvelous park of Skansen, the open-air museum, the Royal Flagship *Vasa* in her museum, and amusement parks and summer restaurants.

Here are the most interesting sights: The Royal Palace, built between 1700 and 1754 by royal architect Nicodemus Tessin and his son, N.T. the Younger, to replace the original palace, which burned down in 1697. The place is huge, and like so many royal properties in the democratic monarchies of Scandinavia, easy of public access; you can stroll into the inner courtyard any time during the day. Interior parts that may be visited are the Hall of State, containing the king's silver throne; the Chapel Royal, with its historic and artistic treasures; the Festival and Bernadotte suites; and Gustav III's collection of classical sculpture. See also the palace museum with its relics of the former palace. The changing of the guard takes place year-round on Wednesday at noon and on Sunday at 1 P.M. and also at noon on Saturday from January through August. The ceremony takes place daily from June through August, usually at noon.

Before leaving the Old Town, pay a visit to the Stortoget, the oldest square in Stockholm, with its tall old houses and the Börsen (Stock Exchange), containing on its second floor the headquarters of the Swedish Academy, which awards the Nobel Prize for literature. And don't miss the Mårten Trotzigs Gränd, one of the narrowest city thoroughfares in the world. It connects the Prästgatan with Västerlånggatan—the latter a shopping street for over 200 years.

Visit also the Cathedral (Storkyrkan) with the wooden sculpture "St. George and the Dragon." During summer months there is a sound and light performance certain days during the week.

One of the city's great attractions is Skansen, Stockholm's unique outdoor playground. To say that it has a museum, a zoo, is merely to give a dull enumeration of its facilities. To say that it is the scene of concerts, and folk dancing, is merely to suggest its enduring liveliness. It's full of open-air dance floors, coffee shops and workshops (handicrafts are demonstrated in the old buildings).

Stockholm is situated on 14 islands. It is the center of the resort area with Lake Mälaren to the west and over 20,000 islands in the Baltic. The famous white boats operated by the Waxholmsbolaget company run an intricate network of routes from downtown Stockholm to the islands and places like the tiny town of Vaxholm with its 16th-century fortress. The Inter-Skerries Card (Båtluffarkortet), costing SEK 140 and available from early June through mid-August, gives 16 days' unlimited travel on the Waxholmsbolaget boats.

PRACTICAL INFORMATION FOR STOCKHOLM

GETTING INTO TOWN FROM THE AIRPORT. There is a bus every 10–15 minutes from Arlanda International Airport, about 26 miles from the center of town and much too far for a taxi. The fare is SEK 35. Buses run to the City Terminal at Klarabergsviadukten above the Central Train Station. A taxi from the airport costs at least SEK 350, but a limousine service to any point in Greater Stockholm run by SAS operates on a shared-taxi basis and costs from SEK 185. For two or three people traveling together in a limousine to the same address one pays the full rate and the others half-price.

HOTELS. It is advisable to reserve rooms well in advance. If you arrive in Stockholm without a reservation, consult the Hotellcentralen in the Central Station. A charge is made for each room reserved. Compass Booking (tel. 667 08 60) operates a free 24-hour hotel booking service. Even the lower-priced hotels are usually spick and span in every respect. Basic hotel rates can be expensive, but a number of bargains are available during the summer when business travelers are on holiday.

The various hotel discount schemes will reduce the cost of accommodations. 46 hotels offer the "Stockholm Package," with accommodations for one night for SEK 260–520 including breakfast, plus the Key to Stockholm card, which gives free transportation within the city, free entrance to museums and discounts on sightseeing. The package is available daily from June 20 through August 19 and weekends year-round. For details write to Stockholm Information Service, Excursion Shop, Box 7542, S–103 93 Stockholm, or telephone The Hotel Center (tel. 08–24 08 80). The Stockholm Package is also bookable through appointed travel agents.

If you are all out to save money you might try a youth hostel or student hotel: some of them are included in our hotel list.

Moderate

Adlon, Vasagatan 42, S-111 20 Stockholm (tel. 24 54 00). 62 rooms.

Anno 1647, Mariagränd 3, S–116 46 Stockholm (tel. 44 04 80). 42 rooms.

Kom, Döbelnsgatan 17, S–111 40 Stockholm(tel. 23 56 30). 91 rooms. Central. Kitchenette with fridge in all rooms; breakfast only. Near subway.

Stockholm, Norrmalmstorg 1, S-111 46 Stockholm (tel. 22 13 20). 92 rooms. Central location. Breakfast only.

Inexpensive

af Chapman, youth hostel on a ship facing the Royal Palace. 130 beds. For bookings write STF, Box 25, S-101 20 Stockholm (tel. 10 37 15). Close by is the new youth hostel **Skeppsholmen** (tel. 20 25 06). With 150 beds. Stays are limited to five nights.

Gustav af Klint, Stadsgårdkajen 153 (tel. 40 40 77). 28 cabins, none with bath. A "hotel ship" moored at Stadsgården quay with hostel-type accommodation and sauna. Near subway.

Hotel Jerum, Studentbacken 21, S-114 89 Stockholm (tel. 63 53 80). 120 rooms. Youth hotel. Open June-Aug. Restaurant. Subway to city.

Långholmen, Gamla Kronohäktet, S–102 72 Stockholm (tel. 668 05 00). 101 rooms. Former prison on the island of Långholmen, built in 1724 and converted into a combined hotel and hostel in 1989.

Mälaren River Boat, Söder Mälarstrand 6, S-117 20 Stockholm (tel. 44 43 85). 28 beds. An old ship converted into a youth hostel and restaurant.

RESTAURANTS. Because prices are high in Stockholm, inexpensive dining will often require that you resort to cafeterias or chain restaurants. But many restaurants offer a SEK 45 lunch, usually consisting of bread and butter, salad, a hot dish, milk or low alcohol beer, coffee and service. At inexpensive restaurants the tab should be about SEK 60 per person, not including drinks. Many restaurants have a "happy hour" between 4 P.M. and 7 P.M., when prices are reduced.

Moderate

Bakfickan, in the Opera House (tel. 24 27 00). Shares facilities with the famous Operakällaren but less expensive.

BZ. Berzelii Park (tel. 24 06 20). Famous dance restaurant.

Glada Laxen, in the Gallerian shopping arcade off Hamngatan (tel. 21 12 90). Central location, popular and crowded at lunchtime. Seafood specialties.

Goldolen, hanging under the gangway of the Katarina elevator at Slussen (tel. 40 20 21). View of the harbor.

Matpalatset, Hamngatan 15 (tel. 20 91 95). Choice of Mexican, Italian, and Swedish food from five different self-service counters.

Mejan Restaurant, Fredsgatan 9, in the Academy of Art building (tel. 20 23 00). Arty atmosphere.

Vau de Ville, Hamngatan 17 (tel. 21 25 22). Chosen as Stockholm's 1986 "Restaurant of the Year." Good food at reasonable prices.

Inexpensive

Central Station Restaurant. This is the place for a big American-type breakfast with a Swedish accent. Get there before 10 A.M.

Örtagården, Nybrogatan 31, above Östermalmshallen market. Generous vegetarian buffet in turn-of-the-century atmosphere.

Teahouse, under the elms in Kungsträdgården. Summer only. Sandwiches.

It's worth trying the cafeterias at large department stores like Åhléns or PUB. There are also popular cafeterias in the Hötorgshallen and Östermalmshallen market places, several specializing in delicious seafood.

GETTING AROUND STOCKHOLM. By Subway/Bus. There is a good subway (T-banan) and many bus routes. The transport area is divided into zones. Tickets may be bought as coupons from ticket counters or from drivers. Children and pensioners travel at half fare. It is cheaper to buy a special discount coupon at *Pressbyrån* newsstands, which gives a significant saving compared with buying separate tickets each time you travel. A journey within one zone costs two coupons. Two children under 7 accompanied by a paying passenger may travel free.

Tourist tickets giving unlimited travel on subway and bus services are also available. A ticket covering the city center area only costs SEK 22 for 24 hours, but a better bargain is probably the ticket that takes in the whole of the Greater Stockholm area and costs SEK 40 for 24 hours or SEK 76 for 72 hours.

The best bet is to buy a Key to Stockholm card *(Stockholmskortet).* As well as giving free transportation throughout Greater Stockholm, it offers free admission to 50 museums in the city plus free sightseeing trips. Cards can be bought at SEK 190 for two days or SEK 285 for three days from a number of outlets, including the Tourist Center at Sweden House and the *Hotellcentralen* accommodations bureau at the central railroad station.

By Taxi. Call 15 00 00 if you want a taxi immediately, or 15 04 00 for advance bookings. The sign "Ledig" shows that a taxi is available for hire. Taxis are expensive and at times unobtainable. Fares are higher at night.

By Bicycle. Bicycles can be hired at Skepp o Hoj, Djurgården Bridge (tel. 60 57 57), open from April through September.

ENTERTAINMENT. A very handy publication is *Stockholm This Week,* which you can get from most hotels and all tourist centers. A pocket-sized, 200-page booklet with maps, *Discover Stockholm,* is available at the Tourist Center at Sweden House, and gives a lot of useful information on excursions and sightseeing attractions. Information in English on current attractions can be obtained on an automatic telephone answering service (22 18 40).

Cinema. English and American movies are often shown at the same time as they are released in London or New York. Foreign films in cinemas and on TV are usually shown in the original language with Swedish subtitles.

Discos. Discos and nightclubs change names, ownership and addresses frequently. Check beforehand. Many restaurants have dancing on some week nights. There are no real bargains. An entrance fee is usually charged, and a minimum age limit is imposed at a number of night-spots.

Café Opera at the Opera House, the "in" place for Stockholmers. No entrance fee until just before midnight, when the disco starts.

Karlsson, Kungsgatan 65. Everything from reggae to disco.

Stampen, Gråmunkegränd 7. Popular club among young people.

There are pianobars at the hotels *Sheraton, Amaranten, Reisen, Continental,* and *Malmen.* The *SAS Royal Viking Hotel* has a SkyJazz bar on the ninth floor, with live performances every evening.

Theaters and Concerts. Stockholm offers visitors a variegated theater and musical life. Its two centers are the *Royal Opera House* and the *Stockholm Concert House* at Hötorget with the Orpheus fountain by Carl Milles. The Royal Opera is located just across the bridge from the Royal Palace. The season runs from mid-August until about June 11. Ballet Festival, first week of June.

The concert season lasts from about the middle of September to about the middle of May. The Stockholm Concert Association Orchestra plays regularly at the Concert House and is fully up to international standards.

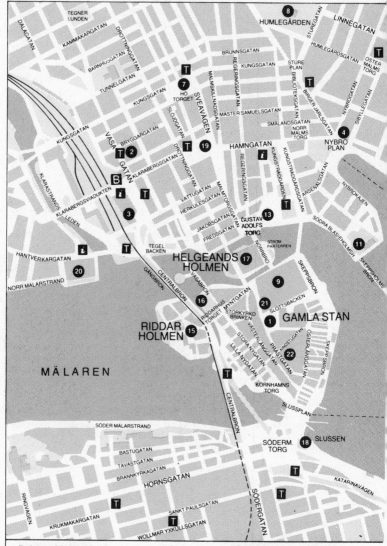

Points of Interest

1 Börsen (Stock Exchange)
2 Centralpostkontoret
  (Central Post Office)
3 Central Rail Station
4 Dramatiska Teatern
  (Royal Dramatic Theater)
5 Historiska Museet (Museum of
  National Antiquities)

6 Kaknästornet (Kaknäs Tower)
7 Konserthuset (Concert Hall)
8 Kungliga Biblioteket
  Royal Library)
9 Kungliga Slottet (Royal Palace);
  Livrustkammaren (Royal Armory)
10 Moderna Museet (Museum of
   Modern Art)
11 Nationalmuseet
   (National Museum)

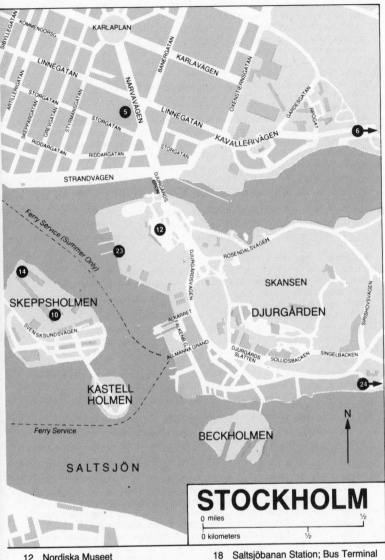

STOCKHOLM

0 miles   ½

0 kilometers   ½

12 Nordiska Museet
    (Nordic Museum)
13 Operan (Royal Opera House)
14 Östasiatiska Museet (Museum of
    Far Eastern Antiquities)
15 Riddarholmskyrkan
    (Riddarholm Church)
16 Riddarhuset (House of Nobility);
    Supreme Court
17 Riksdag (Parliament)

18 Saltsjöbanan Station; Bus Terminal
19 Sergels Torg
20 Stadshuset (Town Hall)
21 Storkyrkan (Cathedral)
22 Tyska Kyrkan (German Church)
23 Vasavarvet (Vasa Museum)
24 Waldemarsudde
T Subway Stations
i Tourist Information Offices

Several theaters specialize in light opera—playing classics and modern musicals. It's great fun hearing and seeing a familiar perennial in a strange theater and a strange language. Season: September to mid-June.

The *Royal Dramatic Theater*—birthplace of the careers of Greta Garbo, Ingrid Bergman—has four seperate stages. Season: mid-Aug. to mid-Jun.

Particularly recommended is the *Court Theater* of Drottningholm Palace. Unsold tickets are sold off one hour before each performance. Another historic theater is *Confidencen* in Ulriksdal Castle Park. Season: mid-May to early Sept.

Folkan, Östermalmstorg, has light entertainment in Broadway style.

Folkoperan, Hornsgatan 72, specializes in classical productions by talented amateur performers.

At a kiosk on Norrmalmstorg unsold tickets to theater productions, concerts, etc. are sold daily at reduced prices. Supper tickets are also available.

Every day during the summer concerts and other kinds of entertainment are held in the open air at *Skansen;* displays of folk dancing and folk music; chamber music recitals in period costume; children's theater every Sat. and Sun.

Between June 15 and end of August, the Stockholm City Council arranges free concerts in the city's many parks. In *Kungsträdgården* (Royal Garden) there are daily gramophone concerts and, three evenings a week at least, free entertainment on the outdoor stage, often featuring leading artists.

The *Gröna Lund* amusement park on Djurgården (bus 47 or ferry from Slussen or Nybroplan) is open from late Apr. to early Sept. Daily open-air performances.

MUSEUMS. The visitor to Stockholm has a choice of museums and places of interest. Entrance fees vary from SEK 5–15, but admission is free at most museums to holders of the Key to Stockholm card. Some museums are closed Mon., so check with the tourist office. Many have a cafeteria.

Drottningholm Palace, on island in Lake Mälaren. The royal residence, a magnificent 17th-century French-style building. Also Theater Museum and China Palace. Fountains play daily 1–6 P.M. The Court Theater is an 18th-century theater that was somehow lost sight of but reopened 50 years ago. The repertoire consists almost entirely of operas and ballets contemporary with it. Performances are held May to September, two to four times a week. Tickets are difficult to obtain.

T-banan to Brommaplan, change to Mälaröarna buses (any line). In summer on weekdays a boat goes from the City Hall Bridge (Stadshusbron).

Guided tours of all buildings every hour, May–Aug. 11–4.30, Sept. 1–3.30 (12–3.30 at weekends).

Etnografiska Museet (Ethnographical Museum), Djurgårdsbrunnsvägen 34, near the Kaknäs Tower. Open 11–5, Tues.–Fri.; 12–4 Sat. and Sun.

Gustav III's Pavilion, Haga Park near Brunnsviken. Bus 515 to Haga (short walk through park). June–Aug. daily except Mon. 12–4; Sept., Sat. and Sun. 1–4.

Hallwyl Museum, Hamngatan 4. A palatial residence from around 1900. Open daily June–Aug. 11–4; Sept.–May daily except Mon. 12–3. (12–4 on weekends). During summer there are musical entertainments in the evenings.

Historiska Museet, Museum of National Antiquities, Narvavägen 13–17. Collections from prehistoric times and the Middle Ages. Open daily 11–4; closed Mon.

Kaknästornet, the Kaknäs Tower, Djurgården. Restaurant and cafeteria. 155 meters high (500 ft.). Mainly built for TV broadcasting. Fine panoramic view. Daily 9–midnight May–Aug.; closes earlier other months.

Kulturhuset, the House of Culture at Sergelstorg with exhibitions on every floor. Usually free. The *Panorama* restaurant on the top floor serves lunch and has a fine view of the Sergels torg. Open year-round Mon., Wed., and Thurs. 11–8; Tues. 11–10; Fri.–Sun. 11–6.

Leksaksmuseet, the Toy Museum, Mariatorget 1 C. One of the largest toy museums in Europe. Open Tues.–Fri. 10–4, Sat. and Sun. 12–4.

Millesgården, Lidingö. Former residence of famous Swedish-American sculptor Carl Milles. Many of his works are exhibited. Apr.–Sept. 10–5 daily; Jan.–Mar. and Oct.–Dec. 11–3 daily. (11–4 on weekends).

Moderna Museet, Museum of Modern Art on Skeppsholmen island. Collections of 20th century sculpture and paintings, one of the most interesting and progressive in the world. Open Tues.–Fri. 11–9, Sat. and Sun. 11–5, closed Mon.

Nationalmuseum, National Museum, near Grand Hotel. Swedish State collections of paintings, sculptures, etc. by Swedish and foreign artists. Temporary exhibitions all year. Open daily except Mon. year-round, Tues. 10–9, other days 10–4.

Nordiska Museet, Nordic Museum, Djurgården. Large and varied collections of objects showing the progress of civilization in Sweden from the 16th century onwards. Open June–Aug., Mon.–Fri. 10–4 open until 8 on Tues.); Sat. and Sun. 12–5.; Jan.–May, Mon.–Thurs. 10–4; Sat. and Sun. 12–5.

Sjöhistoriska Museet, Maritime Museum, Djurgårdsbrunnsvägen near Kaknästornet. Ship models, shipbuilding, etc. Daily 10–5.

Skansen, Djurgården. Opened in 1891, this is the world's oldest open-air museum. Situated on a hill with an excellent view of the city. 150 buildings representing different times. Demonstrations of crafts such as glass blowing, baking, printing, weaving. Zoo with typically Swedish animals: bear, moose, reindeer. Lill-Skansen is a section for children, with small animals. Concerts, folklore, dancing during summer months. Buses 44 and 47, ferry from Slussen, in summer also from Nybroplan. May–Aug., 9 A.M.–10 P.M.; Sept.–Apr., 9–5.

Skattkammaren, the Treasury at the Royal Palace. With 12 royal crowns and other treasures, this is one of the finest collections of regalia in Europe. Open daily 10–4 (Sun. 12–4) May–Sept. Reduced schedule rest of year.

Slottet, the Royal Palace. The State, Guest and Bernadotte apartments are open to the public. Changing of the guard daily at noon (Sun. at 1 P.M.) Jun.–Aug.; on Wed., Sat., and Sun. Jan.–May; Wed. and Sun. Sept.–Dec.

Stadshuset, City Hall. Monumental building completed in 1923. The tower with a wonderful view is open daily 10–3 in summer. The lift goes half way, then there are stairs. Guided tours of City Hall daily at 10; Sat. and Sun. also at 12.

Tekniska Museet, Technical Museum, near Kaknästornet. Collections illustrate the development of technical engineering and industry. Open Mon.-Fri. 10–4, Sat. and Sun. 12–4.

Vasa Museum, Djurgården. This Swedish man-of-war sank in 1628 on her maiden voyage and was raised in 1961. The site where she was on show for many years was closed in 1988 and Vasa is now housed in a new museum. Open mid-June–mid-Aug., daily 9.30–7; mid-August–June, daily 10–5.

SHOPPING. The Swedes have a tradition of handicraft that has survived the present day mechanization of most industries. Jewelry and silver, pewter and stainless steel, glass and ceramics, as well as leather, fabrics, etc. are all good buys in this category.

Along with good workmanship, Sweden is a center for modern industrial design. *Orrefors* and *Kosta* are world-famous for glass tableware, *Svenskt Glas* (Birger Jarlsgatan 8) has a good display and can handle all the details of shipping to your home. Prices, including shipping, insurance, and customs, are about half those in the U.S. A good center for handcrafts, including leather, textiles, and ceramics, is *Stockholms Läns Hemslöjdsförening* (Drottninggatan 14). *Svensk Hemslöjd* (Sveavägen 44) displays the handcrafts of famous artisans and you can see a permanent exhibition of some of Sweden's finest products at the *Form Design Center* there. After that drop by at one of the big department stores such as *Nordiska Kompaniet* (N.K.), one of the world's shopping meccas. Other department stores worth visiting are Åhléns on Klarabergsgatan and PUB on Hötorget.

Tax-free shopping is offered in more than 1,000 shops in Stockholm and at more than 13,000 locations throughout Sweden. Ask for a special receipt for goods to be taken out of the country. At the repayment office at airports or ports you will receive cash in hand, even if you used a credit card originally. A certain percentage is deducted for the service. As the tax is 23% you should take advantage of this service; shops usually require that you buy at least SEK 200 worth of goods to qualify for the reductions. The tax-free service is available only to non-Scandinavian residents.

The newest shopping area is *Sturegallerian,* an undercover area built on the site of the former public baths at Stureplan. There are about 50 shops, plus restaurants and cafés. For food go to *Hötorghallen* and opposite it, *Kungshallen.* Another indoor shopping mall is *Gallerian* at Hamngatan. There is a flea market at Skärholmen open Sat. and Sun., and the biggest shopping mall in Stockholm.

USEFUL ADDRESSES. *U.S. Embassy,* Strandvägen 101 (tel. 783 53 00); *Canadian Embassy,* Tegelbacken 4 (tel. 23 79 20); *British Embassy,* Skarpögatan 6 (tel. 667 01 40); *American Express,* Birger Jarlsgatan 1 (tel. 23 53 30); *Thomas Cook,* Bryggargatan 12A (tel. 762 58 20); *Wagons Lits,* Vasagatan 22 (tel. 762 58 27); *Swedish Tourist Board* and *Stockholm Information Service,* both at Sweden House, Kungsträdgården (tel. 789 20 00); *Swedish Touring Club,* Drottninggatan 33 (tel. 790 31 00).

International Youth Center, Valhallavägen 142, summer only (tel. 664 61 62).

The Regions

Gotland Island in the Baltic is reached by a 40-minute trip by air from Stockholm, or by ferry from Västervik, Nynäshamn, and Oskarshamn. This is a prime holiday area for the Swedes. Many packages are available: the most popular are cycle tours. Here you find the town of Visby with its medieval walls and church ruins. There are many folklore events, the main one being the annual performance of "Petrus de Dacia," a medieval mystery play.

In Dalarna province folklore and tradition mingle. This is a beautiful area with tourism flourishing around Lake Siljan. Music is high on the list of summer events, which include the Rättviksdansen, the play "The Road to Heaven" in Leksand, and "Music around Siljan." The most traditional events are the church boat races, rowing competitions in long boats.

One of the largest lakes in Europe is Lake Vänern. North of the lake is the province of Värmland, a wild and beautiful place. It was here that Selma Lagerlöf, the Nobel Prizewinner, wrote many sagas. On the southern shore of Lake Vänern is Lidköping. Visit the Rörstrand porcelain factory, where there is a permanent exhibition, a shop, and a tour of the factory on weekdays. Close by is Läckö Castle, where cultural exhibitions are held every summer.

Gothenburg is the second largest city in Sweden and the largest seaport. At Liseberg, the largest amusement park in Scandinavia, there are concerts and entertainments in summer. North of Gothenburg you will find at Tanum rock carvings that are 3,000 years old. Visit the fortresses at Varberg and its museum, or Elfsborg at the entrance to Gothenburg harbor. See the locks at Trolhättan, along the Göta Canal, the waterway linking Stockholm with Gothenburg. If you do not have enough time or money for the three-day cruise on the Canal, do not miss a day trip from Töreboda to Karlsborg or vice versa.

On the East Coast is Kalmar and its castle, and beyond is the island of Öland, connected to the mainland by the longest bridge in Europe. Öland is popular for its beaches, flowers, and the Viking village of Eketorp. On Öland there are 16 old fortresses and 34 churches. At the southern end is the Långe Jan (Long John) lighthouse at Ottenby. 197 steps will take you to the top and a wonderful view.

Further south to the west is Skåne with the city of Malmö. The countryside is dotted with 240 fortresses and manor houses. In Kåseberga are the Ales stones, a pile of 57 rocks in the shape of a ship.

The Swedish highlands range from central Sweden to beyond the Arctic circle for a distance of 500 miles. Jämtland is skiing and hiking country. There are well marked trails in winter and summer. There are plenty of good, reasonable mountain resorts, all served by the railway going from Östersund.

PRACTICAL INFORMATION FOR THE REGIONS

Hotels and Restaurants

Borås. *Hotel City* (M), Allégatan 32, S-502 32 Borås (tel. 033–11 75 10). 48 rooms. Near rail station.

Borgholm. *Halltorps Gästgiveri* (M), S-387 00 Borgholm (tel. 0485–850 00). 10 rooms. Attractive old house on the island of Öland.

Gothenburg. *Hotel Carl Johan* (M), Karl Johansgatan 66–70, S-414 55 Gothenburg (tel. 031–42 00 20). 150 rooms. *Royal* (M), Drottninggatan 67 (tel. 031–80 61 00). 80 rooms. Central. Breakfast only.
Restaurants. *Gamle Port,* Östra Larmgatan 18 (tel. 031–11 07 02). Near the tourist office. Swedish cooking. *Räkan,* Lorensbergsgatan 16 (tel. 031–16 98 99). Steer your order to the table in radio-controlled fishing boats!

Gränna. *Hotel Gyllene Uttern* (M), S-563 30 Gränna (tel. 0390–108 00). 53 rooms.

Grythyttan. *Grythyttans Gästgivaregård* (M), S-710 60 Grythyttan (tel. 0591–147 00). 74 rooms. 17th century posting inn.

Kalmar. *Hotel Villa Ängö* (I), Baggensgatan 20, S-392 30 (tel. 0480–854 15). 9 rooms.
Restaurant. *Costas Krog,* Larmgatan 6 (tel. 0480–115 70). Centrally located.

Karlskrona. *Hotel Siesta* (I), Borgmästaregatan 5, S-371 31 Karlskrona (tel. 0455–801 80). 25 rooms.

Karlstad. *Grand Hotel* (I), Västra Torggatan 8, S-652 25 (tel. 054–11 52 40). 70 rooms.
Restaurant. *Tiffany's,* V. Torggatan 19 (tel. 054–15 33 83). Local fish and game specialties.

Kiruna. *Hotel Kebne* (M), Konduktörsgatan 7, S-98 134 (tel. 0980–123 80). 54 rooms.

Lidköping. *Stadshotellet* (M), Gamla Stadens Torg 1, S-531 02 Lidköping (tel. 0510–220–85). 71 rooms.

Malmö. *Hotel Baltzar* (M), Södergatan 20, S-211 34 Malmö (tel. 040–720 05). 41 rooms.

Rättvik. *Motell Rättvikshästen* (I), Nyåkersvägen, S–795 00 Rättvik (tel. 0248–110 15). 40 rooms.

Söderköping. *Brunn* (M), Box 44, S-614 00 Söderköping (tel. 0121–109 00). 108 rooms. Spa hotel on the Göta Canal.

Svartå. *Svartå Herrgård* (M), S-710 11 Svartå (tel. 0585–500 03). 40 rooms.

Tällberg. *Åkerblads Hotel Gästgiveri* (M), S-793 03 Tällberg (tel. 0247–508 00). 64 rooms.

Tanumshede. *Tanums Gestgifveri* (I), S-457 00 Tanumshede, (tel. 0525–290 10). 29 rooms.

Trollhättan. *Hotel Carliz* (I), Garvaregatan 18, S-461 00 (tel. 0520–111 39). 11 rooms.

Visby. *Toftagården* (M), S-621 98 Visby (tel. 0498–654 00). 78 rooms.

Vittaryd. *Toftaholm Herrgårdshotell* (I), S-340 15 Vittaryd (tel. 0370–440 55). 40 rooms.

Switzerland

Switzerland might have been created with the tourist in mind. First, the Swiss themselves have always appealed to the English-speaking people. They are gracious, dignified, reserved and somewhat formal, rather like the British, and, like Americans, they are industrious, thorough, efficient and hard working. Secondly, the country is extraordinarily easy to get around—it has really the most efficient public transport system in the world—while hotels and restaurants, in all price ranges, are both spotlessly clean and very well-run (it goes without saying that they are value for money).

Most of all, Switzerland has an incomparable variety of scenery. The Alps are of course the most notable attraction with their glaciers, rushing torrents and unexpected mountain lakes reflecting the dramatic scenery all around. But to the north there are also wide plains and rolling hills, while to the south beyond the St. Gotthard Pass you'll come across swaying palm trees and two great lakes mirroring the blue of a positively Mediterranean sky. There is similar variety in urban scenery, from the delightful old-world charm of St. Gallen away in the north east or Luzern in the historic heart of Switzerland, to the glistening prosperity of Zürich and the cosmopolitan chic of Geneva. Switzerland also has the advantage of being a resort all year round. You must decide whether you prefer the Alps covered with glistening snow (Switzerland is still Europe's favorite destination for winter sports) or summer flowers, though even in July and August the truly keen skier can satisfy his snowy urges among the permanent white wastes of the highest glaciers. And all this extraordinary variety is contained in a country that is the size of a postage stamp on the map of Europe. (As matter of fact Switzerland is only slightly larger than Massachusetts and only about half the size of Maine).

Prosperous Switzerland's high living standards, the envy of the country's neighbors, give the impression that it is an expensive place to visit. Don't be put off: time spent comparing prices before you buy yields unexpected bargains. Nonetheless, if you're on a tight budget, steer clear of the big international resorts and keep your time in the cities to a minimum. Lodging will be your biggest expense, so campers and youth hostelers have a major advantage. Careful shopping around among restaurants and markets will help keep food costs within reasonable limits.

The places included in this chapter are an arbitrary selection from what can only be described as an embarrassment of riches. No mention has been made of the Rhône valley, the Grisons or the Ticino for example since all these areas are that much farther from the main centers. But they are just as well worth visiting and inexpensive accommodations are easily found there, especially with the help of the nearest Swiss Tourist Office, which is famous for its efficiency. We hope that readers will understand that it is just not possible to cover the whole of Switzerland in the small space available.

PRACTICAL INFORMATION FOR SWITZERLAND

WHAT WILL IT COST. Switzerland is a prosperous country, and you can certainly have an extremely expensive vacation here. But contrary to many expectations, there are ways of keeping your holiday costs within reasonable bounds. Perhaps the most important is to stay away from the big cities and principal international resorts; prices here are appreciably higher than elsewhere. But if you do spend a few days in these places, do not buy anything in the main streets. The shops may be inviting, but they are also very expensive. Try to stay in hotel rooms without bath or shower; they are an average of 15% lower. And never make long distance telephone calls from your hotel room. It can cost 200 to 300% more than the normal rate. Taxis are very expensive—there are exhorbitant minimums in Geneva and Zürich especially—and best avoided if possible.

If you're feeling hardy try hiring a bicycle. They are available from *all* rail stations at reasonable rates and you can return them at any other station. If the weather is fine, why not go on a picnic? *Migros* and *Co-op* stores both have inexpensively-priced foods and you'll probably be able to give yourself a delightful meal for very little money. The Co-op also has a good selection of wines. Hard liquor is excessively expensive in Switzerland. So buy your duty-free drink on the way here and then stick to mineral water and sodas, which you can get in very cheap 4-bottle packs from Migros. Don't forget to get your money back on the empties.

The Swiss unit of currency is the Swiss franc which is divided into 100 *centimes* or *Rappen.* There are coins of 5, 10, 20 and 50 centimes and of 1, 2 and 5 francs. There are notes of 10, 20, 50, 100, 500 and 1,000 francs.

At the time of writing, the exchange rate for the Swiss franc was Fr. 1.50 to the U.S. dollar and Fr. 2.41 to the pound sterling. Check the exchange rate before you leave.

Sample Costs. Cinema (moderate seat) Fr. 15 average; theater (this can vary greatly) up to Fr. 30 for not the best seats; museums are normally free; coffee varies, average Fr. 2; carafe of wine (3 dcl.) Fr. 9 (Swiss wine is very expensive, and cheaper alternatives are rare).

Hairdressers are very expensive in Switzerland, so have your hair done before you come!

NATIONAL TOURIST OFFICE. The *Swiss National Tourist Office,* which has branches in the U.S., Canada and the U.K., will be able to provide you with a wealth of information regarding budget holidays in Switzerland. Within the country there are local tourist offices in all main cities and tourist regions. You will always find someone who speaks English. Remember that tourist offices are called *Verkehrsbüro, Office du Tourisme* or *Ente Turistico* in the German-speaking, French-speaking and Italian-speaking areas of the country respectively.

Addresses of the tourist offices for major Swiss cities are: *Basel,* Blumenrain 2 (tel. 061–25 50 50); *Bern,* Main Station (tel. 031–22 12 12); *Luzern,* Frankenstrasse 1 (tel. 041–51 71 71); *Geneva,* Cornavin Railway Station (tel. 022–738 52 00); *Lausanne,* 2 Av. de Rhodanie (tel. 021–617 73 21); *Interlaken,* Hoeheweg 37 (tel. 036–22 21 21); *Grindelwald* (tel. 036–53 12 12); *Fribourg,* Square-des-Places 1 (tel. 037–81 31 75); *St. Gallen,* Bahnhofplatz la (tel. 071–22 62 62); *Zürich,* at Main Railway Station (tel. 01–211 40 00).

Addresses of the Swiss National Tourist Office overseas are:

In the U.S.: Swiss Center, 608 Fifth Ave., New York, N.Y. 10020 (tel. 212–757–5944); 260 Stockton St., San Francisco, CA 94108-5387 (tel. 415–362–2260).

In Canada: Commerce Court West, Box 215, Commerce Court Postal Station, Toronto M5L 1E8 (tel. 416–868–0584).

In the U.K.: Swiss Center, New Coventry St., London W1V 8EE (tel. 071–734 1921).

WHEN TO COME. There are of course two tourist seasons in Switzerland. The winter sports season runs from mid-December to mid-April, the summer season from late May to mid-September. From the budget point of view, the best times to come are the two weeks before Christmas, January, and March to the week before Easter. Then you avoid the high season. However, the later you come the greater risk of finding the snows have melted or at least that they are only good at the very tops of the mountains.

Late spring and early summer can both be delightful, though chilly at nights at higher elevations. Summer can also be a little wet and cold, so it's as well to bring a few warm clothes. Surprisingly, winter temperatures are not all that low—though one could hardly call them hot—except in the Jura in the northwest which is sometimes called the Swiss Siberia.

The principal advantage of off-season travel is financial, though you will also find the crowds thinner on the ground. However, prices in the cities do not have seasonal variations except during special events. Then they go up.

Average afternoon temperatures in degrees Fahrenheit and centigrade:

Geneva	Jan.	Feb.	Mar.	Apr.	May	June	July	Aug.	Sept.	Oct.	Nov.	Dec.
F°	39	43	51	58	66	73	77	76	69	58	47	40
C°	4	6	11	14	19	23	25	24	21	18	8	4

SPECIAL EVENTS. Switzerland has a vast year-round program of cultural, folklore, sporting and traditional events, often big affairs of international renown, but frequently much smaller, simpler, and relatively local in character. The latter, although drawing fewer spectators, are often the most picturesque. A booklet, *Events in Switzerland,* published twice yearly, is available free from the Swiss National Tourist Offices.

National Holidays. Jan. 1 (New Year's Day); Jan. 2 (Bank Holiday); Mar. 29, 31, Apr. 1 (Easter); May 1* (Labor Day); May 9 (Ascension); May 20 (Whit Monday); Aug. 1* (National Day); Dec. 25, 26. *Not throughout the country.

VISAS. Nationals of the United States, Canada, Australia, New Zealand, EC countries and practically all other European countries do not require visas for entry into Switzerland. You must of course have a valid passport.

HEALTH CERTIFICATES. Not required for entry.

GETTING TO SWITZERLAND. By Plane. *Swissair*—which is regularly voted by European business travelers as the best airline—flies from New York, Boston, Chicago, Atlanta, Toronto and Montreal to Zürich, and also from New York and Toronto to Geneva. *Air Canada* also flies from Montreal and Toronto to Zürich. *PanAm* flies from New York. The Swiss regional airline *Crossair* flies regularly from Swiss cities to various European destinations.

Both Zürich and Geneva are linked to all west European capitals and other major cities. From London *Swissair* and *British Airways* fly to Zürich, Geneva and Basel. *Dan Air* (from Gatwick) has daily service to Bern and Zurich. Some seats on scheduled airlines can be bought for Ł99 and cost even less on charter flights.

By Train. Switzerland is Europe's railway crossroads, with connections to almost every European country, including the U.S.S.R. From the U.K. there are several convenient routes. You can travel by train from London to Switzerland in less than 12 hours, thanks to the Hoverspeed–rail/hovercraft–rail service to Paris, then the superb French *train à grande vitesse.* You leave London (Victoria) at 10 A.M. on the CityLink service to Paris (Gare du Nord), then transfer by Métro/RER to the Gare du Lyon for trains to Switzerland. You'll be in Geneva by 9.15 P.M., Laussane by 10, and Bern by 10.30. Reservations are essential.

If you can't afford the luxury of speed, take an afternoon train to Dover, ferry to Oostende or Calais, then sleep in a couchette (bunk cabin) across the continent; you'll wake up in Basel the next morning, with easy connections to Bern and Züich. The fare is cheaper and connections more direct via Oostende.

By Bus. *National Express-Eurolines* has a through coach service from London (Victoria Coach Station) to Geneva, leaving at 3 P.M. on Monday, Wednesday, and Friday, and arriving in Geneva at 12:05 P.M. the next day. The fare is L45 one way, L79 roundtrip.

CUSTOMS. Except for a restriction to 400 cigarettes or 500 grams of tobacco or 100 cigars plus 2 liters of wine (half these quantities for residents of European countries), plus 1 liter of spirits, all of which should be carried in your hand luggage; nothing intended for personal use is barred. As for exports, there are no limits on Swiss products. You may bring in and take out of the country any amount of any currency.

HOTELS. Swiss hotels are among the finest in the world. They can of course be expensive, especially in major cities and resorts. However, away from these places there are numerous extremely reasonably-priced, comfortable, excellently run and spotlessly clean hotels. Even in the larger and more expensive towns, however, you should be able to find inexpensive accommodations. A good tip is to head for station hotels. They invariably offer good value for money. If you do have difficulty finding accommodations, the local tourist office will almost certainly be able to help; in some places they may ask for a small fee. There is also an excellent booklet called the *Schweizer Hotelführer* (Swiss Hotel Guide) which lists all hotels in the Swiss Hotel Association, to which practically every Swiss hotel belongs. This is available free from tourist offices.

Our hotel grades are divided into two categories, Moderate (M) and Inexpensive (I). Two people in a double room with shower in a Moderate hotel can expect to pay from Fr. 110 to Fr. 180, including breakfast, service and taxes. Two people in an Inexpensive hotel in a double room can expect to pay from Fr. 70 to Fr. 110, including breakfast, service and taxes. In more rural areas these prices are subject to some seasonal variation.

Self-Catering. The Swiss National Tourist Office as well as regional tourist offices in Switzerland can supply details of chalets and apartments in all parts of Switzerland. There are many different types of self-catering accommodations, all offering considerable savings for small parties and families. Winter sports enthusiasts in particular will find these are an excellent way of keeping costs to a minimum. Demand is high, however, especially in the winter sports season and it is advisable to make reservations as early as possible.

Youth Hostels. Youth hostels in Switzerland are generally excellent. There are around 100 hostels (called *Jungendherbergen* in German-speaking areas, *Auberges de la Jeunesse* in French-speaking areas, and *Alloggi per Giovani* in Italian-speaking districts). Rates range from around Fr. 10 per night in remoter rural areas to Fr. 18 in cities. Where meals are available, lunch and dinner cost on average from Fr. 6 to Fr. 9 and breakfast around Fr. 5.50. All hostels require that you use sleeping bags, but at least three quarters supply them as part of the basic charge.

Additional information is available from *Schweizerischer Bund fur Jugendherbergen*, Postfach 3001 Bern (Fr. 4), and of course from the Swiss National Tourist Office, which also supplies a detailed map and list of addresses free of charge.

Camping. There are some 450 camp sites throughout Switzerland, the majority with a good number of facilities. Charges vary a lot but average Fr. 9 to Fr. 18 per person per night. There are reductions for children. Many sites also have facilities for caravans. The majority, however, are closed during the winter. For further details, see the Swiss Camping Guide, published by the Tourist Club of Switzerland (TCS) in cooperation with the Swiss Camping Association and available in bookshops for Fr. 11.80. You can call the TCS direct in Geneva at 022/737–13 36.

RESTAURANTS. Swiss restaurants are in general excellent and, though many can be expensive, you will find a surprisingly large number offering excellent value for money. It goes without saying, however, that, away from bigger cities and main tourist centers, prices are appreciably lower. A good tip is to make for station restaurants (variously called *Bahnhof Buffet, Buffet de la Gare, Restaurant Bahnhof*).

They invariably offer good value for money. Order the daily menus (*tagesteller*) if you want a multi-course meal. A couple of other points to bear in mind are that the expression *à discretion* or a à volonté means you can eat as much as you want of any particular dish—you can really fill your boots for very little if you play this one right—and that, whenever they are available, it is best to order Algerian, Spanish or Italian wine *en carafe,* as the native product, though excellent, is expensive.

We have divided our restaurant listings into two categories, Moderate (M) and Inexpensive (I). One person in a Moderate restaurant can expect to pay from Fr. 30 without wine or beer; one person in an Inexpensive restaurant can expect to pay from Fr. 15 without wine or beer.

Food and Drink. Swiss cuisine (*Küche/Kochkunst* or *cucina,* if you prefer the German or Italian-speaking cantons) is varied, if not especially subtle. The great specialty is *fondue,* the delicious concoction of Gruyère or Emmentaler cheese melted and skillfully mixed with white wine, flour, kirsch and a soupçon of garlic. There are lots of other cheeses and cheese specialties in this dairyland, including Appenzeller, tête de Moine, and the famous raclette, served melted with potatoes and gherkins. For a list of restaurants serving Swiss cheese specialties, try the tourist office's *Guide Fromage Suisse.* If you like pig's feet, don't leave Geneva without ordering *pieds de porc au madère,* a great specialty of this city. A Valais specialty is *viande séchée* (dried beef or pork). The meat is not cured, but dried in airy barns in Alpine valleys. It is also a specialty of the Grisons where it is called *Bündnerfleisch.* Cut wafer-thin, with pickled spring onions and gherkins, it makes a delectable, although somewhat expensive, hors d'oeuvre.

Pork meat in sausage form has a variety of names, each locality having a special recipe for their making: *Knackerli* and *Pantli* (Appenzell), *Mostmöckli,* and *Kalbsleberwurst* (the latter made of calf's liver). The Grisons boasts of its *salsiz* (small salami), *Landjäger, Beinwurst, Engadiner Wurst,* and *Leberwurst.*

Cakes and sweetmeats are equally varied in this part of the world. *Leckerli* are Basel specialties: spiced honey cake, flat and oblong in shape, with a thin coating of sugar icing on top. In Bern, they are sold with a white sugar bear for decoration. *Fastnachtküchli* are sugar-dusted pastries, eaten everywhere during Mardi Gras. *Gugelhopf* are large, high, bunlike cakes with a hollowed center, useful for stuffing with whipped cream. *Schaffhauserzungen,* which as the name implies are made in Schaffhausen, are cream-filled cakes.

The Swiss, especially those of the west and the south, are great wine drinkers. White wine is appreciated as an appetizer in preference to spirits or vermouth and— if only for the sake of your budget—you should at least give it a try; start with the fuller, softer Valais whites (*Johannisberg* or *Fendant*).

TIPPING. By law, an automatic service charge of 15% is included in all hotel, restaurant, café and bar bills as well as hairdressers' charges and taxi fares. This normally covers everything except that some people give the hotel baggage porter up to Fr. 4 for a large amount of baggage. However, if anyone is especially helpful, an appropriate reward would be appreciated. Station porters are hard to come by so if you get one tip him well. At the airport, passengers use trolleys that are plentiful. These are also available at the principal railway stations. In a cloakroom where no fixed charge is made give about 50 centimes per person to the attendant. Ushers and washroom attendants may expect Fr. 1; and if you feel that you have had special service from your hotel maid you can leave her about Fr. 2 extra. Theater ushers get Fr. 2 if they sell you a program.

MAIL. Current rates for letters and postcards (all mail goes airmail) are: for less than 10 grams to the U.S. Fr. 1.40, for less than 20 grams to the U.S. Fr. 1.70; postcards to the U.S. Fr. 1.10; for less than 20 grams to the U.K. Fr. 0.90, postcards Fr. 0.80.

CLOSING TIMES. Usual shop hours are 8 A.M. to 12.15 P.M. and 1.30 P.M. to 6.30 P.M. In Zürich and Bern, shops stay open over lunch. In Geneva, large shops are open over midday, but smaller shops usually close. Banks: hours vary from place to place, but usually 8 A.M. to 4.30 or 5 P.M. on weekdays. Foreign currency exchange windows at airports and larger railway stations are open daily from 10 A.M.

GETTING AROUND SWITZERLAND. By Train. With the most integrated public transport system in Europe—indeed, in the world—getting around Switzerland by rail, and on the allied postal bus and steamer systems, is very easy indeed. Timekeeping is exemplary. Trains, buses and boats are kept immaculately clean. Sign-posting is excellent and often in English. Timetables are available everywhere and are easy to interpret. For the avid sightseer the *Swiss Pass* is indispensible as it gives unlimited travel for a designated period on most trains, all postal buses (a widespread network) and lake steamers as well as reductions of 25% to 50% on many mountain and cable railways. The cost (2nd class only quoted): 8-day pass, Fr. 195; 15-day pass, Fr. 235; 1 month pass, Fr. 335. The new three-day Swiss Flexi Pass (Fr. 160) allows the same unlimited travel options for any three days chosen within a 15-day limit. 24 major Swiss cities have now joined the Swiss Pass Scheme. It is available outside Switzerland from main travel agents and all Swiss National Tourist Offices. Eurailpass and Inter Rail Passes are also valid in Switzerland except on most mountain railways and buses. Always check locally.

In some of the popular tourist areas *Regional Holiday Season Tickets,* valid for 7 to 15 days, can be obtained that allow at least 5 days' unlimited travel by train, mountain railways, lake steamers and Alpine postal buses, with half fare for the rest of the time. These are available only in Switzerland. For example, the Railway Regional Holiday Season Ticket for the Bernese Oberland costs Fr. 110, is valid for 15 days and includes 5 days' unlimited travel.

There is also a half-fare travel card obtainable at a reasonable price, which entitles you to travel at half fare for a period of 30 days. This is becoming increasingly popular with tourists. Enquire at the Swiss National Tourist Office about this and any other inexpensive transportation plans.

By Bus. Probably the best way to sightsee in the countryside is to take any one of the innumerable bus tours available in Switzerland. Local services in rural areas are excellent and use the fabled yellow postal buses; tickets are available at rail stations and main post offices.

By Steamer. There are regular services throughout the year (with reduced winter sailings) on 12 lakes in Switzerland. Other than on some of the smallest vessels, all of these have dining or refreshment services on board. All of these services are included in the *Swiss Holiday Card* (see rail section).

By Bicycle. Bicycles can be rented at all Swiss rail stations. You can return them at any other station. Rates are as follows: with or without a valid train ticket Fr. 14 per day and Fr. 56 per week for a normal bike, Fr. 23 per day for a multi-speed mountain bike. Tandems cost Fr. 30 a day, Fr. 120 a week. If you have a valid ticket, there are special arrangements for families and groups. Families, regardless of size, pay Fr. 36 per day and Fr. 144 per week for all bikes. Groups get reductions according to the number of bikes rented. It is recommended that bikes be reserved by 6 P.M. on the day before they are required, and that groups reserve at least a week in advance.

Bern

Bern was founded in 1191 by Duke Berchtold V of Zähringen. It joined the Swiss Confederation in 1353 and became the Federal Capital in 1848. Today it has a population of 143,000. The city is situated on a natural peninsula surrounded on three sides by the river Aare. It is the seat of the Swiss Parliament and here, too, are most of the governmental institutions as well as 70 embassies and consulates representing foreign countries, the headquarters of the Universal Postal Union and the Central Office for International Railway Transport. The city is easily accessible by the fast inter-city trains from Zürich and Geneva as well as by plane—*Dan-Air* flies direct to Bern's airport, Belp, from London.

There is a long list of sights worth seeing in Bern. The first of these is in the station subway—the Christoffel Tower with the remains of the city wall set up in 1346 when the town was expanded for the third time. On leaving the main railway station and walking in the direction of the old town, the various building phases of the city's history can be traced. Between the station and the Bärenplatz lies the

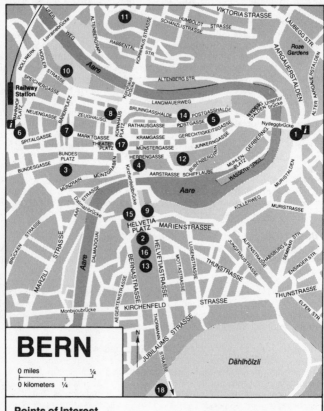

BERN

0 miles   ¼

0 kilometers   ¼

Points of Interest

1 Bärengraben (Bear Pit)
2 Bernisches Historisches
  Museum
3 Bundeshaus
4 Casino
5 Fountain of Justice
6 Heiliggeistkirche
7 Käfigturm
8 Kornhaus
9 Kunsthalle
10 Kunstmuseum

11 Kursaal
12 Münster (Gothic Cathedral)
13 Naturhistorisches Museum
14 Rathaus (Town Hall)
15 Schweizerisches Alpines
   Museum; P.T.T. Museum
16 Schweizerisches
   Schützenmuseum
17 Zeitglockenturm
18 Zoo

i Tourist Information

third and most "recent" part of the city with its street of shops, Spitalgasse, which might very well also be called "Bahnhofstrasse." At the end of Spitalgasse, in Bären-platz, there is the gate to the second-oldest part of the town, the Käfigturm or Prison Tower; to the right, at the end of a prolongation of Bärenplatz, is the Bundeshaus, Switzerland's Houses of Parliament, a vast sandstone edifice built during the late 19th-century. The Käfigturm just mentioned was built much earlier (about 1256) and today houses a museum devoted to Bernese economic and cultural life. Beyond the Käfigturm lies Marktgasse, which is really no more than a prolongation of Spi-talgasse. Here you will find many excellent stores and restaurants. At the end of this street is the Zytglogge (Zeitglocken) Tower, the oldest of the city's gates dating back to the year 1191. Every hour on the hour people assemble around the Zytglog-ge to watch Europe's most famous clock strike. On the clock is a splendid collection of animals and knights in armor, as well as sundry subsidiary characters, who com-bine to strike the hour in a complex and unforgettable fashion.

Just before the Zytglogge Tower is Kornhausplatz, which—as its name sug-gests—houses the old Corn Exchange, where today a variety of specialized exhibi-tions and the National Library (Landesbibliothek) are to be found. Just next door is the recently renovated Municipal Theater, another imposing sandstone edifice dating back to the 17th century.

Virtually every Bernese square and main street has its own historic fountain. On Kornhausplatz, for example, there is the Kindlifrässer Brunnen—the fountain bear-ing a figure of the legendary child-eater.

Beyond the Zytglogge lies the oldest part of the town, at the center of which stands the Gothic Cathedral (Munster) built in 1421. Its 98-meter tower serves as a public lookout point and is accessible via a spiral staircase. Nearby is the Town Hall (Rathaus) built during the years 1406–1416. This seat of local government can be visited only by special arrangement.

Further east the town drops steeply to the point where all the little streets meet near the Nydegg Church, the oldest of Bern's numerous churches. From this point two bridges cross the river Aare: the first of these, now renovated and listed as a national monument, is the Untertor Bridge with the Zähringer Tower and, above it, the more recent Nydegg Bridge. This bridge leads to the Bear Pit—a must on your list of sights. Please remember that the bears should not be fed anything but the carrots you will find on sale at the kiosk nearby.

PRACTICAL INFORMATION FOR BERN

HOTELS. Hotels in Bern are at least as good as those elsewhere in the country. They are easy to find as they all lie within a certain radius and are indicated by a series of brown signposts. There is an accommodations office in the tourist office in the rail station.

Moderate

Astor-Touring, Zieglerstr. 66, Eigerplatz (tel. 45 86 66). 120 beds. Large hotel, but very quiet. Some (I) rooms.

Bristol, Schauplatzgasse 10 (tel. 22 01 01). 140 beds. Spacious and central, ad-joining the Bären.

Krebs, Genferstrasse 8 (tel. 22 49 42). 80 beds Friendly, impeccable, good loca-tion near station. Restaurant downstairs.

Inexpensive

Goldener Adler, Gerechtigkeitsgasse 7 (tel. 22 17 25). Quiet and historic building in old part of town. 40 beds.

Inexpensive

Goldener Schlüssel, Rathausgasse 72 (tel. 22 02 16). 48 beds; with two good res-taurants.

Hospiz zur Heimat, Gerechtigkeitsgasse 50 (tel. 22 04 36). 70 beds. 18th-century facade, excellent Old Town location.

National, Hirschengraben 24 (tel. 25 19 88). 58 beds; with restaurant.

RESTAURANTS. Bern has a wide range of restaurants catering to the varying tastes of federal politicians, international diplomats and the local population. There are a number of good, inexpensive spots in town.

Moderate

Goldener Schlüssel, see Hotel above. Swiss specialties and also simple meals.
Kam Yu, Läuferplatz 6. Chinese cuisine.
Kornhauskeller, Kornhausplatz 18. Historic cellar restaurant with local atmosphere. Swiss specialties.
La Gondola, Bollwerk. Italian specialties. Recommended.
Mövenpick, branches at Waisenhausplatz 28 and Neuengasse 44.
Sternenberg, Schauplatzgasse 22. A wide choice with good service. More expensive meals upstairs while the more budget-minded eat downstairs.
Zytglogge Restaurant, Theaterplatz 8. Excellent cuisine, reasonable prices.

Inexpensive

Bahnhofbuffet Express, Main Station. Cafeteria-type buffet offering variety.
Bäreck, Bärenplatz 2. Wide choice of simple meals.
Klötzlikeller. Gerechtigkeitsgasse 62. Cozy old wine cellar with murals.
Migrolino, the restaurant of the big food chain over the Migros supermarket at Marktgasse 46/Zeughausgasse 31. No alcohol.
Spatz, Bärenplatz 7. Quick meals; hot food served from 11 A.M. till 11 P.M.

GETTING AROUND BERN. By Bus and Tram. Bern has an extensive and inexpensive network of buses and trams, most of which start from the main station. Fares range from 100 Fr. for the shortest trips, to Fr. 1.20. There is a 24-hour ticket, good for the entire network, which costs Fr. 4, and 1-, 2- and 3-day tickets (valid A.M.–P.M. costing Fr. 3, 5, and 7 respectively). These tickets are available from the public transport ticket office in the subway leading down to the main station. Ordinary tickets are available at tram and bus stops; you should buy your ticket before boarding the tram or bus.

There is also a little railway (the only "profitable" one in Switzerland) which runs from the Bundesterrasse (the terrace behind the Houses of Parliament) down to Marzili on the banks of the Aare. This is the Marzili cogwheel railway. It works on the water balance system. The track itself is only 105 meters (320 ft.) long, but during the one-minute trip, it climbs 32 meters (70 ft.). The one-way trip costs 60 centimes.

By Taxi. These are plentiful in Bern but, as elsewhere, expensive.

By Bicycle. Available from the main rail station.

ENTERTAINMENT. Cinema. There are about 20 cinemas in and around Bern. Most have four performances a day and show a range of films wide enough to satisfy all tastes. English-language films are almost always in the original version with French or German subtitles.

Discos and Clubs. The chances of finding good nightlife in Bern are relatively limited, though it should still be possible to have a good night out without spending too much money. In Wallgasse, there is a convincingly English pub, the *Mr. Pickwick,* which is open until after midnight and where you can get a meal at a reasonable price.

There also are a small number of dance halls and discos: the *BaBaLu* near the station, *Bar Club Messy* and *Chikito* in Neuengasse. The *Mocambo* is in Genfergasse 10. Weekdays are much less expensive than weekends. Drinks of all kinds are expensive; a Coke will cost upwards of Fr. 5 and a whiskey will be at least Fr. 15—so go during the week and make a Coke last a long time.

Theaters. Most performances are in German, so unless you speak the language well you may well find a visit to the theater rather a puzzling affair. The *Municipal Theater,* in Kornhausplatz, however, has a wide repertoire of operas, operettas, musicals and ballets. *Käfigturm Theater,* Spitalgasse 4, has ballet, pantomime, cabaret and recitations. *Kleintheater* (little Theater), Kramgasse 6, has modern German-language plays and outstanding acting. For details of what's on, see *This Week in Bern,* which is available free from the tourist office.

Concerts. *Casino Concert Hall,* Casinoplatz. *Conservatoire,* Kramgasse 36 (closed during school holidays). *Radio-Studio Bern,* Schwarztorstrasse 21. *Französische Kirche* (French Church), Zeughausgasse 8. *Bern Cathedral* also presents evening concerts from June to September.

MUSEUMS. Opening hours vary so much and change so often that it's best to consult *This Week in Bern,* which gives full details on all museums. Entrance fees vary from Fr. 1 to 3, though many museums are free. All the principal museums can be reached on foot from the station in about 10 minutes. There's a lot to see, so spread your museum visits out a bit to give yourself time to digest them comfortably.

Art Museum (Kunstmuseum), Hodlerstrasse 12. Entrance 3 Fr. The Museum was reopened in October 1983 after reconstruction. The collection includes works by Cézanne, Picasso, Klee and other artists of the 19th and 20th centuries.

Historical Museum, Helvetiaplatz 5. Entrance 3 Fr. One of Switzerland's most important historical museums with internationally renowned collections on Bernese history and prehistoric times, applied art, ethnology and coin and medal engraving. A major attraction is the fine collection of 15th-century tapestries from the heyday of Burgundian-Dutch culture.

Käfigturm (Prison Tower) **Museum,** Marktgasse 67. Entrance free. Information and exhibition center devoted to the economic and cultural life of Bern. Permanent sound/slide show illustrating the Canton's history, tourism and other cultural and economic aspects.

Municipal Art Gallery (Kunsthalle), Helvetiaplatz 1. Entrance 4 Fr. Temporary exhibitions of national and international art.

Natural History Museum, Bernastrasse 15. Entrance 1 Fr.; some afternoons free. One of Europe's major natural history museums. 220 dioramas showing Swiss and foreign mammals and birds. Extensive collection of minerals, from the Swiss Alps. Most popular exhibit is the preserved St. Bernard rescue dog, Barry.

PTT Museum, Helvetiaplatz 4. Entrance free. Houses one of the most extensive collections of rare stamps open to the public in the world.

Swiss Alpine Museum, Helvetiaplatz 4 (see PTT Museum above; same address). Entrance 1 Fr. Scenery and cultural life in the Swiss Alps, history of mountaineering, collection of reliefs, cartography.

SHOPPING. Bern's proud boast is that its 8 kilometers of arcades makes it Europe's largest all-weather medieval shopping center! The focal points for good shopping lie between the main station and the Zytglogge Tower. You will find watchmakers and jewelers, clothing stores, shops specializing in leather goods, embroidery and stationery, department stores, cafés-cum-cake-shops, etc. The shops all lie so close together that the best thing to do is walk right down the town under the arcades on one side and then up the other to be quite sure not to miss anything. The best stores for you to make for—if you want practical buys—are *EPA* on the left half-way down Marktgasse (toiletries, tights, food department upstairs, etc.), *Bon Marché* and *Globus* in Spitalgasse, both on the right going down the town and *Migros* for literally everything, again on the left going down Marktgasse.

USEFUL ADDRESSES. *U.S. Embassy,* Jubilaumsstrasse 93 (tel. 43 70 11); *British Embassy,* Thunstrasse 50 (tel. 44 50 21); *American Express,* Bubenbergplatz 11 (tel. 22 94 01); *Bern Tourist Office,* main station (tel. 22 76 76).

The Bernese Oberland

The Bernese Oberland is a magnificent area of 1,800 square miles that takes in the old city of Bern, nine valleys, the lovely lakes of Thun and Brienz, and mountains that make this area the aristocrat of the Alps. Rousseau was one of the first who praised the beauties of these wild mountains. In 1816, Lord Byron stayed on the Wengeralp, and Goethe, Shelley, Thackeray, Ruskin, Matthew Arnold, Mark Twain and Longfellow also found inspiration here.

The wide variation in altitude creates a great diversity of scenery. Around the Lake of Thun you will see fig trees and vineyards; barely a couple of hours away are eternal snow and ice. You can take a nice July morning swim in Lake Thun, jump on a train to Jungfraujoch and go skiing in the afternoon.

PRACTICAL INFORMATION FOR THE BERNESE OBERLAND

Hotels and Restaurants

Grindelwald. *Alte Post* (M), tel. 53 42 42. Central; breakfast only. Some (I) rooms. *Grindelwald* (M), tel. 53 21 31. Quiet. *Panorama* (M), tel. 53 20 10. With good restaurant and some (I) rooms. *Alpenblick* (I), tel. 53 44 84. Spare, cozy, all wood, on way to glacier.

Interlaken. *Chalet Oberland* (M), tel. 21 62 21. Central and with good Swiss Chalet restaurant. *Splendid* (M), tel. 22 76 12. Central; has an English pub. *Aarburg* (I), tel. 22 26 15. Lovely riverside setting, on edge of Old Town. *Alfa* (I), tel. 22 69 22. Cozy house in garden setting. Near West Station. Breakfast only.

Zürich

Zürich, with some 360,000 inhabitants, is Switzerland's largest city, and a paradoxical one, too. The famed home of the invisible "Gnomes of Zürich" and of numbered bank accounts, it is one of Europe's most important commercial and banking centers. There is a bank to be seen on most street corners. On the elegant banking and shopping street, the city's Bahnhofstrasse, you are walking over bank vaults containing hoards of gold.

What's more, this financial center lies in a beautiful setting between the shimmering blue water (if it's sunny!) of Lake Zürich and green wooded hills. It's mostly an ultra-modern, spic-and-span city, and downtown Zürich with its plush offices and elegant shops exudes the contented air of prosperity.

Many famous people have lived or worked in Zürich, including Lenin, who used to study at the Sozialarchiv on the Predigerplatz before his famous trip back to Russia in 1917. James Joyce, who is buried in Zürich, wrote many pages of *Ulysses* while sitting in the Pfauen Restaurant. Wagner composed much of *Tristan and Isolde* and Thornton Wilder wrote *Our Town* while in Zürich.

If you arrive in Zürich by train, you haven't far to go to start your sightseeing. Just behind the Bahnhof is the Swiss National Museum. Or you can go down through the "Shop-ville" under the busy Bahnhofplatz and then walk along the Bahnhofstrasse straight to Bürkliplatz on the shore of Lake Zürich.

Towards the end of this elegant street, on the right, is Paradeplatz, around which are clustered some of Europe's biggest banking houses. Leading off Bürkliplatz are the attractive quays with their splendid lawns, flowerbeds and trees. On the General-Guisan-Quai is the Kongresshaus, which is a dozen or more halls with a concert hall, restaurants and a nightclub.

From Bürkliplatz a bridge crosses the Limmat where it leaves the lake, and on the other side is Bellevueplatz, the entertainment center of the city. Walking north away from the square on Limmatquai you pass some of the old guildhalls, many of which are now restaurants. Towering over the quay is the 12th-century Romanesque Grossmünster cathedral with twin 15th-century Gothic towers. It is dedicated to Saints Felix, Regula and Exuperantius, who converted the people of "Turicum" (Zürich) to Christianity in the third century.

Crossing the river again to the west bank, you come to the Fraumünster, dating from the 13th century, though its original cloisters (circa 853 A.D.) are incorporated into the adjacent Stadthaus. Just to the north is Zürich's old parish church, Peterskirche, with its massive tower and gold-faced clock. All around this church is a maze of narrow, winding streets leading up to Lindenhofplatz, site of the old Roman fortress and the statue of the Women of Zürich. This commemorates a medieval battle during which the city's women, to aid the men in the army, appeared in full battle array on the Lindenhof and frightened off the Austrians. This is the most picturesque quarter of town.

Recrossing the Limmat, the visitor can walk back a bit to the old Rathaus or town hall, the seat of the city and cantonal parliaments.

PRACTICAL INFORMATION FOR ZÜRICH

GETTING INTO TOWN FROM THE AIRPORT. There is a frequent and fast train service between the airport and the main rail station in the center of town. The fare is Fr. 4.60 one way.

HOTELS. Hotels in Zürich are generally expensive, but there are nonetheless a number of good inexpensive spots. There is an accommodations office at the rail station that will be able to help should you have difficulty finding a place to stay.

Moderate

Biber, Niederdorfstrasse 7 (tel. 252 22 20). Scrupulously clean and comfortable. No alcohol allowed. Restaurant serves Chinese and Indian food. Not for the high-spirited, but otherwise very good. In the center of the entertainment quarter.

Florhof, Florhofgasse 4 (tel. 47 44 70). 56. beds. Convenient University district.

Franziskaner, Niederdorfstrasse 1 (tel. 252 01 20). 40 beds. Convenient and well-run. In nightlife district.

Seidenhof, Sihlstrasse 9 (tel. 211 65 44). Central location near Bahnhofstrasse. No alcohol allowed. Some rooms are more expensive.

Sternen-Oerlikon, Schaffhauserstrasse 335 (tel. 311 77 77). In suburb of Oerlikon about 4 km. (2½ miles) from the city center. The restaurant is particularly good.

Inexpensive

Bristol, Stampfenbachstrasse 34 (tel. 47 07 00). Large budget hotel that makes a business of catering to students and their families. Breakfast only.

Italia, Zeughausstrasse 61 (tel. 241 05 55). No rooms with bath. Breakfast only.

Splendid, Rosengasse 5 (tel. 252 58 50). No rooms with bath. Central.

RESTAURANTS. While Zürich is famous for food, unfortunately much of it is rather expensive. However, if you are careful it is nonetheless possible to eat well here without committing yourself to the poorhouse.

Moderate

Blockhus, Schifflände 4. Rustic decor, with fondue the specialty of the house. The portions are so big, they can easily be split in two.

Bodega Española, Münstergasse 15. Spanish, of course, in decor and cuisine. The casual atmosphere and carefree waiters make a good change of pace from Swiss restaurants.

Mövenpick. Many locations all over Switzerland. Check in phone book for nearest one. Swiss restaurant chain with wide price range. Seafood and other specialties can be much more than "moderate."

Zunfthaus zur Schmiden, Marktgasse 20. The least expensive of Zürich's many historic guildhouse-restaurants.

Inexpensive

Bierhalle Kropf, In Gassen 16. Great sausages and *leberknodli* served under boar's head and 100-year-old murals.

Mensa, Rämistrasse 71, and **Mensa Polyterrasse,** Leonhardstrasse 34, are student places where you can get rockbottom prices with a student ID card.

Migros. 45 locations throughout Zürich. Cafeterias in economy-priced supermarket chain. Standup and sitdown sections, but sometimes it's cheaper if you stay on your feet.

Zeughauskeller, Bahnhofstrasse 28a, off Paradeplatz. 15th-century stone-and-beam hall with regional meat dishes, beers and wines.

GETTING AROUND ZÜRICH. By Bus and Tram. Buses and tram services are excellent. Most services start from the main rail station in the center of town.

Buy tickets from the machine at the stop before boarding the vehicle. There is also a one-day season ticket that is good for all trips on the Zürich network. A free booklet with maps in English is available from all city transit (VBZ) offices.

By Taxi. Taxis are expensive and not recommended unless you are in a real hurry.

By Bicycle. Bicycles are available for hire at the rail station.

ENTERTAINMENT. Discos and Clubs. Zürich has become much more lively in recent years with visitors often surprised at the degree of entertainment available in what foreigners often have been told is a very staid city. Nightlife centers around the Niederdorf, which is also the Red Light district. You get a traditional nightclub atmosphere at the *Terrasse,* Limmatquai 3, *Red House,* Marktgasse 17, and *Le Privé,* Helvetiaplatz. There is jazz at the *Casa Bar,* Munstergasse 30, and country and western at the *Börse Restaurant,* Bleicherweg 5. There are lots of discos and several singles' bars. For folklore, there is the *Kindli* at the Rennweg.

Nightspots here are anything but permanent institutions, so check them beforehand with your hotel porter or at the tourist office. Remember also that many of them can be expensive, and that drinks are almost always expensive.

Theaters and Concerts. The *Opernhaus,* with its program of opera and operetta throughout most of the year, sets a high standard of performance and innovation. The concerts of the Zürich Tonhalle Orchestra are highly commended. The Zürich Festival, in June, is among Europe's most prestigious, with opera, symphony concerts, recitals, ballet, exhibitions, plays, and films. The *Schauspielhaus* is one of the leading German-speaking theaters in the world. If you are interested in the theater, you will find its productions of classical and modern plays fascinating, even if you don't speak German. The *Bernhard Theater* plays more contemporary works, while the smaller *Theater am Hechtplatz* is experimental.

MUSEUMS. Heidi Weber Private Museum, Höschgasse 8. Last building designed by Swiss-born architect Le Corbusier combines his own paintings, sculpture, and building's design. Opening hours are irregular.

Museum for Form and Function (Kunstgewerbemuseum), Ausstellungstrasse 60. Graphic and applied arts; there is a fine library.

Rietberg Museum. Admirable primitive and Oriental sculptures.

Swiss National Museum (Landesmuseum), Museumstrasse 2. Just behind the main rail station. Especially good for students of Swiss history.

Zürich Art Museum (Kunsthaus), Heimplatz. Small but outstanding permanent collection, especially strong on French moderns.

USEFUL ADDRESSES. *U.S. Consulate,* Zollikerstr. 141 (tel. 55 25 66); *British Consulate,* Dufourstrasse 56 (tel. 47 15 20); *Swiss National Tourist Office,* Bellariastrasse 38 (tel. 202 37 37); *Zürich Tourist Office,* at the Main Railway Station (tel. 211 40 00); *American Express,* Bahnhofstrasse 20 (tel. 211 83 70); *Thomas Cook,* Talacker 42, (211 87 10).

Luzern

Few cities are more delightful to visit than Luzern, with its 15th- and 16th-century houses, its medieval covered bridges and dreamy old-world atmosphere. To enter Luzern is to approach the heart of historic Switzerland, for the deeply indented shoreline of the Vierwaldstättersee (better known as Lake Luzern) was the cradle of the Swiss Confederation in 1291.

You'll have the most fun crossing and recrossing those wonderful wooden bridges, the Kapellbrücke (completed in 1333) with historic scenes painted on its ceiling, and the Spreuerbrücke (built in 1408) where the paintings depict a grim dance of death. The former bridge, incidentally, zigs into the River Reuss diagonally past the picturesque 13th-century water tower, then zags to the southern bank. The Old Town Hall, the city wall, with its fortified towers, and the Hofkirche also number among the city's treasures.

A trip to the Lion Monument (Löwendenkmal) and the Glacier Gardens is mandatory. The first commemorates the Swiss Guards who were slaughtered while defending Louis XVI during the French Revolution. The Glacier Gardens are an open-air display of what an ancient glacier left behind as it melted.

Also not to be missed is the city's splendid transport museum, with historic engines and carriages, an old lake paddle steamer with a restaurant on board, and even a planetarium.

The Lake of Luzern (Vierwaldstättersee) is considered by many to be Europe's most beautiful. It has regular boat services, many in graceful old paddle steamers. Two recommended trips are by boat to Alpnachstad, then by the world's steepest cogwheel railway to the summit of Pilatus (7,000 feet); and by boat to Vitznau, then by mountain railway to the top of Rigi (5,900 feet). A superb day out is to be had by sailing to the end of the lake at Flüelen and back. There are restaurants on board, or take a picnic. The lake is surrounded by picturesque little towns such as Weggis, Brunnen, and Gersau, all of which merit a visit, as well as relics of Switzerland's fight for freedom from the Habsburgs, particularly the adventures of the legendary William Tell.

PRACTICAL INFORMATION FOR LUZERN

HOTELS. Budget accommodations are packed to the roofbeams from April to October so it's essential to book in advance. The Tourist Office will certainly be able to help if you have difficulty making reservations (see below for address). Accommodations here are generally slightly cheaper than in Zürich or Geneva.

Moderate

Diana, Sempacherstrasse 16 (tel. 23 26 23). Central for trains, buses, boats, and the old town. Good accommodations and cuisine.

Johanniter, Bundesplatz 18 (tel. 23 18 55). Historic building

Kolping, Friedenstrasse 8 (tel. 51 23 51). Quiet but central; suitable for families.

Zum Weissen Kreuz, Furrengasse 19 (tel. 51 40 40). All rooms have bath or shower.

Inexpensive

Goldener Stern, Burgerstrasse 35 (tel. 23 08 91). Only rooms with bath or shower available.

SSR Touristenhotel, St. Karliquai 12 (tel. 51 24 74). Central but quiet.

Restaurants

Moderate

Galliker, Kasernenplatz. Specialties include *pot au feu* and fruit tarts. Closed Sun.

Walliser Spycher Le Mazot, Eisengasse 15. Another spot specializing in fondue dishes and *raclette.* Attractive ambience.

Inexpensive

Kunsthaus-Kongresshaus, Bahnhofplatz. Daily specials served at this vast museum restaurant with attractive garden dining area. Near boat-landing point at the Strandbad (beach).

Zunfthaus zu Pfistern, Kornmarkt 4. Local *fondue* specialties served in this spot popular with Americans. Upstairs is a more expensive restaurant serving French food.

ENTERTAINMENT. Cinema. There are nine cinemas, mostly in the city center, showing a wide variety of films.

Nightlife. There is folklore most evenings at the *Stadtkeller,* Sternenplatz 3. There is a nightclub and dancing at the Casino, and pop and rock music at *Gerbern Video-Disco,* Sternenplatz 7. *Mr. Pickwick,* at Rathausquai 6, is an English-style pub. If the weather is fine, a lively time can be had along the Rathausquai and there is sometimes impromptu entertainment.

Concerts and Theater. The highlight of the year is the *Luzern International Festival* every August and September. Launched in 1938 by Arturo Toscanini and Bruno Walter, it is still one of the world's most important musical events, with the Berlin and Vienna Philharmonics and other renowned orchestras.

There are operas, operettas, and plays throughout the year at the *Kunsthaus* and in the churches.

MUSEUMS. Glacier Garden, Denkmalstr. 4. Extraordinary evidence of the glaciers that once covered the whole of this part of the Luzern region. By the Lion Monument.

Museum of Natural History, Kasernenplatz 6. By the southern end of the Spreurbrücke; one of the country's best museums of its type. Geological exhibits from Central Switzerland carefully documented and displayed.

Museum of Swiss National Costumes and Folklore, Utenberg. Colorful national costumes; in the same building as the Federal Yodeler's Club. Open Easter to Nov. only.

Picasso Collection, Am Rhyn-House. Interesting collection of pictures by the great Spanish master; by the old Town Hall.

Richard Wagner Museum, Wagnerweg 27. Delightfully located villa on the south side of the lake where the maestro lived from 1866 to 1872.

Swiss Transport Museum, Lidostr. 5. On the north side of the lake and easily reached by public transport. Outstandingly fine collection of rail locomotives and carriages, airplanes, cars and ships as well as many working models. Also contains Switzerland's only Planetarium and a building for aerospace models. Three restaurants and (strangely) the Hans Erni museums are attached.

USEFUL ADDRESSES. *Luzern Tourist Office,* Frankenstrasse 1 (tel. 51 71 71); *Central Switzerland Tourist Office,* Alpenstrasse 1 (tel. 51 18 91), which is good for information about the lake; *American Express,* Schweizerhofquai 4 (tel. 50 11 77).

St. Gallen

St. Gallen, largest city in the northeast, is among Switzerland's most attractive and the center of one of the loveliest Swiss regions. From it you can easily explore a string of delightful resorts along Bodensee (Lake Constance); the rugged, snowy mountains in the Säntis range, rising to 8,200 feet; and the Appenzell country with its curious folklore customs. It also numbers among the best budget areas of the country.

Barely one hour from Zürich by train, St. Gallen is a modern little metropolis of around 74,000 inhabitants, and an important textile city that also zealously maintains its fine heritage of medieval culture. The city's origins date back to 612, when the Irish missionary Gallus laid the foundation of an abbey that was to become a major cultural center of medieval Europe. The abbey itself was largely destroyed during the Reformation, but in its magnificent Rococo library (rebuilt in the 18th century), containing over 100,000 volumes, visitors can see illuminated manuscripts, a number of which are over a thousand years old.

The splendid twin-towered Rococo cathedral, built in 1756, is the town's most imposing building; its superbly restored interior fairly scintillates with light and color. On the northern side of the cathedral lies the old quarter where ancient houses are rich in oriel windows and frescoes. By way of contrast it is worth visiting the new Municipal Theater and University; both are almost stark in their simplicity, but conceived with great imagination. St. Gallen's long connection with textiles is traced in the Industrie and Gewerbemuseum (embroidery museum) in Vadianstrasse. There you can see lace and embroidery made in St. Gallen from the 16th century to the present day. The collection includes many pieces worn by famous European courtiers as well as some really stunning examples of modern techniques. St. Gallen's citizens love parks and gardens and have many, including the Peter and Paul Deer Park, where you can see ibex, chamois, stags, marmots, deer, wild boars, and also enjoy wonderful views extending from Bodensee to the Säntis mountains.

About seventeen miles west of St. Gallen is Wil, a beautiful 700-year-old town, once part of the estates of the Abbey of St. Gall. The massive 15th-century residence of the Bishop-Princes, the Hof zu Wil, still dominates the old Hofplatz but now houses the local museum. From the terrace of St. Nicolas church you may see the Vorarlberg, Säntis, Churfirsten and Glärnisch Alps.

A fine half-day excursion by road from St. Gallen is about 20 miles southwards to Schwägalp for the cable car, which takes you to within a few feet of the summit of 8,200-ft. Mt. Säntis. Weather permitting, you'll have incredible views not only of the Swiss Alps, but also far beyond the frontiers.

Prices are appreciably lower here, particularly in the mountainous Appenzell region, where you can enjoy folk traditions jealously preserved, and watch the making of the famous Appenzell cheese.

PRACTICAL INFORMATION FOR ST. GALLEN

Hotels and Restaurants

Dom (M), Webergasse 22 (tel. 23 20 44). Quiet, comfortable and friendly; near the Cathedral; breakfast only. *Sonne Rotmonten* (M), Guisanstrasse 94 (tel. 25 68 25). Comfortable. *Vadian* (I), Gallusstrasse 36 (tel. 23 60 80). Breakfast only; very inexpensive.

Restaurants. Apart from the hotels, also try the *Bahnhof Buffet* (M), the *Schützengarten* (M), and the pricier *zum Golden Schäfli* (M) with inexpensive daily plates.

Geneva

Geneva is the home of dozens of international organizations. It is a lively, cosmopolitan city, with formal gardens, broad avenues and lovely views of the lake with Mont Blanc towering in the distance.

You can see many of the attractions of Geneva in a single walk by starting from the railroad station down the rue du Mont-Blanc. At the lakeside, turn right along the quai des Bergues flanking the Rhône, crossing the river on the Pont de l'Ile to the place Bel-Air, from which you follow the rue de la Corraterie to the place Neuve with its Grand Théâtre and the Conservatory of Music. From here, you enter the park, which contains the university and Geneva's most famous monument, the gigantic Reformation memorial to international Protestantism.

Leaving the park, turn left up rue St. Léger into the charming old place Bourg-de-Four, and then take any of the narrow streets, ramps and staircases that lead up to St. Peter's Cathedral. From the top of the north tower you can get a sweeping view of Geneva and its lake.

The winding cobbled streets leading down from the cathedral to the modern city have all the picturesque charm of antiquity. The Grand-rue is the oldest of them; Jean-Jacques Rousseau was born at No. 40 in 1712. See also in this neighborhood the 12th-century house at No. 6 rue de Puits-Saint-Pierre and the 17th-century houses built by Italian religious refugees on the rue de l'Hôtel-de-Ville.

For an interesting contrast to these ancient attractions, go back across the Rhône and out to Ariana Park, where the handsome Palais des Nations, now the European office of the United Nations, the World Health Organization headquarters and other international buildings can be visited by guided tours throughout the year.

One of the joys of 45-mile-long Lac Léman (Lake Geneva) is that along the northern or Swiss side the road never strays far from the shore, providing a succession of lovely views of the lake with France on the other side, mountains and vine-clad hillsides. From Geneva at one end to Villeneuve at the other, the road passes a string of resorts and small towns as well as the ultra-modern city of Lausanne. On the motorway you also have fine views and it is a lot faster for those in a hurry.

At Coppet, eight miles from Geneva, is the lovely old château where the famous Madame de Staël held her literary salons for such notables as Byron, Schlegel, Gibbon and Sismondi. Five miles further is Nyon, founded by Julius Caesar after a battle in 58 B.C. as a camp for war veterans and now an attractive market town.

Three miles beyond the small town of Rolle, with the almost inevitable castle, it is worth turning left at Allaman to visit nearby Aubonne, a village that has remained practically unchanged for 400 years and is graced by a 12th-century castle.

PRACTICAL INFORMATION FOR GENEVA

GETTING INTO TOWN FROM THE AIRPORT. There is a frequent and fast rail service from Geneva airport to Cornavin station in the city center. It takes six minutes and the fare is Fr. 3.60 one way (second class). There is also a regular bus service to Cornarvin station that takes 20 minutes and costs Fr. 1.50.

HOTELS. Rooms can be hard to find if there's an international conference in town, which is pretty often, so it's best to reserve ahead. There's an accommodations office in Cornavin station that should be able to help. Geneva hotel prices are quite high, but it is nonetheless possible to find rooms at reasonable rates.

Moderate

Astoria, 6 place Cornavin (tel. 732 10 25). Opposite the station; breakfast only.
Rivoli, 6 rue des Pâquis (tel. 731 85 50). Between place des Alpes and place Châteaubriand near the lake; breakfast only. Well-managed, pleasant and comfortable.
Strasbourg-Univers, 10 rue Pradier (tel. 732 25 62). Stylish oasis in unsavory station area. Excellent value.
Touring-Balance, Pl. Longmalle 13 (tel. 28 71 22). Sleek decor, ideal setting in heart of luxury shopping, edge of Old Town.

Inexpensive

Bernina, 22 place Cornavin (tel. 731 49 50). Opposite the station; breakfast only; comfortable.
De la Cloche, 6 rue de la Cloche (tel. 32 94 81). Pristine pension in grand old mansion, rock-bottom prices.
Des Tourelles, 2 bd. James-Fazy (tel. 732 44 23). Fading Victorian gem with bay windows, fireplaces, French doors. Rhône views come with traffic roar.

RESTAURANTS. Geneva restaurants are definitely on the expensive side, and, though French cuisine predominates, you will also find many more Chinese, Greek, Italian and other ethnic restaurants than in other Swiss cities.

Moderate

Les Armures, 1 rue du Puits-Saint-Pierre. Geneva's oldest restaurant in historic Old Town building. Great *fondues, raclette* and snacks.
La Bonne Brasserie, 14 rue de Lausanne. Meals till 11 P.M. In front of train station.
Le Cafe du Grutli, Maison Grutli, rue General-Dufour 16. High-tech student canteen for local artists. Trendy meals, snacks till midnight.
Cave Valaisanne, blvd. Georges-Favon (Place du Cirque). Friendly, folksy spot for *raclette* and *fondue.*
Le Chalet Satellite, Ct. Commercial Meyrin. Near Cointrin Airport. Châteaubriand and *raclette* are the specialties of the house.
La Diligence, 2 rue Pécolat. Terrace, traditional cooking. Closed on Sun.
Mövenpick, 17 rue du Cendrier and 40 rue du Rhône. A group of different restaurants varying from grill to deluxe eatery in the same building.

Inexpensive

Brasserie Eaux Vivienne, 3 rue des Eaux-Vives. Italian food with beef flambé as the specialty. Closed Sat. P.M.
Le Centre, 5 place du Molard. On the picturesque place du Molard in town center, this restaurant serves good freshwater fish and seafood.
Cent Suisses, 18 chemin de l'Imperatrice. Historic, bucolic setting for simple lunch in international district. Great fruit tarts.
Au Pied du Cochon, 4 place du Bourg-de-Four. Popular Old Town gathering spot features pigs' feet, a Geneva specialty.

GETTING AROUND GENEVA. By Bus and Tram. Services are frequent and reliable. Tickets should be bought at the automatic machines at the stops before boarding. You can save by buying a *carnet* (booklet) of tickets at a reduced rate at the station.

By Boat. You can explore the lake in a relaxed manner by taking one of the scheduled boat services. Stop off at Montreux, one of the smartest lakeside resorts in Europe, with its flower-decked waterfront and glorious views. From there you can visit the imposing Château de Chillon, the inspiration for Byron's *The Prisoner of Chillon.* The boats stop there, too. There are also boat services to the French shore, and motorboat trips for shorter journeys.

ENTERTAINMENT. Discos and Clubs. There are considerably more lively nightspots in Geneva than in Zürich. Most are reasonably priced. The *Vieille Ville* (Old Town) is the area for a good part of Geneva's nightlife, and there are a number of outdoor cafés around the place Molard. There are bars everywhere.

Popular nightspots in town are *Maxim's,* 2 rue Thalberg, *Ba-Ta-Clan,* 15 rue de la Fontaine, *La Garconniere,* 15 rue de la Cité. Most of Geneva's young would rate *La Macumba,* in St. Julien-en-Genevois just over the French border (cross at Perly) as the most lively nightspot. It claims to be the biggest disco in Europe. *Brasserie Landolt,* rue de la Candolle, is a popular student hangout, with an outside terrace. Since nightspots are anything but permanent institutions and can change their character, it is best to check at your hotel before going. In summer, along the quais there are free open-air concerts; and Thursday and Saturday evenings the CGN steamer company runs dance cruises on the lake.

Theaters and Concerts. Concert halls include *Victoria Hall,* rue General-Dufour, where the famous *Orchestre de la Suisse Romande* gives its symphonic concerts; *Conservatoire de Musique,* place Neuve; *Radio-Suisse Romande,* 66 Boulevard Carl-Vogt. The *Grand Casino,* 19 Quai de Mont Blanc, is a relatively new concert hall and theater in which the world's top musicians give concerts. The *Grand Théâtre* is an opera house with an international reputation, and tickets can be hard to get hold of. In the season on Sunday mornings, there is chamber music in the foyer. In summer, there are open-air recitals in the Old Town, and organ recitals in the Cathedral and other churches. There are ballet performances at the *Grand Casino* and *Grand Théâtre,* and jazz concerts at the *Halles de l'Ile.* For French stage plays get a program from the tourist office. There you can also pick up information on productions in English.

MUSEUMS. The most important collections are listed below. There are over thirty art galleries that have interesting temporary shows. To check on them, see *La Semaine à Genève* (This Week in Geneva).

Art and History, 2 rue Charles-Galland. Fine permanent collection of archeological objects, painting and sculpture; particularly strong in decorative art, with emphasis on Genevese enamels.

Bauer Collection, 8 rue Munier-Romilly. Outstanding collection of Chinese and Japanese ceramics, jades, prints etc., in former private house.

Natural History, 11 route de Malagnou. Splendid collection in new building. There is also a **Botanical Museum and Conservatory** near the United Nations building.

Petit Palais, 2 Terrasse Saint Victor. Impressionist and post-Impressionist paintings.

Rath, place Neuve. Temporary shows, many of them excellent. Notable for watch and jewelry exhibition in September.

USEFUL ADDRESSES. *American Express,* 7 rue du Mont-Blanc (tel. 731 76 00). *Thomas Cook,* 64 rue de Lausanne (tel. 732 45 55). *Tourist office,* at the Main Railway Station (tel. 738 52 00). *American church* (732 80 78) and *American Library* (732 80 97), 3 rue de Monthoux. *Australian Mission,* 58 rue de Moillebeau (tel. 734 62 00). *Canadian Mission,* 1 rue du Pré de la Bichette (tel. 733 90 00). *United States Mission,* 11 rte. de Pregny (tel. 799 02 11). *United Kingdom Mission,* 37 rue de Vermont (tel. 734 38 00).

Turkey

Turkey's recorded history is long and varied, and for much of it the country has occupied center stage in many of the most crucial developments of European civilization. Long before it became Turkey, Asia Minor entered pre-history with a bang when Noah's Ark settled on Mount Ararat in the far northeast of the country. Subsequent Turkish history is less dramatic, but better documented. In the 6th millennium B.C. Paleolithic and Neolithic settlements spread into the southeast of Turkey. By the 2nd century B.C., the Hittites had appeared, ushering in the Bronze Age. Their inland kingdom, which eventually encompassed the whole of Asia Minor, was succeeded by the Phrygians, the "Sea People." In 1230 B.C., the siege of Troy by the Greeks began the unceasing rivalry between Europe and Asia that, to some extent, continues today.

A number of Greeks remained in Asia Minor and founded colonies along the Aegean shore. The earliest stirrings of Western thought originated in these colonies around the 18th century B.C. Some 400 years later, the Greek Alexander the Great swept triumphantly through these settlements leaving as his legacy considerable prosperity, which was only increased by subsequent contact with Hellenistic and, later, Roman civilizations.

As the Roman Empire declined in the 4th century A.D., Asia Minor became increasingly important. First as the center of what was left of the dying Roman Empire—Byzantium became its capital in A.D. 333—and latterly as the hub of the resurgent Byzantine Empire. After several ups and downs, the Empire was weakened by the growing power of the Seljuk Turks, who from the 11th century onward ruled most of Asia Minor, and leaving their mark most notably at Alanya, Antalya, Kayseri and Konya. The Ottoman Turks took over 300 years later, conquering Constantinople in 1453. The Turkish Empire, ruled by the Caliphs, spiritual as well as temporal masters, spread, at its height, over three continents stretching from Algeria in Africa to Iran in Asia and northward into the Balkans and large tracts of southern Russia. Vienna in the center of Europe was twice besieged and escaped only by the narrowest of margins.

Though this imperial grandeur was to last for almost 500 years, when it fell it did so dramatically until by the end of World War I Turkey was known as the "Sick Man of Europe." However, under the leadership of the great general and statesman, Kemal Atatürk, modern-day Turkey—a secular republic in the Turkish heartland of the extinct Islamic caliphate—was successfully established.

Only 3% of Turkey's 296,000 square miles are actually in Europe, but the country's 52 million inhabitants have, at least outwardly, adopted European customs, as well as western political and economic systems. However, the country has undergone considerable political upheavals in the last 15 years or so, culminating in the imposition of martial law by the armed forces in September 1980. Having accomplished the immediate task of pulling the country back from the brink of civil war, the economy was gradually restored by the National Security Council, whose head was elected President for 7 years in 1982, while over 90% approved the new constitution. One year later, the free-enterprise Motherland Party obtained a majority in the election for the Grand National Assembly. Municipal elections in 1984 and

1987 confirmed the preeminence of the Motherland Party. However, local elections in 1988 placed the Motherland Party third, with 21.8% of the votes. Presidential elections in November 1989 voted in former Prime Minister Türgut Özal as president for seven years.

In so large a country, major attractions are plentiful. The west and south coasts offer an unsurpassed wealth of imposing remains of successive civilizations dating back some 4,000 years in splendid setting under the inviting Mediterranean sun. Good roads follow most of this coastline or lead to the outstanding tourist sites, where accommodations are adequate. But off the beaten track, hotels can be basic, especially in the greater part of the Anatolian plateau and eastern areas which, despite great natural beauty, are only for the hardy traveler.

PRACTICAL INFORMATION FOR TURKEY

WHAT WILL IT COST. Turkey is by far the cheapest of the Mediterranean countries, especially outside main towns and coastal resorts. Though inflation hovers between 50% and 70% (down from 120% in 1980), frequent small devaluations of the Turkish *lira* keep prices fairly stable when measured against foreign currencies. Consequently prices in this chapter are quoted in U.S. dollars, which indicate the real cost to the foreign tourist more accurately than the constantly increasing lira prices. But as it is impossible to anticipate government policy, the quotation of prices has been kept to a minimum to avoid misleading approximations.

The monetary unit is the Turkish Lira, TL. At the time of writing, the exchange rate for the lira was about 2,282 lira to U.S. dollar and 3,620 lira to the pound sterling. Check for the latest situation, as there are constant devaluations. Major international credit cards are becoming more widely accepted in the larger cities, but it is unwise to depend on them. Banknotes and traveler's checks can be changed at banks, travel agencies and major hotels. Exchange slips should be retained to reconvert TL into foreign currency—likewise, if the value of purchases taken out exceeds 40,000 TL.

Sample Costs. A haircut from $1.50 at the most basic barber to $10 at an average shop; hairstyling $4–$15. Small bottle of beer, $1–$3; sandwich 50¢–$1.50; a Coke 75¢–$1.80; a small bottle of *raki* $2–$6; glass of tea 20¢–$2.50. Most cinemas have a uniform price, about $1.30, cheaper in the provinces. The only theatrical performances of interest to the non-Turkish speakers would be at various festivals in antique theaters, $2–$5 per seat, somewhat higher for a moderate seat at the Istanbul Art Festival. Museums and archeological sites from $1–$5.50.

NATIONAL TOURIST OFFICE. In Istanbul: Central office, Mesrutiyet Cad. 57/6–7, Galatasary (tel. 1456 593); Hilton Hotel, Cumhuriyet Cad., Harbiye (tel. 1330 592); Karaköy Maritime Station (tel. 1495 776); Atatürk Airport (tel. 5737 399); Sultanahmet Sq. Divan Yolu Cad. 3 (tel. 5224 903). Also in all major towns and coastal regions. Helpful abroad in supplying lists of tour operators, they are essential within Turkey for organizing budget travel, which means mainly buses and advice regarding accommodations and food in out-of-the-way places. The staff is, on the whole, helpful and patient.

Addresses of the Turkish Tourism Information Office overseas are:

In the U.S.: 821 United Nations Plaza, New York, N.Y. 10017 (tel. 212–687–2194); 2010 Massachusetts Ave., Washington D.C. 20036 (tel. 202–429–9844).

In the U.K.: 170–173 Piccadilly, London W1V 9DD (tel. 071–734 8681).

WHEN TO COME. The tourist season lasts from the beginning of April to the end of October. It is at its height in July and August, when some beach hotels raise their prices by 15 to 20%, though mainly only the more expensive ones (never in the inexpensive ranges). These are also the months when it is difficult to find rooms anywhere along the four coasts, the Aegean, Mediterranean, Black Sea and Marmara. Yet except for a holiday entirely devoted to nautical sports, April to June and

September to October are preferable even on the southern coasts and most certainly anywhere inland, where it can become unbearably hot in the south in summer and just as unbearably cold in the winter, especially in the northeast.

Price-wise, there is little to be gained by off-season travel as most beach resort hotels close November through March. A few hotels in Istanbul offer off-season reductions, however.

The climate in Turkey varies a great deal according to the time of the year and the location. On the Anatolian plain summer is hot and dry, winter snowy and cold. The Black Sea coast is mild and damp, with a rainfall of over 90 inches a year, and often warmer in winter than Istanbul and the Sea of Marmara; the Aegean and Mediterranean coasts are blessed with a moderate climate all the year round, except for a few hot and humid days July and August.

Average afternoon temperatures in Fahrenheit and centigrade:

Istanbul

	Jan.	Feb.	Mar.	Apr.	May	June	July	Aug.	Sept.	Oct.	Nov.	Dec.
F°	45	47	52	61	68	77	81	81	75	67	59	51
C°	7	8	11	16	20	25	27	27	24	19	15	11

SPECIAL EVENTS. *January,* Camel Wrestling, Selcuk and Aydin villages; *May,* festivals in the ancient amphitheaters of Ephesus, Silifke and Pergamum (Bergama, near Izmir); *son et lumière* begins at Blue Mosque, Istanbul; *June,* Rose Festival, Konya; *June/July,* Istanbul Arts Festival, Turkey's outstanding cultural event; grease wrestling, Kirkpinar, near Edirne; *July,* Folklore Festival, Bursa; *August, son et lumière,* Atatürk Mausoleum, Ankara; *August/September,* International Fair, Izmir; *December,* Rites of the Whirling Dervishes, Konya.

National Holidays. Jan. 1 (New Year's Day); Apr. 23 (National Independence and Children's Day); sunset Apr. 15 to sunset Apr. 18 (Ramadan Feast, *Seker Bayrami*); May 19 (Youth and Sports Day); sunset June 22 to June 26 *(Kurban Bayrami);* Aug. 30 (Victory Day); Oct. 29 (Republic Day).

VISAS AND HEALTH CERTIFICATES. Not required by citizens of the U.S., Canada, and Commonwealth and EC countries for stays of up to three months. U.K. citizens must obtain a visa, available upon entry for £5.

HEALTH. There is a risk of malaria in the southeastern provinces between July and October; consult local authorities.

CUSTOMS. You may import duty free into Turkey either 400 cigarettes or 50 cigars or 200 grams of tobacco; 2.5 liters of alcoholic drink; and five bottles of perfume. Keep proof of purchase of gifts, souvenirs, and carpets. All valuable personal items should be registered in the owner's passport on entry.

GETTING TO TURKEY. By Plane. *Pan American* flies daily from New York, via Frankfurt, to Istanbul, with connections to Ankara and Izmir. *Turkish Airlines (THY)* fly three times a week from New York to Istanbul via Brussels. All major European and Asian towns are connected daily with Istanbul, less frequently with Ankara, and Izmir. Charter flights in summer to Antalya, Istanbul, Izmir and Dalaman. London is the center for cheap flights to Turkey. *The* cheapest high season scheduled fares on British Airways and Turkish Airlines start at £369 (PEX); charters are about £150, and inclusive holidays begin at £200.

By Boat. There are no sailings from North America. Istanbul is a favorite port of call for cruises both from the U.K. and from Piraeus, Venice and Trieste. Calls by cruise ships are also made at Izmir and Kuşadasi (for Ephesus). Ferries ply between Ancona and Izmir, Venice and Izmir, Piraeus and Izmir/Istanbul, May through September.

By Train. The most convenient route from western Europe is from either Venice or Munich. From both cities there are through 2nd-class bunk beds leaving the former at about 5·P.M. and arriving about 42 hours later (two nights on the train) in Istanbul. From Munich the train leaves at about 9 P.M. and arrives again about 42 hours later. Buffet and refreshments services part of the way. In some months there is a change of trains at Belgrade on both routes. Details in the U.K. from British Rail European Rail Travel Centre, Victoria Station, P.O. Box 303, London SW1Y 1JY (tel. 071–834 2345). Both routes go via Zagreb, Belgrade, Sofia and Svilengrad. From Greece there is a through service that leaves Athens at about 7 A.M. and arrives in Istanbul 8.40 A.M. the following day; 2nd-class day carriages only; goes via Thessaloniki and Pithion. (tel. 071–730 0202).

By Bus. *International Express-Eurolines* (tel-071-730 0202) runs twice weekly to Turkey. One leaves Friday evening from London Victoria coach station and travels via Brussels, Frankfurt, Munich, and Zagreb, with no overnight stop, and costs £185 roundtrip. It arrives in Istanbul late morning on the fourth day. The other leaves Victoria Sunday evening, going via Amiens, Paris, Ljubljana (an overnight stop). It reaches Istanbul late morning on the fourth day. The cost is £177.

HOTELS. Turkish hotels are officially classed HL (deluxe), H1 to H5 (first to 5th class), motels M1 to M2, and P, *pansiyons* (guest houses). Many cheap establishments in the provinces are not classed at all, and for good reasons; yet some of these may be cleaner than 4s or 5s in the capital, and services may be friendlier though hardly more efficient. Prices vary greatly within each category, often for no apparent reason, so that our Moderate (M) based on the official 3 includes several 2s and 4s and our Inexpensive (I)—based on 4 and 5—includes an occasional overrated 2. Prices are prominently displayed in all rooms.

Nearly all Moderate hotels are strictly utilitarian, while Inexpensive hotels are of an austere simplicity; all have private showers, unless otherwise mentioned. All Moderate hotels and most Inexpensive hotels serve breakfast, but only a few of the latter feature a restaurant. Half board, when obtainable, is on the whole the most economical arrangement, full board even more so, if you don't mind being tied down. There is no lack of Moderate and Inexpensive hotels throughout the country; as a matter of fact off-the-beaten-track—which means almost the entire vast interior and eastern areas—they are the only available accommodations. Though all listed have been carefully chosen, a secure system of grading is very difficult as the quality of service varies not only from year to year but from day to day.

Two people in a double room in a Moderate (M) hotel could expect to pay $50 to $80, including breakfast, tax and service charge. Two people in a double room in an Inexpensive (I) hotel or *pansiyon* could expect to pay from under $50, including breakfast, tax and service charge.

Hostels. Student dormitories operate only during the school vacations in July and August. However, there are 50-odd student hostels in Turkey and, if you have an ISTC or FIYTO card you should have no trouble in finding a bed in one of these hotels. For further information, contact ISTC's Turkish representatives in Istanbul: Genç Tur, Yerebatan Cad. 15/3, Sultanahmet; or Intra Tur, Halâskargazi Cad. 111/2, Harbiye. Student card holders are entitled to 10% discounts on Turkish state railways and Turkish Maritime Lines, and usually free entrance to historical sites.

Camping. There are numerous organized camp sites along the coastal roads in western and southern Turkey; open April or May through October. The official *Camping in Turkey* booklet provides all necessary details. The best-equipped camp sites are the *Kervansaray Mocamps.* Rates are about $4 per person per night. Camping outside approved sites is permitted but not advisable. Alternatively, hotels and pensions often have rooftop campbeds available at very cheap rates.

RESTAURANTS. Turkish restaurants are officially classified as 1, 2 and 3; they may be *Restoran, Lokanta* or *Kebapci.* For our listings, 2s correspond to Moderate (M), and 3s to Inexpensive (I). The set menus in Moderate hotels are inexpensive but nearly always deadly dull, while set menus of equal price and quality are served only in a few restaurants in the bigger towns connected in some way with snack bars; these are usually called *Kafes.* On the whole, though by no means always, a Restoran usually has international dishes, while a Lokanta is good for the tastier

Turkish specialties. A Kebapci is a kebab house, a national institution offering a wide variety of meat grilled on charcoal. These are really the best solution for the budget traveler.

The innumerable fish restaurants along the Bosphorus are very tempting, but seafood is more expensive than meat so check the price list at the entrance of these places carefully. If there isn't a price list, the place is either pretty expensive or so cheap that it should be avoided at all costs. Avoidance is also recommended for the fish fried straight from the net at the Istanbul bridges. Obviously it is fresh, but the rancid oil used to fry it in is every bit as uninviting as the unpleasant paper it gets wrapped in.

You'll find that menus are usually written in Turkish only, but you can point out what dish you want from those on display or simmering on the stove. Frequently you are invited into the kitchen where you can choose what you want. Service is generally fast and polite.

There are innumerable pastry shops—strong on syrupy sweets—while nut and candy stores provide desserts. Impecunious nibblers and noshers can indulge in snacks ranging from sesame rolls to roast corn sold by itinerant street sellers; a critical eye for dust will not come amiss for anyone tempted to try them.

One person in a Moderate (M) restaurant, without drinks, can expect to pay from $7 to $19; in an Inexpensive (I) restaurant, expect to pay less than $8.

Food and Drink. Turkish cuisine isn't especially exotic, being based on age-old recipes that are common to the eastern Mediterranean from Egypt to Greece. Dishes include: *kuzu dolmasi* (baked lamb stuffed with rice), *midye dolmasi* (mussels stuffed with rice and spices), *zeytin yagh* and *patlican dolmasi* (eggplant stuffed with rice and spices—*dolmas,* incidentally, means stuffed). *Sis,* or shish in the English spelling, means broiled on a spit; thus *kilic sis* is swordfish (Turkish swordfish is mercury-free) wrapped in bay leaves and duly broiled on a spit. *Imam boyildi* (which means "the Priest fainted") is made up of fried eggplant slices with layers of onion and tomato cooked in olive oil and served cold. Then there is *kadin gobegi* (woman's navel) which is a pleasant dessert. Once you have gotten this familiar with the lady in question, you might as well try *dugun corbasi* (Marriage soup) which is made from meat broth, eggs and lemon juice.

For drinks, there is Turkish red or white wine *(kirmizi sarap* and *beyaz sarap),* which costs from $3 a bottle upwards, and the potent grape brandy called *Raki.* You will also find that someone has given familiar types of alcohol their own distinctive Turkish names; ask for *Viski* or *Votka. Ayran,* sour buttermilk, is very popular and refreshing. Coffee, Turkish or otherwise, is relatively expensive. It has been replaced by *çay* (tea), served without milk in small glasses.

Drinking Water. Tap water is heavily chlorinated and supposedly safe to drink in cities and resorts. It's best to play it safe, however, and drink bottled mineral water *(maden suyu)* which is better tasting and inexpensive.

TIPPING. Except at rockbottom establishments, a service charge of 15% is added to the bill, but does not necessarily find its way to the personnel. Keep this in mind and give a small tip to those who took care of you: waiters expect another 10%; porters, bellhops and washroom attendants as well as movie and theater ushers all expect a small tip. Round off the taxi meter to the next TL 100.

MAIL. Post offices are recognizable by the yellow sign PTT. Postage rates are often adjusted for inflation, but are cheap compared to other countries.

CLOSING TIMES. Most shops are closed daily 1 P.M. to 2 P.M. and all day Sunday. Generally they're open Monday to Saturday, 9.30 to 1 and 2 to 7. In resort areas some shops stay open until 9 P.M. and are often open Sunday. Banks and Public Offices open Monday to Friday 8.30 to 12, 1.30 to 5.

CONVENIENCES. Except at airports and railway stations, these are pretty thin on the ground. You might, however, try the better restaurants. Many lavatories are not only simple but dirty and of the no seat variety.

GETTING AROUND TURKEY. By Plane. *Turkish Airlines (THY)* operate an extensive network of internal services, a number of the routes being summer only. Between Istanbul and Ankara there are up to 8 flights daily on weekdays. THY offers a 10% family discount, even if only husband and wife travel.

By Train. The 5,000 miles of Turkish Railways offer several long distance expresses, but even they are slow. Travel in 1st-class or the one-class diesel trains is cheap enough and there is a 10% student discount and a 30% discount for groups of 24 or more. Daytime trains have buffet or dining cars and overnight expresses carry sleeping cars and 2nd-class couchettes. Whenever possible make advance reservations. This is obligatory on some routes. Reductions are made for roundtrips.

By Bus. Private companies provide frequent and inexpensive day and night services between all towns. They are complemented by equally economic minibuses and dolmuş (shared taxis) on shorter routes, and also in towns on a fixed itinerary. In most cases long distance buses are much quicker than trains.

By Boat. *Turkish Maritime Lines* (Rihtim Cad., Karaköy, tel. 1440 207) operate car ferry and cruise services from Istanbul. U.K. office: Sunquest Holidays Ltd., Aldine House, Aldine St., London W12 8AW (tel. 081–749 9933). No U.S. office.

The Black Sea ferry sails May to September, Istanbul–Samsun–Trabzon–Istanbul, departing from Kabataş or Sarayburn docks in Istanbul three days a week, and represents excellent value.

Mediterranean cruises offer a 10-day trip, calling in at ports between Istanbul and Alanya. They depart every 15 days from May to September.

Overnight car ferries from Istanbul's Sirkeci Dock to Izmir depart on Fridays at 3 P.M., year round. Fares (one person/one way, without meals) range between $15 and $37, and $22 for a car. There are numerous car and passenger services crossing the Sea of Marmara and the Dardanelles, and these can be crowded.

By Car. *Avis, Hertz, Eurocar, Inter Rent,* and *Budget* have offices in most of the following towns and cities: Istanbul, Ankara, Izmir, Kuşadasi, Antalya, Alanya, and Adana. Their rates are international. The main asphalt highways are well maintained but unlit, and not always well signposted. There are still many gravel-chip roads, and travel off-the-beaten-track usually means a dirt road. City roads can be crowded with hooting, speeding vehicles.

By Bicycle. Suicidal in the bigger towns and not without its dangers elsewhere except in the remotest areas, though even then it's a good idea to get off the road at the approach of a car (admittedly a rare occurrence).

Istanbul

Istanbul has a fascinating history. It was founded in the 7th century B.C. by a Greek colonizer and subsequently conquered by the Persians, though soon liberated. The prosperous city-state it had become by the 1st century B.C. then fell to the Romans. It was renamed Constantinople by the first Christian Emperor (Constantine) who made it his capital in A.D. 333. The city was enlarged and beautified by a succession of Roman and Byzantine Emperors and grew to become Europe's most prestigious medieval capital until it was pillaged in the fourth Crusade in 1204. It then languished under the ephemeral Latin Emperors, partly recovered under the last Byzantine dynasty—the Palaeologues—and then entered a new period of imperial grandeur after its conquest by Sultan Mehmet II in 1453.

This was to last nearly 500 years.

However, the transfer of the Republic's capital to Ankara in 1922 heralded another period of decline, albeit a brief one. Since World War II the city has undergone explosive development. Today almost 6 million people are crowded into the vast and unattractive suburbs that sprawl over the northern European and Asian coasts to the Sea of Marmara on the once-lovely shores of the Bosphorus. Further south in Asia, the developments of the last 20 to 30 years have produced even more unfortunate results. Factories line much of the coastal highway for 58 miles all the way to Izmit, producing the atmospheric pollution that only a strong northerly wind can disperse.

Yet the walled old city on its headland between the Marmara Sea and the inlet of the Golden Horn has remained one of the world's outstanding sights, even though this unique site has today been deprived of much of its natural beauty. The three essential places to visit, as well as several other sites almost as important, are all within walking distance of each other on the headland's blunt eastern edge, while scattered throughout the old city are marvelous mosques and palaces, which rise up like a vision from the Arabian Nights.

In the center of the sightseeing area is Ayasofya (St. Sophia), built by Constantine in A.D. 347, destroyed by fire and rebuilt by Justinian in the 6th century A.D. The Turks converted the basilica into a mosque and added the four minarets. It's now a museum where some of the original mosaics have been preserved, and is considered to be one of the most beautiful buildings in the world.

The great dome and minarets established an architectural style that was to dominate the Istanbul skyline. Not far from it stands the Turks' answer to Justinian—the Mosque of Sultan Ahmed I—known, because of the lovely colored tiles in its interior, as the Blue Mosque. (Don the over-sized slippers at the door, and you can enter any mosque in Istanbul.) Near the Blue Mosque are the Fountain of Sultan Ahmed II, built in 1712, and the restored Sultan Hamam (Bath). Both are lovely examples of Turkish rococo.

Only a short distance away is the At Meydani (Hippodrome), laid out by the Roman Emperor Severus in A.D. 203. The chariot races held here often resulted in popular riots, the most famous in 532 started the fire that gutted the entire St. Sophia area (including the great basilica) and nearly cost Justinian the throne. In the middle of the race track stand the obelisk of Pharaoh Thutmes III, which was brought from Egypt by Theodosius the Great, the broken remains of a once even larger obelisk, the bronze Serpent Column taken by Constantine the Great from Delphi and a fountain donated by Kaiser Wilhelm II in 1898. Beyond the Blue Mosque is the Museum of Mosaics, in the partly reconstructed imperial stables whose walls and even floors were magnificently decorated.

A genuinely unusual site near St. Sophia is the Yerebatan Sarayi or Sunken Palace. It's a cistern built by Justinian in 532. Pathways lead through the 336 Corinthian columns. Though there is an older cistern called Binbirdirek, or Thousand and One Columns, it in fact has only 224.

Unless possessed of unusual stamina, a rest is now clearly indicated. There are some inexpensive eating places round the vast At Meydani (Hippodrome Square) but as sightseeing will almost certainly be resumed at Topkapi Palace, the best introduction to this wonder of the East is a lunch at the Topkapi Sarayi, which is on a terrace inside the palace grounds. It's a little expensive, but well worth it for the atmosphere, view and, lastly, food.

Topkapi Palace

Constantine the Great's Sacred Palace remained unequalled in Christendom for 800 years, but could not be maintained by the declining Byzantine empire and was in ruins when Mehmet II began the construction of the first imperial Turkish kiosk in the incomparable position of Topkapi in 1462. This is the Gate of the Cannon, named after the battery that fired the salute from Seraglio Point. Subsequent sultans added elaborate architectural fantasies in marble and stone, many based rather incongruously on the ancestral nomadic tent, till a bewildering conglomeration of buildings extended over four vast courtyards. In the outer Court of the Janissaries is St. Irene, rebuilt by Justinian after the great fire of 532 and now restored for performances of the Istanbul Festival. The ticket office is in the Bab-i-Selam (Gate of Salutation) which once only the sultan was allowed to enter on horseback. The Divan Court is a huge rose garden leading to the Divan, the Council of State. To the left is the Harem, 400 apartments, halls, rooms and terraces; to the right, a unique collection of Chinese porcelain is housed in the kitchens, where meals used to be prepared for 5,000 people.

Each of the kiosks in the third court contains remarkable treasures, though they are outshone by the fabulous jewels of the Treasury itself, a true cave of Aladdin overspilling into four rooms. The Erivan Kiosk in the fourth court was known as the Golden Cage, as the sultan's closest relatives were kept there in close confinement after the custom of murdering all possible rivals for the throne had been abandoned in the 19th century. The views from the eastern and western terraces are equally stunning. Below the outer court is the Archeological Museum where you can say *sic transit gloria,* in front of the supposed sarcophagus of Alexander the Great.

Don't miss the Suleymaniye Mosque at the peak of the third of Istanbul's seven hills. It was raised in the 16th century by Sinan, the greatest of Turkey's architects, and its dome soars to a height of 174 feet. Below is the mighty aqueduct built by the Emperor Valens in A.D. 375.

Three bridges span the Golden Horn and lead to the new town (actually not all that new as the Galata Tower was erected in 1348 as part of the fortifications protecting the Genoese merchant community). After abandoning Topkapi Palace, the sultans lived in the huge 19th-century Dolmabahce Palace at the entrance of the Bosphorus. Kemal Atatürk died there in 1938.

Excursions from Istanbul

The most pleasant is a cruise along the Bosphorus. The ferryboats leave year round from Eminönü (Galata Bridge) on the old Istanbul side and zigzag between Europe and Asia until they reach the Black Sea. They first sail past Rumelihisar, a castle built by Mehmet II two years before the conquest of Istanbul, then under Europe's longest suspension bridge, 3,540 ft., opened on the 50th anniversary of the Republic in October 1973, and then between charming little villages serving delectable seafood. At Sariyer, you can get a bus or a taxi back (the roundtrip by boat takes five hours).

More relaxing can be done on an excursion by boat, also from Galata Bridge, to the Princes' Islands, six miles from the southern end of the Bosphorus in the Sea of Marmara where there are pleasant wooded resort spots with open-air restaurants and the easy pace of the horse-and-buggy age (no cars are allowed). The boat lands at Büyükada, the biggest of the islands.

PRACTICAL INFORMATION FOR ISTANBUL

HOTELS. Though advance booking is recommended by the tourist authorities, especially for high season, there is no certainty that private bookings will be taken or acted upon by hotels, and the more inexpensive the hotel the greater the chance that your booking will be ignored. However, you might have more success if you book through an agency. Though most of the top hotels are in the elegant residential area round Taksim Square, the newer budget establishments are conveniently close to the main sightseeing area in the Old Town; on the whole they are good value if noisy. In winter, only the more expensive hotels are likely to offer reductions. These can be anything up to 20%.

New Town

Moderate

Bale, Refik Saydam Cad. 62, Tepebasi (tel. 1530 700). Fairly central, modern, with 63 rooms, all with bath, and some with fine views.

Büyük Londra Oteli, Meşrutiyet Cad. 117 Tepebasi (tel. 1450 670). 42 rooms; a turn-of-the-century hotel that has grown old gracefully and has faded character.

Dilson, Siraselviler Cad. 49 (tel. 1521 305). 90 rooms, very central.

Keban, Siraselviler Cad. 51 (tel. 1522 504). 87 rooms, off Taksim Square. Small rooms but all modern amenities.

Inexpensive

Çirağan, Müvezzi Cad. 3, Beşiktaş (tel. 1600 230). 64 rooms, quiet; beyond Dolmabahçe Palace.

Opera, Inönü Cad. 38–42, Taksim (tel. 1435 527). 50 rooms, some with pleasant views.

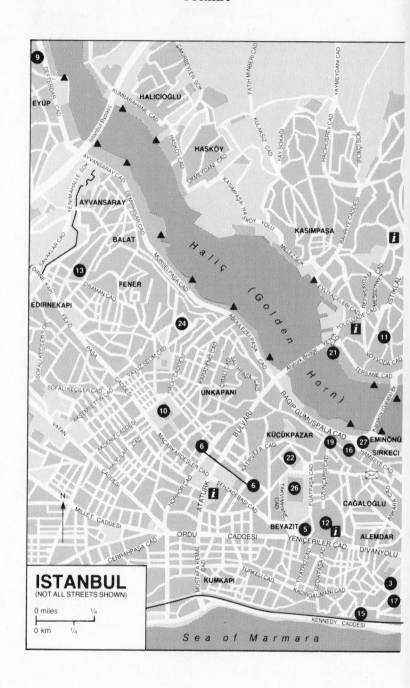

ISTANBUL
(NOT ALL STREETS SHOWN)

0 miles ¼
0 km ¼

Sea of Marmara

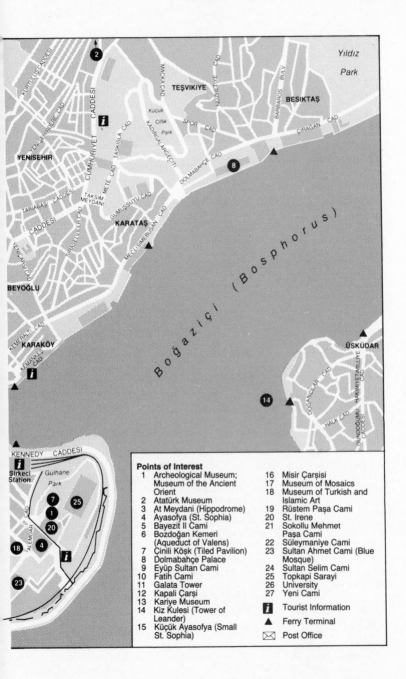

Points of Interest

1 Archeological Museum; Museum of the Ancient Orient
2 Atatürk Museum
3 At Meydani (Hippodrome)
4 Ayasofya (St. Sophia)
5 Bayezit II Cami
6 Bozdoğan Kemeri (Aqueduct of Valens)
7 Çinili Köşk (Tiled Pavilion)
8 Dolmabahçe Palace
9 Eyüp Sultan Cami
10 Fatih Cami
11 Galata Tower
12 Kapali Çarşi
13 Kariye Museum
14 Kiz Kulesi (Tower of Leander)
15 Küçük Ayasofya (Small St. Sophia)

16 Misir Çarşisi
17 Museum of Mosaics
18 Museum of Turkish and Islamic Art
19 Rüstem Paşa Cami
20 St. Irene
21 Sokollu Mehmet Paşa Cami
22 Süleymaniye Cami
23 Sultan Ahmet Cami (Blue Mosque)
24 Sultan Selim Cami
25 Topkapi Sarayi
26 University
27 Yeni Cami

i Tourist Information
▲ Ferry Terminal
✉ Post Office

Plaza, Siraselviler Cad., Arslanyatağı Sok. 19, Taksim (tel. 1453 273). 18 rooms, older-style, views over Bosphorus.

Santral, Siraselviler Cad., Billurcu Sok. (tel. 1511 810). 83 rooms and as central as the name indicates; garage.

Old Town

Moderate

Akgün, Ordu Cad., Haznedar Sok. (tel. 5120 260). 87 rooms. Close to main sights.

Anka, Molla Gürani Cad. 42, Findikzade (tel. 5256 002). 65 airconditioned rooms; garage.

Kalyon, Sahil Yolu, Sultanahmet (tel. 5114 400). 38 rooms on seafront.

Olcay, Millet Cad. 187 (tel. 5853 220). 134 rooms; on the main road to the airport and further from the sightseeing area. Swimming pool.

Inexpensive

Astor, Laleli Cad. 12, Aksaray (tel. 5224 423). 42 rooms and within easy walking distance of the main sightseeing area.

Babaman, Laleli Cad. 19, Aksaray (tel. 5268 238). 53 rooms.

Barin, Fevziye Cad. 25, Sehzadebasi (tel. 5264 440). Good-value, newer hotel with all amenities and English-speaking staff.

Barut's Guesthouse, Ishak Pasa Cad. 8, Sultanahmet (tel. 5201 227). 22 rooms. Quiet, secluded, with roof terrace overlooking the Sea of Mamara. Owned and run by friendly Turkish people.

Berk Guesthouse, Kutlugun Sok. 27, Cankurtaran, Sultanahmet (tel. 5110 737). Warm hospitality in quiet and comfortable 7-room house.

Bern, Millet Cad., Muratpasa Sok. 16, Aksaray (tel. 5232 462). 46 rooms.

Burc, Gencturk Cad., Laleli (tel. 5138 186). 32 rooms.

Eyfel Oteli, Kurultay Sok. 19 Beyazit (tel. 5209 788). 85 rooms.

Hakan, Genctürk Cad. 9, Aksaray (tel. 5122 370). 40 rooms.

Kilim, Millet Cad. 23, Findikzade (tel. 5853 246). 42 rooms and restaurant.

Hostels: *Topkapi Atatürk Student Center,* Londra Asfalti, Cevizlibağ Duragi; and *Kadirga Student Hostel,* Cömertler Sok. 6, Kumkapi. **Camp sites:** open from April to October, and all on the E5 road near Yesilköyairport, at *Ataköy Camping,* on the beach near Bakirköy; *Mocamp Kervansaray Kartaltepe,* 4 miles from the beach; and *Yesilyurt Camping.*

RESTAURANTS. Generally, as both prices and settings in Moderate restaurants, though not the food, would be considered as definitely belonging to Inexpensive categories in most Western towns and cities, we strongly recommend that you stick to this higher category (at least in larger towns and resorts; in more remote provinces Inexpensive restaurants are frequently all there is on offer and, except for the somewhat sleazy get-up, they are normally quite acceptable). Dining rooms in Moderate hotels, which have fixed price menus, are the cheapest and easiest but least interesting solution for budget eating.

New Town

Moderate

Bab, Yeşilçam Sok. 24, Beyoglu. A very conveniently located cafeteria.

Borsa Lokantasi, Halaskargazi Cad. 90, Osmanbey (tel. 1324 200). Open daily 11.30 A.M.–11.30 P.M.

Dört Mevsim, Istiklal Cad. 509, Beyoglu (tel. 1458 941). Well above the average, run by Anglo-Turkish couple. Closed Sun.

Hacibaba, Istiklal Cad. 49, Taksim (tel. 1441 886). Full menu, easily selected from display inside. Tables on the terrace overlook leafy churchyard.

Hanedan Restoran, Ciğdem Sok. 27, Besiktas (tel. 1604 854). 50 yards from Besiktas ferry terminal. Sit outside in summer.

Kaptan, Arnavutköy, 1 Cad. 53 (tel. 1658 487). Worth taking a cab to. A favorite with locals; happy, crowded restaurant across from the Bosphorus. Fish a real treat.

Malta Köskü. 19th-century pavilion in Yildiz Park. Offers stunning views, garden setting, and classical music, but slightly expensive. Good for lunch, teas, and cocktails.

Pizza Prima, Halaskargazi Cad. 40, Osmanbey. Italian of sorts.

Rejans, Olivo Gecidi 15, off Istiklal Cad., Galatasaray (tel. 1441 610): Hidden up stairs at end of a cul-de-sac; founded by three Russian dancing girls fleeing the revolution and immortalized by Hemingway. Celebrated for its Chicken Kievski and lemon vodka.

Swiss Pub, Cumhuriyet Cad. 14. Reasonable prices but short on authenticity.

Zihni, Bronz Sok. 21, Tesvikiye, Macka (tel. 1469 043). Piano bar.

Inexpensive

Cicek Pasaji (Flower Market) is an animated area off Istiklal Cad. with little restaurants and lively bars, where you can be entertained by street musicians and eat inexpensively.

Haci Salih, Alyon Sok., off Istiklal Cad. Popular lunch place for locals. Traditional cooking with vegetarian dishes a specialty. Very simple, clean, and good value. No alcohol.

Old Town

Moderate

Havuzlu Lokanta, Gani Celebi Sokagi, Grand Bazaar, next to Post Office. Courtyard with tables and marble fountain provides restful atmosphere. Also a spacious dining room.

Konyali, Medidiye Kökü, Topkapi Saray (tel. 5139 596). In palace grounds. Lunches only; unbeatable for atmosphere, and the view from the large terrace justifies the more expensive food. Cheaper snack bar below.

Pandeli, Misir Carsisi, Eminönü (tel. 5225 534). Up two flights of stairs, over the main arched gateway to the Egyptian Market. Beautiful tiled, domed alcoves off central room, some with views; long-aproned waiters serve traditional food in style. Lunch only.

On the Bosphorus

The innumerable restaurants, cafés and nightclubs here are, by Turkish standards, uncharacteristically expensive, though not if the high quality of the seafood is taken into account. Among the largest concentration, on the lovely Bay of Tarabya, the *Köşem Bistro,* Kefeliköy Cad. 92, is within the Moderate range. There is also a series of restaurants called *Palet* scattered about, each numbered from one to five. But they are a little more expensive, so check the price list outside carefully; number two is definitely out of the budget category, though perhaps the Janissary band and dancing will prove sufficiently tempting to let you forget your budget. Kumkapi is an area of the Old Town with dozens of little fish restaurants in a network of streets running off Sahil Yolu, due south of Laleli. Prices vary, but fish is generally more expensive than meat. Many have live music.

GETTING AROUND ISTANBUL. By Bus. The City trolley-bus service is efficient but limited, with buses in short supply. Ordinary buses are both antiquated and overcrowded at any time of day. Buses for the European shore of the Bosphorus (No. 40) and of the Marmara (No. 94 for Florya and No. 96 for Yesilköy) leave at frequent intervals from Taksim Square. For the Asian shore of the Bosphorus and the Marmara, buses leave from the landing wharf in Kadiköy, Üsküdar.

The terminal for most overland buses is at Edirnekapi and Topkapi (not to be confused with the palace), both of which are gates in the land ramparts.

By Minibus. With frequent stops along fixed routes, these are essential complements to the inadequate public transport system. They are in fact only slightly more expensive than buses, which is to say that they are still incredibly cheap. At the

Sirkeci rail station and Taksim Square, the main terminals, signposts indicate the various routes and directions; elsewhere, it is difficult for the foreigner to discover routes.

By Taxi. Fares are very reasonable and are metered. Round off to the next TL 100. Taxis have distinctive black and yellow checks around the middle of the car.

By Train. There are electric trains from the Sirkeci rail station to Ataköy and Florya beaches on the Sea of Marmara.

By Boat. There are main boat terminals at both ends of the Galata Bridge, catamarans up the Golden Horn, and ferries to the Bosphorus and the Princes' Islands. There is a car ferry from Kabataş, near the Dolmabahçe Palace, to Üsküdar.

On Foot. Walking anywhere in the Old Town is rewarding, but nowhere more than along the four miles of the ramparts (12 ft. thick and 43 ft. high), with 90 towers and seven monumental gates) begun by Theodosius II in 413. But there is no need to follow their entire length from the Castle of the Seven Towers (Yedikule) on the Sea of Marmara to the Golden Horn as there are buses and minibuses from the Topkapi and Edirnekapi (Gates), about halfway along, to the main sightseeing center round At Meydani (Hippodrome Square). There, the main sights must be visited on foot unless you take an organized tour.

ENTERTAINMENT. Nightlife. The once fabled belly dancers of Istanbul have now mostly gone to America and got jobs in the Catskills. However, there is a species of entertainment called, rather grandly, Turkish Cabaret. But this is unreasonably expensive for what is really no more than provincial striptease. There are some less expensive places, which do not style themselves so grandly, in the lowlife district of Sirkeci behind the rail station where dancing women of mature age do sad turns on wooden platforms to a deafening din (the real show is among the spectators).

There are, however, a few discos and clubs, all moderately priced in the New Town. Among them, *Taksim Belediye Gazinosu,* in Taksim Park, is relatively good value, though of course there is no gambling (a gazino and kulup bear little or no relation to a Western casino or club). Cumhuriyet Cad. has a fairly reasonable choice of spots; *Kulup 33,* at no. 18, has a certain amount of life after 9.30 when the restaurant closes and the disco takes over. *Regine Gazinosu,* at no. 16, is an upscale disco-nightclub open 10 P.M.–4 A.M. *Kulia* Cumhuriyet Cad. 117 (tel. 1469 345), an all-night hangout for actors and writers, offers good piano music. For jazz fans, *Bilsak,* Soganci Sok. 7, Siraselviler Cad. (tel. 1432 899) is an easy-going restaurant and jazz bar where local groups and singers sometimes perform. Closed Sundays.

Cinema. Some films in English are always on show in the cinemas around Taksim Square. Consult the *Daily News* for programs.

Theaters. Straight plays in Turkish need the special setting of Rumeli Hisar Castle on the Bosphorus, or of St. Irene at Topkapi during the *Istanbul Arts Festival* in June and July. Always of interest to the tourist are the opera, ballet and concert performances in the 1,300 seat Atatürk Cultural Palace (box office tel. 1515 600) on Taksim Square.

There are *son et lumière* performances every evening from May to October in front of the Blue Mosque.

MUSEUMS. Mosques can be visited by anyone so long as you wear the felt slippers provided outside over your shoes, or leave your shoes outside. The Topkapi Museum is closed on Tuesday, all others are closed on Monday.

Archeological Museum (Greek and Roman) and **Museum of the Ancient Orient** (Mesopotamia and Hittite), below the Topkapi Palace. Many fine statues and a famous collection of old coins.

Atatürk Museum. Kemal Atatürk's house, unchanged, together with a display of documents and miscellanea charting the history of the Turkish Republic.

Çinili Köşk (Tiled Kiosk), opposite the Archeological Museum. The summer residence of Mehmet II and now the Museum of Tiles.

Kariye Museum (Church of the Holy Savior of the Chora Monastery), near the Edirne Gate. Fine mosaics and frescoes dating from the Byzantine period.

Museum of Aya Sofya (St. Sophia). Remarkable example of Byzantine art; awe-inspiring interior with its dome decorated with magnificent mosaics and marbles.

Museum of Mosaics, stables of the Imperial Palace. In their original setting; mosaic pictures and architectural designs.

Museum of Turkish and Islamic Art, in a restored palace facing the Hippodrome. Treasures of religious art from the Turkish empire.

Topkapi Palace Museum. The maze of the restored harem; a dazzling display of the treasure of the Sultans, together with fine collections of glazed earthenware, china, old weapons and armor, enamels, miniatures and embroidery.

PALACES. The white marble *Dolmabahçe Sarayi* was built by Sultan Abdul Mecit in 1853 in a Turkish-Indian-Baroque style worthy of the Arabian Nights. It has baths, a collection of fabulous reception rooms and halls and a number of 19th-and 20th-century paintings. The *Beylerbeyi Sarayi,* on the Asiatic coast of the Bosphorus, was built in 1865. The interior conforms exactly to Hollywood's ideal of an Oriental palace with gilded walls and floors and outsize Sevres vases. The *Yildiz Sarayi,* in which Abdul Hamid II led his haunted life, consists of several small kiosks connected by underground passages and was built during the last half of the 19th century. There is a workshop of glazed earthenware, a park with beautiful trees (some 500 years old) and a wonderful view over the Bosphorus. The Malta and Kadir kiosks are now pleasant restaurants with Moderate prices.

SHOPPING. The best buys are to be found in some 4,000 minute shops all huddled together under one roof in the *Grand Bazaar,* a labyrinth of 82 streets and alleys, with a mosque, 10 prayer houses and a hammam, near the Bayezit Mosque in the Old Town. All neon and electric signs have recently been removed, a great improvement to the oriental atmosphere but not to the overwhelming variety of mass-produced junk. Yet there are still many good buys, ranging from leather goods to copper and brass ware, rugs and embroideries, onyx jewelry, towels and slippers. But don't get conned into buying so-called antiques whose provenance is not even doubtful in most cases (the cheaper they are the more phony they'll be; in any case, the genuine article, increasingly rare these days, can't be exported without an export license). But for all goods, no matter what the price asked, you are expected to bargain—even if you think the first price reasonable. Bargaining is part of the game, and if there is no deal no one will be offended. Don't be in a hurry, absorb the atmosphere and look around.

As Turkey is considered a developing country, many of the things you buy there will be exempt from U.S. Customs under the G.S.P. plan (details in *Planning Your Trip* at the beginning of the book).

The pungent odors of cinnamon, clove, mint and thyme waft through the Egyptian or Spice Bazaar (Misir Çarşisi) next to the New Mosque (Yeni Cami) at the Galata Bridge. The poisonous-looking green powder is Henna, used to dye hair and nails red. Cured meal spiced with garlic *(pastirma),* huge rounds of cheese, pickled vegetables and wooden frames of Anatolian honey are the best buys.

Halvah loukoum (Turkish Delight) and other enticing candies make welcome presents and do not necessarily have to be eaten on the spot. The best place to look for these is along Istiklal Cad., which has preserved the nostalgic pre-war atmosphere of what used then to be the elegant part of the New Town, below Taksim Square. Bargaining is frowned upon here but practiced nonetheless; but on crossing central Taksim Square and hitting the elegant boutiques of Cumhuriyet Cad. it is definitely not acceptable.

USEFUL ADDRESSES. *Consulates: British,* Mesrutiyet Cad. 34 (tel. 1447 540); *U.S.,* Mesrutiyet Cad. 106 (tel. 1513 602). *Church of England,* British Consulate, Consulate Gardens; *Catholic Church,* St. Espirt, Cumhuriyet Cad., Taksim; *Neve Shalom Synagogue,* Büyük Hendek Cad. 61, Şişhane. *American Hospital,* Güzelbahçe Sok. 20, Nişantaşi (tel. 1314 050). *Turkish Airlines,* Cumhuriyet Cad. 131 (tel. 1452 454); Hilton Hotel entrance, Cumhuriyet Cad. (tel. 1470 121). *American Ex-*

press, Hilton Hotel entrance, Cumhuriyet Cad. (tel. 1481 406). *Wagons Lits Tourisme,* Cumhuriyet 22; nearly all airline and travel agencies are on Cumhuriyet Cad. *Post Office:* Head Office, Yeni Postahane Cad., Eminönü, Old Town; branch offices in Mesrutiyet Cad. near British Consulate, and in Cumhuriyet Cad. near Taksim Square. *Tourist Police (Turizm Polisi),* Mimar Kemalettin Cad., Sirkeci (tel. 5274 503).

Side Trips from Istanbul: Edirne and Bursa

Edirne (the ancient Hadrianople), close to the Bulgarian and Greek borders, is four hours away by bus from Istanbul but well over five hours by train. Outstanding among the splendid edifices around the huge, central Cumhuriyet Square is Sinan's masterpiece, the Selimiye Cami, built between 1568 and 1574 by Sultan Selim II. The Caravanserai of Rustem Pasha, also designed by Sinan, has been expertly restored. The adjoining Eski Cami (Old Mosque) is, as its name suggests, the earliest Turkish monument. It was built by Mehmet I in 1413. Between 1437 and 1447, Murat II added the Üç Şerefeli Cami, the Mosque with the Three Galleries. Next to Ali Pasha's Bazaar, 19 cupolas rise above the Bedesten (Covered Bazaar), another of Sinan's works.

Bursa, the first capital of the Ottoman Empire, is known as Yeşil (Green) Bursa, not only because of its many trees and parks but also because of its Yeşil Cami (Green Mosque) and Yeşil Turbe (Green Mausoleum), which derive their names from their green tiles. Off the town square called Heykel, is the Ulu Cami (Great Mosque) with its 20 domes. Bursa is also the site of Uludag (the Great Mountain), Turkey's most popular skiing resort. Many hotels offer *celiks* (mineral baths). Daily flights take 20 minutes from Istanbul. Express ferries and hydrofoils leave Istanbul's Kabataş dock for Yalova where buses depart from the dock for Bursa.

PRACTICAL INFORMATION FOR EDIRNE AND BURSA

Hotels and Restaurants

Bursa. *Diyar* (M), Çekirge Cad. 47 (tel. 209 786), 35 rooms; *Ada Palas* (I), Murat Cad. 21 (tel. 361 600), 39 rooms, thermal baths; *Huzur* (I), Birinici Murat Camii Bitsigi (tel. 158 021), mineral baths; *Ilman* (I), Kültür Park Karsisi (tel. 206 590), 28 rooms. All the above are in the quieter Çekirge suburb near Kültür Park where the archeological museum is located. *Artic* (I), Fevzi Çakmak Cad. 123 (tel. 219 500), 63 rooms, all with bath, modern and very central, near the Great Mosque.

Restaurants. All (M) and serving particularly tasty doner kebab, leg of lamb broiled on an upright spit, best with yogurt, the local specialty, are: *Özkent,* Kültür Park; and *Sönmez,* Yükseller Mev. (tel. 145 460). Favorite, inexpensive places for lunch where you might have to wait in line (but it's worth it) are: *Kebabçi,* Kayhan Carsis, where the famous kebab originated, in a mosque courtyard; and *Cicek Izgara,* Bazaar Yeri, for delicious *köfte,* in Ottoman-style house behind municipal buildings. Both these are near Ulu Cami mosque.

Edirne. *Balta Otel* (M), Talatpaşa Asfalti (tel. 15210). 80 rooms with bath. *Fifi Lokantasi* (M), Demirkapi Mevkii, is as fanciful as its name. *Kervan* (I), Talatpaşa Cad. 134 (tel. 11382). 48 rooms, garage, good restaurant. *Park Oteli* (I) Maarif Cad. (tel. 14610). *Sultan Oteli* (I), Talatpaşa Cad. 170 (tel. 11372).

The North Aegean Coast

Canakkale, at the northernmost tip of the Aegean Coast, is five and a half hours west of Bursa by bus. This is a good stopping off point if you're heading for the battlefields of Gallipoli.

The ruins of ancient Troy are 40 minutes southwest of Canakkale. Long thought to be simply an imaginary city from Homer's Iliad, Troy was excavated in the 1870s by Heinrich Schliemann, a German amateur archeologist. He found the remains of nine successive civilizations, one on top of the other, dating back 5,000 years. Considering Troy's fame, the site is surprisingly small.

Between Canakkale and Izmir the E24 highway leads around the Gulf of Edremit, an area of olive groves, pine forests, and small seaside resorts. Ayvalik is an ideal place to stay while visiting the ancient site of Pergamum (modern-day Bergama). These Greco-Roman ruins are spread out over several miles, so it's best to take a taxi or *dolmus* (shared taxi) from one site to the next. The most noteworthy places are the Asklepieion, the Archeological Museum, the Red Hall, and the Acropolis, whose library once contained a collection of 200,000 books, all on papyrus.

The fire of 1922 destroyed almost all of the old town, but the traveler will still find much of interest in the Agora (ancient Greek marketplace), the fortress of Kadifekale on Mount Pagos, with its beautiful view over the bay of Izmir, the Archeological Museum in the center of the modern town of over two million inhabitants. Opposite the Clock Tower, built at the beginning of the century, is the small mosque of Konak, with its fine glazed tiles.

For a rest from sightseeing, you might want to go for a swim on the beach at Inciralti, about seven miles out of town toward Çeşme. A pleasant outing is to take the ferry across the bay towards Karşiyaka.

PRACTICAL INFORMATION FOR THE NORTH AEGEAN COAST

Hotels and Restaurants

Ayvalik. *Ankara Oteli* (I), Sarimsakli Mey (tel. 41195). 57 rooms with bath. Located on beach.

Bergama. *Tuscan Bergama Moteli* (M), Izmir Yolu, Cati Mev. (tel. 1173) 42 rooms with bath. On the main road leading into Bergama, the Tuscan has a pool fed by hot springs.

Çeşme. *Ertan* (M), Cumhuriyet Mey 12 (tel. 26795), 60 rooms, on waterfront facing main square. *Turban Ilica Motel* (M), Dereboyu Mev. Boyalik (tel. 32128); beach. *Sahil* (M), outdoor seaside restaurant across the square from the Ertan; good for seafood suppers and leisurely breakfasts.

Izmir. *Anba* (M), Cumhuriyet Bulvari 124 (tel. 144 380). 53 rooms, more pricey but excellent value. *Karaca* (M), 1379 Sok (tel. 144 445). 68 rooms and equally central. *Kilim* (M), Atatük Bulvari (tel. 145 340). 88 rooms, faces the sea. All airconditioned. *Billur* (I), Anafartalar Cad. 783 (tel. 136 250). 60 rooms. *Kaya* (I), Gazi Osman Paşa Bulvari 45 (tel. 139 771). 52 rooms, adequate.

Restaurants. There is good seafood to be had along the waterfront, but it is unusually expensive, perhaps as a result of the large U.S. presence at the nearby NATO command. *Bergama, Imbat* and *Mangal,* all on Atatürk Cad, where the *Golden Restaurant* conforms more to the usual (M) price range. Likewise *Kervansaray* and *Park* in the green oasis of the Kültür Park, next to *Ada Gazinosu* (M) and *Göl Gazinosu* (M), respectable nightspots open in summer only. *Bonjur Gazinosu* (M) and *Nümune Gazinosu* (M) in Cumhuriyet Bulvari, are open all year round.

Troy. 8 miles north, at Intepe, *Tusan-Truva Motel* (M), (tel. 14 61), 64 rooms, most with views over the Dardanelles. Set in a quiet pine forest; beach.

Ephesus and the Aegean Coast

Allow at least a day to tour Ephesus, one of the grandest reconstructed archeological sites in the world. To appreciate the atmosphere of this ancient Greek and Roman city to the full, with its long marble road grooved by chariot wheels, go early or late in the day to miss the bus tours and crowds. There's much remaining of the city's splendors to see, including the ornate, two-story Library of Celsus with its rolls of papyrus in the reading room, the noblemen's houses with terraces and courtyards, a 25,000-seat amphitheater, municipal baths, and a brothel.

In the 11th century B.C. the Ionians arrived at Ephesus and established the city as a powerful trading port as well as a sacred center for the cult of Artemis, Greek goddess of chastity, building a temple in her honor, the foundations of which remain.

St. Paul and St. John both preached here and it is believed that a simple house, five kilometers from Ephesus at Meryemana, is where St. John brought the mother of Christ after the Crucifixion, and from where the Virgin ascended to heaven. Following the visits of Pope Paul VI in 1967 and Pope John Paul in 1979, it has become an increasingly popular place of pilgrimage.

When you are through sightseeing, relax on the sea only 12 miles away. Kuşadasi lies in the middle of a huge landlocked gulf divided by promontories into a series of fine beaches, each provided with modern hotels. This is an ideal center for excursions not only to nearby Priene, Miletus and Didyma (Didim), each remarkable for its antique ruins, but also to Bodrum, ancient Halicarnassus further south, and inland to Pamukkale, the stonework Niagara near the ancient city of Hierapolis.

The coast south of Bodrum, which is now accessible with the opening of Dalaman airport, is pocketed with wooded coves, fishing villages, and the more developed resorts such as Marmaris. It's an ideal place to hire boats from, and to explore the coastline with its remote beaches and archeological sites such as Xanthos, Letoon, and Pinara. Boats from Marmaris will take you up the Dalyan River estuary to ancient Caunus, past Lycian rock tombs, and boats from Kaş will take you to the ancient sunken city of Kekova.

PRACTICAL INFORMATION FOR EPHESUS AND THE AEGEAN COAST

Hotels and Restaurants

Bodrum. A fashionable, crowded yachting center, packed with family-run pensions and small hotels, and with many lively restaurants along the harbor, at the foot of the castle, and in town. *Baraz* (M), (tel. 1857). 24 rooms; *Gozen* (M) (tel. 1602). 20 rooms; *Artemis Pansiyon* (I), (tel. 2530), 22 rooms; *Merhaba Pansiyon,* Akasya Sok. 5 (tel. 2115); hot showers and good roof terrace; *Mylasa Pansiyon,* (tel. 1846); all along Cumhuriyet Cad. Ask for sea view.*Cem Pansiyon* (I), Üçkuyular Cad. 7 (tel. 1757). *Evin Pansiyon* (I), Kumbahçe Mah. Ortanca Sok. 7 (tel. 1312). *Heredot Pansiyon* (I), Neyzen Tevfik Cad. 178 (tel. 1093).

Dalyan. *Kaunos Otel and Restaurant* (I), Posta Kodu 48810 (tel. 1057). On waterfront. *Hotel Turtle* (I), Sultaniye, Koyu (tel. 6114 1487). Telephone for boat to pick you up. On lakeside amongst orchards.

Didyma. *Hotel Makar* (I), 22 rooms, all with shower. Family-run, 50 yards from beach, good restaurant.

Fethiye. Likya Hotel (I), Karagözler Mah. (tel. 1169). *Ülgen Pension* (I), Cumhuriyet Mah. Paspatir Mevki 3 Merdivenli Yokusu (tel. 3491). *Günes* restaurant (M) Likya Cad. 4. Open daily 9 A.M.–late. By harbor, near Yap Kredi Bank. Good fresh Turkish food. *Rafat* restaurant, on the waterfront, is recommended.

Gümbet (two miles from Bodrum) has the largest beach in the area. *Sport Hotel* (M), (tel. 1247). *Tarça Hotel* (M), (tel. 1721 2914). *Bavaria Pansiyon* (I), (tel. 1945).

Kalkan. *Kalkan Han* (M), Koyici Mev. (tel. 151), 16 rooms. Restored house with rooftop breakfast terrace. *Balikçihan Pansiyon,* (I), (tel. 1075), 7 rooms. *Pashas Inn Pansiyon* (I), 10 Sok. 8 (tel. 1077).

Good fish restaurants, such as the *Korsan,* line the small bay. There are more fish restaurants on the road above.

Kaş. *Çan Otel* (M), off Hükümet Cad. (tel. 1441). A wonderfully restored village house with lots of charm. *Kaş Oteli* (M), Hastane Cad. 15 (tel. 1271). Wonderful view over the sea to Castellorizo, but the plumbing could be better. Good swimming off the rocks at the front. *Mimosa Oteli* (M), Elmali Cad. (tel. 1272). 20 rooms; recently built on hillside. *Toros Hotel* (M), (tel. 1923). 22 rooms.

Mercan Restaurant (M), Hükümet Cad. Good fish restaurant on the harbor.

Kuşadası. *Akman* (M), Istiklal Cad. 13 (tel. 11501). 46 rooms, just outside the village and across the road from the beach. *Kustur Tatil Köyü* (M), (tel. 14110). 400 tiny bungalows near beach. *Marti,* (M), Kadinlar Denizi Mevkii (tel. 13650). 113 rooms, more expensive and directly on the beach. *Aran* (I), Kaya Aldoğan Cad. (tel. 11325). 22 rooms. *Filiz Pansiyon* (I), Yavansu Mev. (tel. 12471). *Grup Pansiyon* (I), Istiklal Cad. 3 (tel. 11230). *Posaci Pansiyon* (I), Leylak Sok. 5 (tel. 11151). *Stella* (I), Bezirgan Sok. 44 (tel. 11632). Good views and pleasant bar, breakfast served on the roof. Restaurant-cum-disco is planned.

Restaurant. *Sultan Han* (M), Bahar Sok. 8 (tel. 3849). Traditional food in old Turkish house with courtyard.

Marmaris. Popular beach resort on a lovely bay. *Atlantik,* (tel. 11218), 42 rooms; *Marmaris,* (tel. 11308), 63 rooms; both (M), on noisy seafront across the beach. *Turban Marmaris Tatil Köyü* (M), (tel. 11843). 248 bungalows on a good beach. *Halici Hotel* (M), (tel. 11683). 93 rooms, near beach. *Manolya Pansiyon* (I), Siteler Mah 15 (tel. 12514). *Nalan Pansiyon* (I), Siteler Tek Mev. (tel. 14089).

Restaurants. *Bamboo* (M), *Liman* (M), *Tilla* (M) are the best of the many fish places on the seafront. For nightlife, try *Palmiye* (M) and *Yarasa* (M).

Ölü Deniz. (Fethiye's beach). Camp site facilities along lagoon and beach, some with bungalows. Restaurants line the beach, and they're filled with music and crowds come the evening. *Kebapici Salonu* (I). Behind Han Camp. Grill your own meat at your table in this outdoor restaurant. Meals served with meze, salad, and wine.

Pamukkale. *Motel Koru* (M), 120 rooms, four pools. *Tusan* (M), (tel. 1010). 47 rooms within old ruined fort; large open-air thermal pools and splendid view. *Konak* (I), 16 rooms, small pool, good Turkish meals. *Mistur* (I), 34 rooms, pool, camp attached. *Turizm* (I), 31 rooms around pool above the ruins of the ancient agora.

Selçuk. *Tusan Efes* (M), Efes Yolu 38 (tel. 1060). 12 rooms. *Hülya Pansiyon* (I), Atatürk Cad. Özgür Sok. 15 (tel. 2120). Delightful family house with the option of delicious meals. *Kale Han* (I), Atatürk Cad. 49 (tel. 1154). 18 rooms.

Turgutreis (Bodrum Peninsula). *Mut Hotel* (M), Domalan Mev. (tel. 1241). *Simin Hotel* (M), Akyarlar Köyü (tel. 1313). *Özünal Hotel* (I), Yali Mev. (tel. 1067).

The Turquoise Coast

Few shores can rival the profusion of natural and artistic beauties found along the 400 miles from the Bay of Antalya to the Bay of Mersin.

Antalya, the capital of this Riviera, was a summer resort in the days of the Seljuk Turks 800 years ago, and offers an imposing portal built for the entry of the Emperor Hadrian in A.D. 130, a grooved minaret dating back to 1230, and the Karatay Mosque of 1250. And best of all, is the spectacular view over the gulf to the Lycian mountains above miles of pebble and sand beaches in a semi-tropical setting of banana plantations and orange groves. In season, there is a twice-daily plane service from Istanbul. It's ideal for early or late sunshine; July and August are advisable only if you really like heat.

Near Antalya lies Perge, with the remains of an acropolis. The best-preserved amphitheater of the ancient world (seating capacity 15,000 and it's still used for open-air performances) is at Aspendos, 31 miles to the east. There's an even bigger amphitheater at Side, 19 miles on.

85 miles southeast is Turkey's largest beach resort, Alanya. It sits below an 800-foot cliff that is crowned by an enormous fortress five miles in circumference. Within the third rampart rose the palace of the great Seljuk Sultan Alaeddin Keykubat. A curtain wall still descends to the huge octagonal Red Tower next to the 13th-century shipyards.

PRACTICAL INFORMATION FOR THE TURQUOISE COAST

Hotels and Restaurants

Alanya. *Alaadin* (M), Saray Mahallesi, Atatürk Cad. (tel. 12624). 108 rooms, in town. *Kaptan* (M), Iskele Cad. 62. (tel. 14900). 45 rooms; also in town. Both hotels are on the seafront, but though they claim a beach it is too polluted for bathing. *Günaydin* (I), Kültür Cad. (tel. 11943). 18 rooms. *Özen* (I), Müftüler Cad. 35 (tel. 12220). 28 rooms.

A good choice of hotels extends along the eastern beach. *Banana* (M), (tel. 11548). 350 rooms, pool, beach across the road, tennis and riding. *Panorama* (M), (tel. 1181). 138 rooms, beach. *Merhaba* (I), Keykubat Cad. (tel. 1251). 62 rooms. *Selam* (I), (tel. 1250). 28 rooms. On the less "in" west beach are: *Mini Pansiyon* (I), 10 rooms and *Neslihan Pansiyon* (I), 21 rooms.

Restaurants. *Akdeniz* (M), *Basarka* (M) and *Keykubat* (M) are good for seafood. There are several *kebapci;* all (I).

Antalya. *Lara* (M), Lara Yolu (tel. 190 142). 75 rooms. On a fine beach 7 miles out, pool. *Altun Pansiyon* (I), Kaleici Mev. (tel. 116 624). 15 rooms, very clean and cheerful, near Fluted Minaret. *Büyük* (I), Cumhuriyet Cad. 57 (tel. 111 499). 42 rooms, half with sea view; no restaurant. *Hayat Oteli* (I), Kazim Ozalp Cad. 81 (tel. 11 226). Near bus station.

Restaurants. The old port district has been expertly restored, and the small yacht basin is surrounded by a good choice of (M) restaurants and snack bars. Drink tea from samovars and watch the sunset from the tea garden overlooking the harbor.

Mersin. *Hosta* (M), Fasih Kayabali Cad. 4 (tel. 147 60). 52 rooms. *Nobel Oteli* (M), Istikal Cad. 101 (tel. 11 227). *Savran Oteli* (M), Saguksu Cad. 46 (tel. 24 472). *Toros* (M), Atatürk Cad. 33 (tel. 12 201), 62 rooms.

Restaurants. *Fuar Lokantasi* (M), Yeni Sahil Yolu. *Liman Lokantasi* (M), Liman Binasi Üstü.

Side. *Motel Cennet* (M), Selimiye Köyü, (tel. 11 67). 110 rooms. *Turtel* (M), tel. 22 25. 46 rooms, above average. Both on beach.

Ankara

Ankara has grown into a city of over 3 million inhabitants since it became the Turkish capital in 1923. Atatürk called in leading European town planners, swamps were drained, huge government buildings were raised and wide, airy boulevards and parks were laid out.

The most imposing structure in Ankara is the Atatürk Mausoleum, a vast soaring hall surrounded by colonnades, completed in the early fifties. But the citadel of old Angora still stands with its inner fortress and its white tower. At this crossroads of history, there is the Temple of Augustus, Roman baths and an aqueduct, the Alaeddin and Aslanhane mosques, a model farm founded by Atatürk, the National Opera House and the Turkish National Theater. And last, the splendid Museum of Anatolian Civilizations housed in a former *bedesten* (covered bazaar), where you can admire the most important collection of Hittite art in existence.

Ankara can be your base for excursions into Anatolia, notably to Göreme (center of Cappadocia), Kayseri and Konya.

The Göreme valley is easily accessible, a site unparalleled on earth with its fairy chimneys and honeycombed rocks. This was once a monastic center with 365 churches, many still adorned by amazing frescoes. From the cataclysmic landscape, the gigantic rock needle of Ortahisar thrusts up.

To complete this fairy-tale setting, there are two underground cities. Eight spacious floors, each offering accommodation for 200 people, were carved into the bowels of the earth. At Kaymakli, twelve miles south of Nevşehir, a central airshaft assures perfect ventilation all the 250 feet down to the bottom, from which a tunnel runs 16 miles south to another self-contained city at Derinkuyu.

Kayseri, the ancient Caesarea Mazaca, is a 40-minute flight or morning's drive from Ankara and lies at an altitude of 3,270 feet (Ankara is at 2,900 feet). It offers remains of the civilization of the Seljuk Turks, including a hospital built there in 1204, and the Great Mosque of 1136.

Konya lies 160 miles from Ankara. It was St. Paul's Iconium and the capital of Alaeddin Keykubat, who used 42 columns from Roman temples for his mosque. The monastery round the tomb of the founder of the Whirling Dervishes is now a museum. The 13th-century Karatay Medrese is a ceramics museum; and the Ince Minaret Medrese is a museum of stone and wood carvings.

PRACTICAL INFORMATION FOR ANKARA AND ENVIRONS

Hotels and Restaurants

Ankara. Some of the Moderate and all of the Inexpensive hotels are in the Old Town (Ulus). *Erşan* (M), Mesrutiyet Cad. 13 (tel. 1189 875). 64 rooms. *Yeni* (M), Sanayi Cad. 5, Ulus (tel. 3104 720). 66 rooms, reasonable. *Anit* (I), Gazi Mustafa Kemal Bul. 111 (tel. 2292 144). *As* (I), Rüzgarli Sok. 4, Ulus (tel. 310 3998). 45 rooms. *Efes* (I), Denizciler Cad. 12, Ulus (tel. 3243 211). 40 rooms. *Hanecioğlu* (I), Ulucanlar Cad. 68 (tel. 3202 572). 54 rooms, no restaurant. *Olimpiyat* (I), Rüzgarli Esdost Sok. 18, Ulus (tel. 3243 088). 67 rooms. *Paris* (I), Denizciler Cad. 14 (tel. 3241 283). 30 rooms.

Restaurants. *Anadolu Çiçek Pasaji,* Izmir Cad., *Damla,* Yüksel Cad., *Kizilay, Hüyla,* Hoşdere Cad., Cankaya, and *Kral Çifliği,* Tunalio Hilmi Cad., Kavaklidere, are all oriental-oriented. *Liman Lokantasi,* Izmir Cad. 11. *Piknik Lokantasi,* Tuna Cad., Kizilay, and *Piknik Pub,* Inkilap Sok., Kizilay, are more international. *Pizza Pino,* Tunali Hilmi Cad., more Italian. All these are (M). *Kebapci Bursa Iskender* (I) and *Kebapci Yesil Brusa* (I) specialize in *Bursa Kebap,* a mixed grill served on flat unleavened bread garnished with grilled tomatoes and green peppers and topped with yogurt. *Set,* Kizilay Meydani (I), self-service restaurant and cafeteria in the department store. In the same highrise is the *Set Gazinosu* (M).

Avanos. *Venessa* (M). Orta Mah. (tel. 1201). 76 comfortable rooms.

Göreme. *Melek Pansiyon* (M). Run by a Dutchman, bit off the beaten track; good atmosphere and cozy restaurant. *Peri Pension* (M), a dwelling carved out of the rock, at the turning to the open-air museum.

Kayseri. *Hattat* (M), Cami Kebir Cad. 1 (tel. 19 331). 67 rooms. *Turan* (I), Turan Cad. 8 (tel. 11 968), 68 rooms, restaurant.

Konya. *Özkaymak Park* (M), Otogar Karşisi (tel. 133 770). 90 rooms, near coach terminal. *Yeni Sema* (M), Yeni Meram Yolu (tel. 171 510). 30 rooms; quiet, but a bit out of the way. *Konya* (I), Mevlana Alani (tel. 121 003). 29 rooms, sauna.

Restaurants. Pleasant outdoor dining at *Fuar* (M), Konya Fuari (Luna Park). *Merkez* (I), Hükümet Cad.

Nevşehir. *Göreme* (M), Bankalar Cad. (tel. 17 06), 72 rooms. *Orsan Kapadokya* (M), Kayseri Cad. (tel. 10 35). 80 rooms, pool. *Lale* (I), Gazhane Sok. (tel. 1797), 28 rooms; *Viva* (I), Kayseri Cad. 45 (tel. 1326), 24 rooms. Both with restaurants.

Niğde. *Merkez Turistik* (I), Atatürk Meydani (tel. 1860). 32 rooms, restaurant.

Ortahisar. *Motel Paris* (M), Aksaray Mev. (tel. 1099). 24 rooms, pool.

Ürgüp. *Büyük* (M), (tel. 1060). 48 rooms. *Hotel Hitit* (M), Dumlupinar Cad. 54 (tel. 4868 1481). One of the best small hotels. *Hotel Maria* (M), Kayseri Cad. 10 (tel. 1487). 8 rooms. *Tepe* (M), (tel. 1154). 51 rooms, pool, closed November through March. *Hotel Ozata* (I), Ataturk Bulvari 56 (tel. 1981). 32 rooms, very good standards.

Restaurant. *Hanedan Restaurant* (I), Nevsehir Yolu Uzeri (tel. 1266).

Yugoslavia

This is a country whose scenery varies from rich Alpine valleys, superbly fertile vast plains and rolling green hills, to bare, rocky gorges up to 3,000 feet deep, and forests. Huge expanses of gaunt limestone mountains drop suddenly down to the coast, where a thousand-odd islands reveal the summits of submerged mountain ranges. Climate varies enormously with altitude and location. You can swelter on the coast in late October while snow lies a foot deep 10 miles inland on the nearest mountains. And though rapidly expanding tourism has brought its numerous rashes of smart (and less than smart) modern complexes all over the country, there are still many parts, even along the overdeveloped coast, that have preserved an atmosphere all their own.

Until the 20th century, Yugoslavia as such (it means "land of the South Slavs") did not exist. Its lands, in which the South Slavs arrived around the 6th century A.D., were constantly split in the perpetually changing chessboard of big power politics. For many centuries much of it was under Turkish domination, other chunks came under Austria or Hungary, while parts of the coast were long ruled by Venice.

As the Turks were gradually driven out in the 19th century, the map of Yugoslavia changed radically with the emergence of the independent kingdoms of Serbia and Montenegro. Bosnia-Hercegovina, though freed of the Turks, was transferred to the administration of Austro-Hungary in 1878. Macedonia remained under Turkish domination until the Balkan Wars of 1912/13. Slovenia in the northwest and Croatia, including the entire Dalmatian coast, stayed under Austro-Hungarian rule. When the Kingdom of Yugoslavia was formed in 1918, rivalries between its various component parts remained acute. However, after the horrific losses in World War II, Marshal Tito, the country's leader from 1945 to 1980, succeeded in achieving the apparently impossible: unity and independence.

Modern Yugoslavia is a federation of six independent republics: Serbia, Slovenia, Croatia, Bosnia-Hercegovina, Macedonia and Montenegro, with two autonomous regions, the Vojvodina and Kosovo inside Serbia. A total population of 22 million people, descended from five major and many minor nationalities, are dispersed among them. Although the main language is Serbo-Croat, there are two other major ones (Slovenian and Macedonian). There are also two alphabets (Roman and Cyrillic), three major religions (Orthodox, Catholic and Moslem) and a fascinating cultural mosaic.

Yugoslavia's brand of communism is based principally on a system of workers' self-management under which most enterprises are owned and run by workers. Thus rival organizations running bus services, hotels and so forth compete with each other, and small private enterprises—especially shops, restaurants and workshops—flourish. Nonetheless, the Yugoslav economy is not strong. High inflation, low productivity, and a huge trade deficit have recently grown to such proportions, along with unrest in parts of the country, that the situation is unpredictable as we go to press—though main tourist areas are unaffected and prices tend to be more than ever in the visitor's favor. Thus, it is possible to travel freely, widely and cheaply throughout one of Europe's most varied countries, especially if you use local buses or explore the beautiful islands by local passenger boats, staying in small guest houses or private accommodations which are readily available through local tourist offices.

PRACTICAL INFORMATION FOR YUGOSLAVIA

WHAT WILL IT COST. There are package tour arrangements catering to all pockets, but you can travel at very reasonable cost independently by using public transport and staying in small hotels, guest houses or private accommodations.

The monetary unit is the dinar, divided into 100 paras. By the end of 1989 the inflation rate had been pushing to 2,000% for the year. The government finally stepped in early in 1990 and converted the dinar into a hard currency. At press time the exchange rate was 10.45 dinars to the dollar and 26.15 dinars to the pound sterling. Prices in Yugoslavia have gone up somewhat, but the exhange rate of the dinar against foreign currencies has remained fairly stable and new dinar notes were being printed as fast as possible. Traveler's checks and Eurochecks can be exchanged at banks, exchange bureaus amd travel agencies in all towns and resorts, as well at virtually all hotels. Since Yugoslavia's money is now a hard currency, there are no longer any restrictions on the amount you can bring into or take out of the country. Prices throughout this chapter are quoted in approximate equivalents in dollars.

Sample Costs. Cinema $2; theater (moderate seat) from $3–$4; coffee in café $0.80; beer in café $1; bottle of wine in moderate restaurant from $3, in supermarket from $2.

NATIONAL TOURIST OFFICE. The *Yugoslav National Tourist Office* distributes information on all aspects of tourism through its offices overseas, including a list of travel firms marketing tours to their country. Their head office in Belgrade is Mosě Pijade 8, 4th floor. In addition, there are regional and local tourist offices in most centers, and over a dozen tour operators with branch offices in many towns and resorts.

The addresses of the Yugoslav National Tourist Office overseas are:

In the U.S.: 630 Fifth Ave., Suite 280, New York, N.Y. 10111 (tel. 212–757–2801).

In the U.K.: 143 Regent St., London W1R 8AE (tel. 071–734 5243).

WHEN TO COME. July and August are the most popular months for holidays along the coast. They are also the hottest, the most expensive, and the most crowded. Bathing is possible on the coast from May to early October. Winters are pleasant, though the sky may be overcast up to about May. Summers can be very hot indeed inland, unless you contrive to spend part of your time up in the mountains. Spring and fall are decidedly the best times for the interior. Winters there can be extremely cold. Winter sports in the mountain regions last from November through to May.

Average afternoon temperatures in Fahrenheit and centigrade:

Belgrade	Jan.	Feb.	Mar.	Apr.	May	June	July	Aug.	Sept.	Oct.	Nov.	Dec.
F°	37	41	53	64	74	79	84	83	76	65	52	40
C°	3	5	12	18	23	26	29	28	24	18	11	4

Dubrovnik												
F°	50	52	58	63	70	76	80	79	75	69	60	52
C°	10	11	14	17	21	24	27	26	24	21	16	11

SPECIAL EVENTS. Among a crowded calendar of events, the following are some of the major festivals held each year: *May,* Peasant Wedding folklore event,

Plitvice; *June,* festivals of traditional songs in several centers on Istrian and Croatian Littoral; *June-August/September,* summer festivals in many centers, notably Belgrade, Ljubljana, Ohrid, Opatija, Šibenik, Split, Zagreb; *July,* Galičnik Wedding folklore event, International Review of Original Folklore in Zagreb, Moreška Sword Dance in Korčula (main performance on 27th but held Thursday evenings all summer long), Peasant Wedding folklore event in Bohinj, Festival of Yugoslav Films in Pula; *July 10-August 25,* Dubrovnik Summer Festival, Yugoslavia's main cultural event; *August,* Sinj equestrian tournament; *September,* Belgrade International Theater Festival; *October,* Bemus Music Festival, Belgrade; *October-December,* concert and theater season in all main cities.

National Holidays. Jan. 1 (New Year's Day); Jan. 2; May 1 (Labor Day); May 2; Jul. 4 (Veterans); Nov. 29, 30 (Republic). In addition, in *Serbia:* Jul. 7; in *Macedonia:* Aug. 2, Oct. 11; in *Montenegro:* Jul. 13; in *Slovenia:* Jul. 22, 23; and in *Croatia* and *Bosnia-Hercegovina:* Jul. 27.

VISAS. Nationals of Great Britain and some other countries do not require visas for entry into Yugoslavia, but must have a valid passport of course. Those of the U.S., Canada, Australia and New Zealand do require a visa, available free at Yugoslav embassies and at any Yugoslav frontier post or airport as well.

HEALTH CERTIFICATES. Not required for entry from any country.

GETTING TO YUGOSLAVIA. By Plane. There are flights by *JAT* (Yugoslav Airlines) from New York, Chicago, Los Angeles, Montreal, and Toronto to Belgrade and Zagreb, and from New York to Dubrovnik. *PanAm* offers regular flights by way of New York–Frankfurt, and, with a change of planes, to Zagreb and/or Dubrovnik year-round. In addition, there are services from many European cities to Belgrade, Zagreb, Ljubljana, Split, and Dubrovnik, with extra flights and destinations in summer.

By Train. The most convenient route from the U.K. leaves London at about 1 P.M. and travels via Dover to Oostende, where you join an express train that runs via Köln, Munich, Salzburg and Villach into Yugoslavia. It passes through Ljubljana, Zagreb and Split, reaching the last at about 6 A.M. There are 2nd-class bunk beds from Oostende to Klagenfurt, and a buffet service part of the way. Other services run into Yugoslavia from Germany, Austria and Italy.

By Bus. There are a number of privately operated bus routes from Western Europe (including the U.K.) that pass through Yugoslavia en route to Greece. Some of these will take passengers to Yugoslavia only, but make sure they have the proper licenses. Details from travel agents.

CUSTOMS. There is one level of duty-free allowance for goods imported into Yugoslavia. Travelers over the age of 15 may import 200 cigarettes or 50 cigars or 250 gr. of tobacco; 1 liter of spirits, 1 liter of wine, ¼ liter of eau de cologne and a reasonable quantity of perfume.

HOTELS. A list of hotels giving prices and facilities is available from the Yugoslav National Tourist Offices overseas. Inflation, for the visitor, has been countered by the devaluation of the dinar, and there are plenty of inexpensive accommodations away from popular resorts. Though hotels are classified De luxe, A, B, C, etc., standards and prices within each category vary and are not always strictly comparable with similar categories in western European countries. Expect to pay for a Moderate (M) room $50–$75, for Inexpensive (I) $35–$50 for two in main centers in season. Elsewhere and at other times, these prices will be substantially lower. Private accommodations, graded according to standard, are well organized and offer good value; local tourist offices provide information. Small privately run guest houses have also increased, especially in the north and west of the country (look out for *gostilna* in Slovenia, *gostionica* in Croatia) and are usually very reasonably priced. Self-catering accommodations are shown as "apartments" in the hotel lists.

Youth Hostels. A special organization dealing with holidays and travel for young people is *Karavan-Naromtravel*, Knez Mihailova 50, Belgrade, which also runs several international youth centers. Student hostels, with no age limits, are very low-priced in all main cities and towns (but summer only). Tourist offices can advise.

Camping. A list of sites is available from the Yugoslav National Tourist Office; this also indicates the facilities in each. They get crowded in summer in the popular resort areas and there is no advance booking, so start looking early in the day.

RESTAURANTS. If you use restaurants frequented by tourists, you can expect to pay $10–$15 in a Moderate (M) place, under $10 in an Inexpensive (I) one, without drinks, but there are plenty of snack bars and workaday restaurants where you can eat simply but adequately for less, especially in towns. There are now also many small private-run restaurants, some offering excellent value. But always check prices before you order.

Food and Drink. Yugoslav cooking shows considerable regional differences. Bosnian and Macedonian dishes have the greatest Turkish influence; Slovenian ones have similarities with those of neighboring Austria. Along the Dalmatian coast there is a distinctly Mediterranean flavor. On the whole, meat specialties are better prepared than fish. Here are a few national favorites: *piktije*, jellied pork or duck; *pršut*, smoked ham; *čevapčići*, charcoal-grilled minced meat, and *ražnjiči*, skewered meat; *sarma* or *japrak*, vine or cabbage leaves stuffed with meat and rice; *Bosanski lonac*, an excellent Bosnian meat and vegetable hot-pot. Desserts are heavy and sweet: *štrukli*, nuts and plums stuffed into cheese balls, then boiled; *lokum*, Turkish delight, and *alva*, nuts crushed in honey, are very sweet indeed.

This is a great wine-growing country and wine flows cheaply everywhere. Slovenia's wines are best known: *Ljutomer, Traminer* and *Riesling*. The white *Vugava* grown in Vis is excellent as are red Dalmatian wines such as *Plavac* and *Dingač*. Potent *šlivovica* (slivovitz) plum brandy is the national liquor, and *maraskino*, made of morello cherries, the tastiest liqueur. Coffee in the north is Italian-style *espreso* (black) and *cappuccino* (white); in the south it is usually strong and Turkish style.

TIPPING. In theory there is really no tipping in socialist Yugoslavia. As a rule, Yugoslavs leave only some minor small change when paying restaurant bills. There is positively no tipping at bars. If you feel the service warrants it, you can leave an extra 3%–5% when paying restaurant bills, but no more. Tip cab drivers a maximum of 5% if they have been helpful.

MAIL. At presstime airmail letters to the U.S. cost the equivalent of $0.60, to the U.K. $0.30. These prices will certainly increase. There are lower rates for surface mail but this is extremely slow.

CLOSING TIMES. Business hours in Yugoslavia vary from season to season and from region to region. But general guidelines are as follows: banks 7–7, Sat. 7–1; stores 8 to 12 and 4 to 8, though quite a few are nonstop; restaurants 7 A.M. to midnight; cafés 6 A.M. to 11 P.M. (later for those with music); cinemas 3 P.M. to 11 P.M. and from 10 A.M. in city centers.

GETTING AROUND YUGOSLAVIA. By Plane. *JAT (Yugoslav Airlines)* links 18 centers, *Adria Airways* 12. Flights are frequently booked to capacity, so reserve well ahead.

By Train. With a substantial section of its network now electrified and with the promise of more electrification to come, Yugoslav Railways provide an inexpensive if generally rather crowded method of travel around the country. Trains are classed as *Ekspresni* (Express), *Poslovni* (rapid), *Brzni* (fast) and *Putnički* (slow). Supplementary fares are charged for the first two, unless your tickets were purchased outside the country. Buffet cars are carried on a number of express trains, but always make a point of checking this. Yugoslavia participates in the *Inter Rail* (discounts for youth) but not the Eurail scheme.

The publication *Red Voznje* contains all rail timetables and some ferry and air services. It is only available in Yugoslavia.

By Bus. A comprehensive bus network covers the country, and main routes are serviced by modern, comfortable express buses. They can, however, be crowded, especially during public holidays, so get your ticket in advance and arrive early. In remoter areas or on slower services, buses may well be of rather venerable vintage and roads can be less than smooth. But you get to see the countryside (especially remoter areas) and meet the people—and fares are low.

By Boat. The main operator is *Jadrolinija*, the state shipping line. There are many passenger boat and hydrofoil services linking coastal centers and islands; local tourist offices can advise on timetables. Hydrofoil services on the Danube also operate from Belgrade to the Iron Gates on the Romanian border. Full Danube cruises from Passau or Vienna to the Black Sea call at Yugoslav river ports, including Belgrade, but are expensive.

Belgrade and Serbia

Since Herodotus first mentioned it twenty-five centuries ago the city of Belgrade has been repeatedly destroyed—the price it has had to pay for its strategic position, spread out as it is on hills commanding the junction of the rivers Sava and Danube, a crossroads between the West and the Orient, and the gateway to Central Europe.

Belgrade (Beograd) is in the heart of the Balkans. Since its near-destruction in 1941, it has grown into a modern city of one-and-a-half-million inhabitants. Almost the only ancient building still in existence is parts of the great fortress of Kalemegdan, which dominates the Vojvodina Plain. What remains of the buildings dates mainly from Turkish and Austrian times, but it incorporates remnants of the much earlier Celtic, Roman, and Slav defenses, making it a mute history of the city's life for some 2,000 years. There is an excellent museum, and, from the top of the citadel, the view over the junction of the Sava and Danube rivers and the great sprawl of the city is stunning.

There is acceptable and even occasionally interesting architecture of recent years among the abortive highrise experiments of the 1950s. Across the Sava River lies Novi Beograd whose unimaginative blocks of cement also include the impressive Sava Center (congress complex) and Modern Art Museum.

A general impression of the center of the city can be gained by the following itinerary. Start in Trg Republike, or Republic Square, home of the excellent National Museum. Opposite is the National Theater, where there is an opera season each year. Not far from here is the narrow cobbled street called Skadarlija, a favorite haunt of the Bohemian set in the 19th century. It has now been restored to provide a very popular dining out area with good folk music and lively street entertainment. Pass by the building called Albanija, and you will come to the nerve center of the capital, the street called Terazije. Here two main streets meet, and we follow the Bulevar Revolucije which is 4 miles long. It brings us soon to the impressive National Assembly.

Then we come to the Tašmajdan Park, and glimpse the Church of Sveti Marko (St. Mark): it is a copy of the church at Gračanica.

From Belgrade, the Danube flows east towards and through the Carpathians; it is a little-known area, though there are hydrofoil trips that zoom through the towering gorges (once part of the frontier of the Roman Empire) to the remarkable hydro-electric barrages of the Iron Gates and back; a more leisurely trip is also well worth while.

But among Serbia's most famous features are the medieval monasteries and their frescoes, in varying states of repair, which lie in the mountains to the south, often tucked away in remote valleys and not easy to find. An organized tour is the simplest way of seeing them. This also means you can be sure they are open when you get there. If you have time and patience to sort out local buses, however, you'll undoubtedly have a memorable experience. If you haven't, a compromise would be a visit to the Fresco Gallery in Belgrade, or to Topola (about 50 miles south) where, on Oplenac hill, is the remarkable mausoleum of the Karageorge family.

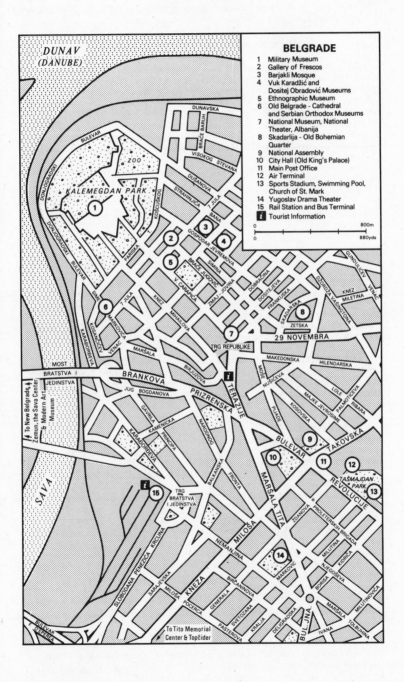

BELGRADE

1 Military Museum
2 Gallery of Frescos
3 Barjakli Mosque
4 Vuk Karadžić and
   Dositej Obradović Museums
5 Ethnographic Museum
6 Old Belgrade - Cathedral
   and Serbian Orthodox Museums
7 National Museum, National
   Theater, Albanija
8 Skadarlija - Old Bohemian
   Quarter
9 National Assembly
10 City Hall (Old King's Palace)
11 Main Post Office
12 Air Terminal
13 Sports Stadium, Swimming Pool,
   Church of St. Mark
14 Yugoslav Drama Theater
15 Rail Station and Bus Terminal
ℹ️ Tourist Information

0   800m
0   880yds

The interior of the church and the crypt are completely covered with mosaics, each a faithful reproduction of a Serbian monastic masterpiece.

PRACTICAL INFORMATION FOR BELGRADE

HOTELS. It is highly desirable to book accommodations in advance in Belgrade. If you have any difficulty, the Tourist Information Office in the Pedestrian Underground Passage at the Albanija Skyscraper, Terazije, or at the railway station, will help (tel. 635–343, 635–622). They can also advise on private accommodations. In low season these offices close early.

Moderate

Kasina, Terazije 25 (tel. 335574). 96 rooms. Central, but noisy.
Park, Njegoševa 4 (tel. 334722). 131 rooms. A short walk from center.
Prag, Narodnog fronta 27 (tel. 687355). 118 rooms, recently renovated. Central, but can be noisy.
Splendid, Dragoslava Jovanovića 5 (tel. 335444). 50 rooms, no restaurant. Central, near Federal Assembly building; recently renovated.
Toplice, 7 jula 56 (tel. 626426). 110 rooms. Central, the nearest to Kalemegdan, but can be noisy.

Inexpensive

Central, Maršala Tita 10 (tel. 191712). In the pleasant old suburb of Zemun, by the Danube.
National, Bežanijska kosa bb. (tel. 601122). 70 rooms. Across the Sava, on the motorway from Zagreb.
Taš, Borisa Kidriča 71 (tel. 343507). Small hotel, recently renovated, in recreation center by Tasmajdan park. Pools.
Union, Kosovska 11 (tel. 187036). 74 rooms. Some Moderate rooms. Central.
Youth accommodations. Mladost, Bulevar JNA 56a. Year-round.

RESTAURANTS. Belgrade's restaurants, outside the hotels, are as varied as you would expect in a capital city. The most popular ones (*not* listed here) are those in the city's old Bohemian quarter centered on Skadarlija close to the city center; prices are quite reasonable if you choose your dishes carefully.

Moderate

Djordje, Šekspirova 29. Attractive private restaurant.
Dušanov grad, Terazije 4. Good for quick meals right in the center.
Jezero, Ada Ciganlija. Near bathing beach on Ada Ciganlija island in Sava river. Good value, sports facilities.
Klub Kniževnika (Writers' Club), Francuska 7. Some of best food in the city. Ignore shabby entrance.
Vuk, Vuka Karadžicá 12. Private restaurant in center; excellent value.

Inexpensive

Atina, Terazije 28. Popular pizzeria. Takeaway *piroški,* excellent for a quick, filling snack.
Kasina, Terazije 25. Self-service express restaurant serving Serbian specialties.
Venecija, Kej oslobodenja bb, Zemun. Fish soups or *paprikaš,* grills; overlooking the Danube.
Two good cafés are **Kod spomenika,** Trg republike 1, and **Moskva,** Balkanska 1, both with sidewalk tables. **Znak "?"** (Café of the Question Mark), 7 jula 6, opposite the Cathedral is in a typical Serbian home of two centuries ago.

GETTING AROUND BELGRADE. Public transport is by trolley bus, bus or tram. You can get tickets on the vehicle or, a little more cheaply, in advance from kiosks. Day tickets, valid for an unlimited number of journeys, are available; also a carnet of 12 tickets.

MUSEUMS. Bajrakli Džamlija, Gospoda Jevremova 11. Built in the 17th century and the only mosque left in the city; converted into a church in the 19th century.

Ethnographic Museum, Studentski Trg 13. Illustrates costumes, household articles and typical peasant house interiors from different parts of the country.

Fresco Gallery, Cara Uroša 20. Shows copies of the finest frescoes of the medieval Serbian and Macedonian monasteries.

Modern Art Museum, in a suitably modern building near the Sava River in New Belgrade. 20th century painting and sculpture with the emphasis on Serbian artists.

Museum of the Serbian Orthodox Church, in the Patriarchate, Sedmog Jula 5. Displays some of the best examples of icons, vestments and other art work from Serbian churches.

National Museum, Trg Republike. Archeological, historical and numismatic collections, as well as a picture gallery. Neolithic material includes stunning gold jewelry, statuettes and the famous Duplja cart; also splendid medieval monastery relics.

Tito Memorial Center. In a quiet district to the south of the center, this includes the tomb of the late President and museums connected with his life; set in pleasant grounds. Entrance from Bulevar oktobarske revolucije.

SHOPPING. A booklet on shopping in Belgrade is available from the Tourist Information Center. Of the major department stores, you can't miss the highrise block of the Beograd Palace on Maršala Tita, which houses the largest of them all, *Beogradjanka.* Another big one, *Beograd,* is at Trg Terazije 15–23, with its drugstore *(Dragstor),* open round the clock. Of particular interest for the foreign visitor is the chain of handicraft shops, known as *Narodna Radinost.* A number of open-air markets (open daily including Sunday) are very lively, selling handicrafts from many parts of the country as well as fresh produce, household goods, clothes—in fact, pretty well everything you can think of. The principal one is at Zeleni Venac.

USEFUL ADDRESSES. *U.S. Embassy,* Kneza Miloša 50 (tel. 645655); *Canadian Embassy,* Kneza Miloša 75 (tel. 644666); *British Embassy,* Generala Ždanova 46 (tel. 645055); *Tourist Information,* Central Railway Station (tel. 646240) and subway passage at end of Terazije below the Albanija building (tel. 635343); *Youth travel,* Karavan-Naromtravel, Knez Mihailova 50; *American Express,* Atlas Travel Agency, Moše Pijade 11 (tel. 341471); *Wagons-Lits, KSR,* Moše Pijade 21 (tel. 335331); *Main Post Office,* Takovska 2.

Ljubljana and Slovenia

Set in Yugoslavia's northwest corner, against Italian and Austrian frontiers, Slovenia is the part of Yugoslavia seen first by most visitors entering the country by road or rail. The north is a continuation of Austria's Alpine region, while rolling hill country begins south of the Julian Alps, and extends to a tiny section of the large Istrian Peninsula's coast south of the Italian border near Trieste.

The thickly-wooded Alpine regions contain many charming lakes, notably Lake Bled, with its 11th-century castle, romantic island and fine modern hotels, and Lake Bohinj, quieter and higher. The outstanding features of the southern inland area are the numerous karst caves. Those of Postojna are Europe's most striking series of vast interconnected underground caverns. Also worth visiting is Lipica where the famous stud for Lippizaner horses, founded 400 years ago, was re-established some years ago. As you approach Slovenia's short section of coast, the vegetation changes abruptly to vines, olives and figs and the climate becomes wholly Mediterranean. Here sophisticated, old-established Portorož rubs shoulders with the newer coast resorts of Koper and Piran, based on old fishing ports. All, however, have many modern hotels and all the facilities that tourists expect.

Ljubljana, Slovenia's capital, is built around its hilltop castle. The Austrian influence is unmistakable, and the city offers pleasant riverside walks, noble houses, fine museums and Baroque churches. Remains of the Roman town of Emona can also be seen, notably on Mirje street. Ljubljana's summer festival, with open-air performances of opera and ballet, is well worth a visit. From here you can visit Ptuj and Celje, the latter with discoveries of Roman art treasures. Maribor, near the Austrian border, is the main center for the Pohorje mountains.

Slovenia is Yugoslavia's best-known winter sports area, largely because the resorts are easily accessible. There are ski lifts at Kranjska Gora to the best slopes of the Vitranc Mountains and lifts at Bohinj to the vast terrain of the Vogel Plateau.

The Pokljuka region provides perfect conditions for beginners. In the Pohorje mountains the ground is even easier—and the prices reasonable. In summer, climbing and walking attract visitors to the same mountains. For kayak enthusiasts Slovenia offers splendid descents, notably on the Krka and Soča rivers. All forms of water sports are practised on the coast.

PRACTICAL INFORMATION FOR LJUBLJANA

Hotels and Restaurants

Kompas (M), Miklošičeva 9 (tel. 326061), 61 rooms. *Slon* (M), Titova 10 (tel. 211232), 185 rooms, central. *Union* (M), Miklošičeva 1 (tel. 212133), 270 rooms. *Park* (I) (tel. 316777), 90 rooms, a little outside the center. *Tikveš Motel* (I), Draga (tel. 557893), 14 rooms. *Turist* (I), Dalmatinova 13 (tel. 322043), 131 rooms.

Guest houses include *Gostilna pri Mraku* (M), *Pension Kanu* (M), *Gostilna Jelen* (I). Very inexpensive accommodations are available in student hostels in summer (no age limit); also private rooms. The Tourist Information Center can advise.

Restaurants. *Mrak* (M), Rimska 4, unpretentious, near center. *Na Brinju* (M), Vodovodna 44, good food, small summer garden, out of center. *Pod Rožnikom* (M), Cesta na Rožnik, Serbian food, pleasant setting, Tivoli Park. *Kresnička* (I), Kolovićeva 8, good value, out of center. *Triglav* (I), Miklošićeva 12, includes self-service section, central.

MUSEUMS. Castle. Still partly under restoration but worth the walk up for the views.

Krizanke, Trg francoske revolucije 2, a 16th-century monastery complex on earlier foundations, was adapted in the 1930s for the Ljubljana Festival.

The National Gallery, Cankarjevo 20, contains the best works of the particularly prolific Baroque school of Slovene artists.

The National Museum, Trg Herojev 1, has one ethnographic and one archeological section. Its greatest treasure is almost certainly the Vače Situle, a bronze urn from the 5th century B.C.

The National and University Library, Turjaska 1, includes first editions of all books printed in Slovene, and a number of interesting incunabula.

USEFUL ADDRESSES. *Tourist Information Center,* Titova cesta 11 (tel. 215412). Slovenia's main travel agency is *Kompas* with several offices, including Titova cesta 12 (tel. 331444).

Zagreb and Inland Croatia

The rich rolling farmlands of Zagorje rise to the north of Zagreb, while to the south an upland region, the Gorski Kotar, leads into the still remote Lika, separated from the sea by the gaunt 50-mile-long, 5,000-foot-high Velebit Range. Almost all Istria's coastline as well as most of the 600 miles of the Croatian Littoral and Dalmatia (covered later in chapter), the narrow beautiful coastal strip and its hundreds of islands extending all the way south to Dubrovnik, belong to Croatia.

In Istria, the 400 years of Venetian rule are evident in most coastal towns and villages, while the succeeding century of Austrian dominion shows clearly in the main coastal resort of Opatija. Tourist complexes (villas, chalets, hotels, bars, restaurants, camp sites and trailer parks, beaches, etc.) have grown up around many previously tiny villages. Being so accessible, this part of the coast is extremely popular. Its beaches are safe for children and there's a wide range of watersports facilities in most centers.

In Crikvenica, on the Croatian Littoral south from Rijeka, modern development overshadows the older buildings. The lovely islands of Krk and Lošinj are well-provided with accommodations. Beautiful Rab, a popular holiday spot for generations, can boast in its capital (of the same name) one of Yugoslavia's loveliest Venetian-style towns. The most popular inland resort in Croatia is Plitvice, with its 16 lakes lying like terraces, one higher than the other, among nature's wonders.

Zagreb, the capital, on the fringe of a fertile plain, is the capital of Croatia and rivals Belgrade in its cultural life. It is largely central European in appearance due to the fact that during the historical see-saw of past centuries, Croatia formed part of the Habsburg Empire. Centuries ago Zagreb comprised two neighboring, but separate towns, one secular and the other religious. Perched on the summit of a hill, the former dominated the latter as it did the whole valley. In the 13th century it was named Gradec, meaning 'fortress', and was walled to protect the citizens against the Tartars. The other town, named Kaptol, was also fortified in the 16th century, at the time of the great Turkish drive to the Danubian plain, though as it happened the enemy never came within 40 miles of the town. It was only in the 19th century the two communities and others that had sprung up in the vicinity at last united into the single city of Zagreb.

The lower town is centered around Ilica, the main street that crosses it for a distance of some 2½ miles. It is full of shops and cafés, and leads you to the center Trg Republike—Republic Square. From there you should climb Radićeva Street and Štrosmajer Promenade to the quarter of the upper town known as Gornji Grad. This route affords fine views. You can also go by funicular, which puts you down near Lotrščak tower from which an ancient cannon is fired daily at noon to commemorate the retreat of the Turks.

Gornji Grad is dominated by St. Mark's Church, its roof brilliant with red, white and blue tiles depicting the emblems of Croatia and Zagreb. The interior has been decorated by the best modern Yugoslav artists, including the sculptor, the late Ivan Meštrović, who lived in the United States. The modern frescoes and various other works of art blend quite harmoniously with the 14th-century Gothic sanctuary.

Down in the Kaptol district, near the Cathedral (largely rebuilt in the 19th century), don't miss the lively open-air market of Dolac, held every morning.

On the outskirts of Zagreb is a cable-car that carries you up to Mount Sljeme, and beyond it there is the whole of the lovely Zagorje region with its old castles and churches, spas and quaint villages, in an unspoiled rural setting. Tito's childhood home at the village of Kumrovec is now a museum.

PRACTICAL INFORMATION FOR ZAGREB

Hotels and Restaurants

Dubrovnik (M), Gajeva 1 (tel. 424222). 279 rooms, recently renovated, very central. *International* (M), Miramarska 24 (tel. 511511). 370 rooms, away from center, nightclub. *Central* (I), Branimirova 3 (tel. 425777). 103 rooms, opposite main rail station. *Jadran* (I), Vlaška 50 (tel. 414600). 48 rooms, near cathedral. *Zagreb Motel* (I), Dubrovačka aleja (tel. 533055). 51 rooms, south of Sava River near fairground.

Private accommodations can be booked through several travel agencies. For youth accommodations, contact *Omladinski turistički centar*, Petrinjska 73, who also run the *Omladinski* (Youth) *Hostel* at Petrinjska 77 (tel. 434964).

Restaurants. Zagreb abounds in snack bars, cafeterias and self-service restaurants, and there are innumerable small places where you can buy the ubiquitous *čevapčići* with some bread and wine for a cheap snack. For something more substantial try:

Dubrovnik put (M), in Tuškanac park, pleasant setting, good value. *Kaptolska klet* (M), Kaptol 5, central and good. *Korčula* (M), Nikole Tesle 17, central, Dalmatian and fish specialties. *Kornati* (M), Gajeva 9, fish specialties. *Pod Mirnim Krovovima* (M), Fijanova 7, a little way from the center. Particularly good lamb-on-the-spit and freshwater fish. *Students' Center* (I), Savska 25. Three good (I) snack bars are *Corso*, Gundulićeva 2, *Medulić*, Medulićeva 2, and *Splendid*, Zrinjevac 15; all central.

MUSEUMS. Archeological Museum, Zrinjski Sq. 19. Covers prehistoric to medieval times and includes a massive coin collection.

Arts Center, Jezuitski trg. Magnificent changing exhibitions in beautifully restored 17th-century Jesuit monastery.

Ethnographic Museum, Mažuranićev Square. Interiors of peasant homes and fine collection of costumes, folk music instruments, etc.

Gallery of Old Paintings, Zrinjski Sq. 11. An impressive collection of paintings, mainly Italian Renaissance.

Gallery of Primitive Art, Ćirilometodska 3, in the Upper Town. A fascinating selection of paintings by "naïve" Croat peasant-painters who have become world famous.

Meštrović Gallery, Mletačka 8. A collection of works by Yugoslavia's world famous sculptor.

Mimara Museum, Rooseveltova trg. Fabulous one-man private collection of art treasures from almost every epoch and most parts of the world.

USEFUL ADDRESSES. *U.S. Consulate,* Braće Kavurića 2; *British Consulate,* Ilica 12; *Tourist Information,* Trg Republike 11 (tel. 278910); Zrinjevac 14 (tel. 411883); in Lotrščak Tower in the Upper Town (tel. 421887); also at central rail station, bus station and airport; *Wagons-Lits,* Nikole Tesle 4.

Dalmatia—Dubrovnik and Split

This long stretch of coast and its numerous islands forms a separate entity, though administratively and ethnically it is part of Croatia. The coastal regions present important differences from the interior, due to geography and still more to their separate historical background. While the Turks occupied much of present-day Yugoslavia, Venice mostly ruled the Adriatic coast until the Napoleonic Wars. Only one Dalmatian city remained independent throughout these stormy centuries, namely Ragusa, today Dubrovnik.

Much of the coast is of breathtaking beauty, its gaunt limestone mountains sloping sharply to the shore—sometimes direct into the sea. Here you have hundreds of small, scrub-covered islands etched against the intense blue of sea and sky, and colorful little villages tucked into bays and inlets, their red pantiled roofs glowing warmly. A number of lovely small stone-built towns, little larger than the villages but embodying high standards of civilized living and whose more ancient remains blend harmoniously with predominantly Venetian architecture, are scattered along the coast. And almost every few miles there are modern hotels or "tourist complexes," with chalets and restaurants, and an ever growing rash of guest houses and private accommodations.

Among the larger historic towns, the walled city of Dubrovnik is an exquisite example of late Renaissance architecture. Split's old center lies within the walls of the monumental palace built by the Roman Emperor Diocletian. Trogir is an unspoilt medieval town and the historic city of Zadar contains impressive Roman and Romanesque remains. In addition there are scores of ancient little towns, some on the islands, where Venice left her imprint, such as Brać, Hvar, Ston, Šibenik and Korčula. For peace and quiet, try the islands of Koločep, Lopud, Brać and Šolta. Dalmatia possesses several colorful traditional ceremonies and customs; if you are in the vicinity, don't miss the Moreška at Korčula, every Thursday in summer, or the Alka at Sinj in August.

We have selected Dubrovnik and Split as our two main centers. Both are crowded in summer and can be expensive, but offer excellent possibilities for exploring more of the coast, the interior and the islands, as well as being of immense interest themselves; and there is always private accommodation to bring down the costs.

The walled city of Dubrovnik is a unique gem and you should begin with a tour of its undamaged medieval walls. Allow at least an hour and remember entry to the walls closes at 6 or 7 P.M. (there is a small fee). If time is short, follow the circuit on the landward side for the best views.

The old city's main thoroughfare is the Placa (or Stradun) which crosses it from one side to the other, and runs along what was once the narrow channel separating Ragusa on its island from Slav Dubrovnik on the mainland. It is here that you will find the principal buildings, though there are of course countless narrow medieval streets leading off it that the visitor will find very well worth exploring.

Two of the most important buildings in Dubrovnik are the Sponza Palace and the Rector's Palace. The first is near the 100-ft. high Clock Tower (recently rebuilt, but originating from 1445); the Palace is in Gothic style with Renaissance elements, its main façade ornamented with an external gallery supported by graceful arches. It has served many purposes over the centuries, including as a Customs House, but today houses the City Archives with some remarkable documents illustrating Ragusa's diplomatic dealings with all the great powers over the centuries. The Rector's Palace, rebuilt in the 15th century after earthquake damage, is a splendid building combining late Gothic and early Renaissance styles. The Council rooms and Rector's apartments now make a fascinating museum. There are innumerable other buildings of interest—palaces, churches, places of learning and of commerce, many of them used as settings for music or drama performances, especially during the famous Dubrovnik Festival. But one of the delights of the city is making your own discoveries amongst the narrow cobbled alleyways (blessedly closed to motorized traffic, by the way).

Split, which lies just about half way between Rijeka and Dubrovnik, does not make the same immediate visual impact as Dubrovnik, for it has become one of Yugoslavia's major industrial centers. Yet all this is spread around the remarkable remains of Diocletian's tremendous palace, which forms the core of the old town.

Work on the Palace was begun in A.D. 295 and it took ten years to complete. As soon as it was ready Diocletian abdicated, though still only 61, and spent the last eight years of his life in the peace of his native Dalmatia. His attempts to secure a stable succession failed, however.

When Solin was sacked by the Avars in A.D. 615, such of the inhabitants as managed to escape fled first to the neighboring islands, and then when the raiders had gone, sought more permanent shelter within the walls of Diocletian's Palace, eventually building houses in the spacious courtyards, with any kind of material that came to hand. The Roman Palatium became medieval Spalato, and in 1918, the modern town of Split.

The enormous palace rectangle covers approximately 30,000 square yards. It is in a surprisingly good state of repair. In the 18th century it inspired the Adam brothers' Adelphi in London. The south front of the palace faces the sea, and it was here that the imperial apartments were placed so that for visitors arriving by sea, the first sight is of the outside of the main hall. The thickness of the walls makes it clear that the palace was originally designed to serve at all times as a fortified castle. Once inside the building you realize that you are looking at a military encampment. There are plenty of relics from those days of antiquity: the underground halls, a 3,500-year-old Egyptian sphinx, a grandiose mausoleum converted into the Cathedral of Our Lady, a Jupiter Temple transformed into a baptistry. Then, under the Venetians, the humble refugee dwellings packed into the palace area gave way to stately mansions, among which is the Gothic-Renaissance Papalić Palace, now housing the outstanding Split Museum (possibly still closed for restoration). This unique blend of antique and medieval splendor contains at least as many inhabitants as in the days of the palace's imperial glory; far from being artificially preserved, it pulsates with the intense life of the 20th century.

There are numerous humble little medieval churches dotted around the city, and the Franciscan Convent contains a superb Stations of the Cross. In the area round the palace you will find much that is picturesque and surprisingly beautiful. The main square of Narodni Trg, with its Venetian Gothic Town Hall, now the Ethnographic Museum, stands immediately outside the palace limits, and a few yards beyond it is the octagonal Hrvoje Tower, once part of the 15th-century defenses. In the little square in front of it is a statue of the poet Marko Marulić by Meštrović, Yugoslavia's foremost sculptor.

Split is excellently placed for exploring the islands for it is not only a port of call on express coastal services, but has numerous links by regular passenger boats and hydrofoils to islands such as Korčula, Hvar, Brač and Šolta.

PRACTICAL INFORMATION FOR DUBROVNIK AND SPLIT

Hotels and Restaurants

Dubrovnik. *Garni Hotel Dubravka* (M), Od Puča 1 (tel. 26293). 22 rooms, the only hotel in the old town. *Garni Hotel Petka* (M), Gruška obala 76 (tel. 24933). 112 rooms, overlooking Gruž harbor. *Jadran* (M), Stonska 4 (tel. 23322). 48 rooms, in Lapad. *Lapad* (M), Lapadska obala 37 (tel. 23473). 71 rooms in former home of Esterhazy family, overlooking Gruž harbor. *Splendid* (M), Masarykov put 10 (tel. 24733). 60 rooms, in Lapad. *Sumratin* (M), Aleja I.L. Ribara 31 (tel. 24722). 70 rooms, in Lapad. *Gruž* (I), Gruška obala 61 (tel. 24777). 40 rooms, overlooking Gruž harbor.

Note that many hotels are some distance from the old walled city—those at Gruž (1½ miles) for example, and at the Lapad peninsula (2–3 miles). However, there are frequent bus services.

The International Youth Center Rašica, Ivanska 14 (tel. 23841) on Lapad peninsula gets heavily booked. Otherwise, private accommodations are the least expensive. Consult the tourist office or a travel agency for details.

Restaurants. All (M) and in or near the old town are: *Dubravka,* Brsalje 1, near Pile Gate; *Gradska Kavana,* Pred Dvorom 3, very popular, prices can be erratic; *Jadran,* P. Miličevića 1, attractive setting in cloisters of former monastery; *Ankora,* Siroka 1, Dalmatian and fish specialties.

Split. *Park* (M), Setaliste 1 maja 15 (tel. 515411). 60 rooms in pleasant Bacvice district. *Slavija* (M), Buvinova 3 (tel. 47053). 32 rooms. Adapted from fine historic buildings in heart of old city. *Central* (I), Narodnitrg (tel. 48242). 48 rooms, in heart of old city. *Bellevue* (M) Ante Jonića 2 (tel. 47175) 46 rooms. On Venetian-style Trg Republike, just outside Palace walls facing waterfront.

Restaurants. All (M) are: *ACY Marina's Pizza Bar,* sharing the same fabulous views of the harbor as the very expensive main restaurant adjoining it. *Kod Joze,* Sredmanuška 4, just northeast of the old town. *Konoba Adriatik,* in the heart of the old town; national dishes. *MAK,* in ultra-modern Koteks shopping center east of the old town. *Sarajevo,* Ilegalace 6, in the old town; Bosnian specialties.

Museums

Dubrovnik. The Ethnographical Museum, Maritime Museum and Aquarium, are in the fortress of St. John.

The Franciscan Monastery has an old pharmacy museum, fine paintings, reliquaries and old manuscripts in its beautiful Gothic cloisters.

The Historical Museum is part of the Rector's Palace, and its exhibits give a picture of life in Dubrovnik from early days up to the downfall of the Republic, especially in the 18th and 19th centuries. There is also a collection of exotic objects brought home by the sailors of the town.

The Icon Collection is in Puča St., opposite the Serbian Orthodox church.

The Rupe Granary is an historical monument of the 15th century, and contains a permanent exhibit of Yugoslav folk art.

The Sponza Palace has changing exhibitions, sometimes including a fascinating display of agreements and guarantees signed by most heads of state of the great powers over the centuries.

Split. Archeological Museum, Zrinjsko-Frankopanska 13. A fine collection of Roman antiquities discovered at Solin.

City Museum (Papalić Palace), Zarkova 5, statues, coins, works of art.

Ethnographic Museum, Narodni trg, folk-art, costumes, embroideries, tools and weapons.

Fine Arts Gallery, plaster casts and sculptures from classical times up to the present period.

Meštrović Gallery, Moše Pijade 39, about 2 km. from center, containing more than 200 sculptures by this famous artist.

Museum of Croatian Archeological Monuments, Ognjen Price. Excellent displays in fine new building on Marjan peninsula, near Meštrović Gallery.

USEFUL ADDRESS. Dubrovnik. *Tourist Information,* P. Miličevića 1; *British Consulate,* Atlas Building, Pile 1. **Split.** *Tourist Information,* Titova obala 12.

Bosnia-Hercegovina—Sarajevo

The domes and slender minarets scattered across the towns of this republic give it an Oriental air, hardly to be wondered at when you recall that it formed part of the Ottoman Empire for four centuries. The Turkish heritage is evident not only in the architecture, for a good many of the inhabitants have kept the faith of their former rulers. Although readily accessible, Bosnia-Hercegovina provides a stimulating contrast to the traveler coming from the Adriatic coast. Between them, they comprise a region of bare rocky hills, deep gorges, and vast game forests. The province offers excellent rock climbing and hunting. The rivers contain trout while trips can be made by kayak and raft down the exciting rapids of the Drina Gorge (several travel firms arrange excursions). The Sutjeska National Park is a particularly wild and beautiful region.

The capital of the combined republic is the picturesquely situated city of Sarajevo, a blend of East and West. Mostar, Hercegovina's principal town, features its hump-backed stone bridge over the Neretva, built by the Turks in 1556, around which are clustered Turkish-era houses and mosques. Other towns in Bosnia are Banja Luka, Jajce, built around an impressive waterfall, and Travnik, the residence of the Turkish vizirs (governors) from 1700 until 1852.

Undoubtedly, Sarajevo is one of the most interesting places in Yugoslavia and, indeed, Europe. The old town, with its narrow streets bordered by Oriental-style houses, is perched on the steep slopes of the Miljačka Valley, and the new quarters have spread in a great sprawl across the plain of Sarajevsko Polje, situated at the mouth of a fortified gorge at a height of over 1,600 feet. More recently the city has expanded enormously with districts of highrise and other modern buildings, and achieved international renown as the venue of the 1984 Winter Olympics. The whole is encircled by mountains gradually dropping down into small hills, upon which are laid out the many delightful Turkish-style gardens for which the city is famous.

One of the most interesting quarters is that of Baščaršija, the bazaar that consists of a maze of narrow alleys seething with a colorful motley crowd and full of craft workshops. In this district is the Baščaršija Mosque, whose dominating aspect makes it even harder to realize that you are still in Europe.

It was the energetic Gazi Husref Bey who built among other things the magnificent Begova Džamija (Mosque of the Bey) in 1530, which you will see from Saraći (Saddlers') Street. It has exquisite Persian carpets and prayer rugs, as well as one of the earliest-known copies of the Koran. There are so many really remarkable mosques to be seen in Sarajevo that a full list would make lengthy reading, but two more at least must be mentioned. The first is the Mosque of Ali Pasha, and the second the Mosque of the Emperor (Careva Džamija); they are close to each other and near the center of the city.

Other points of interest include the pseudo-Oriental building intended by the Austrians to serve as the Town Hall, and the strange little Orthodox Church reconstructed when the Turks were in occupation, with a wall that hid those who visited it from view. It has a superbly carved wooden iconostasis.

Opposite Princip Bridge, on the wall of the Young Bosnia Museum, is a commemorative plaque marking the spot from which the young Gavrilo Princip fired those fateful shots at the Austrian Archduke, that led to World War I.

PRACTICAL INFORMATION FOR SARAJEVO

Hotels and Restaurants

Beograd (M), S. Principa 11 (tel. 532688). 70 rooms, central. *Europa* (M), Jugoslovenske Narodne Armije (tel. 532722). 225 rooms. Service erratic, but well located by lively Baščaršija (bazaar) area. *National* (M), Obala Pariške komune 5 (tel. 532266). 73 rooms, just across the river from the center. *Central* (I), Zrinjskog 8 (tel. 215115). 39 rooms, central. *Zagreb* (I), Valtera Perića 1 (tel. 36680). 43 rooms, in the newer part of town but still quite central.

The 1984 Winter Olympics led to a sharp boost in accommodations, including a number of small privately run hotels (bookings through local travel agencies). There are also plenty of private accommodations (check with the tourist office).

Restaurants. *Dalmacija* (M), Maršala Tita 45, near the old town, specializes in fish, and has pleasant garden. *Koštana* (M), B. Šurbata 16, a little away from center. *Kula,* Gornji Kotorac 99, at Butmir, out near the airport, has a lovely situation, good food and very reasonable prices. *Orijentalni restoran* (I), by the market place in Baščaršija, local dishes, basic, good value. Two central self-service restaurants (I) are *Bosna* and *Marin Dvor* (which also has a waiter-service section), respectively at numbers 36 and 1 Maršala Tita. There are innumerable small eating places and food bars where you can get national or local specialties such as *ćevapčići* or *burek* as quick and inexpensive snacks. Also many excellent pastry shops, and discos packed with the young.

MUSEUMS. Jewish Museum. Maršala Tita Street 98.

The Museum of Young Bosnia, Obala Vojvode Stepe 36. Devoted to the revolutionary student group whose activities sparked off the 1914–18 war.

Old Orthodox Church, Maršala Tita 83. With a rich collection of icons, frescoes etc.

The National Museum of Bosnia-Herzegovina is not far from the Railway Station at Vojvode Putnika 7. The first wing contains a collection of prehistoric, Greek, Roman and medieval objects; while in the left wing there is a really remarkable ethnographic collection, including reproductions of Bosnian peasant houses and feudal Turkish dwellings. In the gardens of the Museum there are a number of the unique burial steles (*stećci*) of the Bogomils.

Svrzo's House, Jovana Kršića 4. Classical example of Moslem home.

USEFUL ADDRESSES. *Tourist information,* Jugoslovenske Narodne Armije (JNA) 50 (tel. 24844); the main local travel agency is *Unis-Tours,* Vase Miškina 16 (tel. 23140). *Vacation Centre,* Zadrugina 17 (tel. 36163) is one of several youth tourism centers for inexpensive accommadations.

Montenegro—Budva

Shut in between Bosnia-Hercegovina, Serbia and Albania, this smallest republic of the federation possesses some 60 miles of coastline dotted with rapidly developed seaside resorts, backed by rocky hills. The interior is dominated by the rugged Black Mountains, the Venetian's Montenegro, which the Yugoslavs call Crna Gora. In the north are some green valleys, and in the south huge Lake Skadar is shared with Albania.

Montenegro's history is one of unceasing struggle ever since the foundation of the medieval Serb state, of which it was a province until 1389. Then, following the Turkish victory at Kosovo, Serbia shrank northwards and finally disappeared. Though isolated, Montenegro resisted all foreign invaders.

From walled Kotor, deep within the splendid triple bay of the same name, a breathtaking road zigzags up Mount Lovćen, offering one of the most startling panoramas in Europe, over the fjord-like Gulf of Kotor, the successive ranges of mountains, and including a distant view of Albania. The former capital Cetinje, which still preserves its pre-World War I atmosphere, lies in a fertile bowl amid soaring bare mountains. In the mighty Durmitor Range to the northeast is the Tara Canyon—55 miles long—one of the most remarkable in Europe. Raft trips can be arranged. Modern beach resorts stretch from Hercegnovi to Ulcinj, from which 11 miles of continuous sand run to the Albanian border. Montenegro's developing port of Bar is now linked by a spectacular railway route from Belgrade, boring its way through dramatic mountainscapes and along the rim of precipitous gorges.

Following the violent earthquake of 1979, all tourist amenities have now been restored or replaced, but the architectural treasures will take longer. The walled towns of Budva and Kotor were particularly badly affected, but the former has now been completely restored. Work on Kotor will take longer, but several of its most interesting monuments (excluding the Cathedral) have been restored and re-opened.

Though Titograd is the capital of Montenegro, this modern city built on the site of ancient Podgorica, which was almost completely destroyed in 1944, is not of particular interest, so we have chosen Budva as our center.

PRACTICAL INFORMATION FOR BUDVA

Hotels and Restaurants

Just outside the walls of the old town is reconstructed *Mogren* (M) (tel. 41022). About 1 km. away by the extensive *Slovenska Plaža* beach (tel. 41044), a new holiday center re-creates a small-village atmosphere and includes moderately-priced accommodations with a range of sports and entertainment. Other hotels and sports facilities are found by Bečići beach, a few km. further, including the large moderately-priced *Bellevue* (tel. 41476), *Mediteran* (tel. 41988), *Montenegro* (tel. 41556), and *Splendid* (tel. 41555). There is also an international youth center. The main travel agency is *Montenegro Express* (tel. 41266, 41388), which has its headquarters in Budva and many branch offices who will be able to advise on self-catering and private accommodations, some now available in the walled town.

Restaurants. These include *Vidikovac* on the main road overlooking the old town; *Sunce* near the harbor; *Starigrad* in the old town; *Jadran* near the marina.

Macedonia—Ohrid and Skopje

The main attraction of this southernmost province is medieval Ohrid, in its lovely lakeside setting. Capital of Tsar Samuel, the medieval churches contain some extraordinary frescoes and icons. There are two other large lakes, Prespa and Dojran, and the countryside holds countless reminders of Greek and Roman times. As in Serbia, there are a great number of medieval monasteries and it is here in Macedonia that you will see some of the earliest and finest frescoes in the country.

The disastrous earthquake of July 1963 destroyed the center of Skopje, a city of 200,000 inhabitants and the capital of Macedonia. However, thanks to the help and cooperation of many nations and organizations, Skopje was rebuilt rapidly; its monuments from Roman times and its later treasures were restored, among them the church of the Holy Savior, with its famous woodcarvings, the Turkish Bath of Daut Pasha, now an art gallery, and Kuršumli han, a 17th-century inn, now housing the archeological section of the Museum of Macedonia.

Skopje makes a good center from which to launch into exploration of Macedonia. You can travel inexpensively by bus in this remote southern extremity of Yugoslavia and, in the process, come into contact with a way of life that is in utter contrast with the more sophisticated conditions further north. It is a beautiful countryside of mountain ranges ribbed by deep valleys or broken by wide cultivated plains. And some of the little towns—if you penetrate the newer districts and find their old core—have considerable if, at times, rather disheveled charm. Markets are places to seek out for colorful characters and costumes.

PRACTICAL INFORMATION FOR OHRID AND SKOPJE

Hotels

Ohrid. *Grand Palace* (M), (tel. 25030). Near lake, only hotel in town. There are much better at **Gorica,** 5 km. (3 miles) south, including *Park* (M), (tel. 22021), 110 rooms, on shore.

Skopje. *Bristol* (M), Maršala Tito (tel. 239821). 33 rooms. Central and recently renovated. *Grand* (M), tel. 239925). Central, beside Vardar river. *Panorama* (M), (tel. 231976). 87 rooms. *Jadran* (I), (tel. 220022). 23 rooms. *Turist* (I), (tel. 236753). 80 rooms.
Youth Hostel, Prolet 25, near the railway station.

USEFUL ADDRESSES. Ohrid. *Tourist Office Biljana,* Partizanska (near the bus station) (tel. 22494). **Skopje.** *Tourist Information,* Dane Gruev bb (tel. 230803, 233843), Gradski zid, blok iii, and at the entrance to the Čaršija (Bazaar), near the Stone Bridge.

Index

The letters H and R indicate hotel and restaurant listings.

Fodor's Travel Guides

U.S. Guides

Alaska
Arizona
Boston
California
Cape Cod
The Carolinas & the
  Georgia Coast
The Chesapeake
  Region
Chicago
Colorado
Disney World & the
  Orlando Area

Florida
Hawaii
The Jersey Shore
Las Vegas
Los Angeles
Maui
Miami & the Keys
New England
New Mexico
New Orleans
New York City
New York City
  (Pocket Guide)

New York State
Pacific North Coast
Philadelphia
The Rockies
San Diego
San Francisco
San Francisco
  (Pocket Guide)
The South
Texas
USA
The Upper Great
  Lakes Region

Virgin Islands
Virginia & Maryland
Waikiki
Washington, D.C.

Foreign Guides

Acapulco
Amsterdam
Australia
Austria
The Bahamas
The Bahamas
  (Pocket Guide)
Baja & the Pacific
  Coast Resorts
Barbados
Belgium &
  Luxembourg
Bermuda
Brazil
Budget Europe
Canada
Canada's Atlantic
  Provinces
Cancun, Cozumel,
  Yucatan Peninsula
Caribbean
Central America
China

Eastern Europe
Egypt
Europe
Europe's Great
  Cities
France
Germany
Great Britain
Greece
The Himalayan
  Countries
Holland
Hong Kong
India
Ireland
Israel
Italy
Italy's Great Cities
Jamaica
Japan
Kenya, Tanzania,
  Seychelles
Korea

Lisbon
London
London Companion
London
  (Pocket Guide)
Madrid & Barcelona
Mexico
Mexico City
Montreal &
  Quebec City
Morocco
Munich
New Zealand
Paris
Paris (Pocket Guide)
Portugal
Puerto Rico
  (Pocket Guide)
Rio de Janeiro
Rome
Saint Martin/
  Sint Maarten
Scandinavia

Scandinavian Cities
Scotland
Singapore
South America
South Pacific
Southeast Asia
Soviet Union
Spain
Sweden
Switzerland
Sydney
Thailand
Tokyo
Toronto
Turkey
Vienna
Yugoslavia

Special-Interest Guides

Bed & Breakfast
  Guide to the Mid-
  Atlantic States

Bed & Breakfast
  Guide to New
  England
Cruises & Ports
  of Call

A Shopper's Guide
  to London
Health & Fitness
  Vacations
Shopping in Europe

Skiing in North
  America
Sunday in New York
Touring Europe